THE COLUMBIA UNIVERSITY

COLLEGE OF

PHYSICIANS AND SURGEONS

COMPLETE HOME MEDICAL GUIDE

THE COLUMBIA UNIVERSITY

COLLEGE OF

PHYSICIANS AND SURGEONS

COMPLETE

HOME

MEDICAL

GUIDE

Prepared in Conjunction with the Columbia-Presbyterian Medical Center

Third Revised Edition

Crown Publishers, Inc. New York

MEDICAL EDITORS

DONALD F. TAPLEY, M.D.

Senior Deputy Vice-President for Health and Sciences and Alumni Professor of Medicine

THOMAS Q. MORRIS, M.D.

Vice Dean, Faculty of Medicine, and Senior Associate Vice President for Health Sciences

LEWIS P. ROWLAND, M.D.

Henry and Lucy Moses Professor and Chairman, Department of Neurology

....

JONATHAN LAPOOK, M.D.

Assistant Professor of Clinical Medicine

....

EDITORIAL DIRECTOR

Genell J. Subak-Sharpe, M.S.

ASSOCIATE EDITOR

Diane M. Goetz

Published by Crown Publishers, Inc., 201 East 50th Street, New York, New York 10022. Member of the Crown Publishing Group.

Random House, Inc. New York, Toronto, London, Sydney, Auckland

CROWN is a trademark of Crown Publishers, Inc.

Manufactured in the United States of America

Design by Lauren Dong

Library of Congress Cataloging-in-Publication Data
The Columbia University College of Physicians and Surgeons complete
    home medical guide. — Rev. 3rd ed.
      p.   cm.
    "Revised and updated ed. of the popular : Complete home medical guide."
    Includes index.
    1. Medicine, Popular. I. Columbia University. College of
  Physicians and Surgeons. II. Complete home medical guide.
  RC81.C716 1995
  613—dc20   94-13101
                                                      CIP

ISBN 0-517-59610-5

10 9 8 7 6 5 4 3 2 1

Third Revised Edition

Contents

Acknowledgments

Over the years, scores of people have been involved in creating *The Columbia University College of Physicians and Surgeons Complete Home Medical Guide.* While it is impossible to cite all of the many dedicated physicians, consultants, writers, editors, illustrators, and others who have contributed so much to this book, there are some whose dedication and efforts deserve special mention.

First and foremost, we acknowledge the support and efforts of the entire College of Physicians and Surgeons community. Almost sixty physician/specialists at P&S have worked with the editors on this volume. In addition to their myriad other duties, they have drafted manuscripts during vacations and at other free moments, without hesitation or complaint.

A team of skilled medical writers and editors has also been involved in creating this book. Diane Goetz merits special mention for her leadership in directing the creative team, recruiting physician contributors, and keeping the book "on track." Carl Lowe headed the effort for this third eddition. Other writers and editors include Diana Benzaia, Susan Carleton, Catherine Caruthers, Dr. Symra Cohn, Victoria Chesler, Kim Dalton, Larry Frederick, Jennifer Freeman, Connie Grzelka, Catherine Heusel, Judith Hoffmann, Christopher Hallowell, Maxine Karpen, Cynthia Keyworth, Dr. Emily Linzer, Susan Lowe, Helene MacLean, Joy Nowlin, Emily Paulsen, Sharon Petzka, Barbara Ravage, Nan Silver, Sarah Subak-Sharpe, Caroline Tapley, Robert Thumin, Dr. Valerie Ulene, Timothy Wetmore, and Lois Wingerson.

We have also worked with a team of leading medical artists, headed by Robert Demarest, John W. Karapelou, and Lauren Keswick from the P&S Audio Visual Service. Illustrations have also been provided by Douglas Cramer, Leonard Dank, Glenna Deutsch, Marsha Dohrmann, Carol Donner, Douglas Dunn, Neil O. Hardy, Kittie Herman, and Beth Willert. In addition, illustrations have been provided by the American Heart Association, the American Cancer Society, and Biomedical Information Corporation. John Bernhartsen of the U.S. Coast Guard and Roger Miller of the Food and Drug Administration have provided valuable help and expertise. Stanley C. Stevens, Sr., of Personal Health Profile designed the medical record charts.

The laborious task of fact-checking, proofreading, and myriad other aspects of manuscript preparation have been handled by Sarah and Hope Subak-Sharpe, Letta Neely, and Arlyn Apollo. They have served above and beyond the call of duty in seeing to the many details in preparing a manuscript of this magnitude.

The staff at Crown, including Rusty Hannon and William Peabody (production), Merri Ann Morrell (composition), Lauren Dong (design), Pamela Stinson (production editor), Durrae Johanek (freelance copy editor), and particularly our editors Betty Prashker, Cressida Connolly, and Laurie Stark, deserve special thanks for their patience, guidance, and invaluable insight. Finally, the many spouses who have done everything from baby-sit and keep dinners waiting to reviewing manuscripts and offering practical suggestions deserve an extra tribute.

Income from this book goes to scholarship funds at the Columbia University College of Physicians and Surgeons.

The Editors and Contributors

Medical Editors

Donald F. Tapley, M.D.
Alumni Professor of Medicine
Senior Deputy Vice President for Health Sciences

Thomas Q. Morris, M.D.
Vice Dean, Faculty of Medicine
Senior Associate Vice President for Health Sciences

Lewis P. Rowland, M.D.
Henry and Lucy Moses Professor and Chairman,
Department of Neurology

Jonathan LaPook, M.D.
Assistant Professor of Clinical Medicine

Editor Emeritus

Robert J. Weiss, M.D.
DeLamar Professor Emeritus and Dean Emeritus,
Columbia University School of Public Health

Editorial Director

Genell S. Subak-Sharpe, M.S.
G. S. Sharpe Communications

Associate Editor

Diane Goetz

Contributors

Karen Antman, M.D.
Professor of Medicine
Chief, Division of Oncology

Jonathan Aviv, M.D.
Florence Irving Assistant Professor of Otolaryngology
Director, Division of Head and Neck Surgery

Arthur Bank, M.D.
Professor of Medicine, and Genetics and
    Development

A. L. Loomis Bell, M.D.
Professor of Clinical Medicine

J. Thomas Bigger, Jr., M.D.
Professor of Medicine and Pharmacology

Rita A. Charon, M.D.
Assistant Professor of Clinical Medicine

William J. Davis, M.D.
Clinical Professor of Pediatrics

Harold M. Dick, M.D.
F. E. Stinchfield Professor and Chairman,
Department of Orthopedic Surgery

Jay Dobkin, M.D.
Associate Professor of Clinical Medicine

Anthony Donn, M.D.
Edwin S. Harkness Professor of Ophthalmology

John Driscoll, M.D.
John Manning Clinical Professor of Pediatrics
Acting Chairman, Pediatrics

Kenneth C. Fine, M.D.
Associate Clinical Professor of Medicine

Glenda Garvey, M.D.
Professor of Clinical Medicine

Elsa-Grace Giardina, M.D.
Professor of Clinical Medicine

Henry Ginsberg, M.D.
Tilden-Weger-Beiler Professor of Medicine

Barry Gurland, M.D.
Director, Center for Geriatrics and Gerontology
John S. Borne Professor of Clinical Psychiatry

Donald A. Holub, M.D.
Professor of Clinical Medicine

Thomas Jacobs, M.D.
Professor of Clinical Medicine

Israeli A. Jaffe, M.D.
Professor of Clinical Medicine

Norman Kahn
Professor of Pharmacology
Edwin C. Robinson Professor of Dental and Oral
  Surgery

Herbert Kleber, M.D.
Professor of Psychiatry

Jonathan LaPook, M.D.
Assistant Professor of Clinical Medicine

Robert Lewy, M.D.
Associate Clinical Professor of Medicine and
  Public Health
Senior Vice President for Medical Affairs

Robert B. Mellins, M.D.
Professor of Pediatrics
Director, Pediatric Pulmonary Division

Jay Meltzer, M.D.
Associate Clinical Professor of Medicine

James R. Morris, M.D., Ph.D.
Postdoctoral Clinical Fellow in Neurology

Thomas Q. Morris, M.D.
Vice Dean, Faculty of Medicine
Senior Associate Vice President for Health Sciences

Harold C. Neu, M.D.
Professor of Medicine and Pharmacology
Chairman, Division of Infectious Diseases

John M. Oldham, M.D.
Professor of Clinical Psychiatry
Director of the New York State Psychiatric Institute

Carl A. Olsson, M.D.
Professor and Chairman of Urology

Timothy A. Pedley, M.D.
Professor and Vice-Chairman, Department of
  Neurology

Steven M. Roser, D.M.D., M.D.
Professor of Clinical Dentistry (Surgery and
  Otolaryngology)
Director of Maxillofacial Surgery/Section of
  Hospital Dentistry
Director, Presbyterian Hospital Dental Service

David J. Rothman, Ph.D.
Bernard Schoenberg Professor of Social Medicine
Director, Center for the Study of Society and Medicine

Lewis P. Rowland, M.D.
Henry and Lucy Moses Professor and Chairman,
Department of Neurology

Ihor S. Sawczuk, M.D.
Associate Professor of Urology

Ridwan Shabsigh, M.D.
Assistant Professor of Urology

Michael Shelanski, M.D.
Michael L. Delafield Professor of Pathology
Chairman, Department of Pathology

Karen Soren, M.D.
Assistant Clinical Professor of Pediatrics

Robert N. Taub, M.D.
Professor of Clinical Medicine

Robert Walther, M.D.
Clinical Professor of Dermatology

Myron L. Weisfeldt, M.D.
Chairman, Department of Medicine
Samuel Bard Professor of Medicine

Andrew L. Witt, Ph.D.
Professor of Pharmacology

The Editors

DONALD F. TAPLEY, M. D., Alumni Professor of Medicine and Senior Deputy Vice-President for the Health Sciences, has spent most of his medical career at the College of Physicians and Surgeons. After completing a fellowship at Oxford University, he joined the P&S faculty as an assistant professor of medicine in 1956, rising to dean in 1974. During his ten-year tenure as dean, Dr. Tapley presided over the tremendous growth of the institution and is widely acknowledged as one of the most notable medical-school deans in the nation. His medical specialty is endocrinology, and over the years he has published a number of papers in this field, with special emphasis on the role of the thyroid hormones.

LEWIS P. ROWLAND, M. D., is a world leader in his medical specialty of neurology. At Columbia, he holds the Henry and Lucy Moses professorship in neurology and is also chairman of the Department of Neurology. After his graduation from the Yale University School of Medicine and an internship at New Haven Hospital, he came to Columbia University's Neurological Institute for advanced training in neurology. After stints at the National Institutes of Health and the University of Pennsylvania Medical School, where he was professor and chairman of the Department of *Neurology,* he returned to Columbia in 1973. In addition to his academic, clinical, and research activities, Dr. Rowland is associated with a number of professional journals and was editor-in-chief of Neurology. He is past president of the Association of University Professors of Neurology, the American Neurological Association, and the American Academy of Neurology. He has been on advisory boards of the National Institute of Neurological Diseases and Stroke, Muscular Dystrophy Association, Multiple Sclerosis Society, and others.

THOMAS Q. MORRIS, M. D., has also spent most of his medical career at the College of Physicians and Surgeons and Columbia-Presbyterian Medical Center—first as a student and trainee and then as a physician, educator, and administrator. His previous positions have included director of the student health service, acting chairman of the Department of Medicine, associate dean for academic affairs, and president of the Presbyterian Hospital. He is now Vice-Dean, Faculty of Medicine, and Senior Associate Vice-President for Health Sciences. His many honors include the Dean's Award for Outstanding Contributions to Teaching. He also serves as senior advisor to the New York Academy of Medicine and as a trustee of the Mary Imogene Bassett Hospital in Cooperstown, New York, and the American University of Beirut.

JONATHAN D. LAPOOK, M. D., is an Assistant Professor of Clinical Medicine at the Columbia-Presbyterian Medical Center, where he has spent most of his medical career. After graduating with honors from Yale University, Dr. LaPook attended Columbia's College of Physicians and Surgeons, followed by a residency in internal medicine and fellowship in gastroenterology at the Columbia-Presbyterian Medical Center. In addition to this teaching and clinical work at the medical center, he maintains a private clinical practice in New York City and is a leader in the field of medical computing. As president of his own company, LaPook Lear Systems, he has developed an acclaimed medical practice management software package called Probity. He has also published a number of scientific papers and has contributed to several medical books.

GENELL J. SUBAK-SHARPE is a medical writer and editor who began her journalism career on the metropolitan staff of the New York Times. Since then, she has served as vice-president of Biomedical Information Company and as editor of a number of publications for both physicians and consumers. As president of G.S. Sharpe Communications Inc., a New York book and editorial production company, she has written, coauthored, or edited more than forty books on health and medicine. She has produced books under the imprimatur of the Columbia University College of Physicians and Surgeons, the Yale University School of Medicine, New York's Mount Sinai Hospital Medical Center, the Cleveland Clinic, the American Cancer Society, and the Animal Center of New York. Many of her books have been translated into Japanese, German, French, and Hebrew, and are sold worldwide.

Foreword

This Third Revised Edition of *The Columbia University College of Physicians and Surgeons Complete Home Medical Guide* reflects many of the changes that have taken place in American medicine since publication of the first edition in 1985. Although our goal—namely, to provide you with a comprehensive home reference that teaches you about your body in sickness and health—remains unchanged, we are placing increased emphasis on disease prevention and your role in maintaining your own good health.

To make this weighty volume easier to use, we have changed the format throughout. Each section now follows a consistent style to help you quickly find the information you need, including self-help guidelines as well as subsections of male/female differences.

Another major change is the inclusion of alternative therapies as well as conventional medical and surgical treatments in the discussions of specific diseases. Increasingly, the gap between some conventional and alternative approaches has narrowed, with each adopting the best of the other. Thus, today's cancer patient will still receive the latest in surgical, drug, radiation, and other conventional treatments, but he or she may also be taught self-hypnosis or visualization to help control pain and foster a sense of well-being. Columbia's new Center for Alternative/Complementary Medicine—the first of its kind at any American medical school—reflects this melding.

HOW TO USE THIS BOOK

This book is divided into six major parts, each one devoted to a particular facet of medicine and health. In part 1 is a guide to our health care system and how to use it. Recognizing that our medical system is undergoing reform and change, we discuss how to get the most for your health care dollar during this time of transition. At this writing, we hesitate to predict the extent of health care reform, but we describe the different options under consideration, and provide guidelines on how to get the optimal care from each. Issues and questions addressed include: How do you decide whether you should join a Health Maintenance Organization or some other managed care system? When should you seek a second opinion and where do you go? Chapter 2 discusses how to meet special needs. How do you prepare for long-term care? What are your options in caring for aging parents? Should you have a living will? Health care proxy?

Part 2 addresses new approaches to wellness, with emphasis on how you go about adopting a healthful lifestyle. Chapter 5 tells how to structure a nutritious diet without destroying the pleasure of eating. It also offers practical guidelines for weight control and nutrition supplements, and discusses the role of diet in preventing disease. Chapter 6 takes on the thorny issues of smoking, alcohol, and illegal drugs, again, with practical suggestions on how to overcome addictions to these substances.

Chapters 7 through 10 address the fundamentals of good health in the different life stages: infancy and childhood, adolescence, and the reproductive years.

Part 3 gives an overview of symptoms and the diagnostic process. In chapter 11, you will find a table listing scores of symptoms, possible causes, and diagnostic studies. Chapter 12 describes dozens of common tests and procedures: When are they indicated? Are there risks? What should you ask your doctor first?

Part 4 deals with first aid and safety. What is the first thing you should do in any medical emergency? How should you assess the situation? Are your CPR techniques up-to-date? This is one section that you should read periodically, and perhaps give yourself and other family members self-tests. Then when confronted with a true emergency, you will know how to proceed.

Part 5—still the largest section in this book, going from chapters 16 through 33—deals with the treatment and prevention of hundreds of diseases, covering everything from the common cold to rare genetic diseases. In these chapters, you'll find the new format especially useful because you can immediately turn to the relevant section to get the information you need.

Part 6 concentrates on drugs and their use. Chapter 34 presents an overview on taking medications, with tables on what you should include in your home medicine chest and first-aid kit. This is followed by an appendix of commonly prescribed drugs. This is where you'll find charts listing drug names, common side effects, and precautions you should follow when taking specific medications. This information is especially important today, as an increasing number of prescription drugs become available on a nonprescription basis.

Also included in the appendixes are a glossary of common terms, an updated and greatly expanded directory of health organizations and resources, and a listing of regional poison control centers. Finally, you will find convenient forms you can use to keep your own family medical records.

In buying *The Complete Home Medical Guide,* you have made a major investment in taking charge of your own health. We think you'll soon find that this is the most used book in your home library. And, as in the past, Columbia University's proceeds from the book go toward scholarships for medical students at the College of Physicians and Surgeons.

—The Editors

Using Our Health Care System

1

How to Get the Care You Need

• • • • • • • • • • • • • • •

THOMAS Q. MORRIS, M.D.
Parts of this chapter are adapted from the chapter by Robert J. Weiss, M.D., which appeared in the revised second edition.

PAYING FOR MEDICAL CARE

Today, the American health care system is poised on the brink of revolutionary change. Exactly what shape this change will take remains unclear, but certain features—such as an increase in managed care and limits on some expensive treatments—are likely to be involved. In the long run, however, changes in health care delivery should result in improved access to health care and lower health care costs for the majority of Americans.

Why is health care reform suddenly the hottest item on the political agenda in the mid-1990s? Mainly because glaring problems in the current system have become impossible to ignore. The past few decades have seen an unprecedented rise in private and government expenditures for health care, yet paradoxically increasing numbers of Americans are unable to obtain basic medical services because they lack insurance. Even those who are insured live in a climate of uncertainty in which a job change or a serious illness can spell loss of coverage and financial ruin. Meanwhile, employers are forced to cut back on the health benefits they offer workers, even as workers themselves see wages eroded by high insurance costs and increasing out-of-pocket payments for care. Here are the facts as of 1994:

- Between 1980 and 1992, American health care spending rose from 9 percent to 14 percent of the Gross Domestic Product (GDP), despite cost-cutting efforts on the part of government, insurers, and businesses.
- Health care costs are projected to reach 19 percent of the GDP—almost one out of every five dollars spent—by 2000 unless changes are made.
- Workers will lose almost $600 per year in wages by 2000 if the health care system is not changed.
- Health costs add about $1,100 to the price of every American-made car.
- If they continue to rise at current rates, health costs will eat up as much as 111 percent of increases in real federal tax revenues during the 1990s.
- Americans spend $2,868 per citizen on health care each year, as compared with just over $1,000 in the United Kingdom and Denmark and just over $1,500 in France and Germany.
- Hospitals and doctors provide more than $25 billion worth of care to uninsured patients. The cost of that care is passed along to those with insurance in the form of higher premiums, deductibles, and copayments.
- More than 37 million Americans—including 9.5 million children—have no health insurance.
- Another 22 million are regarded as underinsured; their coverage is inadequate for their needs.

- More than 2 million Americans lose their health coverage every month.
- Over the course of any 2-year period, 1 in 4 Americans suffers at least a temporary loss of insurance coverage.
- 85 percent of uninsured Americans belong to families that include one employed adult.

Although lawmakers, doctors, insurers, and health care consumers all agree that the situation needs to be remedied, there is wide disagreement on how best to do so. Some advocate the creation of a single government body to pay for and control all health care expenses. Others favor plans that would require employers to provide insurance to all workers at negotiated rates, subject to government regulation if they climb too high. Still others believe that, while insurance should be made available to all, market forces and competition should be allowed to exercise natural restraints on costs.

WHY HEALTH CARE COSTS HAVE SOARED

A number of factors have contributed to the rising cost of health care. One powerful influence is the aging of the population; between 1980 and 1990, America's population between ages 65 and 84 increased by 20 percent, while the number of Americans 85 and over increased 38 percent. Older people have more health problems, and more expensive health problems, than the young.

In addition, there has been a virtual explosion in medical technology in the past few decades. Expensive, high-tech studies such as computed tomography (CT) and magnetic resonance imaging (MRI) are performed routinely, as are costly operations such as coronary bypasses and kidney transplants. New tests that use recombinant DNA to detect minute particles of viruses and antibodies have entered the laboratory arsenal, allowing greater diagnostic precision than ever before—for a hefty price. Some critics charge that while these new technologies have undeniable value, they are often used unnecessarily when a cheaper alternative would work just as well.

Increased paperwork, too, has contributed to rising medical costs. It is estimated that about 20 to 25 percent of our health care dollars are spent on paperwork. A large part of the overhead in doctors' offices and hospitals goes to pay staff whose sole job is to wade through red tape from insurers and government programs. Between 1983 and 1993, the number of health care administrators working in our hospitals and clinics rose by 300 percent.

Medical fraud and malpractice add to rising costs as well. Untold millions are spent each year on fraudulent billing for medical services that either were never rendered or were performed unnecessarily. High jury awards in malpractice cases add to rising costs in two ways: through skyrocketing malpractice premiums, the costs of which are passed on to patients in higher doctors' fees; and through the practice of "defensive" medicine, in which doctors order unneeded tests and procedures to demonstrate their thoroughness in the event of a malpractice case.

What costs the most, though, is the system's focus on treatment rather than prevention of disease. Insurers will reimburse patients and doctors for procedures such as diagnostic tests, surgery, or drugs, but will not cover "well-care," or preventive medicine, both of which are also needed. Prenatal care for expectant mothers could prevent many premature births at a fraction of the cost of caring for tiny, sick newborns in neonatal intensive care units. Immunizing a child against whooping cough or measles costs pennies, while hospitalization for an unimmunized child who contracts such diseases and suffers their complications can run into the tens of thousands of dollars.

The possible examples of savings through prevention are endless, and they cut across all sectors of the economy, not just health care. The parents of the unimmunized child who contracts a preventable disease, for instance, incur not only the medical cost of the illness but also the cost of missed work and lost wages. And the parents' employers lose out as well, through reductions in productivity.

WHAT'S BEING DONE

As of this writing, Congress has debated and rejected several health care reform bills sponsored by representatives from both parties, and as the debate continues, it's impossible to predict what provisions—if any—will be adopted. Clearly, our health care system is in a state of transition, with a growing number of physicians and patients joining prepaid managed care systems such as those described below.

EXISTING PAYMENT OPTIONS

Few Americans can afford to pay the entire cost of an acute episode of illness out of their own pockets. Most people who have insurance for themselves and their families obtain it through their employers, who pay a significant portion of the insurance premium. In an effort to reduce the cost of their employees' medical care, many employers are encouraging employees to join less costly prepaid medical plans, such as health maintenance organizations (HMOs).

Even within the more limited options offered by the new health alliances, consumers should evaluate their medical coverage needs before selecting a plan. While all plans must offer basic benefits, they vary in the extras they cover, such as preventive and corrective dental care for adults or long-term rehabilitation for children with disabilities. Consumers can consult plan administrators or their local health alliance to find out exactly what is and is not covered by various plans. Such advice is particularly important when any lifestyle changes are anticipated—retiring, changing jobs, or setting up a business.

GROUP MEDICAL INSURANCE

This is the traditional or indemnity form of medical coverage, typified by the insurance policies offered by state Blue Cross and Blue Shield plans. Each of them is a separate company and may offer a variety of insurance plans. The plans may differ widely in the procedures covered and the amount they reimburse the patient. Most pay 100 percent of emergency care, such as setting broken bones, and pay varying amounts for elective surgery, prenatal care, eyeglasses, and other services. At present, however, some do not cover outpatient care by physicians. The patient pays a premium on a monthly basis and visits doctors of his or her choice; fees are covered on a fee-for-service basis, with the patient generally responsible for 20 percent of charges.

THE MANAGED CARE CONCEPT

In the past decade, most health insurers have adopted at least some of the practices of managed care, a health services concept aimed at cutting costs while improving quality of care and enhancing subscribers' overall health. While increased quality and decreased cost may seem to rule each other out, managed care enthusiasts say the two goals are actually quite compatible.

Central to managed care is utilization review; in which physician decisions and practice patterns are subject to review by the insurance company. The purpose is not so much to second-guess doctors as to prevent overuse of tests, procedures, and hospital admissions. Because unnecessary procedures and hospitalizations actually put patients at risk of complications, utilization review should ideally be good for patients, although many doctors find it intrusive and time-consuming.

Toward the same goal, many insurance plans now require patients to get second opinions before undergoing certain medical or surgical procedures and to obtain the insurer's permission before hospital admission. If the insurer considers a particular treatment unnecessary or overpriced, payment may be withheld.

Primary-care doctors play a central role in managed care, acting as "gatekeepers" whose authorization must be obtained before a patient can see a specialist—a cardiologist or orthopedic surgeon, for example. Generalists are able to manage most common medical conditions, and they have the added advantage of knowing the patient and understanding various factors—family life, occupation, medical history—that come into play in an illness. Primary care, one of the major goals of the Clinton health plan, is cost effective because primary care is less expensive than specialty care. It also promotes improved health by preventing the fragmented, impersonal care that makes many patients dissatisfied with medicine in general.

Managed care also involves extensive data gathering on practice patterns and on patient outcomes from different treatments. This information is used both as an aid in utilization review and as a basis on which to formulate practice guidelines so that medical care will be more standardized from doctor to doctor and hospital to hospital.

The managed care approach has been used most extensively in two relatively new types of health coverage, HMOs and Preferred Provider Organizations (PPOs).

HEALTH MAINTENANCE ORGANIZATIONS (HMOS)

HMOs charge a single monthly or annual fee that covers all medical expenses, from routine and emergency care to hospitalization. Many also charge a small "copayment," usually about $5 for each visit to the doctor. Although these plans have been around for years, they have begun to grow rapidly as the pressure to cut nationwide medical bills has increased. By the end of 1993, their enrollment was almost 45.2 million—almost three times as large as it was in 1984. HMO enrollees made up 17.4 percent of the total health insurance market in 1993, up from 4 percent in 1980.

HMOs are attractive to employers because their annual medical bill for an average patient may be nearly 30 percent less than that of conventional medical insurers. The savings come from closely monitoring doctors' costs, limiting hospitalizations, and negotiating discounted fees from doctors and hospitals.

The HMO label covers a variety of groups, which may be organized by an employer, a group of doctors, a union, a consumer group, an insurance company, or a for-profit health care company.

Several different types of HMOs are currently in operation. They are:

- **Open-ended or Point of Service.** Enrollees are permitted to use doctors outside the HMO network, but the costs of services are not fully covered.
- **Staff Model.** Physicians are employees of the HMO and enrollees do not have the option of getting outside care, except in emergencies.
- **Group Model.** Physicians belong to an independent medical group that contracts with the HMO to serve members.
- **Network.** Physicians from more than one independent medical group contract with the HMO. A network may contain a few solo practices, but larger groups are the main health care providers.
- **Individual Practice Association (IPA).** Individual doctors in solo or small group practice contract with the HMO to provide care to members.
- **Mixed.** Two or more of the approaches listed above are combined.

PREFERRED PROVIDER ORGANIZATIONS (PPOS)

These organizations combine some of the advantages of conventional health insurance with the total coverage for a single fee provided by HMOs. Patients enrolled in a PPO can select their own doctor from a list of "preferred" physicians and hospitals that are members of the group. As in HMOs, the emphasis is on ambulatory care, in which patients are treated outside the hospital whenever possible. In the past few years, PPO enrollment has soared. Like HMOs, PPOs are recommended by employers and formed by unions, consumer groups, doctors, and for-profit medical companies.

MEDICARE AND MEDICAID

Medicare and Medicaid are federally subsidized health care plans that were established by Congress in the 1960s to help provide health care for citizens 65 and over, and those least able to afford medical insurance on their own. Medicare provides about 40 percent of the cost of acute care for elderly patients. Medicaid programs provide medical assistance to the poor and unemployed who meet the eligibility requirements, which vary greatly from state to state, while benefits for Medicare patients are mandated by the federal government.

LEVELS OF CARE WITHIN THE SYSTEM

What happens when you are sick? How does the complex medical system provide you with the care you need, from routine tests provided by the family doctor to highly specialized types of surgery and diagnosis? The system is divided into three levels: primary, secondary, and tertiary care.

PRIMARY CARE

Primary, or "first contact," care is provided in such settings as doctors' offices, hospital emergency services and outpatient clinics, and freestanding clinics. Internists, family practitioners, and pediatricians are the main providers of primary care, although many women use gynecologists as their primary doctors. A growing number of patients, particularly in HMOs, receive their primary care from nurse practitioners, who have training above the registered nurse level.

Primary care may be obtained by individuals on their own initiative, without referral by a doctor. It includes health maintenance in infants and children, immunizations, screening for infectious and communicable diseases, the monitoring of normal pregnancies, treatment of minor injuries and common complaints, and management of chronic diseases. Referrals from the primary level of care provide access to more specialized levels. The full scope of primary care, and pointers on choosing a primary caregiver, are discussed later in this chapter.

SHOULD YOU JOIN AN HMO?

Few forms of medical coverage are growing more rapidly than Health Maintenance Organizations (HMOs) and their close relatives, Preferred Provider Organizations (PPOs). Managed care plans are widely backed by employers and the federal government because they significantly reduce medical bills, but some consumer groups charge that they compromise patient care, and doctors maintain they interfere with the relationship between physician and patient. HMOs themselves cite studies showing that the care they provide is consistent with that obtained from a family physician.

No doubt, health care is different under HMOs and PPOs than it is under traditional fee-for-service medical insurance plans. While not for everyone, some plans do offer distinct advantages. You should consider an HMO if you:

- Are relatively healthy and very assertive.
- Have a chronic disease that requires regular attention. With regular visits, you can establish a relationship with a physician.

Don't consider an HMO if you:

- Have difficulty demanding attention.
- Go to a doctor only for acute care.

ADVANTAGES

- HMOs provide care at a single, fixed annual fee.
- HMOs provide for all medical needs: routine visits to the doctor, drugs, surgery, and hospitalization.
- There are no bills to submit, forms to fill out, or deductibles to pay.
- At each visit you simply present a membership card and usually make a small copayment.

DISADVANTAGES

- In most cases, the physician is very busy. The HMOs usually pay these doctors a fixed fee for taking care of the medical needs of all their patients. Some are assigned as many as 500 patients.
- For an HMO to pay for a visit to an outside specialist or hospital, you must obtain permission prior to consultation. PPOs are usually more flexible; a patient can consult a specialist, but must pay part of the fee.
- You won't have a trusted physician who has treated you for years, and you do not have total freedom in selecting a new physician. At many HMOs you are assigned a primary-care physician; others let you select from a list. In a PPO, you choose your doctors, both primary-care and specialist, from a list provided by the group. The primary-care physician is always the first doctor you see and the one who will refer you to a specialist, if you need one.
- It may be difficult to see the doctor. Your medical needs are screened when you show up at the office. The doctors supervise, but if you have a problem that can be handled by nurses or other trained staff, they will take care of you.
- Routine diagnostic tests or x-rays will be performed by technicians. Sometimes trained assistants will give routine examinations and injections. The physician may simply consult with and advise the staff, make diagnoses, and prescribe medication.

WHAT IF TESTS INDICATE THAT YOU HAVE SOMETHING POTENTIALLY SERIOUS?

- The primary-care physician decides how to proceed with your care.
- If you need to be hospitalized, you don't select the hospital but will be sent to an HMO-approved one.
- If you need a top-notch specialist some plans will pay for it, but others won't.
- You will be dealing with busy doctors who are encouraged to keep you out of the hospital. That does not mean you will be denied necessary treatment. Studies show that HMO doctors perform as many surgical operations as do other doctors, but they keep their patients in the hospital a shorter time.

SECONDARY CARE

Care at the secondary level is provided by a specialist or subspecialist, often in a community hospital or other similar setting. Specialties that are usually considered secondary level include obstetrics and gynecology, dermatology, otolaryngology, rheumatology, and cardiology. Access to this level of care may require a doctor's referral. Many people, however, refer themselves.

TERTIARY CARE

Tertiary care is highly specialized, high-technology care, oriented toward complex problems and out-of-the-ordinary procedures such as neurological surgery, open-heart surgery, and organ transplantation. Care of this kind requires extended training on the part of physicians, sophisticated equipment for diagnosis and treatment, specialized facilities and, in the great majority of cases, hospitalization for the patient. Tertiary-level care is found at hospitals associated with medical schools, at large regional referral centers, and at hospitals specializing in a particular disease or group of diseases. Physicians practicing at this level of the system are almost always subspecialists, with intensive training and experience in a narrowly defined field.

Third-level care also includes high-technology diagnostic tests that require highly trained technicians and sophisticated equipment that is too costly and complex to be used in smaller hospitals or doctors' offices. These range from cardiac catheterization, which must be done in an operating room, to advanced medical imaging technologies that give doctors a far more precise look at diseased organs than that provided by conventional x-rays. These include such costly medical imaging technologies as positron emission tomography (PET), which requires the use of extremely short-lived radioisotopes that can be obtained only from a cyclotron.

The different levels of care frequently overlap. Many specialists routinely provide primary care, a trend that should intensify with continued efforts to increase the numbers of primary doctors. From the patient's point of view, the important distinctions among the three levels of care may lie in the fact that referral is necessary at some levels within the system, and not at others.

....

HEALTH CARE PROVIDERS

MEDICAL DOCTORS

Although other health professionals are assuming many of the tasks that were once the sole province of medical doctors, the M.D. still plays the central role in the delivery of health care. To obtain an M.D. or Doctor of Osteopathy (D.O.) degree, a student must complete a course of instruction in an approved medical school or college of osteopathy in the United States or abroad. The usual course is four years, the first two largely classroom and laboratory study of the basic medical sciences, and the last two clinical experience, in teaching hospitals and clinics.

Medical school graduates must complete one year of approved postgraduate training before they can be licensed to practice medicine. This postgraduate year (formerly called "internship" and now called "PGY-l") emphasizes one of the major specialties and provides supervised clinical experience on various hospital services, including wards, clinics, emergency service, and, for surgical postgraduates, the operating room.

At the end of this year, the doctor takes the state board examination for a medical license. Students in U.S. medical schools take the National Board Examinations, which are given in three parts: part 1 at the end of the basic science years; part 2 at the end of the clinical or fourth year of medical school; and part 3 after PGY-1. All states except Texas and Arizona now recognize the National Board Examinations for state medical licensure, but they may have some additional requirements. (Doctors must hold a license from each state in which they practice; different states have somewhat differing standards.)

Formerly, many doctors entered general practice after this first year of postgraduate training. Today, most specialize, completing three to six years of additional in-hospital training ("residency" or PGY-2) in preparation for certifying examinations administered by one of the recognized national specialty boards, for example, the American Board of Internal Medicine and the American Board of Surgery. Most of today's family practitioners are in fact specialists, certified by the American Board of Family Practice.

Specialization is the almost inevitable response on the part of doctors to a field of knowledge that has become extremely broad and complex. It provides the opportunity to master a more limited body of material, and to feel confident in applying it to patients' needs. On the other hand, overspecialization is blamed for some of the soaring cost of health care in America. Many critics claim that our physician population is too heavily weighted toward specialists; as of 1993, 60.5 percent of doctors here were specialists and 39.5 percent primary-care physicians, while the ratio is approximately reversed in other industrialized nations.

To remedy the situation, health care reformers are seeking to increase the number of training slots for primary-care physicians and reduce the number of specialty programs. In addition, some medical groups have suggested that many currently practicing specialists could be diverted into primary care with minimal extra training.

Without some change in medical education, there stands to be a severe shortage of primary-care doctors. According to the Council on Graduate Medical Education, even if program slots for primary care increase in the next few years, there may not be enough primary physicians until the year 2040.

PHYSICIANS WHO PROVIDE PRIMARY CARE

Increasing medical specialization has resulted in a marked decrease in long-term contact between individual doctors and patients. Fragmentation of care among specialists—one doctor for this complaint, another for that operation—too often means that routine preventive care and health maintenance are neglected. While specialists' services may be needed on occasion, each individual should have a primary-care doctor. This is important, whether you select a doctor on your own or obtain your medical services from a group practice or an HMO.

The primary-care doctor is the one who oversees general health, both mental and physical, over a period of time, who knows the complete medical history, and who is aware of the individual's family situation, living environment, and occupation, together with any accompanying stresses. These doctors refer their patients to an appropriate specialist when necessary and also act as case manager when a patient is hospitalized, coordinating the actions and recommendations of specialists.

The choice of a primary-care doctor should be made when an individual is healthy and has the time to consider alternatives and evaluate impressions—not, as is so often the case, under conditions of pain and pressure. Until recently, the doctor selected as the primary-care physician was usually a general practitioner (GP). Such nonspecialists are now few and far between; their place has been filled by internists (specialists in general internal medicine) and family practitioners. Family practitioners treat people of all ages, not necessarily families as such.

Both internists and family practitioners, as well as osteopaths, are qualified to provide comprehensive health care and to diagnose physical and mental disease, but their training differs to some degree. Family practitioners and osteopaths have postgraduate training in such fields as internal medicine, minor surgery, orthopedics, and preventive medicine. The postgraduate training of internists places more emphasis on more serious disorders of the heart and lungs, the gastrointestinal and genitourinary tracts, and the endocrine glands, and on chronic diseases such as arthritis and diabetes.

While it is useful for a doctor to have some knowledge of the entire family, a given family may well require more than one primary-care physician. Different members have different needs.

SOURCES OF NAMES

A reliable source of doctors' names is a good hospital, which can provide the names of internists and family practitioners on their staff who practice in the community. A medical school is another good source: Many faculty members, in addition to their teaching responsibilities, practice privately.

A further source of names is the local medical society, which can provide a list of licensed practitioners in the area (the same list may be available at the local library). In some communities, public interest groups provide lists of doctors' names and addresses together with information on office hours and other practical considerations. Some have begun to supply comparative data on doctors' prices for common procedures. Friends and relatives, usually consulted first about a new doctor, are in fact the least reliable of the possible sources of names. They may, however, be able to give useful information about doctors' personalities.

CHECKING A DOCTOR'S QUALIFICATIONS

The next step is to find some assurance that the doctors under consideration have been well trained. Good training is a sine qua non, the basis of future competence. Medical directories, including the *Directory of Medical Specialists* published for the American Board of Medical Specialties, are available at most local libraries. (See the accompanying list of specialties and subspecialties covered in this directory.) From these reference works, you can learn which medical school a doctor attended (it should be fully accredited), and where postgraduate training or residency was done (large, well-known teaching hospitals usually have the best postgraduate training programs). The directory will also tell whether a doctor is board-certified (has passed the examination given by the appropriate American specialty board) or is board-eligible (has finished postgraduate training, but has not yet been in practice for two years, the minimum required before taking the certifying examination, or has not passed the board examination). An older physician may not have gone through the formal certification process; most younger ones have done so, although not all pass the certification examination.

A doctor's hospital appointments, also listed in the medical directories, are an important indicator of qualification and reputation. Most hospitals screen doctors carefully before appointment to the staff; most also periodically reevaluate their staffs' performance. In general, the better the hospital, the better qualified the doctor. Preferably, the doctor's appointment should be with a teaching hospital (one affiliated with a medical school or having a specialty training program), since such hospitals have highly qualified specialists on their staff and are familiar with sophisticated current techniques and equipment. However, many community hospitals enjoy a deservedly high reputation and provide excellent care.

In addition to being initially well trained, a doctor should be up-to-date in knowledge of the field. The American Board of Family Practice, among others, recognizes the importance of this in requiring periodic recertification of its members; for internists, and some other specialists, recertification (with the American Board of Internal Medicine) is on a voluntary basis. Signs that a doctor is keeping abreast of medical progress include attendance at approved continuing education courses, attention to current journals and publications, and participation in weekly hospital rounds. A teaching position at a hospital or medical school is a further and highly reliable indicator that a doctor is up-to-date, and recognized as being so by peers.

If a patient belongs to an HMO or PPO, he or she will probably have to choose from among a list of local participating primary-care physicians, and the primary doctor may be able to make referrals only to participating specialists, except in special circumstances. Even though choice may be somewhat restricted, many HMOs and PPOs have strict quality criteria doctors must meet before they can sign on as providers. Therefore, some of the legwork of checking out a doctor's qualifications may be unnecessary.

PRACTICAL CONSIDERATIONS

Practical considerations play an important part in the choice of a doctor. The doctor's office should be conveniently located, near public transportation, or with easy parking; the hours should be compatible with the patient's schedule. The hospital with which the doctor is affiliated (which is the hospital to which the patient will be admitted if seriously ill) should not be too distant.

If there is a family member who is house-bound, the doctor chosen should be willing to make essential house calls. The patient should also find out who covers when the doctor is not available and how emergencies are handled. A doctor should be willing to go to the hospital emergency room if a patient is admitted there. Other indications of a well-run practice are the efficiency of the doctor's answering service, the cleanliness and orderliness of the office, and the attitudes displayed by the doctor's nurse and secretary.

PERSONAL CONSIDERATIONS

Personal considerations include the doctor's sex and age. Some people have a strong preference for a doctor of the same sex. Regarding age, a younger doctor is more likely to be up-to-date than an older one. Older doctors have more clinical experience, and if they participate in continuing education courses and keep up with the professional literature, they should also be knowledgeable about current techniques.

Finally, there is the all-important factor of the doctor's personality. Once it has been established that the doctor is well trained and competent and that the practice is well run, individual reaction to the doctor as a person should be the decisive factor in the choice. It is usually possible to tell in a brief initial interview whether or not a particular doctor is someone with whom the patient can be comfortable.

THE DOCTOR-PATIENT RELATIONSHIP

A good relationship between patient and doctor demands input from both individuals. When evaluating a new doctor, or reevaluating a current one, the following points should be considered.

Communication. The doctor should give patients undivided attention, treating them courteously and unhurriedly and communicating in language that the patient can understand, avoiding jargon and answering questions willingly and clearly.

Emphasis on Prevention. Questions about smoking, drinking, sleep, and exercise, when accompanied by recommendations for promoting health, indicate that a doctor places due emphasis on the prevention of disease.

Presentation of Alternatives. When recommending a procedure or course of treatment, the doctor should present the alternatives, with a clear explanation of the risks and benefits involved.

Explanation of Tests. The doctor should be willing to explain the purpose of any tests that are ordered, and should report back promptly on test results. Tests should complement physical examination and counseling, not supplant it.

Habits of Referral. If the patient's condition is one that is beyond the doctor's competence, he or she should willingly refer the patient to a specialist. The patient should not, however, be referred to a specialist for routine or minor complaints. Underreferral could endanger the patient's health; overreferral means unnecessary expense. For major surgical procedures, a doctor should be willing, if necessary, to refer out of the community, to a large medical center.

Provision for Follow-up. Doctors should explain clearly what to expect, as far as can be predicted, and should alert the patient to signs or symptoms that indicate a need for a return visit. When a prescription is given, they should explain possible side effects and arrange for follow-up if the need arises. The patient should never be made to feel hesitant about telephoning a doctor.

Scheduling Checkups. The scheduling of routine checkups should reflect the now-solid evidence that the optimum frequency, in the absence of symptoms, is every five years before age 60, every two years between ages 60 and 65, and annually thereafter.

Tolerance of Differences. The patient's priorities and lifestyle may well differ from those of the doctor; the doctor should respect these differences. If the patient makes an informed choice about medical treatment, fully understanding the risks and benefits, the doctor should accept the choice or suggest another physician.

The patient also has responsibilities. Patients who claim a share in the decision making about their health are obligated to be knowledgeable and responsible. They should educate themselves by reading and by asking appropriate questions. They should be accurate and prompt in reporting symptoms and adverse drug reactions. They should follow their doctors' instructions and take medications as directed (a large percentage of patients do not). If they do not understand what a doctor is saying, they should make this clear. Finally, they must take the important preventive measures that only they can take: eating a proper diet, exercising regularly, avoiding excessive alcohol and all tobacco, dealing with stress, and seeing to it that their social lives and their work provide as much pleasure and fulfillment as possible.

THE OFFICE VISIT

A first-time visit to a doctor, or a "complete workup," has two distinct parts: the medical history and the physical examination. These, together with any tests that may be ordered subsequently, provide doctors with baseline information about their patients' physical condition.

The medical history is the single most important communication from the patient to the doctor and is the only part of an office visit that is under the patient's direct control. Frankness is the best guarantee of good care. (See chapter 11 for a more detailed discussion of information gathering.)

The physical examination follows the medical history. A good doctor will respect the patient's modesty, but not at the expense of thoroughness: The breasts, genitals, and anal area should be examined as carefully as other parts of the body. On the basis of the medical history and the physical examination, the doctor may order tests, make recommendations, write prescriptions, or perhaps refer the patient to a specialist. If the patient does not understand what is being said or what is proposed or what to expect, he or she should ask for a clear explanation. Studies show that patients are more dissatisfied about the information they receive from their doctors than about any other aspect of medical care; this can

be rectified with appropriate questioning. The patient may want to take notes on the answers.

THE SECOND OPINION

Getting a second opinion is a common practice among doctors, and many medical insurers are making it mandatory before they will agree to cover the patient. The guidelines are stated in the American Medical Association's principles of medical ethics: "A physician should seek consultation upon request; in doubtful or difficult cases; or whenever it appears that the quality of medical care may be enhanced thereby." Under these circumstances, and with their patients' permission, primary-care physicians consult with colleagues in appropriate fields, or refer their patients to these specialists. Similarly, specialists consult other specialists and subspecialists.

In hospitals, consultation is often automatic and mandatory, although it may be overused. Thus, a hospitalized patient should ask the primary-care physician acting as case manager to intervene if the number of specialists involved seems excessive.

Patients have a right to a second opinion. There are many circumstances in which it is appropriate for them to exercise this right and ask for a referral to a second or even a third doctor for consultation. In doing so, patients are not casting aspersions on a doctor's competence or judgment, but rather are taking a responsible attitude toward their own health and well-being.

A second opinion should always be sought if:

- *Surgery is proposed as the treatment for an ailment, or as an aid to diagnosis.* About 80 percent of all surgery done in this country is elective, that is, nonemergency. One in five of these operations is not indicated by either symptoms or test results. Even when symptoms and tests do indicate intervention, there may be serious questions as to whether the benefits of the surgery, such as enhanced quality or length of life, outweigh its costs and risks.

There is a growing feeling among doctors that, for the elderly in particular, many elective procedures do not enhance the quality of life. Thus, if surgery is recommended, the patient should get valid statistics both on the probable success of the operation and on the quality of life if the surgery is not done. Patients should also ask about other possible medical treatments; if surgery is proposed for diagnostic purposes, they should ask about alternative methods and whether the results will make a difference in treatment or life expectancy. In some cases, it is advisable to get a second opinion from a subspecialist in an appropriate medical field, rather than from another surgeon. However, a second opinion from another qualified surgeon is strongly indicated when the operation proposed is

MEDICAL SPECIALISTS AND SUBSPECIALISTS

Doctors who have completed one year of standard postgraduate training may then go into special postgraduate programs to qualify for one or more of the following medical or surgical specialties or subspecialties.

Allergy and immunology
Anesthesiology
Colon and rectal surgery
Dermatology
Emergency medicine
Family practice
Internal medicine
Cardiology
Endocrinology and metabolism
Gastroenterology
Geriatrics
Hematology
Infectious diseases
Medical oncology
Nephrology
Pulmonary disease
Rheumatology
Neurological surgery
Nuclear medicine

Obstetrics and gynecology
Ophthalmology
Orthopedic surgery
Otolaryngology
Pathology
Blood banking
Pediatrics
Pediatric cardiology
Pediatric endocrinology
Pediatric hematology-oncology
Neonatal-perinatal medicine
Nephrology
Physical medicine and rehabilitation
Plastic surgery
Preventive medicine
Psychiatry and neurology
Psychiatry
Neurology/special competence in child neurology
Child psychiatry
Radiology
Surgery
Thoracic surgery
Urology

one of several that are commonly done unnecessarily: hysterectomy, cholecystectomy (removal of the gallbladder), hernia repair, tonsillectomy, or operations to relieve varicose veins, hemorrhoids, or low back pain.

It may be difficult to get an unbiased opinion from a second doctor on the same hospital staff. If at all possible, go to a doctor in another hospital for a second opinion. In cases of disagreement among specialists, a third opinion may be helpful. Most insurance policies that cover consultation fees allow for this.

- *The diagnosis is of a rare or potentially fatal or disabling disease.* The original diagnosis may have been incorrect. Or, if it is correct, there may be new or experimental treatments available at an institution specializing in the disease.
- *Symptoms persist unrelieved and the doctor can provide no explanation for them.* Some diseases are incurable; the only treatment is palliative, one that alleviates pain and suffering without seeking to cure. Studies show that most people with a fatal disease are aware of their condition; most doctors

will answer a direct question frankly, if asked. In other cases, however, involving both acute and chronic disease, correct diagnosis and treatment should provide some relief of symptoms within a reasonable time.

- *Risks and benefits of proposed procedures are not satisfactorily explained.* The patient has a right to know the risks (including the dollar cost) and the potential benefits of any procedure or test.
- *Diagnostic procedures seem unnecessarily complex, expensive, or both.* Some doctors make excessive use of technology in borderline situations, either out of insecurity or a wish to cover themselves against malpractice actions.
- *The patient lacks confidence in the doctor's ability to do all that can reasonably be done.* Effective treatment demands trust. This is as valid a reason as any other for getting a second opinion.

HOW TO GET A SECOND OPINION

In the great majority of cases, the doctor should willingly supply the name of a specialist for consultation. A primary-care doctor can give the specialist the necessary background information and receive a speedy report and will know what tests and treatments have been done, thus saving repetition. In addition, the doctor is likely to have a good rapport with a specialist; this has important implications for the patient's future care.

The information given earlier in this chapter (see "Sources of Names" and "Checking a Doctor's Qualifications") can be used for finding a specialist if patients must find one on their own.

Any doctor who tries to dissuade a patient from seeking a second opinion should be dropped.

CONTINUING EDUCATION

Continuing medical education is an important part of doctors' on-going training. Many of the specialty boards and societies require periodic recertification of their members, following an examination, evidence of continuing medical education, and at least a brief review of patient records. More than 20 states require that doctors participate in accredited continuing education courses to maintain their medical practice licenses. The most effective way for a physician to keep up to date is to be on the staff of a hospital with an active teaching program. Some states—for example, New York—are considering relicensing examinations for all physicians.

CHOOSING A SURGEON

The question of experience is particularly important when choosing a surgeon. Surgeons must "practice" to maintain their skills. Also important is the hospital where the operation will be done and its experience with the procedure. Necessary equipment and skilled anesthesiologists or technologists will not be found in a hospital where the procedure is done infrequently. Major procedures demand the facilities of a major medical center; less complex surgery can safely be performed in a good community hospital. Finally, in choosing a surgeon, look for one with a good reputation, and one who will operate only if the consequences of surgery are less threatening than the condition that suggests that the procedure should be done.

In most cases, the primary care physician or consulting specialist recommends a surgeon, but patients always have the option of selecting their own.

CHOOSING A PSYCHIATRIST

While there are a wide variety of settings in which psychiatric care is given and a number of different theoretical approaches to the treatment of mental and emotional illness, for most people choosing a psychiatrist means finding a doctor who will provide individual treatment for what are sometimes called "problems of living." One of the best sources of names is a trusted family doctor. The department of psychiatry at a medical center or medical school can also provide names of psychiatrists with private practices, as can members of the clergy, social workers, and, for children, school guidance counselors.

The "match" between doctor and patient is perhaps more important in psychiatry than anywhere else in medicine. Therefore, the first few visits should take place with the understanding that there is no stigma attached to changing therapists if little or no rapport develops. At an early visit, a psychiatrist should take a medical and psychiatric history, and also maintain contact with the family doctor.

Patients should be wary of a psychiatrist who resorts immediately to medications, who "blames the victim," or who is reluctant to permit a second opinion. If visits are scheduled more often than once weekly, patients should ask why. As a general rule, an hour a week is sufficient for treatment, unless the patient feels a need for more time.

Increasingly, people who want psychotherapy are turning to clinical social workers and psychologists rather than to psychiatrists, whose approach is more likely to involve long-term treatment lasting several years. The advent of managed care, which generally places limits on the number of outpatient psychotherapy visits per year, has fueled this trend, as have studies demonstrating that most common mental illnesses—particularly depression and panic attacks—are best treated with short-term therapy and medication. For patients with these illnesses, the psychiatrist's role may be limited to prescribing and monitoring medication.

CHANGING DOCTORS

Common reasons for changing doctors include fees that are too high and complaints that the doctor is not available when needed or fails to give patients enough time. With complaints of this type, it is only fair to give the doctor the benefit of the doubt and discuss the problem; it may be that misinformation or a remediable lack of communication is at the root of the trouble. On the other hand, if the problem is a clash of personalities, discussion is fruitless and the patient should change doctors.

Patients should also change doctors if the doctor abuses power and attempts to tyrannize or bully them. Women should be aware that sexual harassment, while uncommon, does occur and is unacceptable.

Doctors are human and make mistakes; however, incompetence is an obvious reason for changing physicians. Incompetence is hard to define, but some common signs are prescribing over the telephone for new symptoms, acceding to all the patient's demands (no matter how unreasonable), and overtreating—for example, prescribing antibiotics for a cold. A genuinely incompetent doctor should be reported to the state medical society, which has the power to revoke a doctor's license to practice.

When the patient decides to change this should be discussed with the doctor, if the relationship has not deteriorated too far to do so. While the patient should be sensitive to the fact that the relationship with patients is one of the doctor's "rewards," the patient's first responsibility is to his or her own health. Patients who want records transferred to another doctor must give written authorization for this to be done.

DISTRIBUTION OF DOCTORS

In the 1980s, some experts predicted that the United States was facing an oversupply of doctors. The situation, however, has proved to be somewhat self-adjusting. Medical school admissions have declined and the increasing number of older persons has created a greater need for doctors. Physicians now spend 75 percent of their time caring for patients over the age of 65. By the end of the decade, that number is projected to reach 95 percent, which will require a substantial increase in the medical care doctors will have to provide. Already, those older than 65 account for more than 40 percent of days spent in hospitals and 30 percent of all visits to doctors.

The AIDS epidemic is also straining the medical system. It is already one of the largest users of doctors' time and hospital beds in certain areas, and it promises to get worse as the number of cases continues to increase. In addition, while doctors may have to compete for patients in affluent suburbs, there is still a severe shortage of medical care in most rural and impoverished areas. As the more attractive markets become flooded with doctors, perhaps more recent graduates will choose to locate in these underserved areas.

NURSES

The greatest number of health professionals are nurses, and experts believe their role in the health care system will expand as reform measures are put into practice.

EDUCATION OF NURSES

Training for nurses has been undergoing a change in the past few years, with a trend toward more education to provide care commensurate with the sophisticated and complex advances in modern medicine.

There are four educational routes to becoming a registered nurse: associate degree programs (2-year community college programs); diploma programs (3-year hospital-affiliated programs); bachelor's degree programs (4-year university-affiliated programs); and master's degree programs for college graduates who want to become nurses. The associate is a 2-year degree of 60 credits in liberal arts and nursing in which most or all of the clinical education takes place in a hospital setting. The number of 3-year diploma programs is declining as hospitals, in an effort to curtail costs, are withdrawing from the business of educating nurses.

The 4-year baccalaureate degree offers a bachelor's degree in nursing, or a bachelor of science degree with a major in nursing. The bachelor's degree offers a greater knowledge and understanding of community health services, leadership roles, and the psychosocial aspects of patient care than does the associate degree. Although legally all RNs are licensed to engage in the same basic practice, those with a bachelor's degree can make more comprehensive decisions and are prepared to assume clinical management roles. This does not mean a baccalaureate-educated nurse will necessarily leave the bedside, and indeed even nurses with advanced degrees often opt for advanced direct-care roles.

LICENSING

Upon completion of an educational program, a nurse is eligible to take the state licensing examination, which he or she must pass in order to receive a license and practice. Licensing for nurses protects the public by ensuring uniform, basic standards of practice.

EXTENDED ROLES

There has been an increase in formalized programs for the development of specialized nurses who can function in extended roles, taking over much routine screening and providing a partial solution to rising health care costs.

Nurse practitioners are RNs who have specialized in one of 13 primary-care areas, such as geriatrics or midwifery. Specialization is usually obtained through study for a master's degree. The certification examination in the specialty is voluntary, but increasingly it is viewed as necessary in order to practice. Currently, some 130,000 nurse specialists are practicing in hospitals, clinics, nursing homes, HMOs, and home care agencies.

Regulations governing a nurse practitioner's activities vary from state to state. Generally, nurse practitioners provide direct primary and preventive care, conduct routine physical examinations, monitor chronic conditions, provide nutrition and health counseling, and make referrals. They may make house calls, be in charge of a rural health facility, or be on the staff of a hospital, day-care facility, or nursing home. In some states, they can prescribe medication and can work autonomously; in others they are not licensed to prescribe medication and often work in some kind of partnership, however infor-

ALLIED HEALTH WORKERS

The following is a partial listing of health care professionals, excluding doctors and nurses.

Dental hygienists provide services for the maintenance of oral health, including cleaning and scaling of teeth.

Emergency medical technicians (EMTs) are licensed to provide immediate care in emergency situations (see Paramedics).

Home health aides provide personal care services and some nursing to the home-bound sick and disabled. Homemakers provide household services under similar circumstances.

Licensed practical nurses (LPNs) are trained and licensed to provide hands-on nursing care under the supervision of registered nurses or doctors.

Medical records personnel are responsible for keeping patients' records complete, accurate, up-to-date, and confidential.

Medical technologists perform laboratory tests to help in the diagnosis of disease and to determine its extent and possible causes.

Nurses' aides, orderlies, and **attendants** assist nurses in hospitals, nursing homes, and other settings.

Occupational therapists work with disabled patients to help them adapt to their disabilities. This may involve relearning skills needed for daily activities and modifying the physical environment.

Opticians fit corrective glasses and manufacture lenses.

Optometrists measure vision for corrective lenses and prescribe glasses.

Orthotists and **prosthetists** prepare and fit braces and artificial limbs.

Paramedics provide care in emergency situations. They are more highly trained than emergency medical technicians.

Pharmacists are trained and licensed to dispense medications in accordance with a doctor's prescription.

Physical therapists provide services designed to prevent loss of function and to restore function in the disabled. Exercise, heat, cold, and water are among the agents they use.

Physician assistants (PAs) perform physical examinations, provide counseling, and prescribe certain medications under a doctor's supervision.

Podiatrists prevent, diagnose, and treat diseases, injuries, and abnormalities of the feet. They are the only health care practitioners other than physicians who may use drugs and surgery to treat human illness.

Psychologists are trained in the study of human behavior. They provide counseling and testing in areas related to mental health. They also do individual and group therapy.

Radiologic technicians prepare patients for x-rays and take and develop x-ray photographs.

Recreational therapists provide services to improve patients' well-being through music, dance, and other artistic activities.

Registered dietitians (RDs) are licensed to apply dietary principles to the maintenance of health and the treatment of disease.

Respiratory therapists treat breathing disorders according to the doctor's directions, and assist in postoperative rehabilitation.

Social workers help patients with finances, insurance, discharge plans, placement, housing, and other social and family problems arising out of illness or disability. They also do individual and group counseling and therapy.

Speech pathologists and **audiologists** measure hearing ability and treat disorders of verbal communication.

mal, with a doctor. Many nurse practitioners work in underserved areas, which doctors generally do not find attractive, and provide services that are more accessible and less expensive than those provided by physicians.

A nurse midwife has specialty training in the management of essentially normal pregnancies and deliveries, in postpartum care, and continuing gynecological care. There are currently some 6,000 practicing nurse midwives in the United States, up from about 1,500 in the mid-1980s. Most nurse midwives work in collaboration with an obstetrician. By definition, the care given by nurse midwives is low-intervention care, with high priority placed on the preferences of patients, many of whom deliver in special birthing centers, which may be freestanding or associated with a hospital. Nurse midwife care is therefore often less expensive than a doctor's care.

At the other end of the educational scale are licensed practical nurses. Their training involves a one-year vocational program often entered in high school. The licensure is limited, involving a separate examination, and allows for practice of some selected tasks under the supervision of a registered nurse.

IN HOSPITALS

Hospitals employ 67 percent of registered nurses. This is the setting where most people come into contact with nursing care, but few know what to expect of a nurse or how to take advantage of nurses' expertise in planning care after discharge.

Within the hospital, nurses serve not only as the primary givers of care, but also as patients' advocates and coordinators of care, making sure that the correct nursing procedures are performed and the right diet and medications are given. In consultation with the primary physician, a nurse may be able to answer any questions a patient has regarding treatment or medications.

The nurse may act as liaison between the patient and physician, relaying messages or questions to the doctor. Often, hospitalization imposes problems upon family life after discharge. A nurse can give instructions on the use of technology, for instance, or answer questions regarding exercise, medication interactions, nutrition, and general lifestyle changes.

An emerging role in hospital nursing is that of the primary nurse, an RN who is responsible for planning and evaluating the total nursing care of a small number of patients, usually five to ten. A primary nurse works as a member of the health care team and is responsible for all nursing orders and hands-on care, as well as for arrangements after the patient's discharge from the hospital.

One aspect of a nurse's role that is often overlooked is his or her knowledge of community resources available to a patient after discharge. The nurse, in consultation with the primary-care physician, will determine whether a patient will need care after discharge. Before leaving the hospital, every patient should inquire about home care services and whether they are covered by Medicaid, Medicare, or health insurance. Those who will be receiving home care should have the name and telephone number of the home care agency and the date that someone will come. As the trend toward shorter and shorter hospital stays continues, adequate provisions for and understanding of home care has become critically important.

HOME CARE NURSES

The demand for nursing care in the home is increasing. As a less expensive alternative to extended hospital care or a nursing home, at-home nursing care appeals to private and government insurers. As a result of cost-cutting programs such as the federally mandated DRG (diagnosis-related groups) system, which specifies the number of hospital days that will be paid for in every type of hospital admission, patients are being discharged earlier—and oftentimes sicker—than previously. In addition, a growing number of aged individuals with chronic health problems can be ministered to at home for less money and less disruption than would be involved in nursing home admission. Home nursing care may also be appropriate after the birth of a baby or during recuperation from major surgery.

At-home nursing can be obtained in several ways. The patient who does not have a referral from a friend or physician can look in the Yellow Pages of the local phone book under nurses, home health services, or visiting nurses, and in the blue pages for the local health department. Any of these agencies should know whether the services are covered by Medicare, Medicaid, or private insurance policies.

Because such care is being given in a person's home and not in a hospital, a patient has some authority over when and by whom the care is given. The patient should find out in advance what kind of services will be given, over how long a period, during what time of day, and at what price. If an individual is not satisfied with the care, he has a right to a change.

Almost all nurses provided from visiting nurse agencies are baccalaureate educated. These nurses provide professional nursing services only. Ancillary work, such as washing hair, is done by home health aides. If such services are desired, agencies can often provide them. A visiting nurse is an excellent person to ask about community services, such as subsidized travel provided by religious and nonprofit groups or Meals on Wheels programs partially funded from municipal budgets.

Even if home nursing care is covered under Medicare

or Medicaid or private insurance, the services provided might not be sufficient. A family or individual can call a local Medicare office, visiting nurse agency, or the city or county health department and request a nurse to come into the home, assess the patient's needs for home care, and let the patient know what services are provided by insurance, government agencies, or other organizations. Depending on income and insurance coverage, the assessment will be free of charge, on a sliding scale, or provided for a fee for those whom the agencies consider able to pay for it.

ALTERNATIVE PRACTITIONERS

A 1993 report in the *New England Journal of Medicine* of a 1990 survey conducted by the Harvard Medical School found that fully one-third of patients surveyed used unconventional or alternative therapies such as chiropractic or nutrition therapy in the course of a year. These patients were overwhelmingly upper-middle class and educated, and they employed unconventional treatments in conjunction with conventional ones—without telling their physicians.

Medical experts reacted to the study with some dismay; not only were their patients going elsewhere for certain types of care, but they also were doing so without their doctors' knowledge.

NEW AGE MEDICINE ENTERS THE MAINSTREAM

Until fairly recently, any approach to health and illness other than traditional medicine as practiced by M.D.s and D.O.s was officially dismissed as quackery. Today, however, increasing numbers of well-respected physicians have begun to examine the possibility that some so-called alternative therapies—the Chinese techniques of acupuncture and acupressure, for example, as well as meditation and other relaxation techniques—might be valid adjuncts to medication, surgery, and traditional medical therapy.

This change in attitude began in the 1970s, with the development of comprehensive clinics for patients suffering from chronic pain. Recognizing that this type of debilitating, long-term pain stems from complex interactions among physical and emotional factors, pain specialists drew from a variety of disciplines, many of them nontraditional, to design their programs. Instead of focusing solely on pain-relieving medications and surgery to cut nerve pathways involved in certain kinds of pain, pain clinics make liberal use of therapies such as hypnosis, movement therapy (including yoga and the ancient martial art of t'ai chi, which provides relaxation while it enhances strength and flexibility), biofeedback (which allows patients to monitor and gain control over usually involuntary physiological processes such as fluctuations in blood pressure), and meditation.

In the late 1970s, the work of Dr. Herbert Benson, a noted Harvard cardiologist, gave further legitimacy to alternative practices, particularly meditation. Working with mildly hypertensive patients, Dr. Benson demonstrated that daily sessions of meditation were associated with significant decreases in blood pressure—decreases that were reversed once meditation stopped. Meditation and similar techniques, including hypnosis, are also helpful in coping with sleep problems, addictions, and stress-related symptoms.

More recently, Dr. Dean Ornish, and his preventive heart disease program in Sausalito, California, have achieved noteworthy results in treating heart patients with a combination of conventional therapies and a very-low-fat diet, regular exercise, and meditation. Some patients who adhere to his program have actually reversed some of the heart damage resulting from decades of poor health habits, including smoking and eating too much fat.

These and other successes with alternative medicine, along with the public's growing interest in these approaches, have prompted medical researchers to take a new look at the whole area. In 1993, the National Institutes of Health set up an office dedicated to funding well-designed studies that compare alternative and conventional treatments. Several respected teaching institutions, including Montefiore Medical Center in New York City and Tufts University School of Medicine in Boston, offer courses in unconventional medicine. And, in early 1994, Columbia University College of Physicians and Surgeons established its own Center for Alternative/Complementary Medicine in its rehabilitation department. The center will offer a second-year medical school elective course on alternative therapies and set up a data base including every study of these approaches from here and abroad.

USING ALTERNATIVES WISELY

Proponents of alternative medicine cite its distinct advantages over traditional care: It is usually simpler, less expensive, and less disruptive to the body as a whole. In addition, alternative practitioners tend to take a more personal approach to the delivery of care than traditional doctors do, spending more time with each patient and discussing every aspect of patients' physical, emotional, and spiritual lives.

While these merits are undeniable, it is important to remember that alternative medicine embraces a whole spectrum of approaches, from those with proven benefits to

EXAMPLES OF ALTERNATIVE PRACTICES

Discipline	Practitioners and Uses
Acupuncture, an ancient Chinese practice in which fine needles are inserted into body at specific points. Objective is to restore balance of life forces of yin and yang.	Practitioners are trained in traditional Chinese medicine, but 24 states require that they also be licensed medical doctors. In the United States, it is used primarily to treat pain; less commonly, it is used to treat nerve and circulatory disorders, but its efficacy in these areas has not been demonstrated.
Alexander Technique, a method of identifying and correcting faulty posture and movements.	Practitioners are trained and certified by North American Society of Teachers of Alexander Technique. Used mostly to treat back and neck pain arising from poor posture, occupational demands (experienced by violinists and computer operators, for example), arthritis, and structural abnormalities.
Aromatherapy, the use of aromatic oils that are inhaled, massaged into the skin, or added to bath water.	Practitioners are often trained in various massage techniques. Used mostly as a relaxation therapy, although it is also promoted to treat insomnia, headaches, and other stress-related or emotional problems.
Art therapy, the therapeutic use of visual arts such as drawing, painting, sculpture, or clay modeling.	Therapists are often mental health professionals with additional training approved by the American Art Therapy Association. Used to treat mental illness or aid in rehabilitation after a stroke or injury affecting eye-hand coordination.
Ayurveda, an ancient practice that originated in India and is still used there. Emphasis is on balancing three basic life forces, or doshas, to maintain wellness.	Ayurveda practitioners are not licensed in the United States, although chiropractors, physicians, and other licensed practitioners can incorporate its principles into their disciplines after several months of training in an ayurvedic institute. There are now several spas and ayurvedic clinics that teach its principles of maintaining health and well-being.
Biofeedback training, in which a person uses electronic monitors to control certain normally involuntary functions.	Training is offered by physicians, psychologists, physical therapists, and rehabilitation centers. Used mostly to control pain, muscle spasms, and stress-related disorders such as migraine headaches.
Chiropractics, spinal adjustment based on the theory that pain and some illnesses arise from misalignments, or subluxations, of the spine.	Practitioners who complete a course at a chiropractic college are licensed in all states. Used mostly to treat back and neck pain, although some chiropractors also offer nutrition counseling and incorporate other alternative therapies, such as homeopathy, into their practices.
Herbalism, which uses various herbs and other plants for medicinal purposes; a basic aspect of Chinese medicine and folk medicine.	Practitioners are often self-styled or incorporate herbalism into other alternative practices, such as naturopathy, aromatherapy, or homeopathy. Herbal remedies should never be substituted for a prescribed medication, nor should they be used without first checking with a doctor or pharmacist. Caution is needed because many herbal remedies can cause adverse reactions or interact with prescribed medications; some are also highly toxic.
Homeopathy, based on the theory that a minute amount of a substance that produces symptoms similar to those of an illness can stimulate the body's natural defenses to overcome that illness.	Homeopaths are licensed in only Arizona, Nevada, and Connecticut, but chiropractors and some physicians incorporate homeopathy, and homeopathic remedies are now sold in health food stores as well as many pharmacies. Used mostly to treat minor, self-limiting illness or as an adjunct to conventional mecicine. The substances themselves may be toxic but are so diluted that they are barely detectable and are unlikely to be harmful unless used as a substitute for a needed medical treatment.

EXAMPLES OF ALTERNATIVE PRACTICES (Cont.)

DISCIPLINE	PRACTITIONERS AND USES
Hydrotherapy, the use of water in various forms.	Hydrotherapy may be used by physical therapists, nurses, and other health professionals to manage pain and treat various muscle disorders. Therapists may also use water aerobics or other water exercise to maintain muscle tone and fitness in arthritis patients and others who have difficulty exercising on land. May also be used as a relaxation therapy.
Hypnotherapy, the medical use of a trance-like state.	Practitioners may be physicians, dentists, psychiatrists, or alternative practitioners. Used to control pain, overcome phobias, diagnose multiple personalities, and recall a traumatic event or past experience. Self-hypnosis may be taught to control pain or overcome a bad habit such as smoking or overeating.
Light therapy, the medical use of natural or artificial light.	May be administered by a physician, physical therapist, or mental health professional. Used to treat seasonal affective disorder—a type of depression that develops during the winter months—psoriasis and other skin disorders, neonatal jaundice, and sometimes to stimulate vitamin D production in shut-ins who are not exposed to natural sunlight.
Massage therapy, the use of various manipulative techniques.	Practitioners licensed by the American Massage Therapy Association must complete 500 hours of study; techniques are also practiced by physical therapists, osteopaths, chiropractors, sports medicine specialists, and other therapists. Used to alleviate pain and stiffness and overcome stress.
Movement therapies, which may use dance, exercise, and t'ai chi and other martial arts.	Practitioners are trained in their respective disciplines to use movement to achieve fitness, control stress, or, in the case of dance therapy, treat mental illness.
Music therapy, which uses music and rhythm to improve physical or psychological functioning.	Several professional organizations license music therapists, who are usually trained in physical therapy or another medical discipline. Used to improve coordination, encourage social interaction, and aid in rehabilitation. Some studies indicate it may also aid in pain control, but results are not consistent.
Naturopathy, which uses nutrition and other natural remedies to treat illness and maintain health.	Practitioners with an N.D. degree (doctor of naturopathy) have completed courses in one of three American schools, located in Toronto, Seattle, or Portland, Oregon. Regimens often call for high-dose nutrition supplements, herbal remedies, and a variety of "holistic" practices. Should not substitute for conventional medicine in the treatment of disease.
Pet therapy, the therapeutic use of animals.	Psychotherapists, physicians, social workers, special education teachers, and various other practitioners may employ various animals for therapeutic purposes. Used to treat disabled or emotionally disturbed children, withdrawn elderly, and as a part of rehabilitation. Specially trained dogs are also used as aids for the blind or deaf.
Relaxation therapy, which may include meditation, yoga, deep breathing, and guided imagery or visualization.	Practitioners are trained in their respective disciplines; techniques are used by physicians, psychotherapists, and many alternative practitioners. Used to control stress, pain, and stress-related illnesses.

those that can be downright dangerous, especially to individuals with serious illnesses who reject conventional treatments altogether. The extremely restrictive diets promoted by some nutrition therapists are far too low in calories and nutrients for patients with AIDS or cancer, for instance. Likewise, large doses of natural remedies or vitamins can act as drugs in the body, building up to toxic levels and disrupting normal processes.

When considering an alternative therapy, individuals should weigh the risks against the benefits, as they would with any type of medical treatment. For example, willow bark, marketed as an aspirin alternative that is easier on the stomach, contains salicylates, the same active ingredients as in aspirin. Either preparation—"natural" or processed—is contraindicated for use in children with a viral illness because of its association with Reye's syndrome, a potentially fatal condition that affects the brain and liver.

Finally, patients should always tell their physicians if they are consulting any type of alternative practitioner. The physician will know whether the alternative therapy can have adverse effects on conventional treatment, particularly medication. Likewise, physicians can monitor the results of both approaches, possibly becoming advocates for some aspects of alternative care.

AVOIDING MEDICAL FRAUD

Because many alternative practitioners are unregulated and many are unlicensed, charlatans are, unfortunately, overrepresented in unconventional medical fields. Such individuals usually make liberal use of scientific terms and references in promoting the remedy, treatment, or service offered. The press may label them "scientists ahead of their time." They may claim research experience or a degree that turns out to be fictional or one that can be bought without regard to qualifications. The number of adherents is not a reliable guide: Some products whose health claims are scientifically quite unproven have the backing of large and vociferous lobbies.

Here are a few key questions that may help determine whether a service or product is fraudulent.

Who, if anyone, endorses it? An endorsement by "millions of satisfied users" is meaningless. However, the endorsement of a national professional organization or a recognized voluntary health agency is conclusive.

Do experts in the field use or recommend the service or product? If it is worthwhile, they will do so.

Is the service or product guaranteed? No worthwhile medical service is ever guaranteed; a guarantee of success is not possible in medicine.

Does the remedy or treatment make sense? By definition, a fraudulent remedy has a false rationale. Common sense, supplemented by some research in the local library, will usually reveal the weak links.

OFFICE AND CLINIC CARE

According to an annual survey conducted by the U.S. Public Health Service, the average American has five visits a year with a doctor. The survey defines a visit as an encounter with a physician (or another health professional under the doctor's supervision) in the doctor's office, the patient's home (even by telephone), or in another ambulatory-care setting such as a clinic. Half of these visits are initiated by the doctor, as part of follow-up care.

Between the ages of 17 and 75, women tend to see doctors more often than men; before 17 and after 75 the rate is about equal. The number of visits rises steadily with age. Today, the poor, who are sick more, logically tend to see doctors more.

PUBLIC HEALTH SERVICES

Local health departments and voluntary health agencies provide health screening, which varies considerably both in availability and reliability. The services may screen for infectious or parasitic diseases or for chronic disorders such as high blood pressure, sickle cell anemia, or diabetes. Screening programs should offer, or make referrals to, follow-up medical care if needed.

NEIGHBORHOOD AND PRIMARY HEALTH CARE CENTERS

These programs, including migrant health care, date from the 1960s and were established to provide ambulatory care in underserved communities, mainly rural areas and inner-city neighborhoods. Much of the funding for these programs came from the Office of Economic Opportunity, and they were dismantled during the 1980s.

WOMEN, INFANTS, AND CHILDREN

This federally funded program has been estimated to save $3 in future health care costs for every $1 spent on prevention. It provides well-baby care, nutritious food, and nutrition education for pregnant women, infants, and children under 5 whose families' incomes fall below a designated level.

DISEASE PREVENTION AND CONTROL

These programs are usually undertaken by county or city health departments to provide immunization, screening, and follow-up care for communicable diseases. Typically they are concerned with immunization for childhood diseases such as diphtheria, measles, and polio; with

TABLE 1.1: SOURCES OF CARE

Source	Basic Features	Pros/Cons
Office-Based Practices		
Solo practice	One doctor practices alone in his or her own office.	Many doctors find this system less complicated than sharing. For patients, this system offers a more personal relationship with their doctor. For doctors, however, this type of practice usually means a heavier work load and more responsibility. Patients may have to go to a stranger for emergency care if the doctor is not available.
Partnership	Two or more doctors share space, equipment, and office staff.	Lowering the workload and spreading responsibility allows doctors to spend more time with each patient. The partners also share the costs of equipment, space and staff, a savings which may be passed on as lower fees. Patients have a familiar back-up doctor.
Group	A voluntary association of three or more doctors, a group practice may be single or multi-specialty. Hospital clinics provide ambulatory care to patients.	As with partnerships, other physicians are available for education and consultation, and costs are split.
Hospital outpatient department, or clinic		Many hospitals are now setting up first-rate clinics to provide ambulatory care. Clinics have bad reputations for long waits and substandard care, earned in the time when they were staffed mainly with medical students, residents, and volunteers.
Ambulatory Surgical Center, or surgi-centers	This center is used for minor surgery such as D&Cs (dilation and curettage), abortion, hernia repairs, tissue biopsies, and some forms of cosmetic surgery. Some are independent, others are affiliated with a hospital.	These centers offer lower cost alternatives to hospitals because they do not need sophisticated back-up equipment or long hospital stays.
Freestanding emergency center	Also called urgicenters, these facilities, often set up by for-profit, private groups, provide 12-to-24-hour care on a drop-in basis. The centers usually treat cuts requiring stitches, sprains, and bruises, and upper respiratory infections.	Urgicenters can fill several needs in a community when a hospital is far away. They are usually open longer than doctors' offices and can keep costs down because they don't have hospital beds to support. Urgicenters tend to be more expensive than doctors' offices but less than emergency centers. They may tend to overuse procedures, since this is how they make money.
Community Health Facilities		
School health program	In elementary and high school, this program is usually coordinated by a school nurse who administers first aid and may also keep track of vaccinations and provide follow-up and consultation with parents. Most colleges and universities also provide health services, often with ambulatory services.	The comprehensiveness of health services offered varies from one community and school to the next.
Industrial health program	Today, employers are not only the major "third party payers" of health care costs, many also offer direct services on the job ranging from treatment of work-related injuries and minor illnesses to periodic physical exams and general medical and dental care. At some workplaces, services such as alcohol abuse counseling, stop-smoking clinics and fitness programs are also available.	Services offered vary from one company to the next. Some small companies cannot provide health insurance for their employees; some large companies have their own comprehensive health services.

care for tuberculosis and sexually transmitted diseases; and with influenza immunization for the elderly. The programs vary widely from community to community. (For information on community-based programs for people with mental, physical, or emotional disabilities, see appendix C, Directory of Resources.)

HOME CARE

Care at home may be appropriate when a patient has an acute illness or is recovering from an episode of acute illness (as, for example, after hospitalization for a heart attack) or when a person is suffering from a chronic illness. It is also the most common setting for care of the elderly. For that reason, community programs designed to help augment home care, such as adult day-care centers, medical day-care, and mental health day-care, are discussed in chapter 2, Meeting the Health Care Needs of the Aged and Disabled.

HOSPICES

Hospice care for the terminally ill is available in a growing number of communities. A hospice may be an independent, freestanding institution, or a special wing in a hospital, or simply a few hospital beds that can be made available to the program as needed. Many hospice programs are carried on in patients' homes.

Basic to the hospice approach is total care of both patient and family to minimize the two greatest fears associated with dying: fear of isolation and fear of pain. Care is palliative, with emphasis placed on the careful control of pain and the management of other symptoms of terminal illness. Patients remain at home as long as possible; many die there. While the patient is at home, families typically provide much of the care, receiving assistance and support from a team consisting of a physician, nurses, counselors, home health aides, and other workers as needed. When the patient must be admitted to the hospice facility, care by the same team provides continuity. Bereavement counseling and self-help groups may also be provided, but insurance rarely covers them.

Patients are accepted into hospice programs at their own request, with a doctor's referral. A stipulation is that the prognosis be no more than six months of life. This may create difficulties for patients whose illnesses are terminal but unpredictable.

HOSPITALS

Hospitals combine "healing" and "hotel" functions, providing a place where patients with serious illnesses are taken care of. Frequently, the two functions are at odds. When there is a conflict, hospital personnel usually place the hotel function in second place, whereas patients are often inclined to see things differently.

IS HOSPITALIZATION NECESSARY?

More and more often the answer is no. The United States still has one of the highest per capita rates of hospitalization in the world, but efforts to curb increases in medical costs are bringing that rate down. After years of steady increases, in the early 1980s the federal government enacted a program to reduce payments for Medicare patients by putting in a payment schedule known as diagnosis-related groups (DRGs). Since then the number of patients in hospitals has fallen, the price of a hospital room has dropped, thousands of hospital employees have been laid off, and companies that set out to reap huge profits by running hospitals are incurring losses.

Hospitals now often perform easier procedures on an outpatient basis. According to the American Hospital Association, about 54 percent of surgeries in 1992 were performed on an ambulatory basis.

Hospital care is still the most expensive of all care, accounting for $80 of every $100 spent on health care. It can also be dangerous. In one of seven hospitalized patients, some problem arises as a result of the hospitalization. Among these problems are infections, falls and other accidents, adverse reactions to medications, complications of surgery, and problems traceable to mistakes on the part of hospital workers.

The expense of hospitalization, together with greatly improved drug therapies that enable many patients to be treated at the doctor's office, has in fact contributed to the recent drop in hospital use. Another contribution to the decline appears to be a general unwillingness to repeat the hospital experience.

THE TYPES OF HOSPITALS

Hospitals are categorized as acute or extended care depending on the average length of stay.

THE HOSPITAL HIERARCHIES

Because hospitals have both a healing function and a hotel function, they have two coexisting power structures. The two are mutually dependent and often overlap each other. Nevertheless, their focus of interest is different, and clashes are not unknown.

In a community hospital, the head of the medical hierarchy is a physician, whose title may be medical director, chief of staff, or physician-in-chief. This position may be rotated on an annual basis among the physicians on the staff. Alternatively, the medical director may be elected by the other physicians or may be appointed by the hospital's governing body, usually a board of trust-

TABLE 1.2: TYPES OF HOSPITALS

Type of Hospital	Basic Features	Pros and Cons
Community hospitals	The most common type of hospital in the United States. They range in size from 50 to 500 beds; they usually provide secondary-level care and take care of everyday medical and surgical problems. General hospitals may be either nonprofit, and funded by the government and community, or for-profit.	The choice of specialists and facilities offered depends on the hospital; larger hospitals tend to have a fuller complement of specialists and equipment. These hospitals usually provide good personalized secondary-level care.
Teaching hospitals	Hospitals with students in training. Virtually all have ties with a major medical school. They can range in size from a few hundred to several thousand beds. These hospitals provide care at all three levels: primary, secondary and tertiary. They may be owned by the government, university or a for-profit group.	These hospitals offer some of the highest level care available, especially for complex or technically difficult illnesses. Patients may find some drawbacks, however. Patients, by virtue of being in a teaching hospital, are "teaching patients." They usually are examined by students, as well as doctors, and may have to give their medical histories several times and have their case discussed by a group of strangers. Some may find this treatment impersonal.
Public hospitals	Owned by the federal, state, or city governments and operated by the state, city, or county department of health. They include municipal short-term hospitals, which provide care for the indigent, and some teaching hospitals. Other hospitals wholly supported by public funds are county hospitals, public service health hospitals and the hospitals run by the Veterans Affairs Administration.	These hospitals offer excellent care at subsidized prices. However, some might find them crowded and lacking some of the amenities available at private hospitals.

ees. In small hospitals, the medical director is directly responsible for the care given in all the various medical departments, such as surgery, medicine, and pediatrics. In larger hospitals, each of these departments has its own elected or appointed chief of service, who is responsible in turn to the medical director.

The medical director receives a salary from the hospital during his or her tenure in the position. Other doctors usually are not salaried, nor do they pay the hospital for the use of its facilities. In university hospitals, the hierarchical structure is complicated by the superimposition of an academic structure. The chief of staff for surgery, for example, will also be a professor of surgery at the medical school and (usually) chairman of the school's department of surgery.

Doctors practicing at university hospitals are either full-time or part-time. Full-time doctors are employees of the university and spend their time in research and teaching, including bedside teaching and, thus, patient care. Part-timers have some university responsibilities but also see private patients. Postgraduate trainees in university and other teaching hospitals provide the exception to the general rule that hospitals do not pay the doctors who work there.

At the top of the "hotel" hierarchy of the hospital is the chief administrator (often called the chief executive officer). Increasingly, hospital administrators hold advanced degrees in the administrative rather than the medical field, as was the case in the past. For the hospital administration, the hospital is a complicated business enterprise that must function in an efficient and solvent fashion while still serving as a center for patient care and often also as a locus for medical education and clinical research.

The hospital's nursing department, focused toward the healing function, is nevertheless responsible to the hospital administration. Nurses are hired and paid by the hospital. Where a hospital is affiliated with a school of nursing, some of the nurses will be students working under the supervision of the nursing school faculty. However, because of the size of the nursing staff (nurses are needed for three shifts a day, 7 days a week), the great majority of nurses in any hospital are hospital employees.

Nurses' aides and orderlies are also hired and paid by the hospital administration, as are laboratory technicians, members of the housekeeping department, and the business and clerical staff. Clinical support services, for example, physical therapy, occupational therapy, the pharmacy, the blood bank, and diagnostic testing centers such as electrocardiography and electroencephalography, are within the purview of the hospital administration rather than that of the medical staff.

SPECIAL FACILITIES

Emergency Departments. Most hospitals have an emergency service, although it may not be open around the clock, or may not have a team of physicians (or even one physician) present day and night. Emergency departments have the equipment (including resuscitative machinery) necessary for treating common emergency conditions, and they have immediate access to the full range of hospital services. In descending order of priority, emergency departments act first, to save lives immediately endangered; second, to treat illnesses or injuries that might become life threatening; third, to deal with emergency or urgent problems that are not dangerous but require treatment; fourth, to evaluate and treat minor complaints; and fifth, to treat chronic complaints.

In recent years, the hospital emergency department has become a primary-care facility for everyday ailments. Large city hospitals often have a "triage" nurse on duty at the door to divide urgent cases from those that can be cared for in an outpatient clinic. Unless a patient's condition is immediately life threatening, a wait is to be expected. How long the wait is will depend on the urgency of the complaint relative to the urgency of the complaints of other patients.

Emergency rooms may not legally refuse to treat a person in need of true emergency care, even if that person cannot demonstrate an ability to pay. Care given in an emergency room is much more expensive than that given in a doctor's office, and unless the situation is demonstrably an emergency, most insurance policies do not cover the hospital bill.

Intensive Care Units. Almost all large community hospitals, and many smaller ones, have an intensive care unit (ICU); the quality of care provided is variable. Intensive care units provide close monitoring, observation, and quick responsive treatment to patients who need this kind of supervision, among them patients with heart failure, recent stroke victims, and, in hospitals that do not have a shock–trauma center (see below), victims of serious accidents. Certain surgical cases go routinely from the operating room to the intensive care unit; others go routinely if the patient is in a particular age group. The nurse:patient ratio is usually 1:2 (as opposed to 1:8 on regular floors).

With its sophisticated and noisy medical machinery, an intensive care unit can be an alarming place. Patients are often heavily sedated. There is no privacy because of the necessity of constant observation, and patients are allowed no personal possessions except dentures and essential toilet articles. Visits are usually limited to the closest relatives (no children) and restricted to short time spans such as, for example, 5 minutes every 2 hours.

Many patients in special care units experience transient psychiatric difficulties (the "intensive care unit syndrome"). Distortions of reality, sometimes progressing to auditory or visual hallucinations and then to frank paranoia, may evolve after the first 3 to 5 days in an intensive care unit or coronary care unit (CCU). The syndrome appears to be related to sensory deprivation, lack of human contact, and an environment in which night and day are indistinguishable. Some units have added psychiatric social workers to the team to counteract this emotional deterioration. Families can help by making their brief visits as substantive as possible.

Coronary Care Units (or Coronary Observation Units). Only the smallest of the U.S. hospitals now lack a coronary care unit. These units, offshoots of the ICU, have grown enormously in popularity in the past 20 years—past the point, some experts maintain, of cost-effectiveness. Coronary care units provide constant monitoring for people who have had a heart attack or who need observation for a variety of cardiac conditions. Emphasis is placed on rest and the gradual reduction of stress; caffeine and tobacco are banned. Visiting is geared to the needs of the patient.

Neonatal Intensive Care Units. Neonatal intensive care units (NICUs) are found in major medical centers. They specialize in the problems of the newborn, whose fluid requirements, oxygen management, temperature control, and drug dosages are unique. The infants are housed in "isolettes," which both reduce the risk of infection and provide for individualized temperature and oxygen needs. Premature babies weighing as little as 2 pounds have a good chance of survival, given ideal care, in a neonatal intensive care unit. How much physical contact parents may have with their newborn will depend on the infant's condition and the policies of the unit.

Shock-Trauma or Critical Care Centers. These centers, which are generally located in major metropolitan areas, provide specialized care for the victims of serious accidents. An ancillary but vital part of the system is a mechanism for transporting the injured to the center, with life-support equipment and trained personnel available en route. Several centers have established "helivac" units using helicopters.

Shock-trauma centers have a full complement of life-support equipment, immediate access to laboratories, and on-call specialists in every medical field, including the newly recognized field of intensive care.

Other special units that are generally available only in large medical centers include burn units, geared to the special needs of those who have suffered extensive burns; renal dialysis units for the treatment of hospitalized patients and outpatients with chronic kidney disease; neurological injury units that specialize in injuries involving the brain or the spinal cord, or both; and cardiac rehabilitation units for those who have had coronary artery bypass surgery.

ELECTIVE SURGICAL ADMISSIONS: WHAT TO EXPECT

The first questions to ask are: "What are the alternatives?" and "Is this surgery necessary?" If the weight of evidence convinces the patient, then the following expectations should be considered.

An elective procedure is a nonemergency procedure and will therefore be scheduled with several days' or even months' notice. Generally, the preoperative tests—a blood test, a chest x-ray, and blood pressure check at the minimum—are done on an outpatient basis a few days before the operation, and admission takes place the night before or the day of the surgery.

Before admission, patients should check with the hospital's business office about financial obligations. In all likelihood, their health insurance will cover much of the hospital expense; how much, of course, depends on the policy. No insurance policy, however, will cover a private room, which may be as little as $10 or as much as $300 more a day than a semiprivate room. It may not cover such personal expenses as a bedside telephone, or private duty nursing. The insurance policy will also probably cover most of the expense of medication and laboratory work (these are billed separately from the hospital room) and at least some part of the physicians' fees. The patient should ask whether the choice of room will be reflected in the bill: Some doctors charge more when the patient elects a private rather than a semiprivate room.

Also before admission, the patient should contact the admitting office about room preference and be prepared to give the diagnosis, doctor's name, date for which surgery is scheduled, age, and whether he or she smokes. Patients should ask what time they are expected to check in at the admitting office and whether they are expected to make prepayment for private rooms.

Admission Procedures. The basic purpose of these procedures, which can be time-consuming, is to ensure that the admission is voluntary, legal, and financially sound. The patient will be asked to sign several financial forms and the hospital's Conditions of Admission (or Consent to Treatment) form. In signing the latter form, the patient voluntarily consents to treatment; this is the valid consent that precludes the hospital's liability for assault and battery in the event the treatment is unsatisfactory.

The patient should bring the following to the admissions office: insurance card (or a check for partial prepayment of the hospital bill); name, address, and telephone number of employer; social security card; and the name, address, and telephone number of someone who should be informed of any changes in the patient's condition.

Packing should be limited to toilet articles, a bathrobe and slippers, reading materials, a notepad and pencil, and no more than $10 in cash. Jewelry and valuable watches should be left at home. The patient should bring a list of the medications taken routinely, with details as to strength and dosage, but should leave the medications themselves at home.

Preoperative Routines. Preoperative routines include a medical history and physical examination for the hospital records. In a teaching hospital, the history and physical will probably be done by a postgraduate trainee and may be repeated by a medical student. The patient has a right to refuse more than one history and physical. However, one doctor (or student) may see or feel something that another overlooks and it is therefore advisable to agree.

A nurse will repeat many of the questions included in the medical history in order to make a "nursing assessment." Questions about medications, home situation, and the support systems available to patients help provide comprehensive care and give information that will be helpful in discharge planning.

The patient will be asked to sign a form consenting to surgery. This form states that the "nature of the operation" has been explained. Before signing the form, the patient should be sure that he or she has a good understanding of what will be done and what the risks and anticipated benefits of the procedure are. Patients should be certain that the procedure described is the one wanted and that body parts (including "left" or "right") are specified. The surgical consent form may cover a surgeon's options—for example, "left breast biopsy; possible left radical mastectomy." All such options should be explained before surgery.

Consent forms similar to those for surgery are required for invasive tests (for example, cardiac catheterization, angiography, percutaneous liver biopsy). The same type of information should be given to the patient, before signing, as is given before surgery.

Prepping. Prepping for surgery is done the night before the operation or first thing in the morning the day of the surgery. Since hair harbors bacteria, the site of the operation and a large area around it will be shaved and painted with antiseptic. If it is anticipated that a skin graft may be needed, that site will also be prepared.

An anesthesiologist (chosen by the surgeon) should talk to the patient the night before the surgery to inquire about previous experiences with anesthesia and any drug allergies. If there is an option as to the type of anesthesia to be used (local, spinal, or general), this should be explained and the pros and cons of the different types explored.

The Operation. The patient will be allowed nothing to eat or drink for 12 or more hours before the operation. The stomach must be empty when a general anesthetic is given because of the risk of vomiting and aspirating the vomit while anesthetized. Even if the operation is to be done under local anesthetic, the empty stomach precaution will be observed, as unforeseen circumstances may arise, making a general anesthetic necessary.

About 1 hour before the operation, the patient will be given a sedative and will then have to remain in bed. Some 20 minutes later, he or she will be moved onto a gurney (a stretcher on wheels), asked to remove eyeglasses and dentures, and taken to the operating suite.

The patient is more likely to feel dehumanized in the operating room than anywhere else in the hospital. The surgical team—the surgeon, the anesthesiologist, the operating room nurse, and their assistants—is technologically oriented and works with speed. Patients will be closely observed but should not expect much "tender loving care." With general anesthetic, the patient will be completely unaware of what is going on; even with a spinal or local anesthetic, the patient will be less alert because of the preoperative sedation.

After any operation that requires a general anesthetic, patients are taken from the operating room to a special recovery room. Here, vital signs (pulse, temperature, respiration, and blood pressure) will be checked every few minutes for an hour or so, to ensure that the patient is recovering satisfactorily from the anesthetic. In addition, a nurse will call the patient's name and ask him or her to respond, testing the extent to which the anesthesia has worn off.

Recovery. The patient will be taken back to his or her room once the vital signs have stabilized and the anesthesia has begun to wear off. Pain at the site of the operation is to be expected; there may also be nausea and vomiting. Medications are available for the relief of these postoperative symptoms, and patients should make their needs known.

One aftereffect of general anesthesia is an increase in lung secretions and a consequent risk of pneumonia. Turning in bed and breathing deeply will help the patient mobilize these secretions; coughing brings them up. Turning, coughing, and deep breathing (TCDB in nurses' shorthand) may be painful but are essential to keep the lungs clear. Early ambulation has much the same effect and the additional benefit of preventing muscle deterioration, which can begin after only a few days' immobility.

A spinal anesthetic alters the pressure of fluids within the spinal column. It is important for the patient to follow postoperative instructions carefully so as to avoid the headaches that may accompany pressure changes as the spinal fluid readjusts. Usually it is recommended that a patient who has had a spinal anesthetic lie completely flat (on the back, and without a pillow) for 12 hours or more.

If the patient has had an abdominal operation, a nasogastric tube (running from the stomach up through the esophagus and exiting at the nose) will have been put in place at the end of the operation, to remain for several days. This tube carries out stomach gases that might otherwise accumulate and cause great discomfort. Even so, the patient is likely to have some gas pain on the third day after the operation when the gastric juices become active again.

Depending on the operation, the patient may have other tubes that drain excess fluid from the site of the surgery. There may also be an intravenous tube that delivers fluid and possibly nutrients to a vein in the arm.

PATIENTS' RIGHTS

In 1973, following years of bad publicity and pressure from consumer groups, the American Hospital Association formalized a list of the rights of hospitalized patients. This list can be found posted in hospital corridors (in accredited hospitals, it is mandatory to post it), and it is often printed in patient information handbooks (see chapter 3, Medical Decision Making).

The Patient's Bill of Rights was adopted by the American Hospital Association in an attempt to improve relations between patients and hospitals. It has been promoted by many as a legal document, or as a document that has the potential of being legally binding. However, enforcement of any of these rights would be difficult: They deal to a large extent with intangible factors—consideration, respect, confidentiality, reasonableness—that affect the relationship between patients and those who treat them. Nevertheless, patients who feel that their rights have been violated should always raise the issue with their doctors and the hospital staff. (See "Remedying Deficient Hospital Care" later in this chapter.)

THE PATIENT'S ROLE IN THE HOSPITAL

Patients who understand the goals of their medical programs, and cooperate actively with those who are treating them, can make a great difference in the speed of their recovery. Their rights as patients include the right to a full disclosure, in lay language, about their condition and the procedures that are planned. (See the section on patients' rights and the Patient's Bill of Rights in chapter 3.) It is their responsibility to exercise this right by asking questions about anything that is not clear to them. (It may be helpful for them to have written notes about questions to ask and also to make notes on the answers.) A patient has a right to read his or her own medical record.

A patient should ask the doctor in advance for details about recovery—whether there will be discomfort or pain and for how long, when is a reasonable time to expect discharge, and how long activities may be limited afterward. Discharge of the patient as soon as it is medically advisable, with continued convalescence at home, in an extended-care facility, or in a nursing home, is in everyone's best interest, and the patient should be willing to leave as soon as the doctor gives an okay.

IN CASE OF DEATH

If the patient's illness is serious, and there is a possibility of death while in the hospital, there are certain things that should be taken into consideration. The patient may, for example, want to consider donating tissues or body organs (the corneas, skin, bone, pancreas, or kidneys, among others), or the whole body. In many states, patients 18 or older can authorize that all or any parts of their body be used for specified purposes after death, under the Anatomical Gift Act (see chapter 3). Many states now require hospitals to inquire about organ donation when a patient dies in the hospital. Alternatively, the patient can let the immediate family know of his wishes; they can then give the necessary permission. Those wishing to donate their bodies to medical education (dissection of the human body is an essential part of students' training) should contact the department of anatomy, or the dean's office, at any medical school. Usually, bodies used for these purposes are later cremated.

If a member of the family dies while in the hospital, the question of an autopsy may arise. In some hospitals, autopsy is mandatory under certain circumstances, for example, a sudden or unexpected death, or a death during surgery. Usually, however, an autopsy is done at the hospital's request and with the family's permission. (Permission is requested in priority order, from the surviving spouse to more remote relatives.) Many people have trouble deciding whether to authorize an autopsy. There are, however, at least two good reasons for doing so. First, since several diseases are known to have hereditary risk factors, families may be able to take steps to avoid succumbing to the same disease. Although the cause of death may seem to be clear, this is not always the case. There is a reported 40 to 50 percent difference between diagnoses made before death and the findings at autopsy.

Second, an autopsy may contribute indirectly to the health of future generations of the country as a whole. Following an autopsy, the body is returned to the family for disposition.

THE RIGHT TO DIE

In some cases, patients do not recover from surgery, they are not cured by the most advanced treatment, or they experience traumatic injuries that leave them in a comatose condition in which they are totally dependent on life-support machinery.

The much publicized case of Karen Ann Quinlan, a New Jersey woman who failed to regain consciousness after consuming a combination of drugs and alcohol, focused national attention on the use of technology to sustain life. After a lengthy court trial, her family won the right to order her to be disconnected from life-sustaining devices. Since then, the courts have ruled in a similar manner in other cases and some five states have passed laws that set forth the conditions under which a patient or the immediate family can ask that extraordinary measures to sustain life not be taken. Most use the total absence of any activity in the brain to legally signify death.

Both the family and the family physician should be aware of the patient's wishes before such a situation arises. Before they enter the hospital, it is wise for patients to discuss what life-sustaining measures they wish taken. The "living will" is an excellent guide to situations in which extraordinary lifesaving procedures should be halted. (For more information on living wills, see chapter 3.)

HOSPITALS AND CHILDREN

Hospitalization is a traumatic experience for any child, but especially for a child under 5. Fear of abandonment by the mother (normal at this stage of development) will be exaggerated by the event. Studies have shown that trauma can be markedly reduced through play. A doll and some of the hospital supplies used in the child's care (or their play equivalents) provide the child with a vehicle for dealing with inevitable anxiety.

Sick children regress, going back to wetting their beds, or to depending on a favorite blanket or toy. They may become extremely fussy about food and need the reassurance of the familiar. If possible, parents should stay with a very young hospitalized child around the clock; today, most children's hospitals and pediatric wards encourage this practice. A child who is old enough to have a bedside phone and use it properly can be left alone more.

In many hospitals, all children under 16 are accommodated in the same pediatric unit. For an adolescent, this may present a problem.

THE QUALITY OF HOSPITAL CARE

Quality assurances: Most hospitals and nursing homes are accredited (approved) by the Joint Commission on Accreditation of health care organizations. The accreditation process is the major voluntary mechanism for hospital review and assurance of quality. The commission sets optimal rather than minimal standards in numerous areas, including the hospital's compliance with patients' rights; the quality of medical, nursing, dietetic, and other services; pathology reports; drug use; record keeping; the management of the hospital and its long-range planning; the relationship of the hospital to its neighboring community; and the safety and maintenance of buildings and grounds.

Accreditation is usually given for 2 years, after which the hospital is inspected again. A hospital that fails inspection in significant areas, or that fails to take corrective action for problems that have been found, will have its accreditation revoked. While accreditation is an assurance that certain standards have been met, it is no guarantee of quality. However, lack of accreditation, or a recent loss of accreditation, should raise serious questions.

The federal government, acting through Professional Standards Review Organizations (PSROs), also regularly audits the quality of hospital care. These organizations monitor the appropriateness and quality of services provided to patients whose health care is federally financed by reviewing admissions, certifying the need for continuing treatment, conducting medical care review, and reviewing extended or extremely costly treatment. Hospitals that fail to correct deficiencies identified by PSRO audits lose their ability to collect Medicare and Medicaid payments—a financial catastrophe for most hospitals today.

Hospitals also have their own internal review mechanisms. Quality assurance review committees meet regularly and are concerned with such questions as the appropriateness and length of patients' hospitalizations, patients' complaints, and reports on surgical specimens. Many of the questions that concern these internal reviewers also concern the Joint Commission on Accreditation, thus providing a double-check. The caliber of the physicians on a community hospital's staff is largely determined by the staff's medical credentials committee (in teaching hospitals, this function is performed by ad hoc appointments committees). Credentials committees review the qualifications of new applicants for a position on the hospital's staff and deal with requests for hospital privileges.

Although doctors are legally permitted to perform the full range of medical and surgical services once they have been licensed, in point of fact their practice will be largely determined by their hospital privileges, which are in turn determined by the credentials committee. Doctors' hospital privileges limit what types of patients they may treat in the hospital, what procedures they may do, and under what circumstances they must consult with a colleague.

INFORMAL EVALUATIONS

As when choosing a doctor, it is wise to investigate local hospitals ahead of need. Patients have less control here, however, as admission to one hospital rather than another may depend on such factors as their doctors' admitting privileges, the type of disease they have and the kind of treatment it requires, or whether it is an emergency admission. Many doctors, moreover, prefer to limit their practice to one hospital, gathering all their patients under one roof not only for convenience, but because such an arrangement often gives them a better chance of getting a bed when one is needed.

If a patient's doctor has admitting privileges at several hospitals, he or she may be able to give an appraisal of the quality of care at the different institutions. In addition, a local nursing association or nursing agency may provide valuable comparative information about the hospitals in the area: which has the lowest nurse:patient ratio, the lowest turnover of nurses, the highest RN:LPN ratio, and the highest proportion of staff to agency nurses. A hospital's ability to attract and keep good nurses is an excellent indication of quality, and good nursing care is an important factor both in a satisfactory outcome and in comfort while in the hospital.

REMEDYING DEFICIENT HOSPITAL CARE

It is necessary, first, to distinguish substandard care from the kind of annoyance that is an unavoidable part of being a patient in the hospital. Being awakened in the middle of the night to be given an optional sleeping pill, for example, is unnecessary, and a patient should rightfully complain. But being awakened at night for a check on vital signs may be part of the careful, close monitoring that is vital to recovery.

It is also necessary to distinguish between minor and major deficiencies in care. Minor problems are those that interfere with comfort but do not constitute a threat to physical welfare. Some examples are lukewarm food, a longer than anticipated wait for painkilling medication, extra minutes spent on the bedpan. Such grievances can usually be resolved by discussing them (calmly and rationally) with the patient representative or ombudsman, or a member of the social services department.

Alternatively, a discussion with the staff nurse or head nurse will usually solve such problems. If that fails, it may be necessary to complain to the head of the appropriate department: nursing, nutrition, or housekeeping, for example. The complaint should be written, rather than telephoned.

Deficiencies of care that are in effect denials of a patient's right to "considerate and respectful care" are also minor, in the sense that they seldom threaten physical welfare. They have, however, important implications for the quality of care as a whole and every effort should be made to correct them.

Major deficiencies in care are those that seriously threaten well-being. They usually involve potentially dangerous shortcomings on the part of the nursing staff. There are some basic principles of good nursing care: attentiveness to changes in the patient's condition, promptness in answering calls, taking time to ask questions and listen for the answers, calling the doctor if the patient's condition changes or if the patient requests it, and possessing the training and skills appropriate to the patient's illness and condition. If these principles are not being met, the patient's well-being may be jeopardized and he or she should notify the doctor, who should then intervene vigorously on the patient's behalf. A move to another section of the hospital may afford better care, since the quality of nursing often differs greatly between one floor and another. If serious deficiencies in care remain or if you have reason to think that the doctor's care is deficient, a complaint should be made (again, in writing) to the medical director of the hospital, who has the ultimate responsibility for all care given in the institution. In extreme cases of negligent care, the patient may have grounds for suing the doctor or the hospital, or both, for malpractice.

MALPRACTICE

The American Society of Internal Medicine has stated that "a malpractice action is justified when a patient suffers injury, disability, or death as a result of an act of negligence by a physician." However, the society also states that "unanticipated therapeutic outcome which follows appropriate medical care is not malpractice. . . ." The distinction that is made here between a bad result, on one hand, and negligence, on the other, is an important one. Opinions differ in medicine as to what is the best course to pursue, and even the best treatment may have an unpredictable result. Decisions must be made in med-

ical treatment in the face of uncertainty, but negligence is negligence.

There are four standards of care that in effect constitute a doctor's legal obligations toward a patient; violation of any one could be grounds for a lawsuit.

1. The doctor must obtain the patient's informed consent before treatment. This means that a patient must understand the risks involved in a procedure before consenting to it; it does not mean that a doctor must detail every remote possibility, nor that a signed consent form is necessary every time a patient is treated. A signed consent form, however, is required by law before surgery or an invasive diagnostic test. If informed consent is not obtained properly—if, for example, a patient is asked to agree to "any or all" procedures, or the consent is obtained when the patient is sedated just prior to surgery—the doctor is technically open to a charge of assault and battery.

2. In treating a patient, the doctor must use reasonable skill and care in accordance with accepted medical practice, and within the limits of his or her competence. The key words here are *reasonable* and *accepted*. Both are difficult to define, and it has proved to be extremely difficult to establish in court that this standard has been violated, except in cases of extreme negligence.

3. A doctor must adequately supervise those aspects of a patient's care that he or she delegates to others. Doctors customarily delegate to nurses and other health care personnel; this is acceptable legally as long as the doctor assumes responsibility for supervising those who are helping. (Under certain circumstances, hospital nurses and aides, although not in the doctor's employ, are considered to be under the doctor's supervision.)

4. A patient, once accepted by a doctor, cannot be abandoned by the doctor. A doctor is not under any obligation to accept a patient, but once treatment has begun, care for that patient must continue until treatment is no longer needed, until the patient voluntarily leaves the doctor, or until the doctor has properly notified the patient that he or she is no longer responsible for the patient's care.

In an emergency, such as an automobile accident, doctors are expected to give reasonable care as best they can, given the circumstances. A doctor who initiates treatment has the responsibility to see to it that another doctor takes over the care of the victim. Because many doctors have been wary of lawsuits stemming from roadside treatment, most states have enacted "Good Samaritan" laws that exempt physicians from civil liability when emergency care has been given in good faith.

A patient with a legitimate grievance against a doctor should first talk the matter over with the doctor. This may clarify what is perhaps a genuine misunderstanding.

If such a discussion proves fruitless, the patient can contact the grievance committee of the county or state medical society (responsible members of the medical profession take questions of possible professional incompetence seriously), or seek a lawyer. The unpleasantness of taking a doctor to court can often be avoided by using good judgment (getting a second opinion, seeking another doctor) and by being certain that all questions have been answered and doubts resolved before giving consent to a procedure.

EXTENDED-CARE FACILITIES

Extended-care facilities are a relatively recent innovation, providing care that is between that given in an acute-care hospital and that provided in a skilled nursing facility (nursing home). These facilities provide short-term, comprehensive inpatient care, usually following hospitalization, for patients who no longer need the full range of hospital services but still require continuous professional nursing and medical supervision. They may also serve people who are not acutely ill, but who have medical conditions that require skilled care. Most extended-care facilities are physically attached to hospitals so that patients simply move from one wing of the building to another. Others are nursing homes that have met standards set for qualification by the Joint Commission on Accreditation or Medicare. The cost of care in such units may be one-third or one-half that of care in hospitals.

LONG-TERM CARE FACILITIES AND NURSING HOMES

Long-term care facilities provide extended care for patients with conditions that cannot be accommodated in a general hospital. Among these facilities are hospitals for the treatment of tuberculosis, chronic disease hospitals, rehabilitation hospitals, mental retardation facilities, and psychiatric hospitals for both children and adults. In addition, nursing homes of all types provide long-term care. They generally fall into three categories—residential care facilities, intermediate care facilities, and skilled nursing facilities. Services provided range from primarily sheltered living to around-the-clock nursing care.

BEFORE YOU LEAVE THE SPECIALIST'S OFFICE: A CHECKLIST

- Do you understand the doctor's diagnosis?
- If you have been given a prescription, do you:
  —Know the name of the drug?
  —Understand the directions for taking it: how often, how long, etc.?
  —Know what side effects it might produce? What, if any, precautions you should take while on the drug?
- Do you need a follow-up appointment?
- Has the doctor told you when you might expect your condition to improve, and what to do if it doesn't?
- For additional information, see chapter 34, Proper Use of Medication.

2

Meeting the Health Care Needs of the Aged and Disabled

• • • • • • • • • • • • • • • •

BARRY J. GURLAND, M.D., ANN BREUER, M.D., AND ESTHER CHACHKES, A.C.S.W. Parts of this chapter are adapted from the revised second edition.

During the past two decades, the health care professions have vastly improved medical services to the elderly. Previously, most medical professionals were inexperienced in diagnosing and managing the disorders associated with aging. Consequently, geriatric care received little attention from the medical establishment: The elderly were a disadvantaged minority with inadequate access to medical care whose treatable symptoms were often ascribed to the inevitable deterioration of aging.

But times have changed as the elderly segment of the U.S. population has grown dramatically in the past 20 years. The old old (those over 85), the population with the most medical problems, has been the most rapidly expanding demographic group. The swelling numbers of the elderly have created a politically potent force and a medical consumer group with economic clout: The continued availability of Medicare and Medicaid has allowed this growing cohort of elderly persons to afford the costs of a variety of medical services, particularly the very expensive hospital and other institutional services. Today, the average physician who treats adult patients, regardless of specialty, spends about 45 percent of the time treating elderly.

The increasing contact between health care professionals and elderly patients has fostered a better understanding of the distinctions between normal aging processes and changes related to the diseases frequently found in the elderly. Many debilitating conditions previously thought to be the inevitable results of old age can be ameliorated with treatment.

The high cost of caring for the elderly, especially the price of services provided in institutions, has become a controversial public issue. At the same time, medicine has recognized the importance of helping the elderly live independently—without being institutionalized—by means of preventive medicine, early intervention at the first sign of disease, and intensive rehabilitation. No longer content to merely help the elderly live longer, physicians are trying to help them function more effectively and retain good health.

Two major health care disciplines focus on the elderly: geriatrics, which incorporates the art and science of caring for the health problems of the elderly, and gerontology, the study of the aging process from a biological, mental, and social perspective.

Although these two fields are technically distinct, in fact, they share many overlapping concerns.

SPECIAL HEALTH PROBLEMS OF THE ELDERLY

The diverse and complicated health problems of the elderly cut across the disciplines of medicine, psychiatry, social work, and nursing. As a result, they may overwhelm a physician or other health professional without the time or capacity to investigate all the nuances of the situation or secure the full cooperation of the patient and his or her family in treating the illness. Moreover, the main complaint may overshadow other less urgent, but still important, secondary problems.

The multiple and interdisciplinary health demands of the elderly require a coordinated effort from many health care professionals for optimal treatment, otherwise uncoordinated efforts may produce conflicting management plans that hinder each other.

In many cases, the facilities offering one type of service lack others needed by their clients. Elderly with both physical maladies and mental problems may attend a community mental health center where medical services are not available. Similarly, people with a mixture of complaints may only receive services at social service agencies, nutrition sites, or ambulatory medical care clinics.

Added to the difficulty of organizing health services for this age group is their frequent lack of mobility. The elderly may be house-bound, lack access to transportation, reside in a long-term care facility, or simply be unwilling to attempt an excursion outside their usual haunts.

Frequently the cost of the health and related services needed by an elderly person is not reimbursed by medical insurance. Health coverage usually covers acute rather than chronic conditions, medical rather than psychiatric problems, and institutional rather than community-based services. Payments for social care and home care are severely restricted.

But, for the elderly, chronic conditions are usually of chief concern, requiring a different approach than treatment of acute illness.

When the elderly suffer acute illness, it is more likely to occur in the presence of a chronic, complicating malady that may follow or be aggravated by the acute condition and often becomes a serious health problem.

RECOGNIZING SIGNS AND SYMPTOMS

Even in the absence of troubling symptoms, the elderly should generally visit physicians more often than younger people. Beyond age 65, they should receive an annual physical exam. Although there are many normal physical changes that accompany advancing age, new symptoms or physical changes should not be automatically dismissed as the effects of old age. Any change in a person's usual physical or mental state, particularly if the

Acute Illness Requires:	Chronic Conditions Require:
• A highly selective diagnosis	• Comprehensive evaluation of health conditions including psychosocial factors as well as medical disorders
• Rapid cure	• Long-term care
• Prevention of complications or residual effects and avoidance of relapse	• Focus on slowing health declines or producing relatively small gains in wellness
• Vigorous treatments often with bed rest of hospitalization	• Coordination of several disciplines and agencies to deal with all complicating factors
	• Maintenance of as high an activity level as possible and functional capacity

change is relatively rapid, has not been previously experienced, and affects ability to carry out daily activities, should be evaluated by a physician.

Symptoms requiring physician evaluation include:

- Fatigue, sleeplessness, poor appetite, rapid change in weight, constipation or diarrhea
- Headaches and/or dizziness
- Vague aches and pains, swellings around the joints
- Foot problems: ingrown toenails, ulcers, fungus infections, sepsis, undue coldness, unusual color, pain, or inability to walk
- Failing vision or hearing; pain in the eyes
- Persistent rash, growths on the skin or changes in the color of moles, unhealed ulcers, blood in the stool or black stools
- A tendency to fall, shaking of the hands or head, limb weakness
- Sexual problems
- Depression, apathy and loss of interest, slowness of movement or thoughts, forgetfulness and confusion
- Breathlessness, chest pain (especially on exertion)

MEDICATION PROBLEMS

The aged frequently take multiple medications for their multiple medical problems, and these medicines may interact with each other, potentiating side effects or neutralizing each other.

- The elderly react to medications differently than younger people, frequently experiencing more side effects because their bodies allow higher levels of active ingredients into the bloodstream.
- If a physician prescribes medication without knowing that another doctor has prescribed another pharmaceutical, the chance of drug interaction is enhanced.
- When an elderly person takes an over-the-counter medication, borrows medication from a friend, or takes leftover medicine from another prescription, he or she may experience side effects from drug interactions.

Anyone taking medication should follow these guidelines.

1. Take the medication in the proper, prescribed dosage for the recommended amount of time, otherwise the medicine may not be effective.

2. Continue the medication for the recommended period even if the symptoms have apparently abated.

3. Do not continue treatment over or past the point indicated by the safety limits of the medication.

4. Report all medications to all of your physicians.

5. Watch out for specific side effects that indicate drug toxicity and may mean you have to switch medications; try to tolerate other, perhaps discomforting but harmless side effects that accompany certain medications. These may recede as you continue treatment. If you have questions about how to discern between these side effects, ask your doctor.

6. Check with your physician before resuming treatment to deal with a relapse.

The elderly may inadequately comply with treatment when their eyesight is weak and they are unable to read directions, if the prescribed treatment regimens are very complex, if they are too weak to to open bottles or otherwise dispense medications, or if their memories are poor. These difficulties are exacerbated when no one is available at home to assist with treatment.

PROBLEM DRUGS FOR THE ELDERLY

Sedative or Sleeping Agents
Diazepam
Chlordiazepoxide
Flurazepam
Meprobamate
Pentobarbital
Secobarbital

Antidepressants
Amitriptyline

Nonsteroidal Anti-Inflammatory Drugs
Indomethacin
Phenylbutazone

Oral Diabetes Drugs
Chlorpropamide

Analgesics
Propoxyphene
Pentazocine

Dementia Treatments
Isoxsuprine
Cyclandelate

Platelet Inhibitors
Dipyridamole

Muscle Relaxants or Antispasmodic Agents
Cyclobenzaprine
Methocarbamol
Carisoprodol
Orphenadrine

Antiemetic Agents
Trimethobenzamide

Antihypertensives
Propranolol
Methyldopa
Reserpine

Source: *Journal of the American Medical Association*

INVOLVING THE ELDERLY IN THEIR OWN HEALTH CARE

Health care for the elderly must include those being cared for in decision making—the care should be "planned with," rather than "planned for." When the elderly maintain a sense of responsibility for their health care, they retain a healthy feeling of control over their wellness. Otherwise, their morale and welfare may suffer from a pessimistic passivity that may intertwine inextricably with the quality and direction of their lives. However, during acute illness an elderly person may have to assume a passive role during treatment.

The elderly should have a say in where they reside, how vigorously a condition is investigated and treated, who renders the treatment, when treatment is helpful and worthy of continuation, or when side effects or lack of effectiveness necessitates a change of treatment. This involvement means that the elderly should have the rationale and plan for the management of their illness plainly explained so they can cooperate with treatment. Active participation reduces the feeling of helplessness that often undermines disease resistance and the resilience required for recovery.

The most important decision that requires participation by the elderly is the choice of a primary physician. Because the need to see specialists for various disorders often increases with age, it becomes extremely important to engage one primary physician who is both aware of all aspects of a person's health and able to coordinate care among several physicians if necessary. This doctor should also know the family's living conditions and financial resources. This doctor does not have to specialize in the treatment of elderly patients as long as he or she demonstrates an interest in treating the elderly and a willingness to spend the necessary time explaining the patient's condition and course of treatment to both the family and patient.

Each elderly person should choose a "surrogate" decision maker. This person, usually a family member, would choose medical treatment and placement when the patient has become incapable of making these decisions. In addition, an elderly person should discuss preferences for future medical treatment with the primary physician. An attorney should be consulted on executing a living will, a durable power of attorney, and other documents that identify a surrogate. The legal effectiveness of these documents varies depending on individual state laws (see chapter 3).

COST REIMBURSEMENT

As all health care costs have risen, cost-containing strategies have attempted to hold down the reimbursement of medical costs to the elderly by restricting reimbursement eligibility and narrowing the range of health services and locations that qualify for reimbursement. Also, the duration of hospital stays has been curtailed, as well as the total expenditures allowed an institution, and restrictive criteria have been applied to admission to long-term care facilities. Although scrutiny of long-term care has cut back on admissions to hospitals and nursing homes, this restructuring of reimbursement has not resulted in a concomitant expansion of alternative home care services.

Since Medicare coverage is more liberal for hospital care than for community-based services, some elderly are forced into institutions mainly for financial reasons. Medicare (parts A and B) pays for medical costs and hospital services.

Medicaid has broader coverage than Medicare and will, for example, pay for more than 90 days of long-term care, although this may vary from state to state. Both Medicaid and Medicare cover certain health appliances and aids, and certain personal care and housekeeping services to help persons with chronic disabilities to remain at home; however, a means test is required for Medicaid, so that patients have to spend most of their assets in order to be poor enough to qualify. Nevertheless, many elderly who do not qualify for Medicaid are still too poor to afford private services.

Even when using Medicare and Medicaid to their full extent, the average elderly person spends more than $1,000 per year for health care; much more if medically debilitated. Private third-party payers tend to reimburse medical expenses while excluding health-related social services and long-term care institutions. These exclusions may change as insurance companies investigate how much chronic illness actually costs in medical expenses. (More specific information about Medicare and Medicaid reimbursement is provided under "Home Care," "Community Facilities," and "Nursing Homes" in this chapter.)

Religous philanthropies, such as the Jewish Association of Social Agencies, Catholic Charities, and the Federation of Protestant Welfare Agencies, occasionally provide services for those with inadequate insurance coverage.

HEALTH CARE OPTIONS— NEGOTIATING THE SYSTEM

A number of different living situations are available for elderly who need health care. Many, of course, live alone in traditional housing, and some live with relatives, while others dwell in special retirement communities or other facilities specifically for the elderly, or within institutions such as nursing homes.

To make the right choice of living arrangements depends on older citizens or their relatives exhaustively investigating the available options. To facilitate this process, many people hire a case manager—a private social worker specializing in securing and coordinating medical and social services. Case managers provide valuable information on what is available, understand how to cut red tape to gain access to these services, and know how to negotiate for reimbursement. They are especially helpful in making long-distance arrangements for care for a family member who lives in another city or state.

Case managers are expensive, usually charging at least $50 per hour. Since there are no special certification programs for this specialty, you should hire a manager who is a certified social worker. Listings are often available from hospital social workers, religious organizations, or state and regional government offices of the aging.

The Directory of Health Organizations and Resources in appendix B lists local and regional case management organizations. The area agencies on aging are listed in *A Directory of State and Area Agencies on Aging,* available from the U.S. Government Printing Office or at libraries and at local area offices. Family Service America, located in New York, can provide referrals to its more than 270 member agencies throughout the United States and Canada. For information, send a self-addressed, stamped envelope to 254 West 31st Street, 12th floor, New York, NY 10001.

LIVING ARRANGEMENTS

Substantial numbers of the elderly live alone, preferring independence and familiar surroundings to life in a relative's house or in a nursing home or other special facility. Planning by other members of the family is necessary to the success of the elderly's independent living. After hospitalization (12 percent of the elderly are hospitalized each year), the elderly may continue to live at home if careful predischarge plans are made and adequate home health care is available. In most communities, applying for community services such as Meals on Wheels, day-care programs and home health workers before the end of a hospital visit will smooth the transition back home from the institution.

Modifications to their living space can help make life safer and more comfortable for the elderly.

- Outside ramps and railings
- Bright lighting in hallways
- Grab bars in bathrooms
- Low-pile carpeting and nonskid rugs
- Weatherstripping, storm or thermal windows, and insulation to cut down on drafts

Independent living should also include a strategy for quickly communicating when the elderly need emergency help.

This can include:

- **Emergency Alerting Devices.** Systems can be installed that automatically dial police or ambulance service in case of an accident or other mishap.

• **Informal Alert System.** Neighbors, postal workers, or newspaper deliverers can inform a designated person if an elderly resident leaves mail and packages untouched for days. Some communities provide telephone reassurance programs that call seniors daily. An informal arrangement can simply mean a window shade is raised every day to signal neighbors that all is well.

A growing number of retirement communities offer continuing care for the elderly at fees that are partially refundable when residents die or leave. Although early versions of these living centers often failed because of poor planning and financing (residents required more services than anticipated), more than 500 successful facilities are now available in the United States.

For seniors not requiring the care of an institution, but still needing some assistance, other living systems have been devised.

• Shared dwellings: often in close proximity to a nursing home.
• Sheltered or enriched housing: individual apartments specially designed for the frail or handicapped. An on-premises staff member provides emergency help, occasional assistance, and advice. Sometimes, sheltered housing is part of a multilevel campus in which health-related facilities and skilled nursing facilities coexist.
• Family-type homes for adults operated by individuals in private homes may be available in some areas. These often accommodate one or more persons who do not need medical or nursing care but require some personal care service in addition to room and board.

HOME CARE

Most home care for the elderly is provided by family members, even though relatives generally live farther apart than in the past. Caring for the elderly requires family teamwork to keep any individual participant from being overwhelmed with work and responsibility, as well as to share the satisfaction of caring for a dependent member of the family.

As the elderly population grows, most people can expect to have older, sick, or disabled persons in their families. Before embarking on long-term care for an elderly relative, family members should evaluate the extent of their commitment and then periodically reevaluate their efforts in order to avoid elder-care burnout. The needs of all family members (from children to great-grandparents) should be considered so that families do not emotionally, physically, and financially exhaust themselves and persist in providing home care past the point when such care ceases to be appropriate.

Families caring for the elderly should use unskilled and temporary help for parts of each day or weekends or vacations to provide respite from their daily tasks. In addition to skilled home health care (see below), bright and useful part-time help may be available at college and university placement offices. Students may be hired inexpensively to do household chores or provide companionship to seniors.

Despite the society-wide need for home health care and the revived interest on the part of health care providers and reimbursers, this area of health care is underserved. Economic factors may change this lack of services since the cost of home care is considerably cheaper than institutional care. When services are provided in the home, an expensive acute-care bed is freed or a nursing home bed is made available for someone else. For the chronically ill or disabled elderly, however, home care may be more costly if payment is out-of-pocket and not covered by third-party payers. Still, home care offers the advantages of continuity of care, independence, and the maintenance of ties with a familiar place, a family, and community.

Excellent home care requires the intelligent use of available medical and supportive services. Unfortunately, placement in a hospital or nursing home is often an easier task than negotiation of the fragmented and unorganized fabric of home services necessary for maintaining persons in their own houses. Plus, it is easier to obtain third-party reimbursement for skilled medical care than for less technical and less expensive supportive care.

HOME HEALTH SERVICES

Over 5,000 home health agencies provide home health services in the United States, either directly or indirectly under a physician's supervision. These home health agencies may be private, either profit making or nonprofit; hospital-based; or associated with public health agencies, neighborhood health centers, or local and county health departments or community and church groups.

Services fit into two categories.

• **Skilled Services.** Nursing, physical therapy, occupational therapy, speech and hearing therapy, dental care, nutritional counseling, lab services, case management (coordination of services by social workers).
• **Supportive services.** Personal care (bathing, dressing grooming), homemaking (light housekeeping, shopping, meal preparation, and nonskilled nursing by a home health aide), chores, transportation.

Most home health agencies provide services to anyone, accepting private payment or reimbursed, at least partially, by government or individual insurance plans. Information on home health agencies is available from city or county public health and welfare departments, the Area Agency on Aging, the local office of the Social Security Administration, day-care centers, and houses of worship. Other information sources include the United Way and the Yellow Pages (see the listings "Home Health Services" and "Nurses").

Choose an agency capable of providing all needed services and those necessary in the future. Remember, a patient being discharged from the hospital does not have to choose the hospital-based agency: Selection should be based on needs and personal preference.

Some areas of the United States contain only a single home health agency, but where choices are available the elderly and their families should evaluate agencies' services and suitability in meeting particular needs before making a choice. Ask these questions.

- Do the available services meet present and anticipated needs?
- What is the cost per visit for each service? What is the type and rate of reimbursement?
- Are adequate medical supplies and equipment available?
- What are the days and hours when service is provided?
- How are emergencies handled?
- How is supervision organized?
- Is backup service provided when home health workers do not arrive?

VOLUNTARY HEALTH AGENCIES

Organizations like the American Cancer Society and the Easter Seal Society have volunteer "friendly visitor" services that can be of help to the disabled elderly and can provide needed respite for family members. These agencies may also be able to provide specialized equipment and listing of resources available in the community.

PHARMACIES AND MEDICAL SUPPLY HOUSES

These retail outlets are a ready source of specialized equipment and of the more usual sickroom supplies. In many cases, wheelchairs, walkers, portable oxygen equipment, and hospital beds may be rented or purchased. Renting may be preferable if the need for equipment is temporary and the items are expensive.

REIMBURSEMENT FOR HOME HEALTH SERVICES

Expenses for skilled services may be reimbursable through Medicare, Medicaid, and private insurance plans. Some agencies providing supportive services receive federal or state funding; the agency or the social

service department should be contacted to see if the individual meets state-specified need and eligibility requirements.

Medicare. People eligible for Medicare benefits (those age 65 or older and disabled persons receiving social security disability for 24 months) may receive coverage for home health care under this program if the following conditions are met.

1. A physician must certify (and periodically recertify) that there is a need for home health services for the treatment of a medical condition and must set up a treatment plan.
2. The necessary care must be part-time, skilled nursing care, physical therapy, occupational therapy, or speech therapy.
3. The patient must be confined to the house.
4. The home health agency must be certified by Medicare.

If these conditions are met, Medicare will pay the "reasonable cost" (rates of reimbursement are fixed by Medicare and the providers) for an unlimited number of covered home health visits for one year following the patient's most recent discharge from the hospital or skilled nursing facility. In addition, Medicare may pay for some supportive services but only if skilled services are also needed. Medicare does not pay for full-time nursing care at home, drugs, meals delivered to the house, or other services that are designed primarily to help people with their personal or domestic needs. Therefore, it is important to find out how much of the bill will be the patient's responsibility.

Many people assume that Medicare will cover their health needs, both in and out of the hospital, when they reach the age of eligibility, but this is not always so. Most elderly people have chronic health and social problems, but Medicare emphasizes reimbursement for acute care. Many who need help in the home for daily living do not need skilled nursing, but provision of supportive services is contingent on the need for skilled services. Many need assistance with personal care and homemaking but are not home-bound—being home-bound is one of the criteria for Medicare benefits.

Medicaid. States are required to provide home health care services in their Medicaid programs. Those eligible to receive these services are people on public assistance and supplemental security income, as are others who qualify under state means tests (which vary widely from state to state). Not all home health agencies, however, will accept Medicaid patients, since the reimbursement is often less than the actual cost of care. If an agency does accept Medicaid patients, more services, especially personal care services, may be available than under Medicare.

Private Insurance. Until recently, no private insurance plans included coverage for home health services. Some companies now provide partial coverage and some major medical policies cover some home health services in full. However, not all home health agencies will accept private insurance payments and this should be verified before choosing an agency.

HOSPICE PROGRAMS

For elderly persons coping with terminal illness, hospice services are available in many communities and are reimbursed by Medicare. These services offer home visits by a hospice team and include skilled nursing care, physician services, medical social work, counseling services, medical appliances and supplies, and occupational and physical therapy. Home health aides supervised by a nurse can also be placed in the home if needed. Short-term inpatient care is provided in a participating hospital, hospice unit, or skilled nursing facility.

In order to be covered by Medicare, a patient must be certified terminally ill with a medical prognosis that life expectancy is less than 6 months, and palliative care must be deemed the most appropriate form of care. In addition, the patient must know his or her diagnosis. Under Medicare, hospice coverage has a lifetime limitation of two periods of 90 days each and one subsequent period of 30 days.

....

COMMUNITY FACILITIES

For the elderly living at home who are not house-bound, there are a number of community services available that provide care during the day.

ADULT DAY-CARE

A variety of community-based centers conduct adult day-care programs for the elderly, which are an alternative, in many cases, to institutionalization. The services provided in the different types of programs are tailored to meet specific needs, and each type has a different therapeutic objective.

DAY HOSPITALS

Usually located at an extended-care facility or hospital, these facilities provide medical care and supervision to people recovering from acute illness. Where they deal primarily with patients recently discharged from an institution, they are sometimes called after-care clinics. Referral is by a physician, and reimbursement is generally the same as for other hospital services.

MEDICAL DAY-CARE

This service is generally located in a long-term institution or freestanding center and provides health care services such as nursing and other supports to the chronically ill or disabled who do not need frequent medical intervention. Rehabilitation and maintenance are the therapeutic goals. Referral is by a physician and reimbursement is by third-party payment on a sliding scale. In some states, Medicaid pays for this care.

MENTAL HEALTH DAY-CARE

This service is usually located in a psychiatric institution or freestanding center and provides a supervised environment together with mental health services to adults with organic or functional mental illness. The therapeutic goal is supervision, safety, and assistance with coping skills. Referral is by a psychiatrist and reimbursement is by third-party payment on a sliding scale.

SOCIAL ADULT DAY-CARE

Often situated in a freestanding center, this service caters to adults whose social functioning has regressed and who are not able to function independently. Referral is by families and health facilities, but a physician's examination is required prior to admission. Reimbursement is by third-party payment on a sliding scale; many centers are funded through Title XX of the Social Security Act.

The Department of Health and Human Services reports that there are more than 600 adult care programs in operation. Program objectives and services provided are largely dependent on the philosophy of the sponsoring organization and on negotiation with the funding source. Common to most day-care programs is attendance from several hours to a full day, up to 5 days per week, a midday meal, and transportation within a specified area. Services vary from state to state and provider to provider. Selection of a program should be approached with great care to be certain that it is suitable to individual needs.

NUTRITION SERVICES

Meals on Wheels is a community service, offered under voluntary auspices but supported in part by public funds. The program provides at least one hot meal per day at a reasonable charge to home-bound people age 60 and older. Specifics vary from state to state; the state agency administering programs for the elderly should be contacted for additional information.

For the elderly attending senior centers, hot meals provided through the Area Agency on Aging provide not only adequate nutrition but also a chance to socialize. This program allows the agency to keep in touch with clients' physical and social situations and head off potential problems. Referral is open-ended: The elderly can refer themselves. In all cases, the center should be told of any special dietary needs.

EDUCATIONAL AND RECREATIONAL ACTIVITIES

In many communities a variety of educational and recreational activities are available through senior centers, churches, and voluntary and government agencies. These activities reduce loneliness and boredom when medical conditions decrease important social interactions. While some of these programs require a fee, some do not charge. Recreational services for home-bound elderly may also be available.

Some community agencies sponsor self-help programs and support groups for families. Many persons have found that sharing concerns and problems with others makes the burdens and stresses of caregiving easier to bear.

....

NURSING HOMES

A nursing home is a residential facility that provides nursing service, room and board, personal care, and custodial services. The 19,000 nursing homes in the United States provide about 1.5 million beds. Nursing homes outnumber community hospitals 3 to 1; on any given day, twice as many people are in nursing homes as in hospitals. About three-quarters of these, with a million beds, are proprietary (run for profit by individuals, partnerships, or corporations). Fifteen percent, with about 300,000 beds, are run by voluntary nonprofit organizations. The rest are under government auspices.

While nursing homes accommodate some patients with serious congenital illnesses or disorders, as well as patients recently discharged from the hospital after an episode of acute illness, or recovering from strokes or recent surgery, the great majority of residents are the chronically ill elderly. Three out of four nursing home residents are women and the "typical" current nursing home resident is in her eighties, single or widowed, with three or more significant chronic illnesses and considerable mental impairment. Usually her only source of income is her monthly social security check; other assets have long been exhausted. On average, these residents stay in nursing homes for 2.5 years, though one out of four residents stays for 3 years or more. Discharge comes with death or referral to a hospital for a terminal illness.

TYPES OF NURSING HOMES

Federal regulations apply broad standards for the physical environment, medical and nursing requirements, and staffing patterns for three different types of nursing homes. State interpretations of these standards vary widely.

- **Residental-care facilities (RCFs)** provide meals, sheltered living, and some medical monitoring—supervision of medications and surveillance of symptoms and signs of problems. RCFs are appropriate for those unable to manage household chores but not needing intense medical attention.
- **Intermediate-care facilities (ICFs)** provide room and board and regular (not round-the-clock) nursing care for those unable to live independently. May also provide social and recreational activities and rehabilitation programs: physical therapy, occupational therapy, speech therapy, and social work services.
- **Skilled nursing facilities (SNFs)** provide 24-hour nursing care by registered nurses, licensed practical nurses, and nurses' aides. SNFs are for those who need intensive nursing care and rehabilitation. Most ICFs and SNFs are state certified and therefore reimbursable with public funds for their care. Certification does not guarantee quality care, but lack of it usually signals that the nursing home displays grave deficiencies.

REIMBURSEMENT

Few individuals or families can afford to pay for nursing home care out-of-pocket for any period of time—nursing homes cost around $25,000 per year. (The national cost is about $20 billion annually, of which 40 percent is paid privately.) Since reimbursement by private insurance for nursing home care is minimal, much of the financial burden falls on federal, state, and local government programs, mainly Medicaid, which takes over when an individual "spends down" to the point that the cost of services exceeds the patient's income.

While most state Medicare programs reimburse for care in an ICF, and, in some circumstances, in an SNF, they may limit the benefits, require prior authorization for care, and curtail the length of stay and the number of visits by physicians. These limits vary from state to state, but Medicaid still remains the main source of government funding for long-term nursing home care.

Medicare, originally designed to reimburse for acute episodic care, will reimburse for needed care in an SNF for 150 days after hospital discharge (the patient pays coinsurance after the first 20 days) if certain conditions for skilled nursing and rehabilitation care have been met. Although 90 percent of nursing home residents are Medicare beneficiaries, Medicare pays less than 3 percent of nursing home expenses, and while nursing home residents make up only 4 percent of the Medicaid-eligible population, they account for 30 percent of total Medicaid expenditures.

CONSIDERING PLACEMENT

Most nursing home referrals are made by families: More than half of the residents come to long-term facilities directly from their own or their family's home. Selection of a facility or admission to an institution is rarely arranged by a doctor, and the certification of need for care (made to comply with Medicaid reimbursement regulations) is often completed only after the decision is made to place an elderly family member in a home.

Although nursing home admissions have more than doubled in the past 40 years, nursing homes serve only one of three of the elderly requiring regular or continuous nursing care. The others receive care at home from their families and use resources available through home health agencies and community. (See the section "Home Care.")

As a rule, families hesitate to place their elderly in institutions; studies show that families usually try to avoid nursing home placement as long as possible, even at great personal, economic, and physical cost. The large number of people in nursing homes indicates that never before have so many people lived long enough to require intensive care.

Families considering placement of an elderly member in a nursing home should evaluate the alternative to institutional care. Frequently a social worker or other professional with knowledge of community resources can arrange services that avoid or postpone placement. Family service agencies, some voluntary nursing homes, senior citizens' centers, or, if the elderly person is in the hospital, the hospital social service department can provide counseling on the available options.

The older person should be included in planning: The elderly are adults with a right to autonomy to the fullest extent possible and a right to express personal likes or dislikes regarding placement. Do not pretend that a nursing home is some other kind of institution. Misinformation of that type is always discovered and damages the elderly person's well-being and family relationship. Moreover, studies show that participation in decision making aids in subsequent physical and mental adjustment.

CHOOSING A NURSING HOME

Lists of nursing homes can be obtained from a social services counselor, from the local social security office, or from the state or county public social services agency. Some counties publish consumers' handbooks, which supply information on the nursing homes in the area. The home should be licensed, meet appropriate safety regulations, provide the necessary medical and nursing care, and have arrangements for emergencies and transfers to a hospital in case of acute illness. The home should provide a religious and cultural environment similar to that to which the patient is accustomed. It should be close enough for the family to visit conveniently. And it should provide the highest possible quality of care.

While periodic investigations of nursing homes and government inspections and regulations have cut back on cases of extreme neglect in these institutions, moderate levels of neglect are still frequent. While many homes, especially the voluntary institutions, follow high standards, others provide inadequate care. Standards for licensing vary from state to state, and you must choose a home carefully. For example, although all licensed ICFs and SNFs are required to employ at least one full-time registered nurse, this does not guarantee more than minimal nursing care, and even the best homes, in states with the strictest requirements, may have only one registered nurse looking after a unit with 60 beds. Hands-on care in nursing homes is usually provided by aides with little training on staffs with high turnover. The frustrating work, minimal wages, and low employee morale is not conducive to excellent care.

To evaluate a nursing home, make firsthand observations and interview residents, staff, and administrators. Question the skill with which professional (or professionally supervised) services are given, and check the quality of life in the home's living arrangements.

Discuss financial arrangements before deciding on placement.

• Establish whether the patient is eligible for Medicare or Medicaid coverage and how such benefits relate to any private medical or hospitalization insurance policies that the patient may have.

• If the patient has personal funds initially, establish whether the home will keep the patient on at the Medicaid rate when those funds run out.

• Find out whether the cost quoted is inclusive. Many homes charge separately for laundry, medications, dressings, special nursing procedures, and other "extras."

The move to the nursing home is extremely important.

• Families should spend as much time as possible with the patient during the settling-in period (as good judgment indicates).

• Make every effort to continue with familiar routines so that the person entering the home does not feel abandoned by the family (continue usual shopping trips, visits with grandchildren, etc.).

• Bring family pictures or familiar items from home if they can be accommodated in the nursing home.

• Be aware of the sense of loss felt by the elderly entering nursing homes—loss of home, of continuity with the past, of familiar faces and places.

On the other hand, for many elderly and disabled, nursing homes offer a new freedom in living by providing companionship and the reassurance of having help within call at all times.

....

PHYSICAL AND DEVELOPMENTAL DISABILITIES

Physically and developmentally disabled people comprise the largest minority in the world. Since one in ten people worldwide (an estimated 20 to 30 million in the United States) is disabled, it is inevitable that each of us is or will be personally concerned with the welfare of at least one disabled friend or family member. Disability results from:

- Illness
- Accident
- Injury
- Age
- Congenital anomaly

Disability may be single or multiple, and include loss or impairment of manual dexterity, mobility, vision, hearing, and mental or emotional function.

In a sense, everyone is disabled at one time or another and unable to perform a task because of physical limitations or environmental barriers. When this happens, people try to minimize the limitation, modify the environment, or both. For example, to take a job on the hundredth floor of a building requires either sufficient physical stamina to make the climb each day or the use of an adaptive piece of equipment (an elevator). If the elevator is undependable and stamina is inadequate for the climb, the individual having to work in such a location would be handicapped.

Everyone constantly compensates for disabilities by altering or removing handicaps. The inconvenience and fatigue of walking from suburb to city is modified by using a car or a bus. A bridge or a boat makes it possible to cross a river without having to swim.

Resources for the disabled are a means of helping individuals modify their environment so that they are no longer handicapped in doing what they want to do. Elevators, cars, and bridges are taken for granted as necessary for the public good. For those with additional limitations, more modifications—such as braille signs and curb cuts—make it possible to live without being handicapped by the environment.

Although people with physical and developmental disabilities are a vast and diverse group, they are too often lumped together as though they represented a homogeneous group. What they do share is a need for modification of the environment to achieve maximum potential and the most independence. This need presents a challenge for the disabled, their families, and society as a whole.

Until early in the 20th century those with disabilities were often hidden away and cared for within the home or segregated in institutions. Advances in medicine and technology and the exigencies and ravages of modern warfare (which have produced many veterans with disabilities) have changed the picture entirely, but unfortunately, the old attitudes sometimes linger.

Today an entire field of medicine is devoted to the development or restoration of function. Called physical medicine at its inception in the early 1900s, this field is now known as rehabilitation medicine. The doctors who specialize in this field—physiatrists—are first thoroughly trained in general medicine where they master the diagnostic and therapeutic skills of physical medicine. Then they specialize in the comprehensive management of patients with impairment and disability arising from neuromuscular, musculoskeletal, and vascular disorders, including the psychological and social aspects of various conditions. Unlike areas of medicine aimed primarily at amelioration of disease or injury, rehabilitation medicine is concerned with restoration of the individual to a place in society.

Technological advances, particularly the miniaturization resulting from space research, have led to many sophisticated aids promising enormous advances in communication, mobility, and independence for people with various disabilities. Systems are now available that operate with a touch of the chin or a finger, allowing people with minimal mobility to control their wheelchairs, lights, heating systems, and telephones. Soon, voice-activated systems should be perfected, further expanding the horizons of those with restricted movement.

There are advances, too, in attitude, both in society and among persons with disabilities. The government finally recognized the civil rights of disabled persons in the 1973 Rehabilitation Act (Public Law 93-112). Section 504 of the act states: "No otherwise qualified handicapped individual in the United States shall, solely on the basis of his handicap, be excluded from participating in, be denied the benefits of, or be subjected to discrimination under any program or activity receiving federal assistance."

Because the Department of Health and Human Services used to administer most programs serving disabled people (now the Department of Education does), the Secretary of Health and Human Services (then called Health, Education and Welfare) was charged with writing the regulation pertaining to section 504. It took 4 years and massive sit-ins by the disabled in Washington and HHS regional offices to get those regulations written and signed, but on April 28, 1977, it was at last accomplished and the civil rights of the disabled became protected by the law of the land.

In 1990 the Americans with Disabilities Act wrote into law the fact that all new mass transit systems (including trains and buses) must be made accessible to wheelchairs and make available alternate forms of transportation for those unable to board buses and trains. (Older trains and buses also have to make accommodations.) This law also mandated that new retail outlets, restaurants, hotels, and the like had to be accessible to the wheelchair-bound, that the phone company had to provide services to the voice and hearing impaired, and that larger businesses had to renovate their facilities to make them accessible to disabled employees.

Whether children or adults, the disabled themselves and those who care for them require a great deal of special information and perhaps aids of varying cost and complexity to compensate for the impaired function. Finding the correct information or the most appropriate aid can be a monumental task and an ongoing one.

THE PRIMARY RESOURCE

Because the challenge of disability is different for each person and family, each disabled person is the most knowledgeable in what resources are needed to best overcome a disability. With this knowledge, the disabled adult is necessarily his or her own best counselor. It may be necessary to engage the support and assistance of family members or other caregivers, but no one else has as much reason or motivation to secure the best possible life as the affected person. In the case of small children, parents must take charge of care, but even a child is a good judge of what is needed and what is possible.

Very often the necessary services for a disabled person are available via only a few channels, and if one is not associated with a rehabilitation center, finding out which services are best and how they may be obtained can require persistence and detective skills of a high order. This is particularly true for people in rural areas far from large medical centers.

Perhaps the most comprehensive sources of information on services and equipment for the disabled are the computer memory banks. Presently there are several such data banks. One is Accent on Information, a service that will search for specific equipment through the data banks at Illinois State University. Information on use and cost of service is available from Accent on Living, Bloomington, Illinois.

MEDICAL RESOURCES

Many factors affect the acquistion of the best available medical care. The nature of the medical problem, the geographic location of the patient, and the family circumstances all dictate to some degree what kind of medical help is appropriate, beneficial, and practical.

For most physical disabilities, a rehabilitation center or the rehabilitation department in a medical center offers the most comprehensive help. A physiatrist oversees and coordinates the services of a whole battery of health care specialists who may help deal with specific needs. The physiatrist will first work with any medical specialists who may be involved with primary care, such as a neurologist, a rheumatologist, a cardiovascular specialist, an orthopedist, or any other physician involved in the treatment of the disease or injury. With information on the underlying cause of the disability and the prognosis from the primary physicians, the physiatrist may then call on biomedical engineers, physical therapists, speech therapists, occupational therapists, or others specially trained to measure various physical abilities and design ways to improve or enhance them.

If a disability has been incurred suddenly and causes severe psychological problems, a psychiatrist, a psychologist, or a social worker may be recommended for the disabled person or family members who need help. The social worker may be called upon to assist in the transition from hospital to home by finding appropriate community services such as homemakers or medical and social service agencies.

If the disability is not one ordinarily requiring the help of a rehabilitation center, or if traveling to such a center is impractical, every local avenue of assistance should be investigated. The family physician is the first person to be consulted. He or she may be able to make referrals or inquiries that would be difficult for the patient alone to do. Other local or county resources include the visiting nurse service, the social services department of the nearest hospital, and any clinics that deal with the specific disability. Indeed, the visiting nurse services are one of the best sources of help and information available in many local communities.

For those with developmental disabilities, especially in the case of those capable of independent or moderately supervised living, required services may fall more heavily into areas of special education or occupational training rather than medical assistance.

Though developmental disabilities are organically based, they vary in their affect on mental function and the most seriously affected require assistance in decision making as well as daily living.

The quality of service and information varies widely from hospital to hospital and agency to agency. Some are fortunate in finding excellent help all in one place. Others must search diligently and almost never feel adequately served. The search for help should not stop until the quality and quantity of service meet most of the needs of the disabled person and the family.

No single list of all rehabilitation facilities is available. The department of rehabilitation medicine at a university-based hospital usually can tell you what is available in your area.

AT HOME

The average house does not accommodate the needs of the disabled. Even able-bodied people who vary from the norm may find it uncomfortable to manage with cabinets or shower heads too high or too low, steps too narrow or too steep, windows too difficult to adjust, and insufficient light. To make a home safe and comfortable for a disabled person may require only a few inexpensive modifications of existing furnishings, or it could involve costly architectural changes.

Since the cost of changing a house can be significant and mistakes in renovation expensive, it is advisable to research the matter well before starting. The help of a physical or occupational therapist or a rehabilitation engineer may be invaluable. These specialists may be able to suggest specific devices or simple modifications perfectly suited to the problem. (Assistance from such specialists is best obtained through a primary-care physician or a physiatrist.)

For those without access to these professionals, other resources can be found. The nearest local or state chapter of the foundation or society that serves people with such a disability should be contacted first. Most of these associations afford information and referral services that can recommend equipment and suppliers, and sometimes can supply the names of others who have successfully dealt with the problem. The public library or a good bookstore may have books or articles of help.

Once the home environment has been modified as necessary to accommodate a physical disability, the issues of personal mobility and activities of daily living must still be dealt with. A physical therapist specializes in treating mobility problems and is trained to evaluate and improve mobility through wheelchair training, gait training with assistive devices, and recommendation of special accommodations such as wheelchair lifts and bathroom aids, for example. Physiatrists and primary-care physicians may request a periodic consultation with a physical or an occupational therapist to evaluate mobility and to suggest equipment modifications or other changes that the disabled person's condition or environment might warrant. An occupational therapist, an expert in upper extremity function and activities of daily living, can, by evaluation, help a disabled individual gain better control over his or her body and become more self-reliant.

Working under the aegis of a physician, both the physical and occupational therapists can not only prescribe appropriate aids but also can often help in securing them from reliable sources. Since they keep abreast of developments in their fields, they can often bring helpful information to their patients.

The special needs hotline, provided by the American Telephone and Telegraph Company, offers information about devices available for the hearing impaired (800-833-3232), or for people with speech difficulties (800-233-1222).

OUTSIDE THE HOME

While regulations that mandate barrier-free access to public buildings and transport and nondiscrimination in employment have long been in effect, it will still be years before all the older buildings and systems can be modified to accommodate the disabled.

In the meantime, it is useful to find out exactly what the rights of the disabled are, where changes have been made, and how to employ available services to make it possible to enjoy the benefits of public transport, regular employment, cultural and educational opportunities, shopping, travel, and recreation.

First it is important to get local information. Depending on the size of the community, local "access" booklets may be available (your mayor's office is a good source). In cities with large public transport systems, the transport authority will have information on barrier-free or alternative transit services. In smaller areas, the organizations dealing directly with specific disabilities usually know what kind of transportation is available.

Travel for business or pleasure requires particularly careful planning. A wealth of information can be had from the suppliers of services such as airlines, railways, buses, hotels, tourism offices, and so on.

Mainstream is a placement service concerned with disability employment issues. This organization maintains an information center at 3 Bethesda Metro Center, Suite 830, Bethesda, MD 20814; (301) 654-2400.

CENTERS FOR INDEPENDENT LIVING

In 1972, a few disabled citizens in Berkeley, California, started an organization called the Center for Independent Living, which rapidly grew into a large multipurpose community organization offering a wide array of services. Supported by federal, state, and private grants, the Berkeley Center for Independent Living has become the prototype for similar groups across the nation, and these centers are revolutionizing self-help and group mental health for large disabled populations.

The centers, largely staffed by disabled people, offer counseling, education, housing, job placement, health care, wheelchair repair, transportation, attendant referral, financial advocacy, legal assistance, and sex counseling.

The centers stress a holistic approach to living and health. They provide peers as role models and involve disabled individuals completely in deciding on and working toward a suitable, achievable, and gratifying goal. Centers for Independent Living also provide a peer support system, as well as education and counseling for families and the professional community.

Information about the location of centers throughout the country may be obtained from the Berkeley Center, 3539 Telegraph Avenue, Berkeley, CA 94704; (415) 841-4776.

GENERAL PUBLICATIONS

In addition to the publications of organizations concerned with specific disabilities, publications of general interest to people with a variety of disabilities include:

• Accent on Living, P.O. Box 700, Bloomington, IL 61702. A pocket-size quarterly full of practical information on transportation, housing, and other aspects of disabled living.
• Rehabilitation Gazette, 4502 Maryland Avenue, St. Louis, MO 63108. An international journal and information service for disabled people published biannually.
• The Howard A. Rusk Institute of Rehabilitation Medicine, 400 East 34th Street, New York, NY 10016. This institution also has a number of publications of interest.

ADVOCACY GROUPS

Advocacy groups for the disabled are widespread. Many agitate for local compliance with existing laws or regulations. Local newspapers and television programs frequently give information on the activities of such groups. All the Centers for Independent Living have advocacy groups, as do the Paralyzed Veterans of America. Another group, national in scope, is the American Coalition of Citizens with Disabilities, 1201 15th Street NW, Suite 201, Washington, DC 20005.

Several consumer advocacy groups around the country help individuals obtain greater freedom and rights. Included among these are the various Centers for Independent Living, Paralyzed Veterans of America, and the American Coalition of Citizens with Disabilities (see appendix C, Directory of Resources, for a complete list). The Department of Education can provide information on more than 200 federal programs serving disabled people. Call or write the office of Special Education Programs or the Rehabilitation Services Administration. (See Government Assistance for the Handicapped in appendix C.)

The nearest office of the Social Security Administration is another important source of information. For those who encounter difficulties in dealing with this or other federal offices, help can often be found through senatorial or congressional offices.

Every state has a federally mandated Office of Vocational Rehabilitation, though designation will differ from state to state. It may be under the auspices of labor, education, or social services. County and local hospital social work offices have information on the services provided through Vocational Rehabilitation. These include free vocational counseling and referral to training programs or job placement services. For some, tuition and transportation costs may be paid.

The educational services for the home-bound, blind, or deaf include closed-circuit television and telephone hookups to various institutions such as public schools and community colleges. The National Library Service for the Blind and Physically Handicapped of the Library of Congress provides free cassette players and cassettes. A number of other organizations, such as the National Association for Visually Handicapped, supply complimentary services or additional types of equipment.

ORGANIZATIONS FOR PEOPLE WITH SPECIFIC DISABILITIES

Numerous organizations seek to serve the needs of those with a specific disability. Many are national in scope, with state or local chapters; others are local, having been created through the generosity and concern of some family or group. All provide useful public education materials, some have regular publications, and a few offer direct financial aid, equipment, or personal advice.

The directory in appendix C lists the national offices of specific disability groups. They should be able to make referrals to appropriate local affiliates as well as to other agencies that might be more helpful in a particular locale.

The directory is not exhaustive. There are many other sources of assistance and information, and each of the resources can provide names of others as well. With luck this constellation of resources can be found quickly. Many times, however, the search requires persistence and patience.

Any resource guide is apt to be out-of-date soon after it appears in print. Organizations, both public and private, frequently change names and addresses. Groups merge and move. If the names and addresses given in the directory appear to have changed, the information can be quickly updated by seeking help from your local reference librarian. The *Encyclopedia of Associations* is a guide published annually that lists virtually every nongovernmental organization in the United States (federal organizations are similarly listed in the U.S. Government Manual). When names change or groups merge, the old names are retained in the index for a few years. In addition, the information given about the individual organizations in the directory will include former names.

DIRECTORY OF HEALTH ORGANIZATIONS AND RESOURCES

Appendix B includes major organizations and agencies that provide health information and other services. Most are national organizations and many have local chapters not included in this directory. Check your telephone white pages for possible listings. Telephone numbers have been supplied for those organizations able to handle phone inquiries. The others would prefer that inquiries be made by mail. Since organizations frequently move, all addresses are subject to change.

3
Medical Decision Making: Ethical Considerations

DAVID J. ROTHMAN, Ph.D.

Extraordinary advances in medical science and technology have made possible the cure of previously incurable diseases, the repair of organs that seem hopelessly damaged, the survival of tiny, premature infants, and the prolongation of life. They have also raised a host of perplexing questions such as:

Should brain-dead patients be maintained on respirators so that their organs can be transplanted?

When survival can be prolonged almost indefinitely by mechanical means, who decides if the machinery should be disconnected?

Should every effort be made to save all babies with birth defects, no matter how severe?

Our extended medical capabilities create these ethical dilemmas and require the painstaking application of moral principles.

Bioethicists—specialists in the interface of ethics and the biological sciences—generally agree that three important moral principles should guide medical decision making: respect for autonomy, beneficence, and justice.

AUTONOMY

Self-determination is central to the Western regard for individual freedom, privacy, and the acceptance of responsibility for one's actions. Respecting others' autonomy acknowledges their right to their own choices, opinions, values, goals, and freedom to act without interference. In medicine, respect for autonomy allows patients to make their own decisions in consonance with their values.

An autonomous person acts or makes choices after careful evaluation of the alternatives. People unable to make fully deliberate choices (children, the mentally ill, and the retarded) depend on others to decide for them. Consequently, people of diminished autonomy who are mentally incompetent to make their own decisions require someone to speak for them.

BENEFICENCE

The principle of beneficence is best expressed by the simple, authoritative terms of the Hippocratic corpus: *primum non nocere*—"above all, to do no harm." Doctors have a duty not to inflict unnecessary pain or cause other problems. They are also pledged to strive for the best outcome for their patients, using their knowledge and skill to cure disease, restore function, preserve life,

and relieve suffering. They owe these duties both to their own patients and to the population in general. As the World Medical Association stated in 1975: "It is the mission of the medical doctor to safeguard the health of the people."

Traditionally, doctors have argued that the principle of beneficence justified withholding the truth about grim prognoses; in their patients' best interests they kept bad news about disease to themselves. Today, such "benevolent paternalism" has been effectively challenged by those who view it as direct interference with the individual's right of self-determination.

JUSTICE

Justice requires that people be treated fairly: All similar cases should be treated alike, the needs of all should be taken into consideration in allocating scarce resources, and everyone should receive equal access to the benefits of medicine—or an equal liability to the risks of biomedical research. Justice is not served when some receive preferential treatment, when people are denied information or services to which they are entitled, or when the interests of the few prevail over the many.

CONFLICTING PRINCIPLES

No single moral principle has absolute standing in medicine or anywhere else. Principles, and the claims that spring from them, sometimes collide. Although some people bestow more weight to considerations of autonomy than to beneficence, or primarily rely on the principle of justice, it is still no easy matter to resolve many bioethical conundrums. For example:

A bedridden but not terminally ill woman asks the hospital and its physicians to stop feeding her. Are they bound to honor her request in disregard of their mission to preserve her life?

A heart transplant team is trying to rank potential recipients of organs in order of priority. Should the team accept the principle of "first come, first served," or should the sickest patient receive the next available heart?

A patient asks his physician not to tell his fiancée that he has an inherited fatal disease. Should the physician withhold the information?

No set of ethics governs real-life situations without exceptions and qualifications. Conflicting principles can be resolved only by carefully balancing each.

THE PATIENT'S BILL OF RIGHTS

(as established by the American Hospital Association)

The hospital shall establish written policies regarding the rights of patients upon admission for treatment as an inpatient, outpatient, or emergency room patient, and shall develop procedures implementing such policies. These rights, policies, and procedures shall afford patients the right to:

1. Receive emergency medical care, as indicated by the patient's medical condition, upon arrival at a hospital for the purpose of obtaining emergency medical treatment
2. Considerate and respectful care
3. Obtain the name of the physician assigned the responsibility for coordinating his or her care and the right to consult with a private physician and/or a specialist for the type of care being rendered, provided such physician has been accorded hospital staff privileges
4. The name and function of any person providing treatment to the patient
5. Obtain from his or her physician complete current information concerning diagnosis, treatment, and prognosis in terms the patient can reasonably be expected to understand
6. Receive from his or her physician information necessary to give informed consent prior to the start of any nonemergency procedure or treatment or both. An informed consent shall include, as a minimum, the specific procedure or treatment or both, the reasonably foreseeable risks involved, and alternatives for care or treatment, if any, as a reasonable medical practitioner under similar circumstances would disclose
7. Refuse treatment to the extent permitted by law, and to be informed of the medical consequences of his or her action
8. Privacy to the extent consistent with providing adequate medical care to the patient. This shall not preclude discreet discussion of a patient's case or examination of a patient by appropriate health care personnel
9. Privacy and confidentiality of all records pertaining to the patient's treatment, except as otherwise provided by law or third-party payment contract

10. A response by the hospital, in a reasonable manner, to the patient's request for services customarily rendered by the hospital consistent with the patient's treatment
11. Be informed by his or her physician, or designee of the physician, of the patient's continuing health care requirement following discharge, and that before transferring a patient to another facility the hospital first informs the patient of the need for and alternatives to such a transfer
12. The identity, upon request, of other health care and educational institutions that the hospital has authorized to participate in the patient's treatment
13. Refuse to participate in research, and that human experimentation affecting care or treatment shall be performed only with the patient's informed effective consent
14. Examine and receive an explanation of his or her bill, regardless of source of payment
15. Know the hospital rules and regulations that apply to his or her conduct as a patient
16. Treatment without discrimination as to race, color, religion, sex, national origin, or source of payment, except for fiscal capability thereof
17. Designate any private accommodation to which admitted as a nonsmoking area. In the event that private accommodations are not available, a patient shall have a right to be admitted to accommodations that have been designated by the governing authority as a nonsmoking area. It shall be the duty of the governing authority of the hospital to afford priority to the rights of nonsmokers in all semiprivate, ward, and pediatric common patient areas
18. Voice grievances and recommend changes in policies and services to the facility's staff, the governing authority and the state department of health without fear of reprisal.

A copy of the provisions of this section shall be made available to each patient or patient's representatives upon admission for treatment as an inpatient, outpatient, and/or emergency room patient, and posted in conspicuous places within the hospital.

PATIENTS' RIGHTS

In 1973, the American Hospital Association (ASA) formalized a list of hospital patients rights—the Patient's Bill of Rights. Its two objectives are to meet the demands of consumer-protection groups for greater accountability from health care providers and to turn back the rising tide of malpractice suits by making the hospital experience less impersonal and therefore more satisfactory.

This document's use of the language of rights, however, expresses entitlement—a demand by patients for the duties of health care professionals and hospitals. The document must be posted in hospital corridors and is often printed in patient information handbooks. (See box.)

Much of the Patient's Bill of Rights is self-explanatory and straightforward, such as the right to emergency care (1) or the right to information about transfer (11). Other, more general principles deal with the intangible considerations affecting hospital stays, specifically the relationship between hospitalized patients and those who provide care. These include the patient's right to respectful, considerate, and responsive care (2, 10); the right to care that is personal and individualized—if only to the extent that the names and functions of the caregivers are known (3, 4); the right to be treated without prejudice or discrimination (16).

Embedded in this document are outline descriptions of two rights of particular importance. Points 5, 6, and 7 concern the concept of "informed consent," inextricably linked to "necessary information." Points 8 and 9 concern the right to privacy (necessarily qualified by the facts of hospital life) and privacy of information.

Patients' prerogative to see their charts is nowhere mentioned in the bill of rights, but this is a legal right that patients should exercise. (Despite this legal right, a patient's chart is, in fact, the property of the hospital.)

Some doctors argue that patients often cannot cope with the information in their charts (the entries are written by doctors and nurses in medical shorthand as a record for other health care professionals), and charts may not satisfy patients' curiosity about their condition. But charts can serve as useful foundations for conversation between doctors and patients to clear up uncertainties about the purpose of treatment or the prognosis.

PRIVACY AND CONFIDENTIALITY

Confidentiality between patients and their doctors is an ancient tradition in medicine. The Hippocratic oath spells this out: "Whatsoever I shall see or hear in the course of my profession . . . if it be what should not be published abroad, I will never divulge, holding such things to be holy secrets." This tradition is legally recognized by the courts and a patient can generally rest assured that information given to the doctor will not be disclosed. Occasionally, however, major exceptions to this rule occur.

For example, doctors are legally required to report to the Centers for Disease Control and Prevention Public Health Service cases of sexually transmitted diseases that they discover in their practice. In this case, the doctor's obligation to protect others from harm overrides loyalty to the patient.

In other cases where the same principle would seem to apply, the law is less clear. A California Supreme Court decision (*Tarasoff* v. *Regents of the University of California*, 1976) established the principle that psychotherapists "have a duty to exercise reasonable care to protect an individual at risk, or when harm may not be inevitable." Nevertheless, most doctors would not feel obligated to preserve confidentiality if, for example, one of their patients was an airline pilot suffering from blackouts or seizures who refused to ground him or herself.

Other exceptions to the confidentiality rule involve record keeping: While informal exchanges of medical information between doctors usually protect patients' identities, hospital charts are often discussed among doctors and nurses, although strong hospital traditions demand that the details of a patient's case not be discussed with anyone not on the health care team.

Test results and x-rays, as well as all information given to doctors, whether in their offices or in the hospital, automatically become part of a patient's record. Insurance companies are allowed access to medical records before making payments. In practice, they usually receive a summary, but these may very well contain information that the patient would prefer stay out of their hands.

CONFIDENTIALITY AND AIDS

Many people believe that the enormity of the AIDS threat to public health justifies exceptional measures to curb its spread. In particular, some experts urge widespread screening of high-risk groups of people with blood tests for the presence of the AIDS virus (HIV) antibodies. (When these antibodies are present, an individual is infectious, even though no disease symptoms are present.) Counseling and education of those with positive test results may help limit the high-risk behaviors that contribute to transmission of the virus. Routine testing is controversial, not because of test inaccuracies, but due to the patient's right to privacy.

Testing all donated blood and blood products, semen,

organs, and tissues for HIV antibodies is standard medical practice. Testing is mandatory for all members of the armed forces, inmates of federal prisons, state department personnel, and applicants to the Job Corps. On the other hand, mandatory testing before obtaining a marriage license is rare and in most other cases, testing remains voluntary.

The Centers for Disease Control and Prevention recommend that certain groups be "encouraged" to seek testing, including people being treated for intravenous drug use or sexually transmitted diseases, high-risk women of childbearing age, women of childbearing age living in areas where AIDS is prevalent, prostitutes, and those who suspect that they are at risk because they have had multiple sexual partners. It is suggested that people be tested only when the purpose of the test, its range of reliability, and its potential for social harm have been clearly explained, and the individual has given consent. Counseling should be provided for those who practice high-risk behaviors.

However, it is recognized that without strong safeguards of confidentiality, testing only scares away those at highest risk. In the continuing climate of fear about AIDS, third-party knowledge of positive test results may cause stigmatization and jeopardize important civil rights in such areas as housing, employment, and access to health care. (In response to this threat, people with AIDS are now protected by the Americans with Disabilities Act, but discrimination that qualifies for redress is often difficult to prove.)

Currently, many states have confidentiality laws applying specifically to AIDS-related medical records. Most states allow disclosure to the sexual partners of affected individuals (as is true of sexually transmitted diseases in general), but some states still prohibit disclosure of HIV test results without written consent. However, the inclusion of test results in a medical record accessible only to those providing direct care to the patient, does not in itself constitute disclosure. And some states allow disclosure, without a person's consent, to organ banks, blood banks, state health agencies, and the personal physician. In states without disease-specific laws, state statutes on medical record keeping regulate disclosure of HIV test results. (These laws vary widely from state to state.)

The public's interest in providing care to people with a stigmatized medical condition as well as the fear of disclosure that scares away those in need of treatment has led to proposed federal legislation on this topic. Under this legislation, testing and counseling data would be disclosed only to:

> public health officers, if required by state law
> blood, organ, semen, and breast milk banks

> spouses and sexual contacts (the disclosure would be made by a doctor or counselor)
> health care workers who would come in physical contact with infected body fluids

In addition, records could be subpoenaed by a state health officer attempting to stop transmission of the disease. However, as of this writing, no federal legislation specifically restricts the disclosure of HIV test results. Instead, these decisions are regulated by individual state laws.

Because of the cost of care for AIDS (the direct cost, from diagnosis to death, according to the Agency for Healthcare Policy and Research, is about $100,000 per case), insurance companies may not want to cover individuals at risk for AIDS with health or individual life insurance policies. Most jurisdictions currently allow insurers to test for HIV before writing life insurance policies, while some states restrict the use of the test or even prohibit inquiries about past tests prior to writing health care policies.

LEGAL ASPECTS

The idea that individuals must consent to medical intervention before a doctor can treat a patient has a long history in common law. Originally associated with the notion of "assault and battery," a physician was liable for damages if he touched the body of a patient without consent, notwithstanding motive, evil intentions, or consequent injury. Unauthorized "offensive touching," violating bodily integrity, was sufficient to establish liability.

In the early 20th century, the law also recognized that the purpose of obtaining a patient's consent, in addition to authorizing what would otherwise be battery, was to ensure that decisions about medical treatment were consistent with patients' wishes. A legal commentary of 1903 noted: "The patient must be the final arbiter as to whether he shall take his chance with the operation, or take his chances of living without it."

The concept of negligence was introduced somewhat later. Liability for negligence stems from the fiduciary nature of the doctor-patient relationship. Doctors and patients are not equal partners: One is healthy and knowledgeable, the other sick and medically ignorant. The stronger partner—the doctor—thus has a duty to take care of the weaker and can be held liable for any "careless" action or failure to act. Courts held that the doctor's "duty of care" included informing the patient about the nature and consequences of the proposed treatment before asking for consent and that the failure to do so was negligence.

"Consent" became "informed consent" in a landmark

case in 1957, declaring that doctors have a duty to disclose "any facts which are necessary to form the basis of an intelligent consent by the patient to proposed treatment." These "necessary" facts include information about risks and benefits of treatment, and existing alternatives. Only if the patient has had the opportunity to evaluate the available options and weigh their attendant risks and benefits, the court held, can an informed and autonomous choice be made.

The patient's right to self-determination is not absolute. In situations involving the interests of society or where the patient's own welfare is at stake, a doctor is not required to obtain informed consent. Such instances may include:

• *Public health emergencies.* In crisis situations, the health of the population or a part of the population may demand a mass inoculation program or quarantine, even in disregard of an individual's wishes.

• *Medical emergencies.* When it is impossible or impractical to get a patient's informed consent (for example, in cases of serious trauma or a drug overdose), consent to treatment is assumed.

• *When the therapeutic privilege is invoked.* Doctors may claim the "therapeutic privilege" to withhold information on the grounds that disclosing it will have harmful effects on the patient. Some jurisdictions broadly interpret this concept, permitting doctors to withhold information if disclosure will cause *any* deterioration in the patient's physical or mental condition. Others permit nondisclosure only if the consequences of giving information would be so serious as to jeopardize treatment. But the courts have warned that the therapeutic privilege "does not accept the paternalistic notion that the physician may remain silent because divulgence might prompt the patient to forgo therapy the physician feels the patient really needs."

THE CLINICAL CONTEXT

Informed consent is required before surgery, many diagnostic and therapeutic treatments, and before anesthesia is administered. It is also required before a patient participates in any clinical study or experiment (see below). Surgery and tests such as cardiac catheterization that involve considerable intrusion of bodily integrity require lengthy explanations.

A signed consent form stands as evidence that a patient has been informed about, and has given permission for, the treatment described on the form. Consent forms protect the rights of the patient, not those of the doctors, as is often thought. Signing a consent form does not waive the right to sue for malpractice.

For a patient to give, and a doctor to receive, properly informed consent, several requirements must be met.

1. The doctor must give the patient all relevant information about the nature and purpose of the procedure, its risks and benefits, and any alternatives—including the alternative of no treatment—with their associated risks and benefits. Although patients cannot reasonably expect to be told everything about the natural history of their disease (all the possible complications and remote risks of all alternative treatments), they are entitled to the disclosure of all "material" information. To define "material," courts have used a "reasonable-patient" standard, instructing doctors to give such information as a "reasonable person in the patient's position" would want to have, which clearly leaves a great deal to the doctor's judgment. A new standard now seems to be evolving: "Material" information is the information that this patient, in these circumstances, would want to know.

Withholding or distorting information out of concern for a patient's welfare is deception, albeit with a benevolent motive. Even though doctors tend to withhold the truth when a diagnosis of a fatal or terminal illness has been made, such information is obviously "material," and is, moreover, required by respect for a patient's dignity.

Studies have shown that most people would prefer to know the truth when their condition is grave. It has also been established that many patients know the truth without having been formally told. If doctors and family members keep silent, the inevitable result is emotional isolation, not protection, for the patient. While it is clearly wrong to force knowledge on someone who does not want it, doctors generally should give patients as much information as possible.

2. The patient must understand the information, whether it is given orally or written on a consent form. Common barriers to understanding are language problems and the often abstruse wording of consent forms. Fear, denial, and anxiety may also prevent patients from understanding and remembering what they have been told or appreciating its significance.

3. The patient's consent must be given voluntarily, without coercion or undue influence from health care personnel or others. Few doctors deliberately coerce patients into giving consent, but their indirect influence may weigh heavily. Moreover, the dependency engendered by sickness, anxiety, and hospitalization itself tends to impair the patients' ability to act of their own free will. The voluntariness of consent may also be undermined by well-meaning family and friends, or be compromised by strong emotion.

4. The patient must be mentally competent to give consent. There is no universally accepted definition of competence, which is both a legal and a psychological concept. Generally, to be considered mentally competent to give consent, a person must be able to understand what the treatment involves, and its consequences may be fairly minimal standards. At a more sophisticated level, a determination of competency may hinge on the patient's ability to make a "reasonable" decision. What seems reasonable to a patient may appear totally irrational to health care professionals. When a patient's competence is in doubt, consent must be given by a surrogate who has been designated to represent the patient. (See "Role of a Surrogate.")

A DEFINITION OF DEATH

At what point do we say that death has come? Only a few years ago, the answer seemed simple: when heartbeat and breathing stopped. But death is a process; all the body's organs do not fail simultaneously, and today's technology can restore and sustain the function of many organs. Machines can operate for hearts that do not beat and lungs that do not breathe on their own. But even though the question of when death is final has grown complex, it demands an answer.

In medicine, there are two practical reasons for needing a definition of death (the law and society have their own).

- With death all treatment ceases; resources devoted to the deceased can be redeployed for the living and a bed in the intensive care unit can be made available to another patient.
- After death, vital organs for transplantation may be legally taken from the body. To maximize the chances of success, these organs should be removed as soon after death as possible.

A definition of death (brain death) was developed in 1968 by a Harvard Medical School committee. According to this definition, a person is brain dead when he or she has suffered irreversible cessation of the functions of the entire brain, including the brain stem. This is determined by a number of tests that determine total unawareness of all stimuli, no spontaneous muscular movement or respiration, no reflexes of any kind, and a flat electroencephalogram, indicating the cessation of electrical activity in the brain. If after 24 hours there is no change, the patient can be declared dead. The Harvard committee recommended that the declaration of death be made by doctors uninvolved in any way with planned transplantation of organs or tissues from the body, as a protection for both doctor and patient.

Although the "Harvard definition" remains widely accepted, it is recognized that medical criteria and tests for determining death are liable to change as knowledge increases and techniques grow more refined. For this reason, the statute proposed in 1981 by the President's Commission for the Study of Ethical Problems in Medicine relies instead on "accepted medical standards." From this perspective, a person is dead when he or she has sustained "irreversible cessation of circulatory and respiratory functions," or if heartbeat and breathing are being maintained mechanically and "irreversible cessation of all functions of the entire brain, including the brain stem" has occurred. In either case, doctors must determine beyond doubt both the cessation of function and its irreversibility. This statute, endorsed by numerous influential medical and legal associations, has been adopted by many states.

TREATMENT DECISIONS

Physicians' ethics and their professional training strongly emphasize the necessity of positive action to combat disease and preserve life, and the resources of modern medicine provide powerful tools to fulfill these objectives. Yet, respect for autonomy requires them to honor their patients' values and goals and not allow their own values to influence patients' decisions about treatment. Unsurprisingly, conflicts arise when a patient exercises the right to refuse treatment that the doctor feels is necessary.

Refusals of diagnostic tests or treatments may reflect patients' unwillingness to accept risks or willingness to bear pain (as in the refusal of painkillers). Refusals of this kind may not have detrimental consequences, and when they result from careful choice such decisions are usually accepted relatively easily by doctors. However, the patient's request to forgo treatment must be meticulously evaluated when the refusal will almost certainly lead to immediate death.

Sometimes patients' reasons for refusing treatment are religious, as when a Jehovah's Witness refuses a transfusion because of the conviction that "eating blood" violates God's law. Sometimes the motive is a desire to spare the family the emotional and financial strain of a prolonged dying. Most often, however, the basis for refusing treatment (or further treatment) are patients' judgments that the quality of their lives is so poor that they do not wish a prolonged existence. These subjective assessments of the quality of life vary from person to person and may shift at different ages. Some people can accept painful circumstances intolerable to others, and older people may be able to accept restrictions that are unacceptable to the young. While the doctor has the responsibility to use professional judgment and to give advice, patients are best able to judge the acceptability of their quality of life.

Clearly, it is of extreme importance that the decision to refuse treatment, especially when the refusal almost certainly means death, is made by a patient who is mentally competent and fully informed. On the other hand, only informed and caring surrogates should decide for incompetent patients. The decision should involve a probe into the patient's motives and a careful consideration of his or her physical and psychological status. Pain, disease, and depression may warp a patient's judgment; drugs may affect mental ability; wishes may be ambivalent. Competence to decide may be lost and then regained, thus making it necessary to reevaluate decisions. However, doctors should recognize that a patient's refusal of treatment is not in itself reason to question the patient's mental competence.

Although patients retain the right to refuse treatment, some take this a step further and demand euthanasia. A Harris Poll found that while a majority of doctors consider it wrong to comply with a patient's request to end his or her life, the public as a whole does support this concept. Legally, "mercy killing" is murder. However, while euthanasia puts caregivers at risk for prosecution and is morally unacceptable to many of them, few regard the use of narcotics that relieve suffering as wrong. The withdrawal of life-support systems from terminally ill patients, at their request, is generally accepted as well and is not regarded as "killing." Physicians sharply distinguish between "permitting to die" (failing to use extraordinary measures, letting nature take its course) and "causing death" by direct intervention.

Despite polls indicating public support, it is not clear whether the public would, in fact, sanction the practice of active euthanasia by the medical profession. In Michigan, a law that took effect in 1993 made it a felony to help another person commit suicide. The Michigan suicide law, largely a reaction to the much publicized suicide assistance provided to several ostensibly terminally ill people by Jack Kevorkian, M.D., is being challenged by a number of court cases, including one involving Dr. Kevorkian, on constitutional grounds. In November 1994, the state of Oregon passed an initiative that would allow physician-assisted suicide.

In general, while doctors' feelings about preserving life are very strong, and their most compelling ethical principle is to do no harm, the relief of suffering is increasingly being seen as a central tenet of medicine.

CARDIOPULMONARY RESUSCITATION

When someone suffers a cardiac arrest, cardiopulmonary resuscitation (CPR) must be started immediately to have any chance of success. CPR is a very aggressive treatment: In an effort to restart the heart, the chest is massaged forcefully, numerous tubes are rapidly inserted, and electrical shocks are administered to the heart. Unfortunately, this therapy is not often successful. In a study at a major medical center, only 14 percent of those resuscitated survived to leave the hospital. Many feel these studies show CPR is used too often, that its use of resources (expert personnel, time, money, and subsequent intensive care) is disproportionate to its benefits, and that it might often be used inappropriately, thus bringing more harm than good to those subjected to it.

Many hospitals routinely perform CPR on all patients who suffer a cardiac arrest, except those for whom DNR (do not resuscitate) orders have been written. A DNR order means that if a patient's heart stops beating, the staff member who observes this will not "call a code" to bring the CPR team to the bedside, and the patient will be allowed to die (usually within a few minutes).

No order to withhold resuscitation should be written without a competent patient's consent, and patients have the right to accept or refuse any other treatment. When a patient is mentally competent, doctors discuss the possibility of a cardiac arrest with him or her, and explain resuscitation attempts and their consequences. Occasionally, when a doctor feels that such a discussion would adversely affect the patient's condition, he or she will seek a "therapeutic exception," preferring to talk with the family. To prevent abuse or overuse, the use of the therapeutic exception is being increasingly circumscribed. When a patient is not competent, and there is no clear and convincing evidence of what he or she would have wanted, the family (or a surrogate) has to make the decision. Because cardiac arrest is not uncommon in the seriously ill, many doctors are making it a practice to discuss the possible need for CPR early on, when such patients are first hospitalized.

If so instructed, a doctor primarily responsible for a patient's care enters the DNR order in the chart, together with the circumstances that justify it: the diagnosis, the prognosis, and the appropriateness of withholding resuscitation. Discussions with the patient, or the patient's family, or both, are also documented.

A DNR order can be viewed as a decision to withhold a lifesaving treatment *or* as an appropriate part of a decision to pursue a nonaggressive treatment plan. But the decision's morality order depends on how it is decided. When a mentally competent patient or surrogate has participated freely and fully in the decision not to do CPR, the consequent decision is informed and cannot be challenged on moral grounds.

SAMPLE   **ADVANCE DIRECTIVE**

LIVING WILL AND HEALTH CARE PROXY

Death is a part of life. It is a reality like birth, growth, and aging. I am using this advance directive to convey my wishes about medical care to my doctors and other people looking after me at the end of my life. It is called an advance directive because it gives instructions in advance about what I want to happen to me in the future. It expresses my wishes about medical treatment that might keep me alive. I want this to be legally binding.

If I cannot make or communicate decisions about my medical care, those around me should rely on this document for instructions about measures that could keep me alive.

I do not want medical treatment (including feeding and water by tube) that will keep me alive if:

I am unconscious and there is no reasonable prospect that I will ever be conscious again (even if I am not going to die soon in my medical condition), *or*

I am near death from an illness or injury with no reasonable prospect of recovery.

I do want medicine and other care to make me more comfortable and to take care of pain and suffering. I want this even if the pain medicine makes me die sooner.

I want to give some extra instructions. [Here list any special instructions, e.g., some people fear being kept alive after a debilitating stroke. If you have wishes about this, or any other conditions, please write them here.]

The legal language in the box that follows is a health care proxy. It gives another person power to make medical decisions for me.

I name_____, who

lives at _____,

phone number _____,

to make medical decisions for me if I cannot make them myself. This person is called a health care surrogate, agent, proxy, or attorney-in-fact. This power of attorney shall become effective when I become incapable of making or communicating decisions about my medical care. This means that this document stays legal when and if I lose the power to speak for myself, for instance, if I am in a coma or have Alzheimer's disease.

My health care proxy has power to tell others what my advance directive means. This person also has power to make decisions for me, based either on what I would have wanted, or, if this is not known, on what he or she thinks is best for me.

If my first choice health care proxy cannot or decides not to act for me, I name _____,

address _____,

phone number _____, as my second

choice.

I have discussed my wishes with my health care proxy, and with my second choice if I have chosen to appoint a second person. My proxy(ies) has(have) agreed to act for me.

I have thought about this advance directive carefully. I know what it means and want to sign it. I have chosen two witnesses, neither of whom is a member of my family, nor will inherit from me when I die. My witnesses are not the same people as those I named as my health care proxies. I understand that this form should be notarized if I use the box to name (a) health care proxy(ies).

Signature _____

Date _____

Address _____

Witness's signature _____

Witness's printed name _____

Address _____

Witness's signature _____

Witness's printed name _____

Address _____

Notary [to be used if proxy is appointed]

Reprinted by permission of Choice in Dying (formerly Concern for Dying/Society for the Right to Die), 200 Varick Street, 10th Floor, New York, N.Y. 10014-4810, (212) 366-5540.

EVIDENCE OF PATIENTS' WISHES— ADVANCE DIRECTIVES

Advance directives are written documents, often prepared *before* the onset of any serious illness, which state a person's wishes regarding health care and/or the designation of another person to make health care decisions in the event that the ill person is impaired and cannot decide.

THE LIVING WILL

In an effort to implement patients' exercise of autonomy, 47 states have enacted living will laws, beginning with the California Natural Death Act of 1976. The provisions of these laws vary from state to state, but they share a recognition of the living will as a legal document; they also protect doctors acting in accordance with a living will from legal action by families or others. Even in those states that do not have such laws, the living will provides important though not necessarily binding evidence of an individual's wishes.

A living will is a statement made by a mentally competent person as to what he or she wants done in terms of health care if mental incapacitation occurs. An individual can draw up an original will or use a standard form (which varies somewhat among states). These forms can be obtained from Choice in Dying (formerly Concern for Dying/Society for the Right to Die), 200 Varick Street, 10th Floor, New York, N.Y. 10014-4810, (212) 366-5540. (See box for sample of an advance directive.)

Typically, a living will expresses an individual's wish that, when the terminal phase of illness is reached, doctors should refrain from life-sustaining measures that would only prolong dying, and that he or she should be allowed to die with dignity. The wording is necessarily imprecise, since the will is intended to cover unknown future circumstances, but the individual's general intentions and desires are unmistakable. It is incumbent on those to whom the directive is addressed to ensure that any treatment given conforms with those intentions, whether or not they would have chosen this course themselves.

HEALTH CARE PROXY/DURABLE POWER OF ATTORNEY FOR HEALTH CARE

In a number of states, the concept of a durable power of attorney—originally dealing with decisions about property—has been extended to cover health care decisions. A durable power of attorney or health care proxy is usually, but not necessarily, drawn up with a lawyer's help. It may be included as part of the living will or as a separate document. (See samples.)

A durable power of attorney empowers a family member or friend to act on another's behalf, as an "attorney-in-fact." While an ordinary power of attorney becomes invalid if the principal (i.e., the patient) becomes incompetent, a durable power of attorney continues through any future incapacity unless it has been revoked by the individual while still mentally competent.

A health care proxy or durable power of attorney is in many ways preferable to a living will because it extends beyond the prohibitions typical of that document. Decisions can be made based on the appointee's intimate knowledge of the patient's wishes *and* the doctor's recommendations. The appointee is in the position of knowing the patient's condition and prognosis, and receives medical advice on an actual, present set of circumstances. Unfortunately, many people, especially isolated elderly people, have no one to appoint.

It is wise to have several copies of a durable power of attorney prepared, signed, and even notarized, since an institution may retain a copy as a defense against possible legal challenge.

THE PATIENT SELF-DETERMINATION ACT

Advance directives took on increased importance as a result of the the Patient Self-Determination Act, federal legislation that went into effect in December 1991. It requires hospitals, nursing facilities, hospices, home health care programs, and HMOs to provide information to adult patients about their rights under state law to accept or refuse treatment and how to prepare an advance directive. The health care organizations must also document whether patients receiving services have advance directives. (See box.) Violators of the act risk losing Medicare and Medicaid funds.

The Patient Self-Determination Act was inspired by the case of Nancy Cruzan, a Missouri woman injured in a car accident in 1983. The Cruzan family had spent years trying to secure court permission to stop tube feedings to Ms. Cruzan, who had been severely and irreversibly brain damaged as a result of the accident. The U.S. Supreme Court ruled against the family's wishes. The Court noted the lack of clear and convincing evidence of what the patient would want if she were capable of communicating before allowing a step, such as removal of nutrition, that would most certainly cause death.

Eventually, the Cruzans won the right to remove Ms. Cruzan's feeding tube, and she died two weeks after disconnection. However, the long and draining process could have been dramatically shortened if Ms. Cruzan had left behind a statement of her wishes. After witnessing the family's ordeal, Missouri Senator John Danforth

SAMPLE   ## DURABLE POWER OF ATTORNEY FOR HEALTH CARE

I, _____ ,

hereby appoint: _____

Name _____

Home address _____

Home telephone number _____

Work telephone number _____

as my agent to make health care decisions for me if and when I am unable to make my own health care decisions. This gives my agent the power to consent to giving, withholding, or stopping any health care, treatment, service, or diagnostic procedure. My agent also has the authority to talk with health care personnel, get information, and sign forms necessary to carry out those decisions. If the person named as my agent is not available or is unable to act as my agent, then I appoint the following person(s) to serve in the order listed below:

1. Name _____

Home address _____

Home telephone number _____

Work telephone number _____

2. Name _____

Home address _____

Home telephone number _____

Work telephone number _____

By this document I intend to create a power of attorney for health care that shall take effect upon my incapacity to make my own health care decisions and shall continue during that incapacity.

My agent shall make health care decisions as I direct below or as I make known to him or her in some other way.

(a) Statement of desires concerning life-prolonging care, treatment, services, and procedures:

_____

_____

_____

(b) Special provisions and limitations:

_____

_____

_____

BY SIGNING HERE I INDICATE THAT I UNDERSTAND THE PURPOSE AND EFFECT OF THIS DOCUMENT.

I sign my name to this form on _____

My current home address:

_____

_____

(You sign here)

···

WITNESSES

I declare that the person who signed or acknowledged this document is personally known to me, that he/she signed or acknowledged this durable power of attorney in my presence, and that he/she appears to be of sound mind and under no duress, fraud, or undue influence. I am not the person appointed as agent by this document, nor am I the patient's health care provider, or an employee of the patient's health care provider.

First Witness

Signature: _____

Home address: _____

Print name: _____

Date: _____

Second Witness

Signature: _____

Home address: _____

Print name: _____

Date: _____

(At least one of the above witnesses must also sign the following declaration.)

I further declare that I am not related to the patient by blood, marriage, or adoption, and, to the best of my knowledge, I am not entitled to any part of his/her estate under a will now existing or by operation of law.

Signature: _____

Signature: _____

I further declare that I am not related to the patient by blood, marriage, or adoption, and, to the best of my knowledge, I am not entitled to any part of his/her estate under a will now existing or by operation of law.

Signature: _____

Signature: _____

*Check requirements of your area's state statute.

Sample form is from "A Matter of Choice," prepared for the U.S. Senate Special Committee on Aging.

WHAT DOES THE PATIENT SELF-DETERMINATION ACT SAY?

The Patient Self-Determination Act requires all Medicare and Medicaid provider organizations (specifically, hospitals, nursing facilities, home health agencies, hospices, and prepaid health care organizations) to:

1. Provide written information to patients at the time of admission concerning an individual's right under State law (whether statutory or as recognized by the courts of the State) to make decisions concerning . . . medical care, including the right to accept or refuse medical or surgical treatment and the right to formulate advance directives;
2. Maintain written policies and procedures with respect to advance directives (e.g., living wills and health care powers of attorney) and to provide written information to patients about such policies;
3. Document in the individual's medical record whether or not the individual has executed an advance directive;
4. Ensure compliance with the requirements of State law (whether statutory or as recognized by the courts of the State) respecting advance directives at facilities of the provider or organization; and
5. Provide (individually or with others) for education for staff and the community on issues concerning advance directives.

The act also requires providers not to condition the provision of care or otherwise discriminate against an individual based on whether or not the individual has executed a living will or other directive.

Adapted from "What Does the Patient Self-Determination Act Say?" from Choice in Dying.

(R) proposed the Patient Self-Determination Act in an effort to help families avoid such legal battles.

PROBLEMS WITH ADVANCE DIRECTIVES

Despite the promotion of advance directives, most Americans have still not completed one. For those who have completed them, their usefulness is sometimes limited for several reasons: The living will may reflect the desires and expectations of a person's middle years, which are based on values likely to change with age. Unless it has been regularly reviewed and revised, the consent given may not be valid at the time the will comes into effect. This may make doctors and hospitals reluctant to honor it.

Moreover, it may not be clear what treatments are to be thought of as life sustaining or life prolonging, and therefore to be withheld. For example, giving antibiotics to fight an infection is not generally considered life sustaining, but it is a treatment that someone in great pain from terminal cancer, and with a newly developed pneumonia, might prefer to forgo. On the other hand, many people would be reluctant to think of food and water as treatment; they seem, rather, basic to care. But, as evidenced by the final ruling in the Cruzan case, both the courts and the medical profession are increasingly accepting the tube feeding of terminally ill or comatose patients as a life-prolonging measure. Consequently, to make a living will truly effective, it is necessary to be very specific in its provision (although unforeseen future circumstances may make it impossible to cover *all* circumstances). Evaluating every likely variety of future health problem and identifying all possible treatment options is difficult, but your physician and lawyer can help you in this task.

Despite problems with timeliness and lack of precision, however, advance directives are powerful tools. In drawing up the documents, individuals secure the fulfillment of their wishes for a time when, by definition, they no longer have the ability to make their wishes known.

INFORMAL CONVERSATIONS WITH PHYSICIANS

What about informally discussing with your doctors what to do if you become incompetent? Unfortunately, this kind of approach seldom assures you of forgoing unwanted treatment.

- Your doctor may not be available when needed to substantiate your wishes.
- It is impossible to cover all future eventualities (the nature of the illness, the suffering and debilitation that it might entail, the types of treatment that might be available and their relative risks and benefits) with enough precision to make the doctor's record of the conversation of any real use.

Both of these are reasons to take a more formal approach. However, even if you have a prepared advance directive, it is wise to discuss it with your physician because he or she may be in charge when the need arises for lifesaving or life-ending decisions.

WHEN A PATIENT IS NO LONGER COMPETENT

When a patient no longer has the mental ability or the emotional stability to make his or her own decisions, someone must stand ready to protect and exercise the individual's rights. If a living will has been made or a durable power of attorney has been drawn up, those named in the documents have the task of making decisions the patient, if mentally competent, would have chosen. In other circumstances, however, it will be necessary for someone to act as a surrogate.

ROLE OF A SURROGATE

The factors usually considered in picking a surrogate are kin relationship and geographical closeness. However, advice is best given by the person most familiar with the patient's values and most likely to know of prior expressed wishes, whether that person is a relative, a friend, or a significant other. It may be, for example, that the lover of a young man dying of AIDS is a better surrogate than the patient's parent. However, if friends are themselves of doubtful competence and no family can be traced (as is often the case with elderly people who have lived for years in nursing homes), a guardian ad litem (a guardian for an express purpose) will be appointed by the court.

If there are useful clues such as statements made earlier about what the patient would want done, a pattern of past actions, or religious or philosophical beliefs, a surrogate can probably make a "substituted judgment," deciding as the patient would have decided. Often, however, there are no clues at all as to what the patient might have wanted. The surrogate must then try to make a judgment of what appears to be in the patient's best interests, balancing burdens and benefits of treatment alternatives with as much objectivity as possible.

Experts believe that surrogates making life and death decisions should follow a guideline proposed by the New Jersey Supreme Court (*in re* Conroy): Treatment is no longer in a patient's best interests when "the net of burdens of his prolonged life [the pain and suffering of his life with the treatment less the amount and duration of pain the patient would likely suffer if the treatment were withdrawn] markedly outweigh any physical pleasure, emotional enjoyment, or intellectual satisfaction that the patient may still be able to derive from life."

While the Conroy case concerned the withdrawal of treatment from an elderly nursing home patient suffering from many serious and irreversible impairments, the principles invoked by the court equally apply to patients' best interests in all cases involving life-sustaining treatments. Such decisions should be based on considerations of whether continued life would be of benefit *to the patient*. The value of that life to others—friends, family, the community—should not be part of the decision.

Many states have adopted the guideline inspired by the Conroy case, and 23 states have enacted statutes that establish a prioritized hierarchy of people who are to be consulted regarding surrogate decisions. Starting with immediate family members, this list encompasses those people who are most likely to know the wishes of the patient.

Decisions that have life-and-death consequences for mentally incompetent patients are often referred to hospital ethics committees (see "Ethics Committees" in this chapter), and are particularly appropriate for consideration there.

TERMINATING TREATMENT

For a person in a comatose state, the higher functions of the brain—those connected with thought and awareness—are lost. However, the brain stem may be relatively intact, and so the vegetative functions remain: reflexes, breathing, and the circulation of the blood. Food, if supplied, may be digested normally.

Comas may be brief, allowing a victim to recover completely, or they may last for months or years, ending only with death. Patients in a long-term coma are said to be "permanently comatose," or in a "persistent vegetative state." This diagnosis is based on a thorough physical examination and scans of the electrical activity of the brain; the chances of recovery are virtually nil. These circumstances pose an ethical dilemma about how to treat the comatose victim.

Medical treatment ordinarily aims at benefiting the patient by relieving suffering, restoring function, and preserving life. But the permanently comatose can derive no such benefits. No suffering occurs, function can never be regained, and these individuals are not alive in any meaningful sense of the word. Consequently, many argue that expending time and resources on treating the comatose is futile and inappropriate.

Decisions to terminate treatment of irreversibly comatose patients have been supported by the courts in numerous cases since the New Jersey Supreme Court ruled in 1976 that Karen Ann Quinlan's respirator could be unplugged. (Ms. Quinlan had been permanently comatose for more than a year. After the respirator was turned off, she resumed breathing on her own and lived in a vegetative state for nine more years.)

In the Quinlan case, the ruling was based on the patient's constitutional right to privacy, as were many of the subsequent rulings. Such decisions, long supported by responsible physicians, have also received the formal support of organized medicine. In 1986, the American Medical Association stated that it would not be unethical for doctors to withhold life-prolonging medical treatment, including food and water, from patients in an irreversible coma, even when death was not imminent.

ETHICS COMMITTEES

Though ethics committees are still not as widely established as they should be, they are now found in most medium-size and large hospitals. A very large medical center may have several committees, each associated with a different division, including, very importantly, the neonatal nursery. The committees are charged with review of institutional decision making and have, to a considerable extent, substituted for the cumbersome and expensive judicial review of controversial decisions.

There is no "typical" ethics committee. Some have a recognized place within the hospital's administrative structure; some are independent. They may concentrate on setting policy for their institutions, focus on educating staff members about relating ethical principles to specific decisions, or they may serve mainly to confirm medical prognoses (these might be more properly called prognosis committees). Generally, however, a committee counts among its members one or two doctors, a nurse, a hospital administrator or an attorney, a member of the clergy, a bioethicist, a social worker, and one or more laypeople. The inclusion of laypeople is important because they introduce a perspective different from that of the more medically oriented members. The committee meets regularly, but often at short notice and upon the request of doctors or nurses or families (increasingly) when serious differences arise about treatment decisions among health care professionals, or between families and health care professionals.

Cases that go before ethics committees often concern the appropriate level of care for terminally ill patients, and the withholding or withdrawal of life-support measures. Other cases have to do with the disclosure of information, with families who insist on inappropriate treatment for patients, or with patients who refuse treatment yet refuse to be discharged. In neonatal ethics committees, most questions center on the benefits of aggressive, or heroic, versus conservative (for example, maintenance) treatment for seriously ill newborns.

A committee's task is to give advice, not to make decisions. An ethics committee does not supplant the regular decision makers—doctors, patients, and families—nor are its recommendations binding. Rather, it provides for prompt and sensitive review of difficult decisions and ensures that the interests of all concerned—especially those of mentally incompetent patients—are properly considered. When they are directly involved, patients

and their families may be invited to attend the meeting. This is an important opportunity for them to express their views and to hear those of a group that might be said to constitute their "moral community."

If a case concerns disagreements among caregivers—between two doctors, for example, or a doctor and nurse—patients may not be told that the ethics committee is to be consulted. Since details of the patient's condition will be discussed, and the medical record may be quoted, strict confidentiality may be breached. Generally, however, the deliberations of the committee will be governed by the conventions of medical confidentiality as these are observed in a hospital setting.

DECIDING FOR SERIOUSLY ILL NEWBORNS

Of all the children born alive in the United States each year, about 6 percent are so ill that they must be treated in a neonatal intensive care unit (NICU). The great majority of the babies in such units are of low birth weight, weighing 2,500 grams (5.5 pounds) or less. Advances in neonatal care have dramatically improved the survival rate of these tiny babies and of those born weighing less than 1,000 grams (2.2 pounds), half now survive. (Only a couple of decades ago, nine of ten babies of that birth weight would have quickly died.) Other babies in the intensive neonatal unit have severe congenital defects, some caused by defective genes or chromosomal abnormalities, with a grave prognosis. Still others are born very prematurely.

While medicine often has the power to save the lives of infants such as these, should all neonates, regardless of their condition, receive very aggressive treatment? In the NICU, the choices about who shall live and who shall die are frequently more agonizing than anywhere else in the hospital.

Since medical questions regarding infants cannot be decided based on substituted judgment (what the infant would have decided if competent), society generally recognizes parents' rights to autonomy and privacy in making decisions on behalf of their children, and parents almost always speak for the child when choices about treatment must be made. As a result, when infants face severe illness or disability, parents must undertake the extraordinarily difficult task of putting themselves fully in the child's position, and make a decision that is in the best interest of the child both now and in the future.

Neonatologists or pediatricians and neonatology unit nurses must give parents both guidance and information in making these kinds of decisions. The offered information must be up-to-date, as accurate as possible about the prognosis, and frank as to areas of uncertainty. Doctors must make certain that despite the emotional turmoil that surrounds the birth of a seriously ill or defective infant, parents truly grasp the facts of their child's condition and prognosis, and understand the risks, benefits, and long-term implications of the treatment options.

Sometimes the medical facts are clear, the future quality of a child's life can be easily assessed, and the choice of treatment is not difficult: When a child has a mild impairment, all efforts to sustain life should be attempted. On the other hand, for a baby born terminally ill or with a severe and irreparable congenital life-threatening defect, treatment only prolongs suffering. However, between these extremes lies a large zone of uncertainty. Here, the standard proposed by the President's Commission is apt:

> Permanent handicaps justify a decision not to provide life-sustaining treatment only when they are so severe that continued existence would not be a net benefit to the infant. . . . Benefit is absent only if the burdens imposed on the [infants] by the disability or its treatment would lead a competent decision maker to forgo the treatment.

This standard would, for example, lead to a decision to perform surgery for the repair of a blocked intestinal tract in a Down syndrome baby. Although these children have some degree of mental retardation, they are usually both loving and lovable and their quality of life in a caring environment is good.

The standard is, as the Commission notes, a "very restrictive" one, since it specifically excludes any consideration of the negative impact an impaired child's life might have on parents and siblings. The *value* of the life *to the child* must be the basis for all decisions.

Sometimes parents make decisions that others consider detrimental to the welfare of their children. In such cases, parents and those caring for the child will have to try to reach an agreement as to what is to be done. If this effort fails, the hospital's neonatal ethics committee (sometimes called the infant care review committee) should review the case. This committee takes as its premise that it should seek the best interests of the child; to do so it enlists a variety of concerned people to help resolve the impasse. As a last resort—when, for example, physicians wish to continue treatment and parents persist in their refusal—the physicians may turn to a state agency (usually its child welfare bureau) or to the courts. A hearing will be held and a guardian will be appointed to protect the interests of the child.

....

ALLOCATION OF RESOURCES

Even in the United States, with the best-equipped hospitals in the world, assets are sometimes insufficient to meet needs. The scarcity of some resources, such as beds in intensive care units or skilled nurses, may reflect the results of public policy. In other instances, scarcity is an inherent problem, as with organs for transplantation. Allocation decisions—for example, how to decide which of two patients receives the one available bed in the intensive care unit—are among the most difficult in the daily practice of medicine in a hospital.

The principles that rule decisions of this kind (how society's benefits and burdens are to be distributed fairly) are those of distributive justice: Scarce resources are viewed as "society's benefits," items created by society's considerable investment of money, time, and talent. (Within intensive care units, the beds, the floor space, the monitors, respirators, drugs, and skilled nursing are all elements of intensive care.) Because of its investment, society, in the form of the hospital, has a legitimate role in deciding allocation of these resources.

Justice first requires that those competing for scarce resources be compared and judged. In the example of two patients both needing a hospital bed when only one is available, the initial relevant factors to be considered might be each patient's medical history, physical condition, and prognosis. From these, a judgment may be made that one patient would clearly benefit more than the other from intensive care.

However, in many cases, the initial comparison conclusion is that both potential patients are equally good candidates. The evaluators might then be tempted to consider *non-medical factors,* assessing the relative "social worth" of the two patients (their value to others, their past or potential future contribution to society) as a means of weighing society's "return for its investment" in one patient rather than the other. Subjective considerations of this kind, however, are treacherous, both ethically and practically: for instance, consider the question who is of greater social worth, a brilliant middle-aged bachelor scientist or a young woman with two children? Morality and fairness require a method of choosing among candidates that is less likely to be tainted with social bias.

In medicine, when two candidates demonstrate an equal likelihood of benefiting from a particular treatment and only one can receive it, the principle of justice usually used is "first come, first served." No one undergoing dialysis, for example, is terminated because a new patient arrives and the schedule is full. This rule preserves personal dignity by providing equality of opportunity, a basic element of justice.

ORGANS FOR TRANSPLANTATION

In today's medical world, human organs are the scarcest of resources. The standards for selecting recipients of organs for transplantation are rigorous. It must be clear that the patient has a good likelihood of benefiting from the procedure. Among the disqualifying conditions are serious illness (other than that to be remedied by the transplant), persistent health-threatening habits (such as smoking), obesity, and very advanced age.

While considerations of recipients' social worth should not be factored in to the transplantation decision, psychological factors are very important. Some hospitals do not charge for transplants, so financial means may not be a deciding factor, but federal and state medical programs refuse to pay for transplants regarded as experimental, a category including many infant organ transplants.

Patients who qualify for transplant are tissue- or blood-typed for compatibility with donated organs and are placed on the appropriate waiting list, which may be regional or (in the case of heart transplants) include all potential recipients in the United States. Waiting lists are weighted: those in more urgent need go to the top, while those in less serious condition are placed toward the bottom of the list. Final selection for a transplant depends on a compatible organ becoming available at the time a patient reaches the top of the waiting list.

DONATING ORGANS

For a transplant to have a chance of success, transplant tissues must be removed from a donor while still being oxygenated by the donor's circulatory system. Most organs come from accident victims. Defining death as "the irreversible cessation of all functions of the brain, including the brain stem" makes the transplantation of these organs possible.

The Uniform Anatomical Gift Act is the law that governs organ donation. In many states, drivers' licenses designate a person's wish to donate organs under this act—drivers can authorize the removal of "any needed organs or tissues," or specify which may or may not be taken. Whereas this brief statement, which must be witnessed, constitutes consent, many hospitals also require the written consent of the donor's next of kin. In addition, uniform donor cards are available from regional transplant programs (listed in the telephone book) or from the following organizations:

The American Medical Association
515 North State Street
Chicago, IL 60610
(312) 464-5000

Medic Alert Foundation International
P.O. Box 1009
Turlock, CA 95381-1009

National Kidney Foundation
30 East 33rd Street, 11th Floor
New York, NY 10016
(212) 889-2210

The characteristics of donated organs—most important, the blood group and the results of antigen tissue-typing that affect compatibility—are entered into the computer networks that monitor the availability of organs. If a good match is found between an organ and a patient on a waiting list, and if time and distance allow, the donated organ is rushed to the medical center where the operation is to take place.

It is expected that fetal tissue will become increasingly important in transplantation. Under the provisions of the Uniform Anatomical Gift Act (1987 version), permission for the use of fetal tissue for transplantation is usually given by the mother. (For example, some experts believe that fetal insulin-producing cells may be of value to a diabetic dependent upon insulin injections.)

Although spontaneous abortions may provide fetal material, it is most likely to originate from fetuses electively aborted. Those opposed to abortion fear that a demand for fetal tissue may further legitimize the procedure. It has even been suggested that a market for such material might lead women to seek pregnancy with the object of aborting and selling the fetus. But given the very large number of elective abortions performed, this is an extremely unlikely possibility.

··

EXPERIMENTATION ON HUMANS

Before any new drug, device, or procedure is released for general use, it must be tested on humans; animal studies are not sufficient. When drugs or medical devices are new, this testing is considered experimental because of the uncertainty of the new therapy's effectiveness.

Time and again, experiments involving comparatively few people have benefited millions. However, such experiments expose subjects to risks that cannot be fully calculated beforehand. Drugs well-tolerated in lab animals may cause serious side effects in humans. Consequently, when researchers test new drugs and devices, the needs of humanity—for knowledge, new therapies and devices, safe treatment, and so on—may conflict with the interests of the individual test subjects. Government regulations ensure that the subjects of research are adequately protected; possible harm must be minimized, and possible benefits maximized.

Biomedicine distinguishes between therapeutic and nontherapeutic research. Subjects of therapeutic research necessarily bear the risks of the experiment but may reap benefits. For example, if a new drug is found to be more effective than the standard one in treating the pain of arthritis, that drug benefits arthritic patients participating in the research. And if the new drug is not found effective, the standard treatment remains available.

Nontherapeutic studies, on the other hand, offer no direct potential benefit to test subjects. The goal of these studies is to advance basic knowledge, which may or may not have any practical application in the future. An example of this type of research is the investigation of cardiac catheterization, a procedure in which tiny catheters are inserted through the blood vessels into the chambers of the heart. Catheterization was first tried in healthy volunteers who anticipated no possible benefit from the procedure. Only later was the refined technique used to assess the function of heart and lungs in sick patients.

For the most part, those recruited as subjects in therapeutic research projects are patients or outpatients in teaching hospitals. Doctors on staff at such hospitals hold appointments at the affiliated medical schools; research is among their responsibilities as teachers and scientists. In their dual roles as physicians/investigators, conflicts of obligations may arise during research projects. While these researchers must adhere to the strict demands of the research protocol (the written description of the aims and methods of the study), at the same time they must provide optimal care for their patients.

Most of the subjects in nontherapeutic research projects are volunteers. Prison inmates, once used in many studies, are far less commonly recruited today, partly out of concern that this population was disproportionately bearing the burdens of research and was not capable of giving truly informed consent.

DESIGN OF STUDIES

Most studies conducted on hospitalized patients or groups of outpatients are drug trials that compare new (experimental) drugs with standard ones in terms of side effects and effectiveness. Designed as randomized blind or double-blind studies, this research gives one group of subjects, selected by chance, an experimental drug while a second group receives a standard substance. Alternately, the effect of an experimental drug may be compared to that of a placebo (an inert substance with no innate therapeutic value). Occasionally, studies compare a new drug, a standard drug, *and* a placebo.

In a blind study, the subjects do not know what is in the pill they take. In a double-blind study, neither the subjects nor the investigators know which pills are which. A record is kept by a third party not associated with the experiment. In double-blind crossover trials, two groups of subjects switch medications midway through the experiment, again without the knowledge of subjects or investigators.

The word *placebo* comes from the Latin, meaning "I shall please." Traditionally, a placebo was thought of as an inert substance (a sugar pill or saline injection), which "pleased" patients by giving them the impression that doctors were making efforts on their behalf. It is

now agreed that a placebo may be any agent whose effects derive from the subjects' belief that it will work rather than from the substance's inherent qualities, biological or otherwise.

Placebos are essential for distinguishing the effects of drugs from effects associated with drug administration itself. Subjects should be always informed about the placebos if they are used in trials. Otherwise, the experiment would be unethical and should not be performed.

CONSENT REQUIREMENTS

Consent requirements protecting human research subjects predate the Nuremberg Code of Ethics after World War II but were carefully defined in it. Applied at the trials of Nazi criminals accused of "crimes of a medical nature," the Nuremberg Code states:

> The voluntary consent of the human subjects is absolutely essential. This means that the person involved should have legal capacity to give consent; should be so situated as to be able to exercise free power of choice . . . and should have sufficient knowledge and comprehension of the elements of the subject matter involved as to enable him to make an understanding and enlightened decision.

The subject must know the "nature, duration, and purpose" of the experiment and the methods that will be used, and must be told about "all inconveniences and hazards reasonably to be expected." It is the investigator's responsibility to ensure the quality of the subject's consent. Although the requirements for informed consent to research predated those for informed consent to therapy, both types of consent are the same in most essentials.

Because experimental studies investigate the unknown, and, in many cases, no statistically significant data exist on the effects of brand new drugs or devices, it may not be possible to disclose all possible risks to potential test subjects. This fact conflicts with the requirement that all possible hazards be fully disclosed. Another ethical difficulty encountered by researchers concerns the voluntariness of consent. Is the consent of a desperately ill patient truly voluntary? Are prisoners, living with round-the-clock coercion, free to refuse?

THE REGULATION OF RESEARCH

Beginning in 1966, and increasingly through the 1980s and 1990s, the federal government has acted to protect the subjects of biomedical and behavioral research, with strict provisions for monitoring and reviewing procedures. Government actions were prompted in part by exposure of dubiously ethical studies, including experiments with hepatitis viruses conducted on retarded children at the Willowbrook State School in New York without the knowledge or consent of the parents.

The most important reviewing bodies in this process are institutional review boards. These boards are mandatory at all universities, teaching hospitals, and research organizations that receive funds from the Department of Health and Human Services for human experimentation; they are also in place at other institutions such as pharmaceutical companies. Boards include staff physicians, nurses, and administrators as well as investigators and community representatives.

Initially controversial, institutional review boards are now widely acknowledged to play an important role in protecting subjects' interests and prompting self-scrutiny on the part of investigators.

Research protocol must be approved by a review board before work on a project begins. In its analysis, an institutional review board has two main tasks.

- It must ensure that the risk/benefit ratio is satisfactory—the expected benefit must be commensurate with the potential risk to the subjects.
- The board must make certain that subjects are fully informed about the study before consenting to participate. The consent form itself, in which the purpose and methods of the study are outlined, must be complete and comprehensible.

Special attention to consent requirements is needed when, at the time of an experiment, a subject's ability to give consent is impaired (for example, because of sedation). Consent of surrogates is required when subjects are not competent to give it themselves and the research does not pose more than minimal risk. For a child over 7 years of age, parents' consent must be supplemented by the child's "assent"—a positive agreement, not just a lack of objection.

In addition to the reviews conducted by institutional review boards, human experimentation is monitored by the Food and Drug Administration, which is responsible for overseeing all research on drugs and devices, and by the Office for Protection of Health Risks, an arm of the Department of Health and Human Services. This legally mandated supervision helps ensure better compliance.

SUMMING UP

Increasingly difficult bioethical questions arise as part of the patient treatment process. To best ensure that decisions do, indeed, reflect the wishes and best interests of the patients, individuals should take appropriate actions *before* a crisis arises. Legal devices, such as living wills, informed consent, and designation of a durable power of attorney, are among the many tools that have evolved to protect a patient's rights.

PART II

New Approaches to Wellness

4
The Funda-mentals of Good Health

ROBERT LEWY, M.D.
Parts of this chapter are adapted from the chapter by Henry Greenberg, M.D., which appeared in the revised second edition.

THE HUMAN BODY AND HOW IT WORKS

The human body is often likened to a machine, but no machine in the world operates as effectively and efficiently. Although medical scientists have been studying the body for hundreds of years, there is still much we don't fully understand about its normal functioning and about disease processes. Nonetheless, we do know that the various organ systems work in amazing harmony most of the time, thanks to a highly complex internal communications network. Although we tend to describe a single organ system or disease, usually the entire body is affected by an activity or disorder.

We focus considerable attention on disease and organ dysfunction, and yet the large majority of us find our body performs very well despite all of the stress and abuse we subject it to. In later chapters, the major organ systems and the common disorders that affect them will be described in detail. This section presents a brief overview of how these organ systems work in harmony to sustain life, day-to-day activities, and general good health.

HOW ORGAN SYSTEMS WORK TOGETHER

To get an idea of how various body systems work together to accomplish a common activity, consider the complex orchestration that occurs every morning when we wake up and eat breakfast. While asleep, the major organ systems are already working in concert, albeit at a low, basal level. The circulatory and pulmonary systems are providing the oxygen and other nutrients needed by every cell to function. Together, the complex communications networks of the endocrine and nervous systems are regulating heart rate, blood pressure, body temperature, and other involuntary or autonomic processes. Metabolism continues at a slowed pace, involving virtually every body organ. As dawn approaches, the body begins to wake up. Complex circadian rhythms accelerate; hormone levels change; sleep becomes lighter; heart and respiratory rates begin to increase. Finally, we awaken, sometimes prompted by an alarm clock but often without any external stimuli.

Since it has been 8 or more hours since our last meal, one of the first things we feel is hunger. The appetite center, located in the hypothalamus area of the brain, works through an intricate feedback system involving hormones, nerves, and sensory organs to ensure that we eat enough. It's also usual to awaken to a full bladder.

The nervous system conveys the message that the bladder is full, prompting the urge to urinate. To ensure that this urge doesn't awaken us in the middle of the night, the kidneys process fluid differently while we sleep so that the urine is concentrated and therefore of lower volume. That's why morning urine is darker in color than that produced while we're awake.

Even before breakfast is on the table, the major sense organs—the eyes, ears, nose, and then the tongue and mouth—begin preparing the body to receive food. The aroma of, say, eggs sizzling in a frying pan reaches the mucous membranes lining the nose and stimulates olfactory nerve receptors, which transmit the impulse to the brain, where it is recognized as an odor. In response to odor and even just the thought of food, the brain, working through the endocrine and nervous systems, transmits messages to glands in the mouth and stomach, which increase the flow of digestive juices in anticipation. The message also may prompt a physical response; if the smell says the eggs are burning, we quickly act (requiring the coordinated effort of the nervous and muscle systems) to remove the pan from the stove. If the pan handle is too hot, the nerve endings in the skin trigger an automatic protective reaction; without thinking, the hand is jerked from the pan even before the pain sensation is perceived.

The sense of hearing also comes into play. Familiar sounds associated with a meal—for example, juice being poured into a glass or cereal into a bowl—are carried as vibrations through the outer ear, into the eardrum, middle ear, and inner ear and then finally to the hairlike nerve cells that transmit the signals to the brain, where the sound is perceived and registered. If the sound says the coffee is boiling over, the body responds with a coordinated, conscious action: We turn off the coffeepot.

Sight is yet another important sensory response in readying the body for a meal. Light from an object, such as a glass of juice, strikes the lens of the eye and is directed to the retina. The impulse generated by the retina travels along the optic nerve to the brain, where it is perceived. If the image shows a favorite food, our appetite center and digestive system will be further stimulated.

With the first bite of breakfast, two of our senses are stimulated: taste and touch. In the mouth, food comes in contact with the tiny taste buds on the tongue; nerve receptors in these taste organs are transmitted to the brain. All taste sensations are combinations of only four basic responses: sweet, sour, salty, or bitter; these plus the food's odor produce its unique and recognizable flavor.

Touch is also involved in eating. As the food touches nerve endings in the tongue and palate, its texture and temperature further stimulate circulation of blood in the entire digestive system and also help increase the secretion of digestive enzymes.

In a marvelously coordinated, highly complex process

that requires little or no conscious effort aside from chewing or swallowing, our breakfast is transformed into the fuel and other nutrients required by all of our individual cells. Along the way, our food passes through distinctive body structures.

Mouth. The actual digestive process begins with chewing, a conscious effort involving the skeletal muscles of the jaw, mouth, and tongue, coordinated by the nervous system. In the mouth, food is broken into small pieces and mixed with saliva and other digestive juices. Saliva contains an enzyme, ptyalin, that begins to break down starches or complex carbohydrates into simple sugars that can be absorbed easily farther along the digestive tract.

Pharynx. From the back of the mouth, food is squeezed through the pharynx, a funnel-shaped structure, into the esophagus, a foot-long tube that leads to the stomach. In 4 to 8 seconds, the bolus of chewed food passes through the esophagus and into the upper part of the stomach.

Esophagus. The muscles in the lower esophagus, unlike those in the jaw, are involuntary and respond automatically to the stimulus of swallowing. An involuntary series of coordinated muscle waves, a process called peristalsis, moves the food through the esophagus, as well as through the rest of the digestive tract. Rings of muscle that function as a valve between the esophagus and stomach relax to admit the food. These muscular valves then close to prevent a backflow (regurgitation) into the esophagus.

Stomach. Much of the digestive process occurs in the stomach. Four or five times every minute, rippling waves controlled by the autonomic nervous system pass through the muscles of the stomach walls, mixing food with gastric acid and digestive enzymes and further breaking it down. Food is reduced to a thin liquid mass and the digestive juices break down some of the nutrients into forms that can be utilized by the body. Carbohydrates continue to be broken down in the stomach; gastric juices and enzymes also begin breaking down protein and fat into forms that can be absorbed.

Small Intestine. This partially digested liquid food mass moves next through the muscular pyloric valve to the duodenum, the initial portion of the small intestine. The emptying of the stomach is a complex act, requiring an integration of feedback messages to and from the brain carried by the vagus nerve, as well as by intestinal hormones released by changes in volume and acid levels.

As food enters the upper part of the small intestine, hormones stimulated by its arrival coordinate the flow of digestive enzymes from the pancreas and of bile from liver and gallbladder. The pancreatic juices and bile give the duodenum its alkaline environment, in contrast to the acidic environment of the stomach. These digestive secretions complete the breakdown of proteins and fats,

processes that take longer than the digestion of carbohydrate and its conversion to glucose. The small intestine is about 22 feet long, and as the now liquefied and well-mixed food continues its journey, a steady flow of basic nutrients is available to the body.

Villi. The small intestine is lined with villi, fingerlike projections that greatly increase the total surface area of the intestines. The villi also permit each cell to come in contact with a blood capillary. These microscopic blood vessels are only one cell thick, and permit the direct exchange of biological chemicals between the intestine and the blood. (A similar physiological mechanism to increase the surface area for blood-organ interchange occurs in the lungs and kidneys.) Digested nutrients pass through the villi. Sugars (from carbohydrates and some protein) and amino acids (from protein) pass directly into the bloodstream and are carried to the liver or muscles to be further metabolized or used as fuel. The digested fats pass from the villi to blood or the lymphatic system and enter the bloodstream through a vein. Blood rich in digested nutrients flows from the small intestine into the liver, which, acting in concert with the endocrine and other body systems, regulates the amount of nutrients, particularly glucose, that enter the bloodstream for distribution to individual body tissues.

Liver. The liver, the largest of the internal organs, carries on a number of highly complicated chemical processes. It produces bile from old blood cells, which are being reprocessed. One of the breakdown products of hemoglobin gives bile and hence the stool its brown color. Bile is essential to the digestion of fats. The liver manufactures a number of other substances as well, including cholesterol, enzymes, vitamin A, blood coagulation factors, and complex proteins. The liver also acts as a storehouse for blood, certain vitamins and minerals, and fuel, in the form of glycogen, which is readily converted to glucose as the body needs it. It detoxifies alcohol and many other potentially harmful chemicals.

Large Intestine. Finally, food that is not digested moves from the small intestine into the colon or large intestine. In the colon, water is extracted from the waste material and what remains moves via peristalsis through the 3 feet of the large intestine to the rectum for eventual elimination in the form of a bowel movement. Just as the beginning of the digestive process—the chewing of food in the mouth—is controlled by our conscious actions, voluntary control returns at this end of the digestive tract, during elimination.

While all these digestive processes are going on, other body systems are carrying on their respective functions in a finely tuned, coordinated manner.

Lungs. With each breath, the lungs take in oxygen and eliminate carbon dioxide and other gaseous wastes.

Circulatory System. The circulatory system carries oxygenated blood and other nutrients to cells throughout the body and collects their wastes. Each cell comes in direct contact with a blood capillary, which brings it oxygen and other nutrients and takes away cellular waste.

Kidneys. The kidneys filter out the wastes and help regulate blood pressure and internal chemical fluid balance.

Muscles and Bones. The muscles and bones give us shape, movement, and strength and protect the internal organs. The marrow of bones is essential for the manufacture of blood components.

Endocrine System. The endocrine system produces chemical messengers that coordinate many of these processes and control such vital functions as reproduction and growth.

Central Nervous System. The central nervous system provides the seat of our intelligence and emotions. It also coordinates and controls other vital functions, often in concert with the endocrine system.

Immune System. The immune system helps protect the body from invading microorganisms and other foreign substances.

Skin. The skin also protects the body, helps regulate temperature, and carries on a number of important metabolic functions.

This is a highly oversimplified summary; in reality, most organ systems have multiple functions and none acts independently; the smooth functioning of one is highly dependent upon others. A breakdown of one process or system is likely to have an impact throughout the body. Thus, it is important to remember that symptoms affecting one part of the body may have their origin in a quite distant and seemingly unrelated organ.

Few of us truly appreciate just how precise and fine-tuned the body is until something goes awry. Even then, the body often can remedy the situation on its own. This does not mean that maintaining good health requires no effort. For most people, a lifestyle that provides the basics of good nutrition, adequate rest, physical activity, and a commonsense approach to life in general will go a long way toward meeting most health needs. When something does go wrong, being able to recognize warning signs and then seeking proper medical attention will further ensure that you maintain good health.

A HEALTHY LIFESTYLE

Good health is a goal toward which many of us strive. After all, we know that, in great measure, our physical well-being determines the quality of our life. But deciding which approach to a healthy lifestyle will best improve or maintain personal health is no easy task. It is virtually impossible to read a newspaper, watch television, listen to the radio, or browse in a bookstore without being bombarded by information from experts and so-called experts on the art of staying healthy. It is no wonder that confusion abounds.

Are vitamins the elixir of the Fountain of Youth? Will regular attendance at a spa, gym, or fitness center keep us in shape, or is jogging or running more sensible? Should we worry most about our weight, our cholesterol intake, the food we eat, or the air we breathe? If we give up that cocktail before dinner, eat organic foods, get regular medical checkups, and follow the advice in a best-selling exercise manual, are we guaranteed to live a longer, healthier life?

Unfortunately, the answers we hear to these questions too often come from entrepreneurs, advertisers, or well-meaning, but ill-informed advisers rather than medical experts. The truth is that there is no secret or complex trick to optimizing your chances of living a long and healthy life. All it takes is following such simple health habits as avoiding smoking, drinking in moderation, eating a well-balanced diet, controlling weight, reducing stress, and exercising regularly. By understanding the basic principles of healthy living and applying them with sense and moderation, people can vastly improve the quality—and may well increase the length—of their lives.

DIET AND NUTRITION

Diet as a means of disease prevention has—with good reason—received a lot of attention from the medical community and the popular media. An unhealthy diet has been linked in varying degrees to six of the ten leading causes of death in America today: cancer, adult diabetes, atherosclerosis, stroke, heart disease, and cirrhosis of the liver. Of these, heart disease and cancer are responsible for the vast majority of chronic illnesses and premature deaths. Whereas enormous strides have been made in the treatment and cure of these diseases, medical science is now also investigating their prevention, with special emphasis on how dietary modifications affect probability of disease. Obesity, our most common nutrition-related health problem, is a contributing factor in a number of health problems, including high blood pressure, arthritis, certain types of cancer, adult diabetes, and heart attacks.

Our health is influenced not only by how much we eat, but *what* we eat. While many experts have been advocating a low-fat, low-cholesterol, high-complex-carbohydrate diet to combat heart disease, evidence has been mounting that virtually the same diet may also reduce the risk of other diseases.

To control weight and minimize other food-related

health problems, all of us need to become knowledgeable about nutrition. Although Americans are more concerned about eating healthfully today than in the past, the abundance of conflicting, misleading, or outright false information about diet can be bewildering. Indeed, sorting out reliable nutrition advice from the plethora of misinformation (i.e., popular diet books such as *Fit for Life* or *How to Be Your Own Nutritionist*) can be difficult. Chapter 5, The Basics of Good Nutrition, provides a detailed discussion that provides authoritative information on diet and health.

EXERCISE AND FITNESS

Although many more Americans are now walking, running, playing tennis, and engaging in other active sports than in the past, most still do not get sufficient exercise. We drive to work and to malls, use elevators instead of stairs, spectate rather than participate in sports, and do little heavy labor on the job. Inactivity is common among all age groups. Even though several studies have linked a sedentary lifestyle with an increased risk of heart attack, only about 40 percent of all Americans (children as well as adults) exercise with any frequency. Even those who do exercise often don't exercise vigorously enough.

Lack of exercise is a risk factor for heart disease, but the flip side is also true: Adhering to a regular exercise program can help eliminate other known risk factors. Exercise tends to:

- Lower blood pressure.
- Help control weight.
- Increase levels of high-density lipoproteins (the "good" cholesterol) in the blood.
- Help control diabetes.
- Lower stress. In addition to benefiting the cardiovascular system, regular exercise may enhance a person's sense of well-being, improve muscle tone and flexibility, and provide more energy.
- Help people give up smoking.
- Possibly increase longevity. There is a decidedly lower death rate among the elderly who exercise.

AEROBIC EXERCISE

Aerobic exercise is the form of exercise that promotes cardiovascular fitness. During any exertion, muscles work by converting fuel to energy. In aerobic exercises, such as brisk walking, running or jogging, bicycling, swimming, skating, and jumping rope, exertion is sustained long enough to require the heart and cardiovascular system to fuel the muscles with oxygen. Supplying this oxygen makes the heart work harder. Since the heart itself is a muscle, this added exertion makes it more efficient and better conditioned. In anaerobic exercise, the muscles are able to provide the necessary energy through a chemical process that does not involve oxygen. Anaerobic exercises include bowling, golf, weight lifting, doubles tennis, and volleyball. Although some of these sports may seem strenuous, the activity level is not upheld long enough to make the exercise aerobic. But anaerobic sports and activities are also valuable because they promote strength, endurance, flexibility, or physical skill—a combination of coordination, agility, and speed.

DESIGNING A FITNESS PROGRAM

Ideally, a cardiovascular fitness program should be flexible, graduated, tailored to your individual needs, and if necessary, supervised by a fitness expert. The three key factors in designing a program are intensity, duration, and frequency of exercise.

Cardiovascular conditioning requires a sustained effort for at least 30 minutes per day, 3 days per week with your heart rate within its "target zone."

This zone is between 70 and 85 percent of your maximum heart rate—the maximum times your pulse can beat in one minute. Maximum heart rate is calculated by subtracting your age from 220. For example, a 40-year-old's maximum heart rate is 180. The target zone is between 70 and 85 percent of the maximum heart rate, in this example, 126 to 153 beats per minute.

Exercise below 70 percent of the maximum heart rate gives the heart and lungs little conditioning; anything above 85 percent is dangerous. If you're beginning an exercise program, start at approximately 70 percent, slowly increasing to 85 percent as your conditioning improves. If you have not been exercising regularly, be careful to raise your heart rate gradually; it may take several months to raise it above 70 percent.

A simple way to determine if you are reaching your target zone is to take your pulse immediately after exercise. Simply place two or three fingers lightly over the carotid artery, located on the left and right sides of your Adam's apple, count the pulse for 10 seconds, and multiply by 6. If the pulse is below the target zone, increase the rate of exercise; if above, reduce it. Check your pulse rate once a week during the first 3 months of exercising and periodically thereafter.

Another way to assess whether you are meeting your target zone while exercising is to rate your condition on a "perceived exertion" scale of 1 to 10, in which 1 represents "not-at-all fatigued" and 10 signifies "extremely fatigued." While exercising, you should reach level 7 or 8.

Exercisers should be aware that some medications and medical conditions may affect the maximum heart rate and the target zone. For example, some medicines for hypertension lower the maximum heart rate and thus the target zone. Diabetes may also have an effect on these guidelines. If you are taking medications, be sure to consult a physician to determine whether this rate should be adjusted.

When starting an exercise program, aim to work out two to four times a week. Studies show that you need exercise only three times a week to benefit your cardiovascular system. Although the "training effect" on the body increases if you exercise more often than that, your risk of injury also increases, particularly with strenuous exercises like running. You may want to exercise more frequently if your program entails less injury-prone activities such as walking or swimming, or if weight control is one of your exercise goals.

Beginners may have trouble exercising at their target zone for all 30 minutes. If so, work out for as long as possible at the target zone, building up to 30 minutes over time. Exercising at the proper intensity, even if only for 5 or 10 minutes, can provide some training effect. On the other hand, working out at a level below the target zone, even for the full 30 minutes, won't have much of an effect, aside from burning some calories. Moderate interval training, alternating exercise of slightly increased intensity with low intensity or rest periods, is another way to begin a program.

In order to maintain the training effect, you must increase the intensity or duration of exercise as your heart becomes better conditioned. A bicycle rider, for example, may eventually have to pedal longer, faster, or cycle up hills or in a lower gear to push the heart into the target zone. (See below for examples of how to begin and upgrade a training program.)

STRESS TESTING

Before beginning an exercise program, anyone who is over 35 or has a known medical problem should check with a physician. In many cases, the doctor may recommend a stress, or exercise tolerance, test. This test measures the performance of the cardiovascular system during exercise so that a safe, individualized fitness program can be created for you. (A stress test may also be used as a diagnostic tool if certain types of heart disease are suspected.) A physician is most likely to suggest a stress test if you are sedentary, obese, smoke, or have a high cholesterol level or a family history of heart disease. A stress test may also be recommended for anyone under 35 who has high blood pressure, diabetes, or a history of chest pain or other symptoms of heart disease.

A stress test can be performed in the physician's office, a hospital, or a stress-testing facility. During the test, you pedal an exercise bicycle or walk on a treadmill while your pulse rate, blood pressure, and perhaps oxygen consumption are monitored, and an electrocardiogram is

taken. The test will begin slowly and will eventually take you up to your maximum heart rate.

Since this test involves some risk, it is important that it be administered by a trained health professional in a facility that is equipped for any emergency that might arise. If you are at high risk of heart disease or have had any symptoms that might indicate heart disease, it is best to have a physician perform the test. In either case, the results should be interpreted by a physician, preferably a cardiologist.

SAMPLE EXERCISE PROGRAMS

Following are sample exercise programs for three individuals: a healthy 25-year-old man, a healthy 45-year-old woman, and a 65-year-old man who has had a myocardial infarction (heart attack). They are meant only as examples, not prescriptions. Before beginning your own exercise program, consult your doctor.

• **The 25-Year-Old Man.** Running is a good and popular choice for aerobic conditioning, but be cautious if you have not been exercising regularly. Running can prove to be too strenuous for people who are out of shape. Begin a running program by alternating 3-minute walks and 3-minute jogs for 30 minutes up to three times a week. Each week, increase the jog interval by 1 minute and decrease the walk interval by 1 minute until the entire 30 minutes is spent jogging. From this point, you can add 5-minute increments every other week until the jog lasts 46 to 50 minutes. Then you can increase speed by alternating 5 minutes at a fast pace with 5 minutes at a moderate pace.

Although running offers an excellent cardiovascular workout, it does not condition the upper body (arms, shoulders, etc.). For that reason, consider supplementing a running program with workouts on a rowing machine. To start, set the rowing machine at the lowest resistance point. Then increase the setting with each 3-minute set, until you reach a perceived exertion level of 7 or 8. After 2 or 3 weeks, try to begin each set at the second lowest resistance level, assuming it has become comfortable as a base level. If not, keep to the initial setting for a few more weeks.

• **The 45-Year-Old Woman.** Aerobic dance and calisthenics performed at a fast pace are excellent aerobic activities that give the heart a thorough workout and involve most muscle groups. Whether you exercise on your own, in a class, or by following a tape, be sure to warm up and cool down with stretching exercises (often these are built into class or tape routines) every time. If you experience pain in a particular part of the body, avoid specific routines that increase the pain until it abates.

EXERCISE PRECAUTIONS FOR ALL AGES

- Do a few warm-up exercises first to stretch the muscles, tendons, and ligaments, to flex joints, and to increase the blood flow.
- Start slowly and increase speed, distance, and duration gradually.
- Avoid exercise on days when the windchill factor is below 20°F (6.6°C), when the temperature is above 90°F (32.2°C), or when the humidity is above 80 percent.
- Stop exercising if you feel dizzy, breathless, or nauseated, or if you feel pain in a joint or muscle.
- Seek medical help at once if you have pain in the center of your chest that lasts more than 2 minutes and that may be accompanied by pain in the arm, shoulders, neck, or jaw.
- Wait at least 2 hours after a heavy meal before exercising, and at least 4 hours after consuming alcohol. Drinking alcohol before exercise can cause irregularities of the heartbeat and dehydration.
- Drink water before, during, and after exercising, especially on a hot or humid day.

Swimming is an excellent alternate exercise. Both the crawl and the backstroke offer good conditioning. Be sure to alternate with rest periods. As you become stronger, you can add one or two laps.

- **The 65-Year-Old Man.** Walking is an excellent aerobic exercise after a heart attack because it is versatile. It offers benefits to people who are very out of shape, but can also be intensified to keep a physically fit person in peak condition.

Before beginning or resuming any exercise program after a heart attack, it is crucial to have a symptom-limited exercise stress test (meaning the test is stopped as soon as chest pain is felt). Based on the results, the physician should set a target heart rate for you. During exercise, do regular pulse checks (a 10-second pulse multiplied by 6) to make sure you're maintaining—and not exceeding—the target rate.

See a physician immediately if you experience any recurrent chest pain, weakness, dizziness, or excessive fatigue. The doctor may want to do a repeat exercise stress test. If available, a supervised program at a YM/YWCA, YM/YWHA, or community center is preferable to individual exercise, at least for the first year following a heart attack.

Like jogging or running, walking does not usually provide upper-body conditioning. Arm calisthenics are a good alternative to walking. For a post–heart attack patient, they should first be performed with ECG monitoring. A physician should determine the appropriate frequency and number of repetitions for each exercise. Upper-body exercises can include shoulder flex-extend; elbow flex-extend; arm swing, front to back; and arm "bicycle" motion.

DECIDING HOW AND WHERE TO EXERCISE

Thousands of new gyms and physical fitness centers have opened in the past decade, providing a number of options for pursuing an exercise regimen. Although exercising on your own is less costly and time-consuming, a gym does offer some advantages. There is, of course, the financial incentive to use the gym often once you've paid for a membership. If you have a sociable bent, you'll probably find the camaraderie another reason to return regularly. Many gyms also offer convenient places to change and shower, a wide range of modern exercise equipment, and guided instruction.

In evaluating an exercise training center:

- Look for aerobic exercise equipment (treadmills, exercise bicycles with resistance controls, a pool at least 60 feet long, a running track).
- Note the types of instruction available (swimming, running, aerobic dancing, as opposed to yoga, weight lifting, and calisthenics).
- Consider the quality and background of instructors (ideally, they should have a degree in physical education or exercise physiology).
- Note the physical facilities, particularly whether the dressing rooms, showers, and lockers are clean and adequate.
- Visit at least twice at the hour when you would be most likely to use the facilities, to see how crowded they are.

Note: A posh setting or high membership fee does not necessarily mean that the center is oriented toward cardiovascular fitness. There are many inexpensive YM/YWCAs, YM/YWHAs, and municipal facilities that are quite adequate.

EXERCISE IN REHABILITATION

A wide range of patients can benefit by adding exercise to their recovery regimen. Research shows, for example, that patients who exercise regularly after a first heart attack recover more completely and more rapidly than do others. Carefully prescribed aerobic exercises are extremely useful for patients with angina pectoris (chest pain). With exercise, individuals with asthma or chronic lung disease can improve their respiratory capacity, and diabetics may lower their blood sugar levels and insulin requirements. In fact, diabetes often disappears in obese adults once they achieve a healthy weight through regular exercise and a healthy diet.

SMOKING

Cigarette smoking is the single most preventable cause of illness and death in the United States today. Cigarette smoke itself contains more than 4,000 health-threatening compounds, including tar, carbon monoxide, nicotine, and cancer-causing benzopyrene, benzopyrelene, arsenous oxide, and radioactive polonium. The major immediate effects of smoking can range from tachycardia (abnormally fast heartbeat) to arrhythmia (variation of the heart's normal rhythm) to increased blood pressure and bronchial constriction. But by far, the greatest risks the smoker faces are coronary heart disease and cancer.

Smokers have a 70 percent greater chance of developing coronary heart disease than do nonsmokers—the risk increasing in direct proportion to the number of cigarettes smoked per day. Even people who smoke one pack per day have twice the risk of heart attack and five times the risk of stroke as nonsmokers.

Studies have shown that the carbon monoxide ingested by smoking, in addition to reducing the blood's oxygen level, causes changes in body tissues that may leave smokers prone to heart disease. The smoker with a blood level of carbon monoxide above 5 percent faces a 20-fold risk of coronary heart disease over the individual with a level below 3 percent. Smokers who switch to cigarettes with low tar and nicotine will only somewhat lower the level of carbon monoxide in their blood. The heart disease risk of smokers who quit, on the other hand, will begin to decline immediately. Within 10 to 15 years, the ex-smoker's chance of early death from heart attack is no greater than that of someone who never smoked.

Clearly, one of the most important preventive health measures an individual can take is to avoid or give up smoking. There are a number of methods, ranging from cold turkey to hypnosis. Groups like the American Cancer Society run low-cost stop smoking clinics for those who feel they would do better with face-to-face counseling and peer support, and supply literature on quitting for those who want to go it alone. Research has not proven any one method is more successful than the rest, but some do seem to work better for some people than for others.

A relatively newer technique shown to be effective in reducing the addiction to nicotine is its administration in controlled doses, either through chewing gum or a transdermal patch. Especially when used in conjunction with a behavioral modification or support program, this technique can be very helpful in overcoming nicotine addiction.

The notion of what constitutes success when attempting to stop smoking has changed. Many researchers now believe that even gradually reducing the number of cigarettes smoked daily is a positive step and that a certain amount of relapse should be seen as normal and not a sign of irreversible failure. More information on quitting can be found in chapter 6, Smoking, Alcohol, and Substance Abuse.

ALCOHOL

Alcohol is the most commonly used recreational drug in the United States. Taken in moderation, it can be compatible with a healthy lifestyle. But alcohol abuse causes problems that reach far beyond drinkers themselves. The Department of Health and Human Services has defined alcoholism as "the nation's number one health problem"—a major cause of disrupted family life, automobile and industrial accidents, poor job performance, and increasing crime rates.

Cirrhosis of the liver, almost invariably a result of alcohol abuse, is the seventh leading cause of death in the United States. In addition, alcohol has been implicated as a contributor to 50 percent of fatal automobile accidents, 53 percent of fire deaths, 45 percent of drownings, 22 percent of home accidents, and 36 percent of pedestrian accidents. Violent crimes attributed to alcohol abuse include 64 percent of murders, 41 percent of assaults, 34 percent of rapes, 30 percent of suicides, and 60 percent of child abuse.

The financial toll of alcohol abuse is heavy, too. American industry loses over $25 billion per year due to the accidents, absenteeism, and medical expenses of alcoholic workers.

The pregnant woman who drinks heavily risks giving birth to a child with fetal alcohol syndrome (FAS)—a pattern of physical and mental defects that may include malformed facial characteristics, growth deficiency, heart defects, poor neurological coordination, and mental retardation. FAS has become a problem of large proportion, since there are an estimated 1 million alcoholic women of childbearing age in the United States. A 1984 study, funded by the National Institute of Child Health and Human Development, looked at data from more than 31,600 pregnancies and found that consumption of at least one to two drinks daily was associated with a substantially increased risk of producing a growth-retarded infant. Even though an occasional drink may not cause a problem, alcohol has no positive effects on pregnancy to recommend it, and thus pregnant women, or those who wish to get pregnant, are advised not to drink at all.

Finally, the American Cancer Society reports that heavy drinkers, especially those who also smoke cigarettes, are at an unusually high risk for oral cancer and cancers of the larynx and esophagus.

Is it safe to drink at all? For some people, light to moderate drinking does not seem to have any serious effect. The problem is knowing how much is harmless for whom. Some people, for example, can develop cirrhosis of the liver with only one drink per day, while ten drinks per day will not lead to cirrhosis in others (although this amount may have other serious consequences). At what point does social drinking become alcoholism? The accompanying test, from the National Council on Alcoholism, may be helpful in identifying some signs. Those who score 4 or more should seek help promptly.

For those who still want to enjoy an occasional drink, there is much that can be done to promote a healthy, positive attitude toward alcohol. The following suggestions for keeping alcohol use moderate are especially important for parents of teenagers and young adults.

• *Make it clear that drunkenness is not acceptable, and certainly not attractive or chic.* Too many people consider getting "bombed" or "plastered" to be appropriate at social gatherings; in fact, it's the goal of some events. Don't send children the message that getting drunk is tolerated in certain people (e.g., a famous writer or a family member whose drunkenness is found endearing). At the same time, be clear that "holding one's liquor" isn't a sign of prowess for either men or women; if anything, it reveals a dangerously high tolerance that comes from overuse.

• *Put alcohol in its proper place.* Drinking should be enjoyed in moderation at social events and as an accompaniment to meals. It is an adjunct to living, not an end in itself. Parties and family gatherings should be planned around enjoyable activities, good food, and good conversation rather than the liquor. Good hosts and hostesses do not try to push alcohol on their guests; they always take no for an answer.

• *Serve a variety of beverages at social functions.* Whether at home or at the worksite, nonalcoholic alternatives should be available for abstainers and safe drinkers alike. Drinkers can enjoy an alcoholic drink for sociability and for its mellowing effect, then switch to something nonalcoholic for the rest of the evening.

• *Set comfortable drinking patterns.* Some experts suggest avoiding a habitual pattern of drinking. By varying the drink, the time, even the place, the drinker avoids making alcohol an ingrained habit that is intimately associated with a certain time of day or a certain way of drinking. For example, if drinkers find themselves trapped by the after-work ritual of cocktails, they can substitute some other activity for it on occasion. Instead of having a martini, they can try a hot bath or a cool shower, play music, talk to a friend on the phone, or move meal time up 1 hour earlier.

• *Recognize that it's all right to say no.* You should never have to explain why you're not drinking at any particular time. The growing American concern with fitness and with a natural, healthy life has made abstinence acceptable. Safe drinkers can test their own drinking habits by abstaining occasionally, asking themselves: Do I feel perfectly comfortable doing without alcohol?

• *Prohibit driving while drinking.* Partygoers should make return transportation arrangements beforehand. One person can abstain in order to drive home. And friends can tell friends ahead of time, "If I ever have too much to drink, don't let me drive." Never allow an intoxicated friend to take the wheel out of fear of making a scene. Do so and you permit a possible suicide or murder. Not all drunk drivers are alcoholics, but they are all a menace to themselves and others.

• *Present a healthy role model to children.* Alcohol abuse is often related to family drinking patterns. The children of alcohol abusers are at higher risk of becoming alcoholics themselves than are children of moderate drinkers or teetotalers. Because family patterns of drinking—both good and bad—affect children's behavior, parents have ample opportunity to guide their children away from alcohol abuse through their own actions. Parents can talk to their children, without moral overtones, about the problems of alcohol and drug abuse. They can discourage drunkenness in themselves and their friends. They can refuse to drive when they've been drinking. They can present moderation and abstinence as part of a healthy and appealing lifestyle.

• *Avoid drinking alone.* Tests designed to diagnose alcohol abuse often include the question: "Do you drink alone?" It's not that the presence of others magically protects against alcoholism, but drinking alone is a sign that alcohol figures too heavily in a person's life. Drinking alone abandons the social benefits of alcohol. Alcohol abusers often isolate themselves with their drinking. They are having a "love affair" with the bottle and prefer its company to human companionship. Also, solitary drinking makes it easier to over indulge by, for example, gulping drinks and sneaking extra ones.

• *Don't drink to avoid problems.* It may seem tempting to escape family troubles, crises in love relationships, and problems at work with a drink. But no problems are ever solved by a bout with the bottle. "Escapist drinking" is symptomatic of alcoholism; people who find themselves using alcohol in this way should talk to a good friend, loved one, member of the clergy, or doctor they trust.

(For more information, see chapter 6, Smoking, Alcohol, and Substance Abuse.)

DRUG ABUSE

Although the ill effects of drugs have not been entirely defined, there is sufficient evidence to determine that their use is not compatible with a healthy lifestyle. Nevertheless, there is an increasing tendency toward "recreational" drug use in which drugs become part of a social setting just like alcohol.

Although not everyone who tries recreational drugs becomes a regular user, the progression to drug abuse usually follows the same pattern.

- *Experimentation.* The individual has one or perhaps a few experiences with a particular drug out of curiosity or because of peer pressure.
- *Occasional use.* This is usually unplanned and generally occurs in social situations where the drug is readily available.
- *Regular use.* Drug taking becomes routine.
- *Drug dependency.* The individual's psychological and physical well-being is so closely linked to the chosen chemical that it becomes a necessity. At this stage of addiction, physical withdrawal signs occur if the drug is abruptly discontinued.

The most popular drugs are the psychotropics such as marijuana, hashish, and cocaine, which distort sensory experience and produce pleasurable mood swings. According to the National Institute on Drug Abuse, changes in the way marijuana is grown have greatly increased concentrations of THC, its major psychoactive ingredient. Strengths of THC, which were in the range of 0.1 percent to 0.2 percent in the mid-1960s, are now reported in concentrations as high as 13.49 percent. Even the more commonly available marijuana (about 5 percent THC) is 25 to 50 times more potent than the marijuana widely used 30 years ago.

Drug experimentation and use typically begin in adolescence. Among teens, alcohol and marijuana are the most common drugs. Cocaine, on the rise in the 20-to-40 age group, may also be growing more popular among teens. Pediatrician Donald Ian Macdonald of the University of Florida, writing in the *American Journal of Diseases of Children,* has described four stages among adolescents as they begin to experiment with drugs.

- Stage 1: learning the mood swing. Giving in to peer pressure, the teen begins to experiment with a drug and finds the high pleasurable. Once the high is experienced, most teens decide to continue using the drug for enjoyment. However, many of them don't pass beyond this first stage—they may continue to use the drug, but do not become dependent. It can be difficult for parents to detect drug use at this stage, since there are few behav-

ioral changes, other than the effort to cover up the drug use. One clue, according to Dr. Macdonald, is tobacco use. Those adolescents who admit that their friends smoke, even if they deny their own use, are revealing that they are in a high-risk peer group and have friends who have already caved in to peer pressure.

- Stage 2: seeking the mood swing. In this stage, the teen uses drugs to deal with stress and negative feelings rather than to increase positive feelings. These teens may have a predisposition to dependence. Common signs of this stage are deterioration in school performance, lack of motivation, irritability, and dramatic mood swings. The adolescent's group of friends may change as he or she is drawn to others who share the habit. Unfortunately, parents often respond to this stage in inappropriate ways, denying the problem, blaming the child's friends or environment, and refusing to acknowledge that the child may be the source of his or her own problems. All these approaches enable the teenager to continue use.

- Stage 3: preoccupation with the mood swing. Drug use has become a major focus of the teen's life. The adolescent is in trouble in a number of areas and may be paying for a habit through theft, dealing drugs, unwitting or disbelieving parents, or even an afterschool job.

- Stage 4: doing drugs to feel okay. Finally, drugs lose the ability to produce euphoria and are taken just to ward off guilt and depression. At this point, relationships with the family—even the family unit itself—may have broken down completely.

An often overlooked contributing factor to adolescent drug abuse is the underdeveloped value system of people in this age group. Teens are often incapable of the moral judgment that is a strong deterrent to peer pressure. Thus, parents who shrug off their children's experimenting with drugs because "all" teenagers do it are failing to help their children develop good judgment. Teens become addicted—often addicted to combinations of drugs, frequently adding alcohol to their drug addiction—without realizing what is happening to them. (For more information, see chapter 8, The Adolescent Years, and chapter 6, Smoking, Alcohol, and Substance Abuse.)

THE HEALTHY WORKPLACE

Work, jobs, careers, professions—a major part of most of almost everyone's life. It is not only where we spend 40-some hours a week, it is often the major source of our identity as well. In many cities, work becomes the center of social life. For people obsessed with their jobs, work even takes the place of a social life.

The work environment—both social and physical—has a profound effect on our lives. If we derive satisfaction from a job, learn how to control stress, keep frustration to

SOCIAL READJUSTMENT RATING SCALE

Life Event	Mean Value	Life Event	Mean Value
1. Death of a spouse	100	23. Son or daughter leaving home	29
2. Divorce	73	24. Trouble with in-laws	29
3. Marital separation	65	25. Outstanding personal achievement	28
4. Jail term	63	26. Spouse begins or stops work	26
5. Death of close family member	63	27. Begin or end school	26
6. Personal injury or illness	53	28. Change in living conditions	25
7. Marriage	50	29. Revision of personal habits	24
8. Fired at work	47	30. Trouble with boss	23
9. Marital reconciliation	45	31. Change in work hours or conditions	20
10. Retirement	45	32. Change in residence	20
11. Change in health of family member	44	33. Change in schools	20
12. Pregnancy	40	34. Change in recreation	19
13. Sex difficulties	39	35. Change in church activities	19
14. Gain of new family member	39	36. Change in social activities	18
15. Business readjustment	39	37. Mortgage or loan for lesser purpose (car, TV, etc.)	17
16. Change in financial state	38	38. Change in sleeping habits	17
17. Death of a close friend	37	39. Change in number of family get-togethers	16
18. Change to a different line of work	36	40. Change in eating habits	15
19. Change in number of arguments with spouse	35	41. Vacation	13
20. Mortgage or loan for major purpose (home, etc.)	31	42. Christmas	12
21. Foreclosure of mortgage or loan	30	43. Minor violations of the law	11
22. Change in responsibilities at work	29		

Adapted from T. H. Holmes and R. H. Rahe, "The Social Readjustment Scale," *Journal of Psychosomatic Research*, Vol. 2, 1967, 213–218. © 1967, Pergamon Press, Inc. Reprinted with permission.

a minimum, and work in a safe environment, our work can have a positive influence on our health.

STRESS

Job stress has countless sources. It may stem from the nature of the work itself. Air traffic controllers and stock traders, for example, have to make crucial, split-second decisions that produce high stress levels. Having to constantly rotate your work shifts can also add to stress by interrupting your daily sleep-wake cycle. Other stress inducers include boring and repetitive tasks that offer little chance for decision making (such as assembly line work), and positions where you have a good deal of responsibility but little power or control, such as many middle-management posts. Stress may also be created by management practices or be the result of the workers' personalities.

Stress and muscle tension can build up even in nonstressful jobs just from sitting or working in one position for long periods of time. The exercises listed later in this chapter are designed to relieve muscle tension and strain.

Various methods for reducing and coping with stress,

both on and off the job, are discussed in the box "Stress and Health."

OCCUPATIONAL SAFETY

Many American workers are exposed daily to some kind of occupational health hazard—carcinogenic agents, pulmonary irritants, or the job-related pressures of noise, crowding, and stress. Every year, approximately 100,000 Americans die from occupational illness—a figure probably underestimated, since the link between job and disease is often unrecognized or unreported. Nevertheless, this is more than twice the number that die in motor vehicle accidents. There are approximately 390,000 new cases of occupational diseases annually, while 2.2 million workers are stricken by disabling injuries.

Occupational exposure to toxic chemicals, and to the physical hazards of excessive radiation, noise, and vibration, can produce chronic lung disease, cancer, degenerative diseases to vital organs, birth defects, and genetic changes. Some hazards can cause stillbirth, miscarriage, impaired fertility, or sterility.

These health effects are often linked to particular jobs.

STRESS AND HEALTH

by Kenneth A. Frank, Ph.D.

Stress has always been a part of life. But the pervasive, accelerating change that is characteristic of modern times has dramatically increased the amount of stress we face daily. Increasing evidence suggests that how we cope with stress is an important factor in health and illness. Among the most common disorders in which stress is believed to factor are heart disease, ulcers and other digestive disorders, diabetes, asthma, high blood pressure, migraine, arthritis and other diseases with an autoimmune component, dermatitis, recurring attacks of genital herpes, and perhaps even certain cancers, as well as psychological problems.

Definition

Stress is hard to define because it is very subjective: One person's stress may well be another's pleasure. One useful definition of stress describes it as our psychological and physiological reactions to a situation perceived as exceeding our coping resources. Many psychologists distinguish between the situation (the "stress") and our resulting response ("distress"), recognizing that it is the latter that is likely to be detrimental to health and well-being. How negatively we react to stress depends on a number of factors, including how much control we feel over the situation, how predictable and intense the stressor is, and our individual perspective. For example, the hustle and bustle of a crowded city street may be sweet music to one driver and unbearable to another.

Causes

Much of the physical toll stress takes on the body is caused by the "fight-or-flight" response that occurs automatically in reaction to perceived danger: The pituitary gland releases adrenocorticotropic hormone (ACTH), which in turn stimulates the adrenal glands to pour out corticosteroid hormones and epinephrine. These almost instantaneous responses cause the pulse to quicken, muscles to tense, blood pressure to rise, the senses to sharpen, all in preparation to either flee or fight. This reaction may be lifesaving in situations involving real sudden danger but, especially when stress is chronic, may prompt other physical reactions leading to abdominal pains, tension headaches, psychological symptoms, or other illnesses through interactions with the immune system.

Another factor causing stress-related illness may be personality. Over the past 25 years the Type A personality and its role in heart disease risk has been the subject of continuing research and controversy. Type A's are hot-tempered, impatient, competitive people. They are markedly different from the more relaxed, less competitive or driven Type B's. Some studies seem to indicate that certain aspects of the Type A personality are a major factor in heart disease, while others do not. Two long-term studies at Duke University have pinpointed hostility as the key component of the Type A personality that is linked to a higher incidence of heart attacks. Studies also suggest that Type A's may be at greater risk than others because they have higher levels of stress-related hormones, which may have detrimental effects on blood pressure, blood vessels, blood lipids, and other systems.

Diagnosis

It is difficult to measure stress and predict its effect in a given individual. However, one of the most useful self-rating tests is the Social Readjustment Rating Scale, which rates the stressful impact of diverse life events (see box on preceding page). Note that even positive events, such as an outstanding personal achievement, and those that recur regularly, such as Christmas, are regarded as stressful. Studies suggest that an accumulation of 200 or more stress points in a single year greatly increases the likelihood of a major illness; a score of 300 or more carries an 80 percent likelihood of a major illness or accident within two years; and scores of between 150 and 300 translate into a 50-50 risk.

Treatment

Several different types of psychological treatments can help people suffering from stress and stress-related problems.

Cognitive-behavior therapy, a relatively short-term and direct therapy, is based on the concepts that the problem often lies with the way we experience and define our subjective world rather than the actual situations that may stress us; maladaptive behavior may play a role in creating or perpetuating stress. And certain ways of thinking interact with these behaviors to contribute to the maintenance of poor coping patterns. In this therapy, people are helped to develop positive coping skills to replace counterproductive ones.

STRESS AND HEALTH (Cont.)

Psychoanalytic psychotherapy, more costly in time and money, helps people understand the roots of the problem, such as vulnerability resulting from early life experience. Insights into the origins of stress reactions, in addition to the new experience with the therapist, may not only reduce stress but also facilitate development of more realistic and adaptive coping behaviors, as well as deeper and more long-lasting change.

Group therapy can provide needed social support and a feeling that one is not alone in his or her distress. Groups may also provide the opportunity for catharsis, offer members useful information, and promote the acquisition of more adaptive socializing and interpersonal skills. Groups can be particularly helpful to adolescents, the bereaved, newly divorced, and people who have experienced excessive trauma.

Home Remedies and Alternative Treatments

In some cases, excess stress may be avoided by pacing major life changes in a preplanned manner as much as possible, for example, postponing a job change for a year if you're about to get divorced, or waiting a year or two to start a family if you're newly married and burdened with your first mortgage.

While it is unlikely and potentially hazardous for a Type A to transform into a Type B, steps can be taken to avoid the most harmful effects of Type A behaviors by carefully managing yourself. For example, try to avoid situations that evoke hostility; you could go to the bank at off-hours if the long line for the teller angers you. Schedule true work breaks, such as going to an art gallery or bookstore rather than eating at your desk or having a business lunch; and learn to manage time effectively rather than overbooking yourself.

Sometimes effective techniques for easing stress can be learned in adult education classes or through self-help books. The most common methods include:

Relaxation training, which may be as simple as sitting for 15 minutes in a reclining chair with closed eyes while you repeat the word "one" silently each time you exhale, or may utilize a more sophisticated version of progressive relaxation or transcendental meditation.

Exercise, especially vigorous aerobic exercise performed for 30 minutes three or more times a week, which also can facilitate weight control, cardiovascular fitness, and diabetes control.

Biofeedback training, which involves learning to control normally involuntary body functions, such as slowing the heart rate, lowering blood pressure, and halting vascular or muscle spasms that can trigger pain.

Prevention

Stress-management studies have shown that the following coping strategies help people deal with life more effectively and can reduce stress-related illness.

1. Good copers almost immediately seek human attachment to guide priorities and clarify options. For example, a newly diagnosed cancer patient may develop an attachment to a nurse, or a grieving spouse seeks comfort from a neighbor. The importance of social support in times of stress cannot be overemphasized. Numerous studies have found that the people most likely to recover from serious illness or injury are those who have close personal relationships.
2. Good copers emphasize positive expectations for the future, usually hopeful ones, such as looking toward the challenge of a new job rather than bemoaning the job lost.
3. Successful copers tend to regulate the time and amount of stressful information reaching them, so that their transition from denial to acceptance (and fighting) can be gradual.
4. Copers facing several stressful problems at the same time deal with them one at a time, or take a large seemingly unmanageable problem and break it into manageable units.
5. Copers seek information relevant to their problem from a variety of sources and create alternate strategies for achieving their goals.

For example, workers involved in manufacturing the pesticide dibromochloropropane have an infertility rate two to three times that of the general population. It is difficult to estimate how much cancer is linked to the workplace—perhaps as much as 20 percent of all cancers can be traced to occupational exposure. Of the more than 63,000 chemicals manufactured or used in American industry, approximately 160 could meet criteria for proven carcinogens. Among them are arsenic, asbestos, chromium, coal products, dusts, iron oxide, mustard gas, nickel, petroleum, and ionizing radiation. Another 2,000 could be listed as potential carcinogens. Of the 1 million people who have worked in industries where there is heavy asbestos exposure, 30 percent will die from cancer.

The Occupational Safety and Health Act (passed in 1970) established the Occupational Safety and Health Administration (OSHA) in the Department of Labor, with responsibility for mandating and enforcing health and safety standards for the workplace. Scientific support for OSHA is provided by the Department of Health and Human Services' National Institute for Occupational Safety and Health (NIOSH). Although this is a start, NIOSH is dreadfully understaffed to handle the magnitude of its job. The 90 million workers subject to OSHA services are distributed in 5 million workplaces of which over 60 percent (3.1 million) employ fewer than 20 people. Most of the remaining 1.9 million employers have fewer than 100 workers.

It becomes obvious, then, that protection against occupational hazards cannot be left to OSHA, but requires the cooperation of employers, employees, unions, the medical community, and state and local governments to:

• Set and enforce standards
• Educate employees and employers to recognize hazards
• Properly train employees who work with dangerous substances and to monitor their exposure
• Provide protective clothing and equipment
• Design and maintain industrial equipment with safety in mind
• Identify those workers who are at risk and to recognize early signs of disease
• Isolate dangerous processes within the worksite, to limit exposure
• Substitute less hazardous materials whenever possible
• Use specialized ventilation systems to eliminate hazardous fumes and dusts in the work environment

Much of the technology to reduce occupational risk is already at hand; it is a matter of employing it. For some hazards, such as asbestos, the likelihood of disease is very high among exposed workers, so that a concentrated effort in a few industries can produce a large benefit.

Some 20 states have now passed "right-to-know" laws,

mandating that employees be allowed access to information about the chemicals with which they work. If others can't be depended upon to protect the worker, workers themselves must be aware of the risks to which they are exposed. Right-to-know laws encourage workers to assume responsibility for their own health and safety and to inform their doctors about the potential hazards of their workplace.

THE OFFICE ENVIRONMENT

The advent of "office automation" has produced a number of unfounded fears about the effect of computer viewing screens (called VDTs or CRTs) on office workers' health. One major worry can be quickly put to rest: VDTs are not a source of hazardous radiation. Studies show that computer screens give off no more radiation than the minuscule amount produced by fluorescent lights, and less than color TVs.

VDTs have also been accused of damaging the eyes. Again, government and industry studies have found no evidence that this is true. However, under some circumstances VDTs can lead to eyestrain, which is simply soreness of the eye muscles and causes no serious or long-term effects. Precautions can be taken to keep eyestrain to a minimum. Since glare is a major source of strain, screens should not be placed where light from windows or fluorescent fixtures can bounce off them. Screens can also be fitted with an antiglare filter if they don't come equipped with one.

Office lighting may also add to eyestrain. If the light is too bright for the computer screen, it washes out the image, which causes the operator to squint and furthers the eyestrain. To avoid this problem, the American Optometric Association (AOA) recommends that the ambient lighting level should be between 30 and 50 foot-candles, and the brightness control on the VDT screen should be set at four times the level of room light.

Eyestrain can also be induced by constantly refocusing the eye between the computer screen and a sheet of paper on the desk. Therefore, computer and word processing operators should use a copy stand to hold notes and reference materials vertically at the same height and distance from the eyes as the screen. The optimal distance between the eye and the screen is 14 to 24 inches. Finally, NIOSH recommends that operators take a 15-minute break from the VDT every 2 hours.

Fatigue, muscle and back strain, and possibly circulation problems can result from long hours at the VDT. Most of these stem from trying to put today's computers atop yesterday's desks. For example, the best height for keyboards is no more than 26 to 28 inches off the floor. Conventional office desks are 30 to 32 inches. The AOA recommends that VDTs be placed so that the top of the screen is 10 degrees below eye level and the middle of the screen is 20 degrees below. (How high that is, of course, depends upon how far away from the screen the operator sits.)

Proper chairs—ones that allow correct vertical alignment of the vertebrae and provide lower lumbar support—are important in preventing fatigue and back strain. Seat height should be between 16 and 22 inches and the angle between the seat and the backrest should be between 80 and 110 degrees. In order not to restrict circulation to the legs, the ideal chair seat should pitch downward at a slight angle of about 3 degrees and should have a "waterfall edge," dropping off sharply to keep pressure off the underside of the thighs.

PREVENTIVE HEALTH SERVICES

As a nation, Americans are healthier today than ever before. We have a greater knowledge of the causes of health problems, and new methods for the treatment of illness and injury are continually being developed.

We take almost for granted the seemingly miraculous cures available, ranging from vital organ transplant to the reattachment of severed limbs. But the glamour and drama of the "pound of cure" sometimes eclipses the unglamorous "ounce of prevention." Although we may never see headlines proclaiming so, the gains in life expectancy that have occurred in the 20th century were achieved more by prevention and health promotion measures than by treatment and curative medicine. The eradication of smallpox was accomplished not by finding a cure, but by deploying a vaccine that prevented the disease. Medicine is now coming to realize that victory over today's major killers—heart disease, cancer, stroke—must be achieved more by prevention than by cure.

From the viewpoint of cost-effectiveness, prevention of disease is the best investment a nation or a person can make. Yet only a tiny fraction of the annual federal budget is expended in disease prevention.

Most people wait until illness strikes before seeing a physician, and few realize that the means of protecting or promoting their health lies within their own hands. Medicine's capacity for the prevention of disease is steadily increasing, but it is up to the individual to act on this knowledge.

The most effective preventive strategies address the personal health practices of patients, such as appropriate nutrition and exercise and the avoidance of smoking and alcohol and drug abuse. This makes it more important than ever that individuals take great responsibility for their own well-being and that the physician acts as the patient's counselor and educator.

Planned, organized, and scheduled preventive visits to the doctor should be a top priority for all health-conscious people. However, a vital component of preventive medicine is for the doctor to inquire into various areas of life (such as work and home life), not just a specific physical symptom the patient mentions.

ADULT HEALTH SCREENING

Just as every child should receive health supervision on a regularly scheduled basis, adults should also plan for preventive health care. But the concept of the "complete annual physical" for apparently healthy adults is now outmoded. It has been replaced by periodic screenings based on individual risk factors. This is a happy medium between the traditional annual doctor's visit and the habit of seeing the doctor only once illness has struck.

Screening is intended to identify unrecognized disease, to keep track of the progress of recognized disease, and to make any necessary changes in treatment. The frequency of the screening varies with the patient's age and sex, based on the likelihood of a particular disease being present at a particular time. Family history, environmental exposure, and past medical history can, of course, influence the content and frequency of risk factor screening.

A number of factors should determine whether patients should be screened for a particular symptom or disease. These include whether:

- An effective, relatively safe treatment exists
- Early detection can substantially improve the patient's outcome
- The disease or condition is serious and prevalent enough to justify the cost of screening
- The screening process is relatively easy to administer; and resources for follow-up are generally available

If a patient has a family history of a particular disease, the physician is likely to recommend screening for it more frequently or from an earlier age than in other patients. For example, in families with a history of heart disease, even children may evidence hypertension (high blood pressure) and elevated levels of cholesterol. With early detection and with diet modification, serious future problems may be prevented.

When two or more close relatives (parents, children, or siblings) have had cancer or a familial disease that predisposes patients to cancer, early testing will generally be recommended. Heavy smokers and people exposed to environmental hazards (carcinogenic chemicals such as coal tar and asbestos) should also have regular checkups.

TABLE 4.3: PREVENTIVE MEDICINE PROCEDURES FOR HEALTHY ADULTS

(Every 1 to 3 years for ages 19–64; annually for ages 65 and over)

SCREENING

History

Dietary intake
Physical activity
Tobacco, alcohol, drug use
Sexual practices
Functional status at home[1]
Prior symptoms of transient ischemic
    attack[1]

Physical Exam

Height and weight
Blood pressure
Clinical breast exam[2]
Visual acuity[1]
Hearing and hearing aids[1]

High-Risk Groups
Complete oral cavity exam
Palpation for thyroid nodules
Clinical testicular exam[3]
Complete skin exam
Auscultation for carotid bruits[4]

Laboratory Diagnostic Procedures

Nonfasting total blood cholesterol
Papanicolaou smear[5]
Mammogram[6]
Dipstick urinalysis[1]
Thyroid function tests[1]

High-Risk Groups
Fasting plasma glucose
Rubella antibodies[7]
Venereal disease testing
Counseling and testing for HIV
Urinalysis for bacteriuria
Hearing
Tuberculin skin test
Electrocardiogram
Fecal occult blood/
    sigmoidoscopy/colonoscopy
Bone mineral content[4]

COUNSELING

Diet and Exercise

Fat, cholesterol, complex carbohy-
    drates, fiber, sodium, iron,
    calcium
Caloric balance
Selection of exercise program

Substance Use

Tobacco cessation
Alcohol and other drugs
    Limiting alcohol consumption
    Avoiding driving and other dan-
        gerous activities while under in-
        fluence
    Treatment for abuse

High-Risk Groups
Avoiding use/sharing of
    unsterilized needles and
    syringes

Sexual Practices

Sexually transmitted diseases, part-
    ner selection, condom use, anal
    intercourse
Unintended pregnancy and contra-
    ceptive options

Injury Prevention

Safety belts
Safety helmets
Violent behavior
Firearms
Smoke detector
Smoking near bedding or upholstery
Prevention of fall[1]
Water heater temperature[1]

High-Risk Groups
Back conditioning exercises
Prevention of childhood injuries

DENTAL HEALTH

Regular tooth brushing, flossing,
    dental visits

Other Primary Preventive Measures

High-Risks Groups
Skin protection from ultraviolet
    light
Discussion of hemoglobin testing[7]
Discussion of aspirin therapy[4]
Discussion of estrogen replace-
    ment therapy[8]

Immunizations

Tetanus-diphtheria booster

High-Risk Groups
Hepatitis B vaccine
Pneumococcal vaccine
Influenza vaccine
Measles/mumps/rubella vaccine[7]

Remain Alert for:

Depressive symptoms
Suicide risk factors
Abnormal bereavement
Malignant skin lesions
Tooth decay/gingivitis/loose teeth
Signs of physical abuse or neglect
Peripheral arterial disease[4]
Changes in cognitive function[1]
Medications that increase risk of
    falls[1]

[1] Ages 65 and over
[2] Annually for women 40 to 64; every 1 to 3
    years for younger women at high risk
[3] For men ages 19 to 39
[4] Ages 40 and over
[5] Every 1 to 3 years for all women under 65
    and older women at high risk
[6] Every 1 to 2 years for women, starting at 50
    and younger women at high risk
[7] Ages 19 to 39
[8] Women over 40

There are more than 3,000 traits and diseases commonly known to be controlled by heredity, and for many of them preventive measures and early detection can vastly decrease the severity of illness.

Table 4.1, preceding page, lists recommended screening and diagnostic tests, as well as counseling and immunization strategies appropriate for patients who are symptom-free. This list is not exhaustive; it is largely based on topics reviewed by the U.S. Preventive Services Task Force. Physicians may add other preventive services on a routine basis after considering the patient's medical history and other individual circumstances. Examples of conditions not specifically examined by the task force include chronic obstructive pulmonary disease, liver disease, bladder cancer, endometrial disease, travel-related illness, prescription drug abuse, and occupational illness and injuries.

Of course, there are times when a complete physical is still warranted. For adults, it is appropriate at age 18, in order to establish a baseline against which to measure future changes, and may be appropriate at intervals throughout life, depending on the individual's personal and family medical history.

SCREENING FOR CARDIOVASCULAR DISEASE

More Americans die from cardiovascular disease than from any other cause. It is responsible for nearly 50 percent of all deaths, many of which could be prevented by early screening followed by intervention. Men with elevated serum cholesterol levels and elevated blood pressure who are cigarette smokers are at the greatest risk. Diabetes is another major risk factor. Contributing factors to heart disease are physical inactivity, obesity, stress, and family history of heart disease. Before menopause (scientists are not sure why) women have a much smaller risk of coronary heart disease than men. After menopause, their risk begins to rise and approaches that of men.

Screening for heart disease should include blood pressure monitoring for all patients, including children. Adults with normal blood pressure should be rechecked at least every 2 years, while those at risk should be monitored more frequently. HDL and LDL cholesterol levels in the blood (see chapter 16, Heart and Blood Vessel Diseases, for additional information) should be measured periodically in healthy people, and annually for those at risk. A smoking history should be obtained on the initial visit and repeated periodically, and weight should be monitored. Finally, the physician should be aware of stresses that affect the patient.

SCREENING FOR CEREBROVASCULAR DISEASE (STROKE)

Although well over one-quarter million people survive strokes each year, about one-third remain disabled for life with paralysis, speech disorders, and loss of memory. The risk factors for stroke are similar to those for coronary heart disease—high blood pressure, a diet high in saturated fats and cholesterol, diabetes, and smoking. Chief among them is high blood pressure (hypertension), which is responsible for more strokes than any other single cause. Since black people have more than a 40 percent greater chance of having high blood pressure than whites, they are also much more prone to stroke.

CANCER SCREENING

Cancer is the second most common cause of death in this country. Almost half of cancer fatalities come from cancer of the lung, the large intestine, or the breast.

Factors that affect the content and frequency of cancer screening are use of alcohol, smoking habits, diet, exposure to radiation (including sunlight), occupational exposure to chemicals, water and air pollution, and heredity.

Familial forms of cancer include all the major ones—lung, skin, breast, colon, and uterine. This does not mean that every individual who has had a family member with cancer is at a higher risk of developing that disease. "Familial" in this case refers to two or more documented cases of close relatives developing the same form of cancer. There are also familial diseases that predispose patients to cancer, for which early testing should be done.

Virtually every patient with familial polyposis of the colon (multiple polyps in the colon) will develop colon cancer by age 50, and thus should have the stool tested for blood at age 10 rather than at age 40, the recommended age for those at average risk. Young women exposed to the drug DES because their mothers took it during pregnancy are at a higher than normal risk for developing a form of vaginal cancer, and should have a gynecological exam earlier than most teenagers.

Because of the hazards of radiation, a routine chest x-ray is no longer recommended except for patients at risk of lung cancer or who have symptoms. They may require a regular sputum analysis as well.

Breast cancer occurs in one out of every nine women. Modern methods of detection permit early identification before it has spread to the lymph nodes. Women at greater risk include those with family history of breast cancer, women over 50, single women, and those with previous breast cancer. All women over 20 should perform breast self-examination monthly. Between ages 20 and 40, a breast physical examination is recommended every 3 years, and over age 40, annually. Low-dose mammography is recommended for all women over 50, and the American Cancer Society also recommends a baseline mammogram for all women between the ages of 35 and 40.

Cancer of the cervix, if detected early, is curable. The

Pap test detects abnormalities in cervical cells. In low-risk women, after two negative tests a year apart, the Pap smear will be repeated on a less frequent schedule. In higher-risk women (those with family history of cancer, sexually active teenagers, women who began having sexual intercourse at an early age), the Pap smear may be performed on a more frequent schedule.

Cancer of the colon and rectum (colorectal cancer) is the second most common malignancy in America. Early detection of colon cancer by means of digital rectal examination and sigmoidoscopy can reduce mortality. For those over 40, annual digital rectal examination is recommended. Over age 45, a fecal occult blood test to detect polyps or other causes of rectal bleeding is recommended. Over age 50, proctosigmoidoscopy examination (a "procto") is recommended every 3 to 5 years if the patient is free of symptoms. (For additional information, see chapter 17, Cancer.)

IMMUNIZATION OF ADULTS

Even parents who dutifully follow a prescribed immunization schedule for their children often forget about themselves. While most vaccinations do not have to be repeated beyond childhood, some are advisable periodically or when necessary for known exposure, for international travel (see Table 4.1), and for those at high risk of certain diseases.

Tetanus and Diphtheria. While there is little incidence of tetanus (lockjaw) in this country, those cases that do occur (about half of which are fatal) involve a laceration or wound occurring in or around the home or yard. Over two-thirds of these cases occur in people over 50, which would indicate that large numbers of people over 40 are not adequately immunized. Tetanus boosters for adults are recommended every 10 years.

Poliomyelitis (Infantile Paralysis). Although polio has been practically eradicated in this country, outbreaks can occur among unimmunized people, and the traveler to underdeveloped areas may be at further risk. Routine immunization against polio is not recommended for adults over 18, with the exception of travelers to countries where polio exists, members of special population groups with disease caused by wild polio virus, and laboratory and health care workers who may be exposed to polio virus. Three doses of inactive polio virus (trivalent type) should be given at intervals of 1 to 2 months, with a fourth dose 6 to 12 months later. Pregnant women and patients with immunodeficiency diseases should not take oral polio vaccine.

Influenza (Flu) Vaccine. Adults at high risk of influenza A and B should be vaccinated annually. This includes those with chronic heart and respiratory conditions, cancer, kidney disease, diabetes, anemia, or conditions that alter immunity. Influenza vaccine is also advised for those over 65, and for healthy younger adults who work in close contact with persons at high risk. Individuals who are sensitive to eggs should not be given influenza vaccine.

Pneumococcal Vaccine. Patients with certain chronic conditions are at risk of developing pneumococcal infections, principally pneumonia. Those susceptible include patients with sickle-cell anemia, certain malignancies, cirrhosis of the liver, kidney failure, and disorders of the spleen; alcoholics; diabetics; persons with congestive heart failure or chronic pulmonary disease; and those who have had their spleens removed, have had organ transplants, or have immunosuppressive diseases. Immunization consists of a single dose of vaccine. Booster doses should not be given nor should the vaccine be given during pregnancy.

Rubella Vaccine. Rubella (German measles) can cause birth defects if it occurs during the first trimester (first 3 months) of pregnancy. For that reason, women of childbearing age who have never been vaccinated against rubella and who are antibody negative by testing should receive a single dose of vaccine. Pregnancy must be avoided for 3 months following injection, and the vaccine should never be taken by a pregnant woman.

Hepatitis B Vaccine. Health care workers, physicians, dentists, and others who come in contact with contaminated needles are at risk of getting hepatitis B, a viral infection that affects the liver. Others at risk are users of illegal drugs, sexually active male homosexuals, and people with hemophilia who get frequent blood transfusions. The vaccine is administered in three separate doses and provides protective immunity to over 90 percent of vaccinated individuals.

SUMMING UP

How we live our lives has a profound effect on our health. By avoiding smoking, drinking only in moderation, exercising regularly, learning to handle stress, maintaining ideal body weight, and following a prudent diet, we can substantially reduce our risk of premature cardiovascular disease and cancer—together responsible for more than 70 percent of the deaths in this country. By making efforts to control our work environment, we can reduce our risk of occupational diseases. And we can better our chances of surviving those diseases we can't prevent by having periodic screening for diseases likely to occur in our sex and age group.

Prudent living improves our lives immeasurably, bettering our chances of living to enjoy a mobile, productive, and relatively pain-free old age.

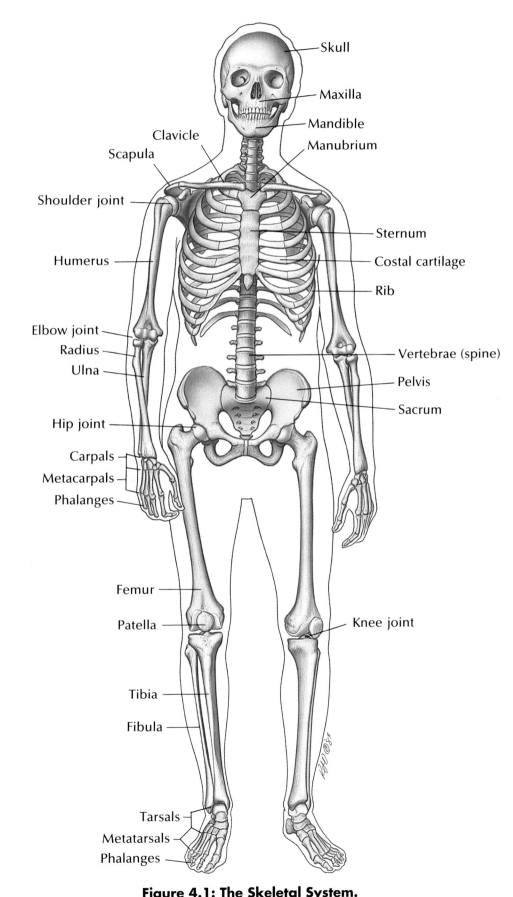

Figure 4.1: The Skeletal System.

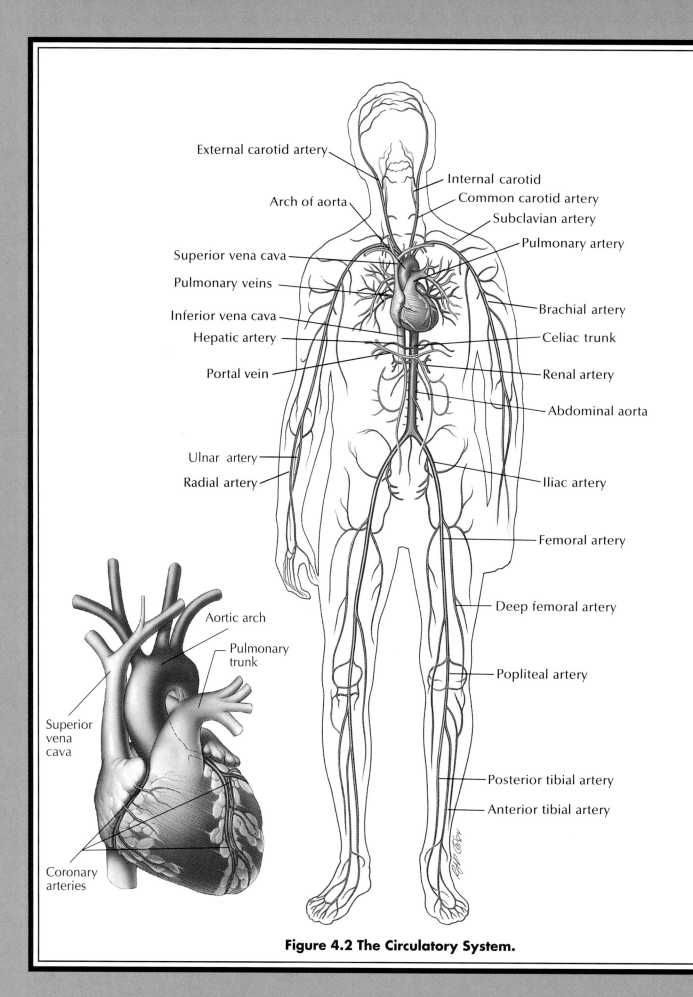

Figure 4.2 The Circulatory System.

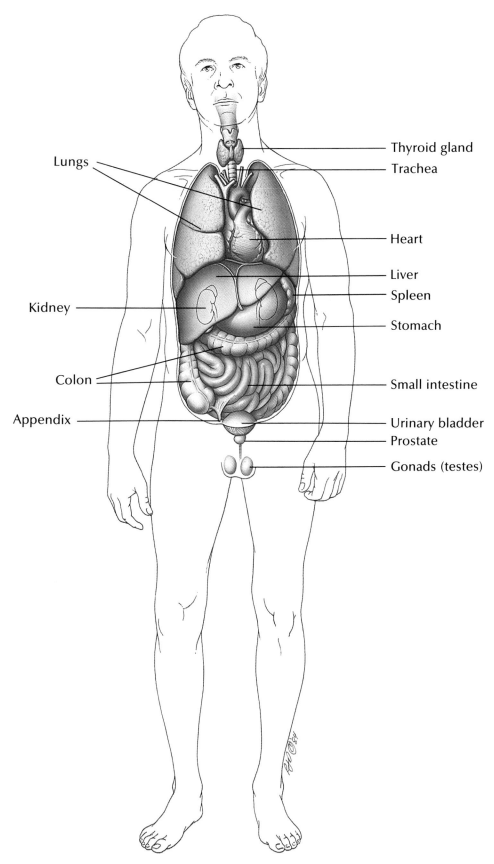

Lungs

Thyroid gland

Trachea

Heart

Liver

Spleen

Kidney

Stomach

Colon

Small intestine

Appendix

Urinary bladder

Prostate

Gonads (testes)

Figure 4.3: The Internal Organs.

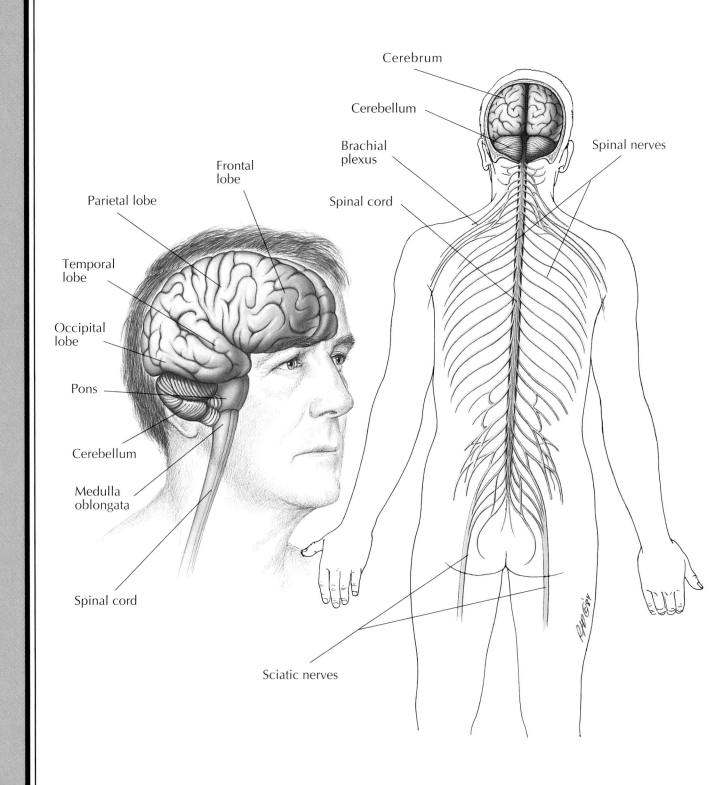

Cerebrum

Cerebellum

Brachial
plexus

Spinal cord

Spinal nerves

Frontal
lobe

Parietal lobe

Temporal
lobe

Occipital
lobe

Pons

Cerebellum

Medulla
oblongata

Spinal cord

Sciatic nerves

Figure 4.4: The Nervous System.

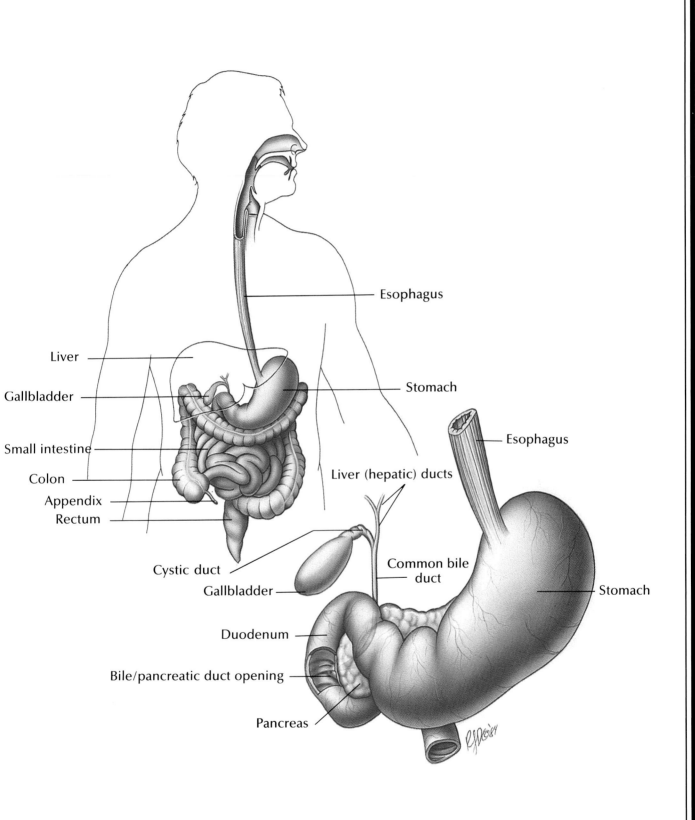

Esophagus

Liver

Gallbladder

Small intestine

Colon

Appendix

Rectum

Cystic duct

Gallbladder

Duodenum

Bile/pancreatic duct opening

Pancreas

Stomach

Esophagus

Liver (hepatic) ducts

Common bile duct

Stomach

Figure 4.5: The Gastrointestinal System.

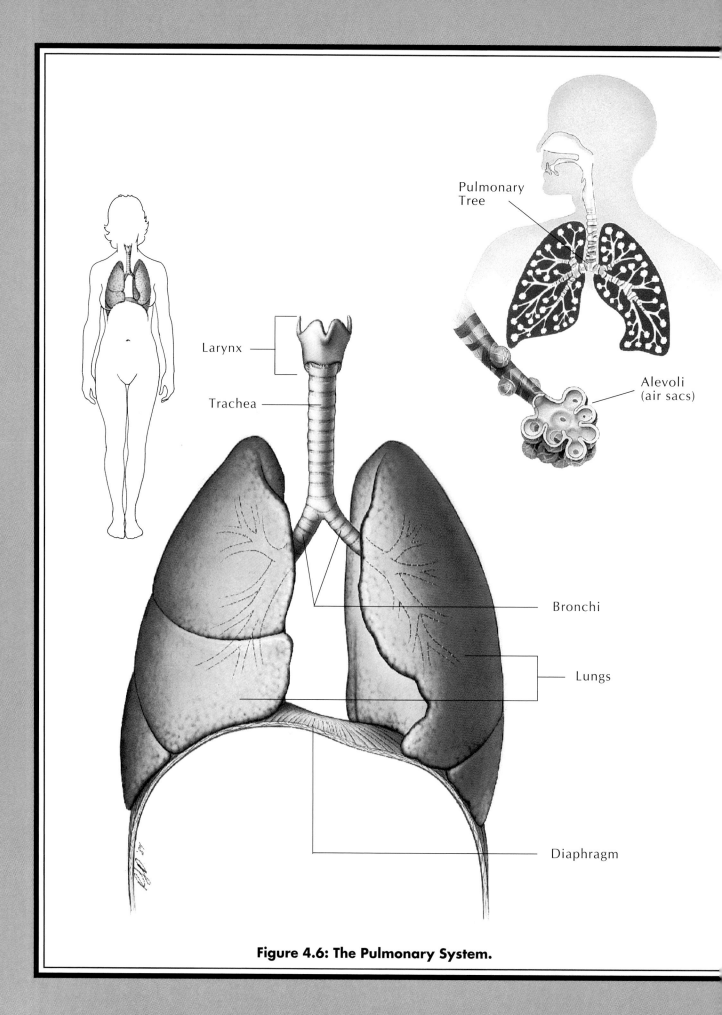

Pulmonary Tree

Alevoli (air sacs)

Larynx

Trachea

Bronchi

Lungs

Diaphragm

Figure 4.6: The Pulmonary System.

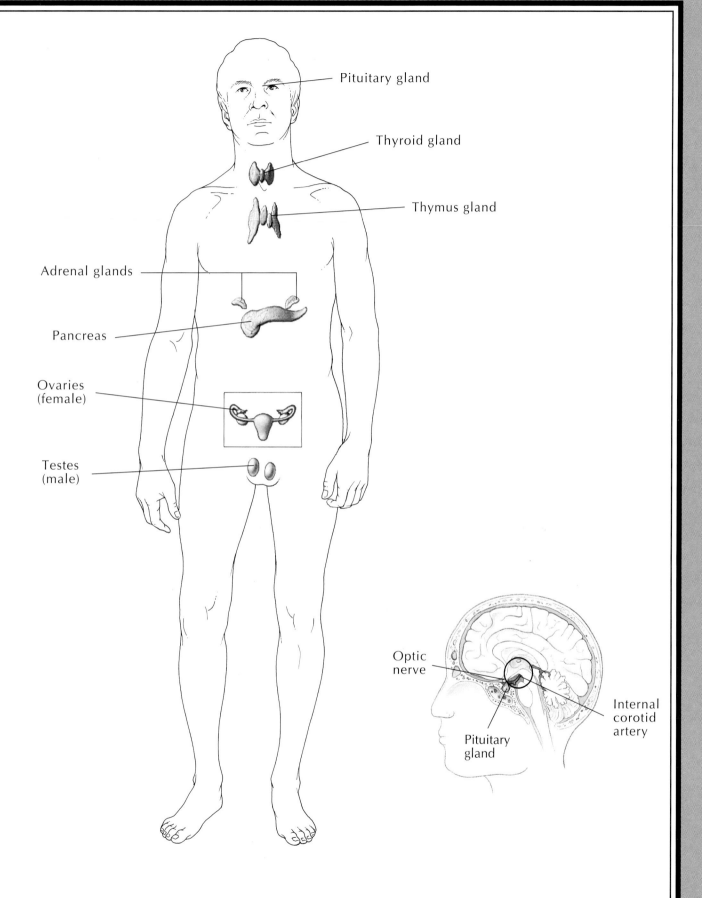

Figure 4.7: The Endocrine System.

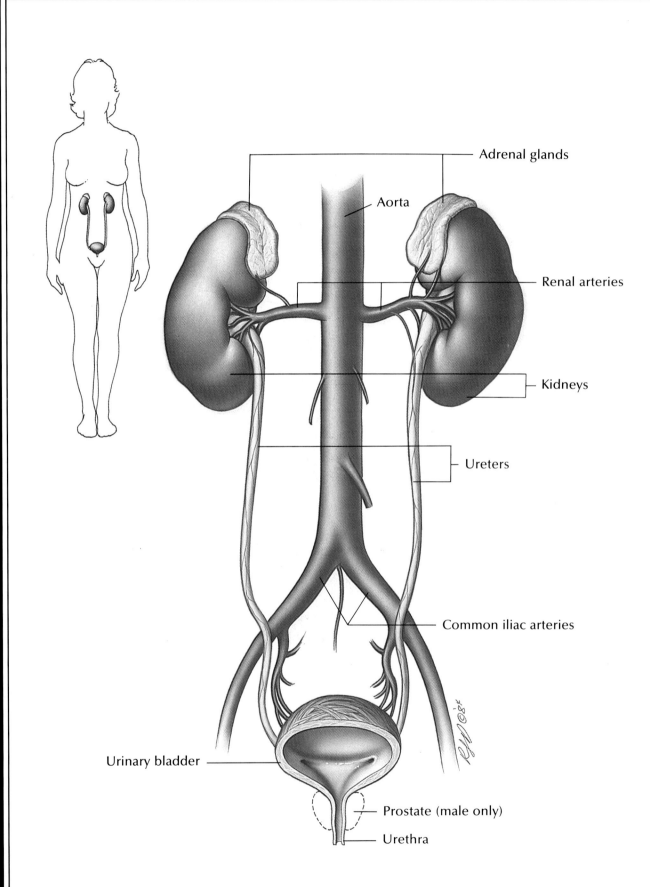

Adrenal glands

Aorta

Renal arteries

Kidneys

Ureters

Common iliac arteries

Urinary bladder

Prostate (male only)

Urethra

Figure 4.8: The Urinary System.

5
The Basics of Good Nutrition

• • • • • • • • • • • • • •

HENRY GINSBERG, M.D.
Parts of this chapter are adapted from the chapter by Theodore B. Van Itallie, M.D., which appeared in the revised second edition.

The medical perspective on nutrition's health effects has undergone a radical transformation in the past two decades. While medical experts have always acknowledged nutritious food as a means of preventing severe, debilitating nutritional deficiencies such as kwashiorkor (protein deficiency), scurvy (vitamin C deficiency), and beriberi (thiamine deficiency), intensive research and large-scale population studies have now provided convincing proof that nutrition can be used to optimize health.

With health costs rising every year, improving health should be every American's concern. While malnutrition and deficiency diseases are still a problem in many underdeveloped countries, these conditions have almost vanished in the United States. The U.S. food supply has improved to the point that despite our tendency to consume suboptimal diets, most Americans get adequate amounts of the basic essential nutrients necessary to sustain "average" health.

The current mainstream awareness of the importance of good nutrition began in the 1960s, a decade when macrobiotic and vegetarian diets enjoyed increasing popularity. The nutrition movement gained momentum with the notion that nutrients, taken in adequate amounts, could not only prevent deficiency diseases but also actually optimize health. At that time, publicity about the supposed benefits of vitamin C kicked off a vitamin-taking frenzy that continues today to expand sales of nutrition supplements.

Public awareness of nutrition's importance received a significant boost in the 1980s as medical research focused on the health significance of cholesterol. At that time the media turned their spotlight on a large, long-term study by Harvard University researchers of the inhabitants of Framingham, Massachusetts, that linked heart disease to increased blood cholesterol levels. The message was clear—many Americans eat a diet that raises cholesterol and the risk of heart disease. This study and other similar research firmly demonstrated the relationship between a poor diet and poor health, demolishing the argument that nutrition's health effects were mere speculation.

Recent polls demonstrate that nutritional awareness continues to grow. When the American Dietetic Association (ADA) surveyed 1,000 people about their knowledge, attitudes, and behavior regarding nutrition, 82 percent of the respondents felt that nutrition was at least moderately important, and 54 percent felt it was highly important—a 5 percent rise from a similar study done just two years earlier.

But while awareness ascends, many people's nutritional beliefs still wallow in misinformation. The ADA poll showed that although 27 percent of people rated themselves as very knowledgeable, very few could correctly answer specific questions about recommended nutritional guidelines. Only 9 percent knew the current recommendations regarding fat consumption and virtually no one could identify the guidelines for daily cholesterol intake.

Perhaps the most disheartening conclusions of the survey regard people's efforts—or lack of interest—in improving eating habits. Despite an increased awareness of nutrition's importance, few people appeared willing to expend a concerted effort to eat right. Less than 40 percent of those questioned claimed they were doing all they could to achieve a healthy diet. Reasons for not doing more included a fear of forsaking favorite foods, overestimation of the time it takes to monitor a diet, and a sense of confusion over what dietary changes were necessary.

This chapter provides tools for making healthy dietary choices by clarifying nutritional facts and demonstrating that good nutrition is really quite a simple concept. Eating well takes very little time and doesn't necessarily mean denying yourself tasty, favorite foods.

THE FOOD GUIDE PYRAMID

People often equate a healthy diet with sacrifice, erroneously believing that a nutritious eating plan leaves no room for sweets, red meat, or fast food and necessitates strict adherence to a series of ascetic eating restrictions. While eating right may impose certain limitations, there are few, if any, absolute prohibitions to which a person in normal health must adhere. In fact, the most important part of a good diet is probably not the excluded foods but those that should be included.

Nutritionists have found that getting enough of certain foods is vital for good health: Cholesterol levels can be lowered by consuming more soluble fiber, cancer risk reduced by eating large quantities of fruits and vegetables, and osteoporosis combated by increasing your intake of foods rich in calcium.

Based upon this philosophy, the U.S. Department of Agriculture has developed a simple scheme, called the Food Guide Pyramid, to help structure a healthy diet. Rather than telling you what to avoid, the Food Pyramid focuses on the types of foods you should be eating and

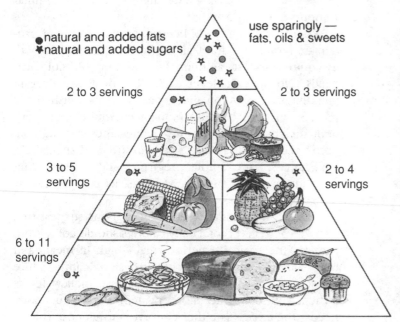

● natural and added fats
✦ natural and added sugars

use sparingly —
fats, oils & sweets

2 to 3 servings

2 to 3 servings

3 to 5
servings

2 to 4
servings

6 to 11
servings

Figure 5.1: The Food Guide Pyramid.

THE FOOD GUIDE PYRAMID

The comparative amounts of each food group you should eat daily include:

Bread, Cereal, Rice, and Pasta	6 to 11 servings
Vegetable Group	3 to 5 servings
Fruit Group	2 to 4 servings
Milk, Yogurt, and Cheese Group	2 to 3 servings
Meat, Poultry, Fish, Dry Beans, Eggs, and Nuts	2 to 3 servings
Fats, Oils, and Sweets	Use sparingly

serves as a guide to how much of each type should be consumed. Foods are classified in six groups.

1. Bread, Cereal, Rice, and Pasta
2. Fruits
3. Vegetables
4. Meat, Poultry, Fish, Dry Beans, Eggs, and Nuts
5. Milk, Yogurt, and Cheese
6. Fats, Oils, and Sweets

The food group that should make up the largest proportion of your diet—breads, cereals, rice, and pasta—forms the foundation of the pyramid. The upper portion of the pyramid is composed of the other food groups sculpted to represent the diminishing amounts of each you should be eating.

The Food Guide Pyramid is meant to help you plan meals and menus. By adhering to the guidelines, your diet is sure to include a variety of foods associated with good health, a diet that provides you with optimal amounts of nutrients rather than merely adequate amounts (see figure 5.1).

ESSENTIAL NUTRIENTS AND THEIR FUNCTIONS

Contained within the food groups included in the food pyramid are more than 40 different nutrients essential to maintaining good health. These fall into six general categories: proteins, carbohydrates, fats, vitamins, minerals, and water.

PROTEINS

Proteins play a variety of important roles throughout the body. As the primary component of numerous tissues, they form much of the body's structure: Muscles are predominantly protein, as are the outer layers of hair, nails, and skin. While the basic framework of the skeleton is composed of calcium, a protein called collagen also makes up a substantial proportion of bone. Proteins also fulfill crucial physiological functions; glands produce specialized proteins called hormones (e.g., the pancreas makes insulin) that transmit messages from one part of the body to another; blood cells manufacture protein antibodies to help combat infection; and cells all over the body synthesize enzymatic proteins responsible for many life-sustaining reactions.

Proteins are composed of compounds called amino acids linked end to end. The number and sequence of different amino acids are what give each protein its unique characteristics. Of the 20 different amino acids, the body can manufacture all but 9; the 9 the body is unable to synthesize on its own are called "essential" amino acids. The term *essential* refers not to the relative importance of these 9 amino acids (all amino acids are necessary for optimal health) but denotes the body's dependency on the diet as a source of these substances. The remaining amino acids that the body is able to synthesize are known as "nonessential."

Animal products such as meat, eggs, and milk provide the richest sources of both essential and nonessential amino acids. Some plant products contain significant amounts of amino acids, but no single plant source can

WHAT IS A "SERVING"?

There are some very serious misconceptions about what "one serving" really is. Many of us imagine that whatever it takes for us to satiate our appetites constitutes a serving; a dinner of pasta and vegetables is one serving of pasta and one serving of vegetables even if we choose to go back for seconds and thirds. But servings as defined in the Food Guide Pyramid are relatively small-size portions.

Listed below are a number of examples of serving sizes in each food group. Use these as a guide in planning your meals. By understanding serving sizes, and the relative amounts of each food group you should consume, you can easily use the pyramid to chart a healthy, well-balanced diet.

FOOD CATEGORY	ONE SERVING EQUALS
Bread, Cereal, Rice, and Pasta	1 slice of bread
	½ bagel or English muffin
	½ hamburger or hot dog bun
	1 corn tortilla
	3 to 4 small crackers
	1 small pancake
	¼ medium waffle
	½ cup of pasta
	½ cup rice
	½ cup hot cereal
	¾ to 1 cup cereal (flakes)
	¼ cup granola
Vegetables	¾ cup vegetable juice
	½ cup broccoli, carrots, green beans, etc.
	1 small potato (size of a large egg)
	1 cob of corn (6″ long)
	⅓ cup yam or sweet potato
Fruits	¾ cup fruit juice
	1 medium apple, banana, orange, or other fruit
	½ medium grapefruit
	⅓ cantaloupe (5″ diameter)
	¼ cup dried fruit
	½ cup canned fruit
Milk, Yogurt, and Cheese	1 cup (8 oz.) milk
	½ cup (4 oz.) evaporated milk
	1 cup yogurt
	½ cup cottage cheese
	1 oz. cheese
Meat, Poultry, Fish, Dry Beans, Eggs, and Nuts	3 oz. fish, lean beef, veal, poultry
	½ cup cooked dry beans
	2 tbsp. peanut butter
	1 egg

provide all of the essential amino acids in optimal amounts and proportions.

Whereas many people believe large amounts of protein are required to fulfill all the body's functions, in reality quite modest amounts satisfy our physiological needs. No specific level of intake, or RDA (Recommended Dietary Allowance), has been established for protein, in part, because individual requirements vary dramatically according to age (babies and growing children need more than adults) and a variety of special circumstances. For example, pregnancy and breast-feeding both increase protein requirements, as does illness or other types of stress.

While current dietary recommendations suggest that 12 to 15 percent of total daily calories should come from protein, the typical American diet—high in meats and other animal products—contains significantly more (closer to 16 to 20 percent). At these dietary levels (when you consume more protein than your body needs) the excess is either converted to glucose (blood sugar) and used by the body as energy or stored in the body in the form of fat.

PROTEIN MYTHS

Because protein has a traditionally healthy image, false myths about this nutrient are widespread.

• Eating additional protein will enhance muscle development, increase strength, and improve athletic performance. Although amino acid supplements are widely promoted, particularly for use among athletes and bodybuilders, they have no proven benefit. In fact, supplements can lead to nutritional imbalances by providing too much of some amino acids and little or none of others.

• Protein is denser in calories than carbohydrates. Protein and carbohydrates have the same caloric density—4 calories per gram—but foods high in protein, such as meats, whole milk, and cheese, may be more fattening than foods rich in carbohydrates because they often contain large amounts of fat (fat provides 9 calories per gram). Because of this association with fat, protein-rich foods need to be selected carefully, with an eye toward consuming low-fat alternatives (e.g., lean cuts of meat, low-fat or nonfat milk, and cheeses made with part-skim milk).

• High-protein diets help reduce weight. High-protein diets used to be extremely popular for quick weight loss. However, much of this weight is water. (More water is required in the metabolism of carbohydrate than in the metabolism of protein, and a low-carbohydrate diet causes water loss.) High-protein diets can be dangerous. Never attempt this sort of diet without a doctor's supervision.

CARBOHYDRATES

Carbohydrates can be classified in three categories: simple carbohydrates, complex carbohydrates, and fiber. All three consist of combinations of sugars (glucose, galactose, or fructose) bound together.

Both simple and complex carbohydrates are easily digested and absorbed by the body for use as a source of energy. While proteins and fats can be broken down and converted into energy, it is generally far more efficient for the body to use carbohydrates for this function. Simple sugars such as sucrose (table sugar), lactose (milk sugar), and maltose (malt sugar) are rapidly broken down, taking only minutes to reach the bloodstream as glucose and galactose, whereas complex carbohydrates may be converted to glucose more slowly, depending on the food in which they are contained and the other foods with which they are eaten. In general, complex carbohydrates are considered healthier foods, because of the other nutrients found along with them—vitamins, minerals, and fiber. The sugary foods that contain the simpler carbohydrates (the sugars) tend to be devoid of other nutrients necessary for good health.

Foods rich in complex carbohydrates include pasta, breads, legumes, and vegetables.

Carbohydrates not used immediately for energy are either converted to glycogen, the stored form of glucose, or converted into and stored as fat.

Carbohydrates serve other vital roles besides being used for energy. In conjunction with proteins, they are used in the formation of antibodies and in the formation and maintenance of cartilage and bones (as well as the fluid that lubricates the joints between them).

FIBER: A SPECIAL CARBOHYDRATE

Unlike other carbohydrates, dietary fiber is unavailable as an energy source. This nutrient cannot be broken down by digestive enzymes and consequently passes through the intestine without being absorbed. Although fiber provides no caloric contribution to the diet, it affects digestion and health in important ways: Some types of fiber bind water, creating a softer stool that passes more rapidly through the colon, reducing the risk of a number of diseases affecting the digestive tract. Certain types of fiber may also lower serum cholesterol, although the mechanism for this function is not well understood. (See the section in this chapter on cholesterol lowering.)

Fiber can be found in abundance in a variety of foods. Unprocessed breads and cereals, fruits and vegetables, and legumes are some of the best sources.

Some types of fiber, such as cellulose and hemicellulose, are made up of simple sugars and considered carbohydrates. Others, such as lignin (a component of the woody parts of plants), cannot technically be considered carbohydrates but, because they are indigestible, are still classified as fiber.

Despite the image you may have of fiber, not all fiber is coarse and rough; fibers vary dramatically in their consistency. While cellulose is generally tough and fibrous, other forms like pectin (a form of hemicellulose) and agar are sticky or gummy.

Scientists divide dietary fiber into two general categories: soluble and insoluble. Soluble fibers dissolve in water and include pectin, guar, carrageenan, gums, mucilage, and oat bran. Soluble fibers are of considerable current interest to researchers because of their apparent role in helping to lower blood cholesterol. Insoluble fibers do not seem to affect serum cholesterol levels, but they do help prevent constipation. Insoluble fibers include cellulose, hemicellulose, and lignin.

GASTROINTESTINAL EFFECTS OF FIBER

High-fiber diets have been advocated to prevent or relieve a wide variety of gastrointestinal problems, from constipation to colon cancer. Apparently, many of these disorders benefit from a softer, bulkier stool that passes more easily and more rapidly through the colon. Insoluble fibers such as hemicellulose absorb large amounts of water as they pass through the intestinal tract and thereby facilitate the stool's passage through the colon. That is why a number of laxatives used to treat constipation are little more than concentrated sources of fiber.

Other common gastrointestinal diseases alleviated with fiber-rich diets include hemorrhoids, diverticulosis, and spastic colon.

COLON CANCER AND FIBER

There has been considerable speculation that a high-fiber diet can help reduce the risk of colon cancer by cutting down the amount of time it takes for the stool to pass through the colon and thereby limiting colon exposure to potential carcinogens harbored in the stool. Unfortunately, scientific studies have not provided conclusive proof that dietary fiber reduces the risk of colon cancer.

WEIGHT CONTROL

Fiber would appear to be a dieter's best friend: Not only is fiber noncaloric (since it is not digested or absorbed by the body) but some forms of fiber can actually cause you to eat less by promoting a feeling of fullness. From a nutritional perspective, however, fiber is relatively lacking since it contains no vitamins or minerals, and substituting fiber for other foods can reduce the nutritional quality of the diet. In addition, fiber may slightly hinder the absorption of essential nutrients such as iron and zinc.

FIBER AND DISEASE PREVENTION

Fiber's beneficial effect on heart disease is mediated by the cholesterol-lowering effect of some types of fiber. Soluble forms of fibers such as oat bran and the fiber in dried beans and other legumes are capable of reducing cholesterol, although the insoluble fibers apparently have no effect whatsoever.

The mechanism by which fiber lowers cholesterol is still not completely understood. It has been proposed that soluble fiber may reduce the amount of cholesterol produced by the liver. Another theory suggests that fiber binds to bile acids, removing them from the body and accelerating the clearance of LDL cholesterol from the body. Research is under way to understand its effects.

Fiber also benefits people with diabetes. Several studies have found that a diet rich in soluble fiber can improve blood sugar control in diabetics and sometimes even help lower insulin requirements.

ADDING FIBER TO YOUR DIET

Abruptly adding large amounts of fiber to your diet can instigate digestive problems, causing bloating and gastrointestinal discomfort with diarrhea and severe cramping. Consequently, you should add fiber to your diet gradually, eating small amounts of fiber-rich foods, or taking small amounts of fiber supplements until your body grows accustomed to its new diet. Additional fiber can then be added slowly until you are consuming a healthy amount.

For most people, fiber supplements may be unnecessary. It is healthier to try first to get fiber from natural food sources by including ample amounts of fruits, vegetables, and whole grains in your diet.

EATING SUFFICIENT FIBER

How much fiber is enough? The question is a difficult one since no RDA exists for fiber and there is disagreement among the experts about how much fiber is adequate for optimal health. But despite the lack of a clear consensus, it is generally agreed that U.S. citizens eat too little: A national diet survey reported that the intake of fiber is quite low, averaging only about 7 grams of fiber per 1,000 calories of food eaten (about 14 grams per day for a typical 2,000-calorie diet).

Calculating the amount of fiber in your diet can be difficult. Food labels can often be helpful, but sometimes they report only the "crude" fiber content of foods rather than total "dietary" fiber. (Dietary fiber is a more accurate measure, showing the fiber that actually passes undigested through the intestine. Crude fiber is an old-fashioned, inaccurate measurement that measures the fiber that withstands chemical dissolution in laboratory tests.) (Table 5.1 lists total dietary fiber and soluble and insoluble components of common foods.)

For most individuals, a diet including a variety of fiber-rich foods, such as whole-grain breads and cereals, fresh fruits and vegetables, and legumes should provide ample amounts of soluble and insoluble fiber.

SIMPLE SUGARS

The most familiar carbohydrates are simple sugars. Our diets contain an abundance of sugars in the form of syrups, table sugar, jellies and jams, and sweets such as cakes, cookies, and candies. Fruits are also rich in simple sugars, but, unlike the sugar in processed foods, fruits also contain healthy amounts of fiber, minerals, and vitamins.

Although no RDA exists for carbohydrates, nutritionists generally recommend that at least 55 percent of calories come from carbohydrates, with an emphasis on complex carbohydrates (only about 10 percent of calories should come from simple carbohydrates). The typical American diet does not conform to these recommendations and provides only about 46 percent of calories from carbohydrates, 18 percent of which is from refined or processed sugars.

CARBOHYDRATE MYTHS

• Carbohydrates are fattening and will make you gain weight. In fact, since starchy foods like bread, pasta, legumes, and vegetables do not generally contain much fat (unless added in the form of butter, cooking oils, or rich sauces), these foods tend to be quite low in calories by weight (carbohydrates contain only 4 calories per gram). Also, research shows that the body less easily turns carbohydrates into body fat than it does oil and other fats.

• Eating too much sugar causes diabetes. Diabetes is not caused by sugar consumption, but people with diabetes may be unable to eat much sugar because either their bodies are incapable of producing adequate amounts of insulin or their bodies are insensitive to the insulin that they do produce. (See chapter 21.) Many people, especially children, who develop diabetes have a history of the disease in their family. In addition, being overweight can greatly increase the likelihood of developing diabetes as an adult.

LIPIDS OR FATS

Lipids are a broad category of substances that includes fats and numerous fatlike compounds such as fatty acids, fatty oils, waxes, and sterols. Although not all lipids are

TABLE 5.1: FIBER CONTENT OF FOODS

Serving Size		Total Fiber (g)	Soluable Fiber (g)	Insoluble Fiber (g)
Breads, Cereals, and Pasta				
White bread	1 slice	0.53	0.03	0.5
Rye bread	1 slice	2.7	0.8	1.9
Whole-grain bread	1 slice	2.9	0.08	2.8
French bread	1 slice	1.0	0.4	0.6
Dinner roll	1 roll	0.8	0.03	0.8
White rice	½ cup cooked	0.5	0.5	0.0
Brown rice	½ cup cooked	1.3	1.3	0.0
Egg noodles	½ cup cooked	0.8	0.3	0.8
Spaghetti	½ cup cooked	0.8	0.02	0.8
Bran (100%) cereal	½ cup	10.0	0.3	9.7
Oats, whole	½ cup cooked	1.6	0.5	1.1
Corn grits	½ cup cooked	1.9	0.61	0.3
Graham crackers	2	1.4	0.04	1.4
Rye wafers	3	2.3	0.06	2.2
Popcorn	3 cups	2.8	0.8	2.0
Fruits				
Apple	1 small	3.9	2.3	1.6
Apricots	2 medium	1.3	0.9	0.4
Banana	1 small	1.3	0.6	0.7
Blackberries	½ cup	3.7	0.7	3.0
Cherries	10	0.9	0.3	0.6
Grapefruit	½ fruit	1.3	0.90	0.4
Peach	1 medium	1.0	0.5	0.5
Pear	1 small	2.5	0.6	1.9
Pineapple	½ cup	0.8	0.2	0.6
Plums	2 medium	2.3	1.3	1.0
Strawberries	¾ cup	2.4	0.9	1.5
Tangerine	1 medium	1.6	1.4	0.4
Legumes				
Kidney beans	½ cup cooked	4.5	0.5	4.0
Lima beans	½ cup cooked	1.4	0.2	1.2
Pinto beans	½ cup cooked	3.0	2.2	0.7
White beans	½ cup cooked	4.2	0.4	3.8
Vegetables				
Broccoli	½ cup cooked	2.6	1.6	1.0
Lettuce	1 cup raw	0.5	0.2	0.3
Parsnips	½ cup cooked	4.4	0.4	4.0
Peas	½ cup cooked	5.2	2.0	3.2
Potatoes	1 small	3.8	2.2	1.6
Squash, summer	½ cup cooked	2.3	1.1	1.2
Zucchini	½ cup cooked	2.5	1.1	1.4

fats, the two terms tend to be used interchangeably and in confusing ways.

Most fat takes the form of triglycerides, the most common form of fat in the diet as well as the most common form of stored fat in the body. While triglycerides exist in a variety of shapes and sizes, all forms share a basic chemical structure: A molecule of glycerol serves as the backbone to which three fatty acids attach, the fatty acids determining the size, shape, and characteristics of the triglyceride. In turn, each fatty acid consists of a series of carbon atoms that bind to hydrogen. If each carbon carries the maximum number of possible hydrogens, it is referred to as "saturated." If two adjoining carbon atoms do not carry their full complement of hydrogens, it is "monounsaturated." "Polyunsaturated" is reserved for fatty acids with multiple (more than two) carbons bound to fewer than the maximum number of hydrogen atoms.

The body manufactures most of the fatty acids it needs from other nutrients, but is unable to make its own linoleic and linolenic acid. Known as "essential" fatty acids, linoleic and linolenic acid should both be consumed daily in small amounts (for instance, 1 teaspoon per day of polyunsaturated fats like corn or safflower oil are sufficient to fulfill the body's requirements).

Cholesterol is a form of lipid called a sterol (technically, cholesterol is not a fat). While some cholesterol is consumed in the diet—but is present only in foods from animals such as meat, butter, and eggs—most of the cholesterol in our bodies is manufactured by the body from fatty acid precursors. (Cholesterol is discussed in depth later in a section of this chapter.)

Although fats have received considerable bad press, a certain amount of fat is essential to maintaining life, and lipids fulfill a variety of important functions within the body. For example, lipids serve as an important energy source necessary to augment carbohydrates, which, although readily available, are quickly depleted during activities such as strenuous exercise.

During exercise the body initially burns carbohydrates taken from glycogen, the body's stored starch. But, after 20 minutes or so of activity, carbohydrate stores are exhausted and the body must turn to its reserves of fat for energy. Other bodily functions of stored lipids include insulation against excessive heat loss and formation of a protective cushion for the skeleton and internal tissues and organs. Dietary fat is needed for the absorption of several nutrients, including vitamins D, E, A, and K. Without fat in the diet, or if your body cannot properly digest fat, you risk a deficiency of these nutrients.

Although cholesterol is found only in foods from animals, fats are found in foods of both plant and animal origin, although animal products, such as meats and dairy foods, are the most well-known fatty foods. Some vegetables like avocados and olives contain significant

TABLE 5.2: SATURATION LEVELS OF COMMON FATS

Mostly Polyunsaturated

Corn oil
Cottonseed oil
Safflower oil
Soybean oil
Sunflower oil
Fish and fish oils
Margarine*

Mostly Monounsaturated

Avocado
Cashews, peanuts, almonds
Peanut butter
Peanut oil
Olives and olive oil

Mostly Saturated

Butter
Cheese
Cocoa butter
Coconut and coconut oil
Palm oil
Red meat
Lard
Vegetable shortening*

*Margarines and vegetable shortenings are actually hydrogenated liquid oils (other oils may also be hydrogenated or partially hydrogenated). Hydrogenation involves adding additional hydrogen atoms to unsaturated fatty acids, increasing their saturation, and causing liquid oils to solidify at room temperature. Some of the fatty acids altered in the hydrogenation process form what are called trans fatty acids, which have been linked to elevations in total blood cholesterol levels and depressions in HDL cholesterol (the "good" cholesterol thought to prevent heart disease).

amounts of fat; nuts, while free of cholesterol, also tend to be fat-laden.

Although the type of fat found in most foods consists of a mixture of saturated, monounsaturated and unsaturated fats, one form usually predominates. As a general rule, fats derived from animal products tend to be more saturated than those derived from vegetables (fish and poultry less so than red meat). Generally, the only fats and oils from plant products that tend to be heavily saturated derive from coconut and palm oil.

TABLE 5.3: FOOD AND NUTRITION BOARD, NATIONAL ACADEMY OF SCIENCES—NATIONAL RESEARCH COUNCIL RECOMMENDED DIETARY ALLOWANCES[a] Revised 1989

Designed for the maintenance of good nutrition of practically all healthy people in the United States

Category	Age (years) or Condition	Weight (kg)	Weight (lb)	Height (cm)	Height (in)	Protein (g)	Fat-Soluble Vitamins Vitamin A (μg RE)[c]	Vitamin D (μg)[d]	Vitamin E (mg α-TE)[e]	Vitamin K (μg)	Water-Soluble Vitamins Vitamin C (mg)	Thiamin (mg)	Riboflavin (mg)	Niacin (mg NE)[f]	Vitamin B6 (mg)	Folate (μg)	Vitamin B12 (μg)	Minerals Calcium (mg)	Phosphorus (mg)	Magnesium (mg)	Iron (mg)	Zinc (mg)	Iodine (μg)	Selenium (μg)
Infants	0.0–0.5	6	13	60	24	13	375	7.5	3	5	30	0.3	0.4	5	0.3	25	0.3	400	300	40	6	5	40	10
	0.5–1.0	9	20	71	28	14	375	10	4	10	35	0.4	0.5	6	0.6	35	0.5	600	500	60	10	5	50	15
Children	1–3	13	29	90	35	16	400	10	6	15	40	0.7	0.8	9	1.0	50	0.7	800	800	80	10	10	70	20
	4–6	20	44	112	44	24	500	10	7	20	45	0.9	1.1	12	1.1	75	1.0	800	800	120	10	10	90	20
	7–10	28	62	132	52	28	700	10	7	30	45	1.0	1.2	13	1.4	100	1.4	800	800	170	10	10	120	30
Males	11–14	45	99	157	62	45	1,000	10	10	45	50	1.3	1.5	17	1.7	150	2.0	1,200	1,200	270	12	15	150	40
	15–18	66	145	176	69	59	1,000	10	10	65	60	1.5	1.8	20	2.0	200	2.0	1,200	1,200	400	12	15	150	50
	19–24	72	160	177	70	58	1,000	10	10	70	60	1.5	1.7	19	2.0	200	2.0	1,200	1,200	350	10	15	150	70
	25–50	79	174	176	70	63	1,000	5	10	80	60	1.5	1.7	19	2.0	200	2.0	800	800	350	10	15	150	70
	51+	77	170	173	68	63	1,000	5	10	80	60	1.2	1.4	15	2.0	200	2.0	800	800	350	10	15	150	70
Females	11–14	46	101	157	62	46	800	10	8	45	50	1.1	1.3	15	1.4	150	2.0	1,200	1,200	280	15	12	150	45
	15–18	55	120	163	64	44	800	10	8	55	60	1.1	1.3	15	1.5	180	2.0	1,200	1,200	300	15	12	150	50
	19–24	58	128	164	65	46	800	10	8	60	60	1.1	1.3	15	1.6	180	2.0	1,200	1,200	280	15	12	150	55
	25–50	63	138	163	64	50	800	5	8	65	60	1.0	1.3	15	1.6	180	2.0	800	800	280	15	12	150	55
	51+	65	143	160	63	50	800	5	8	65	60	1.0	1.2	13	1.6	180	2.0	800	800	280	10	12	150	55
Pregnant						60	800	10	10	65	70	1.5	1.6	17	2.2	400	2.2	1,200	1,200	320	30	15	175	65
Lactating	1st 6 months					65	1,300	10	12	65	95	1.6	1.8	20	2.1	280	2.6	1,200	1,200	355	15	19	200	75
	2nd 6 months					62	1,200	10	11	65	90	1.6	1.7	20	2.1	260	2.6	1,200	1,200	340	15	16	200	75

[a] The allowances, expressed as average daily intakes over time, are intended to provide for individual variations, among most normal persons as they live in the United States under usual environmental stresses. Diets should be based on a variety of common foods in order to provide other nutrients for which human requirements have been less well defined. See text for detailed discussion of allowances and of nutrients not tabulated.

[b] Weights and heights of Reference Adults are actual medians for the U.S. population of the designated age, as reported by NHANES II. The median weights and heights of those under 19 years of age were taken from Hamill et al. (1979). The use of these figures does not imply that the weight-to-height ratios are ideal.

[c] Retinol equivalents. 1 retinol equivalent = 1 μg retinol or 6 μg β-carotene. See text for calculation of vitamin A activity of diets as retinol equivalents.

[d] As cholecalciferol. 10 μg cholecalciferol = 400 IU of vitamin D.

[e] α-Tocopherol equivalents. 1 mg d-α tocopherol = 1 α-TE. See text for variation in allowances and calculation of vitamin E activity of the diet as tocopherol equivalents.

[f] 1 NE (niacin equivalent) is equal to 1 mg of niacin or 60 mg of dietary tryptophan.

And while cholesterol can be found in large amounts in almost all animal fats, the most significant amounts are found in fatty meats, organ meats, egg yolks, and cheese.

Just as there are no RDAs for proteins and carbohydrates, the National Research Council (the government-sponsored group that determines RDAs) has not established RDAs for fat. Current recommendations supported by numerous health care organizations including the National Cancer Society, the American Heart Association, and the National Cholesterol Education Program advocate that (1) no more than 30 percent of total calories in your diet come from fats and (2) only 8 to 10 percent of total calories in your diet should be derived from saturated fats.

Limiting fat in the diet is one of the most important recommendations for optimizing your health. A number of negative effects can result from a diet high in fat.

• Raised cholesterol levels: Saturated fats tend to raise the level of cholesterol circulating in the blood, thereby increasing the risk of developing coronary artery disease and eventually suffering a heart attack. (In fact, saturated fat in the diet has a much stronger effect on blood cholesterol than does cholesterol in the diet.)

• Increased risk of obesity: Diets high in fat are generally high in calories—fats provide 9 calories per gram—and predispose you to weight gain.

• Possible increased risk of cancer: Preliminary evidence suggests an association between a high-fat diet and several forms of cancer, such as cancer of the breast and colon.

VITAMINS

Vitamins are a group of essential organic substances used mainly as coenzymes in physiological processes that usually cannot be synthesized by the body and must therefore be consumed in the diet. Some vitamins, such as vitamin A and niacin, can be consumed in precursor forms (the carotenes in the case of vitamin A and tryptophan in the case of niacin) that are subsequently converted to vitamins in the body. Vitamins (along with minerals) are commonly referred to as "micronutrients" because compared with "macronutrients" such as protein, carbohydrates, and fats, they are needed in relatively microscopic amounts.

Vitamins serve a wide variety of functions. Vitamin A aids in the maintenance of epithelial tissues, boosts the body's resistance to infection, and is essential to good eyesight. Vitamin D promotes the absorption of calcium, vitamin K is necessary for blood clotting, and vitamin C acts as a potent antioxidant. The B vitamins assist enzymes in the breakdown and formation of proteins, carbohydrates, and fats. Unlike most of the other nutrients that have been discussed, vitamins cannot serve as energy sources and they contain no calories, although several of the B vitamins do play a role in taking energy out of other nutrients.

Vitamins fall into two general categories: fat soluble and water soluble. Fat-soluble vitamins include vitamins A, D, E, and K. Insoluble in water (and therefore insoluble in blood), these nutrients require protein carriers to travel through the bloodstream. Fat-soluble vitamins are not readily excreted; rather, excess amounts are stored in the liver and fatty tissue.

Water-soluble vitamins include vitamin C and the eight B vitamins: thiamine (B_1), riboflavin (B_2), niacin (B_3), pyridoxine (B_6), folic acid, cobalamin (B_{12}), biotin (B_7), and pantothenic acid (B_5). Being soluble in water, these vitamins circulate freely in the bloodstream without the need for protein carriers.

Although it used to be thought that megadoses of fat-soluble vitamins were potentially more dangerous than water-soluble vitamins, very high doses of any vitamin, particularly over a long period of time, may cause adverse effects.

Recommended Dietary Allowances (or RDAs—see table 5.3) have been established by the National Research Council for vitamins A, and C, D, E, K, thiamine, riboflavin, niacin, vitamins B_6 and B_{12}, and folate, and Estimated Safe and Adequate Daily Dietary Intakes determined for biotin and pantothenic acid.

The RDAs are intended to reflect safe and adequate levels of vitamin intake. They are general estimations of how much the average body needs to avoid deficiency disease, plus a small amount to account for some special individual needs.

The RDAs frequently come under attack. Many feel that these recommendations are inadequate and that larger amounts of some vitamins confer additional health benefits not accounted for by the RDAs. These critics point to a growing body of scientific literature that suggests that vitamins (and some minerals), in doses higher than are currently recommended, play an important role in the prevention of chronic disease. For instance, evidence now suggests that vitamin E supplementation protects against heart disease, higher doses of vitamins C and E play an important role in cancer and cataract prevention, and supplementary calcium can help prevent osteoporosis (see "Nutrition and Osteoporosis").

Table 5.4 provides a complete listing of vitamins along with their respective sources, functions, and signs of deficiency and toxicity.

MAXIMIZING THE VITAMIN CONTENT OF YOUR DIET

While the fat-soluble vitamin content of food tends to be quite stable and resists degradation, water-soluble vitamins are fragile and easily destroyed by lengthy storage,

TABLE 5.4: VITAMIN FACTS
(See Table 5.3 for U.S. RDA amounts)

Vitamin	Significant Sources	Major Physiological Functions	Symptoms of Deficiency	Symptoms of Overconsumption
Vitamin A	Vitamin A: liver and other organ meats, whole or fortified milk, cheese, butter, egg yolk. Carotenoids: carrots, green leafy vegetables, sweet potatoes, apricots, cantaloupe, acorn squash.	Functions in the visual process. Assists in the development and maintenance of the skin and mucous membranes, thereby increasing resistance to infections. Promotes normal bone development.	Mild: night blindness, increased susceptibility to infections, loss of appetite, weight loss, impaired growth in children. Severe: drying of the cornea, which may lead to ulceration and permanent blindness.	Mild: nausea, vomiting, dryness of mucous membranes, bone and muscle pain. Severe: double vision, headache, enlargement of the liver and spleen, bone abnormalities, increased pressure in the skull. **Warning: Overconsumption during pregnancy may cause birth defects.**
Vitamin D	Fish oils, liver, egg yolks; dairy products fortified with vitamin D—milk, butter, margarine. Vitamin D is also synthesized by the skin upon exposure to sunlight.	Increases the intestinal absorption of calcium. Promotes the development of bones and teeth.	Rickets (children); osteomalacia (adults).	Mild: nausea, loss of appetite, weight loss, irritability, constipation. Severe: mental and physical growth retardation, damage to the kidneys and heart.
Vitamin E	Vegetable oils and the products made from them (margarine and shortening), wheat germ, seeds and nuts, egg yolk.	Functions as an antioxidant, protecting fatty acids from destruction. May play a role in the prevention of atherosclerosis and slow the development of cataracts.	Loss of appetite, stunted growth, reproductive failure, neurological changes.	Relatively nontoxic. May produce headache, fatigue, nausea, and muscular weakness at very high doses.
Vitamin K	Green leafy vegetables, dairy products, eggs, whole grains. Vitamin K is also produced by bacteria in the intestine.	Necessary for the proper clotting of blood. May play a role in normal bone metabolism.	Abnormal blood clotting associated with an increased tendency to bleed.	One form of vitamin K, menadione, can produce severe symptoms, including anemia and infantile jaundice. Other forms are relatively nontoxic.
Vitamin C (Ascorbic Acid)	Green and red peppers, collard greens, broccoli, spinach, strawberries, oranges and other citrus fruits, potatoes, kiwifruit.	Important in the formation of collagen. Increases resistance to infection. Augments the absorption of iron. Accelerates wound healing. Functions as an antioxidant. May reduce the risk of some forms of cancer and help prevent against the development of cataracts.	Mild: fatigue, listlessness, increased susceptibility to infections, loss of appetite, muscular weakness. Severe: Scurvy with easy bruising, poor wound healing, swollen bleeding gums, bone pain, psychological changes.	Vitamin C can be taken in relatively high doses without ill effects; very high doses may cause diarrhea.

TABLE 5.4: VITAMIN FACTS (Cont.)

Vitamin	Significant Sources	Major Physiological Functions	Symptoms of Deficiency	Symptoms of Overconsumption
Thamine (Vitamin B$_1$)	Fortified grains and cereals, seafood, pork, legumes, seeds, and nuts.	Essential in the metabolism of carbohydrates.	Mild: fatigue, constipation, loss of appetite, weight loss, muscular weakness. Severe: Beriberi. Symptoms include wasting of tissues, edema, heart failure, and a host of psychological symptoms ranging from confusion to psychosis.	None reported.
Riboflavin (Vitamin B$_2$)	Meats, including fish and poultry, dairy products, enriched grains and cereals.	Assists the body in using oxygen to release energy from food.	Cracks at the corner of the mouth, sore throat, skin rash, swollen tongue, chapped lips, psychological disturbances.	None reported.
Niacin (Vitamin B$_3$)	Poultry, meat, seafood, fortified grains. Milk and eggs are good sources of tryptophan, which can then be converted to niacin.	Necessary to take energy from food and maintain appetite and digestion. Aids nerve function. When taken in large doses under medical supervision, niacin may be used to lower cholesterol.	Mild: loss of appetite, weight loss, nausea and vomiting, headache. Severe: skin rash, sore tongue, abdominal pain and diarrhea, nervousness and irritability, psychological changes.	Can produce flushing, liver problems, heart arrhythmias, and ulcers and raise blood sugar and uric acid.
Folic Acid	Liver, poultry, yeast, green leafy vegetables, legumes, fruits.	Participates in the synthesis of nucleic acids and the degradation of amino acids. Promotes red blood cell formation. Appears to reduce the risk of neural tube defects in pregnancy.	Loss of weight, diarrhea, anemia, bleeding gums. Red blood cells appear deformed.	Can precipitate convulsions in patients with epilepsy. May obscure forms of anemia.
Vitamin B$_6$	Meat, fish, poultry, grains, spinach, potatoes, bananas, prunes.	Participates in protein and carbohydrate metabolism. Necessary for red blood cell formation and nerve function.	Itchy and scaly skin, depression, confusion, mouth inflammation, and infantile convulsions.	May destroy sensory nerves.
Biotin (Vitamin B$_7$)	Meat, egg yolk, fish, cereals, nuts, seeds, legumes, yeast. Made by intestinal bacteria.	Involved in the breakdown of certain amino acids and the synthesis of fats. Takes part in glucose metabolism.	Nausea, vomiting, loss of appetite, depression, hair loss, dry scaling skin.	None reported.

TABLE 5.4: VITAMIN FACTS (Cont.)

Vitamin	Significant Sources	Major Physiological Functions	Symptoms of Deficiency	Symptoms of Overconsumption
Vitamin B_{12}	Meat, poultry, fish, eggs, milk and milk products. Vitamin B_{12} is not found in plant foods to any significant degree. Vegetarians should take a daily vitamin supplement containing this nutrient.	Necessary for red blood cell formation and creation of genetic material.	Sore tongue, weakness, anemia, neurological symptoms.	None reported.
Pantothenic Acid (Vitamin B_5)	Meats, whole grain cereals, legumes, milk.	Important in the breakdown and synthesis of fats, the release of energy from carbohydrates, and the production of various hormones and neurotransmitters.	Deficiency is rare because this nutrient is widely distributed in foods. Listlessness, fatigue, "burning feet" syndrome.	Virtually nontoxic. May produce diarrhea at very high doses.

high temperatures, processing, and cooking. The following tips can help minimize nutrient losses and maintain the nutritional content of your diet.

• Fruits and vegetables contain their highest level of nutrients when they are harvested at full ripeness and eaten soon thereafter, with only minimal processing. Thus, the most nutritious produce consists of home-grown fruits and vegetables picked at full maturity (avoid picking prematurely and allowing them to ripen off the vine) and eaten immediately.

• Since substantial vegetable gardening is impractical for most people, the next best alternative is to purchase fruits and vegetables properly harvested and stored or processed to preserve their nutritional value. "Fresh" supermarket produce does not always fit this description as it is often picked before fully ripe, shipped long distances, and stored under poor conditions.

• Frequently, frozen foods are a good choice for produce because they are generally picked at their peak, quickly processed, and stored at nutrient-preserving cold temperatures.

• Store foods properly to prevent significant nutritional losses. A cool, dark place is generally best since vitamin degradation accelerates at higher temperatures and several of the water-soluble vitamins, riboflavin and vitamin C in particular, are very light-sensitive.

• Cooking also contributes to vitamin losses, and many water-soluble vitamins are destroyed by heat. Consequently you should occasionally eat fruits and vegetables raw and keep cooking times to the minimum. Avoid boiling or steaming vegetables in large amounts of water; water will remove vitamins. Microwave vegetables without water whenever possible to preserve nutrient content.

MINERALS

Minerals are inorganic substances essential to a number of important physiological processes: Calcium plays a role in the functioning of nerves and muscles and is integral to the structure of teeth and bones. Iron is essential in the formation of red blood cells, while iodine influences the metabolic rate, and chromium is necessary for normal carbohydrate metabolism. Like vitamins, minerals cannot be produced by the body and must be consumed regularly in small amounts in the diet.

Minerals are divided into two general categories according to the quantities present in the body. Major minerals (or macrominerals) are present in the body and required in the diet in significant amounts; these include calcium, phosphorus, magnesium, potassium, sodium, and chloride. Trace elements (or microminerals) are those minerals found in the body in smaller amounts: arsenic, chromium, cobalt, copper, fluoride, iodine, iron, manganese, molybdenum, nickel, selenium, silicon, tin, vanadium, and zinc.

Under normal conditions, even while the amounts of minerals fluctuate in the diet, your body is able to maintain a narrow and rather delicate balance of minerals, absorbing greater amounts from your food or calling

TABLE 5.5: MINERAL FACTS
(See Table 5.3 for USRDA amounts)

Mineral	Significant Sources	Major Physiological Functions	Symptoms of Deficiency	Symptoms of Overconsumption
Calcium	Milk and milk products, green leafy vegetables, canned fish with edible bones, calcium-fortified foods.	Essential in the formation of bones and teeth; helps blood clot; important in nerve transmission and muscle contraction.	Rickets in children; osteoporosis in adults.	Constipation, elevated blood levels of calcium, which can in turn cause drowsiness, lethargy, nausea and vomiting, and the deposition of calcium in tissues.
Chloride	Table salt, foods high in sodium.	Helps maintain water balance inside and outside the cells; upsets body's acid-base and fluid balance.		The body's balance of acids and bases is disrupted.
Chromium	Wheat germ, oysters, liver, brewer's yeast.	Essential in carbohydrate metabolism; may be necessary for insulin to function normally.	Impaired glucose tolerance, muscle wasting, weight loss.	Very low toxicity.
Copper	Organ meats, whole grains and cereals, eggs, legumes, oysters, nuts, and seeds.	Aids in the formation of hemoglobin; essential to normal nerve transmission; acts as a coenzyme in a number of reactions.	Anemia, demineralization of bones, loss of pigmentation in hair and skin. (Deficiency is rarely found in adults, but occasionally seen in children.)	Mild toxicity: provokes nausea and vomiting, abdominal pain, headache, dizziness and weakness. Profound toxicity: leads to high blood pressure, jaundice, coma, and even death.
Fluoride	Fluoridated water and foods cooked in fluoridated water, fish, tea.	Makes teeth more resistant to decay; may help protect bones against osteoporosis.	Tooth decay.	Mottling of tooth enamel.
Iodine	Iodized salt, fish and other seafood.	Component of thyroid hormones.	Enlargement of the thyroid gland, cretinism (infants).	Very low toxicity.
Iron	Liver, meat, fish, egg yolk, green leafy vegetables, enriched bread and cereals.	Constituent of hemoglobin, which carries oxygen from the lungs to tissues throughout the body, and myoglobin, which stores oxygen in muscle.	Anemia, pale skin, weakness and fatigue, shortness of breath, headache.	Constipation. Large doses of iron can be lethal and are the leading cause of fatal supplement overdose in children.
Magnesium	Green leafy vegetables, nuts, legumes, whole grains, soybeans, seafood.	Modulates the activity of muscles and nerves; normal component of bones. Required for the production of energy by the body. Works to activate hundreds of enzymes in the body.	Nausea, muscle weakness, irritability, confusion, personality changes, loss of appetite. Severe deficiency can result in abnormal muscle movements and uncontrolled muscle contraction.	Early symptoms include drowsiness, weakness, nausea, and vomiting. More severe toxicity can result in paralysis, loss of reflexes, and a dangerously slow heart rate.

TABLE 5.5 MINERAL FACTS (Cont.)

Mineral	Significant Sources	Major Physiological Functions	Symptoms of Deficiency	Symptoms of Overconsumption
Manganese	Whole grains and cereals, peas, nuts, and legumes.	Activates several enzymes in the body.	Unknown in humans.	Very low toxicity.
Molybdenum	Meats, whole grains, legumes, organ meats, dark green leafy vegetables.	Coenzyme in numerous enzymatic reactions.	Unknown in humans.	Copper deficiency.
Phosphorus	Meat, poultry, and fish, milk and milk products, legumes and nuts, soft drinks.	Needed in the formation of bones and teeth; critical in the formation of usable forms of energy by the body; component of numerous important compounds such as nucleic acid and lipids.	Bone pain, weakness, anorexia, malaise.	Lowers blood calcium levels but appears to have no significant clinical effects.
Potassium	Bananas, tomatoes, citrus fruiits, potatoes, legumes, deep yellow vegetables, meats.	Helps regulate body fluid balance; important in the transmission of nerve impulses.	Weakness, loss of appetite, nausea, listlessness, drowsiness, irrational behavior.	High levels of potassium can cause cardiac irregularities and may lead to cardiac arrest.
Selenium	Seafood, poultry, meats, grains, mushrooms.	Functions as an antioxidant; acts as a coenzyme in a number of reactions.	Muscular discomfort, weakness.	Hair loss, nail changes, nausea, abdominal pain, diarrhea, fatigue, irritability.
Sodium	Table salt, processed foods.	Helps regulate the body's fluid volume and acid-base balance.	Feelings of weakness, headache, muscle cramps.	High blood pressure (in salt-sensitive people), water retention with bloating.
Sulfur	Foods high in protein such as meat, poultry, fish, eggs, and milk.	Serves as a component of several amino acids. Constituent of thaimine and biotin.	None reported.	None reported, although sulfur salts are poisonous.
Zinc	Organ meats, meat, egg yolk, seafood.	Involved in normal insulin activity; essential for taste; boosts immune function; improved wound healing.	Loss of taste, delayed wound healing, anemia, hair loss, stunted growth (children).	Muscle incoordination, dizziness, drowsiness, vomiting, anemia, and impaired immune function.

upon body stores when levels are low and excreting more when levels climb too high.

But the presence of other nutrients in the diet can affect the proper absorption of some minerals. Vitamin D, for example, is essential for the absorption of calcium while vitamin C substantially enhances the absorption of iron from vegetables and other vegetarian foods. In some cases, nutrients inhibit mineral absorption. For instance, iron and zinc may pass through the digestive tract and are inadequately absorbed when large amounts of fiber are consumed in the diet.

Drugs and illnesses can also disturb mineral balances.

• Severe diarrhea can result in large losses of potassium and chloride.
• The use of diuretics (water pills) may reduce levels of potassium, calcium, and magnesium and can cause potentially serious electrolyte imbalances (electrolytes preserve proper functioning of the heart and other muscles).
• Strenuous exercise can cause excessive loss of zinc through perspiration.

Table 5.5 lists the minerals that are generally recognized as essential (the list changes from time to time as our knowledge about specific minerals increases) along with their respective U.S. RDAs, functions, and signs of deficiencies and overdoses.

WATER

Water is the most plentiful substance in the body, making up about 55 to 65 percent of adult body weight (and even more for infants). While the physiological significance of water is often overlooked, it is in fact the most essential nutrient. While we can live for several weeks or even longer without food, we can survive but a few days without water.

The water in the blood is the chief transportation vehicle for the distribution of essential nutrients and oxygen throughout the body. The aqueous quality of blood also allows it to be filtered through the kidneys, where dangerous waste products are concentrated in the urine to be excreted. In addition, water throughout the body helps regulate body temperature and is essential in a wide array of biochemical processes.

Although most of us try to eat fairly decent diets, few give much thought to the importance of water. On average, a healthy adult needs between one and three liters of water a day. This can be supplied by drinks such as tap or bottled water, coffee, tea, milk, fruit juices, and soft drinks as well as solid foods, such as fruits and vegetables, which may be 90 percent water. Whereas any combination of foods and beverages that provides the needed amount of water is acceptable, many nutritionists recommend 6 to 8 glasses of liquids a day. Anything that increases water losses from the body, such as strenuous exercise, hot weather, diarrhea, or fever, increases the body's need for water.

NUTRITION AND SPECIFIC DISEASES

Recent research indicates that a healthy diet may supply optimal levels of nutrients capable of protecting your health. In this vein is the tremendous current medical interest in nutrition's role in the development and prevention of chronic diseases such as cardiovascular disease, cancer, high blood pressure, diabetes, and osteoporosis.

CARDIOVASCULAR DISEASE

Cardiovascular disease claims the lives of over 500,000 Americans each year. Although many people consider it a male disease because it generally affects men at a relatively young age, one out of three American women will ultimately die as a result of heart disease—more than die from breast cancer. Atherosclerosis, the buildup of cholesterol-laden plaque in the coronary arteries, narrows the arteries, limiting the amount of oxygen-rich blood reaching the heart muscle. When the oxygen supply to the heart drops drastically, sections of the heart muscle die and a heart attack ensues.

While the precise mechanisms of atherosclerotic plaque formation are not fully understood, it is generally agreed that several nutritional factors influence its development. Numerous studies have demonstrated that lowering the cholesterol in your blood by cutting the saturated fat in your diet can significantly reduce your risk of heart disease. Research also indicates that sufficient consumption of so-called antioxidant nutrients (vitamins C, E, and beta-carotene in particular) may protect arteries from damage and buildup of arterial plaque.

CHOLESTEROL

Despite all of the media attention lavished on cholesterol over the past several years, many people misunderstand the dietary and physiological significance of this substance.

Dietary cholesterol is a waxy substance found only in foods of animal origin such as poultry, beef, fish, eggs, and dairy products; fruits and vegetables contain none. Your body does not need to consume cholesterol, as the liver makes all that you need for normal cell processes.

In your body not all cholesterol is undesirable: Your

body requires a certain amount to build cell walls and to manufacture vital substances, such as vitamin D and hormones. In children, cholesterol plays an important role in the development of the brain and nervous system. It is only in diseased arteries, where cholesterol can collect and block the flow of blood, that cholesterol can become life-threatening.

Insoluble in substances like water and blood, cholesterol must first be combined with fats and proteins to form particles called lipoproteins before it can be transported in the blood for normal processes or returned to the liver for processing and removal from the body.

The body contains several different kinds of lipoproteins, varying in both size and composition. Low-density lipoproteins (LDL), commonly referred to as the "bad" cholesterol, are the most abundant, conveying about two-thirds of the circulating cholesterol. High levels of LDL cholesterol are associated with a tendency for cholesterol deposits on the walls of the arteries. On the other hand high-density lipoproteins (HDL), the "good" cholesterol, scavenges excess cholesterol from the bloodstream and carries it to the liver for excretion. Another class of lipoprotein, the very-low-density lipoproteins (VLDL), carries mostly triglycerides throughout the body to be used as energy or stored as fat.

In order to standardize the medical approach to dealing with high cholesterol blood levels, the National Cholesterol Education Program (NCEP) has developed a series of recommendations for treatment and follow-up based upon evaluation of total blood cholesterol levels.

TOTAL BLOOD CHOLESTEROL

Desirable: 199 milligrams/deciliter or less
Borderline-high: 200 to 239 milligrams/deciliter
High: 240 milligrams/deciliter or more

As a refinement to determining cardiovascular risk from cholesterol levels, the NCEP now designates a low level of HDL cholesterol as an independent risk factor for coronary heart disease.

HDL CHOLESTEROL

Low (increased heart disease risk): Less than 35 milligrams/deciliter
High (decreased heart disease risk): 60 milligrams/deciliter or more

The NCEP now recommends that total blood cholesterol and HDL cholesterol be routinely monitored at five-year intervals beginning at age 20. Individuals found to have abnormal cholesterol levels should have a complete lipoprotein analysis, including both LDL cholesterol and tri-

glycerides. Classifications based on LDL cholesterol levels are as follows:

LDL CHOLESTEROL

Desirable: 129 milligrams/deciliter or less
Borderline-high: 130 to 159 milligrams/deciliter
High: Over 160 milligrams/deciliter

While not as much is known about the role of circulating triglycerides as a cardiovascular risk factor, it is thought that very high levels may also contribute to heart disease. For more information on your triglyceride level, consult your doctor.

AN APPROACH TO EVALUATING AND TREATING HIGH CHOLESTEROL IN ADULTS

RISK FACTORS FOR CORONARY HEART DISEASE

Increased risk is associated with

- Age:
  Men 45 or over
  Women 55 or over or women reaching menopause before age 55 without estrogen replacement therapy
- Family history of premature coronary heart disease
- Smoking
- High blood pressure
- Low HDL cholesterol (less than 35 milligrams/deciliter)
- Diabetes

SCREENING AND FOLLOW-UP RECOMMENDATIONS

- Total blood cholesterol and HDL cholesterol should be measured at least once every five years in all adults 20 years of age and older.
- For individuals with desirable blood cholesterol (less than 200), the level of HDL cholesterol determines the appropriate course for follow-up:
  - HDL 35 or greater: Remeasure within 5 years.
  - HDL less than 35: Consult your physician for a lipoprotein analysis; further medical measures will be based on your LDL cholesterol level.
  - For individuals with borderline-high blood cholesterol (200–239):

The level of HDL cholesterol and the presence or absence of CHD risk factor will guide your physician in determining follow-up.

- HDL 35 or greater and fewer than two risk factors for CHD: Your physician should help you with dietary modification, setting up an exercise program and reducing your factors. Your cholesterol should be measured again in 1 to 2 years.

- HDL less than 35 or two or more risk factors for CHD: Your physician should order a lipoprotein analysis and will base further action on your LDL cholesterol level.
- For individuals with high blood cholesterol (240 or more): A complete lipoprotein analysis is essential. Further action will be recommended by your physician based on your LDL level.

WHAT DETERMINES YOUR CHOLESTEROL LEVEL?

The factors known to influence your blood cholesterol level include:

- *Heredity:* Genetic factors play a major role in determining the amount of cholesterol in your blood. While some people can eat a high-fat, high-cholesterol diet and still maintain normal blood cholesterol levels, other individuals display high levels despite eating prudently. Often your genes determine how rapidly cholesterol is cleared from your bloodstream and how quickly it is manufactured by your liver.

An extreme example of genetic influence is an inherited disorder called familial hypercholesterolemia, which causes cholesterol levels to skyrocket—often upwards of 500. These kinds of elevated levels predispose people to atherosclerosis at a very young age, and unless diagnosed and treated early, individuals with familial hypercholesterolemia may suffer heart attacks as early as adolescence. More commonly, however, an inherited tendency toward high cholesterol is not nearly as dramatic and produces only mild to moderate elevations.

- *Diet:* Dietary factors significantly affect blood cholesterol levels, but unlike hereditary influences, diet can be easily controlled. The most important element of the diet that boosts cholesterol levels is saturated fat; secondarily, dietary cholesterol also slightly raises blood cholesterol. (When eaten in excess, cholesterol can contribute significantly to elevated blood cholesterol.)

Fats are classified into three categories based on their chemical structure: saturated, monounsaturated, and polyunsaturated. Saturated fats are used by the liver to manufacture cholesterol, and diets rich in saturated fat cause cholesterol levels to climb. Experts now recommend that less than 10 percent of your total caloric intake should come from saturated fats.

Although dietary cholesterol has a relatively minor effect on blood cholesterol levels, still, if you eat an excess of high-cholesterol food, it can elevate your heart disease risk. The National Cholesterol Education Program recommends that dietary intake of cholesterol be kept below 300 milligrams per day.

But lowering your risk of heart disease is not just a matter of avoidance—a diet rich in some nutrients can actually have a beneficial impact on cholesterol levels. The soluble fiber found in oats and many fruits and vegetables, for example, has been shown to help lower blood cholesterol when consumed in adequate amounts. Although the way in which it does this is still unclear, foods rich in fiber are an important part of any heart-healthy diet.

- *Age:* As you age, your cholesterol level will tend to rise gradually. Consequently, many physicians tend to ignore mildly elevated cholesterol levels in the elderly. However, the NCEP argues against this lackadaisical attitude and recommends a uniform approach to high cholesterol, regardless of age.
- *Sex:* Your gender also influences your cholesterol levels. Men tend to have higher LDL and lower HDL levels than premenopausal women. Following menopause, women's estrogen levels fall, and, as a consequence, their cholesterol profiles become more like their male counterparts. Estrogen replacement therapy helps prevent these female blood cholesterol shifts from occurring by influencing the body's cholesterol production. But this hormone therapy is no panacea—progestins, often taken along with the estrogens, act to reverse some or all of estrogen's beneficial effects.
- *Weight:* Overweight people tend to have high total cholesterol levels and low levels of protective HDL cholesterol; studies show that as weight rises, HDL levels decline and LDL levels creep gradually upward. The good news is that the changes are not irreversible, and losing weight can reduce blood cholesterol.
- *Smoking:* Although most people know that smoking is associated with heart disease, relatively few understand the correlation between smoking and cholesterol. Smoking forces levels of protective HDL cholesterol down while producing many other harmful cardiovascular effects. This harmful combination makes smoking a dangerous habit. (For more information on smoking, see chapter 6, Smoking, Alcohol, and Substance Abuse.)
- *Exercise:* Regular exercise raises HDL levels. While strenuous exercise may be most influential, even light aerobic exercise appears to help somewhat, if done regularly: 45 minutes of brisk walking—or an equivalent activity—three times a week appears to be adequate.
- *Alcohol:* There is some evidence that alcohol can raise HDL cholesterol levels and perhaps protect against coronary heart disease. Large amounts of alcohol are not necessary to achieve these beneficial effects. While few doctors are willing to recommend drinking as a way of raising your HDL levels since the alcohol's potential risks may outweigh potential cardiovascular benefits, studies suggest that a drink or two a day may be beneficial for some people.

THE STEP 1 DIET

CHOOSE	DECREASE OR AVOID
Fish, Meat, and Poultry	
Fish, poultry without skin	Fatty cuts of beef, lamb, pork, spare ribs, organ meats.
Lean cuts of beef, lamb, pork, or veal	Regular cold cuts, sausage, hot dogs
Shellfish	Bacon, sardines, roe
Milk and Dairy Products	
Skim or 1% fat milk (liquid, powdered, evaporated)	Whole milk (4% fat): regular, evaporated, or condensed; cream, half and half, 2% milk, imitation milk products, non-dairy creamers, whipped toppings
Buttermilk	
Nonfat (0%) or low-fat yogurt	
Low-fat cottage cheese (1% or 2% fat)	Whole-milk yogurt
Low-fat cheeses, farmer, or pot cheeses (all should be labeled no more than 2–6 grams fat per oz.)	Whole-milk cottage cheese (4% fat)
	All natural cheese (e.g., blue, cheddar, Swiss, etc.), cream cheese, sour cream, including low-fat or "lite" products
Sherbert, sorbet	
Egg whites (2 egg whites equal 1 whole egg in recipes)	Ice cream
Cholesterol-free egg substitutes	Egg yolks
Fruits and Vegetables	
Fresh, frozen, canned, or dried fruits and vegetables	Vegetables prepared in butter, cream, or other sauces
Breads and Cereals	
Homemade baked goods using unsaturated oils sparingly	Commercial baked goods: pies, cakes, doughnuts, croissants, pastries, muffins, biscuits
Angel food cake	High-fat crackers
Low-fat crackers and cookies	Egg noodles
Rice, pasta	Breads in which eggs are major ingredient
Whole-grain breads and cereals	
Fats and Oils	
Baking cocoa	Chocolate
Unsaturated vegetable oils: corn, olive, rapeseed (canola oil), safflower, sesame, soybean, sunflower	Butter, coconut oil, palm oil, palm kernel oil, lard, bacon fat
Margarine or shortenings made from one of the above unsaturated oils; diet margarine	
Reduced-calorie mayonnaise, salad dressings made with unsaturated oils, low-fat dressing	Dressings made with egg yolk
Seeds and nuts	Coconut

Adapted from the National Cholesterol Education Program.

FOODS HIGH IN ANTIOXIDANTS			
VITAMIN C	SELENIUM	BETA-CAROTENE	VITAMIN E
Oranges	Nuts	Carrots	Brazil nuts
Red peppers	Wheat germ	Sweet potatoes	Seafoods
Green peppers	Corn oil	Squash	Organ meats
Potatoes	Safflower oil	Pumpkin	Meat
Broccoli	Soybean oil	Apricots	Wheat germ
Cantaloupe	Seeds	Peaches	Papaya
Strawberries			

CHOLESTEROL-LOWERING STRATEGIES

The National Cholesterol Education Program guidelines urge that anyone with a total cholesterol over 200 consider a cholesterol-lowering diet; the higher the blood cholesterol, the more important it is to take corrective action.

There is no single cholesterol-lowering diet; instead, there are many possible variations and food choices that can produce the desired results. The following principles should be part of any cholesterol-lowering plan.

• Reduce your intake of fats, particularly saturated fats. The NCEP guidelines recommend that fat intake should constitute no more than 30 percent of the total calories, and saturated fats should constitute no more than 8 to 10 percent of total caloric intake.

• Limit cholesterol intake. Current guidelines suggest that cholesterol intake be limited to no more than 300 milligrams per day.

• Control your total caloric intake to maintain your ideal weight.

• Consume a diet rich in fruits and vegetables containing the antioxidant nutrients beta-carotene, vitamins C and E, and the element selenium. (These foods include carrots, citrus fruits, and broccoli. See table 5.6 for other examples.) Some experts believe that arterial blockage develops in a complicated process involving oxidation of cholesterol. It is possible that increased levels of antioxidants may slow or prevent this process and keep arterial walls from collecting plaque.

NUTRITION AND CANCER

The relationship between diet and cancer is currently under extensive investigation. While certain dietary factors—especially a diet high in fat—increase cancer risk, others, most notably many fruits and vegetables, appear to lower the risk of cancer.

CANCER-PROMOTING NUTRIENTS

ALCOHOL

Heavy alcohol consumption clearly leads to an increase in certain cancers. The National Cancer Institute estimates that alcohol is associated with about 3 percent of all cancers in this country, increasing the risk of cancers of the mouth, throat, larynx, esophagus, pancreas, and liver. Even relatively small amounts of alcohol may be dangerous to women and appear to be associated with an elevated risk of breast cancer.

FOOD ADDITIVES AND CONTAMINANTS

Thousands of agents are continually being added to the food supply. Crops are sprayed routinely with pesticides to kill insects, preservatives added in processing prevent spoilage, dyes enhance food's appearance, and animals are exposed to drugs and pesticides that end up in our burgers and other meats. In addition, some additives migrate from food packaging into the food within.

Although the Food and Drug Administration would like to test the cancer-causing potential of all food additives and contaminants, it is a nearly impossible task. Some chemicals have been banned or restricted to certain uses in food because of tests showing them to be probable carcinogens: certain red dyes, DDT, and cyclamates, for example. In the case of saccharin, an artificial sweetener shown to cause cancer in laboratory animals, the FDA has allowed its use, but requires all saccharin-containing foods to carry warning labels.

TIPS ON CUTTING FAT CONSUMPTION

SHOPPING

- Read labels when you shop. Avoid most food products containing more than 30 percent of their calories from fat (see "Label Reading").
- Choose oils low in saturated fats. Avoid saturated oils such as coconut, palm, and palm kernel oils. Safflower, soybean, cottonseed, sunflower, and canola are healthier alternatives. Avoid oils and fats that have been hydrogenated.
- Buy lean grades of meat.
- Avoid whole milk, using skim or low-fat (1 percent) milk instead.

COOKING

- Substitute fish and poultry for red meat in main dishes. Ground turkey is an excellent replacement for ground beef in hamburgers and chili.
- Wherever possible replace ingredients high in fat with low-fat alternatives. For example, substitute low-fat yogurt or cottage cheese for sour cream in recipes.
- Reduce the amount of fatty ingredients in recipes. You can usually cut the amount of oil you add by one-third to one-half without upsetting the taste of the meal.
- Use low-fat cooking methods. Broil, bake, or roast meat, fish, or poultry instead of pan frying or deep frying.
- Use a nonstick pan and a vegetable-oil pan coating instead of butter, margarine, or oil when sautéing foods.
- Trim excess fat from meats and remove the skin from chicken and other poultry, preferably before it's cooked.
- Prepare soups or stews a day or two in advance, refrigerate them, and skim off excess fat before reheating and serving.

- Use a low-fat spread rather than butter on your toast or bagel in the morning. Jams and jellies are fat-free alternatives.
- Substitute low-fat and part-skim milk cheeses for regular varieties.
- Avoid cream-based recipes and foods, opting for low-fat alternatives. Clear soups like consommés should be chosen over cream-style ones, and tomato-based pasta sauces are better choices than cream sauces.
- Use low-fat milk in coffee or tea. Avoid nondairy creamers, which are high in saturated fats, as are cream, half-and-half, and whole milk.
- Substitute fruits and vegetables for high-fat snacks like potato chips and nuts. Eat air-popped popcorn without butter.
- Choose nonfat or low-fat dressings or make your own low-fat dressing. Avoid dressings made with cheese like blue cheese and Roquefort.
- While breads are generally low in saturated fat, avoid high-fat croissants and sweet rolls. If made with butter or oils high in saturated fats, even bran muffins can be loaded with fat. Have toast and jam instead of a donut.

TIPS FOR DINING OUT

- Ask for all sauces and dressings served on the side and then apply sparingly.
- Ask for dishes steamed rather than cooked in butter, or roasted instead of fried.
- Request vegetarian dishes even if not listed on the menu.
- Choose a green salad as an appetizer, but go easy on the dressing.
- Substitute low-fat sherbet, ice milk, nonfat frozen yogurt, or tofu desserts for ice cream.
- Choose nonfat cakes and cookies instead of the traditional varieties.

In contrast, Red Dye No. 2 was totally banned in the United States when laboratory tests indicated that it was carcinogenic.

ARTIFICIAL SWEETENERS

A number of artificial sweeteners have been implicated as possible cancer-causing substances and one, cyclamate, has actually been banned by the FDA. Many argue

for cyclamate's safety and this chemical is still widely used in many other countries. As for saccharin, some animal research has implicated it as a possible cause of cancer, but this effect has not been well documented in humans. Thus far, the FDA's repeated attempts to ban saccharin have been blocked by Congress pending the results of further investigations. Aspartame (brand name NutraSweet), one of the newest of the artificial sweeteners, has not been linked to cancer in laboratory tests.

CHOLESTEROL/FAT CONTENT OF FOODS

FOOD	CHOLESTEROL (MG)	SATURATED	FATS (GM) MONOUNSATURATED	FATS (GM) POLYUNSATURATED
1 oz. lean beef	26	0.9	0.8	0.1
1 oz. fatty beef	27	2.2	2.0	0.2
1 oz. veal	28	0.9	0.8	0.1
1 oz. chicken (dark meat)	26	0.8	1.0	0.6
1 oz. chicken/turkey (white meat)	22	0.3	0.3	0.2
1 oz. pork	28	0.9	0.8	0.1
1 oz. beef liver	83	0.1	0	0
1 oz. lean fish	28	0	0.1	0.1
1 oz. fatty fish	25	0.9	1.1	1.1
1 oz. water-packed tuna	11	0	0	0
1 oz. lean lamb	17	0.1	0.2	0.2
1 egg	274	1.7	2.2	0.7
1 tsp. margarine (1.6/1.9 poly./sat.)	0	1.4	3.3	2.4
1 tsp. corn oil	0	0.6	1.1	2.6
1 tsp. safflower oil	0	0.4	0.6	3.3
1 tsp. vegetable oil	0	0.7	1.0	2.6
1 tsp. avocado	0	0.8	2.1	1.3
1 tsp. butter	12	1.9	1.4	0.2
2 oz. 5% fat cheese	20	1.6	1.0	0.1
2 oz. cheddar	56	12.0	6.0	0.5
1 cup whole milk	34	4.8	2.4	0.1
1 cup 2% milk	22	2.4	2.0	0.1
1 cup skim milk	4	0.3	0.1	0
1 cup 1% yogurt	14	2.3	1.0	0.1
1 cup ice cream	56	16.8	9.6	0.3

Adapted from *Health and Nutrition Newsletter*, introductory issue, with permission of Columbia University School of Public Health.

FAT

A number of studies have associated a high-fat diet with an increased risk of certain cancers, especially cancer of the colon, prostate, ovary, and breast. Some of the evidence for the carcinogenicity of fat comes from studies of the Japanese, whose traditionally low-fat diet seems to hold down the incidence of many cancers (stomach cancer is the chief exception). Studies seem to show that when Japanese switch to a Western-style, high-fat diet, their cancer rate increases significantly.

The mechanism for fat's cancer-causing effect is not well understood. A leading theory contends that a diet high in fat alters levels of sex hormones that boost the risk of hormonally sensitive tumors.

CALORIES

Excess calories from any source—not just fat—are correlated with an increased risk of cancer. In the lab, researchers have shown that mice eating calorie-restricted diets experience lower cancer rates than those allowed to feed at will. Studies in human populations support these findings and reveal that people at normal or slightly below normal weight are less likely to develop cancer than the obese.

NITRATES AND NITRITES

While many experts believe that consuming nitrites and nitrates can cause cancer, the association is not firmly established. Nitrites and nitrates—often found in drinking water and used to preserve luncheon meats—are in and of themselves relatively benign compounds. But under a variety of conditions they can be converted into N-nitroso compounds, highly carcinogenic substances. Although some studies in animals have demonstrated a causal relationship between dietary intake of nitrates and nitrites and cancer, human studies have been inconclusive.

CANCER-PROTECTIVE NUTRIENTS

FIBER

A diet high in fiber reduces the transit time of food passing through the colon by absorbing large amounts of water, and making stools soft and bulky. In this way, the colon's exposure to potential carcinogens (found in the stool) may be reduced.

While no one has conclusively shown this cancer-protective mechanism really works in this way, population studies demonstrate that diets high in a variety of fibers appear to confer some degree of protection against colon cancer.

VITAMINS

Foods rich in carotenoids—the pigments that make carrots orange and pink grapefruit pink—are thought to protect the body against certain forms of cancer. Studies have found that smokers who consume a diet rich in carotenoids have a lower incidence of lung cancer than smokers consuming low-carotenoid diets. In addition, other research indicates that a diet high in carotenoids may reduce a woman's risk of developing breast cancer.

While beta-carotene, a chemical that can be converted to vitamin A in the body, often receives a great deal of attention, the other carotenoids may also be involved in preventing cancer. Many of the over 500 different carotenoids found in fruits and vegetables function as antioxidants—substances that prevent the possible carcinogenic effects of oxidation—and little research has been done to explore their health benefits.

Vitamins C and E are also antioxidants that appear to protect against some types of cancer. Besides functioning as a potent antioxidant protecting cells against oxidative damage leading to cancer, vitamin C prevents the formation of N-nitroso compounds, the cancer-causing substances formed from nitrates and nitrites found in preserved meats and some drinking water.

MINERALS

As a natural antioxidant, selenium may offer some degree of protection against cancer. Several studies show cancer mortality to be higher in individuals with low levels of selenium in their blood. Preliminary evidence suggests that calcium may also be protective against some forms of cancer, such as colon cancer.

NUTRITION AND HIGH BLOOD PRESSURE

Although the role of nutrition in hypertension is still somewhat unclear, two things are certain: Obesity tends to raise blood pressure, and in some people, high-sodium diets raise blood pressure.

Numerous studies link excessive weight to high blood pressure. But losing excess weight can reverse this problem and can eliminate the need for blood pressure-lowering medications.

Similarly, cutting back on salt may help your blood pressure; excessive amounts of sodium may cause your body to retain extra fluid in order to maintain the concentration of salt in the blood at a steady level. The extra fluid volume requires the heart to work harder and causes blood pressure to rise. Normally the body can excrete excessive sodium in the urine relatively quickly, but for reasons that are not completely clear, people with an inherited tendency for high blood pressure tend to retain this element.

AMERICAN CANCER SOCIETY DIETARY RECOMMENDATIONS

The traditional dietary principles of variety, balance, and moderation are also the basis of a prudent anticancer diet. The American Cancer Society has established the following general dietary guidelines for minimizing risk of cancer related to diet.

- Maintain desirable weight.
- Eat a varied diet.
- Eat a variety of vegetables and fruits daily.
- Eat more high-fiber foods such as whole-grain cereals, breads and pasta, and fruits and vegetables.
- Cut down on total fat intake.
- Limit consumption of alcohol, if you drink at all.
- Limit consumption of salt-cured, smoked, and nitrite-cured foods.

Sometimes a salt-restricted diet is all that is needed to correct this type of volume-dependent hypertension. Unfortunately, the typical American diet provides far more sodium than the body actually needs, and whereas some foods are naturally high in salt, the most common source of salt in our diet is ordinary table salt (sodium chloride). Cutting down on the amount of salt you add to your food, both at the table and in cooking, is the best way to begin limiting salt consumption.

Other nutrients that seem to exert an influence on blood pressure include potassium and calcium. The National Research Council actually recommends including additional amounts of potassium-rich foods in the diet because of potassium's possible protective effect against hypertension. The role of calcium is less clear and continues to be investigated.

NUTRITION AND DIABETES

Diabetes is really two diseases—Type 1 diabetes (insulin-dependent diabetes mellitus [IDDM] or juvenile-onset diabetes) and Type 2 diabetes (noninsulin-dependent diabetes mellitus [NIDDM] or adult-onset diabetes). Type 1 diabetics are unable to manufacture insulin, the hormone that helps regulate the blood sugar level, and are dependent on regular insulin injections. Type 2 diabetics are able to produce insulin but are unable to use it effectively.

Diet is the cornerstone of treating both types of diabetes. People with Type 1 diabetes must pay close attention to their diet, carefully coordinating food intake with insulin injections. Large amounts of sugar in the absence of insulin can send their blood glucose soaring, whereas insulin without sugar can cause glucose levels to fall dangerously low. On the other hand, Type 2 diabetics can often achieve good control of their blood sugar levels solely by restricting their caloric intake and losing weight (although in more severe cases medications are required).

NUTRITION AND OSTEOPOROSIS

Bones need calcium to stay healthy and maintain their strength and hardness. When calcium enters the body, it is absorbed into the bloodstream, and a certain amount of calcium remains in the blood for metabolic use while excess is deposited and stored in the bones (some may also be excreted in urine). When calcium intakes are deficient, calcium is leached from the bone to maintain adequate blood levels. If calcium intake remains insufficient over a long time, bones eventually grow porous and weak, or osteoporotic.

Good nutrition is critical in the prevention and treatment of osteoporosis. Far too many people, particularly women, consume inadequate amounts of calcium to optimally build and maintain bones, thus compromising their bone strength and integrity. Studies show that in many cases an effective preventive measure is simply consuming more calcium. Calcium supplementation, especially in people whose calcium intake is extremely low, has been shown to be effective in reducing bone fragility and preventing fractures. Eating adequate amounts of calcium is especially important during adolescence, a time bones are growing and calcium stores can be built up. (For more information on osteoporosis, see chapter 24.)

NUTRITION AND OTHER DISORDERS

Medical researchers are rapidly discovering that nutrition plays a role in a variety of other diseases. Many intestinal disorders such as gallbladder disease, diverticulosis, and liver disease have important dietary components. Recent attention has focused on a number of new areas including the role of vitamin C in the prevention of cataracts and the use of B vitamins in the reduction of cardiovascular disease.

WEIGHT CONTROL

OBESITY AND WEIGHT LOSS

Obesity is a national epidemic: more than 11 million American adults are 20 percent or more above their ideal weight. The number of obese Americans is expanding as many children and adolescents join the ranks of the obese. Much of the blame for this U.S. weight problem is linked to overindulgence in fatty junk foods and lack of exercise as sedentary hours are spent watching TV.

The long-term public health implications of the growing trend toward obesity are alarming. Obesity is linked to an increased death rate from many diseases including coronary heart disease, high blood pressure, stroke, diabetes, gallbladder disease, and cancers of the breast, prostate, and endometrium.

However, obesity resists treatment and presents a complex and frustrating problem for overweight individuals and the health professionals treating them. Obesity is due to more than simply overeating; genetics, cultural background, physical characteristics, psychological issues, and social and economic status are but a few of the factors giving rise to this condition. Nevertheless, in order to lose weight you must consume fewer dietary calories than your body expends.

Despite their overwhelming lack of success, Americans have made dieting to lose weight a popular American pastime. It's estimated that in any given year, 70 million Americans either plan or go on some sort of weight-loss diet. Frequently, dieters attempt a crash regimen that promises to melt off unwanted pounds. Radical diets, however, although sometimes successful in the short run, have serious disadvantages.

- Crash diets are difficult to maintain. And as soon as you go off the diet, you gain your weight back.
- Crash diets are nutritionally imbalanced and can even be dangerous. Diets that emphasize one category of foods to the exclusion of others can cause serious metabolic imbalances.
- Extreme diets do not change bad eating habits but instead temporarily substitute one unsound dietary pattern for another.

The task for a dieter is not simply losing weight; it is to develop practical, long-term eating habits that will keep your weight down for years, not just days, weeks, or months.

Very-low-calorie diets are especially dangerous and ineffective because they cause the body to become more efficient at energy conservation—it takes less food to keep your weight up because your resting metabolic rate (the calories you burn during normal activity) drops. As a result, many dieters find that periods of severe caloric restriction make it harder to keep weight off. For instance, after a crash diet, people who had previously maintained their weight on 2,000 calories a day may now find they gain weight while consuming merely 1,800 calories a day.

The solution to these problems is twofold.

- Choose a sensible weight-loss program that helps you develop good eating habits that do not make you feel deprived.

TABLE 5.6: DESIRABLE WEIGHT FOR HEIGHT

°Height (in shoes)	Small	FRAME Medium	Large
Men			
5'2"	112–120	118–129	126–141
5'3"	115–123	121–133	129–144
5'4"	118–126	124–136	132–148
5'5"	121–129	127–139	135–152
5'6"	124–133	130–143	138–156
5'7"	128–137	134–147	138–156
5'8"	132–141	138–152	147–166
5'9"	136–145	142–156	151–170
5'10"	140–150	146–160	155–174
5'11"	144–154	150–165	159–179
6'	148–158	154–170	164–184
6'1"	152–162	158–175	168–189
6'2"	156–167	162–180	173–194
6'3"	160–171	167–185	178–199
6'4"	164–175	172–190	182–204
Women			
4'10"	92–98	96–101	104–119
4'11"	94–101	98–110	106–122
5'	96–104	101–113	109–125
5'1"	99–107	104–116	112–128
5'2"	102–110	107–119	115–131
5'3"	105–113	110–122	118–134
5'4"	108–116	113–126	121–138
5'5"	111–119	116–130	125–142
5'6"	114–123	120–135	129–146
5'7"	118–127	124–139	133–150
5'8"	122–131	128–143	137–154
5'9"	126–135	132–147	141–158
5'10"	130–140	136–151	145–163
5'11"	134–144	140–155	149–168
6"	138–148	144–159	153–173

Here's another simple but rather crude way of calculating your ideal body weight.

Females: 100 pounds for first 5 feet and 5 pounds for every inch over 5 feet. (Subtract 4 pounds for each inch under 5 feet.)

Males: 106 pounds for first 5 feet of height plus 6 pounds for every inch over 5 feet. (Subtract 4 pounds for each inch under 5 feet.)

- Use exercise to help burn calories and develop muscle that will raise your resting metabolic rate (even at rest, muscle burns more calories per minute than does body fat).

CALCULATING CALORIC NEEDS

A calorie is a unit of energy—the amount of energy needed to raise the temperature of one kilogram of water one degree Centigrade. Many factors—age, sex, metabolic rate, and physical activity to name a few—influence how many calories your body needs daily. Individuals who eat a balanced diet and maintain a normal weight probably have no need to calculate their caloric intake. But for people interested in losing or gaining weight, determining caloric needs and intake can be used in planning an eating program.

To determine the calories you need in the course of a typical day, first determine your basal metabolic rate (BMR), the number of calories needed to support your body's vital functions such as circulation, respiration, digestion, and temperature maintenance. While it's difficult to account for all of the variables that influence BMR, some relatively simple formulas have been derived that can provide you with a close estimate (see box). Your total daily caloric requirement is merely the sum of the calories you burn maintaining BMR plus the calories you expend in various physical activities.

GUIDELINES FOR SENSIBLE WEIGHT LOSS

No single weight-loss program works for everyone; instead there are several ways to intelligently lose weight.
    Sensible weight-loss programs should:

- Contain a variety of foods and allow for individual food preferences. (Many people are surprised to find that a diet doesn't necessarily mean giving up their favorite foods.)
- Moderately restrict calories—a gradual weight loss of 1 or 2 pounds a week should be the goal.

In developing a weight-loss program you can accommodate, first evaluate the diet you already eat by maintaining a careful food diary for a week or two. Record everything you eat including the amount you ate, the time of day, and the surrounding circumstances. If possible, carry your food diary with you all day, jotting down all food items immediately; do not wait until the end of the day or you will forget much of what you consumed. Your food diary will show not only what you ate and when you ate it but also will identify problem areas and behaviors that may require modification.
    Using the basic principles of good nutrition (see the "Food Guide Pyramid," earlier in this chapter), you can

CALCULATING BASAL METABOLIC RATE (BMR)

This simple formula for calculating basal metabolic rate has been developed by the Food and Nutrition Board, National Academy of Sciences.
    Women: Multiply your weight in pounds by 11 and then subtract 2 percent of the total for every decade you are over 20 years of age.
    Men: Multiply your weight in pounds by 12 and then subtract 2 percent of the total for every decade over 20.

EXAMPLE:

A 40-year-old woman who weighs 135 pounds multiplies 135 3 11 = 1,485, then subtracts 4% of the total: 1,485 2 60 (4% of 1,485) = 1,425 BMR

EXAMPLE:

A 30-year-old man who weighs 165 pounds multiplies 165 3 12 = 1,980 and then subtracts 2% of the total: 1,980 2 40 (2% of 1,980) = 1,940 BMR

APPROXIMATE ENERGY EXPENDITURES DURING 30 MINUTES OF EXERCISE*

Aerobic dancing	210 cal
Basketball	300 cal
Carpentry	120 cal
Cleaning	130 cal
Cycling	190 cal
Gardening	160 cal
Golf	180 cal
Running	360 cal
Swimming	300 cal
Walking	180 cal

*Note: Values vary based on body weight and the vigor with which activities are performed.

then develop your own weight-loss program. In this chapter are sample menus to help illustrate what a well-balanced, calorie-restricted diet should look like (see box Daily Meal Plans at end of chapter). If you prefer to seek guidance from a professional, contact a qualified physician, a dietitian, or a reliable support group, such as Weight Watchers.

EXERCISE FOR WEIGHT LOSS

Regular exercise is a key part of any weight-loss program.

While calorie restriction slows metabolism, exercise raises calorie burning, helping the body consume calories that would otherwise be used to store fat.

Exercise does not have to be overly strenuous to help you lose and keep off weight. Even a moderate amount is useful. For example, a half hour of brisk walking burns about 180 calories. While this may not seem like much, over the course of a year, a daily walk can be the caloric equivalent of more than 18 pounds of body fat.

Besides helping use up calories, additional benefits to regular exercise are suppressing appetite, improving mood and self-esteem, and strengthening the resolve to keep to a calorie-restricted diet.

DIET AIDS

Diet pills and appetite suppressants often contain amphetamines or amphetamine-like substances that act on the central nervous system to suppress appetite. While these medications may be appropriate in some medical situations, they can cause serious problems for the casual user, including possible abuse or addiction. For the vast majority of people, a sensible, gradual weight-loss program that emphasizes permanent changes in eating and exercise habits is the most appropriate approach to losing weight.

THE USE OF VITAMIN SUPPLEMENTS

THE RDAS (RECOMMENDED DIETARY ALLOWANCES)

To help ensure that we consume adequate amounts of all the essential nutrients, a government-sponsored group called the Food and Nutrition Board of the National Research Council periodically establishes Recommended Dietary Allowances, or RDAs, of certain nutrients to be used as "standards to serve as a goal for good nutrition."

The RDAs are generally intended to reflect safe and adequate levels of vitamin and mineral intake, sufficient nutrients to prevent signs of deficiency, and to maintain a "normal" nutrient level in the blood. These numbers are estimates of the body's need for a particular nutrient plus an extra safety margin meant to account for variability between individuals.

Despite the scientific deliberation that goes into devising the RDAs, many experts believe them inadequate. According to the critics, the RDAs are meant for people in good health, and do not sufficiently acknowledge the special nutritional needs of the ill; certain illnesses and numerous medications can affect the way your body absorbs and utilizes various nutrients and can increase

your body's nutritional requirements.

Similarly, the RDAs cannot fully account for the impact that an individual's lifestyle can have on nutritional needs. For instance, the deleterious effect of tobacco means that smokers have a wide variety of extra nutritional needs as compared with nonsmokers. The demands of exercise and other activities as well as heavy drinking or stress may also raise your nutritional needs.

Most important, by the National Research Council's own admission, the RDAs are not necessarily the levels of nutrient intake that optimize health. Over the past several years the scientific literature has been replete with evidence suggesting that vitamins and minerals, in doses higher than the RDAs, play an important role in the prevention of chronic disease.

MEETING YOUR NUTRITIONAL NEEDS

The American public's growing enthusiasm for nutrient supplements has transformed the vitamin pill business into a multibillion-dollar industry. Whereas millions of Americans have popped nutrient supplements for years, only recently has convincing scientific evidence supported their alleged benefits.

Critics opposed to vitamin supplementation point out that the Recommended Dietary Allowances are best met not with supplements but with a well-balanced diet. While in theory carefully planned meals can provide healthy doses of most of the vitamins, in reality, today's highly stressed and rushed environment leave few of us the time to consume the foods we should.

A recent nationwide food-consumption survey found that large numbers of men and women fail to take in even two-thirds of the RDAs for many nutrients. As a matter of fact, only 22 percent of the people surveyed consumed more than two-thirds of the RDAs for all 15 nutrients while more than 70 percent of all men and 80 percent of women reported diets deficient in at least one nutrient.

Of course, the mere consumption of a daily multivitamin supplement does not fully compensate for eating poorly. Supplements cannot substitute for good nutrition but can bolster weak areas of a fairly adequate regimen. So while you should strive to eat as the Food Guide Pyramid instructs, vitamin supplements can be used as a safe and effective means to meet the nutritional goals established by the RDAs.

BEYOND THE RDAS

While satisfying the RDAs is a good beginning to rounding out your nutritional needs, the RDAs are not necessarily optimal levels of nutrient intake. Studies now indicate that increased consumption of selected nutrients (the antioxidant nutrients in particular) may pro-

EASY WAYS TO CUT CALORIES

The best way to cut calories is to reduce your intake of fats, which by weight contain more than twice as many calories as proteins and carbohydrates. (Also see the box Tips on Cutting Fat Consumption.)

SHOPPING

- Always shop with a grocery list and buy only items on the list. Impulse purchases at the supermarket are often fatty junk foods.
- Do not take young children food shopping. They will insist on purchases of candy and other fattening foods.
- Seek out light substitutes for your usual foods. Often these food products are lower in calories.

COOKING

- In most recipes you can reduce the amount of sugar you add by one-third to one-half without significantly changing the flavor or texture.
- Substitute poultry, fish, or vegetarian foods for meat. Do not substitute cheese for meat—cheese is very high in fat, sodium, and calories.
- Cook more pasta and vegetarian dishes instead of meats, cheeses, and other high-fat, high-calorie dishes.
- Do not cook just bland, boring foods, or the taste deprivation may force you off your diet.

LIFESTYLE HABITS

- Do not fast or allow yourself to become too hungry. Skipping meals is likely to result in gorging later on. Eating regular meals and low-calorie snacks throughout the day often adds up to fewer calories than one huge meal consumed when you are famished.
- Eat meals slowly; it takes time to feel full. Wait at least 10 minutes or so before you go back for seconds.

LIQUIDS

- Drink no-cal seltzer or ice water with a slice of lemon instead of sugary soft drinks.
- Avoid hard alcohol, which is very high in calories and has other negative health effects. If you drink beer, choose a light variety.
- Instead of full-strength wine, drink a spritzer using a 50-50 mixture of wine and seltzer.

DINING OUT

- Restaurant portions tend to be overly generous. Request half a portion or save half to take home for the next day.

DESSERT

- Eat fruit for dessert; the natural sugar in fruit can often satisfy your sweet craving at the end of a meal. While fresh fruits are ideal, frozen fruit is often acceptable.
- When eating canned fruit, choose one that is packed in its own juices rather than syrup.

Total Daily Caloric Intake	Suggested Intake of Total Fat (g)	Suggested Intake of Saturated Fat (g)
1,200	40	13
1,500	50	16
1,800	60	20
2,000	67	22
2,500	83	28
3,000	100	33

duce additional health benefits by lowering the risk of several chronic diseases. The possible benefits of supplementation include:

- The antioxidant nutrients vitamins C, E, beta-carotene, and selenium may inhibit damaging oxidative processes. Numerous studies have linked higher intakes of these compounds with a decreased risk of various cancers.
- Vitamins C and E appear to protect the lens of the

eye against oxidative damage and slow the development of cataracts but only when taken in sufficiently high doses several times higher than the RDAs.

- Vitamin E and beta-carotene have successfully reduced mortality from cardiovascular disease in several study populations.
- Folic acid supplementation during pregnancy and the periconceptual period greatly reduces the risk of congenital deformities called neural tube defects (spina bifida and anencephaly). Despite studies suggesting that

at least 0.4 mg are needed both before and during pregnancy to obtain maximum protection, the RDAs for folic acid recommend only 0.18 mg for women of childbearing age except during pregnancy, when the higher level of 0.4 mg is advised. The Centers for Disease Control and Prevention and the American Academy of Pediatrics have adopted folic acid recommendations above the RDAs and suggest that all women of childbearing age take a daily multivitamin supplement containing 0.4 mg of folic acid.

• Calcium: Many researchers argue that the RDA of 800 mg of calcium for women over the age of 24 is inadequate and suggest that higher calcium intake could provide substantial protection against osteoporosis. Whereas many studies have produced conflicting results, the Consensus Conference on Osteoporosis, an expert panel of doctors and scientists, recommends higher calcium intake to confer vital protection against osteoporosis, particularly during the postmenopausal period.

• B vitamins: Mild deficiencies of vitamins B_6, B_{12}, and folate can lead to elevated levels of a homocysteine in the blood, a substance that may increase your risk of cardiovascular disease. Some experts believe that higher intakes of these vitamins, folic acid in particular, can help normalize homocysteine levels and reduce heart disease risk.

....

OTHER DIETARY ELEMENTS

CAFFEINE

Caffeine is probably the most commonly ingested drug in the United States. This regular component of the diet provides stimulation for many workers—a cup of coffee is used to make morning tasks bearable and a caffeinated soda may be used as a pick-me-up later in the day. But, like any drug, when taken in excess caffeine can cause a range of unpleasant side effects such as irritability, nervousness, anxiety, tremors, and sleeplessness. Although caffeine has become an integral of our lives, this drug affects the functioning of numerous systems throughout the body and acts on the central nervous system to increase alertness, enhance sensory perceptions, overcome fatigue, and improve endurance and motor function.

In recent years, a number of investigations have been conducted studying the health effects of caffeine. While most have turned up no significant evidence of serious ill effects, many physicians advise cutting back on excessive caffeine consumption. Specific areas that have been looked at include:

HEART DISEASE

While studies in both animals and humans concerning caffeine's relationship to heart disease appear to contradict one another, experts believe that caffeine, particularly at very high intakes, may place you at increased risk of suffering a heart attack. Some studies indicate that it may do so by exacerbating cardiac risk factors such as raised blood cholesterol levels.

PEPTIC ULCER DISEASE

Caffeine increases the production of stomach acid and can exacerbate peptic ulcer disease.

BIRTH DEFECTS AND PREGNANCY LOSS

Some studies have found that caffeine can cause birth defects when fed to pregnant laboratory animals in large amounts. To date, similar findings have not been reported in humans and in fact some studies have shown that small amounts of caffeine (1 to 2 cups of coffee or 2 to 3 cups of tea per day) during pregnancy appear to be quite safe. Nonetheless, most physicians recommend that caffeine intake be avoided or at least restricted in pregnant women. Despite a lack of conclusive scientific data, caffeine consumption during pregnancy has also been implicated in causing low birth weight, increasing the risk of spontaneous abortion, and increasing the chances of premature delivery.

ANXIETY

In some people particularly sensitive to caffeine, this drug can cause extreme nervousness, insomnia, tremor, and even panic attacks. Eliminating caffeine from the diet usually resolves the problem.

FIBROCYSTIC BREAST DISEASE

Medical studies on the relationship between fibrocystic breast disease and caffeine are conflicting, but many women suffering from fibrocystic breast disease find that eliminating caffeine from their diet relieves symptoms. If you suffer from fibrocystic disease, try a three- to four-month trial of caffeine restriction—you may find it produces dramatic results.

ANXIETY, TREMOR, AND OTHER SIDE EFFECTS

People particularly sensitive to caffeine can develop a variety of symptoms related to its use including panic attacks, extreme nervousness, insomnia, and tremors. Eliminating caffeine from the diet generally resolves these symptoms.

CUTTING BACK ON CAFFEINE

Those who consume very large amounts of caffeine

SOURCES OF CAFFEINE

Source (Amount)	Caffeine (mg)
Coffee (5-oz. cup)	
Drip	146
Percolated	110
Regular instant	53
Decaffeinated instant	2
Tea (5-oz. cup)	
1-minute brew	9–33
3-minute brew	20–46
5-minute brew	20–50
Instant	12–28
Canned iced tea (12 oz.)	22–36
Cocoa and chocolate	
Cocoa from mix (6 oz.)	10
Milk chocolate (1 oz.)	6
Baking chocolate (1 oz.)	35
Soft drinks (12-oz. cans)	
Dr Pepper	39.6
Regular colas	46
Diet colas	46
Mountain Dew	54
Nonprescription Drugs (in recommended dosage)	
Prolamine	280
No Doz, Vivarin	200
Excedrin	130
Midol	65
Anacin	65
Dristan, other cold remedies	20–35

experience mild withdrawal symptoms when cutting back on their consumption. Symptoms include headache, lethargy, nervousness, feelings of depression, and, in rare instances, nausea and vomiting. These unpleasant feelings are usually short-lived and can be minimized or avoided by cutting back gradually instead of abruptly stopping all caffeine.

LOW-CALORIE SWEETENERS

SACCHARIN

Saccharin has been used to sweeten foods and beverages for almost a century; until the 1980s it was actually the only low-calorie sweetener approved for use in the United States.

Saccharin's extreme sweetness, approximately 300 times sweeter than sugar, has supported its long-term

popularity despite the discovery and approval of several newer low-calorie sweeteners. Consequently, saccharin is still commonly used in candy and chewing gum, soft drinks, and as a tabletop sweetener (Sweet'n Low).

Questions concerning the safety of saccharin arose during the 1970s when studies on laboratory animals suggested that high doses of this chemical might be associated with the development of bladder cancer. While the Food and Drug Administration (FDA) proposed to ban saccharin based on these findings, congressional legislation has postponed the ban until more conclusive scientific research is completed. To date, a link between saccharin and cancer in humans has not been clearly documented, but foods containing saccharin are required to carry warning labels questioning its safety.

ASPARTAME

In the 1980s, the introduction of aspartame (brand name NutraSweet) revolutionized low-calorie, sugar-free foods and beverages. The first low-calorie sweetener to be approved by the FDA in over 25 years, aspartame is now added to more than 1,500 different products ranging from yogurt to carbonated beverages.

Although technically less sweet (180 times sweeter than sugar) than saccharin, many consumers prefer aspartame's taste, and, as a result, it has largely replaced saccharin in many products despite its additional cost.

As yet, extensive safety studies have failed to identify significant health risks associated with its use in most people. As the evidence supporting aspartame's safety accumulates, the FDA is gradually expanding the number of ways it can be used.

Warning: People with phenylketonuria (PKU), a genetic disorder in which the amino acid phenylalanine cannot be digested, should not eat or drink foods containing aspartame.

ACESULFAME-K

Approved by the FDA for use in a limited number of products, the sweetener acesulfame-K is an extremely stable compound. Its stability makes it particularly useful in products like baked goods where other less stable sweeteners like aspartame are destroyed during the cooking process. Studies to date show no evidence of any adverse effects stemming from the use of acesulfame-K.

CYCLAMATE

While widely used in other countries, cyclamates were banned from foods in the United States in 1970 on the basis of studies that they caused cancer in laboratory animals.

Prior to the 1970 ban, cyclamates had been widely used in a number of low-calorie foods and beverages, often in combination with saccharin.

FAT REPLACERS

Low-calorie chemicals that taste and behave like fat generally fall into three categories: carbohydrate-based substances, protein-based chemicals, and modified fat products.

Carbohydrate-based fat replacers like cellulose and gums are commonly used in low-fat cheeses and other dairy foods. The most well known, so-called microparticulated protein-based chemical (known as Simplesse) provides only 1 to 2 calories per gram (less than both fat and protein) while lending a rich flavor and creamy texture to foods. So far, however, this substance has not enjoyed wide popularity. While food scientists have developed several sophisticated, chemically modified fats that would not be absorbed when eaten, safety questions have delayed their introduction into the marketplace.

FOOD ADDITIVES AND PRESERVATIVES

Concerns about the safety of food additives and preservatives have bothered consumers since the beginning of the industrial age. In the late 1800s, milk was often diluted with water, charcoal was added to coffee, and cocoa was combined with sawdust. Noxious chemicals like formaldehyde were used as preservatives, and the sale of contaminated milk and rancid meat was commonplace. Consequently, in 1906 the Pure Food and Drug Act empowered the government to set standards for safety and purity of foods. Since then, federal laws have been amended several times in an attempt to better protect the food supply.

But even though our health standards are stricter now than when the Pure Food and Drug Act was passed, doubts persist among consumers and researchers regarding the safety of some food additives. While some concerns are grounded in misconceptions and misinformation, others appear to be well founded. Concerns are fueled by the fact that, periodically, substances formerly considered safe are found to be potential hazards. Further complicating the situation is the scientific jargon used to describe these substances. Few consumers can differentiate between names like dioctyl sodium sulfosuccinate or butylated hydroxyanisole without feeling uneasy about food additives.

Extreme critics of additives argue for their exclusion from our diets altogether. But that argument ignores their beneficial effects in preventing spoilage, improving food texture and consistency, preserving food color and appearance, flavor, and odor enhancement, as well as reducing calories and fat. While some additives, such as

COMMON FAT REPLACERS

CARBOHYDRATE-BASED FAT REPLACERS	FOOD PRODUCTS
Cellulose	Dairy products
	Frozen desserts
	Salad dressings
Gums	Crackers, muffins, and breads
	Salad dressing
	Desserts
	Processed meats
Dextrins	Salad dressings
	Puddings
	Frozen desserts
	Spreads
Maltodextrins	Baked goods
	Dairy products
	Salad dressings
	Spreads and sauces
	Frostings and fillings
Modified food starch	Processed meats
	Salad dressings
	Baked goods
	Fillings and frostings
	Condiments
	Frozen desserts
Polydextrose	Baked goods
	Chewing gum
	Confections
	Gelatins and puddings
	Salad dressings
	Frozen dairy desserts

PROTEIN-BASED FAT REPLACERS	FOOD PRODUCTS
Microparticulated protein	Dairy-type products
	Salad dressing
	Margarine and mayonnaise-type products
	Baked goods
	Soups
	Sauces

FAT-BASED REPLACERS	FOOD PRODUCTS
Emulsifiers	Cake mixes and icings
	Cookies
	Dairy products
Caprenin	Confections
Lipid analogs	Under development. Safety questions may prevent them from ever being used.

COMMON FOOD ADDITIVES

ADDITIVE	PURPOSE	ADDITIVE	PURPOSE
Acacia	Thickening agent	Iodine	Nutrient
Acetic acid	Acidifier, flavoring agent	Iron	Nutrient
Acetone peroxide	Bleaching agent	Iron ammonium citrate	Anticaking agent
Adipic acid	Controls acidity	Karaya gum	Stabilizing and thickening agent
Ammonium alginate	Thickening and stabilizing agent	Lactic acid	Acidifier
Annatto extract	Coloring	Larch gum	Thickening agent
Arabinogalactan	Thickening agent, stabilizer	Lecithin	Emulsifier
		Locust bean gum	Thickening agent
Ascorbic acid	Nutrient, preservative	Maltol	Flavor enhancer
Aspartame	Sweetener (low-calorie)	Mannitol	Sweetener
Azodicarbonamide	Bleaching agent	Modified food starch	Thickener
Benzoyl peroxide	Bleaching agent	Monocalcium phosphate	Leavening agent
Beta-carotene	Nutrient, coloring	Monoglycerides	Emulsifier, stabilizer
Calcium alginate	Thickening and stabilizing agent	Monosodium glutamate (MSG)	Flavor enhancer
Calcium phosphate	Leavening agent	Niacinamide	Nutrient
Calcium silicate	Anticaking agent	Pectin	Gelling agent, thickener
Caramel	Color, flavoring	Phosphoric acid	Acidifier
Carob bean gum	Thickening agent, stabilizer	Polysorbates	Emulsifiers
		Potassium alginate	Thickening and stabilizing agent
Carrageenan	Emulsifier, stabilizer, thickener	Potassium bromate	Bleaching agent
Carrot seed oil	Flavoring, coloring	Potassium iodide	Nutrient
Cellulose	Anticaking agent, thickener, adds texture	Propylene glycol	Humectant
		Riboflavin	Nutrient
Citric acid	Preservative, flavoring	Saccharin	Sweetener (low-calorie)
Corn syrup	Sweetener	Silicon dioxide	Anticaking agent
Dehydrated beets	Coloring	Sodium acetate	Controls acidity
Dextrose	Sweetener	Sodium alginate	Thickening and stabilizing agent
Dioctyl sodium sulfosuccinate	Emulsifier	Sodium aluminum sulfate	Leavening agent
Disodium guanylate	Flavor enhancer	Sodium bicarbonate	Leavening agent
FD&C colors	Coloring	Sodium citrate	Controls acidity
Folic acid	Nutrient	Sodium stearyl fumarate	Bleaching agent
Fructose	Sweetener	Sorbitan monostearate	Emulsifier, stabilizer
Gelatin	Thickening agent	Sorbitol	Sweetener, humectant
Glucose	Sweetener	Tartaric acid	Acidifier
Glycerine	Humectant	Thiamine	Nutrient
Glycerol monostearate	Humectant	Titanium dioxide	Coloring
Guar gum	Thickening and stabilizing agent	Tocopherols (vitamin E)	Nutrient
		Tragacanth gum	Thickening agent
Hydrogen peroxide	Bleaching agent	Vitamin A	Nutrient
Hydrolyzed vegetable protein	Flavor enhancer	Vitamin D	Nutrient

COMMON FOOD PRESERVATIVES

ANTIMICROBIALS	ANTIOXIDANTS
Ascorbic acid (vitamin C)	Ascorbic acid
Benzoic acid	BHA (butylated hydroxyanisole)
Butylparaben	BTA (butylated hydroxytoluene)
Calcium lactate	
Calcium propionate	Citric acid
Calcium sorbate	EDTA (ethylenediamine tetra acetic acid)
Citric acid	
Heptylparaben	Propyl gallate
Lactic acid	TBHQ (tert-butylhydro-
Methylparaben	quinone)
Potassium propionate	Tocopherols
Potassium sorbate	(vitamin E)
Propionic acid	
Propylparaben	
Sodium benzoate	
Sodium diacetate	
Sodium erythorbate	
Sodium nitrate	
Sodium nitrite	
Sodium propionate	
Sodium sorbate	
Sorbic acid	

Copy adapted from Food and Drug Administration: FDA Consumer Report, April 6, 1979.

certain food dyes, may seem fatuous luxuries, chemicals such as preservatives prevent food poisoning from the growth of harmful microorganisms. Still others, like the vitamin D added to milk, the B vitamins added to breakfast cereals, and the iodine added to salt, promote good health by providing nutrients necessary for good health.

According to the FDA, there are nearly 3,000 direct additives—substances intentionally added to foods—and more than 10,000 indirect additives—substances that are unintentionally added to foods during growing, processing, or packaging. The boxes above list some common classes of additives and preservatives along with their functions.

AVOIDING PESTICIDES AND FOOD CONTAMINANTS

To avoid pesticides and other undesirable food additives and contaminants:

1. Wash and scrub fruits and vegetables well. Avoid soaking in water, which may remove or destroy vitamins.
2. Whenever possible, grow your own fruits and vegetables without pesticides.
3. Trim fat off meats and poultry and discard: Many pesticides and other contaminants concentrate in fat tissue.
4. Purchase produce grown in the United States. Domestic fruits and vegetables are less frequently contaminated than imports.
5. Eat a variety of foods to keep from eating too much of any one contaminant.
6. If you have time to bake your own bread, cookies, muffins, and the like, you can avoid the preservatives included in many commercial products.
7. Always read the ingredient labels of foods and be familiar with additives you want to avoid.
8. Contact the Food and Drug Administration (FDA) regarding your questions or concerns. Request a list of additives and preservatives that are "generally recognized as safe" (GRAS).

LABEL READING

Learning to understand food labeling information is the first step in making sensible dietary choices. According to a recent study, more than 85 percent of Americans read food labels, although many consumers tend to look at labels only when buying a product for the first time. However, reading labels has become an important part of shopping—75 percent of label readers say that they will actually pass up products if they don't like what they read.

Frequently, the information on a food label has been difficult to comprehend. Consequently, the FDA implemented new guidelines for food labels, which should make them easier to understand.

Today, food labels carry a list of nutrients and other measurements selected because of their relationship to current health concerns. Some of the label categories are carryovers from previous labeling requirements such as calories, total fat, total carbohydrate, protein, sodium, vitamins A and C, calcium, and iron. But the revised labels include calories from fat, calories from saturated fat, as well as amounts of cholesterol, sugars, and dietary fiber. Unlike the older labels, food packages no longer list vitamins such as thiamine, riboflavin, and niacin since deficiencies of these nutrients are no longer considered significant public health problems in the United States.

The current labels attempt to show the relative significance of foods in the context of the total daily diet. As a result, nutrients are measured not only in terms of the amount per serving but are also described as a percent of a new dietary reference value, called the Daily Value.

Daily Values are derived from two sets of calculations: Daily Reference Values (DRVs) and Reference Daily Intakes (RDIs). RDIs are basically a new name for USRDAs (Recommended Dietary Allowances), the approximate amounts of vitamins and minerals the average person

GLOSSARY OF FOOD LABEL TERMS

-FREE

Sugar-free: less than 0.5 g of sugar per serving

Fat-free: less than 0.5 g of fat per serving

Saturated fat–free: less than 0.5 g of saturated fat per serving, and the level of trans fatty acids does not exceed 1 percent of total fat

Cholesterol-free: less than 2 mg of cholesterol and 2 g or less of saturated fat per serving.

Sodium-free: less than 5 mg of sodium per serving

Calorie-free: fewer than 5 calories per serving

LOW
(OR LITTLE, FEW, CONTAINS A SMALL AMOUNT OF, LOW SOURCE OF)

Low-calorie: 40 calories or less per serving

Low-fat: 3 g of fat or less per serving

Low-saturated-fat: 1 g of fat or less per serving and not more than 15 percent of calories from saturated fatty acids

Low-cholesterol: 20 mg or less of cholesterol and 2 g or less of saturated fat per serving

Low-sodium: less than 140 mg per serving (very low sodium requires that each serving contain 35 mg or less)

LEAN
(USED TO DESCRIBE THE FAT CONTENT OF MEAT, POULTRY, SEAFOOD, AND GAME MEATS)

Less than 10 g of fat, less than 4 g of saturated fat, and less than 95 mg of cholesterol per serving and per 100 g.

EXTRA LEAN
(USED TO DESCRIBE THE FAT CONTENT OF MEAT, POULTRY; SEAFOOD, AND GAME MEATS)

Less than 5 g of fat, less than 2 g of saturated fat, and less than 95 mg of cholesterol per serving and per 100 g.

HIGH
(OR RICH IN, EXCELLENT SOURCE OF)

A serving must contain 20 percent or more of the Daily Value for that nutrient (e.g., a food labeled "high fiber" must contain 5 g or more of fiber per serving).

GOOD SOURCE

A serving must contain 10 to 19 percent of the Daily Value for the nutrient (e.g., a "good source of fiber" must contain 2.5 to 4.9 g per serving).

REDUCED

Reduced sugar: at least 25 percent less sugar per serving than the reference food

Reduced (or fewer) calories: at least 25 percent fewer calories per serving than the reference food

Reduced (or less) fat: at least 25 percent less per serving than the reference food

Reduced (or less) saturated fat: at least 25 percent less per serving than the reference food

Reduced (or less) cholesterol: at least 25 percent less and 2 g or less of saturated fat per serving than the reference food

Reduced (or less) sodium: at least 25 percent less per serving than the reference food

LIGHT (OR LITE)

The product must contain one-third fewer calories or one-half the fat of the product it is being compared to.

FRESH

The term can only be used to describe foods that are raw, have never been frozen or heated, and contain no preservatives.

HEALTHY

The food must meet the standards for "low-fat" and "low-saturated-fat" as well as contain no more than 480 mg of sodium or more than 60 mg of cholesterol per serving or the food must meet the definition for "lean" and contain no more than 480 mg of sodium per serving.

Nutrition Facts		
Serving Size		1 Cup (30g/1.1 oz.)
Servings per Container		17

Amount Per Serving	Cereal	Cereal with ½ Cup Vitamins A & D Skim Milk
Calories	110	150
Fat Calories	0	0
	% Daily Value**	
Total Fat 0g*	0%	0%
Saturated Fat 0g	0%	0%
Cholesterol 0mg	0%	0%
Sodium 330mg	14%	16%
Potassium 35mg	1%	7%
Total Carbohydrate 26g	9%	11%
Dietary Fiber 1g	4%	4%
Sugars 2g		
Other Carbohydrate 23g		
Protein 2g		
Vitamin A	15%	20%
Vitamin C	25%	25%
Calcium	0%	15%
Iron	45%	45%
Vitamin D	10%	25%
Thiamin	25%	30%
Riboflavin	25%	35%
Niacin	25%	25%
Vitamin B$_6$	25%	25%
Folate	25%	25%

*Amount in cereal. One half cup skim milk contributes an additional 40 calories, 65mg sodium, 6g total carbohydrate (6g sugars), and 4g protein.
**Percent Daily Values are based on a 2,000 calorie diet. Your daily values may be higher or lower depending on your calorie needs.

		Calories	2,000	2,500
Total Fat	Less than		65g	80g
Sat. Fat	Less than		20g	25g
Cholesterol	Less than		300mg	300mg
Sodium	Less than		2,400mg	2,400mg
Potassium			3,500mg	3,500mg
Total Carbohydrate			300g	375g
Dietary Fiber			25g	30g

Calories per gram:
Fat 9 • Carbohydrate 4 • Protein 4

Ingredients: Corn, sugar, malt flavoring, corn syrup.
Vitamins and Iron: ascorbic acid (vitamin c), iron, niacinamide, pyridoxine hydrochloride (vitamin B$_6$), riboflavin (vitamin B$_2$), vitamin A palmitate, thiamin hydrochloride (vitamin B$_1$), folic acid, and vitamin D. To maintain quality, BHT has been added to the packaging.

should be consuming daily. DRVs, on the other hand, are the recommended daily amounts of nutrients for which no set of reference standards had previously existed—fat, carbohydrate, protein, fiber, cholesterol, sodium, and potassium. Calculations of how much of these nutrients we should be eating assume that the average person consumes 2,000 calories a day.

- Daily fat calories are 30 percent of 2,000 calories—600 calories of fat.
- Saturated fat calories should be 10 percent of 2,000 calories—200 calories of saturated fat.
- Carbohydrate calories should be 60 percent of 2,000 calories—1,200 calories of carbohydrates.
- Protein calories should be 10 percent of 2,000 calories—200 calories of protein.
- Daily fiber intake should be 12.5 grams per 1,000 calories, or 25 grams.

(For gram totals, see table 5.1.)

The DRVs for cholesterol, sodium, and potassium, which do not contribute any calories, remain independent of caloric intake.

Example: A product that contains 13 grams of fat (about 117 calories) per serving would state on the label that the "Percent Daily Value" for fat is 20 percent. In other words, one serving provides 20 percent of your recommended fat intake for the entire day.

Daily Reference Values (DRVs)
Fat	65 g
Saturated fatty acids	20 g
Cholesterol	300 mg
Total carbohydrate	300 g
Fiber	25 g
Sodium	2,400 mg
Potassium	3,500 mg
Protein*	50 g

These figures are based on a 2,000-calorie diet for adults and children over age 4.

*Values vary for certain populations.

SUMMING UP

Improving the way you eat is a fairly straightforward process that entails applying nutritional knowledge to food purchases, food preparation, and meals. Luckily, basic, healthy, nutritional principles, as demonstrated in the Food Guide Pyramid, are relatively uncomplicated, although they may conflict with some of your long-term eating habits. Good nutrition means far more than just changing the things you put in your mouth.

DAILY MEAL PLANS

DAILY MEAL PLANS—1,200 CALORIES

Breakfast

1 cup fresh strawberries
¾ cup bran flakes
½ pint skim milk

Lunch

2 oz. tuna fish (in water) made with 1 Tbsp.
   low-calorie mayonnaise and ¼ tsp. dill seed
1 whole-wheat roll
1½ cups romaine lettuce and tomato
1 Tbsp. low-calorie French dressing
1 fresh apple

Dinner

2 oz. roasted chicken without skin (1 thigh or a piece
   ⅔ the size of a deck of playing cards)
1 cup chicken consommé with bean sprouts and
   cilantro
½ cup cooked brown rice
½ cup steamed broccoli
½ cup nonfat frozen yogurt

Snacks

1 Tbsp. raisins
10 wheat crackers
1 cup skim milk

15% of calories are from fat (less than 5% from
   saturated fat)
24% of calories are from protein
61% of calories are from carbohydrate
Less than 100 mg of cholesterol

DAILY MEAL PLAN—1,500 CALORIES

Breakfast

1 fresh orange
¾ cup cooked oatmeal made with 1 tsp. honey and
   cinnamon
½ pint skim milk
1 slice cracked-wheat toast with 1 tsp. margarine

Lunch

½ cup minestrone soup
2 oz. turkey breast on two slices rye bread with
   1 Tbsp. light mayonnaise and mustard
½ cup shredded carrot salad
1 kiwifruit

Dinner

1 serving vegetable lasagna
1 cup fresh spinach salad with 1 tsp. olive oil and
   lemon
1 cup cranberry juice spritzer made with ½ cranberry
   juice and ½ club soda
1 cup melon balls

Snacks

1 cup skim milk
1 oz. pretzels

27% of calories are from fat (less than 5% from
   saturated fat)
18% of calories are from protein
55% of calories are from carbohydrate
Less than 100 mg of cholesterol

But the importance of a healthy diet is undisputed—eating a low-fat diet rich in complex carbohydrates can lower your risk of a wide range of chronic diseases as well as help you keep your weight down.

When changing your diet, do not attempt drastic changes—adjust gradually. Otherwise, you may find yourself giving up the effort to switch to a better diet. But always remember: The time and effort spent eating a healthy regimen will probably pay you back with better health. This is one area where most people can improve their well-being at relatively small expense.

DAILY MEAL PLANS

DAILY MEAL PLAN—1,800 CALORIES

Breakfast

6 oz. grapefruit juice
1 medium bagel
1 tsp. margarine
½ pint skim milk

Lunch

1½ cups cooked spaghetti
½ cup marinara sauce
2 Tbsp. grated Parmesan cheese
½ cup cooked carrots
1 serving tossed green salad
1 Tbsp. low-calorie ranch dressing
2 fig bars

Dinner

3 oz. broiled lean steak
1 medium baked potato
½ cup broiled mushrooms made with garlic and
  ½ tsp. corn oil
½ cup roasted peppers made with fresh basil and
  ½ tsp. corn oil
½ cup three-bean salad
1 steamed pear with 2 Tbsp. raspberry sauce

Snacks

1 cup skim milk
1 slice angel food cake
½ cup fresh broccoli and 1 medium tomato with
  ¼ cup nonfat yogurt dip

17% of calories are from fat (less than 5% from
  saturated fat)
19% of calories are from protein
64% of calories are from carbohydrate
Less than 100 mg of cholesterol

DAILY MEAL PLAN—2,000 CALORIES

Breakfast

½ cup strawberries
¾ cup bran flakes
¼ cup low-fat cottage cheese (1%)
1 cup skim milk

Lunch

¾ cup split-pea soup
2 Tbsp. peanut butter on 2 slices of whole-wheat
  bread
1 cup roasted peppers
1 medium orange
3 breadsticks
1 tsp. margarine

Dinner

4 oz. skinless chicken breast made with 1 tsp. oil and
  herbs
1 large baked potato with ¼ cup low-fat yogurt and
  chives
½ cup romaine lettuce and ½ cup tomato
1 tsp. salad oil with basil-flavored vinegar
1 slice of whole-wheat bread
1 cup fruit salad

Snacks

1 cup low-fat blueberry yogurt
1 cinnamon raisin bagel
1 medium oatmeal cookie

23% of calories are from fat (less than 10% from
  saturated fat)
21% of calories are from protein
56% of calories are from carbohydrate
Less than 200 mg of cholesterol

6
Smoking, Alcohol, and Substance Abuse

· · · · · · · · · · · · · · · ·

HERBERT KLEBER, M.D.
Parts of this chapter are adapted from the chapter by Robert Lewy, M.D., and Eric Josephson, Ph.D., which appeared in the revised second edition.

Drug abuse—including the use of tobacco and alcohol—has mushroomed into one of the greatest public health problems of all time. The health and social problems associated with drug abuse present complex difficulties for society as a whole, and for individual abusers and their families. While there is no panacea for the drug problem, efforts to prevent and treat drug abuse can rescue individuals from addiction and help them reclaim their lives.

ABUSE AND ADDICTION

Drugs are substances that alter biological function, and those that alter mood can be abused. Abuse refers to harmful behavior associated with repeated use of the drug. Addiction occurs when one is so reliant on drug use that it becomes the central focus of your behavior in spite of the harm it is causing. Addiction equals compulsive use in spite of harmful effects and inability to stop for any significant period of time. According to Avram Goldstein, M.D., in the book *Addiction,* the addictive drugs can generally be divided into seven categories.

1. Nicotine
2. Alcohol and related drugs
3. Opiates
4. Cocaine and amphetamines
5. Cannabis (marijuana, hashish)
6. Caffeine
7. Hallucinogens

Drug abuse in the United States and around the world has incurred enormous social cost. Despite the public attention paid to illegal drug use, the most harm, by far, actually is derived from legal drugs. The drug nicotine, usually ingested in cigarette smoke, causes about 400,000 premature deaths every year in the United States. In addition to killing smokers, sidestream, or secondhand, smoke (smoke inhaled by bystanders) is responsible for about 53,000 annual deaths. Widespread publicity about the dangers of cigarette smoke has not deterred the more than 50 million Americans who continue to use cigarettes.

The financial cost of nicotine addiction is enormous. In terms of medical care and time lost from work, the U.S. Congress Office of Technology Assessment estimates that smoking costs more than $140 billion every year (more than $4,400 a second).

As for alcohol, the National Institute on Alcohol Abuse and Alcoholism estimates that two of three adults drink alcoholic beverages and that one of ten adults is a problem drinker or an alcoholic. Alcohol-related diseases and accidents claim about 100,000 lives annually, and cost society anywhere from $40 to $100 billion. (Exact estimates are hard to calculate.)

While fewer people use illegal drugs such as heroin, cocaine, and marijuana than use cigarettes or alcohol (because of their illegality), these substances also exact a considerable toll, particularly among the young. Public concern about the "drug problem" tends to focus on illicit substances for several reasons: Young people use them, these drugs are often involved in drug-related crime, and a large amount of public money is spent trying to stamp out use of these drugs. Although the cost of illicit drug use is estimated to be around $100 billion a year, this figure includes the price of drug law enforcement and the cost for imprisoning drug dealers (and users), as well as publicly funded drug rehabilitation programs.

If we include alcohol, tobacco, prescription and over-the-counter mood-altering drugs, and caffeine in our assessment of drug use, virtually every American is a drug user (although not a drug abuser, and most do not suffer harmful effects). Many people take a variety of drugs, and even those who regularly use antidepressants, barbiturates, other sedatives, and amphetamines often ingest a combination of drugs. For example, one-third of those regularly using barbiturates use other prescription drugs; one-half of antidepressant users are multidrug users; and many prescription drug users are regular drinkers.

Many closely related factors determine the drugs people take.

Age: Young people may be more likely to use illicit drugs; older people may take prescription pharmaceuticals.

Gender: Women may be more likely to use tranquilizers.

Heredity: The sons of alcoholics are four times as likely to abuse alcohol as the sons of nonalcoholics.

Religion: Orthodox Jews use alcohol in religious ceremonies and rarely develop alcoholism.

Culture: People in France consume five times as much alcohol and suffer eight times the cirrhosis death rate as do the more moderate citizens of Norway.

SMOKING

Extensive epidemiological and clinical studies have proven smoking to be a high-risk health hazard. In 1982, as a result of investigations into smoking's dangers, the Surgeon General warned "cigarette smoking is clearly identified as the chief preventable cause of death in our society." More than one of three smokers dies prematurely of a smoking-related disease.

Despite this proven evidence of smoking's harm, 50 million Americans still smoke, although the overall percentage has declined during the past three decades. As of 1992, the proportion of men had dropped to 28.6 percent, while 24.6 percent of women smoked. (*Source:* American Lung Association.) Among teenagers, smoking continues to be popular, and adolescent and college-age females are more likely to smoke than are their male counterparts.

Most smokers claim they want to quit, and with good reason: Researchers have found irrefutable evidence that smoking causes cancer.

- Smokers are three times more likely to die of cancer than nonsmokers.
- Since the 1950s lung cancer in women is up by 400 percent.
- More than 80 percent of cancer deaths are linked to cigarettes.
- Smoking is the leading cause of lung cancer.
- Smokers are six times more likely to contract cancer of the mouth, larynx, throat, and esophagus, and the risk is exacerbated by alcohol.
- Smoking contributes to cancer of the bladder, kidney, and pancreas.

Smoking also contributes to heart disease.

- 40 percent of heart disease in people under the age of 65 is linked to smoking, as is 21 percent for the general population.
- Smoking raises blood pressure.

Low-tar, low-nicotine cigarettes are not risk-free. Tests of tar and nicotine levels are faulty because:

- Machines that test cigarettes for tar and nicotine may not inhale as deeply as real smokers.
- Real smokers may cover the ventilation holes in the filter or paper so the smoke is not diluted.
- Smokers of low-tar, low-nicotine cigarettes tend to smoke more cigarettes than smokers of regular cigarettes.
- The smoke from low-tar cigarettes still inflames and clogs lung airways, leading to bronchitis and emphysema.

For these reasons, cancer specialists warn that there is no such thing as a "safe" cigarette.

Pipe and cigar smokers and snuff users reduce lung cancer risk because they usually do not inhale. However, these products carry their own risk.

- Pipe and cigar smokers develop cancers of the mouth, lip, larynx, and esophagus just as often as cigarette smokers.

- Snuff use is associated with cancer of the mouth and oral cavities.
- Those who switch from cigarettes to a pipe or cigars may still inhale tobacco smoke and run an even higher lung cancer risk than cigarette smokers.

Smoking is a social activity. Some of the social reasons smokers continue to smoke include:

- To appear sophisticated: In movies and social situations smoking has been portrayed as a suave activity.
- To equalize emotions: As an emotional crutch, smoking minimizes anger, fear, and shame and enhances enjoyment, excitement, and relaxation.
- To accompany other activities: Some people are conditioned to want a cigarette after eating, while working, or after sexual activity.
- To engage in a ritualistic activity: Activity associated with cigarette smoking is reassuring to many. Tapping a cigarette, using a lighter or matches, gestures with a cigarette—all of these motions can be used as nonverbal communication or as a means for avoiding communication.
- To cope with stress: Smoking can tranquilize or serve as a smoke screen behind which to hide one's feelings.

Beyond the purely social aspects of smoking, cigarettes contain nicotine, a highly addictive drug that smokers' bodies learn to crave. The addiction to nicotine is manifested in increasing tolerance to the drug that progresses in four stages.

1. Beginning smokers overcome their initial aversion to tobacco smoke.
2. Smokers develop a dependency that must be satisfied by an increasing dosage of cigarettes (leveling off at one to four packs per day).
3. Dependency creates a craving when addicted smokers have to abstain for a period of time.
4. Distinct withdrawal symptoms occur when cigarettes are withheld.

As smoke is inhaled, the nicotine passes through the membrane of the lung tissue and is rapidly absorbed into the bloodstream.

1. The heart pumps about 15 percent of the inhaled nicotine directly to the brain, which absorbs all of it within 7 seconds.
2. In the brain, nicotine stimulates the release of substances called catecholamines (one of which is adrenaline).
3. Catecholamines increase the heart rate and the blood pressure, a metabolic shift that induces a mild "lift" in the smoker's feelings.

Every puff of tobacco smoke provides a "shot" or "fix" of nicotine, and smokers unconsciously maintain a satisfactory level of nicotine in their blood and brain by smoking a sufficient number of cigarettes. Smoking is lengthened or shortened to maintain a comfortable feeling without overdosing and suffering side effects such as nausea and dizziness.

If blood and brain nicotine levels fall too low, nicotine withdrawal symptoms ensue, which include headache, nausea, constipation or diarrhea, falling heart rate and blood pressure, fatigue, drowsiness, and insomnia.

Psychological symptoms are inability to concentrate, irritability, anxiety and depression, and craving for a cigarette.

Despite these intimidating withdrawal effects, every tobacco user, no matter how addicted, should remember that he or she can stop smoking. In the effort to quit, smokers should remember the addictive nature of nicotine and be prepared to accept withdrawal symptoms as a natural consequence of stopping. Withdrawal is a temporary condition that, though unpleasant, is not harmful.

Besides nicotine, cigarette smoke contains two other significant components: gases and tars. Of the many different gases (which include hydrogen cyanide, nitrogen oxide, and ammonia) the most dangerous is carbon monoxide (CO), a gas that binds with the hemoglobin in red blood cells 200 times more strongly than does oxygen. CO's dangerous effects include:

- Oxygen deprivation: By occupying red blood cells, CO depletes the body's supply of this precious element. (To increase the danger, a smoker's heart suffers from nicotine's stimulant effects at the same time as CO reduces the coronary oxygen supply.)
- Impaired vision, hearing, and judgment.
- Promotion of plaque deposits in the arteries: While nicotine stimulates the release of free fatty acids in the bloodstream, CO stimulates their deposit on artery walls, leading to atherosclerosis, a leading cause of heart attack, stroke, and other circulatory diseases.

Smoking is one of the three major risk factors for heart disease, along with high blood pressure and high blood cholesterol. Smokers with one (or both) of these other risk factors are in serious danger of heart attack, a danger that rises in proportion to the daily number of cigarettes they smoke. (Heart and blood vessel disease are the leading causes of death for smokers.) Nicotine also constricts blood vessels and is a major risk factor of peripheral vascular disease, in which blood vessels leading to arms and legs narrow and eventually grow blocked, possibly leading to loss of limbs.

The tars and gases in cigarette smoke progressively damage the lung tissue.

- Cigarette smoke produces more mucus in the lungs but anesthetizes the tiny hairs, or cilia, that line the airways and are supposed to sweep the mucus and foreign matter toward the throat. (But as smokers sleep, the cilia partly recover and move some accumulated mucus and impurities out of the lungs to produce the morning smoker's hacking cough.)
- Cigarette smoke impairs the functions of the pulmonary enzyme system and the lymphocytes designed to keep the lungs clean.
- After years of heavy smoking, the lung's cilia are destroyed, allowing mucus to accumulate and frequently become infected with colds, respiratory infections, and chronic bronchitis. Smokers are $2\frac{1}{2}$ times more likely than nonsmokers to suffer acute respiratory illness.
- Impaired lung function may lead to emphysema, an irreversible condition reducing lung elasticity and destroying air sacs that take in oxygen. Normally, 5 percent of an adult's energy is expended for breathing; people with emphysema use 80 percent.

The tars in cigarette smoke are solid chemical particles that condense as sticky resins in the lungs. Tar contains about 4,000 chemicals, a number of which are known to cause cancer. Some are "complete" carcinogens, capable of causing cancer independently. Others are cocarcinogens, synergistically reacting with other cigarette smoke substances to produce cancer, and still others are cancer promoters, causing already formed cancers to progress faster.

Cancers can begin when tars produce abnormal cells in the mouth, larynx, esophagus, and lungs and these irregular cells develop into lesions. When fully developed, these cancers can spread (metastasize) to other parts of the body. Of these cancers, lung cancer is one of the most harmful, often far advanced before symptoms are noted, and usually fatal (only 10 percent of lung cancer victims are cured). The best cure for lung cancer is prevention of the disease by not smoking.

Smoking is particularly harmful for pregnant women and their unborn children.

- Babies of smokers weigh an average of 6 ounces less than the children of nonsmokers. (Reduced birth weight is a result of nicotine's restriction of blood vessels and CO's oxygen depletion.)
- Children of smokers are still smaller at age 7 and may suffer impaired reading ability.
- Mothers who smoke suffer a greater risk of spontaneous abortion and stillbirth. (One or more packs a day increases the risk of infant mortality by 50 percent.)

Smokers hurt not only their own health, but they also may compromise the health of those around them. Sidestream smoke is blamed for 53,000 deaths each year in the United States. Sidestream smoke is unfiltered smoke and may actually contain higher levels of harmful substances than the smoke inhaled by the smoker.

Sidestream smoke may:

- Exacerbate medical conditions such as blood circulation problems and asthma.
- Increase the risk of heart disease and lung cancer.
- Increase the risk of impaired lung function development, respiratory difficulties, and ear infections in children.

The types of lung cancers that nonsmokers suffer as a result of passive smoke appear to be the same as those contracted by smokers. A Swedish study of 27,000 nonsmoking women found the risk of two types of lung cancer associated with cigarette smoking—squamous cell and small cell—increased three times for nonsmoking women living with or married to male smokers.

HEALTH BENEFITS OF QUITTING

According to the American Cancer Society, many of smoking's adverse effects are reversed when smokers quit.

- Immediately: Bronchitis and emphysema improve as breathing eases and lung function deterioration decelerates.
- After 1 year: Risk of heart disease drops significantly.
- After 7 years: Risk of bladder cancer drops to the same level as for nonsmokers.
- After 10 years: Risk of heart disease is the same as nonsmokers.
- After 10 to 15 years: Risk of shortened life expectancy, as well as risk of lung cancer, larynx cancer, and mouth cancer, approaches that of people who have never smoked.

CIGARETTE SMOKING DEPENDENCE

Dependence on cigarettes occurs in stages.

- Initiation: usually occurs prior to age 20. Peer pressure, desire for self-esteem and status, and persuasiveness of advertising lead to experimentation with cigarettes.
- Transition: Psychological and environmental influences motivate the individual to smoke sufficiently to become a full-fledged smoker.
- Maintenance: Psychological and physiological needs, including the desire to avoid nicotine withdrawal and ensure the immediate physical effects of nicotine, promote the long-term smoking habit.

Smoking is learned behavior and its sensations are initially unpleasant. Just as it can be learned, however, it can be unlearned, and situations that "call" for a cigarette can instead become a call for a different activity.

SMOKING SITUATION	ALTERNATIVE ACTIVITIES
At work, smoking provides stimulation.	Brisk walk, yoga, stretches.
In a social setting, smoking keeps the hands busy.	Hold worry beads, pen, pencil, or eyeglasses.
In stressful situations, smoking can tranquilize.	Consume a healthful snack; talk to a friend or family member.
While driving or working, smoking enhances pleasure or relaxes.	Chew gum; find means of becoming more involved in work or volunteer activities.
During the day, smoking becomes habitual and automatic.	Become conscious of smoking; do not unconsciously reach for cigarettes.

THERAPIES FOR STOPPING SMOKING

Effective therapies have been devised to aid smokers determined to quit their addiction. Studies demonstrate that the most effective intervention utilizes several strategies.

- **Nicotine Fading.** Nicotine intake is gradually reduced, low-nicotine cigarettes are substituted for regular cigarettes and the number of cigarettes smoked daily is progressively reduced. Tapering cigarette consumption reduces severity of nicotine withdrawal. Success rate is highest when combined with relapse prevention.
- **Hypnosis.** Effective for smokers highly motivated to quit. Works best with highly individualized sessions where self-hypnosis is learned, and telephone follow-up is implemented. Method's efficacy depends on an individual's degree of hypnotizability (measurable by various tests).
- **Relapse Prevention.** Maintenance strategies use social support interventions with group sessions of ex-smokers who help each other refrain from smoking. A buddy system involving spouses, co-workers, and friends uses telephone contact to deal with the urge to smoke; development of coping skills to resist smoking impulses; changing attitudes and self-perceptions.
- **Self-treatment.** The most inexpensive method of smoking cessation, but the chance of success depends on the individual. Studies suggest that some amount of face-to-face contact with a doctor, other former smokers, or a counselor may improve the chances of staying off cigarettes.

HOW TO QUIT

Of the almost 2 million Americans who quit smoking annually, about 95 percent do it on their own. No single method of quitting works for everyone: Some stop suddenly (cold turkey) while others gradually cut back. Many smokers join low-cost smoking cessation clinics such as those offered by the American Cancer Society, the American Lung Association, the Seventh-Day Adventist Church, local hospitals, or for-profit organizations such as SmokEnders. (Programs are listed in the Yellow Pages.)

Stop smoking clinics generally provide education about smoking, group support, and a firm date for quitting. Other cessation methods utilize individual and group counseling, hypnosis, behavior modification, and the use of nicotine patches or other drugs to mediate withdrawal.

Here are some of the methods smokers have used to quit.

1. List your reasons for quitting. List personally important reasons such as bad breath, embarrassment at smoking in front of your children, and so on. After quitting, if craving and withdrawal make you uncomfortable, use your list to remind yourself of the unacceptable and unappetizing aspects of smoking.

2. Emphasize immediate benefits. If long-term health benefits of quitting are too abstract and removed to motivate quitting, focus on immediate rewards such as better breath, improved stamina, losing the morning smoker's cough, fresher clothes and hair, and the cleanliness of empty ashtrays.

3. Study your smoking habit. Keep a smoking diary to show when and under what circumstances you smoke (waking up, with coffee, with friends). Note your mood when you smoke, and if you are cutting back gradually keep track of each cigarette you smoke on a piece of paper wrapped around your cigarette pack and secured with a rubber band. Unwrapping and recording your cigarettes will help you grow more conscious of your smoking.

4. Plan your quitting. Set a date several weeks in advance and plan ahead. Tapering off before the target date may be helpful to lower nicotine dependency. Talk to friends who have quit and learn what to expect. Ask your doctor for advice.

5. Enlist the help of friends and family. Ask others not to smoke in your presence. When offered a cigarette, politely but firmly decline.

6. Get rid of all cigarettes and other smoking accessories. Get rid of your favorite ashtrays and lighters at home and at work.

7. Eat a better diet. Smoking decreases appetite by dulling taste and smell, so when you quit you can better taste and smell food again. This also may increase your weight as you satisfy your oral craving for food after you quit smoking.

Avoid high-calorie foods and keep low-calorie snacks handy, but do not be obsessed about holding back on calories in the beginning. The early period of quitting is not the time for a stringent diet, since low-calorie dining will create an atmosphere of self-denial that may lead to smoking relapse. But weight gain is not inevitable when you quit smoking. You can return to your normal weight once you are used to a new, healthier lifestyle.

8. Exercise more. Exercise minimizes weight gain and increases a sense of physical well-being, calming the jitters and relieving tension. Some people have quit smoking after they started jogging or swimming and discovered how smoking rendered them breathless.

9. Avoid situations linked to smoking. Identify and avoid the occasions you are most likely to smoke, and plan other activities such as a walk after dinner instead of coffee and a cigarette.

10. Reward yourself. The financial rewards of not spending money on cigarettes are an immediate incentive for quitting, and some ex-smokers save their former cigarette money to pay for trips, CDs, or clothes. Others use the money for special treats like a new book, flowers, or taxi rides home from work. If you quit, pamper yourself. You deserve it. Pampering adds to the immediate satisfaction of knowing that every day you do not smoke, you are overcoming one of the most serious, powerful, and harmful addictions known to medicine.

Pharmacological therapies for smoking (should be used as adjuncts to behavioral therapies listed above):

- **Nicotine Patch.** Replaces nicotine in the bloodstream without the need for cigarettes. Nicotine replacement in this manner may not work for everyone. Side effects may include nausea, skin irritation, and heartburn. Nicotine gum is also available but is harder to use and is not as reliable as patches in releasing a steady amount of nicotine into the blood.
- **Clonidine Therapy.** Antihypertensive drug that studies suggest may be effective in blocking nicotine withdrawal symptoms.
- **Antidepressants.** Used as a substitute for nicotine to ease withdrawal symptoms. Studies show that heavy smokers are more likely to have suffered from episodes of depression than nonsmokers.

Heavy smokers addicted to cigarettes constantly crave cigarette smoke, and some chain-smokers light another cigarette as soon as the previous one is stubbed out. Waking in the morning with a hacking cough, they still reach for a cigarette even before rising. For these types of smokers, quitting may be difficult and generally must be performed cold turkey since gradual nicotine withdrawal causes too much discomfort. Many of these smokers throw away their cigarettes after a frightening discussion of smoking's effects with their doctor or after reading about the health consequences of smoking. These smokers must make a conscious act of will to quit smoking and focus on improving their health with self-control over their habit.

Anyone trying to quit tobacco addiction can take reassurance from the fact that more than 40 million people have quit successfully since the U.S. Surgeon General's first report on the dangers of smoking in 1964. Today, smokers looking to quit can choose from a smorgasbord of therapies, self-help groups, and information.

The box "How to Quit" offers helpful information on quitting on your own. In addition, a number of organizations offer helpful literature.

- Local chapters of the American Cancer Society offer the "7-Day Quitter's Guide."
- American Council on Science and Health distributes "Smoking or Health: It's Your Choice."
- Office of Cancer Communications, National Cancer Institute offers various materials.
- American Lung Association distributes free reports.

(For addresses and phone numbers see appendix B, Directory of Health Organizations and Resources.)

ALTERNATIVE THERAPIES AND HOME REMEDIES

Acupuncturists use tiny needles inserted into the body at prescribed points to alleviate the urge to smoke. Usually these points are in the ear, and small staples may be left in place in the ear to prolong treatment.

Acupuncture's effectiveness in aiding smoking cessation is controversial and research has not always supported its worthiness. While one study showed the technique had about a one in three success rate, another found little or no benefit. Other research has purportedly found that placebos (needles placed at random points) work almost as well.

Self-hypnosis and various relaxation therapies are also used in the battle to give up cigarettes. Since many people smoke as a reaction to stress, progressive relaxation techniques are substituted for smoking. These techniques include meditation, in which the mind is emptied of all thoughts or relaxing images are pictured in the mind, and muscle relaxation, during which muscles are tensed and then relaxed.

None of these techniques is a panacea for the cravings many smokers encounter when they give up tobacco. If you are quitting smoking, you may find that applying several different techniques provides the most effective formula that will help you stay off cigarettes.

OVERVIEW OF ALCOHOL-RELATED PROBLEMS

Alcohol use is widespread, although the per capita consumption has varied from decade to decade. While U.S. consumption of alcoholic beverages increased after World II, since 1981 it has declined slightly. But even with declines in alcohol use, two of three American adults drink alcoholic beverages. About half of all alcohol consumed in this country is ingested by heavy drinkers, estimated to be between 6.5 and 10 percent of the total population. The extent and frequency with which these individuals drink cause serious health and behavioral problems—disrupting their own lives and that of their family, friends, and employers—and also extracts a heavy societal toll.

Alcohol use is involved in:

- One-half of all murders, accidental deaths, and suicides
- One-third of all drownings and boating and aviation deaths
- One-half of all crimes
- Almost half of all fatal automobile accidents

The health problems associated with alcohol include brain damage, cancer, heart disease, and cirrhosis of the liver.

THE GENETICS OF ALCOHOL

Growing evidence supports the theory that heredity predisposes some people toward alcoholism. This research has focused on mutations in the molecular structures of enzymes that metabolize alcohol and may affect the body's ability to excrete alcohol.

Researchers have found that the heredity of a large proportion of Asians may prevent them from drinking: These people possess an enzyme ineffective at removing acetaldehyde, the first by-product of alcohol metabolism. When high levels of acetaldehyde build up after consuming a small amount of alcohol, these people suffer discomfort such as skin flushing and rapid pulse. Consequently, the presence of this enzyme, which limits the alcohol that can be consumed before illness ensues, may at least partly explain the low incidence of alcoholism among Asian populations.

Studies of individuals with either an alcoholic mother or father or both show that even if they are adopted, they still experience a greater risk of developing alcoholism than the general population. Similarly, offspring of nonalcoholic parents when adopted into families with an alcoholic mother or father are less likely to develop alcoholism than the children of alcoholics.

Two types of genetic predispositions have been theorized from research.

1. **Male-limited susceptibility.** Found primarily in males, this condition is passed on frequently and occurs at an early age. It is associated with criminal tendencies and often requires extensive therapy.
2. **Milieu-limited susceptibility.** More prevalent, this condition is found in both males and females, is not as severe as male-limited susceptibility, and does not necessarily involve crime. Although inherited, it must be stimulated by environmental factors to manifest itself.

HOW ALCOHOL WORKS IN THE BODY

Alcohol is a potent nonprescription drug sold to anyone over the national legal drinking age. This drug is a tranquilizer and a member of the family of sedative-hypnotic drugs.

Temperate and occasional users of alcohol who are in normal health do not appear to suffer negative effects from use of alcohol. In moderate doses, alcohol has beneficial effects: relaxation, appetite stimulation, and creation of a mild sense of euphoria.

Consumed in substantial amounts, alcohol's toxicity may be because it acts as a foreign substance in the body's metabolism. The short-term expression of this toxicity is felt as a hangover. The long-term toxicity may develop into alcoholism and alcohol-related diseases such as cirrhosis.

Unlike carbohydrates, fats, and proteins, which can be manufactured by the body, alcohol is an introduced substance that is not synthesized within the body. It is a food because it supplies a concentrated number of calories, but it is not nourishing and does not supply a significant amount of needed nutrients, vitamins, or minerals—these are empty calories.

Most foods are prepared for digestion by the stomach so that their nutrients can be absorbed by the large intestine, but 95 percent of alcohol is absorbed directly through the stomach wall or the walls of the duodenum and the small intestine.

Various factors affect the speed of alcohol's absorption into the body.

- Watery drinks such as beer are absorbed more slowly.
- Foods (especially fatty foods) delay absorption.
- Carbonated beverages speed up the emptying of the stomach into the small intestine, where alcohol is absorbed more quickly.
- The drinker's physical and emotional state (fatigue, stress) and individual body chemistry unpredictably affect absorption.
- Gender: women have less alcohol dehydrogenase, which breaks down alcohol in the stomach, so more alcohol is absorbed into the bloodstream.

Alcohol moves from the bloodstream into every part of the body that contains water, including major organs like the brain, lungs, kidneys, and heart, and distributes itself equally both inside and outside of cells. Only 5 percent of alcohol is eliminated from the body through the breath, urine, or sweat; the rest is oxidized or broken down in the liver.

In the liver:

- Alcohol is broken down in steps by enzymes until only carbon dioxide and water remain as by-products.
- Alcohol is processed at the rate of 0.3 ounce of pure ethanol per hour (less than 1 ounce of whiskey), and unprocessed alcohol circulates in the body. (The alcohol from two cocktails—each about 1.5 ounces—ingested before dinner is still present in the body, in a diminished amount, 3 to 4 hours later.)

The liver's fixed rate of alcohol breakdown means that drinking coffee or taking a cold shower does not speed the sobering process. Therefore, giving coffee to a person who is drunk may produce a wide-awake drunk, a chilling prospect if the drunk and friends are deluded into thinking the drinker is sober enough to drive a car.

Within moments of ingestion, alcohol reaches the brain where it:

1. Stimulates and agitates, initially producing euphoria
2. Depresses and sedates, producing calmness and tranquility
3. Anesthetizes
4. Induces a hypnotic state and sleep

Alcohol quickly depresses inhibitions and judgment. As inhibitions are released the drinker may feel friendlier, more gregarious, and more expansive. The suggestion to "have a drink and loosen up" is based on the biology of alcohol in the body. Sexual inhibitions may be released, which gives alcohol the reputation as an aphrodisiac; in fact, alcohol impairs sexual function and performance, and eventually blunts desire. Increased consumption may produce Jekyll and Hyde personality changes in drinkers, leading to aggressiveness and cruelty. Radical mood changes (such as bouncing from euphoria to self-pity) are also typical characteristics of intoxication.

Alcohol adversely affects motor ability, muscle function, reaction time, eyesight, depth perception, and night vision. Since these are the abilities needed to operate a motor vehicle and since even moderate amounts of alcohol impair these abilities, drivers should never—NEVER—drink and drinkers should not drive.

As a drinker continues to drink, alcohol depresses lung and heart function, slowing breathing and circulation. Death can occur if alcohol completely paralyzes breathing. However, this state is seldom reached because the body rejects alcohol by vomiting, or the drinker becomes comatose before he or she can imbibe a fatal dose. Acute alcohol overdose leading to death occurs most often in situations such as bars or college fraternities where individuals may be encouraged to ingest large amounts of alcohol rapidly.

A hangover is a combination of physical symptoms.

- Headache: Blood vessels in the head, dilated by alcohol, painfully stretch as they return to their normal state.
- Upset stomach: Alcohol irritates the gastric lining, leading to acute gastritis.
- Dehydration: Alcohol acts as a diuretic, stimulating the kidneys to process and pass more water than is ingested.

Hangover is a withdrawal state. If you medicate this withdrawal with more alcohol, the alcohol will continue to circulate in the blood and will not be completely eliminated. Taking amphetamines (uppers) merely masks hangover symptoms.

The best hangover cure is aspirin, liquids, sleep, and time. Bland foods, especially liquids, may also help. The best prevention for a hangover is moderation or abstinence.

PHYSICAL EFFECTS OF ALCOHOL ABUSE

Since alcohol so easily permeates every cell and organ of the body, the physical effects of chronic alcohol abuse are wide-ranging and complex. Large doses of alcohol invade the body's fluids and interfere with metabolism in every cell. Alcohol damages the liver, the central nervous system, the gastrointestinal tract, and the heart. Alcoholics who do not quit drinking decrease life expectancy by 10 to 15 years.

Alcohol also can impair vision, impair sexual function, slow circulation, cause malnutrition, cause water retention (resulting in weight gain and bloating), lead to pancreatitis and skin disorders (such as middle-age acne), dilate blood vessels near the skin causing "brandy nose," weaken the bones and muscles, and decrease immunity.

The liver breaks down alcohol in the body and is therefore the chief site of alcohol damage. Liver damage may occur in three irreversible stages.

- **Fatty Liver.** Liver cells are infiltrated with abnormal fatty tissue, enlarging the liver.
- **Alcoholic Hepatitis.** Liver cells swell, become inflamed, and die, causing blockage. (Causes between 10 and 30 percent mortality rate.)
- **Cirrhosis.** Fibrous scar tissue forms in place of healthy cells, obstructing the flow of blood through the liver. Various functions of the liver deteriorate with often fatal results. (Found in 10 percent of alcoholics.)

A diseased liver:
- Cannot convert stored glycogen into glucose, thus lowering blood sugar and producing hypoglycemia.
- Inefficiently detoxifies the bloodstream and inadequately eliminates drugs, alcohol, and dead red blood cells.
- Cannot manufacture bile (for fat digestion), prothrombin (for blood clotting and bruise prevention), and albumin (for maintaining healthy cells).

Alcohol in the liver also alters the production of digestive enzymes, preventing the absorption of fats and proteins and decreasing the absorption of the vitamins A, D,

E, and K. The decreased production of enzymes also causes diarrhea.

The Brain and Central Nervous System

Alcohol profoundly disturbs the structure and function of the central nervous system, disrupting the ability to retrieve and consolidate information. Even moderate alcohol consumption affects cognitive abilities, while larger amounts interfere with the oxygen supply to the brain, a possible cause of blackout or temporary amnesia during drunkenness. Alcohol abuse destroys brain cells, producing brain deterioration and atrophy, and whether the organic brain damage and neuropsychological impairment linked to alcohol can be reversed is unknown. Alcohol also alters the brain's production of RNA (a genetic "messenger"), and serotonin, endorphins, and natural opiates whose function may be linked to the addictive process.

A neurological disorder called Wernicke-Korsakoff's syndrome results from vitamin B deficiencies produced by alcoholism and the direct action of alcohol on the brain. Symptoms of this condition include amnesia, loss of short-term memory, disorientation, hallucinations, emotional disturbances, double vision, and loss of muscle control. Other effects include mental disorders such as increased aggression, antisocial behavior, depression, and anxiety.

The Digestive System

Large amounts of alcohol may inflame the mouth, esophagus, and stomach, possibly causing cancer in these locations, especially in drinkers who smoke. Alcohol increases the stomach's digestive enzymes, which can irritate the stomach wall, producing heartburn, nausea, gastritis, and ulcers. The stomach of a chronic drinker loses the ability to adequately move food and expel it into the duodenum, leaving some food always in the stomach, causing sluggish digestion and vomiting. Alcohol may also inflame the small and large intestines.

The Heart

Moderate daily drinking may be good for the heart, but for many the risks outweigh the benefits. Even one binge may produce irregular heartbeats, and alcohol abusers experience increased risk of high blood pressure, heart attacks, heart arrhythmia, and heart disease. Alcohol may cause cardiomyopathy (a disease of the heart muscle). Cessation of drinking aids recovery from this condition.

WITHDRAWAL SYMPTOMS

Three to 6 days after a heavy drinker (drinking a fifth of liquor a day) completely stops drinking, alcohol is finally gone from the body, and acute and life-threatening effects may occur. Withdrawal phenomena include sleep disorders such as insomnia, visual and auditory hallucinations, disorientation, alcoholic convulsions, epileptic seizures of the grand mal type, and delirium tremens accompanied by acute anxiety and fear, agitation, fast pulse, fever, and extreme perspiration. Consequently, alcoholics who decide to quit drinking should do so under competent medical supervision.

FETAL ALCOHOL SYNDROME

Definition

Fetal alcohol syndrome (FAS) is a cluster of irreversible birth abnormalities that are the direct result of heavy drinking during pregnancy.

Cause

Alcohol, like most other drugs, passes easily through the mother's placenta and into the fetal bloodstream. In the fetus, the alcohol depresses the central nervous system and must be metabolized by the immature liver of the fetus, which cannot effectively process this toxic substance. The alcohol stays in the fetus's body for a prolonged time (even after leaving the mother's body) and the unborn child remains intoxicated, possibly suffering withdrawal symptoms after the alcohol is no longer present.

Diagnosis

Children born with fetal alcohol syndrome typically are smaller in size, have smaller heads, and suffer deformities of limbs, joints, fingers, and face, as well as heart defects. They may also have cleft palate and poor coordination.

In some children, FAS does not appear until adolescence, when they exhibit hyperactivity and learning and perceptual difficulties. These impairments are symptomatic of minimal brain dysfunction (MBD), which affects between 5 and 19 percent of schoolchildren, according to a study by the National Institute of Alcohol Abuse and Alcoholism. Studies of children with FAS who are now teenagers have uncovered new physical problems—ear infections, hearing and vision loss, and dental problems—that were not identified when the children were first studied at a younger age.

Only a small percentage of the children born to alcoholic women suffer FAS. The reasons for this are unknown, although it is thought that some children have an increased genetic sensitivity to alcohol. Maternal risk factors for this condition include:

- Chronic drinking during pregnancy
- Previous problems with drinking

- Previous children
- Being African-American

Some studies have shown that female light-to-moderate drinkers (so-called social drinkers) give birth to babies with subtle alcohol-related neurological and behavioral problems. Although these problems are less severe than those in children of heavy drinkers, these findings indicate that lesser amounts of alcohol can also cause developmental and behavioral abnormalities.

TREATMENT AND PREVENTION

Pregnant women should abstain from all alcoholic beverages. Women attempting to conceive should also abstain.

PROFILE OF ALCOHOLISM

As noted previously, evidence indicates there may be genetic factors that help determine whether a person will become an alcoholic. A child of an alcoholic has four times the risk of becoming an alcoholic compared with a child of nonalcoholic parents. However, alcoholism is an equal opportunity disease, striking persons of every economic class and race, both genders, and of many ages. Being successful and happy at home or in business is no protection against alcoholism.

For many years, alcoholics were viewed as morally defective persons who were the objects of scorn and pity but were not seen as suffering a disease. While the acceptance of this condition as a disease clears the way for understanding, treatment, and recovery, at the same time alcoholics can and must take responsibility for their own recovery. And since alcoholism, like diabetes, is treatable but not curable, recovery from alcoholism lasts a lifetime.

THE BEGINNING STAGES OF ALCOHOLISM

Like cancer, alcoholism consists of many diseases, and alcoholics develop alcoholism in different ways. Some alcoholics begin drinking to the point of intoxication from their first drink, immediately behaving in ways destructive to health and relationships. Others suffer a progressive disease, beginning with acceptable social drinking. In the early stages of the condition, the alcoholic comes quickly to depend on the mood-altering qualities of alcohol. Drinks aid mood and are used to perk up, calm down, celebrate, mourn, be sociable, or to withdraw. As the disease progresses, the alcoholic does not need a specific reason to drink, and alcohol is ingested every day, or at prescribed periodic times such as weekends.

In the beginning, alcoholics may start a party early by gulping a few quick drinks in the kitchen or they may order doubles when dining out. They feel uncomfortable at social occasions where alcohol is missing. Consumption may be limited and controlled; perhaps to two strong drinks before dinner, moving up to heavier social drinking of three to five a day.

MIDDLE STAGES

In the middle stages of alcoholism, the compulsion to begin drinking manifests itself earlier in the day. The drinker prefers alcohol-related activities and friends who drink. An increasing tolerance for alcohol is accompanied by an increasing lack of control, drunkenness, and blackouts, a type of amnesia that allows functioning (such as making dinner or driving) but which blots out memory of the occasion later on. Drinkers in the middle stages of alcoholism may go in and out of a series of blackouts during one drinking episode.

At this stage of alcoholism, the first drink of the day sets up a craving for more, and the desire for alcohol overwhelms common sense or what is socially appropriate. (Alcoholics Anonymous members say, "It is the first drink that gets you drunk.") Loss of control while drinking may not inevitably cause drunkenness each time (that is a function of the unpredictability of the drinker's behavior), but sooner or later, that "first drink" will lead to an episode of overindulgence. As the disease progresses, the certainty of getting drunk increases.

Drinkers in this stage begin to be secretly ashamed and worried about lack of control. They may try to control their drinking or stop completely, but these attempts often fail. They may switch brands or kinds of alcohol and go from hard liquor to beer. They may seek a "geographic cure," moving to a new city or job in an attempt to cut down, or they may look fruitlessly for some other external formula that will successfully alter their drinking behavior.

Eventually the alcoholic exhibits signs of denial, one of the chief psychological symptoms of alcoholism. By refusing to accept the fact of alcoholism, denial allows the drinker to keep drinking while repressing inner conflict. In the midst of the growing problems linked to alcohol consumption, drinkers blame everything except alcohol for their plight. Rationalizations for drinking become manifest, and unhappy relationships, financial difficulties, and work problems are all blamed for the need to drink. What the drinker fails to comprehend and denies strenuously is that the heavy drinking is not the result of these problems but the cause.

Although drinkers claim they drink to relieve fatigue, anxiety, and depression, alcohol, in large amounts, exacerbates these feelings. Heavy drinking also brings out feelings of anger, self-loathing, and lack of self-esteem and may produce rages expressed against family members and friends.

As drinking progresses, alcoholics experience:

- Stomach upset
- Minor hand tremors
- Increased tolerance for alcohol
- Morning hangover and shaking hands that require tranquilizers or alcohol to treat.

FINAL STAGES

Persons suffering late-stage alcoholism finally grow obsessed with alcohol to the exclusion of almost everything else. They drink despite the pleading of family and the stern advice of doctors. They may begin round-the-clock drinking despite an inability to keep down the first drinks in the morning. Although relationships with family and work may become completely severed, nothing, not even severe health problems, is enough to deter drinking.

The late-stage alcoholic suffers a host of fears, including fear of crowds and public places. Constant remorse and guilt is alleviated with more drinking. On top of mental disturbances, debts, legal problems, and homelessness may complicate his or her life. Late-stage addiction is characterized by cirrhosis and severe withdrawal symptoms if alcohol is withheld (shakes, delirium tremens, and convulsions). Without hospitalization or residency in a therapeutic community, late-stage alcoholics usually succumb to insanity and death.

People suffering alcoholism do not have to "hit bottom" and reach the extreme late stages of alcoholism to decide to get help. Many men and women have recognized their alcohol problems before they lost their jobs or families, or began drinking in the morning, suffered DTs, or had to be hospitalized. For them, the labels "early stage," late stage," "problem drinker," or "alcoholic" were less important than the fact that their growing powerlessness over alcohol was causing them pain.

DIAGNOSIS OF ALCOHOLISM

In some cases, the "diagnosis" of alcoholism is made by the courts, as when a judge hands down a drunk driving sentence that includes a requirement to attend Alcoholics Anonymous (AA), or to enter a rehabilitation program. The emergency rooms of hospitals make such diagnoses when a man or woman appears suffering from alcohol poisoning or withdrawal. Some doctors, however, may miss the diagnosis of alcoholism, in part because patients rarely admit to excessive consumption;

50 percent of persons with alcoholism seen by doctors are incorrectly diagnosed.

Families may diagnose alcoholism when a family member is hospitalized for the disease or when a spouse leaves because of a drinking problem. However, families may suffer from alcoholism denial in which they completely or partially deny the problem.

INITIAL-STAGE DENIAL

- Excuses for the drinker's behavior are made to bosses, friends, colleagues, or subordinates.
- A pattern of lies is woven to cover up for lateness, missed appointments, or irresponsibility.
- The excuses and lies "enable" the alcoholic to continue drinking and avoid consequences of his or her behavior.

LATE-STAGE DENIAL

- Family members lose perspective on the problem.
- The alcoholic promises to stop drinking, then breaks the promise; the alcoholic's spouse makes more demands in an attempt to control the drinking.
- The spouse of the alcoholic grows suspicious, angry, and despairing.
- The home environment grows deeply unhappy.

In late-stage denial, the most helpful action for a spouse, family member, or friend is to stop enabling the alcoholic. Alcoholics must admit their problem, see that they are powerless over alcohol and that alcohol has made their lives unmanageable. This realization is difficult if the people around them protect them from the consequences of their behavior. When family members let alcoholics experience these doses of reality, without covering up, the individual with the drinking problem may arrive at a personal moment of truth.

Families and friends of alcoholics must do several things to help the alcoholic stop drinking.

1. Abandon wishful thinking that the alcoholic will someday be able to drink safely, recognizing that alcoholism is nearly always progressive.
2. Stop enabling the alcoholic to continue drinking (stop covering up for the drinker's irresponsible behavior).
3. Seek information about alcoholism and its treatment as a disease.

TREATMENT OF ALCOHOLISM

Alcoholism enjoys a good recovery rate once the alcoholic stops drinking. Treatment takes many forms because there are many kinds of alcoholics, each with special needs. Treatment sources include hospitals, alcoholism units within hospitals, private clinics designed solely for the care of alcoholics, residential alcoholic rehabilitation facilities, self-help groups such as Alcoholics Anonymous, and private practitioners such as alcoholism counselors, psychologists, psychiatric social workers, and psychiatrists.

For a small number of alcoholics, a brief stay of 3 to 10 days in a detoxification center may be necessary. Candidates for detoxification are those who suffer withdrawal symptoms because of the alcohol addiction. At the detox center (hospital unit, nonmedical alcoholism facility, or other institution) the alcoholic's body can clear itself of the alcohol's toxic effects. The patient is cared for with rest, nutritious diet, abstinence from alcohol, and careful medical attention, which may include medication to reduce anxiety and manage withdrawal symptoms and psychiatric evaluation to determine the presence or absence of treatable psychiatric disorders such as depression or anxiety. Treating these, however, will not treat the alcoholism, but not treating them is likely to be associated with failure of the alcoholism treatment.

For long-term care, the alcoholic can recover at a rehabilitation center or in the inpatient treatment unit of a hospital. These centers provide alcohol-free environments; continued medical care; group, individual, and family therapy; classes about alcoholism; and regular Alcoholics Anonymous meetings.

Alcoholics Anonymous (AA) and its subgroups—Al-Anon for family members of alcoholics and Alateen for teenage children of alcoholics—are self-help organizations that provide experienced advice and support for alcoholics and their families. From 7,000 responses to an informal survey the organization sent to its members in the United States and Canada, 29 percent indicated they had remained sober for more than 5 years, 38 percent for 1 to 5 years, and 33 percent for less than 1 year. Sixty percent of the respondents had sought counseling for alcoholism prior to joining AA. While a scientific analysis of the sobriety success rate for AA is difficult (the organization does not keep membership lists and does not promote itself with sobriety rates), most experts recognize AA as the core of any alcoholic therapy. The "12-step" approach of AA has been widely copied in other self-help groups.

Outpatient care is also available to patients at rehab centers, allowing individuals to return to work and home while receiving therapy. These centers do not "dry out" alcoholics but provide therapeutic settings in which a bridge back to a normal life can be built.

Many alcoholics do not require detox centers or rehab programs but start treatment with a thorough physical exam by a doctor to diagnose possible alcohol-related conditions. The doctor can ease the alcoholic's mind by giving him or her a clean bill of health or by setting up a schedule of continuing care to manage chronic health problems.

Early recovery from alcohol is marked by:

- Occasional thoughts of drinking, especially at times of stress or at cocktail hour. Although the compulsion to drink may be absent, drink desires are a natural reminder of years of drinking and should gradually diminish and need not be alarming.
- Mood swings. Elation may yield to discouragement and tears. Gradually these wide shifts of mood should moderate.

To combat the early problems of recovery, the alcoholic should:

- Receive plenty of patience from friends and family.
- Take adequate rest and a nutritious diet.
- Join a support group such as AA to share experiences with other people suffering alcoholism.

To help with sobriety, some alcoholics receive Antabuse (disulfiram), a drug that intervenes in the liver's alcohol metabolism, preventing the breakdown of acetaldehyde (an intermediate product of alcohol metabolism). After the administration of Antabuse, even a small sip of alcohol produces acetaldehyde accumulation and nausea, vomiting, severe headache, breathing difficulties, blurred vision, lowered blood pressure, and feelings of impending death.

Antabuse use must be consented to by the recovering alcoholic with the clear understanding of its effects. The drug neither alters the alcoholic's mood nor removes urges to drink. Not an instant solution or complete therapy, this drug deters drinking and can play a useful part in treatment if it makes recovering alcoholics feel "protected" from alcohol while learning to stay sober. Antabuse is administered only until the recovering alcoholic feels ready to live without it; it is not taken long term.

The narcotic antagonist Naltrexone has recently been approved by the FDA for use in treating alcoholism. It appears to diminish alcohol's pleasurable effects and thus helps keep a "lapse" from becoming a "relapse." Like Antabuse, it is not a cure-all and should be given in the context of relapse prevention training and supportive counseling.

Mood-altering drugs such as tranquilizers may occasionally be administered during recovery to quell anxiety. However, one drug habit should not be substituted for another—tranquilizers may be addicting. While some emotional conditions such as manic-depressive psychosis require pharmacological solutions, sobriety should generally be drug-free. This should not prevent individuals who need medications, such as for severe depression, from taking them. While some AA groups discourage even lithium or antidepressants, the Central AA Council recognizes the important role such medications can play for some recovering alcoholics.

LIVING SOBER

Quitting drinking is only the first step in recovering from alcoholism. Learning to live without alcohol requires adjustment in attitudes, values, and lifestyles. If serious psychological disturbances have developed because of drinking, psychiatric counseling designed for alcohol abusers may be required. Occupational rehabilitation or vocational guidance also may be necessary.

Abstinence is the absence of alcohol or drugs; sobriety is a way of life. Recovery begins where formal treatment leaves off, and this lifelong process never ends. In developing a new way of life, many factors play a part. Recovering alcoholics should avoid people, places, and objects associated with their drinking. After being sober for some time, alcoholics should make new friends and engage in new activities by going to school, returning to work, learning a new hobby, doing volunteer work, or renewing a lost association with their churches or religious groups.

Positive addictions should be substituted for alcohol addiction: Walking, jogging, sports, or a regular schedule of exercise promotes well-being and self-esteem and provides a healthy outlet for energy. Research indicates that exercise releases brain chemicals that stimulate a natural high. Even a walk after dinner can act as a tranquilizer that helps alleviate the urge for alcohol.

PREVENTION OF ALCOHOL ABUSE

The National Institute on Alcohol Abuse and Alcoholism defines moderate drinking as an average of not more than two drinks per day, and estimates that 15 million adults (15 percent of the drinkers in the United States) consume more than that amount. The 15 percent of men and 3 percent of women who ingest more than four drinks a day risk a serious drinking problem. Anyone, even safe drinkers, can become a statistic when one night's overindulgence leads to a drunk driving incident, a violent family argument, an incapacitating hangover, or some other mishap.

Efforts at moderation do not have to be prohibitionist or puritanical. Americans need to view moderation or abstinence as life-enhancing choices rather than negative self-denial.

In a statement of goals, the U.S. Department of Health and Humans Services has sought:

1. A freeze in the per capita consumption of alcohol
2. No increase in the proportion of adolescent drinkers

3. A reduction in the cirrhosis death rate and the number of deaths from alcohol-related accidents
4. A reduction in the infants born with fetal alcohol syndrome
5. Increased general public and adolescent awareness of the risks associated with alcohol abuse

Because alcohol use is generally accepted in modern society and alcohol is constantly available (while treatment for alcoholism is not always easy to obtain), these goals present a constant challenge. Most problem drinkers are not presently receiving formal treatment apart from what AA offers. The available treatments are most effective for socially stable, middle-class alcoholics and least effective for the homeless without families.

The need to provide increased services of better quality to those with alcoholism is urgent. The major burden of coping with this complex drug problem continues to fall on the individuals and families most directly affected. A further enlightened public policy on alcoholism addressing legal drinking ages, liquor labeling, laws governing drunk drivers, and public education is still necessary.

A variety of sources of information about alcoholism is available. The Yellow Pages lists resources under "Alcoholism." Local chapters of the National Council on Alcoholism provide information and referrals. Alcoholics Anonymous and Al-Anon family groups are listed in both the white and the Yellow Pages of the telephone directory. For printed materials, contact the National Clearinghouse of the National Institute on Alcohol Abuse and Alcoholism. (For more information see appendix B, Directory of Health Organizations and Resources.)

PSYCHOTHERAPEUTIC DRUGS

DEFINITION

Psychotherapeutic drugs are substances that alter mood. The use of these kinds of drugs is an ancient human custom. For example, South American Indians have a long history of coping with the rigors of high-altitude living by chewing coca leaves, from which cocaine is derived. In the 20th century, major pharmacological advances have produced drugs for many purposes: to calm or excite, to decrease or increase appetite, and to alter the senses of seeing, hearing, touching, or tasting. Some of these substances have legitimate uses (see chapter 34, Proper Use of Medication), but for some people, mood-altering drugs create dependency or addiction.

Antianxiety drugs such as Valium or Librium, sedatives and antidepressant drugs such as Elavil and Tofranil are often misused, and these drugs should be taken only as needed under careful medical supervision.

Drug abuse information is available from the National Clearinghouse for Alcohol and Drug Information. (See appendix B, Directory of Health Organizations and Resources.)

SEDATIVE-HYPNOTIC DRUGS

Sedative-hypnotic drugs depress central nervous system function. Used both as tranquilizers and sleeping pills according to the dosage, these pharmaceuticals are prescribed to quell anxiety, produce calm, and promote sleep; in addition, they are used as anticonvulsants and muscle relaxants. They fall into two major categories:

1. Barbiturates (Seconal, Nembutal, Tuinal). These are classed as short acting or long acting, depending on the time it takes for the liver and kidneys to metabolize the drug and how long it circulates in the blood. Abusers tend to prefer short-acting barbiturates such as Seconal and Nembutal, which are also the most addictive and have the most deleterious health consequences.

Barbiturate abusers may also abuse amphetamines in an attempt to balance the sedative effects of barbiturates. Barbiturate hangovers are commonly medicated with "speed" or "uppers" to create a sense of wakefulness and alertness. Cross-addiction of this type produces strenuous and injurious demands on the body.

Because alcohol and barbiturates are so similar in chemical effect, their combination may be fatal and they should never be consumed at the same time. Even small doses of barbiturates combined with alcohol can be dangerous. Lethal overdoses can occur when users become confused and accidentally take a higher dose than intended or deliberately take more to get to sleep.

The effects of overuse include nausea, hangover symptoms, confusion, low blood pressure, and depressed breathing functions.

Barbiturate addicts, like alcoholics, become obsessed with use of the drug and neglect family, work, and health. They can become anxious, insomniac, paranoid, and suicidally depressed.

2. Benzodiazepines (Valium, Librium).

With regular use, these drugs can create psychological and physical dependency similar to that of barbiturates. At first, abusers depend on the drug to medicate normal stresses, enjoy a mild high, and sleep, but as the drugs produce tolerance in the body, larger doses are required to derive sedative effects. Finally, if the drug is discontinued, the user suffers withdrawal symptoms.

Withdrawal from barbiturates and some benzodiazepines (notably Valium) can be severe and life-threatening, resembling alcohol withdrawal with delirium tremens, rapid pulse, weakness, convulsions, anxiety, restlessness, hallucinations, and temporary psychosis. Death can result from seizures and from exhaustion during the psychotic stage. Withdrawal should be attempted only under medical supervision, preferably in a hospital where it can be safely managed by slowly decreasing the amount of the drug in the body.

AMPHETAMINES

DEFINITION

Amphetamines are a group of closely related drugs that stimulate the central and peripheral nervous systems.

First sold as the inhalant Benzedrine in 1932, amphetamines were issued to U.S. troops during World War II as a stimulant to increase endurance and combat fatigue. After the war they were medically prescribed as antidepressants and diet aids, but today their medical uses are mostly limited to combating narcolepsy (a sleep disorder) and hyperactivity in children, in whom the drug has the paradoxical effect of sedation.

Amphetamines produce an intense alertness and false confidence in the user's sense of perseverance, energy, and mental abilities. Users become talkative, excited, and restless, and feel capable of working tirelessly with special insights.

Despite the alertness produced by the drug, this substance does not in fact improve performance or thinking but merely conveys the impression that these functions are boosted. The euphoric effects of these drugs and their ability to counteract fatigue make them particularly popular with long-distance truck drivers, students, performers, athletes, and others who may need to stay awake for long periods of time.

The three classes of amphetamines are amphetamine, dextroamphetamine, and methamphetamine.

These drugs are usually consumed as pills (bennies, pep pills, diet pills, or uppers). They can also be injected for faster and stronger effect, a method often used by chronic abusers ("speed freaks").

EFFECT

Amphetamines activate adrenaline, which stimulates the central nervous system and creates a sensation of energy. Side effects include:

- Decreased appetite
- Decreased saliva and nasal mucus
- Enlarged nasal and bronchial passages
- Increased heart rate and blood pressure and faster breathing

Large doses may induce:

- Irregular heartbeat
- Restlessness and anxiety
- Aggressive or violent behavior

Although amphetamines are physically addictive, the withdrawal symptoms are milder than with alcohol or narcotics. They produce tolerance and a psychological dependence that is greater than the physical one. Users may feel they can function normally only when they are "speeding," and may require larger doses and stay on a speed bender for days. When a bender ends, users "crash," experiencing enormous fatigue, depression, anxiety, and hunger. They may attempt to sleep but have to medicate insomnia with barbiturates, sometimes creating a dual addiction with both amphetamines and sedatives.

Chronic amphetamine abusers suffer:

- Excitability
- Extreme restlessness
- Exhaustion from lack of sleep
- Loss of appetite and malnutrition

Psychological effects include:

- Anxiety
- Depression and thoughts of suicide
- Paranoia and persecution mania

Amphetamine abusers tend to be antisocial and exhibit aggressive or violent behavior. Abstinence from amphetamines results in a slow diminishment of symptoms (6 months to 1 year), but recovery is usually complete.

....

ILLICIT DRUGS

Although use of alcohol, tobacco, and psychotherapeutic drugs is rampant, use of illicit drugs such as marijuana, cocaine, and heroin arouses the most public concern. The dire health consequences of illicit drug use—death from overdose, allergic reactions, and cardiac complications—are more unpredictable and sudden than they are for "legal" drugs. While prolonged use of tobacco can result in death from various diseases and alcohol consumption can damage the heart, liver, gastrointestinal tract, and central nervous system, and both decrease life expectancy, no one worries that one drink or one cigarette is going to be fatal. Conversely, users of illicit drugs constantly risk death, and a novice user of cocaine can die from cardiac arrest caused by a dose normally tolerated by habitual users. Deaths of well-known athletes from cocaine are grim reminders of the vagaries of illicit drug use.

The repercussions of illicit drug use have reverberated through society. The U.S. government has spent billions fighting illegal drugs, attempting to destroy supplies as well as apprehend and prosecute drug dealers. Attempts to destroy drugs at their source has embroiled the government in international conflict with Third World nations whose economies benefit from the drug trade. Trafficking in illegal drugs, especially the trade in cocaine, has burdened society with myriad costs: lost job productivity, lives lost to suicide and violence, disrupted families, medical treatment for addicts and babies born to addicted mothers, and drug-related crime.

In recent years more than two-thirds of those arrested for other than drug-related crimes have tested positive for illegal drugs. One study showed that 92 percent of persons arrested for robbery and 80 percent for burglary had illicit drugs in their systems.

Illicit use of crack—a form of cocaine that is smoked—has had a devastating impact on inner-city neighborhoods and crime. Use of this particular drug is blamed for much of the skyrocketing crime rate responsible for large increases in prison populations.

Babies born to addicted mothers using IV drugs are often born addicted themselves and/or infected with HIV. Of these unfortunate children, many develop AIDS and die; others are abandoned by their mothers and incur immense medical costs at hospitals. In addition to the personal tragedy that these unwanted children represent, the economic burden of their care is another cost to society from illicit drug use.

Some advocate increases in drug treatment programs for addicts to reduce the demand for these substances. It is estimated that a dollar spent on treatment saves $7 elsewhere in the health care system, and is 7 to 20 times more effective in reducing heavy cocaine use than are funds spend on supply reduction activities.

The use of these drugs is not new. Opiates (of which heroin is one type), cocaine, and cannabis (marijuana) have been used in one form or another for centuries around the world. Government surveys show that the total number of U.S. citizens using illicit drugs peaked in the late 1970s and early 1980s. Although antidrug efforts have sharply reduced marijuana use and nonaddictive use of cocaine, heavy cocaine use remains high and may even be increasing. While illicit drugs were used more widely in the 1970s by youth than they are today, use still remains quite high and in some cases is still increasing:

- 4 of 5 Americans in their mid-twenties have used illicit drugs at least once.
- More than 21 million over age 27 have tried illicit drugs at least once.
- 1 of 5 high school seniors uses marijuana. Marijuana use is at the lowest level since the early 1970s

but appears to be on the rise again after decreasing during the 1980s.

- 3 to 6 million people currently use cocaine. Half of them are age 18 to 25. There are an estimated 2 million cocaine addicts.
- 600,000 people are addicted to heroin, and the number appears to be rising as cocaine addicts switch to heroin.

Chronic, heavy users of illicit drugs face serious health hazards including increased danger of accidents and premature death. Even occasional cocaine users face serious consequences. During the past 15 years hospital emergency rooms report sharp increases in cocaine-related visits; the number of individuals entering drug abuse treatment for cocaine has multiplied greatly, as have cocaine-linked deaths.

While use of one drug does not always lead to use of others, heavy consumption opens the user to an environment that may encourage the use of other illicit substances. Studies of these three "gateway drugs"—alcohol, tobacco, and marijuana—show that adolescents who use one or more of these are at greater risk to go on to use cocaine or heroin. The earlier their use, and the more types are used, the greater the risk of progression.

COCAINE

DEFINITION

Cocaine is derived from the leaves of the coca bush, which grows in the Andes of South America. Used for centuries by Indians to combat the effects of hunger, hard work, and thin air, in the mid 1800s its effects were praised by Freud, among others. Until 1906, this substance was a chief ingredient of Coca-Cola and was also used as a topical anesthetic. Widespread use and addiction led to government efforts against cocaine in the early 1900s. The danger associated with cocaine was ignored in the 1970s and early 1980s, and cocaine was proclaimed by many to be safe. With the accumulating medical evidence of cocaine's deleterious effects and the introduction and widespread use of "crack" cocaine, the public and government have become alarmed again about its growing use. To many Americans, especially health care and social workers who deal with crack users and have witnessed the personal and societal devastation it produces, the pervasive use of cocaine is, by far, the most serious drug problem in the United States.

EFFECTS AND METHODS OF INGESTION

Like the amphetamines, cocaine stimulates the central nervous system. This drug is usually ingested in three ways.

1. Sniffing or snorting it into the nose, where it is absorbed by the mucous membranes
2. Injecting it intravenously
3. Freebase smoking

(Occasionally this substance may be swallowed or sprayed from an atomizer into the back of the mouth or throat.)

Crack is smoked in cigarettes or glass pipes and sometimes mixed with marijuana. Much of it is laced with other drugs, such as amphetamines.

The effects of cocaine are pleasurable, immediate, and brief. It produces intense but short-lived euphoria and can make users feel more energetic. Like caffeine, cocaine produces wakefulness and reduces hunger. Psychological effects include feelings of well-being and a grandiose sense of power and ability mixed with anxiety and restlessness. As the drug wears off, these temporary sensations of mastery are replaced by depression.

HEALTH EFFECTS

Even though the public is often regaled with highly publicized accounts of deaths from cocaine, many still mistakenly believe the drug, especially when sniffed, to be nonaddictive and not as harmful as other illicit drugs. Cocaine's immediate physical effects include raised breathing rate, raised blood pressure and body temperature, and dilated pupils.

By causing the coronary arteries to constrict, blood pressure rises and the blood supply to the heart diminishes, possibly causing heart attacks or convulsions within an hour after use. Chronic users and those with hypertension, epilepsy, and cardiovascular disease are at particular risk. Studies show that even those with normal coronary arteriograms risk cardiac complications from cocaine. Increased use may sensitize the brain to the drug's effects so that less of the substance is needed to induce a seizure. Those who inject the drug are at high risk for AIDS and hepatitis when they share needles. Allergic reactions to cocaine or other substances mixed in with the drug may also occur.

Other unpleasant side effects of cocaine include:

- Insomnia and headache
- Nausea and vomiting
- Loss of appetite leading to malnutrition and weight loss
- Cold sweats
- Swelling and bleeding of mucous membranes
- Restlessness and anxiety

In the 1970s cocaine was expensive and considered a "status" drug. The introduction of inexpensive crack increased the accessibility of this substance, and crack has become the drug of choice for many drug users, especially inner-city disadvantaged youth. Crack's convenience, ease of concealment, wide availability, and low cost have increased its use. The fact that it is smoked rather than snorted or injected (ingestion methods associated with the stigma of being a "junkie") has contributed to its popularity.

Crack is particularly dangerous for several reasons.

• Because it is inhaled and rapidly absorbed through the lungs, into the blood, and carried swiftly to the brain, the chances of overdosing and poisoning leading to coma, convulsions, and death are greatly increased over other forms of cocaine ingestion.

• Crack's rapid rush—5 to 7 minutes of intense pleasure—quickly subsides, leading to depression that needs to be relieved by more crack. This cycle enhances the chances of addiction and dependency. Because of the brief high, users are constantly thinking about and devising ways to get more crack.

• Psychologically, the drug reduces concentration, ambition, and drive, and increases confusion and irritability, wreaking havoc on users' professional and personal lives.

• Habitual use may lead to cocaine psychosis, causing paranoia, hallucinations, and a condition known as formication, in which insects or snakes are perceived to be crawling under the skin. The paranoia and depression can instigate violent and suicidal behavior.

The side effects of adulterants increase cocaine's risks. The drug is often cut with one or more of any number of other substances, such as the cheaper drugs procaine, lidocaine, and benzocaine, and substances that pose no serious risks, such as sugars (mannitol and sucrose), or starches. However, when quinine or amphetamines are added, the potential for serious side effects increases dramatically.

TREATMENT

Treatment for cocaine abuse utilizes counseling and rehabilitation. Individuals who are suicidal, psychotic, or very ill may need hospitalization. Several programs, such as Cocaine Anonymous, which uses AA as a model, provide self-help groups. Certain medications are being researched as alternatives for unsuccessful rehabilitative efforts, but no medication has yet been found to be generally effective.

Cocaine is quickly cleared from the body, and detoxification generally takes several days, but feelings of anxiety and depression may last for weeks. Recovering individuals may mourn the loss of a lifestyle and friendships centered around drugs and may have to confront unpleasant family and economic situations.

MARIJUANA

Marijuana is the most widely used illegal drug. Derived from the plant *Cannabis sativa* (the hemp plant), this psychoactive (mind-altering) drug is grown wild and cultivated in many parts of the world.

EFFECTS AND METHODS OF INGESTION

Marijuana can be put in foods and eaten, but generally it is smoked in cigarettes or "joints," made of the dried leaves, flowers, and small stems of the plant. The active ingredient in this drug is delta-9-tetrahydrocannabinol (THC); the average joint may contain up to 6 percent THC, a substantial rise from the 0.4 percent average content of joints in the early 1970s. Hashish, or hash, is the resinous part of *Cannabis*, pressed into cakes that are smoked. This much more potent form of the drug contains between 3 and 8 percent THC.

The psychological effects of marijuana are a mild sense of well-being, a disconnected sense of time, a dreamy consciousness and self-absorption, and a reduced ability to think and communicate clearly.

Undesirable mental and physical effects include:

• Paranoia, panic, anxiety and fear
• Unpleasant hallucination-like distortions of the senses
• Faster heartbeat (increased by up to 50 percent)
• Bloodshot eyes, dry mouth and throat
• Decreased motor abilities and reaction time
• Altered depth perception
• Impaired short-term memory

At doses usually used in this country, marijuana usually does not produce physical addiction, but dependence may result with regular long-term use. The harmfulness of dependence is clearly seen in teen users who suffer impaired learning abilities (both verbal and mathematical), reduced attention span, and lowered problem-solving skills and reading comprehension. Use of this drug between one and three times per day may interfere with acquiring necessary social skills at crucial times of development, and teenagers may turn to the isolation and escapism of the drug rather than developing healthy coping mechanisms.

Teenagers introduced to marijuana by their friends experience social pressure to use the drug, which is reinforced by the ritual of rolling and smoking a joint and by the fact that marijuana is illegal, enhancing its attraction. While marijuana use is often preceded by alcohol use and smoking, the relationship between use of these substances is complex. Heavy marijuana users are more likely than moderate users to use other drugs such as barbiturates, amphetamines, LSD, or cocaine.

Studies show that long-term marijuana use may cause

cancer. Marijuana smoke, like any smoke, inflames the lungs, irritates air passages, and impairs pulmonary function. It contains several carcinogenic tars and because smokers hold the smoke in the lungs deeply, lung tissue is exposed to these toxins for a prolonged period. Chronic marijuana use results in metaplasia, a precancerous condition of lung cells.

Pregnant women should not use marijuana because it enters the baby's bloodstream through the placenta. The drug may cause stillbirth or spontaneous abortion, and fetuses exposed to marijuana may be born at lower weight than babies of nonsmoking mothers. Breast-feeding mothers should also abstain since evidence indicates the drug is transferred to breast milk.

OPIATES

Opiates—derived from the opium poppy, grown mostly in Asia—include opium, morphine, and heroin. Opiates were both legal and widely available in the 1800s and were thought to have beneficial effects on disorders such as diabetes, diarrhea, and "women's troubles." After these drugs were used to relieve pain during the Civil War, many wounded soldiers became addicted.

METHODS OF INGESTION AND EFFECTS

Opiates can be eaten, inhaled, smoked, and injected (sometimes called "mainlining"). They act as painkillers and tranquilizers and produce euphoria in experienced users; pleasurable sensations are not usually reported by first-time users. Long-term users may experience pleasure when administration of opiates quells the drug's withdrawal symptoms such as shakes, sweating, tremors, hot and cold flashes, anxiety, and craving.

Unlike alcohol, which produces alcoholism only in susceptible individuals over a period of time ranging from 5 to 10 years, opiates can rapidly produce addiction in almost any regular user. Effects of chronic use include:

- Tolerance for the drug
- Psychological and physical addiction manifested in intense craving
- Physical ailments such as liver dysfunction, pneumonia, lung abscesses, and brain disorders (these are related to the route of administration and impurities rather than the drug itself)

Injections of opiates may result in:

- Skin abscesses and ulcers
- Phlebitis
- Excessive scarring
- Bacterial endocarditis
- AIDS if an infected needle is used
- Death from overdose when the central nervous system is depressed and the heart rate is arrested

TREATMENT

Heroin addicts are often treated with methadone, a synthetic opiate that eases withdrawal and, when administered as part of a comprehensive outpatient program at a clinic or hospital, may help addicts stay off the street and begin the recovery process. Whereas some heroin addicts are able to do well on methadone, successfully detoxify, and stay drug-free, others must stay on methadone for years in order to remain off heroin. Even though methadone causes physical dependence, chronically maintained individuals can work, refrain from illegal drugs and activities, and appear normal. However, use of other drugs such as cocaine and alcohol is a problem in many methadone programs. The narcotic antagonist Naltrexone is not addicting and blocks the effects of heroin. It has been especially useful in the treatment of employed addicts with family support and needs to be given only three times a week.

Nondrug treatments such as therapeutic communities work well as long as addicts remain in residence, but the dropout rate is high.

Craving for heroin can be triggered in times of stress, anxiety, or depression, even if the addict has been drug-free for years. Research continues on the possible social, psychological, and biological causes of heroin addiction, and on appropriate treatment and recovery programs.

PSYCHEDELIC DRUGS

DEFINITION

The term psychedelic refers to mind-expanding or mind-manifesting substances. The psychedelic drugs include lysergic acid diethylamide (LSD or acid), mescaline derived from the peyote cactus, and psilocybin, which comes from certain mushrooms.

METHODS OF INGESTION AND EFFECTS

These substances are almost always taken orally, although liquid forms of LSD may be injected wtih great potential hazard.

The main effects are psychological rather than physical and vary according to the user's mood and expectations, and the environment in which the drug is ingested. The highly unpredictable effects include:

- Distortion of sense perceptions
- Difficulty in speaking or communicating

- Suspended sense of time
- Feeling of motor paralysis alternating with hyper-activity
- Depressed appetite and loss of sexual desire

Unpleasant experiences on these drugs ("bad trips") may cause paranoia, feeling out of control, panic, and viewing other people as grotesque distortions.

Psychedelics do not produce physical or psychological addiction. However, some individuals may experience prolonged psychosis and may require therapy or institutionalization. Whether these drugs cause this condition or merely expose a previous tendency is unknown.

LSD users are susceptible to "flashbacks" of the drug experience up to a year afterward, and many experience spontaneous recurrence of visual or sensory distortions. The long-term effects of heavy use include impaired mental function and distorted abstract reasoning.

INHALANTS

DEFINITION AND METHODS OF INGESTION

Inhalants are volatile substances that, while never intended to be used as drugs, are abused because of their mind-altering effects. The chief abusers of inhalants are children from 7 to 17, who sniff these household products because they are easily available at home or at the supermarket.

The inhalants include solvents like gasoline, cleaning fluids, liquid shoe polish, lacquer, nail polish remover, and airplane glue; aerosols like spray paint, insecticides, and hair spray; and anesthetics like nitrous oxide (laughing gas). Also abused are the volatile nitrates such as amyl nitrate, which is used to treat chest pains in heart patients by dilating blood vessels and accelerating heart rate. Amyl nitrate is packaged in covered vials (poppers or snappers) that are broken open and inhaled. Butyl nitrate is the over-the-counter version of amyl nitrate.

EFFECTS

Inhalants temporarily stimulate before they depress the central nervous system. Their immediate effects include:

- Dreamy euphoria, which may last from a few minutes to hours
- Mental confusion
- Hallucinations
- Dizziness, nausea, and lack of coordination
- Fatigue

- Loss of appetite
- Blackouts

Death, which can occur from first-time use, may result from instant heart failure, from sniffing substances in high concentrations (oxygen is displaced in the lungs), and suffocation from the depression of respiratory functions. Long-term effects include weight loss, fatigue, muscle fatigue, and, in certain cases, damage to the nervous system, liver, kidneys, blood, and bone marrow.

DRUGS IN THE WORKPLACE

Drugs decrease the efficiency of the American workforce. Used by individuals of all occupations, these substances compromise productivity at great cost.

- The annual cost of employee drug use to businesses is estimated at $60 billion, about half of which is lost productivity.
- Employees working under the influence of drugs are one-third less productive than those who are drug-free.
- Workers impaired by drugs are four times as likely to injure themselves or a co-worker in an accident as those who are drug-free.
- Drug use substantially boosts health claims, worker's compensation claims, and theft and corruption.

Measures often suggested to combat workplace drug use include:

- Explicit drug-free workplace policies
- Pre-employment drug testing
- Random tests of employees and tests of employees suspected of using drugs
- Referral to drug treatment programs for employees who are using drugs
- Dismissal of employees with intractable drug problems

TEENAGERS AND DRUGS

Almost two-thirds of American teenagers experiment with drugs before they finish high school, and more than one-third use an illicit drug other than marijuana. One survey found that 7 percent used marijuana daily, 6 percent drank alcohol daily, and 20 percent smoked cigarettes every day.

In the United States, drug use by teenagers follows a clear-cut sequence.

1. Beer and wine are the initial drugs used by teens.
2. Tobacco and hard liquor are used after introduction to beer and wine.
3. Marijuana is tried, often together with alcohol.
4. Illicit drugs such as psychedelics or heroin may be used after, or in conjunction with, marijuana.

This sequence does not indicate that all teenagers inevitably experience all of these steps. Use of beer or marijuana does not always lead to use of other drugs such as psychedelics, heroin, or cocaine.

Marijuana users are most actively involved with the drug in their early 20s, but use begins to decline by age 23. For many drug users, the process of growing up—marrying, working, or having children—puts a brake on drug use. Other users replace marijuana and illicit drugs with alcohol or abused prescription drugs.

Teenagers are primarily influenced by their parents and their peers through:

• Cigarette smoking: Almost exclusively determined by peer pressure, although parents who smoke increase the chances of children smoking.
• Hard liquor use: Drinking patterns are often learned from parents.
• Marijuana use: Usually initiated through friends and peers.
• Illicit drug use: Usually associated with poor relationships with parents, exposure to parents and peers who misuse drugs, and by depression or psychological distress.

To reduce the chances of children abusing drugs, parents should:

• Provide accurate information about drugs and alcohol before the child reaches adolescence (some children use alcohol by age 10). Present drug information with the same care with which information about sexuality or religion is presented. Avoid lectures or scare tactics.
• Do not abuse alcohol or other drugs—parental drug use forms a model for children's values and behavior.
• Keep lines of communication open; teenagers who cannot talk to their parents may further isolate themselves with drugs.
• Give children a sense of themselves as valuable individuals, capable of making the right choices. Responsibility, self-esteem, and good judgment are better tools for coping with adolescence and its stresses than overprotective parents.

If parents suspect their children are abusing drugs, they should look for behavioral changes that may signal drug involvement. According to the Department of Health and Human Services, these behaviors include an abrupt change in mood or attitude, a sudden decline in attendance or performance at work or school, or associating with a new group of friends, especially friends who use drugs.

Keep in mind that adolescence is a turbulent time and these changes many not necessarily be drug related. Positive proof of drug use may only come from admission by the teenager, by the presence of drug paraphernalia in the teenager's room, or by obvious drug intoxication.

Discussions of drugs with children should avoid accusations, sarcasm, and blame, but should be supportive, understanding, and firm to keep children from feeling isolated and defensive. Parents must create a calm atmosphere, emphasizing mutual caring and reiterating family values on drug and alcohol use. If the drug situation cannot be handled by the family alone, parents can turn to school counselors, the family doctor, adolescent drug treatment centers, mental health professionals, and drug abuse information centers.

THE DRUG USE EPIDEMIC

Will the use of illicit drugs in the United States decline on its own, the way other epidemics have petered out? Experts cannot arrive at a consensus on this question. One theory proposes that drug use runs in cycles: A period of widespread use, as occurred during the 1960s or in the early 1900s, is followed by intolerance and declining use, a result of the recognition of the health and societal consequences of drugs. If this theory is accurate, then the recent public outcry against drugs is an indication of an intolerant period taking place.

But some experts believe that drugs such as marijuana and LSD have become permanent features of the landscape. And whether or not the drug epidemic may die of natural causes, campaigns against drug use—especially drug use among the young—continue.

The battle against the so-called hard drugs such as cocaine and heroin has had its occasional victories but has not brought major decreases in hard core use. Although heroin addicts often have access to a variety of treatment services, such as methadone maintenance programs and drug-free maintenance programs, the relapse rate is large. There are also long waiting lists in many places. It is estimated that only one-fourth of heroin addicts can be treated. The United States' treatment capacity is approximately 1.4 million persons per year, but about double that is needed.

For some addicts—those with the most to gain by forgoing drugs—rehabilitation frequently seems to work. For those alienated from society with few prospects of prosperity, habilitation is necessary, and treatment is not as effective.

··

SUMMING UP

The drug crisis demands strong measures to protect individuals and society from the negative effects of rampant drug abuse. Children not only need education about the dangers inherent in drug abuse but also need access to alternative activities and social networks to substitute for the groups that gravitate to drugs. Children must be inculcated with a sense of their own worth and understand the important role each individual plays in society.

One way to combat drug abuse is to make drugs unavailable—easier said than done, as the current situation amply demonstrates. Another alternative is to restrict the drug's availability as has been done by raising the drinking age, and to cut back the prescription of anti-anxiety drugs.

People must be dissuaded from using drugs for non-medical purposes, or if they have already started abusing drugs, they must be helped to stop. Cessation programs can succeed. Since the Surgeon General's first report in 1964 warning about the health hazards of smoking, more than 40 million Americans have given up cigarettes.

The prevention of some types of drug use has been very successful. The number of Americans using illegal drugs at least monthly is down to half of what it was in the mid-1980s. Treatment of other drug problems has not been as successful: Many dependent on alcohol or heroin (or combinations of drugs) are likely to be involved in broken homes and dysfunctional work situations. Treatment for these unfortunates may require the reconstruction of their lives as well as freeing them from drugs (no easy task).

Treatment for long-term drug abusers takes various forms, including the prescription of substitute or antagonistic drugs, psychological and behavioral treatment, and participation in voluntary support groups of former abusers or addicts. The relative effectiveness of different treatment methods is difficult to assess, and their appropriateness depends on the individual.

The combination of individual determination to end addiction, support from family and friends, and help from health professionals and others who have experienced similar problems can prove beneficial. But even treatment of limited effectiveness is usually better than no treatment at all. Treatment of addiction, while not as effective as one would like, is as successful as, or more successful than, treatment of other chronic diseases such as heart disease, arthritis, and diabetes.

7
Health Concerns During Infancy and Childhood

• • • • • • • • • • • • • • • •

JOHN DRISCOLL, M.D.
Parts of this chapter are adapted from the chapter by Stephen J. Atwood, M.D., which appeared in the revised second edition.

This chapter is divided month by month for the first year, and year by year thereafter. The developmental stages mentioned are only guidelines to what is average. A child may spurt well ahead in some areas and lag behind in others. This is normal, unless a lag persists for a long time. Unfortunately, some parents tend to compare their children with others and get discouraged if their child does not seem to be keeping up in a particular area. In the playground or nursery, emphasis is often placed on motor skills, for instance, so a child who is concentrating on perceptual or language skills, which are more difficult to recognize, may be misunderstood as "slow." Like adults, children learn something best when they are truly interested in it. Attempts to force infants to learn something before they show an independent interest in it may result in a shaky foundation for that skill. Normal babies learn and develop at their own pace.

THE FIRST YEAR

Most of the developments of the first year seem miraculously programmed into an infant's nervous system, with the baby progressing on his or her own through milestones such as smiling, sitting, and transferring items from one hand to the other. Still, loving interaction is essential to a baby's development. Many studies of children who have spent their first years in uncaring situations such as institutions have demonstrated the effects of its absence. Even an infant who is well nourished, clean, and healthy will develop into a passive and uninterested child unless regularly babbled to, cuddled, given toys to grasp and contemplate, and communicated to with eye-to-eye contact.

While no two children are alike in development, the process does follow several general patterns.

1. Development proceeds from generalized activity of the whole body to specific individual responses. Month-old babies move their entire body wildly when they see something they want; older infants simply smile and reach.

2. Large-muscle control proceeds from head to toe. First infants learn to control their head, then they crawl on their belly, dragging their legs by pulling with their arms, and finally they control their legs and feet in walking. Fine-muscle control begins with flexion and proceeds to extension. Newborns are all curled up; by their first year they should be sitting and standing tall and reaching and picking up objects with accuracy.

3. Movements proceed from symmetry to asymmetry. Normal newborns use both arms and legs equally; by the first year children have learned to control each side of the body separately and use the two hands differently.

Some infants and toddlers undergo developmental testing for a specific reason, such as an obvious delay in sitting, walking, or speech. The results of such tests should be interpreted cautiously. While it is important not to delay too long before investigating developmental lags, it is wise to be very certain about a test result before making dire predictions.

THE FIRST MONTH

BIRTH

This is not the beginning, of course, but just a point in a developmental process that began nine months before. Many things that happen to a mother during pregnancy may have an impact on a newborn. (See chapter 9, Special Health Concerns of Women.) For several hours after birth, the medication present in the mother's bloodstream during delivery may continue to affect an infant.

Although it may be a difficult process, what happens during birth rarely harms a baby. All newborns are given Apgar scores, named after the anesthesiologist who devised them. The purpose of this test is twofold: (1) to identify an infant's quality of transition to extrauterine life, and (2) to determine what measures must be taken to support the baby in the first minutes of life. The test measures heart rate, breathing, reflexes, muscle tone, and skin color. The Apgar score is not intended to be a predictor of future development.

Factors often associated with the health of infants after birth include the following:

A baby's head is soft and is normally molded and misshaped during its passage through the birth canal. Newborn infants may also have a soft swelling (caput succedaneum) at the top of the head, which is not a sign of brain damage. The head will form into a pleasing shape over the first two weeks. An abnormally small or large head is often a sign of either brain injury or abnormal development, although a small or large head may occasionally simply be familial. For example, Napoleon, because of the odd shape and size of his head, was thought to be the person in his family least likely to succeed. All babies have a soft spot on their head (the anterior fontanel), which may not close until 18 months. This is the place where the bony skull has not yet joined. The open fontanel gives the skull more flexibility during delivery or when the baby hits his head. The soft spot will pulse with the heartbeat. When an infant is active or has a fever, it will pulse more rapidly. The fontanel may be touched and will not be harmed by gentle poking or washing. A fontanel that bulges outward or is very sunken is abnormal and is reason to see a doctor.

Nearly half of babies are born with the umbilical cord around their neck, but this ordinarily does not cause problems. In the hospital, the stump of the umbilical cord is painted with a disinfectant to kill bacteria. Unless there is a foul odor or inflammation around the stump, there is no cause for worry while it remains in place. In most cases the stump falls off painlessly when an infant is between 7 and 10 days old.

The newborn baby's liver may be temporarily too immature to remove the normal by-products of the breakdown of extra red cells that were needed during the fetal period. As a result, babies may be jaundiced for the first few days, which is normally not a cause for alarm.

For the first few days after birth a baby's skin may be dry. Many newborn babies have skin that is covered with soft, furry hair. This is called lanugo, and gradually disappears.

Infants' fingernails used to be covered with mittens in the hospital nursery to prevent scratches. There is no need to cover the baby's hands at home, but the nails should be trimmed with a blunt-nosed scissors while the baby is asleep.

PERCEPTION

It is not true, as doctors used to think, that babies are deaf and blind at birth. Newborns will focus on a parent's face and follow it with their eyes. Even on the delivery table, they will focus on their mother, and would rather look toward a picture of a normal face than one in which the features have been scrambled. Loud noises will cause newborns to startle or shudder, and they will respond to the sound of a soft, high voice. By 4 weeks of age, babies may show by their behavior that they recognize their mother and father.

REFLEXES

A newborn baby has a remarkable variety of reflexes to test. If you touch the cheek or the skin around the mouth, a newborn will open its mouth and turn toward your finger, "rooting" for a nipple to suck. If you touch a foot or hand, the baby attempts to make a grasp, which may be surprisingly strong. One of the most famous reflexes is the Moro reflex. When an infant's head falls back or he startles, he will throw out his arms and legs,

extend his neck, and cry briefly. Then he will bring his arms together rapidly, as if to clasp the branch of a tree or his mother. It is easy to believe that this reflex evolved because it helped prevent an infant from falling. Another fascinating motion is the walking reflex: If you hold a small baby's legs down and allow one foot to touch a bed, he will lift that foot and set the other down, and so on, in a walking movement. This reflex will disappear completely later in infancy and is not related to learning to walk.

NUTRITION AND FEEDING

The decision to breast-feed or bottle-feed is important, and should ideally be made jointly by both parents. The success of their choice will depend on mutual support. It is advisable to breast-feed. If it is impossible to sustain breast-feeding, whatever breast milk the mother can provide is better than none at all. Breast milk is easier to digest than any other source of food, and contains all the nutrients necessary for normal growth for as long as six months. It also contains immune factors from the mother's body, which are not found in formula and which can help protect an infant from infection while nursing and create favorable conditions inside an infant's digestive tract. Furthermore, breast milk seems to protect an infant against allergies. Breast-feeding also provides a special atmosphere for communication between mother and child.

On the other hand, there are many circumstances that can make breast-feeding impractical or inadvisable, such as the mother's or infant's illness. Mothers who cannot breast-feed should not feel inadequate or guilty. Millions of infants who have been raised on formula have grown into completely healthy and well-adjusted adults. The standard infant formulas are all equally good nutritionally. The prepackaged formulas are more expensive than powdered or concentrated formulas, but the latter run the risk of being nutritionally inadequate if they are not mixed carefully. If there is any reason for concern that tap water may be contaminated, it should be sterilized before mixing with the concentrated or powdered formula. Cow's milk is indigestible to the immature digestive system of most young infants, and may provoke allergies to milk.

Babies should be fed in the first 6 to 12 hours of life, when the sugar in the first breast fluid, called colostrum (or a bottle of sugar water), can "revive" them from the stress of delivery. It takes 3 to 5 days for normal milk to replace colostrum. During the first few weeks, nutritional needs gradually increase. Infants will signal their hunger by crying, eventually assuming a regular schedule, but "demand feeding" is the best policy until that happens. As a rough average, most babies want to eat every 2 to 3 hours at this age, and take about 10 minutes to empty 80 percent of the milk in one breast. They may continue sucking a dry breast much as a bottle-fed baby would suck a pacifier. Because nutrition and cuddling equal love to an infant, fathers should have as much opportunity as possible to share in providing them.

Transient weight loss during the first week is normal, while the baby is losing excess fluid accumulated in utero. After 5 to 7 days, most babies will begin to regularly gain weight. Bottle-fed babies tend to begin to gain weight right away, and parents should be careful not to feed them more than they actually want in order to avoid excessive weight gain. Try to overcome the instinct to urge a baby to finish the bottle. Formula can be kept refrigerated safely for at least 24 hours.

It is not necessary to give infants vitamin supplements, whether they are breast-feeding or drinking formula. Breast milk contains an ample supply of vitamins if the woman who provides it is eating a well-balanced diet with plenty of fruit or fruit juice and vegetables. The vitamin content of prepared formula is carefully controlled to be adequate for an infant's needs. Feeding supplemental vitamins may even be dangerous; there have been isolated reports of toxic reactions to vitamins A and D in infants who were given excessive amounts of them.

It is also unnecessary to give infants water, except perhaps if they seem thirsty on a very hot day. Both formula and breast milk contain as much water as infants need, and extra water may diminish their appetite for nourishing liquids. Once breast-feeding is well established, it is safe to give a supplemental bottle of formula, if you wish, for your convenience or for reassurance that the infant will take from a bottle when you are unable to breast-feed. This supplement of formula is not necessary, however. The same goals may be accomplished by giving the infant expressed breast milk in a bottle. Bottle-feeding of either breast milk or formula gives the father the opportunity to have the important experience of feeding the infant.

Infants need to be burped because air coming in with their food may create a false feeling of fullness and also may contribute to crampy abdominal pains. Bottle-fed babies should be given the bottle in a tilted position with the nipple down, so they always get milk and not air from the nipple. To minimize spitting up after feedings, tilt the baby at a 30-degree angle for a few minutes before burping. That way, the milk tends to settle and air can come up.

BOWEL MOVEMENTS

Many babies strain with each bowel movement, because they cannot employ just the muscles of defecation—it's all muscles or nothing. This will change as the baby develops more control. Many newborns, particularly ones who are breast-fed, have loose greenish or yellowish bowel movements until they are weaned. A bottle-fed baby's stools will begin to appear more normal within a few days. True diarrhea or constipation is rare; breast-fed babies are believed to be particularly free of problems relating to their stools. Four to six stools a day is not unusual in the first month; some babies have one after each feeding.

The two real health concerns at this time are infections and gastrointestinal allergy. When stools are excessively frequent, watery (not just loose), foul smelling, and green, call the doctor. Blood and mucus in stools are further signs of potential trouble, particularly if the blood is reddish black.

SLEEPING

Newborn babies may appear to sleep nearly all the time, but recent studies show that from the beginning some babies sleep as little as 12 hours a day. Their eyes may be closed most of the time, but infants are often aware of what is going on around them.

SPECIAL HEALTH PROBLEMS

Infants who are premature or born with disabilities sometimes are delivered straight into the intensive care unit. Parents whose babies are in intensive care should spend as much time with them as possible, touching and holding them if possible and trying to provide them with meaningful stimulation.

Premature. Infants who are born prematurely are at risk of respiratory distress syndrome, immaturity of the structure and function of some organs, and brain hemorrhage. They sleep more than infants born at term; in fact, they often appear to sleep nearly all the time. Their cries are more feeble and higher pitched, their movements are more jerky, and they often do not indicate when they are hungry. The reflexes of a premature infant are different from those of a term baby.

Small-for-dates. Babies who are born at term but are unusually small used to be lumped together with "preemies," but today it is recognized that these are two different problems with different characteristics. Unusually small size in a term baby often indicates a medical problem in the mother, such as an abnormal placenta, or a problem in the baby, such as abnormal chromosomes.

Infants with disabilities. Some infants are noted at delivery to have any of a variety of conditions or anomalies that will require a lifetime of treatment and may be associated with variable degrees of motor and mental impairment. The news that their child is not completely normal is

BOYS: BIRTH TO 36 MONTHS
PHYSICAL GROWTH
NCHS PERCENTILES[a]

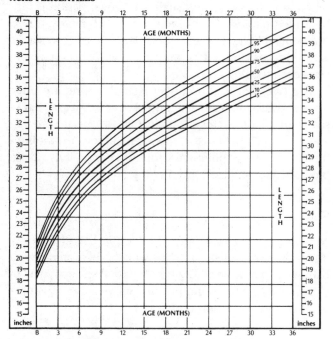

Figure 7.1A. **Growth in Length of Boys.**

GIRLS: BIRTH TO 36 MONTHS
PHYSICAL GROWTH
NCHS PERCENTILES[a]

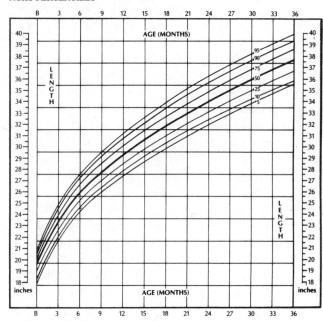

Figure 7.1B. **Growth in Length of Girls.**

Figure 7.1C. **Growth in Weight of Boys.**

BOYS: BIRTH TO 36 MONTHS
PHYSICAL GROWTH
NCHS PERCENTILES[a]

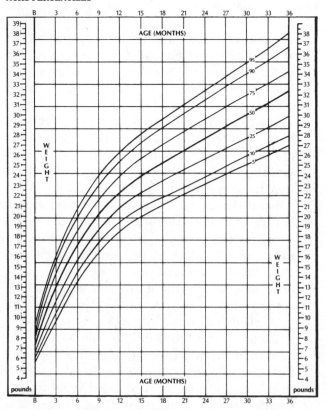

Figure 7.1D. **Growth in Weight of Girls.**

GIRLS: BIRTH TO 36 MONTHS
PHYSICAL GROWTH
NCHS PERCENTILES[a]

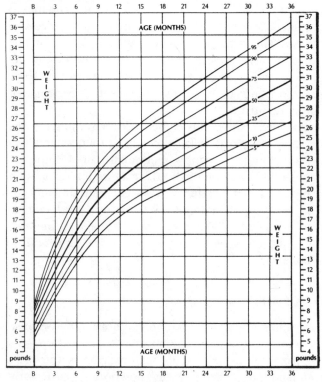

Figure 7.2A. Girls: 2 to 18 Years Physical Growth NCHS Percentiles[a] (Stature).

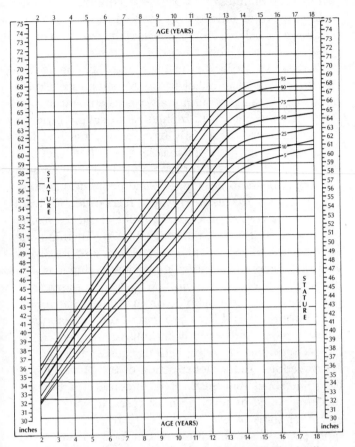

[a]Adapted from: Hamill PVV, Drizd TA, Johnson CL, Reed RB, Roche AF, Moore WM: Physical growth: National Center for Health Statistics percentiles. AM J CLIN NUTR 32:607-629, 1979. Data from the Fels Research Institute, Wright State University School of Medicine, Yellow Springs, Ohio. © 1982 ROSS LABORATORIES

Figure 7.2B. Boys: 2 to 18 Years Physical Growth NCHS Percentiles[a] (Stature).

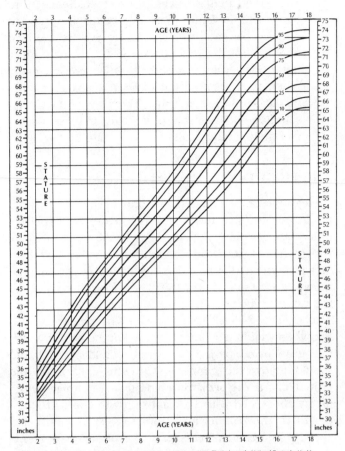

[a]Adapted from: Hamill PVV, Drizd TA, Johnson CL, Reed RB, Roche AF, Moore WM: Physical growth: National Center for Health Statistics percentiles. AM J CLIN NUTR 32:607-629, 1979. Data from the National Center for Health Statistics (NCHS) Hyattsville, Maryland. © 1982 ROSS LABORATORIES

Figure 7.2C. Girls: 2 to 18 Years Physical Growth NCHS Percentiles[a] (Weight).

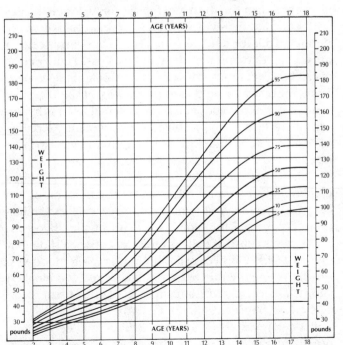

[a]Adapted from: Hamill PVV, Drizd TA, Johnson CL, Reed RB, Roche AF, Moore WM: Physical growth: National Center for Health Statistics percentiles. AM J CLIN NUTR 32:607-629, 1979. Data from the Fels Research Institute, Wright State University School of Medicine, Yellow Springs, Ohio. © 1982 ROSS LABORATORIES

Figure 7.2D. Boys: 2 to 18 Years Physical Growth NCHS Percentiles[a] (Weight).

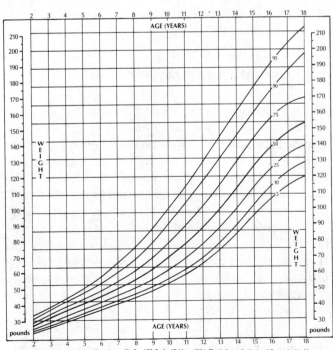

[a]Adapted from: Hamill PVV, Drizd TA, Johnson CL, Reed RB, Roche AF, Moore WM: Physical growth: National Center for Health Statistics percentiles. AM J CLIN NUTR 32:607-629, 1979. Data from the National Center for Health Statistics (NCHS) Hyattsville, Maryland. © 1982 ROSS LABORATORIES

often so devastating to the family that they do not understand the long-term implications of the diagnosis. The pediatrician's greatest challenge is to work with the family to accept the diagnosis and to begin a planning process whose goal is the best outcome for the child. Families often display amazing resiliency and fortitude in the face of adversity when they are told the truth and given ongoing medical and social support. The value of the understanding and available physician for these infants and their families cannot be overstated.

THE FIRST DOCTOR'S VISIT

Sometime near the end of the second week is a good time for infants to have their first visit to the pediatrician's office. At this time the doctor will check the infant's weight, height, and head circumference, and record them on a growth chart appropriate for the baby's age (see the growth charts in this chapter). The curved lines indicate the range within which the measurements for 90 percent of all children will fall at a given age. What matters most is not where children fall on the chart, but the *rate* at which they grow over a period of months. A child's growth rate should follow the gentle upward curve seen on the growth chart. The pediatrician in the first visit will be primarily concerned with an infant's growth and with questions that the parents may want to ask. As mentioned above, whether an infant is growing is about the only predictive statement a pediatrician can make at this time. The doctor can never accurately predict future intelligence or achievements. The most reliable predictors of an infant's future are alertness and responsiveness, qualities that a doctor has no specific way to measure, but which a parent is often able to judge.

THE SECOND MONTH

This is a leveling-off time, when the family has begun to adjust to life with a new baby. The parents get organized and the baby may begin to fall into recognizable behavior patterns (see table 7.1). A baby's "good periods" may alternate with fussy periods during this time, and the infant may find ways of quieting himself from crying: sucking fingers, turning, or looking for and finding a mobile.

Congestion. A normal infant of this age will not breathe through the mouth unless desperate for air. However, infants may develop stuffy noses just like anyone else, due to dry air, dust, or the fuzz from blankets. A humidifier in the baby's room may help. It may also help to elevate the head of the baby's mattress a few inches so the baby can swallow nasal secretions. If a large amount of mucus accumulates in the nose, some

pediatricians recommend that a few drops of a salty solution (¼ teaspoon of salt in 8 ounces of water sterilized by boiling for 3 minutes) be used to wash out the nose. This treatment is not universally accepted, however. Some practitioners believe it only increases the irritation of the nose, leading to further mucus production.

Crying and Colic. In the first months, crying is virtually the only way an infant has to communicate. Crying often signals hunger, but not always. The infant may be too hot or too cold, wet, frightened, or simply irritable. A baby may cry particularly often during the first few days home from the hospital, adjusting to new routines. Young babies often cry for long periods at a time when nothing appears to be wrong. Some pediatricians point out that a baby has no other way to relax or let off steam from the enervating process of learning about the world. Imagine what it is like, not understanding anything one sees or hears, dependent on someone else for every comfort. Of course, life is fatiguing, and crying may simply reflect that. Infants who don't fuss don't appear to sleep as well as those who do. In the United States, serious nutritional problems are rarely the reason for a child's crying, and severely malnourished children are listless and dull. The most serious causes of crying are ear infections, sudden obstruction of the bowel due to gastrointestinal abnormalities, or infections, particularly if accompanied by fever. In most cases, however, there are other signs of the illness. The baby looks sick and often shows a sudden disinterest in food. In such situations the onset of crying is often sudden.

Some infants younger than 4 months of age cry for as long as 12 to 14 hours a day. This distressing problem is known as colic, and it is a condition without a known cause. Typically, colic begins at 2 to 3 weeks of age and clears between the third and fourth month. Some babies with colic let out sudden shrieking cries; others just cry normally, but for hours on end. The infants may seem in great pain, draw up their legs and pass gas. Pediatricians even disagree about whether or not colic is a disease. Some think it may be due to immaturity of the digestive system or chronic abdominal gas; others think it is hypersensitivity to a noisy, turbulent environment. Certainly colic is more common in active, sensitive infants, and can be exacerbated by the tension it causes in parents.

Colic is not dangerous unless it is caused by a serious condition. This can be ruled out by examination of the baby, measurement of temperature, occasional examination of the stool for blood, or x-rays of the abdomen. One serious cause of colic is intussusception, a sliding of one part of the bowel over another, causing blood vessels supplying the bowel to become kinked and blocked and, if not corrected, ultimately leading to tissue damage, bowel blockage, and blood in the stool.

Recent research in Sweden, which studied colic in breast-fed babies, reported that when mothers stopped

TABLE 7.1: PATTERNS OF DEVELOPMENT

At 3 months	Lifts head and chest, with arms extended, from prone position; reaches for (and usually misses) objects; waves at toys; beginning to have some head control when pulled to sitting position; smiles, listens to voices, coos, and says aah and ngah; listens to music.
At 6 months	Rolls over, lifts head, sits briefly; may support most of weight when pulled to standing position; bounces actively; reaches for and grasps objects, transfers them from hand to hand; makes polysyllabic vowel sounds, babbles; responds to change in environment, recognizes parents, prefers mother.
At 9 months	Sits alone with back straight; pulls self to standing position; beginning to crawl; picks up objects with thumb and forefinger; can uncover hidden toy and tries to retrieve dropped objects; says mama and dada, responds to name, plays pat-a-cake, peek-a-boo; waves.
At 12 months	Walks with help; picks up small objects; says a few words; plays simple ball games.
At 15 months	Walks alone, crawls up stairs; stacks 2 blocks; makes lines with crayon; can put small objects in box, names familiar objects; follows simple commands.
At 18 months	Runs stiffly; sits on chair; climbs stairs; stacks 3 blocks, scribbles; empties containers; identifies body parts, pictures; feeds self; asks for help; kisses parents; may complain when needs changing.
At 24 months	Runs well, walks up and down stairs one step at a time; opens doors, climbs; stacks 6 blocks, makes circular scribbling, folds paper; puts 3 words together; handles spoon; listens to stories; helps undress self.
At 30 months	Jumps; stacks 8 blocks; makes vertical and horizontal strokes, tries to draw circles; knows full name and uses pronoun "I" to refer to self; helps put things away; engages in pretend play.
At 36 months	Rides tricycle; balances on one foot; goes up and down stairs alternating feet; uses blocks to build bridges; copies a circle; counts 3 objects; repeats 3 words of short sentence; plays simple games with other children; helps in dressing; washes hands.

Adapted from *Nelson Textbook of Pediatrics*, Richard E. Behrman and Victor C. Vaughn III, editors, W. B. Saunders Co., 1983. Reprinted by permission of the publisher.

eating milk products the baby's colic would disappear, in most cases, within 8 days. The only other treatment for most cases of colic is comfort measures, such as:

- Placing the baby on her stomach
- Swaddling the baby tightly in a blanket
- Holding the baby upright or close to the chest in an infant carrier
- Taking the baby for a car ride or placing him on top of a spinning washing machine to feel the vibrations.

Sometimes drugs are prescribed to prevent intestinal spasm, but they don't always work and it is not desirable to give infants drugs for obscure causes.

Some pediatricians jokingly refer to colic as a condition caused by the baby and affecting the parents. Perhaps one of the more serious problems with colic is that it interferes with the development of a good relationship between parents and baby. It is important to get a break now and then from the stress of a constantly crying baby, either by having parents take turns or by engaging a reliable sitter for a few hours several times a week. Also, it's heartening to know that the problem always resolves itself within a matter of months. For parents, the key with colic is to survive until the infant has reached four months of age, and here reassurance and advice from the pediatrician can help.

Ego Disintegration. Many infants have a spell of fussiness every day in the late afternoon or early evening. The child psychologist Anna Freud referred to this period as "ego disintegration," a time when an infant is fatigued from a long day of trying to come to terms with her environment and herself, and loses control of emotional equilibrium. An infant at this age has no idea how to relax, and thus gets fussy. Unfortunately, this crotchety period often corresponds with the time when the mother and/or father arrives home from work, perhaps suffering some ego disintegration of their own. Parents should understand that this fussiness has nothing to do with the baby rejecting them; rather, it is part of a normal 24-hour cycle. Parents should be encouraged to play with their infants despite the fussiness. It can turn into a gratifying encounter, because the cranky period often evolves into a time of playful alertness.

Falling. A parent should get into the habit of keeping one hand on the baby whenever he is on a changing table or some other place from which he can fall. It is difficult to know when a child will learn to turn over. Fortunately, because their skulls are malleable enough to absorb the impact of a fall, infants typically survive the most frightening falls unharmed. However, if an infant is unresponsive after a fall or vomits, or if the pupils of his eyes do not respond to a direct light, he may have a concussion or some other trauma to the brain, and should be seen by a doctor immediately.

Feeding. It may be very tempting for a parent of a formula-fed infant to prop the bottle in the baby's mouth and then leave her alone. However, this practice should be avoided. The baby could conceivably choke while the parent is out of sight and earshot. In addition, it can seriously interfere with a child's chance for normal development. Feeding is an important time for loving communication for bottle-fed as well as breast-fed infants, and eye-to-eye contact is important. Being left alone with a bottle is a cold, unstimulating way to gain nourishment, and may lead to behavioral problems later on if food becomes an infant's only source of gratification.

Rashes. Sometime between the fourth and tenth weeks, many infants develop an acnelike rash on the face and neck, consisting of pimples with white centers. The rash comes and goes, sometimes becoming worse when the baby is hot or has been crying. It is thought to be associated with hormonal changes as the mother's hormones disappear from the infant's system. Parents need not do anything about this rash, which will disappear spontaneously within a few weeks.

Scratching. Some infants may scratch themselves on the face, but these scratches heal quickly with or without treatment.

Sight. Experts disagree about exactly what an infant can see at this age. Some studies suggest that a baby in his second month cannot see objects 6 or 8 feet away, but many pediatricians and parents think they can, if they are interested.

Smiling. By the end of the second month, the majority of babies smile at something that pleases them, and make noises other than crying.

Sucking. It is normal and very common for a baby this age to begin sucking fingers. This kind of behavior is an early and important sign of self-sufficiency. Finger-sucking is not a sign of inadequate mothering or inadequate nutrition. Nearly every infant needs some extra sucking, and thumbs and fingers are natural sources. A pacifier is an adequate substitute and, some dentists believe, better for future tooth development.

Vaccinations. The baby's second visit to the doctor should take place in the second month. In addition to continuing to measure the baby's growth, the physician will administer the child's first vaccinations. (See the section on vaccinations; a hepatitis B vaccine may have been administered in the hospital shortly after birth.)

THE THIRD MONTH

This is often a magical turning point in a baby's development. Something happens in an infant's nervous system that seems to take the place of the need to cry. The baby gains the ability to interact with the world in other ways.

The importance of this level of achievement is underscored by the fact that this is the age at which children raised in institutions, without getting sufficient stimulation, begin to show signs of deprivation.

Communication. A 3-month-old baby begins to reach out to the world with both arms and, instead of crying, coo and gurgle. The whole body may become involved in the pleasure of seeing a smiling face; the baby may coo, kick, and reach out all at once. A baby of this age may whimper when hungry, rather than crying, and may even be able to wait a few minutes. This ability to wait in anticipation of an expected reward is an important step, representing a level of understanding and trust not present in a younger infant.

Feeding. Feeding time will also become playtime. By now, feeding is the most receptive time, and babies may remove their mouth from the nipple to watch what is going on in the room. Many parents begin to wonder in the third month when to introduce solid foods. The American Academy of Pediatrics recommends delaying the introduction of solid foods until sometime between the fourth and sixth month. For a baby, solid foods are defined as anything that is fed with a spoon: all those pureed baby foods—cereals, fruits, meat, or vegetables—that can be bought in bottles or prepared in a blender. Because the baby gets them by spoon, eating these foods requires a certain level of neurological coordination, a level that very few infants have reached by the age of three months. By far the majority are still at the sucking stage and simply don't know how to work their tongues in order to swallow food from a spoon. Unfortunately, the introduction of solid food is often misguidedly regarded by parents as a sort of landmark in development, and a competition may develop over whose baby is eating solid foods first. This kind of competition is for the benefit of the parents, not the child, and should be avoided.

Solid food should never be put in a bottle, as it may cause an infant to choke. Nor should solid food be mixed with milk, as this represents an increase in calories and may set the stage for later obesity. The best policy is to wait until the baby is ready to swallow food from a spoon.

Physical Progress. An average infant may be able to hold her head up for long periods, and should certainly be able to hold it up for some period without bobbing. She may also be able to help maintain her own shape while sitting up. A 3-month-old infant can usually follow an object with her eyes in a full 180-degree arc.

Playing. By the third month, normal infants may spend long periods lying on their back, playing with fingers or a mobile hung over the crib. They can grab one hand with the other and play with their hands as if they were toys. Babies begin to understand that hands are extensions of themselves.

Sleeping. By the third month, an infant will be alert most of the day, with several daytime naps. Nighttime sleep usually lasts for 10 to 11 hours, although the infant may still require a nighttime feeding. Sleep cycles in infants are consistent with their character: An active, noisy baby may be an active, noisy sleeper. Infant sleep also seems to run in cycles, with periods of deep sleep alternating with periods of semialertness, during which an infant may cry out, suck a finger, rock or bang his head, move about, and settle down again. It is not necessary to respond to all these noises. Most often the infant is not truly awake and begins to fall asleep again without assistance.

Spoiling. Some children seem to cry just to bring a parent to them, and the parent has to decide whether or not to comply. A "spoiled" child is not a bad child, nor are the parents bad parents. The child has simply learned precociously how to manipulate the environment in order to satisfy desires, and crying is a major weapon. Parents are driven to respond to this crying out of guilt, love, or fear of harm to the infant. As a child's demands become ever more difficult to meet, the parents' guilt and anger increase. Some pediatricians feel a baby cannot be spoiled by being picked up every time he or she cries. Others feel this is only true in the first three months. Still others feel that a parent who always responds to a cry will not change after three months of this behavior, so it is better to set limits from the beginning. No doctor would advocate leaving a child to cry without attention, but once a parent is satisfied that nothing obvious is wrong, it may be a good idea simply to let the child cry for a while. A pacifier may help; many babies who do not need food are calmed by suckling.

The Parents. During the third month, some fathers may seem to lose interest in the intimate details of the child's progress and tire of having a wife totally wrapped up in an infant. This is less likely to happen if the father has been involved in the baby's development up to this point. At any rate, this is a good time to locate a babysitter and have an evening away from home.

THE FOURTH MONTH

Curiosity. A 4-month-old is beginning to be aware of both sides of the body, and this may be the end of symmetry in motion. The baby can turn her head to look in any direction and is making a few recognizable noises, primarily vowel sounds such as "ooh" and "aah." As many as four hours a day may be spent sucking (in addition to eating), which may indicate early teething but may be just a normal part of a growing curiosity about things.

Hair. If an infant was born with hair, it probably has begun to fall out by the fourth month, and will continue to come out for several more months. The hair at birth has little relation to the infant's permanent hair and is not an indication of the lifelong color. Because the permanent hair may be growing in at the same time, hair loss may not be noticeable.

Teething. In a few infants, teething begins as early as the fourth month. Teething starts with the lower front incisors. The erupting teeth cause swelling and irritation of the gum, which can be relieved temporarily by rubbing the gum with a clean finger or ice. Sucking actually adds to the infant's distress because it causes blood to rush to the area, and the swelling increases. The baby may begin to rub the gums (which helps to reduce the pain) and may begin to chew. Is distress a sign of teething? If rubbing the gums causes a sudden yowl, the answer is probably yes. Continuing to rub will cause the infant to settle down. Giving a little liquid baby acetaminophen may relieve the pain temporarily. Be aware, though, that the teeth that begin erupting at 4 months may not actually appear for weeks.

Vaccinations. The second set of vaccinations should be administered in the fourth month.

THE FIFTH MONTH

Discovery. This is the age of discovery, of exploring things by manipulating them and by mouthing them. Watching something is no longer enough; a 5-month-old infant wants to feel its shape with both hands and mouth. A child who may seem ready to eat solid foods may still be more interested in mouthing new textures than in consuming the food. The attention span for play increases to more than 1 hour.

Genitals and Diaper Rash. By five months, babies discover and manipulate their genitals. This may be difficult for a parent or grandparent to watch impassively, but it is wise to resist the urge to prevent such behavior, which is a natural part of an infant's exploration. Trying to prohibit it may only heighten the baby's excitement about this newly discovered area. Sores and ulcerations on the genitals are not due to this manipulation but to diaper rash and should be treated vigorously. The solution is to avoid plastic-coated diapers or rubber pants, not to use strong detergents or bleaches when washing the diapers, and to change diapers often (including in the middle of the night). Some (but by no means all) pediatricians recommend using cornstarch or baby powder to absorb ammonia and an antiammonia rinse before drying the diapers. Applying a protective ointment to the sores may also be recommended. Exposing the area to the open air also helps; if possible, let the baby play diaperless on a sheet placed over a waterproof pad. If the problem persists, consult a doctor.

Physical Progress. By the end of the fifth month, most infants can smile spontaneously. They reach for objects and can get a firm grasp when you hand them a rattle. Most infants can perceive and look at an object the size of a raisin, and they laugh and squeal. By this time, particularly active infants will have begun to outgrow their molded chairs, and can easily flop or clamber out of them.

Safety. Infants of this age also begin to be capable of discovering and mouthing objects and substances that are potentially harmful. Any parent who has not baby-proofed the house should do so now (see the section on poisoning and safety in chapter 14). Every house with children in it should contain ipecac syrup, which is used to induce vomiting in case of poisoning, and a list of poisons and their antidotes. Use ipecac only after consulting a doctor or the nearest poison control center. The telephone number of the poison control center should be prominently posted. Ipecac is given as one tablespoon followed by up to six ounces of water or milk, with a repeat dose and feeding 15 minutes later if vomiting has not succeeded.

Sleeping. This is the age when infants begin waking up very early in the morning, at 5:00 or 6:00 A.M. Keeping them up later at night only makes the parent, not the baby, more tired in the morning. Forcing an extra night feeding, which the infant has probably outgrown by now, will not help either. The only thing that may prevent a baby from turning into a human rooster is to install a dark shade in the bedroom.

THE SIXTH MONTH

Babble. By this time, the average child has begun to babble extensively. Although adults may not recognize much of what is said, the 6-month infant can understand a few words, and probably makes two recognizable sounds—mama and dada—although neither has any meaning to the child yet.

Constipation. The introduction of solid foods (see below) may bring on an infant's first bout of constipation. Bright blood in the stool may accompany this, indicating a crack around the anus that is bleeding slightly. The first step in treating this is to soften the stool by feeding the infant prune juice, prunes, or some unrefined sugar like molasses. Next, the anus should be coated with petroleum jelly two or three times a day. If it fails to heal, the infant should be taken to a doctor.

Control. Some babies may have discovered the fascinating game of dropping things, usually before they discover the game of picking them up. The activity usually generates a response from parents, and provides an early experience in cause and effect for the baby, who enjoys this new control over his environment. The activity also represents progress in developing the fine muscles of the hands, which here parallels the development of the large muscles needed for locomotion.

Eyes. By this age, a child's eye color is predictable. Blue eyes will have remained blue. Eyes destined to be brown will be turning a muddy color.

Food. By the sixth month, nearly all babies are ready for solid foods. A sign of readiness is the baby's ability to turn his head or push your hand away when he does not want any more to eat. Some of the reasons for waiting until now to introduce solid foods have been stated earlier. By the age of 6 months, the digestive system is mature enough to handle most foods. Nonetheless, breast milk or formula will remain the mainstay of an infant's diet for many months to come. It is a good idea to introduce foods gradually, a week at a time, starting with a one-grain cereal such as dry rice (a 6-month baby is not ready for wheat). Dilute it approximately 1 part cereal to 6 parts water. Do not use cow's milk as this adds calories and may provoke an allergic reaction. Progress slowly in this fashion to strained vegetables and fruits. By introducing foods at least a week apart, you have time to watch for an allergic reaction.

Strained baby foods may be prepared at home, but care should be taken to make certain the infant gets enough iron. If there is any question about the iron content of the baby's diet, use baby food dry cereals. An infant may balk initially at the idea of solid food because the taste and texture are unfamiliar. Because babies are so interested in manipulating things at this age, it helps to give them a spoon and a cup to play with while feeding by spoon. In any case, children may be more interested in playing with their food than in eating it. The feeding should be fun, not a battle; if a child objects violently to the food, stop trying and wait a few days.

At first, breast milk or formula will continue to be the mainstay of the infant's diet. In order to maintain her milk supply, a breast-feeding mother should let the baby empty one breast, then offer the baby some solid food. She may continue with the other breast if the child is still hungry.

Food Allergies. Allergic reactions to food may appear to be indigestion, but they may also include a runny nose, wheezing, mood changes, and various skin reactions. Using an elimination diet, a parent can withdraw the food suspected of causing the allergy, wait for the symptoms to clear, and then reintroduce it. If the symptoms appear suddenly, the allergy is confirmed. (However, children are often able to tolerate an allergenic food after a wait of several months.) Orange juice is especially likely to cause problems; babies vomit the juice and continue to do so every time it is offered. A day or two later the stools may become frequent and loose, and the child may be fussy and full of gas. Some parents delay the introduction of fruit juices until a baby is able to drink them from a cup, around the ninth or tenth month. Many infants younger than six months are allergic to eggs, and egg whites and meat should be withheld until even later because their proteins are the most difficult to digest.

Physical Progress. At this age, a baby's individual progress should become obvious. A very active child may have begun crawling, drawing her belly and legs along on the ground by pulling with her hands. An active baby may sit for minutes at a time and will enjoy stepping with one leg after the other while being held upright. An average child can roll over alone, and will be able to sit upright without having her head loll one way or another. The average child will be able to move backward and forward, making most babies too active to be fed or diapered easily at this stage. Don't expect an infant of 6 months to stay put.

Safety. Infants ready to eat solid foods are also ready to swallow objects they are playing with. They can choke on biscuits or cookies if they eat them while lying on their back; babies should not be fed anything while lying down, nor should they ever be left unattended while eating. To extract a swallowed object, first whack the infant on the back, holding him face down over your knees. You may try to extract it with your fingers, but this runs the risk of pushing it farther down. As a last resort, try the Heimlich maneuver (see chapter 13, Basics of CPR and Life Support).

Teeth. During this period an infant's invisible secondary or permanent teeth are undergoing enamel formation. Babies at this stage should be given some fluoridated water or fluoride drops along with their usual diet. Fluoride is incorporated into the outer layers of enamel and makes the babies' teeth more resistant to cavities.

Vaccinations. In the sixth month the baby should visit the doctor again and receive the third set of routine vaccinations.

Weaning. When should a breast-fed baby be weaned? The answer is very individual and, for some people, very controversial. Certainly breast milk is the most beneficial form of nutrition for an infant, and in some societies babies breast-feed until age 2 or 3. There is good reason to wean sometime in the second half of the first year, however. Infants adapt to the idea of using a cup more easily before their first birthday than they do afterward. The American Academy of Pediatrics advises that infants weaned from the breast should continue to be given formula until they are 1 year old. One way to begin weaning is to add a supplementary bottle of formula. Used to replace one meal, this bottle a day will start to slow down the flow of milk. However, many mothers prefer to wean their infants directly to a cup, which should happen around the ninth month.

THE SEVENTH MONTH

Feeding. Because of a baby's increasing manual dexterity, feeding time often becomes a game. Babies may want to eat with their hands or to smear food all over the bib or let it ooze slowly down their chin. It's impossible to say whether this represents experimenting with textures or simply teasing Mom. However, what may seem like disinterest in food should probably be viewed as an important stage in the development of independence. Most babies seem more interested in eating with their fingers, and it is wise to go along with this desire. There is not as much need to worry about "good" nutrition at this stage as parents might think. The absolute minimum daily requirements for a healthy diet at this stage are (1) a pint of milk or its equivalent in cheese, low-fat ice milk, or a calcium substitute; (2) 1 ounce of fresh juice or 1 piece of fruit; and (3) 2 ounces of iron-containing protein, such as that in an egg or meat. Rather than turning mealtimes into battles and food into a symbol of something else, a child should start learning to fulfill her own needs. This may be a good time to begin the gradual transition to feeding liquids in a cup. A smart way to start is to offer a baby some expressed milk or formula in a cup, and gradually increase the amount the infant takes from the cup as the amount from a breast or bottle is decreased. By the 10th or 11th month, the baby can be taking most liquids from a cup.

Games. A baby at this age may also have discovered the delightful game of dropping something and calling to a parent to pick it up. Retrieving an object over and over may provide great glee to a child, but doing it is much less entertaining for the parents. There is no way to recommend how often a parent should yield to this obviously manipulative behavior.

Physical Progress. By the seventh month, many infants have begun to move around and can no longer safely be left alone. Crawling ability improves, although some babies prefer to bump across the floor on their buttocks. Many have also begun to pull themselves to a standing position, an experience they may find very exciting but also slightly frightening at first, since they will not yet know how to get themselves down. The scope of the arms and hands is also greatly increased. The baby uses each hand independently, perhaps without a preference for one or the other. Most love to bang toys or other objects together, and to compare differences in their size or shape. The baby may also be interested in poking at things. All unused electric outlets in the home should by now have plastic covers.

Teething and Ears. Teething is usually active during this period. The first tooth, in the lower jaw, is usually the worst. Besides rubbing at the gums and mouth, infants like to put their fingers in their ears. If they persist in tugging at an ear and seem cranky or irritable, they may have an ear infection and should be seen by a doctor.

THE EIGHTH MONTH

Bedtime. Babies of this age may be very stubborn, particularly when they are tired. Few children want to stop playing when bedtime comes, but no baby should be allowed to become exhausted. On the other hand, a very active baby may want to get up in the middle of the night. There is no way to solve this problem. Some parents go along with the baby; others refuse to go into the bedroom after he has been put to bed.

Blankets. By this age, many babies have adopted a toy or blanket that they carry everywhere with them. This habit is perfectly normal and a healthy sign that the child is finding a way to become more emotionally independent as physical independence increases. If the child keeps tripping on a beloved blanket, it will be just as loved if it is cut in half (and one piece can be washed while the other is hugged). If for some reason it is desirable that affection be transferred to another object (for instance, if a special doll or toy has parts that could be swallowed), pin or sew the beloved object to a replacement until the new one begins to take on the same adored, dog-eared, smelly quality.

Feeding. At this point, an infant may begin to use food aggressively, refusing to be strapped in the high chair, throwing food around, and demanding food from other plates. This is no time to try to push food into a child, because she may begin to use food as a way to test parents as well. If a baby is routinely disrupting family meals, it may be better for all concerned to feed her separately.

Physical Progress. How far the average baby has come! By now, most infants can feed themselves crackers and play peek-a-boo. An attempt to take away a toy may be met with resistance; and if something is placed out of sight or reach, the baby will try to find it. The baby can easily pass a toy from one hand to the other and is probably imitating some of the sounds adults make while playing with him. Long since, the baby has learned how to sit without support and to bear some weight while being held upright.

Safety. This is a time of wonderful achievements for the infant, but it may also be a time of frustration and worry for the parents. Most babies are into everything they can reach. If mobile, they can easily get hurt if they become trapped. It is time to reevaluate the entire house in terms of baby safety. It is not a bad idea to get down on the floor and crawl around a little to see what dangers lie on the baby's level. Other young children, sensing the infant's propensity to mouth anything, may start to offer things like worms, pills, and other unsuitable items (see the following section on siblings). As mentioned, babies may get trapped in a standing position and not know how to sit back down; not knowing how to bend, they may fall over straight backward and get a sound bang on the back of the head. Parents are well advised to be sure there is soft carpeting under any piece of furniture the infant may pull herself up by or be placed upon. It may also be wise to teach the infant how to sit down from a standing position, by gently bending her at the waist over and over until she catches on. Buffers in the crib are also a wise investment.

Testing danger is not always unintentional. Infants may have learned how to test their parents by their interest in danger zones, so this is a time for parents to begin learning how to set limits. It is important for the parents to decide which battles are worth fighting, since a persistently strict attitude may be unnecessarily harsh for a baby.

THE NINTH MONTH

Food. Sometime between the ninth and twelfth months, babies who are still breast-feeding may begin to lose interest in it, and this is an appropriate time to take them up on the lapse of interest. In some instances, weaning may actually be psychologically more difficult for the mother, who recognizes the growing independence of her infant. Babies already on solid foods may now be ready to tolerate meats and fruit juices.

Physical Progress. By this point, many infants can sit up by themselves and can reach a standing position with some effort. With this new ability may come an understanding and perhaps a fear of heights. However, children are usually excited about the idea of standing, and may insist on standing up while eating and being dressed. A very active baby may already be crawling and may have learned to crawl up stairs. Coming down is far more frightening than going up, and the baby may get stuck a few steps up. Installing stair carpets is certainly a good idea; putting a gate at the top and bottom of the stairs is essential. With the ability to sit and lean forward with hands free, a 9-month-old baby has complete freedom to explore all of his body and delights in the exercise.

Separation Anxiety. Sometime around this age, almost every infant begins to cry when separated from parents, and may cling desperately or wail piteously at the prospect of separation. Strangers are frightening and not to be trusted, particularly if they stare. Before an "ordeal" such as a visit to relatives, it may help to warn the hosts and talk to the child and hold her close during the visit.

Teeth. Many infants do not develop teeth until near the end of their first year or later. However, the problems that cause unsightly or unhealthy teeth often have their origins in the earliest months or even before birth. Letting a baby fall asleep with a bottle promotes tooth decay, which is caused by the interaction between bacteria in the mouth and sugar in milk or juice. Prolonged exposure to this sugar promotes the formation of plaque, which causes decay. Even though the first teeth are only "baby teeth," destined to fall out at age 6 or 7, their condition sets the stage for permanent teeth. If they fall out prematurely due to decay, the permanent teeth may be displaced and, besides being unattractive, may not function well. Also, decayed teeth at any age are frequently painful and may interfere with normal nutrition. At an early age, a pacifier or nothing at all is better than a bottle for quieting or putting the baby to sleep. If the infant is in the habit of having a bottle at bedtime, try filling it with water. At the least, remove the bottle after the baby has fallen asleep.

Fluoride is an inexpensive and effective way to prevent dental caries. It is most easily administered in the drinking water, but fluoride preparations are available when the water supply is not fluoridated. Breast-fed infants should receive fluoride supplements.

THE TENTH MONTH

Helping. Ten-month-old babies can often begin to help with their dressing, lifting their legs and arms, and many of them can identify body parts by name. However, children of this age are still too young to dress themselves.

Independence. Some babies at this age begin to test out their independence from their parents, creeping away but checking back often to see if the parent is still there, or calling out for reassurance that the parent is still in the next room. Careful babies will try adventures such as standing alone or crawling up stairs, going only as far as the point where they can easily get back down.

Physical Progress. By their tenth month, almost all children can pull themselves up and stand while holding on to something, and many can walk sideways holding on to a piece of furniture such as a sofa. Most babies can pull themselves up to a sitting position from lying down without help. Some can stand alone, at least for a moment. It might seem that babies would first crawl, then creep, next stand, and finally walk. But babies tend to learn to stand and then to creep, as if they feel the need for more experience at ground level before walking erect.

Rocking. Babies only recently weaned may show a very sudden spurt in motor development during the tenth month. They may also begin to rock their bodies, particularly when they go to bed. This is apparently akin to the need to suck the thumb. Trying to stop this rocking behavior goes against the child's needs; if the rocking and banging of the crib is disturbing the rest of the family, oil the crib, install rubber casters, and put a thick carpet under it. A spell in the rocking chair with a parent, and a bedtime story, may also help.

Siblings. Older sisters and brothers are a wonderful asset to a child's development, providing the infant with stimulation and companionship that parents can never offer an only child. They are examples for a baby to copy, and older siblings can offer immeasurable help to a busy mother in caring for an infant. Siblings can also, however, be a problem and even a hazard to a young infant. If a sibling is a preschooler, the introduction of a baby into the home may be cause for jealousy, hostility, and competition. Parents should try to channel these emotions into harmless or even beneficial outlets.

Siblings often want to touch or poke a new baby. Unless they jab extremely hard at the eyes, mouth, ears, or urogenital region, there is little chance of harm. In fact, as soon as the sibling begins to show interest in a baby, it is a good idea to examine the baby together, showing the sibling how to stroke and cuddle the baby gently. If the sibling can be included in everything the parents do with the infant early on, she will not feel left out.

Breast-feeding may be particularly troubling for a preschooler, who may be very jealous of the attention an infant is getting. The sibling may even attempt to feed at the other breast. The appropriate response to this is comfort and cuddling of the sibling, if possible during breast-feeding, rather than horror or scolding. Of course, parents should try to provide a period of single-minded attention to the older sibling as often as they can.

When an infant is at the precarious stage of learning to walk, some siblings take pleasure in distracting the baby or even causing a fall. This may be a sign of intentional competition, and care should be taken to discourage such behavior. But children need a more or less harmless way to express their competitiveness, and the baby will not suffer from having to try again.

On the other hand, children are often fascinated with the games an infant needs in order to practice babbling speech and manual manipulation, and can endure repetition much longer than a parent can. As long as siblings understand how to avoid harming an infant, their play with the baby should be encouraged.

Toilet Training. Many relatives or "old school" baby-sitters may begin to make a younger mother feel inadequate if she is not toilet training her child near the end of his first year. In some cultures, children are routinely forced to learn toilet training in their first year.

The questions surrounding toilet training are always difficult, but it does seem best for the child if the practice is not forced on him. There may be some sphincter control in a 10-month-old baby, but it is still a reflex. Few babies are mature enough to need or understand toilet training in the tenth month. They may passively submit at this age, but the consequence is likely to be rebellious "accidents" and the retention of feces in the second year.

THE ELEVENTH MONTH

Feet and Shoes. The child's feet may look quite peculiar at this stage. Most infants begin to stand on what appear to be rolled-over feet. As they begin to balance with their legs wide apart, their feet splay out and they look like walking ducks. Don't worry: As toddlers learn to walk, they gain balance, no longer need a wide base, and have stronger feet and arches. While learning to walk, toddlers need to be able to grip with their toes; shoes with very soft soles or bare feet are much better than hard soles.

Physical Progress. Most babies of 11 months are well on their way toward the first independent step, although most will not attain it in this month. Many babies of this age will have fashioned their own walker from a lightweight chair or their own stroller. The average baby will be able to drop and pick up toys with one hand while supported by the other. Some child-rearing experts do not recommend the use of walkers since they are associated with many accidents and may be detrimental to the child's neuromuscular development. It may be best to use them sparingly. Many babies wait until this age to start "cruising," walking side to side while pulling themselves along a bed or sofa with their hands. By the 11th month, many children know quite a few words and can identify things by name, although they may still be speaking gibberish. Children this age have a mature grasp, thumb and forefinger, and have little trouble holding small objects like a raisin. They also have no trouble putting small objects into their mouth. It's best to keep such objects out of reach since they are a perfect size to block the windpipe if the child chokes on them. Children at this age may be able to put on their own socks and untie their shoes.

Yes and No. About this age, many babies begin to be aware of the difference between good and naughty, and to test out the word *no*. This is a pattern that will become very familiar in the early part of the second year. Around the first birthday, a baby may begin to say "no" over and over, accompanied by appropriate head shaking. Infants get so taken up with this that they may spend all day refusing to be changed, refusing to eat, refusing a bath, and so on.

THE TWELFTH MONTH

Food. Idiosyncrasies may be common at this time: An infant may absolutely refuse a food eaten enthusiastically 6 weeks earlier. A diet may consist of a good breakfast, a not-so-good lunch, and no dinner at all. Probably the best policy at this time is to let the baby satisfy himself. No child will starve for a harmful period if good food and love are available. As mentioned in the seventh month, a child can be well nourished on a surprisingly small diet.

Negativism. The negativism of the second year begins in earnest now for many children, and is a perplexing behavior. A particularly active child may begin to have tantrums at night and scream inconsolably when faced with even the simplest decision, such as whether to eat a piece of fruit. Most first-time parents are at a loss over some of this behavior, and few parents can really help at these times. The tantrums reflect a child's turmoil in learning to sort out yes from no, mine from yours, and good from bad. It is usually best to let the tantrum run its course, and be ready to reassure an exhausted and confused toddler afterward.

Talking. Do not be discouraged if the baby is not speaking yet. One in four normal, healthy children will not speak three adult words (other than "mama" and "dada") until 4 or 5 months from now. The only reason for concern is if a child is not turning around at the sound of a voice and is not imitating sounds. These may be signs of a hearing problem.

Walking. As they near their first birthday, many children are well into the experiment of trying to walk, although they would rather crawl to get around. When a baby falls over while trying to walk, the resulting tears are more likely from disappointment than pain; reassurance and a new start are what are needed most. In general, babies don't need hard walking shoes, and parents shouldn't buy a 1-year-old baby shoes "large enough to grow into." If the baby is pigeon-toed or seems to stumble too much, have the doctor check her gait. Infants may seem to lose a fraction of an inch as they start to stand because the vertebrae settle with the new posture.

Weight Gain. Weight gain may stabilize for a time because the baby is paying more attention to movement than to eating, and exercising more than before. At the same time, the baby may not yet be digesting solid food completely. All this is normal, and signs of undigested food in the stool are not usually a cause for concern.

TABLE 7.2: RECOMMENDED SCHEDULE FOR ACTIVE IMMUNIZATION OF NORMAL INFANTS AND CHILDREN

Recommended Age[1]	Immunizations[2]	Comments
2 months	DTP, HbCV[3], OPV	DTP and OPV can be initiated as early as 4 weeks after birth in areas of high endemicity or during epidemics.
4 months	DTP, HbCV, OPV	2-month interval (minimum of 6 weeks) desired for OPV to avoid interference from previous dose.
6 months	DTP, HbCV	Third dose of OPV is not indicated in the U.S. but is desirable in other geographic areas where polio is endemic.
15 months	MMR[4], HbCV[5]	Tuberculin testing may be done at this visit.
15–18 months	DTP[6], OPV[7]	
4–6 years	DTP[8], OPV	At or before school entry
11–12 years	MMR	At entry to middle school or junior high unless second dose was given previously
14–16 years	Td	Repeat every 10 years

[1]These recommended ages should not be construed as absolute as, for example, 2 months can be 6 to 10 weeks. However MMR usually should not be given to children under 12 months. (If measles vaccination is indicated, monovalent measles vaccine is recommended, and MMR should be given subsequently, at 15 months.)

[2]DTP = diphtheria and tetanus toxoids with pertussis vaccine; HbCV = Haemophilus b conjugate vaccine; OPV = oral poliovirus containing attenuated poliovirus types 1, 2, 3; MMR = live measles, mumps, and rubella viruses in a combined vaccine; Td = adult tetanus toxoid (full dose) and diphtheria toxoid (reduced dose) for adult use.

[3]As of October 1990, only one HbCV (HbOC) is approved for use in children younger than 15 months.

[4]May be given at 12 months in areas with recurrent measles transmission.

[5]Any licensed Haemophilus b conjugate vaccine may be given.

[6]Should be given 6 to 12 months after third dose and may be given simultaneoulsy with MMR at 15 months.

[7]May be given simultaneoulsy with MMR and HbCV at 15 months or at any time between 12 and 24 months; priority should be given to MMR vaccine at recommended age.

[8]Can be given up to the seventh birthday.

VACCINATIONS

All children should receive vaccinations according to the timetable recommended in table 7.2 beginning in their second month. The goal of vaccination is to mimic the natural infection by stimulating the immune system to react and learn to recognize the infectious agent, but in a way that causes no harm to the person getting vaccinated. Immunization usually provides total protection against a disease, in many cases for a lifetime. For some diseases, such as tetanus, protection from a vaccine is only partial, and revaccination is required some years later.

No vaccine can be completely safe, in part because children's immune systems are not totally predictable. Vaccines often cause transient and trivial side effects, such as fever and rash or tenderness at the site of injec-

tion. An allergic reaction at the site of the injection is rare, but can happen. Serious adverse reactions are exceedingly rare. In any case, any risk to the child from the vaccine is far outweighed by the danger of illness or death from contracting one of the diseases the vaccine would have prevented. When parents or doctors grow lax about vaccination, "forgotten" diseases such as polio and whooping cough can come back to maim and kill unprotected children. In most of the United States, by law children cannot enter school without having completed their vaccinations.

Vaccinations should not be administered when a baby is seriously ill. However, a minor cold or allergy is no reason to suspend a vaccination schedule. In general, immunological abnormalities and any treatments designed to suppress the immune system disqualify the use of vaccines containing live viruses (such as those against measles, mumps, rubella, and polio).

THE SECOND YEAR

By their first birthday, most children are well on the road to their first true independence—the ability to walk. The years before they enter school are a time of increasing emphasis on self-mastery, and a time to begin slowly to understand concepts of social interaction and the difference between private and public behavior. Even more than during the first year, a toddler should be understood in terms of the particular developmental stage. Actual calendar age may be more or less irrelevant, and the age categories listed below should be considered only as rough guides. Of more importance are the subject categories, which represent specific issues in the progress toward maturity.

Child Abuse. The second year is the beginning of the first stage at which child abuse most commonly occurs (the second stage is during adolescence). Child abuse may represent an adult's own turmoil at separation as a child tests his independence. Any parent has undoubtedly been frustrated to the point where he or she can understand why some people succumb to the temptation to abuse a child. But most parents do not abuse their children, and understanding the frustration does not excuse or condone abuse. Most parents who actually give in to this urge have themselves been abused as children.

Falling. No child learns to walk without plenty of spills. Perhaps it is fortunate that at the start of the process, most children appear to be fearless. Also, fortunately, the skull does not close until 18 months of age in most children, so it can absorb much of the impact of a fall without harm to the brain. Nonetheless, a parent should take a fall very seriously. If it causes unconsciousness or a dazed attitude, a doctor should be called without delay. Preventive methods are always preferable to crises. Toddlers can be taught not to fall straight backward like a board by repeatedly bending them from a standing into a sitting position. Children also learn by imitation; showing a toddler how to back down stairs one step at a time may help prevent a fall.

Fears. Sometime during the second year all children become clinging and afraid of strangers, relatives, and particularly doctors. A sensitive doctor will examine a 2-year-old while the child sits on the parent's lap or stands in front of the doctor. A parent should always be nearby. People who stare a toddler in the eye at this stage or ask direct questions are particularly fearsome. This is an entirely normal stage, but relatives should be warned about it before a visit. Many children also develop a fear of the bathtub sometime during their second year. This is serious only if the parents react as if it were serious. To help overcome this fear, a parent should temporarily resume using the bathing table or sink used previously, or take a bath with the child.

Negativism. This is the hallmark of the second year. By saying "no" over and over, and intentionally provoking it from parents, a child sets limits and begins to resolve priorities. Between the ages of 1 and 2, toddlers will often repeatedly do something they know will provoke a parent's anger, and seem to be almost begging for punishment. Why? It is the essence of the child's growing independence, the starting point of the journey that ends years later with separation from the parents. The most important and most difficult job for the parent is to be consistent in the use of "no." Inconsistency will only confuse the child and lead to more testing and negative behavior. Negativism is particularly evident at mealtime. An infant may refuse certain types of food or solid food altogether, and may regress to the bottle or try to breast-feed. These are all signs of confusion about growing independence, and are best met with a sense of humor.

Nutrition and Weight Gain. By the first birthday, a healthy baby will weigh approximately three times the birth weight (large babies may not triple the birth weight). During the second year, the baby will exercise more and, for a variety of reasons, eat less. The diet will also be transformed to include more solid food. A slowing of growth is normal and healthy, as the growth charts in this chapter indicate. The average child will gain only 5 or 6 pounds in her second year.

During the second year, mealtime becomes playtime for most youngsters. A baby will have a great time waving an empty cup, banging a spoon, and all the while picking, pushing, squishing, throwing, or examining the food that was meant to be eaten. More food will actually get into the mouth if it is presented a few bites at a time rather than as a small "mountain" in a bowl. At around 15 months, most babies begin to master eating with a spoon. Avoid helping too much as the baby struggles with the spoon. This is a learning process like any other, and the best way to learn is to practice. It's a good idea, though, to spread some paper or other protective cover under the child's chair.

Eating development provides an excellent demonstration of the way the baby is programmed for each successive stage. In order to be able to master feeding himself, a baby must be able to sit erect and hold his head up firmly. This was learned several months ago. Eating also requires sophisticated use of the hands, which has also progressed from a clumsy pawlike grasp of a block to a delicate thumb-and-forefinger hold on a raisin or pea. (Hard or teething biscuits are particularly appropriate at this stage. They provide something for the baby to hold or rub against sore gums, and they gradually soften in the mouth so they don't need to be chewed.) As teeth develop, a baby progresses from mouthing food to chewing it. By the time a baby can really chew, the digestive system has been thoroughly prepared to handle regular table food.

What is a well-balanced diet for a 1- or 2-year-old? Perhaps the best way to ensure a nutritious diet for a toddler, as for anyone, is to be sure that adequate foods from each of the basic food groups are offered each day. How much food is enough? Trust the child's instincts. As long as children are offered a selection of foods comprising a well-balanced diet, they will consume the proper amounts. Many adult eating problems originate early in life, often as a result of being urged to eat despite a lack of hunger, or because food is used as a reward for good behavior. The more you can avoid confrontations over how much and what to eat, the better. Respect likes and dislikes by giving a child nutritional alternatives. By the time a child is eating table food, some parents switch from whole milk to low-fat milk. Although whether consumption of a low-fat diet at this point in life affects the atherosclerotic process (hardening of the arteries) later on is still controversial, there is no harm in switching to low-fat milk as long as a child eats sufficient meat, eggs, and vegetables to provide essential fatty acids. Changing to skim milk before these other foods are a regular part of the diet, however, can be dangerous and interfere with a child's normal growth.

Obesity. To many parents (and even more grandparents), a healthy baby is one who is chubby, with rolls of body fat. But as the baby begins to walk and exercise more, the body fat should begin to give way to muscle and lean tissue. A grandparent may worry that the baby is getting too skinny, but in the United States overweight is a more serious and common health problem than underweight. Although the precise causes of obesity are unknown, glandular or organic problems are exceedingly rare. Metabolism may play a role, but faulty eating habits or chronic overeating without adequate exercise is what adds the extra pounds. If a 1- or 2-year-old is obese, the best approach is to provide a balanced diet that is lower in calories but still meets nutritional needs and fuels normal growth. Let the child's growth in height catch up with his weight. Achieving this may well require modifying the entire family's eating habits, including preference for snack foods. (It's very hard to mollify a hungry toddler with a carrot when a parent is munching on a cookie!) Another strategy is to increase the child's level of exercise, although most toddlers are active on their own. Exercise alone will not cause significant weight loss in a person who is chronically overeating, but accompanied by diet changes, it will speed weight loss and help control appetite.

Perception. The average 1-year-old is beginning to understand concepts of reality that are quite sophisticated. At this age a youngster can follow the arc of a ball after it has dropped out of the line of sight and understands where it has gone. The same is true of objects that have been purposely hidden from view; at some point at the end of the first year or early in the second year, a child will know enough to go to where something has been hidden, move the obstruction aside, and retrieve it.

Skills. Sometime between their first and second birthdays, most infants master the following skills:

- Imitating housework
- Simple tasks such as putting away toys
- Drinking from a cup and eating with a spoon
- Washing hands
- Scribbling with a crayon
- Building a tower four blocks high that will stand without toppling

The toddler can point to a body part and name familiar objects. By the second birthday, most toddlers can stand, walk forward and backward and up and down stairs, and can kick a ball, as well as throw a ball overhand with rudimentary aim.

Sleep Problems. A 1-year-old eventually tests all limits, including bedtime. A toddler who has tantrums every evening probably is being allowed to stay up too late. Parents should avoid keeping the child up so long that she is exhausted and irritable and asks to go to bed. If this is happening, the parents should begin to be gently firm about an earlier bedtime. A 1-year-old is old enough to sleep through most nights without crying. Any crying bouts, particularly if they are regular and repeated, should not be met with a response that is too quick, too predictable, or overly sympathetic. Unless a child is seriously ill, this is probably another attempt to test parents' limits, and represents a certain vacillation about independence. In many cultures, children are allowed to crawl in and out of the parents' bed freely until the age of 4 or 5. In our society, the practice is less common. Parents need to establish their own response to this activity and work to modify the child's behavior to satisfy her needs, as well as the parents'. The knotty question of when and how to go about removing the child from the bed before she begins to mature psychosexually should always be considered.

Speech. At some point the child will speak three "adult" words, and begin to combine words in pairs. During the second year, toddlers begin to voice some of their wants in intelligible speech. Language develops in a fairly standard pattern: single words in the first 6 months of the year; phrases, adjectives, and adverbs in the second half. Suddenly in the 6 months after the second birthday, many toddlers will erupt into a stream of sentences and ideas that they seem to have been formulating for some time.

If a toddler does not start to speak any words during the second year, a hearing problem may be the reason. There are other possible explanations for delayed speech. A very active child, for whom learning motor skills is most important, may delay speech and then learn to talk in a rush after the second birthday. In large families, the hubbub and activity may cause a toddler to withdraw; gentle encouragement to experiment with sounds is often all that is needed to draw him out. Alternatively, a child with siblings may not feel pressed to speak because he and his companions communicate effectively in other ways. A bilingual family sometimes confuses a small toddler, and often delays the development of speech.

A special problem is the family so intent on having their baby speak that, ironically, they inhibit him. Each utterance may be followed swiftly with an exaggerated response, or a demand for progress, so that the child becomes intimidated. Particularly if a child has started to speak and then stops, a family should consider whether they are exerting too much pressure.

Tantrums. Some children dissolve into tears and inconsolable screams when they realize that their parents are about to leave them temporarily. Other children may kick and scream when denied an opportunity to watch TV. These tantrums, and the fact that the child cares so intensely for something so trivial, may seem inexplicable to an adult. Some people (primarily nonparents) even misunderstand tantrums as a sign of a serious disturbance in a child, or parental neglect. In fact, tantrums are just another sign of a child's mounting confusion about independence. Children having real tantrums at this age can seldom be calmed down or distracted by a parent's coddling. However, they may cool off by themselves quite suddenly, and return to playing placidly with the nearest toy. The best parental approach seems to be to stay nearby or hold the child while the tantrum runs its course, and be available for consolation and cuddling afterward. It is important not to reinforce this behavior by yielding to a child's demands after a tantrum.

Thumb- and Finger-Sucking. Many parents worry that children who continue to suck their thumbs or fingers in their second year may be developing a bad habit. However, this behavior is completely normal and probably essential at this age; in fact, it is one of the few self-reliant ways that a 1-year-old has of handling tension. Some children may also need a comforter, some well-worn beloved object to hold while sucking. Studies have found that finger-sucking increases early in the second year, but begins to subside in the second half of the year. Most children studied showed that none of the problems parents fear occur, such as distorted mouths and a persistent habit of thumb-sucking into the school years.

Toilet Training. While it is possible to rush a 1-year-old to the toilet in time to catch a bowel movement, most experts agree it's not a good idea, probably even less so than it was in younger children. At least a 10-month-old baby is compliant; toddlers in their second year are independent and often resistant, and the toilet, like the high chair, is apt to become a battleground. A child may hold back movements, wet his pants after getting off the potty, or hide in a corner while having a bowel movement—all signals of too much parental control. At a later stage, a child will naturally want to learn toilet habits, and training will be easier and less fraught with implications.

Walking. A toddler's progress in learning to walk can be judged by three factors: width of gait, balance, and the ability to walk and do something else at the same time. The width of gait narrows gradually as walking improves. Balance becomes steadier; it takes a lot of practice to avoid falling after losing one's balance. But walking really becomes a confirmed skill when an infant can stop concentrating on it in order to turn and listen, or bend over to pick something up and examine it. An improving ability to walk brings about a dramatic change in a toddler's posture. At first, a child's feet turn out almost at right angles; soon they begin to draw in toward the parallel. A learning walker balances by thrusting out his belly in front and bottom in back. As the back muscles strengthen, this posture should become more erect, but not until age 4 or 5. One of the things to ask a child's doctor at this stage is for an assessment of the child's gait and whether it will need to be corrected. Standing with slightly bowed legs is also normal for early months of walking.

THE THIRD YEAR

This is the period when the positives of independence begin to outweigh the negatives—even from the child's point of view. Many children by the age of 3 separate from their mothers without any fuss. It is also a time for imitation, and parents can capitalize on this behavior to teach the toddler many important things.

Breath-holding. One of the heart-stopping gambits a toddler may try out at the age of 2 is to stop breathing until the eyes roll up and skin turns grayish blue. Like the tantrums of the previous year, this behavior is a sign of the turmoil going on inside a child. Usually it occurs after a tumble or a reprimand. Unfortunately, the breathing reflexes at this age are not mature enough to force respiration immediately as they would in an adult who attempts breath-holding. However, the brief period without oxygen does not damage the brain and the spell has no permanent effect. Breath-holding does not cause epilepsy, as some people believe. The children who bring on such spells are usually manipulative and overprotected; if encouraged in such behavior with too much sympathy and concern, or compliance to demands, these children will soon learn how to control their parents. This is the time to learn to set limits on a toddler's behavior.

Child Abuse. Child abuse is more widespread than most people realize, and often involves people other than parents. Be particularly aware that baby-sitters can be child abusers. It is also vital to consider child abuse if a child avoids a particular person habitually, or if she shows injuries of a kind that cannot be easily explained. Doctors are often reluctant to point out the possibility of sexual abuse of a child, but if pain in the genital area is not explained by a foreign object or illness, it must be considered. Children at this age are the most common victims of child abuse of all kinds. Every parent has understandable feelings of irritation and wishes for independence from a child, but if these wishes are translated into physical aggression, the parent as well as the child is in dire need of help. Most communities have counseling centers and hot lines to help with child abuse problems; keep the number handy, just in case. Many families affected by child abuse seem to adjust well afterward if they have cooperated with counseling.

Foreign Objects and Pica. Two-year-olds enjoy exploring their own orifices; again, parents must be on guard against their own instinctive negative reactions about manipulation of genitals, which is still a very normal behavior. Manipulating them often includes trying to insert objects into the urethra and rectum, as well as into the nose and ears, not to mention the mouth. Free at last to roam, a 2-year-old can try to put almost any small object almost anywhere. One-sided drainage from the nose and a foul-smelling discharge are warnings that a foreign object may be lodged inside. Use judgment about whether to try to remove such an object yourself; the problem often requires the help of a doctor. It's also amazing what children this age try to swallow. Most foreign objects are probably coughed up without notice, but choking accidents do occur and parents should know how to respond (see Basics of CPR and Life Support, chapter 13). If something small enough to still permit the flow of air is stuck in the larynx, it may be several days before any symptoms appear. The child may then develop hoarseness, a cough, and problems in swallowing and in breathing.

Another potentially serious problem is pica, the propensity of some children to eat nonfood items such as dirt, paint chips, turpentine, and medications. This behavior reaches its peak during the third year. It does not affect all toddlers, but can lead to brain damage from lead paint and a wide range of poisons. Do everything you can to keep such dangerous objects away from toddlers; some 600,000 poisonous ingestions occur in the United States annually, and poisoning and accidents are the leading cause of death in children (see "Poisoning" in chapter 14).

Hyperactivity. What is the difference between an active child and a hyperactive one in need of medical treatment? This question nags teachers, parents, and doctors. Unfortunately, children are sometimes labeled as hyperactive and treated with drugs when the problem does not merit such an approach. Before a child is assumed to be hyperactive, a careful medical evaluation should be done to rule out other problems. At one time hyperactivity was called minimal brain damage, until a number of pediatric specialists pointed out that no connection between hyperactivity and brain damage had ever been detected. The condition is very difficult to define because so many normal children are constantly on the move. However, hyperactive or hyperkinetic children literally never stop. Nothing can hold their attention; they seem to be driven from one activity to the next without completing anything. The accepted treatments for established hyperactivity include drugs such as methylphenidate or dextroamphetamine (Dexedrine). Often, the problem is more psychological than physical; parents may have become so battle-scarred by dealing with a very active child that they frustrate him by their inattention. In other cases, what a teacher takes for hyperactivity may be a learning disability or language problem.

Nutrition. Most children by their third year are eating more or less their parents' diets. For information on a balanced diet, see chapter 5, The Basics of Good Nutrition.

Perception. This is a time of sorting for many children. They learn to group toys by their size and color. They may also, with positive interaction from a parent, begin to learn pronouns and the concepts behind them: his, mine, yours, ours, theirs, sharing, possession.

Skills. During their third year, most children fully master eating with a spoon, undressing and dressing (perhaps with some supervision), and washing their hands. A child of this age typically plays games such as tag with other children, can build a tower of eight blocks—twice as tall as last year—and can draw a line that is almost straight vertically. Motor skills become quite sophisticated: Most children at the age of 3 can jump in place, do a broad jump, pedal a tricycle, and stand on one foot for a second or two.

Speech. At some point nine out of ten normal 2-year-olds begin to combine different words, follow directions, and identify a body part when it is named. Most of them can also name familiar objects in a picture and begin to understand and use plurals. Several reasons for a delay in speech were mentioned in the second year. Other problems to be sensitive to during this year are stuttering, hesitation in speech, and regression to baby talk. It has already been mentioned that parents and older siblings can delay speech by putting too much pressure on a child to learn language. Siblings may mimic or tease a toddler's attempts to speak, or pressure her too hard to imitate them. If parents become aware of this, they may want to limit their own active reinforcement of the toddler's babble, to let up on some of the pressure. The arrival of a new baby in the family can also cause some regression in the speech of a 2-year-old, as she tries to reclaim some of the attention lost to the new sibling.

Toilet Training and Bowel Problems. Most 2-year-olds at some point exhibit an active interest in using the toilet, and it is appropriate to wait for them to express this interest before trying to teach them to do so. This should be the quickest and easiest time for toilet training. But it is wise not to place too much emphasis on the task or make it a focus for attention or rebellion. A child can too easily turn this into a tease. Treated sensitively, a child will come to see toilet training as a very exciting aspect of independence and will be eager to attain it.

There is no one method of toilet training. A straightforward, low-key approach usually works best. When the child seems ready, start by setting him or her fully clothed on the potty seat at a regular time. Next, take the child to the potty when he or she needs changing. Place the stool in the potty to help a child see what is supposed to go into the bowl. Given the chance to imitate older children or parents in the bathroom, a child will soon get the idea. Accompanying parents in the bathroom also helps with some aspects of gender identity. Do not push the child out of diapers too quickly, or attempt night training until the child asks to be helped. Using adult-style pants too soon is risking that the child may be upset by occasional accidents. And if the child has to adjust to a new situation, such as the birth of a sibling or a change of dwelling, expect a regression in toilet skills. The appropriate reaction is to point out that this is all right and you understand why it has happened.

For some children, bowel training seems to represent a threat; they have an unspoken fear about letting part of themselves go down the drain. This translates into retention of bowel movements, so that when the movement finally comes it may be hard and painful. When bowel movements hurt, the sphincter closes reflexively, and the problem becomes a vicious cycle. The most important thing for a parent in this case is to assure the child that the problem will go away, that he need not worry about any failure to perform, and that he may wear diapers again until bowel movements become natural and comfortable. At the same time, the parent should use a stool softener, which will substantiate the promise that bowel movements won't hurt anymore. Occasionally the problem becomes so severe that a suppository or an enema is needed, but this is rare and too harsh a solution for a common problem. They should be avoided whenever possible.

Occasional diarrhea is a very common problem in 2-year-olds. It seems to be brought on by any change in the child's equilibrium: teething, illness, traveling, new foods. Unless the child is failing to gain weight normally, the problem probably reflects the normal immaturity of a 2-year-old's intestinal tract and inability to deal fully with solid foods. If such bowel movements are no more frequent than four or five per day, and unless they contain blood or are accompanied by other symptoms, they probably do not merit serious concern. If they persist or lead to even mild dehydration, a doctor should be consulted.

Toothbrushing. As mentioned, children are great imitators, and that can be used to teach proper toothbrushing, perhaps with the help of the dentist. Like other habits, this one, instilled properly now, should last a lifetime. Cleaning of the teeth should start when the first tooth appears, even if the child is only 7 months old.

THE FOURTH AND FIFTH YEARS

Imagination. The fourth and fifth years are magical times, when a child is able to explore imaginary possibilities and to some extent live in a pretend world where no adults can enter. This is an important time in a child's development. A common part of a youngster's fantasy world is an imaginary friend. Imaginary friends are a good way for a child to try out various personalities without being committed to them. Fantasy companions may be very good or horrendously bad. Sometimes these fantasy friends are blamed for the child's own acts. This is normal, not pathological. For one thing, a child can find out easily what parents will allow by having an imaginary friend do something. A parent should say what he would do if sometime he found the child herself being naughty like that. Many children also try out lying and stealing to see what happens. Of course, such behavior should not go uncorrected, but it is a mistake to interpret it as an indication of a future problem.

Introspection. Before about the third birthday, a preschool toddler has been concentrating on learning physical controls; afterward, the focus changes. The period approaching the start of regular school is one of introspection and attempts to understand the meaning of the child's own achievements. Three- and 4-year-olds are constantly questioning their parents about themselves and the world around them. Their questions become ever more difficult to answer. Why is there sun? When is next week? Where does the wind go? And Why? Why? Why?

Meals. By the time children have fully mastered the use of a spoon and cup, it is appropriate to move them from the high chair to a chair with the family at the dining table. This usually happens sometime at age 3 or 4, and the transition is likely to cause some disruption in family mealtimes. More now than ever, when a child's eating practices are obvious to both parents and siblings, proper eating behavior and standards should be enforced. A child should understand that he should eat what is served, choose from acceptable alternatives, or not eat at all. The further question of table manners now enters the picture. Food should not become a literal weapon any more than it should be a figurative one. The traditional and time-honored response to serious misbehavior at the table is to send a child to his room until he is ready to finish quietly, which usually happens well before dessert is served. Dessert, however, should not be withheld as punishment; temporary banishment from society sends a clearer message.

Night Toilet Training. By the time a child enters kindergarten, daytime toilet training should be complete. The need for a healthy child to wear diapers to kindergarten would, of course, be a cause for ridicule and a sign of serious problems in the child. Before the fifth birthday, most children will probably be night trained, but at their own request. The need to stay dry all night must come from deep within, or night training cannot work, because it is a matter of subconscious control. This may not occur until sometime after the third birthday. But night training is also a matter of physical maturation. Some children with small bladders or incomplete neuromuscular control may continue to wet the bed for several more years. Many normal children wet the bed occasionally even after training.

Sex. No parent should be surprised by stumbling on a group of preschoolers examining each other's genitals or giggling in a nervous, conspiratorial way about some bathroom or primitive sexual joke. Three-year-olds are simply exploring the nature of their physical differences from each other, and are far too immature to understand or act on any of them. As with reactions to masturbation, it may be difficult for an adult to avoid showing shock at such a moment. But children at this age already have some built-in guilt and prohibition about this early sexual exploration, and any effort to scold or prohibit them will increase their guilt and lead to attitudes of shame whose permanent consequences can hardly be imagined. Ideally, a self-assured parent can, in a constructive way, ensure that while the children are exploring each other, the things they deduce are accurate and positive.

Siblings. Many 3- and 4-year-olds suddenly become siblings. It is important to ensure that they receive adequate support and attention while one parent is caring for a newborn infant. When a toddler causes a younger infant to cry in the course of play, the parent's response is often to comfort the infant and shout at the toddler. But it may be the toddler who needs comfort more than the infant. A scolding may be seen as a rejection, and will exacerbate feelings of jealousy toward the infant.

Skills. By the time they start kindergarten, virtually all children can dress themselves without supervision. They understand colors and what to do to relieve hunger, coldness, and fatigue. Most 4-year-olds can tell you what a common word means and what household objects are made of. Average 4-year-olds can balance on one foot for 10 seconds, hop on one foot, and catch a ball bounced to them. Most children have developed handedness by the time they start regular school. Fortunately, few people view left-handedness as a problem anymore; the composer Johann Sebastian Bach and Lewis Carroll, the author of *Alice Through the Looking Glass,* are among the many famous left-handers.

Speech. A 3-year-old child begins to abandon baby talk entirely, although there may still be trouble with certain combinations of sounds. The child by now understands fully the difference between mine and yours. Don't be surprised if a 3-year-old begins to use rude words. He has learned them from older playmates who know they are considered unacceptable. Practicing them at home may be a way of taunting parents, who have two choices: to be firm about the use of dirty words around the house or to avoid paying them too much attention and thereby turning them into attractive taboos.

THE SCHOOL YEARS

Nutrition. For better or worse, a child's eating habits are fairly well established by school age. However, significant new peer pressures will affect a youngster's culinary desires. Before long, a child will want to eat what his peers do, which may not be what the parents have offered previously. In this situation, parents must judge how much of a stigma a child will suffer by not conforming, and weigh this against their nutritional standards. Remember, however, that schoolchildren are likely to trade or scrounge to get what they want to eat. Older children with mobility and an allowance can buy what they like, which usually ends up being candy or fast-food burgers and fries. The best fall-back position is to provide the most nutritious diet for meals that are still consumed at home—breakfast and dinner.

Personality. By the time a child starts school, most of the important early developmental milestones have been passed. The next few years are marked by continued physical growth, but at a slower rate than during infancy and early childhood. Personality traits become more established and, as the child progresses in school, intellectual development broadens. From now on, the best indication of a child's social and intellectual progress will come from teachers. The next few years are generally smooth ones. The next most trying period for both children and parents is puberty and adolescence.

Vaccinations. Another set of vaccinations is needed before a child enters school, at age 4½ or 5. Most states require children to be vaccinated before starting school.

COMMON ILLNESSES OF CHILDHOOD

DIARRHEA

DEFINITION

It is often difficult to tell whether an infant has diarrhea or simply has frequent loose but normal bowel movements. Many infants have a reflex that gives them a bowel movement soon after every meal. Diarrhea is by definition looser than normal bowel movements; therefore, it is important to notice what is *normal* for each child. Too much water may show up as a water ring in the diaper. In less developed countries, diarrhea is the most frequent cause of infant death because of the dehydration it causes. In the United States, however, it is rarely fatal because treatment is readily available.

CAUSE

Diarrhea is most often caused by acute infections that don't affect a child's ability to thrive. If there is malabsorption of fat as well as water, stools may be foul smelling and grayish. This is a condition known as steatorrhea. Children with malabsorption of this type often have unusually large appetites to try and compensate for the calories that are passing right through them. Diarrhea that persists for days and days may be caused by lactose intolerance (which is less common in breast-fed babies than in those given formula), but transient lactose intolerance may also be a *result* of diarrhea.

TREATMENT

The goal of treatment for an infant or small child with diarrhea is to prevent dehydration. For virally induced diarrhea, milk products other than breast milk should be stopped for 24 hours and clear fluids should be given. After 24 hours, clear fluids should be continued as half-strength formula diluted with water, and other binding foods such as bananas, rice cereal, or toast should begin to be introduced. The best clear fluid to use is one of the oral rehydration fluids developed specifically to replace fluid losses, and sold in pharmacies or supermarkets under trade names. There is no place for medicines—either antibiotics or antidiarrheals—in the treatment of the child with acute viral gastroenteritis. If diarrhea is caused by lactose intolerance, the treatment is clear fluids followed by change to a sucrose- or glucose-based formula.

FAILURE TO THRIVE

DEFINITION

Is my baby growing properly? The question troubles nearly all new parents. In a large majority, the answer is yes. Obviously, some children are smaller than others; what matters is the rate at which they grow. As long as a child's growth tends to follow a steady upward curve (see the growth charts in this chapter), the child is growing appropriately, regardless of size. A persistent failure to follow the curve, however, reflects failure to thrive. Therefore, determining true failure to thrive is difficult and usually requires measurements over a period of months.

CAUSE

The major cause of failure to thrive is inadequate nutrition, usually because of some feeding problem. The difficulty may be due to the mother's nervousness during feeding or to chronic overfeeding, which ironically causes the baby to spit up too much of what is eaten. Malabsorption, in which the baby does not properly digest food, is another nutritional cause of failure to thrive. The problem may also be due to disorders of the heart, kidneys, thyroid, lungs, adrenal glands, nervous system, or intestines. Testing for these conditions may require hospitalization, so before resorting to this evaluation, a pediatrician will always ask parents to keep a careful diary of how much the infant is eating and when, in order to rule out nutritional causes.

TREATMENT

Failure to thrive that is caused by nutritional problems is cured relatively easily by finding ways to provide more calories and to reverse the downward trend in growth. Once the underlying cause is detected and corrected, most babies quickly catch up.

FEVER

DEFINITION

The body's normal temperature varies over the course of the day from about 97.6°F (36.4°C) in the morning to about 99.5°F (37.5°C) in the late afternoon, the so-called diurnal variation. Minimal elevations of temperature (100.4°F to 101.3°F or 38°C to 38.5°C) may be caused by hot weather or excessive clothing. Fever is a symptom, not a disease, and generally indicates the presence of infection. Many physicians think that fever is the body's normal response to infection.

Generally, rectal thermometers are used in children under 5 years of age because oral temperatures are difficult to obtain reliably in younger children. The thermometer should be in place for 2 minutes for rectal temperature taking, 3 minutes for oral and 5 minutes for axillary (armpit). Axillary measures are the least reliable. Commercially available temperature strips that are applied to the forehead are inaccurate and often miss fevers. Similarly, touching the forehead often misses fevers.

CAUSE AND DIAGNOSIS

When a child develops a fever, parents should look carefully for signs of the underlying cause.

Is breathing difficult?
Is the baby pulling at his ears?
Does urinating seem to cause pain?
Is there severe diarrhea or a stiff neck?

If the cause is a viral or bacterial infection, it will probably last for 2 to 3 days or else manifest itself in other symptoms, such as rash, swollen lymph nodes, or runny nose that can lead to a specific diagnosis.

TREATMENT

Although a doctor should be consulted, especially if fever exceeds 104°F (40°C) or occurs in infants under 2 months of age, fever alone does not generally require treatment. Many doctors prefer to let a baby's natural defenses fight off mild infections, and reserve treatment such as antibiotics for more serious illnesses. Parents often mistakenly believe that high fever causes brain damage and that fevers left untreated only go higher. As a result of these misconceptions, parents often treat low-grade fevers unnecessarily. Generally, if the fever is greater than 102°F (39°C) acetaminophen can be given orally to children older than 2 months of age. Treatment will usually reduce the temperature by 1 or 2 degrees within 2 hours, but will rarely reduce the temperature to a completely normal level. Ibuprofen has been approved for treatment of children 6 months or older and has the advantage of longer duration of action. However, acetaminophen remains the drug of choice.

The American Academy of Pediatrics has recommended that children under 18 years of age not be treated with aspirin if they have flu symptoms, chickenpox or another viral infection because studies have linked aspirin in this setting to Reye's syndrome. Most physicians have stopped using aspirin to treat fevers.

VOMITING

All babies spit up (regurgitate), and vomiting may be difficult to distinguish from normal regurgitation. If a baby grows normally despite frequent spitting up, there is probably no cause for alarm. But true vomiting is a danger sign, especially if it involves projectile vomiting. If food or formula is vomited forcefully, sometimes shooting across the room, this might be an indication of an obstruction at the stomach outlet (pyloric stenosis), which prevents food from passing into the small intestine. Fortunately, this condition is easy to correct with surgery to open the pyloric sphincter between the stomach and the small intestine. Other causes of vomiting, which should be treated according to individual circumstances, include:

Viral stomach infections
Food allergies
Accidental ingestion of drugs or other toxic substances
Diseases of the liver or kidney

Children who can't keep anything down should be carefully evaluated for signs of dehydration; in severe cases rehydration fluids may need to be given intravenously until the vomiting subsides.

COMMON DISEASES

APPENDICITIS

DEFINITION AND INCIDENCE

Appendicitis is an acute inflammation of the appendix, a dead-end tube that leads from the cecum, where the large intestine begins, in the right lower abdomen. Appendicitis is the most common reason for abdominal surgery in a child, and one of the few indications for emergency surgery in children over the age of 2. About 4 out of every 1,000 children under the age of 14 have to undergo an appendectomy to remove the appendix. Appendicitis is more common in boys than girls, for unknown reasons, and is rare under the age of 2, although when it occurs in very young children it is usually more dangerous. The frequency of appendicitis increases with age and peaks between 15 and 30 years.

CAUSE

The cause of the inflammation is most often an obstruction, although the reasons for the obstruction vary.

DIAGNOSIS

Typically, appendicitis causes pain in the lower right abdomen or occasionally in the right pelvis. Children with acute appendicitis may hold their hands over their navel when asked where it hurts; infants tend to lie quietly with the hips flexed. In young children, the progression of the disease is often so fast that the first sign may be the intense generalized abdominal pain caused by perforation of the wall of the appendix, without the crampy, spasmodic pains and sometimes constipation that may precede it in older children and adults.

TREATMENT

Surgery is the only treatment for acute appendicitis, and only under the most dire circumstances should it be delayed for more than a few hours. Because a ruptured appendix (perforation) causes release of fecal material from the digestive system into the abdominal cavity and secondary infection, surgery should be performed immediately or after antibiotics are administered intravenously when perforation is suspected. However, a doctor must take time to ascertain that the appendix is indeed the problem and avoid unnecessary surgery. Postoperative recovery is rapid, and most children can resume activities within 3 to 4 days. Although the incidence of perforation is high (20 to 40 percent) in children, the prognosis after surgery is excellent, with a mortality rate of less than 1 percent.

ASTHMA

DEFINITION AND INCIDENCE

Asthma is an allergic reaction of the muscles of the airways which affects passage of air through the lungs, making breathing difficult. Asthma affects 5 to 10 percent of children, but a portion of them may outgrow the condition. Some authorities estimate that as many as 30 percent of asthma sufferers recover completely by adolescence. Physically, asthma involves several reactions to a foreign substance perceived by the body as threatening.

Spasm of the muscle walls of the bronchial tubes
Swelling and inflammation of the mucous membranes
Secretion of mucus and other substances into the
    breathing passages

CAUSE

What substance will provoke an attack of asthma in an individual depends on what that individual is allergic to. Animal dander, dust, pollen, and molds are some common allergens. A predisposition to asthma is often inherited, although the specific allergens vary from one individual in a family to another. Emotions and stress may also play a role (for more information, see chapter 29, Allergies).

DIAGNOSIS

About 85 percent of asthmatic children have their first symptoms by the age of 5. The course and severity of the disease are difficult to predict, although most children have only occasional episodes of mild wheezing and coughing.

TREATMENT

The most convenient and popular treatment for asthma is aerosol inhalers containing drugs that help dilate the constricted airways and steroids, which reduce the inflammation. In severe cases where aerosolized therapy has not stopped an attack, injections of epinephrine or intravenous theophylline or corticosteroids may be effective.

PREVENTION

As much as possible, the substances that provoke asthma in a child should be removed from the house and particularly the child's bedroom. Dust and mold, feather pillows, or even pets may have to go, depending on the cause and severity of the asthma. Desensitizing allergy shots may also be helpful in preventing attacks, although these have to be administered regularly for years in order to be effective. The primary goal remains education of the child and the family to understand the disease, to recognize early signs and symptoms, and to initiate therapy in a timely fashion to minimize the severity of each attack. With appropriately aggressive therapy, very few children should require hospitalization for treatment.

CHICKENPOX

DEFINITION

Chickenpox is a common infectious disease characterized by red spots (macules) that evolve into blisters (vesicles) and then pustules. The spots occur predominantly on the trunk and face, but may appear over most of the body. A new vaccine has recently been approved for use, so chickenpox may soon become as rare as whooping cough.

CAUSE

Chickenpox is caused by the varicella zoster virus, a member of the herpesvirus family.

DIAGNOSIS

The incubation period is 10 to 21 days after a child has been exposed to the chickenpox virus. Symptoms usually begin with a slight fever and malaise. A rash then begins to appear, forming small red bumps that progress to a cloudy, fluid-filled blister on top of a small reddish patch. The blisters eventually break and form a scab. The lymph glands may also swell. The severity of the disease ranges from a rash and not much else to many hundreds of bumps and a fever as high as 105°F (40.5°C). The symptoms are usually worse in the first 3 to 4 days, while the rash is erupting. The vast majority of children recover fully in 1 to 2 weeks. Serious complications, such as pneumonia and encephalitis, are rare and seen mostly in adolescents or adults who contract the disease.

TREATMENT

As a viral infection chickenpox does not respond to active treatment; antibiotics have no effect. The usual strategies are aimed at preventing scratching, to minimize scars and the chance of secondary bacterial infection. Recommendations may include:

Keeping a child's fingernails short and perhaps having a young child wear mittens

Regular antiseptic baths and frequent changes of clothing

Topical application of anti-itch preparations such as calamine lotion

Acetaminophen (not aspirin) to control fever

PREVENTION

A child with chickenpox should be isolated until all of the lesions are scabbed over to prevent spreading the disease to others. The role of a relatively new oral antiviral drug, acyclovir, on the course of chickenpox in children is being evaluated.

COLDS

DEFINITION AND INCIDENCE

A cold is a viral illness that strikes almost everyone at some time or other. In the Northern Hemisphere there are three peak cold seasons: September, late January, and April. Colds are most severe in children younger than 4 years, although complications such as persistent sinusitis are more common in older children.

CAUSE

A cold can be caused by a variety of viruses, although sometimes a concurrent bacterial infection may add complications. Why a cold comes on at a particular time is not known. The cold virus is contagious and is spread through the air, so it can be transmitted rapidly in an enclosed space such as a bus or a nursery school classroom.

DIAGNOSIS

The first symptoms of a cold are irritability, restlessness, and sneezing. Young children usually have a fever a few hours before other symptoms appear. During the first three days ears may be congested. Older children generally notice dryness of the nose, followed by sneezing, chills, muscle aches, a runny nose, and often a cough. Most children lose their appetite. Colds generally last 4 to 10 days.

TREATMENT

There is no cure for the common cold. There is no evidence that antibiotics or bed rest affect its course. Children with colds should be given plenty of fluids of their choice to drink. Individual symptoms may also be treated.

Pain and fever can be relieved with saline nose drops and acetaminophen.

Nasal congestion can be relieved using suction devices for infants and commercially available nose drops for older children. The use of nose drops is generally restricted to five days. Suction may be useful in clearing nasal passages so an infant can nurse, but it should not be overused as it can damage nasal mucosa. The best drainage usually comes by laying an infant on his back, tilted up slightly. Nose drops administered 15 minutes before meals and bedtime can help older children eat and get to sleep without breathing difficulties. The addition of antihistamines to cold medicines is only occasionally helpful.

Coughing is the body's way of clearing the throat and lungs, so it is unwise to use anticough medicines with a cold. A humidifier may help ease breathing. If croup occurs, taking a child into a steamy bathroom may relieve the coughing.

PREVENTION

A child who has just recovered from a cold may be unusually susceptible to other infections, so it is wise to restrict contact with other children for a day or two after the symptoms have disappeared.

CONVULSIONS

DEFINITION AND INCIDENCE

Convulsions are an involuntary twitching and jerking of the limbs, sometimes resulting in loss of consciousness. About 3 percent of children have convulsions, most often during an episode of fever at 3 months to 5 years of age. While in a small percentage of children these convulsions may indicate epilepsy or other problems, most children who have one or two convulsions as a young child will never have another.

CAUSE

Convulsions are caused by a sudden increase in electrical activity in the brain. Everyone has a threshold beyond which convulsions will occur, and it varies from individual to individual. The seizure threshold can be lowered by such factors as fever, excitement, lack of sleep, age, chemical factors, lack of oxygen, low calcium levels, head trauma, and genetics.

DIAGNOSIS

Convulsions may include the following symptoms:

> Jerky movements of the arms and legs
> Slow and irregular breathing
> Feeble cries or a gurgling sound
> Rigid neck
> Dilated pupils
> Drooling
> Slight movements of the fingers, toes, and
>   eyelids

A seizure that is "provoked" by acute conditions such as fever or head trauma is less likely to lead to epilepsy than one that is "unprovoked," or cannot be explained by outside circumstances.

TREATMENT

While the seizure is occurring, first aid should consist of making sure that the child does not hurt herself and that airways remain open (see chapter 14, Common First-Aid Procedures). If fever is a cause, lower the temperature by using cool compresses.

As most seizures, especially febrile (fever-induced) seizures, in young children do not indicate an underlying problem, most physicians do not recommend any medical treatment for a child who has had fewer than three seizures. Drugs such as phenobarbital can prevent recurrence of most seizures, but the side effects are powerful, and since most children will not have a repeat convulsion anyway, the benefit does not seem worth the cost. (For more information, see the section on epilepsy in chapter 26, Brain, Nerve, and Muscle Disorders.)

PREVENTION

If a child has had seizures during one or more episodes of fever, attempts should be made to control the fever next time the child gets sick, such as by administering acetaminophen and making sure that the child has adequate rest.

EAR INFECTIONS (OTITIS)

Children are unusually vulnerable to two kinds of ear infections: those of the outer ear (otitis externa) and those of the middle ear (otitis media).

OTITIS EXTERNA
DEFINITION

Otitis externa, also called "swimmer's ear," is an infection of the skin lining the external ear canal, outside the eardrum.

CAUSE

The most common cause of otitis externa is excess water in the ear, leading to maceration of the skin. The most frequent associations are with swimming or excess showering. The most frequent superimposed infections are caused by bacteria.

DIAGNOSIS

Otitis externa often begins with itching and swelling and proceeds to extreme pain in the ear canal. Swelling of the ear canal and a foul-smelling discharge are other signs of external ear infection.

TREATMENT

A child with otitis externa should be taken to a doctor promptly, as medical treatment will cure the infection and ease the pain rapidly. The most common treatment is with topical antibiotics, in the form of ear drops, that usually contain steroids to decrease the swelling. Oral antibiotics are required only when fever and tender lymph nodes accompany the ear symptoms.

PREVENTION

Children who are bothered by frequent outer-ear infections, especially if they swim frequently, may benefit from a preventive ear wash with dilute alcohol or acetic acid immediately after every swim.

OTITIS MEDIA
DEFINITION AND INCIDENCE

Otitis media is an infection of the middle ear. About one-third of all children under the age of 6 develop otitis media at some point.

CAUSE

Otitis media often results from obstruction of the eustachian tube, which provides drainage from the middle ear to the throat and nose. This type of obstruction is common among infants and younger children for reasons that are unknown but may have something to do with poor cartilage development or some other functional abnormality that improves with age. Contamination of the middle ear can also occur during vigorous nose blowing, sneezing, or swallowing while the nose is obstructed.

DIAGNOSIS

The most common signs of middle-ear infection are pain in the ear, fever, and temporary loss of hearing. Through an otoscope, a doctor can see if the eardrum is swollen.

TREATMENT

Treatment usually starts with a broad-spectrum antibiotic, such as trimethoprim-sulfamethoxazole (Bactrim or Septra), since most infecting organisms are sensitive to this drug. Pain medications are usually comforting.

EPIGLOTTITIS

DEFINITION

Epiglottitis is a relatively rare but potentially fatal infection of the epiglottis, the lidlike structure in the throat that prevents food from entering the windpipe.

CAUSE

Infection of the epiglottis may be a complication of an upper respiratory infection. There is now a vaccine for the *Haemophilus influenzae* bacterium that formerly was a leading cause of epiglottitis. The remaining cases in immunized children are most commonly caused by viruses.

DIAGNOSIS

Symptoms include sudden onset of a sore throat, fever, difficulty breathing, and a muffled quality to the child's voice. The sore throat is so severe that children with epiglottitis will not eat and will drool rather than swallow their saliva.

TREATMENT

When epiglottitis occurs, children should be rushed to the hospital for emergency treatment. This will include intravenous antibiotics and may require insertion of a breathing tube or creation of an opening in the trachea to permit breathing in the sickest infants.

HEAD LICE

DEFINITION

Head lice (*Pediculosis capitis*) are a common infestation among schoolchildren. The lice are tiny creatures that usually live in the hair, glue their tiny white egg sacs (nits) to hair shafts, and cause severe itching of the scalp.

CAUSE

Head lice are spread by direct contact and by sharing items such as combs, hair bands, and hats.

DIAGNOSIS

Severe itching is the first and major symptom of head lice. While usually confined to the scalp hair, the lice may also sometimes be found in eyelashes and eyebrows.

TREATMENT

Head lice are easily eradicated with a special pesticide-containing shampoo that can be purchased at a drugstore. A second application of the shampoo may be needed in about 10 days to make sure any remaining lice are destroyed. The nits should be combed out with a metal or fine-tooth comb. Bedding, hats, combs and brushes, and other items that come in contact with hair should be washed in hot, soapy water.

PREVENTION

Children should be kept home from school until the first treatment is completed to avoid spreading lice.

HUMAN IMMUNODEFICIENCY VIRUS (HIV) INFECTIONS AND ACQUIRED IMMUNE DEFICIENCY SYNDROME (AIDS)

DEFINITION AND INCIDENCE

HIV infection undermines the immune system and makes its victims vulnerable to a range of life-threatening illnesses. HIV infections have had a dramatic impact on the health of children over the past decade, becoming one of the leading causes of death in children 1 to 4 years of age. The epidemic is expanding at a greater rate among women and children than in the remainder of the population. HIV infection, which results in immune incompetence, generally manifests itself as a history of frequent illnesses such as recurrent ear infections, chronic cough, chronic diarrhea, and recurrent or persistent yeast infections. Recurrent fever, developmental delay, and failure to thrive are also common in children infected by the HIV virus.

CAUSE

The HIV virus is a retrovirus that infects the cells of the body's immune system, leading to varying degrees of immune incompetence. Infants are infected before birth; about 20 percent of infected mothers pass the virus to their children in the womb. Prior to current screening of blood donors, children could also be infected through transfusions.

DIAGNOSIS

The incubation period for primary infection is 2 to 4 weeks, with the primary illness generally being nonspecific and subclinical. The latent period before AIDS is diagnosed is a median of 3 to 5 years for congenital infections, and even longer for transfusion-acquired disease. It is presumed that every child infected with HIV will ultimately develop AIDS. Infants can be tested for the presence of the HIV virus in the blood or tissue by culture when the mother is known to be infected, although only 20 percent of such children will actually acquire the virus from an infected mother.

TREATMENT

Treatment to date involves an increasing array of retroviral agents that inhibit the replication of the virus. Meticulous attention should be given to every aspect of care for these children, including early recognition and aggressive treatment of infections, prophylactic antibiotics in selected children, appropriate immunization, good nutrition, and recognition and treatment of the psychosocial needs of the child and family.

PREVENTION

The best way to prevent a child's getting AIDS is for the parents to be free of the disease before the child is conceived. AIDS cannot be passed from one person to another except through direct contact with blood or body fluids. While there have been several instances of infected children being barred from attending school with healthy children, there is no evidence of an HIV-infected child ever having passed the disease to another child at school.

INFLUENZA (FLU)

DEFINITION AND INCIDENCE

The flu is a common viral infection. It is often taken lightly precisely because it is so common, but flu is a potentially dangerous disease with many complications, so a child suffering from it should be observed carefully. The highest incidence of flu occurs in children from ages 5 to 14.

CAUSE

Influenza is caused by a variety of viruses. Infection is transmitted from one person to another by virus carried through the air.

DIAGNOSIS

The usual incubation period is about 3 days after an airborne virus comes into contact with a child's nasal passages. The most common symptoms are abrupt onset of fever (102° to 104°F or 38.8° to 41.1°C), chills, headache, muscle pain, and malaise. Some flu sufferers may also develop diarrhea. The fever may last anywhere from 2 to 5 days. Sometime after the second day, respiratory symptoms become predominant and fever and muscle aches subside. A dry, hacking cough usually sets in around the fourth day, and may persist for 1 to 2 weeks. In most cases an attack of the flu is benign, but complications to watch for include febrile convulsions (see "Convulsions" in this chapter), chest pain, and prolonged high fever, which may be a sign of pneumonia.

TREATMENT

Treatment should include bed rest and restricted activity. The patient should drink plenty of fluids, especially during the fever. Acetaminophen is useful for fever control and relief of discomfort, but aspirin should not be given because of the risk of Reye's syndrome when used during a viral infection.

PREVENTION

Vaccinations exist for many strains of influenza virus. Routine immunization is not recommended, however, except for the elderly and children with serious chronic respiratory disorders.

KAWASAKI SYNDROME

DEFINITION

Kawasaki syndrome is an acute inflammatory illness that affects many systems of the body and has a predictable clinical course. It was initially described in Japan by Dr. Kawasaki in 1967.

CAUSE

The cause of Kawasaki syndrome remains unknown, although recent work suggests that the disease may be secondary to production of a bacterial toxin.

DIAGNOSIS

The distinct features of the syndrome include fever, conjunctivitis, changes in the mucous membranes of the mouth, generalized rash, changes in the extremities, and enlarged lymph nodes. The presence of five out of six of these criteria is required to make a firm diagnosis. The illness is also marked by significant cardiovascular complications, including myocardial infarction (heart attack). Because of the devastating complications of the illness, some authorities recommend treatment when there is a high degree of suspicion by the physician even without the presence of five symptoms.

TREATMENT

As soon as the diagnosis is made, the child should be treated with a single infusion of gamma globulin given over 12 hours. The child should also be started on aspirin, which is continued at different doses until about 3 months after the onset of illness.

PREVENTION

Since the cause of the syndrome is unknown, there are no preventive measures.

LYME DISEASE

DEFINITION AND INCIDENCE

Lyme disease is a subacute or chronic infection by a spirochete that is transmitted by the bite of an infected deer tick. It is most common in the northeastern region of the United States.

CAUSE

The culprit spirochete, *Borrelia burgdorferi,* and deer tick transmission were identified during an outbreak in Lyme, Connecticut, in 1977.

DIAGNOSIS

Lyme disease is a clinical diagnosis. A characteristic red bull's-eye rash develops in 70 percent of patients at the site of the deer tick bite. Many children will seem otherwise well, while others will develop fever, aches, and pain. Untreated, the rash may last days or weeks. Half of affected children develop arthritis several weeks or months later, generally involving the knees and other large joints. Neurologic signs may be seen in 25 percent of the cases. Most patients with only a rash have no abnormal laboratory tests. The Lyme spirochete is difficult to culture; it may be detected in blood tests, but the tests should be performed by experienced laboratories.

TREATMENT

Antibiotic treatment is most beneficial when started early, but in all forms of Lyme disease prolonged treatment is necessary. Amoxicillin and penicillin are the most commonly used drugs for children with the bull's-eye rash, but doxycycline may also be used in children older than 9 and where arthritis is present.

PREVENTION

Lyme disease can best be prevented by taking steps to avoid tick bites, such as:

Avoiding endemic areas such as woods and meadows in the U.S. Northeast
Wearing long sleeves and long pants in endemic areas
Carefully inspecting children for the tiny (pinhead-size) deer ticks
Applying tick repellent when going outside

MEASLES

DEFINITION AND INCIDENCE

Measles is a serious viral illness that mainly affects children. Since the introduction of the measles vaccine, the disease has become less frequent in the United States among children; it is more common among adolescents who were not immunized during their early childhood.

CAUSE

Measles is caused by a virus that is spread through the air or by physical contact.

DIAGNOSIS

Early symptoms of measles include:

Low-grade fever
Slight cough
Coldlike symptoms
Conjunctivitis (pinkeye)

Within 2 or 3 days a rash will appear on the face, usually concurrent with an abrupt rise in temperature to about 105°F (40.5°C). For a while the child will appear desperately ill, but within a day or two the symptoms usually subside.

TREATMENT

Treatment for measles includes bed rest, adequate fluid intake and, if laryngitis and cough are excessive, humidification of air. The chief complications of measles are pneumonia and, rarely, encephalitis.

PREVENTION

Measles can be prevented by immunization during infancy.

MONONUCLEOSIS

DEFINITION AND INCIDENCE

Mononucleosis (often simply called "mono") is a viral disease that most commonly affects adolescents and young adults.

CAUSE

Mononucleosis is transmitted via direct contact with saliva. In adolescents it is thus commonly referred to as "the kissing disease," although a younger child may contract it from the saliva of a playmate.

DIAGNOSIS

The incubation period for the mononucleosis virus is vague and may be longer than a month. The first symptoms are malaise, fatigue, headache, nausea, and abdominal pain, which may last for 1 or 2 weeks. A sore throat and fever up to about 102°F (38.8°C) set in later. The lymph glands swell, and a few patients (5 percent) develop a rash. Because of its insidious onset, mononucleosis may first be recognized by its complications: hepatitis and pneumonia.

TREATMENT

There is no specific treatment for mononucleosis, although rest is advised. As long as there are no complications, children will recover by themselves, although fatigue may persist for months after recovery.

MUMPS

DEFINITION

Mumps is a contagious viral disease involving a painful enlargement of the salivary (parotid) glands. Fortunately, an effective vaccine against the disease means there is little need for anyone to suffer mumps anymore.

CAUSE

The mumps virus is spread by direct contact, through saliva containing the virus, and through the air.

DIAGNOSIS

Mumps usually begins with a fever, muscle pain in the neck, headache, and malaise. Pain and swelling develop in the salivary glands in front of and below the ear. Swelling of these glands proceeds rapidly, and is usually visible, reaching a maximum in 1 to 3 days and then subsiding within a week. The swelling may be accompanied by a moderate fever no higher than 103° or 104°F (39.4° or 40°C). Mumps is far more severe if it is contracted in adulthood.

TREATMENT

Treatment for mumps is purely supportive, including acetaminophen and fluids.

PREVENTION

Infants gain a temporary immunity against mumps, lasting from 6 to 18 months, from their mother's immunity through the placenta. A vaccination against mumps should be given at 15 months. If a child does contract mumps, one infection seems sufficient to provide immunity for life.

MALE/FEMALE DIFFERENCES

In men and adolescent boys, the mumps infection may spread to the testes, causing painful swelling and, in some cases, infertility.

RUBELLA (GERMAN MEASLES)

DEFINITION

Rubella is an infection that is very dangerous to a fetus in the womb. It is not particularly dangerous to a child who catches it, but a fetus who contracts rubella may develop severe congenital defects, including blindness, deafness, and heart defects. It is thus very important for any woman who thinks she might be pregnant to avoid exposure to the disease.

CAUSE

Rubella is caused by the rubella virus. It can be spread by air or physical contact.

DIAGNOSIS

The virus may be cultured from the throat or urine from 1 week prior to the onset of a rash to 2 weeks after its appearance.

TREATMENT

There is no drug therapy for rubella. Treatment usually involves bed rest and adequate fluid intake.

PREVENTION

Rubella immunizations given to most children as part of their routine vaccinations prevent these children from getting the disease and passing it to pregnant women. Women who have not been immunized against rubella should get the vaccine before becoming pregnant. The vaccine should not be given, however, if there is any chance that the woman is already or about to become pregnant, as it may then transmit the disease to the fetus.

SCARLET FEVER

DEFINITION

Scarlet fever is a bacterial infection named for the characteristic pink-red rash that appears mainly on the chest and abdomen but may cover the entire body, and "strawberry tongue," with bright red showing through a whitish coating. Before the discovery of antibiotics, scarlet fever was feared as a potentially lethal disease, but this is no longer the case.

CAUSE

Scarlet fever is caused by a strain of *Streptococcus* bacterium and can be transmitted by air or by physical contact.

DIAGNOSIS

Symptoms begin to appear 2 to 5 days after a person is exposed to the bacteria. They include:

High fever (103°–104°F, or 39.4°–40°C)
Vomiting
Sore throat
Chills
Pink-red rash on chest and abdomen or entire body
Strawberry tongue

The fever, chills, sore throat, and vomiting will occur first, with the rash following in 12 to 48 hours. The rash, which feels rough like sandpaper, will fade after a week or so, and the skin will begin to flake and peel, a process that may continue for several weeks.

TREATMENT

Treatment focuses on antibiotics to fight the *Streptococcus* bacteria. Penicillin is usually the drug of choice. Erythromycin may be given to children who cannot take penicillin. Therapy should continue for a full 10 days, even if the symptoms subside. Other susceptible family members should be examined and treated if appropriate. Liquids should be given, especially during the feverish stage. Specific symptoms such as sore throat or headache may be treated with aspirin or acetaminophen.

SORE THROAT (PHARYNGITIS)

DEFINITION AND INCIDENCE

Sore throat, or pharyngitis, is a common complication of upper respiratory tract infections. Although it can occur at all ages, it is most common in children between ages 4 and 7.

CAUSE

Sore throats are most commonly caused by self-limiting viruses. They can also be caused by the *Streptococcus* bacterium, with the associated "strep throat" and the dreaded complication of rheumatic fever, and so must be treated properly (see below).

DIAGNOSIS

Viral sore throat usually comes on fairly gradually, accompanied by fever, malaise, and lack of appetite. Most commonly the sore throat reaches a peak 2 or 3 days after the onset of symptoms. It is often accompanied by hoarseness, cough, and a runny nose. The illness usually lasts less than 24 hours and rarely persists more than 5 days.

Streptococcal sore throat, seen most commonly after the age of 2, often begins with headache, abdominal pain, and vomiting. Fever may go up as high as 104°F (40°C). The throat usually becomes sore a few hours after the first symptoms. The degree of pain ranges from slight to severe enough to impair swallowing. Fever may continue as long as 4 days, and the child may feel ill for 2 weeks. Tonsils may also be involved (see "Tonsillitis" in this chapter).

TREATMENT

Viral sore throats clear spontaneously. Treatment of specific symptoms may include acetaminophen, over-the-counter throat drops, or hot tea with lemon and honey. Gargling with warm salt water, placing warm compresses on the neck, and inhaling steam may also help. Since swallowing may be painful, a child should not be forced to eat. However, liquids should be offered and soup may be soothing.

If a sore throat persists more than a few days, a child should be taken to the doctor for a throat culture, in which cotton swabs are rubbed on the back of the throat and then tested for the *Streptococcus* bacterium. If the throat is infected with *Streptococcus*, penicillin or erythromycin treatment usually relieves the symptoms within a day. However, since strep throat can lead to serious complications, most notably rheumatic fever, it is important to continue the antibiotic therapy for a full 10 days to ensure that the microorganisms have been completely destroyed.

SUDDEN INFANT DEATH SYNDROME (SIDS)

DEFINITION AND INCIDENCE

SIDS is a poorly understood disorder that strikes up to 2 of every 1,000 infants in the United States, making it the leading cause of death in infants in the first month of life. Autopsies can provide a definitive explanation of only 20 percent of such deaths. The peak incidence of SIDS occurs at around 2 months, with most deaths occurring between several weeks and 6 months of age.

CAUSE

The risk of SIDS is not uniform: Asian infants are at a very low risk, while African-American and Native American babies are at particularly high risk. The ratio of males to females affected is 3:2. Factors that increase the risk for SIDS include:

Low birth weight
Teenage or drug-addicted mothers
Maternal smoking
Family history of SIDS

There is also an increase in SIDS associated with respiratory illness season. Most deaths are reported to occur between midnight and 8:00 A.M.

Exactly how and why SIDS occurs remains unknown. There are common findings at autopsy that suggest these infants have had intermittent or chronic hypoxia, or shortage of oxygen to the tissues. The issue of whether the death is due to pulmonary or cardiac failure remains unsolved.

DIAGNOSIS

A baby stricken with SIDS will be discovered to have stopped breathing in his or her sleep.

TREATMENT

For the moment, the most important aspect of dealing with SIDS comes after the tragedy, ensuring that the parents receive understanding and support. The National Sudden Infant Death Syndrome Foundation provides invaluable information about specific parent support groups and counseling services for grieving families.

PREVENTION

The value of home monitoring to prevent SIDS, despite large programs to provide monitoring, is still not estab-lished. Recently the American Academy of Pediatrics made a strong statement about the role of positioning during sleep in SIDS. Based on an expert committee's review of the world literature and the much lower frequency of SIDS in other countries where the common recommendation is that infants sleep in the prone position, the academy recommends that healthy infants, when put down to sleep, be positioned on their side or back.

TONSILLITIS

DEFINITION

Tonsillitis is an infection of the tonsils, which can be either acute or chronic. Located in the throat, the tonsils are important to the development of the immune system.

CAUSE

Tonsillitis is caused by viral or bacterial infection of the tonsils.

DIAGNOSIS

Chronic tonsillitis may cause recurrent or persistent sore throat and obstruction of swallowing or breathing, as well as a sense of dryness or irritation in the throat and sometimes bad breath. The signs of chronic tonsillitis are far from obvious, however, and most doctors are very cautious in making the diagnosis.

TREATMENT

Most tonsillitis is self-limiting and should be treated like a sore throat, with warm compresses, soup, tea, aspirin, saline gargles, and so on. These days, tonsillectomy is usually indicated only in children who have had tonsillar or peritonsillar abscesses, or whose tonsils are so large that they threaten to obstruct breathing or lead to cardiac failure. Only very rarely should a child younger than 2 have a tonsillectomy. Frequent sore throat is not a valid reason for a tonsillectomy; removal of the tonsils has not been proven to solve the problem. Children's tonsils are relatively larger than adults', and just because tonsils seem large is not a reason to remove them if they do not present a threat to breathing or eating.

WHOOPING COUGH (PERTUSSIS)

DEFINITION AND INCIDENCE

Whooping cough is a serious inflammation of the respiratory tract caused by a bacterium. It is now rare, thanks to the widespread DTP immunization during infancy. Still, several thousand cases are reported each year in the

United States. Before immunization, it most commonly attacked very young children and had a very high mortality rate. The most common whooping cough patient in the United States today is an adolescent or young adult who was not properly immunized in the first year or who has an immunological problem. The disease is rarely serious once a child is more than a year old.

CAUSE

Whooping cough is caused by the *Bordetella pertussis* bacterium and is spread through the air.

DIAGNOSIS

Pertussis is from the Latin for "intensive cough," and this is the most striking feature of the disease. At first symptoms may be only a runny nose, mild cough, and low-grade fever. But as the disease progresses, the nasal discharge becomes thicker and more profuse, leading to severe upper respiratory congestion in a young baby. This stage usually lasts 1 to 2 weeks before progressing to a paroxysmal stage. Typically, a child will cough four to five times during a single expiration. This is followed by a sudden intake of air and a whooping sound as it is inhaled through the narrowed glottis. During these coughing spells, the face may turn red or blue, the eyes bulge, and the tongue protrude, and there may be drooling. Vomiting may accompany the coughing. Understandably, these attacks leave the child exhausted. This stage may last 2 to 4 weeks or even longer; weight loss is common. The coughing attacks gradually become less frequent and disappear, but a cough may persist for several months after recovery.

Pneumonia is one of the most serious potential complications of whooping cough, causing more than 90 percent of the deaths from the disease in children under the age of 3.

TREATMENT

Erythromycin given during the early stage of the disease may prevent it from progressing to the paroxysmal or coughing stage. But once the coughing begins, antibiotics do not seem to shorten its duration.

Suction to remove the secretions from the upper nose and upper respiratory tract may be necessary in very young children, and oxygen may also be required. Fluids should be given to prevent dehydration. Nutrition must be maintained, especially in an infant, even though the disease is exhausting and a child may not feel like eating.

PREVENTION

Whooping cough can be prevented through the DTP immunization, which should be given when an infant is

2, 4, 6, and 18 months old, with a booster shot at 4 to 6 years.

WORMS

Infestation with worms is common in children throughout the world. Worms come in many shapes and sizes, from microscopic (pinworms) to several feet long (tapeworms); many reside in the intestinal tract. Following are the most common types of worms found in children in the United States.

PINWORMS (ENTEROBIASIS)

DEFINITION AND INCIDENCE

Pinworms are an essentially harmless infection that often causes more social problems than medical problems. Pinworm infections are particularly common in nursery schools and kindergarten; an entire classroom may be affected in a short period.

CAUSE

Pinworms are transmitted from person to person by ingesting the eggs, which may be carried on fingernails, clothing, bedding, contaminated food, or other objects, or even in dust and air. The worm then matures inside the body. Typically, the female worm crawls out through the anus at night to deposit her eggs. This causes severe itching; the child usually scratches the area and some of the eggs become embedded under the fingernails. The eggs are then transmitted and ingested by someone else, allowing the parasites' life cycle to continue.

DIAGNOSIS

The major symptoms of pinworms are itching in the anal area, restlessness, and difficulty sleeping. Infection can be diagnosed by placing adhesive tape over the anus, removing it, and then examining the tape under a microscope for eggs. Worms may also be observed in the stool. Complications from pinworms can include secondary bacterial infections of the area that is constantly scratched, and vaginal involvement in young girls.

TREATMENT

Treatment for pinworms is a single dose of pyrantel pamoate, followed by a second dose in 2 weeks. Petroleum jelly may be applied to the anal area to relieve the itching. Other family members should also be treated, especially if they have any symptoms. Careful washing of bedding and clothing is advised, but there is no evidence that cleanliness plays a major role in either getting or eradicating pinworms.

ROUNDWORMS (ASCARIASIS)

DEFINITION AND INCIDENCE

Roundworm infections are most common in tropical areas, but as many as 4 million cases, mostly among children, are reported in the United States each year.

CAUSE

Roundworm eggs are passed in the feces and harbored in the soil, where they may remain for months and even years. They are transmitted to humans by hand-to-mouth contact, perhaps by eating without having washed hands that have been in contact with contaminated soil, or by eating raw food that contained roundworm eggs.

DIAGNOSIS

Roundworm infections are diagnosed by examining the stool for eggs. Most people do not suffer any serious consequences from roundworm infections, but in unusual instances the parasite may cause lung problems, intestinal obstruction, or nutritional deficiency.

TREATMENT

Treatment for roundworms is drugs that kill the adult worms in the intestinal tract.

HOOKWORMS

DEFINITION AND INCIDENCE

Hookworms are very common worldwide, but are rarely seen in this country, where they are limited to subtropical areas of the Southeast.

CAUSE

Hookworm eggs are passed in the feces and develop into larvae in the soil. Humans are infected by drinking contaminated water or by coming in direct contact with contaminated soil, usually by walking barefoot, and having the larvae penetrate the skin.

DIAGNOSIS

Diagnosis is made by examining the stool for eggs. Most hookworm infections cause no symptoms. When symptoms do occur, they may include itching where the larvae enter the skin, abdominal pain, loss of appetite, a feeling of fullness, and diarrhea. Anemia may occur in severe cases and represents one of the most serious potential complications of hookwork infection.

TREATMENT

Treatment for hookworms involves giving iron for any anemia and drugs to eradicate the worms from the intestinal tract.

8
The
Adolescent
Years

• • • • • • • • • • • • • • • •

KAREN SOREN, M.D.
Parts of this chapter
are adapted from the
chapter by Andrea
Marks, M.D., which
appeared in the revised
second edition.

An individual progresses from childhood to adulthood during the decade of adolescence—ages 10 to 20. This progression encompasses not only the physical development of puberty but also the psychological and social transition needed to establish an adult identity. This guide for both parents and teenagers outlines the important aspects of adolescent health, describing normal growth and behavior and potential adolescent difficulties.

Adolescence is characterized by change: A young person comes to terms with body changes, copes with the awakening of sexual feelings and development, plans for a societal role, and ultimately achieves independence. Although the biological progression of adolescence has remained relatively fixed over the past few decades, its social context has metamorphosed dramatically. The risk-taking behaviors characteristic of adolescence are now more likely to include substance abuse and experimentation with sexuality, and the daring deeds of teens may unfold in an atmosphere of violence. Such changes have yielded new challenges for teenagers and their families and new problems for the health professionals who care for them. Indeed, these developments have made the emergence of adolescent medicine all the more important because many parents and pediatricians are uncomfortable dealing with the heightened difficulties of adolescence.

While the teenage years often are described as tumultuous, insecure and rebellious, these stereotypes do not characterize all or even most situations. Family surveys reveal many routes through adolescence, and numerous factors determine how well a family handles the changes of adolescence. If prior family life has been harmonious, harmony will probably continue during this period.

Family conflicts at this time often focus on differing values. Parents may forget that adolescents experiment with new ideas and behaviors, opposing traditional or parental values. Meaningful communication between parents and an adolescent may break down. While parents and their teenager often complain, "We can't talk to each other," adolescents still need counsel and advice, and it is particularly important to keep lines of communication open, even in the face of serious disagreement.

With so much emphasis on the psychological and social aspects of adolescence, medical well-being is often taken for granted. Assuming that adolescent years are the healthiest years of life, many people overlook medical problems that may not be readily apparent. Typically, the adolescent no longer undergoes regular pediatric checkups, and many teenagers seldom see a physician except for brief, required checkups (e.g., school sports examinations or when symptoms occur). Both parents and teens should recognize that, although adolescent health problems are different than those during earlier childhood years, professional health care should continue through these years.

PHYSICAL DEVELOPMENT

HEIGHT AND WEIGHT

The adolescent growth rate is second only to that of a newborn infant. Typically, weight almost doubles and height increases by approximately 25 percent. For example, at the age of 11, an average boy may weigh 75 to 80 pounds and stand about 56 inches tall. Within 7 years, the youngster may weigh 150 pounds and measure almost 70 inches. Girls undergo a similar dramatic growth spurt that usually occurs 2 years earlier than in boys. However, growth patterns vary and not all children grow according to established patterns. Similar to adults, adolescents vary considerably in height and weight. In general, a preadolescent child in the upper or lower percentile in height and weight will still be in the same general range after growth is completed, but this is not always the case. Smaller than average youngsters may grow to average or above average height, and vice versa. Heredity, nutrition, and general health are important determinants of growth and size.

SEXUAL DEVELOPMENT

The development of secondary sexual characteristics—a hormonally controlled process—marks puberty's onset. Before visible changes appear, the endocrine glands produce hormones that spur sexual development. This process begins when the hypothalamus, in response to signals not fully understood by researchers, prompts the pituitary to begin secreting gonadotropin hormones. These hormones stimulate the testes in boys, and ovaries in girls to begin production of testosterone (male hormone) and estrogen (female hormone).

Rising levels of these sex hormones cause the physical changes of puberty. For both boys and girls, the changes follow an orderly sequence over the course of several years, although the timing may vary considerably among individuals. At the beginning of puberty, parents often notice that the youngster is sleepier than usual, wanting to stay in bed later in the morning, and perhaps taking a nap after school in the afternoon. This change in the sleep-wake cycle is attributed to the fact that both growth hormones and gonadotropins are released in larger amounts during sleep, and levels of these hormones rise markedly during puberty. The sleepiness usually lasts until growth and sexual development are completed.

Early puberty is also associated with an increased appetite; in fact, parents often comment on the huge amounts of food a teenager can consume and still remain thin. This increased nutrition supports adolescents' tremendous growth.

FEMALE SEXUAL DEVELOPMENT

In girls, the first physical signs of sexual development are the budding of breasts, usually between ages 9 and 13. Not uncommonly, one breast may begin to develop before the other, or the breasts will be asymmetrical. While this may seem a cause for concern, it usually is not a sign of abnormality. Breasts are seldom exactly the same size, and by adulthood they have usually evened out so the differences are barely noticeable. If the breasts remain markedly asymmetrical or, in rare instances, one fails to develop, it can be a source of embarrassment and sensitivity. A visit to a physician may assure a girl with asymmetri-cal breasts that she does not have a disease, and that the problem can be surgically corrected.

At the same time as the breasts develop or shortly thereafter, pubic and other body hair begins to grow. As puberty progresses, girls experience an adolescent growth spurt and begin to accumulate body fat in an adult female pattern: rounded hips and buttocks and a further filling out of the breasts. At the same time, vaginal discharge may increase, a sign of impending menarche, or the onset of menstruation. By the time menstruation is established, the growth spurt is largely completed, although some girls add an inch or two in height after menstruation begins.

The average age of menarche in the United States and other Western countries is now about 12.5 years, although menarche at anytime between the ages of 8 and 16 is considered normal. While the age of menarche has been declining by about 8 months per generation since the turn of the century, this decline appears to have largely ceased. The reasons for the younger age of menarche are unclear, but improved nutrition is believed to be a major factor. Studies have found that when a girl of average height reaches about 105 pounds, menstruation shortly follows. The percentage

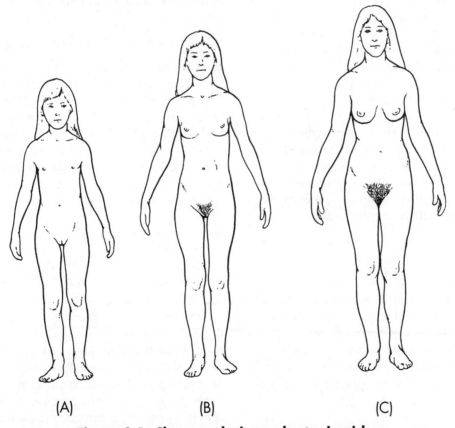

(A)   (B)   (C)

Figure 8.1: Changes during puberty, in girls.
(A) shows a typical girl before the onset of puberty; in (B) the breasts are beginning to develop and there is the beginning of pubic hair. There is also increased height and body fat. (C) shows a fully developed female figure at about age 17 or 18.

of body fat is also believed to be a factor, presumably because a certain amount of fatty tissue is needed for the hormonal changes initiating menstruation. The fact that ballet dancers, long-distance runners, and other girls with low percentages of body fat generally experience menarche at a somewhat later than average age supports this theory.

The onset of menstruation does not necessarily coincide with the beginning of ovulation. Many teenage girls experience irregular and/or very heavy periods for the first year or two—possible signs of absent or irregular ovulation. This is not abnormal but a sign that while enough female sex hormones are being produced to cause a proliferation and shedding of the uterine lining, not enough pituitary stimulating hormone (FSH and LH) is being secreted to result in regular ripening and release of an egg from one of the ovaries. Within 1 or 2 years of menarche, however, most girls ovulate with some degree of regularity.

MENSTRUAL CRAMPS

DEFINITION

Menstrual cramps, medically known as dysmenorrhea, are cramplike pains in the lower abdomen or lower back that begin just before or at the onset of menstruation and usually disappear by the second day of flow. Women of all ages can have menstrual cramps, but the problem is most common among adolescent girls.

CAUSE

Once considered psychosomatic, dysmenorrhea is now recognized to have a true physical cause—generally a high level of prostaglandins, hormonelike substances produced in tissues throughout the body that perform a number of functions. Prostaglandins produced by uterine tissue cause contractions of the uterine muscles, resulting in cramps.

DIAGNOSIS

Teens or their mothers can usually self-diagnose dysmenorrhea based on when and where the discomfort occurs. If any severe pain occurs or continues beyond the first day or so of menstruation, or if the treatments described below fail to relieve the cramps, a thorough examination is advisable to investigate possible organic causes for the pain.

TREATMENT

Menstrual cramps can often be alleviated by the home remedies discussed below. If these measures do not help, a number of medications block prostaglandin production and can relieve up to 90 percent of dysmenorrhea cases. Known as nonsteroidal anti-inflammatory drugs, or NSAIDs, stronger doses of these drugs are available by prescription or, in lesser doses, as over-the-counter medication. Commonly recommended NSAIDs include ibuprofen (Motrin, Advil, Nuprin, and others), naproxen (Anaprox and Naprosyn), and mefenamil acid (Ponstel), which are available in both prescription and nonprescription forms.

Sometimes several forms of NSAIDs must be tried before the most effective is found. Typically, the drugs are administered at the earliest sign of the period and are taken for 1 or 2 days.

In some cases, especially if contraception is needed by a sexually active teen, birth control pills may also be prescribed to lighten menstrual flow and decrease or vanquish cramps.

ALTERNATIVE THERAPIES AND HOME REMEDIES

Some women find that exercise, heating pads, or warm baths, with or without aspirin or acetaminophen, are sufficient to relieve menstrual discomfort. Other remedies that help some women include massage, yoga, meditation, and deep-breathing exercises.

MALE SEXUAL DEVELOPMENT

Boys generally enter puberty an average of 1 year later than girls, usually between the ages of 10 and 14. The first physical signs are growth of the testes and penis, accompanied or followed by growth of pubic and other body hair. A growth spurt follows these initial signs by about 2 years, and because males generally are larger than females, growth during this period may be more pronounced than in girls. Changes in the larynx cause a deepening of the voice and growth of an "Adam's apple." At this time, there also is an increase in facial hair that begins with a mustache and within a few years extends over most of the lower face.

Rising testosterone levels stimulate increased muscle mass during the growth spurt, and male biceps, shoulder, and thigh muscles grow larger than in girls. During the growth spurt, breast tissue may develop in up to two-thirds of adolescent boys, but this usually disappears in about 6 months (although in some it may persist for a year or longer). Occasionally a source of embarrassment, male breast tissue usually is not a sign of any abnormality.

Ejaculations generally begin sometime between the ages of 11 and 15, although anytime between the ages of 8 and 21 is considered normal. Ejaculation may occur during sleep or in response to masturbation or a sexual fantasy.

Although the major events of adolescence in boys

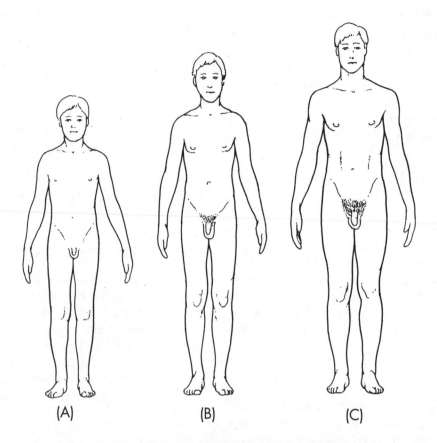

Figure 8.2: Changes during puberty, in boys.
(A) shows a boy at about age 9 before the onset of puberty. In (B) secondary sex characteristics are beginning to develop; e.g., the beginning of pubic hair and enlargement of the penis and testes. There is also increased height and muscle development. (C) shows a fully developed male at about age 18.

are usually completed by the age of 17 or 18, growth may continue (albeit at a slower rate) until the age of 20 or 21.

DELAYED PUBERTY

DEFINITION

Although the rate of adolescent growth and development varies widely, lack of sexual development in girls by age 13 or in boys by age 14 is generally considered an indication of possible delayed puberty.

CAUSE

Delayed puberty may result from organic causes, such as tumors, genetic defects, thyroid or other endocrine diseases, and malnutrition. However, in the vast majority of cases, the delay in puberty is termed "constitutional" (without pathology); these teens will enter puberty without intervention, but at a later time than their peers.

DIAGNOSIS

A complete medical history and physical examination form the basis for an evaluation of possible delayed puberty. In addition, blood tests to screen for multiple contributing factors such as hormone deficiencies and chromosome abnormalities may be performed and x-rays may be used to assess bone age.

TREATMENT

Treatment depends upon the nature of the underlying disorder, if any. Many of these youngsters eventually enter puberty without treatment, but those who have some sort of abnormality, such as a hormonal disorder, require medical therapy. In some cases, puberty can be brought on by hormonal treatments, but these must be administered under careful medical supervision.

If this condition induces psychological difficulties—if the delay in growing larger seems particularly troublesome to the youngster—professional psychological counseling may be appropriate.

Alternative Therapies and Home Remedies

Even if a child is physically normal and simply a "late bloomer," delayed development can cause psychological problems. For example, teenagers may worry that they are abnormal, especially if classmates tower head and shoulders over them. Parental support and reassurance is important during this period. Learning karate or other martial arts techniques may help build self-esteem.

PRECOCIOUS PUBERTY

Definition

Premature, or precocious, puberty—puberty that occurs before the ages of 8 in girls and 9 in boys—is also rare, occurring in about 6 of every 1,000 otherwise normal children. Children who develop premature puberty may initially be taller than their peers, but since their growth is likely to stop early, they may end up abnormally small. The early development also can lead to psychological problems.

Causes

In some instances, the early puberty is hereditary and normal, but more commonly, the premature development is due to an organic disorder. However, a physician should be consulted in all cases.

Diagnosis

A complete medical history and physical examination form the basis for an evaluation of possible precocious puberty. In addition, blood tests may be necessary to evaluate hormone levels, x-rays to assess bone age, and other imaging studies may be ordered to evaluate the abdomen, pelvis, and/or brain.

Treatment

Doctors usually attempt to halt and reverse the premature development, but the treatment depends upon the cause. For example, if the premature puberty is due to a tumor, its removal may resolve the problem. In other situations, hormonal treatments to suppress production of the sex hormones may be attempted. In addition, young people who enter puberty early may require psychological support.

SEXUAL ACTIVITY

Many parents have difficulty discussing sexuality with their teenagers and the subject is often ignored. But adolescents need guidance—the incidence of sexually trans-mitted disease among this age group is disturbingly high. If parents cannot provide useful sexual advice, a physician or some other trusted adult—perhaps an older sibling or relative—should be enlisted as an adviser.

Even when sexuality is ignored by parents, it is a fact of life for most adolescents. By the age of 19, the large majority of adolescents—80 percent of boys and 75 percent of girls—have engaged in sexual intercourse. First sexual experiences are occurring at much younger ages, with more than one of four 15-year-old girls and one of three 15-year-old boys reporting sexual activity. In addition, many junior high school students are sexually active.

ADOLESCENT PREGNANCY

Each year, approximately 1 million teenage girls become pregnant. By the late 1980s, girls under the age of 15 were giving birth to more than 10,000 children a year. Pregnancy among these very young mothers can be both socially and medically devastating, especially when the adolescent does not receive adequate prenatal care. Very young mothers are at increased risk of bearing low-birth-weight babies or suffering stillbirths or miscarriages.

CONTRACEPTION

Despite increased availability of contraceptives in recent decades, large numbers of sexually active teenagers either do not practice birth control or delay seeking it. Few teenagers are prepared to use birth control prior to first intercourse. A recent study showed that teenagers waited an average of 1 year after becoming sexually active before seeking a prescription method of contraception, and many of them made their first inquiries about birth control because they feared they were already pregnant.

Early in adolescence, youngsters should be taught the basics of human reproduction. Parents often assume that their children know the facts of life, but large numbers either do not understand the basics or have mistaken notions about when and how conception takes place. Teens should be taught how to predict the time of ovulation and be counseled on the use of both nonprescription and prescription methods of contraception such as the condom, vaginal sponge, and other barrier methods, and oral contraceptives.

Frequently, teenagers hesitate to seek birth control advice from a physician or clinic: They may not want to consult their regular physician for fear that their parents will find out they are sexually active. In this case, the adolescent's doctor must assure the young person of confidentiality. Also, most cities have Planned Parenthood or other clinics where a young person can go for birth control and/or medical advice, including abortions, and be assured of confidentiality.

Most contraceptive methods available to adults also are safe for adolescents: condoms, foam, contraceptive sponges, diaphragms, birth control pills, subdermal implants (Norplant), depo medroxyprogesterone acetate injection every 3 months, and, in some cases, intrauterine devices. An appropriate method should be chosen in accordance with a teenager's medical history, physical examination, sexual practices, and other behavioral factors.

SEXUAL IDENTITY

Studies consistently show that up to 10 percent of typical population groups are homosexual or bisexual. Sexual identity may be established fairly early in life, but it is during adolescence that the youngster must come to terms with his or her sexual orientation. At this time, the homosexual adolescent may begin to feel different from his or her peers. How well the homosexual adolescent adjusts depends upon many factors, including parental reaction and social environment. Typically, the first homosexual experience takes place during middle or late adolescence.

Since sexually active male homosexuals are at increased risk of a number of health problems, including AIDS, young men must be counseled about protection from sexually transmitted diseases. Health checkups should include screening for sexually transmitted diseases, including hepatitis B. Although immunization against hepatitis B is recommended for virtually all teens, it is particularly important for male homosexuals who test negative for previous hepatitis B infections. HIV testing may be clinically indicated depending upon the adolescent's history of sexual practices and physical examination. Certainly, young homosexual men should be counseled to avoid high-risk sexual practices and to limit the number of sexual partners. (For more information see chapter 19, HIV Infection and AIDS, and chapter 18, Infectious Diseases.)

While some homosexual and bisexual young people are able to come to terms with their sexual orientation more easily than others, psychological and social problems are relatively common for young people in these groups. Parents, too, may find it hard to accept a child's homosexuality, and family conflicts can compound the problems already experienced by the adolescent. Behavior problems such as truancy, drug or alcohol abuse, risk taking, and sexual promiscuity, among others, may develop at this time. Depression and attempted suicide also may occur. Parents and teens can consult support groups and also seek professional counseling, including family therapy.

AIDS

Sexually active adolescents are at increasingly high risk for exposure to AIDS, which is now the sixth leading cause of death among 15-to-24-year-olds. Although the precise prevalence of HIV infection among adolescents is unknown, it can be inferred from AIDS statistics: As of December 1992, although less than 1 percent of all AIDS cases had occurred in 13-to-19-year-olds, 20 percent of cases were in those ages 20 to 29. Because HIV infection is known to have a relatively long incubation period of 10 years or more until full-blown AIDS results, it can be assumed that these young adults were probably infected as teens.

To date, most AIDS occurs within high-risk groups (e.g., intravenous drug users, homosexual and bisexual men and their sex partners, and recipients of blood transfusions contaminated with the AIDS virus). As of December 1992, among 13-to-19-year-olds with AIDS, about 25 percent displayed homosexual behavior, 13 percent were intravenous drug users, 4 percent were both, 33 percent were hemophilia patients who had received contaminated blood products, and 6 percent had received contaminated blood transfusions for other conditions. However, 16 percent had been infected through heterosexual contact, and the source of infection was unknown in 7 percent. A disturbing trend in adolescent AIDS is the relatively higher proportion of heterosexually acquired AIDS in teenage girls as compared with adult women.

Despite the dissemination of information about AIDS among the public and the media, many teenagers are still misinformed or confused about AIDS. Parents should obtain and provide their youngsters with accurate information on AIDS and its transmission. (Detailed information is included in chapter 19, HIV Infection and AIDS.) School intervention programs also can help properly educate teens and dispel rumors and misconceptions about the disease. The use of condoms should be encouraged in teens who are sexually active.

Studies show that of those teens who are aware of the high-risk behaviors associated with HIV infection, very few actually modify their behavior to place themselves at lower risk. Therefore, HIV testing among teens may be appropriate, depending on the teenager's risk factors for infection. Some teens may present with symptoms suggestive of AIDS infection; others may request HIV testing because of incapacitating worry. However, intensive pretest and posttest counseling is necessary to ensure that the youngster understands the meaning of HIV test results and their consequences.

SEXUALLY TRANSMITTED DISEASES AMONG ADOLESCENTS

Disease	Incidence	Risks
Gonorrhea	Nearly 25 percent of gonorrhea cases reported to U.S. public health officials occur in teenagers.	Since gonorrhea can occur without symptoms, all sexually active adolescents should be screened for the gonococcus organism during checkups. Hidden infections in women can lead to pelvic inflammatory disease.
Chlamydia	In recent years, chlamydia—a disease caused by a bacteria-like intracellular parasite—has emerged as the most common sexually transmitted disease.	Chlamydia can cause infections of the urinary and genital tracts of men and is responsible for cervicitis, pelvic inflammatory disease, and fertility problems, including an increased risk of tubal pregnancies, in women.
Condyloma (genital warts)	Genital warts, caused by human papilloma viruses (HPV), are epidemic among American young people.	Some warts are highly visible, resembling small cauliflower-like growths, but others are very small or hidden inside the vagina or penis. (Sexually active teens should be examined for genital warts.) Warts are highly infectious and linked to an increased risk of cervical cancer.
Syphilis	Previously on the decline, syphilis is once again increasing, especially among heterosexuals in some geographic regions.	Sexually active adolescents should be screened periodically for this infection. Adolescents with syphilis may be more susceptible to contracting HIV infection. Syphilis may damage unborn fetuses in pregnant teens.

SEXUALLY TRANSMITTED DISEASES

The fear of AIDS has made physicians and parents more aware of the potential danger of sexual activity, but AIDS is only one of many potentially serious sexually transmitted diseases epidemic among today's young. All sexually active adolescents should be checked for possible venereal diseases during a physical examination; even without symptoms, adolescents may be infected with hidden disease or harbor microorganisms that can be transmitted to others or eventually develop into an active disease. In addition, evidence indicates that girls sexually active at a young age with multiple partners suffer an increased risk of developing cervical cancer later in life and should undergo periodic pelvic examinations and Pap smears.

In addition to the most common sexually transmitted diseases discussed in the box above, sexually active adolescents are susceptible to a number of other problems, including genital herpes, body lice and mites, and a variety of vaginal and urinary tract infections. Most of these disorders produce discomfort that prompts young people to seek medical attention. (Additional information on sexually transmitted diseases can be found in chapter 18, Infectious Diseases.)

PSYCHOSOCIAL AND SOCIAL DEVELOPMENT

Although the aspects of adolescence that adults find most annoying—defiance of parental order, moodiness, frequent flamboyant and outlandish dressing—have been traditionally emphasized, there are many positive aspects to this stage of life. During these years teenagers usually have the time, physical energy, and ability to enjoy athletic or physical activities; companion activities, such as dancing; or more individual pursuits like hiking or horseback riding. Free of the adult responsibilities to come, teenagers often spend large amounts of time in the company of friends; however, the nature and role of friendships may change, as individual personalities and interests develop.

Adolescence is a time for many firsts. During these years a teenager may first seriously think about and question intellectual and spiritual matters such as politics and religion. This may also be a time when lifelong interests—astronomy, botany, or painting, for example—are discovered and developed. And it will be during these years that many will first experience sexual or romantic love.

The newness of adolescent feelings and experiences intensify the accompanying emotions. While undergoing so many powerful emotions and thoughts for the first time can be a heady experience for many, they may overwhelm others. For example, first love may provoke feelings of deep satisfaction, while the dissolution of a love relationship may be extremely confusing and frightening because the individual has no personal experience on which to draw.

Adolescence can also be an impressionable age when different ideas and postures captivate the individual's attention, if only for a short time. By trying on different attitudes a teenager finds out what feels most comfortable. This is an ability many adults have either lost or do not have the liberty to indulge, because of personal and professional pressures and responsibilities. An adolescent's experimentation with ideas, concepts, and feelings, although at times exasperating to parents, helps determine the life he or she will lead as an adult.

GROWTH PATTERNS

During adolescence a young person should make considerable progress in establishing independence, sexual identity, and the notion of a future role in society.

These processes do not transpire all at once, but evolve over a period of years and generally continue well into adulthood. Psychosocial development along these lines usually begins in early puberty, but there is no set pattern that is considered ideal or applies to even a majority of adolescents.

Contrary to much popular belief, maturation during adolescence is not always tumultuous. Dr. Daniel Offer, a psychiatrist at the Michael Reese Medical Center in Chicago, surveyed thousands of "normal" adolescents over a 10-year period. He found three patterns of growth among teenagers: continuous in 23 percent, surgent in 35 percent, and tumultuous in 21 percent, while another 21 percent of his subjects could not be classified. He concluded that there was no preferable or superior route through adolescence, and that the route followed by any given individual results from a number of variables including the family's child-rearing practices, genetic makeup, life experiences, social environment, and psychological makeup. In some instances, the growth may be a steady, relatively smooth process; in others, there may be a series of turbulent changes interspersed with periods of adjustment or even regression.

EARLY ADOLESCENCE

Although there is no universal pattern, typically normal development in early adolescence—generally the junior high school years—displays the greatest pubertal growth and development. At this time, the youngster begins to challenge parental authority, rules, and values and compares his pubertal changes with peers of the same sex. Both girls and boys worry about being different from their friends and go to great lengths to conform to the mores and behavior of other youngsters. "But all the other kids do it," is a common refrain applied to almost every aspect of young life, including hairstyles, dating, manner of dress, or after-school activities. School becomes more challenging not only academically but also socially as a result of increased demands on the teenager's intellectual and social ability. For some, the challenge is stimulating, for others overwhelming.

MIDDLE ADOLESCENCE

During middle adolescence—usually, the high school years—young people spend more time with peers and away from their families. At this time, teens become capable of abstract thinking and consider the future implications of social interactions. As teens begin to mull over college, careers, and plans, the expectations and fantasies may clash with reality, leading to frustration and perhaps depression. The teenage struggle for emancipation often causes parents to feel ignored or challenged. Nonetheless, at least one study shows that while teens are most influenced in behavior by peers, parents exert the most influence on career plans and educational goals.

Dating and narcissistic experimentation often begin at this time, and teens may exhibit risk-taking behavior.

LATE ADOLESCENCE

During late adolescence, as teens enter college or begin their working lives, they more readily accept their parents and may begin to share their views and values. At this time, intimate relationships with other young adults based on companionship and love may develop. Concrete plans for advanced schooling, work, or family life are made, and the person is close to adulthood.

VIOLENCE

Today's teenagers are confronted with an increasingly violent world, and they are affected as observers, victims, and perpetrators of violent crime. In many urban areas devastated by poverty and drug abuse, the streets have become unsafe for everyone. Guns, the weapons of choice, have largely replaced fists and knives. Consequently, conflicts that for previous generations might have ended in bruises and bloody noses now result in shootings and deaths.

A 1990 survey of inner-city youths in Michigan found that 44 percent reported that they could obtain a gun within one day, 42 percent had seen someone shot or knifed, and 22 percent had seen someone killed. Similar situations exist in Baltimore, Chicago, and other cities. Recently, a survey showed 40 percent of all teenagers knew a teen who had been shot. And in most cases the attacker was also a teenager. A 1994, government report noted that children and teenagers are now the most common victims of violence in the United States.

The media have brought violence into virtually every home. Prime time television programs feature gunfire, assaults, rapes, and murders, and children's cartoons display apparently painless violence—people bounce back quickly, giving an unrealistic version of violence's impact. Even news programs and video games are increasingly violent and add to the violent environment that surrounds youngsters.

In this atmosphere, it is not surprising that teenagers may react with fear and paranoia, suffer depression, or become inured to the violence and don't even acknowledge it as unusual and abnormal. Some learn violence and use it as a coping mechanism, perpetrating harmful aggression toward others.

Parents should intermittently question teens about their attitudes toward violence and crime and ascertain their exposure to violence—some parents have no idea what their youngsters see during travels to school and social events. Understanding the media violence that teens experience (in song lyrics, on television, etc.) and discussing this violence with children will help parents better cope—and help their children cope—with this disturbing media environment. In addition, parents who keep guns at home should realize that they are endangering their children by providing easy access to weapons.

PSYCHOLOGICAL PROBLEMS

Because of the potential for disastrous consequences, adults who interact with teenagers must be sensitive to and knowledgeable of the warning signs that signal problem behavior. Adolescence is often the time when some of the serious—although relatively uncommon—mental illnesses of adult life, including schizophrenia, depression, and certain character and personality disorders, first appear.

Among the symptoms that may signal clinical depression that parents should be aware of are:

- Chronic unexplained fatigue
- Psychosomatic illness
- Decreased appetite
- Sleeping difficulties
- Isolation from friends
- Drop in school performance

A 1990 study reported that 16 percent of male adolescents and up to 20 percent of females suffered from depression.

Other warning signs of possible mental illness include alcohol or drug abuse, recklessness, truancy, delinquency, sexual promiscuity, or running away from home. Such symptoms are a signal that the adolescent or parent should seek professional help from a qualified health professional, such as a doctor or psychotherapist.

SUICIDE

The problem of teenage suicide has attracted considerable media and national attention in recent years. Every year at least 5,000 teens commit suicide in the United States, and for every successful suicide, it is estimated 50 to 150 teens try and fail. In 1990, a study reported that 6 percent of young people admitted to suicide attempts and 15 percent said they came very close to trying. Although girls attempt suicide two to three times more often than boys, they are not as likely to succeed since males usually select more lethal means of self-destruction, such as guns or hanging. (In contrast, girls are more likely to attempt suicide with pills.)

While some suicides may be the result of taking unnecessary risks, the major cause, as in adults, is depression. Parents, teachers, physicians, siblings, peers, and others in close contact with adolescents should take special note of signs of depression and make every effort to get professional help for any affected young person. Some teens may exhibit the "classic" symptoms of sadness, fatigue, insomnia, loss of appetite; others may indulge in self-destructive behavior such as drug or alcohol abuse or sexual promiscuity; and still others may be particularly accident prone. Previous suicide attempts or undue fascination with the subject—for example, preoccupation with music, movies, or media reports dealing with suicide—also are serious warning signs of a person who may be at high risk.

In recent years, there have been reports of suicide epidemics in which the death of one teenager or noted personality, such as a rock musician or movie star, seemed to inspire a string of similar suicides. Widespread media coverage of suicides and televised dramatizations of teen suicides have raised many questions about the media's role in aggravating the problem of teen suicide. Research has shown that newspaper reports of suicidal deaths may be associated with increases in the suicide rate among a newspaper's readers and that the increase is proportional to the fame of the person who committed suicide and the prominence given the story.

Some experts believe that if a suicide occurs in a school or community, future suicides may be avoided with small discussion groups in school or community centers where teens discuss their feelings in an intimate setting with trained counselors as well as peers.

In the past, there has been a reluctance to question

young people about suicidal thoughts, fearing that the questions may prompt the act. But today, direct questioning in a nonjudgmental manner is recommended. Simply asking a young person who shows signs of depression or self-destructive behavior: "Have you been feeling so down lately that you have considered killing yourself?" can pave the way for discussion and appropriate action. Whenever a problem of potential suicide is suspected, quick action, for example, seeking the help of a psychiatrist or other professional trained in dealing with suicide, is mandatory. (See chapter 33 for more on depression and suicide.)

RISK-TAKING BEHAVIOR

The most common causes of adolescent death—accidents, suicide, and homicide—often can be attributed to various types of risk-taking behavior. Common examples of risk-taking behavior include cigarette smoking, alcohol and drug abuse, and reckless driving or other daredevil exploits. Risk-taking behavior can also include irresponsible sexual behavior, which can result in pregnancy, sexually transmitted diseases, and emotional problems.

Screening for self-destructive behavior should be part of an adolescent's medical checkup, and parents need to be alert to behavior patterns that can lead to serious injury, long-term health or emotional problems, or even death. There is no single motivation for risk-taking behavior, but some teens may use this behavior to gain attention from their peers or to be accepted as part of a peer group.

The concept of personal physical vulnerability and mortality is difficult for most people to grasp, but is especially so for adolescents who, because of their youth, are generally healthy and strong, and not afflicted with infirmities that expose their physical frailties. The difficulty in perceiving personal vulnerability can lead some adolescents to ignore possible long-term health consequences of certain behaviors such as smoking and alcohol use. For others, risk taking may be associated with an underlying depression or poor relationship with their parents.

DRUG AND ALCOHOL ABUSE

While studies found that illicit drug use among adolescents declined in the United States during the 1980s, it rose again in the 1990s and remains a major problem.

In 1993, 42.9 percent of high school seniors surveyed said that they had used an illicit drug in their lifetimes, with 29 percent having used one within the past year.

Marijuana has been the most prevalent illicit drug used; in 1993, 35.3 percent of high school seniors reported having smoked marijuana during their lives.

Chronic daily or weekly use of marijuana has considerable toxicity, both physical and behavioral side effects, and in adolescence has been associated with short-term memory deficits, a slower rate of learning, apathy, and depression.

Cocaine and crack use in teens has become particularly worrisome over the past few years. In 1993, 6.1 percent of high school seniors reported having used cocaine at least once while 2.6 percent had smoked crack. Crack use is particularly disturbing due to its highly addictive nature, its relatively low cost, its greater accessibility in poor urban areas, and its link to risk-taking behaviors among teens, such as promiscuity, violence, and crime.

Further, 17.4 percent of high school seniors surveyed in 1993 reported using inhalants, such as correction fluid, paint thinner, shoe polish, fuel, antiperspirants, and coronary artery dilaters (nitrates). Unfortunately, many young teens and even preteens experiment with these potent substances. Most teens consider inhalants to be without risks, but side effects can be serious and include confusion, impulsivity, and, at higher doses, seizures and cardiorespiratory arrest. LSD and hallucinogen use may also be on the upswing among certain groups of adolescents, and of the high school seniors surveyed in 1993, 10.9 percent had tried hallucinogens.

The 1993 statistics show that amphetamines were used by 15.1 percent of high school seniors during their lifetimes, heroin by 1.1 percent, barbiturates by 6.4 percent, and tranquilizers by 6.1 percent.

Another type of substance misused by adolescents is anabolic steroids, synthetic derivatives of the male hormone testosterone. (The media have highlighted the muscle-building quality of these substances as well as the medical and legal consequences suffered by several famous athletes who used them.) In 1992, 1.1 percent of high school seniors reported using anabolic steroids. Surveys show that of those who do use these drugs, almost one-half want to enhance athletic performance and one-quarter want to improve physical appearance. Adverse side effects are dependent on the age and frequency of use and the type of drug, but may include masculinization in girls, feminization in boys, psychological symptoms, and acne.

Alcohol is the most prevalent intoxicant used by adolescents, who can certainly become alcoholics. In 1993, 76.8 percent of high school seniors reported using alcohol. About 40 percent of teens are known to initiate alcohol use by eighth grade and 60 percent by ninth grade—13 percent of eighth graders admit to getting drunk at least once every two weeks. One out of 30 high school seniors reported drinking alcohol daily or almost daily.

Multiple risk factors are associated with substance abuse among adolescents. A family history of alcoholism increases the risk of alcoholism in teens, probably secondary to a combination of genetic and environmental factors. Youngsters with behavioral problems, conduct disorders, and aggressiveness tend to abuse illicit drugs and alcohol. School failure in the early years has been linked to later drug and alcohol use. In addition, teens who associate with peers who use drugs have a greater tendency to use drugs and alcohol themselves. Age is an important factor—the earlier a teen begins drug or alcohol use, the greater the risk that she will become a problem user.

Because adolescent psychological development usually involves experimentation with different behaviors and lifestyles, adults may tend to minimize the consequences of illicit drug use. The health care practitioner should assess the adolescent's experimentation and experiences with drugs and alcohol and offer prevention and early intervention services when needed. Although various programs are available for teens with substance abuse problems, many experts believe they are inadequate to deal with the scope of the problem. (For more information, see chapter 6, Smoking, Alcohol, and Substance Abuse.)

TOBACCO USE

Cigarette smoking among American teenagers has declined in the past decade, but the current rate of use is still a major concern. A recent survey of high school seniors found that one of five smoked one or more cigarettes a day within the prior month. Many teens who smoke, when asked, say they will quit within 5 years; however, in fact, experience shows that 5 years later most will still be smokers. More girls than boys now smoke cigarettes, a reversal of past patterns of tobacco use. (However, more boys than girls use illicit drugs and alcohol.)

The long-term health consequences of smoking are well known, but most young people have little concern with the fact that this habit may cause heart disease, cancer, or emphysema in 20 or 30 years. A focus on more immediate health effects—chronic cough, phlegm production, wheezing, prolonged chest infections, the aggravation of asthma, shortness of breath, and diminished endurance and athletic ability—may be more effective persuasion for teens not to smoke. Because adolescents tend to be especially concerned about personal appearance and social acceptability, the fact that smoking yellows teeth and promotes bad breath and generally detracts from personal attractiveness can be used in convincing young people not to smoke. The high cost of cigarettes is also an effective deterrent to teenage smoking.

In recent years, smokeless tobacco in the form of snuff and chewing tobacco have become more popular with adolescent boys, especially young athletes, in part because youngsters believe it harmless. In reality chewing tobacco greatly increases the risk of mouth and throat cancers and promotes gum disease and tooth loss. Attempts are being made to require a warning label on smokeless tobacco and also to limit its sale and promotion to young people.

Nicotine—the stimulant in tobacco—is a powerfully addictive drug. Studies show that the longer and more a person smokes, the more difficult it is to stop. Thus, a young person who has only recently started to smoke should have less difficulty quitting smoking than an older person who has smoked heavily for many years.

An increasing number of schools are instituting smoking-prevention programs aimed at young adolescents, usually seventh and eighth graders who are the most likely to experiment with cigarettes.

Studies also show that when parents smoke children are more likely to take up the habit themselves. Consequently, parental abstention from smoking improves adult health and promotes better health for their adolescents. (See chapter 6, Smoking, Alcohol, and Substance Abuse, for a more detailed discussion of smoking.)

HEALTH CARE OF THE ADOLESCENT

By the time a youngster reaches adolescence in good health, many parents and physicians take the child's state of health for granted. The teenager may undergo routine checkups for school, athletic teams, camp, and other activities, but these physician visits tend to be perfunctory, encompassing little more than a brief conversation, palpation of the abdomen, a blood pressure reading, and perhaps a urine test. This type of medical attention is unlikely to detect the most prevalent and significant health problems of the adolescent (see the box "Special Health Concerns of Adolescents"). If properly focused and thorough, however, an adolescent checkup can detect potential health problems in their early, highly treatable stages. It also provides an opportunity to establish a meaningful relationship between the adolescent and his doctor.

An adequate checkup should include a careful medical and psychosocial history, a thorough physical examination, and selected tests to screen for potential health problems before they become apparent or require medical attention.

In some instances, the tests may signal lifestyle changes that may prevent disease. For example, a blood test showing high cholesterol may signal the need for dietary change to prevent later coronary disease. Other tests may indicate the need for treatment for disease at an early stage before serious symptoms or irreparable damage has occurred. (Table 8.1 outlines the types of questions and

TABLE 8.1: MOST PERTINENT COMPONENTS OF HEALTH ASSESSMENT AND SCREENING DURING ADOLESCENCE

Past medical history provided to a physician should include information about:

Immunizations: diphtheria-tetanus, polio, measles, mumps, rubella, BCG, hepatitis B
Chronic illness
Hospitalizations
Allergies
Medications, including vitamins and birth control pills

Family history should include information about:

Cardiovascular disease or high cholesterol
Cancer, asthma, and collagen vascular disease
Cigarette smoking, substance abuse of household members
HIV infection and TB infection of household members

A medical review of systems (by history) should include:

Dietary habits and weight patterns
Physical activity
Dental and eye care
Menstrual history

Psychosocial history should describe:

Family relationships
Peer relationships
School and/or work performance
Special interests or skills
Feelings about self

Medicosocial history should describe:

Usual mood: problems such as suicidal thoughts
Serious accidents
Legal difficulties
Use of drugs and/or alcohol
Cigarette smoking
Sexual activity: contraception, pregnancy, sexually transmitted disease, homosexuality
Exposure to or participation in violence
Exposure and access to weapons

Physical examination should assess:

Height and weight with percentiles
Blood pressure and pulse
Condition of eyes, ears, nose, mouth, teeth, gums, heart, lungs, abdomen, spine, breasts, external genitalia, skin, thyroid, lymph nodes
Note: Girls should receive a pelvic exam if indicated.

Laboratory tests should include:

Tuberculosis Mantoux skin test
Vision testing
Audiometry
Hemoglobin or hematocrit
Sickle-cell screen (if indicated)
Urinalysis (optional)
Cholesterol testing (if indicated)
Sexually active adolescents should be examined for:
Boys: gonorrhea and chlamydia, serologic test for syphilis
Girls: same as boys, plus wet prep, Pap smear

Adapted from "Health Assessment and Screening" by Andrea Marks, M.D., and Martin Fisher, M.D., in *Pediatrics 80* (July 1987), no. 1.

tests that should be included in an adolescent checkup.)

Because the adolescent progression from childhood to adulthood includes the mental and social changes necessary for a young person to develop an adult identity, an adolescent checkup should also include an assessment of psychological and social development.

FREQUENCY OF HEALTH CHECKUPS

In 1991, the American Academy of Pediatrics Committee on Practice and Ambulatory Medicine recommended that adolescents be evaluated by a physician at least every 2 years at ages 14, 16, 18, and 20. More recently, the Bright Futures Project of the Bureau of Maternal and Child Health, with input from the American Academy of Pediatrics, revised these guidelines to encourage yearly evaluation of adolescents. If complete examinations are not undertaken annually, at least an interval history and examination should be done, with particular attention to risk-taking behaviors.

RESPONSIBILITY FOR ADOLESCENT HEALTH CARE

Traditionally, adolescents, who are neither adults nor children, have not received adequate attention from medical specialists. However, a new specialty in adolescent medicine has been created as an alternative

SPECIAL HEALTH CONCERNS OF ADOLESCENTS

SKIN

Acne afflicts most adolescents with minor pimples, whiteheads and blackheads, and occasionally severe disfiguring cysts and abscesses. This condition usually begins 1 to 2 years before the onset of puberty as a result of the impact of androgenic hormones (that both sexes produce) on sebaceous glands in the skin. Parents should never tease teens about acne since even the smallest pimples appear disfiguring to these youngsters.

Acne should be evaluated by a knowledgeable physician; many effective treatments for quelling serious acne are now available, including topical benzoyl peroxide in gel and cream form, topical antibiotic lotions, oral antibiotics (such as tetracycline, doxycycline, or erythromycin), and topical tretinoin (retin A—especially for inflammatory and cystic acne). Teens must be warned to avoid sun exposure if retin A or tetracycline is prescribed (sun exposure may cause redness or rash).

WEIGHT AND NUTRITION

The concern of many teenagers about excess weight motivates many to indulge in fad diets that compromise nutrition. Teens generally possess the worst nutritional status of all age groups. (See "Nutritional Assessment" later in this chapter.)

EYES

About one of four teenagers requires some form of vision correction. Myopia, or nearsightedness, generally develops during late childhood and early adolescence, and eye examinations for myopia should be performed every 1 to 2 years during adolescence. Teens who need to wear glasses should be encouraged to wear them.

TEETH

If an adolescent practices good dental hygiene and has regular dental checkups throughout childhood, tooth decay should not be a major problem. However, when adolescents consume diets high in sweets, neglect proper brushing and flossing, or live in an area without fluoridated water, they may develop dental cavities. Gum disease also is very common among adolescents.

Dental examinations are recommended at least twice a year. Malocclusion, or poor bite, also may become more pronounced during early adolescence, and may require orthodontia correction. (For more on dental health, see chapter 32.)

SPINE

About 5 percent of teenagers develop scoliosis, a problematic curvature of the spine. Orthopedists vary in their recommendations, sometimes urging watchful waiting and reevaluation and at other times urging exercises or, in more severe cases, the use of a back brace. Girls are at greater risk than boys and all teens should have a yearly screening. (See chapter 24 for a more detailed discussion of this and other back problems.)

REPRODUCTIVE SYSTEMS

Adolescent girls should be taught to perform monthly breast self-examination and boys should learn testicular self-examination. A complete pelvic exam may be performed for teenage girls, usually at about age 17 or 18 or earlier for the sexually active. The examination should include a Pap smear, repeated every year.

Girls also should be questioned about their periods to determine if they have irregularities or an unusual amount of discomfort. Boys should be examined for penis and scrotum abnormalities. Sexually active adolescents also should be counseled regarding birth control. (See "Sexual Activity.")

PELVIC INFLAMMATORY DISEASE

Pelvic inflammatory disease (PID) or salpingitis is an infection of the uterine lining and the fallopian tubes precipitated by sexual activity and related to the presence of sexually transmitted disease in the genital tract. Sexually active teenage girls are at greater risk of PID than adults due to a combination of behavioral and biological factors: Teens with multiple sex partners who do not use condoms or other barrier methods of contraception increase the risk. In addition, the teenage immature genital tract contains certain cell types on the cervix that may be attractive to sexually transmitted diseases, further enhancing PID risk. Acute cases cause severe abdominal pain, fever, and vomiting, usually requiring hospitalization and intravenous antibiotics. But low-grade, chronic PID may have few or no symptoms while causing severe internal damage that leads to infertility, ectopic pregnancy, or chronic abdominal pain. (For a fuller discussion, see chapter 9, Special Health Concerns of Women.)

SPECIAL HEALTH CONCERNS OF ADOLESCENTS (Cont.)

INFECTIOUS MONONUCLEOSIS (MONO)

This viral infectious disease most commonly occurs during adolescence and early adulthood and can be transmitted in many ways, generally by direct contact with an infected person such as kissing (it is often called the kissing disease). Mono causes a sore throat, swollen lymph nodes, fatigue, and, in some cases, a swollen spleen or liver. Most cases resolve themselves with rest and time. If the liver is affected, alcohol and certain drugs should be avoided for a specific period of time. (For more information, see chapter 18, Infectious Diseases.)

CHRONIC DISEASE

It has been reported that about 6 percent of U.S. adolescents suffer from a chronic disease that is disabling or limits activity. These include diabetes, asthma, lupus, rheumatoid arthritis, sickle cell disease, cystic fibrosis, cardiac disease, and cerebral palsy. Since adolescence is a difficult period of life even for the healthy, the chronically ill can find it devastating. Teenagers need to establish independence, but those with chronic illnesses and disabilities may have to depend on others for basic functions. Also, while

teens need to feel attractive and fit in with their peers, conditions that alter their appearance or make them feel conspicuous may damage their self-esteem.

Even if a chronic disease has been well controlled in early childhood, it can cause extra problems during teen years. The hormonal changes or growth spurts that occur during adolescence may exacerbate the course of these diseases, and some teens may refuse to take their medication because of side effects. (Steroids, for example may cause a round face and weight gain.) Adolescents may also refuse to follow self-care and diet regimens, such as those needed in diabetes. In other cases, as teens search for independence, they may challenge the disease and the world that regulates the treatment of the disease to see how far they can go before disease worsens. In such cases, teens may refuse medication, or take less and less to see how little they need.

While the drive for independence is a psychologically important and healthy process, excessive challenge can jeopardize a teen's life and should be discussed with a physician to provide the adolescent with more autonomy and participation in health care decisions. This type of empowerment can help the youth control a disease and maintain a feeling of independence.

---

to pediatricians, general internists, family practitioners, and other primary-care doctors.

Other alternatives to private family physicians include special adolescent-care facilities and clinics at many medical centers around the country. School-based clinics also are becoming more common, especially in areas where families are unlikely to have health insurance. Some of these centers simply perform screening tests for scoliosis, vision or hearing problems, and readiness for competitive sports. Others provide more comprehensive services, including complete physical examinations, laboratory services, immunizations, reproductive health care, and social and mental health services. While most of these centers require parental consent for participation, adolescents can consult counselors about risk-taking behaviors at these facilities in confidentiality.

IMPORTANCE OF CONFIDENTIALITY

A trusting relationship between teenagers and their examining physicians is crucial to adequate medical care. To help doctors understand youngsters' problems parents must provide background information, insights

into new behaviors, and a view of the adolescent's psychological and social development and adjustment. During an initial checkup, the physician may wish to first speak with the parent alone to elicit information. Alternatively, both parent and child may be seen together. For most of the examination, however, the adolescent should be seen alone.

Although it is important for the physician to discuss an adolescent's mental and physical development with parents, teenagers must be assured of confidentiality. Parents should realize the importance of confidentiality and respect a child's privacy; in turn, the adolescent should realize that confidentiality cannot and should not be maintained in serious health or life-threatening situations. While many states have passed laws ensuring a teenager's confidentiality when discussing birth control and abortion, most health assessments and screenings generally require the consent of both the parent and the teenager.

NUTRITIONAL ASSESSMENT

Adolescents have notoriously poor eating habits, and often overindulge on fatty, sweet foods. They tend to skip meals, especially breakfast and lunch, and eat too much right before bedtime. Girls tend to diet excessively to reduce weight, and boys may diet to increase muscle bulk and weight.

The nutritional assessment of an adolescent should measure height and weight and evaluate diet and overall nutritional status. In order for a physician or dietitian to assess nutritional status, the adolescent and/or parents should provide a food diary for a typical day, including portion sizes of all foods and beverages consumed during regular meals and as snacks. From this, the physician or dietitian should be able to determine whether the young person is consuming too many or too few calories and to evaluate whether the diet provides adequate vitamins and minerals in the correct proportions.

Nutritional needs during adolescence may be affected by:

- Puberty's hormonal changes
- Growth rate
- Level of physical activity
- Menstruation
- Pregnancy

Generally, girls in the 13-to-15-year-old group require about 2,200 calories a day, while boys need about 2,800; in the 16-to-18-year-old group, girls require about 2,100 calories daily and boys need about 3,200. (To provide for the accelerated growth of adolescence, the typical teenager requires more calories than an adult of the same size and comparable activity level.)

Eating habits commonly change during adolescence—more meals are consumed outside the traditional family setting, and a significant proportion of nutrition frequently comes from snacks, often in the form of fast food or junk food high in calories, fat, sugar, and salt, and often low in fiber, vitamins, and minerals. Nutrition surveys have found that because of dietary patterns growing adolescents in the United States are susceptible to deficiencies in calcium, iron, and vitamins A and C. These deficiencies may be easily prevented by feeding adolescents a variety of foods in the proportions indicated by the Food Guide Pyramid (see "Nutrition").

The large amounts of calories, salt, saturated fats, and cholesterol in fast foods are dietary factors linked to an increased risk of cardiovascular disease and other health

ANOREXIA NERVOSA AND BULIMIA

DEFINITION

Anorexia nervosa is an eating disorder characterized by a distorted self-image. Even though emaciated, victims consider themselves overweight, starve themselves to shed pounds, and may continue dieting to the point of death. Purging and/or laxative abuse are sometimes used to avoid weight gain. Some victims develop a combination of anorexia and bulimia, eating normal amounts of food and then vomiting to stay extremely thin.

Bulimia is an eating disorder characterized by eating binges followed by purging, typically with self-induced vomiting and/or laxative abuse to prevent weight gain. The victim may appear quite normal and makes a great effort to conceal her illness. In extreme cases, a bulimic may binge and purge daily—usually consuming huge quantities of food. A common sign of bulimia is excessive tooth decay caused by contact with gastric acids during self-induced vomiting.

CAUSE

Both of these conditions are psychological illnesses whose precise causes are unknown. The typical victim is from a middle-class family and is a high-achiever. Both disorders usually begin during adolescence, and may persist well into adulthood or throughout life.

DIAGNOSIS

Bulimics may be of normal weight or slightly over- or underweight, while anorectics are invariably thin.

Failure to menstruate is a common early sign of anorexia. Even though young anorexics consider themselves overweight, they often will go to great lengths to disguise their thinness from parents by, for example, wearing loose-fitting, long-sleeved clothes.

Bulimics may not be diagnosed until a complication of their vomiting occurs, such as dental problems caused by stomach acid or rupture of the esophagus.

TREATMENT

Treatment of these disorders is not simple, and if parents suspect that a teenager has an eating disorder they should seek professional help as soon as possible. Initially, many parents tend to underestimate the seriousness of these disorders—both are potentially life-threatening.

MALE/FEMALE DIFFERENCES

These disorders occur far more commonly among girls than boys.

problems. All young people should be encouraged to follow prudent and healthful eating habits, and special education efforts should be directed to adolescents with a family history of cardiovascular disease, hypertension, high blood cholesterol, or obesity.

Nutritional assessment should investigate a teen's comfort with his body image. If weight is of particular concern, constructive intervention with sensible advice on diet and exercise may help prevent development of an eating disorder.

In addition, an adolescent's height and weight should be measured and compared with standard growth charts. Teenagers who are more than 20 percent above or 10 percent below ideal body weight should be further evaluated. Adolescents who have been losing weight should be assessed to determine if the cause is dieting, depression, illness, or an eating disorder such as anorexia nervosa. (See box on preceding page.) Similarly, unexplained weight gain should be assessed since this may also be a sign of depression, eating disorders, or other illness.

THE SPORTS PHYSICAL EXAMINATION

Every adolescent starting to play a new sport should have a physical examination to detect orthopedic or medical conditions that could affect athletic participation. The screening should include a general medical history, maturational and musculoskeletal assessment, and cardiovascular evaluation, which involves a blood pressure reading and listening to heart sounds.

The medical history should focus on acute or chronic medical conditions that require special management or precautions: asthma, diabetes, epilepsy, and missing or impaired organ, such as an eye or kidney.

In the presence of such conditions, the young athlete may be advised to take special precautions or to avoid certain sports in favor of others. For example, a young person with only one kidney should refrain from playing football and other contact sports, which may damage the working kidney, whereas swimming and other noncontact sports are quite acceptable from a medical standpoint.

SCREENING FOR CARDIOVASCULAR RISK FACTORS

FAMILY HISTORY

The most common forms of heart and blood vessel diseases have a strong hereditary component; experts believe those at high risk should be identified at an early age and undertake a prudent program to prevent these conditions. Adolescent checkups should include screening for high blood pressure and evaluations of other cardiovascular risk factors. Adolescents with a strong family history of heart disease or those who have established risk factors should be counseled against behavior that further increases their risk.

All youngsters at risk for cardiovascular disease should avoid cigarette smoking, which greatly increases the risk of a heart attack; the risk is compounded among people who have other risk factors, such as high blood pressure.

HIGH BLOOD PRESSURE

Blood pressure should be measured when an adolescent is relaxed (not right after rushing to the doctor's office or after discussing a stressful problem). Adolescents should be instructed not to use caffeine, nicotine, alcohol, or other stimulants for several hours before having blood pressure measured.

Doctors now initiate treatment for certain cardiovascular risk factors such as high blood pressure at an earlier age than in the past. Generally, nondrug treatment such as reduced salt intake, weight loss, and increased exercise is attempted initially, especially if the hypertension is in the mild range of 140/90–100. If these measures fail to reduce blood pressure to normal levels, then drug therapy may be initiated.

The National High Blood Pressure Education Program stresses that treatment of high blood pressure at all ages, including adolescence, is associated with increased longevity and a decreased risk of heart attack, stroke, heart failure, and kidney failure. Children and adolescents whose blood pressures are in the high normal range should be checked twice yearly, since they have an increased risk of developing hypertension as adults.

In some unusual instances, high blood pressure among adolescents is secondary to other disorders, such as a hormonal imbalance or kidney disease. In these instances, treatment of the underlying cause may be sufficient to cure the hypertension. (For more information on hypertension, see chapter 16.)

CHOLESTEROL

An elevated serum cholesterol level (hypercholesterolemia)—detected by a relatively simple blood test—is another well-established cardiovascular risk factor now being identified and treated at an earlier age than in the past. Most cases of high cholesterol result from a complex interplay of genetic, dietary, and environmental factors.

The National Cholesterol Education Program urges that children and adolescents with the following risk factors be screened.

- Family history of premature cardiovascular disease (age 55 or under) or parental hypercholesterolemia

- High blood pressure
- Overweight
- Diabetes
- Physically inactive
- Smokers
- A diet high in fat and cholesterol

At least two repeat tests are needed at different times to conclusively establish a diagnosis of hypercholesterolemia. Once a diagnosis is made, a cholesterol-lowering diet is recommended, and for most people dietary modification sufficiently lowers cholesterol. However, some adolescents may require cholesterol-lowering medication in addition to regulating their diet.

While the need for drugs is unusual in childhood and adolescence, young people with an inherited form of familial hypercholesterolemia often need pharmaceutical help in lowering cholesterol. These adolescents tend to have very high levels of blood cholesterol and other lipids. They also have a high risk of suffering an early heart attack—occasionally even during adolescence—that may be forestalled by cholesterol-lowering drugs. (For more information, see chapter 16, Heart and Blood Vessel Diseases.)

OBESITY

Obesity is technically defined as body weight 20 percent above the ideal: 1 of 20 adolescents is obese. However, another 5 to 10 percent of adolescents are moderately overweight—between 10 and 20 percent above ideal weight—and should lose weight.

Obesity increases the risk of heart disease and a number of other serious health problems for adolescents as well as adults. Adolescent girls are more likely to be obese at this age than boys, and those at highest risk are girls of lower socioeconomic background or who have at least one parent who is obese.

Obesity is a complex problem not fully understood. While recent research indicates that genetic factors predispose some people to gain excess weight, increased exercise and a commonsense approach to moderation in food consumption can prevent obesity. Being overweight carries a social stigma, and teenagers are particularly vulnerable to the psychological and emotional problems that can result from obesity. (For more details, see section in chapter 6.)

IMMUNIZATION UPDATES

Evaluation of immunization status of an adolescent is an important part of a health screening: Studies show that as much as 20 percent of adolescents in the United States may be inadequately protected against the infectious diseases for which there are vaccines. At an adolescent checkup, parents should be prepared to document immunizations received during childhood; if they have not kept accurate records themselves, these can be obtained from the pediatrician or clinic that administered the immunizations. Doubts as to whether the young person has immunity to a particular infectious disease, either through adequate immunization or prior exposure, can be resolved with blood tests to determine antibody levels against the disease.

The primary goal of immunization screening is to ensure that the adolescent is adequately protected against specific infectious diseases.

For the most part, routine immunization is completed before adolescence, but booster shots may be needed. Also, if childhood immunization was not fully carried out, it may be done now.

TETANUS AND DIPHTHERIA

Adolescents who have never received immunizations or who are questionably immunized against tetanus and diphtheria should receive a primary series of tetanus-diphtheria (Td) toxoids. This three-dose series, usually given over a period of 12 months with the second dose given 2 months after the first and the final dose administered 6 to 12 months after the initial dose, is different from the one administered to children, which is commonly referred to as DTP (for diphtheria, tetanus, and pertussis). Adolescents do not require pertussis vaccine and receive a lower dose of diphtheria toxoid than younger children.

Adolescents and adults who have been adequately immunized should receive booster shots of diphtheria and tetanus every 10 years. The adolescent who received a complete five-dose series of DTP as a child will require a Td booster at 14 to 16 years of age. (A tetanus shot alone may not have included diphtheria.) Pertussis shots are not given routinely past 6 years of age.

POLIO

Adolescents under the age of 18 who were never or were questionably immunized against polio should generally receive a three-dose primary series of the oral vaccine on the same schedule as for the tetanus/diphtheria immunization. Those younger than 18 who were partially immunized should receive the number of doses required to complete the three-dose series. At present, routine immunization for older adolescents and young adults living in the United States is not recommended.

The oral polio vaccine may be given simultaneously with tetanus-diphtheria vaccine or with measles, mumps, and rubella vaccines. It should not be administered to people with impaired immune systems or to people living in a household with a person with an immune-system disease, since such individuals are at risk of developing polio from the live virus in the vaccine. Under such circumstances, unimmunized adolescents should receive three doses of the inactivated polio virus vaccine (IPV) at an initial visit, then at 1 to 2 months and at 8 to 12 months after the initial dose. IPV also is the preferred mode of vaccinating adolescents and young adults above age 18, although routine immunization of this age group is not indicated. **Neither vaccine should be used during pregnancy.**

MEASLES, MUMPS, AND RUBELLA

Immunity against measles, mumps, and rubella was formerly thought to be provided with a single trivalent MMR vaccine given in childhood. However, recent outbreaks of both measles and mumps in previously vaccinated children and adolescents have raised doubts about the persistence of immunity and have spurred the medical community to recommend booster vaccinations. This booster is currently being given to children before entering elementary school. For those teens who have not received the second dose of MMR, revaccination sometime during adolescence is recommended to ensure immunity. **The MMR vaccine should not be given during pregnancy, and pregnancy should not be attempted for at least 3 months following immunization.**

HEPATITIS B

In an attempt to achieve universal vaccination, all newborns are now being vaccinated against hepatitis B. In another generation, it is hoped that the disease will be eradicated after universal immunity is established.

All adolescents at high risk of infection from injecting drugs or from multiple sex partners should receive hepatitis B vaccine. However, because risk factors often are not identified directly among adolescents, the Centers for Disease Control and Prevention now recommend universal hepatitis B vaccination in communities considered at high risk. Some pediatricians also urge that adolescents be immunized prior to the initiation of sexual activity.

Complete hepatitis B protection requires three doses—the second dose in 1 month after the first and the third 6 months later.

TUBERCULOSIS

Screening for tuberculosis is done by a skin test to determine tuberculin sensitivity. Since the resurgence of TB, widespread screening has become controversial. The American Academy of Pediatrics Committee on Infectious Diseases recommends that most teens be tested at least once during adolescence, between ages 11 and 16, with the Mantoux skin test. Such screening should be done annually for teens at high risk, including those:

- Who have contact with adults with infectious TB
- Who are from or whose parents are from regions of the world where TB is endemic
- With abnormal chest x-rays suggestive of TB
- With clinical evidence of TB
- Who are HIV positive
- With certain other illnesses or medical risk factors that compromise their ability to fight infection
- Exposed to high-risk adults

Adolescents who have a positive skin test should then have a chest x-ray. Their parents, siblings, and other close contacts also should be tested and appropriate prophylactic therapy should be started.

9

Special Health Concerns of Women

• • • • • • • • • • • • • • • •

BY ELSA-GRACE GIARDINA, M.D.

Parts of this chapter are adapted from the chapters by W. Duane Todd, M.D., and Phyllis Leppert, M.D., Ph.D., that appeared in the revised second edition.

As we approach the 21st century, the health status of women is emerging as an issue of vital concern not only to women themselves, but also to the medical profession and those who pay for medical care. Heretofore, women's health has focused mostly on reproductive matters; otherwise, women have been viewed as generally healthy and somehow impervious to heart disease and other major killer diseases. Consequently, research into these diseases has focused primarily on men, without considering whether women might require a different approach.

This began to change in the early 1990s, when the National Institutes of Health—under the leadership of Dr. Bernadine Healy, a prominent heart researcher and the first woman to head that government agency—established the Office for Women's Health Research. This office was given a mandate to ensure that all clinical trials supported by the NIH include adequate numbers of women. Congressional hearings and major conferences were held to raise both physician and public awareness of the health needs of women.

Some of these needs were spelled out in a landmark 1993 report by the Commonweath Fund, a New York–based foundation that concentrates on health issues. This report detailed the nation's first comprehensive survey on women's health, which found a widespread "lack of needed medical care, underuse of preventive services, depression and low self-esteem, abuse, and poor physician communication." Key findings among the 2,500 women and 1,000 men surveyed by Louis Harris and Associates included:

- Each year, 13 percent of women (compared to 9 percent of men) fail to receive needed medical care. (Among uninsured women, the figure rises to 36 percent.)
- In the previous year, more than one-third of the women surveyed failed to have a Pap smear, physician breast and pelvic examination, or a physical check-up; 44 percent of women over 50 did not undergo mammography.
- The lifestyle of many of the women surveyed put them at increased risk, especially for heart disease: 67 percent admitted to being overweight; 31 percent never exercised; 25 percent smoked; and 4 percent said they drank heavily. Only 25 percent of older women were on hormone replacement, a therapy that lowers the risk of both heart disease and osteoporosis (and perhaps Alzheimer's disease); 70 percent did not take calcium supplements, another preventive measure against osteoporosis.
- Depression and low self-esteem were found to be pervasive. Some 40 percent of women said they had recently suffered severe depression (compared to 26 percent of men); 20 percent admitted to low self-esteem.
- Domestic violence is a fact of life for millions of American women. An estimated 30 million suffered some type of child abuse, setting what appears to be a lifelong pattern. More than 20 million women suffer verbal or emotional abuse by their partners, and 7 percent (a total of 4 million women) are physically abused. Yet 92 percent do not discuss the abuse with their doctors, and 57 percent keep it secret from everyone.

Thus, at long last, the medical community and women alike are coming to grips with the fact that women's health has been largely neglected. As the American population ages, the economic implications are staggering. Although women continue to live longer than men, they are more likely to spend their latter years in nursing homes, the victims of costly, debilitating disorders such as Alzheimer's disease, osteoporosis, and arthritis. There is, however, basis for optimism. As women continue to move into a more prominent position in society, they also are taking a greater interest in maintaining their good health and demanding more adequate medical services. The NIH has allocated $625 million for its Women's Health Initiative and Office for Women's Health Research. Over the next decade, these research efforts should begin to define more effective preventive and treatment programs for women. In the meantime, it is important for women to recognize that the other general chapters in this book apply as much to them as to men. They also should undergo regular screening examinations for high blood pressure, breast cancer, cervical cancer, and other diseases that are highly treatable if detected early (see chapters 4 and 12 for specific details).

FINDING THE RIGHT DOCTOR

The Commonweath Fund study cited earlier found that many women are dissatisfied with their medical care, so much so that 41 percent reported changing physicians, largely because of communication problems. Many women are uncertain about who should provide their primary health care—an issue that is debated among doctors themselves. In the past, women relied mostly upon an obstetrician/gynecologist (OB/GYN) as their primary doctor. Although some obstetrician/gynecologists pay attention to other aspects of their patient's health, many tend to concentrate almost exclusively on reproductive issues. This may be adequate during young adulthood, but as women approach their middle years, they are also likely to need a more general doctor such as an internist or family physician. Even young women with a strong family history of heart disease, diabetes, and other chronic diseases may be well advised to have two doctors—one to look after their gynecologic and reproductive matters, and the other to tend to broader health issues and coordinate their care by other medical specialists. Many managed care groups, medical centers, and clinics devoted to women's health are offering this combined approach.

When choosing any medical specialist, it's important to check his or her background and qualifications (see chapter 1), but your level of comfort with the doctor's personal style is paramount. Does the physician take time to listen to your concerns, to ask questions, to provide information? Do you feel comfortable discussing personal matters with this doctor? Are you treated with respect? Is the office staff polite and helpful? If not, seek another doctor with whom you feel totally comfortable.

BROAD ISSUES IN WOMEN'S HEALTH

HEART DISEASE IN WOMEN

Because women live longer than men and are less likely to suffer a fatal heart attack or stroke in the prime of life, many people have assumed that women were somehow immune to cardiovascular diseases. The fact is, women are just as vulnerable as men to heart attacks and stroke. Heart attacks are by far the leading cause of death in women as well as in men. According to the American Heart Association, each year cardiovascular diseases claim the lives of about 448,000 men and 478,000 women. This is more than 10 times the number who die of breast cancer, yet women consistently voice much more concern over the latter.

Women are not alone in discounting the importance of heart disease as their major health problem; many doctors also overlook it in their female patients. Complaints of chest pains, shortness of breath, and other classic symptoms of coronary artery disease are more likely to be dismissed as psychological or trivial when they occur in women than in men.

Women are twice as likely to die after a heart attack than their male counterparts; they also have a higher mortality rate during coronary bypass surgery and angio-

plasty—the two most common treatments for severely blocked coronary arteries. Similarly, more women die of strokes every year than men, even though the stroke rate among men is higher.

No one knows why women do not fare as well as men when they are stricken with a heart attack or stroke. Some think it is because they are diagnosed at a later stage; others believe treatments that work well for men may be less effective in women. Answers to these and other questions are lacking because most medical research in these areas has focused largely on men. Many of the clinical trials for heart medications, for example, have involved mostly male subjects. Fortunately, this is beginning to change.

On average, heart disease develops later in women than in men. But after menopause, the incidence of high blood pressure, coronary artery disease, heart attack, and other cardiovascular disorders rises markedly. There is mounting evidence that estrogen protects against heart disease, accounting for women's lower risk of a heart attack before age 50. And a growing number of studies show that estrogen replacement after menopause extends this protective effect. (See sections on Menopause and Hormone Replacement Therapy in this chapter.)

Of course, women benefit from the same preventive measures advocated for men. They should undergo regular screening examinations for high blood pressure, diabetes, and elevated cholesterol levels, and follow up with appropriate treatment. They also should exercise regularly, maintain ideal weight, and use alcohol in moderation. (For a more detailed discussion, see chapter 16.)

OSTEOPOROSIS AND OTHER MUSCULOSKELETAL DISORDERS

Millions of older women are disabled by chronic bone and joint disorders. According to some estimates, 25 percent of women in nursing homes are there because of musculoskeletal disorders. With proper treatment and rehabilitation, many could live independently or get by with home aid. Rheumatoid arthritis—one of the more severe joint diseases—is more prevalent among women than men and can be painful and crippling. Lupus, another rheumatic disease, also afflicts women more than men. Both are thought to be autoimmune diseases, but why women are so frequently targeted is unknown. (These and other rheumatic disorders are discussed in chapter 25.)

Women also have a much higher incidence of osteoporosis—the progressive loss of bone mass—than men. Studies have found that by age 75, up to 90 percent of women have some degree of osteoporosis, making them vulnerable to fractures, especially of the wrists and hips. Almost 80 percent of hip fractures in the United

States occur in women, and osteoporosis is a factor in a large majority of cases.

Although most people experience some bone loss as they age, such preventive measures as adequate calcium intake, weight-bearing exercise, and estrogen replacement therapy can help keep it in check. (See chapter 24 for more details.)

ALZHEIMER'S DISEASE

The cause of this devastating loss of brain function remains unknown; nor is it understood why women with Alzheimer's outnumber men. But some researchers theorize that hormones may be a factor. One study found that women receiving estrogen replacement had 40 percent less Alzheimer's disease than women who did not receive hormone replacement. More study is needed to determine whether Alzheimer's can be prevented; in the meantime, a growing number of doctors believe that the possibility is another reason to consider estrogen replacement. (See chapters 26 and 33 for more details.)

VIOLENCE AGAINST WOMEN

Millions of American women are victims of violent crimes each year, and the most likely perpetrator is a husband, lover, or close associate. Experts estimate that one-third to one-half of all American women will be the targets of domestic violence during their lifetimes. One study of married couples found that at least one-fourth of the women surveyed had endured at least one incident of domestic violence, and in 1 of 14 of these marriages, the violence was regarded as severe and repetitive. According to the U.S. Department of Justice, more than 25 percent of women who are murdered are killed by a present or former male intimate. Domestic violence is second only to car accidents as a cause for female emergency room visits.

Domestic violence cuts across all social, racial, and economic lines, although in a large number of cases, alcohol and drug use and low income status are contributing factors. A family history of domestic violence is also a risk factor—men who were abused as children or witnessed domestic violence at home are apt to become wife batterers themselves, and women who come from a home where violence was a fact of life are more likely to become victims themselves.

Women caught in a web of domestic violence often feel they have no alternatives, but with increasing awareness of the problem, most communities now have support groups and shelters for battered women. The police, courts, and physicians also are becoming more responsive to the needs of battered women (see Directory of Health Organizations and Resources, appendix B).

CAUSES OF DEATH IN WOMEN

CAUSE	NUMBER OF DEATHS PER YEAR
Heart attack	237,000
Stroke	87,000
Lung cancer	50,000
Breast cancer	43,000
Pneumonia/influenza	37,000
Accidents	30,000

Source: National Center for Health Statistics, 1990.

THE FEMALE BODY

FEMALE REPRODUCTIVE ANATOMY

At birth, a woman has external genitalia and internal reproductive organs, both of which change as she matures, from the time of menstruation until after menopause and into old age. Diagrams (see figure 9.1) can convey a sense of basic structure of these reproductive organs, but every woman differs slightly from the average.

THE GYNECOLOGICAL EXAM

After taking a patient history that includes familial disease history, personal health, and information about menstruation, pregnancy, childbirth, and contraception, a gynecologist performs a physical examination with emphasis on the breasts and the abdominal and pelvic organs. The physician or a staff member will also take your blood pressure, weight, and possibly a blood or a urine sample for analysis.

You commonly sit up while your breasts are examined. The first step is a visual inspection for depressions, bulges, unusual-appearing moles, dark or reddened areas, swelling, sores, or areas of the skin with a rough appearance. The second step is palpation, performed while you lie down. The physician skillfully checks for lumps, thickenings in the breasts, or enlargements in lymph nodes (part of the body's disease-fighting system) in the armpits and other sites. The gynecologist next palpates the abdomen to check for unusual formations in the abdominal cavity, which includes the internal reproductive organs. Then the gynecologist performs an examination of the external genitalia for sores, reddened or crusted areas, or other abnormalities. This is followed by a pelvic examina-

GENITALIA AND REPRODUCTIVE ORGANS

The external genitalia are called the *vulva,* which includes the following parts:

- *Mons veneris* or *"Mount of Venus"*—This pad of fatty tissue covers the pubic bone. At puberty an increased output of two hormones, estrogen from the ovaries and androgen from the adrenal glands, stimulates growth of pubic hair to cover this area. After menopause, when hormone levels decrease, pubic hair may thin out, straighten, or turn gray.
- *Labia majora*—These two folds of fatty tissue touch to protect the urinary and reproductive openings that lie between them.
- *Labia minora*—The inner lips, which usually protrude less than the outer lips, come together at the intersection of the mons veneris. The fused portion, or prepuce, covers the *clitoris,* which is made of erectile tissue and fills with blood and swells during sexual arousal. The clitoris is involved directly or indirectly in all female orgasms.
- *Vestibule*—Within the labia minora are the urethral meatus, through which urine passes, and the vagina, the opening of the reproductive tract. Two small Bartholin's glands, which keep the opening of the vagina moist, are also located here.

The internal reproductive organs include the following:

- *Hymen*—In some women, the hymen is a semicircular strip of mucous membrane at the lower fringe of the vaginal opening (some women are born without a hymen). This membrane may have several openings, or one large one.
- *Vagina*—A woman's vagina is a tube about five inches long with walls that expand during intercourse and expand even more during childbirth. In their normal state, the walls of the vagina gently touch. The vagina produces continuous cleansing secretions that maintain the acidity of its walls and prevent infection. The first third of the vagina is sensitive and the inner two-thirds less so, with fewer nerve endings. The bladder and rectum lie close to the vagina, and pressure on the vaginal walls may be felt in either of these two areas.
- *Cervix*—The cervix is the neck, or lowermost part, of the uterus. Its opening, the cervical os, allows passage of menstrual blood and semen. It is too small to permit tampons or other objects to enter the uterus.
- *Uterus*—About the size and shape of an inverted pear, the uterus is a hollow organ lined with a specialized layer—endometrial tissue—that thickens and is shed each month during the menstrual period. Fertilized ova, or embryos, implant themselves here and grow. In most women, the uterus tilts forward, forming almost a right angle to the vagina and resting on the bladder. In nearly a third of women, however, the uterus tilts backward (a normal condition).
- *Fallopian tubes and ovaries*—The fallopian tubes—two 4- to 5-inch tubes with tiny finger-like projections—extend from the upper portion of the uterus on either side. Nearby are the ovaries, two small oval organs on their own supportive bands of ligament. The ovaries produce hormones that cause the uterine lining to thicken each month, and they produce a ripe egg (usually one, but sometimes more) most commonly every 28 to 32 days. The egg is reached for by a fallopian tube's projections and drawn into the tube. Conception occurs when a man's sperm meets and fertilizes the egg in the fallopian tube.

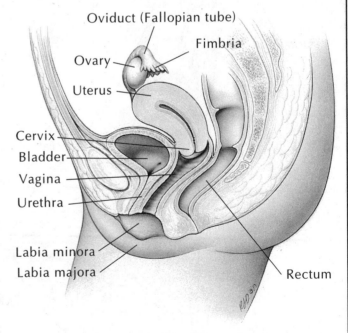

Figure 9.1: Female pelvic organs.

THE BREASTS

The interior of each breast is divided into several sections called lobes, which are further subdivided into lobules. Each lobule contains milk-secreting glands cushioned by fat and fibrous connective tissue. An intricate system of tiny ducts arranged like tree branches carries the milk produced by the glands to a collecting chamber immediately below the nipple. The entire breast is richly supplied with blood vessels, as well as sensory nerves that make them exceptionally sensitive.

Connective tissue attaches the breast to the pectoral muscles of the chest wall. The breast itself contains no muscle tissue; thus exercises purported to increase breast size can only increase pectoral muscle size so the breasts protrude more.

Although breast milk is not normally produced until the infant begins sucking, a woman's body anticipates the possibility of pregnancy every month. During the first half of the menstrual cycle, rising levels of estrogen stimulate the growth of new cells in the glands, ducts, and fibrous tissue of the breast. This increase in cell activity is accompanied by an increase in blood flow to the breasts, which may be experienced as fullness, warmth, and, sometimes, tenderness. After ovulation, the second ovarian hormone, progesterone, is released into the bloodstream. The secreting process then begins in the gland cells. This may cause an increased sensation of warmth, fullness, and tenderness in the breasts.

If pregnancy does not occur, the hormone levels shift again and the breast changes are reversed. Swelling diminishes and breast tissue softens. If pregnancy does occur, the buildup of duct, gland, and fibrous tissue continues. After childbirth, prolactin and oxytocin (hormones produced by the pituitary gland) trigger the production and release of breast milk.

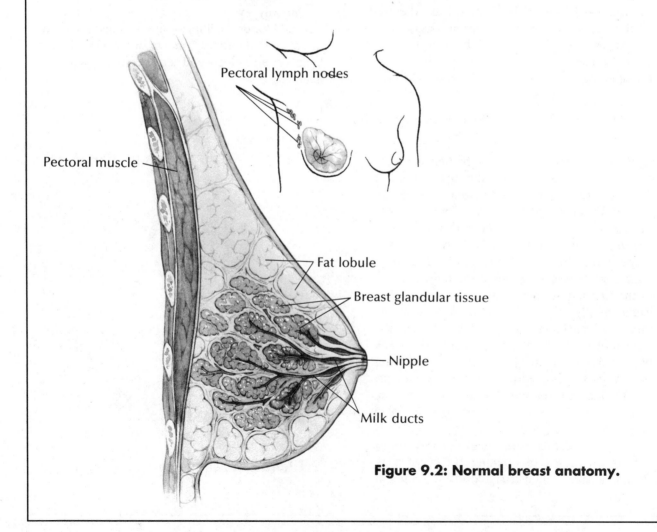

Figure 9.2: Normal breast anatomy.

tion, in which an instrument called a speculum is inserted into the vagina. This should not cause discomfort; if it does, tell the physician. When the speculum is opened, the lower internal reproductive organs can be viewed and also reached with the gynecologist's gloved fingers. The physician will examine the vagina, cervix, and uterus for growths and discolored or hardened spots, will press on the abdomen with one hand while locating the ovaries internally, and will feel for unusual conditions. The physician will also rub a small wooden spatula over the cervix to obtain a smear of secretions to be studied for abnormal cells. The smear may be used for one of several tests, but the most common is the Papanicolaou, or Pap test, an important screening tool for cervical cancers. Finally, the physician will insert a lubricated gloved finger into the rectum, at the same time pressing with the fingers in the vagina to feel for unusual conditions that might have been missed before. If you need to be fitted for a diaphragm or other contraceptive device, the physician or a staff member will probably do so at this time.

The physician should report findings as the examination progresses or immediately afterward in the privacy of his or her office. There should always be an opportunity for you to ask questions.

PUBERTY AND THE ONSET OF MENSTRUATION

Every normal baby girl is born with the potential to reproduce, with 2 million or so primitive ova, or eggs, already in her ovaries. By age 7 about 300,000 remain; the others have been reabsorbed by the body. During puberty, a girl's reproductive organs mature, leading to menarche, the first menstrual period, which usually occurs sometime between the ages of 10 and 16. At this time, the young woman is considered physically capable of becoming pregnant. Before menstruation begins, many developmental changes, visible and invisible, will already have taken place. The hypothalamus, which controls the body's production of hormones, has been sending substances to the pituitary gland, located at the base of the brain. The hormones produced by the pituitary gland stimulate the ovaries to begin secreting estrogen, which causes the eggs to mature. By the time a girl is 8, she will typically be producing small amounts of estrogen. This hormone, along with others, is responsible for a sudden growth spurt, change in body proportions, the growth of pubic and underarm hair, and the development of breasts. In addition, the girl's external genitalia begin to look more like a woman's and the internal organs grow and change so that they can accommodate reproduction.

When a certain level of estrogen production is reached, an egg is released from the ovaries, and the follicle, or egg container within the ovary, begins to secrete progesterone, another hormone. The progesterone and estrogen combination causes the uterine lining to thicken in preparation for nourishing and sustaining a fertilized egg. If pregnancy does not occur, the follicle dies. The progesterone level drops, the uterine lining breaks down and is shed, and the girl has her first menstrual period.

Menstrual cycles tend to be irregular during the first years, and this probably has something to do with the body's need to establish its hormone level patterns. Many adolescent girls do not ovulate every month, and the bleeding is not due to a reduction of progesterone levels, but to the thickness of the uterine lining, which is shed during menstruation. It is wise, however, to assume that if a girl has begun to menstruate, she is ovulating and is able to become pregnant.

It is important for a girl to have an adult who can ease her transition into womanhood with information and understanding. A girl's reactions to menstruation tend to follow the patterns she observes in her immediate environment. If her mother or other people in her life consider menstruation to be a curse or an illness, she is likely to develop the same attitude. If she is taught that menstruation is part of the process of growing up and achieving adulthood, along with the capacity for childbearing, she may have a much more positive attitude.

MENSTRUATION AND THE MATURE WOMAN

Menstruation in a mature woman usually occurs regularly, with cycles averaging 28 to 32 days, although no woman menstruates at exactly the same time each month. Also, some women have longer or shorter cycles than these, and they are also considered normal as long as there is no excessive bleeding and the cycles are fairly regular. Numerous factors involving either physical or emotional stress can cause menstrual irregularities. The menstrual cycle is divided into four phases:

- The bleeding phase, or actual menstrual flow
- The proliferative phase, when the body is preparing itself for pregnancy (there is a slight vaginal discharge at this time)
- The ovulation phase, when the ripe egg is released from the ovary (vaginal discharge increases and the mucus is thicker)
- The secretory phase, which usually lasts for 14 days, after which the menstrual flow starts and the cycle begins again

Menstrual flow usually amounts to 4 to 6 tablespoons of vaginal and cervical secretions of tissue and blood. Some women, particularly after lying down, pass clumps of menstrual tissue that look like clots. Actually, menstrual blood does not clot; the clumps are made up of endometrial tissue. Menstrual fluid has no odor until it comes in contact with air and vaginal bacteria.

At the beginning of the ovulatory phase, an ovum or egg begins a several-day-long journey down one of the four-inch-long fallopian tubes, propelled toward the uterus by thousands of slowly moving hairlike projections called cilia. The ova normally alternate ovaries and fallopian tubes each month. This process is called ovulation. If fertilization occurs, it usually does so in the fallopian tubes. Five days before ovulation, the uterus begins to prepare itself for a possible pregnancy; blood vessels in the area swell, providing a rich supply of blood to nourish the soft, spongy tissue of the uterine lining, which will cushion the egg when it arrives. The uterine glands secrete nutrients to nourish the egg. For the first three days after it enters the uterus, the minuscule egg, a single cell barely visible to the naked eye, floats freely. If it has been fertilized, it will implant itself in the uterine lining and begin to develop into a fetus. Otherwise, the ovaries stop producing the hormones that support the thickened uterine lining. Without these chemical signals, the blood vessels shrink and deprive the uterine lining of its blood supply. The weakened blood vessels open, a few at a time, discharging droplets of blood. More and more drops are released, and the flow of menstrual blood empties the uterus.

Women who have light flow may use as few as one or two menstrual tampons or sanitary pads per day. Women with heavier flow might require eight to ten tampons or pads per day. Menstrual sponges, which can be rinsed out and reused, are also available in drugstores. The size of a tampon or pad refers to its absorption ability; a menstruating woman of any age may use any size tampon that can be inserted comfortably or any size pad that can be worn comfortably. Manufacturers produce tampons in various gradations of absorbency.

CONDITIONS RELATED TO MENSTRUATION

PREMENSTRUAL SYNDROME (PMS)

Definition. Once considered a largely psychological problem, PMS is now recognized as a series of physical and psychological symptoms associated with the normal hormonal fluctuations of the menstrual cycle. Premenstrual symptoms occur to some extent in nearly every woman at one time or another; when extreme, such symptoms can be incapacitating.

PMS occurs in the week to 10 days before the menstrual period begins. More than 150 symptoms have

been identified. The most common are bloating and a feeling of heaviness, headaches, muscle aches, abdominal cramping, breast swelling and tenderness, lethargy, mood swings, acne, and food cravings. Some women experience more beneficial symptoms such as increased energy levels and heightened sexual libido.

Cause. The causes of PMS have been the subject of extensive research but remain unclear. It has been suggested that the estrogen upsurge of the premenstrual phase of the cycle increases water and salt retention, causing the discomforts due to swelling and weight gain. Gastrointestinal disturbances such as diarrhea or constipation may be the result of bloating in combination with the change in steroid hormone levels. In addition, fluctuating steroid levels cause blood vessel changes that render some women susceptible to migraine or vascular headaches.

Diagnosis. Physicians are increasingly recognizing PMS as a legitimate disorder. Diagnosis is based upon the presence of symptoms during the days prior to menstruation and the extent to which they cause discomfort.

Treatment. There is no universal treatment for PMS; rather, the focus should be to alleviate discomfort due to your individual pattern of symptoms.

Medical treatment may include hormone therapies to help restore the body's hormone balance. Natural progesterone suppositories or injections may be prescribed to help offset the increased estrogen-to-progesterone ratio, and thus relieve such symptoms as water retention and irritability. A diuretic such as spironolactone (Aldactone) may be prescribed for bloating, as may thyroid hormone (Synthroid) for depression. If an excess of prolactin is discovered to be the cause of breast tenderness, bromocriptine (Parlodel) may be prescribed; this should be used cautiously, as it has been associated with many undesirable side effects.

Analgesics such as ibuprofen or acetaminophen can be used to help reduce mild headaches and muscle aches. More severe headaches may call for a prescription drug such as propranolol (Inderal). A physician may recommend iron supplements if PMS-related fatigue is believed to be caused by an iron deficiency.

Home Remedies and Alternative Therapies. Nonmedical approaches, such as practicing sensible nutrition prior to menstruation, may be all that is necessary for some women to minimize PMS symptoms. Adhering to a low-salt regimen while increasing intake of fluids and potassium-rich foods is often effective in preventing bloating. It is suggested that women may also experience relief by restricting alcohol and caffeine intake.

The use of dietary supplements has been widely studied, and although results are inconclusive, some correlations have been found. For example, some research suggests that vitamin B supplements may alleviate bloating, depression, and acne, but this remains controversial. Some women with breast tenderness benefit from high doses of Vitamin E.

Because stress may exacerbate certain PMS symptoms, you may find relief in a number of strategies that help relieve tension and feelings of depression. Aerobic exercise may help you to manage stress, provide a satisfying release of energy, and elevate mood; many women who adopt a regular exercise program enjoy reduced premenstrual symptoms. In addition, you may find that yoga, meditation, and sexual activity leading to orgasm provide relaxation and help alleviate PMS discomfort.

An important part of self-treatment is becoming aware of your monthly fluctuations and learning to recognize the symptoms that accompany them. In accepting your hormonal changes, you can plan accordingly, for example, by wearing clothes that are comfortable when you feel bloated, and, if possible, avoiding potentially stressful situations.

MENSTRUAL CRAMPS (DYSMENORRHEA)

Definition. Cramps and other discomfort associated with menstruation is referred to as dysmenorrhea. Most women experience varying degrees of dysmenorrhea; in some, it appears as mild discomfort and fatigue, whereas others suffer pain severe enough to preclude normal activities. Dysmenorrhea is categorized as primary when there is no identifiable cause and as secondary when there is a clear underlying disorder.

Women who do not ovulate are less likely to sustain menstrual cramps; this is often the case in those who have recently started menstruating and those who take birth control pills. Childbirth often changes a woman's menstrual symptoms, often for the better.

Cause. Until recently, dysmenorrhea was dismissed as either psychological or an inescapable aspect of womanhood. Today, doctors know that dysmenorrhea is a distinct medical condition, although the precise cause remains poorly understood. The action of prostaglandins, hormonelike substances that prompt uterine muscles to contract, are instrumental in primary dysmenorrhea. The level of prostaglandins does not appear to correlate with the degree of dysmenorrhea; some women appear to have elevated levels of prostaglandins without ill effects, whereas others with normal levels may suffer severe symptoms. Other factors, including anatomical differences, genetic predisposition, and stress, also may play a role.

The various causes of secondary dysmenorrhea include endometriosis (the growth of normally uterus-lining tissue elsewhere in the pelvic cavity), fibroids or other tumors, and pelvic infection.

Diagnosis. An assessment of dysmenorrhea is based upon the severity of cramps and other discomforts during menstruation. Any change in reproductive health, including painful intercourse and significant changes in volume and length of menstrual flow, warrants a gynecological examination; such changes may identify a cause of secondary dysmenorrhea.

Treatment. Most women with primary dysmenorrhea are helped by taking nonsteroidal anti-inflammatory drugs (NSAIDs), which block the production and action of prostaglandins. These include aspirin and over-the-counter formulations of ibuprofen (Advil, Nuprin, Motrin, and others) and naproxen (Aleve). For more severe cramps, prescription NSAIDs such as naproxen (Naprosyn) or piroxicam (Feldene) may help. Although no one NSAID is superior, people respond differently to each medication. Thus, several may be tried before one that works well is found.

Some physicians prescribe birth control pills to alleviate dysmenorrhea, but this is not considered an appropriate use of these hormonal preparations. However, it may be appropriate treatment for a woman who wants to use this form of birth control. Secondary dysmenorrhea is treated by identifying and then remedying the underlying cause. This may entail taking antibiotics or other drugs, depending upon the specific condition, or other procedures including dilation and curettage (D&C) procedure (see "Menorrhagia").

Home Remedies and Alternative Therapies. In addition to taking nonprescription painkillers, there is much you can do yourself to help reduce menstrual cramps, and with a little experimentation, you should be able to find an approach that brings at least some relief. Heat is an age-old remedy; it can be applied with a heating pad or hot water bottle on the abdomen or lower back. A hot bath may also help.

Some women attain relief through exercise, which not only reduces stress, but also increases the brain's production of endorphins, the body's natural painkillers. Orgasm may also help by reducing tension in the pelvic muscles and therefore bringing relaxation and comfort.

Several yoga positions are said to alleviate menstrual cramps. One is the cat stretch, which involves resting on your hands and knees and then slowly arching the back. Another is the pelvic tilt, in which you lie with the knees bent and then lift the pelvis and buttocks. Simply assuming the fetal position, with your knees pulled up toward your chest while hugging a pillow or heating pad to your abdomen, may help.

An alternative therapy that helps some women involves visualization in which you concentrate on the color of your pain until you gain mastery over it. In addition, aromatherapy and massage may reduce discomfort. Distractions such as listening to music or becoming immersed in a book or movie are still other helpful tactics.

TAMPONS AND TOXIC SHOCK SYNDROME

Toxic shock syndrome (TSS) is a relatively rare disease about which there are still unanswered questions. Toxic shock syndrome most commonly affects menstruating women under the age of 30; however, men and children, as well as nonmenstruating elderly women, have been affected.

Toxic shock is caused by a bacterium that is often found in the nose and mouth. Some women also have this organism in their vaginas. The bacterium produces a toxin that, if sufficient bacteria are present, may be released into the bloodstream, possibly with fatal consequences.

The majority of victims have been tampon users, but medical researchers are not sure what role, if any, tampons play. Toxic shock was first identified in association with use of superabsorbent tampons, which were withdrawn from the market. Most tampons, however, contain some type of superabsorbent fiber. One current theory is that tampons trap the bacteria and provide a breeding ground for them. If a tampon is left in place for an extended time, as is the practice with superabsorbent types, the opportunity for the bacteria to grow and produce toxins is increased. Another theory is that the superabsorbent fibers cause microscopic lacerations in the vagina that enable transmission of the bacteria or toxin to the bloodstream.

Toxic shock syndrome is characterized by a sudden onset of fever, vomiting, and diarrhea, sometimes accompanied by headache, sore throat, and aching muscles. There may be a dramatic drop in blood pressure within a day or two. The woman may go into shock, become disoriented, and suffer kidney failure. At the same time, a red, peeling rash may develop, particularly on the palms and soles of the feet. The disease tends to recur and can be fatal. A woman wearing a tampon who begins to experience symptoms should remove it and seek immediate medical attention. Antibiotics, medication to stabilize blood pressure, and intravenous fluids may be given.

A woman who chooses to use tampons should change them frequently and alternate between the use of tampons and pads. One who has had toxic shock should not use tampons at all.

CONTRACEPTION

No couple should engage in sexual activity unless they first consider the effect that a pregnancy might happen and plan accordingly. This means if prevention of pregnancy is part of a couple's decision, they should agree on the method of birth control and use it consistently. Those whose lifestyles include more than one sexual

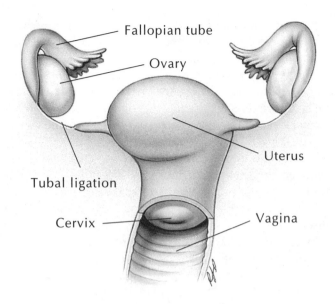

Figure 9.3: In female sterilization, the fallopian tube may be either tied (ligated) or cut and cauterized, to prevent passage of the ovum into the uterus.

partner should be prepared to use contraceptive methods themselves and not assume that their partners will attend to it. Due to the widespread choice of contraceptives, the ability of sexually active people to prevent unwanted pregnancy has increased significantly over the past 25 years. The methods vary in ease of use, safety, and effectiveness. The individual or couple choosing contraception should consider all of these factors.

Contraceptives are available by prescription or over-the-counter in drugstores, from Planned Parenthood, or by mail-order. Despite the relative ease of obtaining contraceptives, and the fact that most states no longer place age restrictions on the purchase of them, there are still many unwanted pregnancies.

Much has been written about the safety and possible dangers of some methods of contraception. Recommendations based on long-term studies of the newer methods are just beginning to appear, along with guidelines for certain age groups or people in certain health categories. Ironically, the methods that have the greatest number of questions about safety are the most convenient. These include the birth control pill and the intrauterine device (IUD). Less convenient and with less health risk potential are the barrier methods: the diaphragm, the cervical sponge, the cervical cap, and the condom.

Permanent contraception—tubal ligation in a woman (figure 9.7) is an increasingly popular alternative for women who have completed their families.

The fact remains that contraception is very much an individual decision, to be made on the basis of the indi-

TABLE 9.1: POSTCOITAL CONTRACEPTION

Type	Composition	Method of Action	Side Effects	Complications
DES (the morning-after pill) or high-estrogen oral contraceptives	Synthetic estrogen	Large doses make the uterine lining inhospitable for implantation of the egg	Nausea, vomiting, headaches, menstrual irregularities, breast tenderness	Possible birth defects in baby if pregnancy is not terminated; increased risk of breast cancer
Postcoital IUD	Copper IUD	Postcoital insertion prevents implantation of the fertilized egg in the uterine wall	Refer to Table 9.2, Contraceptive Devices	Refer to Table 9.2, Contraceptive Devices

vidual's pattern of sexual activity, age, health, desired family size, and religious convictions.

ABORTION

Although abortion was legalized by the United States Supreme Court in 1974, it remains a highly controversial, emotionally charged issue. In addition, the legalization of abortion does not make a woman's or a couple's decision to have an abortion a comfortable choice. Deciding to abort a fetus stimulates emotional, moral, and religious conflicts. A woman or a couple may want to consult a physician or the skilled counselors in a family planning center.

Legal abortion is a relatively safe procedure, the risk of death substantially less than that involved in carrying a pregnancy to term. The most important consideration is the duration of the pregnancy; the later in the pregnancy the abortion is performed, the greater the risk to the woman.

A woman who suspects she is pregnant should have a pregnancy test as soon as possible. Some of the newer tests can detect a pregnancy within a few days of the first missed period. A woman who uses an at-home test should have its results confirmed by a blood test done by a health care professional. Abortions should be performed as early as possible in the pregnancy.

TYPES OF ABORTIONS

Menstrual Extraction. Performed in the first 3 weeks of pregnancy, this procedure involves the use of a syringe to extract the embryo. Dilation of the cervix is not necessary, and anesthesia usually is not used.

Vacuum Abortion. Performed at 4 to 12 weeks of pregnancy. Requires local or general anesthesia. The cervix is dilated, a vacuum tube is inserted, and the fetus is suctioned out.

Vaginal Application of Prostaglandins. Performed between 14 and 20 weeks of pregnancy, it can be accomplished with vaginal suppositories of prostaglandins, which cause uterine contractions and expulsion of the fetus and placenta.

INFERTILITY

Infertility is generally defined as the inability to achieve pregnancy after at least 1 year of regular sexual activity without the use of contraception, or the inability to carry a pregnancy to live birth. (Sterility is defined as the absolute inability to conceive children.) If a pregnancy has never occurred, the condition is called primary infertility, but if a couple cannot initiate another pregnancy after the birth of a first child, it is called secondary infertility. The causes of primary and secondary infertility may differ.

Infertility is fairly common, and about one out of every six couples is infertile at any given time. A woman reaches the height of her fertility in her mid-20s. Her ability to conceive slowly declines until age 30 and drops more rapidly after that. A man's fertility decreases slowly until about the age of 40, and then decreases more rapidly.

Women unable to conceive in their 30s should seek help more quickly than younger women because their chances of getting pregnant are declining more rapidly. Those not menstruating regularly may want to seek treatment as well, since irregular cycles may indicate lack of ovulation; such women are not likely to conceive without treatment. A woman with a history of pelvic disease or a man who had mumps as an adult might also want to seek help quickly.

THE FIRST STEP

Doctors who treat infertility first take a family history of each partner to investigate possible genetic disorders

TABLE 9.2: CONTRACEPTIVE DEVICES

Type	Composition	Method of Action	Side Effects	Complications	Contraindications to Usage	Drug Interactions	Availability
Birth control pills/oral contraceptives	Synthetic hormones	Suppression of hormonal cycle necessary for the maturation and release of the egg	Nausea Cycle weight gain Breast tenderness and swelling Fluid retention Depression Acne Hirsutism or alopecia Headaches Circulatory disorders Reduction in amount and duration of menstrual flow Vaginitis	Venous thrombosis Stroke Heart attack Angina Liver tumors Impaired liver function Diabetes High blood pressure Post pill amenorrhea Breast cancer Cervical cancer Uterine cancer Ovarian cancer Gallbladder disease	Active smoker History of any of the listed complications: Sickle cell anemia Uterine fibroids Pregnancy	Taking the following will decrease the effectiveness of the pill: Ampicillin sulfa drugs (e.g., Bactrim) Antihistamines (e.g., cold tablets) Antidepressants Sedatives/tranquilizers Seizure medication Tuberculosis medication Arthritis	By prescription only from a doctor after a checkup
Combination pill	Synthetic progesterone and synthetic estrogen	Suppression of ovulation					
Mini pill	Synthetic progesterone only	Alteration of the cervical mucus, making a hostile environment for sperm Changes of the endometrium to prevent implantation					
Intrauterine device IUD "Loop" "Coil"	Copper or plastic device inserted into endometrial cavity of uterus, where it may remain for years	Exact mechanism unclear. Suggested mechanisms include: Inflammatory reaction to the presence of a foreign body inhibits implantation of the embryo Destruction and inhibition of sperm transport by local inflammatory response	Risk of pelvic inflammatory disease Heavy or prolonged menstrual bleeding	Uterine perforation Involuntary expulsion without the user's awareness Ectopic pregnancy Pregnancy with complications including: Miscarriage Premature delivery Stillbirth	Suspected pregnancy Current, recent, or recurrent pelvic inflammatory disease Abnormal Pap smear History of uterine cancer Uterine fibroids History of ectopic pregnancy Allergy to copper	None	Placed only by your doctor after a checkup. Placement followed yearly or more often by your doctor.
Diaphragm	Dome-shaped latex rubber with flexible metal spring accompanied by sperm-killing jelly or cream	Physical barrier against the passage of sperm into the cervix Cream or jelly kills sperm on contact	Increased frequency of urinary tract infections	None	Sensitivity to rubber or sperm-killing cream or jelly	None	Fitted by physician or health care professional
Cervical cap	Rubber cap accompanied by sperm-killing jelly or cream	Physical barrier against the passage of sperm into the cervix Cream or jelly kills sperm on contact	None	Possible toxic shock syndrome	Abnormal Pap smear	None	Over-the-counter without a prescription

TABLE 9.2: CONTRACEPTIVE DEVICES (Cont.)

Type	Composition	Method of Action	Side Effects	Complications	Contraindications to Usage	Drug Interactions	Availability
Spermicides	Creams Jellies Aerosol foams	To be used with a diaphragm or cervical cap or condom	None	None	Sensitivity to ingredients	None	Over-the-counter without a prescription
Condoms	Sheath of thin rubber or lamb's gut used over erect penis	Barrier protection preventing ejaculate from entering vagina	Protection for both partners against sexually transmitted diseases including HIV	None	Sensitivity to spermicide	None	Over-the-counter without a prescription
Contraceptive sponge	Polyurethane sponge impregnated with spermicide	Blocks entrance to the cervical canal Spermicide kills sperm Sponge absorbs ejaculate	None	Possible toxic shock syndrome	None	None	Over-the-counter without a prescription
Withdrawal	Coitus interruptus	Withdrawal of penis before ejaculation	None	Highly unreliable for preventing pregnancy	None	None	
Natural family planning—rhythm method	Calendar method Temperature method Mucus inspection method	Abstaining from sexual intercourse during ovulation in the fertile phase Determination of ovulation based on: Monthly cycle record-keeping Body temperature throughout the cycle Examination of changes in the cervical mucus throughout the cycle	None	Highly unreliable for preventing pregnancy	None	None	
Vasectomy	Sterilization of men	The vas deferens, the tube that carries sperm, is cut and cauterized in a 20-minute outpatient procedure under local anesthesia	No effect on a man's virility	Infection, hematoma, epidiymitis, granuloma formation	None	None	Performed by surgeon who specializes in genitourinary procedures
Tubal ligation	Sterilization of women	The fallopian tubes are ligated or tied so they are unable to carry the egg to the uterus for fertilization. Also may be done under local anesthesia as an outpatient	No effect on a woman's femininity	Bleeding, infection, bowel trauma, bladder trauma, uterine trauma	None	None	Performed by an obstetrician/gynecologist

Sample Chart

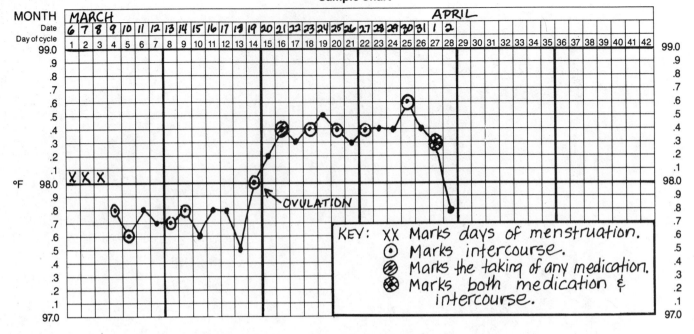

Figure 9.4: Sample temperature chart.

Source: Serano Laboratories, Inc., 100 Longwater Circle, Norwell, Massachusetts 02061.

and medical conditions that might affect fertility: mumps, measles, whooping cough, diphtheria, rubella, thyroid disease, tuberculosis, epilepsy, and the presence of infections. The doctor asks about use of certain medications that may be spermicidal, as well as the use or abuse of alcohol, tobacco, tea, coffee, or recreational drugs, all of which affect sperm count.

A sexual history of each partner follows. Women are asked about when they first menstruated and what their periods are like; whether they suffer pelvic pain between periods (indicative of ovulation); previous pregnancies, miscarriages, and therapeutic abortions. Information is taken about the use of lubricants during intercourse (some, such as Vaseline, retard the movement of sperm) or contraceptives, pain during intercourse, and pelvic infections. (Pelvic inflammatory disease may cause blockages that interfere with the passage of ova through the fallopian tubes.) Women are taught how to measure and record basal body temperature upon awakening each morning. A chart such as the one above will help determine if ovulation is taking place (see figure 9.4).

Questions for men include whether there were problems in the normal descent of testicles; whether surgery (orchiopexy) was necessary to help them descend; whether and at what age circumcision took place; and whether reproductive tract infections have occurred.

Both partners will likely be asked about their sexual behavior: how often they have sex, orgasmic patterns, preferred positions, masturbation, or other sexual tech-

niques. A few infertility cases are solved on the spot when it is learned that the couple is not engaging in intercourse properly or at the appropriate times.

THE PHYSICAL EXAMINATIONS

Both partners undergo extensive physical examinations, during which a doctor looks for normal development of sexual organs and secondary sex characteristics (pubic hair growth and breast development). A careful examination of the woman's abdomen may reveal scars from operations she has not mentioned. A pelvic examination will confirm the presence of a healthy uterus and ovaries, or reveal any problems of shape and size. The man's genitals are examined for abnormal development or displacement of organs. Blood and urine are tested for the presence of sexually transmitted diseases. As the workup progresses, more sophisticated tests are done.

An infertility workup is trying for both men and women. Often, they wonder whether their problem is psychological, a reasonable concern that can be resolved only by going through the workup. When couples are having sexual intercourse continually in an effort to start a pregnancy, the goal of pregnancy may come to dominate their lives and sometimes leads to depression. Intercourse may then become less an expression of interest and affection than a job to be done in preparation for tests or when it is most likely to result in pregnancy. At this time, a woman sometimes becomes less interested in sex and enjoys it less. She develops a new point of view toward her partner, seeing him either as supportive or unsympathetic, cooperative or difficult. Their relationship may be permanently altered by the revelations of this ongoing crisis. A man sometimes questions his own virility because fertility and manliness may be closely intertwined in his mind. Sex-on-schedule becomes a problem for the male partner, who just may not feel like it at the necessary time. Sometimes he develops performance problems or feels anger and resentment toward his partner.

Each partner may feel at various times like a failure. The fertility specialist and the health care team may or may not be sensitive to these problems. Some fertility practices now include a nurse practitioner whose job it is to provide facts and empathic support.

INFERTILITY IN MEN

During an infertility evaluation the male is evaluated first. If the couple's infertility is due to him, the most likely cause is his sperm. In a woman, however, infertility may be due to a variety of causes. Sperm analysis is the first step for the man. (See chapter 10 for a more detailed discussion of diagnosis and treatment of male infertility.)

INFERTILITY IN WOMEN

When no evidence of reproductive dysfunction can be found in the male partner, study of the woman begins. The initial test, the Huhner test, collects cervical mucus, in the doctor's office, within 2 hours of sexual intercourse. Mucus is examined under a microscope to see if sufficient live sperm are present and whether enough mucus is present to ease the passage of sperm through the genital tract and into the fallopian tubes, where fertilization takes place.

PROBLEMS IN FEMALE CONCEPTION

A woman may be unable to conceive because of abnormalities of her uterus, fallopian tubes, or ovaries (see figure 9.5), or if eggs are not being produced.

Sometimes a woman with normal menstrual periods does not produce an ovum with each menstrual cycle. This can be determined by a basal body temperature chart, which a woman creates at home by taking her own temperature before getting up in the morning. If ovulation is taking place, her temperature rises slightly and remains higher in the second half of the menstrual cycle than in the first half. Her chart at the conclusion of a menstrual cycle demonstrates whether this rise takes place. Alternatively, a home ovulation test can determine if and when ovulation takes place.

Female infertility may also result from hormonal imbalance. Normally, many hormones contribute to the successful balance of the female reproductive process, and these substances are necessary for development of viable ova. Blood tests can detect and quantify the necessary hormones, which include both estrogen and progesterone. On the other hand, the hormone prolactin—usually produced when a woman breast-feeds—may be present and preventing both menstruation and ovulation.

Measurements of the hormone progesterone may determine whether her reproductive system is allowing insufficient time for fertilized egg implantation. This condition can be treated with hormones, a treatment

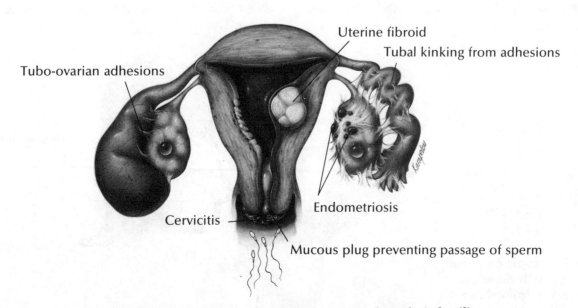

Tubo-ovarian adhesions

Uterine fibroid

Tubal kinking from adhesions

Cervicitis

Endometriosis

Mucous plug preventing passage of sperm

Figure 9.5: Common problems causing female infertility.

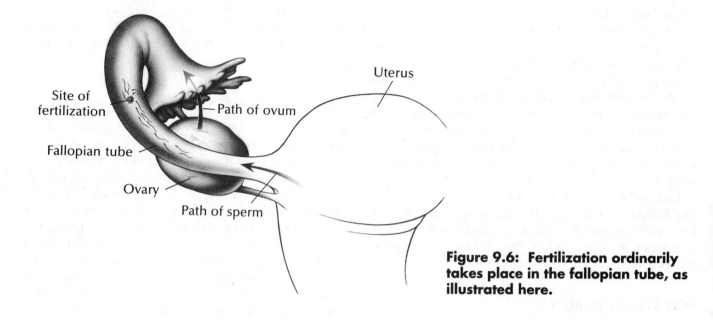

Figure 9.6: Fertilization ordinarily takes place in the fallopian tube, as illustrated here.

that sometimes results in overstimulation of the ovaries, which may produce multiple births.

The Uterus. Several uterine conditions may make pregnancy difficult or impossible.

Fibroids. These are benign tumors that can distort the shape of the uterus. Surgery may be required to remove them.

Tipped uterus. Normal wombs lie with their closed end facing forward and pointing upward. A tipped uterus faces back and down. Surgery to correct the position has had only limited success in improving fertility and is not recommended.

Endometriosis. This condition usually affects women between ages 30 and 40. The endometrium, the same tissue that lines the uterus and is expelled each month during menstruation, may grow elsewhere in the pelvic cavity (for example, in the fallopian tubes or on the ovaries). The misplaced tissue responds to hormonal signals and may cause scarring and adhesions. In some cases, endometriosis may twist the reproductive organs out of their normal alignment, preventing the ova from reaching the fallopian tubes. Otherwise, it is not fully understood how endometriosis interferes with fertility. Research indicates that the errant tissue may have some influence on the ovum after it is released from the ovary. Treatment of endometriosis may include hormonal therapy and/or surgery.

The Fallopian Tubes. Damage to the fallopian tubes makes it difficult or impossible for an ovum to be passed

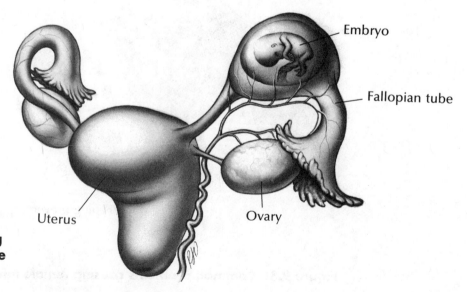

Figure 9.7: Ectopic or tubal pregnancy, with developing embryo in the fallopian tube instead of the uterus.

to the uterus every month, and may prevent conception (see figure 9.6). Sometimes, if the tubes' lining is damaged, conception may occur too high in the tube and pregnancy will begin there instead of in the uterus—an ectopic, or tubal, pregnancy (figure 9.7). This requires surgical removal to prevent rupture of the tube and other serious complications. Some surgeons try to leave the tube intact, but often it is damaged beyond repair. A woman with only one functioning fallopian tube has her chances of pregnancy cut in half.

To determine fallopian tube function, fertility specialists use a variety of tests, including laparoscopy and a hysterosalpingogram (see chapter 12, Diagnostic Tests and Procedures). Before these tests are ordered, however, a doctor may try insufflation of the fallopian tubes, in which carbon dioxide, a gas readily absorbed into the body, is blown gently through the uterus and escapes through the fallopian tubes. This test enables the physician to determine whether the tubes are open. The tubes are muscular, so there is bound to be some resistance to passage of the gas, but properly open tubes accept the gas at a steady rate. Sometimes the physician listens with a stethoscope on the abdomen to determine the rate at which the gas is escaping.

WHEN THE COUPLE REMAINS INFERTILE

A large proportion of couples actually conceive while undergoing fertility tests. Another group will be helped by removal of blockages, treatment of endometriosis, or induction of ovulation with fertility drugs. For some couples, however, the tests reveal an absolute inability to have children. These couples often adopt children.

Another alternative is artificial insemination: The male partner's semen is collected and placed in the cervix or uterus of the female partner around the time of ovulation. Reported pregnancy rates with this technique, however, are low.

Artificial insemination with sperm from a donor should take place only if both partners concur in taking this action. Donors are usually chosen for physical similarities to the couple, and a physical history of potential donors is used to rule out disease and poor semen count. Medical students and residents are often donors. Insemination procedures are usually performed more than once, sometimes with a different donor each time. Often the partner's sperm may be mixed with the donor sample. This method of artificial insemination often produces satisfactory results.

IN VITRO FERTILIZATION

In vitro fertilization has received widespread media attention since the first test-tube baby in 1978. It is still highly experimental and used only when no other alter-

native is acceptable. It requires a woman to be capable of producing ova and ovulating.

During this procedure, the woman receives hormones to stimulate ovarian activity just after her menstrual period in order to produce as many ova as possible. Just before ovulation, the woman enters the hospital, where the ova are removed by laparoscopy. After a short incubation, a sperm sample is added, either from her partner or from a donor and, should fertilization occur, the developing embryos are incubated (in a "test tube"), until the embryo reaches a two- to eight-cell state. The embryos are then transferred to the uterus or fallopian tubes, depending upon the technique being used. The woman may receive more hormones to decrease the possibility of miscarriage. Hormone levels continue to be measured until it is certain that the pregnancy is in progress. In vitro fertilization is expensive—$6,000 or more per attempt.

PREGNANCY

PLANNING PREGNANCY

The best time to have a baby is when you and your partner want one. Pregnancy and parenthood inevitably require considerable adjustment in a couple's lifestyle. Physiologically, the optimal years for childbearing are between ages 18 and 35. Research shows that women who become pregnant in their early teens or after the age of 35 have an increased risk of pregnancy complications. A very young mother has a far greater than average risk of bearing a low-birth-weight infant. After age 35, and particularly after 40, there is a greater risk of having a child with a congenital anomaly, such as Down syndrome. Even in this age group, however, the risk is small and the vast majority of babies are healthy.

Pregnancy is a demanding experience, both physically and emotionally, and it requires time, effort, and money to raise a child. A couple therefore should be very sure that both partners are ready before planning a pregnancy and that the child is not being born to save the marriage, for example, or satisfy demands for a grandchild.

Preferably, a woman should begin to prepare herself before conception for the demanding work of pregnancy and labor. If she is above her ideal weight, she should make every effort to lose weight, and if she is flabby and out of condition, she should exercise and tone her muscles. Since the vulnerable first trimester of intrauterine life may begin before she is aware of it, she should give up smoking and alcohol. Most important, she should check with her doctor about the safety of any drugs, both prescription and over-the-counter, that she may be taking. About 20 percent of birth defects are caused by environmental factors such as drugs, viruses, and vitamin excess and deficiencies, and approximately 60 percent result from the combination of an environmental factor with a genetic predisposition. A woman who is planning a pregnancy, or who is already pregnant, should be aware of these hazards and take all possible measures to guard against them.

Pregnancy is necessarily a time of waiting, but it need not and should not be a time of passive waiting. It is a time to learn as much as possible about what is happening in the body, what will happen in labor, what to expect in caring for the newborn infant and how to prepare.

AM I PREGNANT?

Symptoms of pregnancy result from hormonal changes that take place in a woman's body at the time of conception and in the days and weeks that follow. Not all women experience the same symptoms.

The most common first sign of pregnancy is a missed period. Less common is some slight vaginal spotting about 7 days after conception, called implantation bleeding. Other signs of early pregnancy include full, swollen, and sometimes tingling breasts; sensation of pressure in the pelvic area; and frequent urination. Morning sickness in early pregnancy is common and in fact may occur at any time of day. If a woman has been taking her basal body temperature to determine her date of ovulation, she will note that if conception has occurred her temperature rise, associated with ovulation, will continue for 20 or more days.

THE PREGNANCY TEST

Conception occurs when the egg has been fertilized by the sperm and becomes implanted in the uterus. The tissue surrounding the fertilized egg produces a hormone that enters the mother's bloodstream and is excreted in her urine. The presence of this hormone, chorionic gonadotropin, is the basis for modern pregnancy testing, which can be done as early as 6 to 9 days after a missed menstrual period and in some cases even earlier. Depending on which test is performed, a woman will know within a few hours or days whether she is pregnant. Indeed, if a rapid screening test on urine is done, she will know within a few minutes.

Home pregnancy tests have become quite popular. While the manufacturers of the testing kits claim that they are 96 to 99 percent accurate, such factors as vibration, sunlight, heat, the presence of detergents and some medications, and some medical conditions can influence the test, producing a falsely positive or falsely negative result. It is therefore important that a woman have her pregnancy confirmed by a doctor or in a clinic, where more reliable tests are used.

PROVIDERS OF CARE

Once pregnancy has been confirmed, most women receive their prenatal care from physicians—either obstetricians (doctors who specialize in the care and treatment of women during pregnancy and childbirth) or family practitioners trained to do uncomplicated obstetrics—and deliver their babies in a hospital. About 2 to 3 percent of women are cared for by certified nurse-midwives, registered nurses who have received extra training in the care of normal pregnancy and who work with obstetrician backup in case of complications. A few women receive their care from lay midwives. Some of these women are very competent, but the requirements for licensure vary from state to state. A woman planning to use the services of a lay midwife should check her qualifications carefully, as well as the qualifications of the doctor providing backup. If she chooses a midwife, she should meet with the backup physician several times during pregnancy.

The out-of-hospital childbirth center movement began in the mid-1970s, largely in response to hospital procedures that were perceived as stressing technology at the expense of human needs. Since then, however, the concept of family-centered childbirth has become an integral part of care in most hospitals. Many have childbirth rooms (labor-delivery-recovery rooms), in which the father may stay with the mother throughout labor and delivery and which make the transfer to a delivery room during the second stage of labor unnecessary. As for technology, most women do not object to modern fetal monitoring techniques once they understand the reason for their use.

Delivery in hospitals ensures that problems can be treated speedily; studies show that 10 to 15 percent of women in labor develop a serious problem. Freestanding childbirth centers are equipped to handle only normal births, even though there have been a few cases in which emergency cesarean sections have been performed at childbirth centers. If a complication develops during labor, the woman will have to be sent from the center to a hospital, and precious time may be lost in transit. Births at these centers, however, can be less expensive than hospital births.

If a woman is considering a childbirth center for her prenatal care and for labor and delivery, she should inquire as to the qualifications of the staff and the reputation and nearness of the backup hospital. The center should provide patients with written guidelines detailing the circumstances under which transfer to other facilities will be made. If a woman has any doubts about the

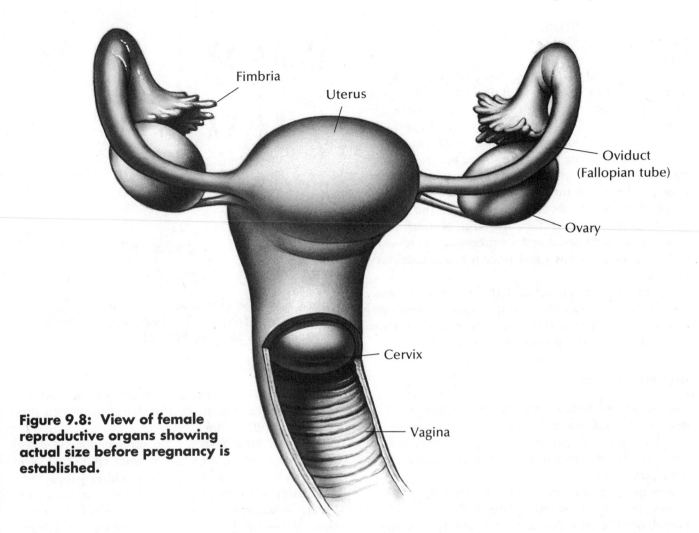

Fimbria

Uterus

Oviduct
(Fallopian tube)

Ovary

Cervix

**Figure 9.8: View of female
reproductive organs showing
actual size before pregnancy is
established.**

Vagina

standard of care, she should check with the local health department.

Home births enjoyed something of a vogue a few years ago but now are less common, perhaps because of growing flexibility of hospital practices. Home delivery is safe only for normal births. In addition, it may be difficult to ensure an adequately germ-free environment to protect both the mother and baby against infection.

PRENATAL EXAMINATIONS

Routine prenatal examinations ensure the health of both mother and fetus. Every study that has considered the impact of regular, consistent prenatal care begun in the first trimester (the first 3 months), shows unequivocally that such care prevents many complications and helps ensure that if they do arise they will be treated before they become serious. Early prenatal care and continued care throughout pregnancy reduces the risk of stillbirth and infant mortality by 75 percent.

The first prenatal examination is usually carried out in the second month of pregnancy and includes a discussion of the woman's medical history (past illnesses and operations, past pregnancies, miscarriages, abortions), her family history of disease (heart and kidney disease, diabetes and hereditary disorders such as sickle cell anemia), the child's father's history of disease, the family history of twins, and the history of the present pregnancy itself. A physical examination is done to assess the woman's health and to check for any general disease. A pelvic examination is performed to check the size of the uterus (see figure 9.8) and to detect any abnormalities or misplacement.

The first prenatal examination includes a Pap smear to detect any possible cancerous or precancerous condition of the cervix, a vaginal culture to check for infection, and a urine sample to check for the presence of protein and glucose. Blood is routinely drawn and tests include a complete blood count, a rubella (German measles) test, blood type and rhesus (Rh) factor tests, and a test for syphilis (which is mandatory in most states). Pregnant women, especially those living in large cities or who have engaged in high-risk behavior, may be advised to be tested for HIV, the virus that causes AIDS. A glucose challenge test to identify possible gestational diabetes is recommended between the 24th and 28th weeks of pregnancy. Depending on the medical history and the findings of the physical examination, other tests may be necessary.

After the initial examination, most women should see their doctor once a month until the 7th month of pregnancy. In the 8th month, two to three visits are usually scheduled; in the final month, weekly visits are the rule.

Frequent follow-up visits monitor weight and blood pressure and measure the growth of the uterus. Between the 10th and 12th weeks of pregnancy the fetal heartbeat can be heard through an ultrasonic fetal stethoscope. This, too, is checked at each visit. The internal pelvic examination of the first visit is usually not repeated until the last month of pregnancy, unless special circumstances, such as a prior premature delivery, dictate it.

Most doctors encourage the father to attend all or any part of the initial examination. It is a good opportunity to discuss problems that may have arisen and to anticipate future concerns, particularly birth plans.

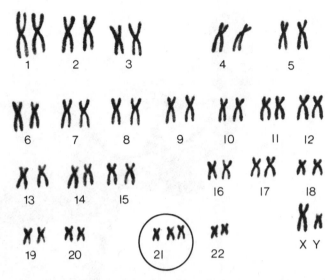

Figure 9.9: The chromosomal pattern of Down syndrome or Trisomy 21. Note the abnormal 3 chromosomes for pair No. 21.

THE DUE DATE

The due date for birth is only an approximation based on physical examination and medical history. This calculation of the due date, or estimated date of confinement, is based on the date of the last menstrual period and the size of the uterus.

A normal pregnancy is usually calculated to last for 40 weeks (280 days) from the first day of the last menstrual period, or 38 weeks (266 days) from the day of conception. A baby may be born anywhere from 3 weeks before the due date to 2 weeks after, and pregnancy will still be completely normal and the baby considered full term. In fact, only 1 baby in 20 arrives precisely on the due date.

Ultrasound, a technique that uses high-frequency sound waves to visualize internal organs, can determine the expected duration of the pregnancy. However, a due date calculated by ultrasound can be off by 10 to 14 days.

Pregnancy is arbitrarily divided into three periods, or trimesters. The first trimester ends at 12 weeks, the second lasts from weeks 13 to 27, and the third from weeks 28 to 40. Most doctors speak of numbers of weeks completed (reckoned from the date of the last menstrual period) rather than of trimesters when referring to the progress of a pregnancy.

GENETIC COUNSELING AND PRENATAL TESTING

The prenatal diagnosis of congenital and genetic defects has become an increasingly important part of modern obstetrical care. The number of conditions that can be diagnosed prenatally has increased greatly. Since it is not feasible to do all possible tests in any one case, it is important to obtain accurate family medical histories from both father and mother to determine which specific tests should be done.

Extra diagnostic tests are usually recommended for women who will be 35 years or older when they give birth or when the family history of either parent indicates a risk of certain hereditary diseases or congenital defects, or when a previous baby has been born with a chromosomal abnormality (Down syndrome, for example; see figure 9.9) or a defect such as spina bifida, in which the spinal neural tube fails to close.

These prenatal tests detect birth defects early enough so that the pregnancy can be terminated before the legal limit for abortion (24 weeks' gestation) if the parents so choose. If a defect is found and the parents decide to proceed with the pregnancy, the knowledge provided by the diagnosis will help them prepare for the special considerations of caring for the child. Approximately 95 percent of these tests reveal no abnormality in the fetus, so prenatal testing also can reassure couples at high risk for a particular abnormality. Prenatal diagnostic testing does not guarantee that a child will be born normal; it can rule out the presence of particular problems, but a tested fetus runs the same risk of birth defects (4 percent) that all babies do.

HIGH-RISK PREGNANCIES

Women with medical conditions such as high blood pressure, diabetes, heart or lung disease, AIDS, or thyroid or neurological problems have an increased risk for a variety of pregnancy complications. Pregnancy may exacerbate the disease and, conversely, the disease may

TABLE 9.3: PRENATAL TESTING

Test	Indication	Procedure	Timing	Results	Follow-up Studies
Alpha fetoprotein screening	Routine	Blood test	12th–18th week	Elevated levels are associated with serious defects in the development of the central nervous system, e.g., spina bifida, anencephaly. Low levels are associated with Down syndrome	Ultrasound Amniocentesis
Amniocentesis	Recommended for women older than 35 or those with a history of fetal abnormalities	Sonography is used to guide a long, thin needle through the abdomen into the uterus to extract a small amount of amniotic fluid, which then is carefully analyzed for abnormalities	8th–12th week	Elevated levels of alpha fetoprotein suggest failure of the brain or spine to close properly; failure of the abdomen to close; obstruction in the urinary or gastrointestinal tract. Detection of chromosomal defects including Down Detection of more than 70 metabolic abnormalities Sex/gestational age	Varies according to findings
Chorionic villus sampling	Same as amniocentesis	Performed through the cervix/vagina or the abdomen with the assistance of sonography to guide the needle.	8th–12th week	Identifies same defects as amniocentesis but much earlier in the pregnancy	Varies according to findings
Blood glucose screening	Routine	Blood test to measure blood glucose after a sugar drink	24th–28th week	Elevated blood glucose level (140 mg/dl or higher) indicates need for additional testing	Detection of gestational diabetes
Ultrasound sonography	Routine	High-frequency, painless sound waves produce a picture of the fetus in the uterus. No radiation exposure to fetus or woman	Varies, but usually during first trimester and near term	Detection of major malformations in fetus Age of fetus Presence of twins	Alpha fetoprotein Amniocentesis

affect the pregnancy and its outcome. Before becoming pregnant, these women should consult with their doctors about having a baby. In some cases, they may be advised against it, but with modern maternal and fetal medical care, many of the complications of high-risk pregnancies can be successfully controlled.

CHANGES DURING PREGNANCY

WEIGHT GAIN

A generation ago, pregnant women were cautioned not to gain much more weight than the probable weight of the baby. But more recent studies have shown that a

APPROXIMATE WEIGHT GAIN OF PREGNANCY

Fetus	7.5 (pounds)
Placenta	1.5
Amniotic fluid	2.0
Uterus	2.5
Breasts	1.0
Extra blood	3.5
Body fluids	2.0
	20.0

minimum weight gain of 24 pounds is better for the mother and for the growth and development of the baby. Women who gain very little (less than four pounds) in pregnancy are more likely to have low-birth-weight babies, who are more vulnerable to infection than babies of normal size. A woman who is underweight when she becomes pregnant should gain more than the minimum—up to 30 pounds. A woman who is overweight should not choose this time to go on a weight-loss diet, even though she is more likely than mothers of appropriate weight to have a difficult labor: Cutting back on nutrients during pregnancy can harm both mother and fetus. Moreover, if body fat is lost, toxins that have accumulated in fatty tissue over time, such as pesticides, will be released into the bloodstream, and these may adversely affect the fetus.

During the first 3 months of pregnancy, a woman should gain 2 to 3 pounds. From the beginning of the 4th month, and until term, a steady gain of about three-quarters of a pound per week is desirable, although a spurt of 2 pounds is not unusual. When the gain is steady, there is no worry about exceeding the optimal weight, and thus no temptation to reduce food intake in the final months when most of the weight gained represents fetal growth.

To gain 20 pounds during her pregnancy, a woman will have to eat somewhat more than usual. If there is no change in her activity level, she will need an extra 300 to 500 calories, bringing the total caloric intake to 2,300 to 2,500. If she is exercising less, she will need proportionally fewer calories.

NUTRITION

While it is true that a pregnant woman is eating for two, her nutritional needs do not double. Instead, she should increase her calorie intake to ensure adequate weight gain, and make sure her diet provides the extra vitamins and minerals needed to support the growing fetus. (See table 9.4.)

Protein is essential for building fetal tissues. A pregnant woman should increase her protein intake to 60 grams daily. For the protein to be used in fetal tissues, sufficient calories must also be consumed to meet the daily energy requirement of both mother and baby.

In order to get sufficient calcium, necessary for the baby's bone and tooth development, pregnant women should drink four cups of milk or the equivalent daily. Young women in their teens and early 20s, who are still developing bone themselves, will need five cups of milk daily to meet their own and their baby's needs.

Iron is necessary for the manufacture of hemoglobin, the molecule within red blood cells that carries oxygen. Not only does the woman's extra blood volume require extra iron, but the fetus must build up a rich reserve of iron in preparation for the first few months of life. Unfortunately, iron is present in only marginal amounts in the average diet and menstruation further depletes a woman's iron. Supplements (30–60 milligrams daily) are frequently prescribed, but consult your doctor before taking these or any other supplements.

Folic acid and pyridoxine, two of the B vitamins, are particularly important in pregnancy. Folic acid is neces-

TABLE 9.4: ESSENTIAL NUTRIENTS DURING PREGNANCY

Nutrients	Food Groups	Minimum Number of Servings Daily During Pregnancy
Protein and iron	Meats, including organ meats, fish, poultry, eggs, nuts, legumes in combination with grains	4
Calcium and protein	Milk (all forms), yogurt, cheese, cottage cheese, ice cream	4
Vitamins A and C	Citrus and other fruits, green leafy vegetables, red and orange vegetables, potatoes and other tubers	5
B vitamins	Whole-grain and enriched grain products, fortified cereals	6
Fluids	Water, unsweetened fruit juices, vegetable juices, beverages	6

sary for protein synthesis in the early months; both vitamins are needed for proper development of the fetal nervous system. A lack of folic acid in the early months of pregnancy has been associated with congenital malformation. Folic acid is the scarcest vitamin in the human diet, however, and reserves may be especially low in women who have been taking birth control pills. Supplements are recommended, either through fortified foods or in tablet form. Your doctor can tell you how much folic acid you should take.

The need for other B vitamins, and for vitamins C, A, and D, also increases in pregnancy, but these are normally present in sufficient quantities in a well-balanced diet. A word of caution: Excessive vitamin A can cause severe birth defects. High-dose vitamin A supplements and Retin-A (tretinoin) should be stopped three or more months before attempting pregnancy.

Liquids are needed in increased quantities during pregnancy. The requirement—over and above milk—is at least 6 glasses a day. Latest studies show that there is no harm in drinking moderate amounts of caffeine-containing products (coffee, tea, cocoa, cola) during pregnancy, but it is wise to limit consumption to a total of two to three cups per day of all caffeine-containing drinks, and to distribute them over the course of the day.

Vegetarian women must pay special attention to nutritional requirements during pregnancy. Those following a strict vegetarian diet with no animal products, such as eggs, cheese and milk, will need vitamin and mineral supplements. Sufficient calories and protein can be obtained from a meatless diet if care is taken to balance foods properly. Complete proteins can be derived from dairy products and from legumes and grains, when these are combined at the same meal to provide a proper balance of amino acids. A woman who consumes no dairy products should eat generous amounts of green leafy vegetables, nuts, and seeds. She should also take supplements containing iron, calcium, vitamin D, and B vitamins (especially vitamin B_{12}, which is found only in animal products).

MEDICATIONS

Eighty-five percent of drugs currently on the market have never been tested for safe use during pregnancy, and virtually all drugs can cross the placenta and thereby reach the fetus. Many drugs are known to be potentially harmful, and some produce serious birth defects. A pregnant woman should take no medication—not even an over-the-counter laxative or cold remedy—unless it has been prescribed or approved by her doctor. The only exceptions to this rule are:

1. Acetaminophen (such as Tylenol) may be taken as directed for the relief of cold or flu symptoms,

TABLE 9.5: NUTRITIONAL NEEDS DURING PREGNANCY

Nutrient	Usual RDA (Age 25–50)	During Pregnancy
Protein (gm)	50	60
Vitamin A (RE)	800	800
Vitamin C (mg)	60	70
Vitamin D (mcg)	5	10
Vitamin E (mg)	8	10
Niacin (mg)	15	17
Riboflavin (mg)	1.3	1.6
Thiamin (mg)	1.1	1.5
Vitamin B_6 (mg)	1.6	2.2
Vitamin B_{12} (mg)	2.0	2.2
Calcium (mg)	800	1,200
Phosphorous (mg)	800	1,200
Iodine (mcg)	150	175
Iron (mg)	15	30
Magnesium (mg)	280	320
Zinc (mg)	12	15
Selenium (mcg)	55	65

headaches, muscle strain or fever. If these symptoms persist for more than a day, however, a pregnant woman should call her doctor. A high fever (over 101°F, or 38.3°C) should be treated by a doctor and should be brought down as quickly as possible. Self-medication with aspirin should be avoided because aspirin interferes with blood clotting and its use can result in bleeding in both mother and fetus. Moreover, aspirin inhibits prostaglandin, a hormonelike substance important in the development of the fetal circulation.

2. Gelusil or Mylanta may be taken for the relief of heartburn if other measures are not effective.

3. Preparation H may be used for relief from hemorrhoids.

The use of these medications should be discussed with the doctor during the regular prenatal visits.

ALCOHOL, TOBACCO, AND OTHER DRUGS

Heavy alcohol consumption during pregnancy retards fetal growth and may result in fetal alcohol syndrome, a constellation of severe birth defects that may include mental retardation. It in not known, however, exactly how the extent of fetal damage relates to the quantity of alcohol consumed. To be on the safe side, pregnant women are advised to abstain from drinking, particularly during the first trimester.

Cigarette smoking during pregnancy interferes with the supply of blood and, consequently, of nutrients to the fetus. Women who smoke have an increased risk of stillbirth and premature, low-birth-weight babies. Some studies have shown that children of mothers who smoke cigarettes during pregnancy score lower on tests of neurological and intellectual function, and are more likely to be hyperactive than children of nonsmokers. There is also a higher incidence of sudden infant death (crib death) among babies born to women who smoke.

Addictive drugs such as heroin, cocaine, and methadone also cross the placental barrier. The infant of an addicted mother will be born addicted and may suffer seizures during the period of withdrawal after birth. Marijuana may cause chromosomal changes in the fetus, with possible growth retardation.

EXERCISE

Keeping fit and promoting good muscle tone is an important part of health care during pregnancy. Exercise prepares the body for labor, promotes good bowel function, aids in sleep, and makes a woman feel better.

As long as the pregnancy is progressing normally, a woman should be encouraged to get regular exercise. If she enjoyed tennis or jogging, for example, before she became pregnant, there is no reason not to continue these activities. However, mind these precautions:

- Late in pregnancy, exercise that puts strain on abdominal muscles, knees, and ankles may be increasingly uncomfortable. Exercise that is not weight-related, swimming or bicycling, for example, is preferable.
- After the fourth month of pregnancy, a woman should avoid exercises performed lying on her back because the pressure might disturb the blood flow to the fetus.
- Hot tubs and saunas (temperature higher than 180°F or 82°C) should be avoided because the heat causes blood vessels to dilate and excessive body fluids to be lost in perspiration.
- Avoid vigorous exercise, especially during hot and humid weather or when the woman has a fever.
- Sports that might result in a heavy fall should be avoided unless a woman is very proficient. A woman should be aware that, as pregnancy progresses, her body's center of gravity shifts forward, and this affects her balance.

Many schools, church halls and Ys, offer special exercise classes for pregnant women. These offer the advantages of a carefully planned program, a trained instructor, and the company of other women. Exercises at these classes generally concentrate on the following areas:

- Strengthening the abdominal muscles to make it easier to support the weight of the fetus, to prepare for labor, and to aid in regaining a flat abdomen after delivery
- Strengthening the muscles of the back to help avoid low back pain
- Strengthening the muscles of the pelvic floor in preparation for labor and to prevent bowel and bladder problems after delivery
- Maintaining good posture, which also helps relieve or prevent back pain

Many instructors also include breathing exercises and specific relaxation techniques.

PERSONAL HYGIENE

Bathing and showering can continue as usual throughout pregnancy. If late in pregnancy, however, the bag of waters (membranes containing the amniotic fluid) has broken, or there appears to be a leak of amniotic fluid, a woman should not take a bath. If she suspects that the membranes have ruptured, she should call her doctor.

A woman should not douche during pregnancy. Not only do many commercial douching preparations contain iodine, which is potentially harmful to the fetus, but douching also may cause an infection present in the vagina to be carried to the uterus. A bothersome vaginal discharge should be reported to the doctor.

SEXUAL INTERCOURSE

Sexual intercourse can continue normally until the last month of pregnancy, unless a woman has been counseled otherwise. If there is vaginal bleeding or a suspected leak from the bag of waters, intercourse should be discontinued until the woman has been checked by her doctor.

It is very common to experience some brief abdominal cramping after intercourse. If this continues or worsens over a 1-hour period, a woman should contact her doctor, since it is possible that the cervix may be dilating. Semen contains prostaglandins, which can initiate uterine contractions.

Especially in the last months, it is important to avoid excessive pressure on the abdomen. Couples should adopt intercourse positions that are comfortable as well as satisfying.

Partners may find that their appetite for sexual relations changes in response to emotional and physical events of pregnancy. Some may desire sexual intimacy more frequently than before, others less often. If there is a conflict, open and honest communication and understanding of the other's needs will help work out the problem.

EMOTIONAL CHANGES

Pregnancy is a time of heightened emotional response. Sudden changes of mood, which may startle both the woman and those around her by their strength and volatility, are completely normal in pregnancy. It is also completely normal to have negative feelings about pregnancy itself. A woman should anticipate that at times she may feel impatient and apprehensive, even resentful about many aspects of pregnancy and the coming birth. It is best to acknowledge these feelings frankly; they are temporary and will not affect a woman's ability to be a loving mother.

Very vivid dreams, some of which may be bizarre or frightening, often occur in pregnancy. Dreaming is one way in which the mind deals with concerns that may not be consciously acknowledged; such concerns are present in most pregnancies and disturbing dreams are entirely normal.

TRAVEL

A healthy pregnant woman can travel as usual, but in the last month she should not travel far from where she plans to give birth. Many airlines will not accept a woman who is more than 32 weeks pregnant as a passenger without a doctor's certificate. When traveling by car, a pregnant woman should adjust her seat belt so that the lower strap lies across the pelvic bones rather than across the abdomen. It also helps to stop every two hours or so, stretching and moving about to relieve pressure from the enlarged uterus on pelvic organs and large blood vessels to the legs.

DENTAL CARE

Good oral hygiene, with brushing and flossing as usual, should continue in pregnancy. If tooth loss is associated with pregnancy (as in the adage, "A tooth is lost for every child"), it is because women tend to neglect their teeth at this time, not because calcium is drawn from the mother's teeth for fetal bone development.

Pregnancy gingivitis—gum inflammation—is common and is due to elevated hormone levels. Gums tend to swell and bleed, and in most cases they return to their previous state after delivery.

Dental x-rays should be kept to a minimum; if they are necessary, the abdomen should be covered with a lead apron. Local anesthesia may be used, but general anesthesia should be avoided if possible because there is a risk of oxygen deprivation for the fetus. A pregnant woman may feel faint in the dental chair due to the weight of the fetus pressing on the inferior vena cava, the main blood vessel returning from the lower limbs. If this is the case, a small pillow or rolled-up towel can be placed under the right hip, tipping the weight of the uterus to the left so that the blood flow is not blocked.

COMMON DISCOMFORTS AND SYMPTOMS

Fatigue is the most widely experienced symptom in the first three to four months of pregnancy. Women may sleep many more hours than usual and still lack energy. This is quite normal and becomes less of a problem during the second trimester of pregnancy.

Morning sickness occurs in about 50 percent of pregnant women during the first trimester. Of these, about a third experience one or more episodes of vomiting. Nausea may occur at any time of the day or may last throughout the day. The cause is still unknown, but hormonal changes are thought to play a role. Morning sickness usually clears up, often suddenly, after the third month. Most doctors prefer to avoid medication for the treatment of simple nausea and vomiting in early pregnancy, but severe or prolonged cases that interfere with good nutrition and normal living require medical intervention.

Heartburn is caused by reflux of stomach contents into the esophagus. Many woman experience a burning sensation in the center of the lower chest or upper abdomen, or an acid taste in the throat. This occurs more frequently in later pregnancy, when there is a higher level of the hormone progesterone, which causes muscle tissue to relax. Thus the muscle that closes off the esophagus from the stomach becomes relatively lax, allowing the stomach contents to back up into the esophagus. Foods that appear to cause heartburn should be avoided. If nighttime heartburn is a problem, elevating the head of the bed slightly or using an extra pillow may be beneficial—gravity will help keep the stomach contents in the stomach. If warranted, Gelusil or Mylanta may be used to relieve the discomfort.

Constipation is a common complaint during pregnancy since the hormone progesterone acts on the smooth muscle of the bowel, causing it to be somewhat more sluggish in its action than usual. Moreover, the uterus, increasing in size, presses on the bowels and displaces them upward and backward, contributing to the likelihood of constipation. The best remedy for this condition is a diet high in foods that promote good elimination. Fresh fruit and vegetables, plenty of fluids, whole-grain breads and cereals, and foods high in bulk and fiber should be included in the diet. Exercise is very effective in keeping the bowels moving regularly. If the problem persists even with proper diet and exercise, the pregnant woman should discuss it with her doctor, who may prescribe a mild laxative.

Backaches may be caused by strain on the muscles carrying the newly acquired weight of both the increased breast tissue and the weight of the uterus. A good support bra and attention to proper posture will often relieve the former problem. Attention to posture and regular exercise to strengthen the muscles of the back and abdomen are helpful in cases of low backache. The back should also be supported when driving or sitting for any length of time. An extra-firm mattress or a bed board may be necessary if the pain becomes severe.

Vaginal discharge, pale and mucuslike, is normal in pregnancy and helps to lubricate the vagina during delivery. However, there are two common causes of an abnormal discharge that may produce discomfort or irritation during pregnancy: The fungus infection *Candida* produces a thin, white discharge; infection with *Trichomonas,* a parasitic protozoan, produces a frothy, yellowish one, often with an unpleasant odor. Both of these conditions should be reported to the doctor. They usually can be remedied easily with vaginal suppositories.

Vaginal bleeding in the form of spotting or staining is common at the time of the first two missed menstrual periods and may continue throughout pregnancy. It may not be cause for alarm but should be reported promptly to the doctor.

Bright red vaginal bleeding is a serious symptom. Bleeding in the early months may indicate a threatened miscarriage or an ectopic pregnancy. (For a discussion of both, see sections earlier in this chapter.) In the later months, bleeding may be a sign that the placenta has partially separated from the uterus, jeopardizing the fetus's survival. Immediate hospitalization is imperative in such a case.

Round ligament pains are quite common in pregnancy and, although uncomfortable, not cause for alarm. As pregnancy progresses and the uterus enlarges, these ligaments become stretched and may at times cramp. The pain is typically sharp and stabbing and is felt on one or both sides of the abdomen and toward the groin area. Massage of the area, the application of heat, or a simple change of position (particularly the assumption of the "fetal position," with knees pulled up to the chest) will be effective in relieving the spasm.

Leg cramps are often bothersome during pregnancy, especially at night. Stretching the leg out as far as possible and pointing and flexing the heel may relieve the muscle cramp, as may standing with all the weight on the affected leg. If these cramps occur frequently, supplemental calcium tablets may be prescribed. Sometimes in late pregnancy, the enlarged uterus presses on nerves extending from the pelvis to the legs, causing pain. Pulling the knee to the chest may help relieve this.

Varicose veins often appear for the first time in pregnancy, usually in the legs but sometimes also around the vulva. Varicose veins in the legs can be prevented to some extent by avoiding socks or stockings with tight bands that constrict the veins. A woman who already has varicose veins when she becomes pregnant should begin to wear good support stockings immediately and should continue to do so throughout her pregnancy. Unless preventive measures are taken, the extra weight, carried on legs whose veins are relaxed by the hormone progesterone, will inevitably cause a worsening of the varicose veins. In addition to wearing support stockings, a woman should put her feet up whenever possible and avoid standing or sitting for long periods of time.

If a varicose vein becomes tender, red, and swollen, a clot may have formed. Medical attention should be sought immediately.

Hemorrhoids are a fairly common complaint during pregnancy and in the days immediately following delivery. They are, in fact, varicose veins of the rectum or anus, causing discomfort and sometimes bleeding. Occasionally they can be very painful. Hemorrhoids are aggravated by constipation and the passing of hard stool. Preventing constipation is therefore the most important preventive measure. Hemorrhoid pain can be relieved by the use of a topical ointment (such as Preparation H).

Sciatic pain, a sharp, needlelike sensation going from the buttocks down the side of the leg, occurs when the expanding uterus presses on the sciatic nerve. Changing position, application of heat, or assuming the knee-to-chest position may temporarily relieve this.

Edema is a swelling of the tissues caused by retention of fluid. All pregnant women normally have some edema. Usually the feet and legs swell the most, since both gravity and weight of the uterus contribute to sluggish circulation of blood and body fluids in the lower limbs. Obviously, standing or sitting for any length of time will worsen the condition. Elevating the legs will help decrease the swelling, as will lying on the left side.

If blood pressure climbs and protein enters the urine, there is a danger of preeclampsia (toxemia of pregnancy), a potentially serious complication of pregnancy (see Table 9.6: The Three Trimesters on the opposite page). Thus, if in the later part of pregnancy a woman experiences edema of the face and hands, together with headaches, blurred vision, and/or abdominal pain, she should see a doctor immediately.

Tingling or sensation of pressure in the vagina is a common problem toward the end of pregnancy. It

TABLE 9.6: THE THREE TRIMESTERS

	Physiology	Complications	Causes of Complications

The First Trimester Weeks 0–12 (See figures 9.14 and 9.15)	Uterus enlarges three times its usual size.
	
	Breasts enlarge noticeably.
	
	Maternal circulating blood volume doubles.
	
	Fetus develops from minute oval disk to recognizable human form with most of its organs and tissues.
		Miscarriage: 20% of all pregnancies end in miscarriage; 75% of these occur in the 1st trimester.
		
		Hydatidiform mole: occurs in 1 in 1,500 pregnancies. Embryo dies or fails to develop due to a chromosomal defect in the fertilized egg. Signs include uterine bleeding and high blood pressure. Diagnosis is confirmed by ultrasound. Treatment is suction curettage.
		
		Ectopic pregnancy: fetus grows in a fallopian tube, in an ovary, or in the wall of the uterus. Signs include vaginal spotting associated with severe unilateral lower abdominal pain. Diagnosis is confirmed by blood tests for human chorionic gonadotropin, ultrasound examination, and pelvic examination. Treatment is with drugs or surgical removal.
			Causes of miscarriage:
			  Fetal abnormalities
			  Structural defects of the uterus
			  Maternal hormonal imbalance
			  Genetic defect of the fetus
			  Maternal syphilis
			  Maternal drug use
			  Severe stress
			  Excessive caffeine
			  Alcohol use/abuse
			  Heavy smoking
			  Poor maternal nutrition

The Second Trimester Weeks 13–27 (See figures 9.16 and 9.17)	Mother becomes conscious of the fetus's movement at about the 20th week. Fetus grows from 3–14 inches in length. By 24 weeks the fetus weighs about 2 pounds.	Premature labor/premature contractions occur in about 5 percent of all pregnancies. Of babies born at 25 weeks (slightly less than 2 pounds), about 50 percent survive. Babies born at least 3 pounds or more have about 95 percent chance of survival.
		
		Signs include the beginning of regular uterine contractions; sometimes there is vaginal bleeding, increased vaginal discharge, or vaginal pressure. Premature rupture of the membranes occurs in 20–30 percent of the premature deliveries and may be the first abnormal sign.
			Causes of premature labor:
			  Poor general health
			  Heavy cigarette smoking
			  Inadequate nutrition
			  Syphilis
			  Preeclampsia
			  Thyroid abnormalities
			  Cocaine abuse
			  Abnormalities of the placenta
			  Physical trauma to the mother

The Third Trimester Weeks 28–36 (See figure 9.18)	Somewhat uncomfortable physically for the mother as the fetus grows from 2 pounds to an average of 7 pounds and the uterus continues to enlarge. A few weeks before the onset of labor the fetus "drops," that is, descends into the pelvic inlet.	Preeclampsia: signs and symptoms include elevated blood pressure, blurred vision, swelling of the face and hands, protein in the urine. Treatment: induce labor or deliver by cesarean section. Placenta previa: painless bleeding is a sign of this condition, in which the placenta lies in an abnormally low position in the uterus. Treatment: strict bedrest and no sexual intercourse. Cesarean section may be necessary for safe labor. Placenta abruptia: this condition is life-threatening for both the mother and the fetus and is an obstetrical emergency. It occurs when the placenta suddenly tears away, producing bleeding, great pain, and shock. Causes include severe anemia, uncontrolled high blood pressure, extremely short umbilical cord, extreme trauma such as a motor vehicle accident. False labor: contractions of the uterine muscles that do not cause the cervix to dilate as in true labor. Contractions can be settled with changing position, walking about, or taking a glass of warm milk. False labor passes as abruptly as it comes on. Premature rupture of the membranes: the membranes rupture, releasing the amniotic fluid before labor begins. Doctors will usually wait for the natural onset of labor but if strong rhythmic contractions have not begun within 24 hours then labor will be chemically induced.	Causes vary or are unknown.

occurs because the position of the fetus puts pressure on the nerves in this area. While uncomfortable, it is no cause for alarm.

Tingling or numbness of the arms, hands, or fingers also occurs in the later months of pregnancy. The nerves that supply these upper extremities traverse the bronchial plexus, which is pressed upon by the enlarging breasts. Shrugging the shoulders or swinging the arms in a circular fashion can help relieve the sensation.

INFECTIOUS DISEASES

German measles (rubella), a mild childhood illness, if contracted during the first 16 weeks of pregnancy, may severely affect the fetus. The risk of fetal blindness, deafness, and a number of congenital defects of the heart and brain is so great that most doctors recommend that the pregnancy be terminated in such cases. Standard tests early in pregnancy include one for past infection with rubella. If a woman is found to lack immunity, she should avoid any possible source of contagion and should be immunized after delivery. (Rubella immunization is not safe during pregnancy because the vaccine contains live viruses that can infect the fetus.)

Another infection that may occur in pregnancy is influenza. Since a high temperature may be fatal to the fetus or cause premature labor, a fever of more than 101°F (38.3°C) that persists for more than 24 hours should be reported to the doctor. (For more information on these diseases see chapter 18, Infectious Diseases.)

LABOR AND DELIVERY

PREPARATION FOR CHILDBIRTH

There are two main general approaches to prepared childbirth—one originated in Great Britain by Dr. Dick-Read and the other developed in Russia by Dr. Lamaze and adapted in the United States by Elizabeth Bing. Both include mental and physical training; however, they differ to some extent in emphasis and technique. Many preparation-for-childbirth classes combine elements or variations of both methods.

The philosophy behind the Dick-Read method is that ignorance of what occurs in childbirth produces fear; this leads in turn to tension and, inevitably, to an increase in the experience of pain. Teachers concentrate on overcoming fear by providing accurate information about the process of childbirth, and by teaching deep relaxation and different breathing techniques appropriate to the different stages of labor. In addition, the classes include information on breast-feeding and exercises to promote suppleness.

Psychoprophylaxis (Lamaze) is a highly structured training that emphasizes breathing techniques, on the premise that intense concentration on breathing patterns reduces the experience of pain. Relaxation is taught in such a way that it becomes a conditioned response. At the start of classes, women are helped to eliminate their fear and doubt about childbirth. They are then taught to respond to labor contractions as helpful stimuli rather than pains. Classes provide information on the anatomy and physiology of pregnancy and labor, and teach exercises to strengthen the abdominal and pelvic floor muscles.

The baby's father is included in most preparation-for-childbirth classes, so that the entire preparation for birth can be shared. The father's support during labor is of even greater benefit if he, too, knows what to expect and is prepared for each stage of the process.

Classes usually start in the seventh month of pregnancy, meeting weekly for one to two hours. Teachers of all methods agree that at least six sessions should be devoted to the labor itself.

For most women who have had training, the pain of labor is experienced as a side effect. With the aid of breathing and relaxation techniques, and with emotional support from their partners and attendants, many are able to cope with the pain without medication. Others require pain relief and should feel no sense of self-reproach about this.

Preparation-for-childbirth classes anticipate and contribute to a normal, easy labor. However, a woman should be aware that not all labors are easy and normal. It may prove necessary to deliver the baby by cesarean section, or by forceps or suction. This does not mean that a woman has failed during labor to apply what she learned in her classes.

THE COURSE OF PREGNANCY BY TRIMESTER

DEVELOPMENT OF THE EMBRYO

Day 9. The inner layers of the cell (endoderm and ectoderm) become differentiated. The amniotic cavity appears.

Days 13-15. The yolk sac develops and the amniotic cavity expands.

Day 20. The fetus is suspended on a body stalk through which it receives nutrients.

Day 28. The body stalk develops into the umbilical cord, joining the placenta and embryo. Oxygen, carbon dioxide, and nutrients are exchanged through the placenta. The amniotic sac expands further and its outer layer merges with the inner layer of the trophoblast. Gallbladder, liver, and stomach begin to form; areas of the brain start to develop.

Day 32. Head parts—nose, mouth, eyes, ears, brain—are developing. Divisions of the heart are recognizable

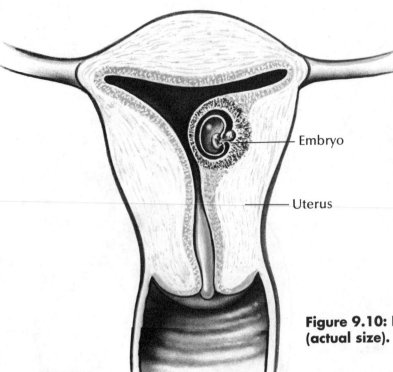

— Embryo

— Uterus

Figure 9.10: Implanted embryo at 6 weeks (actual size).

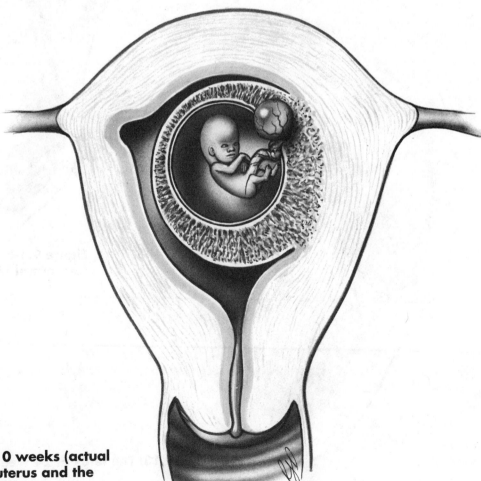

Figure 9.11: The embryo at 10 weeks (actual size). Note enlarged size of uterus and the development of distinct body parts.

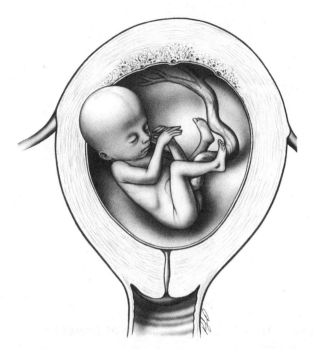

Figure 9.12: The fetus at 14 weeks.

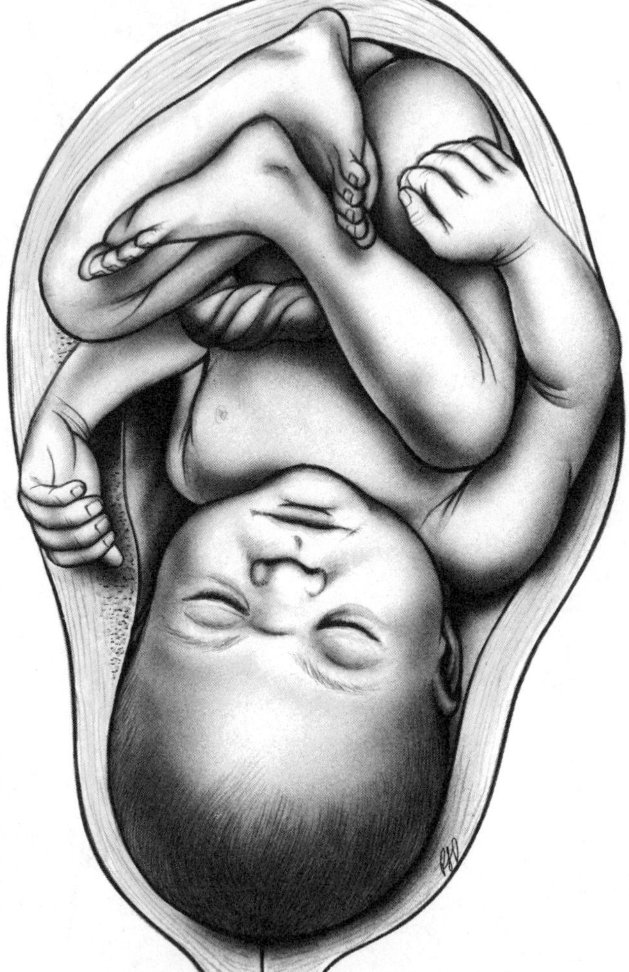

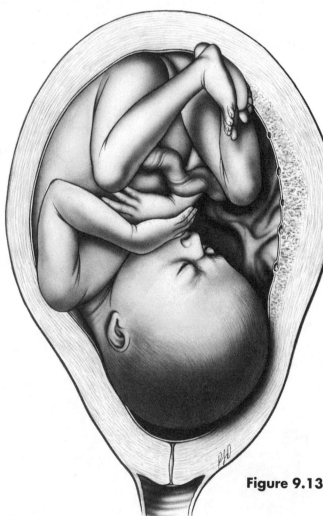

Figure 9.14: Full-term fetus in position for normal birth.

Figure 9.13: The fetus at 24 weeks.

and the first heartbeats occur. Thyroid, larynx, and trachea start to develop.

Days 35–37. Arm and leg buds lengthen. Regional divisions of the brain are recognizable. Lung buds and the kidneys begin to form. The skin and the eyes develop; the nostrils are recognizable.

Days 40–42. The stomach is recognizable. Cells are being laid down to form the skeleton. The heart parts fuse to form the four chambers.

Days 46–49. The beginnings of fingers, toes, and eyelids are evident. The nervous system is forming and muscle fiber begins to develop. Adrenal gland and thyroid cells become more mature. The tail disappears.

FETAL GROWTH AND DEVELOPMENT

Week 8. Centers of bone growth are established and ossification begins. Nose and upper jaw grow rapidly and the two sides of the lips and palate fuse. Tooth buds appear.

Week 12. The eyelids meet and fuse. The inner ear is nearly formed; the lens of the eye develops readily. External genitals are evident as swellings. Hair follicles and the dermis become distinct.

Week 16. The bulge of the forebrain is distinguishable from the cerebellum and brain stem. The epidermis becomes thicker.

Week 20. The ovaries and testes are structurally established. The tubules of the kidneys branch out.

Week 24. Eyebrows and eyelashes are evident; the fetus is covered with downy hair. The bronchial tube continues to branch. The palms of the hands and the soles of the feet develop skin ridges.

Weeks 28–32. The eyelids separate. The testes begin to descend to the scrotum. Fat is deposited under the skin. At 28 weeks, all the vital organs have been formed; further development is mainly that of greater size.

LABOR BEGINS

The onset of labor begins with the body's production of large amounts of prostaglandins, hormonelike substances that initiate uterine contractions. Once labor has begun, the pituitary secretes oxytocin, a hormone that acts on the uterine muscles to strengthen and speed up their contractions.

During a first delivery, normal labor may last up to 24 hours. Subsequent labors are usually shorter, ranging from 3 to 12 hours. At the first signs of labor a woman should inform her doctor or midwife. When uterine contractions occur every 5 minutes it is time to go to the hospital or childbirth center.

THE THREE STAGES OF LABOR

THE FIRST STAGE

The first stage of labor begins with the first rhythmic contractions of the uterine muscles and ends when the cervix is fully open (dilated). This stage is the longest, lasting from 12 to 14 hours on the average for first babies, 8 to 10 hours for subsequent ones (see figure 9.15).

When labor begins a woman will often notice that a plug of mucus and a slightly red-tinged, watery discharge is expelled from the cervix. This is called breaking water.

Contractions usually begin mildly, lasting 10 to 20 seconds, and coming at 20- to 30-minute intervals. As labor progresses and the cervix dilates, the contractions come closer together and last longer. Toward the end of the first stage, they may last 40 to 50 seconds and occur at 1- or 2-minute intervals. Many women find this the most difficult part of labor. If the membranes have not ruptured spontaneously, the doctor may break the bag of waters toward the end of the first stage to help the labor along.

THE SECOND STAGE

The second stage of labor begins when the cervix is fully dilated and ends when the baby is born. This second stage usually takes about 2 hours with a first baby; with subsequent births, it may last only 5 to 30 minutes (see figure 9.16)

Unlike the first stage, when the woman has been largely passive, in the second stage the pressure of the baby's head on the pelvis brings about an urge to push and bear down with the contractions. With the expulsive force of the uterine contractions supplemented by the woman's pushing efforts, the baby passes through the pelvis and is born.

An episiotomy, preceded by a local anesthesia, is frequently performed to shorten the second stage of labor and prevent tears in the skin. There are two types of episiotomy: midline (an incision from the vagina toward the

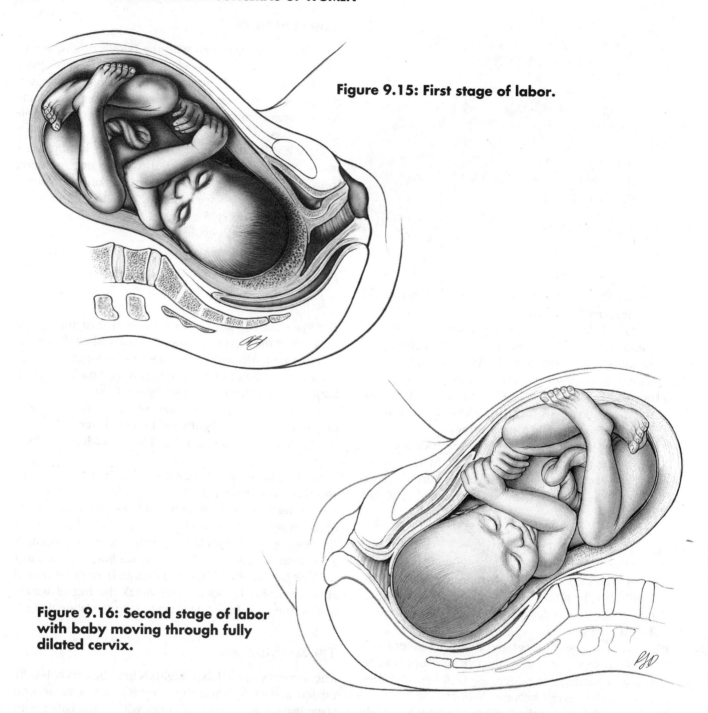

Figure 9.15: First stage of labor.

Figure 9.16: Second stage of labor with baby moving through fully dilated cervix.

rectum) and mediolateral (across the vagina). The mediolateral episiotomy is more painful, but there is usually no threat of splitting to the rectum. In the United States, the midline episiotomy is the procedure most frequently done, although more women now deliver without episiotomies.

THE THIRD STAGE

The third stage of labor is that between the birth of the baby and the delivery of the placenta (afterbirth). Normally, this stage takes only 5 to 10 minutes (see figure 9.17). If the placenta is not delivered within half an hour,

however, the doctor may have to remove it surgically.

After the third stage, the episiotomy (if this incision has been made) is sutured. Usually an injection of oxytocin (Pitocin) is given to the new mother to stimulate uterine contraction and thereby stop the bleeding.

PAIN DURING LABOR AND DELIVERY

Pain-relieving drugs and anesthetics are used conservatively in modern obstetrical practice because any drug given to the mother during labor will traverse the placenta and may adversely affect the newborn.

In early labor and in the second, active phase, medica-

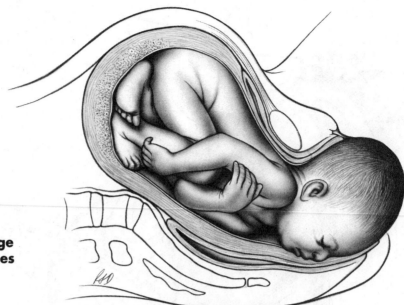

Figure 9.17: In the third stage of labor, birth, the baby faces downward for the journey through the birth canal.

tion such as meperidine (Demerol) may be given by injection to lessen the pain of the contractions. With the pain somewhat relieved, a woman may be able to use relaxation breathing techniques more effectively.

The form of anesthesia generally used to control the pain of labor today is the epidural or peridural block, which is a local anesthetic or in some cases morphine given by injection in the middle of the back. The anesthetic blocks feeling completely from the waist down, not only relieving the woman of pain, but also of the sensation of her contractions. However, with coaching from those attending her, she will be able to bear down in time with the contractions during the second stage of labor.

SPECIAL CONSIDERATIONS AND COMPLICATIONS OF BIRTH

FETAL MONITORING

The fetal heart rate is recorded continuously by Doppler ultrasound, while a tocodynameter records the uterine contraction pattern. These measurements are recorded on a moving strip of paper similar to the familiar ECG record. If electronic fetal monitoring is not available, an attendant will monitor the fetal heart at frequent intervals with a fetoscope.

Continuous monitoring of the fetal heart rate permits early detection of possible complications, so that they can be treated before they become serious. Monitoring is safe, painless, and is considered essential in high-risk pregnancies. The device is held in place by two straps around the woman's abdomen. A woman can change position and even walk about while the monitor is in place (see figure 9.18).

Internal monitoring devices sometimes are implanted if the fetal heart rate suddenly dips, or if there are other signs of fetal distress. A small electrode will be attached to the fetus's scalp by a catheter, which is inserted into the uterus through the vagina. These devices enable the doctor to determine more accurately the pattern of the fetal heart rate and the force of the uterine contractions.

INDUCTION OF LABOR

If there are medical problems such as high blood pressure, or obstetrical problems such as premature rupture of the membranes followed by a long latent period, or if the baby is more than reasonably overdue, labor may be induced. This is done by infusing the hormone oxytocin through an intravenous catheter slowly into the bloodstream in order to initiate contractions. If it is necessary to induce labor when the cervix is hard and thus not easily dilatable, a gel containing prostaglandins may be inserted into the vagina to soften the cervix before the oxytocin infusion.

Once labor has started and the cervix has begun to dilate, an induced labor progresses in the normal fashion. Induction of labor, done properly and for good medical or obstetrical reasons, is an entirely safe procedure.

AUGMENTATION OF LABOR

Labor should progress in a specific time frame. When it slows down or stalls, it is important to expedite it by administering oxytocin to speed up and strengthen contractions. Dysfunctional labor, if allowed to continue without treatment, jeopardizes both the baby and mother.

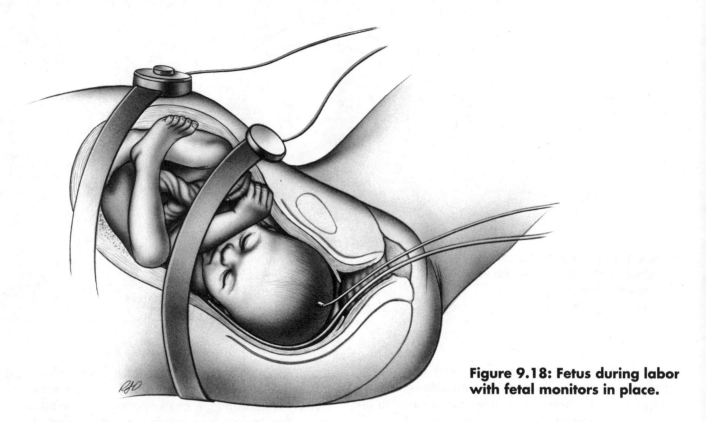

Figure 9.18: Fetus during labor with fetal monitors in place.

CESAREAN BIRTH

Most cesarean births are unexpected, performed because the baby is in distress and must be delivered quickly. A woman who has looked forward to a vaginal delivery may find this extremely disappointing; the father may feel helpless and useless. To help ease the couple's emotional trauma, it is important that the doctor fully explain why the emergency cesarean section was necessary.

Not all cesarean sections are emergencies, of course. In some cases it is known from the beginning that the procedure will be necessary; in others, the necessity becomes apparent late in pregnancy. There are a variety of reasons why a cesarean section may be the safest way to deliver a baby. A serious maternal illness such as diabetes could make labor hazardous to both mother and baby. If the baby is too large to pass safely through the mother's pelvic bones, a cesarean section is necessary.

The major risk to a baby born by cesarean section is premature delivery and the susceptibility to hyaline membrane disease, a life-threatening disease of premature lungs. This may occur when, for instance, the operation is scheduled in advance and the due date is incorrectly estimated. To guard against premature delivery, the doctor draws some amniotic fluid and measures the amounts of two fatty substances, sphingomyelin and lecithin, contained in it. These measurements give an accurate assessment of the maturity of the baby's lungs. In some centers, fetal maturity is determined by ultrasound. Delaying the operation until the beginning of labor is another way to ensure the baby's maturity.

Many cesarean sections are now done under regional (epidural) anesthesia, which is less debilitating than general anesthesia. Some hospitals allow the woman's partner to remain with her during the procedure. The operation is performed by making an incision through the abdominal wall, opening the uterus, and removing the baby and the placenta. The incision on the skin may be lateral (a bikini incision) or an up-and-down midline incision. The former is far less destructive of abdominal muscle tissue, and the scar has the further cosmetic advantage that it can be hidden by even a brief bathing suit. The incision is usually on the lower part of the uterus, and vertical; this reduces risk of rupture should the woman attempt to deliver vaginally in a subsequent pregnancy.

A woman who has had an uncomplicated cesarean delivery will be discharged from the hospital within 4 to 8 days. It will, however, take 4 to 6 weeks before she recovers fully.

Increasingly, babies are being delivered by cesarean section, a procedure that has replaced delivery by forceps, a traumatic procedure that in the past too often resulted in the birth of damaged or stillborn infants. Although surgery is now much safer, some doctors may

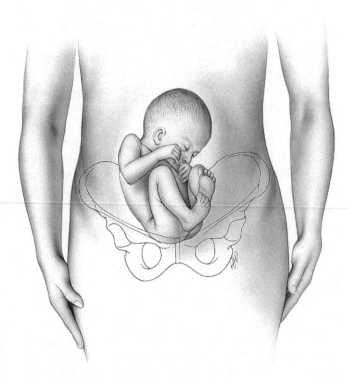

Figure 9.19: Full-term fetus in the breech position.

be too eager to perform it. A desirable rate for cesarean section ranges from 12 to 30 percent of all deliveries, with large teaching hospitals and specialists in maternal-fetal medicine at the high end of the scale because they care for more women with problem pregnancies.

FORCEPS DELIVERY AND VACUUM EXTRACTION

Sometimes it is necessary to deliver a baby with the aid of forceps or a vacuum extractor. The forceps, which is curved in a handlike shape, is placed on either side of the baby's head as it is beginning to come through the vaginal opening. Gently pulling on the forceps, the doctor is then able to lift the baby out. In a vacuum extraction a small plastic suction cup is placed on the baby's head. A vacuum is then created, which enables the doctor to lift the baby out of the birth canal by drawing on the cup.

BREECH BIRTH

A breech birth is one in which the baby emerges with the feet or buttocks rather than the head first (see figure 9.19). If such a baby is small (under 5½ pounds) or large (over 8 pounds), or if the head, as seen by x-ray, is not well tucked into the chest but is extended upright, a vaginal delivery is not safe.

A breech presentation is the one occasion in modern obstetrics in which x-rays are employed to determine the configuration of the woman's pelvic bones. It is important to be sure that the pelvic bones are sufficiently wide apart to allow the baby's head to emerge quickly and easily after the body has emerged.

Dysfunctional or slowed labor occurs more frequently with a breech birth than with the normal head-down presentation; a cesarean delivery may be necessary. In many hospitals, women delivering first babies as breeches routinely have cesarean sections, as they are considered safer.

MULTIPLE BIRTHS

Twins are formed either from one egg (identical twins) or from two fertilized eggs (fraternal twins). Identical twins, less common than fraternal twins, have the exact same genetic makeup and are consequently always of the same sex, though they may differ in size. Examination of the placenta and membranes at the time of birth can help determine if twins of the same sex are fraternal or identical.

Twins occur in about 1 of 80 pregnancies. The likelihood of bearing twins is higher for black women, and for women who were themselves twins or had twins in their immediate families. Twins are also more commonly born to older women and to women with four or more previous pregnancies.

Triplets and other multiple births are rare events, although with the use of fertility drugs more common than in the past. Depending on the circumstances, triplets may be delivered vaginally or by cesarean section. The criteria are always those of the safety of mother and infants.

EMERGENCY DELIVERY

On rare occasions, a baby is born in a car or taxi on the way to the hospital or childbirth center. In such cases, the person accompanying the mother should be as calm and reassuring as possible. No attempt should be made to stop or slow the birth. The mother's perineum should not be touched—doing so could easily lead to infection—and the umbilical cord should not be cut. If the placenta delivers before the hospital is reached, the baby and the placenta should be wrapped together, with the cord intact. The baby should be encouraged to nurse immediately; the sucking action prompts the release of oxytocin, causing the uterus to contract and preventing further bleeding. Almost all babies born unexpectedly in this manner will cry quickly. If there is mucus in the nose or mouth, which may prevent the baby from breathing, the baby should be turned on its side and the back gently rubbed.

THE POSTPARTUM PERIOD

BREAST-FEEDING

Breast milk is nutritionally ideal for a newborn baby and contains antibodies that will help the newborn resist infection in the early months. While most doctors encourage breast-feeding the decision is the new mother's to make. Babies thrive on formula, too.

At first breast-feeding may cause tenseness, anxiety, and fatigue in the new mother. The greatest difficulty in starting breast-feeding is often lack of support from nurses, doctors, other women, and partners. However, once established it is neither difficult nor uncomfortable, and many women find it a very rewarding experience.

CIRCUMCISION

Circumcision, a minor surgical procedure in which the foreskin of the penis is removed, is usually done before the baby leaves the hospital, but not until he is more than 2 days old. Couples of the Jewish faith may wish to have their sons circumcised according to tradition, in a ceremony performed on the eighth day of life. While the procedure is probably painful for the baby (no anesthesia can be used), it does not take long and healing is quick.

Circumcision is not medically necessary, nor is it required by law. Contrary to popular belief, there is no evidence that circumcision prevents penile infection or penile cancer.

POSTPARTUM EMOTIONS

After the long-awaited birth of a child, a woman may experience a range of emotions from exhilaration and relief to disappointment and a sense of anticlimax. These are normal responses. A woman should not reproach herself if the rush of maternal feeling she and others have expected does not immediately occur. Women often feel a little "blue," usually on the third day after the baby is born. This transitory depression is usually a simple emotional rebound from the excitement of the birth.

Serious depression persisting after a birth, or beginning several weeks postpartum, is not common. It may be due to an endocrine imbalance resulting from thyroid disease or to other metabolic and endocrine conditions that are not yet understood. A woman who feels severely depressed in the postpartum period should seek medical help promptly.

POSTPARTUM CHECKUP

The postpartum checkup is as important as the prenatal examinations. At 4 to 6 weeks it is necessary to have a pelvic examination to assess the size of the uterus as well as the proper healing of the perineum. Postpartum exercises to strengthen the abdomen and the muscles of the pelvic floor should be discussed at this time, if they have not already been started. Toning the muscles not only helps a woman to regain her figure but also aids in preventing such problems as prolapse of the uterus later in life. The question of contraception and the planning of future pregnancies should also be discussed at this time. Nursing a baby should not be relied upon as a method of contraception since, although a woman may not have her period during the months that she is nursing, it is quite possible that she may ovulate. Sexual intercourse may be resumed as soon as the placental site is healed—usually in 3 weeks. Some couples prefer to wait until all postpartum bleeding and spotting has ceased.

MENOPAUSE

Menopause marks the cessation of menstruation and ovulation, thereby concluding a woman's reproductive years. Until recently, menopause has been something of a taboo subject, largely because it was regarded as the beginning of old age. This may have been true in the early 1900s when the average age of menopause was 46 and a woman's life expectancy was only 51. Today, even though women enter menopause later, they still have about a third of their life expectancy ahead of them. More importantly, women today often find that these postmenopausal years can be as enjoyable, productive, and rewarding as those that came before.

The growing number of women entering menopause—about 2 million a year—also accounts for changing attitudes. Increasingly, menopause is a topic of conversation, best-selling books, and medical research. This growing openness has helped dispel many myths about menopause; it is also paving the way for increased medical understanding of the effects of menopause on both emotional and physical health.

AGE OF MENOPAUSE

There are two types of menopause—surgical, in which a woman's uterus and/or ovaries are removed resulting in an abrupt cessation of menstruation, and natural menopause, a gradual process that probably begins when a woman is in her 30s as estrogen production begins to fall off. The hormonal changes culminating in menopause accelerate when a woman reaches her mid-40s. Medically, natural menopause is considered complete when a woman has not had a menstrual period for a year; this usually occurs between the ages of 48 and 55. In the United States, the average age of menopause is 52. Sometimes, however, a woman enters menopause in her early 40s, and at the other end of the age scale, a few women continue menstruating until their late 50s.

The age at which menopause will occur is difficult to predict. It is unrelated to menarche—the onset of menstruation—but there appears to be a genetic determination, because women tend to enter menopause at about the same age as their mothers, grandmothers, and other female relatives.

SYMPTOMS OF MENOPAUSE

Menopausal symptoms vary considerably from one woman to another. Typically, however, irregular periods and other menstrual changes are the first obvious symptoms. In some women, periods become lighter and less frequent; in others, bleeding may be heavier, with two or three periods a few weeks apart, and then several months may elapse before another period.

At about this time, a woman may begin to experience hot flashes—a sudden rush of heat to her upper body, often followed by sweating and chills. Hot flashes are caused by vasomotor instability triggered by hormonal changes. About 75 to 80 percent of menopausal women experience at least occasional hot flashes, and in a few, they are so frequent or intense that they interfere with sleep and other normal activities (see Hot Flashes, later in this chapter). In most women, the hot flashes end within a few years of completion of menopause.

Other symptoms or changes associated with menopause include:

• **Vaginal dryness and itching.** These changes usually appear several years after menopause and are marked by a shrinking of the external genitalia, thinning of the vaginal lining, and reduced vaginal secretions. Consequently, a woman may experience itching, increased susceptibility to vaginitis, and painful intercourse. In some instances, application of a vaginal cream or ointment alleviates the problem; in others, estrogen is needed (see Hormone Replacement Therapy).

• **Urinary Tract Symptoms.** The urethra and urinary bladder are also susceptible to tissue thinning, resulting in increased vulnerability to cystitis. Older women, especially those who have had several children, also may experience stress incontinence and other bladder control problems.

• **Palpitations.** Transient episodes of a rapid heartbeat are thought to be caused by the same vasomotor instability that produces hot flashes. Some women experience palpitations along with hot flashes, in others, they occur independently, and still others never have any. If palpitations become troublesome, a beta-blocker or another drug to steady the heartbeat may be prescribed.

• **Depression and Other Emotional Changes.** Some menopausal women experience unexplained mood

TABLE 9.7: SYMPTOMS AND CONDITIONS ASSOCIATED WITH MENOPAUSE

AUTONOMIC

- Hot flashes
- Night sweats and other episodes of heavy perspiration
- Heart palpitations
- Itching

ORGANIC/METABOLIC

- Cessation of menstruation
- Vaginal dryness, itching, and atrophy
- Postmenopausal vaginitis
- Bladder control problems
- Increased urinary tract infections
- Bone thinning (osteoporosis)
- Bloating
- Weight gain
- Headaches
- Joint pain and arthritis
- Muscular weakness
- Shrinking and sagging of breast tissue
- Thinning of scalp and pubic hair; increased growth of facial hair (hirsutism)
- Brittle, slow-growing, and grooved nails
- Thinning, drying, and wrinkling of skin

PSYCHOLOGICAL

- Mood swings
- Irritability
- Depression
- Insomnia
- Anxiety or feelings of apprehension
- Forgetfulness
- Changes in sexual function and desire

Adapted from *Hormones: The Woman's Answerbook*, by Lois Jovanovic, M.D., and Genell Subak-Sharpe, Atheneum, 1987.

swings; others are unaccountably irritable, depressed, or forgetful. It is uncertain whether these psychological symptoms are directly related to menopause or to other circumstances that may coincide with menopause, such as the last child leaving home. Many researchers believe that a combination of hormonal and life-style factors are responsible.

• **Weight Gain.** Many older women experience a redistribution of body fat, with an added accumulation around the abdomen—the so-called middle-age spread. Several factors may account for this. Energy needs decline with age, which can result in weight gain if the person does not reduce food intake or increase physical activity. A woman's increased levels of androgens (male sex hormones) promote abdominal fat deposits. Women who take replacement estrogen may gain weight. Finally, abdominal muscles weakened by repeated pregnancies and inactivity contribute to sagging and the appearance of abdominal weight gain.

DISORDERS LINKED TO MENOPAUSE

During and following menopause, women are more vulnerable to certain diseases, most notably osteoporosis and an increased susceptibility to heart disease. Menopause itself also brings conditions that may require medical treatment.

HOT FLASHES

Definition. A hot flash, or flush, is a sudden sensation of heat that usually starts in the upper chest and neck and spreads to the face. The skin may redden, as when blushing. Some women experience sweating, and chills may precede or follow the flash. Most hot flashes last for only a minute or so, and although the woman herself is acutely aware of what is happening, the changes may not be obvious to others. The frequency and intensity of hot flashes varies greatly from one woman to another—some never have any, and others may have several in an hour. Surveys of menopausal women have found that 50 to 85 percent report having hot flashes, but only 15 percent or so find them troubling. The most bothersome seem to be those that occur at night and are accompanied by heavy, drenching sweats.

Cause. The precise cause of hot flashes is unknown, but researchers theorize that declining estrogen levels signal the hypothalamus, the part of the brain that controls body temperature, to release a chemical that causes a rush of blood to the surface.

Treatment. Estrogen replacement therapy quickly stops hot flashes.

Home Remedies and Alternative Therapies. Many women find they can minimize the effects of hot flashes through commonsense measures such as dressing in light layers that can be removed or added as the need arises. Using a small hand fan helps cool the face. Taking a tepid or cool (not cold) shower before going to bed may help prevent the hot flashes and night sweats that disrupt sleep. Also wear light bedclothes, use thin cotton or wool blankets, and sleep in a cool room. Avoid alcohol and caffeine, especially if they bring on hot flashes.

Sometimes hot flashes are triggered by stress—relaxation techniques such as deep breathing exercises and meditation may be helpful.

Some women maintain that vitamin E supplements help prevent hot flashes, but this has not been proved. Check with your doctor before taking this or any high-dose vitamin or mineral supplement.

VAGINAL DRYNESS

Definition. Reduced vaginal secretions and a thinning of the mucous membranes lining the vagina result in dryness that causes itching and also makes intercourse difficult and painful.

Cause. Declining estrogen levels result in a thinning of the vaginal tissue.

Diagnosis. A gynecologic examination can detect tissue thinning and other changes that contribute to vaginal dryness.

Treatment. Mild vaginal dryness often can be controlled by using a nonprescription lubricant; there are now several brands formulated for menopausal women. If these are insufficient, an estrogen vaginal cream may be prescribed. Other forms of estrogen therapy will also alleviate vaginal dryness. Vaginal itching may be treated with prescription medication that alters the acidity of the vagina.

Home Remedies and Alternative Therapies. Regular sexual activity that results in orgasm also helps counter vaginal dryness, but lubricants may be needed before attempting intercourse. Some women find nonperfumed oils, such as vitamin E oil, cocoa butter, and wheat germ oil, helpful when used as vaginal lubricants. To increase lubrication of the vagina, try inserting a lubricating cream or jelly with a plastic applicator, such as those used to insert spermicidal cream into the vagina.

URINARY INCONTINENCE

Definition. By definition, incontinence involves the involuntary loss of varying amounts of urine, but there are several different types of urinary-control problems. The most common is stress incontinence, the sudden loss of urine that occurs when sneezing, coughing, lifting, or engaging in other activities that increase abdominal pressure on the urinary bladder. Urge incontinence, the sudden, often uncontrollable urge to urinate, most often develops in older women. Overflow incontinence, which is relatively uncommon, is the loss of urine without any sensation or warning that the bladder is full. It often develops when the bladder fails to empty completely during urination. Finally, incontinence may be due to an irritable, or "spastic" bladder—a condition that is often triggered by stress.

Cause. Declining estrogen levels results in a thinning of urethra and bladder tissue and may contribute to bladder-control problems in older women. Also, the female urinary bladder lies in close proximity to the uterus, rectum, and vagina, and any anatomical changes in these organs can affect bladder control. These include a cystocele, in which the bladder protrudes into the vaginal canal; a retrocele, in which the rectal wall presses upon the vaginal canal; and uterine prolapse, in which the uterus descends into the vaginal canal. In all of these conditions, the urinary bladder can be compressed or moved out of its normal position.

Incontinence may be a consequence of a stroke, Alzheimer's disease, spinal cord injury, or other neuromuscular injuries or disorders. Other possible causes include cystitis, an infection and inflammation of the bladder; damage resulting from childbirth, surgery, or trauma; and loss of muscle tone of the urinary sphincter. Some drugs can also trigger or worsen bladder control problems.

Diagnosis. Tests are likely to include a urinalysis and urine culture to rule out infection. A gynecologic examination of the pelvic organs can detect a cystocele and other abnormalities. If nerve damage is suspected, a neurological examination may be ordered. Other possible tests include uroflowmetry, which evaluates the volume and rate of urine flow; cystourethrography, which can detect structural abnormalities of the bladder; and perhaps a pressure-flow study, to detect a urinary obstruction.

Treatment. Treatment varies according to the cause. Estrogen replacement therapy may improve bladder control in some menopausal women. Other drugs, combined with urinary retraining, may alleviate overflow incontinence. If the problem is due to an infection, antibiotics usually produce a cure. A pessary—a rubber, doughnut-shaped device that fits into the upper part of the vagina—helps raise the neck of the bladder, and may be helpful for incontinence related to an anatomical problem. If these conservative approaches are inadequate, surgery may be recommended.

Male/Female Differences. According to some estimates, women with bladder control problems outnumber men about 2 to 1. Although the problem is increasingly common with age, some studies indicate that a large percentage of younger women have some difficulty controlling urinary function.

Home Remedies and Alternative Therapies. Many women with bladder-control problems are embarrassed to seek medical help and instead try to treat themselves. This can be a big mistake because most continence problems can be remedied. Thus, self-help measures should augment, not substitute for, medical consultation and treatment.

Exercises to tone and strengthen the muscles around the bladder may help some types of stress incontinence. Referred to as Kegel exercises for the doctor who developed them, they are intended to strengthen the pelvic floor (pubococcygeal) muscles. To identify these muscles, insert a finger into your vagina and try to squeeze it. Or when urinating, try to stop the flow by tightening your vaginal and anal muscles. To do the Kegel exercises, repeatedly tighten and relax the pelvic floor muscles. Start by tightening the front muscles, then those around the vagina, and finally squeeze the anus. Hold for a count of three, relax, and repeat up to 15 or 20 times, several times a day. You can do the exercises at almost anytime and in any position.

Some people with bladder problems cut back on fluids, which can actually worsen the problem. A better approach is to drink plenty of fluids, but avoid caffeine, alcohol, high-dose vitamin C, and other substances that can irritate the bladder.

Bladder retraining also may be helpful. Don't put off going to the toilet; instead, go when you first feel the urge to urinate. Make a special effort to empty the bladder completely. If you suffer from overflow incontinence, try to urinate every hour or two, rather than waiting until you feel a need to do so.

MENORRHAGIA

Definition. Menorrhagia is a heavy, prolonged menstrual bleeding, which is common among women approaching menopause. (It also occurs in young women who are just beginning to menstruate but have not yet established regular ovulation.)

Cause. Heavy bleeding may occur during menstruation in the absence of ovulation. It may also be associated with fibroids, polyps, or other uterine tumors and use of an IUD.

Diagnosis and Treatment. A D&C (dilation and curettage) may be ordered both as a diagnostic procedure and treatment for menorrhagia. The procedure entails dilating, or widening, the cervix, and then using a sharp, spoon-shaped curette to scrape away part of the uterine lining. In some instances, a doctor will order hysteroscopy before doing a D&C. In this procedure, a lighted viewing device is inserted into the uterus, allowing a doctor to inspect the lining and collect tissue samples for microscopic study. In some instances, laser surgery—a procedure using strong, intense light beams to cauterize or vaporize tissue—is used as an alternative to a D&C.

Prolonged, severe bleeding can cause anemia and other complications. If it cannot be controlled by a D&C and other conservative measures, a hysterectomy may be necessary.

Home Remedies and Alternative Therapies. Severe or prolonged bleeding requires medical attention. During an episode of heavy bleeding, lie down with your feet elevated and apply an ice pack to the abdomen and lower back; this may slow the "flooding." Avoid taking drugs or remedies that promote bleeding; these include aspirin, high doses of vitamin E, garlic pills, and omega 3 fatty acids. During a heavy period, avoid using a heating pad or taking a hot bath, because heat increases blood flow.

Hormone Replacement Therapy

Postmenopausal hormone replacement therapy remains a controversial area. Advocates of hormone replacement point to such benefits as prevention of osteoporosis, a reduced risk of heart disease, and reduction in menopausal symptoms. Opponents maintain that menopause is a natural event in a woman's life, not a deficiency disease, and that long-term hormone replacement may increase the risk of certain cancers.

Even though questions remain, mounting evidence indicates that for many, if not most, women, the potential benefits of hormone replacement outweigh the risks. Further, new ways of administering hormone therapy minimizes the risks.

There is no doubt that estrogen alleviates hot flashes, vaginal dryness, and many other menopausal symptoms. Most commonly, estrogen is prescribed in pill form, preferably in the lowest possible dosage to control the symptoms. If vaginal dryness is the major problem, estrogen can be administered as a topical vaginal cream. Some of the hormone is absorbed into the bloodstream, but not enough to cause adverse reactions (see the box "Side Effects of Hormone (Estrogen) Replacement Therapy"). Estrogen also may be administered through a medicated skin patch that is applied to the abdomen and changed twice a week. This transdermal method appears to produce fewer side effects than oral estrogen.

Increasingly, estrogen is given along with progesterone, an artificial form of another female sex hormone. At one time, estrogen alone was widely prescribed for most menopausal women. Then in the late 1960s, studies showed that women on long-term, unopposed estrogen therapy had an increased incidence of endometrial cancer. Almost overnight, estrogen therapy fell out of favor. It was not until the mid-1980s that a large number of doctors again began advocating hormone replacement therapy, but with a much different regimen. A lower estrogen dosage—typically, 0.625 milligrams a day—was prescribed to be given in combination with progestogen. Precise regimens vary, but the idea is to give enough progestogen to oppose the effects of estrogen on the uterus. Unopposed estrogen results in a buildup of endometrial tissue—a factor that is thought to increase the risk of endometrial cancer. Progestogen prevents this buildup; in fact, many women on this combination therapy experience periodic menstrual-like bleeding for the first few months of therapy.

Although combination hormone replacement therapy appears to lower the risk of endometrial cancer, there are conflicting data regarding a possible increased risk of breast cancer. Some studies show a slightly increased risk and others show no difference. There is also some evidence that progestogen may somewhat reduce the

---

SIDE EFFECTS OF HORMONE (ESTROGEN) REPLACEMENT THERAPY

(Note: Many of these side effects are dose-related, and do not occur with low-dose estrogen.)

BREASTS

Enlargement
Tenderness

CENTRAL NERVOUS SYSTEM

Headaches, including migraines
Dizziness
Depression

DERMATOLOGIC

Acne
Loss of scalp hair
Hirsutism

GASTROINTESTINAL

Nausea and vomiting
Abdominal cramps
Bloating
Gallbladder disease

GENITOURINARY

Breakthrough bleeding (when given with
   progestogen)
Vaginal discharge

OPHTHALMIC

Changes in corneal curvature that may make
   contact lenses intolerable

MISCELLANEOUS

Altered libido
Weight gain or loss
Increased clotting
Fluid retention and edema
Altered glucose tolerance
Possible high blood pressure

---

cardiovascular protective effects of estrogen, but more research is needed to prove this.

Even the staunchest advocates of postmenopausal hormone therapy concede that it is not appropriate for all women. For example, estrogen replacement is contraindicated for women with a history of breast cancer and clotting disorders. It also increases the risk of gall-bladder disease. Others find they cannot tolerate its side effects.

DISORDERS COMMON TO WOMEN

CONDITIONS OF THE BREASTS

The most common breast condition many women deal with once they have begun to menstruate is monthly swelling and sometimes painful tenderness preceding a period. When the period passes, so does the discomfort. This benign condition may be relieved by wearing a bra, switching to a stretchier bra, and avoiding excess salt, sugar, coffee, tea, and alcohol. Sometimes, after the period is over, the lumpiness of the breasts may remain. A certain amount of lumpiness in breast tissue is normal, but new lumps require prompt evaluation by a doctor.

FIBROCYSTIC BREASTS

Fibrocystic breasts result from an exaggeration of the normal monthly changes as a woman's breasts prepare for milk production, anticipating pregnancy. There are two types of fibrocystic condition. One is characterized by lumpiness and tenderness in both breasts, most pronounced in the week before the onset of menstruation. Afterward, the lumpiness and pain lessen. The second type typically occurs in one breast, and is usually characterized by several distinct, round lumps that move easily

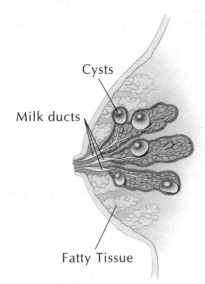

Figure 9.20: Fibrocystic breasts. The lumps in a fibrocystic breast are often filled with fluid, which can be aspirated.

within the breast tissue (see figure 9.20). Although fibrocystic breasts are not a disease, the condition may be associated with intense pain. Treatment involves surgical removal or aspiration of the cyst.

FIBROADENOMAS

Fibroadenomas are benign tumors of the breasts that occur during a woman's reproductive years. They are painless, round, firm tumors with a somewhat rubbery texture that are easily movable and not attached to the skin. They occur singly and most often are found around the nipple or in the upper sides of the breasts. Fibroadenomas are not related to cancer or considered precancerous in any sense. However, possibility of cancer must be eliminated when a breast lump is felt. Treatment of fibroadenomas in older women includes surgical removal of the tumor.

MASTITIS

Mastitis is infection of the breast(s) during nursing of a child. The usual source of the infection is bacteria that enter through a crack or fissure in a nipple. The patient notices swelling, redness, a sensation of heat in the affected area, and pain or tenderness. The overlying skin may be red, and, if the process continues without appropriate treatment, the infected area may become hardened.

In women who are nursing, the diagnosis is fairly simple. It is complicated in non-nursing women by the possibility that the symptoms are produced by a rare form of breast cancer. In a nursing woman, treatment with antibiotics is given for 7 days. Warm compresses can alleviate discomfort. Lancing and drainage may be necessary if an abscess forms. In non-nursing women, a needle biopsy may be necessary to rule out the possibility of cancer.

CONDITIONS OF THE EXTERNAL GENITALIA

WARTS

Genital or venereal warts (*Condyloma acuminatum*) are very common. They are caused by the papillomavirus, and are usually transmitted by direct sexual contact. The warts, which are not painful, appear 1 to 2 months after exposure, usually on the bottom part of the vaginal opening. They also may be found on the vaginal lips, inside the vagina, on the cervix, and around the anus. They may appear as small, dark bumps or grow to assume a cauliflowerlike appearance.

Small warts can be dried by applications of a chemical, applied by a doctor or trained health professional.

SYMPTOMS SUGGESTING GYNECOLOGICAL DISORDERS

Vaginal Discharge (Leukorrhea). Any vaginal discharge associated with itching, burning or irritation should be investigated. In the absence of associated symptoms, it may indicate a minor disorder. When blood is present in the discharge, it may indicate a more serious problem and should be promptly evaluated.

Irritation (Itching or Pruritus). Itching, burning or irritation of the external genitalia usually indicates some local infection of the vagina or external genitalia, commonly yeast, trichomonas, or a nonspecific vaginitis. Occasionally it may be related to local skin conditions, particularly in women beyond menopause.

Abnormal Bleeding. Any bleeding outside of the normal menstrual cycle and flow should be checked. A general guideline is that unusual bleeding superimposed on a normal cycle may indicate a developing disorder such as polyps or leiomyomata (fibroids), but rarely more serious conditions such as cancer. Unusual bleeding in which the normal cycle suddenly changes is most commonly related to minor hormonal changes, such as menstrual cycles without ovulation.

Amenorrhea (Absence of Menses). During the reproductive years in sexually active women, the first consideration should be the possibility of a pregnancy. Other conditions that may be related to amenorrhea are birth control pill use, active breast-feeding and, not infrequently, minor hormonal disturbances such as anovulation (lack of ovulation). Occasionally it may indicate a more serious problem related to the pituitary gland (hyperprolactinemia and adenomas); anorexia nervosa; pelvic tuberculosis; endocrine disturbances arising from the ovary, adrenal gland or thyroid; and some forms of systemic illness.

External Genitalia Pain. The development of pain in the external genitalia most commonly is related to infection. The most common types are an infected sebaceous gland, Bartholin's gland, or a herpes infection.

Lower Abdominal Pain. Pain in the lower abdomen is not necessarily of gynecological origin. It often is related to the gastrointestinal tract or urinary system. Gynecological conditions causing pain include leiomyomata, ovarian cysts, salpingitis (infection in the fallopian tubes), adenomyosis, and endometriosis. The pain in these conditions is usually moderate to severe. Pain related to the physiology of the menstrual cycle, .i.e., mittelschmerz and primary dysmenorrhea, is usually less severe.

Abdominal Swelling. Any noticed growth within the abdomen requires prompt attention. The most common gynecological conditions are leiomyomata and ovarian cysts. Occasionally there may be a progressive enlargement of the entire abdomen, usually related to fluid within the abdominal cavity (ascites). This is not necessarily of gynecological origin, but often is related to ovarian tumors.

Vaginal Protrusion. The sudden or gradual protrusion or bulge at the vaginal opening is usually related to a weakening of the supports of the pelvic structures seen most often in postmenopausal women. It usually represents a cystocele or uterine prolapse.

Painful Intercourse (Dyspareunia). Painful intercourse may occur at any time during a woman's sexual life. It is most common in postmenopausal women due to decreased hormonal effects on the vagina. In menstruating women it is usually related to a vaginal infection. Occasionally it may be due to the involuntary contraction of the muscles of the vaginal outlet (vaginismus).

Warts also can be removed by freezing (cryotherapy) or by laser surgery. They can recur if all warts are not removed, and a woman may catch them again from a sexual partner. Regular Pap smears are important for women who have had genital warts since they are associated with an increased risk of cervical cancer. (For more information on genital warts, see chapter 18.)

VULVITIS

DEFINITION

This general term describes a range of irritations characterized by itching, redness, and swelling of the vulva. The vulva is particularly susceptible to irritation because the area is naturally warm and moist.

CAUSE AND DIAGNOSIS

Allergic vulvitis is the result of the vulva skin's allergic reaction to foreign substances, such as perfumed soaps, laundry detergents used to wash underwear, vaginal sprays and deodorants, and powders. In addition, menstrual blood, feces, and other normal body secretions can cause contact dermatitis, as can medications taken by mouth, injected, or applied to the vulva.

Itching is almost always present with these irritations. Persistent scratching leads to other irritation, and the vulva skin may ooze, scale, crust, or form fluid-filled blisters called vesicles. The scratching may also thicken the skin and give it a whitish appearance, which can be confused with vulvar dystrophy.

TREATMENT

Improved hygiene often cures this condition. Soothing cream may also relieve the irritation.

HOME REMEDIES AND ALTERNATIVE THERAPIES

Cool compresses or sitting in a tepid sitz bath may alleviate itching. Wear white cotton underpants and avoid perfumed soaps, bubble baths, genital deodorants, and other potentially irritating substances.

VULVAR DYSTROPHIES

DEFINITION

This group of diseases causes abnormal changes in the skin of vulva, which if untreated may become malignant. Vulvar dystrophies typically appear in postmenopausal women, but have been reported in younger women.

CAUSE AND DIAGNOSIS

Sometimes caused by changes in the cells in this area, vulvar dystrophy may first appear as dry, thick, reddened areas of skin that eventually turn opaque white. Raised blisters may form white patches on the skin, and the layer of fat under the vulvar lips may flatten out. The skin tends to assume a dry, papery appearance. As the disease progresses the skin may become shiny, the clitoris may shrink, and the vaginal opening may become constricted. Symptoms may vary greatly among women; however, the whitish areas that generally develop result in itching, scratching, irritation, and sometimes superimposed infection.

A vulvar biopsy is necessary for diagnosis. This is done either in the doctor's office using local anesthetic or under general anesthesia in a hospital. The results of the biopsy dictate the treatment.

TREATMENT

If the biopsy reveals abnormal cells, an operation to remove the dystrophic skin may be performed. Often, eliminating the conditions that may have caused the vulvar dystrophy is the treatment of choice. Contributing factors may include a vaginal infection, powders, deodorants, perfumes, or irritating chemicals in synthetic garments. The symptoms are treated with cold soaks and cortisone creams or lotions.

BARTHOLIN'S GLAND ABSCESS

DEFINITION

The Bartholin glands are located on both sides of the vaginal opening. Under normal conditions they are not noticeable. Their job is to secrete a fluid that keeps the vagina moist. If the glands become infected the skin around them may become red, hot, swollen, and unbearably tender. The gland may ooze with pus or, if constricted, may swell with pus to form an abscess.

CAUSE, DIAGNOSIS, AND TREATMENT

The causes of this may include *gonococcus,* the bacterium that causes gonorrhea. Tests for gonorrhea confirm this cause (see chapter 18).

Bed rest, painkillers, ice packs or hot sitz bath, and antibiotics are the treatments of choice. If an abscess has formed the doctor may drain it. If the cysts are very large they may require surgical removal or the creation of a permanent opening/drain called marsupialization.

SEBACEOUS CYSTS

Sebaceous cysts are formed when the oil-producing glands in the skin are blocked. When this occurs in the vulvar area the cysts are prone to infection and abscesses. Hot sitz baths promote their natural drainage, but if they become large and bothersome they should be removed surgically. Therapy is usually not necessary. (For more on sebaceous cysts, see chapter 18.)

DISORDERS OF THE VAGINA

VAGINITIS

In the vagina of every healthy woman there is an acid/base balance maintained by bacteria. Under normal conditions the vagina has a slight discharge made up of cells and secretions from the vaginal walls, uterus, and cervix. The amount, consistency, and color of the discharge change over the course of a woman's monthly cycle and throughout her lifetime. The discharge is usually a clear or milky color, moderate in quantity, thin or slightly viscous, and with a mild odor. It may dry a yellowish color on the underclothes.

DEFINITION

Vaginitis—inflammation of the vagina—develops when the natural acid/base balance in the vagina is disturbed.

CAUSE

Vaginitis may be caused by bacteria or yeast infections. Susceptibility to vaginitis is the result of lowered resistance from a wide variety of causes. These include but are not limited to lack of sleep, poor diet, infection elsewhere in the body, douching that upsets the natural vaginal flora, birth control pills, pregnancy, menopause and other hormonal changes, antibiotics, diabetes or a prediabetic condition, cuts, abrasions, or other irritations to the vagina.

DIAGNOSIS

Symptoms may include an abnormal discharge, mild or severe itching and burning of the vulva, chafing of the thighs, and, occasionally, frequent urination.

TREATMENT

A yeast infection is treated with antifungal suppositories, creams and ointments, which are available in prescription and nonprescription strengths. If vaginitis is caused by infection, antibiotics may clear up the underlying cause. When allergy causes vaginitis, avoiding the allergic agent may end the irritation.

PREVENTION

There are a number of precautions a woman can take to avoid vaginal infections, including:

- Keeping the external genitalia clean and drying carefully after bathing. This prevents odor more safely and effectively than douching.
- Avoiding irritating sprays and soaps.
- Wearing cotton underwear. Nylon underwear and pantyhose retain moisture and heat and aid in the growth of harmful bacteria.
- Avoiding pants that are tight in the crotch and thighs.
- Wiping the anus after defecation from front to back to prevent bacteria from the anus from entering the vagina.
- Changing tampons frequently; some doctors advise their patients to douche after the menstrual period is over to remove any tampon fibers that may remain in the vagina.
- Making sure that sexual partners are clean; use of a condom can provide added protection. Birth control jellies have been found to slow the growth of bacteria that cause certain forms of vaginitis.

HOME REMEDIES AND ALTERNATIVE THERAPIES

Application of plain yogurt made with live lactobacilli culture to the vagina is said to help restore the natural balance of yeast and bacteria, especially if there is an overgrowth of yeast as a result of antibiotic therapy. Taking acidophilus pills may produce similar results and is not as messy as yogurt application.

Women who are prone to vaginal infections may try an occasional acidic douche—for example, two tablespoons of white vinegar added to a quart of warm water or a solution of baking soda and water. Caution is needed, however, because douching itself can promote vaginitis, and many doctors advise against it.

TRICHOMONAS VAGINITIS

DEFINITION AND CAUSE

Trichomonas is a single-celled (protozoan) parasite that is most often contracted through intercourse. A small percentage of women with this infection will be asymptomatic.

DIAGNOSIS

Symptoms include a foul-smelling, thin, foamy, pale green or grayish discharge, vaginal itching and/or burning, frequent urination, and painful intercourse. Diagnosis is made by a physician, who examines the discharge under a microscope and identifies the organism.

TREATMENT

Treatment of both sexual partners is necessary, usually with the antibiotic metronidazole (Flagyl).

CHLAMYDIA

Chlamydia, a bacterium that takes the form of an intracellular parasite, is transmitted through intercourse. It is more common in men than women. Chlamydial infections cause inflammation of the urethra, the tube that conducts urine from the bladder to the outside of the body, characterized by discharge and pain on urination. Women whose male partners have been diagnosed with chlamydia are advised to receive treatment, which involves two weeks of antibiotic therapy. (For more information, see chapter 18.)

OTHER VAGINAL IRRITATIONS

GARDNERELLA VAGINALIS VAGINITIS

This is a nonspecific vaginitis caused by the presence of sexually transmitted bacteria. The most common symptom is a malodorous discharge that may be streaked with blood. Other symptoms include vaginal itching and burning. Diagnosis is made by microscopic examination of the discharge by a physician. Treatment is either with vaginal suppositories containing antibiotics, or oral antibiotics. The patient's sexual partner requires treatment as well.

POSTMENOPAUSAL VAGINITIS

After menopause the tissues of the vagina are no longer being stimulated by estrogen. As a result the walls of the vagina become smooth, drier, and less elastic. There is less lubrication and the entire vaginal canal shrinks. The skin may become dried out and therefore easily injured and prone to infection. Tiny sores may appear in the vaginal wall causing a blood-tinged discharge. Successful treatments range from vinegar douches to estrogen replacement therapy. (See section on menopause.)

VAGINAL CYSTS

Inclusion cysts and Gartner duct cysts are the two most common benign or noncancerous swellings that affect the vagina. Inclusion cysts are found at the lower end of the vagina. They are caused by the inclusion of little tags of skin beneath the skin's surface, usually as the result of imperfect healing of surgical scars, tears, or lacerations acquired during childbirth or through injury. Gartner duct cysts arise from the remnants of an embryonic organ called the Gartner duct. They usually remain small and cause no problems. If they do, the treatment of choice is surgical removal.

DES-INDUCED CHANGES

In the 1950s and 1960s, the synthetic hormone DES was given to millions of pregnant women in the United States to help prevent miscarriage, premature birth, and other pregnancy problems. It has been shown since that DES does not prevent these problems. Moreover, a small number of the daughters of the women who took DES developed a rare form of vaginal cancer called clear cell adenocarcinoma, while others developed abnormalities including vaginal adenosis. Vaginal adenosis is a condition in which the glandular tissue that normally lies in the cervical canal is found in the vaginal cavity. The long-term effects of vaginal adenosis are uncertain, although it may be related to an increased risk of developing cancer. DES daughters also have an increased incidence of undersided or misshapen uteruses, leading to fertility problems. Recent studies indicate that DES sons also have a higher-than-normal incidence of reproductive disorders, including undescended testes.

STRUCTURAL PROBLEMS

CYSTOCELE AND URETHROCELE

Cystocele and urethrocele are conditions in which the bladder and urethra (respectively) have dropped down from their normal positions and bulged into the vagina. These conditions may result from an injury connected with childbirth, a defect in the supportive tissue of the pelvis, or most frequently, aging.

Symptoms range from none at all to a feeling of pelvic fullness or discomfort when bearing down. If symptoms

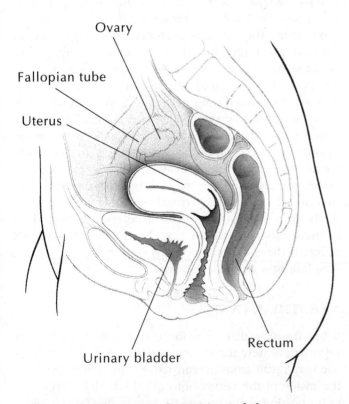

Figure 9.21: Normal position of the uterus.

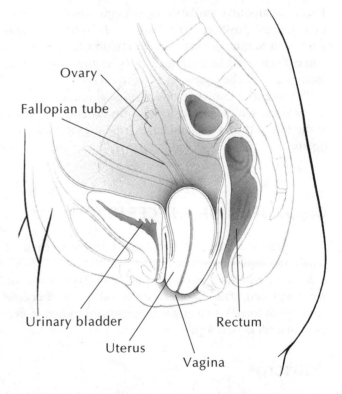

Figure 9.22: Prolasped or tipped uterus.

occur they are usually aggravated by standing for a long time. There may be difficulty emptying the bladder and you may frequently have the urge to urinate. The urine that stays in the bladder provides a breeding ground for bacteria, and infection may develop. It also may become difficult to control the flow of urine, and sudden movements like coughs or sneezes may result in leakage.

Diagnosis usually requires physical examination by a physician. If the condition is bothersome, surgical repair is the treatment of choice. In some cases, special exercises can be very helpful and surgery can be avoided.

RECTOCELE AND ENTEROCELE

Prolapse of the rectum into the back wall of the vagina (rectocele) and prolapse of the small intestine into the upper part of the vagina (enterocele) are a result of weakness in the tissues that support the organs and hold them in place. The weakness may be due to aging, the stress of labor and delivery, or sometimes congenital weakness of that area. Often the conditions occur together. Most rectoceles do not require surgical correction, although it may be recommended for larger ones. The enterocele is somewhat more serious since a loop of intestine may get caught in the bulge that protrudes into the vagina, interfering with the blood supply to that portion of the intestines. Surgical repair is the treatment of choice.

PROLAPSE OF THE VAGINA, UTERUS, AND CERVIX

These organs may prolapse or become displaced from their normal positions (see figures 9.21 and 9.22). This most commonly occurs during childbirth. Symptoms range from a feeling of heaviness in the vagina that increases over the course of a day to no symptoms at all.

Treatment of choice includes surgical repair or a vaginal pessary, which is a device that fits around the cervix at the top of the vagina and helps prop up the prolapsed organs.

DISORDERS OF THE CERVIX

There are two types of tissue in the cervix, each of which normally has its own place, and the two normally meet at one point. Sometimes these two types of tissue are displaced, fail to meet each other, or become infected or torn. When any of these situations occur, cervical disorders develop.

CERVICITIS

Cervicitis is associated with conditions of the vaginal cavity. Most cases of cervicitis are due to infections caused by tears or lacerations of the cervix sustained during childbirth. During acute cervicitis, there is noticeable pus-filled discharge that may be clear, grayish, or yellow. If other organs are involved in the infections, there may be urinary frequency, urgency, and pain, or burning and itching of the external genitalia. Cervicitis due to a tear or laceration will have less discharge. If an infection exists, the physician will try to identify which of a number of possible organisms is causing the condition and will treat it with an appropriate antibiotic. Care must be taken to keep the area clean. Sexual intercourse should be avoided until the condition clears.

CERVICAL EROSION AND CERVICAL EVERSION

Cervical erosion is a condition in which some of the cells on the surface of the cervical opening (os) have been worn away and the glandular surface of the cervix exposed—similar to what happens when skin on the outside of the body is grazed. The causes of these conditions have not been precisely identified. Treatment is variable and ranges from frequent examination to observe any progression of disease (including malignant transformation) to cryosurgery on eroded or everted tissue.

CERVICAL POLYPS

Polyps are small protrusions that grow from a mucous membrane and tend to recur. In the cervix, polyps grow from the mucous membranes of the cervical canal. Only rarely are they cancerous. Polyps may occur as part of the body's effort to heal itself after the cervix has been injured, or they may be formed by hormonal secretions during pregnancy. Small polyps generally do not cause symptoms; larger ones do because they can be irritated by douching, intercourse, pelvic examinations, or straining when going to the bathroom. They may cause heavier periods or bleeding between periods. They may be associated with infection or they may block passage of sperm, making it difficult for a woman to conceive. Polyps are treated by surgical removal, which may be done in a doctor's office. If there are many polyps or they are very thick, hospitalization may be required.

NABOTHIAN CYSTS

When the glandular tissue in the cervix is trapped under regrowth of new tissue, cysts can develop. The new tissue may result from overgrowth of the tissue that lines the inside of the cervix onto the tissue that covers the outer portion of the cervix. Cysts may also form in older women, whose cervical tissue thins out and traps natural secretions. The cysts generally do not become infected unless the entire cervix is infected. They rarely require treatment, although some physicians choose to remove them by cauterization or cryosurgery.

CERVICAL DYSPLASIA (AND CARCINOMA IN SITU)

This condition results from abnormal development of the cells of the cervix. Most authorities consider cervical dysplasia and carcinoma in situ conditions in a continuing process of abnormal cell changes that continue to progress over the years, and therefore may precede cervical cancer. Cervical dysplasia and carcinoma in situ is most frequently found in women ages 25 to 35, but also can occur in women in their teens or early 20s, and in older women as well. A Pap smear will reveal abnormal cell growth.

After one abnormal Pap smear, the smear should be repeated. If the results reveal abnormalities, the patient will undergo an office procedure called colposcopy in which tissue sample (biopsy) is taken for microscopic study. If the biopsy is negative, the woman should still be closely followed and another smear done in 6 months. Dysplasia may be treated by removal of the affected tissue (cone biopsy), cryosurgery, laser surgery, or occasionally hysterectomy. Follow-up after these procedures is important, lest the dysplasia progress or recur.

DISORDERS OF THE UTERUS AND FALLOPIAN TUBES

Several types of disorders can affect the uterus and fallopian tubes: infections that include the uterus and other organs in the pelvic cavity; conditions related to the lining of the uterus; distortions of the normal anatomy, either from birth or as a condition that develops when the woman is grown; and abnormal growths, which may be noncancerous or malignant.

ENDOMETRIOSIS

The endometrium, a type of tissue that nourishes fertilized eggs, normally grows each month within the uterus and, if no egg is implanted, is shed through menstruation.

DEFINITION

Endometriosis is the growth of endometrial tissue in places other than the lining of the uterus. This most often is found elsewhere in the genital tract, but occasionally in other parts of the body (see figure 9.23). It occurs most frequently in women of childbearing age.

CAUSE

The cause of endometriosis is not well understood. The prevalent initial symptom is dull but constant pelvic pain during menstruation. Sometimes there is lower abdominal pain preceding a menstrual period. Other symptoms may include abnormal menstrual bleeding or infertility. Cysts, which may develop when endometrial tissue grows in other parts of the pelvis, can swell and cause severe pain, or burst and release dark brown blood, also painfully.

Irritated by misplaced tissue and cysts, the body may form bands of fibrous material that seal over ruptured cysts. As these adhesions build up, they may literally bind organs together, affecting reproductive organs, the rectum, or intestines. Rarely, endometrial tissue migrates to the lungs or other parts of the body.

DIAGNOSIS AND TREATMENT

Diagnosis of endometriosis requires laparoscopy. The aggressiveness of treatment varies with many factors, including the age and health of the patient, the severity of the symptoms, and the location and extent of the problem. Treated with hormones, endometrial tissue usually sloughs off; sometimes, however, the tissue of the affected organs is surgically removed. The condition is treated more conservatively in older women, since the reduction in estrogen that accompanies menopause can cause the symptoms to remit.

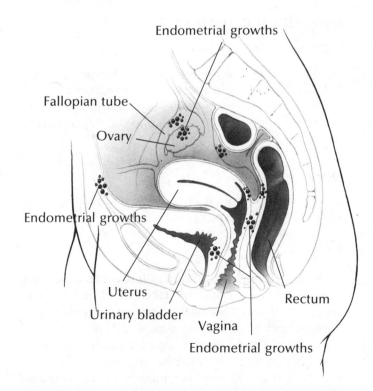

Figure 9.23: Endometriosis, in which tissue that normally grows inside the uterus grows in other parts of the pelvic cavity or internal structures.

ADENOMYOSIS

DEFINITION AND CAUSE

This is a condition in which the endometrial tissue, which usually sloughs off every month during the menstrual period, is instead found growing into the inner muscle wall of the uterus. It is found most often in women in their later childbearing years who have already had children. A woman may have adenomyosis and be symptom-free, with the condition being noted only when the uterus is removed for other reasons. Among those who have them, the chief symptoms are abnormal menstrual bleeding and menstrual pain.

DIAGNOSIS

Diagnosis is usually based on uterine enlargement and cramplike uterine pain that persists throughout the period, becoming worse as the woman gets older.

TREATMENT

The disease is related to hormone production and is relieved once menopause takes place. Painkillers and patience are the most conservative treatment. If the pain is extreme and menopause far away, surgery may be indicated to remove the uterus and possibly the fallopian tubes and ovaries.

ENDOMETRIAL HYPERPLASIA

DEFINITION AND CAUSE

An abnormal condition in which the endometrial lining has grown too thick, endometrial hyperplasia usually occurs at the beginning or end of a woman's reproductive years. The predominant form, cystic hyperplasia, is benign.

DIAGNOSIS

Laboratory examination of a sample of endometrial tissue can reveal this type of hyperplasia.

TREATMENT

A few months on birth control pills may make the menstrual cycle more regular and take care of the problem. Dilation and curettage may be performed on an older woman, and no further treatment will be necessary. However, if the laboratory report indicates adenomatous hyperplasia—hyperplasia is associated with endometrial cancer—hysterectomy is the usual method of treatment, possibly accompanied by removal of the ovaries and fallopian tubes. Sometimes hormone ther-

apy is used instead, with the understanding that this places the woman at risk of having undetected cancer develop.

ENDOMETRIAL POLYPS

DEFINITION AND CAUSE

Polyps, or soft outgrowths, in the endometrial tissue within the uterus are generally small and may grow singly or in clusters. Most common in women of menopausal age, endometrial polyps may cause no symptoms and may be found only in the course of another operation. Infertility may occasionally be traced to polyps that block the passage of sperm. Cancerous polyps are extremely rare.

DIAGNOSIS

If symptomatic this condition may cause abnormal bleeding between periods or in some cases protrude through the cervical opening and be seen by the gynecologist during an examination. Polyps that grow this way may produce cramping because they expand the cervical opening. Polyps that protrude may be injured and bleed or may be twisted and lose their blood supply. Infection can result, and there may be a foul-smelling discharge.

TREATMENT

Protruding polyps are generally removed with dilation of the cervix and curettage (scraping with a blunt instrument).

FIBROIDS

DEFINITION

As noncancerous tumors of the uterus, fibroids (leiomyomatas) grow in the thick muscular uterine wall. They are thought to be very common in women over the age of 30, and less common in young women. They usually shrink after menopause.

CAUSE AND DIAGNOSIS

In pregnant women and those on birth control pills, the rate of fibroid growth may be accelerated, as fibroids appear to be related to hormonal activity. Black women are somewhat more susceptible to fibroids at an earlier age.

Fibroids may have no symptoms and may be discovered by the gynecologist only during a pelvic examination. Symptoms depend on where in the uterus the fibroids are growing. There may be disturbances in urination, severe menstrual pain, excessive menstrual bleeding, and sometimes infertility.

TREATMENT

Most fibroids do not require treatment, particularly if a woman is near menopause. But all fibroids should be carefully followed up with regular checkups. If a fibroid continues to grow or is sufficiently symptomatic, it will require treatment. A malignant fibroid is rare.

Surgical treatment of uterine fibroids is either by removal of the fibroids (myomectomy) or removal of the uterus (hysterectomy), depending on the woman's age, condition, and whether she plans to have children.

CONGENITAL ABNORMALITIES

DEFINITION

The reproductive organs, like any other organ system, are sometimes affected by congenital abnormalities. There may be duplications or partial duplications of internal structures, or structures such as the uterus may be missing or misshapen so that they cannot support pregnancy.

CAUSE, DIAGNOSIS, AND TREATMENT

No one knows why these abnormalities occur; those that cause no symptoms and that do not interfere with pregnancy may not be discovered unless there is an autopsy at death or they are discovered during an operation.

Generally, a doctor will not treat this condition unless a woman is having problems with fertility, pregnancy, or giving birth and no other cause can be found.

PELVIC INFLAMMATORY DISEASE

During pelvic inflammatory disease (PID), a bacterial infection enters the uterus and may spread to the fallopian tubes, ovaries, and other tissues in the pelvic region. The infection may be sexually transmitted and is usually secondary to gonorrhea, chlamydia, or use of an IUD, but it also may develop without obvious cause.

The patient may experience pain in one or both sides of the lower abdomen, pain during intercourse, fever, irregularities in the menstrual period, and possibly a heavy and odorous discharge. Untreated, PID can result in blockage of the fallopian tubes, possibly causing infertility and ectopic pregnancies. In rare cases, the bacteria may enter the bloodstream and cause blood poisoning (septicemia), peritonitis, and inflammation of the joints.

Antibiotics are the usual treatment for PID, along with pain relief, bed rest, and short hospitalization. Complica-

tions may require surgery. (For more information, see chapter 18.)

DISORDERS OF THE OVARIES

POLYCYSTIC OVARIES (STEIN-LEVENTHAL SYNDROME)

DEFINITION AND CAUSE

In polycystic disease, follicles within the ovaries fail to burst through the surface to produce eggs. Instead, they grow and reproduce under the ovarian surface, lacking a signal from the pituitary to cease production. Under normal circumstances, follicles regulated by pituitary hormones break the surface to release an egg to the fallopian tube. Remains of the follicles then produce progesterone, the increase of which causes the pituitary to signal the cessation of egg production.

The failure of this process, in which the follicles do not break the surface of the ovary and receive no signal to cease production, causes the ovaries to fill with cysts, become encased in a thickened capsule, and sometimes to enlarge.

DIAGNOSIS

Polycystic ovaries occur most commonly in women younger than 30. The symptoms include irregular menstruation, abnormal hair growth, excessive weight gain, and infertility (from lack of ovulation). A doctor usually can feel enlarged ovaries, and hormonal assessment tests are subsequently used to detect patterns characteristic of the syndrome.

TREATMENT

Treatment may involve hormones that stimulate a normal menstrual cycle. Rarely, surgery is used to reduce the enlargement of the ovaries.

OVARIAN TUMORS

DEFINITION AND CAUSE

Ovarian tumors can produce a wide range of symptoms or none at all. Some women may experience pain during intercourse, or pressure or fullness in the abdomen or pelvis. Pressure from a tumor can cause irregular functioning of the bladder or bowels. A tumor blocking blood or lymph channels can cause varicose veins, hemorrhoids, or swelling of the legs or vulva. Allowed to

OVARIAN CYSTS

Benign ovarian cysts can rupture during intercourse, childbirth, or surgery, or as a result of a fall. Adhesions—protective banks of tissue—sometimes are produced where the contents of the ruptured cysts accumulate. Rarely, a ruptured cyst can bleed into the pelvic cavity, with very serious consequences.

Physiologic cysts, also known as functional cysts, comprise two types of cysts originating from exaggerations of the ovarian process in women's reproductive years. These are follicular cysts and corpus luteum cysts.

A follicular cyst occurs when a follicle, failing to release its egg, swells with fluid underneath or on the surface of the ovary. A corpus luteum cyst is caused by a malfunction of the corpus luteum, the remains of an erupted follicle that has broken through the surface of the ovary and released its egg. Normally, unless a woman is pregnant, the corpus luteum disintegrates. But in the formation of a corpus luteum cyst, it fills with fluid and remains on the ovary. Sometimes if excessive bleeding occurs in the eruption of the corpus luteum, the cyst fills with blood and is referred to as a corpus luteum hematoma.

Because corpus luteum cysts are relatively small, symptoms may be less clear than those of other ovarian tumors and cysts. The exception is when a corpus luteum cyst bursts, causing pain. This necessitates a laparoscopic examination of the ovaries to differentiate between a ruptured cyst and a ruptured ectopic pregnancy.

FUNCTIONING CYSTS (HORMONE-PRODUCING TUMORS)

Functioning cysts produce hormones that trigger masculinizing or feminizing characteristics, or cause systemic changes characteristic of pregnancy where none exists.

Feminizing ovarian tumors cause varied symptoms. These include early onset of puberty in young girls, abnormal uterine bleeding, irregular periods, or, commonly, endometrial hyperplasia. One type, dysgerminomas, produces hormones that can simulate pregnancy, enlarging the uterus and deregulating menstrual periods.

Masculinizing ovarian tumors are rare. The hormones they produce decrease breast size and the rounded contours of a woman's body while increasing facial and chest hair and the size of the clitoris. They also can deepen the voice. Once a masculinizing tumor is removed, these symptoms disappear.

grow, a tumor can displace the uterus. Some tumors create an irregular menstrual cycle, others cause increased hormone production or masculinizing characteristics. Occasionally, a tumor can twist on its pedicle, causing pain and possibly cutting off its blood supply. If this happens, the parts of the tumor that die can cause swelling, infection, and pain.

DIAGNOSIS

Diagnosis can be elusive. A mass felt by a doctor may be attached to an organ other than the ovary or may merely be a full bladder. Women should therefore urinate before a pelvic exam. Only a biopsy can determine whether an ovarian tumor is benign or malignant. A pathologist examines the tissue taken from the tumor, while a surgeon inspects other organs for signs of malignancy.

TREATMENT

When the patient is a young woman who wants to have children, the surgeon customarily makes every effort to save the ovary; in older women, it is usually removed. This matter should be discussed before surgery.

DISORDERS OF THE URINARY TRACT

INCONTINENCE

A common problem among older women, incontinence is discussed in the section on menopause.

CYSTITIS

DEFINITION AND CAUSE

Cystitis is a urinary tract infection so common that 1 in 5 women have had at least one infection and some women suffer recurrent bouts. Cystitis results from bacteria entering the urinary tract opening just outside the vagina and traveling to the bladder. Its symptoms include the frequent, urgent need to urinate, burning upon urination, sometimes accompanied by a gnawing pain above the pubic bone, and occasionally blood in the urine.

The frequency of cystitis in women is the result of their anatomy. Women's lower urinary tracts (urethras) are short—not more than a few inches—and bacteria can be easily introduced into the bladder. (Men's urinary tracts tend to be considerably longer, giving the bacteria a greater distance to travel.) The urinary opening is located at the site of intercourse, and bacteria may be introduced by the partner's penis; the anus is nearby and fecal bacteria may be introduced into the vagina and then into the urinary tract. If a woman does not urinate frequently or does not completely empty the bladder, the natural contents of urine provide an excellent breeding ground for bacteria.

Other common causes of cystitis include an improperly fitted diaphragm that causes irritation and infection; congenital abnormalities; foreign bodies, such as a catheter in the bladder; lowered resistance from illness, stress, fatigue, or medication; or other medical procedures. In addition, pregnancy, labor, and delivery provide conditions for the development of cystitis. Some women during pregnancy have asymptomatic cystitis that becomes apparent only by a culture.

DIAGNOSIS

Cystitis is diagnosed through urinalysis and culture, with the patient following special procedures to ensure the cleanliness of the specimen. The condition ordinarily is not serious and responds to a short course of antibiotic treatment. Most physicians prescribe drugs to be taken over 3 to 14 days.

TREATMENT

A combination of antibiotics and sulfa drugs such as trimethoprim and sulfamethoxazole (Bactrim, Septra, and others) may be prescribed. Recurrent or resistant infections may require a different antibiotic such as cephalosporin.

HOME REMEDIES AND ALTERNATIVE THERAPIES

During a bout with cystitis, you should avoid food and drinks that may irritate the bladder. These include coffee, tea, juices with high citric acid content, cola, alcoholic beverages, chocolate, and spices. You should drink six to eight glasses of water per day to flush the bladder and urinary tract.

Some women drink cranberry juice or take vitamin C to prevent or help relieve cystitis. Both are useful acidifiers of the urine but have drawbacks. Making the urine acidic can interfere with the action of the medication;

cranberry juice has considerable sugar content; and vitamin C should be taken only in recommended amounts. High doses can also irritate the bladder. It may be more healthful and less expensive just to drink double the usual amount of water.

If cystitis has not cleared up within a week, the physician may change the medication; if a woman has recurrent episodes, the doctor may recommend that she be treated by a urologist.

PREVENTION

Some commonsense preventive measures include:

- Keep the vaginal area clean, including wiping from the front to the back after a bowel movement to prevent contamination of the urinary tract.
- Use tampons, changed every 3 to 4 hours, instead of sanitary pads. (The pads can act as a culture medium for fecal bacteria, which may then be rubbed against the urinary outlet and invade the bladder.)
- Wear cotton undergarments, which allow air circulation and discourage the warm, moist environment that is needed for bacteria growth. Nylon pantyhose should have a cotton crotch.
- Avoid tight clothes in the genital area, such as control-top pantyhose and skin-tight jeans, as well as extended wearing of a wet bathing suit.
- Urinate before intercourse and make sure your partner's hands and penis are clean. Following intercourse, drink a glass of water, wait about an hour, and urinate again to flush out the bladder.
- Drink plenty of fluids and urinate as frequently as the need arises.

SEXUAL DYSFUNCTIONS IN WOMEN

The most significant difference between male and female sexual dysfunction is that women can perform sexually and pretend to have an orgasm, whereas it is impossible for a man to simulate an erection. With increasing sexual awareness among women, however, the level of performance anxiety has risen in both sexes. Women have great capacity for physiological responsiveness in sexual activity—they are able to achieve an orgasm early in the arousal stage and to have more than one orgasm during the same sexual activity—factors that theoretically should protect against sexual problems. Certain attitudes regarding female sexuality, however, have contributed to a variety of sexual dysfunctions.

Anorgasmia. The failure to achieve orgasm is the most common female sexual dysfunction. With the changes in cultural attitudes toward female sexuality and the wider dissemination of sex information, most women now expect to be fully responsive and orgasmic. They are, therefore, concerned if they are not, and are likely to seek professional help.

There are three different types of anorgasmia:

- *Primary:* a woman has never had an orgasm in any sexual situation, including masturbation. Paradoxically, this type is the most responsive to treatment.
- *Secondary:* a woman who has been orgasmic in the past becomes anorgasmic. This is more difficult to treat with sexual therapy alone because psychological and interpersonal factors not directly connected to the sexual experience usually play a role.
- *Situational condition:* anorgasmia occurs under specific conditions, such as when the children are still awake, or with a specific partner. Frequently, these anxiety-provoking concomitants are easily identified and treated.

In some instances, the male partner becomes anxious because he looks upon his partner's inability to climax as a sign of his own sexual inadequacy. Thus, the striving anxious woman and the striving anxious man create a situation in which achieving a specific goal becomes the principal reason for sexual activity, with frustration the inevitable result.

A woman with primary anorgasmia usually is uninformed about her own sexuality and often is apprehensive about expressing her own sexual needs. Treatment includes education about female sexuality and assertiveness in expressing one's own sexual needs, and the use of masturbatory exercises to help the woman become comfortable with her sexuality. She is encouraged to examine her own genitalia by hand and with the use of a mirror, and to identify the position of her clitoris and her other anatomical features. It is also useful for a woman to identify and learn to use the muscles that control the genitourinary area. A woman can identify these muscles by inserting two fingers into the vagina and tightening the muscles around them. Stopping urination midstream is another method of identifying these muscles. Repeated tightening and relaxation of these muscles is recommended both to enhance sexual pleasure and also to overcome incontinence that often occurs following childbirth.

In treatment, women are also encouraged to explore their physiological responses to sexual stimulation by masturbating at times when they are free from interruption and other concerns. The increased knowledge of sexual responsiveness plus the repeated masturbation help most women to become orgasmic by self-pleasuring.

During this period, sexual activity with the partner should be continued and sensate focus exercises by the couple instituted. This allows the woman to practice the knowledge she is gaining through self-exploration and self-stimulation in a couple situation and also avoids resentment on the part of the man, who may feel he is to blame for his partner's lack of responsiveness. The man should also learn about female anatomy and his partner's needs and responses and put this to use. The importance of clitoral stimulation during intercourse should be recognized and practiced. A woman who is easily orgasmic during masturbation but not in intercourse should show her partner her preferences for sexual stimulation.

Arousal Stage Problems. These are often related to the degree of lubrication. Physical changes in the degree of lubrication can occur with illness, certain drugs, aging, and other factors. Most can be treated successfully by the use of creams, oils, and artificial lubricants. Inadequate lubrication in a healthy, premenopausal woman, however, reflects either psychological problems associated with sexual response or inadequate arousal techniques used by the partner. Sensate focus exercises and masturbation also are useful in resolving arousal problems.

Dyspareunia. This is persistent or recurrent genital pain during intercourse. It is rare in men and is usually associated with a penile disorder. Women who experience painful intercourse should be carefully examined for a physical cause that may include vaginitis, urinary tract infection, localized vaginal scarring (as occurs after episiotomy), broad ligament injuries, prolapse, endometriosis, and ovarian tumors. During breast-feeding and after menopause, hormonal changes may result in thinning of vaginal tissues, leading to painful intercourse. If there is no organic cause of the dyspareunia, it is usually associated with inadequate lubrication or other forms of sexual dysfunction, especially vaginismus—the involuntary contraction of the vaginal muscles. Often there is a general aversion to all sexual activity, but particularly to sexual intercourse.

Treatment involves ruling out an organic cause of the dyspareunia and making sure there is adequate stimulation and lubrication before intercourse. If the problem persists, the same approach as for vaginismus (see below) may be recommended.

Vaginismus. This is the sudden contraction of the muscles of the lower outer third of the vagina, which can occur at any point in the sexual response cycle. In some women, it occurs before the sexual response begins and is precipitated by the knowledge that her partner is about to begin sexual activity. Usually, vaginal penetration cannot occur, and when penetration is forced, pain frequently results, leading to further muscle contractions.

The underlying cause of vaginismus, as with many of the other dysfunctions, is anxiety. The causes of the anxiety range from fears associated with earlier painful inter-

BREAST CANCER RISK FACTORS

The risk of breast cancer is greatest for women:

- Over the age of 60
- With a mother, sister, or other close relative who has had breast cancer
- Who have never had children or whose first full-term pregnancy was after the age of 30
- Who have had cancer in one breast, increasing the risk of developing it in the other breast

Other possible risk factors include:

- Early onset of menstruation
- Late menopause
- Obesity, especially in postmenopausal years
- Excessive alcohol use

course, rape or a rapelike situation, or fear of penetration associated with injury, violation, or impregnation.

Vaginismus, when not due to organic factors, usually can be treated by the use of dilators or, in milder cases, the woman's and her partner's own fingers. Both partners should understand the vaginal contraction is an automatic response outside the woman's control and participate in treatment.

Lack of Sexual Desire A significant number of people experience a lack of sexual desire, even though they have normal sexual function. A variety of factors can lead to loss of libido, including physical illness, hormonal abnormalities, depression, and interpersonal problems. Treatment involves identifying the underlying problem and resolving it, perhaps with the help of a qualified sex therapist.

CANCERS COMMON TO WOMEN
By Karen H. Antman, M.D.

BREAST CANCER

DEFINITION

Breast cancer is the most common malignancy among American women, with 183,000 new cases a year and about 46,000 annual deaths. Men also develop breast cancer, but they account for less than 5 percent of cases. In contrast, women face a 1 in 8 lifetime risk of developing breast cancer.

Breast cancer is most common in women over the age of 50, although about one-third of all cases occur in women 39 to 49 years old, and breast cancer occasionally strikes younger women (see box above, "Breast Cancer Risk Factors").

There are several different types of breast cancer, distinguished mostly by their rate of growth and tendency to spread to other organs. Breast cancer often spreads to surrounding lymph nodes under the armpit, under the sternum (breastbone), and under the clavicle (collarbone).

CAUSE

The precise causes of breast cancer are unknown. Recent epidemiologic studies suggest that diet may be a factor; vitamin A may be protective, and a diet high in animal protein and fat intake has been shown to increase risk in some studies but not in others.

Breast cancer can also run in families. Patients who carry abnormal genes called BLCA1 and BLCA2 have a high risk of breast cancer even before age 40.

DIAGNOSIS

Early detection and treatment are extremely important in curing breast cancer.

Mammography. While the role of mammography in women ages 40 to 50 is not well defined and should be discussed with your physician, all women over 50 should have annual mammography. While some women are concerned that the radiation used for mammography might increase the risk of breast cancer, studies involving thousands of women have found the risk of dying of breast cancer significantly decreases for women over 50 who undergo mammography, and there is no evidence that the amount of radiation administered by mammography can actually cause cancer.

Mammography is also recommended for most women who have suspicious breast lumps. The probability that a

WARNING SIGNS OF BREAST CANCER

Any persistent breast changes, such as:

- A lump
- Thickening of tissue
- Dimpling or pulling of the skin
- Any change in breast shape or contour
- Nipple discharge
- Retraction of the nipple
- Scaliness of the nipple
- Pain or tenderness

BREAST SELF-EXAMINATION

Doctors recommend that women start to practice breast self-examination after their first menstrual period, and continue the habit monthly throughout their lives. Most doctors want their patients to learn the technique and will take the time to teach it, or will ask a nurse or physician's assistant to do so. Although breast cancer is rare in women under 30, it is useful for a woman to examine her breasts consistently throughout her life, since there are benign conditions that can occur at any age.

The best time to examine your breasts is about a week after your period. You should examine them monthly, at the same time each month, since the breasts change during the menstrual cycle. Postmenopausal women and others whose periods are irregular should choose one day in the month for breast examination and do their examinations on the same day each month.

Breast self-examination should be done when you are relaxed and not rushed or distracted. The examination begins with inspection and palpation, or feeling. To begin the inspection portion, stand in front of a well-lighted mirror and let your arms hang at your sides. Note shape, depressions or bulges, moles, dimples, dark or reddened areas, swellings, sores, or skin with a rough or orange peel–like texture as well as prominent veins. Observe nipples and areola color changes, scaling, dimpling, or retractions, as well as the direction in which the nipples point. Then repeat the inspection with hands pressing on hips (to make the pectoral muscles bulge in the chest, see figure 9.24) and with hands raised (figure 9.25), placed behind your head, and elbows flexed. Then with one hand behind your head, use the other to examine your breast (figure 9.26). This step can also be done in the shower, with the breast soaped to make it easier to examine. The second part of the breast self-examination is most easily performed in the shower or lying on a couch or bed. Each arm should be raised and the breast felt with the other hand, then examined with the arm at the side (figure 9.27). The breast should be felt gently and systematically with the flat of the fingers of the opposite hand. The goal is to know the individual and unique feel of your breasts so that you can recognize any changes early in their development.

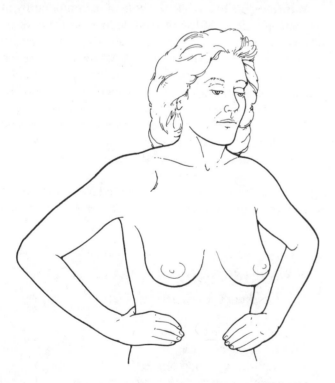

Figure 9.24: Breast self-examination. Start by standing in front of a mirror and carefully observing the breasts for any changes in size or contour, dimpling or puckering of skin, nipple discharge, or other visible abnormality.

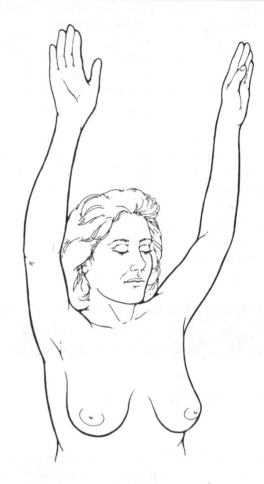

Figure 9.25: Raise your hands above your head and, again, carefully observe the breasts in a mirror for any changes.

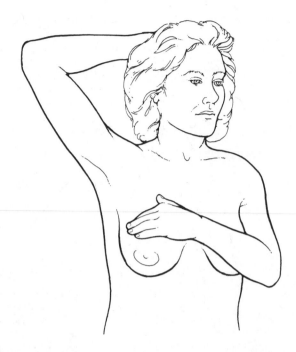

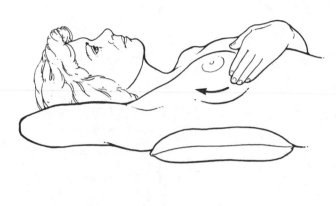

Figure 9.26: With your arms behind your head, carefully examine the breast for any lumps, thickening, or other changes. Repeat on the other side. (This is best done while showering or bathing.)

Figure 9.27: Lying down with one arm tucked behind your head, again carefully examine the breast for any lumps, thickening, or other changes. Repeat on both sides.

lump contains cancer can be estimated, but a biopsy is needed for certain diagnosis.

Biopsy. A doctor can usually perform a needle biopsy in the office. A local anesthetic is injected into the breast, and light suction is applied through a hollow needle inserted into the lump to remove a sample of tissue or aspirate fluid. Disappearance of the lump after fluid is withdrawn usually indicates a benign cyst. Nevertheless,

the fluid is sent to a laboratory for analysis. If no abnormal cells are found, no further tests are required.

In some cases, a surgical biopsy may be necessary. This procedure entails removal of the lump and small amounts of surrounding tissues for laboratory analysis. A surgical biopsy usually is done in a hospital (often as outpatient surgery) using either local or general anesthesia. About 80 percent of biopsies show no cancerous cells.

Additional Tests. When a tumor is found, estrogen-receptor and progesterone-receptor assays are used to determine whether the tumor is dependent on estrogen or progesterone (estrogen- or progesterone-receptor–positive). Additional tests sometimes performed measure the rate at which tumor cells are dividing (DNA flow cytometry) and the presence of abnormal genes such as one called Her 2/Neu.

TREATMENT

A woman with a newly diagnosed breast cancer must discuss the various treatment options with her physician as soon as possible. Recent studies involving thousands of women with 1- to 4-cm (about 2 inches) cancers have found that removal of the lump (lumpectomy) followed by radiation produces a cure rate equivalent to radical or modified radical mastectomy (removal of the breast and underlying tissue). For much larger tumors, mastectomy

BREAST CANCER SUPPORT GROUPS

Volunteer organizations such as Y-ME and Reach to Recovery are designed to help women deal with breast cancer and its treatment. Many YWCA branches and other such organizations also sponsor rehabilitation groups and services for women with breast cancer. Volunteers who have had breast cancer are frequently available to talk to women who have a newly diagnosed breast cancer. To talk to someone who has had breast cancer, ask your physician to arrange a meeting.

Breast cancer is also difficult for the patient's partner and family to deal with; counseling services are usually available for them, too (see appendix B, Directory of Health Organizations and Resources).

Figure 9.28 and 9.29: Simple everyday tasks, such as brushing or combing your hair, can serve as useful postmastectomy exercises. At first, a stack of books or a few pillows may be used to give the arm needed support. Reaching above your head also helps regain use of the arm and prevents swelling. This exercise should be performed standing facing a wall and slowly reaching along the wall until the arms are above the head.

is usually recommended. Chemotherapy and radiation therapy can shrink breast cancers that are initially too large to be removed surgically.

During both lumpectomy and mastectomy, axillary (underarm) lymph nodes are generally removed and examined. Enlarged nodes under the arm may or may not contain cancer. Microscopic examination is required to document spread to lymph nodes. Involvement of lymph nodes in the armpit and under the sternum (breastbone) indicates a significantly aggressive and invasive tumor. An increased number of involved lymph nodes increases the probability of recurrence.

Removal of lymph nodes can result in swelling of the arm on that side. Exercises can help minimize the problem (see figures 9.28 and 9.29). Also, avoid wearing a watch or bracelet, or carrying a handbag on that arm.

Chemotherapy is often recommended for 4 to 8 months after removal of breast cancer. For lesions larger

than 1 cm with negative lymph nodes, CMF (cyclophosphamide, methotrexate, and 5 fluorouracil) chemotherapy or tamoxifen is recommended. Women with positive lymph nodes, particularly if the tumor was estrogen- and progesterone-receptor–negative, often require more intensive regimens using cyclophosphamide, doxorubicin (Adriamycin), and 5 fluorouracil. Such adjuvant therapy decreases the risk of recurrence by about one-third. Patients with many positive lymph nodes have a poor prognosis with conventional therapy and should consider participation in a clinical trial in an attempt to avoid recurrence.

Breast cancer recurring outside the breast and regional lymph nodes also has a poor prognosis. Although strongly estrogen- and progesterone-receptor–positive disease can be controlled with hormones for months to a few years, receptor-negative tumors are treated with chemotherapy with a median duration of response of about a year and a

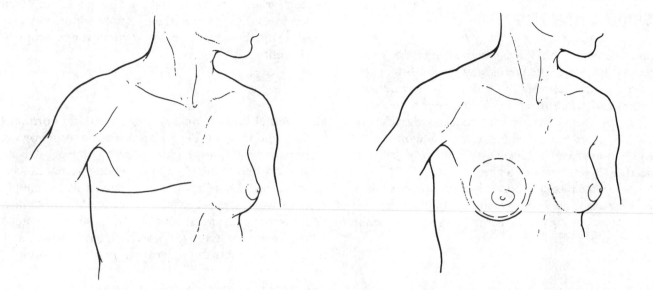

Figure 9.30: Appearance of the chest wall following a simple or modified radical mastectomy. In a simple mastectomy, only the breast is removed. In a modified radical, the breast and lymph nodes from the armpit are removed.

Figure 9.31: Breast reconstruction following a lumpectomy, in which only the tumor and surrounding tissue are removed.

median survival of 2 years. Patients should consider participation in a clinical trial if breast cancer recurs. However, patients whose tumors have not shrunk when treated with conventional therapy are seldom good candidates for new therapies.

Reconstructive Surgery. Mastectomy may be followed by breast reconstruction, which minimizes disfigurement (see figures 9.30 to 9.32). Timing of reconstruction depends upon the extent of the cancer and the preferences of the woman and her surgeon. Although reconstruction can be done at the time of initial surgery, it often follows the mastectomy and any additional therapy, such as radiation therapy. If reconstruction is not performed at the time of the mastectomy, the incision and scar must be placed to facilitate later reconstruction.

Reconstruction may involve implanting a soft saline-containing prosthesis either under the skin or, increasingly, under the pectoral (chest) muscle. Alternatively, a breast may be constructed from fatty tissue that is removed from the abdomen or other part of the body and transplanted to the breast area. Improved plastic surgery techniques and wider acceptance of breast reconstruction by cancer surgeons have made this an increasingly important part of treatment and rehabilitation of mastectomy patients.

A history of breast cancer is often considered a contraindication for the use of oral contraceptives, further pregnancy, or estrogen replacement therapy, although these issues have never been rigorously tested.

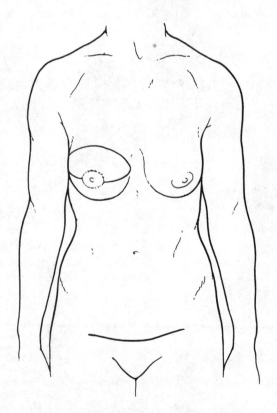

Figure 9.32: Breast reconstruction following a modified radical mastectomy, using an implant of tissue from the abdominal area (a tummy tuck) and reconstructed nipple.

UTERINE CANCERS

Uterine cancers are classified as those originating in the cervix, or the neck of the uterus, and those arising in the endometrium, the lining of the body of the organ. Public education and widespread use of Pap smears to detect early precancerous changes have reduced cervical cancer in the United States, where it was once one of the most common causes of cancer death. However, the rate in the Third World remains high.

Any abnormal bleeding between menstrual periods or after menopause raises a suspicion of uterine cancer. Similarly, any unusual vaginal discharge should be brought to the attention of a physician.

ENDOMETRIAL CANCER

DEFINITION

The endometrium lines the inner surface of the uterus. Endometrial cancer develops mostly in women between the ages of 50 and 64, and an estimated 31,000 new cases of invasive endometrial cancer occur each year in the United States, with 5,700 deaths. If diagnosed and treated early, the 5-year survival rate is 94 percent. When treatment is delayed until the cancer has spread to adjacent organs, however, the 5-year survival rate drops to 68 percent.

CAUSE

Endometrial cancer appears to be related to hormonal factors, and long-term estrogen replacement following menopause without the administration of progesterone apparently boosts the likelihood of endometrial cancer. An increased risk of endometrial cancer also occurs in women who have received long-term adjuvant tamoxifen for breast cancer. Conversely, younger women who take oral contraceptives seem to have a lower incidence of cancer than women who use other forms of birth control.

Although estrogen is linked to endometrial cancer, this hormone is still of great benefit to postmenopausal women, protecting them from heart disease and osteoporosis. Consequently, the fact that endometrial cancer is often diagnosed early and is readily curable and the fact that new doses and scheduling of estrogen replacement reduce the possibility of malignancy leads many experts to believe estrogen's good effects outweigh the risks. However, women on long-term estrogen therapy should have at least annual (some doctors advise twice-a-year) pelvic examinations and report any vaginal bleeding promptly to their doctors.

Similarly, studies have shown that the survival of women receiving tamoxifen significantly improves due to a decreased risk of breast cancer recurrence and a lower incidence of cardiac death. Tamoxifen appears to protect against osteoporosis as well.

DIAGNOSIS

Regular Pap smears—the microscopic examination of cells shed from the surface of the cervix—have detected some cases of endometrial cancer. A yearly pelvic examination by a doctor is an important screening procedure. An endometrial biopsy is used to document endometrial cancer.

TREATMENT

Endometrial cancer is usually treated surgically with removal of the uterus as well as the ovaries and fallopian tubes, but a very young premenopausal woman with endometrial cancer may have an ovary left in place to forestall menopausal symptoms, osteoporosis, and premature cardiovascular disease.

In some cases, radiation may be administered instead of or in addition to surgery. If the cancer has spread, chemotherapy may also be utilized.

TABLE 9.8: SCREENING TESTS FOR UTERINE CANCERS

Who Needs It	How Often
PAP SMEAR	
Women at risk (see "Risk Factors")	Yearly
Women with no risk factors: Beginning at age 18 or onset of sexual activity (whichever is earlier)	Yearly until 3 consecutive Pap smears are normal, then every 2–3 years until age 49
Ages 50–65	Yearly
Ages 66–75	Every 3 years
PELVIC EXAMINATION	
Women at risk (see "Risk Factors")	Yearly
Women who are sexually active and/or ages 18–50	Every 2–3 years
Women over 50	Yearly

Cancers of the vagina are very rare. Young women whose mothers took diethylstilbestrol (DES), an artificial estrogen that was given until about 1970 to prevent miscarriage, are at somewhat higher risk and should have regular gynecological checkups.

PREVENTION

Keeping your weight down is a prudent preventive step. (Obesity is a risk factor for endometrial cancer, perhaps because fat cells produce estrogens.) Discontinuing tamoxifen and estrogen replacement therapy also decreases the risk of endometrial cancer, but this risk must be carefully considered against the benefits afforded by these substances.

CERVICAL CANCER

DEFINITION

Cancer of the cervix, or neck, of the uterus usually occurs at an earlier age than endometrial cancer. At one time, cervical cancer was a leading cause of death among American women. Today, this malignancy is most common in developing countries and in the lower socioeconomic groups that do not have regular Pap smears and pelvic examinations. In the United States there are 13,500 new cases annually and 4,400 deaths.

Warning signs of advanced cervical cancer are the same as for endometrial cancer: abnormal bleeding (between menstrual periods or after menopause) and unusual vaginal discharge. These nonspecific symptoms should be brought to the attention of a physician. (The only real warning sign of early cervical cancer is an abnormal Pap smear.)

Cervical cancer generally takes several years to develop from atypical cells to dysplastic cells to carcinoma in situ and finally to frankly invasive cancer. Although severe dysplasia may need to be treated, women who wish to complete their families can often plan and deliver a subsequent pregnancy if observed carefully before surgical treatment.

In carcinoma in situ, the cells appear malignant under the microscope but they have not yet developed the ability to invade through the membrane below the cells. At this very early stage, no specific symptoms are apparent. Carcinoma in situ is usually detected by an abnormal Pap smear or sometimes visually during a pelvic examination. Women with this condition have a survival rate of close to 100 percent if diagnosed early and treated appropriately. When treatment is delayed until early invasive cancer is present, however, the 5-year survival rate drops to 89 percent. And if cancer has spread to adjacent tissue, the 5-year survival is only 57 percent.

CAUSE

Certain strains of human papillomaviruses (genital warts) appear to cause cervical cancer. These can be spread by sexual contact.

RISK FACTORS FOR CANCERS OF THE FEMALE REPRODUCTIVE SYSTEM

CERVICAL CANCER

- Sexual activity at an early age
- Multiple sex partners
- A history of certain strains of genital Papillomaviruses (genital warts)

ENDOMETRIAL CANCER

- A history of infertility or failure to ovulate
- Late menopause
- Obesity
- Prolonged unopposed estrogen replacement therapy after menopause
- Prolonged tamoxifen therapy
- Genes that increase the risk of uterine cancer

OVARIAN CANCER

- Over age 60
- Childless
- Early onset of menses
- Late menopause
- History of breast cancer
- Genes that increase the risk of ovarian cancer
- Possibly, use of body talc

VAGINAL CANCER

- Daughters of women who took diethylstilbestrol (DES) during pregnancy

DIAGNOSIS

Regular Pap smears are the primary tool for the early diagnosis of cervical cancer. Cells on a Pap smear can appear atypical if the cervix is irritated or if there has recently been an infection; thus an abnormal Pap smear needs to be repeated, because the vast majority subsequently return to normal without treatment.

TREATMENT

Treatment depends upon the age of the woman, extent of the cervical carcinoma, and the probability that the tumor may spread to other parts of the body. If there is no indication of spread, the cancer may be removed by surgery, laser surgery, electrocautery, or cryosurgery. A hysterectomy may be indicated if a large portion of the cervix is involved or if the disease has spread to the uterus; it may be recommended for earlier disease in a postmenopausal woman or a woman who no longer wishes to bear children.

These treatments may be followed by radiation therapy in more advanced cancers to attempt to kill tumor cells that may have spread to nearby tissues.

Cervical cancer that has extended to adjacent organs or spread to other distant organs is sometimes treated with chemotherapy.

PREVENTION

Because of the apparent connection between human papillomavirus infection and cervical cancer, measures to prevent the spread of sexually transmitted disease may decrease cancer risk. These include using a condom during sex and maintaining a mutually monogamous sexual relationship.

OVARIAN CANCER

DEFINITION

Ovarian cancer—with about 22,000 new cases diagnosed each year in the United States—is less common than uterine cancer, but it has a higher mortality rate, resulting in more than 12,000 annual deaths. This cancer is rarely symptomatic in its earlier stages, and the tumor is often locally advanced when diagnosed. There is no screening test for this condition other than an annual pelvic exam for ovarian cancer.

CAUSES

The risk of ovarian cancer increases with the number of ovulation cycles in a woman's lifetime (multiple pregnancies, long-term oral contraceptive use, late onset of menses, and early menopause are protective factors). Because some genes (BRCA1) appear to increase the risk of both breast cancer and ovarian cancer, these two cancers share certain risk factors. The use of body talc has also been associated with a higher risk of ovarian cancer.

DIAGNOSIS

Distention of the abdomen, due to accumulation of fluid, and crampy abdominal discomfort are possible warning signs that should be evaluated by a doctor. But ovarian cancer is difficult to detect in its early stages, largely because the ovaries are deep in the abdomen and an ovarian tumor can grow large before symptoms develop. Vague abdominal discomfort and fullness, the most common symptoms of ovarian cancer, often do not occur until the disease is advanced by which time masses and fluid in the abdomen can be detected by examination or CT scan. Unfortunately there is no simple screening test other than a yearly pelvic examination. Although a mass on an ovary can be felt during a pelvic exam, these usually are benign cysts that occur after ovulation and resolve with the next period. An ultrasound examination may detect suspicious changes, but this is not advocated as a screening procedure.

TREATMENT

Treatment of ovarian cancer is usually with surgery followed by cisplatin or paclitaxel-based chemotherapy or sometimes radiation.

PREVENTION

Multiple pregnancies (or long-term use of oral contraceptives), early menopause, tubal ligation, and surgical removal of both ovaries are preventive measures against ovarian cancer. Use of talcum powder should also be avoided.

A genetic test may soon be available for families with a high incidence of breast and ovarian cancers, to determine if family members are more likely to develop this malignancy. Until such a test is developed, it is recommended that women from high-risk families undergo frequent pelvic examinations for screening.

10

ealth
oncerns

en

• • • • • • • • • • • •

R S. SAWCZUK,
., RIDWAN
BSIGH, M.D., AND
L A. OLSSON, M.D.

In men, more so than in women, the organs of urine excretion and the organs of reproduction—the tissues of the genitourinary system—are intricately interrelated.

Urology is the branch of medicine dedicated to the study and treatment of maladies affecting both urination and reproduction. Urologists, who have postgraduate training in both surgery and urology, have been referred to as "gynecologists for men," because both gynecology and urology deal with the organs of procreation.

Although this chapter focuses on male health concerns, urologists deal with diseases of the urinary tract in both sexes. In fact, relatively recent shifts in social habits and mores have increased the incidence of certain urologic diseases in women (for instance, women's increased rate of smoking has led to an increased incidence of female bladder cancer). Consequently, urologists deal with the diseases of the urinary tract in both males and females as well as disorders of the male reproductive and sexual organs.

ORGANS OF THE URINARY TRACT

The organs of the urinary system include the kidneys, ureters, bladder, and urethra.

The main function of these organs is the production and excretion of urine as a means of ridding the body of waste products.

Urine formation begins in the kidneys, a pair of organs located behind the abdominal cavity and beneath the rib cage on either side of the spine. As the body's cells break down the food we eat and release its energy, they produce chemical by-products collected by the bloodstream. The kidneys cleanse the blood of these waste products and excess water, forming urine, which is transported to the bladder. (The kidneys and their disorders are discussed in chapter 27.)

The ureters, two thin, muscular tubes leading from the center of each kidney, transport urine to the bladder with active waves of contractions (peristalsis). The urine empties into the bladder, a muscular pouch that temporarily stores this liquid before excreting it from the body. Because the bladder walls are elastic, the bladder expands as it fills and contracts forcefully to empty itself of urine.

Although infants empty their bladders involuntarily, urination (or voiding) becomes a voluntary function as the brain and nervous system develop. Continence, or bladder control, is a complex event requiring bladder relaxation as well as proper functioning of the sphincter that controls its opening and closing. Loss of control of either of these coordinated functions may cause incontinence.

MALE AND FEMALE DIFFERENCES

From the bladder, urine is carried out of the body by a thin tube called the urethra. In women, the urethra is about 1 inch long and situated in front of the vaginal wall, ending in the vulvar area.

The male urethra, longer and more resistant to infection, travels through the prostate gland and then through

Figure 10.1: The male genitourinary organs.

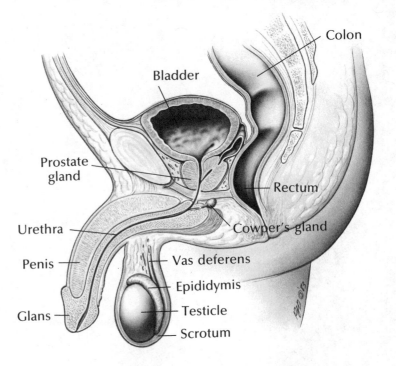

GENERAL SYMPTOMS OF URINARY PROBLEMS

Difficulty in passing urine, as well as changes in its color, are often among the first signs of a urinary infection or other disorders of the urinary tract.

Color. Urine is normally crystal clear and yellow, although the intensity of the color may vary from colorless to dark amber. These variations may be entirely normal and are usually dependent on the amount of fluid consumed and on environmental factors such as extreme heat, which tends to cause dehydration. Normally, the more fluid an individual drinks, the more diluted and lighter the urine becomes, whereas less ingested fluid or more fluid lost through perspiration makes urine more concentrated and darker.

While variations in urine color are not usually a sign of problems, extreme darkening of the urine, however, may indicate a problematic condition.

- Hepatitis, or liver inflammation, can cause urine to become deep orange in color, and will usually be accompanied by pale bowel movements and a general feeling of malaise.
- Urinary tract infection may cause cloudy urine.
- Serious disease may cause small amounts of blood in the urine that cause it to be tea-colored. For example, the development of tea-colored urine soon after a sore throat or upper respiratory illness may indicate a kidney problem that requires an immediate evaluation by a kidney specialist.

Hematuria. The cardinal manifestation of urologic disease is significantly bloody urine, or hematuria, perhaps the most alarming sign of trouble that requires prompt diagnosis and treatment. Pain may or may not accompany hematuria and blood may appear in the first portion of the urination, in the last portion, or throughout the entire stream. The pattern of hematuria may help the physician to make a diagnosis.

Pneumaturia. Bubbles in the urine (as it leaves the bladder) are another sign of trouble. The bubbles may actually be seen or may be noted by the sensation of air passing through the urethra. These result from infection by gas-producing bacteria or from an abnormal connection between the bowel and the bladder.

Pain. In healthy adults, the bladder stores and expels urine voluntarily and without pain. Pain associated with urination (strangury) may indicate an abnormal blockage within the bladder or urethra; burning on urination (dysuria) generally indicates a urinary tract infection.

Urgency. Although a full bladder stimulates the urge to urinate, adults can normally suppress this urge until they encounter an appropriate setting. Then, as urination is voluntarily initiated, the bladder contracts forcefully and the sphincter relaxes, allowing forceful expulsion of the urine.

Conditions that decrease the amount of urine able to be held by the bladder or which cause pain when the bladder is filled can increase urination urgency and cause incontinence.

Frequency. The frequency of urination varies with the consumption of fluids and the production of fluid by the body. Normally, the bladder holds nearly a pint of urine, and the full content of the bladder is expelled with each act of urination. Frequency refers to the need to urinate more often than usual, a possible sign of either incomplete emptying of the bladder (see "Retention," below), a bladder infection, a direct irritation of the bladder (such as a bladder stone), or a neurologic abnormality. Occasionally frequency results from an abnormally high production of urine, which may be due to a kidney problem or diabetes.

Incontinence. Even when the desire to urinate frequently cannot be suppressed, individual acts of urination are still usually controlled. The involuntary loss of urine is called urinary incontinence. This very common condition is not a natural part of the process of aging but indeed can happen at any age and for a variety of causes.

Some causes of incontinence, such as urinary infection, vaginal infection, constipation, and side effects of medications, are temporary. Long-term causes include weakness of bladder suspension, weakness of the urethral sphincter muscle, overactive bladder muscle, bladder outlet obstruction, hormone imbalance in females, and neurologic disease such as multiple sclerosis. The diagnosis and management of incontinence can often be very successful; in many cases, management entails treatment of the underlying problem.

The U.S. Department of Health and Human Services Agency for Health Care Policy and Research's booklet on incontinence titled "Urinary Incontinence in Adults: A Patient's Guide" can be obtained by writing to: National Kidney and Urologic Diseases Information, Box NKUDIC, 9000 Rockville Pike, Bethesda, MD 20892; (301) 654-4415.

Retention. Urinary retention, the inability to empty the bladder of its stored urine, is often excruciatingly painful. Relief is obtained by allowing the urine to drain through a catheter (a rubber or silicon tube) inserted into the bladder via the urethra. While men are afflicted with urinary retention more often than women (most commonly because of an enlarged prostate), urethral stenosis or strictures—areas of narrowing or scarring—are other common causes found in both genders.

Sometimes urinary retention is insidious, with progressively larger volumes of urine retained within the bladder (chronic urinary retention). What may bring the patient to the doctor in this case is incontinence: The bladder capacity is overwhelmed, and small amounts of urine leak continuously, a condition known as overflow incontinence.

Chronic urinary retention may be found in conjunction with bladder stones. If small, stones may be easily passed during urination while larger stones may cause pain and sometimes blood on urination, or an abruptly interrupted urinary stream. The underlying cause of bladder stone formation, such as outlet obstruction due to growth of the prostate, must be dealt with to prevent recurrence.

the undersurface of the penis to the urethral meatus, an opening in the tip of the glans (or head) of the penis.

THE MALE GENITAL SYSTEM

The organs of the male genital system include the prostate, the seminal vesicles, the penis, and, contained in the scrotum, the testicles, epididymides, and vas deferens (see figure 10.1).

Specialized structures within the penis help it accomplish its two major functions: to transport urine and partake in sex. The urethra, which travels within a cylindrical structure (corpus spongiosum) on the undersurface of the penis, transports urine and seminal fluid (semen).

The penis contains also two cylinders of spongy tissue (corpora cavernosa) that fill with blood (engorge) during sexual excitement, causing the penis to expand. Since the fibrous sheath covering the spongy tissues is limited in its ability to expand, the tissues press against the sheath as they fill with blood, making the penis hard.

Though the penis actually extends far into the body, almost to the rectum, it contains no muscles and cannot be enlarged by exercise. However, the internal section is surrounded by muscles that can be strengthened. For most men, the head is the most sensitive part of the penis, especially around the ridge that connects it to the shaft.

Behind the base of the penis is the scrotum, a pendulous sac containing testicles, which produce both sperm and the male hormone testosterone. Each testicle is suspended from a cordlike structure containing blood vessels and a muscular tube called the vas deferens, which carries the sperm from the testicles to the urethra. Connecting the vas to the testicle is the epididymis, a structure important in the maturation of the sperm leaving the testicles.

The sperm travel through the vas deferens and are stored at its upper end until mixed with the secretions of the seminal vesicles and prostate just prior to ejaculation. The exact purpose of the vesicles is unclear, but it is known that they contribute a portion of the ejaculate. The secretions of the prostate comprise most of the seminal fluid or ejaculate, giving it its whitish color, while the sperm actually account for only a tiny fraction of the seminal fluid.

The tiny Cowper's glands empty into the urethra after it passes through the prostate. It is thought that the glands secrete a small amount of clear, sticky fluid that is often visible prior to ejaculation. Since this fluid may contain sperm and is capable of impregnating a woman, withdrawal of the penis from the vagina prior to final ejaculation is an ineffective means of contraception.

Although the prostate serves no purpose in the urinary system, the prostate normally enlarges (hypertrophies) with age and may eventually interfere with the flow of urine through the urethra.

DISORDERS OF THE GENITOURINARY TRACT

General Definition of Genitourinary Tract Problems

Disorders of the genitourinary tract range from infections and structural abnormalities to benign and malignant growths. Disorders will be discussed according to the organs affected. A separate discussion of cancers of the genitourinary tract follows.

Every part of the genitourinary tract is susceptible to infection. Urologists differentiate between upper and lower urinary tract infections, which may have very different long-term outcomes.

Infections of the lower urinary tract, though sometimes frustratingly difficult to cure, rarely cause long-term difficulties. The symptoms are generally more localized than those of upper urinary tract infections; most commonly they are manifested by frequency (the need to urinate again immediately after urination), burning or painful urination, bloody urine, and occasionally an uncontrollable urge to urinate (urgency incontinence). Rarely do simple lower urinary tract infections cause fever and chills.

An upper urinary tract infection (specifically a kidney infection), on the other hand, is usually accompanied by fever, chills, flank or back pain, and malaise. Victims of these infections generally look and feel quite ill and debilitated. (Kidney infections, known as pyelonephritis, are discussed in chapter 27.)

General Causes of Genitourinary Tract Problems

Factors predisposing to recurrent infections vary according to age, gender, and environment, but most involve abnormal drainage of the urine from parts of the urinary system. In children, this may be due to congenital areas of narrowing that prevent the urine from draining from the kidney (congenital ureteropelvic obstruction) or to abnormal backflow of urine from the bladder to the kidney (ureterovesical reflux). In older men, an enlarged prostate results in failure of the bladder to empty, which may predispose to infection. Kidney stones may also prevent proper drainage from the kidney and may lead to infection.

GENERAL DIAGNOSIS OF
GENITOURINARY TRACT PROBLEMS

In addition to a physical examination to evaluate the cause of urinary problems, the urologist may also perform special diagnostic procedures, such as a cystoscopy and urodynamic studies.

During cystoscopy, a cystoscope (a telescopic instrument) is inserted through the urethra, allowing the urologist to visualize the lower urinary tract. These instruments are usually rigid tubes; however, modern advances in fiber-optic technology have led to the development of flexible cystoscopes, which may be used in certain circumstances.

Urodynamic studies involve filling the bladder with specific amounts of fluid or carbon dioxide to determine if the bladder responds normally. (For more information, see chapter 12, Diagnostic Tests and Procedures.)

BLADDER AND URETHRAL PROBLEMS

CYSTITIS

DEFINITION

Cystitis is inflammation of the urinary bladder.

Because the bladder is located completely within the body, it normally is not subject to external bacterial infection: Its lining is resistant to the development of infections and the urine is normally sterile. However, the bladder drains externally via the urethra, whose opening (especially in women) is a breeding ground for bacteria that can, under certain circumstances, travel up to the bladder.

CAUSE

Cystitis in men most often results from an abnormality, such as prostate enlargement, stone disease, or the retention of large amounts of residual urine in the bladder after urination.

(Women, however, are especially prone to cystitis even without anatomic abnormality because the short female urethra allows bacteria more ready access to the bladder.)

DIAGNOSIS

Symptoms of cystitis include frequency of urination and dysuria; the urine may be cloudy, foul smelling, and occasionally bloody. There may also be lower abdominal pain and slight fever.

Finding pus in the urine (discovered during urine analysis), or culturing bacteria from the urine, confirms cystitis. Cystoscopy can also be used to examine infection in the bladder.

URETHRAL STRICTURE

Injury or chronic urethritis may result in scar tissue, which can narrow or, in extreme cases, obstruct the urethra, making urination increasingly difficult and painful. Stricture may be treated by dilation: The urologist inserts a thin, flexible instrument into the urethra to stretch it. The frequency of this treatment varies from patient to patient; however, most strictures do recur.

The area of stricture may also be sharply incised using a cystoscope in an attempt to reduce the blockage. This approach is less traumatic than dilation and may be more successful in preventing recurrence of the narrowing.

Lasers have not been proven more effective in treating urethral strictures than other therapies.

Sometimes strictures are so extensive or unresponsive to dilation or incisional therapy that formal reconstructive surgery is required.

TREATMENT

Although antibiotics usually control the bacterial infection, it is apt to recur if the underlying cause is not diagnosed and treated.

PREVENTION

Sometimes urinary tract infections can be prevented by drinking acidic fluids such as cranberry juice; urinating to completion as the need is felt; and maintaining personal hygiene.

URETHRITIS

DEFINITION

Urethritis is an inflammation of the urethra generally associated with a urethral discharge that may vary in color and consistency from thin and clear to thick and creamy yellow. The major symptoms are urinary frequency and pain on urination or ejaculation.

CAUSE

Urethritis may be due to nonspecific irritants or infections such as sexually transmitted diseases like gonorrhea and chlamydia.

DIAGNOSIS

Gonorrhea organisms are relatively easy to identify with culture techniques. Chlamydia, an organism more difficult to identify, is the most likely cause of nongonococcal (nongonorrheal) urethritis.

TREATMENT

Antibiotics are used to treat urethritis. Generally the symptoms disappear promptly, but since urethritis can be sexually transmitted, the patient's sex partner may require treatment as well. Occasionally, urethritis will be persistent and troublesome to treat, and may cause urethral scarring and stricture. (See box preceding.)

PREVENTION

When due to sexually transmitted infection, urethritis may be prevented by maintaining a mutually monogamous sexual relationship or by the proper and consistent use of condoms.

STONE DISEASE

DEFINITION

Urinary tract stones may form from the various inorganic minerals that under certain conditions can settle out (precipitate) of urine.

Most commonly, a urinary tract stone makes its presence known with the sudden onset of excruciating pain that may result from the stone passing out of the kidney to the bladder. If the stone is in the kidney or ureter, the pain may begin in the flank region and move along the urinary tract to the anterior lower abdomen or, in men, to the tip of the penis. The pain is sharp and colicky (coming in waves) and often associated with profuse sweating, nausea, and vomiting, and sometimes with blood in the urine. Fever does not usually accompany the passage of a stone unless there is a concurrent urinary tract infection.

CAUSE

There are many causes of stones. In some cases, anatomical abnormalities lead to the pooling (stasis) of urine, resulting in the precipitation of various organic and inorganic compounds and stone formation.

Stones can also result from urinary tract infections, which change the acidity or alkalinity (pH) of the urine, and various metabolic abnormalities. Quite often, no cause of the stone formation can be identified. (See chapter 27 for more information on stone formation.)

DIAGNOSIS

The medical evaluation for urinary tract stones depends on the age of the patient and the size and number of stones. Passage of a stone during childhood or early adulthood, a family history of stone disease, or previous history of a stone passage should lead to a thorough anatomic, as well as metabolic, evaluation. Anatomic evaluation may include an intravenous pyelogram (special x-rays of the kidneys and ureters); metabolic evaluation may include blood chemistry analysis, 24-hour urine collection studies, and perhaps special test diets.

TREATMENT

If the stones are large, totally or significantly obstructing the urinary collecting system, or causing other damage, treatment is required to prevent permanent kidney destruction. Small stones may not cause total obstruction and may be monitored without treatment to see if they pass through the tract spontaneously.

Upper Urinary Tract. Traditionally, stones in the upper urinary tract (i.e., the kidney and upper ureter) have been removed by various surgical approaches. A recently developed procedure enables urologists to remove upper tract stones through tubes placed through the flank into the urinary tract (percutaneous stone removal). This new technique avoids large surgical scars, significantly decreases surgical risk, decreases the risk of kidney damage, and decreases postoperative pain and hospitalization. Not all stones, however, can be removed with this technique.

Another noninvasive treatment, extracorporeal shockwave lithotripsy (ESWL)—the "stone bath"—has revolutionized the treatment of upper urinary tract stones. Originally the procedure was performed with either general or epidural anesthesia. Currently, with newer equipment, procedures can be performed with intravenous analgesia and sedation. Occasionally, it can be done completely without medication.

Depending on the type of ESWL unit used, the patient is placed either into a water bath or onto a water cushion system equipped with a shock-wave generator. The stones are located with x-rays or ultrasound, or both, and fragmented into sand-size particles by focused shock waves, which are then passed easily and painlessly in the urine. Postoperative discomfort is minimal, and many patients can resume normal activity within a day of receiving treatment.

In medical centers where ESWL is performed, it can be used successfully on a large percentage of symptomatic patients with upper urinary tract stones. Three months after treatment, 80 percent of patients are free of stones. Because of the extremely low risk and the rapid recovery involved, ESWL is preferred to surgery and other invasive treatments for the removal of urinary stones. A patient's size, weight, and stone burden (i.e., the number and size of the stones) may make this treatment less feasible, however. Furthermore, not all stones are amenable to ESWL, and percutaneous and surgical techniques may still be required.

Lower Urinary Tract. Stones of the lower urinary tract and the bladder can be removed through traditional surgical techniques, as well as with stone basketing. In this technique, either a cystoscope or a ureteroscope is passed into the bladder or through the bladder into the ureter. A basket is attached and used as a snare to engage and extract the stone.

Larger stones may be fragmented with ultrasound, shock wave, or laser techniques.

PREVENTION

Once one has developed a kidney stone, the chance of developing another stone in the future is 50 percent higher than that of someone who has never had a stone.

Prevention depends on the type of stone; after passing a stone, it should be saved and brought to a urologist for analysis. Specific recommendations of diet alteration or medication may be made by the urologist depending on the type of stone, the clinical history, and the results of laboratory tests.

In general, consuming large volumes of water to dilute the urine helps prevent stones. This is especially important in the summer, when a significant amount of water is lost through sweating, leaving less internal water available for the kidney to produce urine. Concentrated urine is more prone to stone formation.

PROSTATE GLAND

The prostate gland, which manufactures some of the components of seminal fluid, encircles the uppermost part of the urethra.

Because the prostate is the organ most often affected by benign or malignant growth processes, urologists spend most of their time dealing with this structure.

BENIGN PROSTATIC HYPERTROPHY (BPH)

DEFINITION

In an adult male, the prostate gland is about the size of a walnut.

At puberty the prostate tissue experiences a growth spurt, but then remains basically stable in size until approximately age 50, when it grows again. As the prostate enlarges—whether benignly or malignantly—the urethra that runs through it becomes progressively compressed, preventing the bladder from adequately emptying. Eventually, if the compression and blockage progress, a man may find himself entirely unable to urinate (urinary retention). Occasionally, due to the inability of the bladder to empty, pressure is transmitted by way of

---

PROSTATE EXAMINATION

Routine yearly examinations of the prostate should be carried out in men over the age of 40, to make early diagnosis of possible cancerous changes. A normal prostate is soft and smooth; if it is irregular, hard, and nodular, prostate cancer should be suspected and a tissue biopsy performed. As with all other tumors, the earlier the diagnosis is made, the better the chance for a cure. (For a detailed discussion of cancer of the prostate and other male genitourinary tract organs, see the section "Cancers Common to Men" later in this chapter.)

---

the ureters back to the kidney, and kidney damage ensues.

SYMPTOMS OF PROSTATE ENLARGEMENT

Growth of the prostate progressively obstructs the flow of urine from the bladder. This in turn leads to the classic symptoms of prostate disease.

- Hesitancy or difficulty initiating the stream of urine
- Frequency (the feeling of incomplete emptying of the bladder)
- Nocturia, or awakening during the night to urinate
- Dribbling at the end of urination

CAUSE

The cause of benign prostatic enlargement is not entirely clear, but the male hormone testosterone seems the most probable answer. (See figures 10.2 and 10.3.)

DIAGNOSIS

A rectal exam usually reveals prostate enlargement. If the prostate is irregular, hard, or nodular, a malignancy may be suspected and a biopsy performed. In addition, blood tests may be used to show kidney function and urine cultured to see if infection is present. The prostate may be examined with pyelography (special pelvic x-rays) and urine flow pressure may be measured.

TREATMENT

Retention. Urinary retention is treated with insertion of a catheter (a hollow tube) through the urethra into the bladder to obtain relief.

Surgery. Surgical treatment may be indicated when an enlarged prostate causes the inability to urinate, or when bleeding or urinary infections have developed.

The most common surgical procedure is the transure-

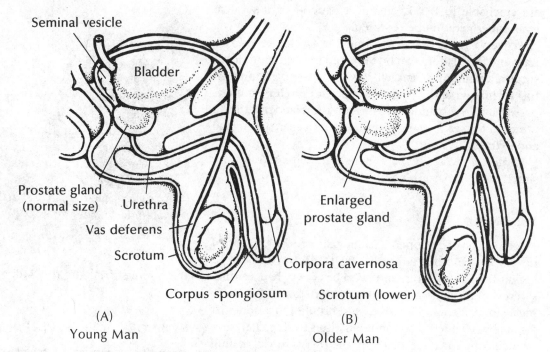

Figure 10.2 and 10.3: Prostate gland in a young man and an enlarged prostate in an older man.

thral resection of the prostate (TURP), in which an instrument called a resectoscope is passed by way of the urethra through the penis into the bladder. Using an electrified loop at the end of the resectoscope, the surgeon carves away the prostate from within to its outermost margins, leaving a hollowed-out shell that gradually shrinks down to form a channel for urine flow from the bladder to the urethra. After the surgery the patient has a catheter in place for a few days. More recently, balloons have been utilized to compress the prostate tissue and open up a wider channel, allowing free flow of urine. This technique affords only transient relief. Stents or tubes, similar to those used to bypass clogged arteries, can also be used to bypass prostatic obstruction, but these methods are usually reserved for elderly patients.

Newer techniques utilizing laser technology are being evaluated for their safety and efficacy as an alternate surgical means of relieving prostatic obstruction.

If the urologist feels the prostate is too large to be removed via the transurethral approach, an open prostatectomy may be carried out. In this technique, an incision is made in the lower abdomen and the prostate is removed through an incision made into the bladder or into the prostate itself. (The particular approach used depends on the personal preference of the surgeon.) These procedures involve hospitalization of a week to 10 days. The major advantage of the transurethral procedure is the shorter recuperative process at home as compared with open prostatectomy.

Drugs. Recent advances in understanding the physiol-

ogy of urination and the action of certain drugs on the voiding process have produced nonsurgical methods for treating benign prostatic enlargement.

Two drugs, with different modes of action, have been approved in the United States for the treatment of BPH:

• Alpha-adrenergic blockers (taken once a day) relax the tightening of the smooth muscles found more abundantly in the enlarged prostate. Although not beneficial for all patients, those with mild or moderate symptoms may obtain relief from taking these agents once daily.

• Finasteride (Proscar) inhibits the formation of the male hormone dihydrotestosterone, which can lead to prostate enlargement. Finasteride can shrink the prostate in most men by 25 percent to 30 percent. It must, however, be taken from 4 to 6 months to produce tangible results.

While the long-term effects of these drugs in the treatment of BPH need further study, for the patient with mild to moderate symptoms of BPH, nonsurgical therapies may give relief.

ACUTE PROSTATITIS

DEFINITION

Acute prostatitis is inflammation of the prostate, a condition often heralded by symptoms similar to those of cystitis: frequent, painful urination and nocturia (awakening from sleep to urinate). There may also be a discharge from the urethra. Prostatitis may also be accompanied by fever, chills, and pain in the perineal region behind the scrotum, the lower back, or above the pubic bone (the suprapubic region).

CAUSE

The most common cause of acute prostatitis is bacterial infection, which can result from infected urine.

DIAGNOSIS

The prostate itself will be very tender, which is evident with a rectal examination. Fever and pain in the area above the pubic bone may be present. Examination of the urine may reveal signs of infection.

TREATMENT

Prostatitis is treated with antibiotics, given orally or intravenously, depending on the severity of the infection. Untreated prostatitis may result in an abscess that is more resistant to antibiotic therapy and may require surgical drainage.

PREVENTION

In the presence of a known urinary tract infection, urologic manipulation, which can cause urosepsis, should be avoided unless necessary.

CHRONIC PROSTATITIS

DEFINITION

The relationship between chronic prostatitis, prostate infection, and acute prostatitis is not clear, but the chronic form may follow an acute episode. Chronic prostatitis usually causes persistent urgency, frequency, and painful urination, but not with a urinary tract infection. Its symptoms often include a feeling of heaviness or pressure behind the scrotum, in the lower abdomen just above the pubic bone, or in the lower back.

CAUSE

The infective process is similar to that seen in acute prostatitis. Occasionally chronic prostatitis can result from untreated acute prostatitis.

DIAGNOSIS

An examination may show an inflamed prostate. Examination of the urine may reveal bacteria, and both urine and prostatic secretions may contain inflammatory cells.

TREATMENT

Treatment usually consists of long courses of the same antibiotics used for acute prostatitis. However, sitz baths and avoidance of alcohol and spicy foods may prevent symptoms.

HOME REMEDIES AND ALTERNATIVE THERAPIES

Sitz baths may relieve symptoms.

PREVENTION

Beyond thorough and effective treatment, there are no preventive measures to be taken for chronic prostatitis.

TESTICLES AND SCROTUM

Any acute swelling or pain in the scrotum requires evaluation by a urologist to differentiate among orchitis, epididymitis, testicular torsion, and other conditions that require immediate attention.

Scrotal Masses. Although a lump in the scrotum can be caused by a number of conditions, anyone with a lump in this region should have it examined by a physician to rule out the possibility of a testicular tumor.

Most lumps are benign, and may be a cyst or other inflammation of the epididymis. Cysts of the epididymis are quite common, especially in men over 40.

EPIDIDYMITIS

DEFINITION

Inflammation of the epididymis, the long, tightly coiled tube that is located behind each testicle and carries sperm from the testicle to the vas deferens, is called epididymitis. This condition causes fever and pain, developing progressively over several hours in the back portion of the testicles, and the scrotum may be enlarged and red.

ORCHITIS

Orchitis is an infection of the testicle that most commonly occurs in conjunction with epididymitis that has not been properly treated. When this occurs, orchitis is a bacterial infection treated with antibiotics.

Occasionally orchitis occurs as a viral infection associated with mumps (mumps orchitis). Although mumps orchitis is a rare phenomenon in the United States, when it does occur it may result in irreversible damage to the testes and infertility.

CAUSE

Epididymitis may be caused by a bacterial or chlamydial infection that travels from the urinary tract to the sperm duct. Occasionally an episode of epididymitis is precipitated by extreme straining, which causes urine to back up the reproductive tract to the epididymis.

DIAGNOSIS

Analysis of the urine may reveal an infection. A scrotal ultrasound may be performed, and occasionally a testicular radionuclide scan is needed to differentiate this condition from testicular torsion.

TREATMENT

Epididymitis is treated primarily with antibiotics. Since some types of epididymitis can result from sexually transmitted bacteria, the patient's sex partner may also require treatment with antibiotics.

HOME REMEDIES AND ALTERNATIVE THERAPIES

Analgesics, bed rest, ice packs, and elevation of the scrotum may be used to relieve pain.

PREVENTION

There are no preventive measures for epididymitis, except when due to sexually transmitted infection. The proper and consistent use of condoms will prevent sexual transmission of infectious agents.

TESTICULAR TORSION

DEFINITION

Testicular torsion is the twisting of the testicle on the spermatic cord (the structure that suspends the testicle within the scrotum, and which contains its blood vessels). (See figure 10.4.) It results in strangulation of the blood supply to the testicle and permanent damage if diagnosis and treatment are delayed. Even if torsion involves only one testicle, the other one may also be at risk for twisting.

The major symptom of this condition is sudden pain, often sufficiently severe to cause nausea and vomiting. Swelling, redness, and tenderness of the scrotum ensue rapidly. Although occasionally the testicle may untwist spontaneously, providing immediate relief, immediate medical attention should still be sought.

CAUSE

Torsion, although more common in adolescence, can happen anytime, at any age, either spontaneously (even

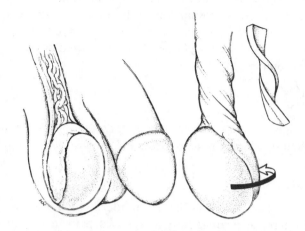

Figure 10.4: Testicular torsion.

during sleep), or following strenuous activity. The underlying cause is faulty "anchoring" of the testes, a congenital condition often manifested in both testicles.

DIAGNOSIS

Diagnosis requires medical expertise, since the symptoms of testicular torsion are often similar to those of epididymitis.

TREATMENT

Even if the physician is able, by gentle manipulation, to return the testicle to its normal position, surgery is usually performed within a few hours to permanently anchor the testicle in place.

Because a testicle whose blood supply has become twisted may be strangulated, necessitating its removal, sudden testicular pain always requires prompt medical attention in order to prevent loss of a testicle.

PREVENTION

While there are no preventive measures to be taken for testicular torsion, if it occurs in one testicle, surgery is performed to anchor both testicles and prevent occurrence in the uninvolved testicle.

SPERMATOCELE

DEFINITION

A spermatocele is a cyst of the epididymis, which can usually be felt as a swelling in the upper portion of the structure, above the testicle.

CAUSE

There is no known cause of spermatocele.

DIAGNOSIS

Spermatoceles can usually be diagnosed by physical examination. If necessary, an ultrasound examination of the scrotum can be performed.

TREATMENT

Unless they grow large enough to cause discomfort, spermatoceles should be left alone. Surgical removal may result in blockage of the epididymis and may impair fertility.

HYDROCELE

DEFINITION

The most common scrotal mass is the hydrocele—an overaccumulation of the fluid normally found between the 2 layers of membrane that envelop the testicle (see figure 10.5).

CAUSE

This excess fluid buildup may result from overproduction or underabsorption of the liquid; the specific cause is often not apparent. Occasionally, the hydrocele results from injury.

DIAGNOSIS

Careful examination and transillumination (shining a bright light) from behind the scrotum to reveal the out-

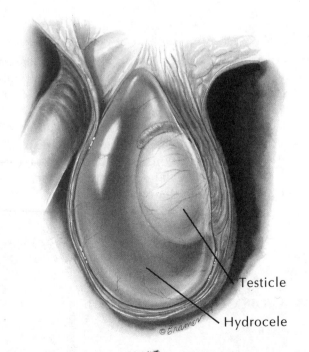

Testicle

Hydrocele

Figure 10.5: Hydrocele, a fluid-filled mass in the scrotum.

line of the mass helps to diagnose a hydrocele. A scrotal ultrasound may be used to determine the nature of the scrotal mass.

TREATMENT

Like cysts, hydroceles rarely require treatment. If the mass becomes so large that it is uncomfortable, surgery is the only effective approach.

VARICOCELE

DEFINITION

A varicocele is an abnormally distended vein that can cause a mass in the scrotum. Normally, the valves in these veins permit blood to drain from the testicle, but not to return. With a varicocele, the blood is allowed to return to the testicle, causing alterations in sperm production.

Although varicoceles are common and generally benign, they are also the most frequent cause of correctable male infertility. Approximately 20 percent of fertile men have a varicocele, but twice as many infertile men have them.

How the condition alters sperm production is not clear, but it may affect the testicle by increasing its temperature.

CAUSE

In most cases, there is no known cause of varicocele.

DIAGNOSIS

Examination of the scrotum with the patient in an upright position can reveal the varicocele, a mass sometimes termed a "bag of worms." The size of the mass may increase when the patient is asked to increase his abdominal pressure by straining and decrease when the patient lies down. Occasionally, Doppler ultrasound is used to diagnose smaller varicoceles.

TREATMENT

Rarely will a varicocele be of such a size that symptoms require intervention. However, if the varicocele is large or unsightly, it can be removed surgically for cosmetic reasons, or more commonly surgery may be performed to correct impaired fertility.

This surgery is relatively simple and can be performed on an outpatient basis or with a short hospital stay: The urologist makes an incision similar to that employed for hernia in the groin, and ties off the abnormal veins, preventing the blood from returning to the testicle via this route. Since other veins take over the drainage function, the testicle is not damaged.

Newer techniques are available to block or plug the varicocele with either balloons or coils that prevent abnormal blood flow. This technique—not widely available—seems to offer no particular benefit over the surgical approach, and its major disadvantage is the possibility that these devices will migrate elsewhere within the body and cause difficulty wherever they finally lodge.

PENIS

PENILE (VENEREAL) WARTS

DEFINITION

Penile warts (*condylomata acuminata*) look like warts found anywhere else on the body, although they may grow more luxuriantly. The warts are generally found on the external genitalia, including the shaft and head of the penis, but occasionally they involve the part of the urethra that travels through the penis.

CAUSE

Like all warts, *condylomata acuminata* are caused by a virus (human papillomavirus). They are contagious and are transmitted through sexual contact.

DIAGNOSIS

External warts can be recognized by their appearance and are diagnosed principally by physical examination. Because of the possibility of internal spread, the urologist may investigate the urethra and bladder by cystoscopy.

Since some types of human papillomaviruses may possibly cause cancers, any unusual lesion should be biopsied.

TREATMENT

Many warts are treated with a topical medication, but extensive warts may require removal by freezing with liquid nitrogen, vaporizing by laser therapy, or surgery. Since warts are usually sexually transmitted, all partners of the affected individual must be treated to prevent reinfection and further spread.

PREVENTION

Because these warts are contagious, sexual abstinence is recommended until they are eradicated. Condoms may provide adequate protection if used carefully.

PARAPHIMOSIS

Paraphimosis is the retraction of the foreskin (in uncircumcised men) behind the head of the penis that cannot be brought forward, resulting in severe swelling. This is a urologic emergency requiring immediate attention. An emergency circumcision or partial circumcision (called a dorsal slit) may be required.

PRIAPISM

DEFINITION

Priapism is a rare and painful condition that produces a prolonged erection unaccompanied by sexual desire. It occurs when blood becomes trapped in the penis, causing its prolonged engorgement.

CAUSE

Priapism may be caused by certain drugs, by blood abnormalities such as leukemia and sickle cell disease, or by an overdose of penile self-injections as treatment for erectile dysfunction.

DIAGNOSIS

This condition is diagnosed by physical examination and medical history. Tests for underlying causes also may be performed.

TREATMENT

Priapism is a serious condition requiring immediate attention. Failure to treat may result in permanent injury to the penis and impairment of the ability to have a normal erection.

The specific cause of priapism may necessitate specific treatment. Among treatments that are used are spinal or caudal anesthesia, surgery to establish new passageways for the blood to escape the penis, anticoagulants to thin the blood, and antihypertensive drugs to lower the blood pressure, as well as blood transfusions to remove damaged blood cells (sickle cells). Recently vasoconstrictors injected directly into the penis have been successfully utilized to treat priapism.

BALANOPOSTHITIS (BALANITIS)

DEFINITION

Balanoposthitis is irritation and inflammation of the glans (tip) of the penis from a variety of causes. In men who have been circumcised, such inflammations are less common and limited to the glans penis (balanitis); in uncircumcised men, the irritation may extend to the foreskin.

Men with diabetes mellitus are particularly susceptible to this condition, and anyone who develops these inflammations should be evaluated for diabetes.

CAUSE

Irritation and inflammation of the glans may result from bacterial or fungal infection, irritation from chemicals in clothing, or an unknown cause.

DIAGNOSIS

Diagnosis is made by physical examination of the penis. If there is discharge, it may be cultured to help choose the appropriate antibiotic.

TREATMENT

Treatment consists of antibiotics for infection, careful cleaning of the glans, and application of topical ointment to relieve the irritation.

PREVENTION

Personal hygiene—keeping the penis clean by washing with soap and water—may at times prevent recurrence. Frequent recurrence in an uncircumcised man may necessitate circumcision.

CANCERS COMMON TO MEN
(Prepared with Karen H. Antman, M.D.)

PROSTATE CANCER

DEFINITION

The prostate gland is the most common cancer site in men, with about 200,000 new cases a year. About 38,000 men die of prostate cancer each year, making it the second leading cause of cancer mortality in men (exceeded only by lung cancer). According to American Cancer Society statistics, the overall 5-year survival rate is 78 percent—a marked improvement from the 50 percent survival rate of the 1960s. About 58 percent of prostate cancer is diagnosed while still localized; in these patients, the 5-year survival rate climbs to 92 percent. In contrast, only 28 percent live 5 years if the cancer has metastasized.

Often early prostate cancer develops without symptoms; in other instances, it produces symptoms similar to those of benign prostate enlargement: a weak or inter-

---

SCREENING FOR PROSTATE CANCER

After age 40, all men should undergo an annual digital examination of the prostate gland. The prostate is the source of an enzyme called prostatic acid phosphatase (PAP). Measurement of this enzyme has been touted as the "male Pap test" for prostate cancer; in reality, it has no value as a screening test, although it may be useful in monitoring the course of prostate cancer. Authorities disagree whether a PSA test should be added to screening and, if added, when it should be done.

---

rupted urinary flow and occasionally blood in the urine or pain and burning during urination. Advanced prostate cancer characteristically spreads to the skeleton, resulting in bone pain, especially in the lower back.

CAUSE

Although the exact cause of prostate cancer is unknown, epidemiological studies point to a number of predisposing factors, including heredity, male sex hormones, infectious agents, environment, and diet.

DIAGNOSIS

A rectal examination, in which a doctor inserts a gloved finger into the rectum to palpate the prostate for any unusual swelling or nodules, remains the most common screening examination for prostate cancer. However, the recent development of a blood test for prostate specific antigen (PSA) is a major advance in early detection of possible prostate cancer. PSA is a protein produced by the prostate gland; when blood tests detect higher than normal levels, prostatic enlargement is likely and further testing is indicated to rule out cancer. These examinations may include an ultrasound examination of the prostate, but only a biopsy of suspicious tissue can diagnose or discount cancer.

Once prostate cancer has been diagnosed, additional tests are needed to determine whether it has metastasized. These usually include bone and CT scans. In some cases, some pelvic lymph nodes may be removed and studied for the presence of cancer.

TREATMENT

Treatment depends upon the stage of the disease. Patients with localized cancer are treated with surgical removal of the prostate (a radical prostatectomy) and/or external beam radiation therapy. In some cases, elderly men with very slow-growing disease may be monitored and treated only if the disease accelerates.

In the past, a radical prostatectomy was associated with a high incidence of impotence, resulting from severing of the pelvic nerves. A new procedure developed in 1982 to treat localized prostate cancer spares the nerves and often preserves sexual function. Even so, the patient will be infertile because the prostate is needed to make components of the seminal fluid that transports sperm. This new technique also makes it easier to reattach the urethra to the bladder, reducing the risk of urinary incontinence. In some patients, incontinence and/or impotence are temporary problems, although it may take a year to regain full function.

Radiation therapy is an alternative to surgery, especially for patients who are too ill or are unwilling to undergo an operation. Typically, the radiation is delivered by an external beam of high-energy rays. Alternatively, radioactive seeds may be inserted into the prostate gland to destroy cancer cells. This form of radiation therapy may be combined with cryosurgery, the use of a freezing technique.

Advanced cancer requires systemic treatment. Because 80 percent of prostate cancers are stimulated by testosterone, hormone therapy to eliminate testosterone is the best form of palliation. This may be achieved by surgical removal of the testes, or by complete androgen blockade. This can be achieved by administering luteinizing-hormone releasing hormone (LHRH), a substance that blocks the chemical signals to produce testosterone from the pituitary to the testes and with an anti-androgen to block testosterone formed from other sites. Estrogen, the major female sex hormone, has a similar effect. All of the treatments cause significant side effects, including loss of libido and impotence. Estrogen can also cause breast swelling, fluid retention, and an increased risk of cardiovascular disease.

PREVENTION

A low-fat diet has been advocated as preventive, but there is no scientific proof that this is so. To date, the best approach to prevention remains annual screening to detect the disease while it is confined to the prostate.

TESTICULAR CANCER

DEFINITION

Cancers of the testes are relatively rare, with only 6,800 cases and 325 deaths a year in the United States. However, it is one of the most common cancers among young men because it typically strikes between the ages of 15 and 34.

Testicular cancers can be seminomas or nonsemino-

mas. Early signs include a lump or swelling of the testicle, and sometimes pain or discomfort.

CAUSE

The cause of testicular cancer is unknown, but the disease occurs more frequently in young men with a history of undescended or late-descended testes.

DIAGNOSIS

All young men, beginning at age 19 or 20, should practice monthly testicular self-examination (see figure 10.6). Suspicious swelling or hard lumps should be checked by a doctor. Also, examination of the testes should be part of any regular physician checkup. If testicular cancer is suspected, an ultrasound examination may be ordered to locate the mass. A definitive diagnosis of cancer requires removal of the testicle for a biopsy. (Biopsy of a testicular mass through the scrotum increases the risk of recurrence and should be avoided.)

If cancer is confirmed, additional tests are needed to determine its stage. These include a chest x-ray, CT scans of the abdomen and pelvis, and blood tests to measure various biochemical markers, including alpha-fetoprotein, beta hCG, and lactic acid dehydrogenase, substances that can be produced by the cancer.

TREATMENT

Surgical removal of the diseased testicle is the primary treatment of localized testicular cancer. However, if the tumor is a seminoma, which is sensitive to radiation, radiation also may be used if there are small enlargements of area lymph nodes. Cell types other than seminoma can be cured by multiple drug chemotherapy regimens, delivered over a 2– to 6-month period, with or without additional surgery.

PENILE CANCER

Cancer of the penis, which is relatively common in many parts of the world, is rare in the United States, probably due to Americans' careful personal hygiene and the widespread practice of male circumcision. Early symptoms include the appearance of a painless nodule, a warty growth, or ulcer on the penis. Pain and bleeding are later symptoms.

Small superficial tumors can be treated by surgical removal or radiation therapy. More extensive cancers may require more extensive surgery, including removal of part or all of the penis.

Testicular cancer has been one of the success stories in the development of adjuvant cancer treatments. If treated in its early stages, nearly all patients can be cured. Even if the disease has spread, surgery and chemotherapy can result in survival rates of 85 percent.

PREVENTION

Boys with undescended testicles should have them surgically placed in the scrotum before the age of 6. Even after surgery, boys should undergo periodic examination for any suspicious changes.

MALE INFERTILITY

Approximately one in six married couples suffer from infertility. While most couples assume that they will be able to have children as desired, both male and female reproductive systems need to be functioning properly to achieve a pregnancy. (For a further discussion of infertility, see chapter 9, Special Health Concerns of Women.)

When couples are frustrated by an inability to have children, anger, frustration, and depression often ensue. Until recently, infertile couples could adopt children without much difficulty and were less inclined to pursue medical solutions to their infertility.

Today, however, adoption opportunities have diminished greatly, and people are more eager to determine and remedy the cause of their infertility.

Figure 10.6: Common causes of male infertility.

DEFINITION

Male infertility is the lack of healthy sperm in the semen.

Problems with male infertility can be broken into three major categories (see figure 10.6):

1. Failure, due to hormonal abnormalities, to produce an adequate number of sperm
2. Failure, due to testicular abnormalities, to produce an adequate number of normally functioning sperm
3. Production of sperm that cannot be deposited in the female genital tract because of ductal obstruction or abnormal sexual function (such as premature ejaculation)

CAUSE

In general, male infertility can be caused by a number of things, including any infection after puberty that causes a high fever: mumps, syphilis, and gonorrhea. Other causes include varicocele, prostatitis, radiation exposure, chemotherapy, pesticides and some industrial chemicals, hormones (such as steroids used by some bodybuilders), abdominal or pelvic surgery, including vasectomy (see figure 10.7), injury to the reproductive organs that could result in a reduction or cutoff of the blood supply to the area and death of the surrounding tissues, erectile and ejaculatory problems as a result of various causes, anatomical abnormalities of any part of the reproductive tract, alcoholism and drug abuse (including long-term use of marijuana), stress, and hormonal imbalance.

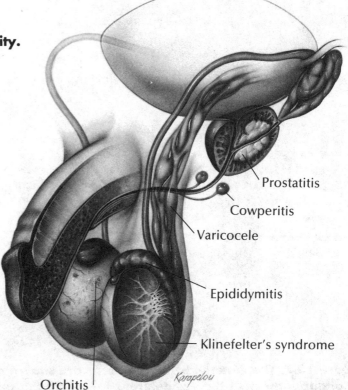

Prostatitis

Cowperitis

Varicocele

Epididymitis

Klinefelter's syndrome

Orchitis

DIAGNOSIS

Semen analysis entails the collection of a specimen either through masturbation into a sterile container or during intercourse into a special condom. The specimen must be brought for analysis within 2 hours of collection to maintain its viability.

While the number of sperm present in semen affects fertility, the quality of the sperm (which can be analyzed under a microscope) is the most important factor. Sperm must move rapidly and easily, and display few abnormalities.

If a man has fewer than 20 million sperm per milliliter of ejaculate (a condition known as oligospermia), he may have difficulty fathering a child. Occasionally, sperm count will reveal the complete absence of live sperm in the semen (azoospermia).

TREATMENT

Underlying causes of infertility must be identified and treated. In cases of low sperm count, artificial insemination with the man's sperm may be attempted.

These conditions may be treated.

Failure to Deliver Sperm: Sexually transmitted diseases may result in blockage of the seminal vesicle or other portions of the male reproductive tract through which sperm pass. In addition, about 500,000 vasectomies are performed in the United States each year, leaving men voluntarily sterile. Blockages can be cleared; vasectomies may sometimes be reversed.

In addition, a small percentage of men have a condition called retrograde ejaculation, in which the sperm enter the bladder instead of continuing on through the urethra. The condition can sometimes be treated.

Impotence (inability to maintain an erection), premature ejaculation, and the inability to ejaculate can all make it impossible for a man to impregnate a woman. These conditions may have an organic cause or a psychological component. Sex therapy has been effective in treating the latter.

Buildup of Sperm Antibodies. Occasionally a man suffers an injury or infection that allows the sperm to enter the surrounding tissue where they are killed by his own antibodies. If the man's injury or infection can be treated, his own antibodies should cease attacking his sperm.

Some women are allergic to sperm and develop antibodies to fight it. This allergy can be somewhat alleviated by using a condom during intercourse for a while,

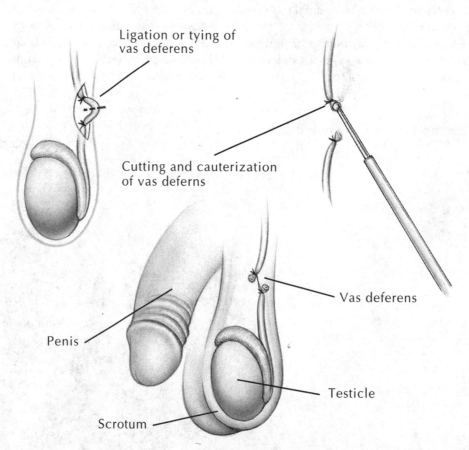

Ligation or tying of vas deferens

Cutting and cauterization of vas deferns

Vas deferens

Penis

Testicle

Scrotum

Figure 10.7: The 2 methods of vasectomy are shown here; the drawing in the middle illustrates the final appearance of the vas deferens following the cutting of the tube and cauterization.

then when her antibodies have lessened, initiate sex without a condom at the time of ovulation.

Undescended Testicles. If a man's testicles did not descend into the scrotal sac before puberty, sperm production will be affected. The testicles function at a slightly lower temperature than the rest of the body's organs and need to be in the scrotal sac to produce sperm. Hormone therapy or surgery can make the testicles descend, but it is best done in childhood. When abnormalities in the testicles themselves affect sperm production, these usually cannot be surgically corrected.

There may be other temporary conditions that a man himself can control—extensive use of hot tubs and saunas, long hot showers, and athletic supporters may all slow growth of sperm. This situation will reverse itself in a short time when the environment changes.

Sperm Immobility. Many of the factors that cause a reduced sperm count may also affect the ability of sperm to move successfully along the female reproductive tract to fertilize the ovum and start a pregnancy. Infections of the prostate gland or surgical removal of the gland will affect sperm mobility. Chronic illness and hormonal problems will also affect the ability of the sperm to move vigorously.

....

MALE SEXUAL DYSFUNCTION

Among men, sexual dysfunction is often associated with anxiety resulting from the misconception that all sexual activity must lead to intercourse, ejaculation, and orgasm. When this expectation is unmet, many men consider the sexual act a failure. Since the sexual response cycle is not under voluntary control, people with this self-imposed expectation are particularly vulnerable to anxieties and a self-fulfilling prophecy of failure.

ERECTILE DYSFUNCTION

DEFINITION

Erectile dysfunction is the inability of the male to obtain and or maintain penile erection sufficient for vaginal penetration and satisfactory intercourse. It is estimated that 10 to 20 million men suffer erectile dysfunction in the United States, and 30 million men suffer partial or temporary erectile dysfunction.

The incidence of erectile dysfunction increases with age. At age 40, about 1 in 20 suffer this condition; at age 65 and older, the incidence is 15 percent to 25 percent.

CAUSE

The causes of erectile dysfunction can generally be classified as either organic or psychological. Although the

---

THE MECHANICS OF ERECTION

Induced by the rapid inflow of blood into the cavernous tissue that makes up most of the penis, erection is a complex event dependent upon the normal functioning of several components, including the vascular, neurologic, hormonal, and psychological systems. Within the confined space of the penile tissues, the increased volume of blood in the erect penis—approximately 11 times that of the blood in the flaccid penis—leads to the increased size and rigidity of the penis.

The integrity of the vascular and neurologic systems appears to be necessary for the regulation of the blood flow into the penis. While hormones are necessary for normal sexual development and, generally speaking, a normal testosterone level is necessary to preserve sexual desire and the capability of the penis to become erect, no specific level of testosterone concentration is associated with improving sexual activity. Instead, a delicate interrelationship among the hormonal, neurologic, and vascular systems has to be maintained, but this process is not yet totally understood.

The mind exercises a great influence on sexual function. Anxiety or stress—even in the psychologically secure—may temporarily deplete the ability to sustain an erection.

---

majority of men with erectile dysfunction are thought to have an organic factor, psychological aspects of anxiety, depression, self-confidence, and partner relationship are important contributing factors. Consequently, many men have a combination of organic and psychological factors.

The organic causes and risk factors of erectile dysfunction include vascular disease, diabetes mellitus, hypertension (high blood pressure), certain medications, neurologic disorders such as multiple sclerosis, chronic alcoholism, prolonged heavy smoking, pelvic trauma and spinal cord injury, pelvic surgery (such as non-nerve-sparing radical prostatectomy, cystectomy, or resection of rectum), Peyronie's disease (buildup of scar tissue in the penis), hormonal abnormalities, and other medical and surgical conditions.

Psychological causes include performance anxiety, stress, depression, and marital conflict.

Although erectile dysfunction is often assumed to be a natural consequence of aging because its incidence increases with age, it is not inevitable. However, many conditions associated with aging—vascular disease, diabetes, cancer, and their treatments—may cause erectile dysfunction.

DIAGNOSIS

Abnormalities in the vascular, neurologic, or endocrine system can be assessed by physical examination and laboratory tests. Adequacy of blood supply to the penis can be ascertained by blood flow or pressure measurements within the penis. Neurologic adequacy is assessed by specialized studies, and endocrine abnormalities are measured in blood tests.

A comprehensive diagnosis of erectile dysfunction often includes nocturnal tumescence monitoring studies that appraise the ability to attain or maintain an erection by measuring episodes of erection that occur normally during sleep. At any age, men should experience spontaneous erections during sleep. The absence of these erections may point to an organic cause for erectile dysfunction.

The urologist usually coordinates efforts to diagnose and treat erectile dysfunction, performing the initial examination and referring the patient for consultations with other health care professionals such as sex therapists, psychologists, psychiatrists, marital counselors, endocrinologists, or neurologists.

TREATMENT

Therapy depends upon the specific cause of erectile dysfunction in the individual patient, his mental, physical, marital, and social conditions, age, interests and goals, and toleration of therapy.

Sex Therapy (Behavioral Therapy). Appropriate for patients without organic cause of erectile dysfunction. This therapy focuses on patient education and reduction of performance anxiety. Involving the partner in the therapy process accelerates the success of behavioral therapy.

Hormones (Such as Testosterone). Indicated only in patients with documented low testosterone levels. Injections with testosterone are generally not very effective and occasionally cause serious side effects, such as prostate enlargement and infertility. Currently, there are no highly effective oral medications.

Penile Self-injections with Vasoactive Drugs. These increase the blood flow into the penis, as well as decrease the blood flow out of the penis. Utilized in the treatment of organic erectile dysfunction, penile injection therapy is a new alternative for diagnosing and treating most organic, but also some psychological, erectile dysfunction.

A full erection lasting for approximately one hour can be achieved by self-injection of a combination of papaverine hydrochloride and phentolamine mesylate, or prostaglandin E-1. The method is successful for approximately 85 percent to 90 percent of affected men, except for those with severe vascular damage. The incidence of complications is low, although some men will experience bruising, pain, and nodule development at the site of the injection. A few men experience priapism, which can be treated with vasoconstrictor medication. (If priapism occurs, this condition must be treated promptly; see "Priapism" earlier in this chapter.)

Any injection-induced erection that lasts longer than 4 hours should be immediately reported to the urologist.

The Vacuum Constriction Device. A nonsurgical, external device that induces erection by applying negative pressure to fill the penis with blood and traps the blood with a rubber ring at the base of the penis. This treatment is simple and noninvasive. Disadvantages include pain, numbness in the penis, dangling erection, and nonacceptance by patient or partner. Main contraindications are hematologic disorders and the use of blood thinners such as coumarin (Coumadin).

Implanted Penile Prostheses. Can be used if intracavernosal injections are impractical or vacuum devices are not successful.

Penile prostheses are very simple semirigid devices that produce a permanent erection; more complex systems with inflatable cylinders can be pumped up or deflated on demand. While semirigid prostheses are least inexpensive, they produce a constant erection, which at times can be cumbersome or embarrassing.

Inflatable prostheses—pumps that manually transfer fluid from a reservoir into cylindrical balloons implanted within the penis—are sophisticated devices that during the nonfunctional, or flaccid, state are indistinguishable from normal penises. When inflated, this type produces an excellent erection, essentially duplicating a normal erection. However, these devices may have problems resulting from a complicated surgical implantation process as well as from mechanical failures.

The technology of penile prostheses has progressed significantly, and recent models have rectified many earlier mechanical difficulties.

Microvascular Surgery. Corrects erectile dysfunction by correcting abnormal blood flow to and from the penis. This innovative treatment works best in young, otherwise healthy patients who have suffered erectile dysfunction as a result of trauma.

PREVENTION

Because of the myriad possible causes of erectile dysfunction, there are no reliable preventive measures. Avoidance of alcohol and prolonged heavy smoking—which may restrict blood flow to the penis—may help prevent erectile dysfunction in some men.

HEMATOSPERMIA

DEFINITION

Hematospermia is the presence of blood in the ejaculate, a frightening urologic phenomenon. While blood usually gives the semen only a slight pink or brownish tinge, at times the ejaculate may appear bright red.

CAUSE AND DIAGNOSIS

Blood in the semen may be the result of inflammation due to a viral or bacterial infection.

TREATMENT

Hematospermia is most often a self-limiting process, and in general no treatment is necessary. If the ejaculate continues to be bloody, the individual should consult a urologist, who will try to determine an underlying cause.

RETROGRADE EJACULATION

DEFINITION

Retrograde ejaculation occurs when at orgasm the ejaculate is propelled back into the bladder rather than through the urethra and out the tip of the penis. Retrograde ejaculation in itself is a harmless phenomenon. If fertility is desired, however, this condition must be corrected.

CAUSE AND DIAGNOSIS

Retrograde ejaculation occurs most often in males with diabetes (due to impairment of nerves in the bladder and bladder neck allowing ejaculate to flow backward). In fact, it may be the first manifestation of abnormal sexual function associated with this disease. Additionally, certain medications, especially those prescribed for mood alteration, may cause ejaculatory abnormalities.

TREATMENT

If this condition is caused by medication, it may be corrected when medication is discontinued. Oral medications that help contract bladder neck muscles (such as Sudafed) may help. Otherwise, sperm may be retrieved from the bladder for artificial insemination.

PREMATURE EJACULATION

DEFINITION

Premature ejaculation is the inability to delay ejaculation long enough to achieve satisfactory sexual function.

CAUSE

Premature ejaculation is not associated with organic or physical abnormalities. Its causes are primarily psycho-

logical. Medication is not associated with premature ejaculation, but drugs such as Prozac may cause retarded ejaculation.

DIAGNOSIS

This condition is generally recognized by the patient's complaint of inability to delay orgasm and maintain erection.

TREATMENT

Premature ejaculation is treated with basic sexual therapy techniques.

When a man first experiences premature ejaculation, he may isolate himself from the sexual act in an attempt to delay ejaculation. This approach is detrimental to gaining better control because he becomes less aware of imminent ejaculation. Rather, he should become more involved with sexual activity so that he can more accurately perceive the feeling of inevitability. When he feels this sensation, he should withdraw his penis (or discontinue stimulation if this occurs during foreplay) and he or his partner should apply gentle pressure to the head of the penis with the index finger and thumb. This suppresses what would otherwise be an inevitable climax, and sexual activity can continue.

With patience, this "squeeze" technique generally results in better ejaculatory control. If, however, this cannot be attained, sex therapy is generally successful in dealing with the problem since premature ejaculation rarely represents a physical malfunction.

SUMMING UP

The genitourinary system is an intricate network of organs with specific functions and interrelationships: The kidneys, ureters, bladder, and urethra in both men and women are necessary for the normal production, storage, and evacuation of urine. Any change in urination should be a warning signal of potential problems and should be brought to the attention of a physician.

The male reproductive system is a complex network dependent upon the proper working of all its components for sexual and reproductive function. The treatment of male infertility and male erectile dysfunction has recently become much more enlightened and sophisticated. Since specialists are now well equipped to deal with problems of male reproductive and sexual function, individuals with these maladies should seek professional help promptly.

Symptoms and Diagnoses

11

Symptoms and the Diagnostic Process

....

MICHAEL SHELANSKI, M.D.

A doctor's diagnosis invariably begins with a review of your medical history and a careful description of any symptoms or signs of disease that you may be experiencing. Your being able to provide complete and accurate information is a critical step in the process, so before you see a doctor, take time to organize medical records and to clarify what is troubling you so you can answer your doctor's questions completely and accurately.

PERSONAL AND FAMILY MEDICAL HISTORY

If you are seeing a new doctor, you will be asked to complete a form detailing your medical history. Typically, you will be asked about everything from childhood illnesses to hospitalizations, operations, and previous or present diseases. Use the forms in appendix D to prepare for this part of your medical visit.

FAMILY TREE

In addition to your own personal medical history, pay particular attention to your family tree. If possible, record any chronic diseases and the cause of death for as many of the preceding generations as you can. This information can provide vital clues to a doctor trying to track down an unusual genetic disease. Perhaps more important, it is also invaluable in developing a preventive approach to health maintenance. A family history of heart disease, high blood pressure, and other common killers that appear to have a hereditary component alerts you and your doctor to your increased vulnerability so that you can tailor your lifestyle to minimize your risk. You may also be advised to undergo more frequent screening examinations. If, for example, you find a family history of colon cancer, you may be advised to undergo periodic colonoscopy or other screening examinations for this disease, even if you are free of symptoms.

Be prepared to do a bit of detective work when filling in the relevant details in your family tree. Even if you never knew your great-grandparents, there are many sources of information you can tap—a family Bible, old scrapbooks, even old photographs, which can provide information about such traits as obesity, osteoporosis, rheumatoid arthritis, and other diseases that are visible. Most families also have an unofficial family historian who can provide information about the health and longevity of previous generations.

MEDICAL RECORDS

If you are uncertain about aspects of your own health history, you have a right to seek access to your medical records from hospitals and physicians. Whether you have a legal right to obtain the records themselves varies from state to state, but in most, you can either request a copy or at least see your medical records. If you are switching doctors or a managed care group, you can request that your current records be transferred to your new health care provider. Of course, it's also a good idea to keep your own medical records. (Again, use the forms in appendix D.)

VITAL INFORMATION

In addition to completing a health history and being prepared to describe any signs or symptoms, be especially diligent about providing information about the following:

- *Allergies.* List all allergies and sensitivities, especially to medicines, foods, and chemicals.
- *Results of previous tests.* If possible, take with you lab reports, x-rays, and other such materials.
- *Medications.* Make a list of all drugs that you now take. Don't overlook oral contraceptives, nonprescription medications such as allergy pills, vitamin and mineral supplements, and alternative remedies such as herbal preparations. Include dosages and brand names. Some experts recommend actually taking all medications with you so a doctor can quickly see what you are taking and whether you might be at risk for an adverse drug interaction. (For more information, see chapter 34.)
- *Previous adverse drug reactions or side effects.* This knowledge is important because many medications are chemically related.
- *Pregnancy.* Let the doctor know if you are pregnant or there is any chance that you might be pregnant.
- *Pacemaker or other implanted device.* This information is important because some examinations, such as magnetic resonance imaging, should not be done on patients who have certain electronic or metal devices in their body.
- *Any forms of treatment you are now undergoing.* In addition to describing other medical treatments, be sure to include any home remedies or alternative therapies, such as dietary remedies, enemas, herbal or natural medicines, chiropractic treatments, and homeopathy.

DESCRIBING YOUR SYMPTOMS

Before going to your doctor, it's a good idea to make an inventory of all signs and symptoms, even if they may seem unrelated to your primary complaint. In addition, be prepared to describe each in as much detail as possible. Use the following guidelines to focus your narrative.

IN GENERAL

- When did the problem develop?
- How did it develop? For example, did it come on suddenly or evolve over time?
- Have you had this problem before? If so, how is it the same (or different)?
- Do other members of your family or close associates have a similar problem?
- What is the pattern or chronological order of your symptoms? For example, do they occur at the same time each day? Are there any warning signs?
- Is there any order in which your symptoms occur? Can you identify any triggering events? For example, do they develop after you eat? Go outdoors? Move about?
- Does anything alleviate your symptoms? Make them worse?

RELATED EVENTS

- What else is going on in your life? For example, are you under unusual stress?
- Have you done anything different or unusual recently? For example, have you traveled? Changed jobs? Acquired a pet or new member of your household?

PAIN

- What is its nature? Is it sharp or dull? Intense or mild? Steady or intermittent? Localized or widespread? Can you alleviate it yourself? If so, how?
- What provokes it? What brings relief?

SIGNS AND SYMPTOMS

In medical terms, a sign is any visible indication of disease; for example, inflammation, swelling, bleeding, a rash or other change in skin color. A symptom is something you experience or feel such as pain, dizziness, nausea, fever, or general malaise. Be prepared to give an accurate and complete description of any sign or symptom, regardless of whether it seems trivial or unrelated to your major complaint.

It's also vital to be as open and honest as possible. Although your doctor will ask questions, don't expect that he or she will stumble on what is truly worrying you. Many people are reluctant to talk about the intimate details of their lives, especially to a doctor or other health professional. Even if you find such openness embarrassing or difficult, try to overcome any reticence. When describing your own symptoms, give as much detail as possible (see box above).

The following box lists common signs and symptoms, their possible causes, and tests or procedures that may be indicated by their presence. Chapter 12 describes what to expect in commonly performed tests and procedures.

TABLE 11.1: COMMON SIGNS AND SYMPTOMS

Note: The following is not a definitive list of all signs and symptoms, nor does it list all of the myriad causes and diagnostic studies. In many instances, a doctor can establish a diagnosis on the basis of a medical history and your description of symptoms. When tests are needed, this table lists some of the possible choices.

Symptom and Site	Possible Causes	Possible Diagnostic Studies
Appetite Loss (*Note:* This is a common component of AIDS, cancer, and many other diseases, and must be studied as part of overall condition)	Depression and other psychological disorders	Psychological testing
	Digestive disorders	Blood studies, GI x-rays, and other studies depending upon underlying cause condition
	Eating disorders	Psychological testing
Belching	Gallbladder disease	Blood studies, CT scan, ultrasonography, x-rays
	Gastritis or indigestion	Possible endoscopy and studies to measure gastric acid
	Malabsorption syndromes	Blood studies, stool analysis, endoscopy, colonoscopy, GI series, possible chromosome studies
Bleeding and Bruises Gums	Peridontal disease	Dental examination
	Vitamin deficiency	Blood studies
Eye hemorrhages	Diabetes	Blood glucose measurements, eye examination
	High blood pressure	Eye examination
	Injuries	Eye examination, possible x-rays
Nose	Clotting disorder	Blood studies
	Injuries	Possible x-rays and other imaging studies
	Polyps and tumors	Examination, possible imaging studies
Skin	Allergies	Allergy tests to identify allergens
	Anemia and other blood and clotting disorders	Blood studies
	Cushing's syndrome and other adrenal disorders	Blood and urine studies, measurement of hormone levels, x-rays or other imaging studies of the adrenal and pituitary glands
	Leukemia	Blood studies, analysis of bone marrow and cerebrospinal fluid
Accompanied by sputum	Lung cancer	Sputum analysis, x-rays, biopsy
	Pneumonia and other lung infections	Sputum analysis, x-rays
	Pulmonary embolism	Blood studies, chest x-rays, lung scan, measurement of arterial blood gases
	Tuberculosis	Tuberculin skin test, sputum and urine cultures, x-rays, possible biopsy

TABLE 11.1: COMMON SIGNS AND SYMPTOMS (Cont.)

Symptom and Site	Possible Causes	Possible Diagnostic Studies
Bleeding and Bruises		
Stool or rectum	Colon cancer, polyps, diverticulitis, colitis, and other intestinal disorders	Colonoscopy or sigmoidoscopy, stool blood tests, biopsy
	Fissure, hemorrhoids, and other rectal disorders	Direct examination, perhaps with an anoscope or sigmoidoscope
	Intestinal parasites	Stool analysis
	Peptic ulcers, severe gastritis	Endoscopy
Urine	Cystitis	Urinalysis, urine culture, cystoscopy
	Kidney or bladder stones	Urine analysis, blood studies, possible x-rays or other imaging studies
	Urinary tract cancer	Urinalysis, cystoscopy, urinary tract and kidney x-rays, possible CT scan, biopsy
	Prostate disorders	Urinalysis, blood studies including PSA (prostate specific antigen) analysis, possible ultrasonography or other imaging studies, possible biopsy
Vagina	Cancer of the cervix, uterus, or vagina	Pap smear, pelvic exam, colposcopy, biopsy
	Cervical erosion, polyps, and other cervical disorders	Pelvic exam, Pap smear, colposcopy
	Hormonal disorders	Blood studies to measure hormone levels, possible imaging studies or laparoscopy
	Infection	Blood studies, pelvic exam, colposcopy, Pap smear and cultures
	Menstrual abnormalities	Blood studies, hormone studies, pelvic exam, possible D&C
	Miscarriage (or induced abortion)	Physical examination, possible D&C
Accompanied by vomit	Cirrhosis of the liver	Blood studies, liver function tests, x-rays or other imaging studies, possible biopsy
	Esophageal tear or varicies	Endoscopy, upper GI series
	Ulcers	Upper GI series and possibly other imaging studies, gastroscopy
Cardiac arrhythmias (*Note:* An ECG and Holter monitoring may be ordered to rule out heart disease regardless of cause)	Anemia	Blood studies
	Anxiety	Psychological testing
	Caffeine	Possible blood and urine studies
	Heart disease	Cardiovascular work-up including ECG, Holter monitoring, heart x-rays, echocardiography, possible tilt-table test, and other heart rhythm studies
	Hypoglycemia	Blood glucose tests
	Menopause	Pelvic examination, hormone studies
	Thyroid disorders	Blood studies, measurement of thyroid hormones

TABLE 11.1: COMMON SIGNS AND SYMPTOMS (Cont.)

Symptom and Site	Possible Causes	Possible Diagnostic Studies
Constipation (*Note:* diet, inactivity, drugs, laxative overuse, and other life-style factors are most common causes)	Appendicitis	Blood studies, urinalysis, possible ultrasonography
	Colon cancer, bowel obstruction	Sigmoidoscopy or colonoscopy
	Hypothyroidism	Thyroid studies
	Irritable bowel syndrome	Blood studies, stool analysis, lower GI series, colonoscopy
Cough	Bronchitis	Sputum analysis, chest x-ray, bronchoscopy, possible pulmonary function tests if problem is chronic
	Common cold, croup, flu, pneumonia, or other respiratory infection	Any of the above depending upon severity of symptoms
	Cystic fibrosis	Laboratory analysis of sweat, stools, and digestive juices
	Lung cancer	Sputum analysis, chest x-ray, bronchoscopy, biopsy
Delirium (*Note:* A high fever and many serious diseases can cause delirium)	Alcohol/drug abuse	Blood and urine studies
	Brain tumor, abscess, or head injury	X-rays and CT or MRI scans, EEG, possible blood studies, and cerebrospinal fluid analysis
	Encephalitis	Blood studies, cerebrospinal fluid analysis, x-rays
	Psychosis or other mental illness	Psychological testing
Diarrhea (*Note:* AIDS and many other diseases include diarrhea as a symptom)	Celiac disease, sprue, and other malabsorption syndromes	Blood and stool studies, x-rays, possible endoscopy, and intestinal biopsy
	Colitis, Crohn's disease, and other inflammatory bowel disorders	Blood studies, GI x-rays, colonoscopy, possible intestinal biopsy
	Food poisoning	Stool analysis
	Giardiasis and other intestinal parasitic disorders	Blood and stood studies
	Traveler's diarrhea and other intestinal infections	Same as above
Fainting	Blood loss and shock	Assessment of vital signs, measurement of blood volume, fluids, and electrolytes
	Cardiac arrhythmias, heart attack or other heart conditions	ECG, Holtor monitoring, tilt-table test and other heart studies depending upon underlying cause
	Hyperventilation	Possible psychological testing and tests to rule out other causes
	Hypoglycemia	Blood glucose measurement
	Stroke	Blood and cerebrospinal fluid studies, x-rays, CT or MRI scans, neurological work-up

TABLE 11.1: COMMON SIGNS AND SYMPTOMS (Cont.)

Symptom and Site	Possible Causes	Possible Diagnostic Studies
Fatigue (*Note:* Fatigue is a common symptom in many chronic and acute diseases, and must be assessed as part of overall condition)	Anemia	Blood studies, possible bone marrow studies, GI studies, and other tests to identify cause
	Cancer	Tests depend upon type of cancer
	Depression	Psychological testing
	Infections, including AIDS, mononucleosis, and numerous other diseases	Blood and urine studies, possible cultures, x-rays, and other tests depending upon site and organism
Fever	Common component of many diseases, and must be assessed as part of overall condition	
Flatulence (*Note:* Diet and other lifestyle factors should be investigated)	Colic	Possible blood studies and other tests to rule out other diseases
	Irritable bowel syndrome and other colon disorders	Blood studies, colonoscopy, lower GI x-ray studies
	Lactose intolerance	Blood studies, lactose tolerance test, possible GI x-rays
	Malabsorption syndromes	Blood and stool studies, GI x-rays, possible chromosome studies
Gait Changes	Arthritis	Blood studies, x-rays, possible analysis of joint fluid
	Back disorders	X-rays, CT or MRI scans
	Multiple sclerosis and other neuromuscular disorders	Blood studies, EEG, x-rays and CT or MRI scans, possible muscle biopsy
	Parkinson's disease	Blood studies, EEG
	Stroke	Blood and cerebrospinal fluid studies, x-rays, CT or MRI scans, neurological work-up
Hirsutism	Cancer	Tests depend upon type of cancer
	Cushing's syndrome and other adrenal disorders	Blood and urine studies, measurement of hormone levels, x-rays or other imaging studies of the adrenal and pituitary glands
	Drug side effects	Blood studies
	Polycystic ovaries and other ovarian or hormonal disorders	Blood studies, laparoscopy, ultrasonography or other imaging studies
Insomnia (*Note:* Insomnia is often related to life-style factors such as jet lag or erratic work hours, which must be considered during diagnosis)	Alcohol or caffeine use	Blood studies
	Anxiety, depression, and other psychological problems	Psychological testing
	Thyroid disorder	Blood studies to measure levels of thyroid hormone

TABLE 11.1: COMMON SIGNS AND SYMPTOMS (Cont.)

Symptom and Site	Possible Causes	Possible Diagnostic Studies
Itching (*Note:* Itching is a common component of numerous skin conditions that may be readily apparent)	Allergies	Skin tests and other allergy studies
	Athlete's foot and other fungal infections	Laboratory analysis of skin or nail samples, Wood's lamp inspection
	Kidney disease	Blood and urine studies, x-rays, and kidney scans
	Liver disease	Blood studies, liver function tests, x-rays, possible liver biopsy
	Polycythemia	Blood and bone marrow studies, kidney x-rays, radioactive chromium studies
	Scabies and other skin parasites	Visual inspection and microscopic study of parasite
	Stress	Psychological testing
	Vaginitis	Pelvic exam, Pap smear, possible culture
Jaundice	Anemia	Blood studies, possible bone marrow studies, GI studies, and other tests to identify type and cause
	Cirrhosis, hepatitis, and other liver disorders	Blood studies, liver function tests, x-rays and other imaging studies, possible liver biopsy
	Gallbladder disease	Blood studies, ultrasonography, possible CT scan and other imaging studies
	Pancreatic disorders	Blood and urine studies, radioisotope scans and x-rays, and possible CT scan of pancreas
Lightheadedness or Dizziness	Alcohol or drug abuse	Blood studies
	Anemia	Blood studies, possible bone marrow studies, GI studies, and other tests to identify type and cause
	Brain tumor and other brain disorders	CT or MRI scans, possible biopsy
	Cardiac arrhythmia and other heart disorders	ECG and other heart tests depending upon underlying problem
	Ear infection	Ear examination, possible cultures and blood studies
	Ménière's disease	Audiometry, head x-rays
	Stroke or ministroke	Blood and cerebrospinal fluid studies, x-rays, CT or MRI scans, neurological work-up
Memory Loss or Mental Confusion	Alcoholism or drug abuse	Blood and urine studies
	Alzheimer's disease	CT or MRI scans and other brain studies
	Depression and other mental illnesses	Psychological testing
	Head injuries	X-rays, CT or MRI scans
	Stroke or ministroke	Blood and cerebrospinal fluid studies, x-rays, CT or MRI scans, neurological work-up

TABLE 11.1: COMMON SIGNS AND SYMPTOMS (Cont.)

Symptom and Site	Possible Causes	Possible Diagnostic Studies
Mood changes	Alcohol or drug abuse	Blood and urine studies
	Depression, stress, and other psychological disorders	Psychological testing
	Diabetes	Blood glucose measurements
	Hormonal disorders	Blood tests, hormone studies, possible imaging studies
	Menopause	Pelvic examination, possible hormone studies
	Premenstrual syndrome	Pelvic examination
Nausea and Vomiting (*Note:* These are components of any illnesses, and must be assessed with other symptoms)	Alcohol or drug abuse	Blood and urine studies
	Appendicitis	Blood studies, urinalysis, possible ultrasonography
	Head injury	X-rays, CT or MRI scans
	Drug reaction	Blood and urine studies
	Ear infection	Ear examination, possible blood tests
	Food poisoning	Blood studies, possible stool analysis
	Gallbladder disease	Blood studies, CT scan, ultrasonography, x-rays
	Gastritis or indigestion	Possible endoscopy and studies to measure gastric acid
	Glaucoma	Tonometry
	Heart attack	ECG, blood pressure measurement, cardiac enzyme levels, possible cardiac catheterization, and other tests
	Hepatitis and other liver disorders	Blood studies, liver function tests, x-rays, possible liver biopsy
	Ménière's disease	Audiometry, water-caloric test, head x-rays, possible CT or MRI scan
	Morning sickness	Pregnancy tests
	Ulcers	Upper GI barium studies, endoscopy
	Vertigo	Audiometry, water-caloric test, head x-rays, possible CT or MRI scan
Nervousness or Anxiety	Alcoholism, drugs	Blood studies, psychological testing
	Panic attacks	Possible psychological testing, otherwise no specific tests
	Premenstrual syndrome	Gynecological examination to rule out organic causes; otherwise no specific tests
	Stress	No specific tests
	Thyroid disorders	Blood tests to measure levels of thyroid hormone

TABLE 11.1: COMMON SIGNS AND SYMPTOMS (Cont.)

Symptom and Site	Possible Causes	Possible Diagnostic Studies
Numbness or Tingling	Bell's palsy	Possible x-rays and CT scan
	Carpal tunnel syndrome	Electromyography, x-rays of hands and wrist
	Circulatory disorders	Blood studies, Doppler ultrasonography, angiography
	Neuropathy	Neurologic studies
	Raynaud's disease	Blood studies, x-rays of hands and feet, possible thermography of hands and feet
	Shingles	No special tests other than physical examination
Pain (*Note:* Pain is a common component of most disorders, and must be assessed in context of location and other symptoms)		
Abdomen	Appendicitis	Blood studies, urinalysis, possible ultrasonography
	Digestive disorders	Gastric acid analysis, x-rays studies, possible endoscopy or colonoscopy
	Gallstones	Blood studies, CT scan, ultrasonography, x-rays
	Gastritis or indigestion	Possible endoscopy and studies to measure gastric acid
	Gynecological disorders	Pelvic examination, possible laparoscopy
	Hepatitis and other liver disorders	Blood studies, liver function tests, x-rays, possible liver biopsy
Back	Arthritis	Blood studies, x-rays, possible arthroscopy
	Muscle spasms or strain	Possible x-rays
	Osteoporosis	Blood studies, x-rays, bone density studies
	Ruptured disk	X-rays, neurological tests, CT or MRI scan
Chest	Angina	ECG, exercise tolerance tests, chest x-ray, possible angiography and other heart tests
	Esophageal disorders	Upper GI barium studies, esophagoscopy, possible endoscopy
	Heart attack	ECG, blood pressure measurement, cardiac enzymes, possible catheterization and other heart studies
	Heartburn	ECG (to rule out a heart attack), upper GI barium studies, gastric acid analysis, possible endoscopy
	Pleurisy	Check x-rays, possible biopsy and analysis of pleural fluid
	Pneumonia	Chest x-rays, blood studies, sputum culture, possible arterial blood gases
	Pneumothorax	Chest x-rays

TABLE 11.1: COMMON SIGNS AND SYMPTOMS (Cont.)

Symptom and Site	Possible Causes	Possible Diagnostic Studies
Pain		
Ear	Infection	Ear examination, blood studies, possible culture of ear discharge
	Foreign body	Ear examination
Eye	Conjunctivitis	Ophthalmoscopy, possible culture of eye discharge
	Glaucoma	Tonometry
	Foreign body	Ophthalmoscopy, possible x-rays or CT scan
	Iritis	Ophthalmoscopy, blood studies and other tests to identify underlying causes
	Sinus infection	X-rays of sinuses
	Injuries	Ophthalmoscopy, x-rays or CT scan
	Sty	Possible culture
	Tumors	Ophthalmoscopy, x-rays or CT scan, possible biopsy
Foot	Arthritis	X-rays
	Bunions	X-rays
	Corns and calluses	Visual examination
	Gout	Blood studies, x-rays
	Neuromas	X-rays
	Warts	Visual examination, possible biopsy
Generalized Aches	Flu	Possible blood studies
	Mononucleosis	Blood studies
	Rheumatoid arthritis	Blood studies, x-rays
	Shingles	Possible blood studies
Head and face	Bell's palsy	Possible x-rays and CT scan
	Brain tumor	Blood and cerebrospinal fluid studies, x-rays, electroencephalography, CT or MRI scan, possible biopsy
	Dental disease	Dental x-rays
	Migraine and other headaches	Blood studies, possible x-rays, CT or MRI scan
	Muscle tension	Possible electromyography
	Sinusitis	X-rays of sinuses
	Stroke	Blood and cerebrospinal fluid studies, x-rays, CT or MRI scans, neurological work-up
	TMJ syndrome	X-rays of temporomandibular joint

TABLE 11.1: COMMON SIGNS AND SYMPTOMS (Cont.)

Symptom and Site	Possible Causes	Possible Diagnostic Studies
Pain		
Joint/muscle	Arthritis	X-rays
	Bursitis	X-rays
	Strains and sprains	X-rays
	Tendinitis	X-rays
Knee	Arthritis	X-rays
	Chondromalacia patella	X-rays, possible arthroscopy
	Lyme disease	Blood studies, possible x-rays
	Strains and other injuries	X-rays
Leg	Circulatory disorders	X-rays, possible angiography, Doppler ultrasonography
	Fractures and other injuries	X-rays
	Phlebitis	Blood studies, ultrasonography, possible radioactive fibrinogen, venography
	Shin splints	X-rays
Mouth	Canker sores	Possible biopsy to rule out oral cancer
	Cold sores	Possible culture to rule out other infections
	Dental cavities and gum disease	X-rays
	Infections	Blood studies, possible cultures
Neck	Arthritis	X-rays
	Meningitis	Blood and cerebrospinal fluid analysis
	Muscle injury	Possible x-rays, electromyography
	Ruptured disk	X-rays, CT or MRI scans
Throat	Cold or flu	Possible culture
	Strep infection	Blood studies, culture of throat secretions
	Tonsillitis or quinsy	Blood studies, possible culture
Painful Intercourse		
In males	Penile warts	Possible laboratory culture
	Prostatic or urethral infection	Blood and urine studies, possible culture
In females	Menopause	Pelvic examination, hormone studies
	Premenstrual syndrome	Pelvic examination
	Vaginitis	Pelvic examination, Pap smear, possible culture of discharge
In both sexes	Chlamydia, genital herpes, gonorrhea, and other sexually transmitted diseases	Blood studies and cultures
	Psychological problems	Psychological testing

TABLE 11.1: COMMON SIGNS AND SYMPTOMS (Cont.)

Symptom and Site	Possible Causes	Possible Diagnostic Studies
Rashes	Allergies	Blood studies, skin tests and other allergy tests
	Dermatitis and eczema	Possible biopsy to rule out other causes
	Drug reactions	Possible blood and urine studies
	Infectious diseases	Blood and urine studies, possible cultures
	Lupus	Blood studies, possible x-rays and other imaging studies if joints or internal organs are involved
	Rosacea	Possible biopsy to rule out other causes
	Toxic shock syndrome	Blood studies, possible blood and other cultures
Seizures	Brain tumor	Blood and cerebrospinal fluid studies, x-rays, electroencephalography, CT or MRI scan, possible biopsy
	Drug side effects	Possible blood and urine studies
	Cerebral palsy	Electroencephalography, mental function tests
	Epilepsy	Blood studies, electroencephalography, x-rays and CT or MRI scan
	Fever	Blood studies and other tests, depending upon underlying cause
	Head injuries	X-rays and CT or MRI scan
	Hypoglycemia	Blood glucose studies
	Kidney failure	Blood and urine studies, renal function tests, x-rays, possible biopsy
	Meningitis	Blood and cerebrospinal fluid studies, possible cultures
	Poisoning	Blood and urine studies
	Toxemia of pregnancy	Blood and urine studies, kidney and liver function tests
Sexual Dysfunction: Male (*Note:* Impotence is often due to drug side effects)	Alcoholism	Blood studies
	Depression and other psychological disorders	Psychological testing
	Diabetes	Blood studies, glucose tolerance test
	Sexually transmitted diseases	Blood studies, possible cultures
	Hormonal disorders	Blood studies to measure hormone levels
	Multiple sclerosis and other neuro-muscular disorders	Blood studies, EEG, x-rays and CT or MRI scans, possible muscle biopsy
	Prostatic cancer and other prostate disorders	Urinalysis, blood studies including PSA (prostate specific antigen) analysis, possible ultrasonography or other imaging studies, possible biopsy
	Thyroid disease	Blood studies to measure thyroid hormone levels

TABLE 11.1: COMMON SIGNS AND SYMPTOMS (Cont.)

Symptom and Site	Possible Causes	Possible Diagnostic Studies
Shortness of Breath	Anemia	Blood studies
	Anxiety	Psychological studies
	Asthma and other lung disorders	Spirometry and other pulmonary function tests
	Heart disease	ECG, exercise tolerance tests, chest x-ray, possible angiography and other heart tests
	Hyperventilation	Possible arterial blood gases, psychological tests
Speech Problems	Alcohol abuse	Possible blood and urine studies
	Alzheimer's disease	CT or MRI scans and other brain studies, mental function tests
	Bell's palsy	Possible x-rays and CT scan
	Multiple sclerosis	Blood studies, EEG, x-rays and CT or MRI scans, possible muscle biopsy
	Parkinson's disease	Blood studies, electroencephalography
	Stroke	Blood and cerebrospinal fluid studies, x-rays, CT or MRI scans, neurological work-up
Swallowing Problems	Anxiety	Psychological testing
	Diphtheria	Throat culture
	Esophageal disorders	Upper GI barium x-ray studies, esophagoscopy, possible gastric acid studies, possible biopsy
	Sore throat	Blood studies, throat culture
	Strep throat	Throat culture
	Tonsillitis and quinsy	Possible throat culture
Sweating	Anxiety	Psychological testing
	Drug reaction	Blood and urine studies
	Fever	Tests depend upon underlying cause
	Heart attack	ECG, blood pressure measurement, cardiac enzymes, possible catheterization and other heart studies
	Infection	Blood studies and possible culture
	Menopause	Pelvic examination, hormone studies
	Stress	Psychological studies
	Thyroid disorders	Blood studies to measure thyroid hormone levels, possible thyroid scan

TABLE 11.1: COMMON SIGNS AND SYMPTOMS (Cont.)

Symptom and Site	Possible Causes	Possible Diagnostic Studies
Swelling and Lumps		
Abdominal	Cancer	Blood tests, imaging studies, biopsy
	Heart failure	Blood and urine studies, ECG, heart x-rays, echocardiography, possible cardiac catheterization, possible heart muscle biopsy
	Hernia	Blood studies, x-rays
	Internal bleeding	Blood volume studies, x-rays, ultrasonography, and other imaging studies
	Intestinal gas	Possible x-ray studies
	Liver disease	Blood studies, liver function tests, x-rays, possible liver biopsy
	Pregnancy	Pregnancy tests
	Uterine tumor	Pelvic examination, ultrasonography, possible D&C
Breast	Cancer	Mammography, biopsy
	Fibrocystic condition	Mammography, possible biopsy
	Mastitis	Possible culture
	Pregnancy	Pregnancy tests
Generalized	Anaphylactic reaction	Blood tests, possible allergy testing after crisis is past to determine cause
	Drug reaction	Blood and urine tests
	Heart failure	Blood and urine studies, ECG, heart x-rays, echocardiography, possible cardiac catheterization, possible heart muscle biopsy
	Hormone disorders	Blood and urine studies, hormone levels, possible imaging studies
	Kidney disease	Blood and urine studies, renal function tests, possible scans
	Liver disease	Blood studies, liver function tests, x-rays, possible liver biopsy
	Thyroid disorders	Blood studies to measure thyroid hormone levels, possible thyroid scan
Joints	Arthritis	X-rays, possible blood studies
	Sprains	X-rays

TABLE 11.1: COMMON SIGNS AND SYMPTOMS (Cont.)

Symptom and Site	Possible Causes	Possible Diagnostic Studies
Swelling and Lumps Skin or body surface	Abscess	Possible cultures, blood studies
	Cysts and other benign growths	Possible biopsy
	Cancer	Blood studies, x-rays and other imaging studies, biopsy
	Enlarged or obstructed lymph glands	Blood studies, x-rays and other imaging studies
	Ganglion	Possible x-rays and biopsy
	Hives	Allergy tests
	Infection	Blood studies and cultures
Taste Changes	Bell's palsy	Possible x-rays and CT scan
	Cancer	Blood studies, x-rays and other imaging studies, biopsy
	Drug reaction	Possible blood and urine studies
	Gastritis	Possible endoscopy and studies to measure gastric acid
	Gum and dental disease	Dental examination and x-rays
	Loss of smell	Possible x-rays and CT or MRI scan
	Pregnancy	Pregnancy tests
	Salivary disorders	Blood studies, possible x-rays or CT scan
Thirst	Anemia	Blood studies
	Diabetes	Blood and urine studies, glucose tolerance test
	Fever	Tests depend upon underlying cause
	Heat exhaustion	Blood tests
	Malaria	Blood tests and cultures
Tinnitus (Ringing in the Ears)	Anemia	Blood tests
	Brain injuries and tumors	X-rays and CT or MRI scan, possible electroencephalography
	Colds and flu	Possible cultures
	Drug side effects	Blood and urine studies
	Ear infections	Ear examination, possible cultures of discharge
	Ménière's disease	Audiometry, head x-rays
	Earwax buildup	Ear examination
	Otosclerosis	Ear examination, hearing tests including audiogram, Rinne test
	Vertigo	Audiometry, water-caloric test, head x-rays, possible CT or MRI scan

TABLE 11.1: COMMON SIGNS AND SYMPTOMS (Cont.)

Symptom and Site	Possible Causes	Possible Diagnostic Studies
Tremor	Alcoholism	Blood and urine tests
	Anxiety	Psychological testing
	Parkinson's disease	Blood studies, electroencephalography
	Thyroid disorders	Blood tests to measure thyroid hormone levels, possible thyroid scan
Urinary Problems		
Discolored urine	Bladder or kidney infection	Blood studies, cystoscopy, possible cultures
	Kidney stones	Blood and urine studies, possible x-rays, or ultrasonography
	Liver disease	Blood studies, liver function tests, x-rays, possible liver biopsy
	Urinary tract cancer	Blood and urine studies, x-rays and other imaging studies, possible laparoscopy, cystoscopy
Incontinence	Aging	Urinalysis, possible nerve and muscle function studies
	Bladder disorder	Urinalysis, cystoscopy
	Nerve deterioration	Nerve studies
	Spinal injury	MRI, nerve studies
	Stroke	Blood and cerebrospinal fluid studies, x-rays, CT or MRI scans, neurological work-up
Urgency	Cystitis	Urinalysis, possible cultures, possible cystoscopy
	Diabetes	Blood and urine studies, glucose tolerance test
	Drug reaction	Blood and urine studies
	Enlarged prostate	Rectal examination, ultrasonography, possible MRI scan, possible biopsy
	Pregnancy	Pregnancy tests
Painful urination	Bladder infection	Urinalysis, possible cultures and cystoscopy
	Gonorrhea and other sexually transmitted diseases	Blood studies and possible cultures
	Kidney infection	Urinalysis, renal scan
	Prostatitis	Rectal examination, possible ultrasonography and biopsy
	Urethritis	Urinalysis and cultures
	Vaginitis	Pelvic examination, Pap smear, possible cultures
Vaginal Discharge	Cancer	Pap smear, biopsy
	Cervicitis	Pap smear, possible cultures
	Gonorrhea and other sexually transmitted diseases	Blood studies and possible cultures
	Pregnancy	Pregnancy tests
	Vaginitis	Pelvic examination, Pap smear, possible cultures or biopsy

TABLE 11.1: COMMON SIGNS AND SYMPTOMS (Cont.)

Symptom and Site	Possible Causes	Possible Diagnostic Studies
Vision Problems	Cataracts	Ophthalmoscopy
	Detached retina	Ophthalmoscopy, possible CT or MRI scan
	Glaucoma	Tonometry
	Iritis	Ophthalmoscopy, possible other tests to find underlying cause
	Macular degeneration	Ophthalmoscopy, vision tests
	Stroke and ministroke	Blood and cerebrospinal fluid studies, x-rays, CT or MRI scans, neurological work-up
	Retinopathy	Ophthalmoscopy
Weakness	Arthritis	X-rays
	Cancer	Blood studies and other tests depending upon site
	Guillain-Barré syndrome	Blood and cerebrospinal fluid studies, neurological examination
	Multiple sclerosis and other neuromuscular disorders	Blood studies, EEG, x-rays and CT or MRI scans, possible muscle biopsy
Weight Changes Unexplained gain	Heart failure	Blood and urine studies, ECG, heart x-rays, echocardiography, possible cardiac catheterization, possible heart muscle biopsy
	Hypothyroidism	Blood studies, thyroid hormone levels
	Liver disease	Blood studies, liver function tests, x-rays, possible liver biopsy
	Toxemia of pregnancy	Blood and urine studies, kidney and liver function studies
Unexplained loss	AIDS	Blood studies
	Anemia	Blood studies
	Cancer	Blood studies and other tests, depending upon site
	Diabetes	Blood and urine studies, glucose tolerance test
	Eating disorders	Psychological testing
	Infection	Blood and urine studies, possible cultures
	Intestinal disorders	Upper and lower GI x-ray series, possible endoscopy, and other studies, depending upon nature of disorder
	Intestinal parasites	Stool analysis
	Malabsorption syndrome	Blood studies, stool analysis, possible colonoscopy, intestinal biopsy
	Ulcers	Upper GI x-ray studies, stool analysis for blood, endscopy

12
Diagnostic Tests and Procedures

MICHAEL SHELANSKI

Parts of this chapter are adapted from the chapter by Raymond Gambino, M.D., which appeared in the revised second edition

Diagnostic tests are an extension of a physical examination and history. They allow the doctor to see things that are not yet visible or to confirm what the doctor or the patient already suspects.

In earliest times, women knew they were pregnant when their bellies grew and they felt their babies move. They soon realized that missing a menstrual period meant the possibility of pregnancy. Then doctors learned that by examining the cervix they could see changes in the color of the cervix and character of the mucus, which signaled pregnancy before the more obvious physical signs.

The famous rabbit test took them one step further, faster. It grew out of the observation that not long after the fertilized egg is implanted in the uterus, the placenta begins to manufacture a hormone called human chorionic gonadotropin. Although the hormone is present in increasing quantities in the pregnant woman's urine, it can't be seen. However, if the urine is injected into the female rabbit, the rabbit's ovaries enlarge and redden. But the test takes 4 or 5 days, won't show results unless the woman is at least 4 weeks pregnant, and means sacrificing the rabbit.

Further research produced an antibody to gonadotropin, which, when mixed with the pregnant woman's blood in a test tube, can detect small amounts of the hormone. It will do this with 99 percent accuracy as early as 9 days after conception, even before the first missed period. Another test produces the same answers using urine, without taking blood and without rabbits.

The second major reason for testing—in fact, the one that accounts for the greatest volume of tests—is therapeutic drug monitoring, that is, keeping track of exactly how a prescribed drug is acting on the patient's system. Is the patient getting too much of the drug? Too little? Is it causing other body chemicals to be out of balance? A familiar example is insulin monitoring in diabetes by measuring blood sugar, a test usually performed daily by diabetics themselves. Many diabetics now test their blood sugar levels before each meal, allowing them to make small insulin adjustments that keep their disease under much better control than ever before possible. One of the goals of scientists in refining test procedures is to develop more tests that patients can do themselves so they can be done more often at less expense and with better therapeutic results.

Another goal is to be able to do more with what we have, and we seem to be making progress. A study over a 10-year period at Columbia Presbyterian Medical Center showed that while the number of new blood tests went up dramatically, the number of blood samples drawn remained constant. Eventually we may be able to test for hundreds of different diseases or conditions from the blood in one small vial.

A third goal is to make the tests simpler and less "invasive" for the patient: A whole new area of simple testing is opening up as scientists realize that saliva—a very easy specimen to collect—can tell a number of things that blood and urine may not about the level in the body of, for example, hormones in a free state.

At the other end of the technology scale from saliva testing is another relatively new noninvasive technique—magnetic resonance imaging (MRI)—which is surpassing many other techniques in sophistication and usefulness. Like the CT scan, MRI produces high-resolution pictures of the structure of various body organs. Using a powerful magnet, it can provide a look at the biochemistry of living cells without the slight risk of x-ray exposure that CT scanning carries. While CT scanners provide anatomical information about the health of organs, MRI measures the health of cells and how well they are functioning.

The more researchers learn about basic science and how the body works, the more sophisticated and accurate laboratory tests become. As we strive to find tests that are more definitive, show results earlier, and create less discomfort for the patient, the number of tests will probably continue to increase. Yet a major consideration in developing new tests is not only what they can tell the doctor about a patient but also what can be done with the knowledge. If there is no treatment for the condition, there is little solace in knowing exactly what the condition is. For this reason, test development will always follow, not lead, basic science, and this is one reason that support for basic science is so important.

BASIC TYPES OF DIAGNOSTIC TESTS

Almost all diagnostic tests fall into four basic categories: those that measure performance (exercise, heart rate, lung function, visual acuity), those that take something out of the body (a specimen) to study, those that look at the body through film or sound (x-ray, scans, ultrasound), and those that use hollow tubes and fiber optics to look inside the body directly (endoscopy).

TABLE 12.1: COMMON DIAGNOSTIC TESTS AND WHEN THEY SHOULD BE PERFORMED

Name of Test	Age at First Test	Comments	Age at Repeat Tests															
			18	19	20	21	22	23	24	25	26	27	28	29	30	31	32	33
Blood tests (anemia, diabetes, thyroid); hyperthyroid	18	Repeat tests not indicated unless symptoms; hyperthyroid for post-menopausal women																
Blood pressure	3–4	Annually	•	•	•	•	•	•	•	•	•	•	•	•	•	•	•	•
Breast exam	20	Should be supplemented by self-exam each month				•		•		•		•		•		•		
Chest x-ray		Not recommended except for those with symptoms or at high risk, such as heavy smokers																
Cholesterol	5						•				•				•		
Color perception (color blindness)	5	Not necessary to repeat																
Dental	3–4	Every 6–12 months; x-rays every 2–3 years	•	•	•	•	•	•	•	•	•	•	•	•	•	•	•	•
Electrocardiogram	20–40	Should be done once as a baseline before age 40. Not necessary to repeat until age 50 unless symptoms. After 50, every 3 years.				•												
Eye (visual accuity)	5	Annually until age 18	•			•			•			•			•			•
Hearing	5	Once during adolescence. No need for further tests unless there are symptoms.																
Mammography	35–40																	
Occult Blood Stool test	40–50																	
Pap test	16–17	Another, 1 year later. If both are negative, then at least every 3 years.					•			•			•			•		•
Pelvic exam	16–17						•		•			•			•		•
Physical exam including history	18						•								•		
Prostate	40																	
Rectal (digital)	30																	
Sigmoidoscopy (also called proctosigmoidoscopy)	50	Again at 51; if both are negative, then every 3–5 years																
Testicular exam	15	This should be supplemented by self-examination each month						•		•			•			•		

| 34 | 35 | 36 | 37 | 38 | 39 | 40 | 41 | 42 | 43 | 44 | 45 | 46 | 47 | 48 | 49 | 50 | 51 | 52 | 53 | 54 | 55 | 56 | 57 | 58 | 59 | 60 | 61 | 62 | 63 | 64 | 65 | 66 | 67 | 68 | 69 | 70 | 71 | 72 | 73 | 74 | 75 |

SPECIMEN TESTS

Purpose. Specimens take a sample of a body substance, ranging from the relatively easy to collect urine, stool, and blood samples, to body fluids that are collected through a hollow needle in a procedure known as centesis, to tissue samples collected with a similar needle through biopsy.

Preparation. Most specimen tests need no preparation. However, some blood tests require fasting for periods of up to 12 hours before the sample is drawn, and other tests may require following a special diet or avoid certain drugs for up to a week prior to the test.

Time. Time ranges from the few seconds needed to draw blood or urinate in a sterile container to a half hour or longer to take a biopsy sample of bone marrow.

Procedure. Specimen tests are usually outpatient procedures, although they are also frequently performed on hospitalized patients. They all work on the same principle. In healthy people the composition of body tissue, fluids, and waste remains relatively constant or within a normal range. When an organ of the body is not "normal" or when there is a change for any reason, from pregnancy to aging to disease, there is certain to be evidence in the body tissue or in one of the body's secretions. Besides the diseases of blood itself, such as anemia or leukemia, which result in changes in the composition or amount of various types of blood cells, there are many other conditions that can be diagnosed by examining blood samples. The same is true of urine and saliva. After the specimen is taken, it is examined by pathologists in a laboratory and may be subjected to various tests.

Risk. Most specimen tests carry little or no risk. Discomfort ranges from that of a minor needle stick to draw blood to significant pain, requiring local or general anesthesia, for certain biopsies.

RADIOGRAPHY

X-ray tests range from simple still pictures, like dental x-rays and those used to tell if a bone has been broken, to moving images of the body at work, called fluoroscopy. These images may be recorded on moving film or videotape (cineradiography), or in a series of stills taken in rapid succession. Radiography is used to show abnormalities in size, shape, position, or functioning of various parts of the body.

While some x-rays are noninvasive, meaning nothing is swallowed or injected into the body, many more sophisticated ones depend on the use of a dye or contrast medium to outline or fill parts of the body that would not ordinarily show up on an x-ray. This contrast medium may be swallowed, injected directly into an artery or vein, or fed in through a thin tube called a catheter, which may enter the body through one of its normal openings or through a small incision.

FLUOROSCOPY

Purpose. Also known as image-intensifier fluoroscopy, this is a type of x-ray image production that enables the body part under study, such as the lungs or stomach, to be observed in motion and seen on a special TV-like screen rather than on film. It is similar to the technology used to examine luggage at airports. In addition to its use as an isolated test, fluoroscopy may be used as part of other tests, such as in bronchoscopy, where it helps the doctor visualize the lung during the procedure, or as an aid in positioning for biopsy of the pancreas, liver, and other organs.

Preparation. You remove any clothing and jewelry covering the area under study. Other preparatory steps may be required, depending on the area to be evaluated.

Time. Duration of the test ranges from a few minutes to an hour, depending on the specific purpose. Results may be available immediately or within a day or two.

Procedure. Fluoroscopy may be performed in a physician's office, a commercial x-ray facility, or a hospital. It may be done by an x-ray technician, usually in the presence of a physician. The fluoroscope is suspended or held over your body to take and transmit continuous images to the video monitor.

Risk. Although radiation exposure is minimal, it is greater than for standard still x-rays. (See "Risks of Radiation" in this chapter.) There is no discomfort because nothing comes in contact with your body.

RADIOISOTOPE SCANS

Purpose. Radioisotope scanning, also called nuclear scanning or radionucleide imaging, is used to obtain information about the condition and functioning of various organs.

Preparation. Most scans need no preparation. However, some require that you fast for periods of up to 12 hours before the test, and others may require that you follow a special diet prior to the test.

Time. The duration of the test depends on the body part under study and the specific scan being performed.

Procedure. Specimen tests are usually outpatient procedures, although they are also frequently performed on hospitalized patients. Although the equipment used and the views of the body shown are similar to a CT scan, radioisotope scanning involves the use of a small amount of radioactive material. It is based on the fact that various organs absorb or concentrate specific minerals or hormones, but these substances do not show up on a regular x-ray. However, if they are made radioactive by the addition of a radioisotope, they can be seen. And if the organ is not functioning properly, too little or too much of the substance will be taken up, or it will be concentrated in some parts of the organ but not in others. The organ will look different on the screen. If a portion of the organ does not show up, it may indicate the presence of a tumor. A rectilinear scanner, gamma camera, or scintoscope is used to read or detect the isotope within the organ.

Risk. The amount of radiation is very low and the isotope disappears within a day or so. (See also "Risks of Radiation" in this chapter.) Rarely, a serious allergic reaction to the isotope occurs. The only mild discomfort involved may be related to intravenous injection of the radioactive material.

COMPUTERIZED AXIAL TOMOGRAPHY SCANS

Purpose. Computerized axial tomography, called CAT or, preferably CT scan for short, was introduced in 1972 and has grown considerably in use because it can detect so many conditions that do not show up on less sophisticated, albeit less expensive, tests. It easily detects calcium deposits often missed by simple radiography and it is more accurate than ultrasound in obese patients, when fat deposits hinder ultrasound waves. Not only can CT scans detect tumors, cysts, and abscesses, but also because of their sensitivity to variations in tissue density, they can even at times distinguish between benign and malignant tumors.

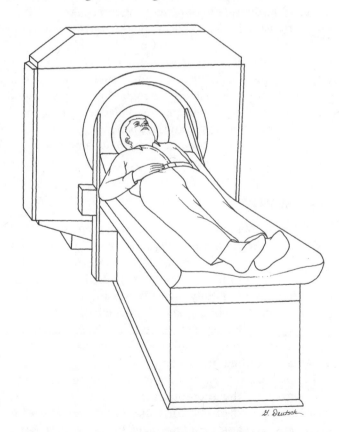

Figure 12.1: Drawing of a patient positioned in a CT scanner for a brain study. The scanning unit can be moved to make CT scans of any part of the body.

Preparation. Preparation depends on the body site under study; often none is needed.

Time. CT generally takes about 20 minutes.

Procedure. Tomography is the focusing of an x-ray on a specific plane of the body, such as a very thin cross section of an organ or the chest cavity. With computerized tomography, the x-ray beam that passes through the cross section is picked up by a detector and fed into the computer, which analyzes the information on tissue density and constructs a picture on a cathode ray tube (CRT) screen (see figure 12.1). Tissues of various density show up as different shades of gray, bone (the most dense) as white, and air and liquid as black. Conventional x-ray films are not used in CT scanning. Instead, the scanner, which both emits and detects rays, is rotated 360 degrees around the patient as he or she lies on the special table that is part of the machine. CT scanning can be used to see inside any of the body's organs, including the brain. It is an outpatient procedure.

Risk. CT is 100 times more sensitive than conventional x-rays and (some brain scans being the only exception) does not expose patients to radioactive contrast media as radioisotope scanning does. The procedure is completely painless and carries only the risk of x-ray exposure, which is minimal.

MAGNETIC RESONANCE IMAGING (MRI)

Purpose. Formally called nuclear magnetic resonance, this technique uses two elements—computer-controlled radio waves and magnetic fields that are up to 25,000 times as strong as the earth's field—to do its very sophisticated analysis. It works like this: A nucleus is the positively charged central core of an atom. Some nuclei behave like magnetic spinning tops. MRI uses a magnetic field to orient the spinning nuclei of the atoms being studied, then temporarily disturbs the orientation with a burst of energy from a radio-frequency transmitter. By measuring the amount of energy released as the spinning tops reorient themselves, scientists can measure the distribution and chemical bonds of the body's abundant hydrogen atoms or, more precisely, the single protons in hydrogen nuclei. These measurements are then translated into three-dimensional images of tissues in the body. In general, motion, such as breathing or the beating of a heart, is not well visualized. The technique is best used in examining the head, central nervous system, and spine, although it can also identify tumors, strokes, degenerative diseases, inflammation, infection, and other abnormalities in other organs and in soft tissue.

Preparation. No special preparation is necessary. Those who are inclined to claustrophobia may request a tranquilizer before the examination or may be able to wear a headset that plays calming music, if the head is not being visualized.

Time. Each MRI view takes about 5 minutes, but multiple views are often required.

Procedure. The patient is placed on a board on a large, circular magnet in a 7-foot-square box for approximately 5 minutes during which the nuclei of hydrogen atoms are excited by radio wave pulses. When the pulse is shut off, the nuclei relax, emitting radio signals that are picked up by an antenna and fed into a computer. Although the patient will not feel anything, he or she will hear loud noises—the grating of metal whipped by magnetic fields—and some may see flashes of light, called magnetic phosphenes. It is an outpatient procedure.

Risk. The magnetic fields can be used repeatedly (except on those with implants containing ferrous metal, particularly pacemakers) without known risks and are considered safer than other diagnostic procedures that expose the patient to radiation or require injection of dye into the veins. However, some people experience claustrophobia while in the device.

POSITRON EMISSION TRANSAXIAL TOMOGRAPHY

Positron emission transaxial tomography, or PET, is similar to CT scanning, but uses substances such as glucose tagged with a positron-emitting isotope to measure some body functions.

ULTRASONOGRAPHY

Purpose. Much like the sonar systems used by ships, ultrasound uses sound waves and their echoes to locate and visualize internal organs. It is particularly useful in looking at soft tissue that does not x-ray well. Although ultrasound costs considerably less and involves less risk than CT scans, it is not always as accurate and is being replaced by CT scans in some cases. But it still has many uses, such as in pregnancy, where unnecessary x-ray exposure to the fetus should be avoided. It is also very useful in examining the heart (echocardiography) because it can show the heart at work, particularly the opening and closing of the valves.

Preparation. All clothing must be removed from the area under study. Depending on the examination, other preparations may be necessary, such as drinking 2 quarts of fluid an hour ahead of time to fill the bladder before a pelvic sonogram in a pregnant woman.

Time. Depending on the area under study, ultrasonography can take from several minutes to a half hour.

Procedure. The area to be examined is first covered with a lubricant such as mineral oil. Then a transducer, a microphone-type machine that both emits sound waves and receives their echoes back again, is passed over the body in contact with the skin. An oscilloscope or computer is used to translate the sound waves into a picture on a television screen. It is an outpatient procedure.

Risk. Ultrasound is a painless and risk-free technique.

ENDOSCOPY

Purpose. Endoscopy is a general name for a number of test procedures that allow the physician to look inside the body through a hollow tube or a fiber-optic device and see internal organs directly. The endoscope, which has various names depending on its length and use, can be used to inflate a body cavity with air in order to see it better, to take samples for a slide culture or biopsy, or even to perform delicate surgery, such as a tubal ligation or repair of joint ligaments.

Preparation. In some hospitals, a mild dose of tranquilizer, such as Valium, lasting about 15 to 20 minutes, is given intravenously during endoscopy to help allay patients' anxiety. For endoscopy of the gastrointestinal system, special dietary measures, fasting, or enemas may be required beforehand.

Time. Duration of the test depends on the area under study but is usually under 30 minutes.

Procedure. The endoscopy tube may be metal and rigid, but more and more, it is likely to be made of threads of fiberglass bunched together like a cable, which transmit light and allow the doctor to see into the body and even around corners. The tube may be inserted through a surgical incision to view joints, or organs in the chest or abdominal cavity. More commonly, the tube is passed through the body's natural openings—the nose, mouth, anus, bladder, or vagina—to view various organs from the inside.

Risk. The level of discomfort and risk depends on the specific site under study.

MANOMETRY

Purpose. Manometry is a test designed to evaluate the functioning of a muscle sphincter. Two of its most common uses are as esophageal motility studies, which may be ordered for those with suspected gastroesophageal reflux or difficulty swallowing, and as anal rectal motility studies, which may be needed for those who have constipation or fecal incontinence for unknown reasons. The technique also can be used to retrain anal muscles to contract more forcefully.

Preparation. Depending on the site under study, you may have the rectum cleaned with an enema or may be required to fast for 8 hours beforehand. Children or very anxious adults may be given a sedative before anal studies. A local anesthetic is sprayed in the nose before esophageal studies.

Time. Depending on the site, manometry may take 20

to 90 minutes. Results may be available as soon as the test is completed or within a day or two.

Procedure. It may be performed in a doctor's office or hospital, usually by a physician who specializes in the area under study. The test measures pressure and movement in the canal under study, as well as sensations and reflexes of the muscle sphincter. In anal studies, a plastic or metal manometry probe is inserted about 4 inches into the rectum and then slowly withdrawn, or a latex manometry balloon may be inserted in the rectum and inflated. These devices transmit information on pressure from rectal muscles as you relax or squeeze, at the doctor's direction. In esophageal studies, a flexible probe is inserted through the nostrils and guided down the esophagus, and you are asked to swallow small amounts of fluid at intervals. The probe transmits information on esophageal contraction at various levels.

Risk. Insertion of a probe into the body carries a minor risk of bleeding. Some people have an allergic reaction to the latex manometry balloon. There may be some discomfort from having a probe inserted in the anus or through the nose into the esophagus.

WHAT TO ASK THE DOCTOR BEFORE A TEST

No one should have any medical test without being fully informed about what it entails and why the doctor is recommending it. Here are some questions a patient should ask the doctor before undergoing a test.

• Why is the test being ordered? Is it to screen for a disease that has no symptoms, such as high blood pressure? Is it because the doctor is pretty certain about a diagnosis but needs the test to confirm it? Is it because the doctor is really puzzled about the diagnosis and is trying to rule out as much as possible? Or is it even, perhaps, to placate the patient?

• How definitive is the test? Will it tell for sure that a condition is or isn't present, or must it be repeated or followed by more sophisticated tests?

• How accurate is the test? What might cause a false positive or false negative or other inaccurate result?

• How much will it cost? Some tests are included as part of a doctor's office fee, others are not. Sometimes a doctor may not charge the patient extra for performing a test, a Pap smear for example, but the patient will receive a bill from the laboratory that does the analysis. Which tests are covered by medical insurance, and to what degree, may vary from policy to policy.

• Is hospitalization required? Sometimes one hospital will require that a patient check in, while another hospital will do the same test on an outpatient basis. While the former may cost more, it also affords the opportunity to monitor the patient more closely for any side effects afterward. Although the doctor's decision will ultimately be based on what is best for the patient's health, finances should be taken into consideration and alternatives discussed.

• Is there any pain? What are the side effects? Most common tests are painless or cause only brief discomfort, such as a pinprick or needle puncture. Others can cause cramps, nausea, headache, or serious discomfort. In these cases, part of the test may involve administering a sedative, or local or general anesthesia. Side effects may last hours or longer, or may only be felt by some patients and not by others.

• What are the risks? This is the most important question. Many common tests have no risks at all. Others have risks that may range from transitory side effects to more serious problems. Invasive tests, that is, those that involve introducing instruments or substances such as barium into the body, generally have some risks. These may include infection, allergic reaction, or injury to the body, either at the site of the incision or to an internal organ. The "normal risk" for some tests may mean 1 in 100 patients will have a problem; other tests may have a long list of very rare risks that affect only 1 in 1,000 or fewer.

• What is the risk of not having the test, and what are the alternatives? This will help the patient to decide whether the risk is one that must be borne because the consequences of an undiagnosed illness may be worse.

FACTORS AFFECTING TEST RESULTS

Hundreds of thousands of diagnostic tests are performed each year, accurately and without problems, but laboratories occasionally make mistakes that lead to inaccurate results. The errors may be technical ones, such as allowing too long a delay from the time a blood sample is collected until it is tested, or unwittingly using equipment that is improperly calibrated. Occasionally, too, there are human failures.

Some errors cannot be controlled. Even a change in the weather can have an effect on test results in some patients. Other patients have genetic traits that cause abnormal results when there is actually nothing wrong.

Another cause of inaccuracy, however unwitting, may be the medicines a patient takes. There are thousands of medications, from aspirin and antacids to birth control pills and other prescription drugs that, taken by patients undergoing tests, can affect the results. Patients should report to their doctors any medication they take regularly and ask if there are any other medications they should avoid (and if so, for how long) before the test.

Instructions about eating and drinking before the test must also be followed very carefully. Results can be affected by ordinary foods like milk, coffee, and table salt. The physician may want the patient to eat specific foods for several days prior to a test, or not to eat anything at all for 6 to 12 hours before the exam.

A patient's mood and physical condition can also affect test results. A patient who is nervous about a test or has not had adequate rest should mention this to the doctor, since either can distort certain measurements. Even environmental exposure to certain chemicals can have an effect.

RISKS OF RADIATION

Medicine has come a long way from the time when fluoroscope machines could be found in every good children's shoe store so mothers could see how their children's feet looked inside new shoes. We now realize that such unnecessary exposure to x-rays is a risk that no one should take.

On the other hand, tremendous advances have been made in early and accurate diagnosis as a result of sophisticated use of radiation technology. X-rays can be lifesaving and, under the right circumstance, a patient should not hesitate to have an x-ray or a radioisotope scan. Nevertheless, there are a number of precautions that the patient and the doctor or radiation technician can take. Parents of children to be x-rayed should be especially vigilant, asking that the x-ray film cassette used be the appropriate size for the child, so that no more of the body is exposed than necessary.

Dental x-rays are probably the most common x-ray and perhaps the most overused. According to the American Dental Association, they should not be a routine part of a dental exam, but their use should be at the discretion of the dentist. The patient should wear a lead apron covering the torso.

Pregnant women should not have x-rays unless there is an absolute medically valid reason for them. (See chapter 9, Health Concerns of Women.) In fact, to guard against exposure to the fetus in an as yet undiagnosed pregnancy, a woman of childbearing age should have elective x-rays of her abdomen or pelvis only during her menstrual period or for a few days afterward. For necessary x-rays of other parts of the body, a pregnant woman should wear a lead apron.

All patients, especially those of reproductive age or younger, should have their genitals protected by a lead shield during any x-rays of the abdomen or intestines.

Since the training and experience of x-ray technicians

can vary, patients should ask whether the technician is accredited (in large hospitals or laboratories, this is usually the case). Properly trained technicians will practice the technique of "collimation"—limiting the x-ray to the specific area to be diagnosed and not including surrounding parts of the body. This is facilitated if the size of the x-ray film cassette is approximately the size of the area to be x-rayed, and not larger.

Finally, patients should keep track of when and where their x-rays were taken, to avoid possible duplication in the future. Since x-ray films and other medical records are routinely destroyed after 7 to 10 years, depending on hospital practice or state law, patients may want to request that the films, or the reports regarding them, be sent to them before that time.

DIRECTORY OF DIAGNOSTIC TESTS

The following tests are listed according to body systems or major disease groups, and are described as they are carried out at many hospitals or laboratories. Since the procedure may vary somewhat from location to location, the patient should check with the doctor about exactly how the test will be performed.

BLOOD TESTS

VENIPUNCTURE

Purpose. This routine procedure is used to obtain one or more small vials of blood for numerous tests involved in diagnosing many conditions other than blood diseases themselves. The most common ones are listed below.

Preparation. The skin is cleaned with antiseptic. Prior to certain blood tests, you must fast for 8 to 12 hours.

Time. Venipuncture takes about 5 minutes.

Procedure. Venipuncture can be done in a doctor's office or laboratory. Usually an arm vein is used, either the right or the left, depending on which one is larger or closer to the surface. A rubber tourniquet is used above the elbow to force blood into the vein and make it even more prominent. The patient may also be asked to repeatedly make a fist and open it, for the same reason. The needle is inserted near the crook of the elbow and one or more vials of blood withdrawn.

Risk. Although the patient may develop a hematoma (black and blue mark), there is virtually no risk involved in this procedure.

COMMON BLOOD ANALYSES

The following are tests commonly done using the blood specimens obtained by venipuncture.

• **Complete Blood Count (CBC).** This series analyzes the various elements within the blood, including hemoglobin concentration, hematocrit, and red and white blood counts. It can diagnose anemia and point the way to other, more specialized tests that may need to be done.

• **CBC with Differential.** Whereas the CBC merely counts white cells, the differential analyzes the type of white cells present to help identify specific infections or diseases.

• **Thyroid-Stimulating Hormone, T$_4$, T$_3$.** These are common tests of thyroid function, especially hypothyroidism and hyperthyroidism.

• **Blood Culture.** In this test, used when septicemia (blood poisoning) is suspected, the blood sample is cultured for bacteria in a laboratory and then tested to see how the bacteria respond to antibiotics.

• **Rubella.** This test identifies antibodies to rubella, also called German measles. It is recommended that all women of childbearing age have this test at least 3 months before trying to become pregnant, thus allowing time for those who do not have antibodies and are therefore not immune to receive a vaccination prior to conception. In addition, the test can determine for each individual whether vaccination will be effective and for how long.

• **Infectious Mononucleosis.** This test identifies antibodies to the Epstein-Barr virus, which causes acute infectious mononucleosis (also known as glandular fever).

• **Prothrombin Time.** This test gives an indication of blood clotting time, although the clotting factors measured are different from those in the thrombin test. "Pro time" is the more common of the two assays and is used primarily to monitor the effects of anticoagulant drugs like Coumadin, which decrease blood clotting and are used in the treatment of cardiovascular and other diseases.

• **Chromosome Analysis.** Also known as chromosome karyotype or cytogenetic testing, this test is best known for its ability to detect chromosomal disorders in the fetus during pregnancy and to evaluate couples who have produced abnormal children. It is also used to seek the cause of birth defects or other problems in children, including questionable gender, to evaluate women who have no menses, to look for the cause of infertility or repeated miscarriages, and to diagnose certain cancers or evaluate their course.

• **Oral Glucose Tolerance Test (OGTT).** This test evaluates the body's tolerance of glucose (blood sugar) and is used in the diagnosis of diabetes and hypoglycemia. You must fast for 10 to 14 hours before the test, which involves drawing several blood samples over a 2- to 3-hour period before and after you drink a glucose solution.

• **Blood Chemistry Group.** This has various commercial names, depending on the testing laboratory, but generally consists of 12 to 25 analyses, including:

Substance	Test For
Blood urea nitrogen	Kidney function
Creatinine	Kidney function
Glucose	Insulin action for the presence of diabetes
Calcium and phosphorus	Kidney function and the patient's nutritional condition
Bilirubin (conjugated and unconjugated)	Liver function
Aminotransferase enzymes	Injury to liver, muscles, heart, presence of hepatitis
Alkaline phosphatase	Liver, bone, and gallbladder diseases
Gamma glutamyl transpeptidase (GGTP)	Liver disease, excess use of alcohol
Total protein and albumin	Water balance, nutrition, liver disease
Uric acid	Gout, kidney disease
Electrolytes: including sodium, potassium, chloride, bicarbonate	Electrolyte balance, for monitoring patients on IV or diuretics
Lipids: including cholesterol, triglycerides, high-density lipoprotein (HDL), low-density lipoprotein (LDL), apolipoprotein B, apolipoprotein B, apolipoprotein A-1	Risk of coronary artery disease

CANCER TESTS

BIOPSY

Purpose. This procedure is used to obtain a tissue specimen for microscopic examination to determine malignancy.

Preparation. No special preparation is usually necessary. However, any anticipated discomfort may be alleviated with local anesthetics or a mild sedative.

Time. The time varies depending on the site and method of tissue removal. For example, taking a skin sample may take less than a minute while renal biopsy takes about 15 minutes.

Procedure. Depending on the type of tissue and its

location, this procedure may be done with a scalpel, needle, or other instrument. In renal biopsy, usually done in a hospital, the patient lies prone, with pillows or sandbags under the abdomen, while a long aspirating needle is injected into one or both kidneys and tissue is withdrawn. The procedure for liver biopsy is similar, but the patient lies on his or her back and the needle is injected between the ribs or under the ribs into the liver. Since biopsies are often done as part of endoscopic exams, they are included in those sections of this chapter and generally not listed separately. (See "Bronchoscopy," "Colonoscopy," "Colposcopy," "Cystourethroscopy," "Gastroscopy.")

Risk. The risk, which is generally small, varies with the procedure for obtaining the specimen, and may include bleeding and infection. In renal biopsy, for example, there is a possibility of bleeding or even the formation and painful passing of blood clots following this procedure.

BONE MARROW ASPIRATION

Purpose. This procedure, also called sternal tap, provides a small amount of bone marrow for analysis and is

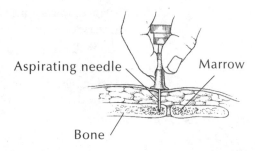

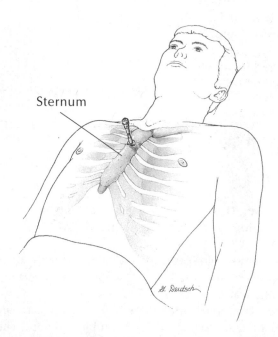

Figure 12.2: These drawings show what is involved in a bone marrow aspiration, in this instance, a sternal tap.

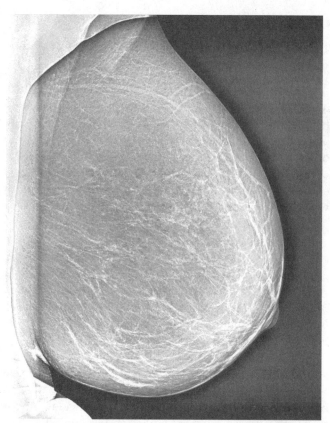

Figure 12.3: Normal mammogram.

used to diagnose leukemia and other cancers, to determine whether various cancers have metastasized, and to evaluate the effectiveness of chemotherapy. Although it is primarily used in cancer diagnosis, it can also be used to diagnose several types of anemia and infections.

Preparation. No special preparation is required. Some patients may be given a tranquilizer. A local anesthetic is given at the site of the puncture.

Time. Aspiration can be done in 5 to 10 minutes.

Procedure. A bone marrow aspiration may be done in a doctor's office or hospital outpatient clinic (see figure 12.2). The site of the puncture may be a bone in the pelvis, a rib, the breastbone, or other bone. A thin aspirating needle is inserted and a small amount of the marrow fluid withdrawn. The specimen is then placed on a slide for microscopic examination.

Risk. Although there may occasionally be some bleeding at the puncture site, more serious risks such as infection or air embolism are rare. Needle insertion and withdrawal may cause a sharp, but brief, pain, followed by some tenderness at the puncture site.

MAMMOGRAPHY

Purpose. This simple procedure provides an x-ray picture of the breast (see figure 12.3) and is used to detect tumors and cysts and to differentiate between benign and malignant tumors.

Preparation. On the day of the test, do not apply any powders, lotions, or perfumes to the breasts or underarms because they could create false-positive results.

Time. Depending on the number of films taken, the procedure may take 5 to 15 minutes. The patient may be asked to wait until the film is developed to be sure the pictures are readable.

Procedure. In an outpatient x-ray facility, the breasts are rested, one at a time, on the film cassette, and x-rays are taken from several angles. The breasts may be compressed against the cassette to get a clear picture.

Risk. Some women find the breast compression uncomfortable. The level of radiation is low, but care should be exercised so that this procedure is not overused. Approximately 90 to 95 percent of malignancies can be detected with this test, but as many as 75 percent of the tests reported as positive may in fact be false positives.

CIRCULATORY SYSTEM TESTS

ANGIOGRAPHY

Purpose. This x-ray visualization of the arteries and veins is used to detect abnormalities such as aneurysms in the blood vessels themselves as well as in the organs they serve. They can be used to locate sites of internal bleeding and blood clots.

Procedure. The procedure generally involves passing a catheter through a vein or artery in the arm or leg to the site to be studied and injecting a contrast medium to make x-ray visualization easier. (For a more specific description of the procedure and risks, see "Cardiac Catheterization" and "Phlebography.")

BONE MARROW ASPIRATION

(See under "Cancer Tests.")

CARDIAC CATHETERIZATION

Purpose. Cardiac catheterization (venous and arterial) allows the visualization of the heart and the coronary arteries that supply blood to the heart muscle. Venous, or right heart catheterization, is used to assess the functioning of the tricuspid and pulmonary valves, and can determine blood pressure and flow in the chambers of the heart and the pulmonary artery. Arterial, or left side catheterization, is used to assess the coronary arteries and the functioning of the mitral and aortic valves and the left ventricle. Since it can show if the arteries are occluded, a major cause of heart attacks, it is often used to determine if bypass surgery is necessary.

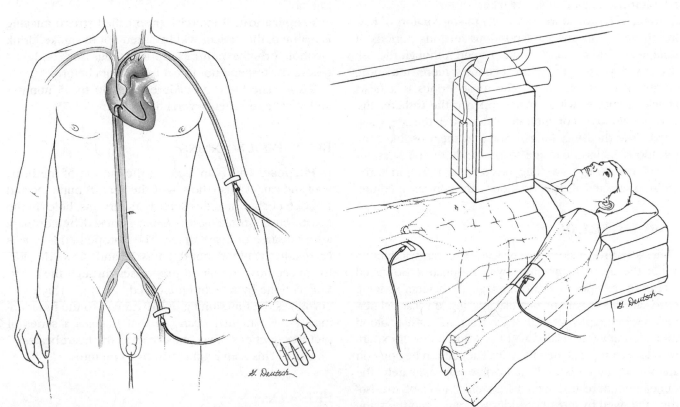

Figure 12.4: These drawings show catheters being threaded through an artery from an incision in the groin into the right side of the heart and through an artery in the arm into the aorta. A fluoroscope is used to guide the doctor into inserting the catheter.

Preparation. The patient is asked to fast for at least 6 hours prior to the test. A mild sedative is given, but the patient remains awake throughout the procedure.

Time. Depending on whether ancillary procedures such as angioplasty are performed, the test may last from 30 minutes to 3 hours. Afterward, the patient requires about 8 hours of rest and observation.

Procedure. Although most patients are hospitalized for the test, it is sometimes done on an outpatient basis. The patient reclines on an examining table positioned under x-ray monitoring equipment. An IV is started in order to administer medication if it is needed during the test. After an injection of local anesthetic, a catheter (a long, very thin, flexible tube) is inserted through a small incision in the arm or groin. For a right heart catheterization, the doctor, using a fluoroscope to help guide the catheter, passes the tube through a vein into the heart through the right atrium and then out again through the pulmonary artery. For a left heart catheterization, the catheter is passed through an artery into the aorta and then the coronary arteries of the left atrium, or both. (See figure 12.4.) Once the catheter is in place, dye is injected through it into the heart or arteries, at which point the patient may feel a hot flash or burning sensation or nausea. The dye, or contrast medium, filters into all parts of the heart or the arteries and gives a clear indication of any abnormalities or obstructions as moving x-ray pictures (angiograms) are taken.

Risk. The procedure, especially the discomfort of having to lie still in awkward positions for long periods of time, may be very tiring for the patient. Although the risk decreases as this procedure becomes more and more common, there are some. The most serious is a heart attack or stroke, which may happen if the catheter dislodges a blood clot or cholesterol deposit in the artery and it travels to the heart, lungs, or brain. Other possible complications include damage to the walls of the heart or blood vessel (rare), swelling, bleeding, or infection at the incision site, and allergic reaction to the contrast medium.

CARDIAC SCANS

There are three major types of scans that can tell doctors about the heart: technetium pyrophosphate (also called infarct or hot spot myocardial imaging), thallium imaging (also called cold spot myocardial imaging, myocardial perfusion scintigraphy, or MIBI stress test), and cardiac blood pool scanning (also called a MUGA scan). A newer experimental technique is the PET scan. They all can be done on an outpatient basis and all involve approximately the same procedure (intravenous administration of the isotope followed by a scan or series of scans), and the same rare risk of radioisotope overdose. (See below and "Radioisotope Scans" under "Basic Types of Diagnostic Tests" for more information.)

TECHNETIUM PYROPHOSPHATE

Purpose. This scan can confirm a recent heart attack (myocardial infarction) and determine the extent and exact location of damage to the heart muscle. The technetium pyrophosphate isotope is bound to a substance that seeks out injured muscle and shows up on the scanner as areas of accumulated radioactivity (called "hot spots").

Time. The isotope is injected 2 to 3 hours before the scan and the scan itself takes 30 to 60 minutes.

THALLIUM

Purpose. In some ways, this is the opposite of a technetium scan, in that the thallium isotope or MIBI accumulates in normal heart muscle, rather than damaged regions, and produces "cold spots" on the screen. The cold spots indicate areas where the coronary arteries are clogged, reducing blood flow to the heart, or where the tissue has been damaged by a heart attack. It is often used before and after bypass surgery. If the MIBI stress test is to follow, a second injection of radioisotope is required. Several hours later, the patient is asked to exercise for 5 to 20 minutes on a treadmill or stationary bicycle to help distinguish between the two conditions. Sometimes the exercise component is done the following day.

Preparation. If exercise (also called stress) imaging is planned, the patient will be asked not to smoke, drink alcohol, or take nonprescription drugs for 24 hours before the test and not to eat for 3 hours before.

Time. The basic procedure takes 30 to 45 minutes and may be repeated several hours later.

BLOOD POOL SCANNING

Purpose. This scan looks at the motion of the heart wall and can evaluate how well the heart is pumping and can detect abnormalities such as aneurysms, holes in the heart, valve problems, or damage caused by coronary artery disease or heart attack. The isotope in this case is carried in the blood, not the muscle, and allows the doctor to see how the blood progresses through the heart. This is done by a technique called "gating," which synchronizes the functioning of the camera to the functioning of the patient's heart, so that it takes a series of pictures fractions of seconds apart as the heart beats.

Time. This scan requires 10 to 15 minutes.

PET SCANS

Purpose. This scan assesses the viability of and blood flow to the heart muscle. It can also evaluate heart muscle metabolism and diagnose coronary artery disease. It uses positron-emitting isotopes that provide more information about the heart muscle than other imaging techniques. Because it can distinguish viable "stunned" heart muscle from dead (infarcted) tissue, PET scans can aid in treatment planning after a heart attack.

Time. This scan takes about 2 hours.

DOPPLER ULTRASONOGRAPHY

Purpose. This is another ultrasound procedure that is similar to echocardiography, but studies blood flow in the major veins and arteries of the arms, legs, and head, rather than the heart. It aids in the diagnosis of various conditions, including chronic venous insufficiency, peripheral artery disease and arterial occlusion, aortic stenosis, and arterial trauma. (See the following section and "Ultrasonography" under "Basic Types of Diagnostic Tests.")

ECHOCARDIOGRAPHY

Purpose. Also known as cardiac echo, this procedure uses sound waves to examine the size, shape, and motion of the heart, and is useful to diagnose abnormalities of the heart valves and to assess cardiac function.

Preparation. There is no special preparation for this test.

Time. Depending on the extent of the study, it may take from 15 to 60 minutes.

Procedure. This is an outpatient procedure. After an oil or gel is applied to the skin over the heart, a pencil-like probe is placed on the skin and then moved and tilted in various directions, using sound waves to send information to a video screen. The patient may be asked to move to different positions. (See "Ultrasonography" under "Basic Types of Diagnostic Tests.")

Risk. As with all ultrasonography procedures, there is no pain or risk.

ELECTROCARDIOGRAMS

Purpose. Electrocardiograms provide basic information about heart function, including unusual rhythms, electrolyte imbalance, enlargement of the chambers, and evidence that the patient has had a heart attack. There are three major types of electrocardiograms (also called ECG or EKG): resting, exercise (also called stress), and long-term ambulatory (also called Holter monitoring). They all involve the recording of the electrical impulses of the heart through electrodes attached to the chest and, in the case of a resting ECG, to the arms and legs. The impulses cause special needles to move over a strip of continuous paper and record the heartbeat as a wavy line whose configuration tells the doctor various things about the heart.

Resting ECG. This is a common diagnostic test, often performed as part of a routine physical, and can be done in a doctor's office in less than 10 minutes. Although it can detect what has happened and what is happening to the heart, it is not a good predictor of what may happen.

Exercise ECG (Stress Test). This test provides more information than a resting ECG by monitoring what happens to the heart when the patient exercises, either on a treadmill or on a stationary bicycle (called an ergometer). It is used to help diagnose chest pain, to determine the functional capacity of the heart after surgery or a heart attack, and to set limits for a person beginning an exercise program. At various intervals during the test, the patient is asked to pedal faster, or the speed or incline of the treadmill is increased. The patient's blood pressure and pulse are monitored, and oxygen intake may also be measured.

Ambulatory ECG (Holter Monitoring). For this test, the patient wears a small portable reel-to-reel or cassette tape recorder attached to electrodes on the chest for 24 hours while he or she goes about normal daily activities. In some cases, the patient may wear a monitor for 5 or 7 days, activating it only at certain times, for example, when symptoms such as chest pain occur. The monitor, which is worn under clothing, can pick up transient symptoms such as arrhythmias, which may not be caught by a resting ECG done for a much shorter period.

Risk. There is no pain or risk with the resting and ambulatory ECG. The exercise ECG can cause fatigue and, in extreme cases, may lead to cardiac arrhythmia or arrest.

ELECTROPHYSIOLOGY STUDIES

Purpose. Also known as EPS, these studies evaluate serious cardiac arrhythmias not adequately controlled by drugs. They also may be done to evaluate fainting that may be caused by arrhythmias, to assess the effectiveness of arrhythmia drugs and their dosages, and prior to implantation of a pacemaker or surgery to correct an arrhythmia.

Preparation. Preparation is the same as for cardiac catheterization. (See above.)

Time. Depending on the extent of the studies, total time may be 1 to 2 hours, including the catheterization.

Procedure. First, cardiac catheterization is done to enable the placement of electrodes into the heart. These electrodes record the heart's electrical activity and pathways and may be stimulated to mimic heartbeat patterns that lead to serious arrhythmias. During such episodes, various drugs can be given and their effectiveness assessed. Sometimes specific abnormal electrical patterns responsible for arrhythmias may be identified and the abnormal pathway may be eliminated with special radio-frequency catheters.

Risk. In addition to the catheterization risks, serious arrhythmias may be provoked. However, they can usually be reversed with an electric shock.

LYMPHANGIOGRAPHY

Purpose. This contrast x-ray procedure is used to diagnose causes of intractable edema (swelling) in the legs and feet, and the presence or spread of cancer in the lymphatic system.

Preparation. No special preparation is necessary.

Time. This procedure takes about 2 to 3 hours the first day and, 24 hours later, another 30 minutes. The contrast medium may remain in the body for 6 months, during which time other x-rays may be taken. The sutures are removed in 7 to 10 days.

Procedure. Lymphangiography may be done on an inpatient or outpatient basis. First, a blue dye is injected between the toes, from where it spreads into the lymphatic system in 15 to 30 minutes and outlines the lymphatic vessels in the feet. Once these vessels can be seen, a local anesthetic is given and a small incision is made in the foot, through which a tube is inserted for injection of the oil-based contrast medium. The lymphatic system is monitored on a fluoroscope as it fills with the contrast dye, a process that can take 1½ to 2 hours. After the tube is removed, the incision is sutured and bandaged. A set of x-rays is taken, followed by a second set the next day. The patient's skin, feces, and urine may have a bluish color for 2 or 3 days until the marker dye disappears.

Risk. Besides the usual risk of infection or allergy to the contrast medium, there is a small risk of oil embolism. The contrast medium eventually seeps from the lymphatic channels into the general circulation, where it may travel to and lodge in the lungs.

PACEMAKER OR AICD FOLLOW-UP

Purpose. Also known as transtelephonic pacemaker monitoring, this test checks an implanted pacemaker or defibrillator (AICD) to make sure it is functioning normally. Although the physician should evaluate the patient in person 2 weeks after such implantations, and again 2 months later, subsequent physical examinations may be alternated with evaluations over a special telephone system.

Preparation. If the test is to be done by telephone from the patient's home, he or she is taught how to use the telemetry equipment. When it is done in the doctor's office or testing center, preparation is the same as for an electrocardiogram.

Time. This test takes only a few minutes.

Procedure. A special device is placed on the chest and linked either to the telephone or to in-office equipment. It transmits electronic signals indicating how the pacemaker and its battery are functioning. The signals are interpreted by a physician or nurse. If there is any indication of equipment failure, a new battery or device must be implanted.

Risk. There is no risk with this test.

PHLEBOGRAPHY

Purpose. Phlebography (also known as venography) allows x-ray visualization of the veins in the legs and the feet and is used to diagnose deep vein thrombosis (which can lead to pulmonary embolism), to distinguish between blood clots and other obstructions (such as tumors), to evaluate congenital abnormalities in the veins, and to locate a suitable vein for a coronary bypass graft.

Preparation. No special preparation is necessary, although the patient may be asked to fast for 4 hours before the test.

Time. The test takes about 30 to 45 minutes.

Procedure. This procedure may be done on an inpatient or outpatient basis. A local anesthetic is given and the contrast medium is injected into a large vein in the leg or foot. The contrast dye may cause a burning sensation in the leg and a general flushing sensation or a feeling of nausea. During the procedure the patient may be asked to blow against a closed fist or push his or her foot against the technician's hand, both of which force blood into the veins, making them more visible.

Risk. Headache and nausea may continue for several hours after the test. Because the contrast medium dilates the veins, there is the possibility of the patient feeling weak and fainting, and there is a less common risk of the procedure actually causing phlebitis or deep venous thrombosis.

TILT-TABLE

Purpose. This test looks for evidence of neurocardiogenic syncope, an abnormal reflex that causes an abrupt fall in blood pressure and a slow heart rate. It is performed on patients who have unexplained fainting episodes.

Preparation. No special preparation is necessary. However, because some patients become nauseated, it may be wise to avoid eating for a few hours before the test.

Time. Depending on patient response and whether the tilt is repeated, the test may take 30 to 60 minutes.

Procedure. The test is performed in a doctor's office or a hospital or commercial laboratory. The patient reclines on a tilt table and is strapped in place with loosely fitting belts. An intravenous line is started, and the patient is monitored with a blood pressure machine and ECG leads. After remaining flat for 15 minutes, the table is suddenly tilted to an upright position. Symptoms of fainting or a fall in blood pressure and heart rate may occur. If no symptoms occur, medication may be administered and the test repeated. After the second tilt, the patient is observed for a short time.

Risk. There are no common major risks associated with the test. However, in the event that an unexpected cardiac event occurs, a defibrillator and crash cart are normally kept nearby.

TRANSESOPHAGEAL ECHOCARDIOGRAPHY

Purpose. Although similar to echocardiography (see above), transesophageal echocardiography provides views of the back of the heart, better definition of its interior structures, and the best view of blood clots in the heart chambers. It also is useful for obese patients or those who have thick chest walls, whose hearts are difficult to visualize with standard echocardiography. In addition, it may be used to monitor heart function during surgery.

Preparation. The patient may be given a mild sedative to help him or her relax. A local anesthetic is sprayed on the back of the throat to reduce the gag reflex.

Time. The test takes 30 to 60 minutes.

Procedure. The test is done in a diagnostic laboratory or a hospital outpatient department. An endoscope containing the ultrasound transducer is passed through the mouth and throat and into the esophagus. During the test, the transducer may be repositioned at different sites in the esophagus. The response to sound waves emitted from the transducer is recorded and analyzed as in other ultrasound evaluations. (See "Ultrasonography" under "Basic Types of Diagnostic Tests.") The patient should not eat or drink until the local anesthetic wears off and the gag reflex returns to normal.

Risk. The patient may experience gagging and discomfort as the tube is passed down the throat and pressure in the chest as the transducer is moved. There also may be a sore throat for a few days after the test. Rarely, bleeding or perforation of the esophagus may occur.

CT Scans

(See under "Basic Types of Diagnostic Tests" in this chapter.)

....

DIGESTIVE SYSTEM TESTS

CHOLANGIOGRAPHY (INTRAVENOUS)

Purpose. Intravenous cholangiography is a contrast x-ray used to detect gallstones, obstructions, or other abnormalities of the gallbladder and bile ducts. The same procedure may be done using a CT scan rather than conventional x-ray.

Preparation. The patient will have a high-fat meal the evening before the test, followed by nothing but water or fat-free liquids. A laxative may be given, since a full bowel can create shadows on the x-ray.

Time. It usually lasts about 2 to 2½ hours, if the bile ducts are not obstructed. If they are, it may take 4 to 24 hours for the contrast medium to concentrate in the gallbladder.

Procedure. The test is almost always done in a hospital. After preliminary x-rays are taken with the patient lying down on a tilting x-ray table, the contrast medium is administered intravenously and more pictures are taken at different angles.

Risk. The only real risk is possible allergic reaction to the contrast medium. To help minimize this, a small amount is administered first and reaction checked before the full dose is given. There may, however, be side effects including nausea, vomiting, hives, or flushing.

CHOLANGIOGRAPHY (PERCUTANEOUS TRANSHEPATIC)

Purpose. This is a contrast x-ray study of the bile duct, often used to diagnose causes of jaundice, in which the contrast medium is administered through a needle directly into the liver. It is especially useful with patients who have had their gallbladders removed because it doesn't depend on the gallbladder to concentrate and excrete the contrast medium.

Preparation. No food is given for about 8 hours before the test.

Time. This procedure lasts about 30 minutes.

Procedure. It is almost always performed in the hospital, since there may be complications and since it is often followed immediately by surgery. The patient lies on a tilting x-ray table and a local anesthetic is injected into the skin covering the liver and the capsule surrounding it. A long, flexible needle guided by a fluoroscope is inserted into the liver in an attempt to find a dilated bile duct, and the contrast medium administered through it. Then a series of x-rays is taken as the table is rotated to different angles.

Risk. A number of complications can result from this procedure, including bleeding, septicemia (a bacterial infection of the blood), and bile peritonitis caused by bile leaking from the punctured duct, but they are rare. Although the radiation exposure from a single cholangiography is small, there is a risk if the procedure is repeated several times. The patient will feel some sting from the needle used for the anesthetic, but will not feel the needle being inserted into the liver. When the dye is injected, there may be a feeling of fullness or pressure. Side effects of the contrast dye sometimes include nausea, vomiting, excessive salivation, hives, and sweating.

CHOLECYSTOGRAPHY

Purpose. Cholecystography (also called oral gallbladder test) is a contrast x-ray study of the gallbladder used to detect gallstones or to diagnose inflammatory disease and tumors.

Preparation. At noon on the day before the test, the patient eats a meal that contains normal amounts of fat, which stimulates release of bile from the gallbladder, emptying it of normal bile and preparing it to accept bile containing a contrast medium. This is followed by a fat-free dinner, which causes the contrast-containing bile to collect in the gallbladder. After dinner, at 5-minute intervals, the patient takes a series of pills containing the contrast dye.

Time. The test takes about 30 to 45 minutes.

Procedure. This outpatient procedure is simply a series of x-ray pictures taken with the patient in different positions. After the initial pictures, the patient may be given a high-fat meal or a pill to produce the same effect, and asked to wait 15 to 20 minutes, after which another set of pictures is taken.

Risk. Except for possible allergic reaction to the contrast medium, there is no risk involved in this test. Some people suffer temporary side effects caused by the pills, most commonly diarrhea and occasionally nausea, vomiting, or difficulty in urinating.

COLONOSCOPY

Purpose. Colonoscopy is the direct examination of the large intestine using a flexible fiber-optic tube inserted through the anus (see figure 12.5). It is used to detect inflammatory or ulcerative bowel disease, to check for polyps or tumors, or to locate the site of gastrointestinal bleeding.

Preparation. The patient is given a liquid diet for 1 to 2 days before the exam, followed by a laxative and one or more enemas to completely empty the bowels. A sedative or tranquilizer may also be given.

Time. This procedure takes 30 to 60 minutes.

Procedure. It can be done as an outpatient procedure, but is usually done in the hospital. With the patient lying on his or her side and knees flexed, a colonoscope is passed through the intestine. Air may be injected to expand the folds of the colon, enabling the doctor to see the entire surface area. When the tube has reached the entire length of the colon, it is slowly withdrawn as the doctor examines the lining for any lesions or polyps. Special attachments allow the removal of some small polyps or the collection of a biopsy sample.

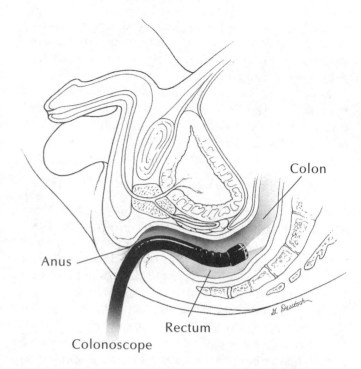

Figure 12.5: This drawing shows an examination of the colon or large intestine, with the fiber-optic scope being inserted through the anus and rectum and threaded into the colon.

Risk. There is very little risk of bowel perforation, but the patient should report any bleeding, dark stool, or abdominal pain. Many patients feel embarrassment and discomfort during this procedure, especially when air is injected and expelled.

DUODENOGRAPHY

Purpose. Duodenography (also called hypotonic duodenography) provides x-ray pictures of the duodenum and the pancreas and is used to diagnose tumors or lesions that may be causes of upper abdominal pain.

Preparation. The patient must fast for 6 to 12 hours before the test.

Time. This test takes about 30 minutes.

Procedure. It can be done on an inpatient or outpatient basis. The patient is seated, and a long, flexible tube called a catheter is passed through the nose into the stomach. The patient then lies down and the doctor, guided by a fluoroscope screen, continues to pass the catheter into the duodenum. A hormone or drug to relax the duodenum is given by injection or IV, and then the contrast medium is administered through the catheter and x-rays are taken from a number of angles. Some of the barium is then withdrawn and air injected through the catheter, which may cause the patient to have cramps. More x-rays are taken before the catheter is removed.

Risk. Risks, which include allergy to the contrast medium or possible internal damage from the introduction of the catheter, are rare. More common are side effects, such as reactions to the hormone or drug, which may include nausea, vomiting, hives, flushing, blurred vision, dry mouth, thirst, irregular heart rhythms, and, especially in patients with prostate problems, urine retention.

ENDOSCOPIC RETROGRADE CHOLANGIOPANCREATOGRAPHY

Purpose. Also known as ERCP, this x-ray visualization of the ducts leading from the pancreas and the gallbladder is used to diagnose the presence of stones or tumors in these ducts.

Preparation. The patient is asked to fast for 12 hours before the test and is usually given a sedative or tranquilizer. A local anesthetic (generally unpleasant tasting) is used in either spray or gargle form to suppress gagging, and it causes the patient to lose some control of saliva. A mouth guard may be inserted to protect the teeth.

Time. ERCP takes about 60 minutes.

Procedure. While it can be done on an outpatient basis, it is usually done on an inpatient basis. The endoscope is inserted into the mouth and down the throat and the patient is instructed to swallow to help pass it down into the esophagus. Guided by a fluoroscope, the doctor then continues to pass it down into the stomach and duodenum, and then injects a drug into the duodenum to relax it. Next the contrast medium is injected through the endoscope and a series of x-rays is taken. Another set may be taken in different positions after the scope is removed. The patient may feel side effects from the drug or hormone used to relax the duodenum and from the contrast medium. These include nausea, hives, blurred vision, dry mouth, urinary retention, and a feeling of burning or flushing. The throat may be sore for 3 or 4 days afterward.

Risk. Besides the slight risk of infection or perforation of internal organs that accompanies any invasive procedure, there is also the problem of urine retention, especially in men with prostate problems. This can usually be avoided by voiding completely before the exam.

ESOPHAGOGRAPHY

Although this test is occasionally done alone, when the doctor is reasonably sure that the problem is confined to the esophagus, it is usually done as part of the upper GI series. (See "Upper GI and Small Bowel Series" in this chapter.)

GASTRIC SECRETION STUDIES

Purpose. This procedure allows the physician to collect and study samples of the gastric juices secreted by the stomach to diagnose causes of epigastric pain or learn more about suspected ulcers before surgery.

Preparation. The patient is usually fed a liquid meal and then asked to fast for 12 hours and to restrict liquids and smoking for 8 hours prior to the test. Part of the test may involve eating, drinking, or chewing to stimulate production of gastric juices.

Time. Although the secretions are all collected in the same manner, the test can last anywhere from 2 to 12 hours, depending on the objective of the test.

Procedure. The longer test requires hospitalization, but the shorter ones may be done on an outpatient basis. The doctor passes a long, flexible tube through a nostril down the patient's throat into the stomach. Once the tube has been started, the patient is asked to swallow until the tube enters the stomach. The gastric juices are then aspirated and collected through the tube over a period of hours.

Risk. The test is uncomfortable and may cause gagging when the tube is initially passed and some irritation in the nostril or throat afterward. Other risks, which are rare, include lung collapse or ulceration of the larynx if the tube is passed into the trachea instead of the esophagus.

GASTROSCOPY

Purpose. Gastroscopy (also called esophagogastroduodenoscopy) allows the doctor a direct view of the lining of the esophagus, stomach, and duodenum through an endoscopic tube. It is used to determine the cause of bleeding, perform a biopsy, or diagnose inflammatory disease, tumors, ulcers, and structural abnormalities.

Preparation. The patient will be asked to fast for 6

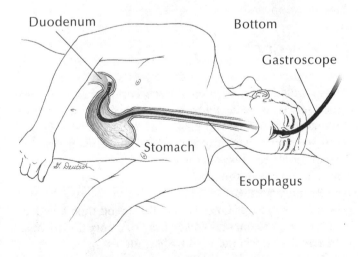

Figure 12.6: During gastroscopy, a flexible fiber-optic tube is inserted into the mouth and threaded through the esophagus, into the stomach and the upper part of the small intestine (duodenum).

to 12 hours beforehand and may be given a sedative or tranquilizer. A local anesthetic is sprayed into the mouth and throat.

Time. The procedure takes about 30 minutes.

Procedure. It may be done on an inpatient or outpatient basis. A flexible fiber-optic tube is passed through the mouth down the esophagus and into the stomach and duodenum (see figure 12.6). The tube, which transmits light and allows the doctor to see the internal structure of various organs, also has attachments that allow the suctioning off of secretions, taking of biopsy samples, and introduction of air, which expands the organs and makes examination easier.

Risk. As with all invasive procedures, there is some risk of internal damage to organs or structures, such as perforation, but this is relatively rare. The patient may feel some gagging, cramps, or fullness as the tube is passed through various organs or when air is introduced, and will probably have a sore throat afterward.

LIVER SCAN

Purpose. This isotope study provides information on the structure and functioning of the liver and is used to detect cirrhosis, abscesses, or growths.

Preparation. No special preparation is necessary.

Time. The procedure takes about 45 to 60 minutes for a structure scan and 30 minutes for each function scan, which are done in a series with the final one after 24 hours.

Procedure. The procedure may be done on an outpatient basis. The isotope is injected and a blocking agent may be used. (See "Radioisotope Scans" under "Basic Types of Diagnostic Tests.")

Risk. There is no risk, other than the remote possibility of isotope overdose.

LOWER GI SERIES

Purpose. Like the upper GI Series, this x-ray exam (also called barium enema) uses barium as a contrast medium to provide fluoroscopic views, in this case of the large intestine. The procedure is used to detect polyps, tumors, gastroenteritis, telescopic bowel, irritable colon or other causes of lower abdominal pain, or blood, mucus, or pus in the stool.

Preparation. Before the examination, the patient may be asked to fast or go on a liquid diet, and then laxatives or one or more enemas will be used to empty the bowels.

Time. The test takes 30 to 45 minutes.

Procedure. It can be done in a doctor's office, testing facility, or hospital outpatient clinic. The barium enema is administered through a tube inserted into the rectum while the patient lies on his side on a tilting x-ray table. The table will be rotated to allow the barium to completely coat the large intestine and x-ray pictures will be

taken. The patient will then be helped to a bathroom or given a bedpan and told to expel as much of the barium as possible. More pictures will then be taken of the thin film that remains on the mucous lining of the intestine. In some cases, this will be followed by a double contrast study, meaning air will be carefully injected into the colon to provide further contrast on the film in order to detect possible polyps.

Risk. Although this procedure is unpleasant and often uncomfortable, there are no serious complications. Risks, such as perforation of the bowel, are rare. The procedure causes some discomfort, including a strong urge to defecate and mild or, especially with the air contrast study, moderate to severe cramps. The stool will be white or light colored for a few days following the test, and the barium may be constipating. For this reason, the test is sometimes followed by a laxative or another enema.

PANCREAS SCAN

Purpose. This radioisotope scan provides information on the structure and functioning of the pancreas to help detect cancer, cysts, or infection.

Preparation. The patient follows a high-protein diet for several days before the test, then fasts for 8 to 12 hours, with the exception of a glass of skim milk a few hours before the test. Another high-protein liquid is given at the time of the test.

Time. A pancreas scan takes 1 to 2 hours.

Procedure. It may be done on an inpatient or outpatient basis. The isotope is given by IV and sometimes causes nausea or vomiting. (See "Radioisotope Scans" under "Basic Types of Diagnostic Tests.")

Risk. There is a rare risk of radioisotope overdose.

PROCTOSIGMOIDOSCOPY

Purpose. A proctoscope exam (also called proctoscopy) allows the doctor to see the rectum and the lower part of the large intestine. It may be used to detect hemorrhoids, polyps, and abscesses or to determine the cause of bleeding. It is routinely used to screen for cancer after age 40, even if there are no symptoms.

Preparation. The patient may be instructed to have a liquid diet or to fast for a few hours, followed by an enema or suppository.

Time. This procedure takes 10 to 20 minutes.

Procedure. It may be carried out in a doctor's office or in a clinic. With the patient in the knee-chest position, the doctor will do a digital rectal exam, using a gloved finger, and then insert the proctoscope, which may be a rigid or a flexible tube. The procedure is similar to the colonoscopy (see "Colonoscopy" earlier in this section), but not as extensive.

Risk. Although the patient may feel some irritation around the anus afterward, this is a routine, safe procedure, with the risk of injury to the large intestine being very rare. The patient may feel some discomfort and the urge to defecate during the procedure.

SIALOGRAPHY

Purpose. This procedure (also called ptyalography) allows x-ray visualization of the salivary glands to diagnose stones in the salivary ducts or other causes of an enlarged or painful salivary gland.

Preparation. No special preparation is required, except possibly fasting for a few hours beforehand. The patient may be given a sedative.

Time. This procedure takes about 45 to 60 minutes.

Procedure. It is usually performed on an outpatient basis. A catheter is inserted through the mouth into the duct of the salivary gland to be studied and a contrast medium is injected through the catheter. The doctor examines the gland using a fluoroscope and may take x-rays. There is some discomfort when the catheter is inserted and pain when the dye reaches the salivary gland.

Risk. As with all invasive procedures, there is a rare risk of internal damage or infection. The patient will continue to taste the contrast dye (which is somewhat unpleasant) and experience some soreness in the mouth after the procedure.

SMALL BOWEL EXAMINATION

This exam is usually done in conjunction with an upper GI series. (See the following description.)

UPPER GI AND SMALL BOWEL SERIES

Purpose. This fluoroscopic examination (also called barium milk shake or barium swallow) of the esophagus, stomach, and small intestine is used to diagnose cases of hiatal hernia, ulcers, tumors, obstruction, or enteritis, and when there are symptoms such as difficulty in swallowing, regurgitation, burning or gnawing abdominal pain, diarrhea, weight loss, or bleeding.

Preparation. The patient may be asked to eat a low-residue diet for 2 or 3 days before the test and will be asked not to eat or smoke for 6 to 12 hours prior to the exam.

Time. It may take anywhere from 30 minutes (for just the esophagus) to 60 minutes (for the esophagus and stomach) to 6 or more hours (if the small intestine is also included).

Procedure. This test may be done in a testing facility or in a hospital on an inpatient or outpatient basis. It begins with the patient swallowing a "barium milk shake," a sweetened, flavored, but nonetheless chalky-tasting substance containing barium sulfate, a contrast medium that outlines the upper digestive tract. Sometimes a more liquid radiopaque material is used. The patient is strapped securely to a tilting x-ray table, which starts in a vertical position with the patient standing, and is tilted at various angles throughout the test to help spread the contrast medium and to get different views on the fluoroscope. Pressure may be applied to the patient's abdomen to spread the medium further. If the test is to include a small bowel exam, the patient will have to wait several hours until the barium filters down into the intestine, and may be able to leave and come back, or to spend the time reading.

Risk. Although the barium is unpleasant tasting and will make the patient's stool white for several days (unless a laxative is given to speed its passing), there is no pain, little discomfort, and virtually no risk with this test, unless it is repeated several times, when radiation then becomes a risk.

NERVE AND MUSCLE SYSTEMS TESTS

BRAIN SCAN

Purpose. This radioisotope study of the brain is used to detect or diagnose tumors, hemorrhage, stroke, or blood vessel abnormalities.

Preparation. No special preparation is necessary.

Time. A brain scan takes about 30 to 60 minutes.

Procedure. It is usually done on an outpatient basis. A blocking agent is used and the isotope is generally given by IV, but may be given orally, and the scan may be done from one or more positions. (See "Radioisotope Scans" under "Basic Types of Diagnostic Tests.")

Risk. There is a rare risk of radioisotope overdose.

CEREBRAL ANGIOGRAPHY

Purpose. Cerebral angiography allows the doctor to see blood circulating through the brain and is used in locating tumors, blood clots, aneurysms, or other abnormalities and in diagnosing stroke.

Procedure. This procedure is virtually the same as angiography of the heart, but the catheter is extended up through the neck into the arteries of the brain. (See "Cardiac Catheterization" under "Basic Types of Diagnostic Tests.")

Risk. The risk is the same as for arterial cardiac catheterization.

CISTERNAL PUNCTURE

Purpose. This procedure, which provides a small amount of cerebrospinal fluid from the base of the brain, is used to diagnose viral or bacterial infections, brain hemorrhage, and tumors.

Procedure. It is done in place of, or in conjunction with, a lumbar puncture (see "Lumbar Puncture" later in this section). The only difference is the puncture site of the needle. With a cisternal tap, the patient's chin is tucked in as far as possible and the needle is inserted in the back of the neck at the base of the brain.

Risks. Although the risks are about the same for the two procedures, there is a little less likelihood of headache following a cisternal puncture.

ELECTROENCEPHALOGRAPHY

Purpose. This test (also known as EEG) records the electrical activity of the brain and is used to diagnose epilepsy, tumors, brain damage, mental retardation, and certain psychological disorders.

Preparation. The patient may be asked not to take any medications that have an effect on the nervous system, for 1 or 2 days before the test.

Time. This procedure usually takes about 1 hour unless a sleep EEG, which takes about 3 hours, is done.

Procedure. This outpatient procedure begins with the attachment of electrodes to the patient's scalp, either with electrode paste or by tiny, virtually painless needles. Very weak electrical current is passed through the electrodes, which produces a mild tingling sensation, and the brain's electrical activity is recorded. After the baseline study is made, the patient is exposed to various stimuli, such as bright or flashing (strobe) lights, noise, or drugs. The patient may be asked to breathe deeply and quickly for 3 minutes or to stare at a black-and-white checkerboard pattern. All of these techniques produce changes in the brain waves. With a sleep EEG, the patient may be kept awake for many hours and then given a sleep-inducing drug or encouraged to sleep during the test.

Risk. There is virtually no risk.

ELECTROMYOGRAPHY

Purpose. Electromyography (also called EMG), which studies the electrical activity of muscles at rest and during contraction, is used to diagnose diseases that affect the muscles, peripheral nerves, and spinal cord.

Preparation. The patient may be asked not to smoke or take caffeine drinks for 2 or 3 hours before the test.

Time. It takes 1 hour or longer, depending on how many muscles are being studied.

Procedure. The study is usually carried out in a hospital. For the first part of the test, to study the nerves, electrodes are placed on the skin and a weak electric current is passed through them while the electrical activity of the nerves and muscles is recorded. For the second

part of the test, thin needles are inserted into the muscles and the electrical activity is again studied and recorded as photographs or tracings on special recording paper.

Risk. Although there may be some pain during and after needle insertion, there is no risk associated with this procedure other than infection, which is rare.

EVOKED RESPONSE

Purpose. Also known as evoked potentials, this test evaluates stimuli delivered through sight, hearing, or touch that evoke minute electrical signals in the appropriate region of the brain. It is used to confirm the diagnosis of multiple sclerosis, assess hearing and eyesight (especially in infants and children), diagnose optic nerve disorders, detect tumors and other brain and spinal cord abnormalities, determine whether limb sensation loss is due to brain or spinal cord injury, monitor brain activity during certain types of surgery, assess brain stem function in coma, and determine brain death.

Preparation. The patient is instructed to wash his or her hair the night before the test and not to use any hair cream, oils, spray, or lacquer afterward. All jewelry and other metal objects must be removed from the body.

Time. The duration of the test depends on the objective of the evaluation.

Procedure. It may be done in a doctor's office or the hospital. Electrodes are placed on the scalp, as in electroencephalography, and, depending on the test, possibly also to the neck, lower back, wrist, knee, or ankle. For visual evoked responses (VER), the patient sits about 3 feet away from a screen and is asked to focus on its center. With one eye closed, the patient focuses on a shifting checkerboard pattern on the screen. The test is repeated with the other eye. For brain stem auditory evoked response (BAER), the patient is seated in a soundproof room. Click sounds are delivered through earphones to each ear. For somatosensory evoked response (SSER), tiny electrical shocks are delivered to the peripheral nerves. Signals produced by the brain in response to the stimuli are recorded.

Risk. No risks are involved.

FLUORESCEIN RETINAL ANGIOGRAPHY

Purpose. This test (also called eye angiography), which allows x-ray visualization of the blood circulation in the retina and the choroid of the eye, is used to diagnose retinopathy, tumors, and circulatory or inflammatory disorders.

Preparation. No special preparation is needed.

Time. Fluorescein angiography takes about 1 hour.

Procedure. It is usually done as an outpatient procedure and may be done in an ophthalmologist's office.

The patient's pupils are dilated with eye drops, much as for a visual acuity test, to prevent the pupils from closing up when the lighted ophthalmoscope is used to examine the eyes. Then the fluorescein dye is injected through a vein in the arm, at which time the patient may feel some nausea or flushing. The patient sits very still with his or her head resting in a special frame to keep it from moving, and a series of x-rays is taken. The patient may be asked to wait 20 or 30 minutes before another set is taken.

Risk. The effects of the dilating drops, light sensitivity, and blurred vision will linger for several hours and the patient's skin and urine may have a yellowish tinge for a day or so. On rare occasions, patients may experience an allergic reaction to the dilating drops (elderly patients may develop acute glaucoma) or to the fluorescein.

INTRATHECAL SCAN

Purpose. This radioisotope study (also called cisternography) allows the doctor to see the flow of cerebrospinal fluid to check for changes, abnormalities, or leaks.

Preparation. No special preparation is necessary.

Time. It may take as long as 72 hours, including waiting time between scans.

Procedure. An intrathecal study is done on an inpatient basis. The isotope is injected by way of a lumbar puncture (see below). Some of the cerebrospinal fluid is withdrawn, mixed with the radioisotope, and reinjected. It takes about 3 hours to fill the subarachnoid space between the brain and the membrane that covers it before the scan can begin. If the doctor is looking for a leak, cotton may be placed in the patient's nose and ears and later checked to see if it has absorbed any of the isotope.

Risk. There is some risk and discomfort associated with the lumbar puncture and there is always the remote risk of radioisotope overdose. (See "Radioisotope Scans" in this chapter.)

LUMBAR PUNCTURE

Purpose. The lumbar puncture (also known as spinal tap) provides a small amount of cerebrospinal fluid for laboratory analysis and is used to diagnose viral or bacterial infections, brain hemorrhage, and tumors or other obstructions.

Preparation. No special preparation is necessary.

Time. This procedure takes about 30 minutes.

Procedure. It may be done on an outpatient basis, but is usually done on an inpatient basis. The patient lies on his or her side, with knees drawn up and chin tucked into the chest in order to provide as much room as possible for the insertion of the needle (see figure 12.7). A

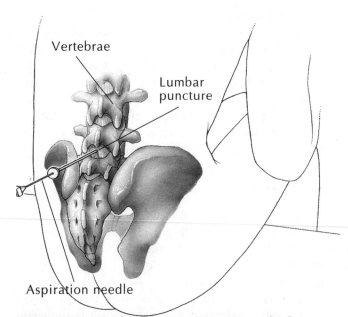

Figure 12.7: A lumbar puncture, in which a hollow needle is inserted between 2 vertebrae and a small amount of spinal fluid is withdrawn for analysis.

local anesthetic is injected, the needle inserted, and a small amount of fluid withdrawn. There may be a feeling of pressure when this is done.

Risk. Although a common aftereffect is a moderate to severe headache (which usually can be relieved by lying flat), there are very few risks associated with this procedure. There is a rare risk of infection from the needle or of leakage of the fluid through a tear in the membranes that surround the spinal cord.

MYELOGRAPHY

Purpose. This procedure allows x-ray visualization of the spinal subarachnoid space—the area between the spinal cord and the arachnoid membrane that covers it—in order to diagnose herniated disks, spinal nerve injury, and tumors.

Preparation. The patient will not be allowed to eat or drink for several hours before the procedure and may be given an enema and a tranquilizer or sedative.

Time. The procedure takes from 30 to 90 minutes.

Procedure. Myelography is usually performed on an inpatient basis. With the patient lying on a tilting x-ray table, a lumbar or cisternal puncture (see "Lumbar Puncture") is performed, a small amount of spinal fluid is removed, and the contrast medium is injected at the same site. A series of x-rays is taken with the table in various positions, and all or part of the contrast medium may be removed by aspiration afterward.

Risk. The patient may find the procedure uncomfortable for several reasons: having to lie still for long periods of time in awkward positions; a feeling of pressure flushing, and nausea and vomiting when the contrast is injected; possibly some pain when it is removed; and the headache that usually accompanies a spinal tap. Although this procedure is uncomfortable, the risk involved is remote. There is always the possibility of infection or allergy to the contrast medium, or the leakage of the dye into the head, but these are rare.

THE TENSILON TEST

Purpose. Also known as the neuromuscular junction test, this procedure can diagnose myasthenia gravis or other disorders in which the muscles weaken because they have lost the ability to pick up signals from the nerves.

Preparation. Because this procedure involves insertion of a catheter into a vein, preparation is similar to cardiac catheterization.

Time. Depending on the number of times the procedure is repeated, the test can last 30 to 60 minutes or longer.

Procedure. A catheter is placed in the patient's vein near the group of muscles affected by weakness. A small dose of the drug edrophonium is injected through the catheter. If the drug does not restore power to the muscles within a minute or two, the dose is increased. When power is restored, the effect lasts only a few minutes. The procedure is repeated 5 to 10 times.

Risk. The drug may temporarily cause nausea, dizziness, slow heartbeat, and blurred vision.

REPRODUCTIVE SYSTEM TESTS

ALPHA-FETOPROTEIN SCREENING

Purpose. Screening for alpha-fetoprotein (a protein produced by the fetus) is used mainly to detect defects of the neural tube, which forms the spinal column and brain, but can also indicate when a fetus is at greater risk for Down syndrome (a term now preferred over Down's syndrome). High levels of alpha-fetoprotein indicate possible spina bifida in the baby. Neural tube defects are the most common birth defect in this country, occurring in about 1 of every 1,000 babies. In about half the cases, the tube is open at the top and the baby is born with a rudimentary brain, or no brain at all, a condition called anencephaly. These babies are born dead or die soon after. The others have spina bifida and may be paralyzed below where the tube is open along the spine, exposing a portion of the nerve column. Some of these children also have hydrocephaly, a con-

dition in which fluid accumulates in the head, which can result in brain damage. Children with spina bifida may be mentally retarded, and frequently have no bowel or bladder control. When a fetus has a neural tube defect, large amounts of alpha-fetoprotein pour out of the open spine or skull into the amniotic fluid. From there it enters the mother's bloodstream, where it can be detected.

Preparation. No special preparation is necessary.

Time. It takes only a minute or two to draw blood by venipuncture.

Procedure. Samples of a woman's blood are taken, between 9 and 22 weeks of pregnancy, when the levels of the protein are sufficient for testing. Those with abnormally high levels, based on gestational age and weight and race of the mother, are given sonograms, pictures of the fetus produced by sound waves to determine whether other reasons, such as multiple fetuses or fetal death, are responsible for the elevated levels of alpha-fetoprotein. If the sonogram reveals no explanation, the woman is given amniocentesis to check her amniotic fluid for alpha-fetoprotein and acetylcholinesterase, a nerve enzyme that is often present when the fetus has a neural tube defect. A low level may indicate a chromosomal defect, the most common of which is Down syndrome and which can be confirmed by further chromosomal studies.

Risk. There is virtually no risk for the blood test. However, most women who go on to have amniocentesis on the basis of the alpha-fetoprotein screening will be found not to be carrying fetuses with Down syndrome. Since in the majority of cases there are no known factors to indicate who might be carrying an affected baby, pregnant women, regardless of age, are being offered this noninvasive test. In California, physicians are required by law to offer it to their patients.

AMNIOCENTESIS

Purpose. Amniocentesis, the withdrawal of a small amount of amniotic fluid from the uterus during pregnancy, is used to test for birth defects and other potential problems. The fluid contains waste materials and skin cells normally sloughed off by the fetus, which can tell a number of things about the fetus's chromosomal makeup. Although the test cannot guarantee that the child will be born without birth defects, there are certain conditions that it can rule out, including Down syndrome, Tay-Sachs disease, amino acid disorders, and neural tube disorders such as spina bifida. It can also determine sex, fetal age and maturity, and give some indications of general health.

Preparation. No special preparation is needed, except that the mother may be asked to void prior to the test.

TESTS FOR SEXUALLY TRANSMITTED DISEASES

A number of safe tests have been developed to detect the presence of sexually transmitted diseases, the best known of which are AIDS, gonorrhea and syphilis, genital herpes, and chlamydia. Blood test results are available within 48 hours, while cultures take 3 to 10 days for a reading. These procedures involve no physical risk to the patient. In some instances, physicians or laboratories are obliged to report the presence of a sexually transmitted disease to a health department or to a spouse or sexual partner. Blood banks routinely test all donations for the presence of antibodies to HIV. For more information on sexually transmitted diseases, see chapter 18, Infectious Diseases, and chapter 19, HIV Infection and AIDS.

Disease	Method	Comments
AIDS and HIV (human immunodeficiency virus)	Blood tests can detect the presence of antibodies to HIV, the human immunodeficiency virus that causes AIDS.	AIDS is a clinical, not a laboratory, diagnosis. Tests can determine only whether someone has been exposed to the virus.
Chlamydia	Diagnosis is determined by blood tests, culturing, the use of an electron microscope, or by various methods of detecting antigens.	A number of sexually transmitted diseases, among them cervicitis, urethritis, pelvic inflammatory disease in women, and epididymitis in men are caused by *Chlamydia trachomatis,* organisms that closely resemble bacteria.
Genital herpes	Diagnosis is made by culturing blood from lesions.	Genital herpes is caused by the herpes simplex Type 2 virus.
Gonorrhea	The *Neisseria gonorrhoeae* organism responsible for the disease is best detected with a culture.	Gonorrhea is usually, but not always, transmitted sexually. It can infect the cervix and vagina of women, and the rectum and urethra of men and women, but sometimes will cause no symptoms.
Syphilis	Depending on the stage of the disease, diagnosis of infection with *Treponema pallidum,* the organism responsible for syphilis, is made by blood tests and by examining scrapings from chancres, ulcer-like lesions, from various parts of the body, which can include the genitals, tongue, lips, and skin.	Syphilis was considered the most serious sexually transmitted disease before the development of AIDS.

Time. The test takes about 15 minutes, but it usually takes about 10 to 21 days for test results to be available.

Procedure. The test is usually performed after the 15th week of pregnancy, when sufficient amniotic fluid has accumulated for a sample to be taken, in the doctor's office or in an outpatient clinic. A local anesthetic is injected into the abdomen, and the small sting from the needle is the only sensation felt. Using ultrasonography (see earlier section in this chapter) as a guide, the doctor inserts a thin, hollow needle into the abdomen and withdraws a small amount of fluid, less than an ounce (see figures 12.8A and B). An alternative procedure is to take a sample of the placental villus cells that are also representative of the fetus. (See "Chorionic Villus Sampling" on the next page.)

Risk. Adverse effects are rare. The only serious risk is accidentally puncturing the placenta with the needle, but the use of ultrasound virtually eliminates this. There is a slight risk of spontaneous abortion and, as with all invasive procedures, there is a risk of infection. Because of these potential complications, this test is not used routinely unless the mother is over 35 or has a family history of genetic disorders, chromosomal defects or mental retardation, or when an Rh factor problem is anticipated.

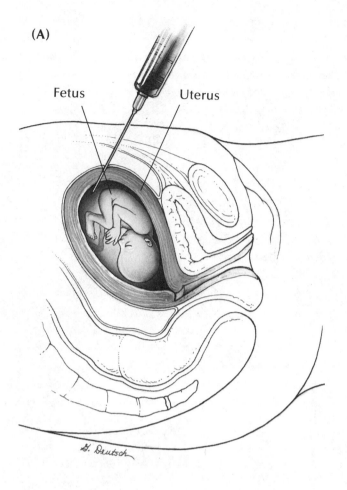

(A)

Fetus   Uterus

G. Deutsch

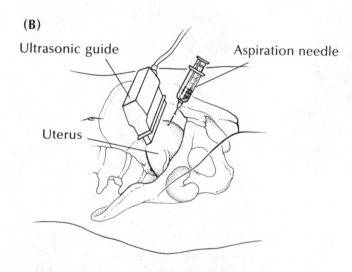

(B)

Ultrasonic guide   Aspiration needle

Uterus

Figure 12.8A and B: The large drawing (12.8A) shows amniocentesis in process, with the aspiration needle inserted into the uterus and amnionic sac to withdraw a small amount of the fluid surrounding the fetus. Ultrasonography (12.8B) is used to guide the procedure to ensure that the fetus is not harmed.

CHORIONIC VILLUS SAMPLING (CVS)

Purpose. Chorionic villus sampling (CVS), the withdrawal of a small amount of tissue from the placenta, is done early in pregnancy to test for damaged chromosomes, which indicate birth defects or other abnormalities. It is used to determine sex, fetal age and maturity, and to detect Down syndrome, Tay-Sachs disease, and fragile X, a cause of mental retardation that is the second most common chromosomal abnormality, as well as other inherited disorders. Although the range of genetic tests is the same with chorionic sampling as with amniocentesis, CVS offers several advantages: It is unlikely to fail and it is done earlier in pregnancy, which allows more time for a decision to be made if an abnormality is detected. It can, however, produce "false negatives" or "mosaics," in which the results yield more than one set of findings.

Preparation. No special preparation is necessary.

Time. The standard vaginal approach takes less than 30 minutes.

Procedure. The test is usually performed between the 8th and 12th weeks of pregnancy. Using a plastic catheter inserted through the vagina and cervix, the doctor withdraws cells from the hairlike projections, or villi, on the placenta. The test can also be performed in a manner similar to that of amniocentesis. With this method, the doctor uses ultrasonography as a guide and inserts a needle into the abdomen instead.

Risk. Some doctors prefer to perform the test transabdominally, believing that by avoiding the vagina and cervix, which harbor bacteria, the risk of infection—a rare but potentially serious complication—will be minimized. In one study a miscarriage rate of 1.9 percent was found with the cervical procedure. It is not known how many of the women would have miscarried anyway, as the procedure is done during the first trimester of pregnancy, when most miscarriages occur.

COLPOSCOPY

Purpose. Colposcopy, which allows the doctor direct visualization of the vagina and cervix, is most often used to confirm cervical cancer (after a positive Pap test) or to perform a biopsy. It is also used to monitor patients whose mothers were given DES during pregnancy.

Preparation. No special preparation is necessary.

Time. This procedure takes about 15 minutes.

Procedure. Colposcopy can be performed in a doctor's office. With the patient lying on her back, her feet in stirrups, a speculum is inserted into the vagina to spread the vaginal walls and allow insertion of a colposcope, a tube equipped with a light that allows the doctor to examine the cervix and to do a biopsy (see figure 12.9).

Risk. There may be some easily controllable bleeding if

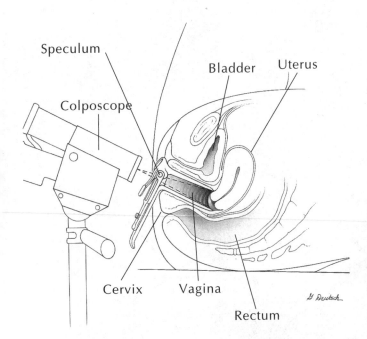

Figure 12.9: **Colposcopy enables a physician to look directly at the vagina and cervix, using a colposcope, a magnifying instrument with special lights.**

a biopsy is done, but there is generally no pain. There is a very slight risk of infection or moderately heavy bleeding.

HYSTEROSALPINGOGRAPHY

Purpose. This x-ray exam of the uterus and fallopian tubes is most often used to confirm tubal abnormalities or obstructions that may be the cause of infertility.

Preparation. The patient may be asked not to eat for several hours before the exam, and may be given a laxative and a sedative.

Time. Hysterosalpingography may last from 15 to 45 minutes.

Procedure. It is usually performed on an outpatient basis. With the patient lying on her back with knees flexed and feet in stirrups, a tube is inserted into the vagina and used to inject contrast medium into the uterus. If the fallopian tubes are not blocked, the medium will flow from the uterus through the tubes and out into the peritoneal cavity. If they are blocked, the point of obstruction will be visible on the fluoroscope.

Risk. The patient may feel some cramping from this procedure and more severe pain if the tubes are blocked. There may be a stinging sensation when the contrast medium reaches the peritoneal cavity. Besides the risk of internal injury associated with any endoscopic procedure, there is a rare risk of intravascular injection of the contrast medium.

LAPAROSCOPY

Purpose. Laparoscopy, which allows the doctor to look directly at the uterus, fallopian tubes, and ovaries, is used to detect endometriosis, ectopic pregnancy, pelvic inflammatory disease or other causes of pelvic pain, or to determine the extent of cancer. It may also be used to perform a tubal ligation (sterilization).

Preparation. The patient is asked to fast for at least 8 hours beforehand.

Time. Diagnostic laparoscopy usually takes less than 30 minutes.

Procedure. This procedure, done under local or general anesthesia, is usually performed in a hospital, but may be done on an outpatient basis. A catheter is inserted into the bladder and a small incision is made in the abdomen just below the navel to allow insertion of the laparoscope. (See figure 12.10.) Carbon dioxide may be injected into the body cavity to distend the abdominal wall and allow more room to see and maneuver. A dye may be used to check for obstructions in the fallopian tubes. (See "Hysterosalpingography," above.)

Risk. As with all invasive procedures, there is a rare risk of infection and damage to internal organs. There also may be some referred pain in the shoulder area until all the gas is eliminated from the body.

MAMMOGRAPHY

(See "Cancer Tests" earlier in this chapter.)

PLACENTAL SCAN

Purpose. This test is performed during pregnancy to determine the cause of vaginal bleeding if problems with the placenta are suspected.

Preparation. No special preparation is necessary other than having the patient void.

Time. It requires about 30 minutes.

Procedure. A placental scan is usually done on an outpatient basis. (See "Radioisotope Scans" under "Basic Types of Diagnostic Tests" for more information.)

Risk. There is no serious risk to either the mother or fetus.

PREGNANCY TEST

This test for determining pregnancy is described in the introduction to this chapter.

SEMEN ANALYSIS

Purpose. Semen analysis (also called sperm count) is primarily used to determine male fertility, but it can also be used in suspected rape cases. Although a number of

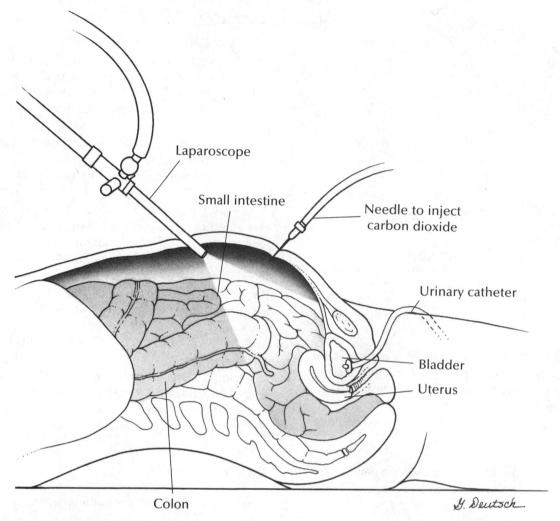

Laparoscope

Small intestine

Needle to inject carbon dioxide

Urinary catheter

Bladder

Uterus

Colon

G. Deutsch

Figure 12.10: Laparoscopy is used to view the pelvic or other abdominal organs through a small incision in the abdominal wall.

substances are present in the semen and analyzed, the sperm count is the best known.

Preparation. The patient will be asked to abstain from intercourse for a specified period, usually 2 to 6 days.

Time. The time needed to collect the specimen varies from one man to the next.

Procedure. The patient obtains a semen specimen by masturbation, which is usually done at the laboratory, but may also be done at home into a sterile container provided by the lab. Although masturbation is the preferred method, coitus interruptus may be used. In rape cases, a semen sample will be drawn from the vagina using an aspirating syringe.

Risk. There is no risk in this procedure.

SONOGRAM

Purpose. This procedure (also called ultrasound or sonography) allows the doctor to see the fetus inside the uterus without the risk of exposure to x-ray. It is used to determine the stage of fetal development when there is a

discrepancy between apparent size and due date, to confirm the presence of more than one fetus, to determine the position of the fetus or placenta, to diagnose causes of vaginal bleeding, and to guide the needle for amniocentesis.

Preparation. There is no preparation needed, but the patient may be asked to drink liquids before the test in order to fill her bladder and create a clearer picture.

Time. The procedure takes about 15 minutes.

Procedure. See "Ultrasonography" under "Basic Types of Diagnostic Tests."

Risk. This is simple and painless. There is virtually no risk involved.

RESPIRATORY SYSTEM TESTS

ARTERIAL PUNCTURE

Purpose. Arterial blood gas sampling measures how well the lungs are functioning in delivering oxygen to the blood and clearing carbon dioxide from it, and how efficient the heart is as a pump. (On the other hand, venous blood—usually taken from a vein in the crook of the elbow—reflects cell metabolism.)

Preparation. No special preparation is necessary.

Time. The test takes less than 5 minutes.

Procedure. The test may be done in a doctor's office, a commercial laboratory, or at the bedside of a hospitalized patient. After the skin is cleansed, a small needle is inserted, usually in the radial artery at the wrist, and a small amount of blood is withdrawn. The radial artery is chosen because the ulnar artery, located on the opposite side of the wrist, serves the same body parts, so that circulation is not interrupted. Since the pressure in the arteries is greater than that in the veins, pressure must be applied to the needle site for several minutes after the needle is withdrawn to be sure that bleeding stops. When frequent sampling is necessary, such as in cardiovascular surgery, an indwelling catheter, or arterial line, may be used. The blood sample is placed in a blood gas analyzer and checked for levels of oxygen, carbon dioxide, and pH.

Risk. Assuming the ulnar artery is functioning, there is virtually no risk involved in this procedure using the radial artery. With an indwelling catheter, there may be a rare risk of infection or of injury to the artery.

BRONCHOGRAPHY

Purpose. Bronchography is an x-ray of the trachea and the bronchial tree used to help locate obstructions, tumors, or cysts in the bronchial tube, or to help guide a bronchoscope during bronchoscopy.

Preparation. To minimize nausea, the patient will be asked not to eat for 6 to 12 hours beforehand.

Time. The test takes about 1 hour.

Procedure. The test is usually done in a hospital but may be done on an outpatient basis. A local anesthetic will be first sprayed and later dripped through a long, thin tube called a catheter, which is passed through the nose or mouth into the throat and down the windpipe. The catheter is used to administer the contrast medium, followed by the taking of the x-ray.

Risk. Complications are generally rare, but as with all invasive procedures involving contrast dye there are risks of infection, damage to the trachea or windpipe from the catheter, and the possibility of allergic reaction to either the anesthetic or dye. The contrast medium will usually dissipate over several hours, but if some of it remains blocked in the ends of the small branches of the bronchial tubes, it can cause irritation and, rarely, lung collapse.

BRONCHOSCOPY

Purpose. Bronchoscopy allows the doctor to see inside the trachea and bronchial tree to check for tumors or foreign bodies, to locate the site of internal bleeding, to remove mucus or a foreign body, or to obtain a tissue or secretion specimen. It may be used to help diagnose cancer, tuberculosis, or other pulmonary diseases caused by bacteria, fungi, or parasites.

Preparation. If local anesthesia is used, a sedative may also be used to help the patient relax. The patient will be asked not to eat for 6 to 12 hours before the test, and to remove any dentures.

Time. The procedure takes about 30 minutes.

Procedure. The procedure is done in the hospital and may involve either general anesthesia, which is inhaled or injected, or local anesthesia, which is generally sprayed into the nose and mouth. For most procedures, the flexible fiber-optic bronchoscope is used, since it allows the doctor to see more and presents less risk of injury to the patient. But the rigid, hollow tube will be used if a foreign body must be removed or if a large biopsy sample is necessary. Various attachments to the bronchoscope allow the suctioning off of excess mucus, the injecting of saline to wash the inner surfaces, and gentle brushing to take samples of cells from the mucous lining. There may be some soreness following the test, especially if a biopsy is taken.

Risk. As with all invasive procedures, there is a risk of injury to the test site, including the teeth, gums, throat, or bronchial tube, although these are relatively rare and less apt to happen with a flexible tube. There is also a risk of allergic reaction to the anesthesia.

LARYNGOSCOPY

Purpose. This procedure allows the doctor to see directly into the larynx to detect foreign bodies, tumors, or other abnormalities.

Procedure. Laryngoscopy is very similar to a bronchoscopy, except that the endoscope does not enter as far into the body. The preparation and risks are generally the same. The patient may experience a sore throat and may cough up blood afterward, but this is generally not serious. (See preceding description.)

LUNG CAPACITY TEST

Purpose. This test (also known as a pulmonary function test) is used to determine the cause of shortness of breath and to detect the presence of diseases or injury. It is often used before surgery or to evaluate disability for insurance purposes.

Preparation. The patient will be told not to eat a heavy meal or smoke for 6 hours before the test and to avoid wearing constricting clothing or taking analgesics.

Time. It takes about 45 to 60 minutes.

Procedure. The test is usually performed in a doctor's office or a laboratory. During the test, the patient wears nose clips (to prevent air from escaping through the nostrils) and breathes into a flexible tube called a spirometer. Various breathing patterns are tested, such as breathing normally, exhaling as fast as possible after inhaling normally, or inhaling and exhaling deeply. The patient may also breathe specific quantities of helium, nitrogen, or pure oxygen.

Risk. Although some patients may find the test tiring, there is no pain or risk.

LUNG SCAN

Purpose. There are two types of lung scans, ventilation and perfusion, which can be used to detect infection, pulmonary embolism, and tumors, and to evaluate emphysema and other breathing problems.

Preparation. No special preparation is necessary.

Time. It takes about 30 minutes.

Procedure. The test is usually done on an outpatient basis. For a perfusion scan, the isotope is given intravenously; for a ventilation scan, it is mixed with a gas and inhaled. (See "Radioisotope Scans" under "Basic Types of Diagnostic Tests" for more information.)

Risk. The only risk, which is rare, is from radioisotope overdose.

MEDIASTINOSCOPY

Purpose. This procedure allows direct visualization of the tissues and organs in the chest cavity behind the breastbone (sternum) and is used to detect or evaluate infections and various types of cancers.

Preparation. Because general anesthesia is used, the patient may be asked to fast for 8 to 12 hours beforehand.

Time. It takes about an hour.

Procedure. Mediastinoscopy is performed in the hospital with the patient under general anesthesia. After an endotracheal tube is inserted, the surgeon makes a small incision in the chest and inserts the mediastinoscope, which is used to collect tissue specimens for analysis.

Risk. After the procedure, the patient will probably experience chest pain, soreness at the incision site, and a sore throat from the endotracheal tube. There is the usual risk that accompanies the use of general anesthesia. Although rare, there are also risks of damage to internal organs, infection, hemorrhage, and laryngeal nerve damage.

THORACENTESIS

Purpose. Thoracentesis (also called pleural tap or pleural fluid analysis) is used to obtain a sample of fluid from the cavity between the lungs and the chest wall in order to diagnose cancer, tuberculosis, blood and lymphatic disorders, or to relieve pressure caused by excess fluid in this area.

Procedure. This procedure, which is usually performed in the hospital, is very similar to amniocentesis (see "Reproductive System Tests" earlier in this chapter), but rather than lying down, the patient is usually seated, leaning forward, and bent over in order to provide as much room as possible between the ribs for insertion of the needle.

Risk. Occasionally a lung is accidentally punctured, which may cause it to collapse, a condition that is not serious and can be readily treated.

SKELETAL SYSTEM TESTS

ARTHROGRAPHY

Purpose. This procedure (also called arthrogram) provides x-ray visualization of a joint, especially the knee or shoulder, used to diagnose abnormalities or injuries to the cartilage, tendons, and ligaments.

Preparation. No special preparation is necessary.

Time. It takes about 1 hour.

Procedure. Arthrography is usually performed on an outpatient basis. A local anesthetic is injected first and then the contrast medium—either dye or air, or both—is injected into the joint. If the knee is being examined, the patient may be asked to walk a few steps in order to spread the contrast medium. The joint is examined using fluoroscopy and x-rays may be taken. For a day or so afterward, there may be some pain and swelling and the patient may be able to hear the liquid moving within the joint when the joint is exercised. The patient will generally be advised to rest and not put any strain on the joint.

Risk. There is little risk in this procedure, other than the slight possibility of infection or allergy to the contrast dye.

ARTHROSCOPY

Purpose. This procedure, which uses a fiber-optic endoscope to see the interior of a joint, is used to diagnose various joint diseases or to perform surgery on the joint.

Preparation. There is no special preparation, but the patient may be asked to fast for 8 to 12 hours beforehand.

Time. It takes about 1 hour.

Procedure. Arthroscopy is usually done on an outpatient basis unless the patient is already hospitalized. The joint, particularly the knee, may be wrapped in an elastic bandage, or a tourniquet may be used to keep as much blood as possible away from the joint. A local anesthetic is injected and a small incision made through which an endoscope—in this instance, an arthroscope—is inserted (see figure 12.11). The joint may be rotated to

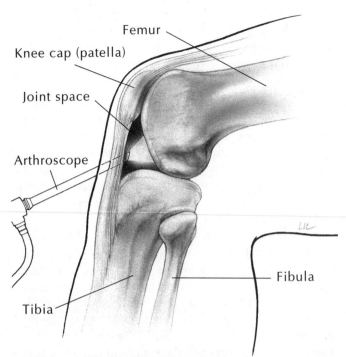

Figure 12.11: Arthroscopy of the knee, in which the arthroscope is inserted directly into the joint space to allow the doctor to see its interior.

Femur
Knee cap (patella)
Joint space
Arthroscope
Tibia
Fibula

several positions of extension and flexion during the procedure. Various attachments to the endoscope may be used to irrigate the joint or take a biopsy specimen. There may be some pressure or discomfort from the tourniquet or the procedure. The incision will be sutured and bandaged and, although the patient may walk or use the joint afterward, excessive use should be avoided for several days.

Risk. As with all invasive procedures, there is always the risk of infection or damage to internal structures, but this is rare.

BONE SCAN

Purpose. This radioisotope test provides a view of the bone useful in diagnosing cancer, bone trauma, and degenerative disorders.

Preparation. No special preparation is required. The patient may be asked to drink several glasses of water or tea before the scan begins.

Time. The isotope is injected and takes about 3 hours to reach the bone, during which time the patient can usually leave. The scan itself takes another hour.

Procedure. A bone scan is usually done on an outpatient basis. Scans are taken with the patient lying in various positions. (See "Radioisotope Scans" under "Basic Types of Diagnostic Tests.")

Risk. Other than the remote possibility of isotope overdose, there is no real risk involved.

DYNAMIC GAIT ANALYSIS

Purpose. The test assesses how people run or play a sport. It is often given to athletes to determine the most efficient use of their athletic abilities.

Preparation. The patient dresses and brings whatever equipment is appropriate for the activity to be analyzed.

Time. Depending on the activity under examination, it usually takes less than 30 minutes.

Procedure. The analysis is done in a doctor's office, exercise laboratory, or physical therapy facility. The patient is asked to perform the activity that is causing discomfort or for which improvement is desired, such as running on a treadmill or pedaling a bicycle. The movements are done at different rates and levels as appropriate. This is recorded on videotape and observed by a sports medicine clinician, such as a physician, physical therapist, or a trained technician. Subsequently, the patient observes the videotape and listens to the clinician's analysis.

Risk. There is no discomfort unless prior pain is reproduced, and there are no risks associated with this analysis.

LIGAMENT TEST

Purpose. Also known as the Stryker test or KT-1000, this test evaluates the strength of knee ligaments by isolating them and comparing their activity with normal joints. It can document physical strength and provide evidence such as might be needed for worker's compensation claims.

Preparation. You will be asked to remain totally relaxed on an examining table.

Time. It takes about 5 minutes.

Procedure. In the physician's office, a ligament tester machine is strapped to the legs. It puts stress on the knee joints by moving them back and forth. Results are printed on a graph and compared with normal findings.

Risk. There are no risks associated with the test.

THYROID TESTS

THYROID SCAN AND IODINE UPTAKE TEST

Purpose. These two radioisotope procedures, often done together, provide information on the size, structure, position, and functioning of the thyroid and are used to aid diagnosis of hyper- and hypothyroidism.

Preparation. In preparation for these tests, the patient is required to discontinue for 2 or 3 days any thyroid hormones and medications and food containing iodine (a list is usually provided by the doctor), and to fast for 8 to 12 hours beforehand.

Time. The thyroid scan takes only about 10 minutes and the uptake procedure involves three separate short scans at 2, 6, and 24 hours, with the patient allowed to leave between scans.

Procedure. These tests are normally done on an outpatient basis. The radioisotope-containing iodine is administered orally. (See "Radioisotope Scans" under "Basic Types of Diagnostic Tests.")

Risk. There is no real risk, other than the remote possibility of a radioisotope overdose.

THYROID ULTRASONOGRAPHY

Purpose. This noninvasive procedure allows the doctor to see the thyroid gland in order to evaluate its structure, monitor its size during therapy, and differentiate between a cyst and a tumor. Ultrasonography is often done in conjunction with thyroid scans.

Preparation. No special preparation is required.

Time. Ultrasonography requires about 30 minutes.

Procedure. It is done on an outpatient basis and is riskless and painless. (See "Ultrasonography" under "Basic Types of Diagnostic Tests" for more information.)

TSH, T_4, T_3

(See the section "Common Blood Analyses" in this chapter.)

URINARY SYSTEM TESTS

CYSTOMETRY

Purpose. This test is used to assess the neuromuscular function of the bladder when there are incontinence problems.

Preparation. It requires no special preparation, but the patient may be asked to void beforehand.

Time. Cystometry takes about 45 minutes.

Procedure. This is usually done on an outpatient basis. The test measures the patient's ability to feel sensations, such as hot, cold, and urgency to void, and the ability to suppress voiding. A catheter is inserted into the bladder and a predetermined amount of sterile water or gas (usually carbon dioxide) is injected into the bladder. The patient is asked to report all sensations, such as when the need to void is first felt; when the feeling can no longer be controlled; whether there is any feeling of fullness, nausea, or flushing; and whether the fluid feels warm or cold. The patient is then asked to urinate and the volume is measured. Any urine that remains in the bladder is drained.

Risk. Although there is always the possibility of infection with catheterization, there is little risk involved in this procedure.

CYSTOURETHROSCOPY

Purpose. This procedure (also called cystoscopy) is used to diagnose urinary tract disorders and provides a direct view of the urethra, bladder, and sometimes the uterus.

Preparation. If general anesthesia is used, the patient will be asked to fast for at least 8 hours beforehand.

Time. It takes about 30 minutes.

Procedure. Cystourethroscopy can be an inpatient or an outpatient procedure using general or local anesthesia. The patient lies on his or her back with knees drawn up while the instrument, which consists of two tubes used separately, the cystoscope and the urethroscope, is inserted into the urethra and then into the bladder (see figures 12.12A and B). Fluid may be injected into the bladder to distend the walls and provide a better view, and urine and biopsy specimens may be taken during the examination.

Risk. If local anesthesia is used, the patient may feel some burning or discomfort when the endoscopes are passed and when the bladder is filled. As with all invasive procedures, there is always the possibility of damage to internal structures, but this is rare.

VOIDING CYSTOURETHROGRAPHY

Purpose. Voiding cystourethrography (also called voiding urethrogram) provides an x-ray picture of the bladder and urethra during urination and is used to diagnose abnormalities, infection, or other disorders of the urinary tract.

Preparation. No special preparation is needed.

Time. The test takes about 30 minutes.

Procedure. The test is usually performed on an outpatient basis. A catheter is inserted into the urethra and into the bladder, which, after it is drained of any urine, is filled with contrast dye until the patient has the urge to void. Still or moving x-ray pictures are taken of the urinary tract as the patient voids.

Risk. There may be some discomfort as the catheter is passed. There are no aftereffects and very little risk associated with this procedure, unless it is repeated several times, in which case there is a risk of excess radiation exposure.

PYELOGRAPHY, INTRAVENOUS

Purpose. This contrast x-ray procedure (also called excretory urography or IVP) allows the doctor to see inside the kidneys, ureters, and bladder to evaluate the functioning of the kidneys and urinary tract.

Preparation. The patient is usually given a laxative or enema and asked to fast for 8 hours beforehand.

Time. It takes about 60 minutes.

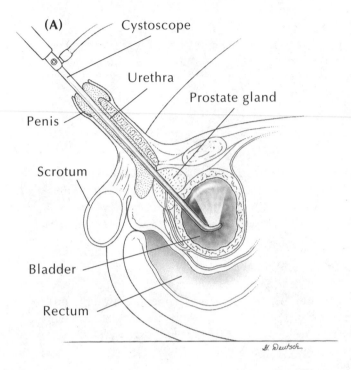

(A)
Cystoscope
Urethra
Prostate gland
Penis
Scrotum
Bladder
Rectum

G. Deutsch

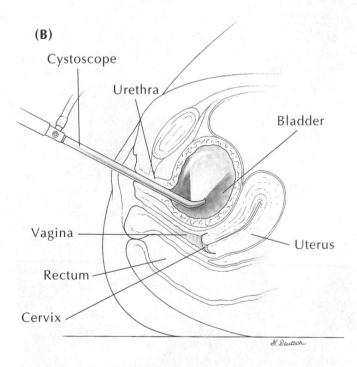

(B)
Cystoscope
Urethra
Bladder
Vagina
Uterus
Rectum
Cervix

G. Deutsch

Figure 12.12A and B. Drawings of cystuorethscopy in both male (12.12A) and female (12.12B). The cystoscope is threaded through the urethra and into the bladder.

Procedure. IVP can be done on an inpatient or outpatient basis. While the patient lies on his or her back on the x-ray table, the contrast medium is injected intravenously and x-rays are taken at regular intervals (5, 10, 15, and 20 minutes) as the dye travels from the kidneys through the urinary tract. The abdomen may be compressed to restrict the dye to the upper urinary tract for the first part of the study. The patient is then asked to void and another x-ray is taken.

Risk. The contrast medium may produce a burning sensation and a fishy or metallic taste in the mouth (even though nothing is swallowed). There is some risk of allergic reaction to the contrast medium, and the patient should report any unusual sensations to the doctor during the test and afterward. There is also a radiation risk if the procedure is repeated several times.

RENAL SCAN AND RENOGRAM

Purpose. These two types of kidney scans, which are often done together, provide information on the size, shape, and position of the kidneys (renal scan) and the flow of blood and production of urine within the kidneys (renogram).

Preparation. No special preparation is necessary.

Time. The procedures take about 50 to 90 minutes.

Procedure. The procedures can be done on an outpatient basis. With the renogram, the patient sits while the scanner is placed against the back over the kidneys. The isotope is administered by IV. With the renal scan, the isotope is injected with the patient lying down. The patient may feel some flushing or nausea when the radioisotope is administered. (See "Radioisotope Scans" under "Basic Types of Diagnostic Tests.")

Risk. there is a rare risk of isotope overdose.

RETROGRADE URETHROGRAPHY

Purpose. This contrast x-ray visualization of the front part of the urethra is used to diagnose abnormalities or injuries. It is done almost exclusively in males.

Preparation. No special preparation is required, but the patient may be given a tranquilizer.

Time. It takes about 30 minutes.

Procedure. Retrograde urethrography is usually done on an outpatient basis. The penis is held in an extended position using a special clamp and a catheter is inserted into the urethra, through which the contrast medium is injected. X-rays are taken of the patient in several positions. If the procedure is done on a woman, a special catheter with a small balloon on each end is inserted into the urethra and the balloon is used to keep the contrast medium from running out.

Risk. There may be some discomfort when the contrast dye is injected. There is a risk of allergic reaction to

HOME TESTING

In recent years a number of at-home tests have been developed that can detect disease, monitor a condition, or provide reassurance if they indicate the absence of a problem. While these tests should not be substituted for care by a physician, they can save the consumer time and money by eliminating unnecessary visits to a doctor. Because they are not 100 percent accurate, when any doubt exists test results should be confirmed independently. Any unusual result or disturbing symptom should be reported to a physician.

A number of tests for different medical conditions, which are marketed under a variety of brand names and are widely available in pharmacies, are considered safe and useful.

Test	Method	Comments
Blood pressure	There are two methods for monitoring blood pressure at home. One uses the traditional arm cuff and stethoscope, the other uses a micro-electronic monitor.	This is a useful monitoring device for those undertaking lifestyle change or taking medication to lower blood pressure. For detailed information, see chapter 16, Heart and Blood Vessel Diseases.
Diabetes	There are two methods available for monitoring blood sugar levels. Both start by pricking the finger to obtain a drop of blood, placing the drop on a plastic treated strip, and waiting a specified period, usually under 2 minutes. One then compares color change on the strip to color panels on the bottle for an estimated blood sugar level. The other uses an electronic device for an exact reading.	Most people with diabetes should monitor their blood sugar at home and adjust their diet, exercise, and medication accordingly to maintain optimum control. For detailed information, see chapter 21, Diabetes and Other Endocrine Disorders.
Hemoccult	This test can detect hidden or microscopic blood in the stool, a possible early sign of colon cancer, or other conditions that cause gastrointestinal bleeding. The Hemoccult test involves either placing a small amount of stool on chemically treated paper and noting a change in color, or dropping a chemically treated pad into the toilet after a bowel movement. If the pad changes color, there may be occult blood in the stool. It is important to follow the instructions carefully before taking the test. Red meat, aspirin, vitamin C pills, and certain other foods and medications should be avoided for several days before the test because they can give false-positive results.	The American Cancer Society advises everyone over the age of 50 to do at least one at-home occult blood test a year. Blood in the stool, however, does not necessarily indicate colorectal cancer. Many conditions, including hemorrhoids, polyps, aspirin use, ulcers, and intestinal bleeding, among others, can produce blood in the stool. Those testing positive should consult a physician for further tests. Anyone with a family history of colorectal cancer should undergo annual screening for the disease.
Ovulation	About 24 hours before a woman ovulates, the level of luteinizing hormone (LH) in her urine increases. The test kit contains several dipsticks that a woman starts using to test her first morning urine about a week after the end of her last menstrual period. Results are available in about 35 minutes.	Home ovulation tests can help women who are trying to become pregnant, especially those having trouble conceiving, by revealing the time of maximum fertility.

HOME TESTING (Cont.)

Test	Method	Comments
Pregnancy	A woman places chemicals (reagents) and a specified number of drops of urine into a test tube, shakes, and waits 10 to 20 minutes. If the hormone is present, the urine changes color.	These self-tests detect hormonal changes associated with pregnancy within 3 days of a missed period. Positive results are 99 percent accurate. Negative results are less reliable. If the test is negative, another test, a few days later, is recommended. For more information, see chapter 9, Health Concerns of Women.
Strep throat	The individual dabs his or her own throat with a cotton swab chemically treated to attract the bacteria, then immerses it in a special solution. If the streptococcal bacteria are present, the swab will turn blue in 10 minutes.	Until recently, the test to detect the streptococcus bacteria that cause strep throat required a visit to the doctor and a wait of several days for the results. However, a positive home test necessitates a visit to the doctor and possibly a repeat test before the individual is treated with antibiotics.
Urinary infections	This test uses either a reagent or chemically treated dipstick that changes color if certain types of bacteria or blood are present in the urine, indications of a possible urinary tract infection.	Although not perfect, the test can detect an infection in its early stages before burning or pain develop. It is particularly useful for women who are prone to recurrent bouts of cystitis. If the test is positive, a physician can telephone a prescription to a pharmacy.
Pap test	Not recommended	All Pap tests to screen for cervical cancer should be done by a physician in conjunction with a physical examination of a woman's cervix.

the contrast medium and, as with all invasive procedures, a risk of internal injury or infection. There will probably be some soreness or irritation at the opening of the urethra.

URINE TESTS

Many of the same substances that are tested for in the blood are also tested for in the urine.

ROUTINE URINE ANALYSIS

A single urine specimen, collected by urinating into a paper cup or other clean receptacle, is used to test for the following:

Substance	Tests for
Blood	Stones, infection, tumors
White blood cells	Infection
Glucose	Diabetes
Ketones	Diabetes
Bile	Liver disease
Protein	Injured glomeruli (blood vessels in the kidneys)
Protein casts	Kidney disease

TIMED URINE SPECIMENS

Some of the substances produced by the body, such as hormones, are excreted in short bursts, rather than continuously. They may show up in the urine, but their presence and quantity will vary throughout the day, and thus one urine sample will not be a reliable indicator. In this case a timed specimen collection is used, with the patient saving all of the urine produced in a 12- or 24-hour period. For example, if the test is to begin at 8:00 A.M., the patient empties his or her bladder at that hour, but does not collect that urine. All of the rest of the urine produced in the next 24 hours is collected in a clean container, and at 8:00 A.M. the next day, the patient urinates and collects the final sample.

Calcium, an indication of kidney stones or gallstones, is one of the substances tested for in this way. Timed collection is also used when a case of high blood pressure is not responding to therapy and the doctor suspects that the condition may be caused by the presence of a tumor known as a pheochromocytoma.

OTHER COLLECTION METHODS

First Void. This is the first urine passed in the morning, sometimes used in testing because, since the patient presumably has not urinated in many hours, the sample will be very concentrated, and may show substances that will not be present later.

Clean Catch, Midstream. This is a method used when an infection is suspected and the doctor is looking for evidence of bacteria. Since the first bit of urine may be contaminated with bacteria that have migrated into the urethra from the outside, it is not a reliable indicator. The patient urinates a little into a toilet or bedpan and then, without interrupting the flow, urinates about an ounce more in the collection vial (finishing urinating into the toilet, if necessary).

PART IV

First Aid and Safety

13
Basics
of CPR
and Life
Support

• • • • • • • • • • • • • •

**MYRON WEISFELDT,
M.D. AND A. L. LOOMIS
BELL, JR., M.D.**

In an emergency situation, life-support techniques can be vital for the survival of a person whose heartbeat or breathing has stopped. However, for adults who have suffered cardiac arrest, the most important lifesaving step is to call for help: Few adults whose hearts have stopped can be saved by cardiopulmonary resuscitation (CPR) without using the equipment employed by professional paramedics. On the other hand, children have a better chance of being revived in an emergency situation. But, in any case, emergency medical help should always be summoned as quickly as possible.

The three most important emergency medical procedures are:

- Artificial respiration (for child drowning victims, this action alone may be life-preserving)
- Cardiopulmonary resuscitation (CPR)
- Clearing obstructed airways from choking (Heimlich maneuver)

CARDIOPULMONARY RESUSCITATION

DEFINITION

Cardiopulmonary resuscitation encompasses more than one simple rescue technique for saving someone whose heart or breathing has stopped. Rather, it is an organized approach to assessing and dealing with a medical emergency. It requires learning the physical skills of artificial respiration (mouth-to-mouth breathing) and closed chest compressions, as well as the proper timing and a specific sequence in which to use the skills.

The American Heart Association, which sets the standards for CPR training, uses the mnemonic "ABC" to represent the three major functions restored by CPR:

- Airway
- Breathing
- Circulation

It is strongly recommended that those who wish to learn CPR take a formal course offered by the American Heart Association or the American Red Cross, which allows adequate time to practice on a training mannequin under close supervision of an instructor.

Always perform life support techniques **as quickly as possible after an injury.** Except under very unusual circumstances, brain damage is likely to occur 4 to 6 minutes after cardiopulmonary arrest and the likelihood and severity of this damage increase each minute there-

after. In the case of a life-threatening medical emergency, life-support techniques should be offered in the following order:

1. Call for help.
2. Restore breathing if breathing has stopped (particularly important for children pulled from the water).
3. Restore circulation if there is no heartbeat or pulse.
4. Stop any bleeding.
5. Treat for shock.

CAUSE

Cardiopulmonary arrest can have many origins. Accidents may result in choking, drowning, suffocation, or electrocution. Strokes, heart attacks, drug overdoses, blood loss, or carbon monoxide poisoning can all lead to a loss of consciousness and cessation of breathing or heartbeat.

DIAGNOSIS: WHEN TO OFFER CPR

CPR should be offered to victims who are unconscious and have no breath or heartbeat. When you approach an apparently unconscious person, call to and jar the victim to determine whether he or she is indeed unconscious or merely sleeping.

If the victim is indeed unconscious, you must be sure that the airway—the passage between the mouth and lungs—is not blocked by the tongue or an object, which would prevent breathing. (If the throat or breathing passage is blocked by an object, see "Choking and Obstructed Airway.") If there is no obstruction, determine if the victim is breathing and if there is a pulse, indicating circulation.

Depending on the state of the victim, you will start mouth-to-mouth breathing alone or chest compressions interspersed with breathing. You must continue until the victim revives, a trained person takes over, or you become exhausted.

TREATMENT: PERFORMING CPR

Treatment must be offered quickly to avoid brain damage from lack of blood and oxygen. To help you establish a sense of timing, and to make sure that you are spending adequate, but not too much, time on each step, the recommended time span for each activity is provided in parentheses.

FIRST STEPS (4–10 SECONDS)

1. ESTABLISH UNRESPONSIVENESS

When presented with a seemingly unconscious victim, first establish unresponsiveness by jarring the person firmly and shouting "Are you okay?" (Okay is understood in virtually every language.) If you get no response,

Figure 13.1: Establish unresponsiveness by shaking the victim gently by the shoulders. At the same time, call out for help.

Figure 13.2: Support the victim's neck with one hand as you turn him over with the other.

shake the person gently by the shoulders and shout again. (See figure 13.1.) It is important to be sure that the person really is unconscious, so that you don't do CPR unnecessarily.

2. CALL FOR HELP

At the same time as you establish unconsciousness, call out for help, even if no one is in sight. This may bring someone within earshot to your aid, and this person, if not trained in CPR, may be able to phone for medical aid. If a second person is present, have her call the Emergency Medical Service (EMS) system. Whoever calls for help should furnish as much information as possible about the victim's condition.

3. POSITION THE VICTIM

For CPR to be effective, the victim must be flat on his

back on a firm surface. If you find the victim lying face down, turn him over, rolling him toward you. First, take the arm that will be on the underside as he rolls and stretch it out straight over his head. Put one of your hands behind his neck to support it as you turn him (see figure 13.2). With your other hand, grasp his upper arm and roll him over gently.

RESTORE BREATHING (3–5 SECONDS)

1. OPEN THE AIRWAY

Once the person is on his back and you are sure he is unconscious, open the airway to be sure that he can breathe. In an unconscious person, the tongue relaxes and falls against the back of the throat, preventing air from getting from the mouth and nose to the lungs (see figures 13.3 and 13.4).

Figure 13.3 and 13.4: The drawing at left shows airway obstruction from the tongue and epiglottis. Figure at right shows the airway obstruction cleared by tilting the head and lifting the chin.

Kneel at right angles to the person's shoulder on whichever side is more convenient or comfortable. Using the hand closer to the victim's head, place your palm across his forehead, and firmly tilt the head backward. Two fingers of the other hand are placed below the bone of the chin and lifted forward. This chin lift tilts the head back and opens the airway (see figure 13.4). Avoid closing the mouth completely as you will need the lips open slightly for mouth-to-mouth breathing.

If an injury to the neck is suspected, the chin lift alone should be used to open the airway. Tilting of the head in the presence of injury to the spine or the neck could cause further injury to the spinal cord.

Practice tip: Lie on the floor and extend your neck back until your chin is pointing straight up and you have trouble swallowing. This is approximately the correct position for opening the airway.

2. CHECK FOR BREATHING

With your hands still in place on the victim's forehead and lifted chin, check for breathing. Looking toward his chest, bend over so that your cheek is almost touching his nose and mouth.

- **Look** to see if his chest is rising and falling.
- **Listen** for sounds of breathing.
- **Feel** if there is expired air on your cheek.

Figure 13.5: When you give rescue breathing, note the chest movements with the breaths.

Look, listen, and feel for several seconds. Sometimes opening the airway is all that is needed and the victim will begin breathing spontaneously. If nothing happens, try opening the airway again. If you see the chest rise and fall, but do not hear or feel air, the victim is attempting to breathe, but the airway is still blocked. See "Choking and Obstructed Airway" in this chapter.)

3. GIVE 2 EVEN BREATHS (3–5 SECONDS)

If there is no evidence of breathing, the victim is not getting any oxygen, and you must get oxygen into the lungs where it can reach the blood. Keep your hands in place on the forehead and lifted chin (see figure 13.5). Using the hand on his forehead, pinch his nostrils together tightly with your thumb and forefinger to keep the air from escaping through his nose.

Take a deep breath, open your mouth wide, and place it completely over the victim's mouth to make a tight seal with your lips. You do not need to press down hard to get a tight seal, only to encircle completely the victim's mouth with your own. Exhale deliberately and evenly 2 breaths of 1 to 1½ seconds each. Take your mouth away to inhale between breaths and to allow air to escape from the victim's lungs (see figure 13.4).

As you administer rescue breathing, note chest movement as an indication of an open airway. Although you will feel some resistance from the victim's lungs, you should be able to feel air going in as you blow and to see the chest rise and fall.

Practice tip: To get a sense of what rescue breathing feels like, blow against your tightly clenched fist. The resistance you feel is akin to the feeling of a blocked airway. Now make a tiny hole in your fist and blow again. You will have to blow forcefully and you will still feel some resistance, but you should feel the air going through.

4. CHECK FOR PULSE (5–10 SECONDS)

Once you have given 2 even breaths, check to see if the victim has a pulse. The easiest place to check a pulse is on either of the carotid arteries, which run down both sides of the neck. Keeping one hand on the forehead, take your hand from under the victim's neck and place 2 fingers on his Adam's apple. Then slide them over into the groove between the Adam's apple and the neck muscle on the side closer to you (see figures 13.6 and 13.7). The carotid pulse should be felt in the space between these structures.

If you don't find a pulse immediately, move your fingers around slightly. Allow adequate time; the pulse may be slow and weak (although it may also be rapid).

Practice tip: Practice finding your own carotid pulse and then try it on someone else.

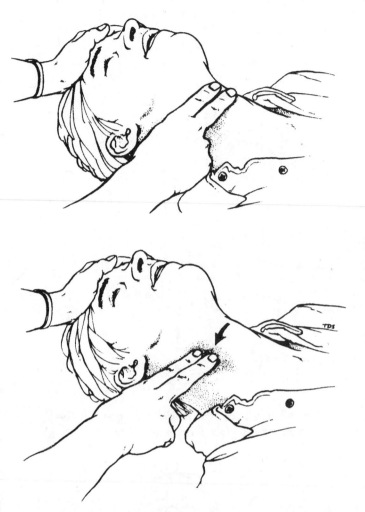

Figure 13.6 and 13.7: Locate the carotid pulse by placing 2 fingers on the Adam's apple, then sliding them into the groove on the side of the neck toward you.

5. GET MEDICAL HELP

If a second person is present, make sure she has called 911 for Emergency Medical Service (EMS). At this point, if someone is calling for help, you can give more complete information about the victim's condition. If you are still alone with the victim and a phone is not nearby, perform CPR for 1 minute before stopping to go call for EMS help yourself. If a phone is handy, CALL FIRST!

6. CONTINUE RESCUE BREATHING

If the victim does not have a pulse, skip this section and go on to Circulation.

If the victim has a pulse but is not breathing, you must now start mouth-to-mouth respiration. Just as you did before, keep your fingers and hand in position on the chin and forehead, pinch the nostrils closed, inhale and

make a seal with your mouth, and exhale air into the victim's lungs. Between breaths, turn your head to the side and look, listen, and feel for the victim's breathing.

Give a breath once every 5 seconds, taking your mouth away between breaths. Continue for 1 minute, or 12 breaths. At this point, check the pulse again. If there is a pulse, continue breathing once every 5 seconds until the victim begins to breathe on his own or medical help arrives. Check the pulse after every 12 breaths.

RESTORE CIRCULATION

If there is no pulse, you will have to create artificial circulation of the blood by compressing and releasing the chest. It may help you to imagine that by pushing down on the chest, you are squeezing the heart between the breastbone and the backbone and forcing blood out through the circulatory system.

The mechanism by which chest compression leads to blood circulation is actually the change of pressure within the chest resulting from each compression. When you push down, chest pressure increases and blood flows outward in the arteries to the brain and other vital organs, while one-way valves in the veins hold blood within the chest. On release, falling pressure in the chest results in the flow of blood into the chest from the venous system.

1. POSITION YOURSELF

Move down a little so you are kneeling next to the victim's chest, about midway between shoulder and waist. To find the correct hand position, first find the bottom margin of the rib cage, down near the abdomen. Using the hand closer to the victim's feet, follow the edge of the ribs as your fingers move up toward the center of the chest. You will feel a notch where the ribs meet the breastbone (see figure 13.8). Put your middle finger on this spot and then put your index finger next to your middle finger (see figure 13.9).

Now place the heel of your other hand next to the index finger (see figure 13.10). Place your other hand on top of the first. You can either interlace your fingers or keep them straight, but at no time should they rest on the chest (see figures 13.11 and 13.12). To avoid injuring the ribs, only the heel of your hand should touch the chest.

2. BEGIN COMPRESSIONS

Shift your weight forward on your knees until your shoulders are directly over your hands and your elbows are locked. Now, bear down and then come up, bear down and come up, keeping your elbows locked. In order to create enough pressure to circulate the blood, you must depress the chest of an average adult $1\frac{1}{2}$ to 2

Figure 13.8: Follow the bottom margin of the rib cage up to the notch where it meets the breastbone.

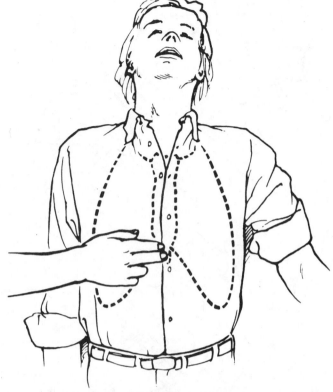

Figure 13.9: Place the middle finger on the notch and the index finger next to it.

inches with each compression. The proper speed is 80 to 100 compressions per minute. To get the right speed and rhythm, count out loud as you do the compressions, saying "1 and 2 and 3 and 4 and 5!" Rest on each "and," then compress on each number. Each series of 5 should take about 3 seconds.

Practice tip: Think of your arms as pistons, moving straight up and down. The compression phase should be about equal in time to the relaxation phase between compressions. Your hands should rest lightly on the chest between compressions to keep them in the proper position.

3. ALTERNATE COMPRESSIONS WITH RESCUE BREATHING

After each 15 compressions (counting to 5, 3 times), perform 2 rescue breaths. Take your hands off the chest, place them on the chin and forehead as before, pinch the nostrils, seal the mouth, and give 2 strong breaths, watching out of the corner of your eye for the chest to rise.

Go back to the chest, find the correct hand position again, and do 15 more compressions, followed by 2 more breaths. Repeat this cycle of 15 and 2 for a total of 4 times, which takes about 1 minute. Then check again

Figure 13.10: Place the heel of the other hand next to the index finger.

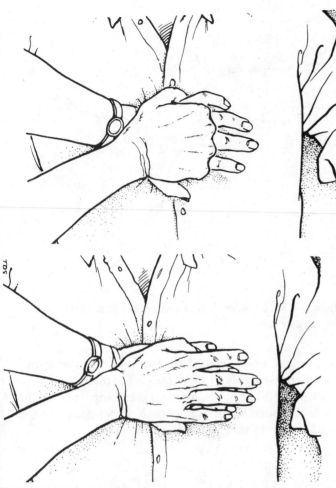

Figure 13.11 and 13.12: Placing one hand on top of the other, either interlock the fingers or keep them straight.

for pulse and breathing. If neither has returned, you must continue alternating compressions and breathing until the patient revives, qualified help comes, or you are too exhausted to continue.

CPR ON INFANTS AND CHILDREN

Although the steps and the sequence in which they are performed remain the same for infants and children as for adults, modifications should be made to compensate for the smaller lung capacity and faster respiration rate of babies. Compressions should be considerably less forceful than those used on adults.

The sequence of CPR for children is as follows:

1. ESTABLISH UNRESPONSIVENESS (4–10 SECONDS)

You must quickly determine if injury is present and determine consciousness. If head, neck, or spinal injury is suspected, great care must be exercised in positioning the child on her back on a firm flat surface. Turn and position the child, supporting the head and neck to

avoid spinal cord injury caused by rolling, twisting, or tilting the head and neck.

A conscious child struggling to breathe will often find the best position to keep a partially obstructed airway open and should be allowed to maintain that position until medical help is available. If the young victim is unresponsive, position the child or infant on the back on a firm, flat surface and begin CPR.

Call for help after conducting CPR for 1 minute as below. If the child is conscious but suffering respiratory distress, do not waste time on CPR maneuvers but get the child to medical help as soon as possible. (Unresponsive children should receive CPR as they are rushed to the hospital.)

2. OPEN THE AIRWAY AND CHECK FOR BREATHING (3–5 SECONDS)

If you are certain the child has not suffered a spinal injury, place your hand on the child's forehead and gently tilt the head slightly backward. In infants especially, excessive backward tilting of the head should be avoided.

Augment the head tilt by placing 1 or 2 fingers from the other hand under the chin and gently lifting upward (see figure 13.13). If you are not sure whether the child is breathing, while maintaining an open airway place your ear near the child's mouth and **listen** for breathing, **look** at the chest and abdomen for movement, and **feel** for air flow from the mouth. If the victim is breathing, maintain the airway; if no breathing is detected, CPR must proceed.

Figure 13.13: To open a child's airway, place your hand that is closest on the child's forehead and tilt back gently while lifting the chin with one or two fingers of the other hand.

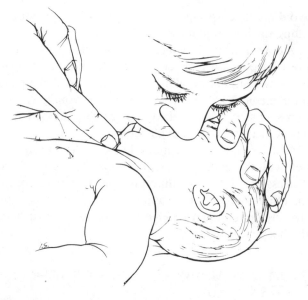

Figure 13.14: The mouth-to-mouth and nose seal on an infant.

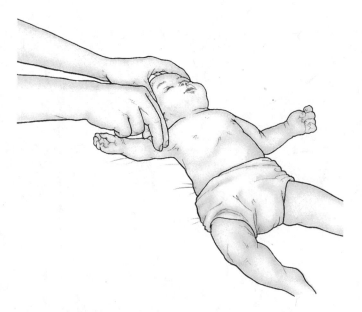

Figure 13.15: Check the pulse on the inside of the upper arm.

3. BREATHE FOR THE VICTIM (3–5 SECONDS)

While continuing to maintain an open airway, take a breath in, then hold it, open your mouth, and seal it over the mouth or the mouth and nose of the victim. In infants it is easier to seal your mouth over both the baby's nose and mouth (see figure 13.14). In larger children a mouth-to-mouth seal is more desirable with the nostrils pinched off by the fingers of the hand holding the forehead, as in adult rescue breathing.

Remember that an infant will need much less air than a larger child. A proper amount of air will move the chest up and down between breaths. A slow, deliberate delivery will reduce the likelihood of forcing air into the stomach, causing distention.

Rescue breathing is the single most important maneuver in rescuing a nonbreathing child or infant. If repeated rescue breathing attempts do not result in airflow into the lungs, evidenced by chest movement, a foreign body obstruction should be suspected. (See "Choking and Obstruction of Airway.")

4. CHECK FOR PULSE (5–10 SECONDS)

Children over 1 year will have a readily palpable carotid artery on the side of the neck between the windpipe and the strap muscles. While maintaining the head tilt with one hand, find the windpipe at the level of the Adam's apple with two fingers of the other hand. Slide the fingers into the groove between the windpipe and neck muscles, as for adults. If no pulse is felt, proceed with chest compression and rescue breathing as below.

Because infants under 1 year have a short neck, the brachial artery may be easier to feel. Place two fingers on the brachial artery located on the inside of the upper arm and press gently to feel a pulse (see figure 13.15).

If a pulse is felt but there is no breathing, initiate and continue rescue breathing about 20 times a minute for an infant and 15 times a minute for a child.

5. CALL EMS

If someone is available to help, have him call the EMS as soon as possible. If you are alone, complete 4 cycles of rescue breathing, or of breathing and chest compression, before taking time to call for help.

6. CHEST COMPRESSIONS

The child must be on her back on a firm surface, not a bed, for chest compressions to be effective. For an infant, the hard surface can be the palm of the hand, with head tilt provided by the weight of the infant's head and slight lift of the shoulders.

To locate the proper position for chest compression on an infant, place index, third, and fourth fingers below an imaginary line drawn between the two nipples and in the middle of the breastbone. The position of the third and fourth fingers denotes the area for chest compression.

The breastbone should be depressed ½ to 1 inch, 100 times per minute, with pressure released between each compression. A smooth compression-relaxation rhythm should be developed; give equal time to each without jerky movements (see figure 13.16).

If the child is over 1 year of age, compression is applied to the breastbone by the heel of one hand, located in the midline, 2 fingers'-breadth above the tip of the breastbone. With one hand, the chest is compressed

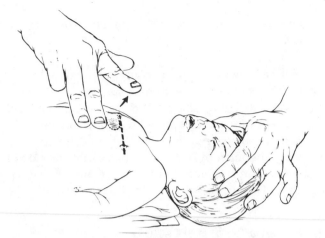

Figure 13.16: Place index, third and fourth fingers between an infant's nipples and in the middle of the breastbone for chest compressions.

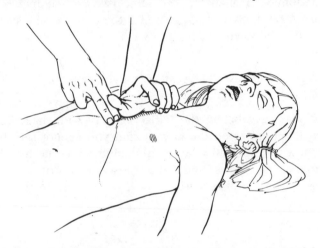

Figure 13.17: For chest compressions on a child over 1 year, use the heel of one hand on the breastbone 2 fingers'-breadth above its tip.

to a depth of 1 to 1½ inches at a rate of 80 to 100 compressions per minute, as for an adult. Compression and relaxation time should be equal and the rhythm smooth and even. The fingers must be kept off the chest (see figure 13.17).

External compression should be accompanied by rescue breathing in a 5:1 ratio of compressions to ventilation breaths for an infant or child. Continue compression and rescue breathing until the child revives, help arrives, or you become too exhausted to continue.

PROFESSIONAL CPR

When doctors and paramedics arrive on the scene of a CPR emergency, they may use a variety of equipment and drugs to assist in cardiopulmonary resuscitation.

Defibrillator. The primary piece of equipment used to restart circulation. Defibrillation—applying specialized electric current to "jump-start" the heart—should

be applied as early as possible to maximize the victim's chances of survival.

Epinephrine. A drug administered intravenously to stimulate the heart.

Note: A new, still experimental technique that has looked promising in early studies uses 4 pairs of trained hands simultaneously: 2 to compress the chest and 2 to interpose compression of the abdomen when the chest compressor is on a "release" beat.

CHOKING AND OBSTRUCTED AIRWAY

DEFINITION AND CAUSE

People who are choking may still be conscious and have circulation but are unable to breathe because something—usually food—is lodged in the throat. Choking on food often occurs after drinking alcohol, which dulls feeling in the throat. Frequently, a choking victim clutches the throat with thumb and forefinger, a universal signal of distress.

Children choke more frequently than adults, usually on a toy or food fragment. Infections such as croup or epiglottitis can produce extreme swelling that blocks the airway. If a child with a fever, a barking cough, or known infection develops an obstructed airway, do not waste time trying to open the obstructed airway—you probably will not be able to clear it. Get the child to a hospital emergency room at once while continuing efforts at mouth-to-mouth breathing.

DIAGNOSIS AND TREATMENT OF A CONSCIOUS VICTIM

Before you do anything to assist a person you think is choking, ask the victim to talk. If talk is possible, the airway is not completely obstructed and it is best to leave the victim alone until he can dislodge the food or object himself by coughing, throat-clearing, or with his fingers.

If the victim cannot talk, the airway is completely obstructed and you should assist in dislodging the obstruction. The technique recommended by the American Heart Association is a series of abdominal thrusts known as the Heimlich maneuver.

ABDOMINAL THRUSTS, OR HEIMLICH MANEUVER (5–6 SECONDS)

1. The victim should be sitting or standing. Grasp the victim from behind with your hands around his waist.

2. Make a fist with one hand and place the thumb side on the victim's abdomen, midway between the waist

and the rib cage. Grasp the fist with your other hand and thrust forcefully inward and upward. Each new thrust should be a separate and distinct movement (see figure 13.18). This maneuver can be done successfully if the victim is sitting in a straight-backed chair (such as in a restaurant).

You can also perform the Heimlich maneuver on yourself.

1. Make a fist with one hand, place the thumb side midline in the upper abdomen above your navel and below your breastbone, grasp the fist with your other hand and then press inward and upward with a quick motion.

2. If this maneuver is unsuccessful, you should press the upper abdomen over the back of a chair, the side of a table, or porch railing. Several such thrusts may be needed to dislodge the object and clear the airway.

CHEST THRUSTS (5–6 SECONDS)

1. If the victim is pregnant or especially obese, it is safer and easier to do a chest thrust rather than an abdominal maneuver. The same two-fist technique is used, but the victim is grasped at the breastbone instead of the abdomen (see figure 13.19).

DIAGNOSIS AND TREATMENT OF AN UNCONSCIOUS VICTIM

If you have begun the initial steps of CPR, including attempts to open the airway, and you cannot see the chest rise and fall when you administer rescue breathing, you should assume that the airway is obstructed and assist the victim as follows.

Figure 13.18: Abdominal thrusts (Heimlich maneuver) on conscious victim.

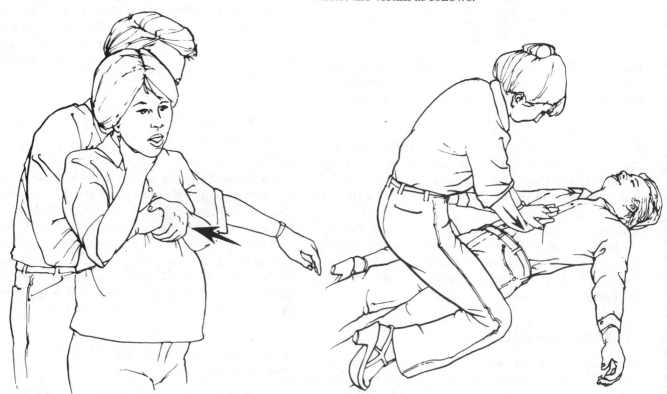

Figure 13.19: Chest thrust for pregnant or obese conscious victims.

Figure 13.20: Abdominal thrusts on an unconscious victim.

1. Abdominal Thrusts (5–6 seconds)

1. Kneeling next to or astride the victim, place the heel of one hand on the abdomen midway between the waist and the rib cage.

2. Place the other hand on top of the first (as you would for chest compressions, but on the abdomen rather than the chest) and thrust inward and upward. Give several quick thrusts (see figure 13.20).

2. Chest Thrusts (5–6 seconds)

1. With an unconscious pregnant or especially obese victim, substitute chest thrusts for abdominal thrusts.

2. Use the same hand position over the breastbone that you would for chest compressions, but do quick downward thrusts (see figure 13.21).

3. Finger Sweep (6–8 seconds)

Sweep the mouth of the victim if abdominal or chest thrusts do not dislodge the obstruction.

1. Open the victim's mouth wide by grasping the chin.
2. Still holding the chin, bend the forefinger of the other hand and with your hooked finger probe deep into

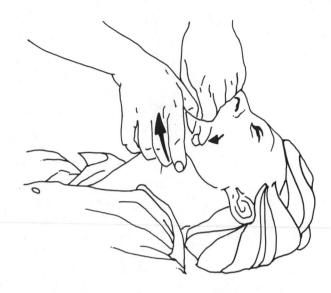

Figure 13.22: Grasp the chin while using the hooked forefinger of the other hand to sweep the mouth for the obstruction.

the mouth along the insides of the cheeks. Then go back to the open airway position and attempt rescue breathing (see figure 13.22).

3. If the airway is still not open, back blows, abdominal (or chest) thrusts, finger sweeps, and rescue breathing should be repeated rapidly as many times as is necessary to remove the obstruction. Occasionally, an open handed blow to the back may dislodge the obstruction and can be tried at this time. The longer the victim goes without oxygen, the more relaxed the muscles become, and this may release the foreign object, so that one of these maneuvers may ultimately be successful.

Obstructed Airway Management in Infants and Children

Infants (Up to 12 Months): Infections sometimes cause swelling that closes the airway in children and infants. In this case you should seek immediate medical attention at a hospital emergency room while providing mouth-to-mouth rescue breathing.

If an infant does not have an infection and the airway is completely obstructed, a combination of back blows and chest thrusts should be used to dislodge the obstruction, whether or not the infant is conscious. If the airway is only partially blocked (the infant can make noise with her voicebox) and the infant is making attempts to breathe and cough, let her continue.

Use a combination of back blows and chest thrusts to dislodge the airway obstruction while straddling the infant on your arm.

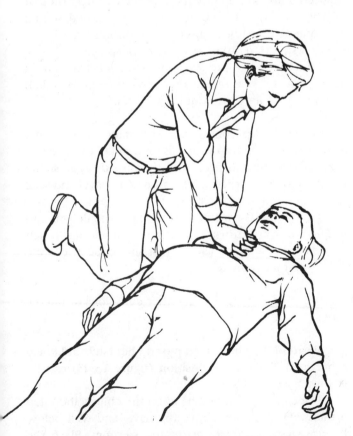

Figure 13.21: Chest thrusts on a pregnant or obese unconscious victim.

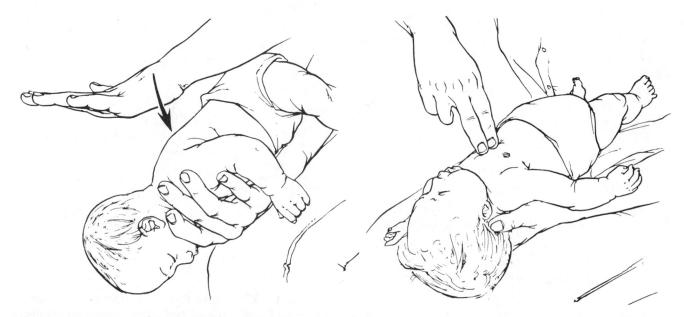

Figure 13.23: Deliver back blows with one hand while you support the infant with the other.

Figure 13.24: Chest thrusts to clear an obstructed airway use the same fingers and position as chest compressions, but a jabbing motion.

BACK BLOWS (4–6 SECONDS)

1. Lay the infant face down along your forearm with her head pointing toward the floor.

2. Support the baby's head with your hand on her jaw and rest your forearm on your thigh.

3. With the heel of your other hand, give the baby 4 rapid blows to the back between the shoulder blades (see figure 13.23).

CHEST THRUSTS (4–6 SECONDS)

1. After delivering the back blows, lay your free forearm along the baby's back with your fingers supporting her head and neck, sandwiching her between your two arms.

2. Turn the baby over so that she is now lying on her back on your other forearm and rest that arm on your thigh. Now that your other hand is free, use your middle and index fingers to give 4 quick chest thrusts in the center of the breastbone (see figure 13.24). (Chest thrusts are administered in the same location and with the same 2 fingers as chest compressions, but they are given with more of a thrusting or jabbing motion than a steady compression.)

3. Alternate back blows and chest thrusts. The finger sweep should not be used on an infant when you cannot see the obstructing object or your large adult finger may force the obstruction deeper into the throat.

4. If you can see the obstructing object, however, you can try to remove it with your fingers, being very careful not to push it farther down into the throat.

CHILDREN (MORE THAN 1 YEAR)

Children who have a known or suspected infection that may be the cause of the airway's being closed should get immediate medical attention—continue mouth-to-mouth respiration on the way to the hospital.

If infection is not the cause of airway obstruction, in children over 1 year of age abdominal thrusts (Heimlich maneuver) are used without back blows.

1. If the child is conscious and is standing or sitting, stand behind and wrap your arms around her waist.

2. Make a fist and place the thumb side against the upper abdomen in the midline above the navel and well below the tip of the breastbone.

3. Grasp your fist with the other hand and deliver 6 to 10 quick upward thrusts. Your hands should not touch the ribs or breastbone. Each thrust should be a separate and distinct movement.

If the child is lying down, either conscious or unconscious:

1. Position the child face up or on her back and kneel at her feet. The astride position (figure 13.25) can be used with larger children.

2. Place the heel of one hand on the child's abdomen in the midline slightly above the navel and well below the rib cage and lower tip of the sternum. Place the other hand on top of the fist and deliver several quick

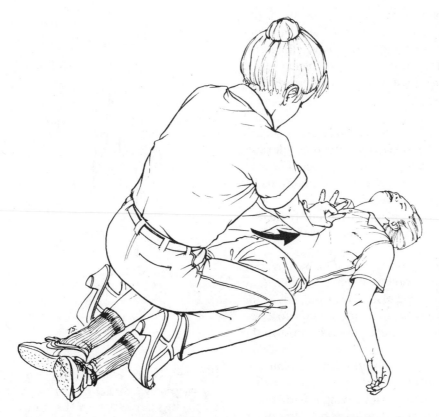

Figure 13.25: The Heimlich maneuver on a child lying down.

upward thrusts. A number of thrusts may be necessary to expel the object.

3. Use the head tilt/chin lift maneuvers to help open the airway (see section on CPR, page 388). It is important not to interfere with the forceful and potentially effective efforts the victim is making to expel the object.

Note: If your initial efforts to dislodge the obstruction are not successful, keep trying. Repeat obstructed airway maneuvers, as deepening anoxia (loss of oxygen) may relax the victim and allow the obstruction to be more easily overcome.

4. If you can see and grasp the obstructing object, remove it. Blind finger sweeps in the mouth (when you cannot see the obstruction), especially in infants and small children, should be avoided as the obstructing object may be pushed down farther.

BLEEDING OR HEMORRHAGE

DEFINITION

After clearing the airways and ensuring respiration and circulation in an emergency, the next major concern is to stop bleeding or hemorrhaging. Bleeding may be external,

from obvious cuts, punctures, or other wounds, or it may occur internally, in which case no obvious signs of hemorrhage will be evident. Internal bleeding, even when not apparent, may still be a critical, life-threatening situation.

TYPES OF EXTERNAL BLEEDING

Depending upon the nature of the wound, bleeding is classified as:

- **Arterial:** blood is bright red and, if the artery is exposed, the blood may escape in spurts synchronized with the pulse. This type of bleeding is the least frequent but the most serious.
- **Venous:** blood is dark red and flows slowly and steadily. This is the type of bleeding associated with most deeper cuts.
- **Capillary:** blood is medium red and oozes slowly. This is the type of bleeding associated with minor scrapes and cuts.

TREATMENT FOR BLEEDING

Bleeding from an ordinary cut or puncture wound usually can be controlled with direct pressure. Whenever tissue is cut, the body releases chemicals that interact with blood components to promote clotting (coagulation) while constricting or narrowing the blood vessels. Applying a bandage or clean cloth to a cut or wound and holding it firmly in place slows blood flow and allows the body's natural clotting mechanism to block bleeding.

When you are confronted with severe bleeding or injuries, follow these steps.

1. Lay the victim down, preferably with head slightly lowered (to prevent fainting) and the legs elevated unless a fracture is suspected or there is bleeding from the nose or mouth. (In those cases follow directions for broken bones and/or internal bleeding.)

2. If possible, expose the wound from under the victim's clothing and elevate the bleeding area to allow gravity to slow the bleeding.

3. Put pressure directly on the wound by covering with a sterile pad, clean cloth, or other suitable (and available) material. If nothing else is available, cover the wound directly with your hand. Don't attempt to clean the wound at this point; it is more important to stop the bleeding.

4. Maintain pressure for 10 minutes. Do not remove a blood-soaked pad or cloth; instead, apply another over it. A bandage can be held in place by tying it with a strip of cloth or stocking, or by wrapping a belt around it. Check for pulse beyond the injury. If you think you are cutting off circulation to areas beyond the wound, release for a few seconds and then resume pressure.

5. Transport the patient to an emergency room.

6. If direct pressure does not control the bleeding, continue to maintain pressure at the site of the wound and, at the same time, apply pressure at the appropriate pressure point over an artery or pulse point located above the wound toward the heart.

For example, if the bleeding is from a wound in the lower arm, apply pressure to the brachial artery, located midway between the armpit and elbow in the groove between the biceps and triceps. Grasp the person's arm in the middle, with your fingers on the inside of the arm and your thumb on the outside, using your fingers to press the flat, inside surface. If the bleeding is in the leg or lower part of the body, the appropriate pressure point is in the crotch area to the side of the pelvic bone. Pressing upon these pressure points will further reduce the flow of blood to the injured area and help promote clotting.

Note: Do not apply pressure to arteries leading to the head or neck, as this may interfere with blood circulation to the brain (see figure 13.26). Immobilize the injured part, leaving the bandages in place, and get the injured person to an emergency room or hospital.

7. Only use a tourniquet for an amputation with bleeding that cannot be controlled by direct or proximal pressure. If a tourniquet is applied, always note the time that it is initially tied. (See "Amputations" in chapter 14.)

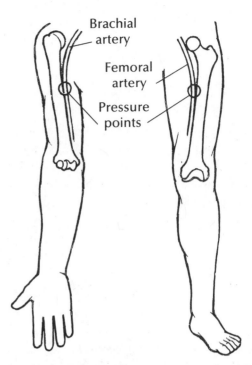

Figure 13.26: Hemorrhaging is controlled either by applying direct pressure to the wound or by applying pressure to the major artery serving the injured area at a point above the cut blood vessel.

BLEEDING FROM AN ABDOMINAL WOUND

Penetration of the abdominal wall is always a serious injury, due to both bleeding and the risk of injury to the abdominal organs. The victim should be taken to an emergency room or hospital as soon as possible after performing the following first aid.

1. Position the victim so that he is lying on his back. If there are no protruding internal organs, follow the steps for controlling the bleeding as outlined above. Cover the wound with a sterile pad or clean cloth and apply pressure to stop bleeding. Tape or bind the bandage in place.

2. If internal organs are exposed, cover the wound with a moist dressing, but avoid touching it or trying to reposition it. Only gentle pressure should be applied if the wound is bleeding.

INTERNAL BLEEDING

Internal bleeding often is not readily apparent, although in some cases there may be coughing or vomiting of blood or bleeding from the rectum, urethra, or vagina, depending upon the location and nature of the injury. Other warning signs are those of hypovolemic shock (shock caused by a very low amount of blood) and include anxiousness, light-headedness, or fainting; a weak, rapid pulse, shallow breathing and shortness of breath; dilated pupils; cold, pale, and clammy skin; and possibly abdominal swelling.

1. If breathing stops, mouth-to-mouth respiration should be started (see section on CPR, page 338). If, in addition, there is no pulse, CPR should be administered, even though this is usually futile if loss of blood is the cause.

2. The victim should lie down and be kept warm and as comfortable as possible, otherwise there are no specific first-aid measures to stop internal bleeding.

3. An ambulance should be called as quickly as possible. If there is a faster way of getting the victim to a hospital emergency room, use it, since prompt medical attention is vital (even though there are instances in which the bleeding may not be as serious as it appears). There is no way to determine the seriousness of the injury until the person is in expert hands; hence, any suspected internal bleeding should be considered a serious medical emergency until proven otherwise.

CARBON MONOXIDE POISONING

DEFINITION AND CAUSES

Unconsciousness from carbon monoxide poisoning is a life-threatening emergency that may require mouth-to-mouth respiration or CPR. Carbon monoxide can cause death by combining with hemoglobin, the oxygen-carrying protein of blood, and therefore depriving the tissues of oxygen. Automobiles, industrial fumes, faulty heating units, and burning buildings are the most common sources of carbon monoxide poisoning.

DIAGNOSIS

Signs of carbon monoxide poisoning include:

- Circumstances that indicate concentrations of carbon monoxide in the air (e.g., a car with a running motor, or a fire in a poorly vented room)
- Severe headache, disorientation, or agitation
- Lethargy, stupor, and coma

TREATMENT

If carbon monoxide poisoning is suspected:

1. Get the victim into the open air as quickly as possible.
2. Check for respiration and pulse. If both are absent, begin CPR.
3. If breathing is absent but there is a pulse, begin

mouth-to-mouth respiration and continue until the victim begins breathing or help arrives.

4. Begin administering oxygen with an oxygen-breathing mask as soon as one can be made available.
5. Get the victim to a hospital as soon as possible. Extended observation and additional emergency care will be required. There may also be other medical problems, especially neurological, cardiac, or pulmonary complications.

DROWNING AND NEAR DROWNING

EVALUATION OF RESCUER'S SKILLS

Plunging into the water to save someone who is drowning or has apparently drowned should be approached with extreme caution. Few nonswimmers can rescue a drowning person; frequently both the original victim and the would-be rescuer drown together. If you cannot swim or if you doubt your ability to get the drowning victim out of the water, it is far better to summon help or try some other tactic other than unthinkingly jumping into the water.

TREATMENT

Pulling the Victim out of the Water: Where swimming to a drowning victim in the water is beyond your swimming capability, the Coast Guard recommends a technique called "throw, row, or tow."

1. From a float, shoreside dock, or moored boat, attach a long rope to a buoyant object such as a life jacket, life preserver, or a large empty plastic bottle that is securely closed and throw it to the floundering swimmer and then pull her to shore.
2. If it is not possible to throw something to the swimmer and a rowboat or other boat is available, row out to the victim as quickly as possible.
3. Give the person an extra oar, rope, or life preserver to hold on to, and tow him or her to shore. Don't try to haul the person into the boat; this may cause it to capsize and you'll both be in the water.

SPECIAL CIRCUMSTANCES

1. If there is a chance the near-drowning victim has a neck or back injury (e.g., from a diving, water-skiing, or boating accident), special care in maintaining neck and back alignment will be needed in getting him to shore. If possible, float the victim onto a board and then pull to shore. If the victim is breathing and a spinal injury is suspected, keep him in the water floating on his back until a board or other support can be brought to you.

2. If the victim has fallen through ice into the water, do not walk on the ice to rescue him. Instead, have the victim, if conscious, try to rest on the edge of the ice, rather than trying to climb out, which may only result in breaking more ice. Throw a rope from shore, or use a long board or stick and try to pull the victim out and across the ice on his belly, to distribute the weight as evenly as possible. If the victim is unconscious, tie the rope around your waist, secure the other end, and slide out on the ice on your belly. If other rescuers are present, form a human chain, with everyone lying down, to reach the victim.

3. If breathing has stopped, begin mouth-to-mouth respiration. This can be done even while the victim is still in the water by giving 4 quick breaths and then a breath every 5 seconds while you are pulling the victim to shore.

AFTER THE RESCUE

1. Once the victim is out of the water, determine if there is a pulse. If not, begin CPR at once and continue until help arrives. Do not attempt to drain water from the lungs. If a back injury is suspected, do not transport the victim except to remove him from the water, and then use a board if possible.

2. Even if the victim is revived, observe carefully for possible complications, such as cardiac arrest, and take the person to a hospital as soon as possible. Water in the lungs decreases their ability to function; the body's salt and fluid balance also may be upset, leading to further complications that may not be immediately apparent. Hospital personnel should be informed as to whether the drowning took place in fresh or salt water; these circumstances may influence the type of medical aftercare.

ELECTROCUTION RESULTING IN CARDIAC ARREST

DEFINITION AND CAUSES

Electric current passing through the body can cause cardiac arrest, generally from ventricular fibrillation (rapid, uncoordinated beating or quivering of the heart muscle). The longer the contact with the electrical current, the less likely are the chances of survival. The source of current may be a downed electrical wire, a defective household appliance, or lightning.

PROTECTING THE RESCUER

1. Approach a victim of suspected electrocution with caution: Until he is free of contact with the current, he is an electrical conductor. Touching someone still in contact with a live circuit may electrocute you. NEVER touch a victim of electric shock until you are sure the power is off or contact between the victim and the electrical source has been broken.

2. If an appliance is the source of electricity, shut off the current at the fuse box, or if you can safely do so unplug the appliance immediately. Simply turning off the appliance is inadequate.

3. If the current cannot be turned off and a live wire is touching the victim, dry your hands completely and insulate them with dry gloves or a dry cloth.

4. Stand on a dry, nonconductive surface, such as a stack of newspapers, a board, or pile of clothes (not on dirt, or anything metallic or wet). If possible, don a pair of dry rubber boots.

5. Decide if it is more practical to push the victim away from the wire or to push the wire from the victim. If your hands are well insulated and you are standing on a dry, nonconductive surface, move the person or the wire using a nonconducting object such as a wooden pole or board. If the wire is clutched in the victim's hand, it may take considerable force to separate the two, but do not directly touch the person or the wire.

TREATMENT

1. Summon help by calling 911.

2. Check whether the victim is breathing or has a heartbeat. If not, begin CPR immediately. Even if the victim does not revive within minutes, continue these measures until help arrives, as recovery from electric shock can be slow.

3. If the victim was struck by lightning, check immediately for breathing and pulse. Since the current has passed through the body and disappeared, the rescuer does not need to worry about sustaining a shock, and treatment can begin immediately.

4. When breathing is reestablished, treat the victim for shock by elevating the feet and covering with a blanket (see "Shock").

5. If the victim is conscious but has fallen from a height, or is a victim of high-tension contact or lightning strike, check for associated injuries, such as skull, spine or extremity fractures, burns, and other injuries. Anyone who has sustained a serious electrical shock should be transported as soon as possible to a hospital emergency room.

SHOCK

DEFINITION AND CAUSE

Traumatic hemorrhagic shock is caused by a blood loss following severe injury: Because of the reduced blood supply to vital organs, life-sustaining functions slow down or stop altogether. The possibility of shock must be guarded against in anyone sustaining serious injury, including hemorrhage or fracture of a large bone. (See the sections on heart attack, allergy, diabetes and infection for more complete discussions of the types of shock caused by those conditions.)

DIAGNOSIS

In the early stages of shock, the body attempts to compensate for blood loss by redistributing the available supply. Blood flow is redirected from the skin, muscles, and soft tissues to the brain, heart, lungs, and vital organs. (Try to determine if the victim takes insulin for diabetes and has possibly suffered insulin shock. For information on insulin shock, see chapter 21.)

In hemorrhagic shock, as well as in shock from other causes, this produces such symptoms as:

- Generalized weakness
- Cold, clammy skin that is very pale or bluish
- Sweating
- Rapid, shallow breathing
- Faint, rapid pulse
- Nausea, sometimes followed by vomiting
- Restlessness

TREATMENT

In the early stages of traumatic shock, the victim may be alert. Do not be misled by this; first aid for shock should begin at once to improve blood circulation, safeguard oxygen supply, and maintain body temperature. Follow these specific steps.

1. Administer basic life support and control bleeding as needed.
2. Summon medical help.
3. Do not move the victim any more than absolutely necessary. The victim should be lying down, with head tilted to one side (unless injury to the cervical spine is suspected).
4. Elevate the feet unless breathing difficulties or pain result. But do not raise the feet or lower the head if the victim has sustained a head, neck, back, or lower extremity injury.
5. Loosen clothing and cover victim with a blanket or whatever else is available to conserve body heat.

6. Keep the victim as calm as possible. Do not ask unnecessary questions.
7. If the victim asks for water, moisten the lips but do not allow him to drink. Do not attempt to give sedatives, hot drinks, or alcoholic beverages.
8. If the victim is diabetic and takes insulin, offer fruit juice or a soft drink. (For more information on diabetic shock, see chapter 21.)
9. If the victim feels nauseated or vomits, roll him to the side so that the vomitus is expelled from the mouth and not inhaled back into the windpipe and lungs.
10. If spinal injury is suspected, keep the head and neck in alignment as you roll.
11. Get the victim to a hospital as soon as possible.

STROKE

DEFINITION AND CAUSE

A stroke results when blood flow to the brain is obstructed by a clot in an artery, or a brain artery bursts and floods brain tissue with hemorrhage and increased pressure. Severe strokes cause loss of speech, sudden weakness or numbness of face, arm, and leg on one side of the body; loss of vision; dizziness or sudden falls; and unconsciousness.

TREATMENT

Rescue breathing and chest compression may be required in some stroke victims who lose consciousness. Stroke victims are approached exactly like any unresponsive person. Determine the need for establishing an airway, and, as necessary, provide rescue breathing and chest compression as outlined in CPR sections. Emergency medical services should be summoned for stroke victims as soon as possible.

In many cases, mild or temporary signs of stroke frequently precede a major life-threatening stroke; medical care of persons suffering a "ministroke" is urgent.

Note: Keep in mind that signs similar to stroke may occur with alcohol or drug excess, insulin reaction, or other diseases.

14
Common First-Aid Procedures

• • • • • • • • • • • • • •

KENNETH C. FINE, M.D.

Hundreds of situations, including small bumps and bruises, mild allergic reactions, and slight burns, are not necessarily life-threatening but still require first aid. Other more serious circumstances necessitate emergency medical treatment and follow-up care. The first part of this chapter outlines three essential components of first aid: summoning help, victim assessment and goals of first aid, and transporting the victim. Following these sections, the most common first-aid occurrences, both life-threatening and less serious, are summarized in alphabetical order. Other situations, such as childbirth emergencies, psychiatric crises, and similar situations involving diseases, are covered in the chapters dealing with specific disorders.

SUMMONING HELP

Knowing how to summon help should an emergency arise is crucial to successful first aid. Clearly post emergency phone numbers on or near all phones. Each family member should know who to call. In most areas, the most important contact will be an Emergency Medical Service (EMS) squad. Some squads operate from hospitals or medical centers, others from fire or police stations. The emergency medical technicians who staff these crews are expertly trained and equipped. In most areas, the EMS can be summoned by telephoning the police emergency number, 911, or by asking the telephone operator to summon an ambulance or rescue squad. Other important numbers to have on hand are the local or regional poison control center (consult the list in appendix C) and the closest major hospital with a well-equipped and staffed emergency department. If you are in doubt about which hospital to choose, ask your family doctor for a recommendation.

In calling for an ambulance or emergency squad, make sure that you give:

- The precise location or address and the telephone number from which you are calling.
- The nature of the emergency.
- The number of people involved.
- The location of the emergency. For example: "I am calling from the corner of Main Street and Second Avenue. My number here is 555-6385. There has been a car accident and two people are badly injured." or "I am at 236 First Avenue South, in apartment 24. My telephone number is 555-4545. My husband is having chest pains and I think he may be having a heart attack."

- Do not hang up until you are certain that the person on the line has all the necessary information and your telephone number should it be necessary to call back. Be prepared to give instructions on how to reach you.
- If it is night, try to have outdoor lights on or someone posted at the driveway or building entrance to give further instructions.

Whenever recommendations are given in this text to transport seriously ill or injured persons, it should be assumed that the best way to do so is by ambulance/rescue vehicle equipped and staffed with personnel trained in stabilization and transport of these victims.

VICTIM ASSESSMENT AND GOALS OF FIRST AID

The effective application of first-aid techniques depends primarily on the ability of the rescuer to assess the situation and to make the proper decisions without delay. These situations can be divided into three types:

- Life-threatening emergencies that require immediate action on the part of the rescuer as well as complex medical follow-up.
- Potentially serious situations that are not life-threatening but that require medical care. This is the most difficult situation for a layperson to judge without first-aid training.
- Those that require simple first aid or self-care.

The goals of first aid are:

1. To restore and maintain vital functions. The ABC of basic life support (open airway, breathing, and circulation) are always the first priority.
2. To prevent further injury or deterioration
3. To reassure the victim and make him or her as comfortable as possible

The order in which first aid should be provided is:

- **First: Assess victim for signs of life.** For an adult if signs of life are absent, dial 911 or otherwise call for help. (For children, attempt rescue breathing for one minute before calling for help.)
- **Second: Restore respiration if breathing has stopped.** (See "Cardiopulminary Resuscitation" and "Choking and Obstructed Airway" in chapter 13.)
- **Third: Restore heart action if there is no discernible heartbeat or pulse.** (See section on circulation in "Cardiopulminary Resuscitation" in chapter 13.)

- **Fourth: Stop bleeding.** (See information on hemorrhage in chapter 13.)
- **Fifth: Treat for shock.** (See "Shock" in chapter 13.)

If there are other bystanders, one should immediately summon help while emergency first aid is being administered. After help has been called, other first-aid measures can then be initiated, depending upon the circumstances.

TRANSPORTING THE VICTIM

A fundamental rule of first aid dictates that the victim should not be moved but should be treated where she lies. However, there are circumstances in which a severely injured person must be moved to prevent further injury from fire, an explosion, fumes, or other potentially life-threatening hazards. Follow these guidelines.

- If possible, short-distance transport should be accomplished on a firm surface such as a stretcher, or a board that will provide even support for the entire body (see figure 14.1).
- If the victim must be dragged to a safe place, pull her lengthwise, not sideways.
- If possible, try to place a blanket under the person so that the edge of the blanket can be pulled carrying her weight. In any situation where spinal injury is suspected and the patient must be moved, the spine and the neck must be kept in alignment. Do not move the neck.

ALLERGIC REACTIONS AND ANAPHYLACTIC SHOCK

An allergic reaction is an exaggerated response or hypersensitivity by the body's immune system to what would otherwise be a harmless substance. Allergic reactions vary from merely annoying symptoms such as itchy eyes and runny nose to life-threatening anaphylactic shock response that may result in death from circulatory collapse or respiratory failure.

In particular, some people are hypersensitive to insect stings, medications, and certain foods and food additives such as sulfites. Anyone who has had a serious allergic reaction should take the necessary precautions to avoid all future contact with the offending substance. Desensitization shots may be recommended if bee stings prompt the response. All allergenic foods and medications should be avoided as well as any drug in the same class or with a similar chemical composition. A Medic Alert bracelet warning of the allergy should be worn.

In many cases, those with a known sensitivity keep what is called an anaphylaxis kit on their person at all times. This kit usually contains epinephrine (adrenaline) and instructions on how to use this medication to combat allergic reactions.

Whenever anyone suffers an extreme allergic reaction, the person should be taken to the hospital as soon as possible even if the symptoms seem to pass. Secondary reactions may occur up to several hours later; consequently, this type of episode warrants close medical observation.

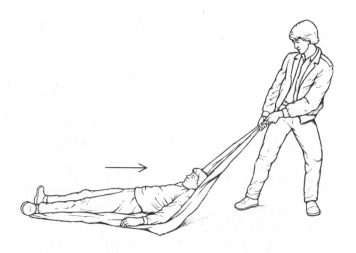

Dragging victim on blanket

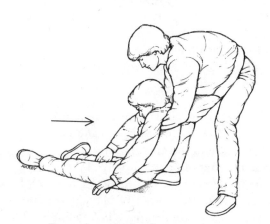

Dragging victim by armpits

Figure 14.1: Transporting the victim. If it is absolutely necessary to remove a victim from an accident scene, try to place the patient on a blanket, and then drag the blanket instead of bodily pulling the injured person. If a blanket is not available, drag the person by the armpits using your body as a support.

SYMPTOMS

- Sudden appearance of hives; widespread, blotchy swelling of the skin.
- Swelling of mucous membranes; the lips, tongue, or mouth.
- Wheezing or difficulty breathing.
- Increased pulse rate or a weak and thin pulse accompanied by drop in blood pressure (shock).
- Nausea, vomiting or abdominal cramps.
- Lightheadedness or fainting.

For a more complete discussion of the mechanisms of allergic reactions, see chapter 29.

TREATMENT

- At the first sign of an anaphylactic reaction, the person should be transported to the nearest emergency room or other medical facility. Call 911.
- If an anaphylaxis kit is available, administer the medications, following the kit's directions, and then take the person to the nearest hospital.
- If the person loses consciousness on the way to the hospital and has no pulse or stops breathing, administer CPR (see chapter 13). Do not waste time; this is a life-threatening situation.

AMPUTATIONS

Amputation—the severing of any body part—is a serious medical emergency. Fortunately, the majority of amputations involve only small parts, such as a fingertip rather than arms or legs. In general, when the tip of a finger or toe is cut off, minor bleeding occurs without major blood loss. These cases can generally be managed easily with the application of a pressure dressing (see the section on bleeding and hemorrhage in chapter 13) and the transportation of the victim and the amputated body part to the hospital. (See information in the box "How to Apply a Tourniquet" for instructions on proper wrapping of severed body parts.) More serious amputations almost always entail significant blood loss and possible shock and other injuries.

TREATMENT

- If the person loses consciousness, check for a pulse and breathing. If appropriate, administer CPR to maintain an open airway, breathing, and circulation (see chapter 13). Do not waste time; this is a life-threatening situation.

- Control bleeding by applying pressure directly to the wound using gauze pads or a clean cloth and elevate the injured extremity. Once the bleeding has been controlled, place several layers of gauze over the severed area and bandage the layers firmly in place. If the bleeding is not controlled by direct pressure, apply pressure to the large feeding artery above the amputation. (See chapter 13.)

HOW TO APPLY A TOURNIQUET

- First make certain that bleeding cannot be controlled with direct pressure or by means of pressure points.
- Use any flat, 1- or 2-inch-wide piece of cloth long enough to go twice around the arm or leg. Rolled bandaging is ideal, but a belt, scarf, strip torn from a shirt, or other similar material may also serve as a tourniquet.
- Place the tourniquet just above the edge of the wound. Do not allow it to touch the wound. If the wound is very close to a joint or directly below a joint, place the tourniquet directly above the joint.
- Wrap the tourniquet tightly twice around the limb and tie a half-knot.
- Place a short, strong stick, ruler, screwdriver, or similar rigid object on top of the half-knot and tie a full knot over it. Note the time when you apply the tourniquet.
- Twist the stick until the bleeding has slowed enough to clot. Secure the stick in place.
- Do not loosen the tourniquet unless a physician tells you to do so.
- As soon as the bleeding is controlled, check for and attend to any other serious injuries, such as fractures, wounds, or damage to the spine, chest, or abdomen. After tending to these, pick up the severed limb and wrap it, ideally in sterile gauze or a towel moistened with saline solution or water, double wrapped in clean, plastic bags.

Place the wrapped part on ice, if possible. If sterile cloth and plastics are not available, a clean cloth, shirt, or other material can be used.

- As soon as possible, take the person to the nearest hospital emergency room, preferably to a hospital or medical center that has a surgery team skilled in microsurgery and reimplantation. Advances in reimplantation techniques in recent years have greatly improved the chances of successfully rejoining severed limbs.

• Avoid applying a tourniquet except as a last resort in controlling massive hemorrhaging. A tourniquet severely increases the risk of tissue damage, reduces the chances for successful reimplantation of the severed part, and may necessitate further amputation of the injured extremity.

• Observe for signs of shock and other injuries. Have the victim lie down with legs slightly elevated. Cover to keep him warm. (See "Shock" in chapter 13.)

BITES AND STINGS

Dog bites are the most common type of animal bites. Dogs attack more than a million Americans annually and about half of these incidents involve children.

All children should be taught to avoid strange dogs, and dog owners should properly restrain their pets at all times, keeping them on leashes when walked and muzzled if they have a propensity to bite. Unleashed dogs should be kept in a secure enclosure at other times. These measures not only protect people from bites but they also benefit pets by preventing them from becoming lost or hit by automobiles—common fates for animals allowed to roam freely.

All animal bites require some level of treatment, depending on the nature and severity of the wound. Animal and human mouths are home to many bacteria that can cause harm when they penetrate the skin.

If the person has not had a tetanus shot in the past 5 years, consult a physician. If the person has circulatory problems or diabetes, a physician should also be consulted, even if the bite appears to be minor.

ANIMAL BITES

To treat a superficial bite from a familiar household pet that is in good health, wash out the wound carefully with soap and water and apply an antiseptic such as hydrogen peroxide and an antibiotic cream.

To treat a deeper bite from a familiar, healthy pet or any bite from a strange animal:

• See a physician as soon as possible if the bite is a puncture wound or large gash; proper cleansing of such wounds is crucial. Stitching may be necessary, depending on the type, location, and severity of the wound. A tetanus shot and antibiotics may also be necessary.

• Consult a physician promptly if there is any subsequent swelling, pain, increasing redness, or drainage.

• Notify the pet owner of the incident and determine the animal's rabies inoculation status. Report vicious animals that are permitted to roam freely to the local animal warden or health department.

RABIES

Rabies is on the increase in the United States. The Southeast, Middle Atlantic and Northeast states report it at epidemic levels among raccoons, skunks, and bats. Less commonly, rabies may be carried by coyotes, foxes, and larger rodents such as ground hogs. Therefore, any bite from a wild animal should be examined promptly by a knowledgeable doctor.

Any wild animal or unfamiliar domestic animal that bites humans, especially without provocation, should be examined promptly by a knowledgeable doctor. If the animal cannot be found, immunization of the bite victim against rabies may be indicated. (In some instances, people who have merely come in contact with the infected animal or pets that have been in a fight with a rabid animal may also need to be immunized.)

The decision to treat for rabies will be based on the type of animal, its behavior, the geographic location, and other factors. All bites should be reported to the local board of health.

A new rabies treatment, consisting of a single dose of rabies-immune globulin and five injections of human diploid cell rabies vaccine, has greatly simplified the anitrabies shots.

Prophylactic immunization may be indicated for certain individuals in high-risk jobs or when traveling to or residing in high-risk areas. Check with your local board of health for current guidelines.

• Any flulike symptoms, fever, swollen glands, or other symptoms following an animal bite or scratch should be investigated promptly by a doctor.

HUMAN BITES

Human bites carry a high risk of infection due to the large number of bacteria residing in the human mouth. All human bites should be checked immediately by a doctor, who may administer antibiotics along with other applicable treatments.

Whenever the skin is broken because of contact with human teeth—including injury to the knuckles after hitting someone in the mouth—the injured area should be treated by a doctor.

BEE STINGS

The great majority of insect stings cause only minor discomfort from a local reaction. About 1 million Americans are severely allergic to the venom of bees, hornets, yellow jackets, and fire ants. Those who are hypersensitive to bee venom should exercise extreme caution in the outdoors during months when bees are active. They should protect themselves with long pants, long-sleeved shirts, and clothing of subdued colors and patterns that do not attract insects. They should not apply colognes or perfumes. If approached by a bee, sensitive individuals should not panic, duck, or move suddenly, but should stay calm and slowly walk away from the insect.

Hypersensitive individuals who spend a great deal of their time in areas populated by bees (farms, orchards, rural parts of the country) should receive desensitization shots. (See "Allergic Reactions and Anaphylactic Shock" for symptoms of hypersensitive reaction.)

TREATMENT FOR HYPERSENSITIVE INDIVIDUALS

- Carry a bee sting (anaphylaxis) treatment kit at all times. (These kits are commercially prepared and available by prescription.) Use a syringe preloaded with adrenaline. After administering adrenaline, call the emergency squad or take the person to the nearest hospital emergency room.
- If a treatment kit is not available, take the person to the nearest hospital emergency room or doctor immediately.
- If any signs or symptoms of generalized reaction to the bite occur before reaching the hospital, tie a light tourniquet 2 to 4 inches above the bite (between the bite and the trunk of the body).
- Remove stinger as instructed below.

TREATMENT FOR THE NONSENSITIVE

- Check the sting site for the venom sac (bee stings only) and stinger. If these are embedded in the skin, remove by scraping over the area with a knife blade, fingernail, or sharp object. Do not try to grasp and pull the stinger out; this action is likely to release more venom into the skin from the venom sac.
- Apply an ice pack to the sting site or flush it with cold water to reduce swelling and relieve pain.
- Dab on calamine lotion or a nonprescription corticosteroid cream to ease itching and swelling. Other remedies include unseasoned meat tenderizer, which contains papain, an enzyme that breaks down toxins in the venom. Aspirin or antihistamines may also be used to alleviate moderate, localized reactions.

JELLYFISH, STINGRAY, AND OTHER MARINE ANIMAL BITES

Stings from marine animals are only rarely life-threatening. However, it is wise to avoid swimming in waters infested with jellyfish or other poisonous sea animals. For symptoms of hypersensitive reaction, see "Allergic Reactions and Anaphylactic Shock."

TREATMENT FOR HYPERSENSITIVE INDIVIDUALS

- Calm and reassure the victim.
- If a jellyfish or Portuguese man-of-war tentacle adheres to the skin, cover it with sand and carefully pull it off—do not rub it off—using a heavy glove, cloth, or towel. Do not touch it with your bare hand or skin. Even when detached from the main organism, this tentacle can sting you.
- Seek medical attention immediately. Jellyfish stings are most serious when they are numerous, or involve the very young or very old.

TREATMENT FOR INDIVIDUALS WHO ARE NOT HYPERSENSITIVE

- Remove tentacle or jellyfish as described above.
- Thoroughly wash the injury and apply rubbing alcohol or vinegar several times, being careful not to touch the sting area with an unprotected hand.
- Apply a thick coat of baking soda paste, which may be shaved or scraped off after 30 minutes, at which time vinegar or rubbing alcohol is reapplied.
- Other remedies that can be applied include diluted household ammonia, lemon juice, and salt water.

TREATMENT FOR STINGRAY BITE

- Wash wound and flush it thoroughly with regular or salt water.
- Immerse wound in hot water as you transport victim to the nearest hospital emergency room.

SPIDER BITES

The two most common poisonous spiders in the United States are the female black widow and brown recluse. Besides these two spiders, most other bites of spiders in North America are harmless, causing minor, localized reactions.

Black Widow Spider. The black widow spider is a small, black spider with a red, hourglass marking on its abdomen.

SYMPTOMS

- There is only a slight local reaction—with some pain—at the site of the bite.
- The neurotoxin injected by the spider may cause pain, muscle spasm, and paralysis in distant parts of the body.
- Vomiting and abdominal cramps.

TREATMENT

- Apply an ice pack to the area of the bite immediately.
- If shock occurs, take appropriate measures. (See "Shock" in chapter 13.)
- Take the victim to the nearest hospital as soon as possible. Treatment usually entails the administration of muscle relaxants and pain medication. Although an antivenin is available, it is not necessary in most cases.

Brown Recluse. The brown recluse is a small spider that has a violin-shaped marking on its upper back. It is usually found in attics and out-of-the-way corners.

SYMPTOMS

- The bite may not become apparent for several hours or days. But then a red lesion appears that becomes a blister.
- The appearance of the blister may be followed by fever, nausea, and a body rash.
- Blister may enlarge into a very painful ulceration.

TREATMENT

- Apply an ice pack to the area of the bite immediately.
- If shock occurs, take appropriate measures. (See "Shock" in chapter 13.)
- Take the victim to the nearest hospital as soon as possible. Medical evaluation is extremely important. Surgery may be necessary to repair the ulcerated area.

SNAKEBITES

While there are about 45,000 snakebites a year in the United States, only about 7,000 of these injuries involve poisonous snakes, resulting in about 10 deaths annually, only one-fourth the number that die from bee stings.

Poisonous snakes are found in every state except Maine and Alaska. Sixty percent of the venomous snakebites are caused by rattlesnakes; the other 40 percent result from bites from copperheads, cottonmouths (water moccasins), and coral snakes. Although not all bites from poisonous snakes result in the release of poison, once the skin is punctured by snake fangs you should assume that poison is present and act accordingly. It is urgent that a snakebite victim be taken to a hospital for antivenin serum as quickly as possible, certainly within 4 hours. (The serum is not effective if administered more than 12 hours after the bite.)

Hikers or campers who plan trips to remote areas without easy access to transportation or medical assistance should carry a snakebite kit and be trained in its proper use. Hikers should also know how to distinguish between two major types of venomous snakes.

- **Pit Vipers.** This family of snakes includes rattlesnakes, copperheads, and cottonmouths. They have triangular heads with a pit between the nostril and eye on both sides of the head, elliptical pupils, and two fangs. All pit viper bites are treated with the same antivenin.
- **Coral Snakes.** Also called the harlequin or bead snake. Coral snakes are banded in red and black interspersed with white or yellow rings. They have teeth, fangs, a black snout, and lack facial pits. An easy way to distinguish this type from nonpoisonous banded snakes: "Red on yellow/kill a fellow;/red on black/good for Jack."

TREATMENT OF SNAKE BITES

- Reassure the person and keep him supine and as quiet as possible.
- Try to identify the snake but do not waste time looking for it if it has disappeared. If you are not sure of the snake's type, but it is easy to kill without danger to yourself, do so with extreme caution. Remember that a snake's biting reflex allows it to still bite up to 60 minutes after it has died. For proper treatment with the correct antivenin, it is especially important to identify an exotic snake from a zoo or one kept as a pet.
- Apply a light constricting band 2 to 4 inches above the bite if it is on an extremity. Do not totally restrict blood flow; check to make sure that a pulse is present below this light tourniquet. If swelling takes place at the level of the band, remove and replace it a few inches above the swelling.
- Do not allow the victim anything to eat or drink. Especially do not allow the ingestion of alcoholic beverages (this includes beer, wine, and wine coolers).
- Bring the victim to the nearest hospital or emergency service.
- If you are far from a hospital, you should suck the venom out of a poisonous snake bite within ten to fifteen minutes after being bitten: Use a sterilized razor to make quarter-inch deep incisions along the fang marks. (But cut lengthwise on arms and legs, not across. And do not make incisions over a coral snake bite.) If available, use the suction cup supplied with snake bite kits to withdraw the venom. Otherwise suck it out by mouth, but do not swallow—spit the venom out. Rinse your mouth afterward, if possible. Do not suck the venom out if you have a cut or sore in your mouth.

After withdrawing the venom, take the victim to an emergency room as soon as possible.

TICKS

Ticks are parasites that feed on warm-blooded vertebrates. Some ticks are harmless; others carry a variety of diseases, including Rocky Mountain spotted fever and Lyme disease. Although the names imply that these diseases are confined to particular geographical areas, in fact, Rocky Mountain spotted fever occurs in all states except Maine, Alaska, and Hawaii, and Lyme disease has been reported in most states.

PREVENTING TICK BITES

- In areas with heavy tick populations such as woods, dense brush, or high grass, stay on well-worn trails.
- Wear proper protective clothing such as long pants, boots, and a long-sleeved shirt. Apply an insect repellant that protects against ticks.
- Keep shirt tucked in to keep insects out of your clothing. Inspect your clothing and skin regularly for the presence of ticks.
- Shower and wash your hair. It takes 4 to 6 hours for most ticks to become firmly attached, and showering is a quick way to rid yourself of loose ticks.
- Inspect pets that venture into tick-infested areas at least daily and remove any ticks.

TREATMENT

- Do not try to remove the tick by rubbing or pulling it out. This may leave the head imbedded in the skin.
- Although experts disagree on this point, we recommend covering the tick with a few drops of thick oil such as olive or mineral oil, or kerosene or gasoline. This will suffocate and immobilize the tick.
- Gently remove the tick with a pair of tweezers, taking care to remove the head. Do not handle or crush the tick between your fingers. (Use the same caution in removing ticks from dogs and other pets.)
- Carefully wash the bite area as well as your hands and the tweezers with soap and water. Apply alcohol or hydrogen peroxide to the area and cover with a sterile bandage.
- Consult a doctor to see if further treatment is needed. Take particular note of symptoms such as fever, rash, generalized aches and pains, headaches, or other signs of illness following a tick bite. If symptoms occur, see a doctor at once.

BURNS

Burns are caused by fire, heated liquids, steam, sun, chemicals, and electricity. In evaluating the type of first aid appropriate for a burn, the source and extent of the injury and degree of the burn should be determined. Burns are generally classified according to their depth and degree of tissue damage.

First-Degree Burns. Limited to the outer layer of the skin (epidermis). The skin is red and tender and there may be swelling without blistering. Not generally considered serious.

Second-Degree Burns. Involve both the epidermis and underlying dermis. In addition to redness, tenderness, and pain, significant blistering occurs. These burns are not serious unless a large area is involved or secondary infection takes place.

Third-Degree Burns. Involve destruction of the full thickness of the skin and also may damage underlying tissue. Skin may be blackened or white and leathery feeling. Although these burns are always serious, there often is no pain because the nerves have been destroyed.

BURNS REQUIRING MEDICAL TREATMENT

- All widespread burns, including extensive sunburn.
- All second-degree burns greater than 2 to 3 inches in diameter or those involving the hands, face, or genitals.
- All-third degree burns regardless of size.

MINOR BURNS

Minor burns include first-degree sunburn and small scalds or burns from hot objects.

TREATMENT FOR FIRST-DEGREE BURNS

- Flush the burned area with cool water from a tap or use cool, wet compresses applied to the skin.
- Cleanse the burned area. Aloe vera cream, aspirin, or ibuprofen may alleviate pain. Usually, further medical care is not necessary.

TREATMENT FOR SECOND-DEGREE BURNS LESS THAN 2 TO 3 INCHES IN DIAMETER

- Rinse the area with cool water, gently wash with soap and water, and rinse again. Spray with an antiseptic spray and cover with sterile dressing.
- Do not apply ointments, petroleum jelly, margarine, grease, oil, butter, or other home remedies.
- Avoid breaking blisters, which increases the risk of

infection. If blisters become infected, seek medical attention.

MAJOR BURNS

TREATMENT

- Remove the victim from the fire or other source of injury. Douse flames or flush chemicals off the skin surface.
- If clothing is ignited, lay the victim down and extinguish flames with water or by covering with a blanket or coat, or by having the victim roll over slowly. Do not allow the victim to run. Running fans the flames and spreads the burns to the upper body and face.
- All larger second-degree burns require medical treatment. In the case of extensive burns, check for respiration, circulation, and signs of shock, and treat appropriately. (See "Shock" in chapter 13.) Then look for other serious injuries and treat.
- Apply cool compresses briefly to bring skin temperature back to normal. Avoid prolonged cooling of a large area because it can lead to excessive body cooling.
- Wrap the victim loosely in a clean sheet and call 911 for an EMS rescue team or, if not available, transport to an emergency room.
- Do not try to remove burned clothing or objects that adhere to the burned area, and do not apply any ointments or other medication.
- Loss of body fluids, pulmonary complications, and infection are major dangers of extensive burns. All extensive burns should be treated in a medical treatment center with a specialized burn facility.

CHEMICAL BURNS

TREATMENT

- If the chemical container contains first-aid instructions, follow them.
- Start treatment immediately by placing the burned area under cool running water and continue flushing for at least 15 minutes or longer.
- If the chemical has splashed into the eye, irrigate the injured eye with cool water. Make sure the eye is open and the head is positioned so the water will not run into the other eye. (If both eyes are involved, flush them simultaneously by tipping the head back and pouring water into both.) Irrigate for at least 15 minutes, then cover the eye with a sterile compress and take the victim to a hospital emergency room.

Note: Not all chemical injuries are burns. Some injuries, such as those caused by liquid hydrocarbon (e.g., Freon), cause freezing. In these cases, the person should be treated for frostbite (see information on frostbite in "Overexposure" later in this chapter). Other chemicals are absorbed through the skin and produce a toxic reaction. When working with hazardous chemicals, wear protective work gloves and other safety clothing. If the skin is exposed to chemicals, wash the exposure area immediately and thoroughly and call your local poison control center for further guidance. (See appendix C for a listing of poison control centers.)

ELECTRICAL BURNS

Electrical burns are often deeper and more serious than they seem.

TREATMENT

- First-aid treatment is the same as for other types of burns. All electrical burns should be examined by a physician.
- Victims of electrical burns should be evaluated for other injuries. When a person is struck by lightning or comes in contact with a high-tension wire, respiratory muscle paralysis, cardiac arrest, and bone fractures may result. These serious injuries must also be cared for.

SUNBURN

Most sunburns are first-degree burns. Although painful, they usually do not require treatment by a doctor unless widespread blistering, systemic symptoms, an unusual rash, or secondary infection occurs. In most cases, cool compresses and taking aspirin, ibuprofen, or another analgesic will ease the temporary discomfort.

CONVULSIONS

Epilepsy is a common cause of seizures; however, seizures that come on suddenly without any prior history of epilepsy may be caused by a high fever, head injury, poisoning, drug overdose, withdrawal from drugs or alcohol, stroke, tumor, low blood sugar, or other causes. In young children with high fevers, convulsions may be due to febrile seizures or diseases such as meningitis. Most seizures last only a short time and stop spontaneously.

Anyone suffering a seizure for the first time should be brought promptly to a hospital emergency room.

SYMPTOMS

- Part of the person's body (or the entire body) may stiffen or jerk.
- The person may urinate and/or defecate.
- Saliva or foam may come out of the mouth.

TREATMENT

Protect the person from injury by laying her gently down on a soft or padded surface. If there is any possibility of a cervical spine injury, take proper precautions. Turn the head to one side, keeping the airway open. Contrary to popular belief, it is not necessary to place anything between the upper and lower teeth.

- Do not restrain the person during the seizure. Instead move to an area where there is no danger of injury.
- If vomiting occurs, turn the person on her side so the vomit is expelled from the mouth and not inhaled into the windpipe and lungs.
- Keep a careful watch and begin mouth-to-mouth resuscitation if breathing stops more than briefly after a seizure. Make sure the airway is not obstructed. Begin CPR immediately if breathing and pulse are absent at any point. (See chapter 13, Basics of CPR and Life Support.)
- If poisoning is suspected, try to identify the source and contact the local poison control center for guidance. (For a listing of centers, see appendix C.)
- If the convulsions are related to a high fever in an infant or child, lower the body temperature by using cool compresses. Do not place in a bathtub and do not use rubbing alcohol.
- Observe the person until she is fully awake, for at least 10 to 20 minutes.
- If the seizure continues for more than a few minutes, or if it recurs in a short time, call for an ambulance.
- Provide first aid for injuries that may have been sustained during the seizure.

MINOR CUTS, SCRAPES, AND BRUISES

TREATMENT

- Wash with cool water and bland soap. Cover with a light protective adhesive bandage (such as a Band-Aid or Telfa strip).
- Use of an antibiotic or antiseptic is optional. Avoid using alcohol. Hydrogen peroxide kills some mi-

croorganisms by generating oxygen at the site of a cut, but it is a weak antiseptic. Stronger substances include iodine complexes such as Betadine and benzalkonium chloride (Zephiran).
- Facial scrapes should be thoroughly washed to remove debris and, after treating with antiseptic or antibiotic cream, should be left unbandaged.
- Treat bruises that involve bleeding into the tissue beneath the outer layer of skin with cold packs to reduce swelling.
- For deeper cuts that go through the skin, control bleeding by direct pressure and elevation. If bleeding persists or recurs, the wound may need a doctor's care to be closed with tape or stitches.

DIABETIC COMA/INSULIN SHOCK

People with diabetes can suffer several types of comas. One of the most common—insulin shock—develops relatively rapidly and is caused by an excess of injected insulin or other sugar-lowering medication that causes a depletion of blood sugar (hypoglycemia). Another type of coma results from inadequate insulin, which leads to too much blood sugar (hyperglycemia) and a buildup of toxic substances called ketoacids (ketoacidosis) in the blood. Both of these situations are serious, but hypoglycemia is of more immediate danger and requires prompt action. If you are unable to tell what is causing a diabetic person to fall into a coma, it is better to treat for low blood sugar. But in both instances, the person should be brought immediately to a hospital emergency room.

HYPOGLYCEMIA (INSULIN SHOCK)

SYMPTOMS OF HYPOGLYCEMIA

- Distress is relatively rapid, usually in a matter of minutes.
- Hunger.
- Sweating.
- Cold, clammy feeling.
- Paleness.
- Trembling, anxiety.
- Rapid heartbeat.
- Feeling of weakness or faintness.
- Irritability and change in mood or personality.
- Loss of consciousness.

TREATMENT

- Feed the person a source of quickly absorbed sugar. If the person is conscious, table sugar, fruit juice, honey, a nondiet soft drink, or any other available sugar source will do. If the person is unconscious, do not try to force sugar or liquid down his throat. Honey, granulated sugar, or a special capsule (such as D-glucose) containing concentrated sugars, which some diabetics carry, can be carefully placed under the tongue where it is absorbed into the body. However, this may be difficult to do.

• Take the person to a hospital emergency room as quickly as possible. Severe insulin reactions can be fatal.

HYPERGLYCEMIA (DIABETIC COMA)

SYMPTOMS OF HYPERGLYCEMIA

• Distress develops gradually.
• Increased thirst and urination, usually for 1 to several days; increasing amounts of sugar are "spilled" into the urine.
• Nausea, vomiting, and abdominal pain.
• Feeling of weakness or fatigue.
• Dehydration (dry mouth and skin, sunken eyes).
• Breath smells fruity.
• Heavy, labored breathing that is rapid and deep.
• Drowsiness or loss of consciousness.

TREATMENT

Take the person to an emergency room as quickly as possible. Any acute change in alertness, consciousness, or mental status in a diabetic warrants immediate medical attention.

DISLOCATIONS

A dislocation disrupts the normal relationship of two bones at the joint. Dislocations most commonly occur in free-moving joints, such as the jaw, shoulder, elbow, fingers, hip, knee, and ankle. A dislocation may be caused by a direct blow, hyperextension, a fall, sports injury or other accident. Torn ligaments, damaged blood vessels or nerves, and a fractured bone may also be present.

SYMPTOMS

• Pain.
• Decreased function and deformity in the appearance of the affected joint.
• Discoloration of the skin and swelling.

TREATMENT

• Check for signs of other injuries or shock and treat accordingly (see "Shock" in chapter 13).

• Splint the joint in the position in which it was found and treat as if it were fractured.
• Improvise a sling if an arm is involved.
• Do not attempt to correct the dislocation or force the bone back into its proper position. This may cause further injury. The person should be taken to an emergency room immediately for x-rays and treatment.

DRUG WITHDRAWAL

People who are dependent on an addictive substance need help, both emotional and often pharmacological, in overcoming their addiction and enduring withdrawal symptoms. Common examples of addictive drugs include alcohol, sedatives, cocaine, amphetamines, nicotine, and other stimulants as well as heroin and other narcotics.

Some people are able to stop taking drugs "cold turkey" without suffering withdrawal problems, but this is unusual. Help for drug addiction is best administered in a specialized treatment facility or clinic, especially since stopping may bring on severe withdrawal symptoms that demand special attention.

WITHDRAWAL SYMPTOMS

Symptoms vary according to the type of drug dependency and may include:
• Cold sweats
• Delusions
• Tremor
• Extreme restlessness and agitation
• Hallucinations
• Convulsions
• Nausea and vomiting
• Anxiety

TREATMENT

Take the person to a hospital emergency room.

FAINTING

Fainting (syncope) occurs when the brain temporarily does not have adequate blood flow, causing the person to black out. When the head is lower than the heart, blood rushes to the head and consciousness is restored. There are many causes of fainting, ranging from benign to very serious. Some people faint at the sight of blood, after experiencing intense pain or emotional shock, or as a result of severe anxiety or fatigue. These spells are due to reflexes that slow the heart and dilate blood vessels, resulting in a drop in blood pressure. Fainting is not uncommon during the early stages of pregnancy. Cardiovascular, neurological, and metabolic problems (such as hypoglycemia) and adverse drug reactions are other causes of fainting. Anyone who experiences a fainting episode or blackout should immediately consult a doctor about the cause.

TREATMENT

• Lay the person on her back with the head lower than the heart and legs. Check for breathing and feel carefully for a pulse, which may be slow and weak immediately after the person faints. If you cannot detect a heartbeat or breathing, begin CPR (see chapter 13).

• If breathing and pulse are present, raise the legs higher than the head to promote the flow of blood to the heart and brain. This should quickly revive the person.

• Loosen clothing and make the victim comfortable.

• When the person revives, color returns to the face, and pulse is normal, suggest lying or sitting quietly for a few minutes before attempting to stand. A weak or "washed out" feeling after a faint is common.

• Determine if there are other symptoms, such as chest pain, palpitations, difficulty breathing, headache, vertigo, weakness or loss of sensation on one side of the body, or difficulty speaking. Try to determine if there is an underlying medical condition such as diabetes or heart disease. If so, or if this is the first episode of fainting or if more than a few minutes elapse before complete recovery, transport the person to a hospital as soon as possible.

• If the faint feeling returns, have the person lie down again.

• Do not give an alcoholic drink or splash cold water on her face. (That works only in the movies.) A cold compress may be applied to the forehead.

FEVER

The average body temperature is about 98.6°F (37°C) when measured with an oral thermometer. Rectal temperatures will generally be about 1°F (1.3 to 2.7°C) higher than oral temperatures. All persons' normal temperatures will be about ½ to 1°F (1.3 to 2.7°C) higher in the late afternoon than in the morning. However, an elevation of more than a degree or two over the normal range is usually a sign of infection or other illness. The fever may be accompanied by other symptoms or, less commonly, the only symptom.

Most fevers disappear in 1 or 2 days and require no special treatment other than taking plenty of fluids to prevent dehydration and perhaps aspirin or acetaminophen to relieve symptoms. Any high fever (103°F [39.4°C] or greater) or one that is accompanied by recurrent shaking or chills, or one that lasts for more than a day, should be evaluated by a doctor.

TREATMENT

• Call the doctor if a very young baby (less than 2 months old) has a fever of more than 101°F (38.3°C), as fewer during this period is unusual.

• A child with a high fever should be lightly dressed and uncovered or covered only with a light blanket.

• If the doctor approves, small amounts of acetaminophen may be given to a child, but follow instructions as to dosage. Aspirin should not be given to children with viral illnesses (flu, chickenpox, etc.) as this may increase the risk of Reye's syndrome, a potentially life-threatening disease affecting the brain and liver.

• If a child's temperature rises to 103°F (39.4°C) he should be sponged with lukewarm water, allowing the water to evaporate from the skin surface. Alternatively, the child should be placed in a tub of lukewarm water. Check the temperature every 25 minutes; continue until the child's temperature falls below 102°F (38.9°C) (do not sponge the child with alcohol, which has potentially harmful side effects; water is safer and just as effective).

• If the fever does not respond or the child has convulsions, consult a doctor.

• A fever accompanied by severe headache, nausea and vomiting, a stiff neck, change in alertness, and hypersensitivity to light may be a sign of meningitis and should be investigated promptly by a doctor.

• Any fever not associated with the usual coldlike or flulike symptoms should be discussed with your doctor.

FOOD POISONING

Food poisoning may be caused by eating foods contaminated by bacteria or their toxins or, less commonly, a substance normally found in the food itself, as in certain mushrooms, plants, or some fish.

Proper preparation and refrigeration of food will prevent most cases of food poisoning.

SYMPTOMS OF FOOD POISIONING

• Severe stomach cramps
• Nausea and vomiting
• Diarrhea, usually within a few hours after eating the offending food
• General weakness and malaise

TREATMENT

• In many cases, the source of discomfort is eliminated from the body by vomiting or diarrhea. So if these occur when food poisoning is suspected, they should not be stopped. In some cases, it is desirable to induce vomiting, but frequently induction of vomiting does not help—symptoms usually strike after the food has already left the stomach and cannot be brought back up.

• Try to identify the source of the poisoning. If it is mushrooms or canned food, take the person to an emergency room without delay. If there are any nervous system symptoms such as difficulty in speaking or swallowing, visual changes, paralysis, or breathing difficulties, the person should also be taken to a hospital as quickly as possible.

• If vomiting or diarrhea is severe or prolonged, watch for signs of dehydration. Offer the person fluids, but do not allow her to eat. Antidiarrheal medication may be prescribed by a doctor if diarrhea is persistent but most often is not indicated if fluid intake is adequate.

• Call a doctor or go to a hospital emergency room if the symptoms persist or are severe or are accompanied by fever, continual, localized abdominal pain, blood in the vomit or stool, or abdominal distention.

FOREIGN BODIES

SMALL OBJECT ON THE SURFACE OF THE EYE

TREATMENT

• Do not rub the eye.
• Wash your hands carefully before touching the eye.
• Pull the lower lid down gently so that its lining is visible; at the same time, have the person look up.

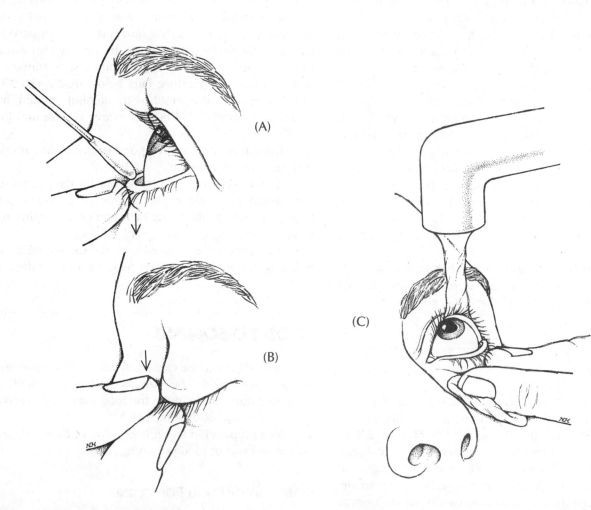

Figure 14.2: Foreign body in the eye. If the foreign object is on the lower lid (A), gently pull the lid down and have the person look upward. Use a moistened cotton swab or corner of a clean handkerchief to remove the object. If the object is not on the lower lid, gently grasp the upper lid (B) and draw it down over the lower. This will produce tears that should wash out the object. Flush out the eye by running lukewarm water directly over it (C).

• If the speck is on the surface of the lower lid, lift it off carefully with a slightly moistened cotton swab or the corner of a clean handkerchief or tissue.

• If the speck is not on the lower lid, gently grasp the lashes of the upper lid between the thumb and forefinger and draw the upper lid out and down over the lower one. The resulting tears may flush out a particle adhering to the upper lid.

• If the object has not drifted to the corner of the eye, lift the upper lid (as shown in figure 14.2) and have the person look down. If the object appears on the inner surface of the upper lid, carefully remove it with a moistened cotton swab or the corner of a clean handkerchief or tissue.

• Flush the eye with lukewarm water or any ophthalmic irrigating solution. If tearing and pain persist, or if vision does not clear, tape a loosely fitting patch over the eye and see a doctor promptly, as there may be an injury such as corneal abrasion.

LARGE OBJECT EMBEDDED IN THE EYE

TREATMENT

• Do not attempt to remove any foreign object that is embedded in the eyeball; instead, cover both eyes with a sterile compress and take the person to an emergency room as quickly as possible.

• If there is difficulty closing the eye because of the size of the foreign body embedded in the eye, protect the eye with a small paper cup placed over it. Tape the cup in place and cover the uninjured eye with a sterile compress. Take the person to an emergency room as soon as possible.

FOREIGN BODY IN THE EAR

The protective structure of the outer ear prevents objects from easily entering its middle and inner parts. However, children (and some adults) often put foreign objects into the ear and occasionally bugs or other objects may accidentally enter.

TREATMENT

• Never attempt to remove a foreign object that has entered the ear canal by poking it with a matchstick, bobby pin, cotton swab, or similar probe. This action may push the object in farther or cause damage to the middle-ear structure.

• A soft object that is not deeply embedded and is clearly visible may be withdrawn carefully with tweezers.

• For all objects that cannot be dislodged by tilting

the head to the side and shaking (not hitting), see a doctor or go to an emergency room promptly.

• Put oil (mineral, vegetable, or baby oil) in the ear only if a live insect becomes lodged in the ear canal. In that case, filling the ear canal with oil will suffocate the insect. Removal by a doctor will then be feasible. If there is any question about material remaining in the ear, a doctor should see the person for a thorough exam.

FOREIGN BODY IN THE NOSE

Most foreign objects lodged in the nose are placed there by curious children or by adults who pack bits of cotton or other substances in their noses to stop bleeding. Sometimes a child will place an organic substance in a nostril and it will not be noticed until it releases an unpleasant smell.

TREATMENT

• Do not attempt to poke at an object in the nose with a toothpick, swab, or similar probe, which can drive it farther into the nose.

• Do not allow the person to inhale forcefully through the nose. Have the person breathe out through the mouth.

• Have the person gently blow his nose two times to see if that dislodges the object. Avoid repeated or very forceful nose-blowing.

• If the object is visible at the entrance to the nose and can be safely reached with tweezers, try to remove it. Do not attempt this on a child who is thrashing and uncooperative.

• If these attempts at removal do not succeed, take the person to an emergency room.

• Any foreign body that has been in place for several hours or days should be removed by a doctor.

FRACTURES

First aid for broken bones generally involves protecting the bone and the rest of the body from further damage. Broken bones always necessitate treatment by a doctor.

GENERAL FRACTURE SYMPTOMS

• Bone can be heard or felt breaking
• Inability to move the injured part
• Pain, tenderness to the touch
• Swelling, discoloration
• Deformity or misalignment
• Bone pokes through the skin (compound fracture)

- Internal bleeding (particularly in the case of broken ribs or pelvis)

GENERAL TREATMENT OF FRACTURES

- Check the ABC's (airway, breathing, circulation). Survey the victim for other injuries and observe closely for signs of shock. Treat accordingly (see "Shock" in chapter 13).
- No attempt should be made to reset or straighten a broken bone; it should be splinted where it lies, with a minimum of movement.
- If the bone has pierced the skin, bleeding should be controlled by direct pressure. Place a sterile dressing over the wound, splint the extremity, and take the victim to an emergency room.
- Call an ambulance. Transport the victim yourself only if an ambulance is not available.

First aid for specific types of fractures is described below.

HEAD INJURIES

Head injuries range from bumps and scrapes to scalp lacerations, skull fractures, concussions, and other brain injuries. They may involve a combination of individual injuries. Minor head injuries such as bumps or abrasions, without any signs of possible brain damage (listed below), can usually be treated by simple first-aid measures. You should always suspect a neck injury in the presence of severe facial or head trauma and follow the directions for treating a head or neck injury. Anyone who has received a blow to the head and has had a loss of consciousness should be brought to a hospital emergency room.

SYMPTOMS OF MILD HEAD INJURY

The person is conscious and shows no sign of brain or neck injury or fracture (see below) but is bleeding from the scalp.

TREATMENT

- Check pulse and respiration. If the person is lying down, do not move or place a pillow or other object under the head.
- Check for signs of brain or neck injury and treat accordingly.
- Control bleeding by placing clean gauze over the injury. (Direct pressure may be applied.) Scalp lacerations can bleed profusely because of the large number of blood vessels in this part of the body, but bleeding can usually be easily controlled with pressure.
- Take the person to a doctor.

SYMPTOMS OF SERIOUS HEAD INJURY

- Large hematoma or depression of the scalp
- Change in mental status such as agitation, confusion, lethargy, or loss of consciousness
- Headache or vomiting
- Amnesia about events before or after the head injury
- Colorless or blood-streaked discharge from the nose or ears
- Speech disturbances
- Convulsions or paralysis
- Eye pupils different in size from each other

TREATMENT

- Administer CPR if breathing stops or if there is no heartbeat. Assume presence of neck injury, use the chin lift or jaw thrust (see CPR in chapter 13) without head tilt to open the airway and for rescue breathing.
- Observe precautions for neck or spine injury (see below). **EXTREMELY IMPORTANT:** Keep the head and neck in alignment with the rest of the spine in cases of suspected spinal injury.
- Watch for signs of shock. Shock generally indicates that there are other injuries and may be the result of spinal injury or internal bleeding.
- Keep the person lying as quietly as possible. Do not move unless absolutely necessary.
- Do not attempt to give any fluids.

NECK OR SPINE FRACTURE

A neck or back injury should always be suspected after any accident or fall in which abnormal forces affect the back (e.g., automobile accident, whiplash, fall from a height where the person lands directly on the feet or back, any accident resulting in serious head and facial trauma).

SYMPTOMS OF A NECK OR SPINE FRACTURE

- Neck or back pain
- Odd position of the head or neck
- Feelings of numbness, weakness, or paralysis in an arm, hand, leg or other part of the body

TREATMENT

- Check for vital signs and perform CPR if necessary (see chapter 13).
- Keep the person absolutely still. Reassure the person if she is conscious, but do not allow her to move the head or neck. Immobilize the individual's head and neck in the position in which she lies. Support the back of the

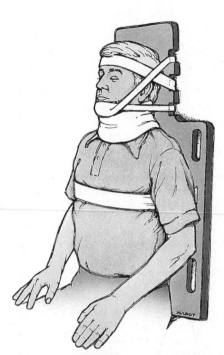

Figure 14.3: Moving a person with a suspected back or neck injury. Before moving, stabilize the cervical spine (neck) with an improvised collar, such as a heavy towel or scarf, and slide a rigid support (door, board, table leaf) under or behind him. Secure the patient to the board with broad straps, such as wide belts or ties.

neck by carefully sliding a rolled pad underneath and by placing pads, pocketbooks, or other stabilizing items at the sides of the head.

• If the person must be moved because of immediate, life-threatening danger (for example, fire, explosion, or noxious fumes), head and spine movement must be prevented. Immobilize head and spine by rolling her onto a firm object such as a stretcher, board, or door. If these are not available, a blanket may be used under the victim and dragged along the ground (see figure 14.1). At all times head and spine movement must be prevented.

• Have several people carefully move the person, making sure the head and neck are held in a direct straight line ("neutral position") with the spine, without any forward or backward bending or sideways turning of the head (see figure 14.3). If you are alone and must act quickly, pull the victim to safety, preferably by the shoulders, using the forearms to maintain the head in a neutral position.

• Summon emergency personnel to transport the victim to the hospital.

HIP OR PELVIS FRACTURE

These fractures are particularly common in the elderly, and may result from even a minor fall. In people with severe osteoporosis (thinning of the bones) the fracture

may occur during normal activity and cause the fall. A person with a suspected fracture of the pelvis should not move, since this can damage pelvic organs.

SYMPTOMS

Pain in the hip, groin, lower back, or pubic area, especially with movement of the leg. With a hip fracture the leg may be shortened and the foot turned outward.

TREATMENT

• Do not move the person unless absolutely necessary.
• If movement is necessary, follow the same procedure as outlined for a spinal injury (see above). Do not permit any movement of the torso and legs. Tie the legs together at the ankles and knees and transport the person on a firm surface (backboard). The leg may appear to be shortened and rotated out. Do not attempt to straighten it.
• Look for signs of shock and treat appropriately. (See "Shock" in chapter 13.)
• Call for emergency medical help and an ambulance.

LIMB FRACTURE

Injuries to the wrist and ankle should be treated the same as the arm or leg until they are x-rayed to determine the extent and nature of the injury.

SYMPTOMS

• Patient describes hearing or feeling the bone break.
• Pain, swelling or discoloration.
• Inability to move, put weight, or use the injured part
• Deformity or misalignment.
• Grating sound or feeling when the bone moves.

TREATMENT

• If the skin is broken at any point along the arm or leg, stop the bleeding by applying direct pressure. Take care, however, not to move the bone. Cover open fractures with a sterile dressing.
• Do not permit the person to use or "test" the injured part.
• If the person is lying down as the result of a fall, do not move, but keep as comfortable as possible by putting a pillow under the head and covering with a blanket.
• Immobilize the injured limb by splinting it in the position in which it is found. Almost any object that is rigid and the correct length can serve as a splint: boards, broom handle, cane, branch, or tightly rolled newspapers

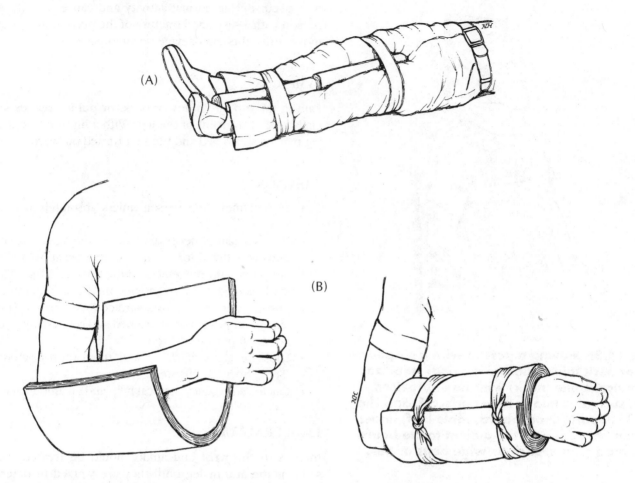

Figure 14.4A and B: Almost any rigid object can be used for a splint. The examples shown here use rolls of thick newspapers.

(as in figure 14.4A and B). In the case of a leg, if a splint is not available, the uninjured leg can serve as a splint with a roll of newspapers placed between the legs.

To make a splint:

1. Make the splint longer than the bone it will support.
2. Pad the splint with soft material such as a sheet, cloth, or clothing before placing it against the fractured bone.
3. Tie the splint to the injured limb snugly but not so tightly that it constricts circulation. Leave the tops of the fingers or toes out and check regularly to make sure circulation is not impeded.
4. Support a fracture of the arm with a sling to prevent further injury and provide pain relief.

OTHER BROKEN BONES

Almost any bone can be broken, including the cheek, nose and other facial bones, the ribs, and small bones of the hands or feet. These bones usually do not have to be splinted. If there is bleeding, it should be controlled. Take care in transporting the person to an emergency room or a doctor who can make the appropriate x-ray studies and initiate treatment.

While it may take up to 6 months or even a year for a broken bone to fully heal in an adult (children heal more quickly), it is not necessary to wear a cast for that long. However, care should be taken to avoid undue stress on the bone until complete healing has occurred.

HEART ATTACKS

A suspected heart attack is always a medical emergency. As quickly as possible, get the person to a hospital with an emergency service and a coronary care unit. Each year, tens of thousands die from heart attacks because they delay seeking medical help. Any unusual or severe chest pain is cause for alarm and should be investigated immediately. The pain may be caused by indigestion or other causes, but only a doctor can make the proper diagnosis.

SYMPTOMS

- Chest pain lasting longer than a few minutes. It may be intense or dull and may feel like squeezing, crushing, or a heavy feeling starting under the breastbone or on the left side of the chest. It often spreads up and to the left arm, although the right arm, shoulders, back, neck, and jaw may also be involved. Unlike the pain typical of angina (see "Angina" in chapter 16), the pain of a heart attack does not subside with rest, although it may fade only to return with greater intensity.
- Shortness of breath
- Fainting
- Sweating
- Nausea and vomiting
- A feeling of impending doom

TREATMENT

- Summon an emergency squad without delay. If this is not practical, transport the person to the nearest emergency room. If you suspect you are having a heart attack and you are alone, call for help; do not try to drive yourself.
- While waiting for help to arrive, reassure the patient, but observe carefully and do not leave him alone.
- Have the patient sit up or lie down, whichever position feels more comfortable.
- If cardiac arrest occurs, start CPR immediately. (See CPR in chapter 13.)
- Do not allow the person to eat or drink unless a doctor specifically instructs you to do so.

OTHER TYPES OF CHEST PAIN

Many conditions besides heart attacks can cause chest pain. If the pain is accompanied by coughing or spitting up blood, pneumonia or some other lung problem may be the cause. A collapsed lung may be signaled by a sudden, sharp pain and shortness of breath. Chest pain that is worsened by movement or deep breathing may be pleurisy or a muscular problem. Indigestion and hiatal hernia are other common causes for chest pain. Any suspicious chest discomfort should be evaluated by a doctor.

NOSEBLEEDS

Nosebleeds are common and usually harmless. Most are caused by minor injuries or from nose-picking. A nose-

bleed may also occur after a few days of nose-blowing during a cold or upon arrival in a high-altitude area. Most stop within a few minutes and require no further treatment.

TREATMENT

- Have the person sit down with head angled slightly forward so the blood doesn't run back into the throat. Swallowed blood may make the person nauseated or gag.
- If the blood comes from only one side, press the fleshy part of the nostril firmly toward the midline; if from both, pinch the nostrils together. Maintain pressure for 5 to 10 minutes.
- If the bleeding continues when pressure is released, insert a twist of sterile gauze or twisted piece of clean cloth torn from a handkerchief or other similar material into the nostril. Make sure the end protrudes for easy removal. Do not use absorbent cotton or facial tissue, which will be difficult to remove.
- Repeat the pressure for about 10 minutes, encouraging the person to breathe through the mouth.
- If bleeding has stopped, the packing may be moistened and gently removed after 30 to 60 minutes. The nose should not be blown (not even gently!) during this time, as this may cause bleeding to resume.
- If the bleeding is profuse or cannot be controlled within 30 minutes, or if nosebleeds recur frequently, go to a hospital emergency service for further care.
- If the bleeding results from direct trauma to the nose, only gentle pressure should be applied and the nose should not be packed with cotton. Apply ice over and above the injury to decrease swelling and promote vasoconstriction.
- If there is persistent bleeding, swelling, change in shape or alignment of the nose, or clear fluid discharges, the injury should be checked at a hospital emergency service.

OVEREXPOSURE

Overexposure to extremes of temperature is often a matter of carelessness or disregard of the dangers of environmental climatic extremes. The very young, the very old, the chronically ill, alcoholics, and drug abusers as well as outdoor enthusiasts are especially vulnerable to overexposure.

FROSTBITE

Frostbite occurs with prolonged exposure to subfreezing temperatures. The risk increases as the temperature declines or the wind (and windchill factor) increases.

SYMPTOMS

- Progressive, painful loss of feeling leading to numbness
- White or blue appearance of the skin
- Firmness of the skin to the touch
- Loss of function

TREATMENT

- Do not try to rewarm the affected parts. Gently wrap the affected parts in a blanket, dry clothing, or several layers of newspaper and transport the person to a hospital as soon as possible.
- Do not rub or massage the frostbitten area with anything, particularly not with snow as some home remedies suggest. Rubbing increases the risk of tissue damage. Snow merely adds to the danger of freezing.
- If treatment must be undertaken outside a hospital, bring the person indoors and begin warming the frostbitten parts immediately by immersing in warm water at a temperature of about 104°–108°F (40°–42°C). Rewarming may take 45 minutes to an hour. Successful rewarming leads to progressive return of function, color, and sensations and may result in blistering, which is normal. This process may be very painful; aspirin or acetaminophen may be given. Do not break the blisters.
- Do not expose frostbitten skin to the intense heat of a stove, radiator, open fire, or heating pad.
- If a hot beverage such as coffee or tea is available, offer it if the person is fully awake. Do not allow the person to drink alcoholic beverages.
- Apply dry, sterile gauze for protection.
- During travel to the hospital or indoors avoid refreezing of the frostbitten part.
- Treat hypothermia (see below) before treating frostbite.

HYPOTHERMIA

Hypothermia refers to subnormal central body temperature that may be due to overexposure to cold temperatures. The very young, the old, alcohol and drug abusers, and outdoor enthusiasts are particularly vulnerable to this condition. In accidental hypothermia, the body temperature lowers progressively, and in extreme cases death from cardiac arrest may result.

MILD HYPOTHERMIA

SYMPTOMS

Shivering, conscious and alert, but may have difficulty speaking or walking. Body temperature is 90 to 95°F (32.2° to 35°C). (Be aware that many household thermometers do not register temperatures below 94°F [34.4°C], so it may be hard to tell what the body temperature is.)

TREATMENT

Wrap person in warm blankets or clothes and remove immediately to a warm shelter. Give warm, nonalcoholic drinks.

SEVERE HYPOTHERMIA

SYMPTOMS

- Body temperature below 90°F (32.2°C)
- Person stops shivering
- Altered mental status ranging from lethargy to unconsciousness

TREATMENT

- Check vital signs: Respiration and pulse may be difficult to detect. *Check carefully.* If they appear completely absent and you are alone, call for help and then begin CPR. (See chapter 13.)
- Take the person to a hospital emergency room immediately. When alone in an isolated area, getting the person to a medical facility is the highest priority.
- If help or a hospital is unavailable, wrap the person in warm blankets and take to a warm shelter. Try to avoid jostling the person when transporting. This may affect heart rhythm.
- Remove wet clothing and wrap the person in warm, dry blankets. Use hot water bottles or another person's body next to the victim to warm the victim.
- Rewarming takes several hours, with some risk of further fall in body temperature as well as shock (see "Shock"), so it is always preferable to take the person to a hospital when possible.

HEAT CRAMPS

SYMPTOMS

Cramps in various parts of the body or muscles during or after exercise as a result of salt (electrolyte) and water losses through sweating.

TREATMENT

- Replenish salt and fluids to alleviate cramps. Administer fluids. If possible, give fluids as ¼ to ½

teaspoon of salt dissolved in a quart of cool fruit juice. Commercial sport drinks with a moderate amount of sugar are also acceptable.
- Stretch cramped muscles.

HEAT EXHAUSTION (HEAT PROSTRATION)

SYMPTOMS

- Pale, moist skin.
- Body temperature is normal or only moderately elevated (102°F/38.9°C).
- Damp skin.
- Nausea, weakness, light headedness, and possibly fainting without prolonged loss of consciousness.
- Very painful cramps may follow strenuous activity.

TREATMENT

- Move the person to a cool, shady, or air-conditioned place and have her lie down with feet elevated.
- Loosen or remove most clothing.
- Apply cool, wet compresses to head and torso.
- Administer fluids as described in the information about heat cramps in the section "Overexposure."

HEAT STROKE

Heat stroke is a medical emergency that occurs most often in hot, very humid weather. This type of heat injury occurs often in healthier people such as athletes and military recruits.

SYMPTOMS

- Person feels hot to the touch and skin is red and dry.
- Body's internal cooling mechanism has ceased to function, so sweating may have stopped and body temperature has climbed to 104°F (40°C) or higher.
- Rapid heartbeat.
- Confusion, and agitation or lethargy, stupor, and loss of consciousness.

TREATMENT

- Summon an ambulance and emergency medical help immediately.
- While waiting for the ambulance, move the person indoors to an air-conditioned area or to a shady place.
- Remove clothing, and cool by spraying the person with cool water. Fan the person to evaporate this water and increase heat loss.
- If a thermometer is available, check the person's temperature and stop cooling measures when it comes down to 102°F (38.9°C).

PREVENTING HEAT STROKE

- Exercise commonsense precautions during hot, humid weather. Wear light clothes, drink plenty of fluids, and avoid overexposure to the sun.
- Take a cool bath or shower once or twice daily.
- Seek air-conditioned places for rest.
- Avoid strenuous activity in very hot and humid weather, particularly during the hottest part of the day.
- Use extreme caution in hot weather if you suffer a chronic disease (cardiovascular disease, neurological problems, or dermatological conditions).
- If you regularly take medication, get your doctor's advice about hot-weather activity. (See chapter 34.)

POISON IVY

Poison ivy, poison sumac, and poison oak are the most common plants producing an allergic contact dermatitis (see figure 14.5). The best way to prevent a reaction is to recognize and avoid all contact with their leaves.

SYMPTOMS

- Skin reaction varies in severity; there may be generalized swelling, rash, itching, and blisters.
- Some people may suffer headache, fever, and malaise.

TREATMENT

- As soon as possible after contact, whether or not a reaction occurs, remove all contaminated clothing, including shoes, and wash all exposed areas thoroughly with strong soap. Apply alcohol and rinse copiously with water.
- If a rash appears, apply calamine or other soothing lotion. Corticosteroid creams or lotions also ease itching and swelling, but follow label instructions. Apply these creams or lotions only to limited areas and do not use them on young children. If you have questions about their application, consult your doctor.
- Cover weeping or oozing blisters with sterile gauze moistened in a mild solution of 1 tablespoon of baking soda in 1 quart of water.
- If fever or severe symptoms such as widespread

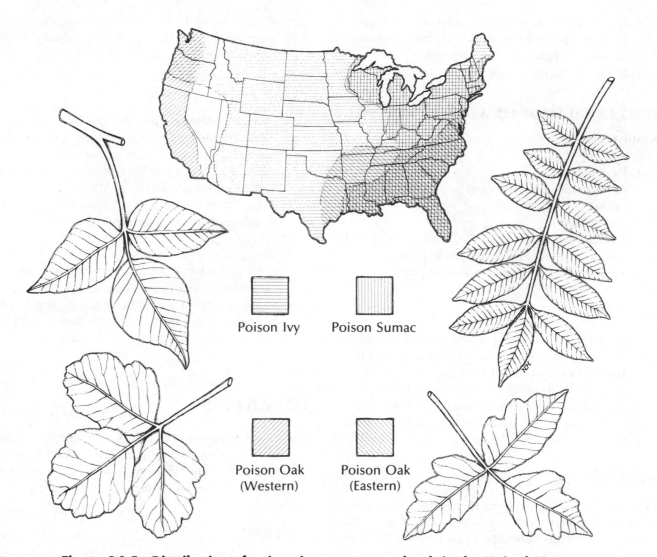

Figure 14.5: Distribution of poison ivy, sumac, and oak in the United States.

Poison Ivy

Poison Sumac

Poison Oak (Western)

Poison Oak (Eastern)

rash or involvement of mouth, eyes or genitals occur, see a doctor. Your doctor may treat the reaction with other medicines, such as prednisone.

• As an alternative therapy, herbalists recommend covering poison ivy blisters with a bandage soaked with tea made from equal portions of white oak bark and lime water.

POISONING

More than 1.5 million calls are made each year to regional poison control centers to report accidental poisonings and more than three-fourths of these incidents involve children under the age of 5. Most poisonings are accidental, but a substantial number are the result of suicide attempts. Although the widespread use of child-proof tops for drug containers sold in this country has reduced poisonings dramatically, children remain the most frequent poisoning victims. The aged are the second most commonly affected group. Failing eyesight, the use of multiple drugs, and confusion or difficulty in remembering whether a medication was taken are among the causes of accidental poisoning in older people.

Other sources of poisonings are drug overdoses among drug abusers—increasingly common incidents, affecting all classes and age groups. Mixing drugs and alcohol or the unwitting use of drugs that interact with each other are yet other sources of accidental poisonings.

This section focuses primarily on ingested poisons; inhalation and chemical spills are discussed elsewhere (see "Inhalation" in chapter 20, Respiratory Diseases and Lung Health.)

HANDLING POISONING EMERGENCIES

Proper management of poisoning requires expert guidance. The most important single resource in handling poisoning emergencies is the local poison control center. A directory of centers appears in appendix C. Your local center is listed in the telephone book white pages or may be obtained from Directory Assistance. Affix this number to all telephones or post it in a conspicuous place, such as a bulletin board next to a telephone. All family members as well as baby-sitters should know when and how to call this number.

When calling the poison control center:

- Be prepared to give as much information as possible. The person answering the phone will want to know your name, location, and telephone number so he can call back in case you are disconnected, or can summon help if needed.
- Give the name of the substance ingested and, if possible, the amount and time of ingestion. If the bottle or package is available, give the trade name and ingredients if they are listed.
- Describe the state of the poisoning victim. Is the victim conscious? Are there any symptoms? What is the person's general appearance, skin color, respiration, breathing difficulties, mental status (alert, sleepy, unusual behavior)? Vomiting? Convulsions?

Using this information, the poison center specialist can give specific first-aid instructions. The majority of the cases called into poison control centers can be handled at home if instructions are followed promptly and correctly.

All households, especially those with children, should have on hand syrup of ipecac to induce vomiting (which is recommended in only certain cases of poisoning). Activated charcoal, when taken by mouth, prevents the intestinal absorption of a large number of ingested substances and is often given by health professionals to treat poisoning. Currently it is recommended for use only by medical personnel. There is no such thing as a universal antidote.

First aid for a poisoning emergency follows the same general guidelines applicable for any injury:

- Check first for vital signs—breathing and pulse—and, if they are absent, call 911, then perform CPR (see chapter 13).
- If there are obvious symptoms of serious poisoning, call 911 or the rescue squad.
- If the person is having convulsions, treat as outlined in the section on convulsions in this chapter.
- If the person is conscious, call the poison control center and follow whatever instructions are given.

- If you are unable to reach a poison control center or a local hospital emergency department for advice, transport the victim to the nearest emergency service.

If you are far from medical assistance (greater than 30 minutes), the following general guidelines should be applied in the absence of specific instructions from a poison control center or other reliable source:

- Determine the nature of the ingested substance. If there are no visible bottles or other clues, examine the mouth for signs of burns, which would indicate an acid or alkali. Smell the breath for a petroleum-like odor.
- Diluting the poison by administering water or milk is advised for most substances. Water is recommended for acid and alkali ingestion if the person can swallow.
- If the substance that has been swallowed is a medication, poisonous plant, pesticide, or other product with significant systemic toxicity and has been ingested within the previous hour, induce vomiting. Give 1 or 2 tablespoons of ipecac syrup (see label instructions for dose) followed by ½ glass to 2 glasses of water. If the first dose does not induce vomiting, this may be repeated in 20 minutes. Vomiting can also be induced by inserting a spoon or finger at the back of the throat to produce a gag reflex. Collect a specimen of the vomitus for analysis by medical personnel.

Do not induce vomiting if:

1. The nature of the substance is unknown.
2. A corrosive substance (house cleaner, lye, bleach, or other acid or alkali product) is suspected.
3. A petroleum product (benzene, kerosene, gasoline, turpentine, paint thinner, other hydrocarbon) is suspected. Vomiting a petroleum product carries the danger of inhaling it into the lungs, causing chemical pneumonia.
4. The person is having seizures, is unconscious or appears to be losing consciousness.
5. The victim is less than 1 year of age.

Take the poisoning victim, along with the bottle or container of whatever was ingested, and any vomitus to the nearest hospital emergency department for further treatment.

ACIDS AND ALKALIS

Household cleaners frequently contain caustic acids and alkalis. They are found in lye, bleaches, and toilet bowl or drain and oven cleaners, and such preparations as hair

POTENTIALLY HARMFUL SUBSTANCES COMMONLY FOUND ABOUT THE HOUSE

Acetaminophen	Drain cleaner	Iodine	Permanent-wave solutions
Ammonia	Fabric softener	Ionic detergents	Rat poison
Aspirin	Floor wax	Laxatives	Room deodorizer
Bleach	Furniture polish	Lighter fluid	Rubbing alcohol
Carpet cleaner	Hairspray	Liquor	Shampoo
Cement and glue	Hair straighteners	Metal polish	Shoe polish
Contraceptive pills	Headache remedies	Nail varnish	Sleeping pills/sleep aids
Deodorants	Heart medicines	Oven cleaner	Tranquilizers
Depilatories	Houseplants	Paint	Turpentine
Diet pills	Ibuprofen	Paint thinner	Vitamins
Diuretics	Insecticides	Perfume	Window cleaning fluid

straighteners. Each year, because of the accessibility of these chemicals, many young children are rushed to emergency rooms after drinking one of these harmful products. Parents and grandparents do not perceive these substances as dangerous since their container labels are almost always marked "poisonous if ingested," and they appear unappetizing to adults. But to young children, their colorful bottles and cans suggest something good to eat or drink.

Many poisonings have also occurred after these chemicals were poured and stored in beverage containers such as milk or soft-drink bottles. **(So never keep harmful substances in containers that are meant for potables!)**

Always make sure these types of chemicals are stored in places inaccessible to children. Ingestions of these poisons are serious incidents. If they occur:

- Take the victim immediately to a hospital emergency service.
- Do not induce vomiting.
- For acid or alkali ingestion, have the victim take water or milk and swallow if possible, or swish it in the mouth once and spit it out. Do not make the person vomit.

PETROLEUM PRODUCTS

Poisonous petroleum products include gasoline, kerosene, benzene, mineral spirits, furniture polishes, paint thinners, and other solvents. In recent years, inhaling or sniffing some of these products has become popular among young people, especially drug users, because the fumes can produce a "high." This can be a deadly practice as evidenced by the number of young people who have died from cardiorespiratory problems or suffered

severe liver damage from sniffing correction fluid, glue, carbon tetrachloride, and other petroleum-based chemicals. Household petroleum products should always be stored out of the reach of children.

If accidental ingestion occurs:

- Call your local poison control center for specific instructions. Serious pulmonary problems may accompany certain types of poisoning.
- Do not induce vomiting unless specifically instructed to do so.

PESTICIDES

Common examples of pesticide poisoning include accidental ingestion of rodent pellets; ant, roach, and other bug poisons; garden sprays; and farm chemicals. Skin contact with these liquid or powdered products may also produce toxicity.

Prevention of pesticide poisoning:

- Avoid the use of pesticides in households where there are young children. Never have pesticide containers lying around where children can reach them.
- If a pesticide must be used, do so when children will be away and make sure that it is a type that does not leave a harmful residue.
- As with all poisonous products, pesticides should be stored in their original containers in a child-proof place.

If ingestion occurs, call your poison control center immediately for instructions or take the child to a hospital emergency service. There are specific antidotes for this type of serious poisoning.

INDUSTRIAL POISONS

Increasing attention and concern are being focused on the fact that industrial poisons are wending their way into food and water supplies. In most instances, the health effects are apt to be delayed. But occasionally the toxic effects are displayed relatively rapidly and may cause irreversible damage or death. Poisonings from lead, mercury, and other heavy metals are graphic examples. A few years ago, mercury poisoning in rural Japan was traced to eating fish taken from waters contaminated by industrial waste. Similarly, lead poisoning among children remains a serious problem in the United States, not only from the practice of eating flaking paint chips that contain lead but also from many other sources, including drinking water contaminated by lead from pipes and brass fixtures. Industrial wastes near factories where lead is used are another source of lead poisoning.

Avoiding exposure is often difficult, since individuals have little or no control over release of these chemicals into the environment. If lead or other such poisoning is suspected, especially in a child, medical consultation should be sought for evaluation and treatment and the local department of health should be notified. In cases of suspected environmental contamination, the Environmental Protection Agency should be notified.

MEDICATIONS AS POISONS

Almost any medication taken in a large enough quantity can have a toxic effect. Aspirin remains one of the leading causes of accidental poisoning in young children, although this danger has diminished because of childproof containers. Iron pills, or multivitamin pills containing iron, are also a major source of childhood poisoning. Acetaminophen (Tylenol, Anacin-3, etc.) is an increasingly frequent source of acute poisoning. Other over-the-counter drugs, including cold preparations, sleep aids, and antihistamines, can be toxic as well. With some drugs, the margin between therapeutic and toxic doses is relatively small; taking a few extra sleeping pills, for example, may be sufficient to cause a coma. Altered metabolism of medications in the elderly may narrow the therapeutic margin.

Take these preventive steps to guard against poisonings with medications.

• Follow label or physician's instructions in taking any medication. Discard leftover prescription drugs unless they are medications taken for chronic or recurring conditions.
• Do not share prescriptions.
• Great caution should be exercised in taking more than one drug at a time, including over-the-counter medications, birth control pills, and vitamin preparations. When taken simultaneously, these substances may have harmful effects. When telling your pharmacist or doctors about your medications, pills, and capsules, list all of them, including nutrient supplements.
• Many accidental poisonings in children involve drugs, usually those taken by their parents. Use containers with childproof tops. As emphasized elsewhere, all medications should be stored in a safe place where children cannot get them. People often overlook the drugs left on a nightstand, in a pocketbook, refrigerator, or other unlikely places, but young children have been victims of poisoning from taking medications left in such spots.
• The elderly or people with failing memories or eyesight may need extra help in keeping track of and in taking prescribed medication. Color-keyed labels, a large-print medication calendar, or a preset alarm may be helpful, but often the best solution is to have a family member, neighbor, visiting nurse, or other reliable person supervise the medication ingestion.
• Patronize a pharmacy capable of properly filling and tracking your prescription medication use as well as identifying unusual side effects or interactions of your prescribed medications.

POISONOUS PLANTS

There are more than 700 plant species in the United States that can cause poisoning if a part of them is swallowed. Depending on the plant, the type and degree of toxicity vary from simple local irritation to serious systemic (widespread) reactions. In some cases, the entire plant is poisonous. In others, there are edible parts attached to segments that are poisonous: Occasionally, it may be the bulb (e.g., daffodils or narcissus) that is hazardous; in other plants, the berries or seeds (mistletoe berries, apple, or apricot seeds) should not be eaten; and in still others, the flower (jasmine), leaves (tomatoes or rhubarb), or roots are toxic. In addition, cooking may alter the toxicity of some plants.

Surveys have found that plants are second only to medicines as the cause of serious poisoning in children under 5. The problem is increasing, according to poison control centers, because of the growing popularity of houseplants, and also the number of families who make foraging for wild food a hobby. Wild mushrooms are particularly notorious. Although only about 100 of the 5,000 species of mushrooms found in the United States are poisonous, some of these, such as the amanitas, are particularly deadly.

To prevent plant poisonings:

• Do not buy houseplants that are poisonous to either humans or pets. Cats and dogs frequently like to chew on plant leaves, and although most

COMMON POISONOUS PLANTS

There are hundreds of poisonous plants in the United States. Following are some of the more common ones that are grown in gardens, used as houseplants, or grow in the wild.

Autumn crocus
Azalea
Belladonna
Bird-of-paradise (seed pod)
Buttercups
Cassava
Castor bean
Chinaberry
Chinese evergreen
Christmas pepper
Corncockle
Daffodil (bulb)
Daphne
Deadly nightshade
Delphinium

Dieffenbachia (also called dumbcane)
English ivy
Foxglove
Grass pea vine
Holly (berries)
Horse chestnuts
Hyacinth (bulbs)
Hydrangea
Iris
Jack-in-the-pulpit
Jasmine (flowers)
Jerusalem cherry
Jimsonweed (also called thornapple)
Lantana
Larkspur
Lily-of-the-valley
Manchineel
Mistletoe (berries)
Monkshood
Mountain laurel

Mushroom
Oleander
Philodendron
Poinsettia
Potato (sprouts, roots, and vines; only the tuber is edible)
Rhododendron
Rhubarb (leaf and roots; only the stalk is edible)
Poison hemlock
Pokeberry
Purple locoweed
Rapeweed
Skunk cabbage
Sweet pea
Tomato plant leaves
Water hemlock
Wisteria (seeds)
Yew (needles, bark, seeds, and berries)

will avoid poisonous plants, kittens and puppies may not be so wise.

- Avoid decorative plants (like the Jerusalem cherry) that have an appetizing appearance but highly poisonous fruits or berries.
- In foraging for food during a hiking or camping trip, don't eat anything that you are unsure about.
- Don't let children nibble on anything that grows wild, including berries you know are safe. Many wild berries look alike and you can't expect a child to make such distinctions when you are not around. Consult the list in the box above for some of the more common poisonous plants.

If someone ingests a poisonous plant:

- Contact a poison control center for information and instructions.
- If you are not sure of the species of plant that has been ingested, bring it and the victim with you to an emergency facility.
- As a general rule, in suspected toxic plant ingestion, if professional advice is unavailable and the victim is fully conscious, the stomach should be emptied by inducing vomiting.

A CAUTION ON HERBS AND HERB MEDICINE

Herbs are mankind's oldest remedies, and many are still used as the basis for modern medicine. But many herbs are also deadly; others are not particularly harmful, but neither do they possess any great healing or curative powers. A medicinal herb should be treated like any medication: Do not take it unless you are completely familiar with its effects or you have checked with your doctor. Be wary of herbalists and home herbal remedies and never try brewing your own. Many plants look alike, and a deadly poison can easily be mistaken for one that is harmless. For example, one bite of water hemlock, which looks very much like parsley, chervil, or coriander (all harmless), can be fatal. Above is a list compiled by the Food and Drug Administration of toxic plants.

SEXUAL ASSAULT

In recent years, more attention has focused on the problems of rape and sexual abuse. There is now greater awareness of the importance of sensitive treatment of rape victims, not only by medical personnel but also by police officials, the courts, the press, friends, and family members. Although women are by far the most common rape victims, men may also be sexually abused.

TREATMENT

• Reassure the victim that she is safe from further harm from the attacker.

• Injuries, such as bleeding and fractures, should be treated appropriately, but the woman should not wash or douche until seen by a doctor. Otherwise, evidence of the attack may be lost.

• Encourage the woman to go to a hospital emergency service as soon as possible. Choose a hospital that offers not only immediate medical and gynecological evaluation but also psychological support, as well as follow-up services in all these areas. If possible, accompany the woman and be willing to offer further assistance and support. At the hospital, she will be checked and treated for any internal as well as external injuries. Vaginal and other specimens will be taken for evidence. Follow-up will include tests for pregnancy and sexually transmitted diseases. Pregnancy prevention may be offered and the woman encouraged to report the attack to the police.

• If the victim is a child, prompt medical evaluation is essential. The youngster also may need extra counseling by an expert in dealing with child abuse, especially if the attack was committed by a family member or friend.

SPRAINS

A sprain is an injury to the ligaments—the fibrous tissue connecting the bones at the joints. A sprain may be relatively mild or quite severe, depending on how badly the joint was wrenched and whether the ligaments were only stretched or were torn.

SYMPTOMS

Same as for a fracture, except for misalignment and deformity (see "Fractures"). A serious sprain cannot be readily distinguished from a fracture without medical evaluation of the injury.

TREATMENT

For a serious sprain, treatment is the same as for a fracture (see "Fractures").

For less serious, less painful sprains:

• Start with RICE—Rest, Ice, Compression, and Elevation. Do not let the victim use the injured body part.

• Apply an ice pack and mild compression with an elastic bandage to the injured part for several hours to keep swelling down.

• Keep the sprain elevated, using pillows or a sling.

• After the first 24 hours, heat may be applied. The injured part should not be used until pain and swelling subside, usually within a couple of days.

• Apply an elastic bandage properly to provide support and immobilization without excessive compression.

• If there is swelling, discoloration, or deformity, consult a doctor.

SUMMING UP

Every capable person should know basic life-support techniques, since first-aid procedures are frequently lifesaving in emergency situations. In many cases, knowing what not to do is just as important as knowing what measures to take. In addition, every family member should know how to summon emergency medical help over the phone. The numbers for the local Emergency Medical Service and poison control center should be permanently affixed to all household telephones.

As is stressed throughout the chapters on first aid, most accidents can be prevented. The checklists in chapter 15 provide a good basis for teaching safety to your family. Households with young children or older adults need extra precautions. The room-by-room survey of major safety features is designed to provide guidance for family safety within the home as well as in yards, garages, and areas outside and around the house.

This section is intended to outline the major first-aid procedures and preventive techniques. It is not intended to cover all of the hundreds of different emergency situations that may arise, but instead to give basic principles enabling readers to evaluate and cope with the most common medical emergencies. For the highest proficiency in dealing with medical emergencies, enroll in the certified CPR, water-safety, and first-aid programs available in your community.

15
The Basics of Safety

KENNETH C. FINE, M.D.

Accidents frequently kill. In the United States, accidents are the leading cause of death for children and young men. For all age groups, accidents are the fourth leading cause of death, claiming more than 150,000 lives a year. In addition, mishaps injure more than 70 million Americans a year seriously enough to require medical care.

The National Safety Council estimates that commonsense precautions could prevent more than one-half of all accidents. Simple precautions such as wearing seat belts in an automobile, keeping your car in good repair, and teaching children proper safety habits are but three ways to forestall unnecessary injuries. This chapter outlines other important preventive techniques for the entire family.

ACCIDENT PREVENTION AND SAFETY PRECAUTIONS IN THE HOME

Most accidents can be prevented. A clear understanding of potential dangers and what can be done to minimize hazards is the first step in securing safety for oneself and family. With this knowledge, you can eliminate or reduce most hazardous conditions in the home, workplace, and elsewhere; other likely problems can be minimized with suitable precautions and good safety habits. This discussion is not an all-inclusive checklist; instead, these major considerations for safety at home and for other circumstances should raise your awareness of possible hazards and stimulate planning for commonsense prevention.

SAFETY AT HOME

More than 4 million disabling accidents occur each year in the home, resulting in 27,000 avoidable deaths. An effective procedure for ensuring safety in the home is a routine room-by-room check for potential dangers. Safety examinations are particularly important to protect small children or older people in the household.

FIRE PREVENTION

Burns annually send 70,000 Americans to the hospital, and cause about 10,000 deaths, a large proportion of them children. Because of the ever-present danger, each family member should know what to do in case of a fire.

Hold periodic family fire drills. In case of a fire, getting all family members out of the house safely is the first priority before summoning help. Never go back into a burning building to save pets or possessions.

Follow these specific fire safety rules.

- Keep fire extinguishers in crucial areas—the kitchen, workroom, and near stairways. Check them periodically, and teach family members how to use them.
- Install smoke detectors, at least one per floor, and keep them in good working order. For instructions on where to install detectors, consult their instructions or check with the local fire department.
- Keep fire ladders, or other means of escape from upper-story windows, in each bedroom.
- Never block fire exits. Use caution when installing bars and other guards on apartment windows that lead to fire escapes. Always provide an easy escape route.
- Use flame-resistant materials for clothing and curtains, particularly for children's sleepwear, clothing, cloth dolls, and toys.
- Never smoke in bed or when sleepy, such as when watching TV and sitting on a couch or upholstered chair; completely extinguish all cigarettes.
- Put protective screens in front of all working fireplaces and have chimneys and flues inspected and cleaned periodically. Never leave a fire unattended; if you have to leave the house, extinguish the fire.
- Use candles with caution since they can set curtains, table linen, clothing, and other objects on fire. Always use a proper candleholder and extinguish the candles before you leave the room.
- Keep matches and lighters out of the reach of children; teach children at an early age not to play with matches or fire of any kind.
- Use extra caution heating with coal and wood stoves; a fire extinguisher should always be nearby. Make sure stoves are properly installed and vented and chimneys are cleaned regularly.
- Place portable heaters away from flammable upholstery and never leave them unattended.
- When cooking, do not let grease and drippings contact flames or sources of heat.
- Check electrical wiring regularly for fraying and wear. Avoid using extension cords on a permanent basis. Install adequate fuses or circuit breakers for electrical circuits. For most households, 15-amp fuses or breakers with a time-delay to allow brief surges for appliances are appropriate. Twenty-amp fuses or breakers should be used only for special heavy-duty circuits; 30-amp fuses for main lines.
- Check the home heating system annually for safe pressure, venting, and wiring.
- Install protective electrical outlet covers if young children are in the household.

FIRST-AID SUPPLIES

Keep basic first-aid supplies readily available. For optimal preparedness, carry a set in the car and have another at home in the medical supply cabinet or shelf. Bring a portable first-aid kit when you backpack, camp, hike, bike, or spend time in a remote and unpopulated area. All boats should carry a first-aid kit wrapped in a waterproof cover. Check these supplies periodically and replenish promptly. The most important items include:

Sterile gauze pads
Adhesive bandages in assorted sizes, including 4-inch-square compress pads
Two rolls of gauze, 1 and 2 inches wide
Roll of adhesive bandage tape, 1 inch wide
Roll of absorbent cotton
Elastic bandages 2 and 3 inches wide
Tissues
Cotton-tipped applicators (swabs)
Precut triangular bandages of various sizes for slings, splints, bandages
Airtight packages of hand-cleansing disposable towels (optional)
Tongue depressors
Several medium-size boards to use as splints
Sharp scissors
Pair of tweezers
Oral thermometer (rectal thermometer for infants and very young children)
Safety pins
Aspirin or acetaminophen
Tightly covered bottle of hydrogen peroxide
Antiseptic spray or cream
Antihistamine tablets
Antidiarrheal medication
Container of ipecac syrup

In addition, these items should be carried at all times in a car or boat:

Folded lightweight insulating blanket (sometimes called a "space" blanket)
Clean, folded sheet
Large waterproof cover (tarpaulin)
Tightly capped plastic bottle of water
Flashlight with fresh batteries

SUPPLIES FOR SPECIAL NEEDS

Persons hypersensitive to insect stings:

Insect sting kit containing a syringe of adrenaline, an antihistamine, and a hypodermic needle (prescribed by and used under the instruction and direction of a physician)

Persons with diabetes:

Reserve supply of insulin
Handy supply of simple sugar, which can be used to treat insulin shock

Persons with heart disease:

Supply of nitroglycerin or other needed medication

All persons with chronic medical conditions:

Medic Alert bracelet, which immediately tells a rescuer that special precautions may be needed

---

• Use extra caution with flammable chemicals such as cleaning fluids, glue, and certain sprays. Make sure there is adequate ventilation; open windows and use fans. Read and follow instructions.

THE KITCHEN

The kitchen is the most dangerous room in the house; frequent kitchen accidents include falls, fires, poisoning, cuts, and electrical shocks. Follow these kitchen safety rules.

• Always use a stepstool or ladder to reach high cabinets; never stand on a chair or counter.
• Don't wear long, loose garments when on a ladder.
• Regularly inspect stepstools and ladders for loose joints, missing rungs, or wobbliness; discard or repair as necessary.
• Consistently check the floor for slippery spots and mop up all spills promptly.
• Ensure adequate clearance between curtains and the stove or other potential sources of fire.
• Don't wear a scarf, a tie, or loose-flowing sleeves when cooking.
• Turn pot handles away from the front of the stove and always use a potholder (not a towel or napkin) to remove hot pots from the stove or oven.
• Use salt or baking soda to quench small stove fires; don't douse with water.
• Keep a fire extinguisher handy in the kitchen that you and other family members know how to use.
• Install a smoke alarm in or near the kitchen.

- Check the safety features of all appliances when you buy them and use only according to instructions.
- Unplug all appliances, especially irons and high-speed food processors, immediately after use.
- Unplug the toaster and make sure that it has cooled off before you poke anything into it.
- Keep knives sharp and always cut away from your body or anybody else.
- Use a cutting board or other appropriate hard surface for cutting and chopping.
- Store sharp knives, including steak knives, in a wall rack or separate case; don't mingle them with other table cutlery or kitchen utensils.
- Keep kitchen and all other matches out of the reach of children; buy only safety matches.
- Check pilot lights periodically and make sure gas appliances are properly installed, vented, and in good working order.
- Store all cleaning materials and compounds in a cabinet with a childproof lock.
- All poisonous materials should be clearly marked; do not transfer poisonous substances to milk bottles or other containers normally used for food or beverages.
- Place only skidproof scatter rugs in the kitchen and other high-traffic areas.
- Keep pesticides and other hazardous materials away from areas where they may contact dishes or contaminate food.

THE BATHROOM

The bathroom is the second most dangerous room in the house, the site of about 200,000 injuries a year, including burns, falls, and electric shocks.

- Never touch or turn on an electric switch or an electrical appliance while standing in the bathtub, shower, or on a damp floor.
- Don't use a portable electric heater in the bathroom.
- Don't use a hair dryer in or near a bathtub containing water.
- Place suction-type mats in bathtubs lacking skid-resistant bottoms.
- Always keep nonskid mats next to bathtubs.
- Install a strong "grab bar" offering solid support for getting into and out of a tub if such a bar is not part of the bathtub installation.
- Keep soap in a soap dish; never leave it on the rim of the tub.
- Never leave a small child alone in the bathtub, even for a brief moment.
- A family with children or children who visit often should remove all locks from the inside of the bath-

room door except for a simple hook arrangement placed high and beyond the reach of small children.
- Install a night-light just outside the bathroom door.
- Used razor blades and other sharp objects should be discarded in their containers, not tossed loose in a wastebasket.

THE MEDICINE CABINET

Drugs, both prescription and over-the-counter medications, should not be stored in the bathroom. (See chapter 34, Proper Use of Medications.) Reserve the bathroom medicine cabinet for toothpaste, shaving supplies, and other toiletries.

THE BEDROOM

Statistically, the bedroom is the most dangerous room in the house, the site of more fatal accidents than any other room. Falls out of bed, stumbles over objects in the dark, fires that kill sleepers—a surprisingly large number of deaths occur in the bedroom.

- Never smoke in bed.
- Unplug heating pads and electric blankets when not in use.
- If you take medicine at night, or need a drug such as nitroglycerin handy, place only one medicine on your bedside table. Always turn on a light and verify that you have the right medicine before taking it.
- Keep a lamp that doesn't tip easily within easy reach of the bed.
- Keep eyeglasses on a bedside table.
- Install retractable fire ladders outside the window of each upstairs bedroom.
- If there are young children in the household, install window guards to prevent falling from upstairs windows. These guards should be easily removable for exit during a fire.
- Install a telephone within easy reach of the bed, especially for people with heart disease, diabetes, or other chronic illnesses.
- Install a special telephone system with preprogrammed emergency dialing and prerecorded emergency messages for anyone with serious illness or disability, particularly if the person lives alone.

THE LIVING ROOM, DEN, AND OTHER ROOMS

- Don't overload electric outlets; make sure electric cords do not obstruct pathways through the house.
- When electric cords lie under rugs or furniture for a long time, check them periodically for frayed or worn spots.

- Use nonskid backing under scatter rugs covering highly polished floors.

ENTRANCE AND STAIRWAYS

- Install railings on stairs. Use banister spindles close enough together to prevent the wedging of children's heads.
- Firmly secure stairway carpeting and regularly inspect it for holes and worn spots.
- Never wax stairs and landings.
- Situate safety gates at both the top and bottom of stairs in a household with young children.
- Always keep stairs free of clutter.
- Locate light switches at the top and bottom of the stairs; never traverse stairs in the dark. Position night-lights at the top and bottom of stairs as an added precaution.
- For visitors, clearly distinguish the door leading to stairs from the one to the bathroom. A surprising number of houseguests suffer serious falls after opening the wrong door.

BASEMENT/UTILITY ROOM/WORKROOM

If you use part of the basement as a laundry room or recreation area, install a fire-resistant ceiling. Keep storage areas free of flammable rags and newspapers. Store all chemicals in clearly labeled jars or metal cans inaccessible to children. Other safety rules:

- Place a conspicuous, all-purpose fire extinguisher on a basement wall.
- Locate electric washers and dryers in a well-lit area where water and dampness do not accumulate. Vent dryers properly; ground all electrical appliances with adequate wiring.
- Follow manufacturers' instructions for washers, dryers, and other appliances and have necessary repairs made promptly by a licensed repairperson.
- Instruct children in the proper operation of laundry appliances and the use of safety switches and emergency procedures before they do a wash.
- Always iron on a strong, well-balanced board with a fireproof cover. Set the iron on its heel during brief intervals between use, and unplug it immediately when ironing is finished.
- Never leave an iron and ironing board unattended.
- Keep all tools out of reach of children. When a child is old enough to handle tools, give the proper instruction and make sure tools are in good repair and properly sharpened. Operate power tools with caution no matter what the age of the user.
- Wear safety goggles when welding, cutting with an electric saw, or using any power tool. Wear proper attire such as heavy gloves and earplugs, tuck in shirttails, and take off ties or other loose articles of clothing.
- Keep pets out of the workroom or other areas where power tools are in use.

GARDEN/GARAGE/BACKYARD

- Never permit a child to operate a power mower.
- Always wear safety goggles when using a power mower, weed cutter, trimmer, or other tool that kicks up stones, twigs, or other objects.
- Never free an object from a mower blade or snow blower while the motor is running.
- Never leave a power mower unattended while the motor is running, even momentarily.
- Always wear protective gloves and goggles when using a power saw. Follow the manufacturer's instructions and make sure the saw is in proper working order and the blades are sharp.
- Roll up an unused garden hose and store it. Never leave it lying in the grass where someone may stumble over it.
- Put away garden tools after use. Store them in a grocery carton or hang them on a wall. Hoes, rakes, and other tools left on the lawn can cause falls and injuries.
- Apply pesticides with extreme care, and spray them downwind. Do not pour them into unlabeled jars; discard leftovers according to instructions, not tossed in the garbage or flushed down the toilet.
- Secure covers on wells, septic tanks, or cisterns sufficiently to prevent removal by children.
- Make garage doors easy to open both from inside and outside. Install electronic doors equipped with an automatic, emergency shutoff that minimizes injury to anyone caught in their way. In case of power failure, garages outfitted with power doors should have an emergency exit.
- Keep the driveway clear of bicycles, motorcycles, children's wagons, and other obstructions. Warn children not to play in the driveway.
- Don't wear loose clothes, a tie, or flowing sleeves when cooking on an outdoor grill.
- Cancel backyard barbecues if there's a high wind or lightning.
- Never pour starter fluid or other flammable liquid onto burning or smoldering charcoal. Use an electric starter instead.
- Keep a fire extinguisher nearby when cooking out. Before lighting a campfire or grill in the woods or open area, dig a fire pit first. Make sure the fire is thoroughly extinguished before leaving it.
- Properly fence in and lock pool areas; never allow children to swim unattended.

SAFETY IN THE WORKPLACE

The workplace is the second most common setting for accidents. Most workplace injuries can be prevented by obeying safety regulations and using common sense. If you work with hazardous chemicals or materials, be particularly diligent in handling them; always change your clothes and shower before leaving the workplace to avoid carrying hazardous residue home. Follow these safety rules.

- If your job requires protective gear, such as goggles, gloves, earplugs, or masks, wear them. Even if your employer does not require or provide a protective outfit, dress in safety clothing whenever you are around potentially harmful substances.
- Never operate machinery or other equipment when drowsy or ill. If you take medication, heed warning labels about operating machinery or driving.
- Alert your supervisor, union representative, or other appropriate official to all potentially hazardous conditions.
- Obey rules regarding smoking in any area where there is a danger of fire.
- If you are pregnant or trying to conceive, avoid exposure to chemicals, or other substances that may be harmful to an unborn child.

FARM AND COUNTRY SAFETY

Agriculture ranks third among all major industries in accidental deaths. The restricted availability of rural emergency medical service creates an acute need for rural residents to understand the hazards they face and the first-aid measures to deal with them.

On farms, ever-present fire hazards and delays in the arrival of firefighting equipment give fire prevention special importance. Follow the fire safety rules at the beginning of this section and comply with these precautions.

- Store all flammable liquids, including sprays and fuel, in adequately ventilated areas away from direct heat and inaccessible to children.
- Don't leave nearly empty gasoline or other fuel containers lying about.
- Don't store fuel, oil-soaked rags, and other highly flammable items in hay barns or other buildings that burn easily.
- Enforce "No Smoking" rules in all potentially dangerous areas, including barns, grain sheds, silos, and fuel-storage areas.

- Keep fire extinguishers in all potentially hazardous areas, including barns and storage areas.
- Drill all family members and farm workers in escaping fires and in locating and operating fire extinguishers.
- Use special caution during lightning and electrical storms. Ground all wiring properly and install wiring and safety circuit breakers in all buildings.

Reduce farm equipment hazards by observing safety rules at all times. Carelessness in handling farm machinery causes more than 1,000 deaths and a larger number of disabling injuries each year.

- Always use a safety belt and overturn bar when operating a tractor.
- Never permit children to play in and around tractors, wagons, and other farm machinery.
- Do not allow children to ride on tractors for fun. Teach older children how to operate farm machinery, but careful adult instruction and supervision should be provided.
- Never leave tractors or other farm machinery unattended with their motors running.
- Never repair or remove a stone or other object from a piece of machinery while the motor is running.
- Wear appropriate clothing (e.g., heavy boots, work pants, and safety goggles) when operating farm machinery.

Farm animals also are a source of danger, especially for unwary or unsuspecting farm visitors.

- Approach any farm animal with considerable caution; even a harmless-looking cow can cause extensive injury if she is startled or is trying to protect her calf. Teach children how to safely approach farm animals and forbid teasing and mistreatment of them.
- Avoid feeding animals from your hands.
- Don't pick up or approach a wounded or sick animal, including a pet or a wild animal, with your bare hands. Securely wrap an injured pet in a towel or blanket and pick it up cautiously to avoid being bitten. Never approach any wild animal that appears sick or is acting strangely; it may have rabies or another serious disease infectious to humans.
- Keep the vaccinations of pets and farm animals up-to-date, especially for diseases contagious to humans.

Sprays and other chemicals are commonly applied to farm fields, but regulations and recommendations governing their use constantly change. Before applying leftover spray, check with your local agriculture agent to learn current instructions for its use. Heed the following precautions.

- Never spray chemicals outdoors on a windy day.
- Protect exposed skin surfaces with clothing, gloves, and goggles. Avoid inhalation of chemicals and other toxic substances by wearing the proper mask.
- Store chemicals in their original containers. After using a chemical spray, carefully wash face and hands (or shower, if possible) and change into fresh clothes before entering the house.
- Allow recommended time between spraying and harvesting of food; wash all food that has been exposed to chemical sprays before eating.

Special note: When visitors are present, clearly explain and enforce all safety rules regarding smoking, animal handling, and the use of equipment.

ROAD AND HIGHWAY SAFETY

Lowering the national speed limit to 55 miles per hour has resulted in a marked decline in the number of highway deaths, but even so, more than 50,000 Americans die in highway accidents each year. About one-half of these deaths are caused by driving while under the influence of alcohol or other drugs, including antihistamines that cause drowsiness or medications that impair reflexes and judgment.

Many lives could be saved or serious injury prevented by universal use of seat belts. Many states now have laws that require proper safety seats for all infants and toddlers, and a growing number are requiring seat belts for adults. Babies and young children always should ride in these seats, even for short distances. Holding a child on your lap is particularly dangerous; should you be thrown against the dashboard or windshield, the child will bear the force of the accident.

All cars should have regular preventive maintenance checks and be checked regularly for any sign of trouble. Brakes and lights should be tested and tires examined before starting on a trip. A spare tire and tire-changing equipment should always be carried in the trunk. A first-aid kit, flares, and a flashlight also should be carried at all times. Additional equipment for special situations, such as winter driving, should be carried as necessary (extra clothing, tire chains, shovel, sand, lock and gas line de-icer, etc.). A cellular phone or CB radio provides direct communication in the event of an emergency. Other car safety rules:

- Never drive when you feel sleepy, tired, or ill. Don't attempt to drive after drinking or taking any drug that may impair reflexes, cause drowsiness, or alter judgment.
- Always wear your safety belt and make sure that all passengers do the same. Babies and young children should always be securely fastened in safety seats (see figure 15.1).
- Know in advance what to do in a crisis. Know how to pull out of a skid on ice or a slippery road.
- Know and observe local safety regulations regarding such things as speed limits and rules of turns.
- Always be aware of what other drivers are doing. Drive defensively and remain calm when dealing with other drivers who are rude, careless, or speeding.
- Watch out for bicycle riders, motorcyclists, joggers, and animals.
- Don't be distracted by conversations, the car radio, arguments, or the scenery.
- Enforce rules regarding horseplay or poor behavior in the car. If necessary, pull off the road and stop the car and put an end to distracting behavior.
- Don't attempt to drive during a heavy downpour, snowstorm, or other bad weather that affects visibility and road conditions. If you must drive at such times, make sure the car is properly equipped with snow tires, chains, or other appropriate devices

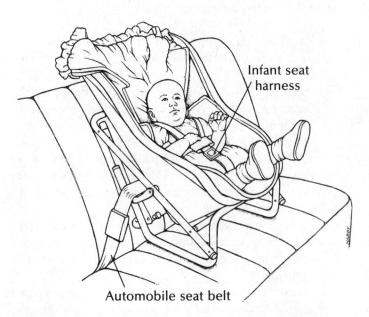

Infant seat harness

Automobile seat belt

Figure 15.1: Babies and young children should always ride in a safety seat, such as the one pictured here. The seat should be belted to the car seat, and the child should be placed in a harness in the carrier.

and that you know what to do in case of skids or other hazardous situations.

- Be sure your view is unobstructed by passengers, packages, or other objects.
- Pets should travel in carrying cases unless they are very well behaved and accustomed to riding quietly in a car. In any event, pets and passengers should not be permitted to ride with heads or other body parts hanging out of the window.
- If you come upon a car accident, proceed with caution. Turn off the motor if it is still running and try to determine if there is danger of a fire or explosion. (Do you smell gas?) If there are injuries, try to treat the victims where they are unless they are in danger of further injury or require basic life-support measures (see chapter 14, Common First-Aid Procedures).

BICYCLE SAFETY

More than 100 million Americans ride bicycles or motorcycles, and each year more than 1 million incur serious injuries. One-half of these accidents involve children under the age of 14; and in 90 percent of all cycling accidents, the cyclist is at fault. Bicycles should be kept in good working order and all cyclists, children and adults alike, should know and follow the rules of the road. This means obeying the same traffic regulations and signals that apply to motor vehicles: stopping for red lights, riding with (never against) traffic, and cycling in the street or road, not on the sidewalk. Follow these safety rules.

- All motorcyclists and bicyclists should wear protective headgear.
- Never wear loose pants or other clothing that is likely to become entangled in a bicycle chain.
- Never permit children or other passengers to ride on the handlebars. Special children's seats should be installed behind the cyclist, and the child should be securely strapped into the seat.
- Bicycles that are ridden at night should be equipped with lights and special reflectors that are clearly visible to motorists.
- Never dart in and out of traffic; if there is a bicycle lane, stay in it. If not, stay to the far right-hand side of the road. When passing a car, follow the same rules and precautions that apply to motor vehicles.
- When cycling with others, ride single-file, not two or three abreast.
- Don't wear radio or tape earphones when cycling; they block out warning sounds from other traffic and are likely to be distracting.

WATER AND BOAT SAFETY

Anyone who goes near the water should know how to swim. Almost everyone can learn, including very young children, older people, and those who are disabled. In addition, swimming is an excellent form of aerobic exercise. Swimming courses are widely available at local Y's, schools, community or recreation centers, health clubs, camps, Red Cross chapters, and other organizations. But even expert swimmers should obey basic water safety rules, including the cardinal one of never swimming alone or in an unattended area. Follow these water safety rules.

- Never permit a child to play alone at the water's edge, including a shallow backyard pool.
- Always use a "buddy system," even when swimming with a group. Anyone, including an expert swimmer, can suffer a cramp or other disabling problem while in the water; this may go unnoticed by others who are not specifically looking out for him.
- Know your limits and don't overdo. Swimming beyond one's depth or capability is a common cause of drowning accidents.
- Don't swim after drinking alcoholic beverages.
- Never dive into a pool or other water unless you have tested the depth first.
- Don't swim in the dark, especially in the ocean.
- Don't swim in boating or fishing areas.
- Be cautious of diving into waves. Pay particular attention to the undertow, especially when the tide is turning. Don't try to swim against an undertow. Swim parallel to shore until you reach a spot where you can swim in toward shore again.
- When storm clouds gather, get out of the water and head for shelter from lightning. Don't stand under a tree, however. Lightning usually strikes at the tallest point and follows the tree trunk down to the ground and then follows the root system. Anyone near the tree or roots can easily be electrocuted.
- Young children and inexperienced swimmers should wear life jackets in the water. Floats, inner tubes, and inflatable water toys are not suitable substitutes; it is easy to fall off them.
- Backyard pools should be fenced with a gate that is locked when unattended. This applies even when the pool has been drained or is iced over.

Boating safety begins with a complete understanding of the capabilities of the particular craft. All boat owners and their families should take a boat handling and safety course such as those sponsored by local units of the Coast Guard, Power Squadron, or boating clubs. Never go out in a boat unless there is someone on board who knows how to handle it; this applies to all craft, from rowboats to sailboats and motorboats. In addition to the general safety rules for swimmers, boaters should also pay attention to the following basics.

- Make sure that each person on the boat is wearing a properly fitted life jacket. Children sleeping on a boat should wear one to bed. Many life jackets come with pockets. Equip each one with a flare and a mirror for signaling, as well as a whistle, which can be heard more easily across water than the voice. Attach strips of reflective tape to the back of the jacket.
- Know and follow the boating regulations that apply to your particular waterway. Watch out for other craft, especially slower moving boats that may not be able to get out of your path, even if you have the right-of-way.
- Water-skiers should always wear a life jacket and there should be two people in the motorboat: one to drive and the other to watch the skier.
- Watch for swimmers who may be in your way.
- Never drink alcoholic beverages when operating a boat.
- Know the capability of your craft; if a storm is coming up, head for safer waters or port.
- Before fueling a boat, make sure that no one is smoking and that all electrical equipment and the motor are shut off. After refueling, check for any gas fumes, especially in low places. Be sure the engine housing is well vented before starting the engine.
- Always carry flares and other warning devices; make sure running lights and the boat radio are in proper working order. If you are an offshore boater, equip your boat with proper communication and navigational equipment, including Loran C and VHP FM radio. An Emergency Position Indicator Radio Beacon (EPIRB) will automatically signal your position on a frequency picked up by ships and planes in the area, as well as by certain satellites. It can be taken into the water with you if the boat capsizes or sinks.
- Be prepared to do everything you can to keep the boat afloat if you begin to take on water. Even if the boat is equipped with an automatic bailing pump, carry extra bailers (gallon and half-gallon plastic bleach or milk containers with the bottoms cut out make good ones). If you spring a leak, stuff it with clothes, mattresses, rags, or whatever else is available. If necessary, go into the water with a rope around your waist to plug the hole from the outside as well.
- If your boat capsizes, do not leave it in an attempt to swim to shore. It will provide a place to rest and it will be more easily spotted by rescuers than a

swimmer in open water. Try to climb onto the hull or stand on the rails to stay out of the water as much as possible.
- If the boat actually sinks, debris such as ice chests, hatch covers, mattresses, and seat cushions will begin to float free as it goes down. Gather them around you to hold on to, to rest on, and to make yourself more easily seen by rescue craft.
- Hypothermia is a serious problem in most U.S. coastal waters. Your respiration, pulse, and blood pressure automatically rise when you first enter cold water, especially that less than 70°F (21.1°C). Try to stay perfectly still for the first 1 to 3 minutes until this reaction begins to subside.
- Even if you are a strong swimmer, do not attempt to swim to shore. The United States Coast Guard reports that many people drown within 10 to 15 feet of a safe haven. Current, water temperature, fatigue, poor swimming ability, and panic may all work against you. Stay with the boat or the debris and try to keep as much of your body out of the water as possible.

HIKING AND CAMPING

Getting back to nature is one of the great pleasures of modern, urban life. But all too often, the hiking or camping trip is marred by an accident that could have been prevented with proper planning and foresight. The cardinal rule for anyone planning a trek into a remote area is: Let someone know where you are and when you plan to return. Arrange regular times when you will call or contact that person; then if you fail to do so, help can be sent. If no one knows you are long overdue, chances are slim that there will be search parties out looking for you.

Another often overlooked but basic rule is always to carry a good map of the area. If you are planning a hiking trip into a wilderness area, contact the area forest service or other official agency and ask for a detailed map of trails, campsites, aid stations, and other important information. Notify this agency of your planned route and estimated date and time of return. Follow these precautions.

- Make sure that you and other members of your party are in suitable physical condition to withstand the rigors of hiking or camping out. Do not hike alone.
- Take along a first-aid kit (see the checklist of first-aid supplies earlier in this chapter), and if medication is needed, make sure you have an extra supply as well as a signed prescription.
- Wear appropriate clothes and pay particular attention to your shoes. They should be sturdy, comfortable,

and appropriate for the terrain; running or jogging shoes may be lightweight and comfortable, but they are not suitable for long hikes or mountain climbing.

• Carry insect repellent and check whether there are any animal- or insect-borne diseases (e.g., Rocky Mountain spotted fever, viral encephalitis, tularemia) endemic in the area you plan to visit. In some instances, vaccination may be appropriate.

• Never eat wild berries, plants, or mushrooms unless you are absolutely certain they are nonpoisonous. Warn children not to eat berries or plants unless they show them to you first.

• If hiking with a party, form a "buddy system" and know where your partner is at all times.

• Watch for poisonous plants such as poison ivy, and avoid contact with them. Even handling shoes or other objects that have come in contact wih poison ivy can cause a reaction.

• Use special caution in exploring caves, abandoned mines, and buildings, and avoid entering them unless you are absolutely certain they are structurally sound and not harboring a wild animal, snakes, or other hazard.

• Don't drink water from unknown sources. If you don't have your own water, boil any taken from a pond or stream for at least 3 minutes before drinking it. If this is not practical, water can be treated with iodine or chlorine bleach. Rainwater captured in a tarpaulin is another good source of potable water.

• Observe and enjoy wild animals, but at a safe distance. Most animals are very wary of humans, but each year several thousand visitors to the wild end up with serious animal bites or even worse consequences. If you are in bear country, be particularly cautious about food supplies. Never keep food in your tent or near your sleeping area and don't sleep in clothes in which you have prepared or eaten food. Food supplies should be placed in a plastic bag and stashed a safe distance from your campsite or placed in a closed car. (Black bears can climb trees and retrieve food hung from branches, as can raccoons.) A special warning to women campers in bear country: The U.S. Park Service has observed that a number of bear attacks have involved women who were menstruating at the time or who were wearing scented cosmetics or hairspray. Apparently bears are attracted to these scents.

• Garbage should be placed in special containers, burned, or carefully packed to carry away with you. Don't leave it strewn around your camp; it not only despoils the area, it also attracts unwelcome insects and animals.

• Before setting up camp, clear the area of leaves, branches, stones, and other hiding places for snakes, spiders, and other potentially hazardous animals or insects. Avoid cave entrances, rock piles, and other places that may be the home of nocturnal animals.

• Don't attempt to feed wild animals. If you come upon a baby animal, don't try to pick it up. Chances are it has a protective mother nearby who will not hesitate to attack if she thinks her offspring is in danger.

• Be wary of any animal—skunk, raccoon, rodent—that is behaving oddly. It may have rabies or some other disease.

• Check on whether there are poisonous snakes in the area, and if so, use special caution. Know what to do in case of a bite from a snake, spider, or other wild creature (see the section on bites in chapter 14, Common First-Aid Procedures).

• If you are hiking in an unfamiliar area, proceed with caution and make sure you are on firm ground. Mountain and rock climbing is tricky and should be undertaken only by experts or under the leadership of an experienced guide.

• Pay attention to the weather. If you are camping in an area where flash floods are a possibility, head for high ground. Avoid camping in dry riverbeds, even if there is no sign of rain. The flood may occur without warning and result from a heavy rainfall miles away. During an electrical storm, stay away from trees, poles, and water.

• Hiking in any wilderness area requires extensive planning and preparation. Top physical condition and the knowledge, skills, and equipment to survive all the potential hazards are essential.

WINTER HAZARDS

It would be a mistake to imply that the major outdoor hazards apply to summer campers only; the increasing popularity of winter outdoor activities has been accompanied by a rise in cold-weather mishaps. The same rules listed for hikers and campers apply to winter sports and outdoor activities. In addition, winter hikers, snowmobilers, cross-country skiers, and hunters, among others, should be skilled in their respective activity and know what to do in case of an emergency.

Weather reports should be heeded; outdoor activity should be avoided during extremes of temperature and wind velocity. Modern weather forecasting has improved, but there is always the possibility of a sudden, unpredicted winter storm and there are still a surprising number of people who venture out without checking a weather report. Obviously, one should always dress appropriately and know what to do if marooned by a storm. Usually, the best advice is to stay in your car or other shelter until the worst is over or until help arrives. Other special precautions for winter enthusiasts include:

• Know your terrain. If you are snowshoeing, cross-country skiing, or hiking in unknown territory, stick to established trails and don't venture out alone.

• Dress appropriately. This means wearing clothing that provides proper insulation against the cold, wind, and wetness, while allowing proper ventilation and circulation. Undergarments should be made of wool or polypropylene. Several layers of loose, nonconstricting wool, down, or synthetic down clothing and an outer layer of windproof/water-repellent material should be worn. Make sure head (an area of potential significant heat loss), hands, and feet are well protected. Mittens worn over gloves provide good protection for hands. Two pairs of socks—one propylene and one wool—and boots covering the ankles provide adequate protection of feet. Wear a wool or polypropylene ski hat and use additional face or neck protection depending on the weather. All clothing should be nonconstricting.

• Before going out onto ice, make sure that it is thick enough to bear your weight. If in doubt, cut a hole in it and measure the thickness. If it is less than 8 inches thick, stay on land or go to a commercial ice rink.

• When sledding or snowmobiling, be particularly wary of crossing roads and railroad tracks. Avoid areas where there may be hidden obstacles, such as fallen branches, trees, fences, or other sources of danger. Check ahead for avalanche conditions.

• In very bright conditions or at high altitude, protect against eye injury from ultraviolet radiation by wearing sunglasses with UV blocking lenses and side panels.

• Don't go out in the cold after drinking alcohol. While you may feel a warm glow from the drink, in reality it makes you more susceptible to the effects of cold and may alter your judgment, decision making, and behavior in a potentially dangerous situation.

SUMMING UP

Most accidents can be prevented with proper knowledge and attention to basic principles of safety. Many of these have been outlined in this chapter. What to do in actual medical emergencies is covered in the proceding chapters.

PART V

Treatment and Prevention of Disease

16
Heart
and
Blood
Vessel
Diseases

• • • • • • • • • • • • • • • •

J. THOMAS BIGGER, JR., M.D.

Despite numerous advances and decades of declining death rates, cardiovascular disease remains the leading health problem in the United States, and the leading cause of death, claiming almost 1 million lives a year. As of 1994, the American Heart Association estimates that more than 56 million people—or 1 in 5 Americans—have some form of heart or blood vessel disease. Of these, millions are free of symptoms; in fact, many do not know that they have a potentially serious illness until they suffer a heart attack, stroke, or sudden death.

The two most common forms of cardiovascular disease are hypertension (high blood pressure), a condition that affects an estimated 50 million Americans, and coronary artery disease, the progressive narrowing of the blood vessels that nourish the heart muscle, which may result in chest pain (angina pectoris) and numerous other outcomes, including heart attacks and sudden death. Very often, the two conditions coexist. Coronary artery disease is the major cause of heart attacks (myocardial infarction), which afflict about 1.5 million Americans each year. High blood pressure increases the risk of a heart attack and is also the leading cause of stroke (cerebrovascular hemorrhage or occlusion), a potentially life-threatening or disabling event suffered by a half-million people each year, with a mortality of some 144,000.

Other major forms of cardiovascular disease include congenital heart defects, rheumatic heart disease and other infections, disorders of the heart valves, and heart muscle disease. Abnormalities such as congestive heart failure or disturbances in heart rhythm (cardiac arrhythmias) also may become life-threatening.

Advances in diagnosing and treating cardiovascular disorders in their earliest stages have greatly improved the prognosis for heart patients in the past few years. For example, rheumatic fever was once a major cause of heart disease, particularly among the young. But the widespread use of antibiotics to treat streptococcal throat infections, the leading cause of rheumatic heart disease, has greatly diminished its incidence and severity. Implantable artificial devices, such as pacemakers and prosthetic heart valves, now make it possible for some people to lead nearly normal lives when only a few years ago they would have been seriously disabled or doomed to an early death. Major advances in heart surgery make possible the repair of most congenital heart defects; other procedures, such as coronary artery bypass operations, can provide often dramatic relief from disabling

angina or may prevent heart attacks and death. In this chapter, the major forms of heart disease and their treatments, risk factors, and possible means of prevention will be discussed.

HOW THE HEART WORKS

The heart is one of nature's most efficient and durable pumps. Throughout life, it beats an average of 60 to 80 times per minute, supplying oxygen and other essential nutrients to every cell in the body and removing waste for elimination through the lungs or kidneys.

The heart itself is a muscular, hollow organ weighing 7 to 10 ounces in the average adult. It is about the size of two clenched fists and is divided into four chambers, the left and right atria and the left and right ventricles (see figures 16.1A and B).

Blood that has circulated through the body flows into the right atrium from the venous system. This blood, which is depleted of oxygen and loaded with carbon dioxide, flows through the tricuspid valve into the right ventricle, which pumps it through the pulmonary valve into the pulmonary artery, which carries it into the lungs. In the lungs, the carbon dioxide is removed and a fresh supply of oxygen is added; the oxygenated blood then travels through the pulmonary vein into the left atrium, then through the mitral valve into the left ventricle. This chamber is the heart's major pump, responsible for pumping the oxygenated blood through the aortic valve into the aorta and, eventually, to all parts of the body through a vast network of arteries, arterioles, and capillaries before it returns via the venules and veins—a total of about 60,000 miles of blood vessels.

In a normal, healthy adult, each ventricle pumps about 3 ounces of blood per beat, which adds up to about 2,100 gallons per day. Normal cardiac rhythm is maintained by the heart's electrical system, centered primarily in the group of specialized pacemaker cells in the sinus node. The impulse that arises in the sinus node is transmitted to specialized atrial conducting fibers to activate the cells in the atrioventricular (AV) node, the gateway to the ventricles. As the electrical impulse enters the AV node, it slows dramatically, but when it emerges from the node into an area called the bundle of His, the conduction speeds up dramatically and excites the network of conducting fibers on the inner surface of the ventricular chambers, thereby stimulating the muscle of the heart's pumping chambers (ventricles) to contract.

A system of valves keeps the blood moving in the right direction through the heart. The coronary arteries, so named because they encircle the heart like a crown,

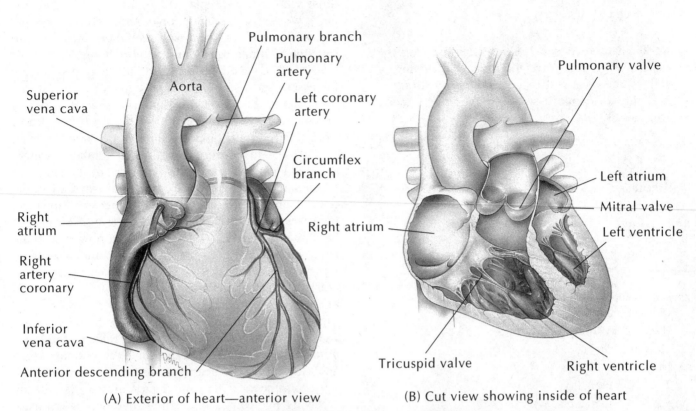

(A) Exterior of heart—anterior view   (B) Cut view showing inside of heart

Figure 16.1A and B: The normal heart.

supply the heart muscle (myocardium) with oxygen and other nutrients.

The aorta forms the main trunk of the arterial system, arching over the heart and then branching to form the abdominal aorta, which carries blood to the abdomen. Smaller arteries branching from the aorta carry blood to all parts of the body. The arteries branch into smaller vessels called arterioles, which conduct blood from the arteries to the capillaries, the smallest blood vessels that carry oxygen and nutrients to the individual body cells and collect waste products to transmit to the venous system for the return journey to the heart and lungs.

....

WHO GETS HEART DISEASE?

Until the middle of this century, most people regarded heart disease as an inevitable part of aging, or the result of events that people had no control over, such as rheumatic fever or congenital defects. This opinion has changed as a result of a number of large-scale population (epidemiologic) studies in which lifestyle and patterns of disease are investigated. One of the most notable and quoted of these has been the Framingham Heart Study, which started in 1948 and has followed more than 5,000 residents of the Boston suburb from which this important

study takes its name. Framingham and other such studies have identified a number of lifestyle habits and other factors that increase the risk of cardiovascular disease (these risk factors are listed in the box on the following page).

Some risk factors, such as being male or advancing age, are beyond our control. In contrast, the controllable risk factors are so designated because they can be altered by changing diet and other habits, or by controlling a disease state. It should be noted that one cannot predict whether a particular individual will have a heart attack on the basis of risk factors; there are always exceptions to the rule. But the chances are increased by the presence of these risk factors, and the more risk factors in an individual, the greater the likelihood.

ALTERING YOUR RISK

HIGH BLOOD PRESSURE

According to the American Heart Association, about 50 million Americans have high blood pressure; most of these do not have any symptoms and would be unaware that they have a potentially life-threatening disease if it were not detected during a routine checkup or examination. There has been marked improvement in the detection and treatment of high blood pressure in recent years, thanks to widespread public education programs.

CARDIOVASCULAR RISK FACTORS

Although there is some disagreement among the experts as to the relative importance of certain risk factors, the ones with asterisks have the strongest scientific evidence associating them with heart attacks.

UNCONTROLLABLE RISK FACTORS

Advancing age*
Male sex*
Heredity*

CONTROLLABLE RISK FACTORS

High blood pressure*
Cigarette smoking*
High blood cholesterol*
Obesity
Diabetes
Type A personality
Environmental stress
Sedentary lifestyle

Even so, substantial numbers of hypertensive Americans are either untreated or are not having their blood pressures adequately controlled.

Sustained high blood pressure has several adverse effects on the cardiovascular system. It causes the heart to work harder and, over a period of time, can lead to an enlarged heart and impairment of pumping function (heart failure). The sustained high pressure against the artery walls promotes arteriosclerosis, or hardening of the arteries. These damaged blood vessels often cannot deliver enough oxygen to vital organs, particularly the brain and the heart itself. Damage to blood vessels in the kidneys is a particularly important and common result of prolonged hypertension; thus, kidney failure is a common complication of untreated high blood pressure. Numerous studies show that these adverse effects of hypertension can be prevented by treating it to keep blood pressure in a normal range. (See "High Blood Pressure.")

CIGARETTE SMOKING

If you are a smoker, the single best thing you can do to improve your heart health is to quit. Although more than 40 million Americans have stopped smoking since the first Surgeon General's report in 1964, an estimated 50 million Americans continue to smoke. Unfortunately, those who stop are replaced by new smokers—increasingly, women and young people. Although most people are well aware of the association between cigarette smoking and lung cancer and other pulmonary diseases, many still do not realize that smoking also greatly increases your risk of a heart attack. In fact, the latest *Surgeon General's Report on Smoking and Health* estimates that more than 250,000 of the American deaths from cardiovascular disease each year are directly related to smoking—many more than the total number of cancer and pulmonary disease deaths attributed to smoking.

Smoking harms your heart in several ways. Nicotine, one of the major addictive substances in tobacco, increases the heart rate and blood pressure, causing the heart to work harder. When nicotine, a powerful stimulant, is inhaled, it goes to work almost immediately by signaling the adrenal glands to pump out epinephrine (adrenaline), which causes the heart to beat faster and blood pressure to rise. It also narrows, or constricts, the capillaries and arterioles, which raises blood pressure and also reduces circulation to the fingers, toes, and other surface areas. At the same time, the amount of oxygen available to the heart is reduced, a potentially serious consequence if your heart muscle is already receiving inadequate blood flow because of coronary artery disease.

Carbon monoxide, an odorless gas that makes up 1 to 5 percent of cigarette smoke, has a great affinity for hemoglobin, the molecule in the red blood cell that carries oxygen. When carbon monoxide is inhaled into the lungs, as it is during smoking, it competes with oxygen in binding to hemoglobin. Because it has a greater affinity for hemoglobin than oxygen, it replaces some of the oxygen that would normally circulate with the blood. When carbon monoxide binds to hemoglobin, it forms a molecule called carboxyhemoglobin; in its presence, oxygen binds even tighter to hemoglobin, further reducing the availability of oxygen to the body cells. Carbon monoxide also may cause degenerative damage to the heart muscle itself, a finding that has been verified in laboratory animals but not humans. Studies also suggest that carbon monoxide may alter blood vessel walls, making them more susceptible to the buildup of cholesterol and other fatty deposits.

Although more studies are needed to verify all these adverse effects, there is clear evidence that the combination of increased levels of adrenal hormones, accelerated heartbeat, and higher blood pressure increases the possibility of anginal attacks and disturbances in heart rhythm. Some researchers believe that this explains the increased incidence in sudden death among smokers. In addition, smokers who have any of the other cardiovascular risk factors have a greatly increased incidence of heart attacks.

The question of passive smoking (inhaling the smoke of others without actually smoking yourself) is one of continuing controversy among both the public and researchers. About one out of three people is sensitive to the tobacco glycoprotein. Research with laboratory animals has found that when this tobacco glycoprotein is inhaled, it increases the clotting activity (platelet clumping) of the blood. This in turn is thought to injure the blood vessel walls and promote the development of atherosclerosis. Since nonsmokers who are exposed to cigarette smoke involuntarily inhale this glycoprotein, it is conceivable that they also suffer from its harmful effects. (The same substance is found in many vegetables, but since it is altered by the digestive process, it does not produce the same effect as when inhaled.) This effect has not been proved in humans, but some researchers feel that the evidence is strong enough to warrant stricter regulation of smoking in public places.

Smokers often ask whether low-tar, low-nicotine cigarettes reduce the cardiovascular risk. The answer appears to be no. In fact, some of the filter cigarettes increase the amount of carbon monoxide that is inhaled, making them even worse for your heart than unfiltered brands.

Nicotine is a powerful addictive substance; no one disputes that quitting is difficult. But many people find that stopping is easier than they had anticipated. About 95 percent who succeed in breaking the habit do so on their own. Quitting cold turkey is the most effective way of stopping, but for many other methods or aids are helpful. (See the box "How to Quit" in chapter 6.)

HIGH BLOOD CHOLESTEROL

Framingham and a number of other studies have consistently found that high levels of cholesterol, a fatty substance that is consumed in the diet and also manufactured by the body, is a major factor in developing atherosclerosis—the narrowing of arteries through a buildup of fatty plaque.

Cholesterol is an essential substance, needed for the function of all cells, reproduction, and other vital roles. Since the body can manufacture all of the cholesterol it needs, it is not necessary to consume any in the diet. The typical American diet, however, tends to be high in cholesterol, which is found in eggs, red meat, whole milk, cheese, and other animal products, especially those high in saturated fats. People who consume large amounts of cholesterol and saturated fats tend to have higher levels of blood cholesterol, as well as a higher incidence of atherosclerotic disease of their coronary and other arteries.

The total amount of blood cholesterol is not the only important factor in assessing the risk of coronary heart disease; the type of molecule on which it is transported is also a factor. Since cholesterol is a fatty substance (lipid) that is not soluble in blood, which is mostly water (and fats and water do not mix), it must be attached to a water-soluble substance before it can travel through the blood.

This substance is a protein, which when combined with the lipid forms a molecule called a lipoprotein.

There are different types of lipoproteins, which are often classified by their size or density. The heaviest is the high-density lipoprotein (HDL), which has the highest portion of protein. The low-density lipoprotein (LDL) is lighter than HDL, and carries a larger amount of cholesterol. The very-low-density lipoprotein (VLDL) carries the largest amount of triglycerides, a lipid that is important in fat metabolism and the manufacture of cholesterol.

Studies indicate that HDL carries lipids away from the blood vessel walls, and is therefore important in preventing the accumulation of cholesterol and other fats along the artery walls. LDL, however, seems to transport cholesterol to the cells, and a high LDL level is thought to be a major factor in developing atherosclerosis. The higher the ratio of HDL to LDL cholesterol, the better. Factors that influence this ratio include heredity, sex, exercise, diet, and cigarette smoking. Some families, for example, exhibit a high level of HDL cholesterol, while others with an inherited disorder called familial hypercholesterolemia have extremely high levels of LDL, and unfortunately often die of heart disease at an early age unless they are identified and treated while still in their teens or young adulthood. Premenopausal women seem to have a higher HDL to LDL ratio than men, a factor some experts think may help explain the lower incidence of heart attacks in younger women. People who engage in very vigorous exercise, such as long-distance runners or swimmers, also have high HDL levels, as do vegetarians. Smokers tend to have low HDL and high LDL cholesterol.

In the United States, the average total cholesterol is about 220 milligrams per deciliter of blood (mg/dl), a figure that is much higher than that found in less-developed countries where there is a low incidence of coronary artery disease. There is no "normal" or "safe" level of blood cholesterol; but above 240 mg/dl, the risk of coronary disease rises sharply. For example, people with a cholesterol measurement of 300 mg/dl or more tend to have a very high incidence of heart attacks.

The National Cholesterol Education Program and the National Heart, Lung and Blood Institute have set physician guidelines for diagnosing and treating high blood cholesterol. These recommendations include:

• All adults over the age of 20 should undergo a blood test to measure total serum cholesterol at least once every 5 years.

• A total serum cholesterol below 200 mg/dl is classified as desirable and requires no further action other than periodic retesting. Individuals whose levels fall within this range may still be given general instructions on how to reduce risk and maintain their desired cholesterol level.

• A total serum cholesterol between 200 and 239 mg/dl is classified as borderline-high. The test should be repeated and averaged with the first. If the average is between 200 and 239 mg/dl, and the person also has coronary disease or two other cardiovascular risk factors, a lipoprotein analysis should be ordered.

• A measurement over 240 mg/dl should be confirmed by retesting. If it is confirmed, treatment to lower it is recommended.

LOWERING HIGH CHOLESTEROL

The benefits of lowering blood cholesterol are substantial. According to studies by the National Heart, Lung and Blood Institute, for every 1 percent lowering in total blood cholesterol, Americans can reduce heart attack risk by 2 percent. For most people, the best way to lower total cholesterol (and improve their HDL:LDL ratio) is to reduce their intake of saturated fats and to increase exercise. The American Heart Association recommends that fats make up no more than 30 percent, with 10 percent or less coming from saturated fats, and polyunsaturated and monounsaturated fats making up the larger portion. The AHA further recommends that cholesterol consumption be limited to no more than 300 mg per day, considerably less than the average of 500 mg that is now consumed.

Although vegetable fats do not contain cholesterol and most are unsaturated, there are exceptions that should be avoided by people who are trying to lower their cholesterol. These include palm and coconut oils and unsaturated fats that have been hardened (hydrogenated) to make solid margarines or vegetable shortenings.

Increasing exercise tends to raise the levels of HDL cholesterol, although there is no evidence that exercise alone lowers total cholesterol. Since losing weight often reduces total cholesterol, this may explain why some people who undertake exercise programs may show a marked lowering of cholesterol. For those people who still have very high cholesterol levels despite dietary and other lifestyle changes, lipid-lowering drugs may be recommended. This is particularly true of people with familial hypercholesterolemia. (For a more detailed discussion, see chapter 5, The Basics of Good Nutrition.)

DIABETES

Diabetes mellitus, defined as an inability to metabolize carbohydrates (and, to a lesser extent, proteins and fat), may be caused either by an insufficiency of insulin or by the body's inability to use effectively the insulin it produces. As a result the level of sugar (glucose) in the blood rises, some of which may be excreted in the urine. Poorly controlled diabetes is characterized by extreme swings in blood sugar, going from very high to very low.

Diabetes greatly increases the risk of heart attacks and other manifestations of cardiovascular disease. People with poorly controlled diabetes tend to have a wide range of related complications, including high blood lipids, coronary disease, high blood pressure, and other circulatory disorders. These affect both the large arteries, causing arteriosclerosis, for example, and the microcirculation, leading to hemorrhages of the tiny blood vessels in the eye and diminished circulation to the extremities, especially the feet.

Most diabetes experts believe the risk of these complications can be minimized by maintaining normal levels of blood sugar. This requires careful attention to diet and exercise and, in patients who require insulin or other antidiabetic drugs, careful self-monitoring to ensure the proper dosages. Not smoking is also doubly important for diabetic patients (see chapter 21, Diabetes and Other Endocrine Disorders).

OBESITY

Obesity, defined as being 20 percent or more above ideal weight (see chapter 4, The Fundamentals of Good Health), has been shown to lead to premature death from a number of causes, including heart disease. Obesity increases the workload on the heart; other ways in which it may directly promote heart disease are unknown. Nonetheless, a report from the Framingham Heart Study asserted that obesity should be considered a major cardiovascular risk factor in its own right, rather than one that contributes to other risk factors such as diabetes or hypertension, as has been the tendency in the past.

TYPE A PERSONALITY

Personality and the ability to cope with stress have long been suspected as important health factors. Some epidemiologic studies conducted over the past 30 years have found that Type A personalities—people who overreact to even minor stresses, who tend to be driven by a heightened sense of time urgency and ambition, and who are often aggressive, hostile, or compulsive—have an above average incidence of heart attacks, when compared with the calmer, more easygoing Type B personality. But the data are conflicting. Other large-scale studies have failed to find any correlation, and a recent study comparing heart attack survivors with those who died found that the so-called Type A's had a higher survival rate than the Type B's.

Although a link between personality type and heart disease is not well defined, recent studies at Duke University Medical Center suggest a possible mechanism.

Researchers found that Type A persons tend to overrespond to any challenge, no matter how large or small. This chronic overresponse is characterized by increases in heart rate and blood pressure, and a surge in adrenal hormones. It is theorized that the frequent surges of epinephrine and other adrenal hormones, which increase stress in the cardiovascular system, may cause minute injuries to the artery walls, making them more susceptible to atherosclerosis.

Modifying Type A behavior is often difficult, especially in our success-oriented society that rewards drive and ambition. Most Type A's actually enjoy their fast-paced lives and are reluctant to change. The key is to identify those aspects of Type A behavior that seem to be the most destructive and to modify them while retaining the more beneficial ones. Learning to relax for varying periods of time and curbing the tendency to overrespond are two important starting points. Regular physical exercise has helped many Type A's modify their behavior. Behavior modification, relaxation techniques, and biofeedback training are among the approaches that are being used to alter the more destructive elements of Type A behavior. (For a further discussion, see chapter 4, The Fundamentals of Good Health.)

STRESS

Our ability to cope with stress is closely related to personality type. Stress in this instance is defined as an imbalance between excessive psychological or physical demands and the ability to cope with them. A certain amount of stress is a normal part of living, and without it, life would be rather dull. But there are some people who overrespond to almost any type of stress. Deciding what to buy at the supermarket, solving a simple problem, and making a major life decision all are approached with the same feelings of intensity and anxiety. Such people have a low capability to cope with their environment.

Of course, there are some types of stress that place almost overwhelming demands on anyone's ability to cope. Examples include the death of a spouse or child, the loss of a job, major illness, or a culmination of stressful events. In any event, stress produces both physical and psychological responses. The heart beats faster, blood pressure rises, muscles tense, the hands become cold and clammy, and we may break into a cold sweat. These physiological responses to stress are characteristic of the "fight or flight" response triggered by the autonomic nervous system—a response that can be lifesaving in times of danger. The psychological effects are characterized by feelings of tension, apprehension, or nervousness.

People who respond appropriately to stress are those who perform well in almost any situation; signs of poor coping include constant feelings of irritation or pessimism. Fatigue, loss of appetite (or overeating), inability to concentrate or perform at usual levels, and vague unexplained symptoms such as headaches or gastrointestinal upsets are other common signs of inability to cope with stress.

The adverse effects of stress on the cardiovascular system are similar to those seen in Type A behavior. Excessive amounts of adrenal hormones are released, heart rate and blood pressure rise, and cardiovascular symptoms, such as palpitations or chest pain, may occur. If these occur only occasionally, they probably do not produce illness or lasting harm. Theoretically, constant inability to cope with stress can lead to serious illness and may set in motion some of the processes that lead to heart disease, but this theory has not been proven.

SEDENTARY LIFESTYLE

Although it has not been proved that a sedentary lifestyle causes heart disease, or that exercise can prevent it, there is a statistical link between physical activity and cardiovascular health, and the American Heart Association now lists inactivity as a cardiovascular risk factor. There is also evidence that exercise and physical fitness result in improved health and longevity. For example, a long-term study of some 40,000 Harvard graduates found that those who exercised regularly lived longer and had a reduced incidence of heart disease. Earlier studies conducted among people whose jobs involve physical activity (dock workers, mail carriers, London bus conductors, among others) also found that they enjoyed a lower than average incidence of heart attacks. These early studies involved mostly men, but more recent studies of women who exercise have found that they may benefit even more than their male counterparts.

Exactly how exercise protects the heart is unknown, but several theories have been advanced: A lack of physical activity can contribute to obesity and an increase in body fat in relationship to lean muscle tissue. It also leads to a lowered capacity in the oxygen transport system, and may affect ability to cope with stress. People who exercise regularly not only have improved cardiovascular function but also have an enhanced sense of well-being.

UNCONTROLLABLE RISK FACTORS

ADVANCING AGE

Although heart disease is not caused by aging per se, it is more common among older people. This is primarily because coronary disease is a progressive disorder; it has been demonstrated that atherosclerosis often begins at an early age and may take 20 or 30 years to progress to the point where the coronary arteries are blocked enough to cause a heart attack or other symptoms. But heart disease is not an inevitable part of aging—many people live to be 90 or more and still have healthy, vigorous hearts, and there are societies in which heart attacks are rare, even among the very aged.

MALE SEX

Men, particularly in middle age, have a higher incidence of heart attacks than women in the same age range. After menopause, however, the incidence rises among women, and after the age of 60, it is about the same as that for men of the same age.

It is not known why younger women enjoy a lower incidence of heart attacks than men. The possible protective role of estrogen and other female sex hormones has been studied extensively, and though there is no conclusive proof, there is a substantial implication that they are responsible for the lower heart attack rate. But there is some conflicting evidence. Women who have their ovaries removed at an early age or who have a premature menopause do not seem to develop heart disease at an earlier age than women who go through menopause in their late 40s or early 50s. But a small number of women who take oral contraceptives containing estrogen have an increased incidence of heart attacks and strokes, especially if they also smoke. Also, men who have been given female hormones do not have a reduction in heart attacks, as might be assumed if they had a protective role.

Other factors may explain the lower incidence in women. They tend to have higher levels of HDL cholesterol, which is considered protective against coronary disease. Until recently, women did not smoke in as great a number or as heavily as men. Now, however, the traditional roles are changing, and it is interesting to note that as many facets of women's lives are undergoing change, their incidence of heart attacks at an earlier age is increasing.

HEREDITY

It has long been recognized that heart disease seems to run in some families. If parents, siblings, or other close family members have suffered heart attacks before the age of 50 or so, the chances of others following suit is significantly increased. Some risk factors, such as high blood pressure or the very high cholesterol that is characteristic of familial hypercholesterolemia, are hereditary. Although family history cannot be changed, steps can be taken to minimize the chances of a heart attack by identifying and then changing these risk factors at an early age.

TYPES OF CARDIOVASCULAR DISEASE

There are many different diseases of the heart and blood vessels, some very serious and others relatively benign. Fortunately, most people, even those with serious heart disease, can lead relatively normal lives, thanks to modern treatment and rehabilitation efforts.

Treatments vary widely according to the type of disease; they may include drugs, surgery, and lifestyle modifications such as increasing exercise and diet changes. But no matter what the form of treatment, it is important that you become an informed partner in your own health care. The past tendency to leave therapeutic decisions entirely up to the doctor is changing; increasingly, the trend is to include patients and often family members in treatment planning.

CORONARY HEART DISEASE

DEFINITION

Coronary heart disease (CHD), also known as coronary artery disease (CAD) or coronary atherosclerosis, involves the progressive narrowing of the arteries that nourish the heart muscle. Often there are no symptoms, but if one or more of these arteries become severely narrowed, angina may develop during exercise, stress, or other times when the heart muscle is not getting enough blood (see "Angina," in this chapter).

CAUSE

The narrowing is due to a buildup of fatty plaque (atheromas) along the artery walls. These deposits are composed mostly of cholesterol, other lipids, and fibrous tissue, such as collagen. Coronary disease appears to be a lifelong process in some people, beginning at an early age and progressing slowly until the vessels become so occluded that the heart muscle no longer gets adequate nourishment. The underlying cause is unknown, although it is seen most frequently in people who live in developed industrialized nations. The various cardiovascular risk factors discussed earlier seem to promote the process.

DIAGNOSIS

A coronary artery must be narrowed to less than 30 percent of its original size before there is a serious reduction in blood flow to the heart muscle served by the vessel (see figure 16.2). Generally, about 5 percent of the total cardiac output of blood goes through the coronary arteries; thus there is adequate coronary blood flow to meet normal demands at rest even if the vessels are 70 to 90 percent occluded. If the coronary arteries are seriously blocked, however, blood flow may not be

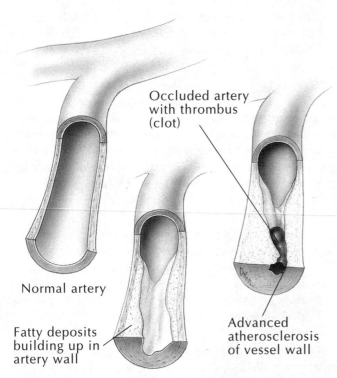

Occluded artery with thrombus (clot)

Normal artery

Fatty deposits building up in artery wall

Advanced atherosclerosis of vessel wall

Figure 16.2: Progression of coronary disease.

adequate for any increased demand, such as that of exercise or an emotional upset. If the heart muscle cannot get enough oxygen—a state known as myocardial ischemia—symptoms such as chest pain (angina) or shortness of breath may result.

A presumptive diagnosis of coronary disease is based on a review of symptoms, health history, an electrocardiogram, and an exercise stress test, perhaps with a thallium scan. A more definitive diagnosis requires cardiac catheterization and angiography.

During an exercise stress test, the patient is hooked up to an electrocardiographic monitor (an ECG or EKG machine) and then asked to walk on a treadmill, peddle a stationary bicycle, or climb steps. The ECG monitor will show whether the heart muscle is getting enough blood. An exercise test also detects silent ischemia, a condition with no symptoms in which heart muscle does not get enough blood.

If severe narrowing is suspected, a coronary angiogram may be needed. This examination entails threading a catheter through a blood vessel into the heart, and then injecting a dye into the coronary arteries to make them visible on x-rays. (These tests are described in detail in chapter 12, Diagnostic Tests and Procedures.)

TREATMENT

Drugs. Various medications constitute the first-line treatment of coronary artery disease. These include:

Beta-Blocking Drugs. These agents act by blocking the effect of the sympathetic nervous system on the heart, slowing heart rate, decreasing blood pressure, and thereby reducing the oxygen demand of the heart. Studies have found that these drugs also can reduce the chances of dying or suffering a recurrent heart attack if they are started shortly after suffering a heart attack and continued for 2 years.

Calcium-Channel-Blocking Drugs. All muscles need varying amounts of calcium in order to contract. By reducing the amount of calcium that enters the muscle cells in the coronary artery walls, spasms can be prevented. Some calcium-channel-blocking drugs also decrease the workload of the heart and some lower the heart rate as well.

Nitrates. Nitroglycerin may be prescribed to both treat and prevent attacks of angina (see the discussion of angina in this chapter).

SURGICAL TREATMENT

Coronary artery bypass surgery. An estimated 170,000 Americans undergo coronary artery bypass surgery each year. This operation, once considered a difficult achievement, is now almost routine in many medical centers. Indeed, there is a good deal of controversy over whether it is now being used unnecessarily to treat coronary disease that could be controlled just as effectively by more conservative, less costly medical therapies.

There remains some disagreement among doctors as to the indications for coronary bypass surgery. Studies have conclusively demonstrated that the operation prolongs life in patients who have a severely blocked left main coronary artery. It is also indicated in most cases in which 3 major arteries are diseased. There is less agreement about when it is appropriate for other patients. In general, it is recommended for people with disabling angina that cannot be controlled by conventional therapy who are also good candidates for surgery.

The operation itself is relatively simple. A segment of healthy blood vessel, usually an artery from the chest (mammary artery) or vein from one of the legs (saphenous vein), is interposed between the aorta and the blocked coronary arteries (see figure 16.3). During the operation, which takes about 2 hours, circulation is maintained by a heart-lung machine. Coronary bypass patients usually spend 2 or 3 days in an intensive care recovery unit following the operation, and another week in the hospital. Costs of the operation vary depending on the individual's condition and geographic locale, but average is $32,000 to $35,000.

Most people who undergo the operation report feeling vastly better afterward. Very often, the patient may have suffered from disabling angina or other cardiac limitations before the operation. With an increased blood supply to the heart muscle, these problems should be

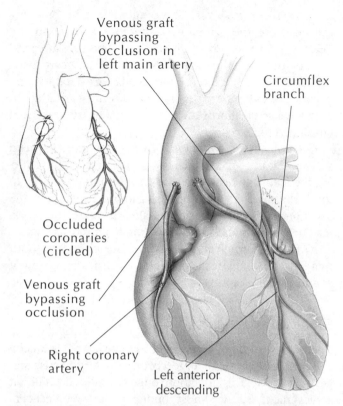

Figure 16.3: Coronary artery bypass surgery. This drawing shows 2 grafts, one of the left anterior descending coronary artery and the other of the right coronary artery.

eliminated or minimized. (It should be noted that not all people with severe coronary disease are suitable candidates for surgery, and also that the operation is not always successful in achieving its intended goals.) As with any surgical procedure, the operation involves some risk; nationwide, about 1 to 3 percent of bypass patients do not survive the operation or recovery period. The risk is highest for people who have heart failure or are debilitated by age or other medical conditions. Women do particularly poorly.

The skill and experience of the surgical and recovery teams also are important considerations. Patients considering coronary bypass surgery always should determine whether the surgeon performs this particular operation regularly (at least 2 or 3 times per week) and whether there is a skilled recovery team and a special recovery unit.

Although bypass surgery greatly improves the way most patients feel, it is not a cure for heart disease. Unless other preventive steps are taken, the processes that caused the artery disease will continue. In fact, the grafts seem to become diseased even faster than the natural coronary arteries. Therefore, it is particularly important for bypass patients to follow a prudent lifestyle following the operation.

Angioplasty. A relatively recent—and increasingly popular—treatment for atherosclerotic arterial diseases is transluminal angioplasty, also referred to as balloon angioplasty. Used to treat severely blocked coronary arteries as well as arteries diseased with atherosclerotic plaque in other parts of the body, this technique involves threading a catheter with an inflatable balloonlike tip through the artery to the area of blockage. The balloon is inflated, flattening the fatty deposits and widening the arterial channel, allowing more blood to reach the heart muscle (see figure 16.4, below).

Angioplasty offers several obvious advantages:

- The operation is performed under local anesthesia.
- Although invasive, it does not involve surgery or the use of a heart-lung machine.
- It is not as costly as coronary bypass surgery, nor does it involve more than 1 or 2 days of hospitalization under ordinary circumstances.

Unfortunately, it is not appropriate for all types of coronary artery disease, nor does it work in all people. For example, studies show that women are not as likely as men to benefit from the operation; they also have a higher mortality rate from the procedure. Some studies have put the success rate at about 60 percent; people who undergo an unsuccessful angioplasty still may require coronary

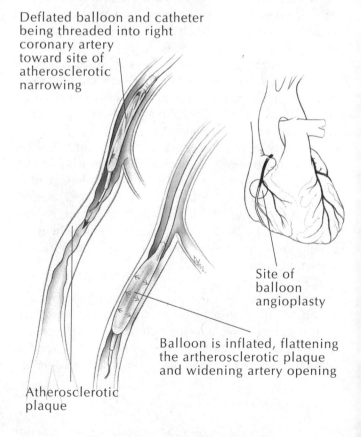

Figure 16.4: Angioplasty.

bypass surgery. As technology advances, the applicability and success rates of angioplasty may improve. It also should be noted that it is not a cure for the disease. In a significant number of patients, the occlusions recur, and a repeat angioplasty may be required after 2 or 3 years.

Angioplasty is also being used to treat blockages in the arteries of the legs and the carotid artery, the major vessel carrying blood to the brain.

A variation of balloon angioplasty uses a tiny drill-like device to shave away fatty deposits, similar to a Roto-Rooter. Another still experimental variation called laser ablation, is performed through a special viewing tube (fiber-optic catheter) that is inserted into the clogged artery. A laser, an intense beam of light, is used to vaporize the plaque.

HOME REMEDIES AND ALTERNATIVE THERAPIES

There is no substitute for medical care when considering a serious—even potentially fatal—condition such as coronary heart disease. The first thing to do if you notice any of the symptoms described earlier is to see your doctor. Medical treatment may be required to prevent heart attack. However, your doctor may recommend nonmedical measures, such as exercise conditioning, relaxation techniques such as yoga, and a low-fat diet, that may help ease the symptoms of coronary heart disease, especially angina, and may help ease the effects of some risk factors. For example, relaxation techniques may help you overcome stress and block pain impulses by refocusing your concentration. These techniques include meditation, yoga, biofeedback training, and self-hypnosis.

For maximum benefit, you should choose a relaxation technique that you are comfortable with and practice it for 20 minutes once or twice a day. In addition to the direct positive effect on your cardiovascular system, relaxation techniques may help you make other lifestyle changes such as stopping smoking and contribute to a general sense of well-being.

Vitamin therapy may also work in conjunction with your medical treatment. High doses of niacin can lower blood cholesterol levels, reducing the buildup of fatty deposits in the arteries. In addition, recent studies indicate that vitamin E, an antioxidant vitamin that also inhibits blood clotting, may help reduce the risk of heart attack. However, do not take any more than the Recommended Dietary Allowance (RDA) of any vitamin without first consulting your doctor; some vitamins in high doses can have toxic effects.

Other more controversial, alternative therapies include garlic, which may be consumed as deodorized pills, and fish oil (omega-3 fatty acid) supplements. Ongoing studies indicate that large amounts of garlic may have a modest cholesterol-lowering effect. Any benefits of fish oil supplements are offset by the increased calorie and fat intake. Thus, experts recommend eating one or two servings of salmon, cod, or other cold-water fish a week rather than taking fish oil pills.

Still other alternative therapies provide no benefit and should be avoided. These include chelation therapy, a technique used to remove heavy metals such as lead from the blood.

ANGINA

DEFINITION

Angina, or angina pectoris, is the medical term for chest pains behind the breastbone. It is a common manifestation of coronary artery disease.

CAUSE

Angina usually occurs when the heart must work harder, and the heart muscle does not get enough oxygen, a condition called myocardial ischemia. Generally, angina is caused by hardening and narrowing of the coronary arteries by deposits of fatty plaque (atherosclerosis). These narrowed arteries may be able to deliver enough blood to the heart muscle to carry out normal activities without symptoms, but any extra demand—for example, climbing stairs, running to catch a bus, getting upset or angry, eating a large meal, or going out on a cold, windy day—may cause angina.

In some cases, angina is caused by spasms of the muscles that control blood flow in the arteries. This is called variant angina. These attacks may occur even when a person is at rest.

DIAGNOSIS

Typically, angina is described as a pressing or squeezing pain that starts in the center of the chest and may spread to the shoulders or arms (most often on the left side although either or both sides may be involved), the neck, jaw, or back.

Often, angina can be diagnosed on the basis of symptoms alone. As part of the diagnostic examination, an exercise tolerance (stress) test may be ordered, and if your doctor suspects more severe narrowing, she may recommend coronary angiography. (See chapter 12, Diagnostic Tests and Procedures, for more information on these tests.)

TREATMENT

Angina attacks usually last for only a few minutes, and most can be relieved by rest. If not, a nitroglycerin tablet slipped under the tongue usually brings prompt relief.

This drug dilates the large coronary arteries, thereby increasing the flow of blood to heart muscle.

PREVENTION

Drugs. Most people with angina learn to adjust their lives to minimize attacks. There are cases, however, when the attacks come frequently and without provocation—a condition known as unstable angina. This is often a prelude to a heart attack and requires special treatment, primarily with aspirin or anticoagulant drugs.

In most instances, drugs are recommended for the prevention of angina before surgery is considered. The major classes of these drugs include the following.

Nitrates. These come in several forms: as nitroglycerin tablets to be slipped under the tongue during or in anticipation of an attack; as ointment to be absorbed through the skin; as long-acting medicated skin patches; or as long-acting tablets. The latter three forms are used mostly to prevent rather than relieve attacks. The nitrates work by reducing the oxygen requirements of the heart muscle.

Beta-Blocking Drugs. See treatment under "Coronary Heart Disease."

Calcium-Channel-Blocking Drugs. These drugs are prescribed to prevent angina that is thought to be caused by coronary artery spasm. They can also be effective for stable angina associated with exercise. (See also treatment under "Coronary Heart Disease.")

Aspirin. Low-dose aspirin halves the chance of a heart attack in patients with angina.

SURGICAL TREATMENTS

Angina that cannot be controlled by drugs and lifestyle changes may require surgery. The two major procedures are coronary bypass surgery and angioplasty. (See treat-

---

ment of Coronary Heart Disease in this chapter and chapter 12, Diagnostic Tests and Procedures.)

HOME REMEDIES AND ALTERNATIVE THERAPIES

The underlying cause of angina requires careful medical treatment to prevent a heart attack. However, some self-care and alternative therapies may be helpful as additional treatments. A number of lifestyle changes may help prevent attacks of angina. For example, angina that occurs after a large meal can be avoided by eating several smaller meals, and avoiding exercise after eating. Other self-care approaches include:

- Stress reduction that may include meditation and biofeedback training
- Exercise conditioning to increase endurance
- Weight control to reduce the heart's workload
- Smoking cessation, which reduces the risk of heart attack (See also treatment under "Coronary Heart Disease")

MALE/FEMALE DIFFERENCES

Angina is more common and more intense in men than in women. Doctors do not know whether this occurs because women tolerate pain better than men, or whether women unconsciously lower their physical activity to avoid attacks of angina.

HEART ATTACK

DEFINITION

A heart attack occurs when a coronary artery becomes completely blocked, either by a clot (coronary thrombus) or by atherosclerotic plaque. The medical term for a heart attack, myocardial infarction, literally means "heart muscle death."

CAUSE

Most heart attacks are a direct manifestation of coronary artery disease.

DIAGNOSIS

Very often, a heart attack occurs without warning; indeed many people who suffer heart attacks are unaware that they have diseased coronary arteries until they are stricken. In some instances, there may have been symptoms, such as chest pain, but they may have been misinterpreted as something else, such as indigestion (see the box, "Recognizing a Heart Attack"). In 10 percent or more of all heart attacks, there may be no

---

RECOGNIZING A HEART ATTACK

The pain of a heart attack differs from that typically associated with other kinds of chest pain such as angina. Any of the following signs and symptoms demand immediate emergency treatment.

- Chest pain that does not recede with rest, lasting 20 or more minutes. The pain may vary from mild to excruciating. It typically begins in the upper middle portion of the chest and may spread to the neck, jaw, back, and arms, especially the left one.
- Sweating.
- Nausea/vomiting.
- Possible dizziness or fainting.
- A feeling of impending doom.

pain or other obvious symptoms. These people usually do not even know they have had a heart attack until it is detected during an electrocardiogram at some later time.

If a heart attack is suspected, it can be confirmed by characteristic changes on an ECG. Blood studies will show elevated levels of certain enzymes that are released by injured or dying heart muscles.

EMERGENCY TREATMENT OF HEART ATTACK

Large numbers of heart attack sufferers die before reaching medical help. Many of these can be saved by prompt administration of cardiopulmonary resuscitation (CPR). This technique combines mouth-to-mouth breathing and external heart massage to maintain circulation until medical help arrives. (For more details, see chapter 13, Basics of CPR and Life Support.)

Until a few years ago, about half of all heart attack patients died, most before they even reached the hospital. These figures have changed dramatically in the past decade; more than two-thirds now survive, thanks in large part to improved medical care both before reaching the hospital and in special coronary care units.

Anyone who suspects a heart attack should seek immediate emergency treatment. The sooner therapy starts, the more heart muscle will be saved and the less the chance of heart failure in the future. The best course is to summon the local emergency medical squad. If one is not available, have someone take you as quickly as possible to the nearest emergency room or hospital that has a coronary care unit. Obviously someone else should drive; you must not try to drive yourself. If possible, you should chew an aspirin on the way to the hospital—aspirin helps stop the clumping of blood platelets, thereby preventing clot formation.

If heart attack patients arrive at the hospital early (less than 4 hours after onset) it is often possible (80 percent of the time) to dissolve the clot in the coronary artery that is responsible for the heart attack by using thrombolytic drugs such as tissue plasminogen activator (TPA) or streptokinase. In fact, the chance of death is cut in half if the patient receives 1 of these drugs within the first hour. A small dose (160 mg or ½ a regular adult tablet) of aspirin also helps reduce the damage to heart muscle and substantially increases the effectiveness of streptokinase. By restoring blood flow before irreversible damage occurs, these drugs decrease heart damage considerably and will also reduce mortality and disability.

Other medications that are administered during this initial period include morphine or meperidine (Demerol) to alleviate pain and anxiety; intravenous nitroglycerin to reduce the heart's oxygen need and improve coronary circulation, and perhaps a beta-blocker. Supplemental oxygen is administered, either via a face mask or nasal prongs.

Depending on the nature and severity of the heart attack, balloon catheterization (angioplasty) or an emergency coronary bypass operation may be performed. In any event, expect to spend a few days under close observation in a coronary care unit. As soon as the crisis is past, you will be encouraged to sit up, and then stand and walk about the room. This early ambulation is now considered an important aspect in a speedy recovery.

CARDIAC REHABILITATION

In general, rehabilitation after a heart attack involves at least the following 4 stages.

- Treatment of and recovery from the acute phase
- Psychological adjustment to the nature of the disorder
- Lifestyle adjustments (for example, stopping smoking, exercise conditioning, dietary changes, behavior modification)
- Long-term maintenance and medical follow-up

The course of treatment is dictated by the nature of the disease. Psychological adjustment is not as clear-cut: Some people accept the situation with determination and optimism; others become very depressed and adopt a defeatist attitude. Still others deny that anything is wrong. Professional counseling or group therapy with other heart patients may be appropriate and should be extended to spouses and other family members if needed.

Cardiovascular rehabilitation is an often neglected aspect of treating heart disease. Once the initial crisis is past and recovery is under way, many doctors and patients avoid discussing what happens next. All too often, a patient will leave the hospital with instructions to "lose weight, stop smoking, and try to get more exercise," without a clear idea of how to go about accomplishing these goals. What's more, heart attack patients are understandably afraid and many harbor misconceptions that are holdovers from past practices. At one time, for example, most heart attack patients were cautioned to avoid exercise, advice that doctors now know is invalid for the majority of patients. In recognition of these shortcomings, a growing number of hospitals, medical centers, physician groups, and organizations are offering formal cardiovascular rehabilitation programs, many of which begin while the patient is still hospitalized and continue after discharge. Unfortunately, most insurance policies do not cover outpatient rehabilitation, so there may be economic stricture on participating on a long-term basis. However, there are alternatives. For example, many YMCAs now offer physician-supervised cardiovascular rehabilitation programs at a modest cost. Local chapters of the American Heart Association usually can provide information about such programs and also can

TABLE 16.1: MODEL EXERCISE CONDITIONING PROGRAM

Weeks	Distance (miles)	Time goal (min/mile; healthy)	Distance (miles)	Time goal(min/mil; heart patients)
1–2	1–2	15	1	20
3–4	2–2.5	12–15	1	17–30
5–6	2.5–3	12	1	15
7–8	3–3.5	12	1.5	15
9–10	3.5–4	12	1.5	14

check on whether they are properly structured and supervised.

EXERCISE CONDITIONING

Exercise conditioning has become a part of many cardio-vascular rehabilitation programs. Exercise programs for heart patients should be directed by a physician experienced in this area and individualized to meet specific patient needs. (Other people undertaking exercise conditioning should follow the precautions outlined in chapter 4, The Fundamentals of Good Health.)

The accompanying tables outline a model exercise conditioning program for both heart patients and healthy people. There should be at least three and preferably five exercise sessions per week. Note: Do not undertake this or any exercise program without appropriate medical clearance.

In each succeeding 2-week period, increase distance and decrease time until the conditioning goal has been reached. To maintain fitness, exercise 20 to 30 minutes in heart target range 4 or 5 times per week. Each session should include 10 minutes of warm-up and 10 minutes of cool-down exercises.

Start by walking; gradually increase the pace as indicated below. If there are no orthopedic problems and if your doctor approves, jogging can be added gradually after 9 or 10 weeks. Start by walking a lap or a couple of blocks, jog for a few yards, then resume walking. If no problems develop, the distance jogged can be increased gradually over a period of 8 to 10 weeks until you are jogging continuously.

RETURNING TO WORK

Following a heart attack, most people can lead a productive, relatively normal life, but some adjustments may be required. Although most survivors can return to work, some may need to change to a different job, especially if it involves the safety of others. For example, airline pilots, firefighters, or police officers usually need to change jobs after a heart attack. Similarly, jobs that require strenuous labor also may be inappropriate.

Lifestyle adjustments are perhaps one of the most important factors in living with heart disease. All too often, heart attack patients assume that they can no longer engage in pleasurable activities of the past, including athletics and sex. For the large majority of patients this is not true. The extremes, such as running a marathon, may no longer be feasible, but then most people who have never had a heart attack cannot do these things, either. The important thing is to examine carefully what is important to making as full a recovery as possible, and then following through in instituting the necessary changes. Stopping smoking is high on the list of necessary lifestyle adjustments for those who smoke and have heart disease. Losing excess weight, altering eating habits to lower cholesterol, and increasing physical activity are examples of other positive lifestyle adjustments that are important in living with heart disease. Some of these require only common sense and determination; others, such as exercise conditioning and dietary changes, may require professional guidance. In fact, no one with heart disease should undertake an exercise program without medical clearance and a diagnostic exercise test (see chapter 12, Diagnostic Tests and Procedures). By the same token, a person should not be afraid to exercise within reason because he has had a heart attack. Heart attack patients who engage in exercise conditioning, either in a supervised setting or individually following a doctor's prescribed regimen, find they not only feel better but also are able to resume previous activities faster and with more confidence. (See table 16.1, Model Exercise Conditioning Program, in this chapter.)

Backsliding to one's former ways is a constant danger, especially as time goes by. Since a previous heart attack is very often a precursor to recurrences, it is important to do everything possible with an eye to prevention. There is no guarantee that adopting a healthier lifestyle will, indeed, prevent future heart attacks or other cardiovascular problems, but it would be foolish not to make the effort.

HIGH BLOOD PRESSURE

DEFINITION

Blood pressure is the amount of force exerted by the blood on your artery walls as it is pumped from the heart and through the circulatory system. Hypertension is the medical term used to describe chronically elevated blood pressure. Chronic high blood pressure damages

TABLE 16.2: RELATIVE MERITS OF VARIOUS EXERCISES IN INDUCING CARDIOVASCULAR FITNESS

Energy Range	Activity	Comment
1.5–2.0 Mets (multiple of resting energy) or 2.0–2.5 cal/min or 120–150 cal/hr	Light housework such as polishing furniture or washing clothes	Minimal cardiovascular benefit; too intermittent to promote endurance
	Strolling 1 mile per hour (mph)	Not sufficiently strenuous to promote endurance unless person's capacity is very low
2.0–2.0 Mets or 2.5–4.0 cal/min or 150–240 cal/hr	Level walking at 2 mph	Same as strolling
	Golf, using power cart	Promotes skill and minimal strength in arm muscles, but not sufficiently vigorous or continuous to promote endurance
3.0–4.0 Mets or 4–5 cal/min or 240–300 cal/hr	Cleaning windows, mopping floors, vacuuming	Adequate conditioning if done continuously for 20–30 minutes
	Bowling	Neither sufficiently vigorous nor continuous to promote endurance
	Walking 3 mph	Adequate dynamic exercise for someone with low capacity
	Cycling 6 mph	As above
	Table tennis, badminton, volleyball	Has endurance benefits if play is vigorous and continuous; intermittent, easy play promotes skill only
4.0–5.0 Mets or 5–6 cal/min or 300–360 cal/hr	Golf/carrying clubs	Promotes strength and skill; enhances endurance only if target heart rate is reached and maintained
	Tennis—doubles	As above
	Calisthenics and ballet exercises	Promotes endurance if exercise is continuous, rhythmic, and repetitive. Isometric exercises such as push-ups and sit-ups probably do not enhance cardiovascular fitness
5.0–6.0 Mets or 6–7 cal/min or 360–420 cal/hr	Walking 4 mph	Dynamic, aerobic, and beneficial
	Cycling 10 mph	As above
	Ice or in-line skating	As above if done continuously
6.0–7.0 Mets or 7–8 cal/min or 420–480 cal/hr	Walking 5 mph	Dynamic, aerobic, and beneficial
	Cycling 11 mph	As above
	Singles tennis	Beneficial if played for at least 30 minutes, especially with an attempt to keep moving
	Water skiing	Total isometrics; very risky for cardiacs, precardiacs (high risk) or normals who are unconditioned
7.0–8.0 Mets or 8–10 cal/min or 480–600 cal/hr	Jogging 5 mph	Dynamic, aerobic, and endurance-building
	Cycling 12 mph	As above
	Downhill skiing	Enhances skill, but ski runs are usually too short to promote endurance significantly; has skill and isometric benefits; stresses of altitude, cold, and exercise may be too great for some cardiacs
	Paddleball	Promotes skill; intermittent and therefore not endurance-building; competition and heat may be dangerous to cardiacs
8.0–9.0 Mets or 10–11 cal/min or 600–660 cal/hr	Running 5.5 mph	Excellent conditioner
	Cycling 13 mph	As above
	Squash or handball (practice session or warmup)	Intermittent and therefore not endurance-building; promotes skill
Above 10 Mets or 11 cal/min or 660 cal/hr	Running 6 miles/hr=10 Mets 7 miles/hr=11.5 8 miles/hr=13.5	Excellent conditioner
	Competitive handball or squash	Competition and heat are dangerous to anyone not in excellent condition

*Met = multiple of the resting energy requirement; e.g., 2 Mets require twice the resting energy cost, 3 Mets, triple, etc. *Note:* Energy range will vary depending on skill of exerciser, pattern of rest pauses, environmental temperature, etc.
Caloric values depend on body size (more for larger person).

From Lenore R. Zohman, M.D., *Beyond Diet: Exercise Your Way to Fitness and Heart Health,* CPC International, Englewood Cliffs, NJ.

HOW TO TAKE YOUR OWN BLOOD PRESSURE

Home monitoring of blood pressure is useful for both patient and physician. By keeping track of daily or weekly changes in blood pressure, you can help your doctor determine whether you should take medication to lower it or if the drugs you are already taking are working. Often, blood pressure readings taken in a doctor's office or clinic will be higher than those taken at home. Once a person has learned to monitor her own blood pressure, it may not be necessary to make repeated trips to a doctor's office or clinic simply for a blood pressure measurement. Most people can quickly learn to take their own blood pressure, especially if one of the several automated sphygmomanometers is used. These devices have a built-in sensing device that removes the need to use a stethoscope.

Following is a step-by-step procedure for taking your blood pressure using a nonautomated sphygmomanometer and stethoscope. A similar procedure is followed if you use an automated device except you do not use a stethoscope and the blood pressure will appear on a digital readout.

1. Pick a quiet spot. You have to use your ears to "hear" the blood pressure. Anything that diminishes your hearing will alter the true reading.
2. It is customary to take the pressure seated and most information on treatment is taken from seated measurements. Blood pressure will vary in the lying, sitting, and standing positions.
3. Sit next to a table so that when you rest your forearm flat on the table, your upper arm (where the cuff will be placed) is at about the same level as your heart. Having your arm above your heart will lower the reading (and vice versa), but the changes are relatively minor.
4. Use your fingertips to locate the brachial artery in the crook of your elbow by feeling for the pulse, a little to the inside of the center of the elbow's crease. Get to know this spot, since it is the best place for the stethoscope. If you can't feel it, just set the stethoscope in the general area just above the elbow crease, to the inside of center.
5. Slip on the deflated cuff, placing the stethoscope over the artery. Use the ring and Velcro wrap to make the cuff snug.
6. Place the stethoscope in your ears. Most people need to have the tips tilted slightly forward, but you may have to experiment to find the position that gives the loudest sound. You can test this before putting on the cuff by gently tapping the stethoscope with your finger and finding the best position for the ear pieces.
7. Once the cuff and stethoscope are set, get the manometer (pressure gauge) in a good viewing position and you are ready to inflate the cuff.
8. You will want to inflate the cuff roughly 30 points (millimeters of mercury [mmHg]) above your expected systolic pressure in order to get the most accurate readings. This value has been determined by trial and error. Since most people know about where their pressure is, it is easy for them to decide how high to inflate.
9. Once the cuff pressure is greater than your systolic pressure, you should not hear any sound in the stethoscope. In effect, you have made a tourniquet for your arm and cut off all of the blood supply. This is why it feels uncomfortable.
10. Now, keeping your eyes on the gauge, gradually release the pressure in the cuff using the release on the bulb. It takes practice to learn how to release slowly so that the pressure falls 2 to 3 points with each heartbeat.
11. As the pressure in the cuff falls, it will continue to act as a tourniquet as long as its pressure is greater than the pressure in the artery. As soon as the cuff pressure drops below the arterial pressure, a pulse beat gets through, and you hear the sound of that pulse in your stethoscope. Read the gauge level when you hear the first sound. The first recorded sound is the systolic pressure. If you also concentrate on feeling, you can learn to sense this first beat. It gives a good check on your sound readings.
12. Continue to let air out. The thumping sound, corresponding to the amount of the pulse wave that gets through the tourniquet, will first get louder as more blood gets by. Then, as the cuff pressure approaches diastolic pressure, the sounds gets faint. Listen carefully until the sounds disappear. The gauge reading at the time of the last sound is the diastolic pressure. Note at this time, you no longer feel a pulse in your arm inside the cuff. This is because the tourniquet effect of the cuff disappears when its pressure is the same as or less than the diastolic pressure.
13. Optional check. Wait a minute and repeat the measurement. This time, readjust your initial cuff pressure to exactly 30 points above your previous systolic pressure. Slow the pressure fall to as close to 2 points per beat as you can.
14. Record date, time, systolic, and diastolic pressures.
15. You can increase the value of the data by also measuring your weight and your pulse. This helps you and your doctor to interpret any changes in pressure. So will notes on any unusual related events such as menstrual periods, taking of other medicines, a recent argument, or physical exertion.

the arteries, although it usually takes years for the detrimental effects to become apparent, and by that time the consequences may be irreversible. Many studies have identified hypertension as a leading risk factor in heart attacks; it is also the major cause of stroke.

A blood pressure measurement is expressed in two numbers, for example, 120/80, which is considered ideal. The higher number is the systolic pressure, or the amount of force (as measured in millimeters of mercury) that is exerted against the artery walls during the heartbeat (contraction). The lower number is the diastolic pressure, which is the force existing while your heart is resting between beats. In the past, experts disagreed as to what constituted high blood pressure; today, most experts agree that consistent readings of 140/85–90 or higher are too high. If your blood pressure is in this range, you should take steps to lower it.

CAUSE

In 90 percent of all cases, the cause is unknown, and is referred to as essential hypertension. Contrary to popular belief, hypertension is not a result of tension or stress, even though blood pressure does go up during periods of stress. Heredity appears to be a factor; the disease tends to run in families, and children of people with hypertension often develop high blood pressure at an early age. Obesity is also a major risk factor for developing hypertension, and losing weight may bring blood pressure into the normal range. High salt intake may play a role in the development of hypertension among people who are genetically sodium sensitive and predisposed to the disease. Conversely, sharply restricting sodium can lower blood pressure in these people.

In about 10 percent of patients, the disease can be traced to specific causes, most commonly kidney abnormalities, adrenal gland tumors, or a congenital narrowing of the aorta. This is called secondary hypertension.

DIAGNOSIS

Consistent blood pressure readings of more than 140/85–90 mmHg lead to a diagnosis of high blood pressure. Most people with high blood pressure do not experience any symptoms unless the disease has progressed to a serious stage. Headaches, visual changes, difficulty in breathing, and other signs of congestive heart failure, ministrokes (transient ischemic attacks), strokes, and kidney failure all are possible outcomes of untreated or poorly controlled hypertension. Many people do not undergo any further testing. Some people have elevated readings because they are nervous about seeing the doctor or because of some other stressful situation. If your doctor suspects this "white-coat hypertension," she may

ASPIRIN—THE "MIRACLE" HEART DRUG

Increasingly, low doses of aspirin are being used both to prevent a heart attack or stroke and also as part of the treatment of a heart attack. A study involving 22,000 middle-aged healthy male physicians found that those who took a single aspirin (325 mg) every other day had 50 percent fewer heart attacks over a 5-year period, compared with the men who took a placebo. When taken in small amounts, aspirin blocks some of the prostaglandin products in platelets, thereby reducing clot formation. It is probably important to keep the dosage small. The beneficial effects may be lost with higher dosages; there also is an increased risk of gastrointestinal bleeding and other adverse effects.

Studies also show that one 325 mg dose of aspirin per day reduces the chance of heart attack by 50 percent in patients with unstable angina. In this condition, the symptoms often are caused by tiny clots that form in the narrowed coronary arteries. Aspirin can prevent these clots from forming, thus easing the symptoms. Low-dose aspirin also is recommended as a preventive measure for people at high risk for suffering a stroke. It is important, however, that blood pressure be brought under control before beginning aspirin therapy in these patients. Conceivably, aspirin taken by a hypertensive person could increase the risk of a hemorrhagic stroke.

recommend that you take your own blood pressure at home (see box "How to Take Your Own Blood Pressure") or wear an ambulatory device that can take 24-hour readings.

If your physician orders additional tests, it is usually to determine an underlying cause of high blood pressure or to assess damage caused by the high blood pressure. Blood and urine tests, computed tomography (CT) scans, magnetic resonance imaging (MRI), radionuclide imaging (such as a thallium scan), or coronary angiography may be ordered in this effort (see chapter 12).

TREATMENT

Cases with specific causes can be treated by correcting the underlying cause. In the remaining 90 percent, the hypertension cannot be cured, but it can be controlled by salt restriction, drugs, and lifestyle changes.

Lifestyle Changes. In the large majority of hypertensives, the disease is classified as mild to moderate, with diastolic pressures between 85 and 104 mmHg. Doctors still do not agree on when to initiate drug treatment for mild hypertension, although most now agree that persistent diastolic readings above 85 mmHg should, at the least, be carefully monitored and treated by lifestyle modification. This will include stopping smoking, losing weight if necessary, exercising, reducing salt intake, and reducing alcohol intake to 2 ounces or less a day. In many people with mild hypertension, this approach will be sufficient to lower the blood pressure to within the normal range.

Drugs. In the past 25 years, a large number of antihypertensive drugs have been developed, and these have truly revolutionized the treatment of the disease. Classes of antihypertensive drugs include the following:

• *Diuretics.* Commonly called "water pills," these drugs lower blood pressure by reducing the body's sodium and water volume. The most commonly used diuretics in treating hypertension are the thiazides; if these fail to lower the blood pressure adequately, a different diuretic or other drugs to take with a thiazide may be prescribed.

• *Beta-Blocking Drugs.* These drugs, which block the sympathetic nervous system hormones to reduce the constriction of blood vessels, may be prescribed alone or with other drugs, usually a thiazide diuretic.

• *Vasodilators.* These drugs relax the muscles in the blood vessel walls, causing them to dilate, or widen. Vasodilators are usually prescribed along with a diuretic or beta-blocking drug.

• *Centrally Acting Drugs.* These agents decrease the heart rate and lower the amount of blood pumped with each beat by decreasing sympathetic nervous system activity, which controls involuntary muscle action. They are usually taken with a thiazide.

• *Angiotensin-Converting Enzyme (ACE) Inhibitors.* These drugs block the formation of angiotensin, a naturally occurring substance that constricts blood vessels. They also decrease the body's ability to retain salt and water. ACE inhibitors are used to treat a number of conditions in addition to high blood pressure. For example, they are now given to treat congestive heart failure, and one study has shown improved survival among patients treated with them.

• *Calcium-Channel-Blocking Agents.* Small amounts of calcium are needed in order for arterial smooth muscles and other muscles to constrict. By blocking some of this vasoconstrictive action, blood vessels are allowed to dilate, and blood pressure falls. A number of calcium-channel-blocking drugs are now approved to treat both high blood pressure and angina.

Drugs prescribed for hypertension should be taken exactly as instructed, and usually for a lifetime. Although they will lower blood pressure, they do not cure the disease; once stopped, the blood pressure will go back up, sometimes higher than before. Side effects or adverse reactions are common with these drugs but usually can be minimized by adjusting the dosage or substituting other drugs. Any side effects, which may include dizziness when standing (orthostatic hypotension), fatigue, depression, and impotence, among others, should be reported to the treating physician. In any event, the patient should not stop taking the drugs or alter the dosage without first contacting his doctor. This is particularly important with the beta-blocking agents because abrupt cessation can provoke a heart attack.

People who are under treatment for hypertension should have their blood pressure checked at periodic intervals (blood pressure machines are now available for home use), and see their doctors regularly.

HOME REMEDIES AND ALTERNATIVE THERAPIES

It is important to work with your doctor to control high blood pressure with lifestyle modification and, if necessary, drug treatment. In addition, relaxation techniques may help. Though there is no conclusive clinical evidence that stress causes high blood pressure, numerous reports indicate that eliciting a relaxation response lowers blood pressure, at least temporarily. In addition, stress management skills provide a general sense of control and well-being, as well as help in implementing other more directly proven risk factor remedies such as stopping smoking. (For more details, see discussion of home remedies and alternative therapies for "Coronary Heart Disease.")

PREVENTION

Because the causes are unknown, it is hard to know how to prevent essential hypertension. There is evidence that proper controlling of weight, exercising regularly, avoiding smoking, limiting salt and alcohol intake, and managing stress may lower your chances of having high blood pressure. However, if you have an uncontrollable risk factor for hypertension, lifestyle modification may not be enough to control it. Examples of these risk factors are advanced age, African-American heritage, and a family history of hypertension.

MALE/FEMALE DIFFERENCES

Though the incidence of hypertension is not necessarily sex-related, the circumstances under which it occurs may be different for women than for men. For example, some women do not experience high blood pressure except during pregnancy or while taking oral contraceptives.

CONGESTIVE HEART FAILURE

DEFINITION

Congestive failure is characterized by an inability of the heart to pump enough blood. The heart muscle is damaged and overworked.

CAUSE

Congestive heart failure may be caused by prolonged high blood pressure, damage from a heart attack, atherosclerosis, a congenital heart defect, a primary disease of the heart muscle (cardiomyopathy), or heart valve disease.

DIAGNOSIS

Early symptoms include difficulty in breathing, especially at night or when lying down, and easy fatigue. When the heart cannot pump enough blood, the body retains salt and water, and blood volume increases, resulting in a backup of fluid into the lungs and other tissues (thus the term congestive failure). Later in the course of heart failure, swelling of the feet and ankles may occur.

Most of the time, symptoms provide enough evidence for diagnosis of congestive heart failure. Diagnostic testing is aimed at determining the underlying cause.

TREATMENT

Lifestyle Changes. Early diagnosis and treatment are important to prevent further deterioration of the heart muscle. Treatment depends upon the cause of the problem and may include salt restriction, weight loss, and a program of exercise and rest.

Drugs. Drugs most commonly used to treat congestive failure are digitalis (cardiac glycosides), diuretics, and vasodilators. Antihypertensive medication may be prescribed to lower high blood pressure.

Surgical Treatments. If heart valve disease is the underlying cause, the patient may require surgery to repair or replace diseased heart valves.

In recent years, the increased availability and improved techniques have made heart transplantation a lifesaving "treatment of last resort" for a growing number of people with end-stage heart disease. Today the major problem is a continuing shortage of suitable donor hearts. Each year many thousands of eligible hearts are lost for transplantation because the prospective donors have not made suitable prior arrangements. Obviously, no one can foresee a fatal accident or some other tragedy. When such events occur, surviving family members often are reluctant to let the heart and other organs be removed for transplantation into other patients. But if a person makes his or her wishes known in advance and has signed an appropriate organ donor card (usually on a driver's license), then such decisions are easier to make should a tragedy occur.

HOME REMEDIES AND ALTERNATIVE THERAPIES

Depending on the underlying cause of congestive heart failure, alternative therapies such as modified exercise conditioning and relaxation techniques may be beneficial if carried out in conjunction with medical treatment. A word of caution, however: Herbal remedies promoted for heart failure should not be used without first consulting a doctor. Some herbs contain substances that can adversely interact with medications a doctor may prescribe. Others are highly toxic.

PREVENTION

Working to prevent the underlying causes, especially high blood pressure and atherosclerosis, may help prevent congestive heart failure. Refraining from smoking, eating a low-fat diet, getting regular exercise, and limiting salt and alcohol intake are important lifestyle modifications.

CARDIAC ARRHYTHMIAS

DEFINITION

Arrhythmias, or irregular heartbeats, are disturbances in the normal beating pattern of the heart. Normal cardiac rhythm results from electrical impulses that begin in the sinus node, the heart's natural pacemaker, and spread through the atria to the AV node. From there, the impulses travel through the His-Purkinje system of specialized fibers and send a powerful electrical jump-start signal to ventricular muscle.

Normally, the heart beats at a steady 60 to 80 beats per minute, although it may speed up to 200 or more beats during periods of intense exercise. Bradycardia is the term used to describe a rate of less than 60 beats per minute. Tachycardia is the term describing a heart rate of more than 100 beats per minute. These arrhythmias are classified by the part of the heart in which they arise. For example, ventricular tachycardias begin in the lower chambers of the heart, and supraventricular tachycardias start higher up, in the upper chambers or middle region.

Most cardiac arrhythmias are temporary and benign; some, however, may be life-threatening and require treatment. A very common chronic arrhythmia is atrial fibrillation, in which the atria beat 400 to 600 times per minute. The ventricles usually beat irregularly at a rate of

170 to 200 times per minute in response to this rhythm. Atrial fibrillation is seen in many types of heart disease; once established, it usually lasts a lifetime.

One of the most serious arrhythmias is sustained ventricular tachycardia, in which there are consecutive impulses that arise from the ventricles at a heart rate of 100 beats or more per minute until stopped by drug treatment or electrical conversion. This type of arrhythmia is dangerous because it may degenerate further into a totally disorganized electrical activity known as ventricular fibrillation, during which the heart's action is so disorganized that it quivers and does not contract, thus failing to pump blood. If the fibrillation is not stopped and normal rhythm restored within 2 or 3 minutes, death will result (see "Sudden Cardiac Death" later in this chapter for a more detailed discussion).

CAUSE

From time to time, everyone experiences a skipped heartbeat, palpitations, or other irregularities, most of which are not serious. The heart speed usually is dictated by the demands placed upon it; when a person is excited or exercising, the heart will beat faster to deliver more blood. In contrast, when we are resting or asleep, the heart slows down. This regulation is primarily accomplished in the autonomic nervous system. When the firing cells of the sinus node do not work properly or when the conduction cells fail to transmit the impulse at the correct rate, arrhythmias occur. A number of factors can disturb the heart's normal rhythm, causing it to beat too fast or too slowly. These include cigarette smoking, anxiety, excessive caffeine, and the use of certain drugs. Some cardiac abnormalities, such as congenital defects, coronary disease, or heart valve disorders, can result in arrhythmias, as can thyroid disease and some lung disorders.

DIAGNOSIS

An electrocardiogram (ECG) is the standard diagnostic tool for arrhythmias. The ECG shows any abnormalities in the atrial and ventricular electrical timing. Sometimes, however, the ECG of a patient with symptoms of an arrhythmia may not show any problem. In these cases, a 24-hour ambulatory ECG machine, a Holter monitor, may be used to record continuously, or the patient may wear an event monitor, which allows monitoring over the telephone.

In some cases, the physician may attempt to induce the arrhythmia, often with an exercise stress test. Another technique, called electrophysiologic testing, involves placing temporary electrode catheters through peripheral blood vessels into the heart and provoking arrhythmias to map the electrical impulses. It is important to find out where the arrhythmia originates to determine the proper treatment.

TREATMENT

Arrhythmias that cause troublesome symptoms or put the patient at risk for more serious complications should be treated with drugs or devices that either slow or speed up the heart rate. These include the following.

Drugs. There are a variety of drugs to treat arrhythmias, and in many cases this is the easiest course of treatment. However, significant side effects may occur, including a phenomenon called proarrhythmia, in which the arrhythmia being treated may actually become more frequent or new arrhythmias may occur. Some of the antiarrhythmia drugs available include:

- *Quinidine and procainamide.* These drugs, which are similar and may be used interchangeably, slow the heart rate by converting abnormal rhythms back to the normal sinus rhythm. They achieve this result by slowing the rate of conduction of electrical impulses and decreasing the excitability of heart muscle.
- *Digitalis.* Drugs derived from digitalis glycosides may be prescribed to decrease the ventricular rate in atrial fibrillation. This slowing of heart rate is achieved by working on the AV node, the structure that governs impulse traffic from the atria to the ventricles.
- *Beta-blocking drugs.* These drugs, commonly used to treat angina and high blood pressure, slow the sinus node firing rate and slow AV conduction. These drugs may be prescribed to treat a variety of supraventricular tachycardias, arrhythmias arising from areas above the ventricle, particularly the atria or the AV node.
- *Amiodarone.* This is a very toxic drug that can control ventricular tachycardia or fibrillation after all other drugs have failed.
- *Lidocaine.* This drug may be used to treat the ventricular arrhythmias that sometimes follow a heart attack or occur during surgery. It can only be given intravenously and is effective and safe when administered by this route.
- *Calcium-channel-blocking drugs.* These agents are used to treat coronary spasm and angina. Two of them, verapamil and diltiazem, also may be used to treat a variety of supraventricular tachycardias.
- *Atropine.* This drug increases heart rate by blocking some of the vagus nerve impulses to the heart. It is sometimes used to treat the bradycardia that may result from a heart attack or other conditions.

SURGICAL AND OTHER TREATMENTS

Pacemakers. Implantable electronic cardiac pacemakers also are used to regulate the heartbeat. These devices, which are implanted under the skin below the collarbone with tiny electrodes leading to the heart, are generally used to control bradycardia. They are tiny, with some as small as a silver dollar. One type of pacemaker, the synchronous model, takes over when the heart rate falls below a certain level. Newer pacemakers pace both the atria and ventricles and provide a reasonable simulation of normal heart rhythm. Modern pacemakers have long-lived batteries and can function for 8 to 12 years before they need changing.

Implantable Cardioverter Defibrillators. Electrical therapy is sometimes used in the treatment of tachycardias. An electric shock is delivered to the heart to restore normal rhythm. Implantable defibrillators accomplish this automatically. These devices consist of electrode patches, leads, or both, which zap the heart in response to the proper signal from another lead that senses the heart's rhythm. The shock is generated by a power pack that is slightly larger than a cigarette package. In some cases, open-heart surgery is required to implant the defibrillators, but newer techniques and devices that do not require direct attachment to the heart are making this a much simpler method of treatment.

Reactions to the device vary. Some people describe the shock as feeling like a hiccup; others liken it to a blow to the chest. Studies in high-risk patients have found that the devices reduce the expected mortality rate from a high of 50 percent down to 2 percent in the first 2 years after implantation of the device.

Ablative Techniques. Some types of serious cardiac arrhythmias can be cured by relatively simple procedures. There are conditions in which the arrhythmias are caused by an abnormal area of heart muscle. By mapping the heart's electrical activity it is possible to locate the abnormal tissue; cutting through it will interrupt the electrical pathway that is causing the arrhythmia, thus eliminating the problem. Until recently, this therapy was possible only through open heart surgery, but now it can be done as part of a catheter procedure under local anesthesia in a cardiac catheterization laboratory. An electrode catheter is inserted into a vein and threaded to the diseased area. Electrocautery removes or disables that section, thus preventing the arrhythmia.

Surgery. If, for some reason, the catheterization approach is not possible, surgery can accomplish the same goal. In the surgical approach, the diseased tissue is removed or destroyed by heating or cooling it. Even though this approach entails the risks of surgery, it may be preferable to lifelong drug therapy, especially in a young person with arrhythmias due to the Wolff-Parkinson-White syndrome, a short circuit between the upper and lower chambers that is sometimes responsible for sudden cardiac death in young people.

PREVENTION

There is no real way of preventing a serious arrhythmia. Sometimes, avoiding products like caffeine, cigarettes, alcohol, and decongestant medication, and avoiding emotional distress and anxiety, all of which may disturb heart rhythm, can help in lessening troublesome symptoms.

HOME REMEDIES AND ALTERNATIVE THERAPIES

By controlling certain nerve impulses, people can sometimes slow down their own heart rates and suppress supraventricular arrhythmias and premature ventricular contractions (PVCs). The following simple techniques may help achieve this result.

- Holding your breath
- Bathing your face in cold water
- Taking a slow drink of water
- Rubbing your neck
- Holding your nostrils closed and blowing out as you would to "pop" your eardrums
- Coughing

In addition, biofeedback training and relaxation techniques may help you cope with stress and anxiety that can exacerbate an arrhythmia.

SUDDEN CARDIAC DEATH

DEFINITION

Every minute, another American succumbs to sudden cardiac death, the abrupt loss of heart function. An age-old phenomenon, sudden cardiac death is often referred to as the major challenge confronting modern medicine. It remains the leading cause of death in industrial countries, striking all ages and social and economic groups.

CAUSE

Sudden cardiac death is the result of an unresuscitated cardiac arrest, which can be caused from almost any form of heart disease. In about 25 percent of all cases, there are no previous symptoms of heart disease. Because most victims of sudden death die outside a hospital, doctors have tended to consider it a complex problem over which they had no control. But in recent years, it has become increasingly clear that most cases of sudden cardiac death are not due to fatal coronary heart attacks, but instead the result of chaotic heart activity such as ventricular fibrillation, which is reversible if treated in time. This realization has led to renewed efforts to identify people who may be at risk of ventricular fibrillation, and to take appropriate preventive action.

DIAGNOSIS

One of the major problems lies in identifying the types of arrhythmias or other circumstances that are most likely to culminate in ventricular fibrillation. A number of studies have shed new light on possible risk factors for fatal arrhythmias. For example, certain patterns of premature ventricular contractions (PVCs) are a warning sign of increased risk of ventricular fibrillation. But PVCs alone do not appear to increase the risk of sudden death significantly in most patients; the situation changes, however, whenthey are accompanied by certain other factors. For example, if these complexes appear in recent heart attack patients or in people with serious coronary artery disease, the risk of sudden death increases. People who have been resuscitated from an episode of sudden cardiac death have a high risk of a repeat episode. People who have ventricular premature complexes during exercise testing or an attack of angina also are at higher risk of sudden death, as are those who have sustained ventricular tachycardia. Episodes of fainting and PVCs in patients with mitral valve disease are still other risk factors.

To date, most of the emphasis in identifying factors that may trigger sudden cardiac death have centered on the heart. A number of researchers propose, however, that there are other triggering mechanisms that should be considered. These include various neurological and psychological factors. The release of adrenal and other hormones can alter heart rhythm; the same is true of certain nervous system responses and interactions. Some re-

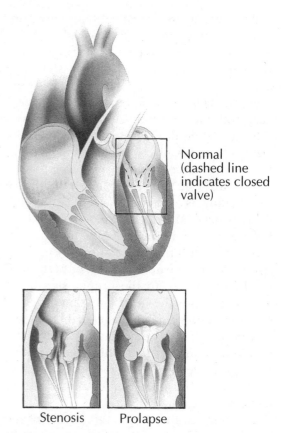

Normal (dashed line indicates closed valve)

Stenosis   Prolapse

Figure 16.6: Mitral valve disorders.

searchers have suggested that the lowered incidence in sudden cardiac death among heart attack patients who take beta-blocking drugs may be explained by the action of these drugs to block the sympathetic nervous system. Studies of laboratory animals indicate that psychological stress also can provoke cardiac arrhythmias. Further studies are needed to define more specifically the mechanisms and factors outside the heart that may provoke sudden death. But even though many questions remain to be answered, a growing number of physicians feel that many cases of sudden death can be prevented or delayed.

TREATMENT OF CONDITIONS LEADING TO SUDDEN CARDIAC DEATH

Implantable cardioverter defibrillators are proving life-saving for people at high risk of sudden death. When the heart goes into ventricular fibrillation, the device detects it and delivers an electrical shock to the heart muscle, which restores normal heart rhythm (see treatment under "Cardiac Arrhythmias")

HOME REMEDIES AND ALTERNATIVE THERAPIES

See alternative therapies under "Cardiac Arrhythmias."

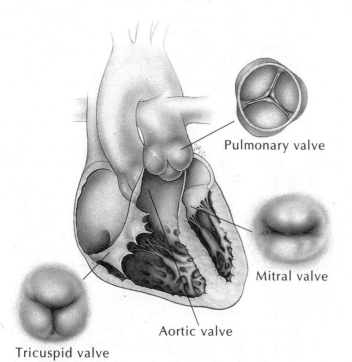

Pulmonary valve

Mitral valve

Aortic valve

Tricuspid valve

Figure 16.5: Normal heart valves.

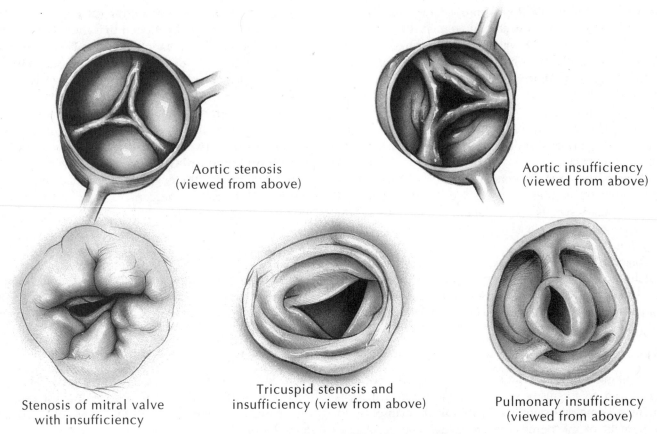

Aortic stenosis
(viewed from above)

Aortic insufficiency
(viewed from above)

Stenosis of mitral valve
with insufficiency

Tricuspid stenosis and
insufficiency (view from above)

Pulmonary insufficiency
(viewed from above)

Figure 16.7: Disorders of the heart valves.

PREVENTION

See prevention under "Cardiac Arrhythmias."

MALE/FEMALE DIFFERENCES

Sudden cardiac death is three to four times more common in men than women; it is the leading cause of death in men 20 to 64 years of age.

HEART VALVE DISEASE

DEFINITION

The heart's 4 valves help direct the flow of blood through its chambers (see figure 16.5). All of these valves are composed of thin leaflets that when closed prevent a backflow of blood and when open permit the blood to move forward to its next destination. When a valve fails to close properly, as is the case in a common disorder called mitral valve prolapse, there is a regurgitation or backflow of blood. A valve that fails to open properly—a condition called valvular stenosis—impairs the forward flow of blood to the body. In either case, the heart has to work harder to pump enough blood to the body, eventually leading to heart muscle damage. Congestive heart failure, syncope (fainting), and arrhythmias are common signs of valve disease.

CAUSE

A number of conditions can lead to heart valve disease. Congenital defects and infections, such as rheumatic fever, are among the most common. Rheumatic heart disease, although greatly diminished since the advent of antibiotics to treat streptococcal infections, still affects more than 1 million Americans and causes about 6,000 deaths per year.

DIAGNOSIS

In many cases, people can have a diseased heart valve for many years without suffering any symptoms or even being aware of the problem. Diseased valves can be detected by murmurs or other unusual sounds heard through a stethoscope. Ultrasound examination of the heart, also called echocardiography, in which sound waves are used to map internal structures, is also helpful. The most precise diagnosis is made by cardiac catheterization and angiocardiography.

Mitral Valve Prolapse. This condition, which is

also referred to as the floppy mitral valve syndrome, is very common, especially among women. In fact, many experts consider it a variation of normal function rather than a disease per se. Mitral valve prolapse is characterized by failure of a mitral valve leaflet to close properly (see figure 16.6). This makes a characteristic clicking sound that a doctor can usually hear. The floppy valve also may allow a backflow of some of the blood that normally should pass through the valve to the left ventricle.

Most of the time, the condition is benign and entirely asymptomatic. In other instances, it can cause a variety of rather vague symptoms, including palpitations, chest pain, easy fatigue, feelings of breathlessness, and perhaps fainting. In rare cases, the person may develop serious cardiac arrhythmias. Recurrences can be prevented by establishing the proper diagnosis—an echocardiogram can detect the abnormal valve—and administering beta-blockers or other medication to control the heart rhythm.

TREATMENT

Depending upon the type of valvular problem, patients often can go for many years without any special treatment. A common example is mitral valve prolapse. Up to 7 percent of the population has mitral valve prolapse, which for unknown reasons is most common in women, particularly those with scoliosis and certain other skeletal abnormalities. In most people, it is not medically serious.

Drugs. Drugs to treat heart valve disease do not provide a cure; they are used to relieve symptoms and prevent complications. For example, in mitral valve prolapse, a beta-blocking drug may be prescribed to treat worrisome symptoms such as palpitations and chest pain, even though the condition itself is not serious.

In other forms of valvular disease, digitalis or other drugs to slow the heartbeat and increase its output may be prescribed. A diuretic may be added to prevent retention of salt and water; a salt-restricted diet may be recommended for the same reason. Anticoagulant drugs may be prescribed to prevent blood clots and antiarrhythmic drugs may be used to maintain a normal heart rate and rhythm.

Since diseased heart valves are highly susceptible to a serious infection called bacterial endocarditis, it is important to take antibiotics before any dental or surgical procedure that may release bacteria into the bloodstream. Depending upon the severity of the disease, a doctor also may recommend avoiding strenuous activities and taking frequent rest periods during the day to minimize the workload on the heart.

Surgical Treatment. When the heart valves are seriously damaged and impairing blood flow to the rest of the body or causing heart muscle damage, surgery to replace the defective valve may be recommended. For example, in rare cases of mitral valve prolapse, the valve may become so weakened that there is excessive backflow of blood or a danger of the valve's rupturing, which can lead to death. In such unusual circumstances, replacement of the defective valve is necessary. A number of durable and highly efficient artificial valves have been developed from animal parts, plastic, and metal. There also are newer surgical techniques to reconstruct defective heart valves.

Balloon Valvuloplasty. To palliate valvular stenosis, a balloon-tipped catheter can be threaded through an artery until it reaches the center of the valve opening, where it is inflated.

HOME REMEDIES AND ALTERNATIVE THERAPIES

Some alternative therapies such as relaxation techniques may be helpful in living with symptoms of heart valve disease, but none exist to actually treat the disease itself.

PREVENTION

Swift and thorough treatment of streptococcal throat infections with antibiotics can prevent most cases of rheumatic fever, one of the leading causes of heart valve disease.

MALE/FEMALE DIFFERENCES

Mitral valve prolapse is much more common in women than in men; otherwise, there are no major differences in the more serious forms of valve disease.

CONGENITAL HEART DEFECTS

DEFINITION

The development of the fetal heart is a very complex process in which a large number of defects may occur. The human heart begins to develop from a single tube in about the 3rd week of pregnancy and starts beating at about the 4th week (even though a fetal heartbeat usually is not detected until the 10th to 12th weeks). The tube twists and divides in such a fashion as to form the 4 chambers, valves, and other parts.

Since the developing fetus gets its oxygen from the mother's blood, the fetal circulation bypasses the lungs via a short vessel linking the aorta and pulmonary artery called the ductus arteriosus. In the normal course of events, this ductus closes shortly after birth and the infant heart, lungs, and circulatory system begin functioning on their own (see figure 16.8). However, since the development of the heart is a complex process that can be adversely affected by many circumstances, it is understandable that defects occur with some frequency.

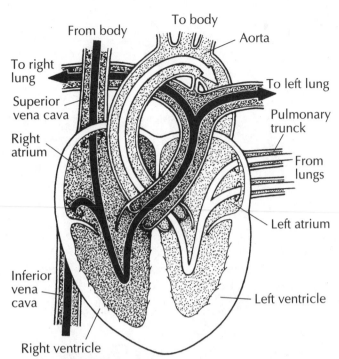

Figure 16.8: Normal blood flow through the heart. Blood from the venous system enters the heart's right atrium, passes into the right ventricle and is pumped to the lungs. Freshly oxygenated blood from the lungs enters the left atrium and passes into the left ventricle, which pumps it into the aorta to begin circulating through the body.

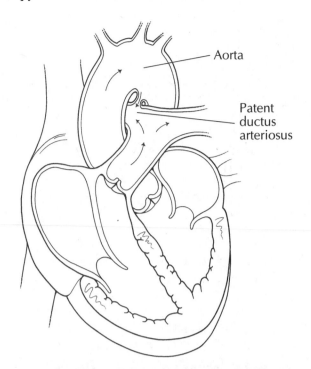

Figure 16.9: Patent ductus arteriosus. Duct between the aorta and the pulmonary artery in fetal heart fails to close after birth.

About 1 in every 120 babies is born each year with some sort of heart defect.

Most congenital heart defects involve either an obstruction to blood flow or an abnormal routing of blood through the heart chambers. A small number of babies are born with disturbances of the heart's normal rhythm; for example, there is a condition called congenital heart block, in which the electrical impulses responsible for normal contractions of heart muscle are blocked in the AV node, where the impulses pass from the atria to the ventricles.

Specific congenital heart defects include the following:

Right-to-Left Shunts (Cyanotic Heart Disease). Some malformations result in an abnormal shunting of blood from the right to the left side of the heart, or a right-to-left shunt. As a result, some of the unoxygenated (venous) blood will flow into the aorta instead of the pulmonary artery, and into the general circulation without first passing through the lungs. Infants with this condition are commonly referred to as "blue babies" because the unoxygenated blood gives a bluish tinge to the lips, skin, and nails.

Specific right-to-left shunts include tetralogy of Fallot, a malformation that has four distinct components:

- An opening between the right and left ventricles (ventricular septal defect).
- A narrowing of the pulmonary artery or valve (pulmonary stenosis).
- An enlargement of the right ventricle.
- A displacement of the aorta toward the right ventricle.

Normally, the aorta—the great blood vessel that arches from the top of the heart and forms the main trunk of the arterial system—receives oxygenated blood from the left ventricle. Another right-to-left shunt, called transposition of the great arteries, occurs when the aorta and pulmonary artery are transposed (e.g., arising from the wrong sides of the heart). Thus, the aorta receives venous blood returning from the body, and the pulmonary artery receives blood from the left ventricle. Transposition of the great arteries will be fatal in a relatively short time unless there is a mixing of oxygenated and venous blood. For example, the channels that are present in the fetal heart that permit blood to circulate without flowing to the lungs may remain open instead of closing, as normally happens shortly after birth.

Still another congenital abnormality resulting in cyanosis is a failure of one or both chambers on the left side of the heart to develop. This defect does not hinder the fetus, but after birth, when the heart and lungs must function on their own, abnormal left heart chambers may mean that the heart is unable to receive blood from

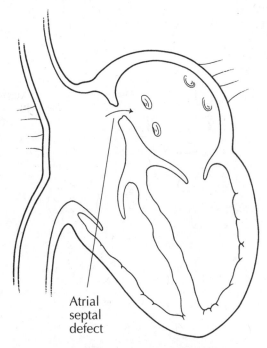

Figure 16.10: Atrial septal defect. An opening in the wall separating the left and right atria results in increased blood volume on the right side of heart, leading to enlargement of the right chamber and pulmonary artery.

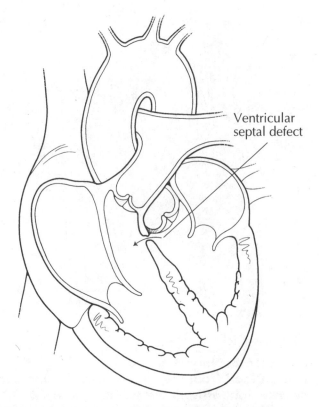

Figure 16.11: Ventricular septal defect. Opening between the right and left ventricles results in movement of some blood from the left to the right ventricle and then out the pulmonary artery.

the lungs and send it to the rest of the body. The outlook for babies born with these types of abnormalities is usually poor.

Left-to-Right Shunts. In a left-to-right shunt, some oxygenated blood will flow back into the right side of the heart through defects in the walls separating the atria and ventricles and/or the great arteries. The most common defects causing left-to-right shunting are:

• Patent ductus arteriosus, in which the duct between the aorta and pulmonary artery in the fetal heart fails to close shortly after birth (see figure 16.9).

• Atrial septal defect and ventricular septal defects, which are abnormalities in the walls separating the left and right heart chambers (see figures 16.10–16.11). Left-to-right shunts do not cause the blue baby syndrome, but as the lungs and vascular system become more developed, symptoms of heart failure may appear.

Valvular Stenosis. Congenital narrowing (stenosis) of one or more of the heart valves, resulting in an obstruction of blood flow. Most commonly, the problem is caused by a fusing of the valve leaflets, which prevents them from opening properly. In order to supply blood to the body, the heart muscle must pump harder than normal, leading to a thickened, overworked heart. This can lead to eventual heart failure.

Coarctation of the Aorta. A congenital deformity in

which the aorta is narrowed between the upper and lower body, leading to high blood pressure in the upper part of the body. This abnormality also causes the heart to overwork.

CAUSE

Disturbances in the mother's oxygen supply, infections, drugs, cigarette smoking, and nutritional deficiencies are among the many factors that can harm the fetal heart, especially if they occur during the first 3 months, when the heart is undergoing its basic formation. Genetics or heredity also may play a role in causing heart defects.

In about 97 percent of babies born with heart defects, the specific cause of the abnormality cannot be identified; in a small minority, the defect can be traced to specific causes, such as the mother's having rubella (German measles) during the first trimester of pregnancy, or chromosomal abnormalities, such as Down syndrome.

Some congenital heart abnormalities may be so mild that they are barely noticeable. Others may correct themselves in time. Still others are serious enough to be life-threatening or to interfere with normal growth and development.

DIAGNOSIS

Proper diagnosis is extremely important because virtually all of the severe congenital heart defects can now be treated surgically. Before an operation can be considered, however, an accurate diagnosis must be obtained. Sometimes a defect is not readily apparent and is recognized only when the baby fails to grow or develop normally or shows symptoms of heart failure. Unusual fatigue, difficulty in breathing, and blueness are signs of possible heart defects. Often a heart murmur can be heard through a stethoscope, but not all children with congenital heart defects have murmurs. Also, many heart murmurs are not significant.

Diagnostic procedures include a careful history taking and physical examination. Depending on individual circumstances, a number of diagnostic tests, such as chest x-rays, electrocardiogram, and echocardiography (a test that uses sound waves to map internal structures), may be required. If these tests are not conclusive, or if surgery is contemplated, cardiac catheterization and angiography are performed (see chapter 12, Diagnostic Tests and Procedures).

TREATMENT

Many congenital deformities can now be corrected surgically at an early age, greatly improving the child's chances of normal development. More than one procedure may be necessary, depending on the defect.

- For septal defects, sewing the defect shut or sewing a patch made of Dacron, Teflon, Gore-Tex, or the patient's own tissue over the hole.
- For stenotic valves, the valve can be widened, often using a balloon-tipped catheter.
- For narrowed vessels, the narrowed segment can be removed.
- For transposition of the great arteries, an arterial switch operation in which the aorta and pulmonary artery are reconnected at the proper locations.
- For patent ductus arteriosus, the defect can be closed by tying or clipping it.

CATHETER PROCEDURES

These procedures do not require open-heart surgery. They are performed under local anesthesia in a catheterization laboratory.

- For patent ductus arteriosus, a miniature umbrella-like device, covered with a Dacron mesh, is moved through the catheter and released at the site of the hole.
- For atrial septal defect, a clamshell-like double-

umbrella device can be implanted under local anesthesia.

HOME REMEDIES AND ALTERNATIVE THERAPIES

There are no alternative therapies for the defects per se, although some, such as exercise conditioning and physical therapy, may be employed in rehabilitation.

PREVENTION

Proper prenatal care, including refraining from smoking, drinking, drugs, and other substances that may harm a growing fetus, may help prevent some congenital heart defects, but there is no guarantee that even the most careful of prospective parents will not have a child with one of these physical problems. Genetic testing prior to conception may predict the possibility of some defects but is certainly not all-inclusive either. In any case, good prenatal care can only help produce a healthier baby, and for those who desire and can afford it, genetic counseling may provide useful information.

MALE/FEMALE DIFFERENCES

Overall, congenital heart defects are slightly more common in males than females, although the ratio varies considerably among specific defects.

STROKE

DEFINITION

Although strokes affect the brain and fall under the province of a neurologist, they are listed among the cardiovascular disorders because most are caused by a vascular problem. Many of the risk factors for a heart attack also apply to stroke.

In recent years, there has been a marked decline in stroke as high blood pressure control has improved; even so, stroke remains the third largest cause of death and the leading cause of serious disability in the United States. (For a detailed discussion of stroke and cerebral hemorrhage see chapter 26, Brain, Nerve, and Muscle Disorders.)

OTHER TYPES OF CARDIOVASCULAR DISEASE

Heart attacks and stroke are the most common of the life-threatening cardiovascular diseases, but there are a number of other conditions that should be considered in any review of this system. Some of these involve diseases aris-

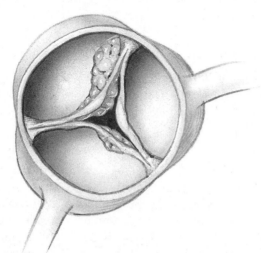

Figure 16.12: Bacterial endocarditis.

ing in other organ systems that affect the cardiovascular system. Examples include diabetes and other endocrine diseases, various blood disorders, chronic pulmonary diseases, kidney failure, certain rheumatoid diseases, syphilis, and some types of cancer. These are discussed in greater detail in the chapters dealing with the primary disorders. Covered in this section are cardiovascular disorders that may not occur as frequently as heart attacks, hypertension, or stroke but are still relatively common or serious enough that people should at least be aware of the warning signs.

INFECTIVE ENDOCARDITIS

DEFINITION

Endocarditis is one of several inflammatory conditions affecting the heart. As its name implies, endocarditis is an inflammation of the heart's inner lining, the endocardium.

CAUSE

In bacterial endocarditis, colonies of microorganisms form wartlike growths on the endocardium, usually the portion that lines the heart valves. These colonies, which also contain blood cells and other material such as fibrin (a protein instrumental in blood clotting), can eventually destroy the heart valves; the bacteria also may travel through the bloodstream to other parts of the body (see figure 16.12). In some cases, emboli may form, resulting in pulmonary embolism, heart attack, or stroke, depending upon where they finally lodge.

Endocarditis most often occurs in people who already have a damaged heart valve or congenital abnormalities of the heart. Artificial heart valves are also likely to become infected. In recent years, there also has been an increase in endocarditis among drug addicts who use contaminated needles and other items.

The most common causative bacterial agents are streptococcus or staphylococcus, but many other bacteria and certain fungi and rickettsiae (parasitic microorganisms that are neither viruses nor bacteria) also may cause endocarditis.

DIAGNOSIS

Possible warning signs include weakness, fatigue, a slight fever, aching joints, and tiny dotlike hemorrhaged areas on the back, chest, fingers, and toes. There is often a heart murmur indicating an abnormal valve or other heart defect. An eye exam may show small hemorrhages in the mucous membranes. In some cases, the disease comes on suddenly, with fever, chills, and rapid destruction of the involved heart valve. Blood tests and cultures should be performed to identify the invading microorganism. An echocardiogram is occasionally used to check heart valves for bacterial growth.

TREATMENT

If endocarditis is recognized and treated in its early stages, the recovery rate is good. Frequently, however, the disease smolders undetected until it has an opportunity to cause serious damage to one or more heart valves. Once the cause of the infection has been determined, aggressive treatment with the most effective antibiotics can begin. This usually requires hospitalization, at least at the onset. Antiobiotic therapy may continue for a month or more. If a heart valve has been seriously damaged, surgery to replace it with an artificial valve may be needed.

PREVENTION

Since the disease is most common in people who already have damaged heart valves, congenital heart defects, or artificial heart valves, it is particularly important that they follow the American Heart Association's guidelines for preventive antibiotic treatment, especially before and after any procedure that may permit bacteria to enter the bloodstream. This includes surgery and routine dental work, such as oral surgery or the cleaning of teeth and gums. Anyone who has had rheumatic fever or valvular disease, or has a congenital heart defect or an artificial heart valve, should be attuned to the warning signs of endocarditis and see a doctor promptly should they appear.

PERICARDITIS

DEFINITION

Pericarditis is an inflammation of the pericardium, the membrane forming the outer covering of the heart. The inflammation causes a thickening and roughening of

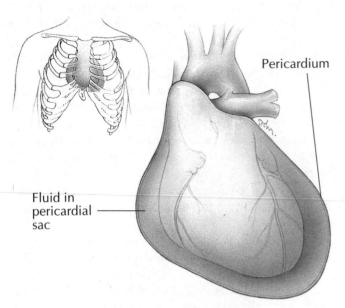

Pericardium

Fluid in pericardial sac

Figure 16.13: Pericarditis.

the membrane and an accumulation of fluid in the sac surrounding the heart (see figure 16.13).

CAUSE

Most pericarditis in this country is caused by a viral infection. The disease also may be caused by bacteria, fungi, or parasites. There is also a noninfectious pericarditis; causes include disease of the underlying heart muscle, injury, and other diseases, such as rheumatoid arthritis, lupus erythematosus, or kidney failure. Cancer radiation therapy to the chest also can cause pericarditis.

DIAGNOSIS

The most common symptom is pain under the breastbone, which may extend to the left side of the chest and to the left shoulder. The pain often becomes worse with a deep breath and is relieved when sitting or leaning forward. When the doctor listens to the heart and chest with a stethoscope, a grating sound can be heard, caused by a rubbing of the roughed pericardium surfaces with each heartbeat.

An electrocardiogram, chest x-ray, and echocardiogram may be performed to confirm the diagnosis. Additional tests, such as blood cultures, skin tests, or tests on the fluid in the sac surrounding the heart, may help determine the cause of pericarditis.

TREATMENT

Treatment includes antibiotic therapy directed at the invading microorganism. Analgesics and anti-inflammatory drugs may be prescribed to relieve pain and inflammation.

In cases caused by a virus, the disease is self-limiting, requiring no further treatment.

Early detection and treatment are important to prevent potentially serious complications. For example, untreated bacterial or chronic pericarditis may cause the pericardium to lose its elasticity, causing a constriction of the heart. If the heart is unable to function normally because of pericardial constriction, surgery to remove part of the pericardium may be required. Another potentially serious complication of pericarditis, especially that caused by a bacterial infection, injury, or tumor, is cardiac tamponade, which is caused by an accumulation of fluid in the pericardial sac, resulting in excessive pressure on the heart. If untreated, blood pressure will drop along with cardiac output. This is an emergency situation that is treated by puncturing the pericardial sac to remove the fluid.

PREVENTION

In many cases, pericarditis cannot be prevented. However, complete and timely treatment of any condition affecting the heart's lining may help.

MYOCARDITIS

DEFINITION

Myocarditis is an inflammation of the heart muscle, usually as a result of other generalized infection or inflammatory disease.

CAUSE

Most cases, especially those in young people, are caused by viruses, such as the coxsackievirus, type B. Other causes include bacteria, rickettsiae, parasites, an adverse drug reaction, arsenic or other toxic substances, or other diseases.

DIAGNOSIS

Myocarditis may start with flulike symptoms over a month or two. The most common additional symptoms are disturbances in heart rhythm. If there is generalized weakening of the heart muscle, there also may be symptoms of heart failure. Myocarditis should be suspected if these symptoms appear during a widespread viral infection, especially if there is no previous history of heart disease. Unfortunately, some cases of myocarditis are diagnosed only after they have advanced to produce heart failure. A physical exam and chest x-ray and echocardiogram then show an enlarged heart and chest congestion. An electrocardiogram may indicate the damage to the heart's function.

TREATMENT

Most cases of myocarditis are self-limiting, and the heart symptoms will clear up as the overriding infection subsides. In some cases, drugs may be prescribed to treat specific cardiac symptoms, such as arrhythmias or heart failure. Rest to reduce the heart's workload is important, as is avoiding alcohol and other substances that may be toxic or irritating to the heart.

PREVENTION

It is almost impossible to consciously avoid myocarditis. Proper hygiene may help you avoid the infectious agents that sometimes manifest in this way.

HEART MUSCLE DISEASE (CARDIOMYOPATHY)

DEFINITION

There are two major categories of cardiomyopathy: primary cardiomyopathy, defined as changes in the structure or function of the heart muscle that cannot be attributed to a specific cause, and secondary, which is associated with disorders of the heart or other organs. Congestive cardiomyopathy is the most common primary form of heart muscle disease. Other types include hypertrophic and restrictive. Heart muscle disease related to coronary artery disease is called ischemic cardiomyopathy.

Cardiomyopathy is relatively uncommon; about 500,000 new cases develop each year in the United States. Instead of afflicting the elderly like most other heart disease, heart muscle disease commonly strikes young people. This group of disorders directly damages the muscle that lines the walls of the heart, impairing its ability to pump blood to other parts of the body.

CAUSE

The causes of primary cardiomyopathy are usually unknown. Some possible causes in congestive cases are infectious or noninfectious heart muscle inflammation, excessive alcohol consumption, nutritional deficiencies, complications of childbirth, and genetic disorders. Hypertrophic cardiomyopathy appears to be an inherited disease. Restrictive cardiomyopathy is usually caused by a disease called amyloidosis, which is associated with cancers of the blood.

DIAGNOSIS

In congestive cardiomyopathy, the heart becomes enlarged and weakened and is unable to pump effectively. Symptoms of heart failure develop. Blood flows more slowly through the heart, causing clots to form on the endocardium (mural thrombi); these may lead to pulmonary embolism, stroke, heart attack, or other circulatory blockages.

Hypertrophic cardiomyopathy, in contrast to the congestive type, involves an enlargement or overgrowth of the heart muscle, usually that of the left ventricle, but sometimes the right chamber is also involved. In one form of hypertrophic disease, the septum—the wall between the two ventricles—becomes enlarged and obstructs the flow of blood from the left ventricle into the aorta. The mitral valve also may be distorted by the thickened septum, leading to mitral insufficiency. The major symptoms are shortness of breath, dizziness or fainting, chest pain, and cardiac arrhythmias.

The condition usually can be diagnosed by characteristic physical findings, electrocardiogram, echocardiogram, and, if doubt still exists, cardiac catheterization and radionuclide angiography. A biopsy of the heart wall tissue may help distinguish between the different types of cardiomyopathy.

TREATMENT

Lifestyle Changes. Patients with cardiomyopathy should avoid cigarette smoking, excessive alcohol intake, excessive salt consumption, and drugs that may have a toxic effect on the heart. Maintaining normal weight and blood pressure are important because this reduces the heart's workload. In some cases of hypertrophic cardiomyopathy, stressful physical activity should be limited.

Drugs. In cases of congestive, restrictive, and ischemic cardiomyopathy, treatment focuses on relieving symptoms and improving function. Drugs include digitalis and digoxin, diuretics, steroids (to relieve inflammation), and ACE inhibitors. For hypertrophic cardiomyopathy, drugs include beta-blockers and calcium-channel blockers.

Surgical Treatment. If drug treatment is inadequate, surgery may be indicated for hypertrophic cardiomyopathy. Sometimes, this involves removal of excess muscle tissue. Selected cases of congestive cardiomyopathy with end-stage heart failure can be treated effectively with heart transplantation.

HOME REMEDIES AND ALTERNATIVE THERAPIES

There are no alternative treatments except for those relaxation techniques that may help in the control of high blood pressure.

PREVENTION

Avoiding smoking and excessive alcohol intake, and ensuring proper nutrition are the only preventive measures. Most cases of cardiomyopathy cannot be prevented.

MALE/FEMALE DIFFERENCES

Men seem to be affected by congestive cardiomyopathy more often.

···

PERIPHERAL BLOOD VESSEL DISEASES

There are two major categories of blood vessel diseases: peripheral arterial diseases, which are disorders of the vessels carrying blood from the heart to all parts of the body, and peripheral venous diseases, which are disorders of the vessels carrying deoxygenated blood back to the heart.

PERIPHERAL ARTERIAL DISEASES; ARTERIOSCLEROSIS OBLITERANS

DEFINITION

Arterial disease may result from obstruction, which impedes the flow of blood; from disorders of the arterial muscles, causing them to either constrict or dilate; or from aneurysms, weakened vessel segments that fill with blood and balloon outward. As discussed earlier, the formation of atherosclerotic, or fatty, deposits along the inner arterial walls is the most common arterial disease. When the coronary arteries become seriously obstructed by these deposits, a heart attack or symptoms of coronary disease are an all too common result; when arteries supplying blood to the brain are blocked, a stroke may

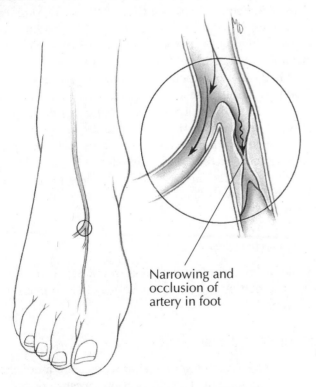

Narrowing and occlusion of artery in foot

Figure 16.14: Arteriosclerosis obliterans.

ensue. Similarly, arteries supplying other parts of the body also may become partially or fully obstructed, leading to a condition referred to as chronic occlusive arterial disease.

When the lower limbs are affected by occlusive arterial disease, the disorder is referred to as arteriosclerosis obliterans (see figure 16.14).

CAUSE

Fatty deposits cause the blockage of the arteries. The typical patient is a man over the age of 50 who smokes, has high blood cholesterol, and who may also have diabetes or high blood sugar. There are, of course, exceptions; people with a family history of early arteriosclerosis and people with diabetes, hypertension, or very high blood lipids may develop arteriosclerosis obliterans at an earlier age.

DIAGNOSIS

In the early stages of arteriosclerosis obliterans, the major arteries carrying blood to the legs and feet become progressively narrowed by fatty deposits. Smaller collateral blood vessels that branch off the major arteries increasingly take over supplying blood to the limb. But these collateral vessels are often inadequate to meet extra demands, such as walking for more than a short distance. Thus, one of the early symptoms of arteriosclerosis obliterans is cramplike pains, aching, or muscle fatigue in the calves that occur during exercise. These symptoms are referred to as intermittent claudication.

The site of the pain is determined by which arteries are occluded. Blockage of the lower abdominal aorta or iliac arteries may cause pain in the hips, thighs, and calves. If the femoral artery is involved, the symptoms are likely to be in the calf; blockages in the popliteal, anterior, or posterior tibial arteries will produce symptoms in the lower leg and foot. As the disease progresses, discomfort may occur even when resting. This disease may also cause a decrease in hair on the extremities.

Eventually, the skin that is chronically deprived of sufficient oxygen and nutrients will begin to break down, resulting in superficial ulcers. These ischemic ulcers are usually small in the beginning and are generally located on the foot, toes, or heel. In severe cases, gangrene may develop, resulting in amputation of the affected part.

Arteriosclerosis obliterans can be diagnosed by feeling the pulses and studying the pattern of circulation to the lower limbs. Pulse volume recordings (PVRs) using Doppler ultrasound measure blood pressure in the legs and feet. Blood pressure cuffs are placed on different parts of the leg and foot to monitor pressures during each cardiac cycle. The sites of occlusion can be located precisely by using ultrasound, contrast arteriography, or magnetic resonance angiography (MRA). (See chapter 12, Diagnostic Tests and Procedures.)

TREATMENT

Drugs. Vasodilating drugs that widen the blood vessels and anticlotting drugs such as aspirin may be prescribed but are usually of little benefit in peripheral vascular disease. A drug called pentoxifylline may help relieve the pain of claudication.

Other Treatment. If the arterial disease is related to other conditions, such as diabetes or high blood pressure, treatment will obviously include controlling these other underlying conditions. (See chapter 21, Diabetes and Other Endocrine Disorders, for a more detailed discussion of the circulatory disorders accompanying this disease.)

Surgical and Other Invasive Treatment. If medical measures are not sufficient, surgery or balloon angioplasty may be advised. There are 2 major types of operations: revascularization, in which the blocked arteries are bypassed with either healthy blood vessels taken from elsewhere in the body (usually a vein in the leg) or synthetic material; or endartectomy, which involves opening portions of the diseased artery and removing the atherosclerotic deposits.

Balloon angioplasty, in which a catheter with a balloon tip is inserted into an artery and inflated to compress the fatty deposits (see figure 16.15), is most successful for people with small segments of blockage. However, the area becomes quickly reclogged in about

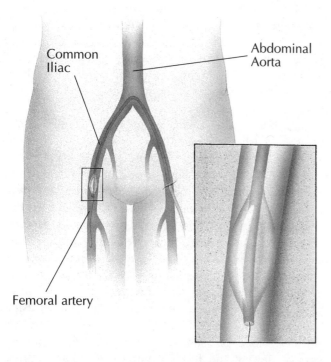

Figure 16.15: Balloon angioplasty. Circulation to the legs and feet may be restored by using a balloon-tipped catheter to flatten fatty plaque and widen the artery's channel.

Common Iliac

Abdominal Aorta

Femoral artery

30 percent of all cases, requiring repeated treatment within a year or two.

Still another technique, laser ablation, which is being used experimentally in major medical centers, entails using a laser instead of a balloon to open the blocked blood vessel. The procedure is similar to balloon angioplasty; the laser catheter has a metal or fiber-optic probe at its tip. The heated probe then ablates, or removes, the fatty deposits layer by layer. Laser surgery has several advantages over conventional surgery: It is faster, entails a shorter hospital stay, and does not require inserting a bypass graft.

HOME REMEDIES AND ALTERNATIVE THERAPIES

If the patient smokes, stopping completely is an essential first step, since smoking not only hinders the delivery of oxygen but also impairs development of collateral circulation. Proper weight control is also very important.

Exercise is an integral part of the overall treatment program. Patients often are instructed to walk or use an exercise bicycle for 30 minutes 2 or 3 times per day, resting if pain or discomfort occurs. Studies have found that following a graduated walking program can improve collateral circulation and improve symptoms in some patients.

Foot care is particularly important for patients with circulatory problems. Wearing comfortable, properly fitted shoes and socks and protecting the feet from injury or infection are crucial. This means inspecting the feet carefully at least once a day and getting prompt medical attention for any problems such as corns, calluses, injuries, or signs of infection. These are trivial, self-healing problems in people with a healthy circulation, but for patients with impaired blood flow to the lower limbs, they can become major infections that threaten the loss of a foot.

Otherwise, arteriosclerosis obliterans is a serious condition requiring close monitoring by a physician or other health care provider. Loss of limb can occur if the condition goes untreated. However, because it is caused by the same factors that result in coronary heart disease, the same alternative therapies—high-dose niacin, vitamin E, and relaxation techniques—may provide some benefit in conjunction with lifestyle modifications and medical treatment.

PREVENTION

Avoiding high-cholesterol diets, refraining from smoking, and getting regular exercise may help prevent this disorder.

MALE/FEMALE DIFFERENCES

As with most atherosclerotic disease, men are more likely to be affected than women, possibly because of protection provided by female hormones such as estrogen.

BUERGER'S DISEASE

DEFINITION

Buerger's disease, or thromboangiitis obliterans, is characterized by an inflammatory response in the arteries, veins, and nerves, which leads to a thickening of the blood vessel walls caused by infiltration of white cells.

CAUSE

The cause of Buerger's disease is unknown, but since it occurs mostly in young men who smoke, it is thought to be a reaction to something in cigarettes or the result of a genetic or autoimmune disorder.

DIAGNOSIS

The first symptoms are usually a bluish cast to a toe or finger and a feeling of coldness in the affected limb. Since the nerves are also inflamed, there may be severe pain and constriction of the small blood vessels controlled by them. Overactive sympathetic nerves also may cause the feet to sweat excessively, even though they feel cold. As the blood vessels become blocked, intermittent claudication and other symptoms similar to those of chronic obstructive arterial disease often appear. Ischemic ulcers and gangrene are common complications of progressive Buerger's disease.

TREATMENT

The most important treatment is to stop smoking; if this is done early in the disease before serious blood vessel or nerve damage has occurred, the symptoms usually improve markedly. If pain and circulatory problems persist, an operation to sever the sympathetic nerves that cause the small blood vessels to constrict may be performed.

HOME REMEDIES AND ALTERNATIVE THERAPIES

Recent studies at the Rusk Institute of Rehabilitation Medicine indicate that acupuncture may help increase blood flow in both Buerger's disease and Raynaud's phenomenon. Otherwise, no alternative therapy really treats the disease.

PREVENTION

Since the disease is almost entirely related to cigarette smoking, refraining from this habit is a most effective preventive measure.

MALE/FEMALE DIFFERENCES

The disease is most common in men between 20 and 40 who smoke cigarettes. Women account for only about 5 percent of all cases.

RAYNAUD'S PHENOMENON

DEFINITION

Raynaud's phenomenon is characterized by spasms of the arteries in the fingers and toes, causing a lack of blood flow to the affected parts.

There are 2 classifications of this disorder: primary, in which there is no evidence of other underlying disease; and secondary, in which the condition is complicated by other disorders, such as lupus erythematosus, rheumatoid arthritis, or scleroderma (hardening of the skin). Sometimes Raynaud's may accompany Buerger's disease. If no other primary cause is determined, the disorder is called Raynaud's disease.

CAUSE

Excessive constriction of the vessels serving the fingers and toes causes spasms, which are usually triggered by cold, smoking cigarettes, or, less frequently, emotional factors. Raynaud's phenomenon may be an indication of an underlying disease.

It also may be job-related; for example, it sometimes occurs in people who work with vibrating machinery, pianists or typists, or people whose circulation is impaired by excessive exposure to a cold, damp environment.

DIAGNOSIS

The symptoms include coldness, blueness, a tingling sensation, numbness, and sometimes pain in the digits. Corresponding fingers on both hands are usually affected. Physicians usually make this diagnosis upon physical examination and medical history, but further tests may be necessary to check for underlying causes.

TREATMENT OF RAYNAUD'S PHENOMENON

Drugs. Primary Raynaud's may be uncomfortable or annoying, but rarely leads to serious problems such as chronic ulcers or gangrene. Many people with Raynaud's phenomenon get some relief by using a calcium-channel blocker such as nifedipine. Another medication called phenoxybenzamine may also help by limiting the constricting effects of adrenaline on the blood vessels. Research continues on drugs that interfere in the biochemical process that leads to blood vessel constriction.

Treatment of Raynaud's that is related to other diseases or environmental conditions is managed by controlling the underlying cause.

HOME REMEDIES AND ALTERNATIVE THERAPIES

Avoiding cold and wearing thick gloves and socks are often all that is needed to control it. The problem is confined to the fingers and toes and, in most cases, can be relieved by rubbing or warming them. In some cases, the circulation may be impaired enough to cause sores or ulcers to form; in a small minority, these may progress to gangrene and amputation.

Biofeedback is sometimes effective in controlling the symptoms of Raynaud's phenomenon. During biofeedback, you learn to elicit the relaxation response and control the specific physiologic factor such as heart rate or skin temperature that produces the stress-related symptoms. Acupuncture may increase blood flow to the limbs affected by Raynaud's.

PREVENTION

Avoiding cold and refraining from smoking are the most important preventive measures.

MALE/FEMALE DIFFERENCES

Raynaud's phenomenon is more common in women, who account for 60 to 90 percent of all cases.

ANEURYSMS

DEFINITION

An aneurysm is a weakened segment of the heart or a blood vessel—usually an artery—that fills with blood, causing it to balloon outward.

CAUSE

Aneurysms may be caused by a congenital weakness in the vessel wall, high blood pressure, arteriosclerosis, injuries, infection, and other diseases.

DIAGNOSIS

Symptoms will depend upon the location of the aneurysm. Common sites include the abdominal aortic artery, the intracranial arteries supplying blood to the brain, and the aorta supplying blood to the chest area. Many aneurysms cause no symptoms and are discovered when a physician palpates the area or on x-ray films or imaging scans done for some other reason. When symptoms occur, they include a pulsating sensation; there may be pain if the bulge is pressing on internal organs. If the aneurysm is in the chest area, for example, there may be pain in the upper back, difficulty in swallowing, coughing, or hoarseness.

A ruptured aneurysm usually produces sudden, severe pain, and, depending upon the location and amount of bleeding, shock, loss of consciousness, and death. In some cases, the aneurysm may leak blood, causing pain without the rapid deterioration characteristic of a rupture. Also, clots often form in the aneurysm, creating a danger of embolisms in distant organs.

In some cases, the aneurysm may dissect into the wall of an artery, blocking some of its branches. Dissecting aneurysms usually occur in the aortic arch, near its origin as it leaves the heart, or start in the descending thoracic portion of the aorta after it gives off the branches

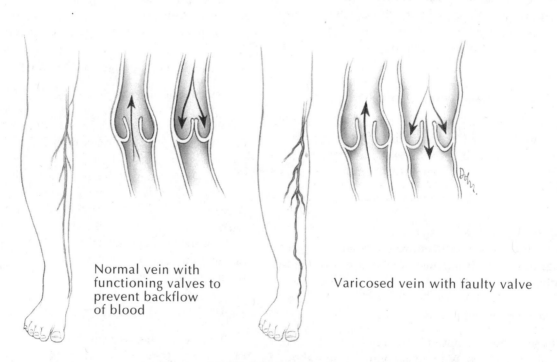

Normal vein with functioning valves to prevent backflow of blood

Varicosed vein with faulty valve

Figure 16.16: Varicose veins.

to the head and arms. Symptoms, which are usually sudden and severe, vary according to the part of the body that is being deprived of blood.

If your physician suspects an aneurysm, he or she will probably recommend an ultrasound test of the area to delineate the size and predict whether it is likely to rupture.

TREATMENT

If an aneurysm is large and the risk of rupture is significant, surgery may be necessary. During surgery, the aorta is clamped to restrict blood flow and the ballooned area is strengthened with a woven Dacron patch or graft. The surgery carries serious risks because the aortic clamping causes stress to the heart. Therefore, periodic ultrasound examinations to monitor the size may be the only course of action for smaller aneurysms.

When an aneurysm ruptures, emergency surgery is necessary to stop the bleeding. Emergency medical treatment of dissecting aneurysms is often quite successful and consists of instantly lowering the blood pressure and keeping it low.

ALTERNATIVE THERAPIES

Because high blood pressure may cause further weakening of the area, any measures that help control blood pressure, such as relaxation techniques, may be helpful if carried out in conjunction with conventional medical therapy. These techniques may also help address the anxiety of aneurysm patients who fear rupture.

PREVENTION

Preventive measures include those of coronary heart disease and high blood pressure—proper weight control, regular exercise, a low-cholesterol diet, stopping smoking, etc. However, many aneurysms are a result of congenital weaknesses, which are completely unavoidable.

....

PERIPHERAL VENOUS DISORDERS

The venous system, which returns the oxygen-depleted blood to the heart via a network of increasingly larger blood vessels, often must work against gravity, especially in returning blood from the lower part of the body. Coordinated muscular contractions and, in medium-size veins, a system of one-way valves help keep the blood flowing in the right direction. But these vessels are not aided by the pumping action of the heart or the elastic tension that enables the arteries to function. Thus, many of the disorders arising in the venous system are related to a breakdown in their ability to maintain blood flow.

VARICOSE VEINS

DEFINITION

Varicose veins are a very common, usually benign, condition that affects one or more of the large veins in the legs. The veins become distended, either because of an inherent weakness in the walls or a malfunction of some of the one-way valves, permitting a backflow and pooling of blood (see figure 16.16).

CAUSE

The reasons varicose veins occur are poorly understood. Obesity, pregnancy, constriction of the veins with garters or tight clothing, and an inherited tendency are among the contributing causes of varicose veins. Contrary to popular belief, sedentary jobs or jobs that involve standing do not, in themselves, seem to cause varicose veins, although they may aggravate a preexisting varicosity.

DIAGNOSIS

The condition produces bulging and discolored veins in the legs, but usually there are few if any symptoms. Sometimes pain or a tingling sensation occurs. The diagnosis is made simply by identification during physical examination.

TREATMENT

Most varicose veins do not require medical treatment. In some cases, however, the circulation may be hindered enough to cause swelling of the foot and ankle, discomfort, or a feeling of heaviness. Itching and scaling may develop in the skin in the affected area; if untreated, this may eventually develop into a skin ulcer.

In such cases, treatment may involve surgical removal. Even when there are no symptoms, some people may be bothered by the cosmetic appearance of the affected veins and want them removed. Pain and development of chronic ulcers also may be an indication for removal. As an alternative to surgery, varicosities may be injected with an irritating (sclerosing) agent and wrapped firmly for a few days. The resulting scarring and blockage of the vein forces surrounding veins to create alternative routes for the blood flow.

HOME REMEDIES AND ALTERNATIVE THERAPIES

For most people with varicose veins, wearing specially fitted elastic stockings is all that is needed. The stockings should be carefully fitted to the individual, providing the most pressure in the lowest part of the leg. The stockings should be put on when first arising in the morning, preferably before getting out of bed. Exercise such as walking or cycling also helps promote better circulation from the lower part of the body. Resting with the legs elevated will help promote circulation; in contrast, sitting with the legs crossed can aggravate the condition.

In conjunction with lifestyle modification, the best alternative to medical treatment, especially if the varicose veins cause nothing more than cosmetic changes, is to concentrate on your attractive attributes and avoid dwelling on these relatively minor blemishes.

PREVENTION

Promoting good circulation may help prevent varicose veins. Exercise and proper weight control, as well as avoiding tight garters and other upper leg–constricting garments, help maintain proper blood flow.

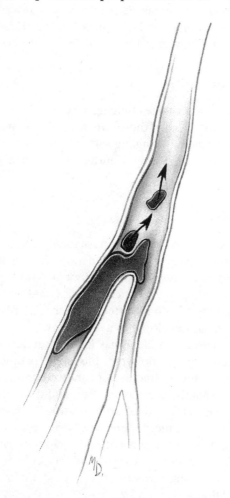

Figure 16.17: Thrombophlebitis. Inflamed vein occluded by a clot (thrombus), with parts of the thrombus breaking off and entering the venous blood flow. This can lead to a life-threatening pulmonary embolism if clots lodge in the lungs.

MALE/FEMALE DIFFERENCES

Women may get varicose veins for the first time during pregnancy; the fetus may place pressure on the abdominal veins, thus forcing blood to pool in the leg veins.

PHLEBITIS

DEFINITION

Phlebitis is a general term used to describe inflammation of a vein. Very often, the inflammation is accompanied by formation of a clot (thrombus), which occludes blood flow through the vein. This condition is known as thrombophlebitis or venous thrombosis (see figure 16.17). There are two general types of thrombophlebitis: a superficial condition that is painful but not life-threatening; and deep thrombophlebitis, a potentially serious condition involving an interior blood vessel. About 300,000 Americans are hospitalized each year because of deep thrombophlebitis, the major danger being that a portion of the clot will break away and travel through the venous system to the lungs, forming a pulmonary embolism. If one of the large pulmonary vessels is blocked, death may result.

CAUSE

Phlebitis is usually caused by an infection or injury. Superficial phlebitis is most likely to develop in people with varicose veins, patients who are bedridden, or in pregnant women.

DIAGNOSIS

There may be obvious swelling and a red streak along the involved vein; there also may be heaviness and pain in the leg. The discomfort is usually eased when the leg is elevated and worsened when it is lowered.

Deep thrombophlebitis is more likely to cause pain, tenderness, and swelling of the entire limb. Unfortunately, deep thrombophlebitis may occur without producing symptoms until a pulmonary embolism signals its presence.

If your doctor suspects deep thrombophlebitis, he or she may recommend a Doppler ultrasound test to determine if a clot exists and to confirm its location.

TREATMENT

Deep thrombophlebitis is usually treated with anticoagulant drugs to reduce the formation of clots and to permit the clots that already have formed to dissolve. Bed rest with the leg elevated may be necessary. Anticoagulant drugs may be prescribed for up to several months to prevent recurrence. If these drugs are used for long-term treatment, patients are cautioned not to take any other medication, especially aspirin, that may interact with them. People on anticoagulants should have periodic blood tests and also should be alert for any signs of abnormal bleeding, such as bloody or tarry stools, blood in the urine, or excessive bleeding of the gums or small cuts.

HOME REMEDIES AND ALTERNATIVE THERAPIES

A doctor must be consulted if phlebitis is suspected. Superficial thrombophlebitis is generally treated at home with periods of rest with the leg elevated, analgesics such as aspirin (which should not be taken for deep thrombophlebitis, figure 16.17) or some other nonsteroidal anti-inflammatory drugs such as indomethacin, and, if needed, antibiotics. Warm compresses may ease the inflammation, and elastic stockings or bandages may be recommended to reduce the swelling. Itching may be relieved with a nonprescription ointment containing zinc oxide.

PREVENTION

People susceptible to phlebitis (or any other circulatory or cardiovascular problem) should not smoke since this promotes clot formation. Moderate physical activity is recommended to maintain muscle tone and promote circulation.

MALE/FEMALE DIFFERENCES

Phlebitis is not sex-related, but superficial phlebitis often occurs in women during pregnancy.

OUTLOOK FOR THE FUTURE

New treatments are constantly being developed that hold great promise for people with heart disease. Artificial hearts, heart and heart-lung transplants, implantable defibrillators, coronary thrombolysis, and new operative procedures, including the use of laser surgery to unclog occluded arteries, are but a few of the advances that are either already being used or are under development. The real hope, however, lies in learning more about the underlying causes of heart disease and then taking the necessary preventive steps.

As stressed earlier, a number of lifestyle factors have been identified that appear to increase the risk of a heart attack. Adopting a prudent lifestyle that avoids or minimizes these risk factors has long been advocated by physicians, the American Heart Association, and others.

Changing the way one lives is not easy, but many people have made major modifications in their diet, exercise, and smoking in recent years. There has also been a marked improvement in detection and treatment of hypertension. There is little doubt that these positive changes have contributed to the halving of premature cardiovascular mortality that has occurred over the past two decades. Science may eventually give us more cures for the many forms of heart disease; in the meantime, there is considerably more that each one of us can do to help minimize the risk of a heart attack or other cardiovascular disease.

SUMMING UP

Cardiovascular disease remains our leading cause of death and sickness in this country. A number of risk factors have been identified that appear to increase the likelihood of heart attacks, strokes, and other cardiovascular diseases; there is increasing evidence that reducing as many of these risk factors as possible also lowers the risk of disease and premature death. Many of these are related to lifestyle: not smoking, maintaining ideal weight, engaging in regular physical exercise, consuming a diet low in saturated fats, cholesterol, and total calories, and controlling stress. Others involve controlling other diseases, such as diabetes or high blood pressure, which contribute to additional cardiovascular disorders. Some, such as advanced age or male sex, are beyond our control but serve as warning signs to pay attention to minimizing the controllable risk factors. Prompt diagnosis and treatment are vital elements in combating cardiovascular disease; the earlier the treatment, the greater the chances of preventing a life-threatening event such as a heart attack or stroke. And early treatment of heart attacks and strokes often can minimize their damage.

In this chapter, we have summarized the major types of cardiovascular disorders. For additional information on cardiovascular complications related to other diseases, such as diabetes, refer to those specific chapters.

17
Cancer

• • • • • • • • • • • • • •

KAREN H. ANTMAN, M.D. AND ROBERT TAUB, M.D.

Cancer is a major public health problem. More than 1.6 million Americans develop cancer each year. The outlook for Americans with cancer has improved steadily since the beginning of the 20th century, when few cancer victims survived for very long. By the 1930s, only one out of five cancer patients survived 5 or more years after treatment and were considered "cured." Since then, the cure rate has climbed in almost every decade: During the 1940s, the 5-year survival improved to one out of four; in the 1960s, it was one out of three; and in the 1970s, 38 percent of cancer patients were cured. Today 51 percent of cancer patients survive for 5 years or more, and the American Cancer Society estimates that an additional 25 percent to 30 percent of cancer deaths could be prevented with earlier diagnosis and treatment.

Yet, despite gains in treating many cancers and improved survival rates, cancer deaths continue to mount. While 143 people per 100,000 died of cancer in 1930, today the figure is nearly 180 per 100,000. Much of this increase is due to increased life expectancy (cancer incidence increases with age) and to marked increases in lung cancer.

Cancer is the second leading cause of death after heart disease in the United States, but it is the major cause of death in women between the ages of 35 and 74. In children under the age of 15, cancer trails only accidents as the leading cause of death. If current trends continue, cancer is expected to be the leading cause of death in the United States by the year 2010. As Americans cut their heart disease rate with healthier cardiovascular lifestyles, more people will survive to suffer and die of cancer.

Many cancer myths persist, exaggerating its worst aspects. Although cancer is reputed to be a hopeless condition, nearly half of all cancer patients can expect to be alive and free of any sign of the disease in 5 years, a much better outlook than that facing most heart attack patients.

Intense anxiety and dread cause some cancer patients to delay seeking a diagnosis until the disease reaches an advanced, less treatable stage. And while cancer treatment is feared for its supposed pain and risk of spreading the disease, recent advances in surgical, radiologic, and chemotherapeutic therapies, and concurrent improvements in medicines to prevent nausea and pain (supportive care), have greatly lessened the uncomfortable side effects of cancer treatment.

Basic and applied research into the causes and cures for cancer continues, including investiga-tions designed to dramatically change screening, diagnosis, and treatment. Two of the most promising areas include the study of cancer on the molecular level and the role of genetics in the development of cancer.

Although cancer therapy is often rigorous, debilitating, and uncomfortable, many people successfully undergo treatment with a minimal disruption of their normal lives. While others are quite ill during the intensive treatment stage, as is true for many diseases, they then recover to resume their careers and other pursuits. And while most people assume that cancer produces intense discomfort, many cancers are associated with little or no pain, or with pain that can often be controlled or minimized. Indeed, less dreaded diseases such as arthritis and certain neurological disorders cause more pain than most forms of cancer.

Overcoming the common cancer fears and misconceptions is important both for individual cancer patients and society as a whole. Cancer must be detected early to obtain the highest probability of cure, but even persistent cancer is often a chronic disease that, although unfortunate, can be effectively treated for many years. Increased information about cancer allows cancer patients and their families to make better decisions about where to go for treatment, how to pick the most appropriate treatments, and what to expect at each step in diagnosis and treatment.

GENERAL DEFINITION OF CANCER

Although cancer is often referred to as a single condition, it actually consists of more than 100 different diseases, all characterized by the uncontrolled growth and spread of abnormal cells. Cancer can arise in many sites and behaves differently depending on its organ of origin. Thus, breast cancer has different characteristics than lung cancer, and breast cancer that spreads to the lungs should not be confused with lung cancer. Even in the lungs, breast cancer continues to behave like breast cancer and, under the microscope, continues to look like breast cancer.

THE CELL BIOLOGY OF CANCER

Each of the organs in the body, such as the lung, breast, colon, and brain, consists of specialized cells that carry out the organ's functions, such as transport of oxygen, digestion of nutrients, excretion of waste materials, locomotion, reproduction, and thinking. For the proper performance of each organ, worn out or injured cells must be replaced, and particular types of cells must increase in response to environmental changes. For example, the bone marrow is able to increase its production of oxygen-carrying red blood cells seven-fold or greater in response to bleeding or high altitude, and certain white blood cells are produced more rapidly during infections. Similarly, the liver or endocrine organs frequently respond to injury by regenerating damaged cells.

Regulation of cell reproduction is complex and varied for each type of tissue. In general, cells are of three types.

Stem Cells—capable of reproduction through multiple divisions.
Committed Cells—divide only a defined number of times, and are limited in capacity for self-renewal.
Specialized Cells—carry out organ function and are incapable of cell division.

An internal feedback system controls cell division by balancing the number of old and dying cells against the progeny of the stem cells. Cells divide until the body or organ reaches a specific—usually adult—size or stage and then cease dividing unless a specific need arises.

Stem cells divide most rapidly in organs where cells are continually shed and replaced such as the skin, bone marrow (which produces blood), and cells lining the intestinal tract. Muscles and bone grow less rapidly (muscles increasing in size in response to use) while

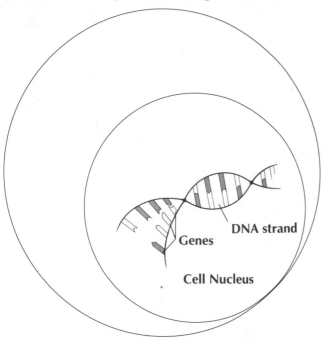

Figure 17.1: Genes are contained on strands of DNA with each cell's nucleus. As malignant tumors develop, additional genes are damaged, leading to cancer.

TUMOR TYPES

In general, cancers fall into four major groups, classified according to the body tissues in which they arise. All types can spread to other types of tissues of the body, while retaining their original cellular characteristics.

Carcinomas—tumors that begin in epithelial tissue, the cells that form the outside surface of the body and line the inner passages
Sarcomas—tumors originating in the connective tissues, principally the muscles, bones, cartilage, and connective tissues
Lymphomas—tumors in the lymphatic system
Leukemias—cancers of the blood-forming tissue

---

bone repairs itself in response to fracture. In contrast, adult nerves, which are composed mainly of specialized cells, hardly grow at all and have only a limited capacity to repair damage from injury or disease.

The presence of feedback control systems and the ability of cells to respond to signals to divide or die distinguish the behavior of normal tissues from cancer cells. Unlike normal cells, cancer cells ignore signals to stop dividing, to specialize, or to die and be shed.

All cancers lose a balance between the number of new cells produced and the number of mature cells that die. In normal adult organs, equal numbers of cells are produced and die each day, and only growing fetuses, children, and regenerating injured tissue produce more new cells than die.

Genes that control the genetics and heredity of each cell are strung like beads on a necklace along the cell's DNA (deoxyribonucleic acid) in the cell nucleus (see figure 17.1). In a benign or malignant tumor, several of the genes regulating these processes are abnormal (mutated). Abnormal genes may be inherited or damaged by carcinogens, viruses, errors in cell division, or as yet unknown factors.

As cancerous malignant tumors develop, additional genes are damaged, leading to:

1. Production of more cells or reduction in normal cell death rate
2. Shedding into the bloodstream of cells capable of spreading and growing in a new location (metastasis)
3. Capacity of metastatic tumor cells to attract the capillary development to feed their growth. Lack of a blood supply would otherwise limit tumor cell growth to a small size that would be of no danger.

Cancer cells do not necessarily grow faster than normal cells, but they persist longer or divide more times during their lifetime. Consequently, cancer cells accumulate, competing with normal, healthy tissue for nutrients, and encroaching on the space and territory of other cells. Many cancers, such as prostate cancer, grow slowly and may be present for many years before causing symptoms. Prostate cancer is rarely evident in men in their 40s, but by age 85 or 90, most men have some cancer cells in their prostate, although this condition is usually localized and not a serious medical problem. Cancer in children, on the other hand, tends to grow more quickly than in adults because children's body tissues generally grow rapidly.

HORMONE-PRODUCING TUMORS

A number of cancers affect the endocrine system, either by directly influencing a specific endocrine gland or by producing an uncontrolled supply of hormones. Since hormonal imbalances can affect virtually every organ and body function, hormone-producing tumors can cause a wide range of symptoms.

• Certain lung cancers can provoke the overproduction of antidiuretic hormone, causing body fluids to accumulate and resulting in severe imbalances of electrolytes (blood salts).

• Metastatic breast cancer, multiple myeloma, bone cancers, and other advanced or metastatic cancers frequently cause hypercalcemia (high calcium levels in the blood) as a result of tumor production of prostaglandins, substances similar to the hormones normally secreted by the parathyroid, and a variety of other hormones (see "Cancer Emergency Symptoms," later in this chapter).

• Tumors of the adrenal cortex may produce excess corticosteroid hormones (Cushing's syndrome).

• Rare tumors of the male or female gonads may produce inappropriate amounts of virilizing or feminizing hormones.

• Tumors that are derived from endocrine tissue such as pancreatic islet cells may produce excessive amounts of insulin or related hormones.

Some cancers disrupt the body's functions with the production of hormonelike substances. For example, the loss of taste and appetite in many people with advanced cancers, resulting in severe wasting of both fatty and lean tissue (cachexia), is due in part to a substance called TNF (tumor necrosis factor).

Cancers of the breast and prostate frequently possess hormone receptors that allow their growth to be stimulated or retarded by specific hormones. For these cancers, hormone treatment may relieve symptoms. Consequently, men with advanced prostate cancer may be administered estrogen and women with advanced breast cancer may be given estrogen or tamoxifen, a drug that blocks estrogen production and uptake. Studies have shown that tamoxifen treatment may decrease the risk of cancer recurrence even for women whose tumors have negative estrogen receptor tests.

GENERAL CAUSES OF CANCER

The common pathway to the development of all forms of cancer is uncontrolled cell division and cell death associated with the accumulation of damage to important regulatory genes. Multiple genes generally must be damaged (mutated) for a cancer to grow and to develop the capacity to spread (metastasize).

GENETICS AND CANCER

Cancers that apparently run in families may develop hereditarily or from similar family exposures. The fact that children may inherit abnormal genes that increase cancer risk is well established. Whereas these children may be at very high risk of developing cancer in the course of their lifetime, not all of them develop cancer, indicating that more than one damaged gene is necessary to produce cancer. Because one gene is already damaged, however, fewer additional mutations need to occur in the course of a lifetime before a tumor is produced. Thus, people with hereditary cancer tend to develop disease at a younger age.

Cancers associated with heredity include:

• Breast cancer
• Colon cancer (especially the type related to familial polyposis)
• Retinoblastoma
• Malignant melanoma
• Lung cancer

Although genetics frequently influence cancer development, environmental factors may also play a substantial role. For example, in families with a pronounced tendency to develop lung cancer, the risk is greatest for family members who smoke or are exposed to asbestos and other environmental factors linked to lung cancer.

Although research into the genetic influence on cancer is in its infancy, researchers have already developed several practical applications for the prevention, diagnosis, and treatment of cancer.

Genetic Markers. These indicate an inherited tendency to develop a specific disease. To date, only a few specific genetic markers for cancer have been identified, but many more are expected. Some genetic markers are readily apparent on physical examination: certain types of moles likely to become malignant melanoma (dysplastic nevi) or a type of colon polyp that develops into cancer (familial polyposis). Other markers can be detected through chemical examination of body cells, the blood, or through screening for specific chromosomal markers.

A person identified as a carrier of a genetic marker can undertake specific preventive action. For example, people with familial polyposis may be advised to have their colons removed before they actually develop colon cancer. More frequent screening to identify precancerous changes or early cancers is recommended for people with an identified genetic susceptibility for specific malignancies, such as those with dysplastic nevi. Persons at high risk also should be particularly diligent about avoiding environmental risk factors. For example, someone with an inherited tendency for lung cancer should avoid tobacco, radon, and asbestos exposure.

Keeping a Family History. Everyone should maintain family health records and construct a medical family tree that diagrams family patterns of disease. If, for example, a family history shows that many female family members in the past have been particularly vulnerable to breast or ovarian cancer, current generations need to be particularly diligent about regular screening examinations for these diseases.

If your family has a particularly high incidence of cancer, especially if cancer develops frequently in family members under 45 years of age or if individuals develop multiple different cancers, a cancer-risk evaluation may be worthwhile. Most universities have designated comprehensive cancer centers you can contact. It is better to be overly cautious than ignore a possible cancer risk—two of every five Americans develop cancer sometime in their lives (generally over the age of 60), and one in five Americans dies of cancer.

HIGH-RISK LESIONS AND CARCINOMA IN SITU

High-risk lesions are abnormal areas or growths that are not yet malignant. When examined under a microscope, cells appear abnormal (dysplastic) and may become malignant in time. High-risk lesions include a type of mole called dysplastic nevus and leukoplakia, whitish patches in the mouth and gums. Dysplastic cells may continue to develop to malignancy or may revert to a normal state without treatment.

Carcinoma in situ is a very early stage of cancer in which malignant cells are confined to the original site, usually the uppermost cell layer of the organ involved. Surgical removal alone is curative.

Gene Therapy. As more is learned about cancer genetics, it may someday be possible to manipulate genes with genetic engineering that blocks or removes cancer-causing genes or, alternatively, implants genes that promote cancer resistance.

EXPOSURES THAT CAUSE CANCER

Many cancers believed to be related to lifestyle or factors in the environment could probably be prevented by judicious changes in personal habits or environmental conditions. Radiation, chemical substances in the air and diet, certain viral infections, and vitamin deficiencies can all damage genes and result in cancer. Research continually expands our understanding of cancer's causes and development.

Smoking. According to the American Cancer Society, one out of every three cancer deaths in the United States today is directly linked to tobacco. Since smoking and chewing tobacco also contribute to 225,000 heart attack deaths a year, this substance is by far the leading cause of preventable death. Besides its association with lung cancer, smoking is also a major factor in causing cancers of the mouth, pharynx, larynx, esophagus, pancreas, and bladder. The complete elimination of smoking would save more than 160,000 lives per year in the United States. Although the dangers of smoking have been widely publicized since the first Surgeon General's report in 1964, 50 million Americans continue to smoke.

Dietary fat. The high-fat diet consumed by most Americans probably contributes to the development of colon cancer, and possibly to cancers of the breast, prostate, and uterus. Dietary fat stimulates the increased production of bile acids, some of which promote colon cancer. In addition, fat-soluble chemical pollutants such as PCBs and dioxin, some of which may be cancer-causing, concentrate in the fat of fish and animals. When consumed in a high-fat diet, these chemicals are stored in human body fat, possibly increasing cancer risk. Body fat also increases the production of certain hormones: People who are overweight tend to have a higher incidence of hormone-related cancers, particularly cancers of the breast, prostate, and uterus.

Environmental Pollutants. Industrial air and water pollution present a persistent health risk, particularly for workers consistently exposed to high levels of carcinogens. The link between occupational exposure to vinyl chloride, industrial dyes, and cancer is well documented.

Ionizing Radiation. While medical diagnosis and even the curative treatment of cancer rely on the use of radiation, the high doses of ionizing radiation used to treat cancers are associated with a low but measurable risk of second tumors. Diagnostic x-rays use about a thousandth of a therapeutic dose.

THE CANCER/DIET CONNECTION

Although definitive evidence linking diet to cancer has not been established, research has focused on these possibilities.

Additives. Food additives' cancer-causing role remains controversial. Some dyes and artificial sweeteners, such as cyclamates, are currently banned from food because they cause cancer in laboratory tests. Meats cured with nitrites and nitrates may increase the risk of cancer, and children and pregnant women should probably limit their consumption of these foods.

Fiber. Epidemiological studies demonstrate that populations consuming high-fiber diets tend to have a low incidence of intestinal cancer. It is thought that fiber mitigates cancer risk by speeding waste through the colon and promoting the excretion of fats and bile acids.

Vitamins. Both human and animal studies suggest an increased susceptibility to several chemically induced cancers if the diet is deficient in vitamin A. However, megadoses of vitamin A should be avoided since it can be toxic in large amounts (see chapter 5, The Basics of Good Nutrition).

Minerals. Iron deficiency has long been associated with an increased risk of esophageal cancer, but a normal diet provides enough of this mineral for most people, and many men already may have too much body iron.

Ultraviolet Radiation. Prolonged exposure to the sun and artificial sources of ultraviolet light such as tanning lamps can cause damage resulting in skin cancer.

Viruses and Other Infectious Agents. Research continues into the role of particular viruses and other disease-causing agents in causing cancer. Some sexually transmitted viral diseases such as venereal warts (human papillomavirus) are associated with an increased risk of cervical cancer, while the AIDS virus (HIV) is associated with both sarcomas and lymphomas. Human T-cell lymphotrophic virus type I (HTLV-I) is associated with some types of leukemia, and Epstein-Barr virus (EBV) with Burkitt's lymphoma.

Despite the myriad carcinogens that surround us, incessant worrying about the cancer-causing potential of everything we eat, drink, or touch is futile. (As a matter of fact, some food additives such as EDTA may decrease the risk of cancer.) However, following a prudent lifestyle that avoids the most well-documented carcinogens is advised. (See section "General Cancer Prevention" later in this chapter.)

GENERAL DIAGNOSIS OF CANCER

Diagnosis of cancer while it is still localized, before the tumor spreads (metastasizes) to other organs, is the goal of screening. Cancers that have not spread to adjacent tissue or distant organs can be cured by surgical removal (and occasionally with radiotherapy alone).

Symptoms depend on the location and type of cancer. The seven classic warning signs listed below are the most common symptoms noted by patients with cancer. They are, however, nonspecific, occurring in people without cancer and absent in many people who have cancer.

Change in bowel or bladder habits
A sore that does not heal
Unusual bleeding or discharge
Thickening or lump in breast or elsewhere
Indigestion or difficulty in swallowing
Obvious change in wart or mole
Nagging cough or hoarseness

Other possible signs:

Persistent, low-grade fever
Pallor
Unusual tiredness
Excessive bruising
Unusual and persistent headaches accompanied by visual or behavior changes and other symptoms
Nagging pain in the bones or elsewhere that has no apparent cause
Appetite and weight loss

NOTE: All of these symptoms may have causes other than cancer.

The diagnosis of any disease necessitates a comprehensive medical checkup that starts with a medical history. In this process, a doctor asks questions about current symptoms, past illnesses, and, since cancer may have a genetic predisposition, family history of disease. Your doctor also needs to know of your environmental exposure to potential carcinogens including the chemicals, asbestos, and other substances in your workplace as well as habits, most notably smoking, that may substantially increase your risk of cancer.

History-taking is followed by a physical examination, focusing particular attention to symptomatic areas. Special diagnostic tests are often required (see chapter 12, Diagnostic Tests and Procedures, for details of specific tests). The most common tests are laboratory analysis of blood, urine, and other body fluids, ultrasonography, x-ray studies of particular organs (e.g., mammography of the breasts; CT scans of the head, chest, or body), or determination of the distribution of injected radioactive tracers, and visual examination of internal organs using a fiber-optic endoscope (e.g., colonoscopy of the large intestine).

Although these tests provide important information and are useful in eliminating the possibility of other disorders, a diagnosis of cancer must be confirmed by microscopic examination of a biopsy specimen or cells shed from the surface of an abnormal area (e.g., Pap smears of the cervix or sputum from the lung) by a pathologist. Depending upon the cancer site, a biopsy may be done in a doctor's office (for superficial cancers) or in an outpatient clinic or hospital.

The results of the microscopic examination of the tumor by a pathologist can also suggest appropriate treatment. For example, tests of breast cancer tissue can determine whether the tumor is dependent for growth on estrogen hormones. By administering the most appropriate treatment, the treating physician can increase the chances of cure.

CANCER STAGING

If a tumor is found to be malignant, the extent or spread (staging) of the tumor must be determined. The tumor stage is generally classified based on the size of the primary tumor, involvement of nearby lymph glands, and evidence of spread to other organs (metastasis). There are several staging classification systems currently in use, and the precise meaning of a particular stage depends on the type of cancer being classified. The extent of the tumor determines the appropriate treatment and the prognosis for cure. For example, breast cancer 1 cm in size (about half an inch) without any lymph gland involvement or evidence of metastasis can be cured in more than 70 percent of cases and is treated more conservatively than a larger cancer or one that has spread to the lymph glands. Similarly, a very early (in situ) cancer of the cervix may be treated with laser surgery, freezing, cauterization, or simple surgical excision, sometimes followed by a short course of radiation therapy to further ensure that the cancer has been totally eliminated. In contrast, a cancer involving a larger portion of the cervix and uterus may require a hysterectomy and perhaps additional radiation treatments or chemotherapy.

GENERAL TREATMENT OF CANCER

After being diagnosed with cancer, patients and their families face important and difficult decisions. While feelings of fear and isolation are normal, numerous sources of medical, psychological, financial, and rehabilitative aid are available. (As a matter of fact, so many sources of assistance are accessible that choosing the right ones can be daunting.) A newly diagnosed cancer patient should be accompanied by one or two particularly close family members or friends during discussions with caregivers. Even though all important decisions ultimately must be made by the patient, the advice and comfort of informed friends or family members provides invaluable emotional support.

Getting a second opinion is often a wise stratagem to confirm the diagnosis and stage of disease, to better inform the patient, and to discuss available treatment options. Indeed, some medical insurers require a confirming second opinion before approving reimbursement for surgery or other treatments. However, some patients incessantly seek a doctor who will echo what they want to hear. But visiting half a dozen physicians in search of an acceptable opinion can be dangerous if it significantly delays treatment of a curable but progressing tumor.

THE TREATMENT TEAM

Most cancers are initially detected by the patient or family physician, but the family physician may not be experienced in cancer care, and cancer generally should be treated by an experienced doctor knowledgeable in current treatments and possessing appropriate resources. The initial treatment of many cancers often requires a team of cancer specialists with a medical oncologist or hematologist coordinating the efforts of a surgical oncologist, a radiation oncologist, and a pathologist as well as nurses, rehabilitation therapists, and psychologists. Often much of the subsequent care can be provided by the family physician working in a community setting, with the original treatment team available for consultation or treatment of complications.

The presence of so many people on the treatment and rehabilitation team increases the importance of the treatment team leader. The patient must be comfortable with and trust this physician, so finding the right doctor for this role may involve interviewing 2 or 3 physicians and carefully checking their qualifications. This process may seem time-consuming, especially when there is urgency to begin treatment, but securing the most suitable doctor is usually not difficult. Very often, a family physician will refer cancer patients to the appropriate oncologist. The criteria for picking a doctor should focus on the doctor's experience in treating other patients with similar problems.

A physician's educational and professional training can easily be checked in one of two medical directories: the *Directory of Medical Specialists* and the *American Medical Association Directory,* both found in most libraries. The state or local county medical society, and the state chapter of either the American College of Physicians or the American Academy of Family Physicians, also can supply background information about doctors and suggest specialists. The National Cancer Institute and local chapters of the American Cancer Society are further sources of names and information (see Directory of Resources, appendix B). Important qualifications include the experience of the physician in the particular type of cancer involved, and whether the physician has access to the most up-to-date resources.

Cancer treatment changes at a rapid rate—many of the cancer therapies available today did not exist even a decade ago—and many doctors simply may not be aware of the most recent advances. Patients should question their doctors about their experience and knowledge to see if they are making the necessary special efforts to keep abreast of new therapies.

WHEN TO GO TO A SPECIALIZED CANCER CENTER

One of the most important early decisions is where to go for treatment. The answer depends upon many factors: the nature of the disease, the patient's locale, economics, and the patient's particular preferences. Although most cancers can be treated locally, a patient may want to seek a referral to a specialized cancer center with a particular expertise in treating certain forms of cancer. Large medical centers or teaching hospitals may be better equipped to handle unusual or complicated cases, and a patient may visit one institution for diagnosis and staging, another for treatment, and still another for follow-up and rehabilitation.

The National Cancer Institute has designated a number of regionally distributed Comprehensive Cancer Centers throughout the United States that carry out investigative cancer treatment and research, and a number of other institutions that are Clinical Cancer Centers or Cancer Research Centers. These centers offer a full range of cancer therapies, including those that are still under investigation. An experimental treatment is not indicated, however, if there is an established therapy that has been proven safe and effective. For information on clinical cancer centers and cancer research centers, contact the National Cancer Institute at 1-800-4-CANCER (422-6237).

TYPES OF CANCER TREATMENT

Cancer therapy falls into two major categories: treatment intended to control the primary tumor (surgery or radiation), and treatment intended to kill cells that have escaped from the primary tumor (drug therapy). Drugs that are used to kill or control tumor cells include chemotherapy and biologicals (hormones, interferons, interleukins, and growth factors).

MANAGING SIDE EFFECTS OF CHEMOTHERAPY TREATMENT

The severity of chemotherapy's side effects depends on which of the more than 20 commonly used drugs is administered, the individual characteristics of the patient, and the drug dosage.

Most side effects resolve once treatment is completed, and some cease even during continued therapy. Whereas decreasing the dose may be required in some cases, even small changes in treatment are usually avoided to insure the treatment's effectiveness.

Minor discomforts and inconveniences (skin problems, edema, weight gain and loss, alterations in sexual performance, digestive disturbances, fatigue) are common and collectively may present a serious problem for the patient. Patients who experience these side effects should bring them to the attention of a member of the treatment team— a simple coping strategy may be sufficient to alleviate the problem. Although the side effects of chemotherapy may be onerous, chemotherapy so far has proven more effective than biologicals (which possess side effects of their own).

Surgery to remove the primary tumor and surrounding tissue is necessary to cure most tumors—about 25 percent of cancers are curable with surgery alone. Radiation therapy by itself can cure an additional 20 percent of cancers such as lymphoma, cervical cancer, and some forms of testicular cancer. And while most leukemias, multiple myeloma, and certain other cancers are treated with chemotherapy alone, cancer is increasingly being treated with combinations of treatments that produce both a higher cure rate and minimize adverse side effects. In this way, radiation therapy may be administered before surgery to reduce the size of a tumor or to decrease the amount of normal tissue that must be removed with the tumor, in some cases averting the need for amputation of a limb. Similarly, anticancer drugs may be combined with surgery or radiation to increase the possibility of curing a cancer that has spread.

Adjuvant therapy describes treatment with radiation, chemotherapy, or biologicals given in addition to, and usually following, primary surgical treatment. It is intended to prevent recurrence by killing malignant cells still present somewhere in the body. For example, following breast cancer surgery, tamoxifen or chemotherapy may be used as adjuvant therapy.

SIDE EFFECTS

As a side effect, all therapy harms normal tissue to some degree, and the powerful drugs used to kill cancer cells inevitably also kill some normal, rapidly growing cells (blood cells, hair, and cells that line the mouth, stomach, and intestines). Both radiation therapy and anticancer drugs damage hair follicles and cause hair loss. However, new surgical techniques, improved methods of administering radiation, and combinations of anticancer drugs have reduced the expected side effects. Reconstructive plastic surgery can minimize the disfigurement of cancer surgery. In addition, breast reconstruction and limb-sparing surgery for bone cancer have improved quality of life without compromising survival rates, and new drugs now control or minimize nausea and vomiting during chemotherapy. (Tetrahydrocannabinol or THC—the active ingredient in marijuana—is also occasionally used to limit nausea.)

Anemia and fatigue, also common side effects of radiation and chemotherapy because of injury to the bone marrow, can be reduced by supplementary blood transfusions and new hematopoietic growth factors such as G-CSF and GM-CSF.

Treatment for cancer can also cause long-term effects such as infertility and an increased risk of developing another cancer. When the risk of almost certain death from cancer is compared with the risk of side effects, most cancer patients choose to be treated.

DEALING WITH THE COMPLICATIONS OF CANCER

Cancer Emergencies. When dealing with cancer, proper therapy is usually more important than prompt therapy. Cancer-related emergencies, however, often require immediate treatment. (In some instances, these emergency situations may be the first obvious sign of underlying cancer.) In an emergency situation, resolving the immediate problem takes precedence over treatment of the cancer itself.

CANCER EMERGENCY SYMPTOMS

Internal bleeding
Intestinal obstruction, which can occur in colon cancer
Spinal cord compression
Metabolic imbalances, such as dangerously high calcium levels
Encroachment on other vital organs such as superior vena cava syndrome, a complication of lung cancer in which the major vein carrying blood to the heart is compressed, building up fluid in the upper part of the body

UNDER INVESTIGATION—NATURAL PRODUCTS TO FIGHT CANCER

BIOLOGICALS

Biologicals are natural products from living organisms that have been isolated and cloned and can be administered in large amounts. Using these substances, some researchers are attempting to stimulate or manipulate the immune system to fight cancer. These attempts are primarily investigational at this time, but there is hope that they represent effective new weapons in the battle against cancer.

A few biologicals have been approved for use in cancer patients, including interleukin-2, a biological that stimulates immune cells (lymphocytes), and interferon, another naturally occurring product. Monoclonal antibodies are also considered to be a type of biological.

MONOCLONAL ANTIBODIES

Monoclonal antibodies are genetically engineered substances able to find and attach themselves to cancer cells. Although most of the therapeutic uses for these antibodies are still being investigated, antibodies designed to react with substances produced by specific types of cancer cells are now used in cancer diagnosis; labeled with a radioactive substance, they can help determine whether a cancer has spread to another site in the body. Soon, researchers hope to attach anticancer drugs to a monoclonal antibody that will carry the medication directly to the cancer cells, increasing the effectiveness of chemotherapy and reducing systemic side effects.

Weight Loss. Because some cancers and therapies interfere with appetite, impair taste, restrict nutrient absorption, and hinder consumption and digestion of food, nutritional support is often necessary to prevent or cope with weight loss. Surgery can cause a decrease in weight, while depression and other emotional turmoil can disrupt appetite and eating patterns. Since nutrition for cancer patients is such a complex issue affected by many factors, a nutritionist or dietitian is often a member of the cancer treatment team.

In general, a diet rich in complex carbohydrates (grains, legumes, and most vegetables), high in antioxidants (especially vitamins A, C, and E, and beta-carotene), and low in fat is best for cancer patients. During brief periods of intensive cancer therapy, however, a balanced diet may not be palatable, and at those times cancer patients should attempt to maintain their weight with foods that can be easily tolerated, such as ice cream, pasta, or other bland dishes. If chewing and swallowing are difficult, soft foods may be necessary. On some occasions, frequent small meals may be the only way to consume sufficient food to maintain one's weight.

During treatment, patients frequently experience food aversions and may avoid temporarily distasteful, even though nutritious, foods. Temporary damage to taste buds often makes patients desire highly seasoned items and unless advised to avoid certain foods, patients may eat whatever is appealing. At the same time, patients should question their physician, nurse, or dietitian about eating problems such as dry or sore mouth, altered taste sensations, and changes in bowel habits.

Pain. Most people assume cancer causes pain, even though there are some types of cancer that cause little or no discomfort. A few forms of cancer may involve a moderate amount of pain, but less intense than the pain experienced in some forms of arthritis, certain nerve disorders, and other less feared diseases. Relaxation training, biofeedback, hypnosis, and cognitive control (behavior modification) as a means of pain control, especially in the milder cases, has attracted attention in many centers.

Drugs remain the main avenue of pain relief for patients suffering from chronic cancer pain. Mild discomfort usually can be controlled by acetaminophen or other nonnarcotic painkillers. About a third of patients undergoing active treatment experience severe pain and require stronger medications, and pain can be more pronounced in people with advanced cancers. Narcotics, properly used, can ease cancer pain for months or years while maintaining the patient in a lucid, functional state. Often, narcotics combined with antidepressant drugs are very effective in controlling pain with little or no impairment of function.

For advanced cancer pain, morphine, methadone, and similar opiate derivatives should be administered in sufficient quantity to relieve pain.

TREATMENT ALTERNATIVES

EXPERIMENTAL TREATMENTS AND DRUG TRIALS

Physicians at the National Cancer Institute, many university-affiliated cancer centers, and Community Cancer Centers are engaged in a continual search for better treatments for all types of cancer. Research is conducted in clinical trials in which new drugs or devices and varying dosages or combinations of drugs are evaluated.

Clinical trials of new treatments are divided into four phases.

Phase 1 trials: Promising new drugs or other remedies are first offered to patients who have not been helped by conventional therapy. These trials are risky because the toxicity to humans of new therapies is unknown, although the effect on animals has previously been evaluated. Phase 1 trials are generally small (10 to 15 patients), but they are important to determine the appropriate drug dosage and schedule and to evaluate side effects.

Phase 2 trials: Tests on about 20 to 40 patients with a single kind of advanced cancer are performed to determine tumor responsiveness to the new therapy.

Phase 3 trials: If the preliminary trials indicate that the new therapy performs better than currently available standard therapies, a phase 3 study compares the new treatment to the standard regimens. (Two groups of patients are gathered; one receives the new treatment and one does not. Neither "randomized" group is supposed to know its treatment status.) Although patients who agree to participate in a phase 3 randomized trial have no guarantee of receiving the new drug or treatment, both the treating physician and the patient often know whether the new treatment is being administered after the groups are chosen.

Phase 4 trials: These studies are used to fine-tune new treatments once they are already known to be effective.

The decision to take part in a treatment or drug trial is a personal decision. Participation in tests of an experimental therapy is often worthwhile if the patient is otherwise healthy and the prognosis is poor with the current standard therapy. Studies are limited in size, and not every willing patient is admitted into clinical trials. The tests rigidly define the types and stages of cancer that are eligible for admission, as well as the patient's general state of health and prognosis. (Information about clinical trials can be had by calling 1-800-4-CANCER [422-6237]. This number allows access to PDQ, a data base, updated monthly, listing current cancer treatments, clinical trials that are recruiting subjects, doctors and hospitals who treat particular types of cancer, and the closest comprehensive cancer center.)

NONTRADITIONAL MEDICINE

Increasing interest in alternative medicine has led many cancer patients and their families to seek nonstandard treatments for cancer. Although acupuncture, homeopathic medicine, nutritional supplements, and other nontraditional approaches may be helpful with other disorders, none have been shown to be effective against cancer. Forgoing mainstream treatments such as surgery

QUESTIONING QUESTIONABLE TREATMENTS

The answers to these questions can clarify the worthiness of alternative or experimental therapies.

Is there documented evidence that this treatment has helped other cancer patients?

Legitimate experimental treatments are carefully monitored and controlled by governmental agencies or peer review committees consisting of physicians and scientists with expertise in the area under study. The experimental drug and research tests are usually provided without cost to the study subjects, although patient care will generally have to be paid by the patients or their insurance. Approach experimental treatments offered outside this control framework with extreme caution or avoid them entirely. Ask if the treatment has been described in medical or other peer-reviewed publications. Be wary of self-published booklets and reports limited to sensational popular publications or news releases.

Is the doctor or treatment center outside the jurisdiction of regulatory agencies?

Clinics in locales outside the jurisdiction of United States authorities always should be viewed with suspicion.

What is the practitioner's background? Are his or her degrees legitimate?

Many alternative cancer practitioners look and act in a smoothly professional manner, and some have medical degrees. Make sure the doctor is indeed a licensed physician. The *American Medical Association Directory*, the *Directory of Medical Specialists*, or the county medical society can provide this information. A large number of alternative practitioners use the title "doctor" but have degrees in areas that are unrelated to medicine, such as doctor of metaphysics (Ms.D.) and doctor of naturopathy (N.D.). Others claim membership in obscure organizations or purport to be nutritionists, a "degree" held by large numbers of fringe practitioners.

Is there a logical rationale for the treatment?

Although many laypeople may lack the medical knowledge to understand fully or judge treatments, a physician should be able to explain it in such a way that the patient and family can comprehend its rationale. But be cautious: Many practitioners deliver convincing salespitches for their treatments and can make even the most illogical regimen sound legitimate. However, a "secret" approach that the practitioner does not want to reveal to the general medical community suggests quackery.

Does the practitioner claim that his or her treatment is boycotted by the medical establishment or persecution by organized medicine?

A common ploy is to claim that the medical establishment fears loss of income, prestige or power because of the effectiveness of his or her "revolutionary" treatment. These claims are bogus although common.

While these questions reveal much about unproved therapy, you should also consult your family physician or local medical society for more information about a practitioner's background and qualifications.

and drug or radiation therapy in favor of alternative medicine is risky—these treatments may do nothing to slow tumor progression, making the cancer much more difficult to treat.

Although alternative treatments do not cure cancer, some cancer patients successfully use these therapies to improve their nutritional and emotional well-being, and counteract some of the negative side effects of treatment. Acupuncture, hypnosis, yoga and other forms of meditation, visualization, and imagery may help cancer patients cope with discomfort and pain. By easing anxiety and depression, they may improve the patient's outlook and quality of life.

AVOIDING UNORTHODOX CANCER THERAPY

Unorthodox cancer therapy is a multibillion-dollar-a-year business. Because many purveyors of unorthodox treatments appear to be caring, sincere people eager to help where established medical treatment has failed, thousands of cancer patients and their families pay for useless or unproven treatments. In desperation, even well-educated, otherwise sophisticated people undertake unproven treatments, sometimes at the expense of lifesaving therapy. Unproven treatments with megavitamins, vaccines, and devices continue to thrive despite their uselessness.

LIVING WITH CANCER

Optimistic attitude and emotional fortitude are important elements in successfully fighting cancer. Numerous studies show that patients who best cope with the stress of cancer are ones who assume responsibility for seeking treatment, ask questions, and participate in decision making. Even during intense treatment, each day should yield a modicum of pleasure and diversion. The ability to at least temporarily lose oneself in music, books, or hobbies is vital for maintaining a healthy outlook, and family and friends are vital in providing support.

Many people refuse to discuss the disease and its prognosis to keep from worrying or burdening others. In reality, silence erects a wall between patients and their families, and candid discussions about the possibility of death decrease the tensions between patients, friends, and families.

SUPPORT GROUPS

Several studies demonstrate that cancer patients belonging to support groups cope better than similarly ill patients who are isolated. Verbalizing fears, as well as sharing information about coping strategies, treatments, doctors, hospitals, and other medical resources, enormously benefits cancer patients and their families. Practical assistance with day-to-day problems of living is also available through these groups.

Nationwide, many support groups operate under the aegis of the American Cancer Society (ACS); specific information can be obtained through ACS (1-800-ACS [227]-2345) or your local ACS chapter. Information about these and other groups is also available at 1-800-4-CANCER (422-6237).

CANCER REHABILITATION

Although more than half of all cancer patients will be alive and free of the disease 5 or more years after treatment, many are plagued by physical reminders of their ordeal and lingering fears of cancer's recurrence. Treatment can alter body functions, requiring new ways of speaking, walking, and eliminating body wastes. Consequently, rehabilitation forms an essential element of modern cancer therapy and, in most cases, should be planned as part of the overall treatment.

The first large-scale cancer rehabilitation program began in 1952 with the founding of the International Association of Laryngectomies, an organization dedicated to teaching new ways of speaking to people who have had their larynx removed. Another well-known rehabilitation program, Reach to Recovery, also founded in the 1950s, helps women cope after a mastectomy to treat breast cancer. Today, programs for ostomy patients, amputees, and the terminally ill are also available. (See Directory of Resources, appendix B.) Staffed by volunteers who have experienced the disease, these associations offer help and advice from people who share the experience of being cancer patients.

All cancer rehabilitation programs try to return patients to their best possible level of function. Many return to their former jobs, but some are rebuffed by employers reluctant to hire former cancer patients. Cancer patients often encounter hostility of fellow workers because of absences for treatment, are excluded from promotions, or are unable to change jobs because new health insurance will not cover their preexisting condition. Employers may assume that cancer patients will continue to require time off, even though studies show that recovered cancer patients often have better work records than those never suffering the disease.

Children who have undergone cancer treatment also encounter difficulty returning to school or normal activities. Counseling for patients, teachers, employers, and co-workers can help overcome misconceptions and rehabilitation problems.

In addition to volunteer efforts, legislation has been passed to promote cancer rehabilitation and to prevent job discrimination against former cancer patients.

THE HOSPICE MOVEMENT

All discussions of cancer must recognize that death is the outcome in almost half of all cases. In today's society, death is increasingly a topic of open discussion not only among health professionals but also among patients and their families. The resurgence of the concept of "death with dignity" and all its attendant ethical and moral considerations reflects changing attitudes toward death and dying.

Modern medical technology can now prolong life far longer than ever before, and this technology, often enormously expensive, can save otherwise healthy patients from life-threatening acute events. Cancer patients with life-threatening infections can now frequently survive their illness and go on to a complete cure.

At the same time, many have questioned whether so-called heroic high-tech methods should be used to prolong the life of patients facing inevitable death without hope for an enjoyable life. While some argue that human life is precious, to be maintained at any cost, the subject attracts massive controversy.

The hospice movement attempts to resolve the conflict for patients and families facing death. Designed for patients who can no longer be treated, hospices provide comfort and an atmosphere that makes death less threat-

PREVENTIVE STRATEGIES

Avoid smoking and tobacco products. The most effective step anyone can take in preventing premature death from many causes is to stop smoking, or better still, never start. (See "How to Quit" in chapter 6.)

Adopt and maintain a healthy diet. A diet including abundant fresh fruits and vegetables, grains, and legumes provides fiber and antioxidant vitamins. While most Americans eat a high-fat diet, switching to low-fat foods may forestall some forms of cancer.

Avoid workplace and other environmental exposures. Protecting workers and the public at large from carcinogenic substances at a less than prohibitive cost has become a major social and economic challenge. Passage of the Occupational Safety and Health Act and creation of the Occupational Safety and Health Administration (OSHA) and the National Institute for Occupational Safety and Health (NIOSH) in 1970 formalized the government's role in protecting workers from occupational hazards. The Environmental Protection Agency (EPA) is charged with minimizing the presence of harmful environmental pollutants. Although these governmental agencies are constantly attacked for excess stringency or laxness, they represent the basic framework for reduction of environmental and occupational hazards.

Avoid or limit radiation exposure. Radiation's potential benefits must always be weighed against possible risks. Routine chest x-rays are no longer recommended as part of an annual physical exam without clear indications of their benefit. Radiation therapy is no longer used for relatively benign conditions such as acne or tonsillitis because of the increased risk of cancer. In addition, radiation dosage administered by modern x-ray machines has been reduced markedly.

Avoid unprotected sun exposure. Ultraviolet light, which causes cellular damage, is the most common cause of skin cancer. A commonsense approach to sun exposure can prevent most cases of this potentially disfiguring cancer. People with fair skin should be particularly careful to limit their sun exposure. Although most skin cancers are not life-threatening, the increase in malignant melanoma, a potentially lethal condition, is thought to be due to increases in sun exposure.

Avoid unsafe sexual practices. Because of the role of sexually transmitted diseases in the development of some types of cancer, condom use, avoiding the exchange of bodily fluids, and maintaining mutually monogamous sexual relationships are prudent preventive measures.

ening. The hospice may be located in a special section of a hospital, a separate facility, or even in the patient's home, with medical personnel and help available as needed. (For a more complete discussion, see chapter 1, How to Get the Care You Need.)

GENERAL CANCER PREVENTION

Most cancers in the United States are thought to be related to lifestyle or environmental factors, and large numbers undoubtedly could be prevented by judicious changes in personal habits or avoidance of exposure to environmental carcinogens. Research constantly reveals new facts about cancer's causes, and as we learn the biological processes involved the potential for preventing cancer increases substantially.

Preventive measures for specific cancers, when they exist, are discussed in the sections below. Unless a definite cause has been identified for a particular type of cancer, little if anything can be done to prevent it. Iden-

tification of risk factors and increased surveillance for those at risk may lead to earlier diagnosis and prompt treatment.

The best means of reducing cancer risk is to avoid unnecessary exposure to known cancer-causing agents. Some preventive strategies are applicable to more than one type of cancer, as well as to other life-threatening conditions such as heart disease.

TYPES OF CANCER

Of the more than 100 different types of cancer, most are distinctly different diseases. The following sections briefly review the most common types that occur in both men and women. Cancers of the breast, uterus, ovaries and other female reproductive organs are discussed in chapter 9, "Special Health Concerns of Women," and cancers of the prostate and male reproductive organs are covered in chapter 10, "Health Concerns of Men."

RESPIRATORY TRACT CANCERS

LUNG CANCER

DEFINITION

Lung cancer is the most common form of cancer seen in the United States, annually accounting for about 170,000 new cases and 149,000 deaths, according to the American Cancer Society. Lung cancer was rare before World War I, but as the popularity of smoking increased among men, partially as a result of cigarette distribution to soldiers, so did the incidence of lung cancer. About 7 percent of smokers die of lung cancer.

The overall cure rate for this cancer is low. About 9 percent survive 5 or more years.

Microscopic examination of lung cancer cells reveals four main variants: small-cell, squamous cell, adenocarcinoma, and undifferentiated large-cell cancer. The majority are squamous cell and adenocarcinoma.

- Small-cell: Comprising about 20 percent of lung cancers, small-cell lung cancer is one of the most aggressive of all lung cancers, but also the most sensitive to chemotherapy. Spread to distant organs usually has occurred by the time of diagnosis. Median survival is 2 years, and only about 10 to 15 percent of patients with localized disease can be cured.
- Squamous cell: Tends to develop mostly in the central part of the lung and does not spread to other parts of the body as rapidly as other types of lung cancer. Only squamous cell has an identified precancerous stage, during which abnormal precancerous cells can be detected in the sputum.
- Adenocarcinoma: Frequently arises in the smaller bronchi and spreads into the pleural spaces between the lung and chest wall.
- Large-cell: The rarest form of lung cancer. It is believed to be a variation of squamous cell or adenocarcinoma.

CAUSE

Smoking is a prime cause of lung cancer, and smokers with a family history of lung cancer have a significantly higher risk of this disease. Lung cancer mortality increases with number of cigarettes smoked per day and the number of years an individual smokes, although smoking low-tar, low-nicotine brands of cigarettes conveys a somewhat lower risk than regular brands. An asbestos worker who smokes runs a 25 percent risk of death from lung cancer. Uranium workers are also at an increased risk of lung cancer, particularly if they smoke.

DIAGNOSIS

Early diagnosis of lung cancer is difficult because a lung tumor big enough to cause symptoms is usually advanced. Occasionally, lung cancer is detected as a shadow on a routine chest x-ray.

Lung cancer symptoms include:

- Persistent cough
- Blood-streaked sputum
- Chest pain
- Recurring pneumonia or bronchitis

TREATMENT

Treatment of lung cancer depends on the tumor type and the extent of invasion. Of the four types, squamous cell cancer is the most easily treated with surgery and radiation. Because small-cell lung cancers usually have metastasized by the time of diagnosis, the initial treatment is generally combination chemotherapy followed in some patients by radiotherapy. Surgery is occasionally appropriate. For other lung cancers, surgical removal of the tumor is the major treatment. If the cancer has invaded the chest wall, removal of ribs and part of the supporting structures may be required, followed by extensive repair and reconstruction using a meshlike substance or muscle and skin grafts. However, this extensive surgery rarely eliminates the disease, and surgery may be followed by radiation therapy or chemotherapy.

Many lung cancer patients also suffer coexisting heart or pulmonary dysfunction related either to smoking or age, which limits the possible intensity of cancer therapy. Occasionally both coronary artery bypass and lung cancer surgery may be performed during the same operation.

Patients can expect to be discharged from the hospital 7 to 10 days after surgery, although full recovery may take several weeks or longer, depending upon the extent of the surgery and the patient's general physical condition. Many patients can resume normal or near-normal physical activities following lung surgery

---

LUNG CANCER RISK FACTORS

- Smoking
- Family history of lung cancer
- Working with asbestos (risk exacerbated by smoking)
- Working with uranium (risk exacerbated by smoking)
- Long-term exposure to radon

depending on the amount of lung removed and the condition of the remaining lung.

If cancer recurs after surgery, the prognosis is generally poor. Combination chemotherapy occasionally can reduce the size of the tumor, alleviate pain and other symptoms, and possibly prolong survival.

PREVENTION

Stopping smoking (or never starting) is the best preventive measure against lung cancer; those who cannot stop are advised to switch to low-tar, low-nicotine brands and to reduce the total number of cigarettes they smoke. Avoid asbestos exposure.

MALE/FEMALE DIFFERENCES

While lung cancer rates have leveled off in men, the incidence in women is rising steeply. Women with lung cancer usually live somewhat longer than men, but the overall mortality is about the same.

CANCERS OF THE UPPER AERODIGESTIVE TRACT

DEFINITION

These cancers of the oral cavity and larynx account for about 3 percent of all cancers; each year in the United States, there are about 30,000 new cases of oral cancer, with about 7,700 deaths, and 12,600 cases of larynx cancer, with 3,800 deaths.

Whitish patches (leukoplakia) or reddened, velvety patches (erythroplakia) on the mucosal lining of the mouth and throat are often precancerous lesions. Untreated, these patches ulcerate and invade underlying structures. Any sore or ulceration that does not heal in 2 weeks should be seen by a doctor. (Canker sores are common and harmless, though painful; they generally heal in a week.) Examination of the mouth and throat should be part of a regular checkup for all adults, particularly for those who smoke or use tobacco products or who consume alcohol in greater than moderate quantities.

Symptoms of cancer of the pharynx (the area behind the nasal cavity, the soft palate, and the back wall of the throat) include a mild sore throat, difficulty in swallowing, and blood-flecked sputum. The eustachian tube, which connects the nasopharynx and the middle ear, may be compressed by the tumor, leading to the sensation of a blocked ear. If symptoms persist for more than 2 weeks, they should be checked by a doctor.

Hoarseness is the major symptom of cancer of the larynx (voice box); however, less serious conditions, including infection, allergy, and injuries, also can produce hoarseness. Any persistent hoarseness lasting more

than a few weeks should be evaluated by a doctor, particularly if the person smokes or uses tobacco. Cancers arising on the vocal cords are not painful until late in the disease, or unless adjacent structures are involved. By that time, there also may be a chronic cough and difficulty in breathing.

For all of these cancers of the head and neck, the first symptom may be a hard lump on one side of the neck. This suggests that cancer has spread to the lymph nodes from unknown primary lesions, and prompt medical attention is required.

CAUSE

Most people with head and neck cancers have used tobacco in some form (smoking, chewing tobacco, or snuff). Heavy alcohol use also increases the risk, especially for cancer of the pharynx.

DIAGNOSIS

Cancers of the mouth and pharynx are easy to see and are often diagnosed by a dentist who observes ulceration or a mass arising from a surface of the mouth or pharynx. Cancer of the larynx can be seen by direct examination through a laryngoscope. Biopsy is necessary to confirm the diagnosis.

Symptoms of cancer of the upper aerodigestive tract include:

White or red patches on the mouth and throat
Persistent hoarseness or dry cough
Difficulty swallowing
Mild but persistent sore throat
A persistent blocked feeling in the ear in the absence of a cold

TREATMENT

Depending upon the size and location of the tumor, initial treatment may be surgical removal of the tumor and surrounding tissue, followed by radiation therapy. For larger lesions, chemotherapy or radiotherapy may be used to shrink the tumor before surgery to allow for adequate removal with a more pleasing cosmetic result. Lymph nodes in the neck are often removed because of the high probability of spread to these areas.

Radiation may be administered externally or through radioactive needles implanted into the tumor and surrounding tissue. Radiation may include treatment of both the primary lesion and the neck.

If the cancer is confined to the vocal cords, more than 85 percent can be treated successfully with radiation therapy. Some early cancers can also be treated by limited laser beam surgery that removes the cancer yet preserves normal speaking ability. Removal of the larynx (laryngectomy) is usually necessary in more advanced cancer, or disease that persists despite radiation therapy. Although laryngectomy usually cures the cancer, it destroys normal speech ability and necessitates learning other means of speaking via electronic or vibrating aids, or trapping air in the throat or esophagus and using the tongue, lips, and cheeks to produce sounds, skills taught by speech therapists.

PREVENTION

Tobacco and excess alcohol use should be avoided.

MALE/FEMALE DIFFERENCES

These cancers are seen most often in men over the age of 45, generally in smokers.

GASTROINTESTINAL CANCERS

Cancers appear in many gastrointestinal organs. In the United States colon cancer is common, whereas gastric (stomach) and esophageal cancers are less commonly seen, and hepatoma (liver cancer) is rare. In contrast, gastric and esophageal cancers are common in Japan, and, worldwide, liver cancer is one of the most prevalent malignancies, especially in areas where hepatitis is endemic.

Sites most commonly affected by cancer in the gastrointestinal tract are the colon, pancreas, stomach, liver, and esophagus, in that order.

COLON AND RECTAL CANCERS

(Prepared with Jonathan LaPook, M.D.)

DEFINITION

Cancers of the large bowel, which includes the colon and rectum, affect 149,000 people in the United States per year and cause 56,000 deaths. Colorectal cancers are highly curable when detected and treated in an early stage, but many people delay seeking medical attention, despite symptoms.

A small cancer may be present in the colon for years without producing symptoms, and the symptoms that do appear depend on the location of the tumor: A cancer growing on the right side of the colon near the small intestine tends to grow into the interior of the intestine (the lumen), sometimes producing right-sided pain and characteristically causing slow internal bleeding, eventually resulting in iron-deficiency anemia. (Unexplained anemia in an older person is often caused by right-sided colon cancer.) The lumen on the left side of the colon is narrower, and cancer developing in this area tends to encircle the intestinal wall, causing partial intestinal blockage, marked by increasing constipation, abdominal bloating, or distention. But while cancers on the left side of the colon also may cause bleeding, anemia is less common than with right-sided tumors.

Rectal cancers are often associated with diarrhea, often streaked with blood. A sense of fullness or urgency may also cause repeated attempts to have a bowel movement, as the sensation caused by the cancerous growth is perceived as an incomplete bowel movement.

CAUSE

Colon cancer is unusual in that there is a clearly defined, benign precursor that can usually easily be removed. A recent large trial of patients with polyps suggested that removing such polyps significantly decreases the chances of developing colon cancer.

At least 30 percent of colon cancers occur in people with known hereditary risk. There is clearly a genetic component to colon cancer, with first-degree relatives having four times the incidence. Having two first-degree relatives with colon cancer raises your risk to eight times normal. Recently, genes have been isolated that cause familial polyposis (a condition in which patients develop hundreds of polyps and almost uniformly develop cancer if the condition is not treated) and cause colon cancer in families without multiple polyps.

People who have experienced ulcerative colitis or Crohn's disease are also at increased risk of developing colorectal cancers; the risk of colorectal cancer increases with age.

DIAGNOSIS

Especially in the elderly, anemia, abdominal pain, or bleeding warrants evaluation for colorectal cancer. Colonoscopy is more accurate than a barium enema in the detection of colon polyps and cancers. As more than half of patients with cancers of the colon or rectum will

RISK FACTORS OF COLORECTAL CANCER

- Family history of colorectal cancer
- Personal or family history of polyps in the colon or rectum
- Personal history of ulcerative colitis and other colon disorders
- Diet high in fat and low in fiber

have multiple lesions, full colonoscopic examination must be undertaken if any cancer is detected.

SYMPTOMS OF COLORECTAL CANCER

- A change in bowel habits (e.g., any change in the frequency, shape, or size of stools)
- Blood in the stool
- Rectal bleeding
- Lower abdominal pain
- A feeling of discomfort or the constant urge to defecate
- Difficulty in passing stools
- Intestinal blockage
- Unexplained weight loss
- Abdominal pain
- Unexplained iron-deficiency anemia

SCREENING TESTS

Who should receive endoscopic screening, how much of the colon should be examined, at what age to begin screening, and how often to perform the examination are all topics of debate. Stool cards are only about 60 to 70 percent sensitive at detecting colon cancer and are extremely poor at detecting colon polyps. Nevertheless, use of six stool cards annually has been shown to decrease mortality from colon cancer by about 33 percent.

Most physicians agree that at age 50 patients should receive at least a screening with flexible sigmoidoscopy. Such examination has been shown to lower mortality from colon cancer by about 40 percent. Since flexible sigmoidoscopy examines only the lower one-third of the colon, higher polyps and tumors may be missed.

In addition, a routine annual physical exam should include a digital rectal examination, which can help detect rectal lesions as well as prostate cancer.

The most effective means of preventing colon cancer involves a total colonoscopy. However, this is a relatively expensive examination and the resources do not pres-

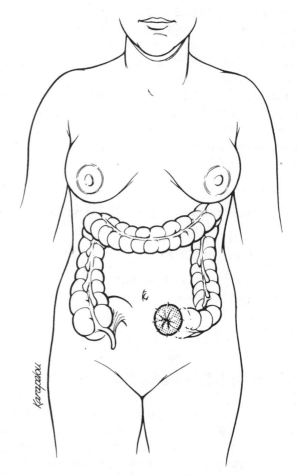

Figure 17. 2: Front view of a stoma opening in the abdominal wall for emptying of colon.

ently exist to routinely screen everybody. In addition, complications such as perforation—though uncommon—do occur. Therefore, criteria have been developed to select those patients at high risk for colon cancer who should receive colonoscopy.

People with first-degree relatives (parents, siblings, children) with colon cancer should receive screening. Patients with chronic inflammatory bowel disease are periodically

SCREENING TESTS FOR BOWEL CANCER

The American Cancer Society recommends the following schedule of screening tests:

Test	Frequency	Who Should Be Tested
Digital rectal examination	Yearly	Everyone over 40; high-risk individuals over 35
Stool guaiac (fecal occult blood)	Yearly	Everyone over 50; high-risk individuals over 40
Sigmoidoscopy or colonoscopy	3–5 years	Everyone over 50; high-risk individuals over 35
	More frequently (varies with the individual)	Individuals with abnormal findings on previous exam, familial polyposis, and some types of ulcerative colitis

examined with the hope of detecting and treating incipient colorectal cancers prior to metastasis. In the future it may be possible to use genetic analysis to select those patients at high risk for developing colon cancer.

If any of these tests is positive, further examinations of the entire colon may be needed. These include a barium enema, in which a chalky, opaque substance that can be visualized on x-ray film is infused into the colon.

TREATMENT

Treatment for bowel cancer generally necessitates surgical removal of the tumor and surrounding colon. In some cases, this means creation of a colostomy, an artificial opening in the abdomen for elimination of body wastes. The colostomy may be temporary to give the colon a chance to heal, or permanent (in 10 to 15 percent of cases) if the lower part of the rectum has to be removed (see figure 17.2). Most patients can lead normal lives once they learn to manage their colostomies.

The risk of recurrence and death from colon cancer is reduced by approximately one-third through the use of chemotherapy if the tumor involves lymph nodes.

Laser removal of very early superficial tumors of the colon through the colonoscope or sigmoidoscope, especially in elderly patients who might not tolerate major operations, is now under investigation.

Advanced or recurrent bowel cancer is usually not surgically treatable and responds poorly to radiation therapy or chemotherapy.

PREVENTION

Reducing the consumption of fats, especially from animal sources, and increasing consumption of grains, legumes, and fresh fruits and vegetables may lower the risk of colorectal cancer. Several studies have found that low-dose aspirin—one tablet every day or two—may reduce the risk of colorectal cancer.

For people with death from familial polyposis and ulcerative colitis, prophylactic removal of the colon may be recommended.

CANCER OF THE PANCREAS

DEFINITION

The pancreas is a dual-purpose gland with exocrine cells that produce digestive juices and enzymes and endocrine cells that produce the hormones insulin and glucagon in "islets of Langerhans," small dots of tissue scattered throughout the larger gland. Cancer of the exocrine portion is more common and usually occurs during middle age.

The past few decades have witnessed a marked increase in cancers of the pancreas, but the reasons for this are unknown. According to the American Cancer Society, there are about 27,700 new cases of pancreatic cancer and 25,000 deaths each year.

CAUSE

The causes of pancreatic cancer have not been established, but smoking has been implicated in the development of this disease.

DIAGNOSIS

Symptoms of pancreatic cancer include severe upper abdominal pain, often radiating to the back; weight loss; jaundice and severe itching; or gastrointestinal bleeding, depending upon the location of the tumor. Various digestive symptoms such as nausea and vomiting, loss of appetite, and loose stools also occur.

The less common endocrine pancreatic cancers may cause a variety of symptoms related to hormonal imbalance: overproduction of insulin resulting in low blood sugar (hypoglycemia), severe diarrhea, or diabetes.

The diagnosis of exocrine pancreatic cancer can usually be made with a CT scan of the abdomen or by x-ray photography after dye infusion into an artery (angiography). Endocrine pancreatic cancers are often suggested by a blood test showing elevated levels of insulin, VIP (vasoactive intestinal peptide), or other hormones. Because endocrine tumors are small, they may not be visible on CT scans; a laparotomy may be necessary to find and remove them. These tumors tend to be indolent, and even if untreated, survival may be measured in years.

TREATMENT

The general outlook for exocrine pancreatic cancer is poor. By the time most of these cancers are diagnosed, they have already metastasized to lymph nodes, liver, or lungs, or invaded other vital structures that cannot be removed. Treatment consists of radiation therapy, chemotherapy, and, if indicated, surgery to relieve symptoms such as duct obstruction. Nonetheless, survival is short, generally less than 6 months.

If the cancer is confined to the pancreas, the gland may be surgically removed, followed by radiation therapy, chemotherapy, or both. The diabetes resulting from removal of the pancreas is treated with insulin injections, and pancreatin is administered to replace the natural pancreatic enzymes needed for digestion. But despite aggressive treatment, most patients relapse.

PREVENTION

Quitting smoking may reduce the risk of pancreatic cancer.

MALE/FEMALE DIFFERENCES

Pancreatic cancer is slightly more common in men than women.

STOMACH CANCER

DEFINITION

Worldwide, stomach cancer is quite common, particularly in Japan, Chile, and parts of eastern Europe, but this disease has declined markedly in the United States during the past 45 years. Japanese migrating to the United States continue to have a high incidence of stomach cancer, but it is less common among their children and in succeeding generations.

This condition is rarely seen in Americans under the age of 40. The American Cancer Society estimates that there are about 24,000 cases of stomach (gastric) cancer with 13,600 deaths yearly.

CAUSE

Epidemiologic studies have implicated diet and other environmental factors in the development of stomach cancer. Studies in humans suggest that chemicals formed by spoiled food (aflatoxins) and some strains of bacteria (*H. pylori*) cause gastric cancer. Stomach cancer can be induced in laboratory animals by feeding them large amounts of nitrates and nitrites, compounds found naturally in certain foods and which are also used to make bacon and other cured meats.

A family history of stomach cancer increases the risk of this disease, as does gastritis. A stomach ulcer does not seem to be a predisposing factor, although patients who had part of their stomachs removed years earlier because of peptic ulcers have a higher incidence of stomach cancer than other people.

DIAGNOSIS

Stomach cancers cause few or minimal symptoms in their early stage. Later symptoms are often similar to ulcer symptoms or may include vague feelings of fullness, loss of appetite, indigestion, weight loss, nausea, and anemia and fatigue.

After inserting a gastroscope to view the inside of the stomach, doctors remove tissue samples from abnormal areas for biopsy to confirm the diagnosis.

TREATMENT

If the detected cancer is still localized, surgical removal can be curative. Very often, however, the cancer has spread to other organs by the time of diagnosis and chemotherapy and/or radiation therapy can be used to reduce the tumor size and palliate symptoms, but survival is generally not prolonged.

PREVENTION

Antibiotic therapy for people infected with *H. pylori*, and avoidance of spoiled foods (aflatoxins) may help prevent gastric cancer. Frequent checkups for people with low gastric acidity are recommended.

In a population of Chinese with low vitamin levels (compared to U.S. citizens) and a high incidence of cancer, supplementation with beta-carotene, vitamin E, and selenium for at least 5 years led to a statistically significant decreased risk of cancer, particularly gastric and esophageal cancer. Whether this would decrease the risk for relatively well-nourished Americans is unknown.

MALE/FEMALE DIFFERENCES

Stomach cancer occurs twice as often in men as in women.

LIVER CANCER

DEFINITION

Cancer originating in the liver is relatively rare in the United States, accounting for only 1 to 2 percent of all cancers; far more common is invasion of the liver by cancers metastasizing from other areas of the body. In some regions of the world, however, especially parts of Africa and Asia where hepatitis is common, 20 to 30 percent of all malignancies begin in the liver. (Liver cancer is the leading cause of cancer fatalities in some of these areas.)

In the United States, liver cancer occurs most often after the age of 40 or 50. The American Cancer Society estimates that about 15,800 cases of liver and biliary cancer and 12,600 deaths occur yearly.

Because its symptoms are often thought to be due to cirrhosis or other preexisting disease, liver cancer is often undiagnosed until an autopsy after the victim has died.

CAUSE

Liver cancer develops most frequently in people who have had certain kinds of viral hepatitis, particularly chronic hepatitis, but it also occurs in people with other chronic liver diseases, including cirrhosis. The consumption of mycotoxins, substances produced by certain molds and fungi (for example, aflatoxin is a product of a mold found on peanuts), is another possible cause. Male sex hormones may similarly contribute to liver cancer, but this has not been proven.

DIAGNOSIS

Pain and swelling in the upper abdomen are among the most common symptoms of this condition. Jaundice may occur if the tumor blocks a bile duct; anemia and elevated enzymes made by the liver detectable with blood tests are other signs of possible liver cancer.

CT scanning can locate tumor sites; a biopsy is required, however, to confirm a diagnosis of liver cancer.

TREATMENT

Advanced liver cancer is almost always fatal within a few months, though the outlook has improved slightly for patients with small, localized tumors that are surgically removed, followed by chemotherapy. Surgical removal in some cases has required a liver transplant, a new approach that has been attempted only for very small lesions.

MALE/FEMALE DIFFERENCES

This condition is more common in men than women.

PREVENTION

Vaccination against hepatitis is recommended. Hepatitis can be contracted from contaminated blood, body fluids, uncooked foods washed with contaminated water in endemic areas, and uncooked seafood, particularly clams and oysters. Also avoid excessive alcohol use.

CANCER OF THE ESOPHAGUS

DEFINITION

Esophageal cancer is relatively rare in the United States, but common elsewhere, most notably in sections of Asia. The American Cancer Society estimates that there are about 11,300 cases of esophageal cancer each year in the United States and 10,200 deaths.

About half of all esophageal cancers begin in the middle portion of the esophagus, and the rest originate in either the upper or lower third. In many cases involving the lower portion of the esophagus, cancer actually originates in stomach tissue that has migrated into the lower esophagus. The probability of cure is best for cancers in the lower portion of the esophagus and poorest for those in the upper portion.

CAUSE

Smoking, drinking alcohol, and other activities that damage the lining of the esophagus, such as consumption of hot liquids, or scarring, are associated with esophageal cancer. Iron deficiency has long been connected with an increased risk of esophageal cancer, but a normal diet provides sufficient iron for most people.

DIAGNOSIS

Early diagnosis and treatment is important because rapid spread to surrounding vital organs, lymph nodes, and the liver and lungs is common.

Difficulty in swallowing (dysphagia) is the most common and often only symptom of esophageal cancer. Any swallowing problem, even one that occurs intermittently, should be checked promptly by a doctor. Other possible symptoms include pain in the chest, back or neck, and spitting up of blood-flecked food.

Diagnosis is made by placing a fiber-optic tube down the esophagus to inspect its lining; pieces of abnormal tissue are removed for microscopic examination.

TREATMENT

Esophageal cancer is often first treated with chemotherapy, radiation, or both to shrink the tumor. Patients with esophageal cancer have often been unable to eat, and poor nutrition makes them too weak initially for surgery. However, shrinking the tumor and allowing the patient to eat and gain weight often provide the strength to withstand a surgical procedure. Cancers that arise in the lower esophagus may be surgically removed and the resulting gap filled by pulling up the stomach. Removal of cancers that involve the upper portion is more difficult or impossible, so survival rates are poor.

PREVENTION

Alcohol, smoking, very hot liquids, and spoiled foods (which may contain aflatoxins) should be avoided.

In a population of Chinese with low vitamin levels by Western standards and a high incidence of cancer, beta-carotene, vitamin E, and selenium supplementation for at least 5 years led to a significant decreased risk of gastric and esophageal cancer. Whether supplementation with these nutrients would decrease the risk for relatively well-nourished Westerners is unknown.

MALE/FEMALE DIFFERENCES

This cancer occurs more frequently in men than in women both in the United States and in endemic areas.

CANCER OF THE SMALL INTESTINE

DEFINITION

Cancer in the small intestine is rare; in the United States only about 3,600 cases occur each year and result in about 1,000 deaths. Most lesions in this part of the body are adenocarcinomas, sarcomas, or lymphomas. The risk appears to be increased by chronic small intestine disorders such as celiac sprue or regional enteritis.

CAUSE

The causes of small intestine cancer are unknown but may be similar to colorectal cancer since their incidence appears parallel.

DIAGNOSIS

Symptoms include fever, intestinal bleeding, loss of weight and appetite, and abdominal pain. Malignancies can be seen on an upper gastrointestinal series of x-rays only when additional x-rays are taken to visualize the small bowel. To confirm the diagnosis, surgery or occasionally endoscopy (visualization with a long tube) is required.

TREATMENT

Adenocarcinomas and sarcomas. The affected area is surgically removed. Radiation may be administered, but is very toxic; normal tissues in this area are more sensitive to radiation than are these tumors. No adjuvant chemotherapy is known to be effective. Chemotherapy may be administered for recurrent disease, but is not particularly effective. New drugs are being investigated.

Lymphomas. Gastrointestinal lymphomas have often spread at the time of diagnosis, but some types of lymphoma can still be cured (see "Malignancies of Lymphocytes"). Lymphomas are usually very responsive to chemotherapy and radiation.

PREVENTION

Because there are no established causes for cancers of the small bowel, no preventive measures can be recommended.

....

URINARY TRACT CANCERS

SYMPTOMS OF URINARY TRACT CANCERS

In their earliest stages these cancers often either have no symptoms or produce effects similar to those of benign enlargement of the prostate and urinary tract infections. Regular examination by a physician is more likely to discover cancer, but all of the following should be investigated as possible signs of prostate or other urinary tract cancer.

Inability to urinate
Frequent need to urinate
Difficulty initiating or stopping urine flow

Weak or interrupted urine flow
Pain or burning on urination
Blood in the urine
Persistent lower back, upper thigh, or pelvic pain

Note: Cancers of the prostate gland, penis, and testes are discussed in chapter 10, "Health Concerns of Men."

BLADDER CANCER

DEFINITION

Bladder cancers account for 52,300 cases per year with 9,900 deaths. When treated and detected early, the 5-year survival rate is 90 percent. Disease that has spread to adjacent organs has a 5-year survival rate of 46 percent; to distant organs, only 9 percent.

The most common symptom is blood in the urine (hematuria); other symptoms include urinary urgency, painful urination, abdominal or back pain, and loss of weight and appetite.

CAUSE

Tobacco use and exposure to certain industrial chemicals and dyes are associated with an increased risk of bladder cancer.

DIAGNOSIS

The bladder lining can be directly examined with a cystoscope, and suspicious tissue can be biopsied. Additional tests such as chest x-rays and bone scans also may be performed to check for spread of the cancer.

TREATMENT

If the cancer is in an early, superficial stage, transurethral installation of BCG (bacilluse Calmette-Guérin) or certain chemotherapeutic drugs can be curative. Alternatively, electrocautery can be performed: a long, fiber-optic instrument is passed through the urethra into the bladder, and electrical current is used to cut away the tumor. Electrocautery can be repeated if needed to control regrowth of the tumors.

Regular follow-up is advised for life since the recurrence frequency of superficial bladder cancer exceeds 60 percent.

PREVENTION

Abstention from smoking can decrease the risk of this disease. According to the American Cancer Society, smoking is responsible for approximately 47 percent of bladder cancer deaths among men and 37 percent among women.

Occupational exposure to certain dyes, rubber, and leather increases the risk of bladder cancer, so use appropriate precautions to limit exposure.

MALE/FEMALE DIFFERENCES

Men are affected more often than women, and whites more often than blacks.

KIDNEY CANCER

DEFINITION

In the United States, there are 27,200 new cases of kidney cancer each year, with about 10,900 deaths. When treated early, the 5-year survival rate is 85 percent but drops to 56 percent when the disease has spread to adjacent organs, and to 9 percent for distant metastases.

CAUSE

There are no established causes for kidney cancer.

DIAGNOSIS

The most common symptom is blood in the urine (hematuria); other symptoms include abdominal or back pain, loss of weight and appetite, persistent fever, and anemia. Tests for kidney tumors include an intravenous pyelogram or abdominal CT scanning (see chapter 12, Diagnostic Tests and Procedures).

TREATMENT

Since most kidney cancers affect only one kidney, localized kidney cancer is best treated by removal of the involved kidney. (The remaining kidney can sufficiently filter wastes from the blood.) If cancer affects both kidneys, tumors may be removed and sufficient functioning kidney tissue salvaged to avoid the need for dialysis. Thus far, no curative therapy exists for metastatic kidney cancer. Interleukin-2 can induce remissions, but the substance is highly toxic. Chemotherapy and hormone manipulation are rarely successful.

PREVENTION

Because the causes of kidney cancer are unknown, no effective preventive measures have been found.

LEUKEMIAS

DEFINITION

Leukemias are malignancies characterized by the production of abnormal or immature white blood cells (leukocytes). Leukemias are classified as either lymphoid leukemias (involving lymphocytes) or myeloid leukemias (involving granulocytes and monocytes). Either type of leukemia can be acute (rapidly progressing) or chronic (relatively slow growing).

As leukemia progresses, abnormal white cells eventually interfere with the production and function of the healthy white blood cells (defenders against bacteria, viruses, and other infections), red blood cells (oxygen transporters), and platelets (clotting agents).

About 29,300 new cases of leukemia occur per year in the United States, 26,700 in adults and 2,600 in children. The death toll is around 18,600 yearly. Although leukemias are less common in children than in adults, they are the most prevalent childhood malignant disease. Children with Down syndrome (mongolism) and some other genetic diseases are at increased risk of leukemia. Acute lymphocytic leukemia (ALL) is the most common leukemia in children. In adults, acute myeloid leukemia (AML) and chronic lymphatic leukemia (CLL) are the most frequent.

The symptoms of leukemia are vague and similar to symptoms produced by other less serious diseases. Fatigue and pallor (from anemia), bruising and nosebleeds (because of inadequate platelets), and fever and other signs of infection such as a sore throat are indications. Enlarged lymph nodes, spleen, and liver, caused by the accumulation of leukemic cells, are more frequent in children. Pain, especially in the joints; swollen and bleeding gums; and various skin lesions also occur.

In acute leukemias, symptoms develop quickly in days or a few weeks, whereas symptoms in chronic leukemia progress more gradually over months or years. However, chronic myeloid leukemia can become a difficult to treat acute leukemia, often fatal within a few months.

The probability of cure of childhood acute lymphocytic leukemia treated at a major cancer center is currently about 80 percent; children with a better or worse prognosis can be identified at the time of diagnosis and treated appropriately. The outlook is not as optimistic for acute lymphocytic leukemia or acute myelocytic leukemia in adults (see also the Leukemia section in chapter 23, Blood Disorders).

CAUSE

Leukemias, like other cancers, are caused by specific genetic changes due to DNA damage that may be inherited or result from exposure to radiation, chemicals (e.g., benzene), viruses (HTLV-I), or drugs.

DIAGNOSIS

Leukemia may be diagnosed by an abnormal amount of one type of blood cell on a blood count or from the appearance of abnormal cells on a blood smear under the microscope. The blood smear or the blood count may show only mild abnormalities, however.

The diagnosis can be made reliably by examining cells taken from the bone marrow, usually removed by needle from the back of the pelvic bones near the hip. (For more information on this test, see chapter 12, "Diagnostic Tests and Procedures.") The marrow in leukemia usually contains too many cells, many of which look abnormal. Special chemical and immunologic stains as well as an examination of the karyotype (gene structure) of the leukemia cells aid in determining the exact type of leukemia and the appropriate treatment.

Leukemias are usually best diagnosed and treated at large centers because of the sophisticated stains and cytogenetics required for accurate diagnosis and the complex supportive care needed during recovery from intensive therapy.

TREATMENT

Acute Leukemias. Because leukemia is so serious (leukemic blood cells generally compromise the body's ability to fight infection and clot blood), patients with acute conditions are immediately admitted to the hospital, the diagnosis of the exact type of leukemia established, and chemotherapy treatment begun quickly, generally within 24 hours of admission.

The first step in controlling leukemia is to obtain a complete remission with induction chemotherapy. These drugs kill both leukemic cells and many normal bone marrow cells, but since most leukemic cells divide more slowly than their normal counterparts, healthy regenerating cells are more likely to repopulate the marrow after treatment. Marrow recovery after a cycle of induction therapy often takes 2 to 3 weeks, and two cycles of induction chemotherapy are frequently required to produce a complete remission. Remission induction may require 5 to 8 weeks in the hospital. Because the white blood count and platelet counts are very low during this period (rendering leukemic patients susceptible to infection and bleeding), antibiotics and platelet transfusions, as well as transfusions of red blood cells for anemia, are usually administered.

A rare variant of acute myeloid leukemia—acute promyelocytic leukemia—is often treated with a vitamin analog (all-trans retinoic acid) followed by chemotherapy.

After marrow recovery and bone marrow confirmation of complete remission, induction therapy is generally followed by further intermittent intensive chemotherapy lasting an additional 4 to 8 months in adults, often longer in children.

Failure to achieve a complete remission (or relapse after remission) is associated with a very poor prognosis. Repeated remission inductions result in progressively poorer responses to therapy and progressively shorter duration of remissions.

Chronic Leukemia. Some of the chronic leukemias can be managed conservatively without drugs or with relatively gentle chemotherapy for many years. The only curative treatment for chronic myeloid leukemia is an allogeneic bone marrow transplant, generally recommended for patients under 50 with a matched sibling marrow donor.

Bone Marrow Transplantation. Bone marrow transplants have been used to treat selected patients with relapsed acute leukemia and is now the only curative treatment for chronic myeloid leukemia. Patients are treated with very high doses of radiation or chemotherapy (up to ten times the conventional dose of chemotherapy) to remove even resistant leukemia cells from the bone marrow. Bone marrow cells removed from a compatible, matched donor are injected to reseed the marrow with healthy cells (an allogeneic transplant). In some patients lacking a compatible donor, marrow may be taken from the patient (autologous transplantation), treated outside the body with drugs to remove leukemia cells ("purged"), and reinjected into the patient.

The side effects of a marrow transplant are substantial: the grafted bone marrow may be rejected, or the marrow's immunocompetent cells may mount a "graft versus host" reaction against the patient, sometimes with a fatal outcome.

Despite these possibilities, a relatively young patient faced with an invariably fatal disease will often be administered this toxic but potentially curative therapy.

PREVENTION

Avoidance of exposure to radiation, chemicals (e.g., benzene), viruses (HTLV-I), and drugs associated with the development of leukemias may lower the risk of this disease.

MALIGNANCIES OF LYMPHOCYTES

These cancers include non-Hodgkin's lymphomas, Hodgkin's disease, and multiple myeloma.

DEFINITION

Lymphocytes are the white cells that circulate through the blood, bone marrow, lymph nodes, thymus, liver, and spleen, all the while searching for infections and producing antibodies. After initial contact with an infectious agent, lymphocytes develop an immunity memory that wards off reinfection. Mature lymphocytes actively producing antibodies are called plasma cells and may become the cancerous cells in myeloma.

Non-Hodgkin's lymphomas are the most common lymphomas, affecting 43,000 Americans each year and resulting in more than 20,000 deaths. Hodgkin's disease accounts for nearly 8,000 new cases each year and 1,500 deaths, while there are nearly 13,000 new cases of myeloma yearly and 9,400 deaths.

Hodgkin's disease can strike at any age but is most common in young adults or adults over age 50. It often begins as a lymph node swelling in the neck or just under the collarbone that tends to spread to contiguous lymph nodes, involving those in the chest, and then the spleen and lymph nodes in the abdomen and pelvis. If the spleen is involved, the liver may also be affected. Symptoms include fever, night sweats, and weight loss.

The overall 5-year survival rate for Hodgkin's disease depends on the cell type and which organs are invaded by lymphoma. Even if the disease has affected the lungs or liver, cure is still possible in about 50 percent of young adults.

Myeloma, a cancer of plasma cells, occurs most often after the age of 50. The abnormal cells continue to function, manufacturing antibodies and releasing them into the bloodstream, but expansion of the cancerous plasma cells in the bone marrow causes destruction of the surrounding bone and localized pain. The bone destruction can cause an abnormally high calcium level in the blood and urine, leading to confusion, constipation, kidney damage, and, if untreated, coma and heart abnormalities. As the plasma cells proliferate, they crowd out normal white and red blood cells, resulting in anemia and decreased levels of normal antibodies, increasing vulnerability to infection. The average survival is now 4 years (see also chapter 23, Blood Disorders).

CAUSE

Lymphomas are increasing in incidence in the United States. Exposure to farm chemicals and certain viruses, such as EBV (Burkitt's lymphoma), HTLV, and HIV (AIDS), increases the risk of lymphoma.

DIAGNOSIS

Patients generally present with swollen lymph nodes. Swollen lymph nodes raise a suspicion of lymphoma, especially if there are other symptoms, such as fever, night sweats, and weight loss. The diagnosis entails a biopsy of involved tissue. Myeloma is often diagnosed by a blood test that detects abnormal amounts of gamma globulin.

TREATMENT

There are many different non-Hodgkin's lymphomas (NHL), some aggressive and some more indolent. The treatment and the prognosis depend on the type of lymphoma and the extent of disease. Treatment may include chemotheraphy, radiation therapy, and a bone marrow transplant.

Hodgkin's disease and some forms of non-Hodgkin's lymphomas are curable with chemotherapy, radiation therapy, or a combination of both.

Myeloma can be treated with chemotherapy and radiation therapy. Treatment may involve radiation therapy to the involved bone, and, depending upon the extent of the disease, chemotherapy.

PREVENTION

Avoidance of viruses and environmental toxins associated with the development of lymphomas may lower the risk of this disease. Because AIDS increases the risk of lymphomas, avoiding exposure to body fluids and other AIDS avoidance techniques decreases the risk of lymphoma.

SARCOMAS

These are cancers of the bone and connective tissue.

DEFINITION

Sarcomas are relatively uncommon, with only about 2,000 new bone cancers and 1,050 deaths a year in the United States, and 6,000 connective tissue cancers resulting in 3,100 annual deaths. Most occur in young adults; the median age of patients is 40.

Osteosarcoma, which originates in bone, usually causes a painful mass, most commonly in the legs, especially above or below the knee. Ewing's sarcoma, which also develops in bone, usually affects the shafts of long bones or the pelvis. Both bone tumors develop predominantly in adolescents and young adults. Pain and swelling in the affected bone are the most common symptoms of bone cancer. Patients with Ewing's sarcoma may also have fever, weight loss, and generalized malaise and fatigue.

Soft-tissue sarcomas (connective-tissue cancers) generally develop as a painless mass in the thigh, on the trunk, or in the abdomen, although other locations are possible. Kaposi's sarcoma, which generally appears as red lesions on the lower extremities of elderly men, is a rare, generally indolent tumor managed with surgery, superficial radiotherapy or low-dose, gentle chemotherapy. However, a variant that arises in HIV-infected patients is considerably more aggressive, developing in mucosa of the mouth and gastrointestinal tract, and in internal organs. (See chapter 19, HIV Infection and AIDS.)

CAUSE

Patients with certain specific genetic abnormalities are at higher risk of developing sarcomas. These include familial retinoblastoma, neurofibromatosis, and a syndrome characterized by a hereditary predisposition to breast cancer and sarcomas. Radiation (given for treatment of a prior malignancy) can result in the development of sarcomas in the location that was radiated. Exposure to certain chemicals—such as the dioxin in Agent Orange, agricultural herbicides, asbestos, and arsenic—result in a higher incidence of certain sarcomas. Kaposi's sarcoma is associated with HIV infection, though the causative mechanism has not been identified.

DIAGNOSIS

Diagnostic tests include a small biopsy of any suspicious lesion. A CT scan is generally necessary to detect sarcomas hidden in the abdomen, and a CT scan of the lungs is important to detect spread.

TREATMENT

Soft-Tissue Sarcoma. Surgery and often radiotherapy are generally required. The risk of relapse depends on adequately removing the tumor with a margin of normal tissue around it (local recurrence) and on the size and aggressiveness of the tumor (its spread to other organs, particularly the lungs). Lesions less than 5 cm in size (about 2 inches) are generally cured when appropriately removed, as are moderately large, low-grade (relatively nonaggressive) lesions. The prognosis for high-grade (aggressive) tumors is less favorable with larger tumors.

Osteosarcoma. In some cases, the affected extremity can be salvaged by removing only the tumor and inserting a metal replacement joint. The survival rate for patients with localized osteosarcoma treated with surgery and chemotherapy is about 50 percent.

Ewing's sarcoma is treated with combination chemotherapy and radiation. Sometimes surgery is used as well.

PREVENTION

Avoid exposure to identified causes of sarcoma, including agricultural herbicides, asbestos, and arsenic. Taking steps to avoid infection with the HIV virus also lowers risk, although the causative mechanism has not been identified.

MALE/FEMALE DIFFERENCES

These conditions are slightly more prevalent in men than women.

THYROID CANCER

DEFINITION

Thyroid cancer is the second most common of the malignancies affecting the endocrine glands (after cancer of the ovaries). About 12,700 new cases are diagnosed in the United States each year. But the outlook is generally good; about 1,050 deaths each year are caused by this type of cancer because thyroid cancer is generally cured or adequately controlled.

Thyroid cancer occurs more commonly in women than in men and may affect young adults. Most thyroid cancers grow relatively slowly. Spread to distant organs is unusual, at least in the early stage of the disease. Types of thyroid cancer are as follows:

Papillary Carcinoma. The most common type of thyroid cancer. Cells form short cordlike structures interspersed with abnormal cancerous thyroid gland tissue (follicles). This tumor often remains localized for years, then may spread to lymph nodes in the neck, and then to the lungs.

Follicular Thyroid Cancer. More common in older people, especially women who have had earlier radiation therapy of the neck. The cells of this tissue form follicles resembling those on the normal thyroid, but this type of thyroid cancer spreads to other organs more frequently than other types.

Medullary (Solid) Thyroid Cancer. Cells do not form recognizable thyroidlike structures. This disease tends to run in families.

CAUSE

Radiation to the neck increases the risk of thyroid cancer. Medullary thyroid cancer is familial and often is associated with multiple endocrine tumors; because of this inherited tendency, siblings of the patient and other family members should be screened periodically.

DIAGNOSIS

The most common sign of thyroid cancer is a painless lump in the neck that, unlike the more common goiters and benign nodules, usually forms a single mass with a hard consistency. Recent and rapid enlargement of the thyroid and/or childhood x-ray treatments to the neck also increase the possibility of thyroid cancer.

Diagnosis is confirmed by biopsy.

TREATMENT

Treatment depends upon the type and location of the cancer.

Papillary Tumor. Small tumors confined to a single thyroid lobe are treated by removal of the affected lobe. Since this type of cancer often develops in an under-functioning lobe and is stimulated by thyroid-stimulating hormone (TSH) secreted in response to low thyroid hormone levels, treatment also may involve giving thyroid hormone to suppress growth of tumor cells. Larger papillary tumors require more extensive surgery, often including removal of the entire thyroid gland and destruction of any remaining tissue with radioactive iodine followed by lifetime replacement with thyroid hormone.

Medullary Cancer. The entire thyroid is removed; if the parathyroid glands are involved, they too are removed. In cases with multiple familial endocrine tumors, the adrenal glands (small, hormone-producing glands located above each kidney) should be checked for pheochromocytomas, which need to be removed prior to thyroid surgery.

Follicular Cancer. Treatment is similar to papillary cancer; metastases may be treated with radioactive iodine or chemotherapy.

PREVENTION

Avoid radiation of the neck.

....

CANCERS OF THE CENTRAL NERVOUS SYSTEM

DEFINITION

Each part of the central nervous system is vulnerable to a particular form of cancer. The most common type of brain cancer is a glioma, a tumor that arises in the supportive tissue of the brain. Other malignancies of the central nervous system include tumors of the pituitary (an endocrine gland at the base of the brain), tumors of the meninges (the membranes surrounding and covering the brain and spinal cord), and cancer in the cranial nerves. Cancers confined to the spinal cord are much less common than brain tumors and usually involve the meninges.

Brain cancer can occur at any age, but is most common among young and middle-aged adults. In the United States, about 17,500 brain cancers are diagnosed each year, causing about 12,100 deaths. For unknown reasons, the incidence of brain tumors is increasing.

CAUSE

The causes of cancers of the central nervous system are unknown.

DIAGNOSIS

The most common symptoms of brain tumor result from increased intracranial pressure, either from the tumor mass or swelling. Symptoms include headache, nausea, visual changes, convulsions, lethargy, personality changes, psychotic episodes, or confusion. The most common early symptoms of spinal cord cancers are pain from compression of the nerve roots; sensory loss, muscular weakness and wasting; and finally paralysis with more advanced disease.

Brain and spinal tumors usually can be detected with CT or MRI scans. Other tests determine if cancers are elsewhere in the body since the brain is a frequent target of metastasis.

TREATMENT

Drugs to reduce brain swelling are generally given immediately to relieve symptoms. Surgical removal of as much of the cancer as possible is followed by radiation therapy or chemotherapy, or both.

Survival depends on the grade of the tumor, which is determined by microscopic inspection. The median survival for patients with high-grade gliomas is about 2 years whereas more indolent tumors are associated with longer survival.

Inoperable cancers are treated with radiation therapy and chemotherapy to reduce the size of the tumor.

Tumors on the surface of the spinal cord may be removed surgically, depending upon their location and degree of damage; inoperable cancers are treated with radiation therapy.

PREVENTION

There are no established causes for central nervous system cancer and no known preventive measures.

....

RETINOBLASTOMA

DEFINITION

Retinoblastoma is a rare cancer of the retina that usually develops in children under the age of 3. About half of all cases are hereditary. Because "sporadic" cases result from new genetic mutations, siblings of patients should be examined periodically. When diagnosed and treated early, 80 percent of all cases can be cured.

CAUSE

Retinoblastoma can be caused by deletion or damage to both Rb genes on chromosome 13. Rb is a tumor-suppressor gene. If damaged or absent, cancers develop more readily. In familial cases, one chromosome already is inherited with the abnormal Rb gene and the other must be damaged to produce a tumor. In sporadic cases, both Rbs on chromosomes 13 in the same retinal cell become damaged.

DIAGNOSIS

Signs include crossed eyes (strabismus) or a yellow or white spot in the pupil. Inherited cases—about 50 percent of all cases—usually affect both eyes. The tumors often can be visualized by careful examination of the eye. A CT scan also may detect other small tumors in other parts of the eye.

TREATMENT

Treatment depends upon the extent of the cancer. One involved eye can be removed along with as much of the optic nerve as possible and the other eye examined periodically. If both eyes are involved, the one with the more extensive disease often will be removed and the other treated with laser surgery, freezing (cryotherapy), radiation, and chemotherapy in an effort to eliminate the cancer while preserving as much eyesight as possible.

Following treatment, the child needs periodic follow-up to determine if the cancer has spread to other organs or reappeared in the other eye.

PREVENTION

Children in families that carry an abnormal Rb gene must be screened periodically for retinoblastoma.

....

SKIN CANCER

DEFINITION

Skin cancer, the most common of all human malignancies, strikes 700,000 Americans each year and causes more than 9,000 deaths.

The most dangerous type of skin cancer is malignant melanoma, a cancer of melanocytes, the cells that produce skin and retinal pigment. Melanomas can start in any skin area that contains pigment-producing cells, but body moles are common sites. Some superficial melanomas spread mainly along the skin surface, but a more aggressive type—nodular melanoma—is raised and lumpy and tends to invade the underlying tissue earlier in the course of the disease. Melanoma affects about 32,000 people a year and results in 6,700 deaths. Its incidence is increasing and is expected to double in the next 10 years.

SKIN CANCER FACTORS

People who are a high risk of skin cancer include.

- Light-haired, blue-eyed, fair-skinned individuals
- Outdoor workers
- Anyone with signs of sun-induced skin damage
- Those with workplace exposure to ionizing radiation or polycyclic hydrocarbons
- Individuals born with many abnormal moles (dysplastic nevi)

The two more common types of skin cancer are basal cell carcinoma, by far the most frequent variety, and squamous cell carcinoma. These cancers, 18 times more common than melanoma, are rarely fatal.

The 5-year survival rate for melanoma when treated early is 91 percent. Once the disease has spread to lymph nodes, however, survival is 54 percent, and advanced melanoma has a survival rate of only 13 percent.

Periodic examination of the skin (particularly moles and other pigmented marks) may improve the prognosis of melanoma because the disease is highly curable when treated in its earliest stage.

CAUSE

Most skin cancers are caused by sun exposure; in the United States skin cancer is most common in the South and Southwest, where the sun is strong and people spend more time outdoors with little protective clothing.

Melanoma occurs most often in fair-skinned whites who spend a good deal of time in the sun. Families with dysplastic nevi have a hereditary predisposition to developing melanoma. Some very large moles present at birth also have the potential to become melanoma, and are often removed in early childhood.

Occupational exposure to ionizing radiation and polycyclic hydrocarbons has been implicated in the development of skin cancer.

DIAGNOSIS AND SYMPTOMS OF MALIGNANT MELANOMA

Any mole or other pigmented mark that exhibits any of the following features should be examined by a physician, preferably a dermatologist.

- An irregular shape. If the mole could be folded in half, the sides would not match.
- Jagged border rather than smooth.

- A change in color or development of nonuniform shading (paler or darker in some areas or with tones of red, blue, or black in addition to brown).
- Greater than 7 mm (about the size of a pencil eraser).

Change in the texture, color, shape, and size of an existing pigmented mark and any mole that appears after the age of 30, or that is tender, itches, or bleeds should be seen promptly by a dermatologist. Diagnosis of skin cancer is done by biopsy.

TREATMENT

Nonmelanoma skin cancers usually can be treated easily with topical anticancer drugs or removal with a blade, freezing, or laser.

Melanomas are treated by surgical removal of the cancer and some surrounding normal tissues. Although recurrent melanoma can be removed, metastatic melanoma is difficult to treat with chemotherapy or radiation.

PREVENTION

Skin cancer is one of the most preventable cancers. Ultraviolet light from the sun causes cellular damage resulting in skin cancer, so lifelong sun protection is the key to prevention. Everyone (but particularly fair-skinned individuals and others at risk) should avoid excessive exposure to the sun and when outside should wear protective clothing and sunscreens rated SPF 15 or greater.

Also avoid tanning salons and other exposure to intense artificial ultraviolet light. Workplace exposure to substances known to cause skin cancer should be avoided and you should consider prophylactic removal of large or other atypical moles.

Paradoxically, by allowing longer exposures without sunburn, the use of sunscreens may actually be increasing sun exposure. Do not overdo sun exposure even when wearing sunscreen.

SUMMING UP

Cancer remains the second leading cause of death among Americans and statistics suggest that by the year 2010, cancer will be the leading cause of death in the United States. Individuals can significantly decrease their risk of cancer by changing everyday habits and can reduce their chances of dying of cancer by following simple screening procedures for common cancers.

More than 1 of 3 of all lives lost to cancer could be saved by eliminating all tobacco use. Thousands of other cases could potentially be prevented by changes in diet (see chapter 5, "The Basics of Good Nutrition") or reducing environmental carcinogens.

Medical advances provide hope for the future: We now have a substantial understanding of how cancer cells develop, and have even located some of the specific genes involved. Individuals with these genes and thus at high risk for certain tumors can be screened at regular intervals or undergo prophylactic removal of organs at risk, if appropriate. Although more than half of all Americans who are diagnosed with cancer this year will be cured, the best prospect for cure is to try to avoid developing the disease.

18
Infectious Diseases

· · · · · · · · · · · · · · · ·

**HAROLD C. NEU, M.D.
AND GLENDA GARVEY,
M.D.**

Large numbers of bacteria, viruses, and fungal spores fill the air, cover our skin, cling to our hair follicles, and dwell at the base of our teeth. The intestines harbor billions of useful bacteria that promote proper digestion and elimination. Our intimate partnership with these minuscule microbes is mostly one of mutual tolerance, and often beneficial symbiosis, but as in many close associations relations occasionally go awry. The frequent result: infection. This chapter presents a broad overview of the more common infectious diseases, some of which are also discussed in chapters dealing with specific organ systems.

CAUSES OF INFECTION

What happens to upset the usual harmonious balance between our bodies and microbes? Two events are necessary for infection to occur.

1. A virulent microbe—one of the small number of microbes capable of producing disease—must invade the body via the skin or the mucous membranes.
2. The immune system, which normally attacks and destroys invading germs, must be in a weakened or compromised condition.

BACTERIAL INFECTION

Each of the body surfaces—the skin, the conjunctiva or outer surface of the eye, the mucous membranes of the upper and lower respiratory tract, and the lining of the genital tract—is home to a characteristic group of bacterial flora unique to that part of the body (bacteria are one-celled creatures that lack nuclei). When a bacterial infection begins, a pathogenic (disease-producing) bacterium first survives at one of these sites amidst and in competition with the normal flora already present. Then, for the infection to proceed, the organism must employ a means of penetrating deeper into the tissues and producing harm. For instance, recent research demonstrates that some bacterial pathogens infiltrate the body by attaching to mucosal cells through specific surface-to-surface interactions. Other bacteria cause disease by multiplying on the epithelial cells (the surface covering of the skin, organs, and other internal tissue) and then secreting toxins (poisonous substances) that diffuse throughout the body and foment illness. For example, *Corynebacterium diphtheriae* infects the lin-

ing of the throat, generating a toxin that enters the body, sometimes damaging the heart.

Some toxins produce disease locally without diffusing into other body structures. For instance, *Vibrio cholerae* yields a toxin harmless to the lining of the intestine but which disrupts the enzymes enabling the intestines to retain water. The result is the severe diarrhea characteristic of cholera. Other bacteria penetrate our mucosal barriers, multiplying and killing the local cells. An example is the *shigella* bacterium that causes dysentery, another severe diarrheal disease. Yet other destructive bacteria, such as streptococcal pharyngitis (commonly referred to as strep throat), can penetrate into subepithelial cells; still others actually spread throughout the body, as is the case with the typhoid bacillus.

Some virulent microorganisms establish themselves as part of our stable bacterial flora in one part of the body but cause disease when they spread to another location. *Streptococcus pneumoniae,* for example, colonizes in the throat during the winter, usually producing no noticeable symptoms or disease until it enters the lung. Another organism, *Branhamella catarrhalis,* lives harmlessly in many throats but can cause disease in the ears of children or in the sinuses of some adults.

A sinister talent of some virulent microbes (including the tuberculosis bacterium) is the ability to survive ingestion by the very cells supposed to destroy them—the white blood cells and the macrophages. Other microorganisms produce poisons called endotoxins as a component of their own cell wall, causing severe damage to humans when these organisms die or are killed in the body by the immune system; endotoxins are associated with the life-threatening shock that sometimes ensues after bacteria pour into the bloodstream from an infection.

VIRUS INVASIONS

As for viruses, they cause as many diseases as bacteria, ranging from severe encephalitis (inflammation of the brain), to hepatitis and sexually transmitted diseases. Structurally less complex than bacteria, viruses' effects primarily stem from their attachment to surface structures and their influence on the genetic system. Unlike bacteria, viruses are parasitic and grow only within other cells. They can cause great harm as they invade cells, multiply within, and kill host cells before moving on to the conquest of other cells.

A virus's damaging parasitic ability depends on its coating or surface. This reliance renders viruses vulnerable to simple substances like hypochlorous acid, or household bleach, which destroys these pathogens by damaging their all-important surface properties. Conversely, antibiotics are ineffective against viruses and destroy only bacteria.

Viruses are able to grow only in certain types of cells. Influenza virus, for example, is restricted to respiratory epithelium; it cannot multiply in other tissue cells. The polio virus has an affinity for the nervous system. Herpes simplex, Type 1 virus prefers areas in and around the mouth; herpes simplex, Type 2 lives in and around the genital organs.

Cellular reactions to viral invasions vary widely. Cells may accept a virus and live symbiotically with it, or at the other extreme, cells may succumb after viruses take them over and kill them by changing their genetic structure (this genetic change is called hyperplasia). Alternatively, hyperplasia may cause cells to grow malignantly, generating tumor formation. The length of time between viral invasion and the appearance of a disease can extend from hours to years; slow-acting viruses, known as "slow viruses," are responsible for devastating diseases of the central nervous system.

FUNGUS GROWTH

The third major group of infection-causing organisms is the fungi (plural for *fungus,* Latin term for "mushroom"). This family of organisms includes yeasts, molds, and mushrooms. Though lacking chlorophyll, fungi structurally resemble plants, with nucleated cells, mitochondria, and more than one chromosome (bacteria lack these traits). Extremely diverse, the fungi family lives on soil, on plants, and in water. When fungi attack humans, they generate many diseases, both on the skin and within the body.

THE BODY'S DEFENSES AGAINST INFECTION

The body possesses many defenses against microbe invasion.

- **Skin:** Forms an effective physical barrier to bacterial, viral, and fungal invasion. Its specific antimicrobial properties are not well understood, but its mild acidity and normal bacteria population deter opportunistic microbes.
- **Membranes:** Within the body, membranes are bathed in secretions, such as cervical mucus, prostatic fluid, and tears, that are toxic to many organisms.
- **Respiratory tract:** Possesses an aerodynamic filtering system in the tracheal-bronchial tree. Small hairs (cilia) in the nose continually sweep out invaders. A layer of mucus traps invaders, and coughing expels organisms. Ninety percent of inhaled microbes are expelled within 1 hour.

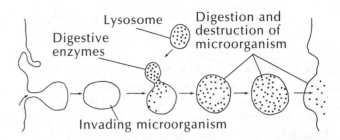

Figure 18.1: During phagocytosis, the macrophage travels to the site of infection and first adheres to the invading agent and then proceeds to surround and ingest it. It then releases enzymes that kill the bacteria.

- **Gastrointestinal tract:** Hostile environment to invading microbes. Acid in the stomach destroys many, while enzymes secreted by the pancreas and intestines are lethal to others. Cells on the surface of the intestine slough off continuously, purging unwanted visitors. The specialized contractions (peristalsis) of the intestines discourage microorganism colonization.
- **Urinary tract:** Defended by local antibodies and a very frequent and effective flushing via urination.
- **Kidneys:** Create a chemical environment particularly hostile to bacteria.
- **Prostate gland:** In men this gland's secretions destroy microbes.
- **Vagina:** No particular cleansing ability, but estrogen stimulates increased deposits of glycogen,

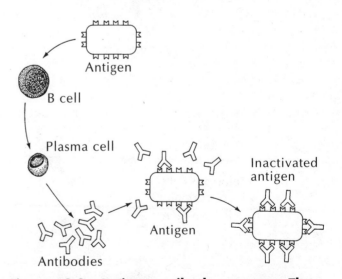

Figure 18.2: Antigen-antibody response. The antigen stimulates a B cell, which has been programmed to recognize it, to transform itself into a plasma cell, which in turn produces antibodies. These antibodies attach to the antigen, making it harmless.

which nourishes beneficial bacteria. Lactobacillus' lactic acid production inhibits harmful bacteria.

The Immune System. When physical and biochemical barriers fail to expel or neutralize an invasion by dangerous microbes, the second line of defense—the immune-defense system—engages invading organisms. This complicated group of organs, nodes, vessels, specialized cells, and blood proteins stands ready to mount a rapid reaction to disease-producing organisms and the toxins they generate. Basically, this system encompasses several types of white blood cells and a blood protein called complement.

White Blood Cells. Manufactured by the billions in the bone marrow, these leukocytes sense, trap, engulf, and destroy unwanted agents, a process known as phagocytosis (see figure 18.1). White blood cells known as lymphocytes manufacture antibodies or instruct other white blood cells called macrophages to kill bacteria (though sometimes they have other specialized functions).

Antibodies. Proteins that circulate in the blood and in fluids between tissues. Antibodies bind to invading organisms, neutralizing their pathologic effects and enhancing their destruction by phagocytic white blood cells.

Lymphocytes. Leukocytes that possess the unique ability to "remember" each and every specific invader.

After the pathogens have been destroyed, a few lymphocytes imprint their identity and pass this information along to other "memory" lymphocytes for an indefinite period of time. If the same type of microbe tries to invade again, the memory lymphocytes quickly spring into action before serious infection sets in. This so-called acquired immunity makes vaccination possible (see figure 18.2).

Complement System. Activated by antibodies, this part of the complex immune defense consists of distinct proteins that, like antibodies, circulate in the bloodstream and in the fluid between tissues. Normally present in low amounts, these proteins multiply rapidly when activated and help the white blood cells ingest invading organisms. In certain circumstances, complement attacks and kills bacteria and other microbes by chemically poking holes in their cell walls.

Cellular and Humoral Immunity. Cellular or cell-mediated immunity describes the action of T cells, lymphocytes that kill or deactivate microbes by attaching to them (figure 18.3). Humoral immunity—deactivation of invading organisms via antibodies dissolved in blood and other body fluids—is carried on by what are called B cells.

B cells are the major components of the lymphoid tissue, which is located in the lymph nodes, spleen, gastrointestinal tract, and bone marrow—all sites that are

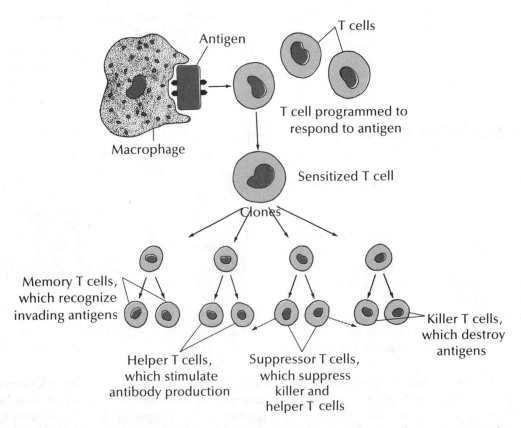

Figure 18.3: After an antigen is released by a macrophage, the T cell programmed to respond to it becomes sensitized. It enlarges and divides, forming 4 types of T cells, each with a specific function in cellular immunity.

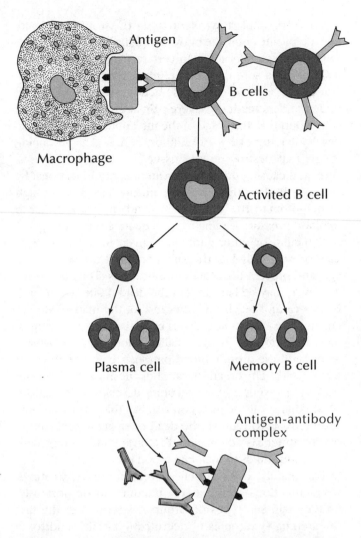

Antigen

B cells

Macrophage

Activited B cell

Plasma cell

Memory B cell

Antigen-antibody complex

Figure 18.4: An antigen released by a macrophage activates a B cell programmed to recognize it. The activated B cell divides, producing B cells that form plasma cells, which in turn produce antibodies and memory cells, which seek out the specific invading antigen. The antibodies produced by the plasma cells go on to produce the antigen-antibody complexes that are instrumental in humoral immunity.

ideally suited to timely intervention against invading organisms.

Cellular immunity is most effective against invaders such as parasites, cancer cells, transplants of foreign tissue, and fungi, whereas humoral immunity comes into play during bacterial or viral infections.

There are thousands of different T cells, each one programmed to respond to a particular antigen. Following phagocytosis (the surrounding of an invader), T-cell sensitization takes place: Sensitized T cells grow and divide, producing a clone population prepared to fight off further invasion by a specific agent (see figure 18.3). Within the clone population there are subsets of T cells:

suppressor, helper, killer, and memory T cells, so named because of their individual functions in combating microbe onslaught.

There also are thousands of different B cells (see figure 18.4), and like T cells each is programmed to respond to a specific antigen by producing specific antibodies. These antibodies travel through the blood and lymph to the specific site of foreign invasion where they attack and destroy the harmful microbes.

B cells need T cells to activate them; in some immune disorders such as AIDS, harmful bacteria (such as those that cause pneumonia) can multiply rapidly when damaged T cells fail to communicate effectively with B cells. In children, T cells are immature, so vaccines designed to encourage development of T-cell-dependent antibodies may not be effective in conveying immunity.

When a pathogenic microbe successfully evades all the body's defense mechanisms, the resultant infection usually causes local inflammation, generalized fever, and a host of other reactions depending on the particular type and site of infection. Fortunately, antibiotics can usually stave off harmful bacteria, and help the body regain health. The following sections discuss the major infectious diseases affecting organ systems.

NEW OR EMERGING INFECTIONS

By Glenda Garvey, M.D.

From time to time, important new infectious diseases make headlines and raise public concern. AIDS, or acquired immune deficiency disease, is the most dramatic recent example. This disease is caused by a previously unidentified virus, a member of the family of retroviruses that has been named the human immunodeficiency virus, or HIV (see chapter 19).

Organisms, including bacteria and viruses, are constantly changing, or mutating. This makes it possible for a previously harmless organism to evolve into one that can cause infections, which at times are life-threatening, in humans.

Other seemingly new diseases are not necessarily caused by new organisms; instead, changing circumstances allow existing microbes to invade humans. A notable example is Legionnaires' disease—the bacterial pneumonia that made headlines in 1976 when a number of people attending an American Legion convention in Philadelphia died of a mysterious type of pneumonia. The cause of the pneumonia was later traced to a bacterium named *Legionella pneumophilium*—an organism that normally lives in fresh-water lakes or streams, but which also thrives in water used in air-conditioning systems and similar reservoirs, where it can spread to humans.

The Centers for Disease Control and Prevention (CDC) in Atlanta tracks new and emerging diseases worldwide to provide an early warning system of diseases that might become a new threat to humans. Although many of these diseases are in developing countries that lack proper sanitation, industrialized countries like the United States are by no means immune from new or re-emerging infectious diseases. Three recent examples are Group A streptococci, the so-called "flesh-eating" bacteria that made headlines in 1994; a newly recognized strain of *Escherichia coli* that can cause fatal blood and kidney complications; and a type of hanta virus, a newly identified organism that is spread by mice and other small rodents and that causes a severe, often fatal respiratory disease.

GROUP A STREPTOCOCCI

This organism causes a broad spectrum of infections; the most common is "strep throat." Complications of this throat infection can include rheumatic fever; less common are severe infections of the skin and muscles. There appears to be a waxing and waning of the severity of Group A streptococcal infections. The last major peak of severity occurred during World War II, and then almost disappeared from our continent. This decline preceded the use of penicillin and appears to be part of cyclical changes in the virulence of the organism.

In the mid-1980s, outbreaks of acute rheumatic fever as complications of Group A strep throat were again noted in the United States and other parts of the world. In the 1990s, outbreaks of severe, invasive infections with this organism have been reported. Of particular note are two complications: necrotizing fasciitis, an infeciton of the skin and underlying tissue, including the muscle, and a type of shock that is like that of toxic shock syndrome, an infection that was first reported with a strain of staphylococcal bacteria. These two manifestations are associated with specific subsets, or serotypes, of the Group A streptococcus. These serotypes are not new, but have re-emerged in greater numbers as the result of a poorly understood evolutionary process. These subsets of Group A streptococci have acquired new virulence due, at least in part, to the mutation of a specific protein in the cell wall of the Group A streptococcus. Some of these mutated streptococci have, as well, incorporated genetic material that allows the production of toxins, including one that causes the toxic shock syndrome.

Group A strep infections that cause necrotizing fasciitis and toxic shock are particularly alarming because, although still rare, they have a high mortality rate—up to 30 to 50 percent, according to some researchers—and survivors may require removal of large amounts of muscle tissue or amputation to halt the infection's destructive course.

These particularly virulent types of Group A streptococci typically enter the body through a break in the skin; for example, a minor cut. In very rare instances, they are linked with a sore throat. The initial symptoms are a flu-like illness with fever, muscle aches, swelling of lymph nodes, and increasingly severe pain at the site of the initial skin wound. At this stage of the infection, the streptococcus is dividing every 45 minutes, and is also producing toxins that destroy muscle tissue, lowering blood pressure, and causing other life-threatening complications. By the fourth day, the patient typically has a very high fever—often to 103° F (39.4° C)—and experiences a drop in blood pressure leading to inadequate circulation.

Penicillin or other antibiotics given in the first three days or so usually halt the infection, limit the tissue damage, and prevent the other complications. The organisms, however, may be harbored in the dead tissue where antibiotics cannot reach them because of the inadequate circulation to the tissue. The bacteria trigger changes, including clotting in the smallest blood vessels which, along with the drop in blood pressure, combine to cause tissue death. The organisms are not "flesh eating," as popularly portrayed; a more accurate description would be "flesh killing." If the infection reaches this stage, the only alternative is to remove the dead or dying tissue. Antibiotic treatment is administered intravaneously along with intravenous fluids to maintain blood pressure.

Fortunately, even during a cyclic increase, Group A strep infections are relatively uncommon. Importantly, only certain serotypes of Group A strep cause the life-threatening syndromes of necrotizing fasciitis and toxic shock. The most common Group A strep infection, strep throat, which occurs predominantly in children, is not typically associated with the more virulent Group A strep serotypes. However, cases have been reported of the shock syndrome in association with a strep throat. Therefore, it does not pay to "play the odds," given the rapid, often devastating course of some Group A strep infections. Any rapidly rising fever accompanied by swollen lymph nodes, a rash, an increasingly painful sore throat or wound and other symptoms suggesting Group A strep infection warrants consulting a doctor immediately.

E. COLI TYPE 0157:H7

There are numerous strains of *E. coli,* including many that are relatively harmless. These rod-shaped bacteria live in the intestinal tracts of warm-blooded animals, including human beings.

Although many *E. coli* strains do not produce disease in humans, a notable exception is Type 0157:H7. This is the organism that made headlines in 1994 when several children fell deathly ill after eating undercooked hamburgers. Investigators traced the illnesses to the 0157:H7 strain of *E. coli* that was first recognized in 1982. This strain of *E. coli* lives in the intestines of healthy cattle and may contaminate the meat during slaughtering. This *E. coli* can cause severe diarrhea that may or may not be bloody, along with abdominal cramps. In severe cases, the infection precipitates the hemolytic uremic syndrome, characterized by the acute breakdown of red blood cells and a rapid deterioration of kidney function.

Humans contract this type of *E. coli* from eating undercooked beef, usually hamburgers or other types of ground beef. Occasionally other foods have been associated with the infection, including roast beef and, in rare instances, unpasteurized milk. Children, the elderly, or people with compromised immune systems are especially vulnerable. The organism can also spread directly from person to person, and outbreaks have been reported in day-care centers and nursing homes.

Antibiotics have little effect on the infection; treatment focuses more on giving replacement fluids and electrolytes. Hospitalization is usually necessary, especially if the patient is a child or other high-risk person.

Public health officials note that this type of *E. coli* infection can be prevented by making sure all meat, especially ground beef, is cooked until it is well done— gray, not pink—and using only pasteurized milk and milk products. When caring for an infected person, frequent handwashing and other hygienic practices can reduce the risk of person-to-person spread.

HANTA VIRUS—THE SIN NOMBRE VIRUS

A type of acute respiratory illness first made headlines in 1993, with an outbreak of cases among young, healthy Native Americans in the Southwest. CDC investigators identified the cause of this rapidly progressive, often fatal pulmonary illness as a virus related to the hanta virus. This virus, however, is distinct from the other known hanta viruses and has been named Sin Nombre Virus. The virus, like many of the other hanta viruses, is inhaled from the urine or droppings of infected small rodents, mostly deer mice, and cotton rats. The infected rodents do not appear to be ill, but in humans, the virus causes a distinct pulmonary syndrome, characterized by fever, muscle aches, headache, cough, and increasing shortness of breath. About half of those infected die from severe lung complications.

The sudden appearance and clustering of cases in the "four corner" states of the Southwest (New Mexico, Colorado, Arizona, and Utah) has been traced to climate changes that led to an increase in the rodent population, peaking in 1993. Co-evolution of the virus and its rodent reservoir appears to have occurred. So far the number of cases is small—about 25 in 1994—but the CDC predicts that number will double in 1995. Of importance is the fact that the range of the virus appears to be expanding, perhaps indicating its ability to survive in an increasing

variety of small rodents. It has been identified in 20 states; most are in the West, but it has also been found in New York, Rhode Island, and other northern states.

Because the initial reports of the disease affected Native Americans, there was speculation that this group was especially vulnerable to this virus. This has been disproved; the virus can infect all people of both sexes and of any age, race, or ethnic background. The one constant is exposure to mice and other rodents. The CDC recommends the following preventive measures, especially for people who live in rural areas populated by deer mice and other small rodents.

- Take measures to prevent rodent infestation of homes. Seal off holes and openings through which mice can enter a home. Store food and garbage in rodent-proof containers and dispose of trash and clutter.
- Use caution when cleaning rodent droppings. Spray droppings or rodent nests with a household disinfectant and wear rubber gloves for the cleanup. Steam clean carpets and clean other surfaces and floors with a disinfectant. Launder any possibly contaminated clothing or bedding with hot water and detergent.
- Call in a professional to clean and disinfect a heavily infested area, especially if hanta virus has been reported in the vicinity. This work calls for wearing protective clothing and breathing masks.
- When hiking or camping in areas where hanta virus has been reported, avoid sleeping on the bare ground. Do not pitch a tent near rodent burrows or possible shelters, such as a woodpile. Keep food in rodent-proof containers and get rid of garbage promptly. If a shelter or cabin appears to be rodent-infested, do not use it until it has been properly cleaned and disinfected. Use only bottled water or water that has been properly disinfected by boiling, chlorine, or iodine treatment. (To obtain more detailed faxed information on the hanta virus from the CDC, call 404-332-4565 and follow the prompts.)

INFECTIONS OF THE UPPER RESPIRATORY TRACT

THE COMMON COLD

DEFINITION

A viral infection of the respiratory tract, the common cold is the most frequent disease striking this part of the body. Although the common cold is a relatively mild infection and clears up without treatment, it is the leading cause of visits to physicians and of student and employee absenteeism.

CAUSE

Rhinoviruses cause 40 to 50 percent of all colds. Other viruses such as coronaviruses account for 10 percent, and parainfluenza, influenza and adenovirus, and respiratory syncytial virus (in children) cause most of the rest. During infection these viruses attach to the epithelial cells lining the nasal passage and sinuses, provoking the discharge of large amounts of mucus. The same virus can reinfect the same person time and again.

The cold season in the United States begins in late August or early September, continues through the winter, and fades away in April and May. Researchers don't know why colds tend to be seasonal but speculate that the congregation of children in schools during the colder months may be an important factor in the proliferation of winter infections. Cold weather also may dry the lining of the nasal passages and increase susceptibility to viral invasion.

Young children are the most vulnerable to colds, and therefore these diseases usually spread rapidly through schools and households with youngsters. Cold viruses probably disseminate through manual contact when children rub their runny noses, pick up the virus on their fingers, and then transfer the virus to another when they touch hands. After you make contact with a cold virus, the cold usually takes about 2 to 3 days to manifest itself.

DIAGNOSIS

Symptoms include nasal discharge, obstruction of nasal breathing, swelling of the sinuses, sneezing, and a sore, scratchy throat that prompts occasional coughs. Fever is usually slight but can climb to 102° F (38.9° C) among infants and young children.

TREATMENT

Colds usually last about 1 week, but about 25 percent of them persist for 2 weeks; smoking can prolong the infection. A few colds are complicated by bacterial infections of the sinuses or middle ear, necessitating prompt antibiotic therapy, but most colds require no drug treatment.

A physician can do nothing for the uncomplicated cold. Culturing the infectious virus for identification is pointless since there are no effective drugs against cold viruses, and both antibiotics and antihistamines are useless except for symptomatic relief. Some over-the-counter cold remedies—especially those containing phenylephrine or epinephrine—help promote nasal secretions and relieve obstruction, but decongestants should not be used for more than a few days.

Some colds are accompanied by allergic reactions that may be relieved with antihistamines, but in general antihistamines are of little use against cold symptoms. Single-ingredient over-the-counter decongestants sometimes relieve congestion, while single-ingredient analgesics such as acetaminophen and aspirin can relieve aches and pains. Multi-ingredient cold preparations are generally more expensive, contain unnecessary ingredients, and may have long-term adverse effects for some cold sufferers.

Patients with other medical conditions, including asthma, should consult their physician when they contract a cold. A physician should also be consulted if there is no relief in the cold symptoms after several days. Bacterial infections, bronchitis (inflammation of the lining of the bronchial tubes, which connect the windpipe with the lungs), or pneumonia can sometimes follow a cold because of the body's lowered resistance.

While a cold is a self-limiting illness that lasts only a few days in a normally healthy person, it may be more serious in the very young, the elderly, or in people with a chronic disease, such as diabetes, heart disease, or chronic obstructive pulmonary disease, or whose immune systems have been weakened by chemotherapy or disease. These persons should contact a doctor when they have a cold because treatment may be required to prevent complications.

HOME REMEDIES AND ALTERNATIVE THERAPIES

Drinking extra fluids helps thin mucus and ease congestion. In particular, consuming chicken soup or other hot beverages has been shown to relieve some of the respiratory symptoms of colds. Although use of large doses of vitamin C has not been shown to effectively prevent colds, vitamin C may slightly shorten the duration of a cold.

A sore throat is best relieved by warm gargle solutions, hot liquids, or cough drops with cough-suppressing activity. Aspirin or acetaminophen and bed rest can help relieve headaches or generalized muscle pain.

ASPIRIN WARNING

Do not give aspirin to children under 16 if the cold is due to influenza or chickenpox. Administer acetaminophen instead. Aspirin treatment for children has been associated with a disease called Reye's syndrome. (See chapter 7, Health Concerns During Infancy and Childhood.)

PREVENTION

To avoid spreading a cold, cold sufferers should frequently wash their hands with soap and water. Despite popular opinion, it's doubtful that exposed family members or co-workers can gain any protection by taking large doses of vitamin C; most careful studies fail to show any benefit from this tactic. (Even doses as high as 3 g per day failed to prevent colds among volunteers exposed to rhinovirus.) The best way to sidestep a cold is to avoid finger-to-nose or finger-to-eye contact, especially after contact with a cold sufferer. Wash your hands regularly, and if you do catch a cold, protect others by disposing of used tissues and covering your mouth and nose when coughing and sneezing.

No vaccine against the common cold may ever exist—more than 100 viruses cause colds.

INFLUENZA (FLU)

DEFINITION

Similar to the common cold, influenza is an acute viral infection of the upper respiratory tract, but it causes greater illness and discomfort. In fact, flu remains a major cause of death worldwide, especially among the aged and those afflicted with chronic, debilitating diseases.

CAUSE

Whereas scores of viruses provoke colds, most flu is caused by two main classes of viruses—influenza A and influenza B—two microbes that continuously mutate to form new strains named for their assumed place of origin (thus the Russian or the Hong Kong flu). New types of influenza A cause epidemics every 2 to 4 years, whereas influenza B appears sporadically or in localized outbreaks. Type B is also associated with the development of Reye's syndrome in children (a rare but dangerous disease affecting the brain and the liver). A third type, influenza C, is relatively mild, rare, and poorly understood.

Flu viruses spread from person to person easily, via inhalation of airborne microbes or by direct contact when you handle articles that an infected person has contaminated with nasal secretions, sneezes, or coughs. Flu symptoms appear after an incubation period of 1 to 2 days.

These viruses infect the nose, throat, and trachea and can enter the small airways in the lung. Like the cold viruses, flu viruses most easily spread in places where people congregate indoors, such as schools and nursing homes, and are thus most likely to cause illness in the winter and spring. Reinfection by the same strain of virus is rare since the body builds up immunity after each attack.

Influenza strikes people of all ages at unpredictable intervals. Its most serious side effect is the reduction of resistance to bacterial infection, especially among the elderly and those with chronic lung disease, often causing bacterial bronchitis or potentially fatal bacterial pneumonia.

DIAGNOSIS

The flu starts abruptly, usually with a high fever (up to 103°F [39.4°C]), a dry cough, and a headache. Muscle and back pain ensue, and flu victims often are too sick to get out of bed. The cough eventually produces mucus, the nose may become congested, the throat sore, and eyes sensitive to light. Nausea and vomiting may also be present. The fever lasts for 2 to 3 days while the other symptoms persist for a week to 10 days, leaving the patient feeling tired for a few days longer.

TREATMENT

Unless a flu sufferer is vulnerable to bacterial complications, a visit to the doctor is usually unnecessary, especially since no drug can eliminate the virus. Flu patients need plenty of bed rest; vaporizers can ease congestion, and aspirin or other analgesics relieve muscle pain and headache. Cigarettes and alcohol should be avoided: Smoking worsens coughing and alcohol depresses white blood cells and increases the risk of bacterial pneumonia. This is of particular concern to elderly people vulnerable to serious complications such as pneumonia.

Lots of nonalcoholic fluids, however, are recommended; they help loosen the secretions in the respiratory tract and decrease the chances of complications like bronchitis, ear infection, and sinusitis. They can also counter the dehydration that may accompany a fever.

PREVENTION

People susceptible to developing serious complications of the flu should have an annual vaccination. The vaccine, periodically reformulated to match the newest strains of the influenza viruses, has improved in effectiveness and the possibility of serious side effects has been reduced. The U.S. Centers for Disease Control and Prevention recommends the vaccine for any person over the age of 65 and for all residents of nursing homes. In addition, people with chronic respiratory disease, cardiopulmonary disease, or any disease involving the blood, kidneys, or body chemistry (metabolism), as well as medical and nursing home personnel, should also be vaccinated. The best time for vaccination is in late fall or early winter: October to December. The vaccine is not recommended for children or for people allergic to eggs.

A prophylactic antiviral prescription drug for the flu—amantadine—is also available, but it is effective only against the influenza A virus. If a flu epidemic strikes before a person in a high-risk group has been vaccinated, he or she should start taking amantadine and be inoculated as soon as possible. The amantadine should be taken for 2 weeks following vaccination to provide protection until appropriate antibodies develop.

HOME REMEDIES AND ALTERNATIVE THERAPIES

See those for the common cold.

ACUTE SORE THROAT (PHARYNGITIS)

DEFINITION

Pharyngitis is a sore throat that can make breathing, swallowing, and speaking painful and difficult.

CAUSE

Both bacterial and viral invasion can cause inflammation of the pharynx, the section of the throat between the nasal passages and the larynx, or voice box. A frequent cause is group A streptococcus. Among young adults infectious mononucleosis commonly causes pharyngitis. Additionally, gonorrhea bacteria can cause pharyngitis among those who practice oral sex.

DIAGNOSIS

For appropriate medical treatment, a physician must differentiate between viral and bacterial infections; bacterial infections can lead to serious complications. Illness from streptococcal bacteria, for example, can result in rheumatic fever and heart damage or acute nephritis, damaging the kidneys. Therefore, physicians usually grow a culture to determine the cause of pharyngitis when an infection lasts more than a few days.

A large proportion of people with a cold or the flu develop pharyngitis symptoms. Like colds and the flu, most throat infections occur during the colder months, the peak respiratory disease season. These infections are most prevalent among school-age children.

If infectious mononucleosis is the cause of pharyngitis, the symptoms may include fever, nasal passage enlargement, headache, generalized body ache, and, occasionally, enlargement of the spleen.

TREATMENT

The bacterial organism that causes pharyngitis, group A streptococcus, has changed, or mutated, in the past few years so that it may resist antibiotics, and also may assume a more virulent form. While doctors previously considered treatment of sore throats optional, today it is urgent to quickly treat this infection to forestall the development of other group A infections such as rheumatic fever, a condition capable of damaging heart valves. Untreated, these infections can be fatal, as was the virulent bacteria, group A streptococcus, that caused pneumonia in Jim Henson, the creator of the Muppets. The well-publicized pneumonia to which he succumbed resulted from an untreated sore throat. If pharyngitis is caused by a virus, no prescription drug can treat it, but when it stems from bacteria an antibiotic can quickly overcome it.

The most often prescribed drug for a sore throat caused by a streptococcal bacterium (strep throat) is oral penicillin. Some physicians prefer injecting a long-acting penicillin—benzathine—since 1 shot lasts 2 weeks and the patient is freed of having to take penicillin pills several times a day. Persons allergic to penicillin receive erythromycin instead.

If a doctor prescribes an oral antibiotic, it is vital that you take the full 10-day course of the drug even though the symptoms may disappear earlier than that. Failure to take the full 10-day course of drugs, especially in the case of streptococcus infection, can result in secondary rheumatic fever.

Penicillin may not be effective in people with very large tonsils: The bacteria called *Bacteroides* that reside in these glands produce a penicillin-destroying enzyme called beta-lactamase. In these cases (mostly children) a cephalosporin drug is usually prescribed.

PREVENTION

Children who attend school or day-care are more likely to bring these virulent microorganisms home. Good hygiene, however, can limit the spread within the family, and caution should also be taken with family pets. For example, a dog may carry group A streptococcus in its mouth and transfer it to a child or adult through licking. If you think your family pet is sick, take it to a veterinarian for a checkup and treatment, if necessary.

HOME REMEDIES AND ALTERNATIVE THERAPIES

Gargling with warm salt water or a diluted solution of hydrogen peroxide can provide temporary relief.

ACUTE LARYNGITIS

DEFINITION

Laryngitis, a very common condition, is an infection and inflammation of the larynx, or voice box.

CAUSE

This malady is usually caused by one of the viruses that also cause the common cold.

DIAGNOSIS

The main symptom is hoarseness, which may escalate into voice loss for a few days.

TREATMENT

The only effective treatment is resting the voice for a few days. (Do not talk or whisper at all!) Avoid throat irritants such as tobacco smoke and alcohol.

PREVENTION

It is difficult to prevent the spread of the viruses responsible for laryngitis, but limiting hand-to-face contact, washing your hands often, and avoiding throat irritants such as tobacco and alcohol may help limit infection.

Often the viruses that cause laryngitis are brought home by a school-age child who has acquired immunity after extensive contact with these microbes. Unfortunately, younger children at home without acquired immunity may still catch these viruses and suffer symptoms. While it is difficult to prevent this spread, teaching older children proper hygienic habits may limit infections.

Note: Always exercise caution when using nebulizers or vaporizers in treating upper respiratory distress; these devices and their filters should be cleaned and replaced regularly to avoid buildup of infection-causing fungi.

CROUP

DEFINITION

Croup, or acute laryngotracheobronchitis, is an upper respiratory infection.

CAUSE

Croup is usually caused by a virus such as *Parainfluenza* type 1, 2, or 3, influenza A, or, infrequently, respiratory syncytial virus (RSV). Croup primarily affects children 3 months to 3 years of age, but most frequently strikes 2-year-olds. In older children the infectious agent may be a bacterium, usually a pneumonia microbe, *Mycoplasma pneumoniae.*

DIAGNOSIS

The infection inflames and swells the nasal passages, larynx, and trachea (the windpipe) and results in hoarseness, cough, and a labored, shrill breathing sound. Attacks usually occur at night, awakening and alarming the child, who sits forward and coughs with a characteristic crowing or barking sound.

The symptoms of croup fluctuate rapidly and unpredictably. From hour to hour, a child's breathing may be normal and then grow loud and uncomfortable; morning may bring relief only to be followed by a worsening at night. Fortunately the symptoms usually clear up in 3 or 4 days, although they can sometimes persist for a week.

If croup stems from a virus, it is generally not dangerous, but if the causative agent is a bacterium called *Haemophilus influenzae,* or if the condition is actually a masked case of epiglottitis, it may be life-threatening. (Epiglottitis is inflammation of the epiglottis, the structure in the throat that prevents food from entering the windpipe. Since epiglottitis impairs breathing and swallowing, it is a life-threatening condition that necessitates immediate, emergency medical assistance.)

TREATMENT

Fortunately, both bacterial conditions linked to croup are readily treated with antibiotics. Besides the administration of medicine, a panicky child should be comforted so that his or her anxiety is reduced as much as possible.

Nasal prongs may help open up the nasal passages, allowing the person to breathe more easily. If that is not sufficient, delivery of inhaled nasal oxygen and, especially in cases caused by RSV, an aerosol mist inhalation of a drug called ribaviran for about 4 days may be beneficial. It is very expensive, however, costing as much as $600 a day. It is also teratogenic, meaning it may cause damage to a growing fetus, so it must not be administered by a pregnant woman.

HOME REMEDIES AND ALTERNATIVE THERAPIES

The best home treatment is to use a steam kettle, vaporizer, or steam from a shower to relieve congestion, although this therapy has no scientifically proven benefit.

Warning: If a child's breathing appears dangerously impaired, and especially if his or her lips start turning blue, the child should be rushed to the hospital.

PREVENTION

Respiratory syncytial virus may be brought into the home by an apparently healthy adult or older children who have developed immunity that younger children may lack. As with other viral illness, promoting good hygiene in the home may help limit the spread within a family. However, the virus sticks to surfaces and is very difficult to eradicate. Whenever possible, try to avoid bringing a young child into the hospital or into another viral environment during the winter when this virus is most often present.

EAR INFECTIONS

SWIMMER'S EAR

DEFINITION

Swimmer's ear is a superficial bacterial infection of the external ear canal.

CAUSE

This infection frequently results from excess moisture or from an infection of the inner ear. It may be caused by the bacterium *Pseudomonas aeruginosa,* which lives in the inadequately chlorinated water of an overcrowded public pool.

DIAGNOSIS

Symptoms include pain and swelling of the external ear that make it difficult to see the eardrum behind the swollen area. The doctor must differentiate this condition from otitis media.

TREATMENT

Unless there is extensive inflammation, the only treatment necessary is ciprofloxacin ear drops. Often, diluted household vinegar suffices. In cases of severe swelling, the physician may place a cotton wick with a 50 percent aluminum solution (Burrow's solution) in the ear for 1 or 2 days before starting topical treatment. Antibiotic drops should be discontinued as soon as there is improvement or they may cause dermatitis.

PREVENTION

Whenever possible, avoid swimming in inadequately chlorinated pool water. After swimming in nonchlorinated water, try to clear the ear of water and administer diluted vinegar ear drops.

MALE/FEMALE DIFFERENCES

Men develop swimmer's ear more often than women, probably because they do not wear bathing caps, and they put their heads under water more often.

MALIGNANT EXTERNAL OTITIS

DEFINITION

Despite its name, this condition is not a malignancy, but a bacterial infection of the external canal that spreads into surrounding tissue and results in persistent draining of fluid from the ear.

CAUSE

This form of otitis is caused by *Pseudomonas aeruginosa,* the same bacterium responsible for swimmer's ear.

DIAGNOSIS

This condition results in severe pain and tenderness, but rarely fever or an increase in white blood cell count (a common sign of infection). An elevated result for a blood test called erythrocyte sedimentation rate (ESR) may indicate malignant external otitis. This infection can cause damage to the facial nerve on the side adjacent to the affected ear, resulting in paralysis of that side of the face. In rare instances, it also causes osteomyelitis (bone inflammation) and even brain abscess and death.

This condition is most prevalent among the elderly who pick at the ear canal and is also common in people with diabetes whose immune systems are not effective in healing tissue damage from picking at the ear with a hairpin or other instrument.

TREATMENT

Malignant external otitis is treated with antibiotics and local surgical removal of wasted tissue. The treatment takes up to 3 months with a large dose of the antibiotic ciprofloxacin. If untreated, the infection can cause facial paralysis or a brain abscess. Since some physicians are unfamiliar with this illness, any person with persistent ear pain should see an ear specialist (otolaryngologist) or infectious disease expert.

PREVENTION

Do not use foreign objects to clean the ears, and do not introduce anything—not even a cotton swab—into the inner ear canal.

OTITIS MEDIA

DEFINITION

This is an infection of the middle ear accounting for more pediatrician visits than any other condition, with an average of 3 episodes per year per child.

CAUSE

Most children between the ages of 6 months and 3 years experience at least one episode of otitis media. Like colds and flu, this illness is seasonal, striking most often in winter. It can be caused by an allergy or a functional anatomic abnormality, but usually results from infection. Children who have their initial attack during their first year are much more likely to have recurrent bouts throughout childhood.

The most common cause of otitis media is infection by 1 of 3 kinds of bacteria: *Streptococcus pneumoniae, Haemophilus influenzae* (nontypeable), and *Branhamella catarrhalis.*

DIAGNOSIS

Local symptoms include earache, hearing impairment, disturbance of balance, and vertigo, while generalized signs are fever, irritability, and vomiting. Otitis should be suspected in any small child with unexplained fever, particularly if a tug on the ear elicits pain. Examination of the color, contour, and structural changes of the middle ear enables a physician to diagnose otitis media. In most cases, the inflamed eardrum cannot be moved, and fluid buildup is evident.

TREATMENT

The most common treatment is an oral antibiotic. The drug used depends on two factors: if the child is allergic to penicillin or amoxicillin, and if bacterial drug resistance to penicillin or amoxicillin is a strong possibility.

If the child is allergic to penicillin, a cephalosporin drug such as cefaclor may be used. A drug mixture of amoxicillin and clavulanate (Augmentin) may be prescribed to treat the 20 percent of cases caused by *H. influenzae* (nontypeable) that are resistant to amoxicillin treatment. If the condition is serious or persistent, the doctor may suction fluids using a small needle (aspiration). When ear pain or fever continues for 48 hours after drug treatment starts, the inner-ear fluid should be cultured to ensure the proper medication is being used. Decongestants do little good for this condition and, in fact, may prolong an attack.

Because half of all children with otitis suffer from persistent fluid within the middle ear even after an acute infection has cleared, all children should make follow-up visits to the physician. Even though this fluid in the ear does not harbor bacteria, it can impair hearing at a crucial language-learning stage of development. If fluid is found during the follow-up visit, the doctor will probably prescribe another course of drug therapy or may recommend that an otolaryngologist implant small drainage tubes.

PREVENTION

To prevent recurrent infections, the dry winter air in the home should be moisturized with a humidifier. Infants should not be fed while lying down. Prophylactic sulfonamide drugs may be prescribed for people such as Eskimos and Native Americans who may be genetically inclined to otitis media because of their flat eustachian tubes. (Also see discussions in chapter 7, Health Concerns During Infancy and Childhood; chapter 20, Respiratory Diseases and Lung Health; and chapter 31, Diseases of the Ear, Nose, and Throat.)

SINUSITIS

DEFINITION

Sinusitis is an acute infection of the sinuses' mucous membranes.

CAUSE

Sinusitis is usually a complication of a cold or other viral infection of the nose and throat, although some cases may follow dental treatment. In a few instances, sinusitis is associated with hay fever or anatomical obstructions that block drainage of fluids. The organisms causing sinusitis are *Streptococcus pneumoniae, Haemophilus influenzae* (nontypeable), and *Branhamella catarrhalis.*

Even though it usually follows a viral infection, sinusitis most often is a bacterial infection. This condition occurs after viruses change the characteristics of the cells lining the sinuses, allowing normally harmless bacteria that enter through the nose and mouth to settle and multiply. Long episodes of infection can lead to irreversible changes in the mucosal lining of the sinuses and result in chronic sinusitis.

If a person has undergone a Caldwell-Luc procedure (an emergency treatment to drain the sinuses), the mouth bacteria, which can grow in the absence of air (anaerobic), may migrate to the sinus cavities and cause a different type of sinusitis.

DIAGNOSIS

The symptoms of sinusitis are facial pain, headache, yellowish discharge from the nose, obstruction of smell, and a nasal speaking tone. If the frontal sinuses over the eyes are involved, there can be swelling of the eyelids and excessive tearing. In almost all older children and in about half of adults, there will also be fever.

Sinusitis is difficult to distinguish from a cold. The doctor should carefully examine the throat, nose, ears, sinuses, and teeth. In a dark room, the doctor will shine a light in the mouth to see if it shows up in the maxillary sinuses behind the cheekbones and in the frontal sinuses. Lack of "transillumination" probably indicates infection. X-rays will reveal trapped air and fluid and thickened mucosal walls of the sinuses. Culturing nasal secretions is of little value. In severe cases, a fluid sample will be taken from the sinuses via a needle passed through an anesthetized facial area; this will relieve pressure and provide material for a culture so that the infectious agent can be identified.

TREATMENT

If the infection is bacterial, an antibiotic such as amoxicillin or a cephalosporin will be prescribed. In severe cases, the sufferer may be hospitalized for intravenous administration of more powerful antibiotics. All drugs must be taken for at least 10 days. If the pain is severe, codeine may be prescribed. Using decongestant nose drops and inhaling steam may be helpful in many cases.

Unfortunately, once sinusitis becomes chronic, there often is permanent mucosal damage. This may require surgery to promote drainage and remove excess mucosal tissues.

PREVENTION

There are no proven ways to prevent acute sinusitis. Prompt administration of decongestants when sinusitis symptoms develop or during bouts of the common cold, flu, and other upper respiratory infections may be helpful. Allergies should be well controlled. Good dental hygiene and prompt treatment of tooth problems will reduce the chance of sinusitis developing as a complication of dental disease.

Some people are anatomically predisposed to sinusitis and may need surgery to correct the initial problem and prevent this condition.

EPIGLOTTITIS

DEFINITION

Epiglottitis is inflammation of the tiny epiglottis, a lidlike protuberance in the throat supposed to block the entrance to the lungs when we swallow. Fortunately, this structure usually functions normally, but infection can produce a life-threatening condition when breathing becomes completely obstructed.

CAUSE

The causative agent is almost always the bacterium *Haemophilus influenzae*.

DIAGNOSIS

The typical patient is a child under the age of 5 who has a sore throat and unexplained fever for several hours; suddenly the child experiences severe difficulty in breathing. The condition is often confused with croup, but croup, which generally strikes younger children, produces a barking cough and difficulty in speaking, whereas epiglottitis cuts off all breathing. (Epiglottitis also occasionally causes a serious, possibly fatal condition in elderly individuals who are heavy smokers.)

When infected, the epiglottis appears markedly swollen and cherry red. X-rays of the neck can confirm the enlargement, but since this is a medical emergency, treatment must begin even if the evidence for the condition is not conclusive.

There should be only one medical examination of the epiglottis; continued examination may cause this structure to swell more, possibly closing the airway and making it impossible for the person to breathe.

TREATMENT

Treatment may involve emergency placement of a tube into the windpipe to facilitate breathing. Intravenous antibiotics such as cefotaxime or ceftriaxone are also administered as quickly as possible. Dramatic improvement usually occurs within 2 days.

INFECTIONS OF THE MOUTH

GINGIVITIS AND PERIODONTITIS

DEFINITION

Both gingivitis and periodontitis involve a buildup of destructive plaque on the gums and between the gums and teeth.

CAUSE

The organism *Streptococcus mutans* causes gingivitis and periodontitis by secreting a substance called dextran that allows microbes to adhere and damage the teeth and gums. Other organisms involved in this condition are called *Actinomyces*.

DIAGNOSIS

A dentist who scrapes off the plaque caused by this condition can diagnose the infection without culturing the sample. Before you have plaque scraped, you must notify the dentist of any underlying heart disease; scraping the plaque releases bacteria that can cause endocarditis (a heart infection). Prophylactic antibiotics taken before dental procedures prevent endocarditis, and to ensure proper treatment, the dentist should consult the person's cardiologist or family doctor to get a complete history of the heart disease. (See "Infective Endocarditis" in this chapter and chapter 16, Heart and Blood Vessel Diseases.)

TREATMENT

Antibiotics are reserved for severe cases of ulceration and tissue death. Otherwise, removal of the plaque is sufficient.

HOME REMEDIES AND ALTERNATIVE THERAPIES

Gargling with an antibiotic mouthwash such as a tetracycline mix may help fight gingivitis and periodontitis.

PREVENTION

Good dental hygiene, including gum maintenance (daily flossing and brushing of the teeth) and not smoking, are the best preventive tactics (see chapter 32, Maintaining Oral Health, for more details).

STOMATITIS

DEFINITION

Stomatitis, commonly referred to as canker sores, is an inflammation of the mouth's membrane lining (the oral mucosa) with attendant painful and recurrent chancre-like sores.

CAUSE

Easily confused with herpes simplex infections, stomatitis, like herpes, often flares during periods of stress. The cause is unknown, though it is suspected to be an autoimmune disorder.

DIAGNOSIS

Stomatitis is characterized by painful canker sores.

TREATMENT

Since the cause of stomatitis remains unknown—researchers are not even sure an infectious organism is to blame—there is no proven treatment. In the past, doctors used silver nitrate sticks to "burn off" the sores, but research has proven this to be ineffective and possibly harmful.

HOME REMEDIES AND ALTERNATIVE THERAPIES

Gargling with a tetracycline (or other antibiotic) mouthwash is an unproven alternative therapy that some people claim helps their condition.

HAIRY TONGUE

DEFINITION

This discoloration of the tongue is thought to denote a change in the body's natural bacterial balance.

CAUSE

Hairy tongue may be caused by infection, but the specific cause has yet to be identified. The condition often follows the use of antibiotics or certain mouthwashes.

DIAGNOSIS

The tongue becomes discolored and appears to be yellow or black.

TREATMENT

There is no known treatment, but hairy tongue goes away without treatment.

PREVENTION

The only prevention for hairy tongue is to avoid taking antibiotics or other medications that upset the bacterial balance of the body.

MOLAR ABSCESSES

DEFINITION

A molar abscess is an infection below the oral ligament, which ends at the second molar tooth.

CAUSE

A decayed tooth is the precursor to the infection, which is caused by anaerobic oral bacteria.

DIAGNOSIS

The diagnosis is made on the basis of pain in the tooth area and a dental x-ray that reveals infection.

TREATMENT

Infection from these sores can spread into the body, producing serious and even life-threatening conditions. For that reason the involved tooth should be removed, the infection promptly treated with antibiotics such as amoxicillin/clavulanate or clindamycin (which kill anaerobic organisms), and the pus drained.

PREVENTION

Good dental hygiene and routine visits to a dentist may help prevent this problem.

MALE/FEMALE DIFFERENCES

Men are more likely to get molar abscesses, and, in general, tooth development (dentition) in men is more complicated than in women.

COLD SORES (HERPES SIMPLEX TYPE 1)

DEFINITION

This is a viral infection that causes cold sores or fever blisters.

CAUSE

The cold sores or fever blisters caused by the herpes simplex virus most often occur among children ages 1 to 5 and among young adults.

DIAGNOSIS

Besides oral pain, an attack causes sudden fever, chills, and irritability often accompanied by a sore throat and sensitive gums. The blisters themselves appear on the lips, tongue, and the floor and roof of the mouth; they eventually come together to form irregularly shaped ulcers.

The initial episode may not be distinguishable from acute pharyngitis when it occurs on the tonsils and within the throat.

TREATMENT

In initial or primary infections, fever and pain may persist up to 1 week and the sores take as long as 2 weeks to heal. The first attack may last up to 21 days and initially be mistaken for strep throat or mononucleosis. The oral drug acyclovir speeds the healing of the sores.

HOME REMEDIES AND ALTERNATIVE THERAPIES

There are none. Vitamin C and amino acid solutions are ineffective against this infection.

PREVENTION

Even though an outbreak of herpes will completely clear, the herpesvirus remains dormant in the body, able to precipitate new attacks at almost any time since the virus cannot be completely killed. Recurrent attacks, which often follow emotional stress, sunburn, or fever caused by another infection, may be prevented by routine administration of acyclovir. Acyclovir drug can be taken for several years with no side effects.

EPSTEIN-BARR VIRUS (EBV)

DEFINITION

The Epstein-Barr virus, a herpesvirus, causes infectious mononucleosis. It is of low contagion and usually affects young adults. The onset of the illness can be sudden or gradual, over a few days.

DIAGNOSIS

Symptoms include fever, sore throat, enlarged lymph nodes (particularly in the neck), general malaise, and occasionally aplastic anemia and enlargement of the spleen. Enlarged spleens can rupture following trauma, so contact sports should be avoided. Hepatitis, if it develops, usually does not extend beyond the duration of the illness. Loss of taste for cigarettes is common as are headaches behind the eye. Very rarely there are neurological manifestations, such as encephalitis, Guillain-Barré syndrome (paralysis due to nerve inflammation), or Bell's palsy. A rash can develop and is very common in those given ampicillin (not part of treatment for EBV; see below).

Diagnosis is made by testing the blood for an increase in atypical lymphocytes and antibodies. Sometimes, in the presence of the virus, the test is false negative and the diagnosis is made after an unexplained fever that lasts for up to a month.

The illness normally persists for between 1 and 4 weeks, but can last up to 3 months. In the past several years, however, researchers have proposed the existence of chronic mononucleosis in individuals suffering mononucleosis-like symptoms that persist for a long period of time.

Testing for the presence of the Epstein-Barr virus in the chronically ill is problematic. After the acute phase of the illness (when the level of antibodies is highly elevated) the antibodies always remain in the blood in lower but still detectable levels throughout life. At this point, a positive blood test merely reveals past history of the disease, not necessarily its continuing presence. Chronic fatigue, headaches, depression, sleep disorders, and muscular pain—symptoms claimed as signs of chronic mononucleosis—can have many other causes. Thus, many experts believe that if chronic mononucleosis does exist, it is extremely rare and most symptoms of chronic mononucleosis are actually psychosomatic. However, more research is needed to determine whether the psyche can affect the immune system to produce symptoms of immune disorder. Symptoms that seem to suggest chronic mononucleosis should be investigated as manifestations of other conditions.

TREATMENT

Because this condition is caused by a virus and not bacteria, patients should not be treated with antibiotics. Steroids should also be avoided, unless fever persists beyond 2 weeks.

Most patients will recover with no complications and fatalities are rare. When fever and fatigue are present, bed rest is recommended. If the spleen is enlarged, excessive exercise should be avoided.

BRONCHIAL INFECTIONS

ACUTE BRONCHITIS

DEFINITION

Acute bronchitis is an inflammatory disease of the tracheal-bronchial tree, which consists of the trachea (the windpipe) and the large branch-off tubes in the lungs (the bronchi).

CAUSE

Associated with acute upper respiratory tract infections, this disorder occurs mostly in the winter. The usual cause is a cold virus or, occasionally, influenza virus, adenovirus or *Mycoplasma pneumoniae.* Rarely, *Bordetella pertussis* or mycoplasma infection is responsible. This infection is most likely in those not vaccinated for pertussis or those for whom many years have passed since vaccination and whose immunity has waned.

DIAGNOSIS

The major symptom is a cough that begins dry but eventually produces a thick mucous discharge, or sputum. During deep breathing there may be pain below the breastbone (sternum).

In cases of pertussis infection, the diagnosis can be made by culturing a throat sample. However, because pertussis is rare, doctors hardly ever perform this test unless alerted to the possibility of lowered immunity to *Bordetella pertussis.*

TREATMENT

Since there is no effective drug for infectious viruses, treatment relies on cough control with codeine preparations and plenty of fluids to prevent dehydration. Adding moisture to the air helps clear the bronchi as well as the nasal passages. But if the cause is a bacterium, antibiotics, usually erythromycin, clarithromycin, or zithromycin, are effective.

PREVENTION

A vaccine developed especially for adults who work with children has been designed to restore waning immunity to *Bordetella pertussis* without side effects.

CHRONIC BRONCHITIS

DEFINITION

Chronic bronchitis is a persistent inflammatory disease of the tracheal-bronchial tree, which consists of the trachea (the windpipe) and the large branch-off tubes in the lungs (the bronchi).

CAUSE

Chronic bronchitis is usually linked to smoking or recurrent bouts of acute bronchitis and develops slowly and insidiously over many years. The organisms causing chronic bronchitis are *Streptococcus pneumoniae, Haemophilus influenzae* (nontypeable), and *Branhamella catarrhalis.*

DIAGNOSIS

This condition is characterized by a chronic cough that produces gradually increasing amounts of sputum or phlegm without odor. (If the phlegm smells bad, it is due to an anaerobic organism and may be a sign of a lung abscess. A chest x-ray should be performed if this is suspected.) The condition usually worsens in the winter and is often exacerbated by acute invasions of bacteria.

TREATMENT

The infections caused by invading bacteria should be cleared promptly with antibiotics such as amoxicillin or a cephalosporin, which should be taken for at least 10 days. If the victim of chronic bronchitis is a cigarette smoker, breaking the smoking habit should be the first step in the treatment plan. Cough suppressants should not be used since coughing removes secretions. In fact, the physician may suggest regular postural drainage—lying with the head lower than the chest—to expedite clearance of the sputum. Bronchodilators may also be used. (See also Respiratory Diseases and Lung Health, chapter 20.)

PREVENTION

You should quit smoking to prevent this condition. Also make sure that your home's vaporizers are clean; fungal buildup from vaporizers can exacerbate the condition.

LUNG INFECTIONS

PNEUMONIA

DEFINITION

Pneumonia is an inflammation of the working tissue in the lungs (see figure 18.5). White cells in the lungs occur in a pattern that prevents the alveoli, the air-exchanging

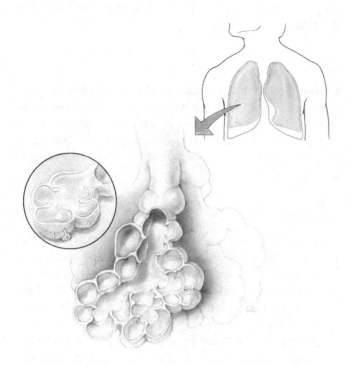

Figure 18.5: Lungs affected by pneumonia. The enlargement shows a close-up of inflamed lung tissue, with an accumulation of mucus and fluid.

part of the lungs, from performing properly. This condition is potentially life-threatening since you need this air exchange function to live.

Cause

This condition is caused by a wide variety of bacteria, viruses, fungi, and other types of organisms that evade the impressive range of defenses against them in the upper respiratory tract or enter through the mouth, evading the epiglottis. Infectious agents may enter through the mouth if you lose consciousness, have an inadequate cough, have a seizure or stroke, or undergo general anesthesia: These events can weaken or paralyze the reaction of the epiglottis and permit microbes into the windpipe, wending their way down into the lung during respiration. Smoking contributes to pneumonia since it damages the small hairs (cilia) that line the respiratory tract and sweep out invading germs.

Malnutrition or conditions like kidney failure or sickle cell disease also impair the lung's ability to get rid of microorganisms that cause pneumonia. And viral infections of the upper respiratory tract can predispose a person to pneumonia because the viruses paralyze the protective cilia.

Among children 12 and under, the most frequent cause of pneumonia is the pneumococcus bacterium. Among adolescents and young adults, the most frequent

infective agent is a bacteria-like microbe called *Mycoplasma pneumoniae.*

Bacterial pneumonia can also ensue as a complication of influenza A; secondary infections are most often caused by *Streptococcus pneumoniae, Haemophilus influenzae,* or (most serious of all) *Staphylococcus aureus.*

A recently discovered form of pneumonia is Legionnaires' disease, caused by the *Legionella pneumophila* bacterium. This disease can occur sporadically or in epidemics as the first known one did, in 1976, at an American Legionnaires' convention in Philadelphia. The sporadic cases may be caused by exposure to an air-conditioning system or water tap carrying the bacteria. Legionnaires' disease is very common in certain cities such as Los Angeles and Pittsburgh and in some states such as Montana.

Diagnosis

To diagnose pneumonia, a physician first listens to a patient's chest, checking for fine, crackling noises, and characteristic dull thuds when it is tapped. A definitive diagnosis cannot be made, however, without chest x-rays, which show patches in the lung where air sacs are filled with fluid and debris instead of air. To determine the particular infective agent, lab tests can be done on sputum, urine, and blood samples, but these tests are not completely reliable.

Most viral pneumonias are mild. Symptoms include fever, headache, malaise, chills, and cough. Bacterial pneumonia, which is more dangerous, usually causes attacks of shaking chills, high temperature (up to 105°F [40.6° C]), rapid breathing, and coughing, at first dry but then producing rust-colored sputum. Headache, nausea, and vomiting may also occur. The symptoms of bacterial pneumonia at first resemble those of a chest cold, with a dry cough and then a sputum-producing cough.

When bacterial pneumonia occurs as a complication of influenza A, flu symptoms often disappear before the patient suddenly worsens with fever, cough, and shortness of breath.

In the case of Legionnaires' disease, after an incubation period of 2 to 10 days, the patient develops fever, general muscular pain, chills, abdominal pain, diarrhea, nonproductive cough, sore throat, and sometimes headache and confusion. This disease can cause renal failure and may appear to be kidney disease. The diagnosis is made by testing the sputum or urine for particular antigens. A blood test is of little value since the disease must have progressed for some time before the blood tests positive.

Pneumonia caused by bacteria that usually live in the mouth but have been aspirated into the lung (during unconsciousness for example) develops slowly and is difficult to diagnose. Initially, bacterial pneumonia causes people to lose their appetites, lose weight, and run a fever before they develop foul-smelling sputum.

TREATMENT

Fortunately, antibiotics are effective against bacterial pneumonia, but even after the infection has cleared, coughing can persist for several days or weeks. If a person is very ill, a test of arterial blood gases should be performed to ensure that he or she is getting adequate oxygen. Otherwise the person should be hospitalized in an intensive care unit and receive oxygen. The organisms that cause pneumonia do not directly cause death, but may dangerously limit oxygen intake with fatal consequences.

When pneumonia is caused by *Streptococcus pneumoniae, Haemophilus influenzae,* or *Staphylococcus aureus,* antibiotics that kill all three organisms are usually prescribed to prevent further bacterial infection (*Staphylococcus* in particular is very dangerous).

Legionnaires' disease progresses rapidly and requires hospitalization. The usual treatment is administration of the antibiotic erythromycin (or similar drugs that cause fewer side effects, such as clarithromycin or zithromycin) or rifampin.

When pneumonia is caused by bacteria that usually live in the mouth but are aspirated into the lung, patients require hospitalization so that intravenous antibiotics can be given for 2 or 3 weeks. After release from the hospital, oral antibiotics should be continued for up to several months.

In all cases, the treating doctor must know where the organism was contracted in order to prescribe the correct antibiotic. In each geographical area, there are strains of bacteria that have become resistant to certain antibiotics. For example, if someone takes a trip to Boston and comes back with a bacterial pneumonia due to *H. influenzae,* the doctor would be less likely to prescribe ampicillin because at the present time, 50 percent of such cases in Boston are resistant to ampicillin.

PREVENTION

Pneumonia caused by *Pneumococcus*—by far the most prevalent type of bacterial pneumonia—can now be prevented with a vaccine. The vaccine also protects against the 22 other most prevalent causes of bacterial pneumonia. (All together there are 83 pneumococci, but 23 of them cause the majority of illnesses.)

People who should be vaccinated include:

- Anyone with chronic lung disease
- Anyone over the age of 60
- Anyone who has had his or her spleen removed or damaged
- Anyone with sickle-cell anemia

In addition, if cost is not a concern, it is now recommended that people receive the vaccine at age 50 since research indicates people develop more antibodies if they receive the vaccine earlier. (Also see chapter 20, Respiratory Diseases and Lung Health.)

MALE/FEMALE DIFFERENCES

Statistically, males get more pneumonia because of their heavier use of alcohol; alcohol lowers the body's resistance to infection, and people who abuse this drug are more prone to a number of infections than those who abstain.

TUBERCULOSIS

DEFINITION

Tuberculosis (TB) is an infectious disease most often affecting the lungs but which can also affect other parts of the body. This deadly disease (formerly known as consumption) has plagued humans since the time of the early Egyptians and, until recently, was on the decline in industrialized nations because of improved housing conditions, nutrition, and the effectiveness of the drug isoniazid available since 1951. Worldwide, however, the disease claims 3 million lives a year, and it has been on the increase in the United States since 1986, especially in large cities such as New York, where the incidence is now 41 cases per 100,000 people.

In this recent U.S. outbreak, tuberculosis is seen most often in older nonwhite males, in immigrants from Asia or the Caribbean areas, or in people with AIDS. It is also spreading among the homeless and urban poor.

CAUSE

Tuberculosis is spread when small salivary droplets containing the *Mycobacterium tuberculosis* bacillus are passed through the air and inhaled. The droplets evaporate, leaving the tubercle bacilli, which penetrate to the alveoli and multiply. The probability of acquiring tuberculosis increases as the concentration of the organisms in the air increases, and the seriousness of the disease is determined by the amount of bacteria with which a victim is infected.

DIAGNOSIS

The symptoms of tuberculosis are quite general and include loss of appetite and consequent weight loss, low-grade fever, fatigue, chills, night sweats, and coughing. Many people have no symptoms and are unaware of infection until the disease is discovered accidentally during a routine chest x-ray.

Babies and adults with impaired immunity are most susceptible to TB, but anyone living with a tuberculosis patient should be examined for infection as soon as possible.

Besides sputum analysis, a skin test called a PPD (purified protein derivative) test is the most useful diagnostic tool. In addition, a Tine test, which pricks the skin with four small tines coated with old, weak tuberculin, is used in large screening, but it is not appropriate for children in urban areas or for health care workers.

Tuberculin tests produce swelling and hardness at the injection site within two days if the bacillus is present in the body. The tests miss about 10 percent of cases, and people taking steroids will not have a positive reaction even if they have tuberculosis. Tuberculin skin tests performed during a viral illness or shortly after vaccination with measles (or another virus) will also produce a false-negative result.

When skin tests are inconclusive, bronchoscopy is often used to obtain a specimen for culture. Liver biopsy may also be useful for diagnosis, since 50 percent of adult TB patients suffer liver complications.

TREATMENT

Two highly effective drugs—isoniazid and rifampin—treat tuberculosis. In 2 weeks they reduce coughing and infectivity, but they must be taken for 6 months to eradicate the disease. Other drugs that may be used include streptomycin, ethambutol, and pyrazinamide.

Drug resistance has become a serious problem in treating TB in some populations, including people from the Caribbean, the Far East, and people who began therapy but failed to take their drugs properly or long enough. Intravenous drug users, alcohol abusers, and the homeless often fail to take the full course of prescribed drugs after their symptoms abate, making them vulnerable to further TB complications and infection with drug-resistant TB organisms.

PREVENTION

Health care workers must wear masks and other protective wear to limit the spread of the organism, and tuberculosis patients should be isolated from others in a hospital. However, if the organism is in the air, ultraviolet lights may prevent the spread of the infection.

Preventive treatment with the drug isoniazid to limit the spread of tuberculosis has been used since the end of the 1950s, but those treated must be observed for signs of toxicity, which occurs in about 1 percent of the population. Prophylactic treatment is recommended for people who have been exposed to tuberculosis, those who are newly infected, those with past tuberculosis who did not receive adequate therapy, and some people who have positive tests and other risk factors. If you have any questions about your susceptibility to TB, consult your doctor.

In some parts of the world, the 13CG vaccine is still used against tuberculosis, but it is not used for this purpose in the United States.

....

CARDIOVASCULAR INFECTIONS

INFECTIVE ENDOCARDITIS

DEFINITION

Endocarditis is a bacterial infection of the endocardium, a thick membrane covering the surface of the heart valves and the heart's chambers. This condition can cause the heart's valves to distort, leading to heart failure and death. Fortunately, such infections are uncommon, but the increasing amount of open-heart surgery has increased the incidence of endocarditis.

CAUSE

The most common causative agents of this condition are *Streptococcus* or *Staphylococcus aureus.* The use of intravenous drugs, preexisting heart valve disease, and advancing age are other risk factors (in later years, aging valves stiffen and become more susceptible to infection).

DIAGNOSIS

Infective endocarditis usually develops slowly and may produce weeks of general ill health, fever, fatigue, weight loss, and muscle aches before an accurate diagnosis is made. Most patients also have heart murmur. Definitive diagnosis is made by a blood culture.

TREATMENT

Effective treatment requires the use of high dosages of a powerful antibiotic or a combination of 2 drugs, usually for 4 to 6 weeks.

PREVENTION

The only way to prevent endocarditis is to give antibiotics prophylactically at least 30 to 60 minutes before a highly susceptible person—anyone with heart valve disease or a prosthetic valve—undergoes any procedure that might enable bacteria to enter the bloodstream. These procedures include tooth extraction, oral surgery, dilation and curettage (D&C), IUD insertion, cesarean delivery or abortion, gum treatments, and many other surgical procedures.

Amoxicillin or erythromycin taken 6 hours after the procedure is also recommended to temporarily lower the amount of bacteria in the blood and alter the surface properties of the bacteria so they do not stick to the heart valves. After administration of these drugs, it takes about 12 hours for the bacteria to begin growing normally. (See chapter 16, Heart and Blood Vessel Diseases.)

MYOCARDITIS AND PERICARDITIS

DEFINITION

These infections attack either the tough thin membrane around the outside of the heart (the pericardium) or the external sac and the heart wall (myocardium) itself. Myocarditis, an inflammation of the heart muscle, is fortunately rare since it may lead to irregular pulse and circulatory disturbances.

CAUSE

These conditions are caused by bacteria, fungi, and viruses, but viruses are the most frequent culprits, especially coxsackie B. Attacks usually occur in the summer, or can result as complications of other diseases.

DIAGNOSIS

The main symptom of both disorders is pain in the center of the chest, which may radiate to the neck, shoulders, and upper arms. Diagnosis is made by isolating the virus from a stool sample and comparing an initial blood sample to one taken 4 weeks later, which, in the case of infection, shows a four-fold increase in antibodies to that particular organism.

TREATMENT

Most myocarditis and pericarditis are viral, and the main treatment is complete bed rest under a doctor's observation. Unfortunately, even after a patient rests, myocarditis may still cause permanent damage to the heart muscle. (See chapter 16, Heart and Blood Vessel Diseases.)

INFECTIONS OF THE NERVOUS SYSTEM

MENINGITIS

DEFINITION

Difficult to prevent or diagnose, meningitis is an infection and inflammation of the membranes covering the brain and spinal cord (the meninges). It is an extremely serious disease that frequently causes permanent disability or death unless swiftly diagnosed and treated. Children are the main victims but it can strike at any age.

CAUSE

In most cases, meningitis is caused by 1 of 3 bacteria: *Neisseria meningitidis* (or meningococcus), *Streptococcus pneumoniae* (or pneumococcus), or *Haemophilus influenzae*. These microbes reach the meninges via the bloodstream from a distant infection in the lung, intestine, heart, or other organ, or by direct invasion from an infection already in the nervous system. In premature infants and babies, the invading bacteria are usually strains of what are called group B *Streptococcus* and *Escherichia coli*, organisms that grow normally in the vaginas of mothers. Among children 3 months to 5 years of age, the most common agents are *H. influenzae* and *S. pneumoniae*. In the United States, there has been a marked reduction in meningitis caused by *H. influenzae* because of a recently introduced vaccine.

Viral meningitis tends to be less serious than the bacterial variety. Most common in the summer, viral meningitis can be caused by viruses also responsible for summer diarrhea or by a microbe transmitted by hamsters and other rodents.

DIAGNOSIS

The symptoms of meningitis include high fever, stiff neck, nausea, and confusion. A definitive diagnosis requires a lumbar puncture or spinal tap to examine the cerebrospinal fluid for the telltale microbe.

In most viral meningitis cases, patients recover on their own without aftereffects. Even so, a spinal tap should be done to ensure that the person does not have a bacterial disease requiring antibiotics.

TREATMENT

Fortunately, doctors have a large number of effective drugs for meningitis, including the relatively new cephalosporin antibiotics, which enable them to treat successfully nearly all cases in their early stage.

PREVENTION

Vaccines to help protect against meningitis caused by *H. influenzae*, which predominantly infects children, should be administered to all youngsters. Prophylactic rifampin should be given to children 5 and under who are not immunized and who live with or have had close physical contact with someone suffering meningitis.

If a person has meningitis caused by the bacterium *Meningococcus (N. meningitidis)*, people in close contact with him or her should receive prophylactic antibiotics, rifampin or a sulfonamide, for 2 days. A vaccine is also available that covers the A, C, and W types of meningitis as well as 135 other types. (It does not cover what are known as meningitis B types.) This vaccine is recommended for people traveling to areas where this bacterium is common—some areas of South America or the Himalayan area—or to an area where an outbreak has occurred.

ENCEPHALITIS

DEFINITION

Encephalitis is a rare but very serious infection and inflammation of the brain cells.

CAUSE

Encephalitis often results when a long-standing herpes simplex Type 1 virus attacks the brain instead of migrating to the body's surface and producing a cold sore. Normally, a person infected with this virus will harbor it within a ganglion (a cell next to a nerve cell) after an initial infectious episode; from this base of operations, the virus periodically reactivates, traveling along the nerve to the skin or mucous membrane. During encephalitis, the virus changes direction, moving to the temporal or parietal lobe of the brain, causing infection and inflammation.

DIAGNOSIS

Symptoms include fever, headache, drowsiness, and confusion; cold sores are usually absent. A diagnosis of encephalitis caused by the herpes simplex Type 1 virus can be made by magnetic resonance imaging (MRI) or electroencephalogram (EEG), which shows abnormalities in the parietal-temporal lobes. By taking a sample of brain tissue—brain biopsy—the diagnosis can be confirmed.

TREATMENT

In general, there is no treatment for encephalitis caused by various viruses. However, the drug acyclovir given by intravenous drip in the hospital can successfully treat encephalitis caused by the herpes simplex Type 1 virus (the microbe that causes cold sores). (The genital herpesvirus—herpes simplex Type 2—causes encephalitis only in newborns whose mothers carry the virus, and in about 10 percent of cases infection leads to viral meningitis.)

PREVENTION

This disease cannot be prevented in adults, but a woman suffering a first episode of herpes simplex infection should deliver by cesarean section to prevent encephalitis in her child.

INFECTIONS OF THE SKIN AND SOFT TISSUES

Superficial skin infections such as cold sores and other viral infections, minor bacterial infections, and parasitic infestations are covered in chapter 28, Skin Diseases.

IMPETIGO

DEFINITION

Impetigo is a skin infection that can occur anywhere on the body, but often appears on the area around the nose and mouth of children.

CAUSE

Impetigo is caused by *Streptococcus pyogenes* or *Staphylococcus aureus* bacteria.

DIAGNOSIS

After the skin reddens and becomes itchy, small blisters and pustules form, resembling chickenpox. Then these break, leaving a tan crust.

TREATMENT

The crust should be removed by gentle washing, followed by application of an antibiotic ointment. If infection persists or spreads, an oral antibiotic may be prescribed such as penicillin or erythromycin.

PREVENTION

Impetigo is highly contagious; infected persons should wash their hands often and try not to scratch their sores. To limit spread, skin abrasions, cuts, and insect bites, which predispose one to impetigo, should be kept clean with antiseptics. Thick clothing may help protect against cuts and bites.

TOXIC SHOCK SYNDROME

DEFINITION

Toxic shock syndrome is a bacterial skin infection predominantly striking hospital patients following surgery, intravenous drug users, and women who use highly absorbent tampons.

CAUSE

Toxic shock syndrome is caused by toxins from the *S. aureus* bacteria, which are believed to enter the body through a break in the skin. First associated with use of highly absorbent tampons in young women, this condition has now been observed in children, older women, and men. Although it is not considered a sexually transmitted disorder, some cases of toxic shock have been associated with vaginal barrier contraceptives (diaphragms or contraceptive sponges), and there have been reports of sexual partners both contracting the disease. In fact, this condition now most commonly occurs following surgery or in intravenous drug addicts.

DIAGNOSIS

The condition causes a general reddening of the skin, especially on the palms of the hands, and fever and often produces diarrhea, vomiting, and confusion. A drop in blood pressure and diminished circulation to the hands and feet also may take place. Diagnosis is made by culturing the blood and vaginal secretions.

TREATMENT

Treatment is with an antibiotic, preferably a semisynthetic penicillin or a cephalosporin.

PREVENTION

Cuts and abrasions should be kept to a minimum so the bacteria cannot be introduced into the blood. Tampons should be changed frequently and intravenous drugs should be avoided.

ERYSIPELAS

DEFINITION

Erysipelas is a superficial skin disorder that affects mainly children and the elderly.

CAUSE

It is caused by a toxin of the *S. pyogenes* bacterium (also referred to as group A strep).

DIAGNOSIS

This condition usually breaks out on the bridge of the nose and on the cheeks; the painful rash is bright red with elevated edges. Fever is also usually present.

TREATMENT

Penicillin, or its substitute, erythromycin, will usually cure this condition.

PREVENTION

Avoid blowing your nose too energetically—bacteria located in your nose or on your hands can be introduced to the skin through a small abrasion.

CELLULITIS

DEFINITION

Cellulitis is a serious skin infection that usually affects underlying tissues.

CAUSE

Cellulitis occurs when bacteria infect deep levels of the skin. Group A streptococci or *S. aureus* microbes enter the skin through a cut, puncture, ulcer, or sore, producing enzymes that break down the skin cells.

DIAGNOSIS

The infected area becomes hot, red, and swollen, and patients suffer fever, chills, and a general ill feeling. In contrast to erysipelas sores, the skin eruption caused by cellulitis does not produce elevated edges.

TREATMENT

Because it tends to spread via the lymph nodes to other parts of the body, cellulitis is a serious disorder requiring prompt therapy either with penicillin or erythromycin.

PREVENTION

Since this infection enters the skin through deep puncture wounds, extreme care should be taken when working in the kitchen with sharp knives or doing home hobbies with drills and saws. Protective clothing and gloves should be worn to minimize the risk of cuts and abrasions.

GAS GANGRENE

DEFINITION

Gas gangrene is tissue death resulting from microbial contamination of devitalized muscle.

CAUSE

Gas gangrene is caused by infection with the bacterium *Clostridium perfringens*. The microbe usually enters the body through a wound or cut. It can develop after bowel or biliary surgery or in an extremity that has poor blood circulation.

DIAGNOSIS

When infection begins up to 2 days after introduction of the microbes, localized pain can be intense and accompanied by high fever, marked swelling, skin discoloration, and a watery discharge. Unlike other types of gangrene, this condition does not produce an offensive odor.

TREATMENT

Potentially a very serious infection, gas gangrene must be treated promptly with extensive surgery to remove all involved skin, subcutaneous tissues, and muscle. Antibiotics are also necessary. Antitoxin has not been shown to be effective. In some cases, high-pressure oxygen therapy (hyperbaric oxygen) is beneficial. Tetanus toxin should be administered to individuals who have not received a tetanus booster within 10 years.

PREVENTION

Be careful to avoid deep wounds; this rare condition is most likely to occur when you step on a sharp object, allowing a contaminated piece of wood or metal to enter the body, or when you suffer a wound in a pond where the causative bacterium grows.

LYMPHADENITIS

DEFINITION

Lymphadenitis is an infection and inflammation of 1 or more of the lymph nodes.

CAUSE

Lymphadenitis usually results from an infection that begins near a lymph node. Often caused by *Staphylococcus aureus* bacteria, this condition affects the nodes in the neck, groin, and armpit. It sometimes strikes individuals who have had coronary artery bypasses using a saphenous vein from the leg: The removal of this vein is accompanied by removal of related structures of the lymphatic system, lowering immunity to infection.

DIAGNOSIS

Painful lymph nodes may swell to several times their normal size.
Note: There are many causes for swollen lymph nodes, including tuberculosis, cancer, cat-scratch fever, sexually transmitted disease, and other illnesses such as AIDS; any persistently swollen lymph gland requires careful diagnostic study.

TREATMENT

Antibiotics successfully cure this bacterial infection.

PREVENTION

Prophylactic doses of antibiotics administered to those whose saphenous vein has been removed and those who have defects in the lymph drainage system may prevent this condition.

MALE/FEMALE DIFFERENCES

Statistically, more males get lymphadenitis than females, because males more often undergo coronary artery bypass or engage in work that causes abrasions.

BITES

Bites are a very common form of infected wound. More than 1 million people per year are bitten. But this type of injury can have dangerous consequences when infectious agents are deposited below the skin.

INFECTION CAUSED BY BITES

DEFINITION

Animal and human bites that penetrate the skin can convey infectious agents causing serious disease. All penetrating bites should receive immediate medical attention.

CAUSE

Bites inoculate the skin with infectious bacteria from the mouth of animals or humans. "Closed-fist bites," resulting when someone hits another person in the mouth, can be the most serious due to the varied bacteria residing in human mouths. Dogs and cat bites generally convey the bacterium *Pasteurella multocida.*

DIAGNOSIS

All bite victims should visit a doctor or hospital emergency room. Usually, no diagnostic tests are necessary unless rabies is suspected. (See chapter 14, Common First-Aid Procedures.)

TREATMENT

A bite that tears open tissues should immediately be washed with soap and water and kept under running water for a few minutes to wash out remaining saliva. A bite victim should be taken promptly to a physician's office or hospital emergency room, where the damaged tissue will be removed and antibiotic therapy initiated.

If the bite is from a wild animal or a stray dog or cat, rabies infection is a possibility; immunization should be started immediately if the animal is found to be infected or appeared sick at the time of attack. If the animal cannot be examined, a physician should decide if immunization is necessary. (See chapter 14, Common First-Aid Procedures.)

Most bites should be treated for several days with an antibiotic that can kill the bacteria *P. multocida,* which is found in the mouths of dogs and cats.

PREVENTION

Never approach strange animals. Avoid confrontations and overly aggressive behavior that instigates hostility with other people.

....

GASTROINTESTINAL INFECTIONS

Although rare among adults in industrialized nations, gastrointestinal infections associated with diarrhea are a leading cause of death among small children in all countries, including the United States. Epidemics of gastrointestinal infections caused by bacteria, viruses, fungi, or parasites sometimes break out in the United States following floods and other disasters that contaminate drinking water.

Eating raw meat or fish and unwashed raw fruits and vegetables increases the chances of intestinal infection as does the excessive consumption of antacids, which disrupts the normal acid-alkali balance in the stomach and intestines. Drugs that halt diarrhea or reduce intestinal motility and cause constipation boost the risk of infection by slowing the passage of bacteria-laden fecal matter. (For information on hepatitis, a serious inflammation of the liver, see chapter 22, Disorders of the Digestive System.)

TRAVELER'S DIARRHEA (TURISTA)

DEFINITION

Traveler's diarrhea, also referred to by many nicknames, is any acute intestinal infection striking tourists who lack immunity to local microorganisms. About 20 to 50 percent of all Americans who travel to Mexico and other developing countries contract traveler's diarrhea. Despite its supposed humorous connotations, this condition is no laughing matter; a third of its patients take to bed and another 40 percent are forced to suspend scheduled activities.

CAUSE

The leading causes of traveler's diarrhea are strains of the *Escherichia coli* bacterium, which normally comprise a portion of intestinal flora. Foreign variants of this microbe to which our bodies are unaccustomed produce toxins interfering with the intestine's ability to absorb water. Other causative bacteria include *Vibrio parahemolyticus* (found in shellfish, lobsters, shrimp, and crab), *Shigella,* and *Salmonella. Salmonella* bacteria contaminate many foods, particularly chicken and eggs and sometimes processed meats.

Recently problematic has been a toxin-producing *E. coli* of a special type that has been contracted from improperly cooked hamburger meat. In the very young or the very old these bacteria can cause an illness resulting in kidney failure from the toxin.

DIAGNOSIS

Typically, 4 to 6 days after arrival in another locale this illness begins with an abrupt attack of abdominal cramps and watery diarrhea (3 to 15 stools per day). In about 3 to 5 days the diarrhea decreases and the traveler can gradually resume normal activity. Some beleaguered tourists suffer repeated episodes on the same journey.

Shigella and *Salmonella* usually cause fever as well as diarrhea, and *Salmonella* and *Vibrio* can cause vomiting. The special form of the bacterium *E. coli* that infects hamburger meat causes bloody diarrhea without fever.

TREATMENT

Taking antibiotics can shorten attacks of this condition. Three drugs, norfloxacin, ofloxacin, and ciprofloxacin, taken twice a day for 2 days will cure most traveler's diarrhea. Over-the-counter agents like Kaopectate are of little help and can actually exacerbate the condition, especially if the diarrhea is bloody. Loperamide (Immodium) combined with an antibiotic can reduce the duration of symptoms from 36 hours to 9 hours.

PREVENTION

Avoid the local drinking water and ice cubes when traveling in high-risk areas; wine, beer, and carbonated sodas are safe. Brushing your teeth with the hotel tap water is safe since most toothpastes contain antibacterial substances, but don't swallow any of the water while gargling. Do not eat raw foods, but fruits and vegetables are permitted if peeled just before consumption.

Most doctors now discourage the use of antibiotics taken prophylactically before a trip, but it may be helpful to travel with an antibiotic to be taken after your first loose stool.

Since raw meat often is contaminated with salmonella, improper food handling can cause intestinal distress. Never prepare other foods on a surface on which raw chicken, turkey, or duck has been cut; wash such surfaces thoroughly with hot water and soap.

CAMPYLOBACTER INFECTION

DEFINITION

This bacterium, which apparently is becoming more widespread, is found worldwide and is usually passed on to humans from puppies and kittens. It can also contaminate water, milk, and some foods.

CAUSE

The bacterium is usually contracted while cleaning up after a pet.

DIAGNOSIS

One to 7 days after exposure, the bacterium colonizes the intestines, sometimes causing diarrhea so severe that doctors mistake it for ulcerative colitis. But this illness is milder, although marked by fever, abdominal pain, nausea, vomiting, malaise, and diarrhea (often bloody). Because this condition resembles ulcerative colitis, a culture may be performed to confirm the diagnosis.

TREATMENT

The condition usually clears up within a week even without treatment. The drug erythromycin may be administered, however, when campylobacter disease spreads through nursery schools and other institutions; this drug reduces the infectious organisms shed in the feces and thus helps contain the epidemic. The antimicrobials, ciprofloxacin, norfloxacin, and ofloxacin, have also proved to be effective therapy.

PREVENTION

Good hygiene including frequently washing your hands helps prevent the spread of this bacterium. Be especially fastidious about washing your hands after cleaning up your pet's feces.

STAPHYLOCOCCUS AUREUS FOOD POISONING

DEFINITION

Gastroenteritis from *S. aureus* is the most common form of food poisoning seen in the United States. Its common name, "ptomaine poisoning," is a misnomer: Ptomaines are an end product of protein decomposition and are unrelated to food poisoning.

CAUSE

S. aureus is often introduced into food by food preparers with unclean hands. Unfortunately, even the use of plastic gloves cannot ensure against infection since preparers may rub their noses with gloves and then touch the food, thereby spreading the bacteria.

DIAGNOSIS

Symptoms often include severe vomiting and diarrhea, beginning 2 to 6 hours after eating contaminated food. The vomiting usually begins first, with the diarrhea following soon after.

TREATMENT

In most cases, the illness is self-limiting and resolves itself in 12 to 24 hours without treatment.

PREVENTION

Foods contaminated with staphylococcus are difficult to detect, as they superficially appear to be normal. Foods most commonly contaminated with staphylococcus include salad dressings, milk products, and cream pastries, but many other foods can also harbor the organism. This staph organism multiplies rapidly at room temperature; prompt refrigeration after preparation can prevent infection.

The most important measure to combat this infection is good hygiene: Limit hand-to-face contact during food preparation, and restrict your dining out to clean establishments.

ROTAVIRUS INFECTION

DEFINITION

Rotavirus is an airborne infectious agent that causes about one-half of all diarrheal illness among infants while occasionally striking adults and older children.

CAUSE

This rotavirus spreads through the air much like the viruses causing the common cold.

DIAGNOSIS

Rotaviral infections usually affect infants and toddlers between the ages of 6 and 24 months, causing low-grade fever, vomiting, and watery diarrhea.

TREATMENT

No medication is available to shorten this illness. Fluids must be given in adequate amounts to replace those lost through the bowels: In severe attacks, this can require intravenous administration of electrolyte solutions in the hospital.

PREVENTION

The best preventive measure is breast-feeding; mothers' milk contains antibodies protective against the rotavirus in most cases. Vaccines under development for this condition have failed thus far.

NORWALK VIRUS INFECTION

DEFINITION

This organism, named for the place it was first isolated, Norwalk, Ohio, causes sporadic outbreaks as well as epidemics of diarrheal illness among both adults and school-age children, usually in the winter and spring.

CAUSE

The infectious organism is spread by contaminated water (including swimming pools) and foodstuffs, especially oysters and other shellfish.

DIAGNOSIS

Symptoms, which set in after an incubation period of 12 to 48 hours, vary widely, ranging from loss of appetite, nausea, and vomiting to fever, severe abdominal cramps, severe diarrhea, and headache.

TREATMENT

Normally, the attack fades quickly and complete recovery occurs without treatment. Fluids must be given in adequate amounts to replace those lost through the bowels; in severe attacks, this can require intravenous administration of electrolyte solutions in the hospital. Among the debilitated elderly and infants, the course of the disease can be threatening because of drastic loss of fluid.

PREVENTION

Good hygiene may help prevent the spread of the virus.

TYPHOID FEVER

DEFINITION

Typhoid fever is a diarrheal disease contracted mainly by visitors to developing countries.

CAUSE

This illness is caused by the *Salmonella typhi* bacterium, which spreads via food or water contaminated with infected human waste; dairy products and undercooked meats are the most common sources. The condition is more common in people who take antacid medication such as cimetidine or ranitidine, which lower the body's defenses against this bacterium.

DIAGNOSIS

Sickness usually develops after an incubation period of 1 or 2 weeks but can be delayed for up to 60 days after exposure. Symptoms appear gradually, starting with dull headache, lethargy, and sometimes either constipation or diarrhea. Fever increases for 2 days and reaches a very high plateau of about 105°F (40.6°C); frequently, it will remain there for about 3 weeks. Diagnosis of typhoid can be made by a culture of the blood and stool and by blood tests.

TREATMENT

Four drugs are effective against typhoid, but after therapy begins fever still takes a week to recede. When the illness clears, periodic testing for typhoid should continue for up to 6 months to make certain the patient is not still harboring the microbes and acting as an unwitting "silent" carrier of the disease. This is especially true of those with gallstones, a common nesting site for *Salmonella typhi*.

PREVENTION

Do not drink the water or place ice cubes in your drinks when visiting a country where the typhus bacterium thrives; imbibe only bottled, carbonated beverages.

DIARRHEA CAUSED BY ANTIBIOTICS

DEFINITION

Occasionally, taking antibiotics disturbs the normal bacterial balance in the body and causes mild diarrhea. In a few cases, the condition may be serious.

CAUSE

When antibiotics suppress normal intestinal bacteria, a

type of clostridium bacteria sometimes overgrows in the intestines, producing a toxin that damages the colon.

DIAGNOSIS

This is the most common cause of diarrhea among hospital patients. The diarrhea is watery and profuse and there may be abdominal pain and high fever.

TREATMENT

Antibiotic use should be discontinued; metronidazole or vancomycin are used to treat this condition.

....

INFECTIONS OF THE JOINTS AND BONES

INFECTIOUS ARTHRITIS

DEFINITION

Although uncommon, bacteria can invade a joint and give rise to infectious arthritis.

CAUSE

In children, infectious arthritis is usually a complication of a preexisting infection or wound; in adults, preexisting osteoarthritis or rheumatoid arthritis is a common predisposing factor. Many bacteria may cause this condition, including *Gonococcus.*

DIAGNOSIS

These infections may be confined to a single joint, causing swelling, tenderness, and pain during joint movement. While mumps, chickenpox, rheumatic fever, and other disorders can cause similar joint swelling and pain, those discomforts are unrelated to infectious arthritis and clear when the disease is cured.

The gonococcus bacteria have a unique tendency to cause red sores on the hands and feet, especially among young women, and may also cause severe pain in the wrists and ankles. In men, the gonococcus will often attack a single joint, usually the knee.

A diagnosis of infectious arthritis is confirmed by culturing fluid from an affected joint.

TREATMENT

Left untreated, infectious arthritis can permanently damage affected joints. For most cases, antibiotics should be administered in large doses, preferably intravenously in a

hospital setting, while the fluid surrounding the joints should be drained regularly. Arthritis due to gonococcus, however, can be treated with oral ampicillin. Surgery is generally not necessary or particularly helpful. (See chapter 25, Arthritis, for more details.)

MALE/FEMALE DIFFERENCES

The gonococcus bacteria may cause different symptoms in women than in men: Women may develop red sores on the hands and feet, in addition to severe pain in the wrists and ankles. In men, the gonococcus will frequently attack only a single joint, most often the knee.

LYME DISEASE

DEFINITION

This tick-borne infection can cause arthritis and, in severe cases, heart and/or central nervous system complications. Although first identified in the late 1970s in Lyme, Connecticut, it has since been identified in the Midwest and West Coast and in northern European countries.

CAUSE

The causative organism, a spirochete called *Borelia burgdorferi,* is transmitted to humans via the deer tick—a tiny insect found not only on deer, but squirrels, rabbits, other rodents, birds, and household pets.

DIAGNOSIS

An infection typically begins with a flulike illness, often accompanied by a rash around the site of the tick bite. Often people are unaware that they have been bitten by a tick, and will not be accurately diagnosed early in the disease.

TREATMENT

If caught and treated with antibiotics in its early stages, the disease usually can be cured with no lasting effects. If untreated, however, it can result in arthritis and other complications. Intensive antibiotic treatment in these later stages may provide relief, but a certain number of patients experience recurrent bouts of fatigue, joint pain, and other symptoms. (See chapter 25, Arthritis.)

PREVENTION

Dress in protective clothing when entering tick-infested areas: Wear a long-sleeved, high-neck shirt with multiple layers of clothing and a hat, and tuck pantlegs into socks.

Check for ticks after excursions and be especially vigilant in areas known to contain large populations of Lyme-carrying ticks.

OSTEOMYELITIS

DEFINITION

Osteomyelitis is a bacterial infection of the bone and bone marrow.

CAUSE

Osteomyelitis is usually a secondary infection following an infection elsewhere in the body; the primary infection is usually caused by a wound, surgery, an open fracture of a bone, or the presence of a foreign body, such as a bullet or surgical plate.

In both children and adults, osteomyelitis can follow a puncture wound of the heel. A bacterium, *Pseudomonas aeruginosa*, lives in old athletic shoes and can cause the infection.

DIAGNOSIS

This malady strikes children more often than adults, causing severe pain and tenderness, particularly when the joint near the infected area is flexed. Fever, drowsiness, and dehydration also occur. If osteomyelitis is caused by a heel puncture wound, the heel will hurt and swell and the victim will probably not experience a fever.

Osteomyelitis is confirmed with blood tests, x-rays, and radionuclide bone scans. For some forms of the disease, such as infection of the vertebrae, a biopsy may be necessary.

TREATMENT

This condition is treated with long-term (4 to 6 weeks) administration of antibiotics and, sometimes, surgery to remove the infected bone. Recurrences are common, and the disease can become chronic. For osteomyelitis caused by heel puncture wounds, surgery and antibiotics are necessary to prevent long-term damage.

....

URINARY TRACT INFECTIONS

INFECTIONS OF THE URETHRA AND BLADDER

DEFINITION

Second to respiratory tract illness, urinary tract infections (UTIs) are the leading cause of physician visits in the United States. Women are affected far more frequently than are men (except among the elderly), and it has been estimated that as many as 10 percent of women suffer an infection of the urethra, bladder, ureters, or kidneys every year.

CAUSE

The infectious agents, usually bacteria, commonly gain access to the urinary tract by migrating up the urethra, the tube carrying urine from the bladder to be eliminated outside the body.

Urination, an effective flushing mechanism, is usually adequate protection against UTIs, but bacteria invade when the urethra or bladder becomes swollen or irritated, or when an obstruction, such as a swollen prostate gland in men and pregnancy in women, prevents complete emptying of the bladder. UTIs can result from sexual intercourse, bubble baths, and use of diaphragms, douches, or other irritants; in many instances, however, there is no identifiable activity associated with the infection.

Nearly 85 percent of urinary infections are caused by *Escherichia coli (E. coli)*, a bacterium normally present in the intestines; other bacteria and chlamydia also cause UTIs in sexually active young women, but *E. coli* can be easily transferred from the anus to the urethra of women.

DIAGNOSIS

Lower abdominal pain and a burning sensation during urination are the principal symptoms among children; adults also experience painful and frequent urination, and the urine will often be bloody and foul-smelling. When the kidneys are infected, fever and pain in the flanks may also occur; men may experience lower back pain, and women can experience malaise. Occasionally, the infection is symptomless, especially if the infection is in the kidneys.

Accurately diagnosing a UTI depends on analysis and culture of the urine. But while proper collection is crucial it is infrequently performed: a "clean catch" specimen requires urine collection only at midstream, and ideally, the urine should have been in the bladder for several hours.

TREATMENT

If you have had the symptoms of UTI for 2 days or less, the condition is usually cured by 3 days of antibiotics. Drugs that have been used include Bactrim or Septra, and the fluoroquinolones such as ciprofloxacin or ofloxacin. If a woman has had the illness for more than 2 days, or if she has hemorrhagic cystitis (severe infection of the bladder), or if a culture taken 2 days after the single dose reveals the continued presence of infecting microbes, then a conventional 4- to 7-day course of antibiotics is recommended. With all therapy, the patient should consume plenty of water.

PREVENTION

Measures that seem to help women avoid repeated infections:

- Drink plenty of fluids to increase frequency of urination and completely empty the bladder during each voiding.
- Keep the genital and anal areas clean by washing with mild soap and water; after a bowel movement, wipe from front to back to avoid introducing bacteria from the anus into the vagina.
- Empty the bladder before and immediately after intercourse.

If these preventive measures fail, and infections are related to sexual intercourse, prophylactic antibiotics may be prescribed. An antibiotic, $\frac{1}{2}$ tablet of Bactrim or Septra, can be taken after intercourse or three times weekly. Conversely, at the first symptom of infection a single large dose of antibiotic can be taken. (See also chapter 9, Special Health Concerns of Women.)

MALE/FEMALE DIFFERENCES

Women are more susceptible to infection in this part of the body because microbes easily traverse their 1.5-inch urethra while finding it difficult to penetrate the 8- to 9-inch male tube. Women's urethral openings are also near anal and vaginal sources of infectious agents, and women lack the men's protective prostate fluid.

KIDNEY INFECTION

DEFINITION

This very serious urinary tract infection often requires hospitalization.

CAUSE

Infectious organisms almost always reach the kidneys by migrating up the urinary tract, although they are occasionally borne via the bloodstream from another infection site in the body.

DIAGNOSIS

Fever accompanying kidney infection rises rapidly and often reaches 104°F (40°C), producing chills and trembling, sometimes accompanied by nausea and vomiting.

Some sufferers experience the urge to urinate constantly even after the bladder is empty. The urine is cloudy and may be tinged with blood. Pain, usually sudden and intense, is felt in the back just above the waist and gradually spreads down into the groin.

TREATMENT

Initial treatment consists of several days of hospitalization and intramuscular or intravenous administration of antibiotics. If these medications produce marked improvement, oral antibiotic therapy may be continued at home for 2 weeks. Two days after the last dosage, a urine culture should be performed to check for residual bacteria (up to 30 percent of patients relapse after apparent recovery). If the examination reveals persistent infection, antibiotics should then be taken for 4 to 6 more weeks.

MALE/FEMALE DIFFERENCES

Unlike urinary infections, which most often affect women, kidney infections strike men and women in equal numbers.

PROSTATE GLAND INFECTION

DEFINITION

Because the prostate gland encircles the male urethra, an infection of this gland interferes with discharge of urine and semen. (Women do not possess a comparable anatomical structure.)

CAUSE

Bacteria infect the gland after migrating up the urethra.

DIAGNOSIS

Symptoms of this infection include fever, pain in the lower back and groin, and frequent, painful urination. The prostate becomes very tender and sensitive to the touch—a fact revealed when a physician examines the gland by reaching a gloved finger through the anus.

A diagnosis of prostate infection is confirmed by examining specimens of urine and prostate secretions. The secretions are gathered by massaging the prostate after the bladder is empty and catching the few drops that trickle down the urethra.

TREATMENT

Treatment of acute prostatitis with antibiotics is usually rapidly effective. Chronic prostatitis requires antibiotic therapy for up to 3 months.

PREVENTION

Proper hygiene—frequent washing of the genitals with soap and water—can limit entry of bacteria to the urethra.

....

SEXUALLY TRANSMITTED DISEASES

GONORRHEA

DEFINITION

This condition is a sexually transmitted disease characterized by inflammation of the urethra, difficulty in urination (in males), and inflammation of the cervix (in females). With 2.5 million cases per year, gonorrhea is one of the most common communicable diseases in the United States.

CAUSE

Caused by the *Neisseria gonorrhoeae* bacterium, this illness is confined largely to sexually active adults between the ages of 20 and 30 but can affect anyone of any age. Many people carry the gonorrhoeae bacterium without any signs of illness; in one study, 2 percent of all women studied at random were asymptomatic carriers.

Though sexual intercourse is the predominant means of transmission, gonorrhea bacteria may spread through casual contact; the bacteria can survive for up to 4 hours on dry, inorganic surfaces.

If a pregnant woman is infected, the disease may be passed to her baby during delivery and cause blindness unless antibiotic drops are applied to the infant's eyes.

DIAGNOSIS

Gonorrhea manifests itself 2 to 6 days after the bacteria invade the urethra. Among men, the main symptoms include burning upon urination and discharge from the penis of a puslike purulent, yellowish liquid. Women may produce a cloudy discharge from the vagina, and experience discomfort in the lower abdomen, abnormal bleeding from the vagina, or pain during urination. Frequently, there will be no noticeable symptoms, and an infected person becomes a silent carrier of the disease.

Among people who engage in oral or anal sex, the mouth, throat, and rectum can also become infected; infection at these sites may cause only very mild symptoms or none at all. If the throat is infected, symptoms may include a sore throat and tonsillitis; anal gonorrhea produces a constant urge to move the bowels and an associated purulent discharge.

The major complication of gonorrhea in women is pelvic inflammatory disease (PID), a major cause of infertility. PID results when bacteria travel up from the cervix to infect the fallopian tubes through which the eggs pass on their way to the uterus. Fallopian infection occurs in nearly 15 percent of women with gonorrhea and takes place soon after initial infection or during menstruation. If untreated, gonorrhea can spread through the bloodstream and infect other parts of the body.

A definitive diagnosis of gonorrhea does not require a culture. DNA probes have made it possible to make a rapid diagnosis of gonorrhea and chlamydia. In men, however, a doctor can usually make an accurate assessment on the basis of symptoms and a microscopic examination of the puslike discharge. However, a similar diagnosis via visual exam should not be used with women: Many bacteria normally inhabiting the vagina resemble gonorrhea under the microscope.

TREATMENT

Initial treatment is with ceftriaxone, 125 mg or 250 mg by injection plus 100 mg doxycycline daily for 7 days. This treats a simultaneous infection with *Neisseria gonorrheae* and *Chlamydia trachomatis.* Unfortunately, many individuals fail to complete the doxycycline therapy, and therefore a new macolide (antibacterial agent), azituromycin, is given orally at a dose of 1 gram to treat gonorrhea and chlamydia infections.

Because of the growing problem of drug-resistant infections, a repeat culture should be taken within 1 week after all penicillin treatments to be sure the microbes have been eliminated. This is especially important if the infection was anal, a particularly difficult treatment site. Disappearance of symptoms does not necessarily signify cure.

Treatment of gonorrhea should be accompanied by a course of tetracycline to eradicate *Chlamydia trachomatis,* a microbe that often simultaneously invades the genital tract along with *N. gonorrheae.* An alternative therapy is with azituromycin, a new macrolide antibiotic given in a single dose.

In every case, all sexual partners must be treated; otherwise reinfection will probably occur.

PREVENTION

Use of a condom during sexual intercourse can help prevent the spread of gonorrhea and most sexually transmitted diseases. Babies should receive antibiotic eye drops to avoid contracting this disease from their mothers.

MALE/FEMALE DIFFERENCES

This disease causes different symptoms in men and women (see "Diagnosis" above).

CHLAMYDIAL INFECTIONS

DEFINITION

This increasingly common sexually transmitted infection can affect almost any part of the genital tract as well as the anus of both men and women. Chlamydia causes nonspecific urethritis, cervicitis, epididymitis, and other problems. When these organisms infect the fallopian tubes, sterility may result. The condition can also be transmitted to newborns, causing eye infections or pneumonia. It is the most common cause of pelvic inflammatory disease (PID) in young women.

DIAGNOSIS

Any sexually active young woman who has abdominal pain, vaginal discharge, and fever should make certain that her gynecologist checks for chlamydia.

The most common conditions caused by chlamydia include:

• *Nonspecific urethritis (NSU).* Sometimes referred to as nongonococcal or postgonococcal urethritis, this illness resembles gonorrhea but cultures fail to identify *N. gonorrheae.* Definitive diagnosis can be made only by culturing the discharge and identifying chlamydia—a task only recently made possible by the development of advanced diagnostic equipment.

• *Rectal infections.* Chlamydia can cause rectal infections after anal intercourse. The condition leads to rectal bleeding, severe soreness and swelling of lymph nodes in the pelvic area, as well as malaise, fever, and a general feeling of ill health. Untreated, this illness causes serious complications in the genital area.

TREATMENT

Oral doxycycline (100 mg) twice a day for 1 to 2 weeks clears up most cases of chlamydia. In every case, all sexual partners must be treated, otherwise reinfection will probably occur.

PREVENTION

Use of a condom during sexual intercourse can help prevent the spread of chlamydia and most sexually transmitted diseases.

MALE/FEMALE DIFFERENCES

This illness is more common in women.

SYPHILIS

DEFINITION

Syphilis is a serious sexually transmitted disease that is far less common than gonorrhea.

CAUSE

Caused by the bacterium *Treponema pallidum,* a bacterial spirochete that affects only humans.

DIAGNOSIS

The incubation period usually lasts 2 to 3 weeks but can be as long as 8 weeks. The first sign of infection is a hard, painless, red, protruding sore or ulcer called a chancre (pronounced "shanker") at the primary infection site (usually on the genitals or occasionally the rectum or on the tongue, lips, or breast). In women, if the sore develops in the vagina or cervix it may go unnoticed. The lymph nodes near the chancre usually swell and a definitive diagnosis can be made by microscopic examination of the bacterium scraped from the chancre.

Secondary syphilis develops 2 to 6 weeks after the chancre heals and is marked by flulike symptoms: fever, headache, loss of appetite, general malaise sometimes accompanied by enlarged lymph nodes, joint pain, and a skin rash of small, red, scaling bumps that do not itch. At this stage a blood test can be used to diagnose the disease.

During the third and final stage of the disease—latent or late syphilis—the disease can lie dormant for years until it flares without warning, attacking almost any organ and mimicking many chronic conditions. At this point, syphilis frequently affects the brain, causing paralysis, senility, insanity, loss of sensation in the legs, and blindness (rare); nerves to a joint can be destroyed. The large blood vessel leading from the heart (the aorta) can be damaged, as can the heart valves. Syphilis rarely progresses to the third stage in the United States.

Syphilis can also be congenital—passed along by a mother to her newborn. The usual signs of congenital infection in a newborn are skin sores or lesions, a runny nose, severe tenderness over the bones, and deafness. The diagnosis can be made by examining umbilical cord blood at the time of birth.

TREATMENT

For babies, immediate antibiotic therapy can quickly eliminate infection, preventing any serious aftereffects. Among adults, injections of penicillin will readily cure syphilis. If the nerves are infected, the physician may hospitalize the patient so that megadoses of antibiotic can be administered intravenously.

PREVENTION

Syphilis is highly contagious during its first and second stages; any person who suspects or knows he or she has an infection should immediately notify all sexual partners. Use of a condom during sexual intercourse can help prevent its spread. Pregnant women with syphilis must give birth by cesarean section to avoid passing it on to the newborn.

MALE/FEMALE DIFFERENCES

In women, the characteristic sores may be internal and thus may not be noticed.

GENITAL HERPES

DEFINITION

Genital herpes is a recurrent, sexually transmitted viral infection that may be contagious even when its characteristic sores are absent.

Because genital herpes is incurable, considerable stigma and emotional trauma have been associated with the disease. While no one relishes the thought of having an incurable, recurring disease, much of the hysteria over herpes is unwarranted. Except in unusual circumstances, the disease is more uncomfortable than serious.

New cases of genital herpes develop among hundreds of thousands of Americans every year, striking all social and economic classes in epidemic proportions.

CAUSE

Genital herpes is caused by the herpes simplex Type 2 virus, a close cousin of the Type 1 virus that causes cold sores. Herpes usually spreads to sexual partners during active manifestation of the disease but herpes carriers can still spread the disease in the absence of lesions and other symptoms. Though most people suffer recurrences, most successive episodes are briefer and milder. Among many people, recurrences eventually cease.

Spread by any form of sexual contact, the herpesvirus invades the body through tiny breaks in mucosal linings. About 6 days after infection, the first symptoms—lesions—surface. After the symptoms go away, the virus travels along the nerves to the deep nerve centers (ganglia) at the base of the spinal cord near the buttocks and enters a silent period of inactivity or latency. When reactivated, it travels back down the nerves, causing a new outbreak in the same area involved in the initial attack and sometimes on the buttocks, thighs, and abdomen as well. Anywhere from 50 to 75 percent of people with herpes will suffer a recurrent infection within 3 months of the initial episode. As time passes, attacks are farther apart and less severe.

The precise mechanism causing reactivation of the latent viruses is not known, but chronically ill or stressed people seem to have the most attacks. Other precipitating factors are thought to be menstruation, pregnancy, emotional distress, local trauma to the genitals, and even sexual intercourse.

DIAGNOSIS

Mild tingling and burning may precede the actual appearance of herpes skin sores; within a matter of hours, fluid-filled blisters develop, often extensively. In women, the blisters, or vesicles, usually involve the external genitalia (the labia, skin around the rectum, and foreskin of the clitoris) as well as the vagina and cervix, which protrudes into the vaginal canal of the end of the uterus. There is often watery discharge and pain during urination. Among men, the blisters break out on the penis and sometimes on the thighs.

Both men and women may experience low-grade fever, headache, generalized muscle ache, and tender, swollen lymph nodes in the groin. In about 2 days, the vesicles become pustular (pus-producing) and coalesce into large, painful ulcerlike sores. These crust over, dry, and heal without treatment (and leave no scars). Although the entire episode, from the appearance of the blisters to the disappearance of all symptoms, lasts about 3 weeks, the herpes can still be contagious for up to 2 weeks after symptoms fade. (The virus is most infectious in the blistering stage but can also be transferred during the tingling period just before the sores appear.)

Genital herpes can be definitively diagnosed by a microscopic examination of a scraping from a sore and by culturing such a specimen in a laboratory.

TREATMENT

Although no drug cures herpes, acyclovir taken orally relieves discomfort and reduces contagion by shortening the period during which viruses are shed. Local anesthetics such as lidocaine and drying agents may also relieve symptoms.

PREVENTION

Sexual activity should be curtailed at the first sign of an imminent attack and should not be resumed until 1 week after all symptoms have disappeared (2 weeks in the case of the initial infection). The use of a condom is wise but not a guarantee of preventing spread.

Oral acyclovir can prevent recurrent attacks but once the drug is stopped herpes may strike again.

MALE/FEMALE DIFFERENCES

Women are at greatest risk from complications of genital herpes: Herpes (as well as other viral genital infections) increase the risk of later cervical cancer, and any woman who has suffered the disease should have periodic Pap smears to detect cervical cancer at its earliest stages. Herpes may also be passed to a baby born during an active infection, possibly causing serious difficulties including blindness, neurological problems, mental retardation, and even death. So pregnant women should be watched closely for signs of an active infection near the time of delivery. If there is danger of passing the infection to the baby, a cesarean section is advised.

VAGINITIS

DEFINITION

Vaginitis is an infection of the vagina without involvement of the urinary tract.

CAUSE

This condition can afflict all women, but is most common among the sexually active. A variety of microbes cause the disease, including the protozoan *Trichomonas vaginalis,* the fungus *Candida albicans,* and the bacterium *Gardnerella vaginalis* (also known as *Haemophilus vaginalis* or *Corynebacterium vaginale* and associated with nonspecific vaginitis).

DIAGNOSIS

No matter which microbe causes this condition, the symptoms are similar: vaginal discharge, itching and burning, pain during intercourse, and vaginal odor.

Infections caused by *T. vaginalis* produce a profuse, malodorous, yellow, purulent, and often frothy discharge; sores can develop on the cervix.

- Fungal vaginitis caused by *C. albicans* results in a white discharge resembling cottage cheese with no distinct odor. The predominant symptom is itching of the vulva.
- Vaginitis caused by *G. vaginalis* produces a white or grayish foul-smelling discharge that coats the vaginal walls. The vagina may also burn and itch.

TREATMENT

For infections caused by *T. vaginalis,* treatment consists of a large single dose of metronidazole (sexual partners must also be treated to prevent reinfection). Fungal vaginitis is treated with one of several drugs or ointments and antibiotics are used for vaginitis caused by *G. vaginalis.*

PREVENTION

Limiting the number of sexual partners and using condoms during sexual intercourse may prevent the spread of the bacteria that cause vaginitis.

ACQUIRED IMMUNE DEFICIENCY SYNDROME (AIDS)

DEFINITION

AIDS is a lethal disease characterized by a severely compromised immune system as a result of infection with human immunodeficiency virus (HIV). In the United States, this condition used to afflict mostly male homosexuals and intravenous drug users but is now attacking the general heterosexual population, especially women, in growing numbers. The only persons not at risk for AIDS are those who never use intravenous drugs and either totally abstain from sex or have sex only with a mutually monogamous, nondrug-using partner who has tested negative for the AIDS virus.

CAUSE

The HIV associated with AIDS is usually transmitted sexually or via contaminated syringes that cause direct contact with blood, semen, or possibly other body fluids containing the virus. (There have been reports of infants contracting the virus from breast milk. The virus has been found in saliva, but it is doubtful that it can be contracted by contact with it.)

The disease's primary characteristic is a severe disruption and failure of the immune system. The suspected virus itself is not lethal, but its gross weakening of the immune system opens the body to devastating "opportunistic" infections and disorders that the body cannot defeat. The most common of these diseases are

- Pneumonia, caused by the protozoa *Pneumocystis carinii;* meningitis, due to the fungus *Cryptococcus*
- Brain abscess due to toxoplasmosis
- Herpes simplex infections
- Other serious, normally rare bacterial, viral, and fungal conditions

DIAGNOSIS

AIDS usually begins with a fever of unknown origin, weight loss, fatigue, shortness of breath, diarrhea, and neurological disorders. Sometimes the lymph nodes swell and breathing difficulties may progress slowly or rapidly. A blood test detects the virus.

TREATMENT

Although the bacterial infections and some of the other opportunistic diseases that plague AIDS patients can usually be treated successfully, these infections frequently recur. At the present time, AIDS is incurable, although some antiviral drugs are being used to improve the quality of life for AIDS patients.

PREVENTION

Because there is no cure for this condition, measures to prevent infection are crucial. Use of a condom during sexual intercourse is imperative to prevent the spread of the AIDS virus. (For a more complete discussion of prevention, see chapter 19.)

....

INFECTIONS CAUSED BY FUNGI

HISTOPLASMOSIS

DEFINITION

This fungal infection is a benign and self-limiting disease in 80 percent of all cases. However, some people develop a chronic form of this condition and suffer from severe lung disease.

CAUSE

This disease is caused by the inhalation of the fungus *Histoplasma capsulatum,* an organism widespread in the Mississippi, Ohio, and Missouri river valleys that flourishes in soil enriched by bird, chicken, and bat droppings (see figure 18.6). *Histoplasma capsulatum* can remain dormant in the body and reactivate when the immune system is compromised, as in AIDS.

DIAGNOSIS

The disease is marked by headache, chills, fever, and sometimes lumps on the leg. There is also a cough and some chest pain, but unless a culture is performed, physicians are likely to mistake the condition for a viral infection. Some people with histoplasmosis develop a severe lung disease (which may be fatal if untreated).

TREATMENT

In most cases, no treatment is necessary. In the few cases that progress to severe lung disease, antifungal medication such as amphotericin B usually effects a complete cure. In AIDS patients, fluconazole or itraconazole will have to be taken orally for a lifetime.

COCCIDIOIDOMYCOSIS

DEFINITION

This acute respiratory disease endemic to the southwestern United States is caused by inhaled fungal spores.

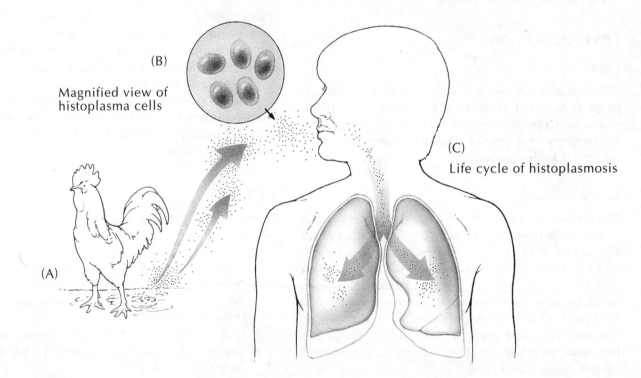

(B)
Magnified view of histoplasma cells

(C)
Life cycle of histoplasmosis

(A)

Figure 18.6: Life cycle of histoplasmosis. (A) The histoplasma fungus grows in soil enriched by droppings from infected chickens, birds, bats, or other animals. (B) The spores are released into the air. (C) When the spores are inhaled, they migrate to the lungs, resulting in symptoms typical of histoplasmosis.

CAUSE

This condition is caused by inhaling the fungus *Coccidioides immitis,* a microbe found primarily in California's San Joaquin Valley (the disease is often called San Joaquin or Valley Fever), but the disease can occur in California as far north as San Francisco. As with histoplasmosis, the organism can remain dormant in the body and reactivate in individuals who are immunocompromised.

DIAGNOSIS

About 2 weeks after inhaling the fungal spores, the person develops fever and a nonproductive cough, and starts to lose weight. There may be pain when taking deep breaths (pleurisy), and lumps on the legs. Diagnosis is confirmed by identifying the fungi in sputum, pleural fluid, skin tissue, or other specimens.

TREATMENT

Most patients recover without treatment and with only minor lung scarring. In a few people, though, the disease is progressive and can lead to a dangerous form of chronic meningitis. This requires therapy with a very potent antibiotic, amphotericin B, which must sometimes be administered via a special chamber implanted in the head. Fluconazole or itraconazole is administered orally for a lifetime in an AIDS patient.

CRYPTOCOCCOSIS

DEFINITION

This fungal infection may cause pneumonia and can progress to other more serious conditions. Until the spread of AIDS, this infection was uncommon; the lowered immune response of AIDS sufferers renders them vulnerable to this fungus.

CAUSE

The fungus that causes this disease—*Cryptococcus neoformans*—is found throughout the world, often occurring in pigeon droppings. When inhaled by someone in normal health, the fungus is usually destroyed by the lung's T-cell lymphocytes. If immunity has been compromised by AIDS and T cells are depleted, the fungus may produce a slow-growing pneumonitis or a granuloma that takes years to develop. If the organisms spread from the lungs, they may infect the meninges, resulting in a chronic form of meningitis.

DIAGNOSIS

In most people, this fungus causes a simple form of pneumonia that clears up by itself. In a few people, it leads to chronic meningitis manifested by chronic headaches, afternoon fever, personality changes, and other nonspecific symptoms. Meningitis usually develops among those who have a complicating condition such as Hodgkin's disease, leukemia, or AIDS. Diagnosis is confirmed by examination of the spinal fluid detecting cryptococcae antigen.

TREATMENT

Treatment is initially with the antifungal amphotericin B and then subsequently with oral fluconazole.

PREVENTION

Avoid areas with dense pigeon populations.

CANDIDA

DEFINITION

A common fungal infection sometimes referred to as thrush or vaginitis (depending on the site of infection), candida results from an imbalance of the body's normal fungi.

CAUSE

This condition is caused by *Candida albicans,* a ubiquitous fungus. When this organism proliferates, it may produce symptomatic infections of the mouth, intestines, vagina, or skin. Infections of the mouth or vagina are commonly called thrush.

Vaginitis caused by *Candida* often afflicts women on birth control pills or antibiotics. Among people abusing intravenous drugs, *Candida* infections can lead to heart valve inflammation.

DIAGNOSIS

Symptoms vary, depending on the part of the body affected.

- In the mouth, oral thrush causes pustules (collections of pus) and is a major problem for HIV-infected individuals and others with compromised immune systems.
- In the intestines, the infection causes gastric upset.
- On the skin, the infection produces a skin irritation (may form a red rash).
- In the vagina, the condition causes itching and a white, cheesy discharge.

Diagnosis of *Candida* infections is confirmed by cultures and blood tests.

TREATMENT

Treatment in normal individuals is with nystatin or clotrimazole, or miconazole topically. Claims for any benefit from special diets or chronic antifungal agents are not supported by reliable research. There is no evidence that *Candida* in the intestine of normal individuals leads to disease; everyone at one time or another has *Candida* present in their intestines. *Candida* should be treated with either intravenous amphotericin B or intravenous fluconazole, followed by a brief course of either intravenous amphotericin or oral fluconazole.

PREVENTION

Candida infection can be prevented in a medical setting by careful attention to intravenous lines, urethral catheters, and skin care. Prophylaxis with antifungal agents prevents disease in people with suppressed immune systems.

ASPERGILLOSIS

DEFINITION

This fungal lung infection usually strikes people whose immune system has been weakened.

CAUSE

This condition is caused by the widespread *Aspergillus* fungus and occurs most often among those with compromised immune systems—people with AIDS, cancer (Hodgkin's and leukemia particularly), or who have had a kidney transplant. The infection also may produce symptoms in people hypersensitive to the fungus.

These minuscule fungi contaminate air systems, construction materials, and fireproofing materials as well as decaying vegetation and marijuana. Inhaled, the small size of the microbe enables it to enter the alveoli, where it is normally destroyed. In damaged lungs, however, the fungus may survive and grow or accumulate in the nasal sinuses and can be inoculated directly into other body tissues.

DIAGNOSIS

This infection produces fever and cough. Diagnosis is difficult; only 10 percent of cases yield positive cultures. There are no satisfactory blood, serum, or skin tests; diagnosis is best made by biopsy of infected tissue.

TREATMENT

Treatment is with amphotericin B. In some cases, surgery may be needed to remove the fungus ball. If the disease is a hypersensitivity phenomenon, it should be treated with corticosteroids.

PREVENTION

Prevention requires use of high-efficiency airflow systems in areas inhabited by people with suppressed immune systems, monitoring of spore counts at hospital construction sites, and warning people at risk about home hazards involving this ubiquitous fungus.

SPOROTRICHOSIS

DEFINITION

A chronic condition caused by a fungus common to soil and decaying vegetation, sporotrichosis occurs most often among gardeners and farmers.

CAUSE

The infectious spores of *Sporothrix*—the fungus that causes this condition—can be picked up from rose thorns, sphagnum moss, and splinters of rotting wood.

DIAGNOSIS

A painless but nonhealing and gradually expanding sore or ulcer appears at the puncture site, and infection spreads to the nearest lymph nodes. Diagnosis can be confirmed by a laboratory exam of a pus sample.

TREATMENT

Treatment is with potassium iodide taken orally. Today, the disease can also be treated with oral fluconazole or itraconazole.

PREVENTION

Gardeners, farmers, and horticulturists should always wear gloves when working to prevent punctures and abrasions.

RINGWORM

DEFINITION

This condition is not due to a worm but results from fungal infection. Referred to medically as tinea, this highly infectious disease mainly afflicts children; ringworm of the scalp can reach epidemic proportions within a school or community.

CAUSE

The infection is usually caused by a species of *Trichophyton* fungus.

DIAGNOSIS

On the scalp, these fungi cause round, bald, scaly patches that itch and flake. Diagnosis is made with an ultraviolet light or by examining a hair under the microscope.

Body ringworm appears as a reddish round or oval sore that scales and itches. The patch gradually grows to about an inch across and the central area heals, leaving a red ring on the skin.

TREATMENT

Antifungal oral and topical drug treatments are used for ringworm of the body or scalp.

ATHLETE'S FOOT

DEFINITION

Athlete's foot is a form of ringworm that grows between the toes.

CAUSE

Caused by *Trichophyton mentagrophytes,* athlete's foot often strikes those who spend many hours in sweaty socks and shoes.

DIAGNOSIS

This condition causes a dry scaling and fissuring of the skin between the toes and on the arch; it can also produce scaling and thickening of the soles. Secondary bacterial infections are common.

TREATMENT

Avoid ointments, sterilization of footwear, and antifungal foot baths—these are of little benefit. The best strategy is to keep the feet dry (especially the skin between the toes), air the feet often, use dry, absorbent socks, and wash the feet daily. If possible, wear sandals or open-toe shoes. If the infection persists, consult a doctor for antifungal medication.

PREVENTION

Keep feet dry by wearing absorbent socks during exercise, letting shoes dry between wearings, and applying talcum powder.

RICKETTSIAL INFECTIONS

Rickettsiae are microorganisms that are bigger than viruses but smaller than bacteria. They live within the cells of ticks and other insects that pass these microbes to humans. Rickettsiae cause a variety of relatively uncommon illnesses characterized by fever, headache, malaise, and rash.

ROCKY MOUNTAIN SPOTTED FEVER

DEFINITION

This rickettsial infection is spread by ticks. Despite its name, Rocky Mountain spotted fever is much more common in the Carolinas, Long Island, and in the islands off Massachusetts than in the western mountain region of the United States.

CAUSE

These rickettsiae are transmitted by tick bites, so the disease appears mainly between May and Labor Day, when adult ticks are active and people are most apt to be camping or hiking in the woods.

DIAGNOSIS

After an incubation period of about 1 week, a victim will experience abrupt and severe headache, chills, prostration, and muscular pains. Fever reaches 104°F (40°C) within a few days and remains high, though morning remissions can occur. On about the fourth day of fever, a rash appears on the ankles, wrists, palms, and soles, and moves on to the trunk.

A physician can make a diagnosis with a blood test, but the test is often negative early in the course of illness.

TREATMENT

Even if a blood test for this condition is negative, anyone over the age of 8 suspected of suffering Rocky Mountain spotted fever should begin treatment with tetracycline. Children under 8 should not be treated with tetracycline but should receive chloramphenicol. Delay in starting antimicrobial therapy is dangerous for this rapidly progressing and potentially fatal disease.

PREVENTION

Wear protective clothing when entering tick-infested areas, especially in locales where the risk of infection is high. Always check your body for ticks after hiking or camping.

TYPHUS

DEFINITION

The potentially fatal infectious diseases known as typhus are all caused by the same organism—*Rickettsia pro-*

wazekii. Relatively uncommon, these diseases still exist in parts of Yugoslavia, Russia, and other places where people are crowded together in conditions of poor hygiene.

CAUSE

The typhus organism, *R. prowazekii,* is transmitted to humans from lice.

DIAGNOSIS

About 2 weeks after infection, the patient suffers a severe headache and high fever; after 3 or 4 more days, a pinkish rash spreads over the body (except for the face).

TREATMENT

Early treatment with tetracycline or chloramphenicol is highly effective in curtailing this disease.

PREVENTION

Since it is transmitted by lice, proper hygiene—frequent washing of clothes and bedsheets—and avoidance of lice infestation prevent the spread of typhus.

....

PARASITIC INFECTIONS

Several tiny and not-so-tiny members of the animal kingdom can invade our bodies and cause serious illness. These parasites include tapeworms, roundworms, flukes, and single-cell organisms called protozoa. Once a parasite establishes itself within the body, treatment is almost always necessary to eliminate the infection, which is relatively rare in the United States. Americans are mainly at risk from parasitic infection when they travel abroad.

MALARIA

DEFINITION

This parasitic infection, spread by mosquitoes, is rare in the industrialized world but fairly common in many tropical countries.

CAUSE

Malaria is caused by the protozoa *Plasmodium,* transmitted by the bite of an infected anopheles mosquito. Once inside a human, this protozoa may multiply in the liver and then reenter the bloodstream, rupturing red blood cells.

DIAGNOSIS

Anywhere from 10 to 40 days after being bitten by an infected mosquito, the person's red blood cells rupture and characteristic chills, high fever (up to 106°F [41.1°C]), and sweating take place, often accompanied by headache, weariness, and nausea.

A diagnosis of malaria is confirmed by a blood test and observation of the plasmodium in the blood. The best time to observe the parasite in a blood sample is before the fever goes up.

TREATMENT

Treatment is with one of several effective drugs now available such as quinine or a sulfa drug. If plasmodium falciparum is suspected, treatment should be initiated with quinine or quinidine. If plasmodium vivax is the etiology of the malaria, chloroquine is the accepted therapy, followed by a 2-week course of privaquin.

PREVENTION

For people planning to travel to malarial areas, the drug chloroquine should be administered prophylactically; when traveling to Colombia, Southeast Asia, and Kenya, where chloroquine-resistant protozoa have evolved, bring the drug Fansidar, which should be used if you develop a fever. In general, preventive drugs have to be started before departure and continued for 6 weeks after returning: Consult your physician before traveling to high-risk parts of the world. You should also bring and use insect repellents during travels to these parts of the world.

AMEBIASIS

DEFINITION

This protozoan infection affects the human intestinal tract.

CAUSE

Amebiasis is caused by the tiny protozoa *Endamoeba histolytica,* which spreads from person to person or indirectly via contaminated food or water. The organism, which dwells in the colon and rectum, where it produces ulcers and inflammation, primarily afflicts homosexual men and visitors to countries with poor sanitation.

DIAGNOSIS

This disease produces a gradual onset of symptoms including fever, local bowel tenderness, and cramping abdominal pain. Bowel movements increase, reaching as many as 15 per day. Stools are semisolid to liquid and often carry blood. If microbes invade the liver, the patient will experience tenderness over this organ.

Diagnosis is confirmed by identifying the parasite in a fresh stool specimen. The specimen should be examined before antibiotics, antacids, antidiarrheal agents, enemas, and intestinal radiocontrast agents (used in colon x-rays) are administered—all these treatments interfere with recovery of the parasite. A successful diagnosis may require examination of several stool specimens.

TREATMENT

The drug metronidazole almost always cures amebiasis.

PREVENTION

Proper hygiene and sanitary living conditions usually prevent the spread of this disease.

MALE/FEMALE DIFFERENCES

This parasite is more common in men than in women.

GIARDIASIS

DEFINITION

Giardiasis is a parasitic infection of the small intestine.

CAUSE

Caused by the protozoa *Giardia lamblia,* this disease is spread by fecal-oral routes, during sexual activity, or via contaminated food or water. It occurs most often among male homosexuals, travelers to Russia and other countries with polluted water, or campers who drink from streams contaminated by beavers and other wildlife.

DIAGNOSIS

The symptoms of this infection include abdominal discomfort, extreme flatulence, and foul-smelling stools that float. The parasite can be identified in a fresh stool specimen.

Some people who suffer recurrent, unexplained abdominal discomfort may have the *Giardia* parasite lodged in their duodenum, just below the stomach. This can be confirmed from an examination of the duodenal contents, obtained either by aspirations through a gastric tube or by having the patient swallow a nylon string to which the parasites attach themselves.

TREATMENT

The infection can be cured with the antibiotic metronidazole.

PREVENTION

Proper hygiene (including frequent washing of hands), and sanitary living conditions can help prevent the spread of giardiasis. When camping, boil all drinking water drawn from streams or ponds.

PINWORMS

DEFINITION

Pinworms are parasites that dwell in the intestines; these microbes are the most common parasitic disorder among children in the United States.

CAUSE

This parasite colonizes the lower intestinal tract of children, and, at night, the female worm crawls out to deposit eggs within skin folds. After an infected child scratches the irritated anus, the eggs spread from hand contact between children, or on toys and other objects handled by children.

DIAGNOSIS

The depositing of eggs leads to the characteristic sign of this infection—intense anal itching. Diagnosis can be made from identifying eggs picked up by a piece of cellophane tape placed in the area around the anus.

TREATMENT

Infections will clear on their own, but reinfection is common. A single dose of pyrantel pamoate eradicates pinworms in about 90 percent of cases; a follow-up dosage should be administered 2 weeks after the first.

PREVENTION

When children catch pinworms, everyone in the family must be treated to wipe out the infestation. All sheets should be washed frequently to kill eggs and worms.

HOOKWORMS

DEFINITION

Hookworms are parasites that inhabit the small intestines of nearly 25 percent of the world's population, but the parasites are now relatively rare in the United States.

CAUSE

Hookworms are contracted primarily by walking barefoot in soil contaminated with hookworm larvae; larvae penetrate the skin and migrate to the intestine, where they attach by their mouths and suck blood.

DIAGNOSIS

The most common symptom is abdominal pain, but hookworms can cause a silent anemia that is severe and can stunt the growth of children. Diagnosis is by laboratory detection of the hookworms' eggs in the stool.

TREATMENT

Several effective drugs such as mebendazole are used to kill hookworm.

PREVENTION

Always wear shoes outdoors to prevent hookworm infestation.

THREADWORM (STRONGYLOIDIASIS)

DEFINITION

Threadworm, or Strongyloides, is a parasite that lives in the intestines. Endemic in the tropics, this worm is generally found in the same climate and unsanitary conditions favorable to the spread of hookworm.

CAUSE

Like the hookworm, the threadworm is usually contracted when larvae in the soil attach themselves to bare feet and then enter the body. After entering its human host, this parasite's larvae are either released into the intestines and passed with stools, or attach to the intestinal wall and prolong the infection.

DIAGNOSIS

This parasite causes epigastric pain and tenderness, vomiting, and diarrhea. Diagnosis is made by detecting the larvae in the stool. The disease can persist for decades: Many American soldiers who contracted the disease in Burma during World War II carried the parasite undetected for 30 years. In all that time they suffered intermittent, unexplained abdominal pain that was not diagnosed and treated until the 1970s.

TREATMENT

Treatment is with oral thiabendazole.

SUMMING UP

While vaccines, antibiotics, and a wide range of drugs have been devised for combating many disease-causing microbes, the war against infectious disease is far from over. Drug resistance among microorganisms has expanded widely in recent years. Incurable conditions such as AIDS have complicated treatment of what were once rare infections. Consequently, diligence in identifying, treating, and preventing infectious disease is now more important than ever for doctors and laypeople.

19
HIV Infection and AIDS

JAY DOBKIN, M.D.

Parts of this chapter are adapted from the chapter by Michael Wilkes, M.D., which appeared in the revised second edition.

During the past decade, more than 300,000 individuals in the United States have been diagnosed with Acquired Immune Deficiency Syndrome—AIDS; more than 60 percent of them have already died. AIDS is now the eighth leading cause of death in America and the leading cause of death for adults under the age of 40. According to the Centers for Disease Control and Prevention, at least 1 million Americans are infected with HIV (the virus associated with AIDS), and over 40,000 new HIV infections are occurring each year.

Worldwide, the figures are even more astounding. The World Health Organization (WHO) has projected that, as of 1994, 30 to 40 million men, women, and children have been infected with HIV and that about 5,000 new infections occur every day.

AIDS has been a disease predominantly affecting younger people. Over 86 percent of Americans with AIDS are 20 to 50 years old. An additional 7 percent are between the ages of 50 and 60.

Initially, in this country AIDS mostly infected homosexual and bisexual men and intravenous drug users (a predominantly male population), as well as hemophiliacs who received HIV-contaminated blood products. But over time the female sex partners of bisexual men and men using intravenous drugs have become infected, steadily raising the number of infected women. Women comprised 7 percent of AIDS cases in 1985; by 1991, the figure had risen to 13 percent.

It is clear that AIDS will persist. Millions more are likely to become infected with HIV, and many, if not all, are likely to die of the disease unless effective treatments or a cure is found. Until this happens, the most effective means of fighting this deadly virus is education about its spread, and preventive measures to curtail the epidemic.

HISTORICAL REVIEW

Although AIDS was not recognized as a clinical entity until 1981, HIV infections occurred in the United States as early as 1979. The disease first aroused attention in 1980 with the diagnosis of a cluster of cases of an unusual type of pneumonia. Ordinarily this type of pneumonia (caused by an organism called *Pneumocystis carinii*) is very rare, attacking only people whose immune systems have been compromised (often with immunosuppressive drugs). But in these new cases, the agent compromising the immune system was unknown. At

AIDS: WHO HAS IT IN THE UNITED STATES?

Centers for Disease Control and Prevention statistics (through March 1993)

ADULT/ADOLESCENT POPULATION

Men who have sex with men	160,345
Individuals who use intravenous drugs	65,778
Men who have sex with men and inject drugs	18,041
Hemophilia/Coagulation disorders	2,519
Heterosexual contact	9,676
Recipient of blood transfusion, blood components, or tissue	5,384
Other/Undetermined	13,595

PEDIATRIC POPULATION

Hemophilia/Coagulation disorder	194
Mother with/at risk of HIV infection	3,887
Recipient of blood transfusion, blood components, or tissue	315
Other/Undetermined	84

about the same time, Kaposi's sarcoma, an equally rare form of cancer, also began to appear with increasing frequency. The common denominator in all these cases was the fact that they were striking homosexual men. By mid-1981, the Centers for Disease Control and Prevention (CDC) had identified a sufficient number of *P. carinii* pneumonia and Kaposi's sarcoma cases to suspect the appearance of a new disease. Medical surveillance programs were formed to monitor the new cases, and research efforts began into the disease's method of transmission.

Identifying the sexual contacts of AIDS patients revealed that many men with AIDS were linked by sexual exposure. For a brief period, AIDS was thought to be a sexually transmitted disease confined to homosexual men, allowing much of the heterosexual population to remain relatively unconcerned and insensitive to the issue of AIDS.

But as the epidemic developed, new risk groups and new modes of transmission were identified. Intravenous drug users contracted the HIV virus at very high rates, suggesting that the virus could be transmitted through contact with infected blood. At the end of 1982, the CDC reported the first transfusion-related AIDS case, and within a few years thousands of people with hemophilia had become infected through the receipt of contaminated blood products.

Evidence from Africa showed that HIV infection was transmitted through heterosexual sexual contact, and in 1983 the CDC reported on two women in the United States who appeared to have AIDS: One woman's sexual partner was bisexual, the other woman's lover used intravenous drugs. Heterosexual transmission is now a well-established means of the spread of HIV.

By the middle of the 1980s, 10,000 Americans had developed AIDS and tens of thousands more were thought to already be infected with HIV. An intense search for the agent responsible for the spread of the disease yielded rapid results.

By 1984 the virus responsible for causing AIDS was isolated by several different research groups, including the National Cancer Institute and the Pasteur Institute in France. In 1986 a task force officially dubbed the virus human immunodeficiency virus, or HIV.

HOW THE VIRUS WORKS

THE IMMUNE SYSTEM

Understanding AIDS requires a basic understanding of the immune system: The immune system consists of a group of specialized cells that protect the body against infections and help guard against the growth of some tumors. Infections from most bacterial, viral, and fungal organisms as well as many parasites are usually curtailed by a well-functioning immune system. But when the immune system is compromised and not functioning efficiently, susceptibility to many of these infections and some types of malignancies increases substantially.

A type of white blood cell called a lymphocyte is an important component of the immune system. Of the numerous different types of lymphocytes, two of the most important are B cells and T cells. B cells are important in the production of antibodies, specialized proteins that aid in the fight against infection.

There are several different types of T cells, each of which plays a unique role within the immune system: T helper cells recognize infectious agents and release toxic substances to help destroy them; T suppressor cells regulate the activity of the T helper cells and determine the strength and duration of the helper cell response.

Under normal circumstances, there are about twice as many helper cells as suppressor cells. HIV infection upsets this balance, reduces the number of T helper cells, and effective immune response decreases.

How the Virus Works on the Immune System

Viruses cause many illnesses including common colds, warts, and AIDS. A virus is much smaller and simpler than a human cell and typically consists of nothing more than a piece of genetic material (RNA or DNA) surrounded by a protein coat. Upon infecting a cell, a virus uses the cell's machinery to replicate itself and produce many new viruses capable of infecting other cells. The polio virus, for example, infects certain types of nerve cells, and if allowed to multiply and progressively infect more and more cells, polio ultimately causes irreversible nerve damage leading to paralysis.

The human immunodeficiency virus primarily infects the T helper cells of the immune system. As HIV infection progresses, more and more cells are destroyed, the number of T helper cells falls, and the immune system gradually deteriorates. Consequently, the predominant manifestations of AIDS are not caused directly by the human immunodeficiency virus but rather are secondary infections that follow this progressive destruction of the immune system.

The process is as follows:

- The HIV attaches to a specialized protein found primarily on the surface of T helper cells.
- Following attachment, the virus enters the cell.
- The virus's genetic material, in the form of RNA, is translated into DNA by a special enzyme manufactured by the virus called reverse transcriptase.
- The viral DNA is integrated into the chromosome of the infected cell.
- The virus then can either remain silent (latent) inside the infected cell, or it can be activated and begin to produce new viral particles.
- If the virus remains latent, the viral DNA remains incorporated in the cell's chromosome and is duplicated along with it every time the cell divides. The virus may be activated at some point in the future.
- When the virus is activated, the viral DNA stimu-

lates the production of numerous viral proteins necessary for the manufacture of new viruses.

- Viral proteins are produced, assembled into new viral particles, and released from the cell, killing the host cell in the process.
- Released viral particles can infect other T helper cells ultimately destroying an increasing number of T helper cells.
- The immune system is gradually crippled by the progressive destruction of T helper cells.

THE DIFFERENCE BETWEEN HIV AND AIDS

For many people the difference between HIV and AIDS is confusing:

HIV stands for human immunodeficiency virus, the virus that causes AIDS. Currently, two types of HIV have been identified—HIV1 and HIV2. Almost all infections in the United States are caused by HIV1; for the most part HIV2 is confined to West Africa.

AIDS (acquired immune deficiency syndrome) is the end result of HIV infection. AIDS manifests itself in a wide variety of ways, including rare infections and cancers. While the manifestations of AIDS may vary, their underlying cause is always the immune destruction caused by the human immunodeficiency virus.

The Centers for Disease Control and Prevention have developed a systematic way of differentiating HIV infection from AIDS with a list of 26 different diseases commonly seen in patients with severe immunodeficiency associated with HIV infection. When present in an HIV-infected individual, these diseases are considered to be sufficient to make a diagnosis of AIDS. Because a small number of people with severe immunodeficiency remain asymptomatic, the CDC definition of AIDS victims also includes all HIV-infected individuals whose blood tests show a T helper count of less than 200, whether disease symptoms are present or not.

The AIDS case definition is mainly used for epidemiological analysis (to keep track of the number and characteristics of AIDS cases) and sometimes to determine benefits eligibility. An AIDS-defining diagnosis does not necessarily mean that a patient's disease status or prognosis has changed drastically. Some AIDS diagnoses, such as Kaposi's sarcoma, can occur when the patient's T helper count is still quite high and the immune system is relatively functional. In fact, patients like this often live longer than non-AIDS patients (patients infected with HIV who have not yet developed an AIDS-defining illness) with lower T helper counts.

AIDS-related complex (ARC) or pre-AIDS conditions refer to symptomatic disease that does not meet the case

definition of AIDS. These nonspecific terms describe an HIV-infected individual with clinical symptoms suggestive (but not diagnostic) of AIDS. Symptoms include involuntary weight loss, fever, night sweats, weakness, diarrhea, swollen lymph nodes, and easy bruising.

DISEASES THAT INDICATE POSSIBLE AIDS

INFECTIONS

- Bacterial infections such as pneumonia, meningitis, bone or joint infection, abscesses (any combination of 2 within a 2-year period)
- Bacterial pneumonia (more than 2 episodes)
- Candidiasis (involving the esophagus)
- Coccidioidomycosis (involving a site other than the lungs)
- Cryptococcosis (involving a site other than the lungs)
- Cryptosporidiosis (diarrhea persisting over 1 month)
- Cytomegalovirus (involving the retina)
- Herpes simplex virus (lesions lasting longer than 1 month)
- Histoplasmosis (involving a site other than the lungs or lymph nodes)
- Isosporiasis (diarrhea persisting over 1 month)
- Mycobacterial disease caused by mycobacteria other than *M. tuberculosis* (involving a site other than the lungs, skin, or lymph nodes)
- *Pneumocystis carinii* pneumonia
- Salmonella (more than 1 episode)
- Toxoplasmosis (involving the brain)
- Tuberculosis (involving either the lungs or other sites)

TUMORS

- Cervical cancer
- Kaposi's sarcoma
- Non-Hodgkin's lymphoma (certain subtypes)
- Lymphoma (involving the brain)

OTHER

- HIV encephalopathy ("HIV dementia" or "AIDS dementia")
- HIV wasting syndrome ("slim disease" or emaciation)
- Lymphoid interstitial pneumonia and/or pulmonary lymphoid hyperplasia
- Progressive multifocal leukoencephalopathy

THE COURSE OF AIDS

While AIDS is thought by most people to be a universally fatal disease, this has not been established. The amount of time from the diagnosis of AIDS until death varies dramatically. Some people have lived as long as 13 years with a diagnosis of AIDS while others have succumbed rapidly to a serious illness.

Several factors appear to affect the survival of people with AIDS including:

- Age: Young adults tend to survive longer than older people.
- Gender: Men seem to survive longer than women.
- Ethnicity: Whites commonly live longer than their black or Hispanic counterparts.
- Initial complications: Those with an initial manifestation of Kaposi's tend to live significantly longer than those who first present with other types of illnesses, such as toxoplasmosis, that are commonly fatal.

HIGH-RISK GROUPS

Because the first identified cases of AIDS occurred in homosexual men, AIDS was originally thought of as a "gay" disease—transmitted from one man to another by sexual contact. Today it is recognized that AIDS can be transmitted in a variety of ways.

HOMOSEXUAL AND BISEXUAL MEN

During the early stages of the AIDS epidemic in the United States, the groups at greatest risk of contracting HIV were homosexual and bisexual men. According to the CDC, of the estimated 1 to 1.5 million people infected with the AIDS virus, about half are homosexual or bisexual men.

Because of efforts by the homosexual community to promote safer sexual practices—education stressing the importance of using condoms and limiting the number of sexual partners—the rates of HIV infection among homosexual men have recently begun to fall.

HETEROSEXUAL CONTACTS OF PEOPLE INFECTED WITH HIV

HIV can be transmitted through heterosexual contact with a person infected with HIV, although the efficiency with which HIV is spread in this fashion is unclear. In the United States, over 19,000 people are thought to have contracted the disease through heterosexual contact, and heterosexual cases now represent about 7 percent of the total number of U.S. AIDS cases.

INDIVIDUALS AT HIGHEST RISK OF HIV INFECTION

ADULTS

- Homosexual or bisexual men
- Intravenous drug users
- Persons with hemophilia or other coagulation disorders
- Heterosexual men and women who have:
  - sex with an IV drug user
  - sex with a bisexual male
  - sex with a person with hemophilia
  - sex with a person born in an endemic area
  - sex with a transfusion recipient
  - sex with an HIV-infected individual, risk not otherwise specified
- Recipient of transfusion of blood, blood components, or tissue

CHILDREN

- Individuals with hemophilia or other coagulation disorder
- Those with an infected mother or mother at risk for HIV infection

During sexual activity, small abrasions in the vaginal wall allow HIV present in semen to penetrate the bloodstream of women. Open sores (such as those caused by many venereal diseases) or small cuts on the penis provide a route of infection to male sex partners. But, while transmission can occur in either direction, studies suggest that male to female transmission is nearly twice as frequent as female to male transmission.

For men and women alike, transmission through heterosexual contact is a growing problem, particularly within the adolescent population. Sexual discovery and experimentation, although a natural part of adolescence, can lead to high-risk behaviors such as unprotected sexual intercourse. This type of high-risk behavior has caused the number of adolescent AIDS cases to nearly quadruple in the past few years.

INTRAVENOUS DRUG USERS

According to the CDC, over 20 percent of reported AIDS cases occur among people whose only known risk factor is drug use. Drug users may share drug paraphernalia, often using needles and syringes contaminated with others' blood. Small amounts of blood remaining in the needle or syringe after it's been used may subsequently be injected directly into the bloodstream of another individual. When the initial user is infected with the HIV virus, transmission is highly likely. This type of activity has caused intravenous drug users to become the second largest group at risk for AIDS.

In addition to infecting one another, IV drug users also can infect those otherwise not at risk: Infected female drug users can infect their offspring during pregnancy, and both male and female drug users can infect sexual partners.

BLOOD TRANSFUSION RECIPIENTS (FROM 1979 THROUGH 1985)

Although blood contaminated with HIV was transfused as early as 1979, it wasn't until 1982 that the first transfusion-related case of AIDS was identified. In 1985, HIV screening became available, and the blood supply was once again considered safe. During this 6-year period, from 1979 to 1985, thousands of people contracted HIV through blood transfusions. (By 1993, over 5,300 transfusion-related AIDS cases had already been identified.)

Even today, while the blood supply is rigorously screened, a minute amount of infected blood can escape the testing process during the brief period of time immediately after a person is infected that tests fail to reveal the infection. As a result, many people undergoing elective surgery choose to self-donate blood several weeks ahead of time (autologous donation), and have units of blood withdrawn before the operation. This blood is then stored and transfused during surgery if necessary.

Many people still wrongly believe that they can contract AIDS while donating blood—a virtual impossibility since sterile needles are used on each donor and are disposed of immediately. The persistent shortage of blood in the United States means that all people in normal health may donate and no one should be discouraged from donating from an unrealistic fear of contracting AIDS.

HEMOPHILIACS

People with hemophilia (a hereditary disease that prevents blood from clotting properly) require large amounts of blood products to prevent bleeding, including regular infusions of a blood component called Factor VIII. By pooling blood from hundreds or even thousands of donors, Factor VIII is concentrated and used more effectively, but the risk of HIV contamination was increased before a screening test became available in 1985. If just one of the thousands of blood donors contributing to this blood product was infected, the entire specimen became contaminated.

When the problem was recognized, people believed to be at high risk were asked to either forego donating blood or identify themselves as at risk so their blood

HOW AIDS IS SPREAD

MAJOR ROUTES OF HIV TRANSMISSION

- Intimate sexual contact with an individual infected with HIV
  Homosexual
  Heterosexual
- Exposure to infected blood
  Sharing of drug apparatus.
  Transfusion.
- Mother to fetus or newborn
  In utero
  During labor and delivery (It is not known whether the mode of delivery—cesarean section versus vaginal birth—affects the rate of transmission.)

OTHER ROUTES OF SPREAD

- Oral sex
- Breast-feeding
- Artificial insemination from an infected donor
- Organ transplantation from an infected donor

could be used for purposes other than transfusion. When a reliable screening test was developed, blood banks began aggressive screening programs, testing all donors for HIV infection.

Since blood bank screening programs were instituted, infection rates among hemophiliacs have fallen dramatically. Currently, 75 percent of adults and more than 50 percent of children with hemophilia are thought to be infected, and while this number is expected to fall it will be difficult to eliminate the risk entirely as long as blood products are necessary to control this disease.

INFANTS AND CHILDREN BORN TO MOTHERS INFECTED WITH HIV

Currently more than 4,400 children under the age of 13 have been diagnosed with AIDS, the great majority infected in utero or during birth by mothers who harbor the virus. Some of these women use intravenous drugs, and others have been unknowingly infected by their sex partners. About 7 percent of the children with AIDS develop the disease through a blood transfusion and 4 percent are hemophiliacs who contracted the virus after receiving contaminated blood products.

Children, particularly those infected before birth, tend to become symptomatic and develop full-blown AIDS more rapidly than adults, and once the diagnosis of

THE RISK OF EXPOSURE TO HIV AT THE WORKPLACE

For some occupations, the health care field in particular, the workplace risk of contracting HIV requires protective measures. Exposure to blood and other body fluids is a regular part of the job for doctors, nurses, lab technicians, and many other health care workers.

Most occupationally related HIV infections have been associated with exposure to blood, probably because it is thought to harbor more AIDS viruses than other body fluids like urine, saliva, and sputum. In most cases of workplace infection, the blood of an infected patient is introduced directly into the bloodstream of the health care worker through an accidental needlestick or other mishap. Exposing unbroken skin to infected blood does not appear to be sufficient to cause infection, and if the skin is intact without cuts, scrapes, or open sores, it appears to protect against viral transmission. Exposing the mucous membranes to infected blood also apparently poses a risk, albeit much smaller, and there have been reported cases of HIV infection after an individual has been splashed in the eyes or mouth with blood.

But while thousands of health care workers have been accidentally stuck with contaminated needles, only a small percentage of them—about 1 in 250—have become infected with HIV. While this phenomenon has not been completely explained, it is thought that a number of factors interact to determine whether an exposure leads to infection.

• The amount of virus transferred during exposure is probably of utmost importance. Although the body may be able to destroy small amounts of the virus, larger quantities may overwhelm the capabilities of the immune system. The amount of virus transferred depends upon the type of body fluid involved (blood and semen are more potent than others) and the stage of infection of the source patient (advanced disease may produce larger amounts of the virus).

• Whether or not infection occurs may also depend on the strength of the immune system of the individual exposed.

PREVENTING HIV TRANSMISSION IN THE HEALTH CARE SETTING

Properly instituted safety precautions could greatly reduce the number of occupational exposures to HIV contaminants.

• Accidental needlesticks must be prevented.

• Contamination of mucous membranes and open or broken skin must be avoided with the use of gloves when contact with blood or potentially dangerous body fluids is anticipated, masks or protective eyewear when splatter is expected, and protective garments or gowns when clothing may be splashed.

AIDS is made, their expected years of survival are substantially shorter. While opportunistic infections such as PCP (pneumocystic pneumonia) are common in children, Kaposi's sarcoma and many other complications seen in adults are rare in the pediatric population.

DIAGNOSING HIV INFECTION

The blood tests most commonly employed to test for HIV infection—the ELISA test and the Western blot analysis—do not identify HIV, but detect antibodies to the virus. These antibodies are produced by the body in response to HIV infection to combat the virus.

Because it can take several weeks after initial infection for the body to produce a measurable amount of antibodies, these tests can produce false-negative results—falsely showing that a person is not infected even though the virus is in fact growing in the body. But once antibodies have been manufactured, the tests,

when properly performed by well-trained technicians, are more than 99 percent accurate.

THE ELISA TEST

ELISA—enzyme-linked immunosorbent assay—is a relatively inexpensive and very accurate test (though not 100 percent). In this test (generally the first test performed), a blood sample is taken and spun at high speed, allowing blood serum to be separated from solid particles such as blood cells. After the ELISA reagent is added to the serum, a chemical reaction that colors the solution indicates the presence of HIV antibodies.

THE WESTERN BLOT TEST

Because the Western blot analysis is relatively expensive and technically difficult to perform, it is rarely used as the first test but, instead, confirms positive or equivocal ELISA results.

During this analysis, various viral components occupy discrete bands on special test paper that is incubated with the serum of the individual being tested. If the serum contains HIV antibodies, they will bind to the viral bands, causing them to change color.

Although HIV testing is now extremely accessible, widespread screening remains controversial.

• False positives: Tests can be wrong in a small percentage of cases and with either the ELISA or the Western blot test. It is possible to obtain a slight color change in some individuals who have not been exposed to HIV and incorrectly identify them as being HIV positive.

• False negatives: The tests can occasionally fail to produce any color change despite the presence of antibodies, thereby erroneously identifying someone who has been infected by the virus as HIV negative.

Public health officials urge cautious use of these tests and counseling both before and after testing to ensure that everyone understands the meaning of the results.

THE STAGES OF HIV INFECTION

THE ASYMPTOMATIC (SYMPTOM-FREE) PHASE

Following infection with HIV many, but not all, people develop an acute flulike illness. Those who experience symptoms commonly develop fever, nausea and vomiting, diarrhea, fatigue, swollen lymph nodes, and muscle and joint aches and pains. These symptoms generally resolve within a few weeks (possibly because the body generates an immune response against the virus) and most people enter a symptom-free phase.

The asymptomatic phase (the latent period) starts at the time of seroconversion—the time when antibodies to the virus first develop—and ends when symptoms of AIDS manifest themselves. While numerous studies have investigated the length of the latent period, the results have varied substantially. The length of the latency period apparently depends on a number of different factors: the strength of the individual's immune system, the method of infection, and the amount of virus transferred during infection.

Despite an absence of symptoms, the immune system progressively deteriorates during the latent period and the number of T helper cells gradually declines (see figure 19.1).

THE SYMPTOMATIC PHASE

As the number of T helper cells dwindles (the T helper count falls below 200 while normally it should range from 800 to 1,200), symptoms such as fever, weight loss, and diarrhea appear.

Frequently, the first indication of illness is the appear-

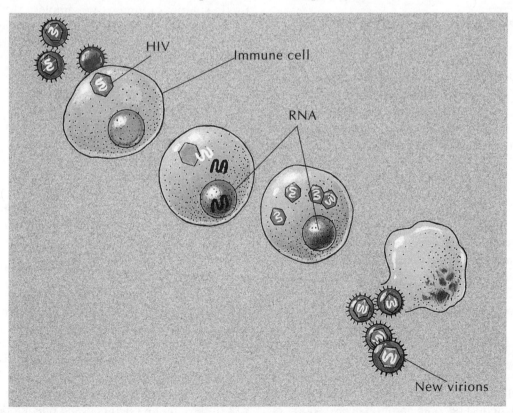

Figure 19.1: The HIV organism enters human immune cells and alters the genetic material found there, eventually destroying the cell and releasing additional virus.

ance of a white curdlike buildup on the tongue or the sides of the mouth or a throat condition called oral thrush. Kaposi's sarcoma can also appear early in the course of the disease and is occasionally the first sign of the immune system's collapse. Infrequently, a serious opportunistic infection like toxoplasmosis afflicts a person who had otherwise been well.

As the immune system further deteriorates, the risk of opportunistic infection increases. These infections, caused by viruses, bacteria, fungi, and parasites normally quashed by the body's immune system without symptoms, cause severe and even life-threatening illnesses when the immune system is not properly functioning.

AIDS-RELATED OPPORTUNISTIC INFECTIONS

Opportunistic infections—the hallmark of AIDS—either directly or indirectly are associated with about 90 percent of AIDS-related deaths.

PARASITIC INFECTIONS

PNEUMOCYSTIS CARINII PNEUMONIA (PCP)

DEFINITION

This lung infection is currently the most common initial opportunistic infection seen in American AIDS patients; almost 75 percent develop it during the course of their illness. Due to the potentially serious nature of the infection, PCP is also the most common cause of death in AIDS patients.

CAUSE

This infection is caused by a widespread parasite. Most people possess antibodies to *Pneumocystis carinii* and harbor small amounts of it in their bodies. While normal immune systems keep the parasite under control, the flagging immune system of AIDS patients allows it to grow and multiply.

DIAGNOSIS

Early symptoms of PCP include fever and a persistent cough generally devoid of sputum. As the infection progresses, patients become progressively short of breath and ultimately have difficulty breathing even while at rest.

AZT (AZIDOTHYMIDINE)

AZT, or azidothymidine, is a member of the drug family called dideoxynucleosides—substances that have been found to have activity against HIV. Early drug trials showed that AZT could induce clinical improvements and prolong the life of individuals with AIDS. Initial enthusiasm over these findings convinced AIDS patients, desperate for any effective treatment, to lobby for the drug's immediate approval. While the FDA's approval process is usually long and cumbersome, AZT was approved very quickly and became available to the public in just over 2 years.

Although some of the initial fervor for AZT has quieted, this drug remains an important therapy for patients with AIDS. AZT is thought to work by disabling the virus and slowing the rate at which it multiplies. While this drug cannot halt the disease, it does appear to slow its progress.

Chest x-rays are helpful in the diagnosis of PCP, but because the abnormalities that show up on film are nonspecific and could indicate other lung infections, the diagnosis must be confirmed by identifying the organism in sputum or lung tissue samples. Although sputum studies alone may be sufficient, the tiny organisms are often difficult to isolate, and special procedures are sometimes required in order to make the diagnosis. Bronchoscopy, a procedure in which a hollow, flexible tube with a fiber-optic viewing device is inserted into the airways, is commonly used to collect sputum from deep in the airways or obtain tissue samples to confirm the diagnosis of PCP.

TREATMENT

In HIV-infected patients, untreated PCP is invariably fatal. Treatment utilizes powerful antibiotics. The most commonly used drugs—trimethoprim-sulfamethoxazole (Bactrim or Septra) and pentamidine—have been shown to be 80 percent effective.

PREVENTION

Antibiotics can be used not only to treat PCP infection but also can actually be taken preventively (prophylactically). The medication of choice for prophylaxis against PCP is Bactrim or Septra, which has been shown to reduce the risk of developing pneumocystic pneumonia by 60 to 80 percent. In general, this antibiotic is administered to all HIV-infected individuals with low T helper cell counts (less than 200) and individuals with higher counts but who display symptoms of immunosuppression.

CRYPTOSPORIDIOSIS

DEFINITION

Cryptosporidium is a parasite that infects the gastrointestinal tract. For those with an intact immune system, infection with *Cryptosporidium* causes diarrhea, abdominal pain, and fatigue, which usually resolve spontaneously within a week or two. For the individual with AIDS, though, the manifestations of cryptosporidiosis are far more severe. Diarrhea can become profuse, leading to dehydration and dangerous metabolic imbalances.

DIAGNOSIS

As with PCP, the diagnosis of cryptosporidiosis depends on identification of the parasite. *Cryptosporidium* can be isolated from stool samples; special staining techniques highlight the parasite and allow it to be identified microscopically.

TREATMENT

No antibiotic has been proven to be effective against *Cryptosporidium*. Antidiarrheal agents, which do nothing to treat the underlying cause of the illness, can actually make the problem worse. Treatment is therefore largely supportive and consists principally of replacing the fluids lost as a result of diarrhea.

TOXOPLASMOSIS

DEFINITION AND CAUSE

Infection with *Toxoplasma gondii* is a common protozoan infection affecting nearly one-third of the general population. Most commonly contracted by eating undercooked contaminated meat or less commonly by contact with the feces of infected cats, it causes only a minor illness in most people. However, in patients with AIDS, infection can overwhelm an unstable immune system and produce a variety of symptoms.

DIAGNOSIS

Toxoplasmosis encephalitis (infection of the brain tissue) is the most common manifestation of *T. gondii* infection in people with AIDS, although infection can involve other sites, such as the lung, as well.

Symptoms of toxoplasmosis encephalitis include fever, headache, and neurologic abnormalities such as seizures. The diagnosis can generally be made with a CT or MRI scan to reveal characteristic parasitic lesions. While definitive diagnosis requires isolating the organism from the lesions (e.g., a brain biopsy in the case of toxoplasmosis encephalitis), in most cases this is thought to be unnecessary, and treatment is initiated on the basis of test results and symptoms alone.

TREATMENT

Pyrimethamine, an antiparasitic agent, and either sulfadiazine or clindamycin, both antibiotics, are most commonly employed, with improvement seen in up to 85 percent of patients. Because small amounts of the parasite remain even after aggressive treatment, low-dose drug therapy must be continued indefinitely to suppress its growth and prevent a recurrence.

PREVENTION

Not eating undercooked meat and avoiding contact with animal feces may lower the chances of infection. However, *T. gondii* is widespread, and contact with this microorganism may be difficult to avoid.

FUNGAL INFECTIONS

CANDIDIASIS

DEFINITION AND CAUSE

Candidiasis, also called thrush, is a fungal, or yeast, infection caused by *Candida albicans*. Although *Candida* is frequently present in the mouth and along the gastrointestinal tract, it does not usually cause illness in people with healthy immune systems. In people with an impaired immune system, however, it often overgrows, producing a characteristic thick, whitish coating.

DIAGNOSIS

While candidiasis usually remains confined to the mouth, it can spread to the esophagus and other parts of the gastrointestinal tract and to the respiratory system, posing more serious problems. Esophageal candidiasis, for example, can be extraordinarily uncomfortable, making swallowing difficult and eating painful or, in some cases, impossible.

Diagnosis is made by examining the characteristic thick, whitish coating or discharge.

TREATMENT

Thrush is treated with antifungal drugs such as nystatin, which are applied directly to the surface of the mouth, or ketoconazole and fluconazole, which are taken orally.

CRYPTOCOCCOSIS

DEFINITION AND CAUSE

A yeast, *Cryptococcus neoformans,* is responsible for causing cryptococcosis infection. Although cryptococcosis can infect numerous organs, including the lung, skin, blood, bone marrow, prostate, and genitourinary tract, more than half the time it manifests itself as meningitis, or infection and inflammation of the brain.

DIAGNOSIS

The symptoms of cryptococcal meningitis can often be subtle, with nonspecific symptoms such as fever and headache. When cryptococcal infection is suspected, special tests are performed to detect the organism in blood or cerebrospinal fluid (the fluid that surrounds and cushions the brain and spinal cord). Alternatively, blood or cerebrospinal fluid samples can be incubated so that the yeast may grow and be easily identified.

TREATMENT

Amphotericin B (Fungizone), an antifungal agent, is used to treat most cryptococcal infections. While this treatment is quite effective, the organism is never entirely eradicated, and relapse rates are high. For this reason, medications are never entirely withdrawn; instead, patients are switched to fluconazole (Diflucan), which they continue to take indefinitely to suppress regrowth of the organism.

HISTOPLASMOSIS

DEFINITION AND CAUSE

Histoplasmosis is caused by infection with the *Histoplasma capsulatum* fungus, which thrives in the soil of several specific regions, principally the central river valleys. (It is also found in areas of the Caribbean and Central and South America.) When contaminated soil is disturbed, the fungus can be airborne and subsequently inhaled. In a healthy person, the infection usually is confined to the lungs, causing only mild symptoms. In the patient with AIDS, however, the infection can be far more severe, spreading to the bloodstream and infecting organs throughout the body, a condition referred to as disseminated histoplasmosis.

DIAGNOSIS

Symptoms of disseminated disease typically include fever, cough, shortness of breath, and substantial weight loss. A diagnosis of histoplasmosis is confirmed by isolating the fungus from the blood, bone marrow, sputum, urine, or body tissues. A skin test (similar to the one for tuberculosis) can sometimes be helpful in diagnosis, but the presence of AIDS often makes the test result unreliable.

TREATMENT

Amphotericin B (Fungizone) is used to treat disseminated infections, but even with aggressive therapy mortality rates are high.

COCCIDIOIDOMYCOSIS

DEFINITION AND CAUSE

Coccidioides immitis, the fungus that causes coccidioidomycosis, thrives in the soil of the southwestern United States, Mexico, and Central and South America. Like the fungus that causes histoplasmosis, *C. immitis* spores arising from contaminated soil can be inhaled. When the immune system is intact, the infection is usually confined to the lungs and produces few if any symptoms, whereas in people with AIDS spread of the infection beyond the lungs (dissemination) is common.

DIAGNOSIS

Blood tests that detect antibodies to the fungus can aid the diagnosis of coccidioidomycosis. But a sure diagnosis requires culturing the organism from body fluids or tissues.

TREATMENT

Treatment is with the antifungal agent amphotericin B. While there is often some improvement in symptoms, incomplete recovery and relapse are quite common.

VIRAL INFECTIONS

CYTOMEGALOVIRUS (CMV) INFECTION

DEFINITION AND CAUSE

CMV is the most common life-threatening viral opportunistic infection associated with severe immunodeficiency in AIDS. As with other opportunistic infections,

CMV is usually benign in a healthy person, but infection in an individual with AIDS can be life-threatening.

DIAGNOSIS

In a person with AIDS, the most common sites of disease are the retina and colon, but the esophagus, stomach, lungs, brain, heart, pancreas, thyroid, kidneys, liver, gallbladder, and adrenal glands are also susceptible to attack. Infection of the retina produces visual changes and can lead to blindness; disease involving the colon typically causes diarrhea and crampy abdominal pain. In the lungs, CMV can cause a severe pneumonia; in the central nervous system it can lead to inflammation of the brain, causing headache and personality changes.

TREATMENT

Two drugs—ganciclovir and foscarnet—are currently available to treat CMV infection of the retina. Both drugs can help resolve an acute infection but cannot rid the body of the virus; thus, recurrences are common and long-term treatment is often needed.

HERPES SIMPLEX INFECTION

DEFINITION AND CAUSE

Herpes simplex virus, or HSV, causes clusters of small, painful blisters (cold sores) most commonly over the mouth and lips and genital area. It is estimated that at least 30 percent of the U.S. population has been exposed to the herpesvirus.

After an initial herpes infection, small reserves of the virus remain harbored silently in the body and can later be reactivated. Even with an intact immune system, recurrent herpes infections can be bothersome, and in individuals with AIDS recurrences are even more frequent and often far more severe. In a healthy person, lesions usually heal spontaneously in a week or two, but healing is often delayed in the person with AIDS.

DIAGNOSIS

Herpes blisters are generally easily identified, but to confirm the diagnosis, the virus must be cultured from fluid from the lesions.

TREATMENT

Acyclovir (Zovirax), an antiviral agent, is used to treat an acute outbreak of herpes. In individuals with persistent or recurrent infections, acyclovir can be continued even after the acute infection has resolved in order to help prevent future attacks.

VARICELLA ZOSTER VIRUS INFECTION

DEFINITION AND CAUSE

The varicella zoster virus causes chickenpox, which may reemerge to cause shingles, a disease most commonly seen in the elderly. Shingles, which can also cause inflammation of the lungs, liver, and nerves, is often an early sign of HIV infection. Sometimes the infection can spread, causing serious infections involving various organs throughout the body.

DIAGNOSIS

A physical examination of the shingles rash is usually sufficient to identify the infectious agent.

TREATMENT

Shingles may be treated with acylovir; other drugs may be prescribed to control nerve pain and other complications.

....

BACTERIAL INFECTIONS

TUBERCULOSIS (TB)

DEFINITION AND CAUSE

Over the past decade, there has been a resurgence of tuberculosis in the United States paralleling the AIDS epidemic. By destroying normal immune defenses, HIV infection increases both the frequency and severity of this disease.

DIAGNOSIS

Because of the immunosuppression caused by AIDS, many people have a negative reaction to the PPD test, the skin test most commonly used to test for tuberculosis. While chest x-rays and other tests can help in the diagnosis, only isolation of the bacteria definitively confirms the presence of TB. In pulmonary tuberculosis, sputum samples often contain significant amounts of the causative bacteria, and urine specimens can be used to detect disease involving the urinary tract.

TREATMENT

A variety of medications are used in the treatment of tuberculosis including isoniazid, rifampin, pyrazinamide, and ethambutol. Usually more than one drug, and quite commonly all four, are used simultaneously.

Because TB bacteria are difficult to eradicate, particularly in people with AIDS, therapy is prolonged and generally lasts 9 months to a year. (See chapter 18, Infectious Diseases, for a more complete discussion.)

PREVENTION

To reduce the risk of TB, a course of isoniazid is recommended for people infected with HIV who may have been exposed to tuberculosis, even in the absence of symptoms.

SALMONELLA

DEFINITION AND CAUSE

Salmonella infections are extremely common among people with AIDS. In healthy people, *Salmonella* infections are generally limited to the gastrointestinal tract, producing the diarrhea and abdominal pain typical of food poisoning. The immune defects caused by HIV allow a rapid overgrowth of the bacteria, often leading to dangerous infections of the blood. Once in the bloodstream, *Salmonella* can go on to infect organs throughout the body, including the heart, lungs, and bones.

DIAGNOSIS

The bacteria can often be identified by culturing feces, vomit, or blood if the infection has spread to the circulatory system.

TREATMENT

Although salmonella infections are usually easily controlled with antibiotics, relapse rates are notoriously high in people with AIDS after therapy is stopped.

PREVENTION

Proper hygiene when preparing food may prevent some cases of salmonella.

MALIGNANCIES/CANCERS

Because the immune system normally plays an important role in recognizing and ridding the body of cancer cells, the risk of some types of cancers is increased in people with AIDS.

KAPOSI'S SARCOMA

DEFINITION AND CAUSE

Before the emergence of AIDS, Kaposi's sarcoma (KS) was a rare, relatively harmless form of skin cancer seen mostly in elderly men and kidney transplant patients. Now it is the most common malignancy in people with AIDS. Not all AIDS patients appear to be at equal risk of developing KS; for reasons that are yet unclear, the cancer is more common among homosexual men than other groups of HIV-infected patients. Columbia University researchers have tentatively identified a type of herpes virus that may cause Kaposi's sarcoma.

DIAGNOSIS

Kaposi's typically begins as a single brown, purple, or reddish lesion, often on the lower legs or feet, face, chest, back, or abdomen and progresses slowly. As the original lesion grows bigger, additional lesions appear on other parts of the body. As the disease progresses, the gastrointestinal tract, lungs, liver, and heart may become involved and lead to life-threatening complications.

KS is diagnosed by microscopic examination of a biopsy specimen from a skin lesion.

TREATMENT

While small areas of localized disease can often be controlled with radiation therapy or chemotherapy, treatment of widespread lesions can be difficult. Unfortunately, chemotherapeutic regimens tend to further destroy the immune system.

Radiation therapy is sometimes employed as are various drugs that attempt to strengthen the body's natural immune response. One such drug—alpha interferon—reduces both the size and number of KS lesions in AIDS patients.

OTHER TUMORS

AIDS is also linked with several other forms of cancer. For example, lymphomas, cancers of the lymph system, and cancer of the cervix are more prevalent among people with AIDS. (For more information on these cancers, see chapter 17, Cancer.)

MISCONCEPTIONS ABOUT HOW AIDS IS SPREAD

All evidence points to the transmission of AIDS through the exchange of bodily fluids such as blood, semen, and

WHO CAN TRANSMIT HIV?

Anyone infected with HIV can transmit the virus to others. Individuals can be contagious even if they do not display signs of illness. In fact, some people may not even know that they have the virus but are still infectious and may pass the virus on to others.

breast milk. There is no evidence that the virus can be transmitted through casual contact with an infected individual. Activities like hugging, kissing, and touching are all considered to be safe (although intimate kissing—where there is an exchange of saliva—may pose some degree of risk).

While some people speculate that biting insects such as mosquitoes may spread HIV, in fact, this does not seem to be the case: Either the virus is unable to survive in mosquitoes and other blood-drinking insects, or the amount of blood the insect transfers from one individual to the next is too small to pass an infection.

Public misunderstanding of HIV and AIDS has led to other unnecessary anxieties about viral transmission. Controversies have arisen among workers about infected colleagues, and some parents have refused to send their children to school with infected children. Similarly, health workers have expressed anxieties about contracting the disease by caring for AIDS patients, and some athletes refuse to compete against HIV-infected players. Some people even hesitate to dine out for fear of catching the virus from infected food handlers or contaminated dinnerware.

While this concern is understandable, it is also unfounded. In some ways, HIV is a fragile virus and generally does not survive well outside the human body. Many researchers believe this fragility explains why, unlike many widespread hardy viruses such as those that cause the common cold, HIV does not rapidly infect the population at large.

PREVENTION

Despite the millions of dollars spent on AIDS research, effective drugs against AIDS or a protective vaccine are unlikely to become available soon. In the meantime, the only way to control the spread of HIV is prevention of viral transmission from person to person.

EDUCATION

AIDS education is aimed at two primary groups:

- Uninfected people, who must learn how to remain

free of HIV, and follow the guidelines for avoiding infection.
- Individuals infected with HIV, who must learn how to live full lives without infecting others.

In spite of the obvious need, AIDS education, especially of young people, is fraught with controversy and has sparked debate among religious, community, and governmental groups. Some groups support only those education programs that emphasize sexual abstinence outside of marriage. Others advocate that even very young children be fully instructed in safe sexual practices and that adolescents be given access to condoms. In any case, while individual religious and moral principles should be respected, it must be recognized that AIDS is an incurable disease that will take millions of lives unless its spread is halted.

Many parents fear that by talking about sex with their children they will appear to be condoning sexual activity at a young age. But in fact studies suggest that just the opposite may be true: In today's society, children quickly learn about sex despite parental silence on the subject. Consequently, parents should make sure they receive reliable information—it could save their lives.

TESTING

One of the first steps in slowing the spread of the AIDS virus is for all people who may have been exposed to HIV to learn whether they carry the virus. Blood screening tests now make rapid, accurate testing possible.

In most states, testing can be performed confidentially or anonymously.

In confidential testing, the name of the individual being tested is known only to the health care professional ordering the test, who promises not to share the information with others without permission. With anonymous testing, a code number is generally assigned to the tested individual (not identified by name), and not even the doctor or nurse ordering the test can match the results to a name.

In several states, however, laws now mandate that all positive test results be reported to the health department and confidentiality cannot be guaranteed. Before being tested, find out about the laws in your area by contacting your local health department.

Test results, whether positive or negative, should not be disregarded. A positive test indicates that you have been infected with the AIDS virus and mandates lifestyle changes both to improve your own health and protect the health of others. Negative test results do not represent permission to behave in irresponsible ways. Even a negative HIV test can indicate a need to moderate your lifestyle.

SAFER SEX

Although some people may be willing to forego sexual activity to protect themselves against HIV infection, many do not feel that the risk of disease warrants such drastic measures. However, it is essential that steps be taken to reduce the risk as much as possible. At a minimum, you should:

- Limit your number of sexual partners
- Use condoms
- Refrain from high-risk sexual practices

While these actions can greatly reduce your risk of contracting HIV, it's important to point out that they do not decrease the risk to zero (only total abstinence can do that).

RISKY SEXUAL PRACTICES

Anal or Vaginal Intercourse. Anal and vaginal intercourse are considered to be sexual practices that carry a high risk of HIV transmission.

Although many experts regard anal intercourse as intrinsically riskier than vaginal intercourse, sexual activity in either area can cause small cuts or abrasions. Semen containing HIV can gain exposure to the bloodstream through these areas when the normal protective barriers are damaged. Although most experts agree that the receptive partner is at greatest risk of being infected, the insertive partner is certainly at risk, too. During sexual activity small abrasions can form over the skin of the penis, and any bleeding from the lining of the vagina or rectum (or blood in the stool in the case of anal intercourse) can introduce HIV into the bloodstream. Preexisting sores or lesions (e.g., from a sexually transmitted disease) on the penis or in or around the vagina or rectum further increase the risk of transmission.

When used correctly, condoms help prevent the mixing of body fluids from one partner with those of the other during vaginal or anal intercourse. Lubrication is also important during either vaginal or anal intercourse: A lubricant can help prevent tissue damage, which increases the risk of viral transmission.

Moderate-risk sexual practices are those where the chances of transmitting HIV are lower but still significant if one of the sexual partners is infected with the virus. To be absolutely safe, these practices should also be avoided. Should you choose to engage in them, they should be performed with some form of barrier protection (e.g., a condom when performing oral sex on a man) whenever possible.

Oral Sex. Fellatio (use of the mouth to stimulate or maneuver the penis) is particularly risky when one partner ejaculates into the other's mouth. Small cuts or sores in the mucous membranes of the mouth provide a route for HIV-infected semen to contact the blood. Even if the penis is removed from the partner's mouth before ejaculation, small amounts of preejaculatory fluid may contain substantial amounts of virus, and can potentially cause infection.

Cunnilingus (oral stimulation of the vagina) is risky because vaginal secretions may contain HIV, and abrasions in the mouth (even small ones such as those from brushing or flossing) can provide the virus contained in these secretions access to the bloodstream.

Intimate Kissing (also known as French kissing or tongue kissing). Small amounts of HIV are thought to be present in saliva, and although the amount may be insufficient to transmit infection, cuts or sores in the mucous membranes of the mouth can potentially provide a route of entry for the virus.

While there have been no cases of AIDS attributable

RECOMMENDATIONS FOR CONDOM USE

The U.S. Preventive Services Task Force recommends that condoms be used in accordance with the following guidelines:

- Latex condoms, rather than natural membrane condoms, should be used. Torn condoms, those in damaged packages, or those with signs of age (brittle, sticky, discolored) should not be used.
- The condom should be put on an erect penis, before any intimate contact, and should be unrolled completely to the base.
- A space should be left at the tip of the condom to collect semen; air pockets in the space should be removed by pressing the air out toward the base.
- Use water-based lubricants. Avoid those made with petroleum jelly, mineral oil, cold cream, and other oil-based lubricants, which may damage the condom.
- Insertion of nonoxynol 9 in the condom increases protection, and vaginal application in addition to condom use is likely to provide greater protection.
- If a condom breaks, it should be replaced immediately.
- After ejaculation and while the penis is still erect, the penis should be withdrawn while carefully holding the condom against the base of the penis so that the condom remains in place.
- Condoms should not be reused.

solely to kissing, it should be avoided if there is any possibility that your partner is infected.

Urine Exposure. Certain sexual practices involve urinating on a sexual partner's skin or in the mouth. Because research indicates that urine can contain HIV, allowing urine to contact the mucous membranes of the mouth or nonintact skin carries the risk of infection.

Some sexual activities carry virtually no risk of transmitting HIV:

- Any erotic activity that does not involve the exchange of body fluids or place one partner's mucous membranes (e.g., mouth, vagina, rectum) in contact with body fluids (e.g., semen, vaginal secretions, saliva, urine) from the other partner is considered to be perfectly safe.

HOW TO CLEAN UP BLOOD OR OTHER POTENTIALLY DANGEROUS BODY FLUIDS

1. Always wear waterproof gloves to prevent direct contact with potentially contaminated fluids.
2. Bleach and water mixed in a 1:10 ratio should be used to wipe up the spill. A solution containing bleach kills the virus but water alone does not.

- Mutual masturbation (provided that the skin is intact).
- Massage and rubbing bodies (provided that the skin is intact).
- Kissing on the face or skin (provided that the skin is intact).

DRUG TREATMENT/DRUG EDUCATION

Currently, many intravenous drug users are believed to share their needles and syringes. In several major cities, needle exchange programs have attempted to eliminate this practice. In addition, educational campaigns have instructed drug users on methods for cleaning needles and syringes before reuse: Flushing them adequately with a mixture of bleach and water kills the virus and renders the instrument much safer for the next user. Further efforts of this kind are being planned to communicate with this difficult to reach segment of the population.

Drug treatment programs should also be expanded. Currently, in New York City and some other large cities, entry into a drug rehabilitation program may take months because of long waiting lists. While only a small percentage of the people who enter drug rehabilitation programs permanently stop using drugs, enrollees are much more successful at drug abstinence than those who try to stop on their own.

HOPE FOR THE FUTURE

IS AN AIDS VACCINE POSSIBLE?

Vaccines use virus fragments, dead virus, or inactivated virus to enable the immune system of vaccinated individuals to develop immunity to a disease without contracting the infection. If a vaccinated person is later infected with the virus, the body recognizes it immediately and promptly eliminates and destroys it.

Since the human immunodeficiency virus was first

TABLE 19.1: U.S. AIDS CASES BY AGE AT DIAGNOSIS
(Cases reported to CDC through December 31, 1993)

Age	Cases
Under 5	4,221
5–12	1,007
13–19	1,554
20–24	13,890
25–29	54,593
30–34	84,557
35–39	79,929
40–44	54,871
45–49	30,279
50–54	16,380
55–59	9,513
60–64	5,446
65 or older	4,921
Total	361,164

Of this total, the number of cases in adult and adolescent males was 311,579, and females, 44,357. There were 5,228 cases in children under 13. Total reported deaths in persons with AIDS was 220,726, including 217,917 adults and adolescents and 2,819 children.

isolated and identified, teams of scientists around the world have worked to create a vaccine that would help to prevent the spread of AIDS. While vaccines against many viruses have been successfully developed and administered (rubella, mumps, and polio, for example), HIV has proven a more formidable opponent. This unique virus escapes destruction by the immune system in several ways that complicate vaccine development. For instance, its ability to constantly mutate and undergo subtle changes that hide it from the body's immune surveillance system means that previous immunity, such as that derived from a vaccine, is unreliable.

While a vaccine may seem like the ideal solution to this epidemic, AIDS research has pursued other promising areas. Some researchers are trying to modify cells by gene manipulation to make them resistant to HIV infection. Others are developing immunomodulators, substances that modify the immune system and counter the deleterious effects of HIV infection. Although a cure for AIDS is not on the horizon, increasing knowledge about HIV may someday provide better treatments and bring us closer to a cure.

SUMMING UP

Although at least a million Americans may already be infected with the AIDS virus, the knowledge is available to halt this epidemic. Widespread education for self-protection could be provided to everyone: Adolescents, for example, can be instructed in the potential dangers of sex and be taught the proper use of condoms. Drug users should know how to sterilize their needles and syringes or be allowed to exchange them for clean ones.

But before effective action will take place, the general public must first recognize the real threat of AIDS. This condition is no longer restricted to homosexuals, drug users, and hemophiliacs. AIDS has spread to children, adolescents, and heterosexual adults, attacking regardless of age or economic status.

No one is immune from AIDS, but as long as people continue to believe that AIDS is someone else's problem, this incurable condition will continue to spread at a depressingly rapid rate.

20

Respiratory Diseases and Lung Health

. . . .

ROBERT B. MELLINS, M.D.

The human respiratory system—from the openings of the mouth and nose to the myriad components of the lungs—begins functioning within moments of birth. From that time on, the respiratory system supplies the body with the oxygen it needs to survive. It accomplishes this task by bringing clean, filtered air to the lungs, where oxygen is absorbed into the circulatory system. The lungs also remove used air, eliminate impurities, and enable us to speak. With luck and some care, these crucial organs will serve a long lifetime.

Air enters the respiratory system when the chest expands. Since the lungs themselves have no skeletal muscle, both inhalation and exhalation are controlled by the chest and thoracic cavity muscles; when these muscles are damaged, the lungs cannot function normally. If the chest cavity is punctured and opened to the outside world, the lungs collapse. Under normal conditions, this is prevented by the protection of the rib cage and the chest wall muscles and diaphragm.

With each inhaled breath, air passes through the nostrils or mouth to the throat (pharynx) and past the tonsils and adenoids, which filter the incoming air and guard against infectious agents. The air then passes through the voice box (larynx) and the windpipe (trachea), where it is warmed or cooled to body temperature before entering the branching system of bronchial tubes in each lung. There, oxygen is absorbed and waste gases are expelled as the lungs retract or deflate to their original size. This process, which relies on both the flexibility and the permeability of the lungs, takes place about 15 times per minute in an adult (see figure 20.1).

Within the breathing passages, air is further filtered and inhaled impurities are trapped by mucus—a sticky fluid produced by tiny gland cells in the passage linings. Mucus also moistens the air so that the delicate tissues of the lungs will not be dried by the airflow. Cilia filter the mucus of these collected impurities.

Cilia are microscopic, hairlike projections growing out of the passageway walls. Millions of cilia inhabit every square inch of the respiratory tract's mucous membranes. The cilia's coordinated movement transports the mucus from the bottom of the lungs toward the throat. Impurities are carried up and out of the peripheral parts of the lung to the larger central airways and the throat so that they can be swallowed, expelled from the mouth by coughing, or sneezed out of the nasal passages. Injured cilia cannot efficiently carry out this func-

tion, and certain substances—including cigarette smoke and various airborne pollutants—damage or slow down the cilia, making the respiratory tract more vulnerable to disease.

Purified air reaches the innermost portion of the lungs through the bronchial passages. Each lung's bronchus divides into two secondary bronchi, which further divide into 20 bronchial branches and finally into more than a million small passageways called bronchioles. The bronchioles deliver air to 300 million alveoli—small sacs with thin, highly permeable walls through which the vital gas exchanges proceed.

Capillaries (tiny blood vessels) surround the alveoli. Oxygen flows from the alveoli directly through the alveolar walls into the blood of the capillaries, allowing the bloodstream to convey oxygen to the cells of the body. Flowing the other way is carbon dioxide, a by-product of physiological actions taking place throughout the organism. Carried in the blood, carbon dioxide travels to the alveoli, up the bronchial tree, through the throat and nasal passages, and out the mouth or nose.

In addition to gas exchange, the lungs serve several other metabolic functions that combat infection and process the various chemicals carried to the lungs by the circulatory system. One of the lungs' most important tasks is the formation of angiotensin II, a powerful natural substance involved in the maintenance of blood pressure. The lungs also inactivate excessive amounts of substances involved in blood clotting and inflammation.

THREATS TO RESPIRATORY FUNCTION

The average human takes about 7.8 million breaths a year, each of which brings the lungs in contact with a wide range of substances that can temporarily or permanently impair respiratory function. Environmental threats to respiratory function occur in the form of gases, particulates, and fibers. The damage wrought on the respiratory tract depends on several factors, including:

- Degree of exposure to the pollutant
- Extent to which the pollutant penetrates the respiratory tract (penetration)
- Length of time the pollutant is retained within the respiratory tissues (retention)
- Rate at which the pollutant is cleared by the body's natural defenses

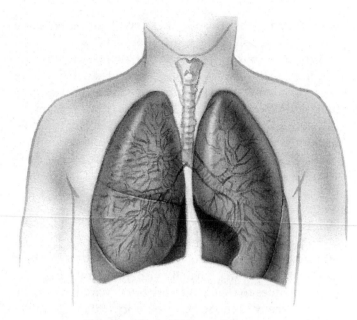

Figure 20.1: Normal lungs

the air quality of the United States. However, even with these advances, many threats to the air supply remain. Motor vehicle emissions—black clouds of smoke from trucks, waves of vapor rising from a typical rush hour traffic jam—contaminate areas around roads. Factory fumes, smoke, or chemicals regularly pollute neighborhoods, and industrial accidents inadvertently release heavy concentrations of toxic, airborne substances. Despite improved regulation of industry, several common types of pollutants continue to have a significant negative impact on respiratory health in this nation.

• Sulfur oxide/small-particle pollutants created as a result of burning sulfur-containing fuels, most particularly from fossil-fueled (oil and coal) power plants.
• Pollutants emitted by motor vehicle exhaust: carbon monoxide, oxides of nitrogen, ozone, and light-reactive compounds.
• Localized, hazardous pollutants such as arsenic, asbestos, beryllium, cadmium, hydrogen sulfide, lead, and mercury emitted by local manufacturing plants, refineries, and smelters.
• Gases and outdoor pollutants that invade the home or which are created by home heating, cooking, or by household products. The recent increase in the use of wood-burning stoves has led to an increase in indoor pollution and represents a special hazard to people with asthma and other lung problems.
• Tobacco smoke.

The widespread nature of these pollutants in the atmosphere makes it difficult to link individual pollutants to particular diseases, but researchers have combined statistical evaluation of pollutant exposures, animal studies, controlled human-exposure studies, and clinical observation to evaluate the ill effects of air pollution on health. Epidemiological studies reveal that air pollution causes:

• Increased deaths among people with cardiac and respiratory disease. Acute air pollution episodes in this country and others since World War II have produced striking increases in deaths in the affected communities, particularly among persons already suffering heart and chronic lung disease.
• Increased incidence of chronic respiratory disease. Ozone and nitrous oxide have been shown to induce changes in the lungs similar to emphysema. Along with cigarette smoking, recurrent infections, and occupational lung hazard exposure, air pollution (particularly ozone and nitrous oxide) is considered responsible for chronic bronchitis, emphysema, and other chronic lung conditions.

• Individual characteristics of the person exposed to the pollutant

Two of these factors—penetration and retention—are determined by the physical and chemical characteristics of the pollutant, most important its size and water solubility. Large, highly soluble particles are more easily filtered out in the upper airways, while smaller, insoluble particles penetrate down to the bronchial passages and alveoli.

Every day, in virtually every American community, airborne contaminants that can adversely affect respiratory health are released into the indoor and outdoor atmosphere. They emanate from combustion processes in industries, motor vehicles, and homes. Depending on weather conditions, they may:

• Be absorbed into the atmosphere, where they are temporarily inactivated.
• Give rise to potentially dangerous pockets of air pollution. (Rural areas are not exempt from air pollution, but the higher levels of industrial and motor vehicle activity of urban communities increases their potential for pollution.)
• Be blown or carried by clouds hundreds of miles to another location, where they pollute that community's atmosphere.

AIR POLLUTION

Government regulation of air pollution has produced a definite improvement over the past two decades in

• Increased severity of asthma attacks. Air pollutants make asthma patients more susceptible to other asthma-producing stimuli.

• Higher incidence of acute bronchitis, pneumonia, and other respiratory ailments among children and adults in areas of high fossil-fuel pollution.

• Increased, temporary difficulty in breathing in otherwise healthy children and adults.

• Lung cancer. (When combined with cigarette smoking, air pollution is seen as a probable contributor to lung cancer.)

• Increased mortality of heart attack victims. Angina pain may be exacerbated by high levels of air pollution.

• Irritation of the eyes, nose, and throat and changes in behavior and heart function. Ozone, the major component of smog, irritates the pharynx and trachea, causing a burning sensation in the upper part of the chest. Increased concentrations of carbon monoxide in the blood have been shown to reduce attention span; inhalation of airborne lead in sizable amounts can damage the nervous system.

INDOOR POLLUTANTS

Indoor air pollution is a mixture of pollutants from the outdoors (including ozone and carbon dioxide) as well as substances generated indoors. Faulty heating devices, for example, can produce carbon monoxide and cause carbon monoxide poisoning. Cooking with natural gas results in nitrous oxide, implicated as a respiratory irritant. In addition, some building materials can contaminate the air with chemicals like the formaldehyde used in binding agents for wallboard; formaldehyde causes skin or respiratory irritations in some individuals. In the workplace, aerosol propellants have been associated with short-term respiratory or cardiac effects. When misused—deliberately inhaled—these chemicals can cause sudden deaths from heart arrhythmias.

Of all indoor air pollutants, tobacco smoke is perhaps the most pervasive and dangerous for both smokers and nonsmokers. Studies indicate that children from homes where the caretaking parent smokes develop decreased lung function compared with children from nonsmoking homes and suffer increased respiratory diseases in the first year of life. In addition, children with asthma need more frequent emergency room care when parents smoke. Adults also suffer from sidestream smoke: Middle-aged nonsmokers exposed to workplace smokers experience reduced lung function.

But smoking is most dangerous for smokers. Besides lung cancer and other respiratory disease, smoking has been conclusively linked to the development of cancers of the esophagus, bladder, kidney, and pancreas, and also to an increased likelihood of having a low-birth weight baby. Despite these risks, however, some 53 million people—one-third of all adult Americans—continue to smoke. Every year, 340,000 people die prematurely from diseases caused by cigarette smoking. Cigarette smoking accounts for an estimated $13 billion in direct health care expenses every year: medical, surgical, nursing, hospital, and home-care costs. In addition, the American economy loses $25 billion every year through lost productivity from workers who fall ill from smoking-related diseases. Clearly, quitting smoking is the best thing anyone who smokes can do to promote lung health. (See box "How to Quit" in chapter 6.)

Tobacco is not the only addictive drug smoked and inhaled; certain forms of cocaine, as well as hashish and marijuana, are inhaled with numerous negative consequences to the respiratory tract. Marijuana smoke contains many of the same respiratory irritants found in tobacco smoke. In addition, it contains other substances, such as delta-9-tetrahydrocannabinol (THC) and other compounds, some of which irritate the lungs.

More than 30,000 studies document the irritant and disease-producing effects of tobacco smoke on the lungs. Although marijuana smoke has not received the same amount of attention, experts suspect that methods of marijuana smoking intensify the health risk: Smoke concentrators—called "bongs," "carburetors," "power hitters," and "buzz bombs"—concentrate the smoke and deliver it under pressure to the lungs, thereby delivering a higher dose of THC and other constituents that are potentially very detrimental to the respiratory tract.

In the United States, where illicit marijuana is relatively expensive, marijuana smokers puff deeply and hold the smoke in the lungs for 10 to 60 seconds to increase drug absorption. This practice probably inflames the airways, and makes the lungs and respiratory system more vulnerable to infection and disease from fungus and bacteria contamination of the marijuana. The presence of known carcinogens in marijuana smoke suggests that inhalation of the smoke from marijuana into the lungs has the potential for causing lung cancer. (And if you smoke both marijuana and tobacco, there is evidence showing that you suffer a still greater risk of respiratory disease. For more details; see chapter 6, Smoking, Alcohol, and Substance Abuse.)

RESPIRATORY INFECTIONS

Infections, ranging from the common cold and flu to life-threatening pneumonia and tuberculosis, are among the most common cause of respiratory problems among all age groups. Viruses, bacteria, fungi, and parasites are among the organisms that are inhaled into the lungs and find an environment in which they can thrive. For detailed discussions of respiratory infections, see chapter 18, Infectious Diseases.

RESPIRATORY DYSFUNCTION

As the only major internal organ of the body continually exposed to the outside environment, the lungs—particularly those of children, the elderly, and those with chronic medical conditions—are particularly vulnerable to environmental insult. When particles are inhaled (from cigarette smoke, polluted air, or someone else's sneeze or cough) they are trapped in the bronchial passages by mucus, prompting a variety of physiological processes associated with acute or chronic respiratory problems.

SHORTNESS OF BREATH (DYSPNEA)

The most common symptom of respiratory dysfunction is a feeling of breathlessness or shortness of breath (dyspnea). This relatively common and unpleasant sensation may stem from asthma, bronchitis, or other respiratory disorders including heart disease and defects in the lungs or chest wall.

There are two types of dyspnea:

• **Obstructive dyspnea.** Caused by obstruction of the air passages due to bronchial constriction, mucus accumulation, or other inflammatory processes in the lining or walls of the airways.
• **Restrictive dyspnea.** Usually due to defects in the lung or chest that prevent the lungs from totally expanding. In restrictive disorders, there usually is no difficulty in breathing when the person is at rest, but even moderate physical activity may produce labored breathing and a feeling of breathlessness.

Dyspnea may be linked to:

• **Heart disease.** When the heart muscle receives inadequate amounts of oxygenated blood, or when the heart itself is unable to pump enough blood to meet the needs of the brain and other vital organs, a feeling of breathlessness results.
• **Anemia.** The blood's lack of sufficient hemoglobin to transport oxygen may lead to a breathless feeling. (See chapter 23, Blood Disorders.)
• **Abnormal changes in body chemistry** (such as the acidic state that occurs in diabetic acidosis).

Whatever the underlying cause, feelings of breathlessness or difficulty in breathing are always a warning sign to seek medical attention. Treatment of shortness of breath depends upon the cause. In diabetic acidosis, for example, restoring the normal acid/alkaline balance of the body's chemistry will stop the dyspnea.

RESPIRATORY PROBLEMS THAT AFFECT ALL AGES

ASTHMA

As many as 12 million Americans—4 million of them children under 16—suffer asthma today or have had asthmatic attacks in the past. This represents a 66 percent increase since 1980. Asthma is largely hereditary, tending to strike each generation of a family, and possibly occuring in more than one member of the family.

In children, asthma may be diagnosed at age 3 or younger. In infants, asthma may be the aftermath of flu, a cold, or virus infection. Bronchiolitis (a viral inflammation of the small airways that occurs in young children during the cold months) is sometimes followed by asthma, and the symptoms of asthma resemble those of the viral infection. Although wheezing represents the hallmark of asthma, this breathing problem can also be caused by other respiratory disorders, so most physicians do not diagnose asthma until they carefully examine a child and note more than two asthma episodes.

For many, asthma fades over time. About half of all children with asthma lose all symptoms as they enter their middle teens. Many evidence improvement once they reach age 6 or so, when the airways normally widen.

Although asthma is rarely fatal, it can be disruptive. For although it can be controlled through medication and other means, it cannot be cured. Asthma episodes are responsible for 8 million school days lost each year, 24 million days of restricted activity for both children and adults, and 12 million bed rest days.

DEFINITION

The word *asthma* is derived from a Greek word meaning "breathlessness" or "panting," both of which accurately describe an asthma attack. The sense of breathlessness during an asthma episode results from a hyperactive response of the breathing tubes: The bronchial tubes narrow due to muscle spasms in the bronchioles and swelling of the bronchial tissues, mucus clogs the smaller tubes, and stale air is trapped in the struggling lungs (see figure 20.2).

Asthma episodes range from mild or severe, lasting anywhere from a few minutes to a few days. When the episode is over, breathing usually returns to normal.

CAUSE

Asthma episodes can be triggered by a variety of factors, most notably allergens, infections, environmental pollutants, and nonspecific stimuli such as exercise and emotional states.

Between 50 and 70 percent of adults with asthma suffer from allergies. In children under 3 years of age, viral infections are likely to be the most common trigger. After 3 years, allergies also begin to play an increasing role as a trigger. After 20 years of age, occupational exposure to toxic substances and allergens also can be important triggers for asthma.

Common allergens associated with asthmatic responses are:

- Foods: nuts, peanuts, chocolate, eggs, citrus fruits, milk
- Plants or plant products: pollens, grasses, mold spores
- Animal or insect materials: dust mites, animal danders, feathers, canine or feline saliva

Infections—usually viral—are often the initiating event for asthma, and almost always aggravate the condition in patients with preexisting asthma.

The most common infectious forerunners of asthma are influenza, colds, upper respiratory infections and bronchitis.

Numerous environmental pollutants and common chemical agents have also been linked to asthma episodes. Airborne chemicals can irritate the sensitive tissues of the respiratory tract and make the airways hypersensitive to subsequent exposures. Exposure to airborne irritants can worsen asthma, or cause asthma to develop in "normal" individuals. It is believed that occupational exposure to chemicals and contaminants causes up to 15 percent of adult-onset asthma in men.

Environmental risk factors include tobacco smoke, toluene, and sulfur dioxides (sulfites).

Many chemicals commonly found in the home have been known to trigger asthma attacks. Persons with a history of asthma should avoid inhaling fumes from any household cleaning product, and should wear a mask when working with any chemical substance.

Common household chemicals that have been associated with asthmatic responses include:

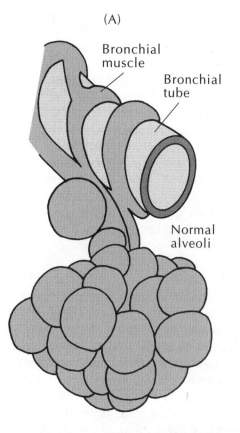

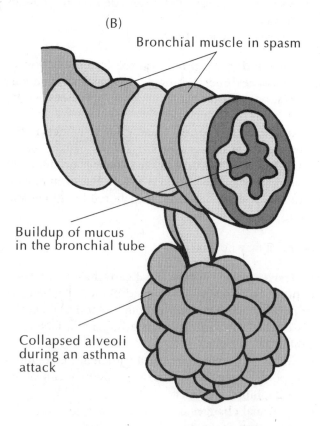

Figure 20.2A and B: The normal bronchial tube and alveoli and the same structures during an asthma attack are shown. The spasm prevents the vital exchange of air in the tiny alveoli, leading to the gasping feeling of not being able to breathe properly. Complete airway obstruction leads to alveolar collapse; partial obstruction leads to air-trapping and overinflation.

- Paints and pain thinner
- Hairspray
- Chlorine bleach
- Spray starch
- Room deodorizers
- Spray furniture polish
- Cleaning solvents
- Perfumes

In some individuals, chemicals in foods—particularly sulfites—can prompt severe, potentially fatal asthmatic episodes. Sulfite-sensitive persons should wear a medical alert bracelet at all times and carry both a bronchodilator inhaler and injectable epinephrine.

Asthma episodes can also be triggered or worsened by nonspecific stimuli, particularly exercise and exposure to cold, dry air. Exercise-induced asthma is fairly common in children and adolescents and usually begins within 6 to 10 minutes of the start of exercise, or shortly after exercise is completed.

Emotional factors can intensify asthma episodes—excitement, sadness, worry, laughing too hard, crying, coughing, and anger have been associated with asthma responses.

MANAGEMENT

Treatment of asthma begins with identification and avoidance of known triggers when possible. A clear understanding of the pathogenesis, namely the underlying airway inflammation, increased mucus production, and bronchoconstriction, leads the patient to accept a long term plan to prevent or suppress inflammation as well as to promote to bronchodiation with acute therapy using a bronchodilator. For very mild asthma, use of bronchodilators as necessary may be sufficient. For asthma of moderate or greater severity, a daily or continuous regimen is necessary.

Treatment of an acute asthma attack is critical. The goal is to alleviate the airway obstruction by reducing airway inflammation, mucus secretion, and bronchial muscle constriction that block the airways and restore normal breathing. If left untreated, an asthma attack can lead to hyperinflation of the lungs and trapping of used air within the bronchial sacs. The lack of adequate ventilation with fresh air can lead to a potentially fatal deficiency of oxygen in the body's tissues as well as retention of carbon dioxide with severe acidosis. For this reason, acute asthma episodes should be taken very seriously and treated immediately. In general, the following steps should be taken.

- Inhalation or injection of a bronchodilating drug (see box). Although some over-the-counter medications may help alleviate a mild asthma episode, most of these

ASTHMA MEDICATIONS

Epinephrine or Adrenaline. A substance, which is also made by the body's own adrenal glands, that helps open airways quickly. As a medication, it is given by injection or inhalation for severe asthma or an acute attack of asthma. Since it has side effects that must be overseen by a physician, it is usually reserved for emergencies only. It used to be the most common way a severe attack was treated but it has, for the most part, been replaced by inhaled bronchodilators.

Inhaled Bronchodilators. Agents used in aerosol form or in handheld metered dose inhalers. They resemble adrenaline and include albuterol, terbutaline, isoproterenol, metaproterenol, and isoetharine. Using 1 or 2 puffs of these bronchodilator agents may relieve spasm and wheezing of the acute episode and are particularly helpful for exercise-induced wheezing. Very recently a long-acting (12 hours) inhaled bronchodilator called salmeterol (serevent) has become available.

Theophylline Bronchodilator. Liquid, tablet, or capsule medicines that help relax and open the airways, available in rapid-acting and sustained-release forms. Sustained-release preparations are especially useful for individuals who develop increased symptoms in the early hours of the morning. Coffee and tea have been known for centuries to provide relief for adults with asthma, presumably because the body can convert caffeine to theophylline.

Oral Bronchodilators. Inhaled agents also available in pill or liquid form and useful for those who cannot use inhaled medication or tolerate theophylline. These include metaproterenol, albuterol, and terbutaline.

Cromolyn Sodium and Nedocromil. Substances, used in aerosol form or in a metered dose inhaler, that are not bronchodilators and must be taken regularly. As prophylactic or asthma-preventing agents these chemicals control allergic asthma. They also seem to stabilize the overreactive airways characteristic of asthma.

Corticosteroids. Very effective anti-inflammatory agents that may be used by aerosol spray as beclomethasone (Vanceril or Beclovent), flunisolide (Aerobid), or triamcinolone (Azmacort), and in tablet or liquid form as methylprednisolone (Medrol), dexanethasone (Decadron) or prednisolone (Pediapred, Prelone). Intravenous cortisone is also used in severe problems. The side effects, which can include weight gain and hypertension and growth suppression in children, generally occur when high doses are used over long periods of time (weeks or months). Short courses (less than a week) generally do not cause serious problems.

THE ASTHMATIC CHILD IN SCHOOL AND THE COMMUNITY

Parents of children with asthma should inform the child's teacher of the condition, what triggers it, and what needs to be done for the child in case of an episode. A child's friends should also be told. They can be very supportive, and their knowledge helps the child feel more accepted.

Children, with their physicians' approval, can participate in many sports and activities, typically those that are not carried out in dusty or pollen-laden areas, and which enable the child brief rest periods. For example, baseball, cheerleading, and bicycling are all appropriate activities; swimming is considered especially good exercise for children with asthma. Before engaging in strenuous physical activity, children should perform warm-up exercises to prepare their bodies for activity. Children with asthma should not be excused from chores or school responsibilities. Those who suffer breathing problems during vigorous exercise generally are able to prevent wheezing by taking medication just before the activity. Indeed several well-known individuals with asthma have won Olympic gold medals. With appropriate care and use of inhalers, children and adults with asthma should be able to engage in normal physical activity, and this should always be a goal of therapy.

medications are of little use against acute attacks and cause unpleasant side effects such as nervousness, tremors, or heart palpitations.

• If inhaled bronchodilators fail to have an effect, the person should be rushed to an emergency care facility for further treatment.

• If the person suffers from oxygen deprivation (becomes blue around the lips, fingers, or toes), warm humidified oxygen should be administered.

For children suffering an asthmatic attack, the American Lung Association suggests these steps

• Reassure the child by the tone of voice, and by acting calm and self-confident.
• Give medication prescribed by the physician for the start of an episode.
• Give liquids to prevent dehydration (the amount necessary varies from patient to patient).
• Let the child do his favorite relaxation exercises.
• Try to determine what triggered the episode and remove it—or the child—from the area.

• Decide whether the physician needs to be called, or whether the episode is under control.

PREVENTION

The first step in preventing asthma episodes is determining the factor(s) that trigger the asthmatic response. Allergy testing can identify many environmental allergens, and food challenge techniques can be used to identify foods that less commonly prompt an asthmatic reaction. (See Food Allergies, chapter 29.) Once identified, causative factors should be avoided as much as possible. Immunotherapy (allergy shots) can also be initiated to desensitize allergic individuals who do not respond to the usual therapy.

Drug treatment for asthma can be directed at either acutely relieving the symptom of airflow obstruction (using bronchodilator medications) or at preventing the underlying process that leads to obstruction (administering, cromolyn, nedocromil, and corticosteroids). (See box on preceding page.)

In addition to medication, many asthma sufferers respond well to behavioral and psychological interventions such as:

• Relaxation exercises
• Airway-clearing exercises

For more information about physician-patient partnership and learning self-help techniques for living with asthma, contact your local American Lung Association chapter.

HOME REMEDIES AND ALTERNATIVE THERAPIES

Some alternative therapies may be useful adjuncts to conventional treatment of asthma, but caution is needed in using them. For example, herbal remedies may contain the very substances that trigger allergic asthma.

So-called anti-asthma diets often eliminate entire food groups, resulting in possible nutritional deficiencies.

The naturally occurring stimulants found in coffee and tea may provide some relief to some asthma sufferers, presumably because the body can convert caffeine to theophylline. But these stimulants should not be considered a substitute for needed asthma medications.

Many people with asthma can benefit from medically supervised exercise conditioning, but again, caution is needed because exercise is a common asthma trigger. Patients should be taught how to use preventive medications prior to exercise, and also helped to select appropriate activities. In general, endurance activities such as long-distance running should be avoided. Using a stationary cycle or swimming in an appropriate environment are generally good choices.

Meditation, yoga, deep breathing and other relaxation therapies may help counter stress; although it plays a lesser role in asthma than was previously thought, stress may be a factor in some asthma attacks. Before engaging in any alternative therapy, inform your primary-care physician, who can alert you to possible hazards.

MALE/FEMALE DIFFERENCES

Many more boys than girls suffer asthma, although the reasons for this phenomenon have not been explained.

······························

OTHER LUNG COMPLICATIONS

PNEUMOTHORAX

DEFINITION

Pneumothorax is a break in the seal of the pleural membrane covering the lung that allows the air to pass out of the lung, thus opening up a space between the two pleural membranes and resulting in collapse of the lung.

CAUSE

In older children and adults (see "Newborns" in section "Pneumothorax in Newborns" in section "Lung Diseases in Infants and Children," later in this chapter), pneumothorax is most often due to trauma or injury to the chest, but it can occur spontaneously in otherwise healthy, vigorous individuals (see figure 20.3). It is also seen as a complication of mechanical ventilation of especially stiff or diseased lungs when high pressures are required to maintain adequate ventilation.

- **Open Pneumothorax:** a penetrating chest wound enabling air to rush in and cause the lungs to collapse.
- **Closed Pneumothorax:** air leak from a ruptured bronchus or perforated esophagus that eventually ruptures into the pleural space.
- **Pulmonary Barotrauma:** injury to the lining of the airways or lung tissue from excessive air pressure as air is forced into the lungs by a respirator; this can lead to pneumothorax.

Pneumothorax may also occur spontaneously (mainly in healthy men but also in women ages 20 to 40) when a symptomless weak point—a bubblelike structure—develops in the lung. Other respiratory conditions such as asthma, cystic fibrosis, or tuberculosis may be predisposing factors to pneumothorax.

DIAGNOSIS

Symptoms, which vary, include sharp chest pain, shortness of breath, and a dry, hacking cough. A chest x-ray or CT scan usually identifies pneumothorax and may reveal any other complicating lung disease.

TREATMENT

A small, spontaneous pneumothorax requires no treatment and usually heals by itself. But in major ruptures, where tension of air in the chest becomes severe, pushing other vital organs to the side, the air must be removed by an emergency surgical procedure. In some cases, surgery may also be used to effectively close the leak and eliminate the pleural cavity.

MALE/FEMALE DIFFERENCES

Pneumothorax is much more common in men than women.

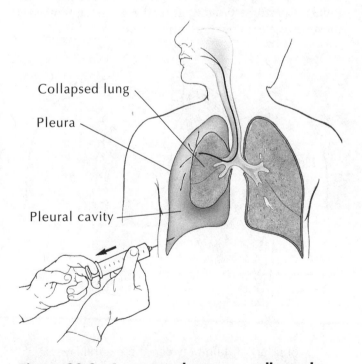

Collapsed lung

Pleura

Pleural cavity

Figure 20.3: A pneumothorax, or collapsed lung, may result from an injury or weakness causing a rupture of a bronchus, or an air sac, that causes air to leak out of the lungs. If the collapse is extensive or seems to be progressing, air may be withdrawn from the surrounding pleural cavity to permit the lung to reinflate.

PULMONARY ALVEOLAR PROTEINOSIS

DEFINITION AND CAUSE

In healthy lungs, the alveoli, some 300 million small sacs with walls the thickness of bubbles, are the terminal spaces through which oxygen flows to the blood vessels in the lungs and to the rest of the circulatory system. Pulmonary alveolar proteinosis is a condition in which these spaces fill with granular material consisting mostly of fat and protein from the blood.

DIAGNOSIS

Sometimes the disease can be diagnosed by x-ray, or by tests that show a reduction in breathing function and the ability to use oxygen.

TREATMENT

This condition may be localized in one of the lungs, or spread throughout one or both. It may progress, remain stable throughout the patient's life, or clear up spontaneously. Indeed, there may be no symptoms. But the condition may cause a nonproductive cough, severe breathing difficulties during physical activity, and fatigue. In severe cases, bronchopulmonary lavage (surgical rinsing of the lungs) is performed under general anesthesia; however, most cases clear up without treatment.

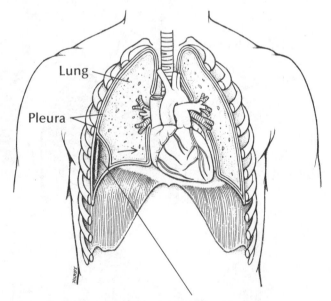

Buildup of fluid between the pleural layers

Figure 20.4: Pleurisy is a painful disorder in which fluid builds up between the layers of the pleura, the double-layer membrane surrounding the lung and lining the chest cavity. Inflammation of the pleura may occur; if bacteria or other microorganisms invade the pleural space, a serious infection may result.

RESPIRATORY DIFFICULTIES

AUTOIMMUNE DISORDERS OF THE LUNGS

Autoimmune processes related to antibody (disease-fighting factor) formation in the body are characterized by lung hemorrhage (pulmonary hemosiderosis) and may be associated with renal disease (Goodpastures Syndrome). These conditions occur most frequently in young adult males and can be rapidly fatal. Autoimmune diseases like lupus and periarteritis scleroderma can also affect the lungs. Treatment by immune suppression such as corticosteroids may help, but not always.

ATELECTASIS

In the normal respiratory process, gas passes through the terminal air spaces of the lungs (the alveoli) and into the bloodstream. If the respiration process is interrupted due to bronchial obstruction, pneumothorax, or other conditions, or enlargement of structures adjacent to the lungs, the gas in the alveoli may be absorbed and not replaced, leading to collapse of a portion of the lungs. This condition is known as atelectasis. Often, the shadow on a chest x-ray caused by atelectasis is very difficult to distinguish from evidence of pneumonia.

LUNG CANCER

Lung cancer is now the most frequent cause of cancer deaths in both men and women. For a detailed discussion of lung cancer, see chapter 17.

MALE/FEMALE DIFFERENCES

Alveolar proteinosis occurs in previously healthy people, primarily men between the ages of 20 and 50.

CHRONIC PULMONARY DISEASES

Many acute respiratory conditions can become chronic, particularly when aggravated by environmental factors such as cigarette smoke or air pollution. Almost everyone has known someone with chronic lung problems like breathlessness on exertion, "smoker's cough," lingering coughs and respiratory problems after a cold, as well as frequent colds. Pulmonary diseases such as

PLEURISY AND PLEURAL EFFUSION

In a small number of patients, the aftermath of a lung infection such as pneumonia is pleurisy, an inflammation of the pleura, the two-ply membrane that encloses each lung and lines the chest cavity. Pleurisy can also be a complication of tuberculosis or a chest injury. With the universal use of antibiotics, it is less common but still occurs.

The layers of the pleura join at the edges so that the pleura resemble a balloon, completely empty of air and wrapped tightly around each of the lungs. Normally, only a thin lubricating layer of fluid lies between the inner and outer pleural linings, and the lungs move freely within the pleura during breathing.

If the pleura becomes inflamed or roughened by infection, the movement of the lung may be restricted, and breathing, especially deep breathing, will be painful (see figure 20.4).

Sometimes excess fluid seeps into the pleural space, a condition known as pleural effusion. Although pain may stop (and be replaced by breathlessness) because there is no longer any friction between the two layers, pleural effusion is a serious matter that may recur if not promptly attended to. As with pleurisy, it is treated by draining the effusion and treating the underlying condition—the pneumonia or other lung infection that caused the pleural condition.

chronic bronchitis and emphysema (chronic obstructive pulmonary disease [COPD]) are more serious examples of pulmonary lung problems. Those with COPD have limitations on their lungs' ability to function, and their respiratory systems have undergone significant changes (see figure 20.5).

CHRONIC BRONCHITIS

DEFINITION

Many people suffer brief attacks of acute bronchitis, or inflammations of the airways with fever, coughing, and spitting up mucus (phlegm) when they have colds. Chronic bronchitis denotes long-term spitting and coughing continuing for months and returning each year, lasting longer each time. In chronic bronchitis, the airways have become narrowed and partly clogged with mucus that is not moving along as it should (propelled by cilia). Because of the obstruction, chronic bronchitis sufferers have continual difficulty breathing.

CAUSE

Cigarette smoke has been associated with irritating the airways, causing them to narrow and paralyzing the cilia. Those who quit smoking find that chronic bronchitis is lessened after a while. Chronic bronchitis can progress to a life-threatening lung disease, emphysema.

DIAGNOSIS

Blood tests, chest x-ray, an analysis of sputum, and tests of pulmonary function are all used to diagnose chronic bronchitis. Although the breathing difficulties symptomatic of this condition are similar to asthma, asthmatic breathing difficulties appear and disappear while chronic bronchitis stubbornly persists.

TREATMENT

This condition is treated with bronchodilators (drugs that widen the breathing passages) and anti-inflammatory drugs delivered with an inhaler. Oxygen may also be administered. Antibiotics may be prescribed to check bacterial infections. Atrovent by inhalation can block the nerves in the airways, helping to reduce cough.

PREVENTION

Not smoking and avoiding air pollution are the best ways to prevent chronic bronchitis.

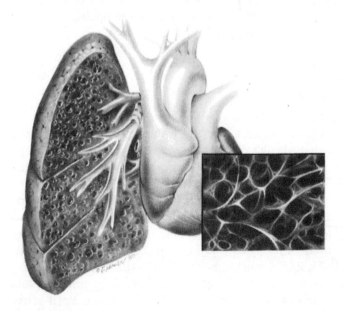

Figure 20.5: A cross section of lung tissue and enlargement showing the characteristic breakdown of alveolar sacs that occurs in chronic obstructive lung diseases.

In the past, about twice as many men as women developed chronic bronchitis. With the increase in smoking by young women, an increase in bronchitis, emphysema, and lung cancer is being recognized in women.

EMPHYSEMA

DEFINITION

Emphysema reduces the normal elasticity of the lung that helps to hold the airways open. The lung can be thought of as a mesh (much like a stocking) stretching from the airways to the pleural surface of the lung. When the elasticity of the lung is impaired, the inflating lung does not pull the airways open. With progressive inelasticity, the lung's small airways collapse on expiration, making it impossible to fully exhale stale air. Almost all emphysema patients are habitual, heavy smokers.

Half of the people in this country who have emphysema are over 65; nearly all the rest are over 45. Frequently, those with emphysema live in areas where pollution is a constant problem.

CAUSE

A major cause of both chronic bronchitis and emphysema is smoking. Air pollution may also hasten the development of this disease. Less commonly, an imbalance in lung chemistry contributes to the condition—some people lack alpha[1]-antitrypsin, a chemical that prevents disease-fighting substances called proteases from destroying lung tissue.

DIAGNOSIS

Emphysema makes its presence known gradually. In the beginning stages, a person with emphysema often suffers very bad colds each winter for a few years, each accompanied by a heavy cough and perhaps chronic bronchitis. The cough frequently persists and becomes chronic.

As the disease progresses, slight morning and evening breathing difficulties may worsen until breathlessness interferes with daily life. A short walk brings on breathlessness; walking up stairs is difficult. Eventually, as the lungs become less and less able to inhale, exhale, and exchange gases, there may come a point when every breath is a major effort and normal activities become impossible.

Shortness of breath is the symptom that most commonly prompts a person to seek medical attention. The patient may mistake the problem for asthma or heart disease. In fact, emphysema may lead to serious cardiovascular problems. Because the disease interferes with the passage of blood through the lungs and into the circulation, the heart must work harder. It may enlarge and eventually suffer heart failure.

Diagnosing emphysema entails a physical exam, medical history, laboratory tests that measure oxygen and carbon dioxide levels in the blood, and pulmonary function tests that measure lung volumes and airflow rates.

TREATMENT

A new form of therapy offers promise of curing emphysema caused by a congenital deficiency of alpha[1]-antitrypsin. Studies are now underway to determine whether administration of alpha[1]-antitrypsin (developed using new molecular biological techniques) can prevent lung destruction.

Although other types of emphysema cannot be cured, a number of measures enable patients to live more comfortably with the disease.

- Smoking cessation and air pollution avoidance
- Controlled breathing to ease the task of ventilating the lungs
- Exercises that strengthen the diaphragm and abdominal muscles to help in the breathing process
- Special positions for sleeping and lying down that clear the lungs of excess mucus
- A walking and exercise program to build strength
- Appropriate combinations of medicines, breathing aids, and living patterns to make life more comfortable (some medications strengthen the force of the respiratory muscles)

MALE/FEMALE DIFFERENCES

The people in the United States with emphysema are primarily men between 50 and 70 who have been heavy smokers for years. As more and more women take up smoking, their emphysema rate is expected eventually to equal the male rate.

BRONCHIECTASIS

DEFINITION

Bronchiectasis is a relatively rare disorder in which the bronchi are chronically dilated or expanded as a result of chronic infection and inflammation. This impairs their function and leads to accumulation of mucus in the breathing tubes, predisposing to further infection, inflammation and destruction of the walls of the airways, and pneumonia.

CAUSE

Although bronchiectasis may be caused by a congenital abnormality, more often it is the result of other diseases. At one time, tuberculosis was a common cause; today, more likely causes include chronic pneumonia, cystic fibrosis, chronic bronchitis, emphysema, measles, silicosis, lung abscess, lung cancer, or a congenital defect in the immune system predisposing the airways to a chronic destructive infection. Aspiration of foreign objects into the lungs, especially common in children, or the inhaling of vomitus into the lungs during surgery also may cause bronchiectasis.

DIAGNOSIS

The affected areas may be localized and confined to one portion of the lung, or they may be scattered throughout both lobes. Only in rare instances will the entire lung be involved. As the disease progresses, the bronchi become thick-walled sacs, with cystlike spaces. The normal structures of the bronchial walls may eventually be destroyed, leading to a spread of the infection and hemorrhage.

The most common symptom of bronchiectasis is a chronic cough, which may produce large amounts of thick, foul-smelling sputum. (In some cases, however, there is very little coughing and minimal production of sputum.) The foul smell is caused by death of the affected lung tissue.

Complications of bronchiectasis include recurring pneumonia, abnormal lung function, and frequent lung infections. The onset is often insidious; the disease may follow a bout of severe flu, whooping cough, or pneumonia. At first, the cough occurs sporadically, usually in the morning, late afternoon, or after going to bed. A change in posture may provoke a spell of coughing. Initially, the cough may be dry, but as the disease progresses it is likely to produce increasing amounts of sputum. Shortness of breath during exercise may occur. Other signs include a clubbing or thickening of the fingertips.

Previously, the diagnosis was made through bronchography but now is made with CT scans of the chest. The sputum should be studied to identify the presence and type of infecting microorganisms.

TREATMENT

Treatment usually requires controlling the infection with antibiotics and promoting drainage of infected material by postural drainage and use of inhaled bronchodilators and anti-inflammatory agents. In some instances, the diseased area may be removed surgically if it is confined to one area of the lung. Patients should be alert to signs of recurring episodes so that antibiotic therapy can be resumed promptly. In some cases of chronic bronchiectasis, long-term antibiotics may be given as a preventive measure.

HEART AND LUNG DISEASE

COR PULMONALE

DEFINITION

Cor pulmonale is failure of the right side of the heart due to lung dysfunction caused by emphysema, silicosis, or other severe lung disease.

CAUSE

The heart and the lungs are close in anatomical position and function. Reserves of blood in the lungs, and the lungs' ability to move that blood through the circulatory system and assist the heart's functions during violent exertion, tie the heart and lungs together as an integrated system.

Normally, the pressure on the right side of the heart is much lower than the left, since the pressure required to push blood through the lungs is much less than that required to pump blood to the rest of the body. The lungs not only keep the blood well oxygenated, they also produce and inactivate substances that control circulation.

When the lungs fail and the blood is not well oxygenated, the blood vessels in the lung constrict. Initially this may be protective, since it will divert blood from poorly ventilated or diseased portions of lung to healthy portions. However, if too many pulmonary blood vessels constrict, it puts excessive load on the right side of the heart, the part responsible for pumping blood into the lungs. As the pressure required to pump the blood through the constricted blood vessels increases, the heart muscle becomes overdeveloped to compensate. Eventually, the load on the heart becomes too great, causing failure of the right side of the heart.

DIAGNOSIS

Outward signs of this problem include swelling (edema) of the liver, abdomen, and lower extremities.

TREATMENT

Treating and reversing the underlying lung disease and improving the oxygenation of the blood are an essential first step. In addition, diuretics may reduce edema.

LUNG EMBOLISM AND INFARCTION

DEFINITION

The cardiopulmonary system circulates blood through the body in a continuing, uninterrupted manner. But sometimes matter foreign to the bloodstream—an embolus usually made up of a blood clot—plugs an artery. Infarction refers to the tissue damage caused by the interruption of the blood supply due to embolus or thrombosis (local clotting).

CAUSE

The lung is the organ most subject to embolism because all of the blood returning to the heart from every part of the body must pass through it first before circulating to the rest of the body. Thus it is a kind of filter for the body. Fortunately it is less vulnerable to infarction, unless already damaged by pulmonary or cardiac disease, because of a double blood supply. (Thrombosis does occur in the lung arteries. See figure 20.6.)

Emboli affecting the lungs most often form in the wall of the heart. They may also be created in the lower extremities after an operation, a prolonged stay in bed, or following an injury. Any sort of prolonged inactivity increases the clotting of blood in the deep veins of the leg, and tiny pieces of these clots may break away, travel through the venous system, and lodge in the lungs. Preventing clotting is an important reason to be up and about as soon as possible after surgery, or, if this is not possible, to keep your legs elevated, thus avoiding stasis of the blood in the extremities.

DIAGNOSIS

If a large embolus enters the lungs, or smaller emboli invade lungs already congested by lung disease, considerable infarction may cause the patient to quickly fall unconscious and die. For those who survive a first embolism, normal function may be restored in a few weeks. But patients who survive an initial embolism are vulnerable to further clots; the source of the original emboli may release others.

The majority of lung embolisms are accompanied by heart disease or occur postoperatively. Others may follow trauma, infections, pregnancies, one-side paralysis (usually from stroke), cancer, and varicose veins.

TREATMENT

Infarction may be treated medically with anticoagulants, relief of chest pain, and cough control. Oxygen is often administered. Under exceptional conditions where a surgical team can be mobilized immediately, the clot or clots

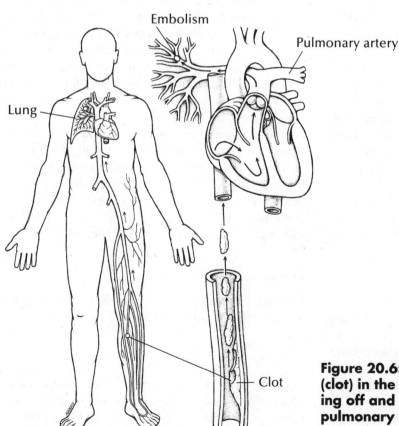

Figure 20.6: Development of a thrombosis (clot) in the leg, with a piece of the clot breaking off and traveling through the heart and the pulmonary artery to lodge in the lungs, which causes a pulmonary embolism.

may be removed from the pulmonary artery. Open-heart surgery and surgery to remove thrombi from the lining of the heart or from major arteries are also performed.

PREVENTION

Circulation of blood in the extremities is reduced when the body remains in one position for a long time, predisposing people to peripheral embolism. After an operation, you should move about as soon as possible. Stand and walk or do exercises periodically to break up periods of confinement such as long airplane rides.

MALE/FEMALE DIFFERENCES

Lung embolism is more frequent in women than in men, and occurs most often in people over age 45.

....

LUNG DISEASES IN INFANTS AND CHILDREN

Lungs are problem organs for the young: Episodes of illness related to breathing cause more children's hospitalizations, time lost from school, and family disruption than any other category of disease.

Babies possess only a small fraction of the air sacs they will have as adults. Lung injuries or disease suffered early in life can therefore have serious repercussions. Young children also may suffer many severe lung infections like pneumonia, bronchiolitis, or croup. They are also vulnerable to chronic conditions like asthma. Serious diseases like cystic fibrosis and sickle cell anemia similarly manifest themselves in childhood.

Adding to their vulnerability, children are fearless explorers prone to accidents in which they swallow or inhale (aspirate) various objects such as peanuts, which contain very irritating oils. Choking may result or, if an object is retained in the respiratory system, the child can become extremely ill from severe damage to the lungs.

RESPIRATORY DISTRESS SYNDROME

DEFINITION

Respiratory distress syndrome (RDS), also known as hyaline membrane disease, is a lung dysfunction that interferes with breathing and causes a potentially fatal lack of oxygen in the blood. The syndrome once claimed the lives of as many as 25,000 to 30,000 infants each year, but better medical understanding and treatment of the condition have reduced fatality rates considerably. Instead of the 65 or 75 percent mortality rate in RDS babies of the past, many medical centers are now reporting that 75 percent or more of the infants with RDS live.

CAUSE

Premature birth makes infants more vulnerable to RDS, but it also may occur in the full-term infants of diabetic mothers or those who deliver by cesarean section. In some newborn infants, RDS may be linked to a lack of a vital substance—surfactant—that reduces surface tension and prevents the alveoli from collapsing every time the infant exhales. To some extent, alveoli with surfactant are like soap bubbles in that they stay open. Without this soaplike substance they would collapse.

DIAGNOSIS

RDS infants show signs of respiratory distress within the first hours after birth, perhaps even in the delivery room. A chest x-ray displays abnormalities in the lungs, and blood tests reveal low levels of oxygen.

TREATMENT

Treatment includes administering carefully measured concentrations of oxygen, maintaining hydration and nutrition, using artificial surfactant, and sometimes using mechanical breathing apparatus to keep the lungs from collapsing: Constant Positive Airway Pressure (CPAP) is one very effective way of keeping the alveoli from collapsing until the body learns to make its own surfactant. After a few days, over two-thirds of RDS babies improve greatly as their breathing grows less strained, their activity increases, and their serum oxygen levels reach normal.

But about 25 percent of RDS infants simply do not respond to treatment. In some cases, tiny premature infants (often weighing less than a pound) are born with such underdeveloped lungs (pulmonary hypoplasia) that they are unable to survive.

BRONCHOPULMONARY DYSPLASIA

DEFINITION AND CAUSE

Bronchopulmonary dysplasia (BPD) is a form of chronic unresolved lung injury in early life. It is a reaction in the infant's lungs to lifesaving intensive treatment with oxygen and mechanical ventilators. The lungs are both stiff and obstructed and are very difficult to ventilate. Chest retractions are grossly visible with each breath as the infant struggles to suck air into the damaged lungs and airway. The levels of oxygen and carbon dioxide in the lungs may be abnormal for months or longer. BPD develops primarily in infants who have been treated for RDS,

LUNG PROBLEMS OF THE NEWBORN

Congenital Lobar Emphysema

The bronchial tubes to one lobe of the lung may be improperly developed so that they are softer than normal and collapse on expiration, trapping air. In the affected lobe of the lung, air is able to enter but cannot leave. As a result, the lobe becomes overdistended and may compress the adjacent normal lung. The baby, who is usually between 1 week and 1 month old, experiences shortness of breath and wheezes. She may begin to show signs of cyanosis (bluish lips and fingernail beds). In some cases, emergency surgery on the lung is necessary. The abnormal lobe is removed in order to preserve the function of the normal lung. When not severe, the abnormal lobe functions more normally with age.

Perinatal Asphyxia

Although newborns can survive with insufficient oxygen for longer periods than can adults (by utilizing energy sources that do not require oxygen), long and difficult labor can harm neonates by cutting off their oxygen supply for a prolonged period. Asphyxia may occur when the fetus is positioned abnormally in the birth canal so his backside or leg is born first, or when the second-born of twins suffers a decreased oxygen supply for an especially long time. Sometimes the mother may have a condition such as high blood pressure, which may affect the fetal blood supply. Maternal smoking is also associated with this condition. The result is that the newborn is not able to start up the lungs without help.

It takes coordinated effort on the part of the health care team to see that such babies are born fairly rapidly and that their lungs are activated. Fetal monitoring gives the team information about the existence of fetal asphyxia. Emergency resuscitation procedures are carried out. Ideally, mothers-to-be at high risk for this condition should give birth in a large medical facility where skilled help is available.

Choanal Atresia

Infants can breathe only through the nose for the first few months. When an infant is born with choanal atresia—a bony obstruction in the nasal passage—respiration can be difficult and the obstruction must be surgically removed.

Stridor

Stridor is a medium-pitched, almost musical sound originating primarily in the larynx or trachea and produced by some babies when they inhale. When it is congenital, the condition usually improves and disappears with age, but can take as long as a year. Although troubling to parents, it is usually not serious and does not require treatment. When associated with croup, as it often is, it is self-limiting. Occasionally other problems such as a misproportioned blood vessel or cyst pressing on the airways contribute to stridor. Correction of the associated problem will eliminate the stridor.

Drug Withdrawal

Drugs taken by pregnant mothers may compromise their babies' breathing. The newborn of a mother who is a drug addict may be born with an imbalanced metabolism that may continue for several weeks until the drugs have completely disappeared from the infant's body.

Structural Malformations

Defects in the face, mouth, chest wall, diaphragm, heart, and major blood vessels may lead to respiratory problems in an infant. Great care in feeding and positioning and possible correction by surgery are indicated.

Sudden Infant Death Syndrome

Sudden infant death syndrome (SIDS) is the largest single cause of infant mortality beyond the newborn period; every year, some 10,000 seemingly healthy infants are put to bed and are later found dead. This occurs in about 2 infants out of 1,000.

SIDS infants are usually 2 to 4 months old. The syndrome is rarely seen after the age of 6 months. Boys die more often than girls, and there are fewer cases in the summer. Although significant numbers of SIDS infants have low birth weights, maternal smoking is now recognized as a greater risk factor.

Low socioeconomic status is also a predisposing factor (perhaps because of poor conditions such as crowding), although SIDS occurs in all population groups. Genetic factors have not been demonstrated, but there is a tendency for SIDS to occur multiple times in families. Other risk factors may include a young, unmarried mother and insufficient prenatal care.

Sometimes a sleeping child is found not breathing (in an apneic condition) and may be resuscitated. The relationship between these apparently life-threatening events and actual SIDS cases is uncertain.

Many suggested causes of SIDS are under investigation; however, the precise cause remains elusive. At present, a disturbance of normal sleep patterns and a combination of biochemical and neurological abnormalities or immaturity of cardiorespiratory control are the focal points of most research.

Families who want to know more about SIDS or who want to share their experiences with other families who have lost a child to SIDS may want to contact the National Foundation for Sudden Infant Death Syndrome or its local chapters.

Bronchiolitis

An infant's small airways (bronchioles), which carry air into the lungs, are much narrower than in later childhood or in adult life. An acute infection due to a virus, bronchiolitis leads to inflammation, swelling, and partial or complete obstruction of the airways; the infant can have great difficulty taking in fresh air and may incompletely expel used air from the lungs. Bronchiolitis is characterized by wheezing, strong inspiratory efforts producing retractions or sucking in of the chest, strong efforts to clear the lungs by exhaling heavily, and rapid breathing.

Most cases of bronchiolitis are reported in January and February, and another household member usually suffers a respiratory infection at the same time or shortly before the infant gets sick.

When bronchiolitis is severe, the infant is usually hospitalized and observed carefully. Oxygen may be administered and intensive care is provided if complications develop. Bronchiolitis, though frightening, is rarely fatal. The course can be either relatively short (2 or 3 days) or prolonged.

with only a small percentage of cases occurring in other infants.

DIAGNOSIS

Bronchopulmonary dysplasia is diagnosed by x-raying the baby's chest while he or she recovers from respiratory distress syndrome.

TREATMENT

Once diagnosed, there is no special or speedy cure. The baby's lungs will repair themselves over time, usually over months if further injury is not superimposed, but the infant may require continued hospitalization. Parents of babies with bronchopulmonary dysplasia need to be patient, loving, and careful with their babies after discharge, since the lungs are somewhat more vulnerable than those of other babies for an extended period of time. This is especially true when colds and other respiratory infections occur.

Note: Other lung conditions may occur as a result of the birth process. The delivery room procedure of suctioning the infant immediately after birth helps avoid respiratory problems related to aspiration of substances present in the birth canal.

PNEUMOTHORAX IN NEWBORNS

DEFINITION AND CAUSE

Pneumothorax in the newborn is a small air leak from the lungs into other parts of the chest cavity. This often results when pressure is exerted in the chest cavity to inflate the lungs for the first breath of life. In 1 to 2 percent of all newborns, the alveoli (tiny breathing sacs in the lungs) rupture.

DIAGNOSIS

A chest x-ray confirms the presence of pneumothorax.

TREATMENT

The leaked air may be removed from the chest cavity by needle or chest tube when the pneumothorax is large; the continuous removal of leaked air is sometimes necessary until the ruptures heal. The traditional technique of treating RDS, called continuous distending airway pressure, keeps the lungs from collapsing, but it may occasionally precipitate air leaks, especially when higher pressures are superimposed to mechanically ventilate the lungs. Newer techniques, which ventilate the lungs at lower pressures, are now being developed.

CYSTIC FIBROSIS

DEFINITION

Cystic fibrosis is a severe, genetically determined disease involving both the lungs and gastrointestinal tract, as well as other organs. It occurs in about 1 in 2,000 live births among white children and at a far lower rate in black and Asian children.

At present, only 50 percent of those diagnosed as having cystic fibrosis as infants or young children live beyond their late twenties. However, this precentage is rising as an increasing number of children and young adults with cystic fibrosis are only mildly affected and survive into adult life. Intensive research into the disease continues in the United States, Canada, Australia, and Europe.

CAUSE

Cystic fibrosis can be transmitted to a child when both parents carry the same recessive gene for the disease but do not suffer the disease themselves. In this situation each child inherits a 25 percent chance of developing cystic fibrosis, a 50 percent chance of carrying but not suffering the disease, and a 25 percent chance of being totally unaffected.

DIAGNOSIS

This disease affects the glands that secrete sweat and mucus. The mucus is very thick and sticky and blocks airways and bile ducts. In addition, the sweat is very salty, and the child may suffer from salt depletion while sweating during hot weather. Children with cystic fibrosis suffer repeated pulmonary infections, and in time the lungs of most patients are infiltrated with *Pseudomonas* bacteria, an infectious agent very difficult to eradicate. Fever, cough, difficulty in breathing, fast respiration, flaring of the nostrils, poor appetite, and reduced activity are typical features of acute cystic fibrosis. Lung collapse, excessive mucus in the bronchi, or abscesses are possible. Sometimes, because of the air that is chronically trapped in the chest, the child gets a barrel-chested appearance.

Cystic fibrosis is diagnosed with a sweat test, which measures the amount of salt in perspiration. If that test is positive, it should be confirmed with a second test. Since a child's siblings run an increased risk of also having cystic fibrosis, they should also be tested.

TREATMENT

Cystic fibrosis is often treated at home with antibiotics, special exercises for draining of sputum—including physical therapy for the chest, physical exercise, and aerosols—as well as diet therapy, which emphasizes the replacement of deficient digestive enzymes. Surgery is sometimes performed to correct physical complications. Because some of the tenacity of the mucus and secretions results from increased amounts of DNA, a new approach is the administration of Pulmozyme, which contains an enzyme that breaks down the DNA, thereby liquefying the secretions and making it easier to clear them.

Scientists have recently isolated the gene responsible for cystic fibrosis and have begun developing treatment techniques that will repair the genetic defect in a patient's lung tissue. Researchers have also identified an abnormality in the regulation of a cellular channel through which chloride ions move that may play a role in the disease. Both of these scientific discoveries promise better understanding of cystic fibrosis, better forms of treatment, and possible prevention.

MALE/FEMALE DIFFERENCES

Boys and girls get cystic fibrosis equally.

CROUP

DEFINITION

Croup is a dramatic and frightening but short-lived respiratory inflammation in children brought on by a cold. This viral illness is characterized by extremely labored noisy breathing and a harsh cough.

Children with croup need gentle handling and reassurance. Parents should feel free to ask the pediatrician questions to assure their own understanding of what has happened so they can comfort the child. Croup is rarely fatal. (For a detailed discussion, see chapter 18, Infectious Diseases.)

DIAGNOSIS

When an infant or young child develops a cold with a cough, runny nose, and a low-grade fever, then wakes up several nights later with difficult, noisy breathing and a harsh cough, he or she has developed the viral infection called croup. Other symptoms may include rapid breathing, pulled in breastbone, vomiting, and a sore throat.

In one form of severe croup, which has a bacterial rather than a viral cause, the child's airway may swell and start to close. This condition is called epiglottitis, an extremely dangerous condition that necessitates immediate emergency medical care. Epiglottitis can be fatal.

TREATMENT

Steam from a hot shower in a closed bathroom can quickly relieve the symptoms of most croup, as can cool night air. Mild viral croup unaccompanied by fever can usually be treated at home if the child's pediatrician agrees. Using moist heat (humidification) at home is usually sufficient to relieve mild viral croup in a few days.

Children suffering croup with fever or who show signs of severe breathing difficulties, restlessness, or signs of insufficient oxygen like cyanosis (blue lips or nails), should be taken to a hospital emergency room as quickly as possible. There, moist air is given with a face mask or croup tent and vital signs and arterial blood gases monitored closely. Oxygen is often given, and some hospitals also give inhaled medications to relax airways and shrink swollen membranes lining the upper airways.

In cases of epiglottitis, an artificial airway may have to be inserted through the nose past the pharynx to the larynx to enable the child to breathe, or an airway is created surgically. The child will be placed in intensive care in the hospital for observation and given antibiotics.

OCCUPATIONAL LUNG DISEASES

Each year, more than 65,000 adult Americans develop a respiratory disease related to their work environment, and 25,000 workers die. Most people's lungs can withstand temporary or occasional exposure to hazardous substances; those who develop occupational lung disorders do so over a long period of time, with repeated exposure to a hazardous substance. Only occasionally does disease develop when a worker's lungs are acutely overwhelmed by fumes, smoke, or other substances.

Many occupational lung diseases take 20 or more years to develop; by that time, the worker may have retired or changed jobs, making the original cause of the disease less apparent. There are 2 basic types of occupational lung disease: those caused by dust in the lungs (pneumoconiosis) and those caused by hypersensitivity to substances at the worksite. In addition, some lung cancers are thought to be triggered by exposure to certain substances in the workplace, and there are some diseases, such as byssinosis, which afflicts cotton workers, that are linked to both hypersensitivity and dust exposure.

PNEUMOCONIOSIS

DEFINITION AND CAUSE

Over the years, this disease has had a number of names: grinder's rot, miner's phthisis, and miner's asthma are but a few. While the specific causes and manifestations may vary, all forms of pneumoconiosis are caused by industrial dust that accumulates in the lungs and eventually interferes with lung function.

TYPES OF PNEUMOCONIOSIS

Silicosis. More than 1 million American workers are at risk for silicosis. Silicon is the most common mineral on earth and silica is used in many industrial processes, including foundry work, pottery making, and the manufacture of glass, tiles, and bricks. Finely ground silica, especially dangerous when inhaled, is used in abrasive soaps, polishes, and filters. Stonemasons and sandblasters may also be affected by silicosis.

Chronic Silicosis. Chronic silicosis is seen in workers who have inhaled relatively low concentrations of industrial dust for 10 to 20 years. The accumulated dust causes a tissue reaction that results in the formation of small, whorl-shaped nodules scattered throughout the lungs. The nodules may remain in a worker's lungs throughout his entire life, having absolutely no effect. Or they may enlarge, increase in number, and join together. Breathlessness becomes a problem, and there may be a cough and sputum production.

Twenty to 30 percent of all chronic silicosis patients progress to complicated illness. At that stage, fibrous tissue replaces soft lung tissue, restricting the lungs' function and leading to breathlessness, weakness, chest pain, a cough, and sputum production. The patient becomes a respiratory cripple, likely to die of heart failure caused by the lung disease (cor pulmonale).

Acute Silicosis. Sometimes workers exposed to considerable silica dust over a short period of time, like sandblasters, tunnelers, and drillers, develop acute silicosis. It is rapidly progressive, as unremediable as lung cancer, disabling, and likely to be fatal within 5 years. The disease is characterized by difficulty in breathing, loss of weight, fever, and coughing. The alveoli become inflamed and fibrosis (scar tissue) develops in the lungs. Many sufferers of acute silicosis are young, active people. When TB was more widespread, it occurred as a common complication of silicosis.

To prevent silicosis, dust control is necessary. This may mean wetting down mines and improving ventilation, or special suits and breathing apparatus. Experts disagree on whether the protection now given workers is adequate.

Coal Workers' Pneumoconiosis. Coal workers' pneumoconiosis, commonly called black lung disease, is a potential danger for all coal miners. The simple form of the disease affects an estimated 10 to 30 percent of these workers. The condition is more prevalent in miners of anthracite coal than in miners of bituminous coal. Silica, kaolin, mica, beryllium, copper, basalt, cobalt, and other minerals have also been found in miners' lungs. When

DANGEROUS GASES ON THE JOB

FOR FIREFIGHTERS

Polyvinyl chloride, of which furniture and decorations are often constructed, becomes a major menace to lung health during a fire. A product of modern plastics, this substance releases hydrogen chloride, phosgene, and carbon monoxide on combustion, all injurious to the lungs. Phosgene is extremely poisonous and has been used as poison gas in warfare. Modern climate-controlled buildings with airtight windows trap smoke, increasing toxic content. Regular exposure to some of these substances may cause emphysema, bronchitis, asthma, and shortness of breath.

FOR CHEMICAL WORKERS AND THOSE INVOLVED IN HIGH-HEAT OPERATIONS

Poisonous gases may be generated by chemical reactions and high-heat operations like welding, brazing, pottery making, smelting, oven drying, and furnace work. It is important that conditions in the workplace that are hazardous to lungs be prevented by changing ingredients, work practices, or machinery; by improving ventilation; and by training workers.

Fumes may result when solids such as metals are heated to become vapors, then cooled quickly and condensed into fine solid particles in the air. Fumes that cause lung disease may come from nickel, cadmium, chromium, and beryllium, among others. Breathed into the lungs, these particles cause lung inflammation, bronchitis, metal fume fever, and lung cancer.

FOR OFFICE WORKERS

Sometimes even the climate in an office building can be hazardous to health. Underground garages, ice-skating rinks that use motorized equipment to scrape the ice, buildings straddling highways, or environmentally sealed buildings may present problems associated with high carbon monoxide levels. Wood-burning stoves, currently used as an economical way to produce heat, are responsible for indoor pollution and have induced exacerbations of asthma.

the condition becomes legally compensable, it is called black lung.

In black lung disease, industrial dust accumulates in the lungs and is visible in x-rays. This dust may cause no difficulties for the worker, but in about 3 percent of miners with dust accumulation in the lungs, fibrosis develops. Each fibrotic area grows, then merges with others. Eventually, most of the lungs fill with stiff scar tissue that prevents breathing. Black lung disease patients may die from respiratory failure, heart failure, or severe infection.

DIAGNOSIS

These conditions are diagnosed using chest x-rays, tests of pulmonary function, medical history and records of dust exposure.

TREATMENT

Treatment for these conditions consists of treating infections and problems that accompany the pneumoconiosis. Otherwise, there is no effective treatment for these diseases.

PREVENTION

Dust control on the job site is essential to prevent these diseases.

ASBESTOS-RELATED LUNG DISEASE

DEFINITION AND CAUSE

Lung damage from asbestos-related lung diseases results from inhalation of the dust of asbestos, a widely used building material prized for its fire resistance and insulation characteristics.

Asbestos may cause lung cancer and fibrosis in anyone exposed to it. According to the National Cancer Institute, among some groups of workers who are heavily exposed to asbestos, as much as 20 to 25 percent of all deaths are due to lung cancer. (In the general population, lung cancer causes only about 5 percent of all deaths.)

But asbestos exposure is not limited to workers. Asbestos, a virtually indestructible fiber, has been used broadly in construction, insulation, and other building materials for many years. Its much prized durability may make it a hazard for those who live, work, or go to school in buildings that were built with asbestos products. Demolition workers and do-it-yourselfers who renovate older buildings run the risk of extensive asbestos exposure. Public buildings—including schools in Wyoming, New York, and New Jersey, as well as university buildings in Connecticut and California—were temporarily closed because asbestos was flaking from the walls or ceilings.

Asbestos occurs in several different forms. The medically significant ones are crocidolite and amosite.

TYPES OF ASBESTOS-RELATED LUNG DISEASES

Asbestosis. This is fibrosis caused by asbestos and begins when asbestos fibers accumulate around the lungs' terminal bronchioles. The body surrounds these fibers with tissues called fibroids. When these fibroids increase and begin to merge, the results may include cough, sputum, weight loss, and increasing breathlessness. Asbestosis patients usually die about 15 years from the onset of the disease.

Lung Cancer. The asbestos worker who smokes is estimated to be 90 times as likely to get lung cancer as the smoker who has never worked with asbestos. (For more information on lung cancer, see chapter 17.)

Mesothelioma. Mesothelioma (cancer of the pleura or chest lining surrounding the lungs) accounts for 7 to 10 percent of the deaths among asbestos workers. It is inoperable and invariably fatal. Most cases of mesothelioma occur when workers are exposed to crocidolite fibers, which are fine and straight. The disease has also been reported in those with very little exposure to crocidolite fibers, such as spouses of asbestos workers and people living near asbestos plants.

Other Cancers. Asbestos workers have a higher than average rate of other cancers, particularly of the esophagus, stomach, and intestines. Asbestos-contaminated mucus, cleared from the lungs and swallowed, is thought

OCCUPATIONAL LUNG CANCER

Cigarette smoking is acknowledged to be the single most important cause of lung cancer. But considerable evidence now suggests that workplace air pollutants are significant causes as well. Many cancers, including lung cancer, occur more frequently in industrialized areas than in rural areas. And lung cancer occurs more frequently among workers handling a variety of substances, including arsenic, bis-chloromethyl ether, coal tar and pitch volatiles, petroleum, mustard gas, coal carbonization products, chromates, asbestos, x-rays, radium uranium, nickel, and isopropyl oil. Chemists, painters, and printers also seem to have an increased risk of lung cancer.

Cigarette smoking, added to the effects of industrial cancer-inducing agents, greatly increases the incidence of lung cancer in workers. Lung cancer, although very seldom curable, is largely preventable. Cigarettes are the single most important factor in lung cancer, but occupational substances that produce cancer can be controlled or replaced.

to be to blame. In recent years, the number of asbestos-related diseases has been increasing. Much tighter controls on all uses of asbestos are clearly needed as well as the use of substitute materials wherever possible.

DIAGNOSIS

Chest x-rays and tests of pulmonary function are used to diagnose asbestos-related lung disease.

TREATMENT

There is no treatment for these diseases. They are invariably fatal.

OTHER DUST-RELATED CONDITIONS

Many other dusts may accumulate in workers' lungs. At this point, most are not regarded as being disease-producing. But a number, such as aluminum, beryllium, carbon black, fiberglass, fuller's earth, kaolin, mica, talc, and tungsten carbide, have recognized adverse effects on lung health.

Some workers may be exposed to a variety of dusts; their worksites may include several different types of dust-producing materials. Other workers change industries and inhale first one kind of dust, then another. Pneumoconiosis caused by a mixture of dusts can be difficult to diagnose. As a general rule, the amount of fibrosis present is dependent on how much silica has been inhaled.

HYPERSENSITIVITY DISEASES

DEFINITION AND CAUSE

When a worker suffers an allergic reaction to substances in the work environment, he is considered to be suffering from a hypersensitivity disease, a condition classified as an occupational lung disease. Depending on its severity, it can be an annoyance or a precursor of serious illness.

Hypersensitivity reactions can occur in the large airways (bronchi), in the smallest airways (bronchioles), or in the alveoli, the terminal respiratory sacs. In general, the finer the dust inhaled, the smaller the passages into which it will go to cause a reaction.

TYPES OF OCCUPATIONAL HYPERSENSITIVITY

Occupational Asthma. About 10 percent of the population has a genetic tendency to develop allergies. These workers will be more likely to develop occupational asthma—an asthma attack in reaction to a substance in the workplace—than would others.

DIAGNOSIS

Some substances are known to provoke allergic reactions if there is sensitivity: detergent enzymes, platinum salts, cereals and grains, certain wood dusts, isocyanide chemicals used in polyurethane paints, some printing industry chemicals, and some pesticides. In the presence of these and other agents, the membranes lining the airways become swollen and inflamed, the victim's airways contract, and excess mucus makes respiration difficult.

TREATMENT

Once away from the source of distress, the person with occupational asthma should find relief. The obvious solution is for such a person to avoid employment that involves exposure to allergenic substances.

Allergic Alveolitis. "Farmer's lung" is the best known example of this hypersensitivity disease that is caused by fine organic dust inhaled into the alveoli, the lungs' smallest air spaces. The allergic reaction is caused by moldy hay, as well as by dusts from other organic substances, including moldy sugar cane, barley, maple bark, cork, animal hair, bird feathers and droppings, mushroom compost, coffee beans, and paprika. Isocyanide paint chemicals also have been shown to induce allergic alveolitis.

DIAGNOSIS

The allergic alveolitis reaction is characterized by a tired feeling, shortness of breath, dry cough, fever, and chills. The symptoms may last for 1 to 10 days. Sometimes emergency treatment and hospitalization are needed for acute attacks.

TREATMENT

Acute attacks may be treated with steroids and other drugs. Recovery from an episode can take up to 6 weeks, and there may be some lung damage. The farmer should change occupations or avoid storage techniques that promote mold—the trigger for the hypersensitive reaction.

Byssinosis. This hypersensitivity reaction occurs in cotton workers and among those in the flax and hemp industries. Commonly known as "Monday fever" or "brown lung," byssinosis is caused by parts of the cotton plant that are found in bales of cotton brought to the work environment for initial processing. Those who open fresh bales of cotton or those who do the first cleaning are at greatest risk for byssinosis.

DIAGNOSIS

The worker first experiences a feeling of tightness in the chest upon returning to work on Monday after a weekend away from the processing plant. (At no time is a fever associated with Monday fever.) Eventually, the tightness begins to persist into Tuesday, then into the rest of the workweek, and finally into weekends and other time off.

TREATMENT

If a worker leaves the industry, he or she generally recovers completely. Continued exposure, however, increases the risk of chronic bronchitis and emphysema. Under similar conditions, some people never develop Monday fever whereas others develop it soon after starting on the job. The progress of the disease also varies from worker to worker.

Industrial Bronchitis. A controversial disease, industrial bronchitis is either an entity caused by substances in the workplace or a misnomer for bronchitis produced by other irritants in various aspects of the worker's life, including cigarette smoking. The medical community has established that bronchitis is much more prevalent in industrialized areas and that occupational lung hazards do contribute to its development.

....

SUMMING UP: PREVENTION OF RESPIRATORY PROBLEMS

The human respiratory system not only provides oxygen to each cell of the body but also removes body wastes, filters out infectious agents, and provides the air needed for speech. Although the lungs are able to withstand abuse in the form of smoke and other pollutants, a number of disorders impair lung function. Some of these maladies are temporary and relatively harmless; others may be life-threatening. Any chronic breathing problem or other symptom such as blood in the sputum or a chronic cough should be checked promptly by a doctor.

The message is: Take care of your lungs and they will take care of you. Avoid pollutants, including tobacco smoke. Keep the body fit through good nutrition and appropriate exercise for your age and abilities. These measures, consistently carried out, promote resistance to airborne disease.

In addition to these personal measures, we can also take political measures to protect the quality of the air supply on which our lungs depend. Support the federal Environmental Protection Agency (EPA), which develops and maintains standards of ambient (outdoor) air

To improve your personal indoor air quality:

- **At Home.** If you have a room air purifier use it correctly: These machines require the user to breathe just in front of them to obtain the maximum benefit. The room must be tightly closed, and the machine selected must be powerful enough to adequately clean the air in the selected room. If room conditions are right, the most effective recirculating filters, according to the American Lung Association, are those that incorporate a chemical filter and a high-efficiency particulate filter. Regular maintenance—cleaning and filter replacement—is essential.
- **At the Office.** Install an air-purifying device for a building equipped with central air-conditioning. An engineering study should analyze the proper type and placement, particularly for large buildings.

quality under the Clean Air Act of 1970. This legislation is designed to protect the most sensitive individuals: those with allergic sensitivities, those for whom it has been determined pollutants are a health hazard, and those whose bodies and lungs are still developing and need defense.

In the workplace, the Department of Labor, through the Occupational Safety and Health Administration (OSHA), develops and maintains safe air-quality standards. The pollutant levels permitted in the workplace, presumably among healthy workers, are generally higher than those that are permissible in the general population.

With offices in Washington and major cities throughout the country, both agencies can answer questions about air quality. Other sources for information about air-quality standards are the National Clean Air Coalition in Washington and local affiliates of the American Lung Association. We all must learn what air pollution control laws are in effect in our local communities and report industries and individuals who violate these laws. At the same time, every responsible citizen should:

- Support regulation by participating in public hearings.
- Work with others for less-polluting solid waste disposal.
- Support public transportation; it can reduce auto pollution levels.
- Be sure that air pollution devices on the family car are working. Some states require emissions inspections of all motor vehicles.

- Check home heating systems to be sure they are operating properly.
- Refrain from burning trash. Many communities forbid garbage incineration.
- Keep house heat low; use electrical appliances as infrequently as possible. Use the car only when necessary.

- Use the appropriate grade of gasoline. Some areas require gasoline to have additives that reduce pollutants.
- Use the face mask provided by your employer. Be sure it fits your face well and filters the contaminants you are exposed to.

21
Diabetes and Other Endocrine Disorders

••••••••••••••••

DONALD A. HOLUB, M.D., AND THOMAS JACOBS, M.D.

The endocrine system is a complex network of glands or glandular tissue that secretes chemical messengers called hormones, which control many vital functions and affect virtually every organ system and part of the body. Among other functions, hormones control or regulate reproduction, growth, metabolism, and maintenance of the body's fluid balance. In conjunction with the nervous system, hormones enable us to react to both internal and external changes in our environment.

We still don't understand many facets of the endocrine system; periodically, researchers discover new facts about familiar hormones and uncover previously unidentified hormones.

HORMONES

These tissues or glands secrete hormones:

- Pituitary gland
- Thyroid gland
- Adrenal glands
- Parathyroid glands
- Ovaries
- Testes
- Pancreatic islets of Langerhans
- Thymus
- Kidneys
- Hypothalamus
- Gastrointestinal mucosa
- Pineal body

In general, the hormones produced in these glands and tissues (see figure 21.1) travel through the bloodstream and affect organs and tissues away from their origin. Other tissues produce "local" hormones or hormonelike substances, such as prostaglandins, with specific, localized functions, many of which are unknown or poorly understood.

Chemical derivation is used to classify many different types of hormones and their wide array of functions.

1. **Steroid hormones derived from cholesterol.** Steroid hormones include the sex hormones (testosterone, estrogen, progesterone, adrenal androgens); mineralocorticoids, which regulate the body's fluid and salt balance; and glucocorticoids, important regulators of glucose metabolism, which include cortisol, a so-called stress hormone. These hormones pass through their target cell membranes and act directly on the cell nuclei.

2. **Hormones derived from protein, peptides, or amino acids.** These include insulin, growth hormone, epinephrine (adrenaline), and many others that do not actually enter the target cells but attach themselves to specific receptor sites on the cell surface and work through other media—one of the most common is a substance called cyclic AMP—to perform their given functions.

The release of hormones may be triggered by nerve impulses, elaborate feedback systems involving other hormones or body substances, or a combination of the two. The various hormones circulate in very small quantities and have very specific target cells or receptors. All in all, the endocrine system is one of the body's most complex and finely tuned control systems; so long as the hormones maintain their delicate balance, you are not aware of just how many vital functions are being performed with amazing efficiency and interdependence. But when the system goes awry, usually because of too much or too little of one or more hormones, the resulting symptoms are often dramatic and even life-threatening.

In recent decades, tremendous gains have been made in diagnosing and treating many endocrine disorders. The discovery of insulin for the treatment of diabetes has saved hundreds of thousands of people from early death, and techniques for screening newborn infants for thyroid deficiency now help prevent cretinism, a particularly severe form of mental retardation. New tests capable of measuring even very minute hormone levels make it possible to diagnose endocrine disorders more accurately and to monitor treatment more effectively. This chapter describes common endocrine disorders.

DIABETES

DIABETES MELLITUS

General Definition

Diabetes mellitus is a chronic disease that renders the body unable to use carbohydrate properly, causing it to rely too predominantly on protein and fat for fuel. This condition affects many organs and body functions, especially those involved in metabolism.

Diabetes is the most common endocrine disorder, affecting about 13 million Americans, more than half of whom are unaware of their condition. Diabetes contributes to about 162,000 deaths per year, either directly or from kidney failure or cardiovascular disease, making it the seventh leading cause of death in the United States.

GENERAL CAUSES OF DIABETES

Diabetes mellitus is caused either by a lack of the hormone insulin (Type 1 diabetes) or the body's inability to use insulin (Type 2).

The insulin hormone is essential in carbohydrate metabolism, the process by which sugar and starches are broken down into glucose (blood sugar), the body's principal fuel. Insulin is produced by the pancreas, an endocrine gland located in the upper-middle abdomen. Scattered through the pancreas are clusters of hormone-producing tissue called the islets of Langerhans containing two types of cells: beta, which produce insulin, and alpha, which make glucagon. Normally these two hormones regulate blood glucose levels, causing almost all carbohydrate and about 50 to 60 percent of protein to be converted into glucose, which is consumed as fuel by almost every type of body cell (see figure 21.2).

NORMAL HORMONAL REGULATION OF GLUCOSE

After eating, almost all of the carbohydrate absorbed from food passes through the liver, where 55 to 60 per-

cent is stored as glycogen and the rest is returned to the circulation as glucose for use by the brain, red blood cells, muscle, and fat tissue. When glucose rises after a meal, the pancreas secretes insulin, which increases the uptake of glucose by body tissues or promotes its conversion to fatty tissue (see figure 21.3).

Insulin uptake by the cells is a complicated process not fully understood. Cells requiring insulin in order to utilize glucose have specific insulin receptors; when insulin binds to these receptors, changes take place within the cell that enables it to burn glucose.

When the glucose level drops, the pancreas releases glucagon, which stimulates the liver to release stored glycogen, convert it back to glucose, and raise the blood sugar level.

DIABETIC (ABNORMAL) HANDLING OF GLUCOSE

If you are diabetic, your cells are unable to use the glucose circulating in the bloodstream. Thinking it's starving, your body begins burning its own fat and muscle—a potentially dangerous process. Acidic by-products of the breakdown of fat, such as ketones, may accumulate in

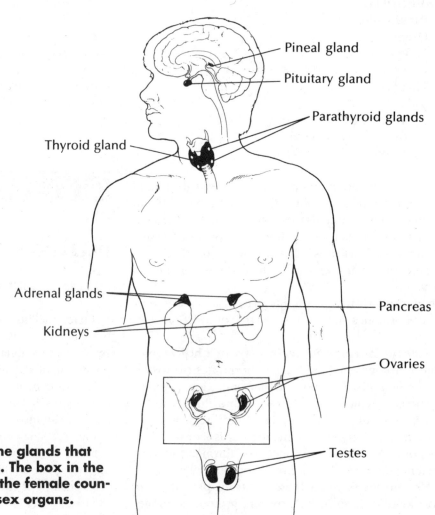

Figure 21.1: Shown here are the glands that make up the endocrine system. The box in the abdomen of this figure shows the female counterpart of the male endocrine sex organs.

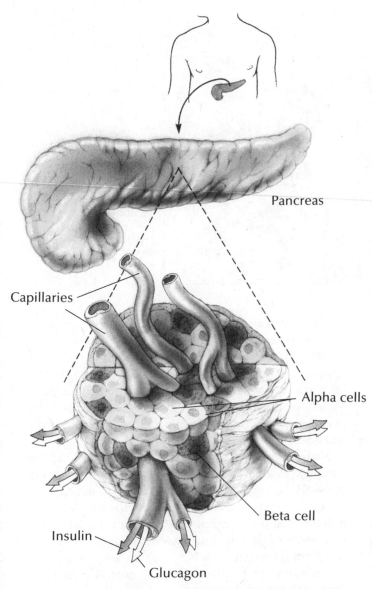

Pancreas

Capillaries

Alpha cells

Beta cell

Insulin

Glucagon

Figure 21.2: Insulin is manufactured in tiny clusters of cells known as islets of Langerhans, which are scattered throughout the pancreas. Within these islets are alpha cells, which secrete glucagon, and beta cells, which secrete insulin. This schematic drawing shows an islet, with the capillaries entering and insulin being released into these minute blood vessels, which carry it throughout the body.

the blood, causing a condition called ketoacidosis, which if untreated can lead to coma and death.

TYPES OF DIABETES

There are two distinct types of diabetes mellitus: Type 1, in which the beta cells cease to produce insulin, and Type 2, in which the beta cells produce varying amounts

of insulin (there may or may not be a shortage), but the body is unable to use it effectively.

Type 1, also referred to as juvenile diabetes, insulin-dependent diabetes, or ketosis-prone diabetes, usually begins in the first three decades of life, but there are exceptions; a small percentage develop the disease after the age of 30. Type 1 is the more serious form of diabetes; before the discovery of insulin in the early 1920s, most Type 1 diabetic patients died of ketoacidosis or other complications of the disease within a few years of its onset.

People with Type 2 diabetes outnumber those with Type 1 about 9 to 1, and most of the estimated 6.5 million undiagnosed diabetics also fall into this category. The majority of Type 2 diabetics are middle-aged or older and overweight.

RISK FACTORS FOR DIABETES MELLITUS

Although the reasons for the malfunctions that result in either Type 1 and Type 2 diabetes are unknown, a number of predisposing and precipitating factors have been identified.

1. **Family History of Diabetes.** Increases the risk for both types of diabetes, indicating a possible genetic predisposition for the condition.

2. **Fault in the Immune System.** May be a factor in Type 1 diabetes. Some researchers believe that in certain genetically susceptible people, an infection of the pancreas may prompt the immune system, in effect, to turn on itself and destroy the insulin-producing beta cells. This theory is bolstered by the fact that diabetes often ensues soon after a viral infection, such as the flu, chickenpox, or bad cold. Antibodies from the immune system designed to attack beta cells of the pancreas can be found in the blood of most people destined to develop Type 1 diabetes.

3. **Pregnancy.** Pregnancy may precipitate diabetes, particularly in obese women over the age of 30 who have a family history of diabetes. About half of these women develop Type 1 diabetes later in life.

4. **Insulin Resistance.** Because the pancreas continues to produce at least some insulin in Type 2 diabetes, this form of the disease is blamed more on insulin resistance (the body is not using the hormone effectively) than on insulin deficiency or pancreatic failure. Studies have found that some Type 2 patients actually produce normal or higher than normal amounts of insulin.

Studies have found patients with Type 2 diabetes may have abnormal insulin receptors, but this is not a universal finding, indicating that there are still other factors involved. Also, some Type 2 patients produce progressively less insulin and, in time, may require insulin replacement.

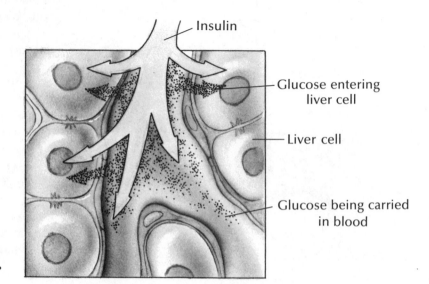

Insulin

Glucose entering liver cell

Liver cell

Glucose being carried in blood

Figure 21.3: Schematic drawing showing the role of insulin in regulating blood sugar. In the presence of insulin, glucose is absorbed from the blood into the body cells, which require it for fuel.

5. Obesity. Fat tissue is known to increase insulin resistance, and since people with Type 2 diabetes are often overweight there has been a tendency to attribute their diabetes to obesity. However, this now appears to be an oversimplification, and factors other than the obesity are also believed to be involved, although these have not been clearly identified.

6. Certain Drugs, Infection, and Trauma. Linked to the onset of Type 2 diabetes in some patients.

GENERAL DIAGNOSIS OF DIABETES

Diabetes is an ancient disease, documented as far back as 1500 B.C. in Egypt. Greek physicians gave the disease its name based on its symptoms: *diabetes* means "siphon" or "fountain," referring to the copious urination characteristic of the disease in its early, untreated state. These early doctors also observed that diabetic urine had a sweet odor and taste; therefore the term *mellitus,* which comes from the Latin word for "honey." As glucose builds up in the blood, some of it spills over into the urine and is excreted. The earliest tests for diabetes involved smelling and even tasting the urine for sweetness; even today, cases of unsuspected diabetes may be first discovered by finding sugar in a routine urine test.

If you have one or more of these symptoms, you may have diabetes:

1. Unexplainable, excessive, almost insatiable thirst
2. Frequent urination
3. Unusual hunger
4. Unexplainable weight loss

You may also feel weak; experience mood swings; suffer an increased vulnerability to infection (such as slow-healing cuts or increased vaginal infections in women); fatigue; leg cramps or pins and needles sensations in the toes and fingers; impotence; blurred vision. Sometimes these symptoms are ignored until the approach of ketoacidosis (acid blood), which is marked by a fruity, sweetish breath odor, tremendous thirst, weakness, dryness of the tongue and skin, nausea, and vomiting. Untreated, this can progress to diabetic coma and death.

Many symptoms of diabetes do not appear until an advanced stage of the disease, and large numbers of people with mild diabetes (usually Type 2) do not have any noticeable signs of the disease. A doctor may be alerted to the condition when routine blood or urine tests show high levels of glucose, but sugar in the urine (glycosuria) is not always a sign of diabetes; it may simply mean that the kidneys are unable to handle normal amounts of sugar and are excreting some of it in the urine. Conversely, some people with diabetes do not have glycosuria, or have it only erratically. Therefore, urine tests do not give a definitive diagnosis of diabetes; instead, diabetes is determined by testing the blood for glucose.

To tell whether you have diabetes, you may have to take several measurements of blood sugar. In Type 1 diabetic patients, diagnosis is usually straightforward because the pancreas is producing little or no insulin. Here's what to expect from the diagnostic tests for diabetes:

1. Fasting Blood Glucose. After an overnight fast and before eating anything in the morning, you give a morning blood sample. If two separate tests are positive (more than 140 milligrams of glucose per deciliter of blood [140 mg/dl]), a diagnosis of diabetes is established.

2. Elevated Fasting Blood Glucose. If your fasting blood glucose is high, more than 115 mg/dl, but less than 140 mg/dl, you might have to take additional tests if you have symptoms that suggest diabetes. No symptoms and no family history of the disease may mean no further tests at this point, but you will be asked to return for periodic blood sugar measurements. If you are overweight, you may be instructed to go on a weight-reduction diet and increase exercise.

3. **Oral Glucose Tolerance Test.** If further tests are indicated, you are given an oral glucose tolerance test. This test measures the body's reaction to consumption of a large amount of sugar or glucose. To help ensure accurate results, it is important that you follow specific instructions for several days before the test. Prior to the glucose tolerance test you should consume at least 100 to 150 g of carbohydrate per day for the 3 preceding days. (See food table later in this chapter for carbohydrate content of typical foods and portions.)

Lack of exercise also can skew the results of a glucose tolerance test. If you are sedentary—particularly if you are hospitalized or confined to bed—your blood glucose will be higher than in normally active people. Pregnancy also alters glucose levels; therefore, different criteria are used to diagnose diabetes at this time. In addition, liver disorders, previous gastrointestinal surgery, and certain other illnesses and a number of drugs can alter the results of a glucose tolerance test.

Before undergoing a glucose tolerance test, ask your doctor to detail special instructions you should follow; also be sure your doctor is aware of your medical history and any drugs you are taking.

A positive glucose tolerance test still does not definitively establish that you have or will develop overt diabetes. Studies involving several hundred patients found that only 22.9 percent of the 401 patients who had positive results actually developed symptomatic diabetes over the next 5 years, and most of these patients were in the top range, with very high blood glucose (200 mg/dl) after 2 or 3 hours, or they had other risk factors, such as a family history of the disease, were over the age of 50, or were overweight. At one time, doctors labeled many of these borderline cases "prediabetic," a term now discouraged for its inaccuracy (most of these people never developed diabetes) and detrimental psychological and economic effects.

- People with diabetes (or "prediabetic") often cannot get insurance or are charged very high premiums.
- Some employers are reluctant to hire or promote employees with diabetes even though their work and attendance records may be superior to those of a nondiabetic peer.

Although these borderline patients should undergo periodic testing and follow commonsense preventive measures, they should not be considered sick. Oral glucose tolerance tests are now rarely used because of their ambiguous results.

TREATMENT

The specific treatments for the two types of diabetes are quite different.

1. Type 1 diabetes requires insulin injections coordinated with diet and exercise to control blood glucose.
2. Most people with Type 2 diabetes do not require insulin injections (although there are exceptions); instead, most can initially be treated by diet, exercise, and, if needed, drugs that increase the body's ability to utilize insulin. (Later in life, however, most require insulin.)

Although there is no cure for diabetes, most people with diabetes can adequately control their disease and lead relatively normal, productive lives. Today, the majority of Type 1 diabetes patients can lead reasonably normal lives by taking regular insulin injections. Fortunately, of the two types of diabetes, the more serious Type 1 is less common, affecting about 10 percent of the total diabetic population.

With some exceptions, Type 2 diabetes occurs most frequently during middle age or pregnancy. This condition is more prevalent in overweight people, and most cases can be controlled by weight loss, diet, and exercise. Oral hypoglycemics, drugs that help the body make more effective use of its own insulin, may be prescribed with or without supplementary insulin for Type 2 diabetic patients whose disease is not adequately controlled by diet and exercise.

The goals of treating both Type 1 and Type 2 diabetes are essentially the same: to minimize both short- and long-term complications by normalizing levels of blood glucose. Normal blood glucose for a nonfasting test is defined as falling between a low of 50 mg/dl and a high of 140 mg/dl. Some doctors are more permissive about the upper level, and consider blood sugars hovering in around 200 mg/dl acceptable. Studies have found, however, that complications are most likely to be minimized if blood glucose can be controlled in the 50 to 140 mg/dl range.

LIFESTYLE MODIFICATIONS

A moderate lifestyle, which is increasingly advocated by physicians and other health professionals for the entire population, is an important aspect of living with diabetes. Even though diabetes demands constant attention, people with diabetes still can do almost anything in moderation; many of the restrictions enforced in the past have yielded to new understanding of the disease and its control. As a result of this freedom, people with diabetes have risen to the top of their chosen careers in business, politics, sports, and many other fields.

The good health habits described throughout this book apply to everyone, both the healthy and those with diabetes. But there are some areas that are particularly important if you have diabetes.

- **Smoking.** Cigarette smoking compounds many of the complications of diabetes: It hinders circulation, promotes heart disease, and damages numerous other body systems that already are increasingly vulnerable because of diabetes. While no one interested in good health should smoke, this is doubly true if you are diabetic, particularly if you suffer circulatory or cardiovascular complications.
- **Diet.** In moderation, those with diabetes can now enjoy foods that were once forbidden on most diabetic diets. Some planning and food preparation may have to be made, but there are now few foods or activities that are strictly forbidden.

EMERGENCY TREATMENT

People with diabetes—and anyone else with a hidden medical condition—should always carry an obvious form of identification to alert doctors or other caregivers to the disorder.

Medic Alert, one such system, is organized by the Medic Alert Foundation, a nonprofit organization founded by a California physician. Medic Alert provides identification emblems that members wear, as well as a wallet card and other identification material that immediately indicate the wearer has a medical problem that may require prompt treatment. Identification is especially important if a person with diabetes lapses into unconsciousness or is injured in an accident and is unable to speak. The Medic Alert bracelet and card contain the wearer's identification number and a telephone number that can be called collect for specific medical information about the person. A lifelong membership covers the cost of the Medic Alert bracelet or necklace, the wallet card that is reissued annually, and the 24-hour emergency telephone service. The fee is tax-deductible. Information is available from Medic Alert Foundation International, P.O. Box 1009, Turlock, CA 95381.

TYPE 1 DIABETES

DEFINITION

See "General Definition" of diabetes in this chapter.

DIAGNOSIS

For symptoms and diagnosis, see "General Diagnosis of Diabetes."

TREATMENT

Insulin Treatment. Before two Canadian researchers discovered insulin in 1921, the only treatment for Type 1 diabetes, in which the beta cells cease to produce insulin, was a rigorous diet low in calories and carbohydrate. This approach prolonged the lives of some diabetic patients, but without insulin, most died of the disease within a few months or years. While the discovery of insulin represented great progress, it is not a cure and must be injected regularly for a lifetime.

Stomach acid destroys proteins like insulin, so the hormone cannot be taken orally but must be injected. Most people with Type 1 diabetes inject insulin into the subcutaneous tissue just under the skin but some use insulin pumps, portable computerized devices designed to administer constant small amounts of insulin (as well as larger amounts after meals and in other circumstances) through an indwelling needle and catheter. These devices are still experimental and are not appropriate for certain types of patients. Other possible methods of insulin administration, such as by inhalation or in an oral form that would not be degraded by digestive juices, are under study but are not yet available.

There are three basic types of insulin.

1. Fast-acting (e.g., Regular or Semilente), which takes effect in 30 to 60 minutes and has a total duration of action lasting 4 to 6 hours
2. Intermediate-acting (e.g., NPH or Lente), which takes effect in 3 to 4 hours and has a total duration of 20 to 24 hours
3. Long-acting (e.g., Ultralente or PZI), which takes effect in 6 to 8 hours and lasts 32 hours or longer.

If your diabetes is mild, it may take only a single daily insulin dose combining a fast-acting and intermediate- or long-acting insulin to keep the condition under control. Increasingly, however, experts recommend multiple daily injections, frequently a combination of fast- and intermediate-acting insulin to prevent the highs and lows in blood glucose common with single-dose regimens and allow for a more flexible lifestyle. In any event, persons with diabetes should recognize the different types of insulins, know when each will reach its peak of action (see table 21.1), and understand how to match insulin with food and exercise to maintain as normal a level of blood glucose as possible.

Physicians differ on the best insulin strategy, and no one regimen works for all or even most patients. Each treatment schedule must be customized to meet the needs and lifestyle of each individual; schedules may need to be adjusted frequently as circumstances change. For example, insulin needs rise during periods of physiological stress or infection. Insulin requirements rise markedly during pregnancy, the adolescent growth

TABLE 21.1: ORAL HYPOGLYCEMIC AGENTS

Generic Name	Brand Name	Times Taken (Per Day)	Onset of Action	Duration of Action (Hr)
Acetohexamide	Dymelor	1–2	1–2 hr	12–24
Chlorpropamide	Diabinese	1	Several days	60
Glipizide	Glucotrol	1–3	30 min	Up to 24
Glyburide	Micronase, DiaBeta	1–2	30 min	12 or more
Tolazamide	Tolinase	1–2	3–4 hr	12–24
Tolbutamide	Orinase	2–3	1 hr	6–8

spurt, and during periods of insulin resistance or acidosis, while those who exercise require a good deal less insulin than sedentary or even normally active people.

These many variables may be confusing and discouraging for those newly diagnosed with diabetes. But most people with diabetes quickly understand how to adjust insulin, food, and exercise to control blood sugar; learn to monitor blood glucose; and test their urine periodically for sugar and ketones.

LIFESTYLE MODIFICATIONS

Diet. Diet is a crucial factor in the overall management of Type 1 diabetes. The precise diet depends upon the individual, the physician, and the consulting dietitian, but most regimens recommend that 50 to 60 percent of the total calories come from carbohydrates, mainly in the form of starches or complex carbohydrates. The remaining calories break down as 20 to 25 percent from protein, and 20 to 30 percent from fats. In addition to counting calories and distributing them among the nutrient groups, it is also important to follow a regular meal/snack pattern that often consists of three meals and one to three snacks consumed throughout the day. (For more information on planning a healthy diet, see chapter 5.)

The eating schedule for someone with diabetes depends upon the type of insulin used and other needs. Once blood sugar is normalized, most people find they can adopt a diet and meal pattern suitable for their individual lifestyle and food preferences. But diet planning often requires careful planning with a dietitian, physician, or diabetes educator.

Counseling. People who are diagnosed with Type 1 diabetes often feel overwhelmed by the number of facts and techniques they are called upon to master. To overcome this feeling, many physicians feel that patient education is best accomplished in a hospital setting, where diabetes can be brought under control while being supervised by health professionals. At the same time, the doctor, diabetes educator, dietitian, exercise physiologist, and other involved health professionals can spend the time needed to teach the basics and monitoring techniques that are important in ongoing treatment. Although close supervision by and rapport with the treating physician are vital elements in successful diabetes control, in the final analysis, day-to-day treatment is the patient's responsibility.

Even children as young as 7 or 8 years of age with diabetes should learn how to inject their own insulin and how to monitor blood and urine. Although many people are reluctant to inject themselves, this is one of the first techniques that must be practiced. Once mastered, most people find the injections relatively painless and almost routine. (Figures 21.4–21.15 show how to mix and inject insulin.)

Even when diabetes is being well controlled, most patients occasionally experience episodes of hyperglycemia (high blood sugar) or hypoglycemia (low blood sugar). Knowing how to handle these episodes is important for self-management: Dealing with high blood sugar, for example, may require skipping a meal, exercising for a few minutes, or increasing the insulin dosage. (In general, a unit of insulin will lower blood glucose by 20 to 60 mg/dl, depending upon the cause of the hyperglycemia and individual response to insulin. But if a urine test shows the presence of ketones, a doctor should be consulted immediately.)

Hypoglycemia, or low blood sugar, can result from too much insulin, a delayed meal, or an unusual amount of exercise and usually causes sudden weakness, faintness, sweating, and tremors or palpitations. Usually this condition can be successfully handled by consuming a source of simple sugar. To prevent bouncing—oscillating between states of hyper- and hypoglycemia—the simple sugar should be combined with a protein source to provide a delayed, slower infusion of glucose. One method is to drink a few ounces of orange juice (a

TABLE 21.2: CARBOHYDRATE CONTENT OF COMMON FOODS

These charts list the approximate carbohydrate content per serving for common foods. (Since a substantial amount of protein is also converted to glucose during metabolism, the protein content is also indicated.)

Milk and Milk Products

Skim Milk
8 oz. cup contains:
Carbohydrate: 12 grams
Protein: 8 grams
Calories: 80

Whole Milk
8 oz. cup contains:
Carbohydrate: 12 grams
Protein: 8 grams
Calories: 150

Consult nutritional labels for carbohydrate content of yogurt and other milk products.

Nonstarchy Vegetables

Serving size: ½ cup cooked
Carbohydrate: 5 grams
Protein: 2 grams

Asparagus	Greens (cooked)
Bean sprouts	Kale
Beets	Mushrooms
Broccoli	Mustard
Brussels sprouts	Okra
Cabbage	Onions
Carrots	Rutabaga
Cauliflower	Sauerkraut
Chards	Spinach
Collards	String beans
Dandelion	Summer squash
Eggplant	Tomatoes
Green beans	Turnips
Green pepper	Zucchini

Serving size: 1 cup raw

Cabbage	Watercress
Celery	Spinach
Chinese cabbage	Starches: breads, cereals, grains, and starchy vegetables
Cucumber	
Endive	
Escarole	Tomatoes
Lettuce	Tomato juice (½ cup)
Parsley	Vegetable juice cocktail (½ cup)
Radishes	

For more precise amounts, consult nutritional labels. Many items, particularly breads and cereals, very greatly in carbohydrate content. If labels are not available, the following can be used to calculate approximate amounts.

Nonstarred items contain:
Carbohydrate: 16 grams per serving

Starred items contain:
Carbohydrate: 20 grams per serving
Protein: 2 grams per serving

Item	Serving Size
Bread	
White, Italian, French, whole wheat, rye, pumpernickel, raisin	1 average slice
Pita bread	½ large or 1 small
Bagel, small	1 oz. (about ⅓)
English muffin	½
Plain roll, small	1 oz.
Frankfurter roll	1 oz. (about 1 roll)
Hamburger roll	1 oz. (about ½ roll)
Tortilla, 6 in. diameter	1 oz. (approx. 1)
Biscuit, 2 in. diameter	1 oz.
Bread crumbs	¼ cup
Bread sticks	¾ oz.
Bread stuffing*	½ cup
Cornbread stuffing	⅛ cup
Croutons	¾ oz.
Corn bread stuffing	⅛ cup
Croutons	¾ oz.
Corn bread	1.5 oz.
Corn or bran muffin	1 oz. (½ muffin)
Popover	2 oz.
Crackers (serving sizes are numbers of crackers)	
Animal crackers	10
Arrowroot	2
Graham crackers, 2.5 in. square	3
Matzo, 6 in. square	⅔
Melba toast, thin slice	5
Oyster	21
Ritz	7
Rye wafers, 2 in. by 3.25 in.	3
Saltines	7
Soda	3
Triscuits	5
Uneeda Biscuits	4
Vanilla Wafers	5
Wheat Thins	12
Zwieback	3

TABLE 21.2: CARBOHYDRATE CONTENT OF COMMON FOODS (Cont.)

Item	Serving Size	Item	Serving Size
Cereal		**Starchy Vegetables**	
Bran flakes	½ cup	Baked beans	⅓ cup
Puffed cereal	1 cup	Dried lentils	½ cup
Cooked cereal	½ cup	Kidney beans	⅓ cup
Cooked grits*	⅓ cup	Corn niblets (cooked)	½ cup
		Corn on the cob	½ ear
Grains		Lima beans	⅔ cup
Barley, cooked	½ cup	Mixed vegetables	⅔ cup
Rice, soaked*	½ cup	Parsnips, diced	⅔ cup
Pasta	½ cup	Peas, green	¾ cup
Popcorn, air popped	3 cups	Plantain, green, 5 in. long	½ fruit
Cornstarch	2 Tbs.	Potato, white with skin	3 oz
Flour, all purpose	2.5 Tbs.	Mashed potato with milk	⅔ cup
Wheat germ	3 Tbs.	Pumpkin, canned	¾ cup
Pancake, 5-in. diameter	1.5 oz.	Squash, acorn	¾ cup
Couscous*	½ cup	Yam/Sweet potato, with skin	⅓ cup

quick source of sugar) followed by a glass of milk or a slice of bread and cheese to provide a slower, more sustained release of glucose. This should be followed by a blood sugar measurement 15 or 20 minutes after eating to ensure that blood glucose has returned to normal. If blood sugar is still too low, an additional juice or a second glass of milk may be necessary. Because individuals differ in their metabolism, what works for one person may not be best for another. Most people with diabetes devise a strategy that works best for them; any individual with Type 1 diabetes should always have a convenient, quickly accessible source of simple sugar available at all times (such as sugar cubes, candy, orange juice, or similar foods). Bear in mind, however, that eating a simple sugar alone may cause the undesired yo-yo effect while combining the simple sugar with a protein, and perhaps a complex carbohydrate such as a slice of bread, will often moderate the change in blood sugar status.

Self-Monitoring. In recent years, the treatment of diabetes, particularly Type 1, has been revolutionized by the development of simple, relatively inexpensive tests that enable both physician and patient to determine the effectiveness of treatment. Previously, patients monitored their diabetes with daily urine tests for the presence of sugar and ketones. Although these tests can detect markedly out-of-control diabetes and the presence of ketones, they are not very meaningful for day-to-day diabetes management or in tracking an episode of hypoglycemia. Even when their blood glucose climbs, not everyone with diabetes "spills" sugar into the urine. Conversely, others, such as pregnant diabetics, with altered kidney function may have sugar in the urine even though blood levels are in the normal range, and still others do not even show sugar in the urine until blood levels have already returned to normal. Consequently, urine tests are not very helpful in indicating the present level of blood glucose and therefore are not useful in revealing what immediate or long-term action, if any, should be taken.

Today it is possible to self-test—measure your own blood sugar—something that previously required laboratory analysis. The procedure takes just 2 or 3 minutes, is low cost (requiring a modest expenditure for chemically treated strips, a glucose meter, and pads or tissues), is easy enough for a child to master, and can be carried out in most places and situations.

In this test, you prick a finger with a spring loaded lancet device, draw a couple of drops of blood, and follow the simple instructions included with the test. The test results reveal whether blood sugar is too high or too low at any given moment so you can take appropriate corrective action.

Self-monitoring—with a daily diary recording blood glucose measurements, food intake, and other relevant facts (see figure 21.16)—is crucial for long-term treatment. This diary forms a permanent record from which both your doctor and you can draw an overall picture of treatment effectiveness and discern problem situations. The diary helps you plan more effectively; if you know that a certain event or situation is likely to raise or lower blood sugar, you can take preventive measures, a practice that gives you mastery over the disease and a feeling that you, not the disease, are in control.

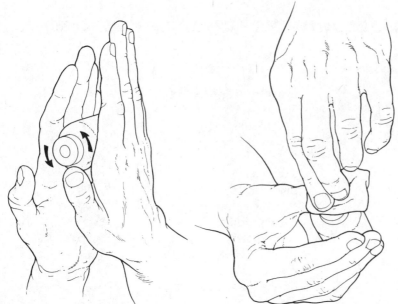

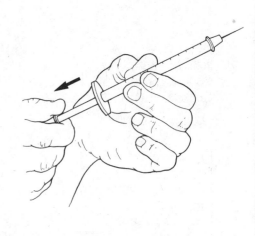

Figure 21.4: To mix the insulin, gently roll the bottle, but do not shake—this will cause air bubbles to form.

Figure 21.5: Wipe the bottle top with an alcohol swab to minimize contamination and chance of infection.

Figure 21.6: After checking the syringe, withdraw the plunger to the needed dosage and draw air into the syringe.

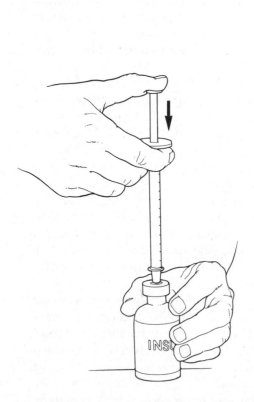

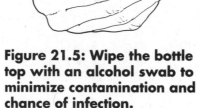

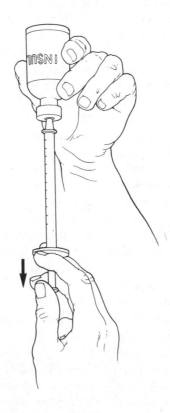

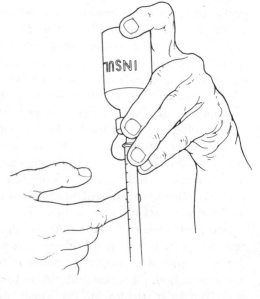

Figure 21.7: Insert the syringe needle into the insulin bottle and push the plunger down to inject air into the bottle.

Figure 21.8: With the bottle upside down, pull out plunger until it is about five units beyond dosage.

Figure 21.9: Carefully examine the syringe to make sure there are no air bubbles. If there are, gently tap the syringe until the bubbles move to the top. Now push the plunger back to the exact dosage and remove the syringe from the bottle. You are now ready to inject the insulin.

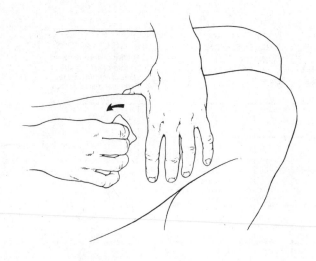

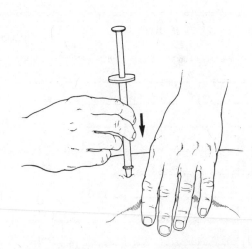

Figure 21.10: Select a site that has not been used recently and carefully wash it with an alcohol swab.

Figure 21.11: Gather up a fold of skin and insert the needle at a 45° to 90° angle.

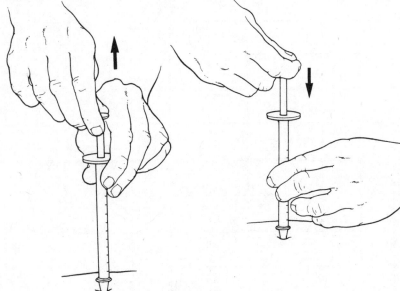

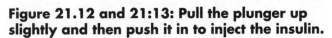

Figure 21.14: Remove the needle and gently cleanse the site with an alcohol swab. Do not rub, however, as this may hasten insulin uptake.

Figure 21.12 and 21:13: Pull the plunger up slightly and then push it in to inject the insulin.

Figure 21.15: Injection sites should be rotated to prevent damage to any particular area from too frequent shots. Insulin may be injected in any of the shaded areas indicated on the figures at right. Most patients work out a rotation schedule (e.g., the right forearm, left forearm, abdomen, right thigh front, left thigh front, and then a similar rotation for the back), altering it to avoid areas that may become lumpy or hard. Any signs of inflammation or infection at an injection site should be checked promptly by a doctor.

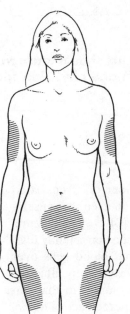
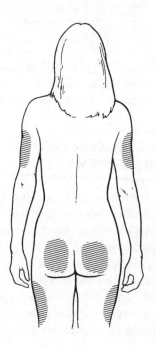

DATE AND WEIGHT		INSULIN				AM Ketones		URINE AND BLOOD GLUCOSE TESTS									EXPLANATIONS: Activity, illness, time and change of eating patterns, time of insulin reactions with blood sugar and treatment.
		Morning	Lunch	Supper	Bed Time			BREAKFAST		LUNCH		DINNER		Bed Time	During Night		
								Before	2 Hrs. After	Before	2 Hrs. After	Before	2 Hrs. After				
	S						B/G										
	I																
Supp. Insulin							S/A										
	S						B/G										
	I																
Supp. Insulin							S/A										
	S						B/G										
	I																
Supp. Insulin							S/A										
	S						B/G										
	I																
Supp. Insulin							S/A										
	S						B/G										
	I																
Supp. Insulin							S/A										
	S						B/G										
	I																
Supp. Insulin							S/A										
	S						B/G										
	I																
Supp. Insulin							S/A										

Figure 21.16: All diabetic patients should learn to keep a careful diary, such as the model shown here. This will help both patient and physician spot patterns that are likely to cause problems and to take corrective action.

GLYCOSYLATED HEMOGLOBIN MEASUREMENT

Physicians find that the measurement of glycosylated hemoglobin from a blood sample is an even more useful test of overall blood glucose control. Glycosylated hemoglobin is a compound that forms when consistently high levels of blood glucose alter the red blood cells over time (glucose molecules become permanently attached to hemoglobin, the red blood cell component that carries oxygen). Normally, only a small percentage of hemoglobin is glycosylated, but in poorly controlled diabetes, the level of glycosylated hemoglobin, expressed as hemoglobin Alc, climbs much higher, often to 12 percent or more. A high reading in this test indicates blood glucose levels elevated over the previous month or 6 weeks; a reading in the normal range means that blood glucose has been normal during that period. A Type 1 diabetic is tested about every 3 months; a Type 2 diabetic, every 3 to 6 months. Regular self-monitoring combined with periodic measurements of glycosylated hemoglobin provide a valuable indication of how well diabetes is being controlled.

DIABETES IN CHILDHOOD AND ADOLESCENCE

Type 1 diabetes very often appears during childhood or adolescence, creating special problems for the entire family. Before the discovery of insulin, few diabetic children survived to adulthood; today, the large majority not only survive but also are able to participate in school and other normal childhood activities, although they face many medical and emotional difficulties along the way. Designing effective treatment often involves counseling the entire family, since the attitudes of parents, siblings, and even close friends are crucial in creating an environment for healthy development and also for treating a difficult disease requiring almost constant attention.

If your child has diabetes, it is vital that you and your child establish a good rapport with the physician overseeing treatment. The treating physician may be a pediatrician experienced in dealing with diabetes, an endocrinologist, internist, or family physician who is accustomed to treating diabetic children. Many doctors are attuned to treating short-term diseases or medical crises; diabetes, however, is a lifelong disease that may involve occasional emergencies but is more likely to demand careful day-to-day attention, support, and patient education. In addition, childhood or adolescent diabetes creates its own special problems related to growth.

Insulin dosages are often difficult to gauge; the viral infections, growth spurts, emotional instability, and erratic exercise and eating patterns typical of childhood can have a profound effect on insulin requirements. Your youngster should understand that diabetes is serious but can be managed in such a way that he or she can participate in normal family, school, and social activities and responsibilities. Take care not to let the disease hamper normal development but try to find a reasonable course of action allowing a normal lifestyle, while complying with necessary treatment.

The treatment program is often conceived while the child is hospitalized, allowing doctors, dietitians, and other members of the treatment team a chance both to stabilize the disease and teach the child and family the basics of diabetes management. While your child is very young, the burden of treatment rests with the parents; both parents and child must overcome fears of getting and giving injections. In most instances, the injections quickly become a part of daily routine and cease to be a source of fear or anxiety. As soon as possible, children should learn to administer their own injections, usually by the time they are 7 or 8 years old, although parental supervision may still be needed. At the same time, children of this age can be taught the basics of testing their own blood and urine.

Adolescence creates a new set of problems, both among those who acquired diabetes at an earlier age and among the newly diagnosed. One of life's most turbulent periods, adolescence results in hormonal changes, growth spurts, and emotional instability that sometimes triggers diabetes; these occurrences all make the disease more difficult to manage. At this stage of life, young people need to declare their independence; a diabetic child who has managed very well up to this point may suddenly rebel and let the disease slip out of control. Peer pressures and the need for peer acceptance become very important. Parents are understandably worried about the consequences of poorly controlled diabetes; at the same time, the adolescent has a compelling need to become independent of parental control.

Until recently, tight control of blood glucose was not the major objective in treating young diabetics; instead, the strategy was to get the patient through the difficult growing and adolescent years, and then to try to establish a better treatment program during young adulthood. A major drawback of this approach was the frequent onset of serious kidney disease, eye problems, and other long-term complications by adulthood. Today physicians place more emphasis on working with the child and family to normalize blood glucose as much as possible and still permit normal development. Again, self-monitoring is an important part of this strategy because by learning what is involved in good diabetes control and having the tools to monitor progress, children are more likely to assume the responsibility for self-treatment. Adolescent support groups are very helpful for aiding young people in their struggles with their disease and the instability typical of their age.

TYPE 2 DIABETES

DEFINITION

See "General Definition" of diabetes.

DIAGNOSIS

For symptoms and diagnosis of Type 2 diabetes, see "General Diagnosis of Diabetes."

TREATMENT

In Type 2 diabetes the beta cells of the pancreas produce varying amounts of insulin, but the body is unable to use it effectively. Although this type of diabetes may not carry the same risk of death from ketoacidosis, it does involve many of the same risks of complications as Type 1 diabetes. The goal of treatment is to normalize blood glucose in an attempt to prevent or minimize these complications.

People with Type 2 diabetes may experience marked hyperglycemia, but most do not require insulin injections. In fact, 80 percent of all Type 2 diabetes patients can be treated with diet, exercise, and, if needed, oral drugs to lower blood sugar (hypoglycemic agents).

LIFESTYLE MODIFICATIONS

Diet. If you have Type 2 diabetes and do not require insulin you don't have to follow the dietary restrictions of Type 1. For instance, you don't need to distribute your total calories over a specific number of meals and snacks, nor is it so important to distribute the calories among the 3 nutrient groups. But you should lower your fat consumption while increasing consumption of complex carbohydrates and fiber. Hypoglycemia is not a problem in Type 2 diabetes; therefore, you don't need to eat extra food to prevent low blood sugar while exercising.

Type 2 diabetes does necessitate restriction of total calories unless your weight is normal. (If you don't need to lose weight, you may have to take oral hypoglycemic drugs.) These restricted-calorie diets are difficult for many to adhere to, as anyone who has repeatedly tried to diet knows. To cope with the difficulty of dieting, people with Type 2 diabetes are given various techniques: behavior modification, peer support groups, hypnosis, group therapy, and intensive patient education. While any one of these approaches works for some people, the overall success rate remains low.

Exercise. Regular aerobic exercise is an important method for treating both Type 1 and Type 2 diabetes since it decreases insulin resistance and helps burn excessive glucose. Regular exercise also may help lower blood lipids and reduce some effects of stress, both important factors in treating diabetes and preventing complications.

Drugs. Oral hypoglycemic drugs may be prescribed for normal-weight people with Type 2 diabetes or for those patients whose blood glucose is not controlled by diet and exercise. These drugs fall into two categories:

1. Diguanides (phenformin): rarely used in the United States anymore because of their potential for serious side effects.
2. Sulfonylureal agents: widely used and available under several different brand names with somewhat different formulations. As their name indicates, these drugs are closely related to the sulfa drugs, which were the major antibiotics before penicillin was discovered. These drugs have been used to lower blood glucose in diabetes since the

1950s (studies during World War II had found that laboratory animals given sulfa drugs developed severe hypoglycemia). These drugs do not help people with Type 1 diabetes, but they can be quite effective for individuals who still produce some insulin. Initially, the drugs appear to stimulate the pancreas to produce more insulin, but after the insulin production returns to previous levels (or goes even lower) the drugs' continued effectiveness is probably due to lowered insulin resistance, which enables the body to make better use of the insulin it produces.

Types of Sulfonylureal Drugs. The sulfonylureal drugs now available in this country are tolbutamide (Orinase), chlorpropamide (Diabinese), acetohexamide (Dymelor), tolazamide (Tolinase), glipizide (Glucotrol), and glyburide (Micronase or Diaβeta). The major differences among them involves their durations of action. Table 21.1 summarizes the major features of these oral hypoglycemic drugs.

Since individuals respond differently to these drugs, it sometimes takes several trial weeks to discover the most effective dosage. The usual strategy is to start with a small dose and, depending upon effect on blood glucose, to increase the dosage and/or number of times it is taken each day until blood glucose is normalized.

Drug Interactions. If you take antidiabetes drugs, be careful to avoid taking other drugs that may interact and cause blood sugar to drop even lower. (Discuss all medications with your doctor and pharmacist.) Specific drugs that should be avoided include sulfa drugs used as antibiotics, chloramphenicol (e.g., Chloromycetin), bishydroxycoumarin (Dicumarol), phenylbutazone (e.g., Butazolidin), and clofibrate (Atromid-S).

PREVENTION

There is no way to guarantee prevention of either Type 1 or Type 2 diabetes mellitus. However, there is evidence linking Type 2 diabetes and impaired glucose tolerance with hypertension, high triglyceride and low HDL ("good") cholesterol levels, and accelerated atherosclerosis (hardening of the arteries with fatty deposits). It is possible that by lowering your risk factors for heart disease, you may also be lowering your risk of adult-onset diabetes. Lifestyle changes that may help are stopping smoking, maintaining proper weight for your height, exercising regularly, and limiting fat in your diet. Research continues to explore the possibility of prevention.

If you have already been diagnosed with diabetes mellitus, you may prevent further progress of the disease by following your doctor's prescription and the recommendations of this chapter.

COMPLICATIONS OF DIABETES

Since the metabolic problems associated with diabetes affect the entire body, the complications of the disease are wide-ranging and affect many different organ systems. The primary complications, which occur most commonly in Type 1 diabetes, may appear relatively rapidly and are directly related to the level of blood glucose.

Long-term complications may not become evident for several years or even decades after the onset of diabetes. A number of recent studies indicate that secondary complications often may be minimized or even prevented by maintaining normal blood glucose, but there are enough exceptions to make development of complications highly unpredictable. Not all people with diabetes develop secondary complications; in some people the type and severity of problems seem unrelated to either the duration of the diabetes or the degree of control.

As noted earlier, many different organ systems are affected by diabetes and the type of complications vary from patient to patient. Some of the more common complications—both short- and long-term—are summarized below.

HYPERGLYCEMIA AND KETOACIDOSIS

DEFINITION

Hyperglycemia is a very high level of blood glucose that can lead to ketoacidosis, a potentially fatal acidity of the body fluids caused by by-products of ketone bodies.

CAUSES

If the blood glucose is too high (hyperglycemia) and inadequate insulin is available to utilize the sugar, the body begins to break down fat and muscle tissue for fuel. By-products of the breakdown of stored fat for fuel are acidic compounds called ketone bodies, which are carried in the blood and excreted in the urine in combination with a base (sodium). Eventually, the body's sodium stores drop, causing ketoacidosis, a drop in the pH of blood and other body fluids (they become more acidic).

DIAGNOSIS

Signs of hyperglycemia usually ensue over a period of time and may go unnoticed until they progress to serious ketoacidosis. The warning signs of hyperglycemia and ketoacidosis include:

- Increased thirst and urination
- Nausea and vomiting

Feeling of weakness or fatigue
Large amounts of ketones in the urine
Blood sugar measurement of more than 300 mg/dl
Signs of dehydration, such as dry mouth and dry skin
A fruity breath odor
Heavy, labored breathing that is also rapid and deep
Fixed, dilated pupils and difficulty in focusing
Loss of consciousness

TREATMENT

Emergency treatment includes immediate administration of insulin, as well as intravenous fluids that restore the body's acid/base balance.

PREVENTION OF HYPERGLYCEMIA AND KETOACIDOSIS

To guard against these conditions, those with diabetes should regularly monitor blood sugar and urine for ketones (discussed in the following section).

HYPOGLYCEMIA

DEFINITION

Hypoglycemia is low blood sugar, a condition that can pose serious problems for the patient with diabetes, especially one who requires insulin injections.

CAUSE

Taking too much insulin may lead to rapid depletion of available blood glucose, resulting in an insulin reaction or shock.

DIAGNOSIS

Warning signs of hypoglycemia from an insulin reaction include:

A cold, clammy feeling
Tingling sensation of the mouth, fingers, or other parts of the body
Excessive sweating
Headache
Hunger
Irritability and change in mood or personality
Impaired vision
Trembling
A rapid heartbeat
Sudden feeling of drowsiness
Sudden awakening from sleep accompanied by other symptoms, especially a cold sweat

Loss of consciousness and coma
Inability to waken diabetic patient

TREATMENT OF HYPOGLYCEMIA FROM AN INSULIN REACTION

To counter an insulin reaction, someone with diabetes should take a simple sugar, such as a glass of orange juice or soda (not sugar-free or diet), candy, or fruit. In the case of rapid deterioration or loss of consciousness, a glucagon injection, which almost immediately converts glycogen stored in the liver to glucose, should be administered. If glucagon is unavailable and a person with diabetes loses consciousness, honey, sugar syrup, or other absorbable simple sugar should be placed under the tongue where it will be absorbed into the body. Persons who cannot be roused or cannot eat or drink should be brought to an emergency medical facility immediately.

PREVENTION

Careful determination of the correct insulin dosage can help prevent hypoglycemia.

INFECTIONS AND DIABETES

DEFINITION

When you suffer from diabetes, infection is a special hazard. You are not only more susceptible to infection, but the infection, in turn, exacerbates diabetes. Types of infections that are particularly common among people with diabetes include:

Urinary tract infections
Thrush, gum disease, and other mouth infections
Both superficial and systemic fungal infections
Vaginitis
Wound infections

Even a trivial cut or sore may prove difficult to heal and develop into a serious, life-threatening problem for someone with diabetes. In addition, infection markedly increases the need for insulin; in fact, blood sugar often rises even before there are any symptoms of infection. If you experience nausea, vomiting, or diarrhea, keeping blood sugar under control may prove doubly challenging because you may be unable to eat normally. Don't mistakenly think that because you are unable to eat, you don't need to take insulin while ill—that may cause ketoacidosis. Even if no food is consumed, the body requires insulin for metabolism.

CAUSE

Diabetes lowers the body's natural resistance to infection in a number of ways: Type 1 diabetes may be caused by a defect in the immune system, a flaw that may compromise other disease-fighting mechanisms. Poorly controlled diabetes appears to hinder the ability of white blood cells (leukocytes) to destroy invading microorganisms, making you more susceptible to infections, both from invading bacteria, fungi, and other foreign organisms, as well as from normally benign organisms that usually inhabit the body or environment without causing disease.

DIAGNOSIS

A high white blood cell count, fever, and swelling of the lymph glands are all signs of infection.

TREATMENT

If indicated, treatment should include antibiotic therapy to kill the invading organisms.

PREVENTION

Call your doctor at the first sign of even a trivial illness such as a common cold or upset stomach for guidance in managing the illness and the diabetes.

EYE DISORDERS ASSOCIATED WITH DIABETES

Diabetes has an adverse effect on almost every part of the eye and is now the leading cause of adult blindness in the United States. Although only a small percentage of people with diabetes totally lose their eyesight, most have some evidence of eye damage after 10 years. The most serious complications are those involving the retina and the lens, although other parts of the eye also may be damaged.

GENERAL PREVENTION OF EYE DISORDERS

Although most people with diabetes encounter only relatively minor eye problems, everyone with diabetes should see an ophthalmologist regularly. Depending upon individual circumstances, people with diabetes may go as often as every 2 or 3 months, or every 6 months or year with a minimal or slowly progressing eye condition. In addition, they should check any symptoms such as blurring of vision, hemorrhages, or other changes promptly. In many instances, prompt treatment in an early stage can prevent further or permanent loss of vision.

DIABETIC RETINOPATHY

DEFINITION

Diabetic retinopathy, degeneration of the retina (the layer of light-sensitive cells lining the back of the eyeball), is potentially one of the more serious eye complications. More than 70 percent of diabetic patients have some degree of retinopathy after 10 years of having diabetes but most do not suffer serious loss of vision.

CAUSE

Retinopathy most commonly affects the tiny capillaries nourishing the retina. The walls of these blood vessels weaken and form tiny aneurysms (ballooned-out areas that may leak blood) resulting in dot or flame hemorrhages, which reduce the sharpness of vision. Eventually, some of these weakened blood vessels die, and if the retina does not get enough oxygen and other nutrients, some of its tissue also dies. This dead tissue forms minute clumps called cotton wool exudates.

In some eyes, new blood vessels overgrow the retina, a condition called proliferative retinopathy. These vessels are often very fragile and can suddenly leak blood into the vitreous humor (the jellylike substance inside the eyeball), dimming vision or causing temporary blindness, which disappears when the blood is reabsorbed. Permanent loss of vision may occur, however, if scar tissue forms and damages the retina.

DIAGNOSIS

An eye exam shows the characteristic damaged red blood vessels or signs of leaking or blocked vessels.

TREATMENT

Fortunately, there are a number of new treatments for diabetic retinopathy that can help prevent blindness or minimize vision loss. Many of these treatments utilize lasers, concentrated light that surgically destroys some of the excess or weakened blood vessels. In some cases, the laser beams may be used to destroy tiny portions of the retina, thinning out the tissue to increase the underlying blood flow. If blood has leaked into the vitreous humor, it may be removed (vitrectomy) and replaced with an artificial substance to restore eyesight. Advances in eye microsurgery have enabled doctors to repair detached retinas and other abnormalities caused by progressive retinopathy.

CATARACTS AND DIABETES

DEFINITION

Diabetes can cause cataracts, loss of transparency of the eye lens or its capsule. In many instances, these cataracts are similar to those that commonly occur in older people; however, in diabetic patients, the cataracts form earlier and develop more rapidly.

CAUSE

Cataracts result from a loss of function of the lens tissue.

DIAGNOSIS

An eye exam reveals a gray-white film in the lens, behind the pupil.

TREATMENT

Cataracts can usually be treated with an operation that removes the diseased lens. Glasses, contact lenses, or implanted artificial lenses are used to overcome the farsightedness that occurs when the natural lens is removed.

CIRCULATORY AND CARDIOVASCULAR COMPLICATIONS OF DIABETES

DEFINITION

People with diabetes have a much higher rate of heart disease and circulatory disorders than the general population; cardiovascular complications cause about three-fourths of the deaths among diabetic patients.

Risk factors for heart disease appear at an earlier age and advance more rapidly in people with diabetes. These factors include hardening of the arteries (arteriosclerosis), buildups of fatty deposits (atherosclerosis), low levels of HDL ("good") cholesterol and elevated triglycerides, and high blood pressure. As a result, people with diabetes are at increased risk of heart attack, stroke, and impaired circulation involving both large and small blood vessels. Premenopausal women with diabetes, who would otherwise expect to have lower blood lipid levels and a lower incidence of heart disease than men, often have very high levels of blood lipids.

CAUSE

How diabetes promotes cardiovascular and circulatory abnormalities is unclear, but research suggests that the cause is linked to abnormally high blood glucose. High blood glucose affects the chemical structure of several blood components, particularly red blood cells and perhaps the platelets, abnormalities that may play a role in the development of arteriosclerosis. (See chapter 16, Heart and Blood Vessel Diseases, for more information.)

Insulin appears to increase lipid synthesis in the artery walls, which may help promote the buildup of fatty deposits. Since many Type 2 diabetics actually have high levels of insulin that their bodies cannot effectively utilize, some researchers believe their high insulin level may promote atherosclerosis. For Type 1 diabetes, however, insulin therapy inhibits the atherosclerotic process by normalizing blood sugar.

Diabetes also damages the capillaries, or microcirculation, which nourish the individual body cells and cause a thickening of the basement membranes, the substances that separate the epithelial cells lining the various body surfaces and the underlying structures. When the capillary basement membranes thicken, the vessels often are unable to carry adequate blood to the tissues they serve, resulting in poor circulation. The limbs are particularly vulnerable to these circulatory problems, and poor circulation to the lower limbs is particularly common in diabetes, resulting in chronic skin ulcers.

DIAGNOSIS

Diagnosis of cardiac and circulatory complications takes place after such tests as an electrocardiogram (ECG), echocardiogram, or exercise stress test to determine heart function and Doppler ultrasound to check blood flow through the outlying vascular system. (See chapter 16, Heart and Blood Vessel Diseases, for details.)

TREATMENT

Treatment for cardiovascular complications can take many forms. Lifestyle changes such as stopping smoking, adopting a low-fat diet, exercising regularly, and avoiding excess salt and alcohol should be a part of a diabetic's treatment plan. In addition, drugs to treat high blood pressure, high cholesterol, blood-clotting disorder, arrhythmias, and other heart and blood vessels disorders may be prescribed. (See chapter 16.)

ALTERNATIVE THERAPIES AND HOME REMEDIES

Relaxation techniques such as meditation or biofeedback may help control high blood pressure and arrhythmias. (See chapter 16.)

PREVENTION

In addition to the lifestyle changes listed earlier, precautions to prevent complications of circulatory disorders must be taken by those with diabetes. Leg cramps or pain, especially when walking or climbing stairs, and, in some cases, gangrene and amputation can be prevented by early treatment of infections or other problems.

FOOT CARE AND DIABETES

Careful attention to the feet is essential for those with diabetes. Ordinarily trivial ailments like corns, calluses, blisters, bunions, cuts or other injuries, and ingrown toenails can become major medical problems possibly leading to serious foot infections, gangrene, and amputation; fortunately, many of these problems can be prevented by meticulous foot care.

Several diabetic complications conspire to make the feet particularly vulnerable to serious problems.

Increased Incidence of Infection. Since the feet are frequently injured just by wearing shoes or walking around, hard-to-heal foot infections are common.

Impaired Circulation. Particularly pronounced in the feet and lower legs. This also slows the healing process. The poor delivery of oxygen makes the lower limbs more susceptible to certain microorganisms that thrive in an oxygen-poor environment.

Nerve Damage. This common complication of diabetes further compromises the feet by reducing sensitivity to pain and discomfort. People in normal health who develop corns, calluses, sores, and other foot problems are driven by the resulting discomfort to take corrective action. But if you suffer from diabetes, you may not perceive any pain and be unaware of the problem until it develops into an infected ulcer or other major disorder. Damage to the motor nerves, which in turn promotes a weakening and shrinking of muscles, also may promote the development of certain foot deformities, such as hammertoes or clawfoot. These deformities also make the feet more vulnerable to infection.

Damage to the Autonomic Nerves. These nerves control sweat glands. This can cause overly dry skin that develops tiny cracks where bacteria and fungi can thrive, leading to infection.

Regular preventive foot care should include having regular checkups by a foot specialist and paying special attention to personal foot hygiene.

Shoes. Make sure shoes are comfortable and properly fitted. Foot deformities or other problems require custom-made shoes; shoes should be fitted by a knowledgeable salesperson and should be made of a soft, pliable material such as leather. Use moleskin or lamb's wool to prevent rubbing and relieve pressure. Special shoe inserts should be fitted by a specialist. Avoid walking barefoot, even at home, to reduce the risk of splinters and injuries. Sandals or open shoes also may not offer adequate foot protection.

Stockings. Wear good-fitting stockings made of absorbent, nonbinding material. Discard stockings with holes or rough spots.

Daily Care. Feet should be inspected at least once a day for signs of reddening or discoloration, blisters, or other irritations. Promptly attend to skin problems, such as cracking or dryness. A foot specialist or other health professional should treat ingrown toenails, corns, and calluses; don't remove or pare corns by yourself and do not apply chemical corn removers. Feet should be washed, and a fine brush or pumice stone used to remove dead skin gently, without excessive rubbing. Rinse and dry thoroughly; apply a lubricating lotion to dry skin.

Toenails. Groom toenails regularly with nail clippers, emery boards, or files (not scissors). Trim the nails straight across and avoid cutting into the corners, which may promote ingrown toenails. Those with poor eyesight or poor coordination should let someone else tend to regular foot grooming.

DIABETIC NEUROPATHY

DEFINITION

This condition consists of nervous system complications associated with diabetes.

CAUSE

It's not clear exactly why diabetes damages the nervous system, but high blood glucose is the likely cause.

DIAGNOSIS

Diabetes-related disorders of the nervous system (diabetic neuropathy) cause a variety of symptoms including slowed reflexes, sexual impotence, loss of sensation, intermittent episodes of pain, and exacerbation of circulatory disorders. The early signs of diabetic neuropathy include tingling sensations in the fingers and toes, feelings of muscular weakness, and, in a large percentage of men, impotence. The neuropathy may compound other diabetes-related complications by causing a loss of sensation and diminished circulation of blood that reduces awareness of injury or infection until serious open ulcers ensue.

Pain—ranging from minor discomfort or tingling to severe aches—is a common feature of diabetic neuropathy. Sharp stabbing pains may come and go, deep aches make sleep or normal activities difficult, and very sensitive skin reacts to even a slight touch.

Although symptoms of diabetic neuropathy may not become evident for years, recently developed, highly sensitive nerve function tests have found that nerve deterioration often begins in the early stages of both types of diabetes. Both sensory and motor nerves may deteriorate and produce symptoms that vary greatly from person to person. In some, symptoms never become apparent though tests may reveal nerve fiber damage; for others, symptoms appear early in the disease and progress rapidly. In many instances, the neuropathy expresses itself by affecting systems controlled by the autonomic nervous system. Sexual impotence, gastrointestinal problems, bladder disorders, irregular heartbeats, or blood pressure abnormalities may be traced to autonomic nervous system problems.

TREATMENT

Diabetic neuropathy is best treated by normalizing blood glucose, relieving specific symptoms, and controlling the underlying diabetes. For example, painkilling drugs can alleviate associated neuropathy discomfort, while mechanical devices are used to cope with loss of muscle control, such as foot drop or ankle weakness.

Impotence is an embarrassing problem for many men with diabetes, who are often reluctant to talk to their doctors about the problem. In recent years, implanted devices to help men with organic impotence achieve and maintain an erection have enabled many diabetic patients to regain the ability to have sexual intercourse. Information about these prostheses is available from primary physicians who treat diabetes or from urologists experienced in treating sexual problems in diabetic men.

PREVENTION

Good control of the underlying diabetes is the best preventive measure of diabetic neuropathy.

DIABETES INSIPIDUS

DEFINITION

Chronic excretion of large amounts of pale urine, which causes dehydration and extreme thirst.

CAUSE

This disorder is caused by lack of vasopressin, sometimes called the antidiuretic hormone, or ADH. Low levels of this hormone cause the kidneys to secrete excessive amounts of water.

DIAGNOSIS

Excessive thirst and urination are the primary symptoms. (The disorder should not be confused with diabetes mellitus, which is caused by a lack of insulin and resultant metabolic abnormalities.) A test measuring a low level of ADH in the blood confirms the diagnosis.

TREATMENT

The disorder can be treated by taking ADH, either by injection or via a nasal spray.

KIDNEY FAILURE CAUSED BY DIABETES

DEFINITION

Kidney failure—the inability to adequately excrete waste products—is another serious potential complication of long-standing diabetes. The kidneys, complex, highly efficient organs that filter waste material from the blood for disposal from the body, each contain more than 1 million nephrons (minute filtering systems) susceptible to damage from diabetes.

CAUSE

Damage to the tiny blood vessels in the nephrons can eventually lead to progressive kidney failure, characterized by the excretion of protein and other nutrients in the urine. Diabetes also increases the kidney's vulnerability to infections.

DIAGNOSIS

Symptoms of kidney or urinary tract infections (flank pain, difficult or burning urination, urgency to urinate, passage of urine discolored by blood) should be promptly evaluated by a doctor. Examination of a urine specimen is necessary in most cases.

TREATMENT

Improved treatment of kidney failure with hemodialysis using an artificial kidney and replacement of diseased kidneys with healthy transplants have greatly improved the outlook for patients with advanced diabetic kidney disease (diabetic nephropathy). But these measures do not cure the underlying disease, and kidneys transplanted in patients with poorly controlled diabetes develop diabetic nephropathy within a few years. For people with mild forms of diabetic kidney disease, controlling blood pressure with an ACE inhibitor slows kidney damage. (For more on kidney problems, see chapter 27.)

PREVENTION

There is evidence that bringing elevated blood glucose into the normal range can reduce kidney damage and optimizing control of blood glucose may prevent kidney damage from ever starting. Controlling hypertension also may prevent kidney damage. Recent studies also indicate that taking captopril (Capoten) may prevent diabetic kidney failure.

PSYCHOLOGICAL EFFECTS OF DIABETES

DEFINITION

Any chronic disease carries the potential for profound emotional effects on the patient, as well as family, lovers, and friends. This is particularly true of diabetes, a lifelong disease in which the person has to pay particular attention to almost every aspect of day-to-day life. Anger, depression, anxiety, and feelings of deep frustration are common reactions. Poorly controlled diabetes, with its abnormal swings from high to low blood sugar, also pro-duces mood changes and feelings of irritability, anxiety, depression, and euphoria.

CAUSE

Emotional stress can evolve into a vicious cycle: Poorly controlled diabetes can produce negative psychological responses that in turn can further exacerbate the disease. It is well known that emotional stress has a profound effect on blood glucose, triggering the classic fight-or-flight response, increasing heart rate, blood pressure, blood glucose, and epinephrine and other adrenal hormones, such as cortisone. These automatic responses are intended to provide the extra energy to overcome a dangerous situation. A certain amount of stress is unavoidable and desirable, but when people with diabetes overreact to trivial daily events, a roller coaster ride of hormonal changes may inhibit the action of insulin at a time when the body is releasing more blood glucose.

TREATMENT

Seeking professional counseling or joining a support group for diabetics or other people with long-term illness may help you deal with your disease. Sometimes it helps to talk to fellow patients who understand your anxieties and empathize with your feelings.

ALTERNATIVE THERAPIES AND HOME REMEDIES

Learning effective ways to cope with the stress of living with an illness like diabetes may help alleviate the psychological effects. Relaxation techniques such as meditation, yoga, and guided imagery often contribute to a increased sense of well-being.

PREVENTION

Achieving an equilibrium of emotional well-being is particularly important for the diabetic patient, even though many factors and circumstances may make this difficult.

Studies have found that better blood glucose control can enhance feelings of well-being. An increased feeling of control can result from using the recently improved techniques in self-monitoring that enable patients to normalize blood glucose and better match insulin, food, and exercise to lifestyle. (See "Self-Monitoring" in this chapter.)

DIABETES AND PREGNANCY

Before the discovery of insulin, there is no record of any woman with Type 1 diabetes having a baby that survived. It is highly unlikely that a woman with uncontrolled diabetes could even become pregnant, and if she did the disease was virtually certain to be fatal to the fetus and often to her. Today, the widespread use of insulin has improved the outlook for women with this condition.

TYPE 1 DIABETES AND PREGNANCY

Recent studies have found that much of the risk to both mother and baby can be minimized by a program of strict care that maintains blood glucose between 70 and 140 mg/dl, with a mean of 80 to 87 mg/dl throughout pregnancy. Ideally, the maintenance program begins before pregnancy is attempted; most experts agree that women should have normal blood sugar for at least 2 months before conception and diabetic complications such as retinopathy, kidney problems, high blood pressure, or other cardiovascular disorders should be minimal and under control.

LIFESTYLE CHANGES

For prospective mothers with diabetes, giving birth to a full-term, healthy baby without suffering serious problems is a tremendous amount of work not to be taken lightly. Both mother and doctor must diligently monitor the pregnancy and fully understand how to adjust insulin and food intake to maintain normal blood sugar. Throughout the pregnancy, frequent self-testing of blood sugar—usually six or seven times per day—is a must, and urine should be checked at least once a day for ketone bodies.

DRUGS

Insulin needs increase throughout the course of pregnancy. Glucose in the mother's blood passes freely to the fetus but insulin does not. If the fetal blood glucose is too high, the baby will begin producing insulin, which acts as a growth hormone that can cause the baby to grow too large. The extra insulin and high blood glucose tend to lower the fetus's potassium, resulting in flaccid muscles and potentially fatal arrhythmias.

INTERVENTION

As the pregnancy nears term, both mother and doctor must carefully monitor the baby. Mother should perform daily fetal movement checks, or "kick counts." (A decrease in movements may be a sign of fetal distress.) Since near-term fetal death is common in diabetic pregnancies, most doctors are anxious to deliver the baby as soon as it is clear that it is mature enough to do well. Thus, during the 36th or 37th weeks of pregnancy, the

doctor may test the amniotic fluid to determine whether the fetal lungs are fully developed and may also test the fetal heart. As soon as the lungs are mature enough to function independently, most doctors prefer to deliver the baby, either by inducing labor or cesarean section. Increased knowledge about maintaining normal blood glucose throughout pregnancy, natural labor, and delivery has reduced the number of cesareans among diabetic mothers. Since managing a diabetic pregnancy is demanding for both mother and physician, anyone in this situation should seek an obstetrician experienced in this area or who works in collaboration with an endocrinologist or internist specializing in diabetes. In addition, a neonatologist or pediatrician should be engaged who specializes in high-risk babies.

Although an increasing number of babies born to diabetic mothers are perfectly normal, an increased risk of birth defects and other problems still persists. The baby should be carefully examined shortly after birth, and then taken to a high-risk nursery for observation for 24 hours. If no problems develop in this time, chances are good that the baby can go back to its mother or a regular nursery.

GESTATIONAL DIABETES

DEFINITION

Gestational diabetes is a condition that appears in normal women during pregnancy and usually, but not always, disappears immediately following delivery. It sometimes goes unnoticed, especially if blood glucose is not checked periodically. Gestational diabetes is most common among women over the age of 35 who are overweight, who have already had a large (over 9 pounds) baby or were big babies themselves, and who have a family history of diabetes.

CAUSE

Gestational diabetes occurs in about 2 percent of all pregnant women. It usually shows up during the second or third trimester, when levels of some hormones increase, making insulin resistance more likely to occur. Its causes are unknown, though it tends to be inherited and eventually develops into Type 2 diabetes in about 30 to 40 percent of the women who have it.

DIAGNOSIS

Although gestational diabetes may be so mild that it causes no obvious symptoms, it poses many of the same hazards to the fetus as other types of preexisting diabetes. Gestational diabetes is usually discovered as a result of screening tests that should be performed on all women between the 24th and 28th weeks of pregnancy. These tests include a plasma glucose test 2 hours after eating, and, if necessary, an oral glucose tolerance test.

For more information on these tests, see "General Diagnosis of Diabetes." The guidelines for diagnosis are similar, but the values may be different for pregnant women—fasting plasma glucose levels tend to be lower and levels following oral glucose tolerance tests are usually higher.

TREATMENT

The mother and baby must be protected by maintaining normal maternal blood glucose. Diet alone usually works; if this is inadequate, insulin injections are necessary. In either event, mothers must learn how to self-test blood glucose and practice the same careful monitoring outlined above.

PREVENTION

Because the tendency toward glucose intolerance is probably hereditary, there is little to be done to prevent it. However, maintaining a proper weight may help prevent the development of gestational diabetes or at least lessen its severity as well as the probability of other health problems during pregnancy.

OTHER ENDOCRINE DISORDERS

Many essential endocrine functions are controlled by the hypothalamus, located at the base of the lower brain, and the pituitary, a tiny gland connected to the hypothalamus and located in a bony portion of the base of the skull. The hypothalamus links the endocrine and nervous systems; it controls appetite, temperature, sleep, sexual function, and fluid balance. In many instances, the hypothalamus influences these functions by releasing hormones sent to the pituitary for distribution to other parts of the body or which stimulate the pituitary to release still more hormones.

Specific hormones of these and other glands (and their functions) include:

Vasopressin. Produced in the hypothalamus and released by the posterior lobe of the pituitary. Sometimes called the antidiuretic hormone or ADH, it prevents the kidneys from excreting too much water, thus helping to maintain the body's fluid balance and constrict, or narrow, the small blood vessels.

Oxytocin. Produced in the hypothalamus and released by the posterior lobe. Induces labor by causing the uterus to contract when pregnancy reaches full term. This hormone also promotes the production of milk and therefore plays an important role in breast-feeding.

Prolactin. Produced in the anterior lobe of the pituitary. Stimulates the breasts to produce milk at the end of pregnancy.

Growth Hormone (Somatotropin). Produced in the pituitary's anterior lobe. Stimulates muscle and bone growth in children and adolescents.

Some pituitary hormones act as tropins, meaning they stimulate other endocrine glands to produce their respective hormones.

ACTH (Adrenocorticotropic Hormone). Stimulates the adrenal glands to produce glucosteroid hormones (cortisol) and male-type hormones.

TSH (Thyrotropin). Stimulates the thyroid to grow and to secrete thyroxine and triiodothyronines.

LH (Luteinizing Hormone). In men, stimulates the testes to secrete male hormones; in women, stimulates the ovaries to produce estrogen.

FSH (Follicle-Stimulating Hormone). In men, stimulates the testicular tubules to produce sperm; in women, stimulates the ovarian follicles to produce a ripened ovum (egg).

MSH (Melanocyte-Stimulating Hormone). Stimulates the production of pigment cells in the skin.

Disorders of the hypothalamus and pituitary are relatively rare and often involve tumors that either cause an over- or underproduction of hormones. If the pituitary gland ceases to produce its hormones (panhypopituitarism), the target glands are affected usually in sequence, beginning with the gonads, then the thyroid, and finally the adrenals. In addition to signs of underfunction of the various endocrine glands, there also may be headaches and visual symptoms. If the disorder is less generalized, affecting the secretion of some hormones but not total pituitary deficiency, the symptoms will be related to the specific hormone(s). Following are disorders resulting from hypothalamus or pituitary dysfunction.

GROWTH ABNORMALITIES

ACROMEGALY/GIGANTISM

DEFINITION

Acromegaly or gigantism is a disease characterized by excessively large hands, feet, and jaw. In fact, this condition causes enlargement of all the tissues in the body. Although most very tall children do not have a hormonal disorder (they are simply genetically programmed to grow tall), those suffering acromegaly or gigantism endure growth in height and weight far above normal standards.

CAUSE

An overproduction of growth hormone and insulin-like growth factor-I (IGF-I) in adults can cause acromegaly, which results in distorted appearance by causing some bones to broaden while the long bones, fused and unable to grow, remain the same. This condition is usually linked to a tumor of the anterior lobe of the pituitary.

In children, excessive growth—gigantism—may be linked to the same factors, although appearance is less distorted because the long bones, still unfused, also grow in proportion to other growth.

DIAGNOSIS

This disorder may first show up on x-rays of the hands, feet, or other affected bones. Blood tests measuring abnormally high growth hormone and IGF-I levels and high growth hormone levels following a glucose tolerance test confirm diagnosis. However, further tests are usually necessary to determine the underlying cause. These usually include a magnetic resonance imaging (MRI) scan of the pituitary gland and other tests of anterior pituitary function.

TREATMENT

Acromegaly and gigantism can usually be treated by surgical removal of the tumor, radiation therapy directed to that area of the pituitary gland, or, rarely, by drugs to control the release of the hormone.

DWARFISM

DEFINITION

In dwarfism—also referred to as restricted growth—a hormonal deficiency causes a failure to grow. (Although for most short children diminutive stature is genetic.)

CAUSE

This condition may be caused by the failure of the pituitary to secrete adequate growth hormone, or by any number of other causes, including thyroid disorders, malnutrition, and other illnesses.

DIAGNOSIS

Dwarfism due to inadequate growth hormone is diagnosed by measuring the level of this hormone and IGF-I in the blood.

TREATMENT

Hormone therapy during the growing years usually can stimulate normal growth.

PREVENTION

Dwarfism can be prevented with adequate hormone therapy during a child's growing years.

....

ABNORMALITIES OF SEXUAL DEVELOPMENT

An excess or deficiency of hormones produced by the gonads (testes or ovaries) can cause infertility, delayed or premature puberty, failure to menstruate, development of inappropriate gender characteristics, and numerous other disorders related to sexual development. Numerous chromosomal abnormalities also may cause these problems. These disorders are relatively rare, but some of the more common ones are briefly reviewed here.

Since the pituitary gland secretes vital gonadotropic hormones that stimulate the testes and ovaries to produce their respective sex hormones, many problems involving sexual development can be traced to pituitary dysfunction.

PREMATURE OR PRECOCIOUS PUBERTY

DEFINITION

Normally, the hypothalamus initiates puberty by stimulating the pituitary to release gonadotropins. If this occurs prematurely, a very young child may develop secondary sexual characteristics and proceed to sexual maturity. Puberty is considered precocious if it begins in girls before age 8 or in boys before age 9.

CAUSE

Premature release of gonadotropins such as luteinizing hormone (LH), follicle-stimulating hormone (FSH), and/or gonadotropin-releasing hormone (Gn-RH) is a primary cause of precocious puberty, although it also may be caused by disorders involving other endocrine glands.

DIAGNOSIS

Signs of precocious puberty are revealed by a physical examination. Blood tests showing higher than normal levels of gonadotropins and sex hormones confirm the diagnosis.

TREATMENT

Children can take hormones that suppress precocious puberty until the appropriate time of onset. In addition, psychological support is advised to help these children adjust to any premature changes that have already taken place.

PREVENTION

Timely, proper hormone therapy can prevent most problems associated with precocious puberty.

SEXUAL INFANTILISM

DEFINITION

Sexual infantilism is the failure to develop sexually. If a child reaches the age of 15 or 16 and shows no signs of puberty, a careful examination by an endocrinologist may be in order.

CAUSE

Sexual infantilism occurs when the testes or ovaries fail to function because of either lack of gonadotropins or another endocrine disorder. In males, this condition may be linked to a failure of the testes to produce male hormones, which can cause delayed puberty. In females, deficient gonadotropins from the pituitary or the failure of the ovaries to produce female hormones causes sexual infantilism.

DIAGNOSIS

If this dates from childhood, the boy is likely to grow taller than expected without development of the usual secondary sex characteristics, deepening of voice, and muscular development. The failure of testes to produce sperm and a lack of sex drive result in infertility.

In young girls, signs of sexual development that may be absent in those with sexual infantilism include menstruation, breast development, and pubic hair growth.

In both cases, physical exam and blood tests showing abnormally low levels of sex hormones confirm diagnosis. Further tests may be necessary to seek the underlying cause, which may be an endocrine problem, genetic trait, abnormal physical condition, or a number of other disorders.

TREATMENT

This problem is rare and can usually be resolved by taking the appropriate hormones.

In males, administration of male sex hormones (appropriate gonadotropins) can correct most of the problems, but will not produce fertility. Treatment for infertility is available (human gonadotropin injections) when fertility is desired.

In females, sex hormone therapy usually stimulates the maturation process.

PREVENTION

Most problems associated with sexual infantilism can be prevented with proper hormone therapy during the teenage years.

UNDESCENDED TESTES

DEFINITION

A male condition in which one or both of the testicles fail to descend to their proper position in the scrotum.

CAUSE

Many cases are caused by subtle endocrine malfunctions, such as inadequate luteinizing hormone (LH) production in utero. Other causes include developmental abnormalities such as an inguinal hernia.

DIAGNOSIS

Physical exam confirms the diagnosis, but determining the cause for and the position of the undescended testicle requires further testing such as serum testosterone level following stimulation of other hormones and ultrasound. There may also be acute pain at the site of the undescended testicle.

TREATMENT

About 3 percent of newborn boys will have undescended testes; within the first year of life, the problem will correct itself in all but about one half of 1 percent. This may be corrected by injection of gonadotropin, but if the testis still does not descend to its proper position in the scrotum, surgery to reposition it may be required. The purpose of such surgery in childhood is to preserve future fertility and to prevent the later development of testicular tumors.

....

MILK-PRODUCTION ABNORMALITIES

GALACTORRHEA

DEFINITION

This condition occurs when milk is produced in a woman who is not nursing, or in a man.

CAUSE

The problem is caused by excessive production of prolactin. This may be a condition of a pituitary gland tumor.

DIAGNOSIS

Diagnosis is based on symptoms and an abnormally high level of prolactin in the blood. A magnetic resonance imaging (MRI) scan of the pituitary gland and other tests may be ordered to determine the specific cause of the overproduction. Many times, no cause is found for this condition.

TREATMENT

Galactorrhea may be treated with the drug bromocriptine and/or with surgical removal of any identifiable tumor or radiation therapy applied directly to the gland.

MALE/FEMALE DIFFERENCES

This disorder is found eight times more often in women than in men.

AMENORRHEA

DEFINITION

Failure of a premenopausal woman to menstruate.

CAUSE

Amenorrhea may have a number of causes, including hormonal imbalance, structural abnormalities of the ovaries, malnutrition, emotional problems, chronic illness, excessive exercise, and certain drugs. Sometimes hormonal imbalances cause other symptoms in addition to the menstrual failure or irregularity. One example is a condition known as polycystic ovary or Stein-Leventhal syndrome, a disorder in which the ovaries secrete an excessive amount of male hormone. Despite normal female hormone secretion, the imbalance causes signs of virilism, including excessive body and facial hair, acne, weight gain, and either failure to menstruate or extreme irregularity. The condition is thought to be caused by faulty pituitary gonadotropin regulation. Excessive production of prolactin caused by a pituitary tumor is another hormonal cause of amenorrhea.

DIAGNOSIS

Diagnosis is based on the history of menstruation cessation or irregularity. Testing levels of hormones produced by the pituitary gland may also help determine if the cause is related to abnormal functioning of the pituitary or the ovaries.

TREATMENT

In the case of polycystic ovary or Stein-Leventhal syndrome, treatment consists of taking female hormones for the hairiness and acne, and "fertility" hormones if pregnancy proves to be impossible.

If the prolactin overproduction is caused by a pituitary tumor, treatment options include using the drug bromocriptine, radiation therapy applied to the gland, and/or surgery to remove the tumor.

PREVENTION

Maintaining proper nutrition and a normal level of exercise will help prevent amenorrhea in some cases, but there is no way to prevent an endocrine disorder.

INFERTILITY RELATED TO ENDOCRINE SYSTEM MALFUNCTION

DEFINITION

Infertility is defined as the failure of a couple to conceive after a year of trying for a pregnancy.

CAUSES OF FEMALE INFERTILITY

Endocrinologic factors cause female infertility in about 30 to 40 percent of all cases. Abnormalities involving the hormones progesterone, thyroid-stimulating hormone, prolactin, luteinizing hormone (LH), follicle-stimulating hormone (FSH), human chorionic gonadotropin (hCG), and/or human menopausal gonadotropin (hMG) may result in infertility. The problem may be caused by the presence of a pituitary tumor or anatomic abnormalities of the uterus or fallopian tubes.

DIAGNOSIS OF FEMALE INFERTILITY

The only way to tell whether an endocrinologic malfunction is causing menstrual or fertility problems is by hormone testing. In addition, a variety of imaging tests may be used to assess the endocrine glands, uterus, and fallopian tubes.

TREATMENT OF FEMALE INFERTILITY

Treatment with the missing hormone, with a hormone that may suppress the overproduction of another hormone, drug treatment, or treatment of a tumor may restore fertility in a woman. For instance, a prolactin overproduction may be treated with bromocriptine. Or if lack of progesterone is implicated, ovulation may not occur until treatment with the hormone restores it.

CAUSES OF MALE INFERTILITY

There are many causes for male infertility, most of which are unrelated to hormonal imbalances. (See chapter 10, Health Concerns of Men.) However, endocrinologic causes include hypothalamic-pituitary malfunction or insensitivity to the male hormone androgen.

DIAGNOSIS OF MALE INFERTILITY

An evaluation of male infertility with endocrinologic causes begins with testing for blood levels of the hormones testosterone, follicle-stimulating hormone, luteinizing hormone, and prolactin. Any abnormality in these results can help determine the need for further testing such as ultrasound or magnetic resonance imaging to detect tumors on a specific endocrine gland.

TREATMENT OF MALE INFERTILITY

Hormone therapy, treatment with other drugs such as bromocriptine, or surgery or radiation therapy to treat glandular tumors may restore fertility. In many cases, however, such as some disorders involving overproduction of gonadotropins, the condition is not treatable.

....

THYROID DISORDERS

The thyroid is a small, butterfly-shaped gland that lies over the trachea (windpipe) just below the larynx (see figure 21.17). The thyroid differs from other endocrine glands in that it requires an outside substance, iodine, to produce its hormone, thyroxine. Thyrotropin, a pituitary hormone, stimulates the thyroid to secrete thyroxine. A well-functioning thyroid requires a properly functioning pituitary, a small but steady supply of iodine, and, of course, normal pathways of hormone synthesis.

Thyroid hormone affects virtually all metabolic processes; too much thyroid hormone speeds up metabolism while too little slows it down. In either instance, the disorder may be caused by an enlargement of the thyroid gland itself, known as goiter. In the past, iodine deficiency was the most common cause of thyroid disease, but today iodine is readily available, either from foods or in supplements added to salt in areas where foods are deficient in this mineral.

OVERACTIVE THYROID (HYPERTHYROIDISM, GRAVES' DISEASE)

DEFINITION/CAUSE

An overactive thyroid, or hyperthyroidism, is caused by excessive production of thyroid hormone; the most common condition is a disorder known as Graves' disease. The cause of Graves' disease is not known for certain, but it may be related to genetic factors affecting the immune system. Hyperthyroidism is less commonly due to tumors of the pituitary, thyroid, or placenta.

DIAGNOSIS

Hyperthyroidism causes one or more of these symptoms:

Weight loss (due to the speeded up metabolism)
Rapid heart rate
Muscle weakness

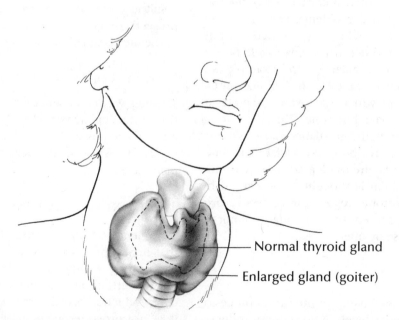

Normal thyroid gland

Enlarged gland (goiter)

Figure 21.17: A normal thyroid gland and the enlargement typical of a goiter.

Tremor
Increased sensitivity to heat
Hot, flushed skin
Feelings of anxiety and nervousness
Bulging eyes and a staring appearance
Goiter

TREATMENT

The choice of treatment depends upon the age and over-all condition of the patient, the size of the thyroid itself, and the preference of the patient. Overactive thyroid disease may be treated by:

Drugs that inhibit production of thyroid hormone
Radioactive iodine to destroy part of the thyroid gland and thereby reduce hormone production
Surgical removal of part of the gland

MALE/FEMALE DIFFERENCES

Overactive thyroid disease is more common in women than in men.

UNDERACTIVE THYROID (HYPOTHYROIDISM, MYXEDEMA)

DEFINITION/CAUSE

The most common cause of underactive thyroid (also known as hypothyroidism or myxedema) is an autoimmune disorder in which the gland is slowly destroyed by the body's immune system. Other causes include lack of TSH from the pituitary, or a congenital defect in which a baby is born with no thyroid or one that does not produce enough hormone.

DIAGNOSIS

Diagnosis of underactive thyroid disease occurs following abnormal results for tests of levels of thyroid hormones in the blood.

Detecting congenital hypothyroidism is particularly important to prevent the severe mental retardation and growth problems it causes. Without adequate thyroid hormone, the brain does not develop properly, resulting in cretinism. Babies with this condition tend to be very lethargic and they fail to thrive or grow properly. Screening for thyroid hormone in newborns can detect this disorder early enough to prevent most if not all of the problems caused by infantile thyroid deficiency. Hypothyroidism is characterized by a slowing down of all body processes. At first, you may barely notice the symptoms: a feeling of lethargy, aching muscles, growing intolerance to cold, or constipation. In fact, you may attribute them to other causes. Also, you may gain weight, even if you reduce food intake. As the disorder progresses, the face becomes puffy and the skin dry. The voice deepens. Feelings of depression and increasing lethargy also are common.

TREATMENT

Treatment consists of thyroid hormone replacement therapy.

GOITER

DEFINITION

Goiter refers to any swelling or overgrowth of the thyroid gland.

CAUSE

The most common causes are the development of benign nodules or chronic (Hashimito's) thyroiditis, an inflammation of the gland due to an autoimmune disease. Rarer causes of goiter include benign or malignant tumors, congenital thyroid enzyme deficiency, and iodine deficiency.

DIAGNOSIS

A goiter is evident upon physical exam. However, testing of hormones produced by the thyroid gland is necessary to determine its cause. In addition, ultrasound or other imaging tests are used to assess the nodules that accompany a goiter.

TREATMENT

Treatment of the goiter depends upon the cause. Nodular goiter, a condition occurring most commonly in middle-aged women who suddenly develop an overgrowth or swelling of part of the gland, may require biopsy or surgical removal of the diseased portion, or administration of thyroid hormone to shrink the nodules. In such cases, careful evaluation is needed to determine whether the growth is due to nodular goiter or a tumor. (For information on thyroid cancer see chapter 17.)

PREVENTION

One preventable cause of goiter is iodine deficiency. Now that iodine is added to salt and other foods such as bread, this is a rare problem in the United States.

MALE/FEMALE DIFFERENCES

Nodular goiter is more common in women than in men.

PARATHYROID DISORDERS

The parathyroid glands are located on the back and side of each thyroid lobe. They secrete a hormone that controls the level of calcium in the blood. If blood calcium falls, a rise in parathyroid hormone releases small amounts of this mineral—vital to proper muscle and circulatory function—from the bones. (Calcitonin, a hormone produced by special cells in the thyroid, may help regulate levels of blood calcium by promoting its storage in the bones.)

EXCESSIVE PARATHYROID HORMONE DISEASE

DEFINITION

This is a condition in which too much parathyroid hormone is released. Because parathyroid hormone acts to keep calcium levels constant in body tissues, an overproduction (hyperparathyroidism) may cause an excess of calcium (hypercalcemia). Primary hyperparathyroidism is one of the most common of all endocrine disorders and occurs in about 1 out of 1,000 adults.

CAUSE

Excessive parathyroid activity usually results from benign tumors on the glands.

DIAGNOSIS

Many people never exhibit symptoms, but discover they have excessive parathyroid hormone disease upon routine calcium screening. Symptoms may include kidney stones, headache, fatigue, increased urination, and thirst. High levels of parathyroid hormone and calcium in the blood and a high level of calcium in the urine confirm the diagnosis.

TREATMENT

The condition can be treated by removing the tumors surgically.

MALE/FEMALE DIFFERENCES

Women are twice as likely to have primary hyperparathyroidism.

DEFICIENT PARATHYROID HORMONE DISEASE

DEFINITION/CAUSE

This is a condition in which there is a lack or severe underproduction of parathyroid hormone (hypoparathyroidism). It is usually associated with removal of the thyroid gland or with an autoimmune disorder affecting the parathyroids.

DIAGNOSIS

Muscle contraction or spasms and convulsions caused by lack of calcium in the blood are the major symptoms.

TREATMENT

Because they no longer have parathyroid hormone to release calcium to the blood, people with this deficiency must take calcium and vitamin D supplements for the rest of their lives.

ADRENAL DISORDERS

The adrenal glands are triangular-shaped and rest atop each kidney. Each has two parts:

1. The cortex, which produces the steroid hormones, such as aldosterone and cortisol.
2. The medulla, which secretes catecholamine hormones, such as epinephrine (adrenaline) and norepinephrine. Since catecholamines are produced by many other body tissues, the adrenal medulla is not essential to maintain life.

In contrast, the cortex, which makes up the outer layers of the gland, secretes hormones that are essential to a number of body functions:

Aldosterone, which helps maintain fluid balance by retaining salt in the body.

Sex steroids, which function similarly to the hormones produced by the ovaries and testes.

Glucocorticoids, which are involved in sugar and protein metabolism, maintenance of blood pressure, and respond to physical stress. They also are involved in an intricate feedback relationship that triggers the release of certain pituitary hormones.

Specific disorders related to adrenal failure include the following conditions.

ADDISON'S DISEASE

DEFINITION

This term applies to the gradual destruction of the adrenal glands.

CAUSE

Addison's disease is usually caused by an autoimmune disorder, but may also be due to other diseases, such as tuberculosis.

DIAGNOSIS

Symptoms include increasing fatigue, loss of appetite, abdominal pains, nausea, dizziness or fainting, a darkening of the skin, and inability to cope with even minor physical stresses. One of the major dangers involves an inability to overcome even a minor infection, which may precipitate extreme weakness, shock, and death.

Diagnosis is confirmed with tests showing low levels of the hormone cortisol in the blood and urine after administering adrenocorticotropic hormone (ACTH).

TREATMENT

Treatment involves replacement of the missing adrenal hormone, cortisol, either with cortisol or cortisone tablets and an aldosterone substitute, such as Florinef.

MALE/FEMALE DIFFERENCES

Addison's disease is slightly more prevalent in women than in men.

CUSHING'S SYNDROME

DEFINITION/CAUSE

This disorder is caused by excessive glucocorticoids, usually the result of an ACTH-producing tumor of the pituitary gland. Other causes are excessive ACTH from malignant or benign tumors of various glands, or tumors of the adrenal glands.

DIAGNOSIS

The major symptoms are:

  Muscle wasting and weakness
  Accumulation of fat on the face, trunk, and neck (sometimes leading to a humped appearance)
  Thinning of the skin, leading to bruising and stretch marks
  Reddening of the skin and excessive hair growth

As the disease progresses, there may be high blood pressure, increased susceptibility to infection, and diabetes mellitus.

Confirmed diagnosis of Cushing's syndrome depends on abnormally high results from tests of cortisol levels in blood and urine and evidence of a tumor detected by a CT or MRI scan of the adrenal glands or pituitary gland.

TREATMENT

Treatment depends upon the cause. If there is an adrenal tumor, its removal is imperative. If the problem lies in the pituitary, the pituitary tumor may be removed surgi-cally or treated with radiation to stop its overproduction of ACTH. If the entire pituitary gland is removed, as is occasionally necessary, then replacement therapy for hypopituitarism (cortisol, thyroxine, sex hormones) is necessary.

DRUG-RELATED ADRENAL INSUFFICIENCY

DEFINITION/CAUSE

The most common cause of adrenal insufficiency (adrenal glands underproducing hormones) is due to steroid therapy for nonendocrine diseases, such as asthma or arthritis. Long-term steroid therapy causes atrophy (shrinking) of the adrenal glands and lowered ACTH secretion. ACTH is the pituitary hormone that stimulates the adrenal gland to produce certain hormones.

DIAGNOSIS

Blood tests showing lowered levels of ACTH and a history of taking the drugs that cause this disorder are necessary for diagnosis.

TREATMENT

Recovery of adrenal function may take 6 to 12 months following withdrawal of steroid therapy; during this time, patients are at high risk for shock during physical stresses (surgery, anesthesia, infections, etc.) because of their cortisol deficiency and they must receive supplementary steroids for these stress factors.

ALTERNATIVE THERAPIES

Because withdrawal from medications for asthma and arthritis may be necessary to treat this condition, alternative therapies for these other problems may be helpful. (See chapters 20 and 25 for details on alternative therapies for asthma and arthritis.)

PREVENTION

This disorder can be prevented by avoiding long-term steroid use.

HYPERALDOSTERONISM (CONN'S SYNDROME)

DEFINITION/CAUSE

This disorder, marked by overproduction of aldosterone, is usually caused by small hormone-producing tumors. Aldosterone is a steroid hormone produced by the adrenal cortex.

DIAGNOSIS

Since aldosterone is the most powerful of the salt-retaining hormones, its excess leads to high blood pressure and a depletion of potassium, which is essential for proper muscle function and maintaining the body's biochemical balance. Symptoms of hyperaldosteronism, in addition to high blood pressure, include muscle weakness and cramps and sometimes excessive urination at night. A high blood serum level of aldosterone confirms diagnosis.

TREATMENT

Treatment involves removing the aldosterone-producing tumor. There are some cases that can be controlled by drugs, especially if both adrenals are secreting excessive aldosterone (primary adrenal hyperplasia).

SUMMING UP

Thanks to the endocrine system we can adapt and respond to our internal and external environment. This highly complex system uses intricate feedback networks and chemical or neural signals to keep the various hormones in proper balance. Diabetes is the most common endocrine disorder, while thyroid disease also occurs frequently. The other disorders are relatively rare, but when they occur they can cause a wide range of symptoms affecting all organ systems as well as psychological responses.

Advances in measuring levels of the various hormones now make it easier to diagnose many endocrine disorders accurately. Most can be treated either by replacing deficient hormones or curtailing the overproduction of others.

22
Disorders of the Digestive System

JONATHAN LaPOOK, M.D.

Parts of this chapter are adapted from the chapter by Lewis P. Schneider, M.D., in the revised second edition.

Digestion exists for health, and health exists for life, and life exists for the love of music or beautiful things.
—G.K. Chesterton, "On Misunderstanding," *Generally Speaking (1928).*

One barium enema is worth a year of psychoanalysis.
—Robert Whitlock, M.D., lecture to medical students at Columbia College of Physicians and Surgeons (1978).

Gastroenterology is an intricate mixture of psychiatry, medicine, and surgery. A typical complaint such as abdominal pain could result from a wide variety of causes ranging from stage fright to a ruptured aortic aneurysm. It is the job of the physician to combine medical knowledge with a carefully performed patient history and physical examination to arrive at a likely diagnosis and associated therapeutic plan.

How can a patient help the physician arrive at the correct diagnosis and therapy? Learning some basic facts about digestion can improve your ability to describe your symptoms, understand the explanations of a physician, and participate in the management of your illness. In addition, understanding how your body works can help you establish a lifestyle that will help prevent problems from developing in the first place.

To help understand how "things go wrong" it is useful to first explore how "things go right." In health, the digestive system is a wonderfully interrelated system involved in the orchestration of many different organs to perform diverse functions including nutrition, immunity, hormonal regulation, and the elimination of waste products.

To fulfill these functions, digestion mechanically and chemically alters food in a complex process controlled by intricate feedback systems involving the nervous and endocrine systems. After food is chewed and swallowed, it is broken down and liquefied as it moves through the stomach and small intestine and then solidified in the large intestine where the waste materials are prepared for elimination.

ANATOMY OF THE DIGESTIVE SYSTEM

The digestive tract is basically a 25- to 30-foot hollow tube, stretching from the mouth to the anus, whose sections each accomplish distinct tasks (see figure 22.1). Food is pushed through the digestive tract by both peri-

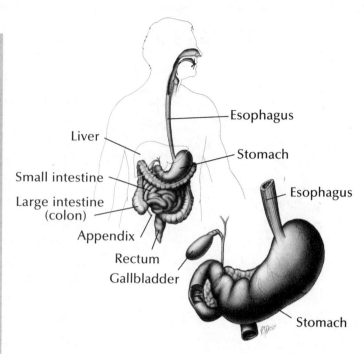

Figure 22.1: The normal gastrointestinal tract is shown here from its beginning in the mouth to its end in the anus.

stalsis, a coordinated series of wavelike muscular contractions, and, to a lesser extent, gravity. The digestive tract branches off into the digestive organs and glands, including the liver, gallbladder, and pancreas. Ingested food follows the basic path of:

1. **The mouth:** In the mouth, food is chewed, broken into small pieces between the teeth, and mixed with saliva. Saliva is produced by six salivary glands, located in pairs on each side of the face. Saliva contains amylase, the first of many digestive enzymes that break down food into its component parts as it moves through the digestive tract. Amylase begins the breakdown of complex carbohydrates, or starches, into the simple sugars that are used by the body for fuel.

2. **Pathway to the stomach:** After food is chewed, it is swallowed, beginning the journey to the stomach. Swallowing is an almost unconscious effort that begins with a carefully coordinated closing of the larynx to prevent food from going into the windpipe as it moves into the pharynx, a funnel-shaped structure leading to the esophagus. The esophagus, a muscular tube about a foot long between the mouth and the stomach, connects to the stomach through an opening in the diaphragm, the muscle wall separating the chest and abdominal cavities. The esophageal sphincter, a valve standing guard at the juncture of the esophagus and stomach, relaxes as chewed food approaches, allowing the food to pass into the stomach, and then contracts to prevent a backflow or regurgitation of stomach contents into the esophagus.

3. **The stomach:** The stomach mixes, stores, and partially digests food. A muscular organ, located mostly on the left-hand side below the lower ribs, consists of several parts:

1. *Cardia:* the part immediately adjoining the esophagus
2. *Fundus:* the upper, dome-shaped part of the stomach
3. *The body (or corpus):* the middle stomach section
4. *Antrum:* the lower third of the stomach

The acid-secreting parietal cells are located in the body and fundus. The antrum contains the cells that make the hormone gastrin, which stimulates the parietal cells to produce hydrochloric acid. Stomach acid kills most bacteria and other microorganisms present in food. A special mucous coating protects the stomach wall and other intestinal organs from being burned by this gastric acid.

The stomach's 3 layers of muscle, running up and down, horizontally, and crosswise, contract to produce a churning action that mixes food with digestive enzymes and hydrochloric acid. The gastric chemicals help break down complex nutrients—carbohydrates, proteins, and fats—into their components. However, the mixture (chyme), which leaves the stomach, must be further processed by the small intestine to be adequately absorbed.

4. **The small intestine:** By the time food is ready to leave the stomach, it has been transformed into a thin liquid. Digestion in the stomach generates signals to the brain via the vagus nerve. An intricate combination of neural, chemical, and hormonal factors controls the rate at which stomach contents flow out through the pyloric valve and the pyloric canal. The pyloric valve releases only a small amount of partially digested food at a time to the small intestine. The small intestine in an adult is 12 to 22 feet long and lies coiled in neat loops below the stomach, surrounded by the colon (large intestine). Consisting of three sections—the duodenum, jejunum, and ileum—the small intestine completes the digestive process and absorbs nutrients. Stimulated by hormones produced in response to the presence of food, bile from the liver and gallbladder empty into the duodenum along with digestive juices from the pancreas. Millions of tiny fingerlike projections called villi on the intestinal wall absorb digested food into capillaries or, in the case of most fats, into lymph channels.

5. **The large intestine:** Undigested food, water, and other intestinal waste passes from the ileum through the ileocecal valve into the cecum, a pouch-shaped chamber located in the lower right part of the abdomen. Projecting out from the cecum is the appendix, a thin finger-shaped organ of unknown function in humans (see fig-

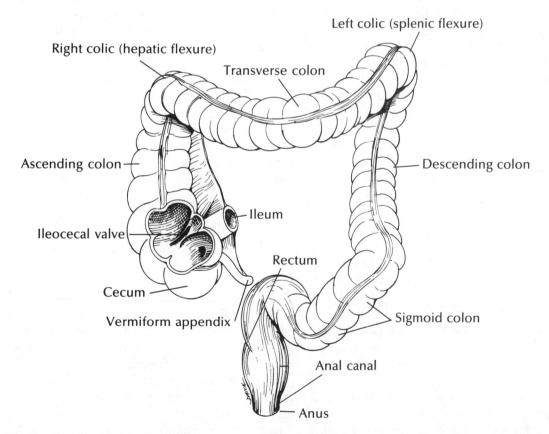

Figure 22.2: The colon, or large intestine, begins on the lower right side and curves up, across, and then down the abdominal cavity, ending at the anus.

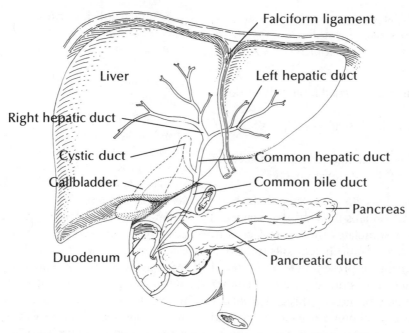

Figure 22.3: The liver performs a number of vital functions, including many that are closely associated with adjacent digestive organs.

ure 22.2). From the cecum, the 4- to 5-foot colon makes 4 broad turns:

- The ascending colon extends upward into the upper right part of the abdomen just below the liver.
- The transverse colon turns at the liver (the hepatic flexure) and crosses to the opposite side of the body cavity.
- The descending colon turns downward at the spleen (the splenic flexure) and descends into the lower left part of the abdomen.
- From the descending colon, the sigmoid colon makes an S-shaped curve, passing through the lower left and midline aspects of the abdomen before emptying into the rectum.

In the colon, much of the water and salt is extracted from the undigested waste products and returned to the circulation, transforming the liquid mass to more solid feces. When you are born, your colon is devoid of microorganisms but soon acquires large amounts of bacteria that break down dietary material not digested by the stomach or small intestine. Changes in this intestinal "flora" can cause diarrhea when antibiotic therapy disrupts its growth and overgrowth after certain types of intestinal surgery.

6. **The rectum and anus:** The rectum is located at the bottom of the large intestine in a straight section, about 6 inches in length. From the rectum the stool passes through the anus, the opening at the lowermost end of the digestive tract, through which it is finally excreted. The internal sphincter and the external sphincter, two muscles at the bottom of the anus, must relax in order for stool to be evacuated.

7. **Digestive organs:** Branching off the intestinal tract are the major digestive organs, the liver and pancreas, and the gallbladder, which stores bile produced in the liver for later release into the duodenum.

- *The liver:* One of the body's largest, most versatile, and complex organs, the liver manufactures bile, cholesterol, vitamin A, clotting factors, and complex proteins, while regulating the amount of glucose and protein entering the bloodstream for distribution to body tissues. The liver also detoxifies alcohol and other potentially harmful chemicals and stores minerals (including iron), fat-soluble vitamins, and glycogen—a starch readily transformed into glucose to fuel body tissues (see figure 22.3).
- *The gallbladder:* A small sac linked by ducts to both the liver and duodenum, the gallbladder concentrates and stores bile, which is needed to digest fats.
- *The pancreas:* About 8 inches long, with its head adjacent to the duodenum and its tail extending up under the stomach and next to the spleen, the larger portion of the pancreas manufactures digestive juice containing enzymes for breaking down carbohydrates, proteins, and fats. Scattered throughout the pancreas are tiny clusters of cells—the islets of Langerhans—which produce the hormones insulin and glucagon, essential for metabolizing carbohydrates (and to a lesser extent, proteins and fats) and regulating blood sugar (glucose). (See chapter 21 for a more detailed discussion.)

Although each portion of the intestinal tract fulfills a unique function, there is enough overlap and duplication so that almost normal digestion can continue even when large portions are removed because of disease or injury. For example, even if your entire stomach were removed, you could continue to eat a reasonably normal diet and lead a normal life. Similarly, portions of the small intestine and all of the colon and the gallbladder can be taken out, if necessary, and, although the pancreas produces essential hormones, these can be replaced by injection if the pancreas ceases functioning or is removed. In addition, the pancreatic enzymes required for metabolism of carbohydrates, proteins, and fats may be supplied as oral medication.

The liver, however, is the exception among the digestive organs: Its functions are irreplaceable and absolutely essential to maintain life.

COMMON GASTROINTESTINAL COMPLAINTS

From time to time, most people experience a mild digestive upset, such as constipation, diarrhea, heartburn, indigestion, or nausea and vomiting. Most of these are self-limiting and often require only commonsense remedies, such as avoiding foods that seem invariably to produce discomfort, modifying eating habits, or waiting until a mild illness passes. If the symptoms are recurrent or become progressively worse, a physician should be consulted.

By actively participating in your own health care you can help your physician arrive at a correct diagnosis. Before your office visit, try to organize your observations concerning your symptoms or illness. Keeping a "symptom diary" with time, place, and surrounding events (food, stress) can be extremely helpful, especially when trying to pin down a specific cause such as lactose intolerance. If you have been previously seen elsewhere for the problem, be sure to have your medical records sent to your new physician prior to your office visit. In addition to the questions listed in "Describing Your Symptoms" in chapter 11, try to have answers for the following questions.

1. Is there any relationship to food? Which foods?
2. Do the symptoms vary with time of day? Do they wake you up?
3. Does moving your bowels relieve or increase pain?
4. If you have diarrhea, does fasting make the diarrhea better?
5. Does any close contact have a similar problem? Is there a family history of gastrointestinal disease?
6. Have there been any recent changes in your lifestyle (e.g., job, family, stress, travel)?

7. What medications are you taking? Do not forget to describe over-the-counter medications, especially ones such as Alka-Seltzer, which contains aspirin. Remember that Pepto-Bismol can turn your stool dark or black.

GASTROINTESTINAL BLEEDING

DEFINITION

Gastrointestinal bleeding, often the first sign that an abnormality exists in the gastrointestinal tract, may be manifested in several ways.

- Hematemesis: Bloody vomitus, either bright red or older, resembling coffee grounds.
- Melena: Shiny, black, sticky, foul-smelling stool. Melena is usually caused by bleeding from an upper intestinal source.
- Hematochezia: Bright red or maroon blood excreted from the rectum, either in the form of pure blood or mixed with formed stool or diarrhea.
- Occult bleeding, which can only be detected through stool testing with a chemical reagent.
- Symptoms of blood loss (such as dizziness) without direct symptoms of bleeding.

CAUSE

While the vomiting of blood suggests an upper intestinal source, the passage of blood from the rectum can be secondary to an upper or lower intestinal source. Blood in the form of dark, tarry stool (melena) is usually secondary to an upper intestinal source such as peptic ulcer. Bright red blood (hematochezia) is usually secondary to a lower gastrointestinal source such as hemorrhoids, diverticulosis, or arteriovenous malformation; however, hematochezia may also be secondary to rapid transit of blood through the intestine from an actively bleeding upper intestinal source such as peptic ulcer or varices.

UPPER GASTROINTESTINAL BLEEDING

Causes of upper gastrointestinal bleeding include:

- Peptic ulcers: the most common cause of upper gastrointestinal bleeding, peptic ulcers can develop in the stomach or duodenum.
- Gastritis: stomach inflammation.
- Mallory-Weiss tear: a tear of the lining of the esophagus and/or upper stomach secondary to retching.
- Esophagitis: inflammation of the esophagus, often secondary to acid reflux.
- Large hiatal hernias: bleeding from around or near the hernia may be associated with chronic, low-

grade blood loss and anemia. Such blood loss is often invisible upon examination of the stool and must be detected by special chemical testing of the stool (e.g., Hemoccult).

- Benign and malignant tumors.
- Varices: distended veins (like varicose veins) that form in the GI tract, often as a result of liver disease (cirrhosis), creating extra pressure in vessels. When varices bleed, the blood loss can be profuse.

LOWER GASTROINTESTINAL BLEEDING

Causes of lower gastrointestinal bleeding include:

- Hemorrhoids: prominent veins in the anus that can sometimes become irritated and bleed.
- Fissures: a "cut" in the lining of the anus, often caused by irritation from passing a hard stool.
- Diverticulosis: outpouchings of the colon that can sometimes bleed profusely. A rare type of diverticulum called a Meckel's diverticulum is a cause of acute bleeding in children.
- Vascular anomalies: abnormal blood vessels that can either bleed rapidly or slowly ooze. Slow, intermittent oozing can indicate chronic, low-grade blood loss and iron deficiency anemia. Acquired vascular anomalies tend to occur in elderly patients while congenital anomalies such as those seen in Rendu-Osler-Weber tend to occur in younger patients.
- Colon tumors
- Inflammatory bowel disease
- Infectious colitis
- Unusual causes of gastrointestinal bleeding: invisible (occult) bleeding and iron deficiency have been seen in marathon runners; the cause is unclear but may have to do with decreased blood supply (ischemia) to the intestine during active exercise. Other unusual causes of bleeding include vasculitis, amyloidosis, Whipple's disease, and solitary ulcers.

Eating beets or other red-colored food may result in bright red fluid excreted from the rectum that can be mistaken for bleeding. True rectal bleeding can indicate serious conditions, however, and rectal bleeding should be evaluated by a physician to exclude abnormalities of the small and large intestines.

DIAGNOSIS

While stools that are black and tarry frequently signal upper gastrointestinal bleeding, black stools may also be caused by iron or the bismuth found in medications such as Pepto-Bismol. Black stools caused by degradation of blood may be the only clue of bleeding from the stom-

ach, esophagus, or duodenum. The appropriate tests to diagnose the cause of an episode of gastrointestinal bleeding depend on the symptoms and on whether the bleeding seems acute or chronic.

The more common tests for gastrointestinal bleeding include:

- *Upper endoscopy or gastroscopy:* examination of the upper GI tract with a fiber-optic instrument inserted through the mouth, enabling an examiner to visually spot problems such as a shallow ulcer or inflamed area, collect tissue samples, or cauterize an area to stop bleeding. Upper endoscopy is the most effective test for diagnosing the cause of upper intestinal bleeding. Endoscopy is contraindicated for persons who have recently suffered heart attacks.
- *Barium swallow (upper GI series):* provides the contrast necessary for x-rays to show ulcers, inflammation, tumors, or obstruction in the esophagus, stomach, or small intestine.
- *Colonoscopy:* examination of the colon or large intestine with a fiber-optic instrument inserted through the rectum. The colon is first cleansed with 2 days of liquid diet followed by consumption of a special cleansing solution. Colonoscopy is normally used if a barium enema does not explain bleeding or if tests indicate an inflammatory, polypoid, or possibly malignant abnormality in the large intestine. A colonoscope can also be used to collect tissue samples and, in some cases, to remove polyps.
- *Proctoscopy, or proctosigmoidoscopy:* allows a view of the rectum and lower part of the colon with a fiber-optic instrument, to check for signs of rectal cancer or diagnose polyps, internal hemorrhoids, and abscesses as causes of lower intestinal bleeding.
- *Barium enema (lower GI series):* allows x-rays to show abnormalities in the colon or large intestine indicating polyps, tumors, diverticulosis pouches, or other structural abnormalities.
- *Occult bleeding tests:* detect invisible or hidden blood in stool samples (e.g., Hemoccult cards).

In cases of severe or unexplained rectal bleeding, an angiogram (arteriogram) or a nuclear scan of the blood vessels leading to the intestine and stomach may help identify the site of bleeding.

TREATMENT

Treatment of gastrointestinal bleeding depends on the suspected cause:

- *Bipolar electrocoagulation (BPEC), heater probe, and laser:* endoscopic technique using heat to coagulate small blood vessels such as those in a bleeding gastric ulcer.

- *Epinephrine or sclerosing agents:* injected into the base of an ulcer to stop bleeding.
- *Sclerotherapy:* a series of injections administered through an endoscope to stop variceal bleeding.
- *Surgery:* used to treat cases of acute bleeding that do not respond to more conservative treatment. The extent of surgery must be individualized. In the case of a bleeding ulcer, such surgery may vary from a simple oversewing of the ulcer to removal of half the stomach (a hemigastrectomy). Patients usually function quite well following surgery but may suffer from complications such as scarring (adhesions)—with associated pain or obstruction—and diarrhea (dumping syndrome).
- *Medication:* with the exception of vasopressin and somatostatin, which may slow bleeding from varices, no medication has been shown to actually slow bleeding from an intestinal source. The role of medication is to heal the source of bleeding to prevent recurrent hemorrhage. A most common example is the use of H_2-blockers (Tagamet, Zantac, Pepcid) to treat bleeding ulcers. It has been shown that most duodenal ulcers are associated with a bacterium called *Helicobacter pylori* infection and may recur unless the bacteria is treated (although the long-term recurrence rate is unknown).

CONSTIPATION

DEFINITION

Constipation is a decrease in the frequency of stool, or difficulty in formation or passage of the stool. Frequency of bowel movements varies widely from person to person within populations, and from one country to another. Many Americans believe they need one stool daily, but no medical evidence support this conviction. Each person has an individual bowel pattern, and frequency of "normal" evacuation may range from three bowel movements per day to only three per week. If this frequency decreases considerably, if there is pain, or if the stools passed are very hard, an individual can be considered constipated.

CAUSE

The number of stools per day may be influenced by diet and activity. People leading a sedentary life or confined to bed will sometimes become constipated, possibly because of decreased contractions of the intestine and of decreased liquid intake, causing hard stool. Often a diet very low in fiber (with few fruits and vegetables) causes constipation. Other causes of constipation include:

- Abnormality in the contractions or motility of bowel muscles, sometimes related to changes of pressure in the intestine or to irritable bowel syndrome. Neu-

rological and endocrine disorders, such as underactive thyroid gland or diabetes mellitus, can also influence contractions of the intestine and cause constipation.

- Medication, including analgesics such as narcotics (Demerol, morphine, codeine), anticonvulsants, antidepressants, anticholinergics, and antacids containing calcium and aluminum compounds. Medications may be especially constipating for elderly patients. Extended use of laxatives may cause constipation by damaging nerves in the colon. Laxative abuse with anthracene cathartics such as cascara agrada, senna, aloe, rhubarb, and frangula cause deposition of black pigment in the colon, a condition called melanosis coli. It is not certain whether the pigment itself is toxic to the colon.
- Blockage of the path of the intestines from a stricture (narrowed area), or by a malignant or benign tumor or polyp, or from diverticulitis.
- External causes, in which an organ or tissue mass presses on the intestine from the outside, such as an enlarged prostate pressing on the rectum, or endometriosis, a gynecologic condition in which endometrial lining growing outside its usual uterine location can compress the large intestine.
- Depression, or neurologic causes such as spinal cord injury.

DIAGNOSIS

If you are constipated, particularly if this represents a change in your bowel habits, you should see a physician for an abdominal and rectal examination to check for blood in the stool, and get blood tests to check for anemia, electrolyte disorders, hypothyroidism, and diabetes. In some cases, further evaluation with lower endoscopy or barium enema may be warranted.

TREATMENT

If no reason for the constipation is found, the amount of fiber or bran in the diet should be cautiously increased, starting with fruits (such as bananas) and vegetables containing large amounts of pulp or fiber. Increased abdominal gas and bloating are likely to occur in the first weeks of a high-fiber diet and usually diminish with time. Fiber intake should be increased gradually and adjusted as tolerated. Patients with diverticulosis should avoid popcorn, nuts, and fruits and vegetables that contain seeds or pits.

HOME REMEDIES AND ALTERNATIVE THERAPIES

- Increased walking and physical activity
- Eating slowly, rather than rushing through meals
- Adding stool softeners to the diet
- Increased consumption of liquids

- Breakfasting on fruit such as prunes or apricots, or fruit juices, often in conjunction with bran or psyllium preparations cereals
- Occasional use of laxatives, particularly in elderly patients, or for people who are temporarily bedridden while recovering from an illness. Laxatives fall into several categories:

  Bulk-forming agents: high in fiber such as methylcellulose and psyllium, e.g., Metamucil, Citrucel, Fibercon

  Emollient laxatives: stool softeners, e.g., Colace, Surfak

  Lubricants: mineral oil

  Magnesia-containing medications: milk of magnesia or citrate of magnesia

  Stimulant: Carter's Little Pills, Ex-Lax, Senokot

  Hyperosmotic: lactulose (taken orally), glycerine suppositories

- Enemas (such as Fleet sodium phosphate enema) may be recommended under the supervision of a physician.
- Behavior therapy and biofeedback. Techniques try to encourage relaxation rather than contraction of the pelvic floor during straining.
- Medication. Cisapride is a new gastrointestinal prokinetic medication that may be helpful in patients with constipation.

If a physician discovers an impacted stool in the anal area, as can occur especially in elderly or bedridden patients, digital disimpaction or enemas are often very important as the first step of treatment.

PREVENTION

Maintaining an exercise regimen and a healthy diet with plenty of fruit, vegetables, and adequate liquids may help prevent recurrence of constipation.

MALE/FEMALE DIFFERENCES

Pregnant women often suffer constipation, but they should consult their doctors before taking any medication, including laxatives.

DIARRHEA

DEFINITION

Diarrhea is an increase in the frequency, volume, or liquid content of the stool.

CAUSE

Diarrhea can result from the inability of the intestine to absorb nutrients, salt, and water properly, or from a number of conditions that cause the intestine to lose (secrete) fluid and salt.

- Infections of the gastrointestinal tract in otherwise healthy people. Viruses (e.g., rotavirus, adenovirus, Norwalk virus), bacteria (e.g., *Campylobacter, Salmonella, Shigella, E. coli, Vibrio cholerae*), and parasites (e.g., *Giardia,* amoeba) can each cause diarrhea. Various strains of *E. coli* are typical causes of traveler's diarrhea.
- Infections in immunocompromised hosts such as patients with AIDS or patients receiving immunosuppressive medication. In addition to getting the "usual" infections listed above, immunocompromised patients may become infected with more "unusual" organisms such as *Mycobacterium avium* and cytomegalovirus.
- Food poisoning and drug or food allergies.
- Acute conditions such as inflammation of the large or small intestine, as with ileitis or colitis, pelvic inflammation, and toxic shock syndrome.
- Rectal sexually transmitted diseases, especially in homosexual men.
- Chronic or recurrent diarrhea may be caused by irritable bowel syndrome, inflammatory bowel disease, parasitic and fungal infections, food allergies, colon cancer, diverticulitis, malabsorption syndromes, and heavy metal poisoning.
- Tumors, whether benign or malignant, can damage the cells of the intestine or cause the intestines to actively secrete increased amounts of salt and water, as with rare tumors found in carcinoid syndrome and Zollinger-Ellison syndrome.
- Antibiotics can cause alteration of the normal intestinal flora and production of colitis secondary to *Clostridium difficile* toxin.
- Other medications, such as quinidine, magnesium-containing antacids (Maalox, Mylanta), chemotherapy, bile acids, laxatives, potassium, and prostaglandins.
- Alcohol can increase intestinal contraction and cause diarrhea.
- Running. "Runner's diarrhea" can occur during or immediately after jogging or running. The cause is unclear but may be related to diet (intake of sugar, causing an osmotic diarrhea, or fiber), abnormal gastric emptying and intestinal fluid absorption, or release of neuropeptides or prostaglandins during exercise. Preventive measures include gradually increasing exercise rather than plunging into a strenuous regimen, avoiding food for several hours prior to a run, and attempting to have a bowel movement prior to exercise. Under the guidance of a physician, medication may be attempted.
- Cystic fibrosis, chronic pancreatitis, and other diseases of the pancreas, an organ responsible for making digestive enzymes, can cause a decrease in enzyme formation, which can in turn lead to malabsorption, diarrhea, and malnutrition.

• Endocrine disorders such as hyperthyroidism, Addison's disease, and in some cases diabetes mellitus (which may also cause constipation).

DIAGNOSIS

If you have diarrhea, you pass watery or loose stools (2–4 small unformed bowel movements daily are diarrhea). Often, the causes of diarrhea can be traced in a medical history. A variety of physical and laboratory tests, such as rectal examination to exclude occult blood in the stool, sigmoidoscopy, and culture of the stool for bacteria and parasites, may be undertaken depending on the circumstances. Patients should try to note whether the diarrhea stops during fasting, because this may establish malabsorption as a cause rather than a secretory disorder. Food poisoning may be suggested if multiple people eating the same meal develop diarrhea or vomiting.

TREATMENT

Most bouts of diarrhea are not associated with fever or intestinal bleeding and are self-limited—they last a limited time and then cease without treatment. Unless significant dehydration occurs, it may be best not to treat mild diarrhea for the first few hours, since the body may be purging itself of an intestinal infection. If diarrhea persists, use of a kaolin-pectin preparation or bismuth is often helpful. Aluminum-containing antacid (such as Amphojel) can also give symptomatic relief. Temporarily avoiding high-fiber foods, dairy products, and sugar-containing drinks may also help until a self-limited infection is resolved.

If these medications don't relieve the diarrhea promptly, or if there is fever, vomiting, abdominal pain, or blood in the stool, the patient should consult a doctor. In cases of severe diarrhea, the first line of treatment may be fluids for rehydration and to restore electrolyte balance.

Diarrhea is sometimes caused by antibiotics and may necessitate their discontinuation. If *C. difficile* toxin is a cause, treatment with Vancomycin or Flagyl is usually prescribed. Infectious diarrhea may necessitate treatment with antibiotics; however, often the infection is self-limited and does not require treatment. Some physicians prescribe yogurt or lactobacillus as a way of restoring the normal ecological balance of the intestines by replacing intestinal bacteria destroyed by the antibiotics. Pregnant women should consult their doctors before taking any medication.

HOME REMEDIES AND ALTERNATIVE THERAPY

Yogurt or lactobacillus may alleviate some cases of diarrhea, and rice may also be helpful. Oral hydration is extremely important, especially in infants, who may quickly become dehydrated. Chicken soup with rice is excellent because the glucose and amino acids help transport sodium and water from the intestine to the bloodstream. Rice-ORS (oral rehydration solution) has been found extremely effective in treating dehydration due to diarrhea and is a valuable form of treatment in underdeveloped countries. All cases of protracted diarrhea should be evaluated by a physician.

PREVENTION

If you have problems with periodic diarrhea, keeping a food diary may enable you to correlate diarrhea with ingestion of a particular food. Avoiding the offending food may then alleviate future diarrhea episodes.

HEARTBURN

DEFINITION

Heartburn, or acid indigestion, is a burning sensation—not usually directly related to the heart—arising behind the sternum (breastbone) often spreading to the throat, jaw, or mouth (see figure 22.4). Because the symptoms of heartburn resemble heart disease, and the reflux of heartburn can raise the heart rate and lead to angina, a physician must carefully consider both diagnoses. (See "Hiatal Hernia" for discussion of reflux.)

INDIGESTION (DYSPEPSIA)

DEFINITION

Indigestion (dyspepsia) is a general term describing a feeling of discomfort in the gastrointestinal tract.

DIAGNOSIS

The term "indigestion" can include epigastric burning, heartburn, abdominal pain, bloating, belching, nausea and vomiting, and sometimes diarrhea. Because it is such an ill-defined term, "indigestion" is not as useful a symptom to a physician as more precise descriptions such as "upper abdominal burning." In describing your symptoms, try to define where in your abdomen the discomfort usually occurs; simply reporting that the pain is in "my stomach" is not detailed enough, especially since patients often incorrectly use the term "stomach" when they mean abdomen (the stomach takes up only a small portion of the abdominal cavity).

CAUSE

Sometimes digestive problems have an identifiable cause, such as peptic ulcer, esophagitis, gallbladder or

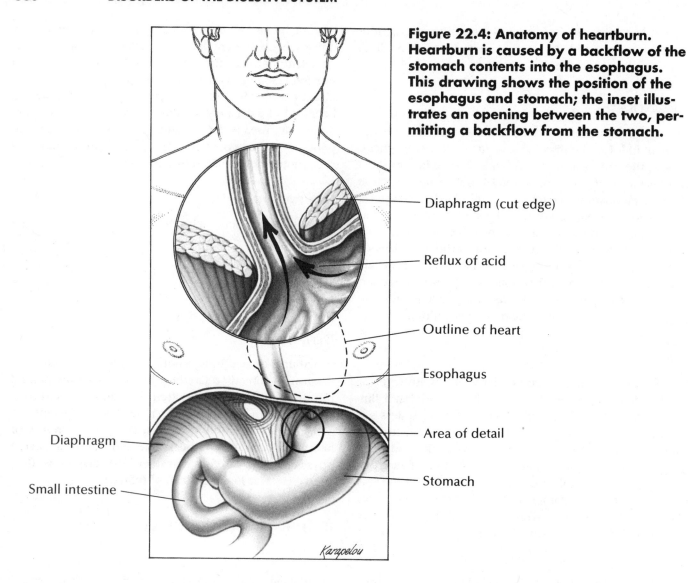

Figure 22.4: Anatomy of heartburn. Heartburn is caused by a backflow of the stomach contents into the esophagus. This drawing shows the position of the esophagus and stomach; the inset illustrates an opening between the two, permitting a backflow from the stomach.

Diaphragm (cut edge)

Reflux of acid

Outline of heart

Esophagus

Area of detail

Stomach

Diaphragm

Small intestine

Karapelou

liver disease, bacterial or viral infections, or the use of certain medications, and these possible causes should be investigated in recurrent indigestion. Often, however, there is no obvious organic cause for the problem. Excessive air swallowing may contribute to feeling bloated and to excessive belching. Stress, caffeine, tobacco, and alcohol can all exacerbate underlying conditions such as hiatal hernias and reflux, and thus may appear to "cause" indigestion.

Stomach problems also may be of psychological origin, or may be an attention-getting device, albeit an unconscious one. Complaints of "my stomach hurts" are often heard from children who do not want to go to school or perform an unpleasant task. On the other hand, school-aged children are also prime targets for appendicitis, and therefore organic causes for abdominal pain must always be considered.

Abdominal pain may occur in adults who have difficulty coping with stress. Such pain is usually quite real and not a sign of malingering (see "Irritable Bowel Syndrome").

TREATMENT

Many cases of indigestion do not require medical treatment and will often resolve themselves in a matter of hours. If symptoms persist or grow worse, a physician should be consulted. Indigestion is actually a symptom rather than a disease, so treatment depends on the underlying cause.

PREVENTION

Keeping a food diary is often useful in tracking down specific foods that cause indigestion. Evaluating lifestyle or emotional factors may also help if these are associated with the problem.

HOME REMEDIES AND ALTERNATIVE THERAPIES

A review of eating habits (chewing with the mouth open, talking while chewing, gulping down food) may reveal a tendency to swallow too much air. Drinking fluids after, rather than during a meal, and avoiding eating late at night may alleviate discomfort. Avoid spicy foods and alcoholic beverages. Do not smoke. Stop taking aspirin if it causes problems—switch to acetaminophen. Relaxation exercises after a meal may also help.

NAUSEA AND VOMITING

DEFINITION

Nausea and vomiting are not diseases but symptoms of many disorders. At some point, almost everyone experiences the queasy feeling of nausea or the uncontrolled, forceful regurgitation of food characteristic of vomiting. The sensation of nausea may be triggered in nerves of the middle ear, the gastrointestinal tract, or the brain. When these impulses are received by the brain's "vomiting center," a sequence of responses is set in motion.

- The esophageal sphincter relaxes.
- The diaphragm and abdominal muscles contract.
- The larynx (windpipe) closes.
- The lower (pyloric) part of the stomach contracts.
- The contents of the stomach are expelled through the esophagus and mouth.

CAUSE

The feeling of nausea and the vomiting reflex may be triggered by a wide range of stimuli or circumstances, including:

- Motion sickness
- Viral or bacterial illness
- Food allergies
- Unpleasant odors or sights
- Food poisoning
- Medications
- Emotional distress
- Chemical toxins

Sometimes nausea and vomiting are symptoms of specific diseases, including infections, heart attacks, kidney or liver disorders, central nervous system disorders, brain tumors, and some types of cancer.

Babies and young children also may be particularly susceptible to nausea and vomiting, and this should not be confused with the common "spitting up" that occurs when a baby eats too much or has air bubbles. Vomiting in an infant may be the result of many factors, including:

- Mild stomach upset
- Intestinal obstruction
- Posture after meals

- Viral infection
- Narcotic addiction
- Milk allergy
- Congenital defect
- Intracranial hemorrhage
- Meningitis
- Metabolic disorders

Nausea and vomiting are also common in women during the first 3 months of pregnancy.

DIAGNOSIS

The timing of nausea or vomiting can indicate their causes: Repeated vomiting during or shortly after a meal may indicate a psychogenic disorder or a peptic ulcer near the pyloric channel. When nausea or vomiting is caused by "preformed toxins," then the reaction is likely to occur within 1 to 8 hours of exposure. When the cause is disease, or bacteria such as salmonella that need time to incubate, the reaction may take longer.

In general, if nausea and vomiting are short-lived and related to an identifiable cause—spoiled food, car sickness, or a viral illness, for instance—they probably are not cause for concern. Accompanied by other symptoms—high fever, pain, diarrhea, profuse sweating—prolonged or recurrent nausea and vomiting should be evaluated by a doctor. Unusual-appearing vomitus may indicate an underlying disease.

- Undigested food may indicate esophageal outpouching (diverticulum).
- Blood may be from a bleeding ulcer or from a tear in the esophagus (Mallory-Weiss tear) due to retching.
- Vomit emitting a fecal odor indicates intestinal obstruction.

TREATMENT

Dehydration is perhaps the most dangerous effect of prolonged vomiting, especially in a young child or if it is accompanied by diarrhea, so liquid should be ingested after vomiting if possible. If the condition persists, oral rehydration solutions or intravenous rehydration liquids may be needed to restore liquids and electrolyte balance.

Regurgitation is common in infants until 9 to 12 months, when they normally become upright for much of their waking hours. If posture is a cause of vomiting in infants, placing the child in an infant seat for an hour after meals may help. Diagnosis of vomiting in an infant should include inquiring about passage of the meconium (a mucousy material in the intestines of newborns) and careful examination for signs of abdominal distention. X-rays of the abdomen or GI tract may also be helpful in determining digestive tract problems.

Vomiting associated with surgery, radiation therapy, or drugs, such as anticancer drugs, alcohol, or morphine, often can be controlled by other drugs. There also are a number of drugs available to prevent the nausea and vomiting associated with pregnancy, motion sickness, and vertigo. If the nausea and vomiting stem from other organic conditions, treatment should focus on identifying and treating those conditions.

MALE/FEMALE DIFFERENCES

Nausea and vomiting during pregnancy are, of course, conditions limited to women. Nausea occurs in 50 to 90 percent of pregnancies, while vomiting occurs in 25 to 55 percent. Nausea usually begins shortly after the first missed period, and disappears after the fourth month of pregnancy. The causes of nausea and vomiting during pregnancy are unclear, but there is no evidence of any ill effect on the fetus. Although some antihistamines may be effective in treating morning sickness, in most cases no treatment is indicated (in some cases eating frequent small meals instead of large ones may be helpful).

HOME REMEDIES AND ALTERNATIVE THERAPY

Soothing drinks, such as ginger ale or chamomile tea, may help settle a mild case of nausea such as one accompanying a virus. Chewing a piece of fresh or candied ginger is another home remedy that works for some people. Many pregnant women find that dry crackers relieve nausea. The nausea associated with motion sickness may be prevented by wearing an "acupressure" seasickness bracelet, which has a device that presses upon an acupressure point on the inner wrist. If nausea is caused by nerves or psychological factors, relaxation techniques may also help.

....

COLON DISORDERS

COLORECTAL CANCER

Colorectal cancer is the third most common cancer in the United States after breast and lung cancer, constituting 14 percent of newly diagnosed cancers in both men and women and about 22 percent of all cancer deaths. In 1994 there were 149,000 new cases in the United States and 56,000 related deaths—second only to lung cancer. Colon cancer will affect approximately 6 percent of the current U.S. population. The rate is much lower in other parts of the world, including South America, Asia, and Africa. While colorectal cancer will metastasize (spread) in about half of all cases, most often to the liver, many colon cancer patients who are diagnosed early in the

course of the disease have a good prognosis. For a detailed discussion on diagnosis, treatment, and prevention, see chapter 17, Cancer.

INFLAMMATORY BOWEL DISEASE

Inflammatory bowel disease is a serious but treatable disease. Inflammation of the lining of the gastrointestinal tract is the major finding. Diarrhea, fever, and abdominal pain are typical symptoms. There are two major types of inflammatory bowel disease: Crohn's disease and ulcerative colitis. Crohn's disease can involve both the large intestine (colon) and small intestine, whereas ulcerative colitis involves only the colon (hence the term "colitis"). The cause is unknown but may involve an autoimmune process. Symptoms tend to come and go unpredictably. The disease can sometimes cause joint pain, skin nodules or ulceration, or inflammation of the eyes. Occasionally there are mild abnormalities of liver enzymes. In Crohn's disease there is a higher incidence of kidney stones.

The treatments of Crohn's disease and ulcerative colitis are very similar. Several drugs have been found to be of use. Traditionally, patients with inflammatory bowel disease have been treated with a medication called Sulfasalazine (Azulfidine), composed of a sulfa medicine (sulfapyridine) and 5-aminosalicylic acid (5-ASA), a medication very close to aspirin in structure. However, side effects from the sulfa limit its use in a large number of patients. More recently, medications have been developed that deliver the aspirin to the small and large intestines without the use of sulfa. Such medications include Asacol and Pentasa. Other medicines such as steroids can be used but do have more side effects. Side effects of steroids include weight gain, high blood pressure, high blood sugar, weakened bones, depression, glaucoma, and skin changes.

For treatment of proctitis (rectal inflammation) or inflammation of the lower colon (sigmoid), steroid foam or enemas, 5-ASA enemas (Asacol), or suppositories containing these medications may be helpful.

In severe cases of inflammatory bowel disease, immunosuppression with Azathioprine and 6-mercaptopurine (6-MP) may be used. Cycolosporine is being used in ulcerative colitis but controlled trials are still pending.

Maintaining a good level of nutrition is important. However, there is no specific diet that is recommended for inflammatory bowel disease. In general, a low-fat, high-fiber diet is recommended.

The Crohn's and Colitis Foundation is a wonderful source of information on inflammatory bowel disease. The address and number is: 444 Park Avenue South, New York, NY 10016 (212) 679-1570 or (800) 343-3637.

Close medical follow-up is extremely important. Successful management involves keeping your physician aware of changes in symptoms and asking any questions that arise. There is an increased incidence of colon cancer in inflammatory bowel disease (greater for ulcerative colitis than for Crohn's). Cancer of the ileum appears somewhat increased in patients with chronic ileitis. The risk tends to increase with duration of the disease. Therefore, it is important to perform periodic colonoscopies or barium enemas to screen for any suspicious changes especially if you've had the disease for more than 10 years.

CROHN'S DISEASE (REGIONAL ILEITIS OR CROHN'S COLITIS)

DEFINITION

Crohn's disease is a chronic inflammation that may affect any part of the digestive tract. About one-third of Crohn's cases involve the large intestine (colon), one-third the small intestine, and one-third involve both the large and small intestines. Ileitis indicates inflammation of the ileum—the last part of the small intestine. The ileum is the most common area of small intestine to be affected by Crohn's disease. However, all parts of the intestinal tract, including the stomach, may be affected by Crohn's disease.

Crohn's disease often begins before age 30 and may cause only one or two attacks or may recur periodically throughout life. Children sometimes experience ileitis and ileocolitis and may display few symptoms other than malnutrition or general failure to grow and develop.

The inflammation of Crohn's disease can be either continuous along the digestive tract or discontinuous, causing "skip lesions" in which inflamed areas of colon alternate with normal areas. Some patients with Crohn's disease suffer associated "extraintestinal" abnormalities, such as eye inflammation (uveitis), joint pains, back pain, kidney stones or gallstones, and certain rare types of skin rashes.

CAUSE

The cause of Crohn's disease (named for an American, Dr. Burrill Crohn, who first described the disorder) is unknown. It appears to run in families and is somewhat more common among persons of Jewish descent. An autoimmune process may play a role.

DIAGNOSIS

Crohn's disease generally causes diarrhea and weight loss, and often abdominal pain, fever, and nausea, but the symptoms can vary. Since the last part of the ileum is near the appendix, ileitis can mimic appendicitis and a surgeon may be surprised to find a normal appendix near a region of inflamed small intestine.

Unlike ulcerative colitis, which involves only the inside lining of the colon, Crohn's disease involves all layers of the colon, including the muscle wall. As a result, abnormal connections from one part of the colon to another (fistulas) may develop as the inflammation bores through the colon wall and reaches the outside lining of the colon.

The swelling and inflammation also cause varying degrees of intestinal obstruction in some patients. Certain blood tests, including sedimentation rate and white blood count, may indicate Crohn's disease but tests such as sigmoidoscopy, barium enema, colonoscopy, CT scan, and barium x-rays of the upper gastrointestinal tract and small intestine are needed to identify the disease. Biopsy of the intestine via the colonoscope or sigmoidoscope helps confirm the diagnosis. Collections of white blood cells called granulomas are indicative of Crohn's disease but are found in only 25 to 50 percent of patients with the disease.

Associated nutritional absorption problems may lead to deficiencies of calcium, vitamin B_{12}, and folic acid. Blood loss can cause iron deficiency.·

TREATMENT

(See "Inflammatory Bowel Disease" for discussion of medication.) In addition to medicines such as Azulfidine, Pentasa, Asacol, Rowasa, and steroid enemas, antibiotics may be used. Flagyl is especially helpful in treatment of perianal disease and in healing fistulas.

Nutritional deficiencies caused by the disease are treated with iron, folic acid, vitamin B_{12}, and calcium supplements, and some studies show fish oil supplements to be beneficial. Elemental (low-fiber) diets may also help, primarily by resting the colon, but these diets, which some people find unpalatable, should be designed with the help of a dietitian.

Most Crohn's patients can be treated as outpatients, but in some cases, hospitalization for diagnostic testing, nutritional support, and intravenous therapy may be necessary. If the patient does not respond to medical treatment, part of the intestine may be removed. However, since the disease tends to recur after surgery, medical treatment is preferred to surgical intervention.

ULCERATIVE COLITIS

DEFINITION

Ulcerative colitis is a chronic inflammation of the rectum and colon with similarities to Crohn's colitis; in fact, in some patients it is difficult to differentiate between the two in diagnosing the condition.

CAUSE

As in Crohn's, persons with ulcerative colitis often have a family history of either ileitis or colitis. The cause of ulcerative colitis is unknown; an autoimmune process may be involved.

DIAGNOSIS

In general, the inflammation associated with ulcerative colitis is continuous from the anus to a specific level of the large intestine (the level varies with the individual). In contrast, Crohn's colitis tends to spare the rectum. Ulcerative colitis is generally limited to the colon, though a few centimeters of small intestine may be involved in "backwash ileitis." Patients with ulcerative colitis tend to suffer more rectal bleeding and watery diarrhea and dehydration, but less severe malnutrition than patients with Crohn's. Findings in ulcerative colitis may include abdominal pain, fever, anemia, and an elevated white blood count. Sigmoidoscopy shows redness and inflammation in the lining of the colon.

A biopsy of the rectum obtained through a sigmoidoscope or a colonoscope may be helpful in confirming inflammation and in excluding infection, which can mimic both ulcerative colitis and Crohn's disease. Stool specimens for special smear and culture analysis are needed to rule out bacterial dysentery and parasitic infections.

TREATMENT

Medical treatment of ulcerative colitis is similar to that for Crohn's: 5-ASA (Asacol), sulfasalazine (Azulfidine), or steroids (prednisone) are administered. A limited, less serious type of ulcerative colitis, called ulcerative proctitis, which attacks only the lower few inches of the rectum, may respond to mesalamine (Rowasa) enemas or suppositories, topical cortisone suppositories, cortisone foam, or so-called cortisone enemas. These preparations appear to have fewer long-term side effects than oral steroids because their action is primarily local (topical) on the colon rather than systemic (involving the whole body). Patients with ulcerative colitis and Crohn's disease are often able to relieve symptoms somewhat with a modified low-fiber diet.

Noninvasive treatment is used whenever possible, but those few patients who continue to have severe diarrhea, bleeding, and anemia may require surgery to remove the diseased section of the intestine. Although the idea of a colectomy may initially be frightening to a patient with chronic ulcerative colitis, patients who have been ill for years with the disease tend to accept the operation well, since they are "cured" after removal of their colon. In addition, the operation removes the threat of colon cancer. If the entire colon is removed, the operation most often creates a hole, or stoma, in the abdominal wall, to which a bag is attached. Rather than emptying into the colon, the last part of small intestine (ileum) empties into the bag. This procedure is called an ileostomy. Some new operations remove the colon but keep the gastrointestinal tract continuous.

PREVENTION

Patients who have had ulcerative colitis involving most of the large intestine for at least 10 years, and especially those afflicted for more than 20 years, are at an in-creased risk for developing malignant tumors of the colon. The incidence of cancer varies from study to study; after the first decade of colitis, the risk tends to rise with incidence of 0.5 to 1.0 percent per year. Many physicians feel that these patients should be periodically screened with colonoscopy and biopsy, although there is some disagreement about the frequency and characteristics of this screening. In any case, patients who have had ulcerative colitis for a number of years require close medical attention to watch for tumors and narrowing of the colon.

IRRITABLE BOWEL SYNDROME

DEFINITION

Irritable bowel syndrome (IBS) is a chronic intestinal disorder characterized by altered bowel habits or abdominal pain. Current thinking is that IBS is a condition in which contraction of intestinal muscle is abnormal. It is thought that intestinal nerves are overly sensitive, overreacting to a number of stimuli, including infection and emotional stress. Thus, it's not surprising that symptoms tend to come and go. There is no evidence that IBS leads to more serious problems such as colitis or cancer or that it affects life span in any way.

CAUSE

IBS can be extremely frustrating to treat because although it is one of the most commonly encountered gastrointestinal problems, it is also one of the least understood. However, it's clear that the spasm and pain are quite real. In fact, it's been possible in laboratory studies to measure the increased spasm.

DIAGNOSIS

The symptoms of irritable bowel syndrome include lower abdominal pain, which is often relieved by belching or bowel movement, although the bowel movements themselves may be painful. Constipation, diarrhea, or both may be present. Some patients also have other gastrointestinal symptoms such as esophageal spasm or dyspepsia and are said to have functional bowel disease. People often suffer with this condition for many years without seeking medical treatment and generally do not exhibit signs of organic disease such as anemia, rectal bleeding, or weight loss.

In middle-aged or older patients where other diseases may be likely, diagnostic tests will usually include routine blood tests, barium x-rays or lower endoscopy, and tests for lactose tolerance or a trial of a lactose-free diet. Patients should keep a food diary to help trace what foods or activities trigger symptoms.

THERAPY

Dietary factors that can exacerbate the symptoms of IBS include lactose, caffeine, fructose (such as in cola drinks), foods or beverages rich in sorbitol or sucrose (such as apples, cherries, peaches, pears, plums, prunes, or any of these fruit juices), and the brassica vegetables (such as cabbage, broccoli, cauliflower, asparagus, brussels sprouts). A high-fiber diet (including bran) is often helpful; however, in some patients bran itself may exacerbate symptoms. Keeping a diary of symptoms and food intake is extremely helpful in determining which foods are offensive. However, no diet has been found that controls all symptoms.

Aside from diet, many different treatments have been used and the results have varied from person to person. Therapies include exercise, a heating pad, and various drugs that relax the intestinal muscle. Psychotherapy is sometimes helpful in reducing intestinal spasm secondary to stress.

PREVENTION

Stress may be associated with a recurrence of symptoms. Therefore, stress reduction, relaxation techniques, yoga, supervised exercise when the physician feels it is safe, or rest may help prevent IBS. In addition, symptoms may be prevented by following a high-fiber diet and avoiding offending foods. (Your doctor should be able to reassure you that irritable bowel syndrome can be controlled.)

DIVERTICULOSIS

DEFINITION

Diverticulosis is an outpouching of the intestinal wall, most commonly in the colon (see figure 22.5). When pouches occasionally become acutely inflamed, the condition is known as diverticulitis.

CAUSE

Diverticulosis pouches are caused by weakness in the intestinal wall, often at the sites where blood vessels pass through muscle. This intestinal wall weakness is often associated with age, but in young people diverticula have been associated with connective tissue disorders. The most common site of diverticula is the sigmoid (the last third), which is involved in 95 percent of cases. The frequency of diverticulosis increases with age, reaching 50 percent or more by the ninth decade. Since only 4 to 5 percent of patients with diverticula develop diverticular inflammation (diverticulitis) and only 10 to 30 percent develop diverticular bleeding, the majority of patients with diverticulosis remain asymptomatic.

A Meckel's diverticulum is the most frequent congenital anomaly of the intestine, occurring in about 0.3 to 3.0 percent of people, depending on the study. It occurs in the last part of small intestine (ileum) and presents with bleeding and obstruction—most often in children.

DIAGNOSIS

Abdominal pain and fever are the primary symptoms of acute diverticulitis. The pain tends to be worse after eating and may be removed by passing stool or gas. Unless the pouches become inflamed, however, diverticulosis of the colon may occur for years without symptoms. The diagnosis is often helped by barium enema or lower endoscopy.

Diverticular bleeding can be dramatic. In contrast to diverticulitis, which tends to occur in the left colon (sigmoid, descending), diverticular bleeding tends to occur in the right colon (cecum, ascending). Bleeding can be localized by bleeding scan (technetium-labeled sulfur colloid or red blood cells) and angiography. Occasionally a bleeding site can be identified at colonoscopy, but colonoscopy performed during active lower intestinal bleeding tends to be technically difficult.

Diagnosis of a Meckel's diverticulum can be extremely difficult. Technetium-99m scan is often helpful, but the test has false positives and negatives. Because of the lack of reliable diagnostic tests, a high level of clinical suspicion is necessary.

TREATMENT

Diverticulitis may be improved by a low-fiber diet, a liquid diet, antibiotics, bed rest, hospitalization, or a combination of all of these. Stool softener and antispasmodics may be of help. Long-term treatment of patients with noninflamed diverticulosis often involves a moderate increase in the consumption of bran or fiber, although nuts, popcorn, raisins, seeded grapes, and other foods with pits may need to be excluded from the diet since they can lodge in the diverticular pouches and cause inflammation.

The majority of diverticulosis patients do not need surgery, but a few with recurrent attacks of bleeding or severe inflammation may require removal of part of the intestine.

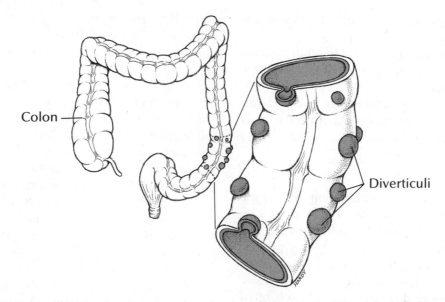

Colon

Diverticuli

Figure 22.5: A drawing showing diverticuli along the colon wall. These outputches sometimes become filled with fecal material, leading to infection and the possibility of rupture.

In most cases, diverticular bleeding stops spontaneously. In cases where the bleeding continues and a bleeding site is identified with angiography, intra-arterial vasopressin can be used to constrict the bleeding artery. If bleeding continues, surgical resection of the involved segment of colon may be necessary.

Treatment of a Meckel's diverticulum is surgical.

APPENDICITIS

DEFINITION

The appendix, an extension of the cecum (the beginning of the large intestine) in the lower right side of the abdomen, has no identifiable function, although its construction of lymphoid tissue suggests that it may be involved in immunity. Appendicitis occurs when the appendix becomes inflamed. Acute appendicitis is the most common abdominal emergency situation requiring surgery, occurring in 7 to 12 percent of the population. Although peak incidence is in the second and third decades, it may occur at any age.

CAUSE

The cause of appendicitis, like the function of the appendix itself, is unknown. Because the incidence of appendicitis rose in Western countries in the early part of this century, then declined in the 1930s, it may be related to the amount of fiber in the diet or hygiene. Appendicitis is believed to be caused by an obstruction in the appendix (most often by hardened stool), with subsequent bacterial infection.

DIAGNOSIS

Appendicitis generally affects children, teenagers, and young adults. The initial symptom is often pain beginning in the upper-middle abdomen that after several hours subsides and then moves to the lower right part of the abdomen. Eventually, the pain becomes a progressively severe ache made worse by movement. Other symptoms may include nausea and vomiting, loss of appetite, constipation, and fever. Appendicitis may mimic various other conditions, including gastroenteritis, diverticulitis, regional ileitis (Crohn's disease), or gynecologic pathology (e.g., ruptured ovarian cyst [mittelschmerz], infection of a fallopian tube, ruptured ectopic pregnancy). Often a blood test will show elevated white blood count and sedimentation rate, but these are relatively nonspecific findings.

Diagnosis of typical appendicitis can usually be made by analyzing the progression of symptoms and making a physical examination for localized tenderness. In atypical cases or in very young or elderly patients, radiographic tests or ultrasonography can help distinguish an inflamed appendix from other diseases. Despite all efforts, up to 30 percent of patients with preoperative diagnosis of appendicitis end up having a normal appendix at operation.

TREATMENT

The standard treatment of appendicitis is prompt surgical removal, sometimes accompanied by antibiotics. If the appendix ruptures into the abdomen, peritonitis (inflammation of the abdominal lining) and abscess formation may occur, increasing the risk of surgery.

MALE/FEMALE DIFFERENCES

For unknown reasons, appendicitis is 1.3 to 1.6 times more common in men than in women.

....

ESOPHAGUS DISORDERS

DYSPHAGIA (SWALLOWING DIFFICULTY)

DEFINITION

Dysphagia is difficulty in swallowing. This condition often causes the feeling that food is being prevented from traveling from the mouth to the stomach. Patients describe food as "sticking" and will point to an area anywhere between the neck and xiphoid (junction of the chest and abdomen). Dysphagia may be due to problems with either the esophagus or the pharynx.

CAUSE

Any persistent difficulty in swallowing should be promptly investigated by a doctor since dysphagia can be a symptom of esophageal cancer, a type of cancer difficult to treat in advanced stages. Fortunately, esophageal cancer is relatively rare and dysphagia usually has other causes. (See chapter 17.)

Other possible causes of dysphagia include:

• Smooth muscle spasm, which may interfere with normal muscular contractions and sphincter control that provide for the orderly movement of food through the esophagus. In some cases, spasm may be caused by acid reflux from the stomach.

• Achalasia, a condition in which the lower esophageal sphincter does not sufficiently relax.

• Structural problems such as rings and webs. A Schatzki's ring is a narrowing at the junction of the esophagus and stomach. It is felt to be related to irritation from acid reflux. A typical symptom is the sticking of food (such as chicken or bread). A web is a thin membrane that can block the lumen (opening) of the esophagus; it is often treated by the passage of an endoscopy or dilator.

• Esophageal ulcers, accompanied by scarring and adhesions, may narrow the passage to the stomach enough to cause difficulty swallowing solid foods such as meat or bread. If swallowing is difficult when eating solids but not liquids, then mechanical narrowing or obstruction should be suspected.

• Esophageal diverticulum (see figure 22.7). Such outpouchings occur in 3 areas of the esophagus: upper (Zenker's), mid (traction), and lower (epiphrenic). Treatment is mainly surgical.

• Infection. In immunocompromised patients such as patients with AIDS, such infections include cytomegalovirus, herpes, and fungus. Fungus (*Candida*) may also occur as a secondary process in patients with peptic ulceration of the esophagus.

• Reflux of stomach acid and contents.

• Myasthenia gravis, a muscle disorder that may also affect adjacent organs.

• Scleroderma, a connective tissue disease associated with abnormalities of the esophagus including abnormal motility, reflux, and diverticula.

• Parkinsonism.

• Certain types of strokes, which weaken pharynx swallowing muscles.

DIAGNOSIS

Typically, the swallowing difficulties cause people to complain that food "seems to get stuck" or takes too long going down, which may be accompanied by pain or burning. Intermittent dysphagia, in which food won't go down after the first swallow but must be regurgitated and swallowed again, is a common sign of a lower esophageal ring.

In many instances, a physician will be able to make a diagnosis based on taking a careful history of the symptoms. If tests are needed, these may include x-ray studies, viewing the inside of the esophagus through an endoscope (flexible tube equipped with fiber-optic devices), and an analysis of secretions in the esophagus. Tests of muscle and sphincter tone and function (manometry) also may be performed. If a Schatzki's ring is suspected, radiography may be performed to confirm the diagnosis.

TREATMENT

Treatment of esophageal dysphagia depends on the cause: When due to a benign stricture formed as a result of acid refluxing from the stomach to the esophagus, the stricture may be stretched by a method called bougienage (metal or rubber tubes of increasing caliber are passed into the mouth and driven through the stricture until dilation is achieved). If dysphagia and pain are caused by spasm in the esophagus, then medication that relaxes the muscle is frequently effective.

Mechanical dilation is also used to treat achalasia, a disorder characterized by an unusually high pressure in the gastroesophageal sphincter. If this fails, surgery may be recommended.

Acid reflux is treated by a variety of medications, including antacids, H_2 blockers, Prilosec, and cisapride.

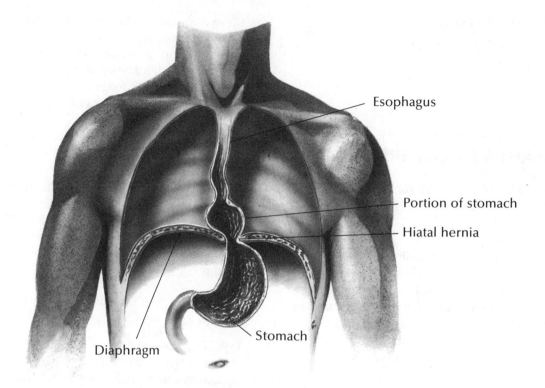

Figure 22.6: View of a hiatal hernia, with a portion of the stomach squeezed above the opening in the diaphragm.

HIATAL HERNIA

DEFINITION

A hiatal hernia means that a small portion of the stomach slips through the muscle that separates the stomach from the chest (this muscle is called the diaphragm). The part of the stomach slipping through the diaphragm may actually sit in the chest instead of the abdomen. This condition is often associated with a weakening of the valve that separates the esophagus from the stomach. When the valve is weakened, stomach acid can bubble up into the esophagus and cause inflammation and pain (see figure 22.6).

CAUSE

The condition associated with hiatal hernia is called "reflux esophagitis" (inflammation of the esophagus caused by acid bubbling up into the esophagus). Persistent exposure of the esophageal tissue to gastric acid also can cause inflammation (esophagitis) and even ulcers. Substances that aggravate reflux esophagitis include caffeine, chocolate, tobacco, fatty food, and alcohol. Avoiding these substances can help reduce symptoms.

A number of common eating habits and practices aggravate hiatal hernia.

- Eating a large meal at night and then lying down or going to bed early promotes the backflow of food and gastric acid from the stomach to the esophagus.
- Unconscious air swallowing—from drinking carbonated beverages, talking while eating, chewing gum, etc.—increases discomfort.
- Pregnancy or obesity.
- Stooping or bending over, especially after eating, may promote reflux.
- Wearing constrictive clothing.

DIAGNOSIS

A hiatal hernia can be diagnosed with x-ray studies following a barium swallow or with endoscopy. Chest pain from hiatal hernia and/or esophageal spasm may be extremely difficult to distinguish from chest pain of cardiac origin, especially since the symptoms of pain spreading from below the sternum (breastbone) to the neck, jaw, and perhaps arms can mimic the symptoms of coronary artery disease. The evaluation is complicated by the fact that in patients with simultaneous heart disease and reflux, acid reflux may increase the workload of the heart and therefore precipitate angina.

Severe reflux may cause acid to bubble up from the

stomach into the windpipe (trachea) and lungs, causing respiratory difficulty such as wheezing (asthma).

TREATMENT

Antacids may be taken 1 hour or so after eating to neutralize stomach acids. H_2-receptor blockers (blockers of histamine receptors, which trigger acid production) have been extremely helpful and include medications such as Tagamet, Zantac, and Pepcid. A major advance is the approval of two relatively new medications, Omeprazole (Prilosec) and cisapride (Propulsid). Omeprazole directly stops the proton pump responsible for pumping acid into the stomach and is more effective in lowering stomach acid than the antacids Tagamet and Zantac. However, Prilosec is currently approved for only 8 weeks at a time.

Cisapride (Propulsid) is a new medication that helps tighten the valve between the stomach and chest. In addition, the medicine helps to empty the stomach of its contents. The result is to lessen the amount of stomach fluid that bubbles up from the stomach to the chest.

Reducing stomach acid by losing excess weight and not wearing tight belts, girdles, or other constrictive clothing also is recommended. If these conservative measures fail, surgery can tighten the hiatal opening. Only a small number of patients with hiatal hernia require surgery.

PREVENTION

Eating frequent, small meals may help prevent reflux in patients with hiatal hernias, as will avoiding lying down or going to bed soon after eating. Elevating the head of the bed a few inches also may help to prevent reflux. Avoiding caffeine, alcohol, nicotine, fatty food, and chocolate tends to help diminish symptoms.

ESOPHAGEAL DIVERTICULA

DEFINITION AND CAUSE

Diverticulosis of the esophagus is a relatively rare condition in which weakened segments in the esophagus form small outpouches (see figure 22.7). These outpouches sometimes fill with food that may be regurgitated when you lie down or bend over. If such regurgitation occurs at night and the material is drawn into the lungs, aspiration pneumonia—a potentially life-threatening condition—may result.

DIAGNOSIS

Esophageal diverticula are diagnosed with x-ray studies taken following a barium swallow.

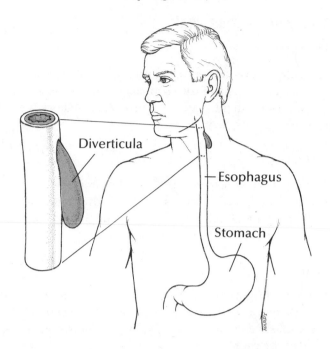

Figure 22.7: Esophageal diverticula are outpouches that develop in weakened segments of the esophagus.

TREATMENT

Most cases do not require specific treatment unless the pouches are large enough to interfere with swallowing or there are other serious symptoms. In these unusual circumstances, surgical removal of the diverticula may be required.

ESOPHAGEAL DEFECTS

DEFINITION

Several congenital malformations of the esophagus occur in a small number of infants. The most common is tracheoesophageal fistula, in which there is an abnormal connection between the windpipe (trachea) and the esophagus. Perhaps the most serious is esophageal atresia, in which the esophagus ends in a "blind," self-contained pouch rather than leading to the stomach. Other congenital malformations include narrowing or strictures of the esophagus, which make it difficult for the infant to swallow, especially when solid foods are introduced into the diet.

TREATMENT

Tracheoesophageal fistula and esophageal atresia require surgery shortly after birth to link the esophagus and stomach and permit the normal flow of food. Strictures often can be corrected by mechanical dilation.

MALLORY-WEISS TEAR

DEFINITION

A Mallory-Weiss tear is the rupturing or tearing of the mucous membrane of the esophagus at its junction with the stomach. An infrequent occurrence, a Mallory-Weiss tear may cause heavy bleeding.

CAUSE

A Mallory-Weiss tear may be caused by repeated vomiting and retching, or any other event that raises intra-abdominal pressure, including a hiatal hernia, severe hiccoughing, heavy lifting, or childbirth.

DIAGNOSIS

Vomiting bright red blood is a sign of a Mallory-Weiss tear. Diagnosis of the size and location of the tear is best accomplished with endoscopy, which allows a direct view of the rupture.

TREATMENT

In about 90 percent of cases, the bleeding stops spontaneously and the tear heals within several days. In cases of continued bleeding, possible therapy includes cautery with bipolar or heater probe during endoscopy, and injection therapy with medications such as epinephrine to constrict the bleeding blood vessel. Angiography is often effective, either via intra-arterial vasopressin (a blood vessel constrictor) or transcatheter embolization (clotting) of the bleeding artery.

....

GALLBLADDER DISEASE

DEFINITION

The gallbladder, linked by small ducts to the liver and small intestine, stores bile, a substance produced by the liver from cholesterol and used in fat digestion. About 1 of 10 Americans form gallstones (cholelithiasis), the most common manifestation of gallbladder disease, whose incidence increases with age. In 1990, the diagnosis and treatment of gallstone disease, including half a million operations, accounted for more than $5 billion in the United States.

CAUSE

Most gallstones form because of high serum cholesterol and obesity, but even thin people with normal cholesterol can get them. High blood cholesterol levels increase their incidence. Noncholesterol stones are either black or brown pigment stones consisting of cal-

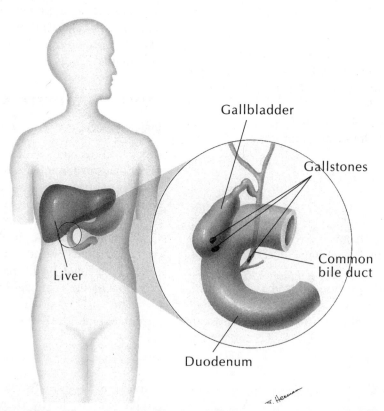

Figure 22.8: A diseased gallbladder with a gallstone blocking the common bile duct that connects the liver, gallbladder, and duodenum of the small intestine.

cium salts of bilirubin. Black pigment stones are more common in patients with cirrhosis or hemolytic conditions such as thalassemias and possibly sickle cell anemia. After gallstones are present, fatty meals or alcohol may provoke painful attacks.

DIAGNOSIS

In most people, gallstones are silent, producing no symptoms, but others cause bloating, gas, abdominal discomfort, and assorted symptoms similar to indigestion. In a significant number of people, multiple stones appear, causing attacks of severe colicky pain, starting in the upper abdomen and often radiating through the right side up to the right shoulder blade. Occasionally, a stone lodges in the common bile duct, which is shared by the liver and gallbladder, leading to elevated liver enzymes, jaundice, and sometimes infection (cholangitis) (see figure 22.8). Passage of gallstones can also cause pancreatitis by an unclear mechanism, perhaps by causing obstruction of the pancreatic duct.

An inflamed gallbladder (cholecystitis) with or without gallstones can cause nausea, loss of appetite, gassiness, and upper right abdominal pain of varying severity. Acute attacks of cholecystitis—often occurring at night after a fatty meal—may be provoked by a gallstone blocking the duct, infection, or irritation from digestive enzymes and can be mistaken for indigestion or hiatal hernia. But severe cholecystitis can progress to tissue death and gangrene of the organ, followed by perforation, although this is uncommon.

Only about 15 percent of gallstones contain enough calcium to be visible on a plain x-ray. Ultrasound is the procedure of choice for establishing the presence of gallstones, although CT scan can also be effective. However, the mere presence of gallstones does not establish the diagnosis of cholecystitis (gallbladder inflammation). Ultrasound and CT scans may detect findings suggestive of inflammation and swelling around the gallbladder.

Nuclear scanning (cholescintigraphy) with technetium-99m helps detect blockage in the cystic duct (the connection between the gallbladder and the common bile duct). Blockage of this duct occurs in acute cholecystitis. Cholescintigraphy has an extremely high sensitivity and specificity of about 95 percent.

Oral cholecystography, in which an iodinated contrast agent is given orally the day before an x-ray examination, has fallen out of use in recent years as newer, more effective tests have emerged. However, it is sometimes useful when other tests are equivocal.

TREATMENT

The treatment of gallstones is currently recommended mostly for symptomatic patients. Some exceptions include children, patients with sickle-cell anemia, and perhaps patients of Native American ancestry who have large stones.

Laparoscopic cholecystectomy is now the surgical technique of choice, allowing the operation to be performed through small incisions in the abdomen through which gallstones and the gallbladder are removed. Laparoscopic cholecystectomy reduces the number of hospital days, pain, and disability when compared with the traditional operation (open cholecystectomy) in which the abdominal cavity is opened and the gallbladder removed under direct visualization rather than through a laparoscope.

Endoscopic retrograde cholangeopancreatography (ERCP) is an important adjunct to surgery, especially for those too sick to undergo an operation or in cases of acute cholangitis. During this procedure, an endoscope (viewing instrument) is inserted down the esophagus into the digestive tract and advanced into a position near the ampulla of Vater, the valve that separates the intestine from the biliary tract. It is at the ampulla that stones often become impacted, causing jaundice and infection of the bile tract (cholangitis). Via a small cut (papillotomy) in the ampulla, stones can be extracted and obstruction can often be relieved.

Nonsurgical therapy is becoming increasingly infrequent and is limited to those patients who cannot undergo laparoscopy. Such therapy includes gallstone dissolution with cheno- or ursodeoxycholic acid and extracorporeal shock-wave lithotripsy in which high-amplitude sound waves are used to fragment stones.

PREVENTION

Maintaining low blood cholesterol levels and a moderately low-fat diet can help prevent gallstones.

MALE/FEMALE DIFFERENCES

Gallstones are more common in women than men and their incidence increases with age. Female to male ratio is approximately 2:1 in younger groups and increases with age. After age 60, about 10 to 15 percent of men and 20 to 40 percent of women have gallstones.

··

INTESTINAL DISORDERS

DIVERTICULOSIS: See Previous Discussion

GAS

DEFINITION

Excessive intestinal gas may be manifested in three ways: belching, abdominal bloating and pain, and the passage of rectal gas (flatus).

CAUSE

1. *High-fiber diet:* Fruits and vegetables leave large amounts of unabsorbable materials, such as pectin and cellulose (the cell walls of these foods), in the intestines. A high-fiber diet is beneficial—lowering cholesterol, and possibly reducing the risk of colon and breast cancer—but it also feeds intestinal bacteria that produce gas by-products. Beans, cucumbers, and pickles may especially increase the amount of rectal gas.

2. *Swallowing air:* Anxiety or certain lung diseases may cause hyperventilation and breathing through the mouth, resulting in belches after large gulps of air. Swallowed air travels partway down the esophagus and is then forced back up, or may enter the stomach, forming a bubble, enlarging with each new addition of air that is the source of belches and a bloated feeling.

3. *Lactose and other malabsorption problems:* Can produce excessive rectal gas; very often, however, the gas is not linked to any disease or abnormality.

4. *Gastrointestinal infections:* May lead to increased gas as a bacteria by-product.

5. *Drinking beer or carbonated beverages:* Excess gas can be released from the swallowed carbonated liquid.

6. *Fermentation by bacteria of nitrogenous and other waste products in the intestine:* Occasionally produces more than normal amounts of methane, nitrogen, and carbon dioxide, which escape through the rectum.

DIAGNOSIS

Intestinal gas accompanied by other symptoms should be investigated by a doctor, as should gassiness not relieved by dietary changes and other conservative measures. Diagnosis is usually via observance of symptoms, but excessive abdominal gas should be investigated to exclude such serious causes as lactose intolerance, intestinal infection, or malabsorption diseases.

TREATMENT

Some people simply produce more gas than others. Gas by itself is not a health hazard and may be relieved by avoiding foods that produce gas and by exercising moderately following a meal (exercise helps stimulate the movement of gas through the digestive tract). Over-the-counter products such as Beano, Gas-X, and charcoal are sometimes helpful. If a fiber-rich diet is eaten daily, the body will often adjust and produce less gas after a time.

Decreasing intake of carbonated beverages and not drinking through a straw may help reduce gas. If dietary fiber is temporarily reduced, gradual reintroduction of fiber in the diet can start with well-cooked canned vegetables or canned fruit cup (with low fiber content) and then, if you are able to tolerate it, cooked frozen vegetables or peeled fruits (moderate fiber content). Finally, if additional fiber is desired and can be readily tolerated, fresh vegetables or salads and fresh fruits, including the skin, may be added (high fiber content).

INFECTION

DEFINITION

Many different infections affect the gastrointestinal tract, a significant number lumped under the term gastroenteritis, commonly referred to as stomach flu.

CAUSE

Most cases of gastroenteritis are caused by viruses, although the upset also may be due to toxic substances, antibiotics (or other drugs altering the bacterial population of the lower gastrointestinal tract), or a reaction to certain foods. In addition, other microorganisms, such as *Salmonella* bacteria, *Shigella* bacillus, and intestinal parasites, may cause gastroenteritis. Typhoid fever and cholera are rare in the United States and other industrialized societies, but still occur in underdeveloped areas where food and water may be contaminated by unsanitary conditions.

Parasite infections, including giardiasis and amebiasis, commonly cause a variety of digestive illnesses. These parasites may be passed by food handlers or through sexual or other close contact. Giardia is common in the United States and is often spread through contaminated water or other unknown ways.

DIAGNOSIS

Nausea, vomiting, diarrhea, abdominal pains or cramps, and fever are the most common symptoms of gastroenteritis. Bacteria and parasites are usually diagnosed by testing the stool. In some cases, blood tests, such as an amoebic antibody test, may be helpful in diagnosing amebiasis. Aspiration of fluids from the small intestine is sometimes necessary to diagnose giardiasis if the presence of parasites is still suspected after a negative stool screening, a test which may simplify diagnosis. Giardia antigen can now be detected in the stool. Since amoebic dysentery can sometimes mimic colitis, sigmoidoscopy and rectal biopsy may help distinguish the two.

For diagnosis of viral infections as well as typhoid and cholera, see chapter 18, Infectious Diseases. For typhoid and cholera, see chapter 18.

TREATMENT

Repeated vomiting and diarrhea can quickly lead to dehydration, especially in an infant or young child, so fluid replacement is often the most important part of treatment. Oral rehydration solution (ORS) is the mainstay of rehydration treatment throughout the Third World. ORS contains water, glucose, and salt (sodium chloride, sodium bicarbonate, potassium chloride) in order to facilitate the absorption of salt and water from the intestine. An excellent home remedy equivalent to ORS is chicken soup with rice.

Most healthy people recover from a mild attack of gastroenteritis in 1 or 2 days without any special treatment. Solid food should not be eaten while the symptoms persist, but extra fluids should be consumed, especially in the presence of vomiting and diarrhea. Antidiarrheal drugs may help and, if vomiting persists, an antiemetic drug may be prescribed. If the symptoms persist or there are signs of dehydration, consult a doctor as soon as possible. Symptoms of dehydration include dry mouth, extreme thirst, inelastic skin, sunken eyes, and lethargy. Also, bloody diarrhea, especially in a person who has recently traveled to underdeveloped countries or the tropics, should be investigated by a physician to rule out amoebic or bacillary dysentery.

Travelers may treat infections symptomatically with antidiarrheal medications containing kaolin and pectin, or bismuth. If the condition persists, antibiotics may help, although they must be prescribed by a physician.

PREVENTION

Since gastroenteritis is often the result of poor hygiene and can quickly spread to other family members, preventive measures such as carefully washing hands after going to the bathroom, not sharing eating utensils or dishes, and other commonsense measures should be practiced.

Travelers should be particularly careful to avoid eating fresh fruits and vegetables, salads, and other uncooked foods, and should drink only bottled water. Avoid beverages such as lemonade that contain unbottled water, and do not use ice made of unsterilized water. The causes of traveler's diarrhea are not fully understood, but experts feel that many cases can be prevented by following these precautions. Pepto-Bismol may be taken as a prophylactic, although the large quantities necessary may be difficult to carry on long trips. It is not recommended that antibiotics be taken prophylactically, since infection with resistant organisms may occur. However, antibiotics taken at the start of symptoms while traveling may shorten the illness.

People living in the household of someone who develops dysentery may need to be tested for dysenteric infection in order to prevent its spread.

OBSTRUCTION

DEFINITION

Intestinal obstruction occurs when food is prevented from moving through the digestive tract.

CAUSE

Intestinal obstruction can result from either a mechanical blockage or from intestinal paralysis (adynamic ileus) that stops peristalsis. Mechanical blockages result from tumors, adhesions or scarring, congenital abnormalities, and strangulated hernia, among other factors. Paralytic ileus may be caused by infection, surgery or other trauma, medications (such as narcotics), or certain metabolic disorders that affect muscle function, such as potassium deficiency (hypokalemia).

DIAGNOSIS

The obstruction may be complete or partial; in either instance, symptoms are likely to include vomiting, bloating, and abdominal cramps.

If the obstruction is high in the intestinal tract, vomiting is likely to be more severe and may result in a biochemical imbalance and shock. Complete obstruction may cause vomitus resembling feces as well as constipation and severe bloating caused by a buildup of intestinal gas. Generally a patient with a sudden blockage of the colon will have a distended abdomen and no stools and no flatus for days. These symptoms also may be present to a lesser degree in a partial obstruction. Obstruction caused by a strangulated section of intestine, usually the result of a hernia, may lead to gangrene and perforation of the intestine, a life-threatening situation. All of these symptoms should be evaluated by a doctor as soon as possible.

Diagnosis is based on symptoms, x-ray studies to locate the site of obstruction, and possibly colonoscopy.

TREATMENT

The obstruction must be eliminated as soon as possible, especially if it involves a strangulated hernia or other condition likely to lead to tissue death. Nonoperative therapy depends on the location and cause of the obstruction; colonoscopy may alleviate conditions such as megacolon (grossly distended colon), while long nasogastric tubes may be inserted to clear other problems. Surgery is needed if nonoperative methods are not suitable. Antibiotics may be given to prevent or treat infection. All patients with this condition should be rushed to the hospital immediately.

LIVER DISORDERS

The number and variety of functions performed by the liver—and its complexity—leave this organ susceptible to a number of disorders. Some experts find it surprising that liver disease is not more common in light of the liver's exposure to so many toxins and potentially dangerous microorganisms. But the liver is protected by its amazing capacity for self-regeneration and its division into semiindependent individual units called hepatic acini: The organ can undergo substantial injury and the uninjured units are still able to function.

Common symptoms from which liver disease may be diagnosed include:

- Jaundice: yellowish hue in the skin, whites of the eye, and other tissues. Jaundice may cause the urine to darken. Jaundice is caused by an excess of the bile pigments (bilirubin) produced by the liver during the breakdown of red blood cells. When these pigments don't follow their usual excretion route through the bile duct and intestines, they gather in the blood.
- Liver enlargement: this condition is called hepatomegaly.
- Liver tenderness or pain: usually a deep aching sensation is felt when the organ is palpated.
- Accumulation of fluid (ascites): marked by a buildup of fluid in the peritoneal cavity. Ascites also may develop from conditions unrelated to the liver, such as congestive heart failure, thyroid disorders, pancreatic and kidney diseases, or cancer that has started in or spread to the peritoneum (the thin layer of tissue covering the intestines).

Sometimes extensive liver disease does not cause obvious symptoms, or produces vague effects similar to the characteristics of other diseases such as loss of appetite, fever, general malaise, fatigue, anemia and other blood and circulatory disorders, changes in body chemistry, kidney failure, and even coma. Thus, before ascribing symptoms to liver disease, a physician must consider other possible causes of the symptoms.

BILIARY CIRRHOSIS

DEFINITION

Biliary cirrhosis is a disorder affecting bile secretion from the liver.

CAUSE

There are two types of biliary cirrhosis:

Primary biliary cirrhosis: a disorder in which the liver's bile ducts are destroyed by a poorly understood process (probably autoimmune).
Secondary biliary cirrhosis: a disorder in which the bile ducts are destroyed as a result of long-standing

obstruction of the biliary tree. Causes include gallstones in the common bile duct and chronic pancreatitis (which can cause the last part of the common bile duct to become narrowed).

DIAGNOSIS

Primary Biliary Cirrhosis (PBC). Because of elevated alkaline phosphatase measurements noted as part of routine blood testing, the diagnosis of primary biliary cirrhosis is being made much earlier than in the past. Cholesterol levels are usually high and there may be fatty deposits under the skin (xanthomas). Osteomalacia or osteoporosis may develop, probably related to malabsorption of vitamin D and calcium.

A major initial symptom is itching (pruritus), possibly related to the backup of bile salts in the liver and subsequent increased deposition of bile salts in the skin. Other symptoms include jaundice, darkened urine, pale stools, and darkening of the skin. Alkaline phosphatase, a bile duct enzyme, is usually the first lab abnormality noticed and often occurs prior to any symptoms.

Ninety percent of patients are female. A special blood test called antimitochondrial antibody is positive in about 90 percent of patients.

PBC is associated with a variety of immune disorders including Sjögren's syndrome (dry eyes and mouth), scleroderma and the CREST syndrome (calcinosis, Raynaud's phenomenon, esophageal hypomotility, sclerodactyly, telangiectasia), and arthritis.

The large bile ducts are normal; therefore, ultrasound will usually reveal no obvious obstruction. Liver function tests can confirm the presence of liver cell abnormality. However, liver biopsy is necessary both to confirm the diagnosis of primary biliary cirrhosis and to establish the degree of damage present in the liver.

Secondary Biliary Cirrhosis. As with primary biliary cirrhosis, initial symptoms are related to bile duct obstruction and include itching, jaundice, and fatty stools. Bone disease may develop. Since secondary biliary cirrhosis follows long-standing bile duct disease, ultrasound may reveal enlargement of the ducts of the biliary system (extrahepatic obstruction). However, low-grade chronic obstruction can cause secondary biliary cirrhosis without enlargement of the ducts; thus, a normal ultrasound does not rule out the presence of secondary biliary cirrhosis.

TREATMENT

Medical therapy of PBC has been disappointing. However, trials have included D-penicillamine, azathioprine, ursodeoxycholic acid, and colchicine with mixed results. Supportive treatment involves replacement of the nutrients lost through malabsorption, including vitamin

D and calcium. Special formulations of fat called medium chain triglycerides can help provide fat in a form that is able to be absorbed, thus allowing for a lowering of dietary fat intake and reduced diarrhea from malabsorption. Cholestyramine and colestipol help bind bile salts in the intestine and can reduce itching.

In secondary biliary cirrhosis, the obstruction of the bile ducts must be removed—either by surgery or by endoscopy (ERCP)—to prevent further damage to the liver. Existing cirrhosis (cell damage), however, is not reversible.

Male/Female Differences

For unknown reasons, primary biliary cirrhosis occurs most frequently in middle-aged women. Ninety percent of patients are female.

CIRRHOSIS

Definition

Cirrhosis describes liver cell damage resulting from a number of different liver disorders and is characterized by progressive destruction of liver tissue and development of scarring, fibrosis, and fatty deposits.

Cause

In the United States, the most common cause is alcoholism. Normally, the liver can detoxify moderate amounts of alcohol without problems but consumption of large amounts, such as a pint of whiskey per day for several years, invariably produces liver damage. Chronic viral hepatitis—specifically hepatitis B and hepatitis C—can also evolve into cirrhosis (see chapter 18). In addition, cirrhosis can be caused by autoimmune hepatitis, biliary tract disease, hemochromatosis, Wilson's disease, alpha₁-antitrypsin globulin deficiency, and cardiac disease (secondary to backup of fluid from the right side of the heart; see chapter 16).

Diagnosis

In its early stages, liver disease may not cause any obvious symptoms, but as the disease progresses the liver may shrink and harden, the spleen may enlarge, and there may be loss of appetite, fatigue, weakness, accumulation of fluid, jaundice, a reddening of the palms, and development of spider nevi (networks of tiny, spiderlike blood vessels under the skin). Other lesions include testicular atrophy, enlargement of the breasts in men (gynecomastia), and bronze discoloration of the skin. Portal hypertension (high blood pressure involving the liver's circulatory system) may also occur, sometimes leading to bleeding from prominent veins in the esophagus (varices). Anemia and various metabolic abnormalities may develop.

Confirming whether cirrhosis is the cause of these symptoms may require a number of laboratory tests and also may involve imaging the liver with a radionuclide liver scan, CT scan, MRI, or liver biopsy. (See chapter 12, Diagnostic Tests and Procedures.)

Treatment

There is no specific cure for cirrhosis. Prognosis depends on the natural history of the underlying disorder and on the effectiveness of specific therapy directed at the underlying disorder.

Cirrhosis related to chronic viral hepatitis is difficult to arrest. Recent trials have suggested a role for alpha interferon in the treatment of both hepatitis B and hepatitis C. Other drugs such as levamisole are being investigated.

Cirrhosis related to alcoholism may be halted if it is detected at an early stage and the patient abstains from alcohol.

Hemochromatosis is treated by removal of blood through phlebotomy and/or by medication (deferoxamine) which removes iron from the body.

In general, diet should be high-fiber, low-fat, and low-salt. Supplemental vitamins and minerals may be recommended by your physician. Other treatments depend upon specific symptoms. Edema or swelling can be treated with diuretics such as Aldactone. If needed, ascites can be treated by carefully withdrawing fluid from the abdomen with a special instrument.

Prevention

Avoidance of alcohol abuse is the most effective step to halt or prevent cirrhosis of the liver. The hepatitis B vaccine is effective in preventing hepatitis B and its complications, including cirrhosis.

FATTY LIVER DISEASE

Cause

A buildup of fatty deposits in the liver can have many causes, including metabolic disorders, diabetes, Reye's syndrome, pregnancy, obesity, and a toxic response to certain drugs and chemicals, particularly carbon tetrachloride, alcohol, and corticosteroids.

Diagnosis

Very often, this condition produces no obvious symptoms, but an enlarged liver may be noted during a physical examination. In some patients, jaundice and pain in the upper right-hand side of the abdomen may be present. Diagnosis is made by noting the abnormal presence of fatty deposits in a liver tissue sample.

Acute fatty liver of pregnancy occurs in late pregnancy (after the 30th week) and resolves with delivery. Symptoms include abdominal pain, jaundice, and encephalopathy. Acute fatty liver of pregnancy is different from cholestasis of pregnancy, in which patients develop elevated liver enzymes, itching, and sometimes jaundice in the last 4 months of gestation.

TREATMENT

Treatment depends upon identifying and correcting the underlying cause. (For more information refer to the appropriate disease.)

HEPATITIS

DEFINITION

Hepatitis, one of the most common of all liver diseases, is a liver inflammation that destroys patches of liver tissue.

CAUSE

Most hepatitis is caused by viruses, but alcohol, drugs, and a variety of bacterial, fungal, or parasitic infections also can inflame the liver.

Researchers have named hepatitis viruses alphabetically. Thus, discovery of hepatitis A was followed by discovery of hepatitis B. When a type of hepatitis was described testing negative for A and B, it was called non-A, non-B. Subsequently, hepatitis C was isolated, replacing non-A, non-B. Recently, hepatitis D and E have been described and undoubtedly the list will continue to grow.

The incubation period is about 2 to 6 weeks for hepatitis A, 4 to 25 weeks for B, and 5 to 10 weeks for C.

Hepatitis A is spread most commonly by foods that have been contaminated with fecal material; an infected person may transmit the virus by handling food with unwashed hands. Epidemics of hepatitis A are also spread by shellfish taken from waters polluted by sewage or by direct physical contact with a person carrying an active infection. After infection, a person produces antibodies against the disease, which are protective for life. Studies have found antibodies against hepatitis A in people who have not had clinical symptoms of the disease, indicating that many people have unknowingly suffered mild hepatitis A.

Hepatitis B, sometimes referred to as serum hepatitis, is spread by direct contact with infected blood. Blood transfusions used to be the most common source of hepatitis B, but screening tests for contaminated blood have eliminated this source. Today the use of contaminated needles by drug abusers is a more common source of the disease, but the disease may be spread by other direct contact (sexual contact, particularly among homosexuals, is a common route of infection). Unlike with hepatitis A, a person harboring hepatitis B can spread it to others even without being actively infected. In fact, the world-wide large pool of asymptomatic carriers is estimated at several hundred million, probably a result of maternal-fetal transmission.

Hepatitis C is associated with transfusions and the use of contaminated needles by drug abusers. As with other forms of hepatitis, the disease may also be spread through sexual contact. Hepatitis C may also be "community-acquired" by patients who have no obvious risk factors for the infection. Patients with hepatitis C have a relatively high incidence of chronic hepatitis.

Hepatitis D occurs only in patients with hepatitis B and can cause a more severe form of hepatitis than in patients with hepatitis B alone.

Hepatitis E is responsible for epidemics of acute hepatitis in developing countries.

Many other viruses can involve the liver, including cytomegalovirus and Epstein-Barr virus. Tuberculosis, which is once again a major public health problem, is another organism that can infect the liver. Typhoid fever (from *Salmonella typhi*) can affect the liver. Parasites affecting the liver include ascaris, roundworm (*Toxocara canis* and *T. cati*), amoeba, Strongyloides, echinococcus, schistosomiasis, toxoplasma, trypanosoma, and malaria. Unusual causes of hepatic bacterial infection include syphilis, brucellosis, Legionnaires' disease, leptospirosis (Weil's disease), and leprosy. Fungal causes include histoplasma (in eastern and central United States) and coccidiodes (in southwestern United States).

Autoimmune hepatitis is a condition in which the liver is attacked by the body's immune system for unclear reasons. Chronic hepatitis and cirrhosis can develop.

Granulomatous hepatitis is a condition in which abnormal collections of white blood cells collect in the liver. There are many causes, with sarcoidosis and tuberculosis accounting for about two-thirds of cases.

Medications are a frequent cause of elevated liver enzymes and may occur at any time after administration of the medication.

Reye's syndrome is a serious systemic disorder that follows viral infection in children and which can cause encephalopathy and fatty liver.

DIAGNOSIS

Symptoms of hepatitis vary from mild, flulike symptoms to severe liver failure and ensuing coma and death. Typically, hepatitis A begins with loss of appetite, nausea and vomiting, fever, and, among smokers, a distaste for cigarettes. There may also be itching, hives, and joint pain. After a few days, the urine may become dark and the skin and eye whites may become yellowish while stools are light yellow and may be looser than normal. A physical examination may show an enlarged, tender liver. Most patients with hepatitis A recover completely; rarely, however, fulminant hepatitis with a high morbidity can develop. A specific diagnosis is made by identifying the viral serum antibodies in a blood test.

Hepatitis B may follow a course similar to hepatitis A. However, it is more likely to evolve into liver failure. A large number of hepatitis B patients also develop a chronic, subacute form of the disease without obvious symptoms. In some people, this subacute hepatitis is relatively benign; in others, however, there is continuing liver damage that may progress to cirrhosis or liver cancer. In population groups where hepatitis B is endemic, liver cancer is common and is thought to be related to the disease. Diagnosis of hepatitis B is confirmed by specific patterns of antibody and antigens found in a hepatitis serology panel. Patients who are immune to hepatitis B test positive for hepatitis B antibody (core and/or surface) while patients with chronic hepatitis test positive for hepatitis B antigen. The presence of hepatitis B antigen (E antigen) suggests infectivity.

Hepatitis C follows a course similar to hepatitis B but has a higher rate of chronic hepatitis (about 50 percent). Diagnosis is made by detecting antibody to hepatitis C. In contrast to hepatitis B, the presence of antibody to hepatitis C does not imply immunity to the virus.

Hepatitis associated with systemic infection (e.g., tuberculosis) is established by isolating or identifying the underlying organism.

Diagnostic tools include liver enzymes, viral serologies, special blood tests for infection (e.g., amoebic serology), ultrasound and CT scan, and liver biopsy. Prior to a liver biopsy, the ability of the blood to clot will be measured, since hepatitis can cause problems with coagulation.

TREATMENT

Most cases of hepatitis A resolve spontaneously. Hepatitis B and C may also resolve spontaneously but have a relatively high rate of developing into chronic hepatitis. Recent studies have suggested a role for alpha interferon in the treatment of hepatitis B and C. Other medications, such as levamisole, are being studied.

Hepatitis that presents as part of a systemic illness (tuberculosis, sarcoid) is treated by addressing the underlying problem.

Autoimmune hepatitis has been successfully treated with immunosuppressive medication including steroid (prednisone), azathioprine, and 6-mercaptopurine (6-MP). However, the medication usually must be given chronically to prevent relapse.

Hepatitis patients should avoid alcohol and certain drugs metabolized in the liver. Rest is also important and bed rest is advised during the symptomatic stage, while a reduced schedule may be recommended for several weeks or even months following recovery.

PREVENTION

In the case of hepatitis A, family members and other people exposed to the disease may be given immune serum globulin (protective antibodies) as a preventive measure. This also may be advised for people traveling for limited time periods to areas where hepatitis A is endemic. In such areas travelers should eat in clean establishments where dishes are washed with boiling water to kill microorganisms.

Hepatitis B immune globulin is effective in preventing hepatitis in exposed individuals (e.g., needlestick victims, sexual partners of patients with acute hepatitis B, infants born to infected mothers). It may be combined with hepatitis B vaccine.

The development of an effective vaccine against hepatitis B was a major breakthrough and promises to improve the long-term outlook against this disease by preventing it from ever occurring. There is currently no vaccine against hepatitis C.

MALABSORPTION SYNDROMES

INTRODUCTION

Malabsorption syndromes are difficulties in taking nutrients out of certain foods and absorbing them usefully into the body. Many conditions affect the ability of the small intestine to absorb nutrients adequately, including:

- Deficiency of enzymes needed to break down particular foods
- Structural defects or tumors in the intestine
- Inflammation
- Intestinal infections such as giardia
- Bacterial overgrowth
- Injury or surgical removal of portions of the small intestine
- Diseases such as tropical or celiac (nontropical) sprue, AIDS, Crohn's, and Whipple's disease
- Congestive heart failure
- Scleroderma
- Intestinal lymphoma
- Liver disease
- Bacterial overgrowth
- Intestinal damage from radiation therapy or certain drugs

Symptoms vary according to the cause, but the most common are:

- Weight loss
- Abdominal discomfort including cramps, gas, and bloating
- Diarrhea
- Abnormal stools
- Nutritional deficiencies
- Anemia
- Children's failure to thrive or grow

Whenever there is unexplained weight loss, abdominal discomfort or symptoms, and nutritional deficiencies, malabsorption should be suspected. Specific malabsorption disorders are listed below.

CELIAC DISEASE (NONTROPICAL SPRUE)

DEFINITION

Celiac disease is an intolerance to gluten, a protein found in wheat and rye flours. The disease, which causes damage to the small intestine, usually appears in childhood, although there are cases in which it is not diagnosed until adulthood. Giardia infection can produce malabsorption identical to celiac disease.

CAUSE

Celiac disease may be a hereditary disorder or may result from early viral infection.

DIAGNOSIS

Symptoms include a failure to grow in childhood, weight loss, abdominal bloating and discomfort, anemia, and the passage of fatty, foul-smelling stools that may float to the top of the toilet water (although floating stools may not necessarily signify disease). The disorder often can be diagnosed on the basis of symptoms and confirmed by examining a small sample of intestinal tissue. If there is no family history of celiac disease, tests for giardia should be conducted through stool samples or microscopic examination of duodenal contents.

As the disease progresses, the fingerlike villi that line the intestinal walls flatten. Normally, villi help absorb nutrients into the bloodstream. Damaged villi can only incompletely absorb nutrients, resulting in the weight loss and nutritional deficiencies common to celiac disease.

TREATMENT

Celiac sufferers must consume a gluten-free diet, avoiding breads and foods that contain wheat or rye flours, as well as soups, gravies, ice cream, and other commercial products to which gluten is added. Food labels must be carefully examined for gluten or grain products.

People with celiac disease often benefit from nutritional counseling, especially since the disorder can cause a variety of nutritional deficiencies—including anemia and iron and B_{12} deficiency—that require vitamin and mineral supplements. In severe cases, steroid drugs may be prescribed to help promote recovery of the intestine.

LACTOSE INTOLERANCE

DEFINITION

Lactose intolerance—the inability to break down the sugar in cow's milk—is a very common disorder, especially among people of non-Caucasian origin. Up to 75 percent of all adults, excluding those of northern European extraction, have some degree of lactose intolerance. The ubiquitousness of this condition causes some to feel that it is not really a disease among adults. In fact, a decrease of lactase could be considered a normal part of aging.

CAUSE

Lactase is an intestinal enzyme that helps digest lactose, a sugar that is found in many foods, especially dairy products. Diarrhea, gas, and abdominal pain can occur when there is not enough lactase to digest milk products. Babies or young children fed mostly cow's milk may lose or fail to gain weight. Although lactase deficiency is the most common carbohydrate malabsorption syndrome, other enzymes needed to absorb various sugars (disaccharides) may be deficient instead of lactase, resulting in symptoms similar to those of lactose intolerance.

DIAGNOSIS

Lactose intolerance is indicated by gastrointestinal symptoms invariably occurring after the consumption of milk or milk products. A lactose tolerance test—the administration of a lactose drink followed by monitoring for gastrointestinal symptoms—confirms the diagnosis. During this test, the blood may also be tested for glucose (sugar), which rises in the lactose-tolerant. Other confirming tests include stool analysis for a high acid content, which signifies intolerance.

TREATMENT

Adults should limit intake of dairy products. Lactaid or Dairy-Ease are two brands of lactase enzyme supplements and enzyme-treated milk with the lactose predigested. Babies receive a soy-based formula or other milk substitutes, or milk with lactase enzyme added. Symptoms of lactose intolerance can be prevented by avoiding cow's milk and other foods that contain lactose, such as cake and pizza. People with lactose intolerance can often tolerate certain strains of yogurt and certain cheeses because the lactose in these foods may already have been broken down by beneficial microorganisms.

TROPICAL SPRUE

DEFINITION

Tropical sprue is a malabsorption syndrome uncommon in the United States; it is seen occasionally among people from the Caribbean, India, and Southeast Asia.

CAUSE

The cause of this syndrome is unknown, although it is believed to be related in some way to nutritional deficiency and environmental factors, including infection, intestinal parasites, or perhaps consumption of certain food toxins.

DIAGNOSIS

Tropical sprue causes varied symptoms, including anemia and other nutritional deficiencies, weight loss, and diarrhea. A sore tongue also is common, as are symptoms of other malabsorption syndromes, such as passage of fatty stools. Diagnosis is based on an analysis of intestinal tissue samples, which display deformities in the intestinal villi.

TREATMENT

Tropical sprue is treated with folic acid and antibiotics (e.g., tetracycline). If vitamin B_{12} is deficient, B_{12} supplementation is given. Treatment may be continued for several months or longer, depending upon the severity of the disease.

WHIPPLE'S DISEASE

DEFINITION

Whipple's disease is a relatively rare malabsorption disorder, mostly affecting middle-aged men.

CAUSE

The cause of Whipple's disease is unknown, although it is believed to be related to a bacterial infection.

DIAGNOSIS

Besides severe malabsorption, symptoms include nutritional deficiencies, chronic low-grade fever, diarrhea, joint pain, weight loss, and darkening of the skin pigmentation. Organs such as the brain, heart, lungs, and eyes may be adversely affected.

TREATMENT

At one time, the disease was invariably fatal; now, however, most cases can be cured or effectively controlled with antibiotics such as tetracycline and nutritional supplements. The antibiotic of choice appears to be trimethoprim-sulfamethoxazole and should be given for at least a year and probably indefinitely.

....

METABOLIC DISORDERS

HEMOCHROMATOSIS (IRON OVERLOAD)

DEFINITION

Iron overload is a metabolic disorder that causes excess deposits of iron in the liver, pancreas, and other iron-storing organs. Iron overload causing tissue damage is hemochromatosis; without damage, the condition is called hemosiderosis.

CAUSE

Hemochromatosis is uncommon and rarely occurs before middle age, although it may occur congenitally. It is inherited as a recessive trait. It is ten times more common in males than in females. Symptoms usually develop between ages 40 and 60 in men and after menopause in women (menstrual bleeding probably prevents women from developing iron overload prior to menopause). This condition can also result from blood transfusions and overconsumption of dietary iron, especially among people with a genetic predisposition to accumulate iron. In South Africa, iron overload is found in the Bantu tribe where iron migrates from utensils into beer, cereal, and other foods.

Hemosiderosis can occur during hemolytic anemia (see chapter 23) or when unnecessary iron has been taken as a diet supplement for an extended time. Alcohol abuse can lead to increased hepatic levels of iron.

DIAGNOSIS

Iron deposition can cause damage to a number of organs. Hemochromatosis can cause cirrhosis of the liver, jaundice, diabetes, an enlarged heart, congestive heart failure, and irregular heartbeat (arrhythmia). Other less common symptoms include abdominal pain, arthritis, and pseudogout. Diagnosis is confirmed by blood tests for iron, transferrin and ferritin, and liver biopsy with special stains to detect elevated iron content. Iron overload victims should be screened for this condition.

TREATMENT

To bring the plasma iron level down, 500 milliliters (about 15 ounces) of blood are removed weekly. After a normal level is reestablished, blood is removed every 3 to 4 months to prevent an iron rise. When anemia results from the removal of the blood, the chelating agent deferoxamine may be given to remove iron without taking out blood. Patients should also adhere to a low-iron diet, avoiding foods such as liver, red meats, or iron-enriched breads and cereals. The addition of ascorbic acid can help increase urinary iron excretion.

WILSON'S DISEASE

DEFINITION

Wilson's disease, or hepatolenticular degeneration, is a relatively rare metabolic disorder of copper metabolism during which a progressive accumulation of copper builds up in the liver, kidneys, brain, and other body organs.

CAUSE

Wilson's disease is caused by inheriting a defective recessive gene from each parent.

DIAGNOSIS

Although this genetic defect is present at birth, symptoms usually do not appear for about 5 years. At that time, copper released into the red blood cells from a copper-saturated liver often results in severe and recurring anemia; cirrhosis may also occur.

A gold-brown or gray-green ring called a Kayser-Fleischer ring at the edge of the cornea is commonly seen and neurologic symptoms, including tremors of the upper extremities, slurred speech, and personality changes, may appear as excessive copper accumulates in the brain. Copper in the kidney may also cause renal dysfunction. Tests reveal an absent or decreased level of ceruloplasmin (a blood protein) and increase in urinary copper level. Liver biopsies with special stains to detect copper content aid in the diagnosis.

TREATMENT

If not treated, Wilson's disease is usually fatal due to liver failure or infection. Treatment reduces copper accumulation. Copper-rich foods (shellfish, organ meats, legumes, nuts, whole-grain cereals, chocolate) are taken out of the diet and penicillamine (Cuprimine or Depen)—a chelating agent that binds with the copper and eliminates it from the body—is administered. For the one-third of all patients allergic to penicillamine and who suffer rash, fever, and deficient white blood cells, the drug is usually discontinued and reintroduced with corticosteroids. Since penicillamine binds with iron and other minerals, iron supplements and pyridoxine may be given to prevent deficiency. Throughout therapy, which most physicians believe should be lifelong, patients must be closely monitored for platelet and white blood cell counts.

If penicillamine cannot be tolerated, oral zinc therapy may be considered. Zinc increases fecal copper loss in patients with Wilson's disease; however, the long-term usefulness of zinc therapy is unclear.

RECTAL DISORDERS

ANAL FISSURE

DEFINITION

Anal fissures are shallow, thin, often painful ulcers of the anal canal.

CAUSE

Anal fissure can result from passage of large, hard stools or may be a secondary result of anal surgery, proctitis, or other diseases. Since the surface of the skin at the anus has been worn away, defecation irritates the fissure and may cause the sphincter muscles to spasm, resulting in intense pain. Fissures are often associated with constipation or inadequately emptied stools, and may also be linked to stress or hemorrhoids.

DIAGNOSIS

During a physical examination to locate the source of pain, the fissure can usually be seen, although anoscopy, in which a small plastic or metal instrument called an anoscope is inserted into the lower few inches of the rectum, may be used to confirm the findings. Flexible endoscopy is also useful in establishing a diagnosis.

TREATMENT

Anal fissures are treated with warm baths and topical creams; stool softeners (brans such as psyllium) are added to the diet. Surgery is generally unnecessary but may be recommended in severe cases. After the fissure heals—which may take 2 to 3 weeks—a sigmoidoscopy may be performed to check for other rectal problems.

ANORECTAL FISTULA

DEFINITION

An anorectal fistula is a hollow, fibrous tract (opening) leading from the anal canal or rectum to the skin through which watery pus drains, irritating the skin and causing itching and discomfort.

CAUSE

Anorectal fistula may develop after inflammation (as from Crohn's colitis) or may be found occasionally in association with trauma, rectal infection (including chlamydia), carcinoma, and radiation therapy.

DIAGNOSIS

Itching and discomfort are the primary symptoms of anal fistula in the early stages, and subsequently drainage of pus, blood and mucus, and occasionally stool occur. Physical examination identifies the problem, but the precise location of the fistula's source can be ascertained through anoscopy. Proctosigmoidoscopy is necessary to exclude inflammation or underlying intestinal disease. Imaging techniques such as barium enema or CT scan may be needed to examine complex fistulas that may accompany Crohn's disease.

TREATMENT

Medications directed against the underlying condition can be effective in healing fistulas. For example, Flagyl is helpful in healing fistulas secondary to Crohn's disease. Some fistulas need surgical repair.

MALE/FEMALE DIFFERENCES

Rectovaginal fistulas (openings from the vagina to the rectum) may occur in women as the result of perineal injury during childbirth, as well as from other forms of trauma such as cancer or Crohn's disease. Rectovaginal fistulas cause passage of flatus and sometimes feces through the vagina.

HEMORRHOIDS

DEFINITION

Hemorrhoids are abnormal enlargements of what are otherwise normal veins in the anal area (see figure 22.9).

CAUSE

Hemorrhoids are often caused by increased pressure during defecation and are associated with constipation, obesity, and pregnancy. Hemorrhoids occasionally occur along with a liver disease, such as cirrhosis, because of increased pressure in the veins of the intestine.

DIAGNOSIS

When hemorrhoids bleed, the blood appears as fresh red stains on the toilet tissue when wiping, rather than as darker blood mixed with the stool. Because of the possibility of a more serious condition, rectal bleeding should not be ascribed to hemorrhoids without further medical investigation. The diagnosis may involve anoscopy, in which an anoscope is inserted into the lower few inches of the rectum to allow the doctor to detect the presence of hemorrhoids and associated local inflammation (cryptitis). Lower endoscopy or barium enema may be needed to look farther up the colon to rule out other diseases that cause bleeding or rectal pain.

TREATMENT

- Application of topical creams and suppositories to soothe the anal area
- Cortisone creams and suppositories, which are helpful and are now available without prescription

Because of the possibility of a mistaken diagnosis, patients should not treat themselves for presumed hemorrhoidal bleeding. Medication should be used under the supervision of a physician.

When hemorrhoids do not respond to medical treatment, surgery by a gastrointestinal or colorectal surgeon may be required.

Surgical methods include:

- Rubber bands used to ligate, or tie off, the hemorrhoid so that it atrophies and drops off
- Injection of a chemical into a hemorrhoid to sclerose it (encourages the growth of fibrous tissue that lessens its blood supply)
- Removal of a clot from the hemorrhoid
- Hemorrhoidectomy, removal of the entire hemorrhoid
- Laser treatment

HOME REMEDIES AND ALTERNATIVE THERAPIES

Methods to reduce the incidence of hemorrhoid flare-ups and to soothe inflammation and itching include:

- Increasing the intake of liquids to prevent the stool from getting too hard or from getting impacted
- High fiber diet

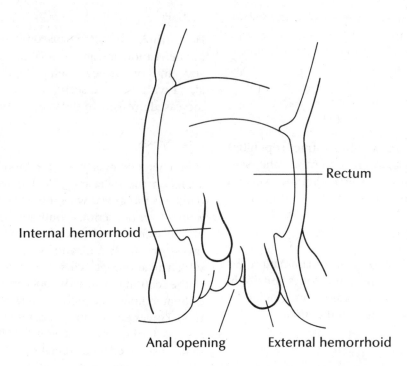

Figure 22.9: A cross section of the lower rectum showing both internal and external hemorrhoids.

- Adding stool softeners, such as colace, to the diet
- Warm baths to soothe the anal area
- Weight loss to reduce straining during defecation

MALE/FEMALE DIFFERENCES

Before taking any medication for hemorrhoids that flare up during pregnancy, a woman should first consult her physician.

STOMACH DISORDERS

GASTRITIS

DEFINITION

Gastritis is an inflammation of the stomach lining. Not a distinctive disease, gastritis can be a result of many diseases or merely a condition whose underlying cause is elusive.

CAUSE

Acute attacks of gastritis can be brought on by:

- *Helicobacter pylori* bacteria
- Drugs (such as aspirin or some antibiotics)

- Ingestion of corrosive substances
- Shock
- Allergic response
- Trauma from surgery
- Alcohol abuse

DIAGNOSIS

Gastritis symptoms include loss of appetite, nausea, vomiting, and/or bleeding and pain similar to gastric ulcer symptoms. Many patients, however, just suffer general discomfort.

Gastritis is often diagnosed by viewing the stomach interior through an endoscope and examining a biopsied tissue sample. Tissue examination may show swelling, ulcerated areas, and destruction of portions of the lining. Alternatively, there may be tissue shrinkage, a condition called atrophic gastritis. In hypertrophic gastritis—a rare form of the condition—the stomach lining and glands overgrow. Special stains can reveal the presence of *H. pylori* organisms.

TREATMENT

Treatment depends upon the underlying cause of gastritis. Specific foods or medications such as alcohol or aspirin that cause irritation should be avoided. In some cases treatment of gastritis is similar to that of ulcers: antacid therapy, omeprazole, sucralfate, cimetidine, or ranitidine. The optimal regimen for eradicating *H. pylori* bacteria is not yet clear, but success has been achieved using a combination of two antibiotics (tetracycline or amoxicillin plus Flagyl) plus bismuth subsalicylate. Use of a single antibiotic combined with omeprazole is being investigated.

PANCREATITIS

DEFINITION

The pancreas serves two main functions:

- Exocrine cells produce many of the digestive enzymes needed to break down proteins and carbohydrates.
- Endocrine cells produce insulin and glucagon, which regulate blood sugar. (For more on the pancreas see chapter 21.)

Pancreatitis, an inflammation of the pancreas, may occur as an acute, painful attack, or it may be a chronic condition resulting in gradual symptoms over a long time.

CAUSE

Pancreatitis is caused by a buildup of digestive enzymes within the pancreas. In the United States, gallstones (perhaps via obstruction of the pancreatic duct) and alcohol are major causes of pancreatitis. However, a large number of cases have no obvious cause (idiopathic); perhaps viral infection is responsible. Other causes include drugs (azathioprine, 6-MP, valproic acid), elevated triglycerides, infection (ascariasis, hepatitis A and B, coxsackie B, Epstein-Barr), Reye's syndrome, cystic fibrosis, and vasculitis. Rarely, duodenal ulcers and physical injury may bring on acute pancreatitis.

DIAGNOSIS

Acute pancreatitis is characterized by severe, steady pain in the upper-middle part of the abdomen; often the pain radiates to the back. Associated symptoms include nausea, vomiting, fever, lowered blood pressure, fast heart rate, and clammy skin. Hypotension (low blood pressure) or circulatory shock may follow these symptoms. The disorder is diagnosed on the basis of symptoms and blood tests (elevated amylase and lipase levels). Ultrasonography or CT scans help determine whether biliary tract disease is present and also provide information by detecting the presence of swelling, abscess, or cyst in the pancreas as well as free fluid

(pancreatic ascites) in the abdomen. Once the acute episode has resolved, endoscopy (ERCP) may help define the cause.

Chronic pancreatitis is usually due to long-term alcohol abuse, but, as with acute pancreatitis, no obvious cause may be found. Symptoms may develop over a period of time without the sudden, dramatic occurrence of an acute attack. Fat digestion is impaired, resulting in fatty stools. Recurrent abdominal pain may be accompanied by nausea, weight loss, and other symptoms. X-rays may find stones or areas of calcified tissue within the pancreas.

TREATMENT

If the problem is due to a partially obstructed pancreatic duct, it may be resolved by ERCP or surgery. Ultrasound treatment via extracorporeal shock-wave lithotripsy of larger stones followed by endoscopic removal may be helpful. During acute pancreatitis, the flow of pancreatic enzymes is decreased as much as possible by abstention from eating or drinking (eating would stimulate enzyme secretion), although intravenous fluids usually are necessary to maintain the body's biochemical balance. Resuming oral feeding too soon can lead to a recurrence of pancreatitis, and therefore sufficient time must pass before attempting small feedings of a diet high in carbohydrates and low in fats. If the attack is linked to gallbladder disease, a cholecystectomy may be performed but usually not until the pancreatitis subsides. Other treatments depend upon symptoms and complications.

PEPTIC ULCERS

DEFINITION

A peptic ulcer is a chronic sore or crater extending through the protective mucous membrane lining and penetrating the underlying muscular tissue of the gastrointestinal tract. An ulcer can form in any area exposed to gastric acid and pepsin, a digestive enzyme instrumental in the breakdown of protein and hence the derivation of the term "peptic ulcer." The areas most commonly affected are the upper part of the duodenum (duodenal ulcer), the stomach itself (gastric ulcer), and, less commonly, the esophagus.

CAUSE

The bacterium *Helicobacter pylori*, or *H. pylori*, has recently been shown to be strongly associated with ulcers and gastritis, although the precise cause of gastrointestinal ulcers is still unknown.

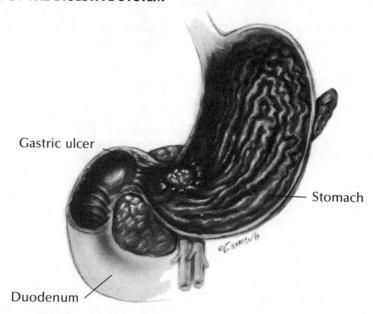

Gastric ulcer

Stomach

Duodenum

Figure 22.10: Cross section of the stomach showing a gastric ulcer in the lower portion.

Although hydrochloric acid in the stomach is required for the development of a peptic ulcer, levels of stomach acid are not necessarily elevated. About 30 to 40 percent of patients with duodenal ulcers have increased acid secretion while most patients with gastric ulcer have either normal or below normal acid secretion rates.

The development of an ulcer is probably related to a combination of factors, including acid production, "cytoprotection" (including protective mucus production), and presence or absence of *Helicobacter* (see figure 22.10). Heredity probably also plays a role.

Stress and the use of nonsteroidal anti-inflammatory drugs such as aspirin may cause ulceration by interfering with cytoprotection.

Stress is by no means a universal factor in causing peptic ulcer disorders. Many people subjected to enormous stress are ulcer-free, whereas many calm people who seemingly lead quiet, relatively stress-free lives develop ulcers. Cigarette smoking may cause duodenal ulcers and has been shown to delay ulcer healing.

Alcohol can cause irritation of the lining of the stomach but has not been proven to cause duodenal ulceration. Also, contrary to popular belief, spicy foods do not appear to cause peptic ulcers. Whether steroids cause ulcers has been a topic of debate; although there seems to be an increased incidence of ulcers in patients taking large doses of steroids chronically, the exact relationship is still unclear.

DIAGNOSIS

Ulcers may occur at any age. Abdominal pain is a common symptom, usually described as a gnawing ache or burning sensation relieved by milk or antacids. The location and type of pain also depend upon the type of ulcer.

- **Duodenal Ulcer.** Produces recurring pain, usually 2 or 3 hours after eating, and the discomfort is relieved by eating.
- **Stomach Ulcer.** Eating may provoke rather than relieve pain; should be biopsied to exclude the possibility of cancer.
- **Prepyloric Ulcers.** Symptoms similar to duodenal ulcers; often caused by aspirin-like medicines and usually heal quickly when these medicines are stopped.
- **Pyloric Channel Ulcer.** In the lowermost stomach section where food passes through the pyloric sphincter into the duodenum; symptoms are likely to include bloating, nausea, and vomiting.
- **Esophageal Ulcer.** Likely to cause discomfort when swallowing or lying down.

Unfortunately, history and physical examination are not reliable in establishing a diagnosis of peptic ulcer disease and therefore further evaluation is necessary. Often a patient with classic symptoms suggestive of peptic ulcer disease will have another cause for the pain.

Up to 50 percent of ulcer sufferers never experience abdominal pain, and recognize their condition only when other symptoms such as gastrointestinal bleeding or obstruction occur. Occasionally, ulcer pain may mistakenly be attributed to other causes such as indigestion or an irritable bowel.

Endoscopy, in which a long, flexible tube with fiberoptic viewing devices is threaded through the mouth and into the intestinal tract, may be used to establish a definitive ulcer diagnosis. Alternatively, an ulcer may be seen on x-ray studies using a barium swallow. In most cases, endoscopy is superior to x-ray study because of increased ability to detect conditions in which there is no crater or obvious defect but only increased redness. In addition, endoscopic biopsies can greatly aid in diagnosis (e.g., detection of gastric cancer and *H. pylori*).

TREATMENT

Although gastrointestinal ulcers may heal by themselves, they are treated to end discomfort and forestall complications such as iron deficiency or hemorrhage.

Strategies include:

1. Eradication of *Helicobacter pylori*
   - The optimal regimen for eradicating *H. pylori* bacteria is not yet clear, but success has been achieved using a combination of two antibiotics (tetracycline or amoxicillin plus Flagyl) plus bismuth subsalicylate. Use of a single antibiotic combined with omeprazole is being investigated.
2. Acid Reduction
   - *Antacids:* help ulcers heal by neutralizing or absorbing gastric acid.
   - *H_2 blocking agents (cimetidine, ranitidine, and famotidine):* lower the production of gastric acid. Although these drugs usually provide relief from symptoms in about a week, healing may take 6 to 8 weeks or longer; also, small doses may be prescribed over a prolonged period to prevent recurrence.
   - *Omeprazole (Prilosec):* directly blocks the pumping of acid into the stomach.
3. Cytoprotection
   - *Sucralfate:* forms a protective coating over ulcers and allows healing without disrupting the flow of gastric acid.
   - *Misoprostol (Cytotec):* prostaglandin treats and helps prevent stomach ulcers associated with aspirin. Side effect includes induction of abortions; patients must be carefully informed about this side effect.

While pharmacologic treatment of ulcers has reduced the need for ulcer surgery, an operation may be required to treat:

- Perforated ulcer: a medical emergency, usually requiring surgery and intensive treatment to prevent peritonitis. A perforated ulcer breaks through the intestinal wall, spilling the contents into the abdominal cavity.
- Recurrent gastrointestinal bleeding.

- Intestinal obstruction that is recurrent or is not relieved by other treatments.
- Gastrointestinal malignancy.
- Ulcers unresponsive to medications or changes in diet.

Ulcer sufferers should quit smoking to speed healing and avoid alcohol and caffeine, which stimulate the production of irritating gastric acid. Decaffeinated coffee and caffeine-free tea or soft drinks may be less irritating to the stomach lining. However, both regular and decaffeinated coffee can increase stomach acid. Drugs such as aspirin should be avoided or used sparingly. If stress is a factor, changes in lifestyle or the development of more effective coping techniques may help. (See chapter 4, The Fundamentals of Good Health.)

Although the traditional dietary treatment of ulcers required bland foods, heavy emphasis on milk products, and frequent, small meals, it has been shown that these foods do not relieve discomfort in all ulcer patients. Highly spiced dishes, fatty foods, or fruit juice can provoke ulcer symptoms but may be consumed freely if they do not.

PREVENTION

Antibiotics, administered as treatment to eradicate *H. pylori* bacteria, have been shown to prevent recurrence of ulcers associated with *H. pylori* infection. In the past, chronic treatment—often with an H_2 receptor blocker—has been advocated to help prevent recurrence of duodenal ulcer. It is possible that eradication of *H. pylori* may reduce the need for chronic preventive therapy.

MALE/FEMALE DIFFERENCES

More men than women develop ulcers for unknown reasons. But the tendency to develop ulcers is genetic and may be passed to both men and women.

PERITONITIS

DEFINITION

The abdominal cavity is lined by a two-layered membrane, the peritoneum. Peritonitis is an inflammation of this membrane.

CAUSE

Peritonitis is usually the result of injury or infection caused by a ruptured appendix, perforated ulcer, diverticulitis, or as a result of abdominal surgery. Occasionally, peritonitis is the result of inflammation related to a systemic process such as vasculitis or familial Mediterranean fever.

TREATMENT

Peritonitis is always a serious situation, calling for immediate therapy that depends on the cause.

MALE/FEMALE DIFFERENCES

In women, pelvic inflammatory disease involving the fallopian tubes, which lie over the peritoneum, may cause peritonitis.

....

POLYPS

DEFINITION

Polyps are small growths of varying size and shape that may have a stalk (pedunculated polyp) or be flat (sessile polyp) and occur mostly in the colon but may be found in the upper intestine (see figure 22.11). There are several different types of polyps, as well as pseudopolyps (normal areas that appear to be polyps because of surrounding colitis). Since some polyps can be malignant or premalignant, they should be investigated and treated as early as possible.

CAUSE

It is not known why some people develop polyps, although there is a hereditary element involved. Recently a gene has been isolated, which is responsible for the development of a condition called familial polyposis in which patients develop hundreds of polyps.

DIAGNOSIS

Polyps usually produce no visible symptoms, although in some cases patients may have rectal bleeding. Rarely, invisible blood in the stool occurs. There is a tendency for polyps to run in families, and a patient who develops one colon polyp is at increased statistical risk of developing colon polyps in the future especially if the polyp is adenomatous.

Diagnosis is primarily made with colonoscopy and barium enema. Many polyps can be removed with a tiny instrument threaded through the colonoscope, making more complicated surgery unnecessary. Risks of colonoscopy include perforation and bleeding of the intestine, but these risks have been reduced with advances in technical design of the colonoscope. Some polyps, such as those that are very large or without a stalk, cannot be removed via a colonoscope. In these cases, the section of the colon containing the polyp may have to be surgically removed. Laser treatment via the colonoscope can be helpful in treating large or sessile polyps. Generally, the larger the polyp, the greater the chance that it will be malignant. Polyps over 2 centimeters in diameter have a greater than 50 percent chance of being malignant. Very tiny polyps have a very small risk of malignancy. Research suggests that polyps should be removed whenever possible, since some polyps may grow, develop malignant features, and bleed. Adenomatous, a type of glandular tumor, and villous

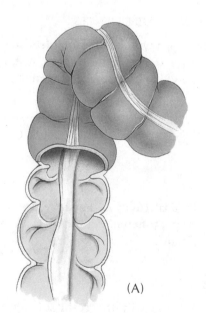

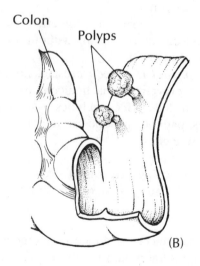

Colon

Polyps

(A)

(B)

Figure 22.11A and B: (A) Normal colon. (B) Intestinal polyps are mushroomlike growths that form along the colon wall.

polyps appear more likely to be linked to some premalignant potential than do hyperplastic polyps.

PREVENTION

Patients with a history of adenomatous or villous colonic polyps need regular, close follow-up by a physician. There is some difference of opinion on how often this follow-up should be scheduled, but current guidelines call for colonoscopy approximately every 3 years in patients who have had polyps.

Close relatives (adult siblings and adult offspring) of patients who have adenomatous or villous polyps should see a physician for periodic rectal exams, stool tests for occult blood, and possibly periodic colonoscopy. Such guidelines at present are under study and are being further developed; patients should check with their personal physician for updated guidelines.

23

Blood Disorders

• • • • • • • • • • • • • • • •

ARTHUR BANK, M.D.

When people are told by doctors that their blood tests are abnormal, they often assume the tests reveal a serious disease like leukemia. But while the ever expanding use of blood tests increases the likelihood that any single test may be abnormal, the odds are small that a single, unusual result is due to a serious disorder. More likely, it represents a value (result) only a bit outside the normal range or reflects a relatively minor condition.

The most common blood abnormalities are not serious but are usually reactions of the body to infections or deficiencies that are treatable. With proper treatment, many sufferers of malignant, severe, and life-threatening diseases survive a long time or, in some cases, are cured. While an internist or generalist can often treat common blood disorders, a hematologist is needed for more severe and complex cases.

THE BLOOD AND ITS COMPONENTS

Ten and one-half pints of blood circulate constantly through the body of the average adult, bringing to each cell the oxygen, nutrients, and chemical substances necessary for proper functioning and, at the same time, removing waste products.

The blood consists of two basic parts: the formed cells, or corpuscles, and the fluid plasma conveying these cells. Blood cells are formed in the bone marrow found in cavities primarily within the flat bones, such as the ribs and the breastbone (sternum). As a fetus, the human body can produce blood in "extramedullary" sites such as the liver, spleen, and lymph nodes, but blood production in these areas is highly unusual after birth.

Most blood cells are red cells, or erythrocytes, whose major function is carrying oxygen from the lungs to other parts of the body. Their distinctive red color comes from the pigment hemoglobin, their major chemical component that combines with oxygen and carries it in the blood throughout the body. The oxygen conveyed by hemoglobin is released to the cells of various tissues and used for the cells' energy-producing processes, vital to the continued function of the tissues and organs. When the body exerts a large amount of energy, such as with exercise, it consumes oxygen rapidly and the muscle cells begin to accumulate acidic by-products of activity. To deal with this physiological phenomenon, breathing quickens, oxygen intake accelerates, and the heart beats faster to pump more blood with its supply of oxygen-containing hemoglobin throughout the body. The tissues in turn receive more oxygen and release a

portion of their acidic waste products to the blood (including carbon dioxide, which is carried to the lungs and exhaled).

Red blood cells in the circulating blood outnumber white cells, or leukocytes, 500:1. The several different types of white blood cells form the body's main defense against disease and foreign invaders. The major type of white cell that fights infection is called the phagocyte or granulocyte, so named because it contains granules. The granulocytes are stored primarily in the bone marrow to be rapidly released in large numbers into the bloodstream in response to infection, foreign substances, trauma, or tissue damage. These cells engulf and destroy bacteria and other toxic products. In contrast to the red blood cells, which survive an average of 120 days, the granulocytes live less than a week in the circulating blood.

The lymphocyte, another type of white blood cell, produces antibodies and provides specific immunologic defenses against foreign substances (antigens). Lymphocytes are stored primarily in the lymph glands, part of the lymphatic system, which drains wastes from the skin and other tissues and provides protection against foreign substances and bacteria. During infection, the swollen glands caused by the proliferation of lymphocytes are an example of lymph node immune response. The lymphocytes produced and stored in the lymph nodes circulate in the blood and then recirculate through the lymph nodes. Many of these cells are extremely long-lived, and contain "biochemical memories" of exposure of the body to various foreign substances, allowing them to combat these substances more rapidly if the invaders return. (For more information on immune response, see chapter 29, Allergies.)

Platelets, which also circulate in the blood, are not true cells but are fragments of cells called megakaryocytes, which are found only in the bone marrow. Together with the blood vessel walls and substances in the plasma called coagulation factors, platelets clot the blood, forming a major protection against continued bleeding when a blood vessel is damaged or severed. Platelets disintegrate as they function in the clotting process; otherwise, they survive an average of 10 days.

Plasma, the yellowish fluid in which all of these cells circulate, contains many other substances like salts, various proteins, antibodies, and blood-clotting factors.

DIAGNOSIS OF BLOOD DISORDERS

A close examination of blood can reveal myriad conditions. These include not only possible blood disorders but also diseases of many other organs such as a bacterial infection (which can cause a high granulocyte count) or colon cancer (which can cause anemia). Blood samples for diagnostic tests are collected from a vein in the arm in a procedure known as a venipuncture. A single sample of blood can be used for a large number of tests; the most common of these tests are the blood counts.

Routine blood counts are usually performed on an automated machine, and are often called the ABC (automated blood count). The ABC includes a measurement of the red blood cells as either a precise number of red blood cells, as in a red blood count (RBC), or as a "relative" number of red blood cells. The relative number of red blood cells can be determined either as the hematocrit (HCT), the amount of blood cells found in a given volume of blood; or the hemoglobin concentration (HGB), which is the amount of hemoglobin present in a given amount of blood.

The RBC, HCT, and HGB all basically look at the same thing: the number of red blood cells present in a given sample of blood. A significant decrease in the RBC, HCT, or the HGB is known as anemia, and can reflect a variety of diseases affecting the entire body, as well as conditions localized in the blood system.

The white blood cell count (WBC) is another part of the ABC; changes in the WBC reflect the presence of infection and diseases affecting the blood-forming system or other systems of the body and can indicate possible disease in many organs. Platelet counts are still another part of the ABC in most cases. Elevations or depressions of the platelet count can indicate diseases of the blood system or of other organs (certain conditions cause increases in the number of platelets, while others cause decreases).

When you are ill, the values obtained in the blood counts are often useful to physicians in determining which particular system of the body is affected. A normal blood count is reassuring and rules out such disorders as leukemia, anemia, and coagulation abnormalities but does not necessarily eliminate the possibility of diseases such as cancer, heart disease, high blood pressure, and degenerative disorders, which do not significantly change blood count levels.

Microscopic examination of a blood smear is routinely performed following abnormal values found in the ABC. Abnormalities in the appearance of the red blood cells and white blood cells often point to specific disease states such as iron deficiency anemia or leukemia. The number of platelets can also be estimated from a blood smear.

Many more specialized blood tests can be performed on a blood sample if certain problems are suspected. For example, clotting time, the time it takes for a blood sample to clot under certain defined conditions, can be used as a diagnostic test and may indicate deficiencies of the blood coagulation factors. Another test, the erythrocyte sedimentation rate, or ESR, measures the rate at which red cells in a blood sample settle to the bottom of a glass tube. The ESR may be useful in determining whether something is generally wrong, although it usually does not specifically diagnose a disease. Other tests commonly performed on the blood do not involve the cells in the blood themselves, but rather measure substances in the plasma including:

- Chemicals that circulate in the plasma, including the electrolytes, sodium, and potassium
- Other metal ions in the blood, such as calcium
- Proteins such as albumin and gamma globulins

Abnormalities in these substances often reflect diseases of the kidney, liver, and other organs.

BONE MARROW EXAMINATION

A bone marrow examination is a major type of test often performed by a hematologist on patients with abnormalities in the ABC. The bone marrow is normally an intricately regulated organ system in which red blood cell production is regulated according to normal needs, white blood cell production and release are tightly controlled, and platelet production is determined by the need for platelets in blood coagulation.

Abnormalities seen on bone marrow examination are often helpful diagnostic clues, and sometimes lead to diagnosis of disorders of the blood or other systems. Certain forms of anemia, leukemia, and other forms of cancer, for example, can be diagnosed by bone marrow examination. Routine bone marrow examination is done under local anesthesia; a needle is inserted into the pelvis or sternum and a small amount of marrow fluid is withdrawn (aspirated) for microscopic examination. This simple procedure can be performed in an office, and in the hands of a skilled operator it is virtually painless.

A bone marrow biopsy—removal of a small core of bone and marrow—is often performed at the same time as bone marrow aspiration. The biopsy provides additional useful information regarding possible abnormalities in the bone marrow not always revealed by aspiration. For example, when leukemia or cancer invades the bone marrow, sticky, abnormal cells may not be extracted with aspiration and remain undetected unless removed in a biopsy.

BLOOD TYPES

Each person's blood contains a specific and inherited set of antigens, or proteins, on the surface of their red blood cells. Paired with red cell antigens, your plasma contains a specific set of antibodies that will attack antigens attached to the surface of red blood cells of another blood "type." Consequently, successful blood transfusion requires the "matching" of blood to avoid giving blood cells to a person whose plasma contains antibodies to the antigens on the blood cells of the transfused blood. If samples of two such "incompatible" types of blood are mixed, the antibodies of one will cause the red cells of the other to clump together (agglutinate). When this happens inside the body, the incompatible red cells will be broken open (lysed), and severe anemia can result.

Blood types are classified in several ways; one system is the ABO blood group system, which divides blood into four types: A, B, AB, and O. In the United States, 45 percent of the population is type O; 40 percent is type A; 10 percent is type B; and 5 percent is type AB. People have antibodies only against antigens their red blood cells lack. In other words, individuals with type A blood have A antigens on their red cells and antibodies against type B antigens in their plasma, while those with type B have B antigens on their cells and antibodies against blood group A in their plasma. People with AB blood types have both A and B antigens on their cells, and no A or B antibodies in their plasma; lacking any antibodies, they can receive any type of blood, and are known as "universal recipients." Those with type O blood have neither A nor B antigens on their cells; their blood cells, therefore, will not be agglutinated by any recipient's antibodies. Thus, they are known as "universal donors." On the other hand, they have both A and B antibodies in their plasma and can receive only O type blood.

Another major blood determinant system is the rhesus system, which divides the population into either Rh positive or Rh negative individuals, depending on whether a so-called rhesus antigen or factor is present on the surface of the red cells. People who are Rh positive are far more common than those who are Rh negative, accounting for 85 percent of all blood. (For more information about the rhesus factor, see chapter 9, Special Health Concerns of Women.)

Your blood type is not particularly important to your health until you need a transfusion; in that case it is crucial that the transfused blood be of the same ABO type (matched) as yours or type O cells. Otherwise mismatched blood can cause agglutination and destruction of the red cells, which may lead to serious medical complications.

....

DISORDERS OF THE RED BLOOD CELLS

ANEMIA (OVERVIEW)

DEFINITION

Anemia, the most common disorder of the red blood cells, is a decrease in the number of red blood cells.

CAUSE

There are three general causes of anemia:

> Decreased red cell production by the bone marrow
> Increased red cell destruction
> Bleeding or blood loss

Deficiencies of iron and vitamins B_{12} and folic acid can lead to inadequate red cell production and anemia. Since iron is needed to form hemoglobin, an inadequate supply can result in an underproduction of hemoglobin and thus to iron deficiency anemia. Underproduction of red cells may also result from invasion of the bone marrow by cancer, leukemia, lymphoma, or from scarring (fibrosis) of the marrow.

In other anemias, the red blood cells may be produced at a normal rate only to be broken down (hemolyzed) too quickly, a condition termed hemolytic anemia. Hemolytic anemias may be caused by the presence of antibodies in the blood resulting from infections, from the action of certain drugs, or from a variety of inherited conditions, such as sickle cell anemia or thalassemia in which the abnormal properties of the red blood cells themselves lead to their accelerated destruction (usually in the spleen). Anemia can also result from blood loss due to trauma or bleeding ulcers.

DIAGNOSIS

A simple and valuable blood test called the reticulocyte count can distinguish anemias due to decreased blood cell production (which cause a low reticulocyte count) from other types of anemia (which display a high count). The reticulocytes that are counted in this test are very young red cells whose levels reflect bone marrow activity.

Regardless of the cause, the symptoms of anemia are usually the same: Weakness and fatigue are common complaints, and, in more severe instances, palpitations and shortness of breath occur as the heart rate increases and the lungs try to bring in more oxygen to compensate for the paucity of red cells. Pallor of the skin, the gums, eyes, and nailbeds is another common feature of anemia.

In hemolytic anemia, jaundice of the skin and whites of the eyes may result from the excessive rate of breakdown of the red cells, a process that releases yellow bilirubin pigments. Severe anemia can precipitate heart failure or chest pain due to cardiac disease.

In most cases, anemia is only a sign of some underlying disease, and the cause of the anemia must be determined by other blood tests and x-rays, as well as by clues provided by physical examination and a detailed patient history.

IRON DEFICIENCY ANEMIA

DEFINITION

Iron deficiency anemia can result from a lack of iron reserves. Iron is usually stored in sufficient amounts in the bone marrow, liver, and spleen to be regularly withdrawn for the manufacture of hemoglobin. The used-up iron is replenished when foods are eaten that contain the mineral or when the red blood cells break down and the iron in them is recycled. When an event occurs that disrupts this replenishment, anemia results.

CAUSE

A lack of adequate iron reserves is most commonly caused by bleeding, since the red blood cells themselves are the major reservoir for iron in the body. In women, iron deficiency anemia is commonly caused by menstrual bleeding; even normal menstruation can deplete iron reserves over a period of months and cause severe iron deficiency anemia.

Iron deficiency anemia can also result from blood loss via the gastrointestinal tract due to either ulcers, tumors, or inflammatory conditions. Bleeding from hemorrhoids may sometimes be severe enough to cause anemia, while blood loss from the urinary tract or from the respiratory tract is also possible, but rare. Similarly, it is extremely rare to have an iron deficiency anemia result from an inadequate amount of iron in the diet alone.

Generally, iron deficiency anemia in men or non-menstruating women must be investigated to find its hidden cause because a silent colon cancer or other similar serious condition causing blood loss may be present. Bleeding from the gastrointestinal tract can sometimes be detected by bowel movements that are black or tarry or that contain red blood, but it also can be occult (hidden) and asymptomatic, especially if the blood loss is slow (chronic).

DIAGNOSIS

The diagnosis of iron deficiency anemia is indicated when blood loss and anemia are present. Iron deficiency anemia is often accompanied by red blood cells that are smaller than normal (microcytic) and below normal hemoglobin (hypochromic). The diagnosis of iron deficiency anemia is confirmed by chemical tests showing decreased amounts of iron in the body. The most commonly used tests are measurements of ferritin, an iron-containing compound in the blood plasma, and serum iron, both of which are low during iron deficiency anemia. Bone marrow examination in iron deficiency anemia will always show the absence of iron on specific staining of the marrow smear for iron. However, bone marrow testing is usually unnecessary to diagnose iron

deficiency anemia, since the ferritin and serum iron confirm the diagnosis.

TREATMENT

Treatment of iron deficiency anemia includes taking iron supplements, but this is usually inadequate; it is imperative to find the underlying cause of iron deficiency anemia especially in all men and nonmenstruating women. The additional treatment of this type of anemia depends on the specific cause of bleeding: An ulcer must be treated in one way, a colon cancer in another. In the absence of continued bleeding, the anemia is treated simply with iron supplements taken orally for 12 months not only to correct the anemia but also to replenish the body's iron stores.

In severe cases of iron deficiency anemia associated with continued bleeding or signs of heart failure, blood transfusions are also required.

PREVENTION

Iron deficiency as a result of menstruation can usually be prevented with the use of iron supplements. Routine use of iron supplements also prevents most cases of iron deficiency anemia during pregnancy (once a common problem). As mentioned earlier, inadequate iron reserves are only rarely due to insufficient iron in the diet. Adequate iron intake is provided by diets that include meats and dark green leafy vegetables. (See chapter 5, The Basics of Good Nutrition.)

MALE/FEMALE DIFFERENCES

Iron deficiency anemia occurs more often in women than in men because of blood loss due to menstruation.

PERNICIOUS ANEMIA DUE TO VITAMIN B$_{12}$ DEFICIENCY

DEFINITION

Pernicious anemia, a type of anemia known as megaloblastic anemia, stems from vitamin B$_{12}$ deficiency due to an inability to absorb it from the intestinal track.

CAUSE

Since vitamin B$_{12}$ is readily absorbed from meats and easily stored in the liver, most healthy people other than strict vegetarians have a 3- to 5-year reserve of this nutrient in their bodies. A B$_{12}$ deficiency occurs when the stomach fails to secrete a substance called "intrinsic factor," which is necessary for B$_{12}$ absorption in the ileum (a section of the small intestine), although other causes can inhibit digestive tract absorption of B$_{12}$.

Vitamin B_{12} deficiency can also result from surgical removal of the stomach or ileum.

DIAGNOSIS

In addition to the usual symptoms of anemia, this condition often causes decreased appetite, weight loss, intermittent constipation and diarrhea, abdominal pain, and a swollen or burning tongue. There may be neurologic involvement, evidenced by tingling sensations in the hands and feet, difficulty in balance, and lack of coordination; alternatively the primary symptoms may be psychological disturbances such as depression, irritability, and confusion.

The diagnosis of vitamin B_{12} deficiency is indicated by the presence of anemia and the finding of large red blood cells (macrocytes) and other abnormalities on the blood smear; it is confirmed by the presence of abnormal red blood cell precursors in the bone marrow, megaloblasts, and low vitamin B_{12} levels in the blood. Additionally, other special tests can be used to document the lack of vitamin B_{12} absorption.

TREATMENT

Initially, vitamin B_{12} deficiency can be treated by intramuscular injections of this nutrient several times a week to restore the body's reserves, and then less often as reserves accumulate. Eventually, the injections are given once a month, but they usually must be continued throughout life. Although many of the symptoms begin to disappear shortly after the first injections, improvement of neurological symptoms can take many months.

ANEMIA DUE TO FOLIC ACID (FOLATE) DEFICIENCY

DEFINITION

A lack of folic acid (one of the B vitamins) may cause another type of megaloblastic anemia.

CAUSE

This anemia is usually caused by a poor diet, and is a particular problem for people who drink large amounts of alcohol. Aside from the abysmal dietary habits that accompany alcoholism, alcohol interferes with folate absorption. Folate deficiency can, however, also occur in cancer patients and people suffering celiac disease (a malabsorption problem), among other disorders.

DIAGNOSIS

As in vitamin B_{12} deficiency, folate deficiency often is associated with large red cells and other abnormalities on the blood smear as well as bone marrow abnormalities. But folate deficiency seldom produces neurological symptoms, and the diagnosis of folate deficiency is confirmed by low levels of folate in the blood. Folate and B_{12} deficiencies can both be present simultaneously.

TREATMENT

Folate deficiency can be corrected by eating foods high in folate, decreasing alcohol intake, and taking folic acid supplements orally or by injection if there is intestinal malabsorption. When vitamin B_{12} deficiency is mistakenly treated with folate, anemia symptoms decrease but neurologic problems persist and often worsen.

HEMOLYTIC ANEMIA

DEFINITION

Hemolytic anemia is an anemia resulting from an increased rate of red blood cell destruction from any cause.

CAUSE

Hemolytic anemias can be caused by both inherited and acquired conditions. The inherited conditions generally are those that interfere with normal red blood cell production. These include hereditary spherocytosis, in which the cells are small and round (spherocytic); sickle cell anemia; thalassemia; and several rarer disorders.

Other inherited diseases of red cells warp their energy metabolism and cause their premature destruction. A deficiency of glucose-6-phosphate dehydrogenase is the most common energy metabolism disorder. Hemolytic anemia can also be caused by antibodies in the blood, which bind to the red cells and cause their premature destruction in the spleen (the spleen is the most active site of normal and abnormal red cell destruction). The combination of many different drugs, taken for other medical conditions, is the most common cause of the development of these antibodies, but antibodies can also form for no discernible reason.

Another cause of hemolytic anemia is a large and active spleen, which destroys red cells rapidly (hypersplenism). Hypersplenism can result from a variety of spleen disorders.

DIAGNOSIS

Hemolytic anemia causes the same symptoms as other anemias, but it also may produce jaundice in the skin and eyes from the production of yellow bilirubin, a substance formed when red blood cells break down and release their hemoglobin. The spleen, in which red blood cells are normally destroyed, may become enlarged from an overaccumulation of cells (this organ can be felt on physical examination of the upper left side of the abdomen). Signs of heart failure and an enlarged liver indicate severe anemia.

TREATMENT

In some cases, particularly hereditary spherocytosis, removal of the spleen (splenectomy) may produce a cure. In others, the liver and other phagocytic cells (blood cells supposed to ingest foreign invaders) may continue to destroy the abnormal red cells even after splenectomy. For hemolytic anemias due to antibodies, adrenal steroids are often effective. In sickle-cell disease and thalassemia, blood transfusions are indicated if the anemia is severe.

GLUCOSE-6-PHOSPHATE DEHYDROGENASE (G6PD) DEFICIENCY

DEFINITION

This is an enzyme deficiency of the red blood cells, which can cause a hemolytic anemia.

CAUSE

This sex-linked, inherited disorder is caused by abnormalities in G6PD, an enzyme required to keep red blood cell function intact. It affects about 10 percent of black males in the United States, a smaller number of black females, and to a lesser degree Caucasian ethnic groups. A number of drugs, most commonly sulfa and antimalarials, as well as viral and bacterial infections, stress red cell metabolic processes and precipitate the hemolysis of G6PD-deficient cells in individuals who have this deficiency.

DIAGNOSIS

Several blood tests detect G6PD deficiency in red blood cells.

TREATMENT

In the most common and relatively mild form of the disease in blacks, the hemolysis affects only older cells and is relatively self-limited since younger red cells with higher amounts of G6PD are unaffected. Nevertheless, the drugs causing the condition should be identified and avoided if possible. In Caucasians, G6PD deficiency is often more serious, since their type of G6PD anemia affects even young red cells that have low and insufficient amounts of functioning G6PD.

MALE/FEMALE DIFFERENCES

Since G6PD deficiency is sex-linked (caused by a gene on the X chromosome), males (with only one X chromosome) are more likely to have this anemia than women.

SICKLE CELL ANEMIA

DEFINITION

Sickle cell anemia causes an abnormal hemoglobin called sickle hemoglobin to be carried by the red blood cells.

CAUSE

Sickle cell anemia is inherited and can be expressed as either sickle cell trait—when the gene is derived from only one parent—or as a full-blown anemia when both parents carry the recessive gene.

In areas of the world where malaria is common, individuals with sickle cell trait tend to have a survival advantage over those without the trait, strongly suggesting that the sickle cell mutation is a favorable adaptational response to malaria. But children who inherit the sickle cell gene from both parents possess primarily abnormal sickle hemoglobin that gels when the red cells are subjected to low oxygen conditions. The gel causes the red cells to become deformed, taking on a sickle shape. The anemia of sickle cell anemia may be mild to severe and is due to hemolysis of the sickle red cells. People with sickle cell anemia are prone to painful episodes or crises when the capillaries, the smallest blood vessels in the body, clog with misshapen, densely packed sickled cells. This capillary traffic jam prevents oxygen from reaching tissues or organs, causing more sickling and tissue damage. The lack of oxygen, which causes pain, tends to occur during infections, but can also happen in the absence of other disease.

DIAGNOSIS

The diagnosis of sickle cell disease is made with a simple blood test, hemoglobin electrophoresis, in which normal and abnormal hemoglobins (including sickle cell hemoglobin) are separated and precisely identified. Less serious variants of sickle cell disease arise when one of the hemoglobin genes is not a sickle gene, but rather a gene for another abnormal hemoglobin, or a thalassemia gene. (See "Thalassemia.")

TREATMENT

Sickle cell anemia varies greatly in severity. The treatment of painful crises deals largely with symptoms, employing analgesia and fluids to alleviate pain and dehydration. Severe anemia is treated with blood transfusions. In many cases, blood production in patients with this anemia is increased to such an extent that transfusions are not routinely required. Bone marrow transplantation can cure the disease if a compatible donor is available.

PREVENTION

Blacks who are known to have sickle trait in their families are usually advised to seek genetic counseling before or early in pregnancy, since the presence or absence of sickle cell anemia can be accurately diagnosed prior to birth.

THALASSEMIA

DEFINITION

The thalassemia syndromes are a group of anemias due to defects in the genes producing hemoglobin.

CAUSE

These anemias are inherited and found most often in people of Mediterranean background, although cases occur in most areas of the world. Like sickle cell trait, thalassemia trait can be inherited from one parent (which is generally mild) or both parents, when it is called thalassemia major. Statistically, the chances are 1 in 4 that a child will inherit the thalassemia gene from both parents if the parents are carriers.

The two main types of thalassemia are known as alpha and beta. In rare cases, the severe form of alpha thalassemia trait is inherited from both parents, and the result is death of the fetus, a condition that is most prevalent in Southeast Asia. By contrast, blacks with alpha thalassemia essentially never have the severe form, even if inherited from both parents. If the beta thalassemia trait is inherited from both parents, as is common in Mediterranean populations, it usually results in a severe, eventually fatal condition known as Cooley's anemia (or homozygous beta thalassemia).

TREATMENT

Children who develop Cooley's anemia need repeated blood transfusions; this can lead to the buildup of iron in the body, often resulting in damage to the liver, heart failure, and premature death. Fortunately, recent advances in understanding and treating thalassemias have increased long-term survival rates. Harmful iron buildup is limited by iron chelaters, chemical substances capable of removing excess iron from the body. The chelating agent is most effectively administered by a mechanical syringe that continuously pumps the agent

underneath the skin while the child is asleep. Bone marrow transplantation can cure the disease if a compatible donor is available.

PREVENTION

Prenatal diagnosis can distinguish severely affected fetuses from those with thalassemia trait or normal hemoglobin genes.

APLASTIC ANEMIA

DEFINITION

Aplastic anemia is a relatively rare disease in which the bone marrow does not function normally, limiting the production of all blood cells including WBCs and platelets.

CAUSE

In so-called primary aplastic anemia, the cause is unknown. Secondary aplasia is generally caused by drugs or toxic substances such as benzene and arsenic, exposure to radiation, or many of the chemotherapeutic drugs used in cancer treatment.

DIAGNOSIS

Aplastic anemia generally develops slowly, its symptoms depending on which types of blood cells are most severely affected. A decrease in red cell production brings on the usual symptoms of anemia, while a decrease in white cells increases susceptibility to infections, and a decrease in platelets increases the chances of spontaneous bruising and bleeding.

Bone marrow biopsy usually indicates the diagnosis by revealing decreased numbers of blood cells and increased fat and scarring.

TREATMENT

The most common treatment for aplastic anemia is blood transfusion. If the aplasia is caused by a toxic agent, removal of the agent may result in recovery. Androgenic steroids may also alleviate the condition.

In patients under age 40 with severe disease, bone marrow transplantation can be curative if a compatible donor is available. Aplastic anemias of unknown origin (idiopathic) have a poorer prognosis.

OTHER ANEMIAS

Anemia may be caused by a wide range of other conditions, the most common of which is anemia associated with chronic diseases such as rheumatoid arthritis, tuberculosis, and cancer. These conditions cause anemia by limiting the bone marrow's ability to use iron, which is present in normally adequate amounts, to make enough red cells. This condition can be distinguished from iron deficiency anemia (with which it is sometimes confused) by blood tests revealing the presence of adequate iron stores.

Chronic kidney disease, another relatively common cause of anemia, can be treated with high doses of erythropoietin, the hormone normally responsible for red cell production. Erythropoietin is now produced by recombinant DNA technology.

Other rarer anemias can be either inherited or acquired. A large number of anemias are caused by rarer abnormalities in red blood cell enzymes, hemoglobin, and membrane components. When evaluation of an anemia does not reveal an obvious cause, the hematologist can use several other blood and marrow tests to diagnose these rarer anemias.

OVERPRODUCTION OF RED BLOOD CELLS (ERYTHREMIA, POLYCYTHEMIA)

POLYCYTHEMIA VERA

DEFINITION

Polycythemia vera is a blood disorder that usually results in an increase in all blood cells, although the red cells are the most severely affected. The increase in circulating red blood cells makes the blood more viscous, impeding its usual rapid flow through the blood vessels and often leading to strokes or tissue and organ damage.

CAUSE

Polycythemia vera is caused by an unknown acquired mutation in a subset or clone of normal bone marrow cells called stem cells. The mutation leads to abnormal excessive production of blood cells.

DIAGNOSIS

The diagnosis of polycythemia vera is made by observing the presence of increased numbers of red blood cells in the body and finding no other cause. In diagnosing polycythemia vera, the physician must distinguish it from other conditions in which the red blood count is increased for known (secondary) reasons.

For example, when certain cardiac and respiratory diseases reduce the amount of oxygen reaching tissues, the body increases its supply of oxygen-carrying red blood cells by stimulating an increase in erythropoietin, the hormone regulating red blood cell production. Secondary polycythemia (more accurately called erythremia since only the red blood cells are affected) can occur in people who live at high altitudes, where the air is low in oxygen.

Certain tumors, especially those of the cerebellum, the kidney, liver, and ovaries, can also cause an increased number of red cells due to either abnormally high erythropoietin production or unknown causes.

Polycythemia vera may be characterized by an increase in just the red cells; in both the red and white cells; or in the red cells, white cells, and the platelets. An increase in the number of platelets due to any cause can result in clotting or, paradoxically, increased bleeding. Physical signs of polycythemia vera include headaches, dizziness, shortness of breath, difficulty in concentration, night sweats, a flushed complexion, and itchy skin, especially after a hot bath. Usually the spleen becomes enlarged, and there may be attacks of gout. Occasionally, there may be cases in which there are no symptoms at all.

TREATMENT

Polycythemia vera can be treated in several ways: When only the red blood cells are affected, blood removal (venesection or phlebotomy) is the most common treatment. If the red blood cells, white cells, and platelets are increased, radioactive phosphorus or chemotherapy may be effective in suppressing the abnormal and excessive blood cell production.

DISORDERS OF THE WHITE BLOOD CELLS

Since white blood cells primarily protect the body against outside invaders, an increase in production of these cells can be a normal physiological response. The two general categories of white blood cells that can become abnormal are granulocytes (or phagocytes) and lymphocytes. Bacterial infections are the major cause of an increase in the number of granulocytes (granulocytosis), cells that seek out and destroy bacteria, but viral infections or other organism invasions can also cause granulocytosis. In addition, burns, poisons, drug reactions, excessive strenuous exercise, and heart attacks can boost the number of granulocytes.

Increases in the white blood count are often accompanied by symptoms and signs of an underlying condition, such as fatigue, weakness, fever, sweating, weight loss, and lack of appetite. These symptoms can also be seen with infections, tissue damage, and certain malignant disorders such as acute leukemia, chronic leukemia, lymphoma, and other forms of cancer. The extensive variety of benign and malignant conditions that cause granulocytosis or abnormal white blood counts complicates the diagnosis of the underlying problem.

INFECTIOUS MONONUCLEOSIS

DEFINITION

Infectious mononucleosis (mono) is a benign viral condition causing many of the same symptoms as acute leukemia.

CAUSE

Infectious mononucleosis is associated with the presence of Epstein-Barr (EB) virus, but the precise relationship between EB virus infection and infectious mononucleosis is uncertain; many people evidence EB virus infection but never develop mononucleosis. In addition, other viruses can also cause infectious mononucleosis or diseases resembling it.

DIAGNOSIS

This condition occurs primarily in the young, and its most common symptoms include fatigue, weakness, sore throat, fever, weight loss, enlarged lymph nodes, and an enlarged spleen. To complicate things further, many of these symptoms are also present in cases of infectious hepatitis, another viral disorder.

In infectious mononucleosis, there are bizarre-looking, atypical white blood cells (mono cells) seen on blood smears. While the malignant white blood cells of acute leukemia can be confused with the abnormal mono cells, leukemia is usually characterized by anemia and platelet decrease, two conditions rare in mono. In addition, bone marrow examination is normal in people with mono but always shows the leukemia cells in acute leukemia. Special antibody tests performed on the blood confirm a diagnosis of mononucleosis.

TREATMENT

The treatment of infectious mononucleosis is largely supportive rather than curative since it is a self-limited disease. Rest, fluids, and treatment of complicating infections are the mainstays of therapy. (For more information, see chapter 18.)

LEUKEMIAS (OVERVIEW)

DEFINITION

Leukemias are cancers or malignancies caused by the production of abnormal numbers and/or types of white blood cells.

CAUSE

The cause of most leukemias is not known. Radiation and drug exposure account for some cases, but the others have no known cause (idiopathic).

Normally, the number of white blood cells in the body remains constant, with just enough new cells produced to offset the number that die. During leukemia, abnormal white cells are either unnecessarily overproduced or not destroyed at the normal time. In all leukemias, abnormal white cells circulate through the body and often interfere with normal functions.

The two broad classes of leukemia are:

Acute Leukemia. A subset (or clone) of immature blood cells called blast cells proliferate. These leukemic cells crowd out and impede normal bone marrow elements and interfere with the production of normal cells. Consequently, a decrease in red blood cells causes anemia, a decrease in white cells makes the patient more susceptible to infection, and the change in production of megakaryocytes and platelets causes bleeding.

Chronic Leukemia. The abnormal white blood cells in the circulating blood and marrow may not be as invasive as in acute leukemia. The total number of white cells is usually high: often 100,000 to 200,000 or more per cubic millimeter of blood, instead of the normal 5,000 to 10,000 per cubic millimeter. But the abnormal properties of these cells may not be apparent for long periods of time.

Acute and chronic leukemias can be further classified according to whether they originate from granulocyte precursors (also called myeloid or myelogenous cells) or from lymphocyte precursors, in which case they are called lymphocytic.

The most common types of acute leukemia are acute myeloid or myelocytic leukemia (AML), which occurs primarily in adults, and acute lymphocytic leukemia (ALL), which is a disease primarily of children. The most common types of chronic leukemia are chronic lymphocytic leukemia (CLL) and chronic myelogenous leukemia (CML), both of which usually occur in adults.

TREATMENT

Many forms of leukemia can now be effectively treated and sometimes cured, but people with leukemia need the strong emotional and professional support of families, friends, physicians, and hospital personnel. They should be cared for in a calm, confident environment by medical professionals experienced in treating leukemia.

Although leukemia is a frightening disease, there is cause for optimism. Today, successful outcome of treatment for acute leukemia usually results in a normal blood count and a well patient. As discussed in the sections below, each type of leukemia requires a specialized therapy. (For more information on all types of leukemia, see chapter 17.)

ACUTE LYMPHOCYTIC LEUKEMIA (ALL)

DIAGNOSIS

Acute leukemia is usually suspected when abnormal white blood cells are seen on a blood smear. There may also be anemia and decreased platelets. The diagnosis of acute leukemia is usually made by bone marrow examination (see section in this chapter), which reveals an increased number of monotonous-appearing, abnormal blast (immature) cells. It is possible to distinguish between different acute leukemias by the types of cells seen on blood and marrow examination, by measuring levels of enzymes in the leukemic cells, and by using special stains that react differently to various types of leukemic cells.

TREATMENT

The outlook (or prognosis) in childhood ALL is extremely good when cared for at special medical centers providing the most advanced therapy. ALL is treated with combinations of antileukemia drugs (chemotherapy) designed to kill all the malignant leukemia cells. This treatment often results temporarily in increased anemia, infections, and bleeding before the leukemia cells are all gone and normal blood cells return. Close and expert hospital management is mandatory, since along with antibiotics, blood and platelet transfusions are often needed. In addition, the brain and spinal cord are also treated with radiation and drugs to eradicate and prevent the reemergence of leukemia cells in these "sanctuaries." Bone marrow transplantation is also often considered during the course of treatment of ALL.

ACUTE MYELOGENOUS LEUKEMIA (AML)

DIAGNOSIS

The diagnosis of AML and its variants is made primarily by the detection of the abnormal cells in the blood and bone marrow. Special stains and antibodies confirm the diagnosis. Each type of AML is named for the developmental stage of the abnormal white cells causing the leukemia. In the most common type of AML, responsible for most adult leukemia and some cases in children, the abnormal cells have granules that can be detected by special stains; in addition, some of the abnormal cells in the blood and marrow may have characteristic abnormal rodlike structures called Averrods.

TREATMENT

Since AML is treated with intensive chemotherapy, using different drugs than for ALL, precise identification of the type of acute leukemia to be treated is critical. Unfortunately, the prognosis for treating AML with chemotherapy is not as promising as in ALL, but newer drug combinations are constantly being tried. In addition, bone marrow transplantation in association with high-dose chemotherapy is also being used extensively in the treatment of AML.

CHRONIC MYELOGENOUS LEUKEMIA (CML)

DIAGNOSIS

Unlike acute leukemia, CML occurs primarily in men between the ages of 20 and 50, and usually develops gradually and insidiously. In this disease, the number of granulocytes in the blood and bone marrow markedly increases, as do the number of immature cells in the peripheral blood and bone marrow. The range of symptoms of CML varies greatly among individuals. Some people may experience no discomfort and only discover their illness after a routine blood test or the finding of an enlarged spleen. Others encounter only anemia or general malaise, and still others suffer weight loss, night sweats, fatigue, and discomfort in the left side of the abdomen from an enlarged spleen.

A diagnosis of CML is usually made after finding increased numbers of immature granulocytes in the blood smear and bone marrow. The diagnosis is verified by tests measuring the level of an enzyme called leukocyte alkaline phosphatase (which is markedly reduced in CML patients) and the presence of a chromosomal abnormality called the Philadelphia (Ph) chromosome, which occurs in 90 percent of people with CML.

TREATMENT

Chemotherapy can produce a remission in CML and allow the affected person to live a relatively normal life for years. Unfortunately, most cases eventually progress to an acute stage and result in death within 3 to 4 years after initial diagnosis. Bone marrow transplantation during the chronic and early phase of the disease has resulted in a 50 percent long-term, disease-free rate, and thus is strongly recommended.

MALE/FEMALE DIFFERENCES

This condition primarily affects men.

CHRONIC LYMPHOCYTIC LEUKEMIA (CLL)

DIAGNOSIS

CLL generally affects people at 40 to 70 years of age, with most cases beginning after age 60. It results from proliferating defective white blood cells (lymphocytes).

In more advanced stages, the abnormal lymphocytes invade the bone marrow and various organs, interfering with the production of red cells, normal white cells, and platelets, and causing anemia, infections, and increased bleeding. The beginning of this process may take several years and not produce any symptoms.

When CLL does produce symptoms, they may resemble myelogenous leukemia: increased fatigue, decreased appetite, weight loss, and night sweats. In other cases, the initial symptoms may be swelling of the lymph glands or spleen or anemia; recurrent infections may be the first indication in still other cases.

The diagnosis of CLL is made after finding the characteristic population of lymphocytes in blood and bone marrow. Specific antibodies are used to classify CLL based on the type of lymphocyte present.

TREATMENT

Treatment of CLL includes the use of steroids, chemotherapy, and radiotherapy. The prognosis for CLL is much better than for CML. People with CLL often survive 5 to 10 years after the initial diagnosis, many requiring little or no treatment.

AGNOGENIC MYELOID METAPLASIA

DEFINITION

Agnogenic (meaning of unknown origin) myeloid metaplasia is a disorder in which the bone marrow becomes progressively fibrotic (filled with fibrous tissue).

CAUSE

The causes are unknown. This disease is considered part of the group of so-called myeloproliferative disorders that may develop into acute leukemia and involve an abnormal proliferation of bone marrow elements (in this case fibroblasts).

DIAGNOSIS

Red cells, white cells, and platelets are produced outside the bone marrow (in extramedullary sites) in the spleen and liver, either of which can grow markedly enlarged. There can be severe anemia, and the white blood cell and platelet counts may be abnormal as well. The diagnosis of agnogenic myeloid metaplasia is made by bone marrow biopsy demonstrating replacement of marrow with fibrous tissue.

TREATMENT

Treatment, which may relieve symptoms but does not produce a cure, includes radiotherapy, chemotherapy, and sometimes removal of the spleen. The prognosis for this condition is poor, and often patients die because of the development of acute myelogenous leukemia.

GRANULOCYTOPENIA

DEFINITION

This condition is characterized by a decrease in the number of granulocytes. In its extreme form, it is known as agranulocytosis.

CAUSE

Granulocytopenia can be due to either decreased production of granulocytes by the bone marrow or increased destruction of these cells. Certain types of drugs, especially those treating thyroid problems and cancer, can markedly decrease white blood cell production. Infiltration of the bone marrow with cancer or leukemia cells and aplastic anemia can also lead to decreased granulocyte production.

Increased destruction of granulocytes is usually due to drugs, which induce the production of antibodies to granulocytes, or to increased destruction of cells by an enlarged and/or abnormal spleen. Whenever a person is treated with a drug known to cause either bone marrow suppression or production of antibodies, which can react with the granulocytes, the white blood count must be carefully monitored to ensure that granulocytopenia does not occur.

DIAGNOSIS

Granulocytopenia is usually mild and very rare, affecting only 1 person in every 100,000. It often manifests itself by frequent infections. The diagnosis is made following a low white blood cell count caused by drugs or spleen malfunction.

TREATMENT

If the condition is due to a drug reaction, it is usually reversed without treatment 7 to 10 days after the drug is stopped. Infections resulting from granulocytopenia are treated with antibiotics.

DISORDERS OF LYMPHOCYTES

Lymphocytes are white blood cells that control the immune reactions of the body. The two main types of lymphocytes are:

- B lymphocytes: produce antibodies that help fight invading organisms like bacteria.

- T lymphocytes: interact with the B lymphocytes to help them produce antibodies, and also help the body recognize foreign substances.

Both types of lymphocytes must function normally for the immune system to work properly.

There are two types of T cells:

- T helper cells (or CD4 cells): increase the production of T cells and interact with B cells to produce antibodies.
- T suppressor cells (or CD8 cells): kill T helper cells, and reduce T cell responsiveness.

During infectious mononucleosis and other viral diseases, the number of T suppressor cells increase and make individuals suffering from these diseases susceptible to a variety of other infections as well.

There is a similar increase in T suppressor cells in acquired immune deficiency syndrome (AIDS). In AIDS, CD4 T helper cell suppression is very severe and irreversible because the HIV virus that causes AIDS preferentially attacks and kills these cells. This suppression puts people with AIDS at great risk for infection with agents that do not ordinarily infect immune-competent individuals. These so-called opportunistic infections include pneumocystis carinii and toxoplasmosis as well as a rare form of cancer, Kaposi's sarcoma, that is also commonly seen in AIDS patients. (See chapter 19, HIV Infection and AIDS.)

....

LYMPHOMAS

DEFINITION

Lymphomas are cancers of the lymphatic system, especially of the lymph nodes.

CAUSE

Lymphomas can occur because of immune incompetence, in the presence of decreased T helper cells resulting from AIDS, or because of other conditions. However, lymphomas can also begin without evidence of T cell suppression, and most lymphomas are of unknown origin. While lymph nodes normally contain T and B cells, a clone of either type of cell can become malignant, proliferate, and take over the entire node. In more advanced cases, the malignant lymphocytes spread to other organs in the body. Lymphomas are named according to the type of lymphocyte clone that becomes malignant, including T cell lymphomas, B cell lymphomas, and mixed cell lymphomas composed of both B and T cells.

DIAGNOSIS

Hodgkin's Disease. Hodgkin's disease is a form of lymphoma diagnosed by the characteristic presence in the lymph nodes of a unique cell called the Reed-Sternberg cell. Hodgkin's disease represents a special class of lymphoma whose spread is predictable and whose response to treatment dramatic. The disease usually begins in the lymph nodes in the neck, spreads to the lymph nodes in the chest and armpits (axillae), then to the spleen and the liver or nodes bordering the aorta in the abdomen and farther down into the body.

Hodgkin's disease affects those 15 to 35 years old and over 50 years of age. If the disease has begun to spread, fever, night sweats, weight loss, and bone pain may also occur.

Non-Hodgkin's Lymphomas. Somewhat more common than Hodgkin's disease, these lymphomas are classified by the appearance of the lymphocytes in the biopsy material. Non-Hodgkin's lymphomas may start in the same way as Hodgkin's, with swelling of the lymph glands in the neck, axillae, or groin, but in contrast to Hodgkin's, spread is unpredictable. Several lymph node areas may be involved early in the disease and there may also be an enlarged spleen, anemia, and general malaise. Weight loss, night sweats, and fever are indications that the disease has spread.

TREATMENT

Lymphomas can be treated with radiation and chemotherapy. (For more details, see the lymphoma section in chapter 17.)

Hodgkin's disease, if caught early before it has entered other parts of the body, has a 90 to 95 percent cure rate with radiotherapy. If the disease has spread, chemotherapy using a combination of drugs or radiation together with chemotherapy may also produce a cure, although not as often. In advanced cases, patients become resistant to chemotherapeutic drugs and eventually succumb to infection or other complications.

In contrast to Hodgkin's disease, non-Hodgkin's lymphomas usually are advanced when the initial diagnosis is made, making cure more difficult. These conditions are usually treated by combination chemotherapy, since radiotherapy is not often successful. Chemotherapy and steroids may result in remission in about 50 percent of cases, but the remission period is usually shorter than in Hodgkin's. Bone marrow transplantation is also used in certain cases of Hodgkin's and non-Hodgkin's lymphomas.

MALE/FEMALE DIFFERENCES

Hodgkin's disease is more common in men than women.

MULTIPLE MYELOMA

DEFINITION

Multiple myeloma is a malignancy of plasma cells, specialized lymphocytes that normally produce antibodies.

CAUSE

In multiple myeloma, a clone of malignant plasma cells multiplies uncontrollably until it takes over the marrow and spills out into other parts of the body. As these cells multiply inside the marrow cavities of bones, they disrupt production of normal blood cells and destroy the bone, often causing severe bone pain as well. (For more information on lymphocytic disorders, see chapter 17, Cancer.)

DIAGNOSIS

While anemia and increased vulnerability to infection may be the first signs of this cancer, the most characteristic symptom is bone pain and fracture of bones, especially the vertebrae. These symptoms are caused by invasion and destruction of bone by proliferating plasma cells. Myeloma affects those mainly over age 50.

TREATMENT

Although there is no cure for myeloma, chemotherapy can prolong life for several years, until the patient becomes resistant to treatment. Radiotherapy may be used to relieve the bone pain, while transfusions can ameliorate the anemia. Bone marrow transplantation is also useful in some cases.

MALE/FEMALE DIFFERENCES

Myeloma is twice as likely to occur in men as in women.

DISORDERS OF BLOOD COAGULATION

Blood coagulation, or blood clotting, is a complex process involving platelets, coagulation factors circulating in the blood, and blood vessels. The primary defense against bleeding is the response of the injured blood vessel and the formation of a platelet plug: When a large vessel is cut, it contracts to limit bleeding, and platelets rush to the site to form a plug. After this immediate response, coagulation begins as a number of enzymes or coagulation factors in the blood plasma are activated and eventually lead to the formation of fibrin, a strong cross-linked protein that becomes part of the clot (the physical barrier to bleeding). Significant abnormalities in the platelets, in the coagulation factors that regulate fibrin formation, or defects in the blood vessels themselves can all lead to excessive bleeding.

THROMBOCYTOPENIA

DEFINITION

Thrombocytopenia is a decrease in the number of platelets.

CAUSE

The most common form of this condition is idiopathic (of unknown cause), although most cases are believed to be due to the presence of excess antibodies against platelets that break them down at an abnormal rate. This can occur in AIDS, viral infections, and in association with lymphomas and other disorders such as lupus erythematosus. A number of drugs, especially quinine and quinidine, can stimulate the production of antibodies against platelets and result in thrombocytopenia. These drugs should be stopped immediately when thrombocytopenia occurs.

Alternatively, thrombocytopenia can result from decreased production of platelets by the bone marrow, either due to aplastic anemia or to invasion of the bone marrow by leukemia, lymphoma, or marrow fibrosis.

DIAGNOSIS

Thrombocytopenia causes bleeding from small blood vessels; the bleeding usually appears as pinpoint bleeding spots (called petechiae) in the skin and mucous membranes. However, the appearance of a few petechiae on the lower legs of young women is common and does not necessarily mean the disease is present. The diagnosis of thrombocytopenia is made by a platelet count.

TREATMENT

Thrombocytopenia due to antibodies is usually treated with adrenal steroids or immune gamma globulin. Splenectomy (spleen removal) is necessary in some cases of increased destruction of platelets or when other treatments fail. When low platelet production causes thrombocytopenia, platelet transfusions are used.

COAGULATION FACTOR DEFICIENCIES

DEFINITION

Coagulation factors are numerous proteins that circulate in the blood and transform from inactive to active forms whenever blood clotting is required. Deficiencies in any of these factors can result in prolonged bleeding.

CAUSE

Coagulation factor disorders, such as the hemophilias, can be inherited, or acquired, such as conditions like disseminated intravascular coagulation (DIC). Diseases affecting the liver, such as alcoholic cirrhosis and acute and chronic hepatitis, are associated with numerous clotting abnormalities, since this organ produces many of the coagulation factors.

DIAGNOSIS

Hemophilias. The best known of the inherited disorders of coagulation are hemophilia A and B, associated with a decrease in the activity of Factor VIII or IX, respectively. The severity of the disorder depends on depletion of the clotting factors. Severe cases are manifested early in life, and children with hemophilia usually show easy bleeding in large joints, such as the knees, and marked defects in clot formation. In milder forms, hemophilia may not be evident until later in life.

Disseminated Intravascular Coagulation (DIC). This special group of coagulation disorders is associated with bleeding from many sites. These syndromes begin with increased and overactive clotting activity that eventually stimulates the activity of plasmin, a "fibrinolytic" enzyme that dissolves clots and results in excessive bleeding.

DIC usually occurs as a consequence of the presence of a number of specific conditions, including overwhelming infection, certain forms of cancer, leukemia, certain obstetrical conditions, and shock.

The diagnosis of factor deficiencies in DIC is made by a variety of coagulation tests including measurements of clotting time, prothrombin time, the levels of individual clotting factors, fibrinogen, and fibrin products.

Other Coagulation Disorders. Many other conditions can cause coagulation disorders, including liver disease.

TREATMENT

Treatment of hemophilias generally consists of transfusions of concentrates of blood products in which there is a large amount of coagulation factors VIII or IX. While many hemophiliacs can lead a relatively normal life, extra precautions must be taken in engaging in sports and during surgery or dental care. Unfortunately, 10 percent of people with hemophilia develop antibodies to Factor VIII and become difficult to treat.

The primary treatment of disseminated intravascular

coagulation is successful therapy for the underlying condition, whether it is shock, sepsis (blood infection), or cancer. Replacement of the missing coagulation factors is often necessary by infusion of fresh frozen plasma and platelets.

MALE/FEMALE DIFFERENCES

Hemophilias are X-linked diseases (sex-linked) and occur mainly in men (who possess only one X chromosome). Women may be carriers, but they do not develop the diseases themselves, even when they have below-normal levels of Factor VIII in their blood.

DISORDERS OF EXCESS CLOTTING

DEFINITION

Excess clotting frequently causes venous and arterial thrombosis (clots that obstruct veins and arteries).

CAUSE

Venous thrombosis can be caused by disease or injury to the veins in the legs, which leads to pooling (stasis) of blood and clotting. Varicose veins are a common condition associated with venous thrombosis. Clots in the legs can break loose and travel to the lungs, causing pulmonary clots that can result in respiratory distress, pain, and, in extreme cases, death.

Arterial thrombosis occurs primarily from atherosclerosis of blood vessels; clots may form on abnormal blood vessel surfaces. This occurs commonly in the coronary arteries, leading to heart attacks, but can occur in the cerebral circulation, leading to strokes or lack of oxygen to other organs.

DIAGNOSIS

Several tests, some using dye injection and catheterization, can diagnose the presence of arterial and venous thrombosis.

TREATMENT

Severe, venous thrombosis is treated with anticoagulant drugs such as heparin and the coumadins. A filter can be placed in large veins to prevent pulmonary clots from occurring.

Arterial thrombosis can be treated with catheters that expand the lumen (width) of the involved vessels. Arterial clots can be dissolved by drugs such as tissue plasminogen activator (TPA) or enzymes such as streptokinase.

SAFETY OF BLOOD TRANSFUSIONS

Current blood testing has drastically reduced the risk of acquiring HIV from blood transfusions. However, a small risk is always present. But in a life-threatening situation, the benefit of receiving a transfusion greatly outweighs the very slight risk of AIDS.

Of course, AIDS is not the only blood-borne disease that can be contracted from transfusions. Other contagious diseases include forms of hepatitis C (formerly called non-A, non-B), hepatitis B, cytomegalovirus, and other rarer disorders.

AUTOLOGOUS DONATIONS

Although the risk of getting AIDS and other diseases from a blood transfusion is extremely low, rather than risk infection some people have blood taken out and stored for their own possible future use. These "donations," called autologous, eliminate the risk (and worry) of contracting blood-borne diseases, or of suffering immunological reactions from donor blood. Autologous transfusions are most appropriate for otherwise healthy people who are facing elective surgery that may result in heavy blood loss.

24

Disorders of the Musculo-skeletal System

HAROLD M. DICK, M.D.

Although we often take for granted the ability to walk, run, use our arms, or climb stairs, we should cherish the intricate workings of our musculoskeletal system that make free movement possible. When a bone problem, muscle disorder, or disease interferes with this delicate machinery, our movement may be painfully limited, our daily activity severely compromised.

BONE DISORDERS

Musculoskeletal disorders—those affecting the skeleton and its system of joints—disrupt the normal quality of life more frequently than any other type of disease. More than 20 million Americans must cope with limited activity, significant disability, or restricted movement due to orthopedic problems.

The human body contains 206 bones constituting about one-tenth of the total body weight (see figure 24.1). The bones' framework supports and protects many vital organs. For instance, the skull shields delicate brain tissue. The spinal column encases the spinal cord, the main pathway of nerves carrying messages between the body and the brain. The rib cage guards the heart, lungs, liver, and kidneys. Bones in the pelvic area anchor the spine, encircle the bladder and, in women, protect the reproductive organs and the developing fetus.

Many people mistakenly view their skeleton as a static and unchanging entity. In fact, the skeleton continually resculpts itself. Every day of your life, bone tissue cells called osteoblasts and osteoclasts constantly create new bone and break down the old in a process called remodeling.

LOW BACK PAIN

Low back pain is a frequent orthopedic problem; few people avoid all low back discomfort. While most pain in this area is mild and clears up on its own, for many it is recurrent and incapacitating.

Pain in the lower back arises from either the spine, the muscles, or one of the many nerves in the area. An analysis of the back's anatomy and its normal, pain-free function demonstrates how pain often develops.

ANATOMY OF THE SPINE

Thirty-three bony blocks, or vertebrae, arranged in five sections link up in the spine. A complex system of ligaments, cartilage, and muscle maintains these vertebrae in proper position. Working smoothly together, this sys-

tem's components provide enormous strength and flexibility, helping to support your weight and maintain your upright position while resisting the jarring physical rigors of daily life. But a damaged link anywhere in the system weakens the spine, threatens its stability, and may make movement difficult and painful. (See figure 24.2.)

The five sections of the spine are:

Cervical Spine. These 7 vertebrae in the region of the neck support the head and protect the uppermost portion of the spinal cord.

Thoracic Vertebrae. The 12 thoracic vertebrae of the upper back each connect a pair of ribs to the spine.

Lumbar Vertebrae. The 5 lumbar vertebrae of the lower back bear most of the weight and stress of the upper body.

Sacral Vertebrae. At the base of the spine the 5 sacral vertebrae fuse into one bone, known as the sacrum.

Coccygeal Vertebrae. These 7 sections comprise the tailbone.

The interior of each vertebra is a thick cylindrical hollow-core bone from which three bony pieces thrust out—one to each side and one toward the rear. The bony prominences join with those of the adjacent vertebrae at a joint called a facet. When thrown out of align-

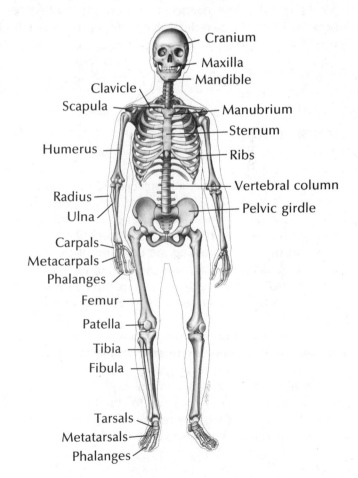

Figure 24.1: An overview of the skeletal system.

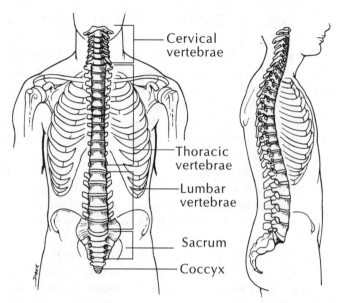

Figure 24.2: The spinal column and its divisions.

ment, the facet presses on nerve tissue and causes pain. When the vertebrae are properly aligned, their cylindrical centers form a canal through which the spinal cord passes; spinal nerves, connecting the cord to the body's network of nerves, pass through openings between each vertebra. Vertebral fractures or pressure from protruding disks at the point where nerves pass through spinal openings can impinge or "pinch" the nerves, causing damage and pain.

POOR POSTURE

DEFINITION

Poor posture results from a misplacement of the body's center of gravity while standing or sitting (see figure 24.3). Normally, a person's center of gravity is such that a plumb line dropped from ear level should fall straight down to the ankle, crossing the outer tip of the shoulder, the middle of the hip, and the back of the kneecap. Your normal center of gravity, though, can be shifted by rounding your shoulders, swaying your back, or sticking out your buttocks.

Poor posture alters the normal curvature of the spine and stresses its supporting muscles and ligaments. With poor posture your center of gravity is shifted forward or backward and the muscles of the back are forced to work abnormally to compensate for the body's weight shift. The resulting strain is the most common underlying malfunction that results in back pain.

CAUSE

During early fetal development, the spine assumes a C-shape; after birth, several important spinal curves form.

At the top, the cervical spine begins to curve forward. This is called normal cervical lordosis and is essential in keeping the head properly positioned. Meanwhile, the thoracic spine develops a backward curve known as a kyphosis, and the lower lumbar region assumes a forward, lordotic configuration. When these normal curves are altered too much, the resultant stress on the vertebrae can cause pain.

There are several variations of abnormality that warp the normal shape of the spine. An abnormal kyphosis causes rounded shoulders and a caved-in appearance around the chest. This postural strain on muscles and ligaments often leads to backache. When the normal forward curve of the lumbar spine is exaggerated, a condition termed hyperlordosis, a huge strain builds on the vertebrae and the small joints between them. Lordosis, or swayback, forces the abdomen and buttocks to jut out, weakens muscle tone, and ultimately produces back pain.

Poor posture habits usually begin in childhood. Years of slouching eventually produce a variety of problems, ranging from back pain to more complicated disorders such as osteoarthritis or disk problems.

DIAGNOSIS

Poor posture is diagnosed with a visual examination; rounding the back, sticking out the buttocks, and arch-

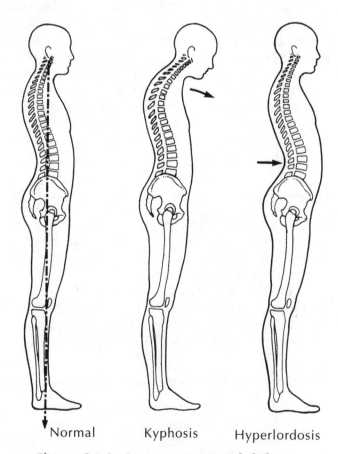

Normal   Kyphosis   Hyperlordosis

Figure 24.3: Common postural defects.

ing the back are the most common signs. An imaginary plumb line from the level of the ear should pass through points over the tip of the shoulder, the middle of the hip, and back of the knee.

TREATMENT AND PREVENTION

Good posture can prevent potential back problems. Whether you are standing, sitting, or sleeping, practice improves your posture. When poor posture has been a longtime habit, the muscles that keep you erect have to be retrained to perform their postural duties. It's essential to stand tall, holding the head straight and keeping the abdomen in. Avoid allowing the buttocks to protrude or the back to swoop inward in a swayback fashion. Focus on keeping good muscle tone in your abdominal muscles.

HOME REMEDIES AND ALTERNATIVE THERAPIES

Exercise therapy: Because poor posture often results from muscles weakened with disuse, strengthening the muscles of the abdomen and back with regular exercise can help bring the body back into alignment. Develop an appropriate exercise routine under the direction of your doctor or physical therapist.

Alexander technique: This method of correcting poor posture habits relies on the guidance of an experienced teacher who provides both verbal and hands-on instruction, gently guiding the body into proper alignment. (See

"Back Care Basics" for more tips on managing posture and back pain.)

BACK CARE BASICS

Protecting the back through proper alignment can be aided by following these simple rules.

• Lifting heavy objects: Don't bend over from the waist even if the object you lift is light. Instead, squat down with your back straight and knees bent (see figures 24.4 and 24.5). Then slowly rise, letting the quadriceps muscles in the thighs perform most of the lifting.

• Standing: Stand up straight with the shoulders back, the abdomen pulled in, the chin in, the small of the back flat, and the pelvis straight (see figure 24.6). If an imaginary line dropped from ear level does not pass directly across the outer tip of the shoulder, the middle of the hip, the back of the kneecap, and the front of the ankle bone, then your posture is out of alignment and needs correction. When standing for long periods of time, move around frequently and shift your weight from one foot to another. Wear flat shoes whenever possible. High heels cause the pelvis to tilt forward and strain the muscles of the back.

• Sitting: Sitting is quite stressful on the back even when performed properly. A straight-back chair with good low-back support is the best choice. Elevating one or both feet flattens the lumbar spine and prevents the back from assuming a swayback position. During long-

24.4   24.5

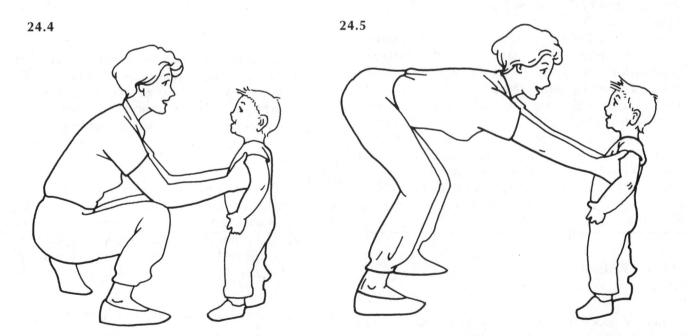

Figure 24.4 and 24.5: The right and wrong way to lift heavy objects. Squat with knees bent and use the strength of your legs to lift, as illustrated in 24.4. Do not bend from the waist and force your arms and back to do the lifting, as shown in 24.5.

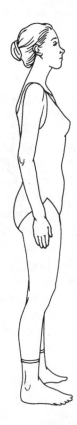

Figure 24.6: When standing, hold the shoulders back, with the abdomen pulled in, the small of the back flat, and hips straight.

distance travel, take regular stretch breaks. On car trips, placing a small pillow behind the lower back reduces muscle fatigue.

• Sleeping: Lying down is the least stressful posture, when done properly. A firm mattress or bed board under the mattress can provide the proper support the back needs. The fetal position (lying on the side with the knees bent at right angles to the body and the neck straight) is the best position to sleep in. Avoid sleeping on your stomach: This position causes the lower back to sway. Sleeping on your back can be restful when a small pillow is placed behind the neck and another pillow just under the knees. Choose your pillows carefully. A pillow that is too high behind your head can strain the neck as well as the arms and shoulders.

BACK TRAUMA

DEFINITION

Traumatic back injuries include any back damage resulting from direct blows to the back, banging into objects, or falling. They may be simple bruises or debilitating bone breaks.

Most commonly, traumatic injuries to the back affect the lower, lumbar region. Occasionally a fall may fracture a vertebra. Compression fractures, in which the vertebrae collapse into a wedge shape, usually occur in bones weakened by osteoporosis in people over 60. More severe vertebral fractures or burst fractures can occur when large compressive forces are placed upon the spine (a fall from a height, for example). If bony fragments impinge upon or damage the spinal cord, neurologic problems including paralysis may result.

The vertebrae are not the only part of the back susceptible to traumatic injury; the soft tissues supporting the spine are also at risk. Commonly, small tears within a muscle or strains produce significant discomfort. While an acute lumbar strain occurs suddenly, another form of trauma, chronic lumbar strain, is the result of repeated smaller strains.

Strain injuries are distinct from sprains:

Strain. A small tear within the muscles
Sprain. An injury to a ligament that holds bone to bone

CAUSE

Traumatic back injuries can occur in a variety of ways. A direct blow to the back, the most obvious kind of traumatic back injury, is probably one of the least common. More frequently, falls, which include tumbling down a flight of stairs or tripping over the edge of a rug, and car accidents traumatize the back. Even simply bending over and picking something up (especially a weighty object) may strain the back and cause spasm and pain.

DIAGNOSIS

If a fracture is suspected, an x-ray should be taken. If the x-ray reveals a fracture, more sophisticated tests, like computed axial tomography (CAT or CT scan, see chapter 12, Diagnostic Tests and Procedures), may then be warranted to more closely evaluate the fracture.

TREATMENT

Treatment of spinal fractures varies depending on the type, location, and severity of the break. Some fractures require immobilization of the spine while others necessitate surgery. Despite their apparent severity, some vertebral fractures heal by themselves and require no treatment at all.

HOME REMEDIES AND ALTERNATIVE THERAPIES

Back strains usually heal themselves without much medical help. When you suffer an acute incapacitating back strain, the following are usually recommended and will help speed along your recovery:

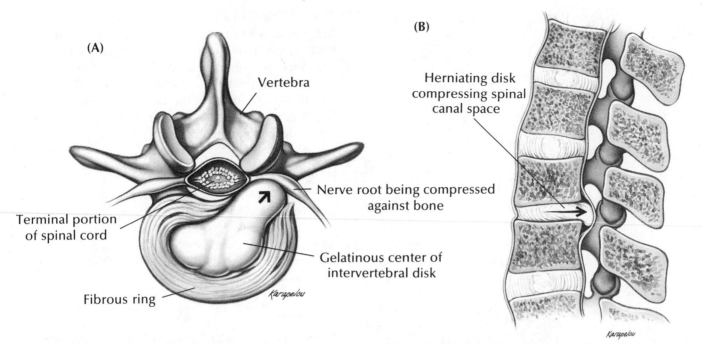

(A)

Vertebra

Terminal portion
of spinal cord

Fibrous ring

Nerve root being compressed
against bone

Gelatinous center of
intervertebral disk

Karapelou

(B)

Herniating disk
compressing spinal
canal space

Karapelou

Figure 24.7A and B: Herniated disk as viewed from a cross section of a lumbar vertebra as seen from above (A), and a side view showing the herniated disk pressing into the spinal canal space (B).

- Absolute bedrest
- Warm tub baths and applications of heating pads
- Anti-inflammatory agents such as ibuprofen
- Massages (consult your doctor; appropriate only in selected cases)
- A corset (appropriate only in selected cases)
- An exercise program to strengthen weakened muscles as your back improves

Those suffering from chronic back strains may also benefit by:

- Undertaking a weight-loss program.
- Correcting poor posture.
- Sleeping on a firm mattress.
- Beginning a daily regimen of exercises to strengthen the lower back.
- Sitting: Sit with your head and hips in alignment. If necessary, use a chair support or a pillow to support the small of your back. (See figure 24.8.)
- Massage therapy: A variety of different massage techniques may relieve muscular discomfort. By improving circulation to the muscles, massage helps eliminate toxic substances accumulated in the injured area while increasing the delivery of oxygen and energy, critical components in the healing process.
- Heat therapy: Heat applied to strained muscles helps relieve discomfort. The increased temperature of the affected area boosts blood flow and accelerates the healing process.

- Rehabilitative therapy: After a serious traumatic injury such as a fracture, a regimen of strengthening and stretching is critical. These activities should be supervised by a trained rehabilitation therapist to ensure maximum benefit and avoid exacerbating the injury.

HERNIATED DISK

DEFINITION

The spinal disks are flat circles of cartilage and fibrous tissue located between the pairs of vertebrae, soaking up the everyday shocks and bounces that jar the spine. Each disk consists of two parts:

- **Annulus Fibrosis.** The disk's tough, fibrous outer portion
- **Nucleus Pulposus.** The disk's gelatinous inner portion

Disks herniate when their gelatinous interior leaks through the fibrous walls (see figure 24.7). Though this condition is popularly known as a slipped disk, in fact, no slippage takes place. Instead, the affected disk simply balloons out from between the bony parts of the vertebrae.

If the bulging, or herniated, area is large enough, it may press on a nerve causing severe, sometimes incapacitating, pain. The protruding disk may press on the sciatic nerve, which begins in the lower back and branches

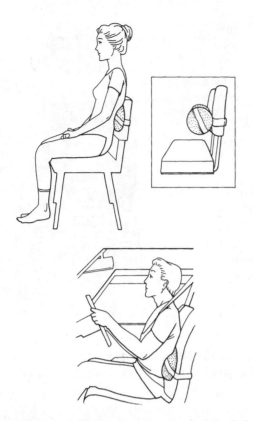

Figure 24.8: A pillow or support behind the small of the back can help prevent back strain when sitting or driving.

down the length of each leg to the foot. This causes sciatic pain or sciatica, lower back pain radiating down the sciatic nerve, over the buttock, down the back of one or both legs, and sometimes into the feet. While herniation most frequently affects the lower back (usually the fourth and fifth disks in the lumbar region), it can also occur in the uppermost vertebrae (cervical) and inflict severe neck pain extending down the arms.

CAUSE

Although it is still not clearly understood why disks herniate, changes in the annulus fibrosis due to aging may weaken the capsule and ultimately allow the disk to bulge. Trauma may cause similar changes and even minor stress, such as lifting if frequently repeated, may eventually result in herniation.

DIAGNOSIS

Despite popular belief, an x-ray of the back does not detect herniated disks. While the vertebrae are clearly delineated on an x-ray, the disks themselves remain indistinguishable from surrounding tissues. Both CT scans and MRIs are commonly used in diagnosing disk problems. (For more on these tests, see chapter 12.) Unlike x-rays, these tests clearly reveal the condition of disks, revealing any abnormalities.

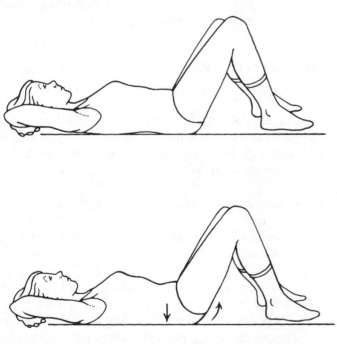

Figure 24.9: Lying down on the back with knees bent and hands behind the head can often relieve back pain. Pushing the small of the back into the floor and holding that position helps release lower back stress.

Figure 24.10: The cat stretch exercise can also alleviate back pain.

TREATMENT

Pain from a herniated disk can be relieved with inactivity, bedrest, muscle relaxants, and anti-inflammatory drugs. Traction and spinal manipulation may be recommended in some cases. Surgery should generally be reserved for selected patients in whom more conservative therapy fails.

PREVENTION

Herniated disks can often be prevented by keeping body weight down with exercise and proper diet. Exercise also tones the muscles.

HOME REMEDIES AND ALTERNATIVE THERAPIES

Bedrest at home is one of the most important measures for initially recovering from a herniated disk.

Other measures include:

Exercise Therapy. Recurrent bouts of back pain from a herniated disk can often be prevented with regular back exercises. Special exercises can keep the back limber and strong, reducing risk of future problems (see figures 24.9 and 24.10).

Hydrotherapy. Exercises performed in the water are particularly helpful for many back problems, building strength without the constant jolting and jarring experienced with so many other forms of exercise like running and aerobics.

Chiropractic Care. Chiropractic manipulation of the vertebrae can relieve pressure on the involved disks, alleviating pain.

Osteopathic Care. Many people find osteopathic treatment very effective in relieving the symptoms of a herniated disk. Osteopaths first apply gentle pressure to the back to relax tensed muscles, then the back is stretched to lessen pressure.

UNSTABLE VERTEBRAE

DEFINITION

Normally, vertebrae, tethered to one another through a complex network of ligaments, remain in relatively fixed positions with respect to one another. An unstable vertebra, though, shifts backward and forward on the vertebra beneath it and can cause severe back pain. Most commonly, vertebral instability occurs in the lower, lumbar spine, although it can also affect the cervical or thoracic regions.

CAUSE

Abnormalities in the ligaments supporting the spine cause this type of instability. Usually, abnormalities in the ligaments are the direct result of a traumatic injury to the back.

TUMORS

Tumors growing in and around the spine also cause back pain. While these tumors tend to be benign and are rarely life-threatening, they cause pain when they impinge upon a nerve root. Enlargement of a tumor in the thoracic or cervical spine often presses on the spinal cord, potentially causing muscle weakness and, in rare cases, paralysis. The development of back pain not relieved by rest indicates a possible tumor, since most other sources of back pain disappear when the pressure is taken off the vertebrae.

DIAGNOSIS

X-rays are helpful in detecting spinal instability. Generally, several x-rays are taken of the body bent in a variety of postures. Only by picturing the body in this way can abnormal movements between the vertebrae be detected.

TREATMENT

Spinal exercises and the use of a special corset markedly improve most cases of unstable vertebrae. While surgery rarely offers a cure, surgical fusion to weld the unstable vertebra to the one above and the one below it can sometimes provide relief for persistent pain.

HOME REMEDIES AND ALTERNATIVE THERAPIES

Exercise. The alignment of unstable vertebrae can be improved by strengthening the surrounding and supporting muscles. Back exercises should always be done with extreme caution and expert guidance to avoid further injury.

Chiropractic medicine. Chiropractic care centers on spinal manipulation, which moves the vertebrae into their normal positions, realigning unstable vertebrae and relieving the discomfort caused by them.

FRACTURES

DEFINITION

A fracture is a break in a bone (see figure 24.11). The physical force producing the fracture can also injure the surrounding muscles, ligaments, and other soft tissue.

Normally bones are strong and hard, but they are also somewhat elastic, particularly in children. Bones in young children bend much like the soft branch of a beech tree, developing cracks without actually breaking

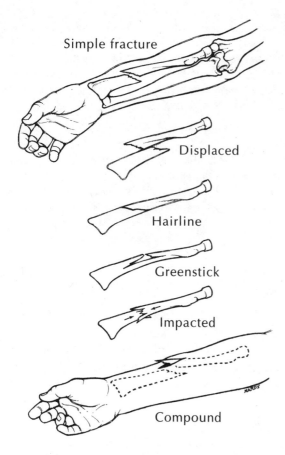

Simple fracture

Displaced

Hairline

Greenstick

Impacted

Compound

Figure 24.11: Types of fractures.

(green-stick fracture). The bones in older adults tend to be more brittle so that when bent or twisted they break either crosswise or at an angle.

TYPES OF FRACTURES

- **Simple Fracture.** The bone is broken with minimal damage to the surrounding skin and tissue.
- **Open (Compound) Fracture.** The broken bone protrudes through the skin.
- **Comminuted Fracture.** The bone is crushed into several pieces at the fracture site.
- **Compression Fractures.** The bone is compacted by a crushing force. Falls can collapse vertebrae into wedge-shaped compression fractures.
- **Stress Fracture.** Hairline crack in a bone caused by repeated stress. X-rays may not detect stress fractures until several weeks after they occur. Rest is the best treatment for this type of fracture.

DIAGNOSING A FRACTURE

Broken bones may occur just about anywhere and any-time—on the ski slopes, during an automobile accident, or in the home. The usual symptoms include:

- Localized pain made worse by movement
- Inability to use the affected area
- Tenderness and swelling
- Deformity of the area around the fracture
- Muscle spasm with slight movement
- Feeling the bone ends grate together

An x-ray of the involved bone(s) is usually needed to confirm the diagnosis. Outward appearances are deceptive; some apparent fractures are not breaks.

Infrequently, even x-rays are not conclusive. Mistakes most commonly occur in the diagnosis of stress fractures. If a fracture is suspected but not seen on x-ray, repeat films, 10 to 14 days later, or special studies such as a bone scan or an MRI may be needed to identify the fracture. (For more on these tests, see chapter 12.)

TREATMENT OF FRACTURES

After a fracture has been diagnosed, treatment begins by realigning, or "reducing," the affected bones.

Closed Reduction. Without cutting open the fracture site, an orthopedist uses the sense of touch to feel the fracture beneath the skin and, with the help of three-dimensional x-rays, realigns the bone. Once the bone is back in position, a plaster cast immobilizes the area.

Open Reduction. A doctor surgically exposes the fracture site, manipulates and realigns the exposed bones, and inserts an internal metallic device such as a plate or pin to maintain rigidity. Hip fractures may require replacement with a prosthesis. During surgery, the operating doctor carefully protects undamaged tissue in the area and preserves the blood supply to the fractured bone fragments.

Some fractures in which bones are not severely displaced are treated by external splinting without bone manipulation. Other fractures may require only a protective device such as an arm sling. Open fractures require specialized emergency treatment to minimize the risk of infection.

Once bones are realigned, they must be immobilized until healed. Healing takes place when the tissues produce a substance called callus, which binds the bony fragments together. Plaster of paris casts may be used to immobilize smaller fractures in extremities (such as a broken arm), whereas traction may be necessary to immobilize larger areas, such as a fractured thigh bone.

The time required to heal a fracture varies with age, the location, type of fracture, and the blood supply to the area. Fractures heal more rapidly in children—a fracture that take 3 weeks to heal in a 4-year-old would take up to 3 months to fully mend in her mother. A long and slanting fracture knits faster than one that runs directly across the bone, a result of its larger surface area available for healing.

Immobilization of a joint carries risks: The surrounding muscles may atrophy causing stiffness. A physical therapist can recommend exercises to keep the muscles and joints in good condition and speed recovery.

HOME REMEDIES AND ALTERNATIVE THERAPIES

Rehabilitation therapy: While immobilization is the only method for encouraging fractures to mend, paradoxically, movement is also an essential component of the final healing process. After casts and pins are removed, the muscles of the affected area are stiff and atrophied. Graduated exercises improve both strength and flexibility, allowing you to regain full use of the area. Exercises, however, should be approached cautiously or you will suffer injuries to unconditioned muscles and ligaments.

OSTEOPOROSIS

DEFINITION

Osteoporosis means weakened or porous bones. Bones incorporate calcium to maintain strength and hardness. When you eat foods containing this mineral it is absorbed into the bloodstream to be distributed throughout the body; calcium in excess of metabolic needs is deposited in the bones (some is also excreted in urine). When calcium intakes are deficient, calcium leaches from the bone to supply physiological processes. If calcium intake remains insufficient over a long period of time, bones lose more and more calcium and eventually become porous and weak, or osteoporotic. Bones weakened by osteoporosis are thin and brittle and highly susceptible to fracture.

Osteoporosis frequently affects the spinal column. As bone porosity increases, the vertebrae can collapse (in a compression fracture) and cause sudden and severe back pain. Gradual collapse contributes to the loss of height that comes with age. Wrist and hip fractures are also common to people suffering osteoporosis.

CAUSE

An inadequate intake of calcium is only one factor contributing to the development of osteoporosis. Others include:

- **Vitamin D Deficiency.** Lack of vitamin D decreases the bones' absorption of calcium.
- **Estrogen Deficiency.** Without estrogen, bone demineralization accelerates.
- **Inactivity.** Weight-bearing exercise is necessary to stimulate bone strengthening. Lack of exercise may contribute to a loss of bone calcium.
- **Smoking.** Smokers experience an increased risk of osteoporosis.

- **Gender.** Women are at greater risk of losing bone strength than men.
- **Heredity.** This disease runs in families—if your mother or grandmother had osteoporosis, your risk is increased. Women of northern European or Asian descent have an increased risk of osteoporosis.
- **Age.** As you reach middle age, bone density decreases. In women, osteoporosis risk increases after menopause, when hormonal changes, particularly the decrease in estrogen, boost the loss of calcium from the skeletal system.

DIAGNOSIS

Osteoporosis usually is diagnosed only after a fracture occurs. X-rays in the absence of a fracture are not very accurate in detecting bone losses and may fail to identify losses of up to 40 percent. Although several more accurate measures of bone density have been developed (e.g., dual photon absorptiometry), they are not widely available for screening.

TREATMENT

The treatment of osteoporosis is designed to prevent further bone loss. In postmenopausal women, estrogen replacement is probably the best therapy currently available. While estrogen can greatly reduce the rate of bone loss, its effects may be transient, and bone loss may resume after several years.

Increased calcium intake and exercise are believed to slow osteoporosis. Exercise, particularly weight-bearing activities such as running, walking, or aerobics, places a healthy stress on bones, which stimulates bone formation and reduces susceptibility to fracture. While consistent exercise throughout life is optimal for healthy bones, beginning an exercise program in middle age or even later may still convey benefits. Some experts believe that regular exercise may slow the progression of osteoporosis even after bones begin to thin.

In Western society, many people, particularly women, consume inadequate amounts of calcium for optimal bone formation. Without sufficient calcium, bones fail to mineralize properly, and their strength and integrity suffer. Research indicates that calcium supplementation, especially in people whose calcium intake is extremely low, may be effective in reducing bone fragility and preventing fractures. The most important time of life for eating adequate amounts of calcium is during adolescence. Calcium stores built up in the teens may delay the harmful effects of osteoporosis decades later in middle age.

PREVENTION

Because bones increase in size and strength only until about age 30, the best time to prevent osteoporosis is early in life, during your teens and 20s. The zenith of your bone weight and strength is reached in your 30s; ever afterward, your bone mass decreases. A high peak bone mass early in life reduces the risk of problematic bone loss in later years. Eating a calcium-rich diet may help maximize bone stores: The Recommended Dietary Allowance of calcium currently stands at 1,200 mg per day for both men and women until the age of 24 and falls to 800 mg per day thereafter. (For more on eating sufficient calcium, see chapter 5, The Basics of Good Nutrition.)

Exercise has been found to be important throughout life for building strong, healthy bones. A lifelong, regular routine of weight-bearing exercises—such as running, walking, aerobics, and weight lifting—stimulates bones to grow stronger.

Women concerned about developing osteoporosis should consider starting hormone replacement therapy around the time of menopause. Replenishing sagging estrogen levels may prevent or at least delay some of the most severe bone losses that occur at that time.

MALE/FEMALE DIFFERENCES

Osteoporosis affects women far more commonly than men. Men generally reach a higher peak bone mass than women, exercise more frequently, and eat more calcium-rich foods. Over their lifetimes, women generally lose between 30 and 50 percent of their bone mass whereas men lose only about two-thirds of this amount. Women experience their most rapid losses during the first few years following menopause, a time when estrogen levels fall off dramatically.

HOME REMEDIES AND ALTERNATIVE THERAPIES

Dietary Changes. Increase foods high in calcium and make certain you consume adequate vitamin D.

Exercise. Weight-bearing activities such as walking and aerobics stimulate bone growth.

OSTEOMALACIA

DEFINITION

Osteomalacia means soft bone. While osteoporosis weakens bones by causing an overall loss in bone mass, in osteomalacia bone mass is retained, but a defect in the bone itself causes a loss in strength; bones fail to mineralize or calcify properly, resulting in softer bone more susceptible to fracture.

CAUSE

Osteomalacia is usually a result of a vitamin D deficiency. Vitamin D participates in the body's absorption of cal-

cium, and a lack of this vitamin prevents the bones from getting the calcium that they need. Normally, milk, egg yolks, butter, fish oil, and liver are good sources of vitamin D. However, food is not the only source of vitamin D—it is also produced by the skin when exposed to sunlight. But some experts believe that as you age your skin loses some of its ability to produce this nutrient.

DIAGNOSIS

General symptoms such as tender bones and muscular weakness may be signs of osteomalacia. Fractures occurring after trivial falls or blows may also be signs of the disease and signal the need for skeletal evaluation.

X-rays are helpful in the diagnosis of osteomalacia; there are specific radiologic findings that can be used to diagnose the condition. Blood tests, including measurement of vitamin D levels, can sometimes aid in the diagnosis.

TREATMENT

The treatment of osteomalacia involves correcting the underlying vitamin deficiency with large doses of vitamin D supplements. In some cases, the condition may be caused by a problem in dietary fat absorption that interferes with the uptake of vitamin D from the diet.

PREVENTION

Adequate vitamin D usually prevents osteomalacia. Adequate sunshine also prevents this condition. But if you spend most of your time indoors or always shield yourself from the sun when outdoors, try to include more vitamin D–rich foods in your diet. Fish oils, egg yolks, butter, and milk (commonly fortified with vitamin D) all serve as good sources. (Keep in mind that these should be added in moderation due to their high fat content.)

HOME REMEDIES AND ALTERNATIVE THERAPIES

Dietary and Lifestyle Changes. Consume foods rich in vitamin D such as fortified milk. Spend more time outdoors—the skin makes vitamin D from sunlight. (However, do not overexpose yourself to the sun.) A multivitamin supplement with the U.S. Recommended Dietary Allowance of vitamin D should also suffice. Do not take megadoses of this vitamin, however; it may be toxic in high doses.

PAGET'S DISEASE

DEFINITION

Paget's disease is an increased and irregular formation of bone; bone cells responsible for dissolving old bone and replacing it with new bone begin to work at an accelerated rate. Eventually the deformed new bone formation is larger, weaker, and has more blood vessels than normal bone. Whereas normal bone has its own structured architecture, bone affected by Paget's disease develops a markedly irregular pattern.

The primary bones affected by Paget's disease are the shin bone (tibia), thigh bone (femur), hip bone (pelvis), the vertebrae, and the skull. The disease may be limited to one bone or it may spread to involve skeletal areas.

Mild forms of this disease have no symptoms. In severe cases, pain may be intense. As the disease progresses, the legs may bow, the skull may grow larger, and the spine may bend slightly, making the person appear to be leaning to one side. As bones enlarge, they may compress against adjacent nerves. Severe skull enlargement can impinge on the auditory nerve and cause a loss of hearing.

CAUSE

The cause of Paget's disease remains unknown.

TREATMENT

Currently, treatment includes administration of medications to reduce the abnormal bone resorption and production and to relieve the pain. Surgery is sometimes required to correct severe deformities caused by Paget's.

SCOLIOSIS

DEFINITION

Scoliosis is a lateral and rotational curvature of the spine occurring in the thoracic and/or lumbar regions (see figure 24.12A and 24.12B). Scoliosis may begin during infancy, the juvenile years (ages 3 to 10), or in adolescence.

Infantile scoliosis more commonly affects males and, for unknown reasons, does not commonly occur in the United States. Juvenile scoliosis equally affects both boys and girls: Whereas a curve may begin to form as early as age 3, some cases of juvenile scoliosis do not become noticeable until the child reaches adolescence, the curve becoming increasingly apparent as the skeleton matures.

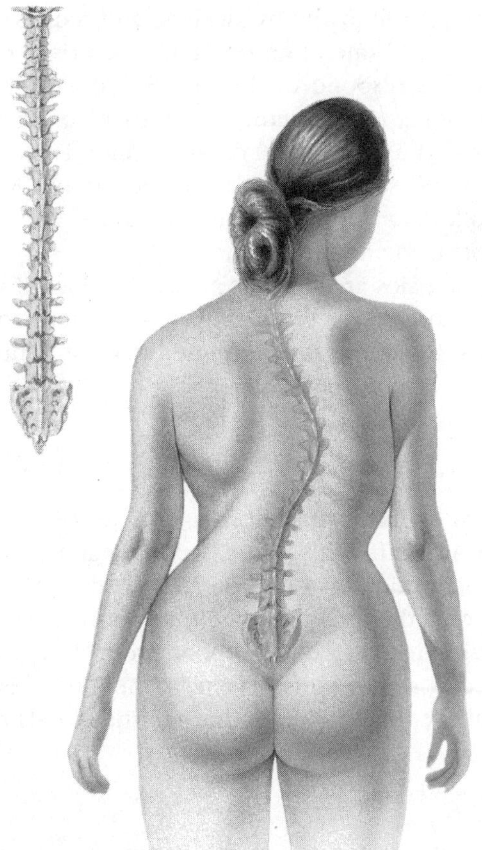

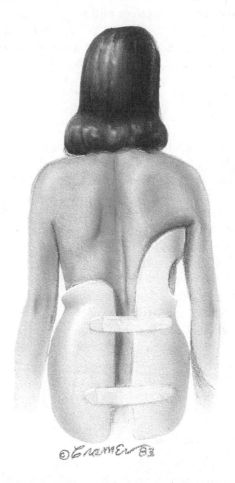

Figure 24.12A: A curvature typical of severe scoliosis.

Figure 24.12B: The type of brace commonly used to treat scoliosis. These are molded to fit the body and are concealed by clothing.

Adolescent scoliosis is the most common form and is severe far more frequently in teenage girls than in their male counterparts.

As scoliosis progresses, the vertebrae rotate, causing the ribs to crowd together on one side while ribs on the other side widely separate. The curvature may force the spaces between the spinal disks to narrow and the vertebrae to thicken along the outer edge of the curve. Kyphosis, characterized by rounded shoulders and sunken chest, and lordosis (swayback) often develop simultaneously with scoliosis.

CAUSE

A small number of cases result from habitually poor posture or from a leg-length discrepancy (one leg shorter than the other). However, the majority of cases have an unknown cause and are considered to be genetic in origin.

DIAGNOSIS

Although the benefits of school screening clinics are controversial, many children with scoliosis have been diagnosed this way. Parents should watch for signs of scoliosis. Any obvious curves in the spine or asymmetry in a child's pelvis (hip bones) or shoulders should be evaluated by a physician.

TREATMENT

A spinal brace can halt the progression of the curvature in the majority of scoliosis cases. In more severe cases, surgical correction may be necessary. In this procedure, specially designed hooks are implanted above and below the curve attached to an instrument known as the Harrington rod. The spine is adjusted into a straight line while the area around the rod is packed with small pieces of bone taken from the pelvis. As healing progresses, the rod and bone fragments fuse into a single unit straightening the spine permanently.

Scoliosis is a progressive disease and is not outgrown in adulthood. Scoliosis sufferers should be examined at least once a year to monitor the condition. Deterioration in the condition necessitates immediate treatment; a progressing case of scoliosis can lead to cardiac and lung problems in later years.

MALE/FEMALE DIFFERENCES

The various forms of scoliosis affect males and females differently. Boys are afflicted with infantile scoliosis more frequently than girls, but both sexes appear to be equally at risk for juvenile scoliosis. Although girls develop adolescent scoliosis only slightly more frequently than their male counterparts, the curvature is far more likely to be severe enough to require treatment in girls.

PREVENTION

Scoliosis cannot be prevented before the condition begins. Routine checkups with a pediatrician should be used to make sure scoliosis is not affecting your child.

OSTEOMYELITIS

DEFINITION AND CAUSE

Osteomyelitis is a bone infection caused by the entry of bacteria into bone. The infection ensues when bacteria from the environment contact bone through the blood or areas of exposed bone such as open fractures. In children, organisms (frequently staphylococcus bacteria) may enter the body via an infection of the mucous membranes in the throat, or an infected sore on the body.

DIAGNOSIS

Symptoms include constant and severe, often excruciating, bone pain followed by swelling and redness. X-rays of the affected bone often reveal characteristic changes as the bones respond to the invading organism. However, x-rays may fail to detect the disease during its earliest stages—the first 7 to 10 days—when it is most easily treated. Bone scans also offer diagnostic aid: Radioisotopes collect in portions of inflamed bone and create a "hot spot" evident in the scan.

Bone biopsies are an important aid in identifying the infectious organism. From biopsy specimens, bacteria are grown in culture to determine the most appropriate antibiotics to treat the infection.

TREATMENT

Hard tissue, like bone, resists antibiotics, rendering osteomyelitis difficult to cure. Upon diagnosis, immediate hospitalization for a prolonged course of intravenous antibiotics is the treatment of choice; only early, aggressive treatment can save the bone from destruction. If untreated, osteomyelitis damages the bone, and the infection eventually spreads through the bloodstream.

BONE TUMORS

Malignant bone tumors rarely originate in the bone; these growths usually arise from cancer cells that have migrated (metastasized) from malignancies in other organs such as the lungs or breasts. Treatment of metastatic tumors must reduce and eliminate tumor growth in both the bone and elsewhere in the body with a combination of surgery, radiation, and chemotherapy. (For a complete discussion of malignant bone tumors and their treatment see chapter 17.)

Benign tumors originate in the bone itself or the surrounding soft tissues. Two common benign tumors affecting the soft tissues are:

- **Lipomas.** Small fatty tumors frequently found on the back. Although they may feel tender, they need not be removed unless they continue to grow.
- **Ganglion Cysts.** Benign growths characteristically present in and around the wrist area. Although they frequently change in size and may become quite large (marble size), they are generally not painful and most resolve spontaneously. Uncomfortable cysts may be surgically excised.

Bony tumors are less frequent than soft tissue growth. Painful but not dangerous, a bony tumor known as an osteoid osteoma often appears in the vertebrae or long bones. Although aspirin is generally effective at relieving the pain, surgical removal of this type of tumor may be necessary to eliminate discomfort.

SPONDYLOSIS

DEFINITION

Spondylosis is a degenerative narrowing of the disk that serves as a cushion between the vertebral bodies. This condition is linked to aging: Many people over 40 suffer from spondylosis. Although most people with spondylosis experience no discomfort, those with severe disease may lose spinal column flexibility and ultimately develop lower back pain and, occasionally, neck pain.

CAUSE

The degenerative changes of spondylosis are a normal consequence of the wear and tear of everyday living. As the body ages, the disks in the back gradually dry out and lose much of their ability to cushion the bony vertebrae from one another. As this protection breaks down, the spine itself ultimately undergoes degenerative changes.

DIAGNOSIS

As this disease progresses, x-rays reveal degenerative changes in the vertebrae.

TREATMENT

Nonsteroidal anti-inflammatory medications are commonly used to alleviate discomfort. Physical therapy is also used to strengthen the muscles of the back.

HOME REMEDIES AND ALTERNATIVE THERAPIES

Chiropractic Care. Some experts claim that the degenerative process of this condition can be slowed if the spine is kept in proper alignment with regular chiropractic manipulations. Manipulations may also help spondylosis sufferers by relieving pain.

Osteopathic Care. Osteopaths employ treatment similar to chiropractors. Spinal manipulations and various forms of massage correct underlying spinal abnormalities that might otherwise accelerate or exacerbate the disease process.

Exercise Therapy. Regular movement in the form of stretching and strengthening exercise is the best way to combat the degenerative process. While a simple stretching routine will help, many people prefer incorporating more interesting and rewarding activities such as yoga or t'ai chi into their exercise programs.

ANKYLOSING SPONDYLITIS

DEFINITION

Ankylosing spondylitis, also known as Marie-Strümpell disease, is a form of rheumatoid arthritis attacking the tendons, ligaments, and fibrous joint capsules around the spine. This condition causes these normally soft tissues in the sacroiliac and intervertebral joints to ossify, or turn to bone. As ossification progresses, the vertebral bodies fuse together, turning the spine into a rigid piece of bone. The stiffened spine may make it impossible to stand up straight or turn the head completely.

Low back pain not relieved by rest is an early sign of ankylosing spondylitis. Morning stiffness also may be present. Joints between the rib cage and vertebrae become inflamed, causing pain and loss of motion, and, when the vertebrae ultimately fuse, breathing becomes difficult.

CAUSE

Ankylosing spondylitis is believed to be a form of chronic inflammatory arthritis. While its precise cause remains unknown, heredity probably plays an important part in the development of this condition.

DIAGNOSIS

Although early in the disease x-rays may appear normal, as the disease progresses they reveal dramatic changes: A severely affected spine has an appearance similar to a bamboo pole. Consequently the condition has been called "bamboo spine."

TREATMENT

While treatment cannot halt the course of ankylosing spondylitis, specially prescribed exercise regimens can minimize spinal deformity whereas drugs can provide some symptomatic relief. Nonsteroidal anti-inflammatory drugs, especially indomethacin (Indocin), are most commonly used. Surgery can be helpful in selected cases.

MALE/FEMALE DIFFERENCES

Men tend to be affected by ankylosing spondylitis far more commonly than women.

HOME REMEDIES AND ALTERNATIVE THERAPIES

Exercise therapy: Stretching exercises should be performed routinely to minimize losses in flexibility. Exercises such as yoga or t'ai chi, which promote full range of movement, are helpful. Sleeping fully stretched out on a firm mattress may prevent some of the stooped posture.

BUNIONS

DEFINITION

A bunion is an inflammation of a small, fluid-filled sac at the base of the big toe. This type of sac, known as a bursa, is found around most joints, generally in areas where tendons or muscles pass directly over bone. The bursae help minimize friction between constantly moving body parts and thereby facilitate motion.

CAUSE

The tendency to develop bunions is inherited. Bunions occur when the big toe is pushed inward into a position where it overlaps the second toe. The base of the toe is forced outward, beyond the normal alignment of the foot, resulting in the prominence characteristic of a bunion. Long periods of pressure from a tight-fitting shoe are a common cause of the inflammation and pain.

DIAGNOSIS

While bunions can usually be correctly identified by visual examination, x-rays may be used to assess their severity.

TREATMENT

You can alleviate bunion pain by relieving pressure on the affected area of the foot. If a bunion persists, surgical removal may be necessary (see figure 24.13).

MALE/FEMALE DIFFERENCES

Because fashion dictates that women squeeze their feet into ill-fitting, stylish shoes, bunions tend to be far more common among women than among men.

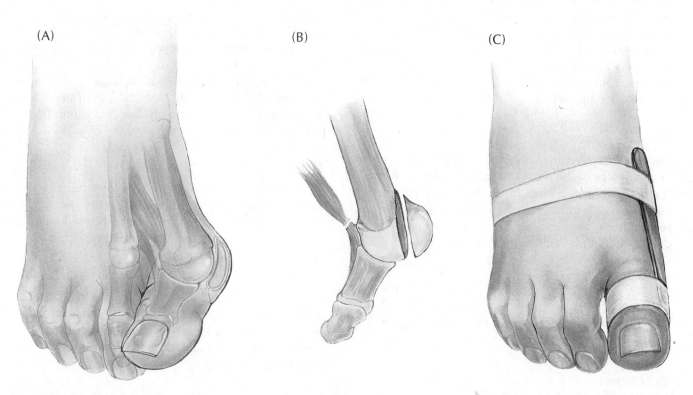

(A)   (B)   (C)

Figure 24.13A, B, and C: In a bunion, the bursa of the big toe becomes inflamed, forcing the toe out of proper alignment (A). Corrective measures include surgery (B) to remove a portion of the toe joint or splinting (C) to force the toe into proper position.

PREVENTION

Proper footwear that incorporates a wide toebox and low heel prevents bunions.

HOME REMEDIES AND ALTERNATIVE THERAPIES

Wearing larger shoes or cutting out a portion of the shoe around the point of pressure should eliminate some of the forces causing the bunion. Do not wear high-heeled or pointed-toe shoes.

HAMMERTOES

DEFINITION

A hammertoe is an uncomfortable deformity usually affecting the second toe in which the toe assumes a painfully bent position.

CAUSE

Shoes that are too short for your foot cause a hammertoe by forcing the toe into a bent position and causing a painful callus to develop at the tip.

TREATMENT

Special orthotic appliances worn in the shoe redistribute pressure and often help relieve painful symptoms. In severe cases, surgery to correct the deformity may be recommended (see figure 24.14).

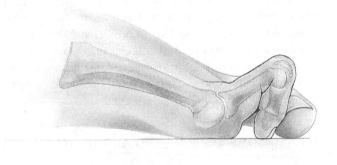

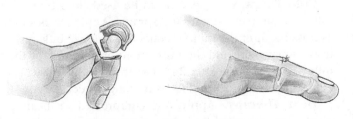

Figure 24.14: Hammertoes.

CLAWTOES

DEFINITION

Similar to hammertoe, clawtoe produces clawlike deformities in all or some of the smaller toes.

CAUSE

Unlike hammertoe, which is usually caused by incorrectly fitted shoes, clawtoe is often associated with more serious underlying medical conditions such as neuromuscular disease or arthritis.

TREATMENT

Surgical correction may be required if symptoms are severe and are not relieved with more conservative treatment (e.g., open-toed shoes). In addition, the underlying cause of the symptoms must be identified and treated.

HOME REMEDIES AND ALTERNATIVE THERAPIES

In some cases, clawtoe may be relieved by wearing open-toed shoes. However, if a serious underlying condition is causing the problem, a change in footwear will not stop the discomfort.

BONE TRANSPLANT

Most bone transplants replace bone riddled with cancer or fractured bones that refuse to heal. This procedure saves limbs; often amputation is the only alternative to a transplant. During the bone transplant procedure, termed a vascularized fibula transplant, the diseased portion of bone is removed and replaced with the fibula (the thin bone that extends from the knee joint to the ankle). The surgeon reattaches blood vessels under an operating microscope to restore blood flow to the transplanted bone tissue and to promote healing. The fibula is used in transplants because its removal does not significantly weaken the leg; the remaining thick leg bone, the tibia, is able to support body weight on its own. Though the fibula often has a much smaller diameter than the segment of bone it replaces, the transplanted bone tissue adjusts to its new location by growing wider.

Cadaveric bone (called an allograft) may be transplanted in some cases, but allografts tend to dissolve, shrink, and break after a few years. Cadaveric bone may also be rejected by the body's immune system, a potential hazard that transplanted bone coming from the patient's own body (called an autograft) does not face.

TOTAL JOINT REPLACEMENT

Degenerative diseases of the joints, such as rheumatoid arthritis and osteoarthritis (see chapter 25), affect millions of Americans. The swelling and inflammation of these diseases can make simple activities like walking or shaking hands difficult, if not impossible. When symptoms become debilitating, joint replacement surgery can restore function.

Recent technological development has made new prostheses available to replace almost every joint in the body, including the hip, knee, shoulder, elbow, wrist, and finger. The ball-and-socket hip prosthesis (made of polyethylene plastic and metal alloys) is most commonly implanted. While this procedure is usually reserved for older patients who are not likely to place undue stress on the artificial hip, the same procedure is performed in younger patients with congenital deformities or other serious problems.

Joint replacements now enjoy a high success rate. Many patients who have had one artificial hip implanted are so pleased with the results they agree to have the other hip replaced. Knee replacements restore walking ability to patients hobbled by arthritis; finger joints made of silicon eliminate uncomfortable friction, allowing hands once paralyzed by pain to move freely again.

MUSCLE DISORDERS AND SPORTS INJURIES

Over 600 muscles drape the human skeleton and give the body its characteristic form. They enable us to walk down the street, throw a ball, and stand up straight. The muscles we are most aware of are called skeletal or striated muscles. Skeletal muscles are most obvious to us visually (they are the muscles that lie just beneath the skin's surface) and they are also the only muscles that we can consciously flex and relax (voluntary muscles).

There are three types of muscles:

Striated Muscles. Capable of voluntary movement and connected to the bones by tough tissue called tendons. When you consciously move a part of your body, you use striated muscles.

Smooth Muscles. Associated with many of the internal organs such as the stomach, intestines, uterus, and blood vessels. These muscles move food through the intestines, cause the uterus to contract during labor, and allow the body's vessels to dilate and contract.

Cardiac Muscle. Not under conscious control, this muscle tissue is found only in the heart.

The great majority of muscle disorders are caused by unaccustomed exertion or strain. While exercisers frequently experience muscle problems, these disorders are by no means restricted to those who work out. A pedestrian forced into a sprint to avoid traffic may suffer

the same muscle strain as an experienced runner. The injuries discussed in this section can result from any sudden exertion.

Do not let the risk of injury dissuade you from exercising. Despite exercise's risks, a consistent physical fitness program promotes healthy bones and other aspects of well-being. Athletes and those who regularly exercise tend to have greater muscle and bone mass than those who are sedentary. Their risk of many chronic illnesses like osteoporosis and heart disease is significantly lower than that of their sedentary counterparts.

Guidelines for safe exercising are as follows:

• Perform exercise regularly. Vigorous exercise on the weekend after a sedentary week working at a desk increases your risk of injury. If you cannot engage in your favorite sport regularly, you should at least work out by running or by doing calisthenics during the week. Whether you favor golf, tennis, or racquetball, you should develop a program that requires exercise at least three times each week. Proper conditioning minimizes the risk of injury.

• Prepare the body for exercise with a 10-minute warm-up session followed by gentle stretching. Warm-ups start blood flow to the muscles and prepare them for the physical stress that will follow. A runner who fails to warm up and stretch before sprinting greatly increases the likelihood of suffering a muscle tear or strain due to tight muscles.

• If you suffer a muscle injury, wait until the pain disappears before using the muscle again; otherwise, the injured area is more susceptible to further damage. Whether this is a sprain, strain, or fracture, make sure that the affected area has regained sufficient strength and flexibility to withstand repeated motions.

• When you have low back pain, avoid activities such as football and soccer that require sudden stops, bends, twists, and turns. The bending and twisting of bowling can also strain the back. Softball also requires sudden movements, such as running to catch a pop ball or sprinting to a base, which is risky for weak or tight back muscles.

GENERAL HOME REMEDIES AND ALTERNATIVE THERAPIES FOR SPORTS INJURIES

Cold Therapy. Ice packs can be used almost universally to treat acute strains and sprains. Apply ice as soon as possible after the injury occurs to minimize inflammation and swelling and then use ice intermittently for the following 24 hours. After 24 hours the inflammatory process usually subsides and ice is no longer necessary.

Heat Therapy. Apply hot compresses or heating pads after the initial 24 hours of on-again, off-again ice treatments. Increasing the local temperature stimulates blood flow, carrying much needed oxygen and energy to the area.

Rest. People who exercise regularly often loathe a layoff, but rest is essential for injury recovery. Inadequate rest slows the healing process and increases the risk of further damage.

Massage. Massage relieves the aches and pains of sports injuries by stimulating blood flow to the affected area. Although deep massage techniques may be painful for strained muscles, many gentler massage techniques are soothing.

ACHILLES TENDINITIS

DEFINITION AND CAUSE

Achilles tendinitis is an inflammation in the large tendon at the back of the leg attached at the heel. Tightness in the soleus muscle above this area may cause the Achilles tendon to tear or rupture completely during strenuous exercise.

TREATMENT

Rest and anti-inflammatory medication are the best treatment for strains of the Achilles. A lift inserted in the shoe heel of the affected leg may help relieve stress on the tendon. If the Achilles tendon is actually torn, surgery is usually necessary to repair it.

PREVENTION

This injury is usually caused by overuse, so moderating exercise is the best prevention. Heel lifts may relieve some of the stress on the tendon.

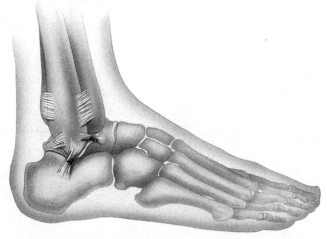

Figure 24.15: The ankle is supported by sets of ligaments that hold the bones together while allowing flexibility.

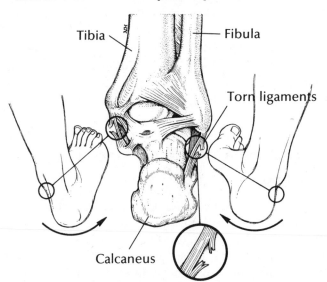

Tibia — Fibula — Torn ligaments — Calcaneus

Figure 24.16: This shows the tears in the ligaments of the ankle typical of a sprain.

ANKLE SPRAIN

DEFINITION AND CAUSE

A sprain is a stretch or tear of the ligaments, the tissue that attaches one bone to another. Most ankle injuries occur when the ankle twists inward, stretching the ligaments along the outside of the ankle (see figures 24.15 and 24.16). If an ankle sprain is severe, it is accompanied by pain, swelling, tenderness, and an inability to move the joint.

TREATMENT

Mild sprains can be treated with rest, ice, and elevation within the first 24 hours after the injury to relieve the pain. If pain and swelling persist for more than 2 or 3 days, consult a doctor. Most sprains heal within 2 to 4 weeks.

PREVENTION

Women should avoid high-heeled shoes. Whenever you exercise, wear shoes that provide adequate ankle support.

ARCH SPRAIN

DEFINITION AND CAUSE

The main arch of the foot, called the longitudinal arch, is subject to sprain when the ligaments are overextended.

TREATMENT

Applying ice to the area initially and then covering with an elastic bandage are helpful in treating this type of sprain.

PREVENTION

Wear shoes with adequate arch support and discard worn-out athletic shoes. If you have trouble finding shoes that fit properly, specially designed orthotic devices can be fitted to your foot at a reasonable cost.

BASEBALL FINGER (MALLET FINGER)

DEFINITION AND CAUSE

Baseball finger occurs when the tip of the finger is hit forcefully (with a ball or other object) and the tendon attached to the tip of the finger ruptures. After this injury, the tip of the finger cannot be fully straightened and assumes a slightly bent position. Because we rarely perform tasks requiring our fingers to be completely straight, the injury causes no functional disability and is often overlooked.

TREATMENT

To aid in recovery, the finger is immobilized in a finger splint for several weeks.

PREVENTION

Wear a mitt or gloves to protect your hands when playing baseball or other sports where your fingers are subject to impact.

BURSITIS

DEFINITION AND CAUSE

Bursitis is the inflammation of the bursae, small fluid-filled sacs located at points of friction around joints, generally in areas where tendons or muscles pass directly over bone such as the shoulder, knee, elbow, and hip. Normally, bursae help minimize friction between the constantly moving body parts in these areas and thereby facilitate motion.

TREATMENT

Splinting the affected area, rest, and cortisone therapy, usually by injections directly into the inflamed bursa, control the inflammation.

PREVENTION

Vary your activity to avoid overusing particular muscle groups and irritating bursae.

CHARLEY HORSE

DEFINITION AND CAUSE

A charley horse occurs when a muscle suffers an acute strain or sprain due to sudden stretching. The muscle fibers tear, and blood collects in a small area under the skin. Tenderness, pain, and local swelling are generally present.

TREATMENT

Resting the area and taping it with adhesive strapping can help relieve the pain. The charley horse generally takes about 1 to 2 weeks to heal.

PREVENTION

Warm up gently and then stretch. (Stretching is most effective when performed after a light aerobic warm-up.) Do not bounce when stretching (ballistic stretching).

COSTOCHONDRITIS

DEFINITION AND CAUSE

Costochondritis, also called Tietze's syndrome, is an inflammation of the cartilage of one or more ribs, most commonly the second and third ribs. The condition may occur at any age but is more common in young adults. While the cause is unknown, costochondritis may develop after a severe blow to the chest. The condition may also be linked to generalized polyarthritis. The pain accompanying this disorder is usually intensified by any movement that shifts rib position: bending, lying down, sneezing, coughing, and the like. The inflammation also renders the chest sensitive to the touch. Because of the chest pain, an affected person may presume he or she is experiencing a heart attack. The fact that pressing on the chest causes pain confirms costochondritis in most cases.

TREATMENT

This inflammatory disorder is usually self-limited and of short duration. Treatment when necessary entails a short course of corticosteroid injections or anti-inflammatory drugs. A person with the disorder sometimes needs to be reassured that the condition is not related to the heart and is not dangerous.

DISLOCATION

DEFINITION AND CAUSE

Dislocations take place when joint ligaments tear and bones that should fit next to each other suddenly separate. A severe blow to the shoulder, a fall, or a twisting of the arm can cause a dislocated shoulder—a frequent occurrence in sports. A dislocated joint is characterized by pain and swelling, and discoloration of the surrounding tissue. The body area becomes misshapen, and the affected area cannot be moved.

TREATMENT

The joint must first be relocated by a trained physician and then immobilized to allow for healing.

LITTLE LEAGUER'S ELBOW

DEFINITION AND CAUSE

This overuse syndrome is a painful inflammation of the elbow in youngsters that occurs due to excessive pitching or other sports participation. Children whose bones are still growing can chronically strain their elbows when throwing a ball for a prolonged time, as often occurs in Little League baseball games. If unattended, this injury can become a serious fracture.

TREATMENT

When a youngster suffers a sore elbow from pitching a baseball, further pitching must be stopped until the area is fully healed.

PREVENTION

Most Little League teams now restrict the number of innings any youngster can pitch. If your children play on a team, make sure these limitations are adhered to.

MUSCLE CRAMPS

DEFINITION AND CAUSE

Cramps are a prolonged, painful, involuntary contraction (spasm) of a muscle. Spasms may be caused by a direct injury, excessive stretching, or an inadequate blood supply to the affected area.

TREATMENT

When cramps occur, gently but firmly rub the painful area. Gentle stretching can also be helpful, but do not attempt to stretch very far or you run the risk of further injuring the muscle.

PREVENTION

Ease into exercise with a period of warm-up, allowing blood flow to your muscles to gradually increase. Even a stretching routine should be approached with caution.

Do not attempt demanding stretches until your body is fully warmed up.

MYOFASCITIS

DEFINITION AND CAUSE

This inflammation of the muscles and the sheaths (the fascia) that enclose them is frequently the result of unaccustomed muscular exertion and unusual posture. Firm, tender knots develop in the muscle tissue, causing locally severe but ill-defined pain. Myofascitis is usually triggered by overuse of the affected muscles, especially in people with poor muscle tone who attempt strenuous activity. Other causes include exposure to cold air or a draft.

TREATMENT

While medications such as cortisone alleviate pain, more lasting relief can be achieved by improving posture, reducing body weight, and exercising regularly.

PULLED HAMSTRINGS

DEFINITION AND CAUSE

The hamstring muscles run from the buttock across the back of the thigh. Inadequate conditioning, a sudden stop, or a sudden burst of activity can strain or pull the hamstring muscle.

TREATMENT

Rest alone is usually adequate to relieve the symptoms.

PREVENTION

Stretching after a gentle warm-up before strenuous exercise helps prevent pulls and strains.

RUNNER'S KNEE

DEFINITION AND CAUSE

Runner's knee is generally a sprain involving the ligaments of the knee, a common occurrence among runners. This sprain produces pain upon movement and local swelling.

TREATMENT

Swelling can be reduced by packing the knee in ice and wrapping it with an elastic bandage. More severe sprains may be associated with tears in the cartilage, which require immediate medical attention.

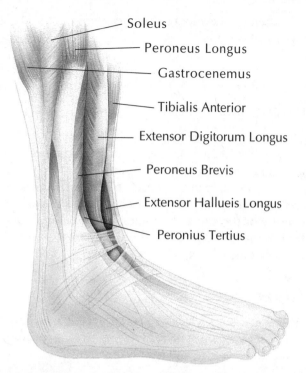

- Soleus
- Peroneus Longus
- Gastrocenemus
- Tibialis Anterior
- Extensor Digitorum Longus
- Peroneus Brevis
- Extensor Hallueis Longus
- Peronius Tertius

Figure 24.17: Shinsplints often affect beginning runners, or athletes who increase the intensity of their workouts.

PREVENTION

Runners should invest in a good pair of running shoes with adequate support and cushioning. Always discard worn-out shoes. Running on soft surfaces as much as possible will also minimize the jarring forces on your knees. Avoid uneven surfaces, which may cause you to twist your knee or fall.

SHINSPLINTS

DEFINITION AND CAUSE

Shinsplints are an inflammation and swelling of the tough, fibrous membrane surrounding the bone and attaching it to the muscles along the tibia (the main bone in the lower leg) (see figure 24.17). Shinsplints may result from improper conditioning or running on a very hard surface such as concrete.

TREATMENT

Rest and heat generally relieve the pain. Specific lower-leg conditioning exercises and stretches can help.

PREVENTION

Avoid shinsplints by stretching after each workout. Always run on soft surfaces such as grass, dirt, or a padded track, and wear running shoes with adequate cushioning.

TENNIS ELBOW

DEFINITION AND CAUSE

Tennis elbow is inflammation and tenderness where the muscles of the forearm attach to the elbow. This syndrome, while common to tennis players, also affects many people who perform frequent rotary motions of the forearm while the hand and wrist remain in a fixed position. The constant grasping and twisting motions cause chronic irritation of the tendons along the outside of the elbow. Tennis elbow begins with an ache over the outer part of the elbow and gradually progresses to involve the forearm.

TREATMENT

Immobilizing the forearm in a splint and applying moist heat can relieve the symptoms. Steroid injections may be administered in more severe cases. Anti-inflammatory medication often helps.

PREVENTION

Improve the mechanics of your swing by taking tennis lessons from an experienced teacher.

25
Arthritis

· · · · · · · · · · · · · · · ·

ISRAELI JAFFE, M.D.

Arthritis is the leading cause of physical disability in the United States, afflicting about 30 million people and annually sending more than half to seek professional help in alleviating arthritic aches and pains. Of this number, arthritis forces about 3 to 4 million to restrict their normal activities in some way. Fortunately, new medications, novel treatment approaches, and an improved insight into the nature of this disease have helped arthritis sufferers cope with their disease.

The word *arthritis* means "joint inflammation." Together with the rheumatic diseases that affect soft tissues, arthritis encompasses more than 100 different conditions. Of these, the most widespread is degenerative joint disease (sometimes referred to as osteoarthritis), which is most common among older people. With increasing life expectancy, the number of people living long enough to suffer degenerative joint disease keeps growing. Rheumatoid arthritis, which may occur at any age, is one of the most destructive of the joint diseases. Of the rheumatic diseases, treatment has been most successfully developed for gout. These arthritic conditions and the other most frequent forms of arthritis will be discussed in this chapter.

Arthritis occurs in all geographic locations, climates, and ages. The skeletons of prehistoric people evidence this disease, and it is common among most warm-blooded animals. Even though the causes of most forms of arthritis elude medical researchers, significant advances in diagnostic techniques, medications, and surgical procedures now enable most arthritis sufferers to live reasonably active, productive lives.

Arthritis may stem from a wide variety of circumstances: genetic predisposition, biochemical abnormalities, endocrine disorders, as a complication of other diseases, and, most probably, a fundamental defect in the immune system. In some cases, infection, athletic injury, or surgery directly or indirectly causes arthritis. The earlier the symptoms are recognized and treated, the better the chances for treatment.

JOINT STRUCTURE

Arthritis disrupts the structure and function of joints, the connections between bones (see figure 25.1). Under normal circumstances, to facilitate free joint movement, the bone ends are covered with cartilage—a protective cushion of tough, slippery material. The bones are connected to each other by ligaments—tough bands of tissue that hold the joints in place and reinforce the joint capsules.

Tendons, bands of tissue longer than ligaments, attach muscles to the bones. Each joint is lined by a synovial membrane, a sac containing synovial fluid, which acts as a lubricant, enabling the joint surfaces to function in a smooth, friction-free way. In healthy joints, the fluid is viscous, clear, and nearly colorless, and it provides nourishment for the cartilage, which contains no blood vessels.

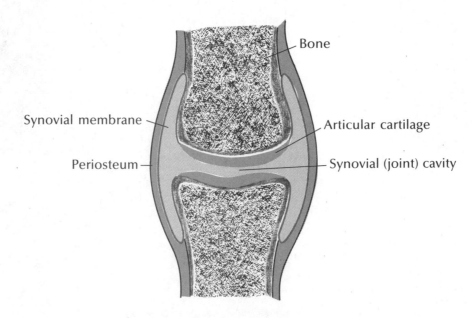

Figure 25.1: Structure of a normal joint.

CLASSIFICATION OF ARTHRITIS

While many physicians group the various types of arthritis according to the structures affected, a common way to categorize the disease's forms is by its pathology and mechanisms.

Most Common Feature	Examples	Comments
Inflammation of the joint membrane	Rheumatoid arthritis	Characterized by inflammation of the synovial membrane, which lines the joint.
Cartilage breakdown	Degenerative joint disease (osteoarthritis)	Usually associated with aging or "wear and tear" and most common in middle-aged and older people.
Metabolic disorder	Gout	Tiny urate crystals, deposited in the joint space, lead to inflammation and pain.
Infection	Lyme disease, gonococcal arthritis	May be caused by bacteria (particularly gonococci and staphylococci), viruses, fungi, and parasites.
Trauma	Tennis elbow, runner's knee	Athletes and others who place undue stress on joints are susceptible. Inflammation often involves tendons and muscles but may be temporary and disappear with rest and corrective measures.
Spine involvement	Ankylosing spondylitis	May occur by itself or as a component of other diseases, such as ulcerative colitis, psoriasis, or Reiter's syndrome.
Collagen vascular disorders	Systemic lupus erythematosus, scleroderma, dermatomyositis	Have many features in common with rheumatoid arthritis, but often involve skin and vital internal organs (heart, kidney, lungs), leading to potentially more serious problems.
Other diseases	Hemophilia, sickle cell anemia, diabetes, hepatitis, inflammatory bowel disease, psoriasis, thyroid disease	Many diseases involve the joints, causing considerable pain and inflammation; treatment of the underlying disorder usually alleviates the arthritis symptoms.
Psychological factors	Diverse	Psychological factors are sometimes associated with arthritis-like symptoms; stress and tension can produce generalized aching, which may be mistaken for arthritis.

Arthritis can attack all of these structures, causing them to break down, cease to function smoothly, become infected, inflamed, or otherwise malfunction.

WHEN TO CONSULT A PHYSICIAN

From time to time, everyone suffers aches and pains similar to those caused by a rheumatic or arthritic disorder. In most instances, these uncomfortable twinges are temporary and do not require medical attention. In contrast, most forms of arthritis persist chronically. While arthritis pain may subside for long periods of symptom-free remission, there is usually no permanent cure. Most types of arthritis can be controlled with proper diagnosis and treatment; the earlier the diagnosis, the better. Therefore, anyone experiencing symptoms or signs suggestive of arthritis should see a physician promptly. These symptoms include:

- Persistent joint pain interfering with normal activities
- Persistent pain and stiffness on arising in the morning
- Soreness and swelling in any joint or in a symmetrical (both sides of the body) pair of joints
- Joint pain that interferes with sleep
- Loss of weight, fatigue, and fever accompanied by joint pains

THE RIGHT DOCTOR

Initially, an internist or family practitioner can often diagnose arthritis based upon your medical history, physical examination, x-rays, and laboratory tests. When the diagnosis is questionable, or when rheumatoid arthritis, lupus, or other more serious and uncommon forms of the disease are suspected, you may be referred to a specialist for further evaluation. Since there are only about 3,000 rheumatologists in the United States, you may have to travel to a major medical center or university hospital. However, people living in many smaller communities and rural areas now have access to arthritis treatment centers that provide doctors, specialized clinics, and related services.

As with any chronic disease, long-term management of arthritis requires a good rapport and working relationship with the doctor in charge of overall treatment. The physician should be experienced in treating the particular type of arthritis; he or she should also be a person with whom both the patient and family members feel comfortable. The many unanswered questions about what causes arthritis make the stress of living with this chronic disease physically and emotionally trying for both doctors and their patients. Feelings of fear, anger, frustration, or depression are common and should be recognized and dealt with, not ignored.

THE TREATMENT TEAM

In treating arthritis, care is a team effort between the person who has the disease and his or her physician. The arthritis sufferer, who has the responsibility for following the day-to-day regimen, is the most important member of the team. Members of the treatment team also include medical specialists, physical therapists who design a program for maintaining joint and muscle function, visiting nurses or other home health aides, and orthopedic surgeons. Increasingly, those with arthritis consult occupational therapists to help with the practical mechanics of everyday activities: dressing and undressing, coping in the kitchen, learning new ways of entering and exiting a car, performing job-related tasks, and maintaining the maximum possible mobility.

A comparatively new specialist on the arthritis scene is a person trained in the fitting of splints, braces, and orthotics, special foot supports. These appliances of lightweight metal or plastic, which often are worn during sleep or for a few hours in the daytime, support joints in ways that can retard the development of permanent deformity.

Many arthritis patients and their families receive emo-tional support from psychiatric social workers and family counselors. Among its many types of emotional sustenance, supportive therapy helps adults adjust to not being able to handle children or perform at work, and it aids adolescents distressed over the disruption of their social, academic, and athletic lives.

AN OVERVIEW OF TREATMENT

Treatment for arthritis has several goals: pain relief, reduction of stiffness, control of inflammation, maintenance of joint mobility, and prevention of deformity. Very often, these goals require a combination of therapies, including drug therapy, a regimen of rest and exercise, physical therapy, the use of heat and cold, and, if indicated, surgical correction of deformed joints or their replacement with artificial ones. For example, an obese patient may be advised to lose weight to relieve stress on weight-bearing joints. In some instances, to accomplish this type of goal, a doctor or therapist will recommend changes in lifestyle and a shifting of responsibilities at home, on the job, or at school.

DRUG THERAPY

Aspirin, nonsteroidal anti-inflammatory drugs (NSAIDs), and corticosteroids are the most common medications for the treatment of many types of arthritis. Medications prescribed for only one or a few types of arthritis are discussed in this chapter under the particular diseases.

ASPIRIN

Advantages. Aspirin functions as both a painkiller (analgesic) and an anti-inflammatory, depending on dosage. Maximum analgesic effect is achieved with 2 regular (5-grain) aspirin tablets taken about every 4 hours. A much higher dose—usually 16 to 24 5-grain tablets per day—is required to control joint inflammation.

Most Common Side Effects. Ringing in the ears, nausea, abdominal pain, stomach or duodenal ulcers, and gastrointestinal bleeding. Aspirin also reduces the blood's clotting ability, which may cause bleeding problems.

To Minimize Adverse Reaction. Reducing the dosage and taking aspirin with food (for example, milk and bread) or antacids helps protect the stomach.

Most Effective Form. Ordinary, generic aspirin. Although pharmaceutical companies spend millions promoting time-release, arthritis-strength, and other "special" aspirin formulations for the treatment of arthritis, many experts feel these forms are only slightly better or more protective than ordinary aspirin. Extra-strength aspirin simply contains more acetylsalicylic acid, the active ingredient in the drug. The same medicinal effect can be achieved by taking an equivalent amount of regular 5-grain or 325-milligram tablets. While some doctors recommend buffered aspirin, which contains an antacid, the same effect can be achieved at a lower cost by using regular aspirin and an antacid or milk to protect the stomach.

ACETAMINOPHEN

Tylenol is one of the branded forms of acetaminophen, the major over-the-counter nonaspirin painkiller. They are analgesics with virtually no anti-inflammatory effects even at very high dosages. Recent adverse publicity about the side effects of long-term acetaminophen use on the kidneys was not based on adequate studies. The drug is remarkably safe.

Advantages. Relieves minor arthritis pain without aspirin's side effects of hindering clotting and gastric upset.

Disadvantages. Not as effective as high-dose aspirin in controlling inflammation.

NONSTEROIDAL ANTI-INFLAMMATORY DRUGS (NSAIDS)

Advantages. NSAIDs are as effective as, or more effective than, aspirin, and they are less likely to cause gastrointestinal irritation and bleeding. They may therefore be tolerated by people who cannot take aspirin in the required dosage.

Side Effects. Gastrointestinal bleeding, nausea, heartburn, ulcers of the GI tract, rash, itching, disturbance of kidney function, sedation, headache, and mood changes. If you suffer any of these side effects report them promptly to your doctor, who may change the dosage or the drug.

NSAIDs interfere with the production of prostaglandins, substances like hormones thought to play a role in the inflammatory process (among many other functions).

Most Effective Form. All drugs in this category are believed to be similar in their mechanism of action, but individuals differ unpredictably in their response to each. Trial and error is usually needed to arrive at the most effective drug and dosage. NSAIDs act fairly rapidly, and after 7 to 10 days of administration it is usually apparent if a particular drug is of value. After prolonged use, these drugs may lose their effectiveness and others may have to be substituted.

Warning: One of the oldest nonsteroidal anti-inflammatory drugs, phenylbutazone (Butazolidin), should rarely be used in the treatment of chronic rheumatoid arthritis because of its potential for serious toxic effects, particularly suppression of the bone marrow. It is not marketed in the United States at this time.

COMMON NONSTEROIDAL ANTI-INFLAMMATORY AGENTS

Specific NSAIDs, with brand names in parentheses, listed alphabetically by generic name include:

Diclofenac (Voltaren)
Diflunisal (Dolobid)
Etodolac (Lodine)
Fenoprofen calcium (Nalfon)
Flurbiprofen (Ansaid)
Ibuprofen (Motrin, Rufen, or in an over-the-counter, nonprescription strength, Advil, Motrin, Nuprin, and others)
Indomethacin (Indocin)
Ketoprofen (Orudis or Oruvail)
Meclofenamate sodium (Meclomen)
Nabumetone (Relafen)
Naproxen (Naprosyn or in an OTC, nonprescription strength, Aleve)
Oxaprozin (Daypro)
Pheylbutazone (Butazolidin)
Piroxicam (Feldene)
Sulindac (Clinoril)
Tolmetin sodium (Tolectin)

CORTICOSTEROIDS

Advantages. These powerful drugs suppress inflammation and are used to treat inflammatory types of arthritis, such as rheumatoid arthritis and lupus. Steroids may produce dramatic initial relief of the pain, swelling, and inflammation of arthritis.

Disadvantages. Originally thought to offer a cure for arthritis, the beneficial effects tend to be temporary; long-term use produces a host of serious adverse effects including puffing or rounding of the face, acne, increase in facial hair and weight gain, lowered resistance to infection, a thinning of the bones (osteoporosis) and skin, gastrointestinal ulcers and bleeding, mental changes (nervousness, insomnia, depression, and psychosis), diabetes, and cataracts.

To Minimize Adverse Reaction. Take the drugs on alternate days (not always possible, depending on the individual and the particular disease).

Inject small amounts of a steroid directly into the inflamed joint to avoid systemic administration, but the number of injections tolerated by a particular joint in a given time period is limited.

Note: Systemic steroids should be used cautiously and under careful medical supervision. The

adrenal glands undergo a temporary loss of function during (and after) prolonged steroid therapy, and supplementary or additional steroids must be taken in the event of stressful situations, such as surgery, infection, or injury.

REST AND EXERCISE

A balanced schedule of rest and exercise is an important component in treating inflammatory arthritis. Long periods of bed rest are discouraged because this can increase muscle wasting and stiffening of the joints. Similarly, excessive or improper exercise exacerbates the inflammatory process and increases joint damage. A careful regimen that alternates rest with exercises to promote and maintain joint mobility without undue stress should be designed to meet individual needs.

In addition to a special exercise regimen designed by a physical therapist, many people find physical and psychological benefits in recreational exercise that does not stress the joints, such as walking, swimming, and t'ai chi.

HEAT AND COLD

Heat, in the form of warm baths or wet compresses, is one of the oldest methods of relieving chronic pain. Starting the day with a warm bath or shower relieves morning stiffness; heat both before and after exercise also alleviates pain. Hot wax treatments, during which a painful hand is placed in melted paraffin wax, is an old remedy that brings relief to many people with arthritis.

Cold alleviates acute pain, particularly after injury to a joint or its surrounding ligaments and tendons. Apply a plastic bag filled with ice directly to the inflamed area for a short period of time.

"Contrast baths"—applying first heat and then cold to a joint or taking a hot bath followed by a cold shower— are often more effective than heat or cold alone in dealing with pain.

SURGERY

In recent years, major advances have been made in developing artificial joints to replace those severely damaged by arthritis. Perhaps the most successful to date are the artificial hip, knee, shoulder, elbow, and finger joints. Although the implantation of these devices has gained a good deal of public attention and surgeons now perform them widely throughout the industrialized world—even some professional athletes sport implanted hips—joint replacement is normally reserved for advanced disease. While artificial joints are effective in restoring joint function, they do not operate as well as natural ones, and increase the risk of infection and other complications. Therefore, joint replacement is generally considered a treatment of last resort. Nonetheless, total hip replacement and total knee replacement represent a major milestone in arthritis therapy, and many individuals are highly functional members of society today only because of this surgery.

Other operations effective in reducing deformity and restoring function include synovectomy (removal of the diseased synovial membrane) and orthopedic procedures to realign deformed toes or fingers.

EXPERIMENTAL TREATMENTS

Researchers constantly test new treatments for arthritis in the search for more effective approaches to the disease, especially those types that involve autoimmune attack, such as rheumatoid arthritis and lupus. Although experimenters have abandoned once promising techniques such as plasmapheresis, a procedure in which the blood is circulated through a machine to filter out components thought to contribute to the inflammatory process, and total body irradiation, which was meant to kill the lymphoid cells that implicate antibodies in causing arthritis, they are pursuing other techniques.

One of the most promising new approaches involves a group of compounds called "biologicals." They are so named because they are made biologically from living cells, rather than through chemical synthesis. They are designed to neutralize biological mediators of the immune process, including naturally occurring inflammatory substances in the joint.

One such experimental approach is called targeted immunosuppression. Researchers form a protein consisting of interleukin-2 (IL-2) and diphtheria toxin, and inject this substance into the patient. The protein is taken up by the activated lymphocytes believed to be essential in mediating the immune process that leads to rheumatoid arthritis. When the IL-2 is taken up, the diphtheria toxin is liberated within these cells and destroys them.

Another technique involves monoclonal antibodies, which are substances made in the laboratory to destroy particular cells. A monoclonal antibody to the CD-4 lymphocyte, believed to be essential for the development of rheumatoid arthritis and which may also play a role in lupus, is given intravenously over a period of days; CD-4 cell counts in the blood are markedly reduced and improvement may ensue for many months. While this technique sometimes results in severe allergic reactions to the antibody, researchers are trying to reformulate the antibody to prevent such occurrences.

Yet another treatment under study for rheumatoid arthritis is called oral tolerization. It involves the oral administration of an extract of type II collagen, the major protein constituent of articular cartilage (the prime site of rheumatoid arthritis tissue damage). This nontoxic substance is extracted from chicken cartilage and other sources. While its mechanism of action is unclear, investigators believe that it desensitizes the immune mediated inflammatory and destructive attack against the type II collagen present in the diseased joint cartilage. If the results of continued studies support the early observations that this treatment may be effective, it could be available for general use in the near future.

Warning: Do not use commercial preparations of cartilage to treat arthritis. These preparations do not have the same characteristics as the material used by researchers.

One of the newest approaches involves one of the cytokines—chemical messengers that mediate inflammation. One of the main examples is called tumor necrosis factor-alpha (TNF-alpha), which is normally produced by the body as a protective response to infection. But patients with rheumatoid arthritis seem to either make too much TNF-alpha, or lack sufficient amounts of a natural substance to neutralize its actions. Laboratory-made monoclonal antibodies that block the action of TNF-alpha have already proven effective in the treatment of rheumatoid arthritis, and this has been confirmed in controlled clinical trials.

QUACKERY

In sharp contrast to legitimate experimental treatments, many arthritis victims embrace a wide variety of unproven therapies, most of which are outright quackery with no real medical merit or benefit. Unfortunately, chronic diseases with no satisfactory treatment or cure have always attracted unscrupulous individuals who prey upon its victims. Consequently, each year hundreds of millions of dollars are spent on worthless quack remedies by desperate people. Rheumatoid arthritis sufferers seem to be particularly susceptible to quackery, perhaps because the disease often comes and goes spontaneously and because conventional therapies are often so unsatisfactory. If a period of remission happens to coincide with a quack treatment, there is a natural tendency to credit the therapy, even if it did not cause the improvement.

Common arthritis quackery includes the use of copper bracelets, bee venom, flu shots, megavitamins, and a variety of balms or salves. None of these has any beneficial property aside from a possible placebo effect.

People who resort to such obviously worthless remedies often defend their action by saying: "I've tried everything my doctor recommends and I still have arthritis. What do I have to lose?" Aside from the money, time, and energy that could be better spent, people who resort to arthritis quackery run the risk of suffering injury from treatments less harmless than copper bracelets. The arthritis pills and shots offered by clinics on the Mexican border, for example, frequently consist of large doses of steroids, which can have very serious side effects. DMSO, an industrial solvent absorbed through the skin, is widely available as an arthritis remedy without FDA approval. Animal studies have shown DMSO to be potentially harmful and the FDA has rejected it for human use. (When DMSO is applied in a diluted solution on the skin, it is not harmful, but it may be highly toxic when taken internally.) Nevertheless, faddist publications continue to promote it as a "miracle" drug being suppressed by the medical establishment in much the same way that Laetrile is allegedly suppressed for cancer therapy. But researchers have found no evidence supporting claims that either DMSO or Laetrile is of any medical value, and people who resort to treatment with either are victims of an expensive hoax.

HOME REMEDIES AND ALTERNATIVE THERAPIES

Alternative therapies are not recommended as the primary treatment for arthritis because these diseases require careful medical monitoring and therapy. However, some home remedies and alternative therapies may be helpful as additional treatments, especially for the inflammatory types of arthritis, such as rheumatoid arthritis, ankylosing spondylitis, and lupus. These include:

Fatty Acid Supplements. Recent research suggests that high doses of an omega-6 essential fatty acid known as gamma linolenic acid (GLA) can help reduce joint inflammation. It is believed GLA replaces arachidonic acid as a building block for prostaglandins, hormones that are important mediators of inflammation. GLA is found in plant seed oils, such as those from evening primrose, borage, black currants, and hemp; capsules are available in health food stores. Studies have found beneficial effects with twice daily doses of 240 mg. of GLA. Research also suggests that these benefits may be enhanced by further supplementation with omega-3 fatty acids, which are plentiful in cold-water fish, and also available in health food stores.

Dietary Modification. Although many fad diets have been promoted for the relief of arthritis, none has been proven to help all sufferers. Nonetheless, individuals have sometimes found that eliminating one or more foods from the diet may decrease arthritis flare-ups. With this in mind, you should keep a daily food diary that correlates your discomfort with your meals. With time, you may find that particular foods apparently contribute to your pain and stiffness, and eliminating those foods may bring some relief.

Relaxation Techniques. Although no one fully understands the physiological mechanisms that trigger flares of inflammatory arthritis, undue excessive physical or emotional stress is believed to play a role in its development. Therefore, the regular use of relaxation techniques—such as progressive relaxation, self-hypnosis, and visualization—may help reduce the frequency and severity of flares.

Acupuncture. Studies have shown this traditional technique of Chinese medicine to be very effective for many types of pain relief. Although researchers do not understand the underlying mechanisms that explain why needles applied to specific points on the body alleviate pain, some patients have experienced significant reduction in arthritis symptoms. Acupuncture does not reduce inflammation.

Self-Help Devices. Devices that conserve energy or protect joints from stress are useful in everyday activities. These include portable telephones to save steps at home, reaching pincers for retrieving objects from high shelves, stools to facilitate sitting in the shower, and writing and eating utensils with special handles easy to grip.

Support Groups. Specialty hospitals or local chapters of the Arthritis Foundation often sponsor discussion groups composed of patients with certain types of arthritis, such as lupus or rheumatoid arthritis. These groups often meet monthly to discuss techniques for coping with the disease and/or to hear health professionals speak about aspects of the disease. Participation in a support group can help you become more knowledgeable about your condition and feel less isolated.

PREVENTION

Since the underlying causes of most types of arthritis remain unknown, nothing can be recommended to prevent them. The primary exceptions are for the forms of arthritis caused by infection, when prompt treatment of infectious diseases with the appropriate agent, such as antibiotics for bacterial infections, usually prevents or rapidly cures infected joints. In addition, learning proper techniques for sports or other activities that stress joints may help prevent or delay degenerative joint disease.

COMMON TYPES OF ARTHRITIS

RHEUMATOID ARTHRITIS

DEFINITION

Rheumatoid arthritis is an inflammatory type of arthritis that causes joint problems as well as damage to other organs throughout the body. As in many types of arthritis, pain and stiffness are major symptoms of rheumatoid arthritis; in this form of arthritis, however, these symptoms are characteristically worse upon arising in the morning and lessen as the day progresses. This pain and stiffness are symptoms of inflamed joints, and inflammation is the hallmark of rheumatoid arthritis. Its early symptoms are usually redness, swelling, and warmth in the affected joint. There is probably no other disease that causes body tissues to suffer such prolonged and sustained inflammation. Initially, the inflammation is confined to the synovium, the delicate membrane that lines the joint. While synovitis is not unique to rheumatoid arthritis, the rheumatoid type of synovitis usually persists and leads to destruction of the articular cartilage, which serves as a cushion or shock absorber between the opposing ends of bone in the joint.

The rheumatoid synovial membrane undergoes a large degree of swelling and enlargement, mostly due to an accumulation of cells devoted to sustaining the inflammation and producing various types of antibodies. In addition, other cells produce cytokines, chemical substances that may directly damage joint tissues. The thickened and active synovial membrane begins to attack the articular cartilage. Until the articular cartilage in a given joint is completely destroyed, the rheumatoid synovitis never fully subsides. Researchers believe there may an unidentified substance in the articular cartilage itself that incites this intense synovial inflammatory reaction (see figure 25.2).

In addition to inflammation of the synovial membrane, fluid accumulates within the joint space itself. Both of these developments produce pain. Intense inflammation causes the body to immobilize or rest the inflamed area. In the case of an inflamed joint, the reaction is muscle spasm or muscle stiffness, which makes motion about the joint even more difficult and painful for the rheumatoid patient. For arthritis, the stiffness is counterproductive. Although the response is intended to splint or rest the joint, it renders use of the joint all the more difficult; too much immobilization results in loss of function.

As the articular cartilage progressively deteriorates—the process may take many years—the edges of bone meet each other. When this occurs, the inflammation tends to subside as the bones fuse together and the joint can no longer function. After a rheumatoid joint has completely fused, either naturally or in some cases surgically, the painful process subsides in that particular area. But joint mobility is completely lost.

This disease affects the entire body, not just the inflamed joints; it is a systemic disorder. Rheumatoid arthritis makes its victims truly sick. They very often experience weakness and listlessness; they tire easily and may lose appetite and weight. These symptoms reflect the body's response to toxic products resulting from chronic, sustained inflammation. People with this disease often feel exhausted by 3 or 4 o'clock in the afternoon, even after doing little work. Furthermore,

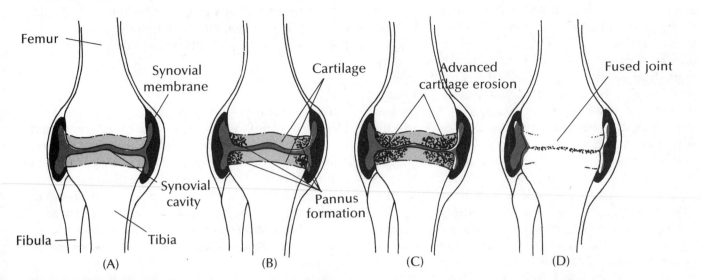

Figure 25.2: Progression of rheumatoid arthritis. The process begins with the inflammation of the synovial membrane (A) and progresses to pannus formation and erosion of cartilage (B). In the more advanced stages, pannus formation continues and there is further erosion of cartilage (C). Finally, the joint cavity is destroyed and the articulating bones become fused (D).

rheumatoid inflammation may extend beyond the joints themselves, involving major organs of the body such as the eyes, heart, or lungs, and their protective membranes. The muscles also may be affected.

Rheumatoid arthritis is the most common form of crippling arthritis; an estimated 2 to 4 million Americans suffer the disease. Rheumatoid arthritis occurs at any age from infancy to late adulthood, but for the most part it tends to strike during the prime of life in the 30s and 40s. The severity of rheumatoid arthritis varies, and many people experience it in a very mild form. It often waxes and wanes, sometimes seeming to disappear almost entirely. Often, though, the disease is progressive, with attacks striking at more frequent intervals and remissions becoming shorter and shorter in duration.

CAUSE

While we do not know the cause of rheumatoid arthritis, we now understand much about the inflammatory process that destroys the joint structures. Rheumatoid factor, a substance found in the blood and joint fluid of about 80 percent of adult patients with rheumatoid arthritis, is a gamma globulin or antibody directed against the patient's normal gamma globulin. This factor operates as an autoantibody directed against a natural body constituent. The detection of rheumatoid factor in the joint fluid, synovial membrane, and blood of arthritis patients has led researchers to theorize that it plays a role in inducing or sustaining the characteristic inflammation. In those persons with rheumatoid arthritis, the

antibody is made by certain synovial cells and is released directly into the joint space. There, it interacts with already present gamma globulin, forming an immune complex, which can itself cause inflammation. This occurs by invoking another body constituent called complement, a very complex substance composed of many fractions.

Complement attracts inflammatory cells into the joint space to engulf these immune complexes. These scavenger cells often rupture, liberating enzymes that can destroy joint tissue. Thus, the body's effort to eliminate immune complexes results in inflammation, and the consequences of this inflammation destroy tissue. Substances released by these dying tissues cause more inflammation as the body attempts to clear away the debris. Hence, there appears to be a circular process in the rheumatoid joint that feeds upon itself and which results in increasing tissue destruction.

The synovial lining cells multiply rapidly and begin to resemble "factories" for antibody production, making more and more of the immune complexes. Furthermore, the synovial membrane itself then begins to attack the articular cartilage directly. The synovial membrane forms what is called a pannus, which progressively envelopes the articular cartilage and grows around it. As the pannus derived from the rheumatoid synovial membrane comes into contact with the articular cartilage, the cells of the pannus make an enzyme called collagenase, which "opens the door" to the articular cartilage itself, thereby allowing tissue-destructive enzymes to enter and destroy the cartilage further.

As yet, we do not know what sets the process in motion or what is responsible for the formation of the rheumatoid factor and the immune complexes. Some researchers believe that a virus or other infective agent may be responsible. Others believe that there may be more than one inciting cause, and that it might be just a portion of a bacterium that has passed innocently through the body and joint tissues. This foreign substance could perhaps become lodged or hidden in the articular cartilage, and in the body's attempt to rid itself of this "antigen," the cartilage is destroyed. Genetic factors have also been implicated. Rheumatoid arthritis patients who carry a genetic marker designated HLA-DR4 are most likely to have severe, destructive disease.

Surprisingly, some patients with rheumatoid arthritis do not have detectable levels of rheumatoid factor either in the blood or the synovial fluid. How can arthritis occur without the factor? So far, this question is unanswered. Some people may have unusual rheumatoid factors, different from the classical type, that are not detected by the usual laboratory tests. Of the approximately 20 percent of the patients with rheumatoid arthritis who test negative for the rheumatoid factor in its usual form, a large percentage have less readily detectable rheumatoid factors, which may initiate and maintain rheumatoid joint inflammation. Furthermore, the destructive pannus does not require rheumatoid factor to exert its deleterious effects.

DIAGNOSIS

An analysis of your medical history, a physical examination, and blood tests are used to diagnose rheumatoid arthritis. For example, rheumatoid arthritis usually attacks joints in a symmetrical fashion. A doctor will suspect this disease when the same finger joints on both hands are involved, though not necessarily simultaneously. In the affected joints, there are usually pain and swelling and morning stiffness, perhaps the most sensitive measure of the degree of inflammation.

In addition to blood tests for rheumatoid factor, other laboratory tests are used to measure the amount of inflammation. The sedimentation rate measures the rate at which red blood cells fall in 1 hour within a specially calibrated tube. An elevated sedimentation rate does not necessarily lead to a diagnosis of rheumatoid arthritis, since the test measures inflammation anywhere in the body, but it is highly indicative of the degree of the inflammation in the rheumatoid joint. A fall in the sedimentation rate usually corresponds to a decrease in inflammation and an improvement in the disease, and the converse is also true.

Moderate anemia often accompanies rheumatoid arthritis, a result of the suppressive effect of the chronic inflammation on the blood-forming organs. This anemia is not materially helped by iron or vitamins, although food supplements may help a superimposed iron deficiency due to hidden bleeding from the gastrointestinal tract caused by the anti-inflammatory drugs.

TREATMENT

Drug Therapy. As in any chronic disease without an identified cause, effective treatment of rheumatoid arthritis tends to be difficult. While many drugs relieve symptoms, treatment to prevent joint destruction and deformity by controlling the underlying disease process is only partially effective. Nevertheless, there is ground for optimism; as our understanding of the mechanism of rheumatoid inflammation expands, the chances for the development of more drugs to interrupt this process also increase.

Since a basic hallmark of the disease is inflammation, drugs whose major function is the suppression of inflammation clearly have a place in the treatment program of patients with rheumatoid arthritis. As noted in the introductory section of this chapter, aspirin or NSAIDs are usually the first line of therapy for rheumatoid arthritis, with corticosteroids reserved for those with more serious disease.

GOLD SALTS

In the 1930s, it was discovered by chance that soluble salts of metallic gold helped arrest rheumatoid arthritis.

Advantages. Unlike cortisone and nonsteroidal anti-inflammatory drugs, gold seems to suppress the disease process at a very fundamental level, although how this occurs is unknown. It must be administered for a prolonged time—usually 3 or 4 months—before its benefits become apparent—but even after the injections have been discontinued, these effects usually persist for many months. This is in sharp contrast to the anti-inflammatory drugs that work within hours following their administration only to have the effects disappear shortly after the last dose.

About 70 percent of all patients receiving gold benefit, and in such patients it is accepted practice to continue maintenance treatment with an injection every 3 or 4 weeks for an indefinite period in order to sustain the improvement. This is particularly important because a second or third course of gold is often less effective than the initial one, and the maintenance gold injections are usually associated with very little risk. A true remission induced by gold is similar to that which occurs naturally in the evolution of the disease; unfortunately, this does not occur in all patients. Those who respond will experience a decrease in morning stiffness, an increase in strength and a sense of well-being, and a decrease in signs of inflammation in the joints with less swelling and less limitation of motion. These patients can usually reduce their dosage of nonsteroidal drugs or corticosteroids.

Disadvantages. In time, the favorable effects of gold may be lost despite maintenance therapy. In addition, there are patients who are not helped by gold or who cannot tolerate it because of toxicity.

Most Common Side Effects. Gold injections may cause a number of adverse reactions, including skin rashes and damage to the blood-forming organs and the kidneys. With an improved understanding of the proper method of gold dosage, most of these side effects have been greatly decreased, and gold treatment has become an accepted standard treatment for severe rheumatoid arthritis.

To Minimize Adverse Effects. A newer form of gold (auranofin or Ridaura), taken by mouth, produces fewer side effects but is not quite as effective as the injections. For patients who cannot tolerate the injections, however, it may be a possible alternative.

ANTIMALARIAL AGENTS

While agents such as chloroquine and hydroxychloroquine (Plaquenil) are effective in controlling the inflammation of rheumatoid arthritis, it is not known how the drugs work.

Advantages. Usually well tolerated.

Disadvantages. Possibility of eye damage.

Most Common Side Effects. Major potential side effect involves damage to the retina; arthritis patients taking antimalarial drugs are advised to see an ophthalmologist every 6 months for a careful eye examination.

PENICILLAMINE

Penicillamine is yet another of the slow-acting drugs which may be used for progressive arthritis that is not adequately controlled by other medications. This drug, which is taken by mouth, is a chelating agent normally used to remove excessive lead, copper, or other metals from the body or to treat cystinuria.

Advantages. Penicillamine was first studied in rheumatoid arthritis because it caused a disappearance of rheumatoid factor from the blood. Some of these patients went into a remission similar to that which could be induced by gold. Penicillamine has been under extensive clinical study for nearly 20 years, and it has been found to be as effective as gold in producing improvement in rheumatoid arthritis. It has the advantage that it can be taken by mouth, thereby avoiding the discomfort of weekly injections. In some instances, it can be used as an alternative to gold when that drug can no longer be tolerated or has become ineffective.

Disadvantages. Many side effects, some of which are

similar to those produced by gold, as well as a variety of autoimmune syndromes.

Most Common Side Effects. Same as gold.

Note: Since antimalarial drugs, gold, and penicillamine are all slow in onset of effectiveness, they should be taken along with aspirin or an NSAID.

METHOTREXATE (RHEUMATREX)

This substance is a cytotoxic drug (which inhibits cell duplication) that has been used for more than four decades in cancer chemotherapy. It was first applied to rheumatic disease in the treatment of psoriatic arthritis (discussed later in this chapter), and the favorable results obtained prompted the studies of methotrexate in rheumatoid arthritis, where it has also been found highly effective.

Advantages. It is unique in that it is taken only 1 day per week—so-called pulse therapy—and this mode of administration affords much greater safety than daily dosing, with almost comparable efficacy. The drug has a relatively rapid onset of action, with benefit often noted as early as 3 weeks after treatment has begun. It is also safer than intramuscular gold or penicillamine. Therefore, it is increasingly introduced earlier in the course of treatment.

Disadvantages. A major flare-up in the arthritis will predictably occur when the drug is discontinued, even after many years of use. This suggests that it acts primarily as an anti-inflammatory agent, without remission-inducing properties, and that the commitment to use it implies an indefinite course of treatment.

To Minimize Adverse Reactions. With strict and careful monitoring of the blood count and liver function, this drug is perhaps less toxic than some of the other drugs derived from cancer chemotherapy. The physician may add 1 mg. of folic acid daily to the treatment regimen. This can minimize certain adverse reactions, such as oral ulcers, liver inflammation, and some of the side effects on the blood. It is important that the folic acid not be taken at the same time as the methotrexate, which may lower the effectiveness of the methotrexate.

SULFASALAZINE (AZULFIDINE)

Used to treat inflammatory bowel diseases such as ulcerative colitis and Crohn's disease, this drug also has a suppressive effect in some rheumatoid arthritis patients.

Advantages. May be capable of producing remission similar to gold, hyrdoxychloroquine, and penicillamine.

Disadvantages. Side effects may be serious and limit its usefulness.

Most Common Side Effects. Stomach irritation, skin rashes, and possible depression of the bone marrow.

To Minimize Adverse Reactions. Strict and careful medical monitoring of bone marrow function is necessary.

AZATHIOPRINE (IMURAN)

This is an immunosuppressive drug which is designed to inhibit the immunologic processes responsible for tissue destruction.

Advantages. May work in certain situations where other drugs have failed.

Disadvantages. Must be carefully monitored because of potential for side effects, particularly on the blood and liver.

Most Common Side Effects. Loss of appetite, nausea, depression of blood elements, and liver inflammation.

PHYSICAL THERAPY

Physical therapy plays a major role in the treatment of rheumatoid arthritis. Applied during the acute phase of the disease, techniques such as heat, rest, and gentle massage reduce inflammation. In addition, physical measures can help prevent deformity and restore function.

Physical therapy helps most effectively when drug therapy has successfully suppressed the basic inflammatory process. Vigorous physical therapy designed to restore joint function cannot be applied until inflammation has been controlled, otherwise it aggravates the disease process. Many physiotherapeutic measures can be carried out by the patient at home, and these greatly facilitate restoration of joint function and rehabilitation.

SURGERY

Orthopedic surgery grows increasingly important in the overall treatment of rheumatoid arthritis. Certainly the most exciting and revolutionary progress has been made in the area of total joint replacement. This technique was pioneered initially for the hip joint, which remains the most successful of the total joint replacement procedures. Replacement of the knee is a newer development, but results have proven as satisfactory as the hip.

During both of these operations doctors remove the diseased joint, taking out as much of the synovium as possible. This removal explains the excellent results for the hip operation, for there are no remnants of the aggressive, diseased synovial tissue left to continue their destructive process (see figure 25.3). In the total knee replacement, all synovium cannot be removed, and low-grade arthritis activity continues around the prosthesis. In some patients, both hips and knees have been successfully replaced with a remarkable restoration of function. Recent results of total shoulder and elbow replacement give cause for optimism that these joints as well will be increasingly benefited by surgery.

For other joints, particularly the wrist and hand (see figure 25.4), surgical treatment is directed mostly toward removing as much diseased synovium as possible, repair of ruptured tendons, and correction of deformities with plastic implants. Results are sometimes very

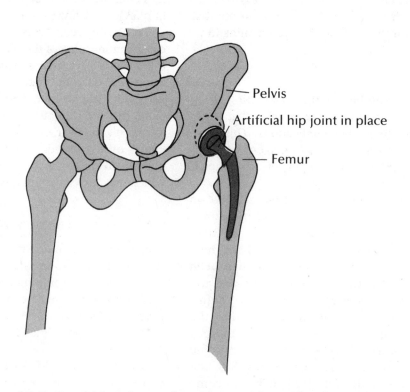

Pelvis

Artificial hip joint in place

Femur

Figure 25.3: Total hip joint replacement with artificial prosthesis.

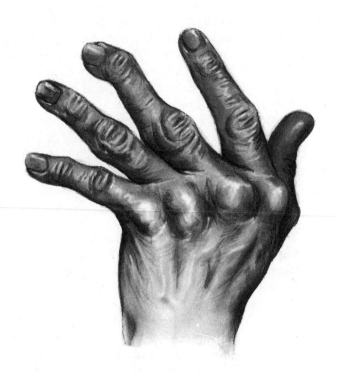

Figure 25.4: Hand deformed by rheumatoid arthritis.

satisfactory, but the success rate is not nearly as consistent as in larger joint replacement. Even though the orthopedic surgeon may achieve a very good cosmetic result in a rheumatoid hand—that is, it may look much less deformed—function is not always improved to a comparable degree. On balance, though, the increasing application of sophisticated orthopedic procedures to the patient with rheumatoid arthritis promises more exciting progress.

MALE/FEMALE DIFFERENCES

For unknown reasons, rheumatoid arthritis occurs two to three times more commonly in women than in men and also may be more severe in women.

DEGENERATIVE JOINT DISEASE

DEFINITION

Degenerative joint disease, sometimes called osteoarthritis, may involve any joint. It often affects weight-bearing joints, particularly the knees and hips, causing considerable pain and loss of function, and sometimes requiring corrective surgery. But most instances of degenerative joint disease do not significantly interfere with activities of daily living and do not cause systemic complications, making this disease much easier to live with than rheu-

matoid and other types of chronic inflammatory arthritis. Degenerative joint disease is by far the most common of all the arthritic disorders. More than half of the adult population over the age of 30 has some feature of this disease, evident either by symptoms or on x-ray examination. If you live long enough, you are bound to develop some form of degenerative joint disease, but usually it is very mild, producing few if any noticeable symptoms.

While the terms degenerative joint disease and osteoarthritis used to be interchangeable, today rheumatologists reserve the term osteoarthritis for a less common inflammatory variety of the disease—called primary osteoarthritis. The condition causes more pain, swelling, and redness than the more common degenerative joint disease.

Hands. Degenerative joint disease commonly affects the small joints of the hands. In the fingers, the disease largely remains in the end joints. As the cartilage of these terminal joints degenerates and the bones begin to rub against each other, new bone is produced as part of the reparative process, forming bony spurs called Heberden's nodes (see figure 25.5). This new bone growth is usually symptomless, at least in the early stages, but sometimes Heberden's nodes are very red and tender. With time, they gradually heal and remain as bony protrusions, somewhat unsightly in appearance, but not limiting function because the middle joints, often involved in the rheumatoid process, are frequently unaffected. In contrast, primary or inflammatory osteoarthritis may involve these middle joints, causing a much greater degree of disability. The considerable inflammation caused by primary osteoarthritis causes it to be sometimes confused with rheumatoid arthritis.

Spine. Degenerative joint disease of the spine also results in cartilage degeneration and new bone formation, or spurs. In this part of the body, bony overgrowths narrow the openings (the exit foramina) through which nerve roots emerge from the spinal canal. Even a very

Heberden node

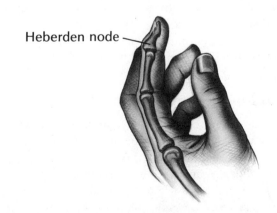

Figure 25.5: A drawing showing the bony spurs of Heberden's nodes, which form on the terminal finger joints.

slight bony protrusion into this space puts direct pressure on the sensitive nerve roots. Here, spinal degenerative joint disease can be very severe and almost totally incapacitating, not because of local effect upon the spinal joints themselves but due to the direct pressure on the nerves. The painful symptoms are similar to those of a ruptured (herniated) disk. As this pressure irritates nerve tissue, the nerves swell, further increasing the nerve compression. Bony spurs in the lower spine may compress nerves to the lower trunk and legs, causing sciatica, a pain radiating from the lower back to the thigh and leg. Muscle weakness and loss of reflexes may also occur.

Hip and Knee. Degenerative joint disease often involves the weight-bearing joints, particularly the hip and knee. The process may take many years to produce symptoms, even after x-rays show joint degeneration. Simultaneously, there may be long periods of remission during which the disease process is halted for reasons that are not yet understood. The condition usually appears predominantly on one side, at least initially. As the disease progresses, pain, stiffness, and resistance to motion due to mechanical factors grow increasingly severe.

CAUSE

As its name implies, degenerative joint disease results from a breakdown of tissue—in this instance, the articular cartilage between the two bony surfaces making up a joint. The primary defect appears to be in the cartilage itself and, as far as we know, it is due to various, poorly understood biochemical and mechanical factors.

The disease frequently appears in response to repetitive trauma or injury to a given joint. For example, pneumatic hammer operators very often develop severe degenerative arthritis of the shoulder joint, but only on the side used to hold the hammer. Pianists or typists frequently develop degenerative joint disease of the fingers.

Degeneration of the articular cartilage cannot simply be blamed on age, physical abuse, or overusage. When the disease involves the hips, for example, it will frequently be predominantly or entirely on one side, even though both hips bear equal weight and stress.

DIAGNOSIS

Doctors diagnose degenerative joint disease by analysis of your medical history and physical examination. In contrast to rheumatoid arthritis, degenerative joint disease tends to involve joints asymmetrically; if finger joints on one hand are involved, for example, it is not necessary that the same joints on the other hand also will be affected. Osteoarthritis almost always attacks the base of the thumb, a helpful characteristic in diagnosis. Also, the bony growth associated with all forms of

degenerative joint disease produces very hard nodules that are very different from the soft, spongy swelling found in the rheumatoid joint. Primary osteoarthritis also tends to run in families. X-ray studies, as well as certain laboratory tests, differentiate this type of osteoarthritis from rheumatoid arthritis.

While degenerative joint disease most commonly produces most of its pain and stiffness at the end of the day (in contrast to rheumatoid arthritis, which is invariably worse in the morning), in the advanced stages there is often morning stiffness as well.

TREATMENT

Drug Therapy. The goal of drug therapy in degenerative joint disease is suppression of inflammation and relief of pain. Pain and stiffness usually can be relieved by analgesics, which simply blunt the pain impulses to the brain, and by anti-inflammatory drugs, which temporarily suppress inflammation. Again, aspirin, which combines both properties, is a mainstay of treatment. For those who cannot tolerate aspirin, nonsteroidal anti-inflammatory drugs may be prescribed. In many instances, they are superior to aspirin and are better tolerated. (See "Overview of Treatment.")

Among the many nonsteroidal anti-inflammatory drugs, indomethacin (Indocin) is unusually effective in degenerative joint disease involving the hip. Cortisone or other steroids should not be used except for those instances when they may be injected directly into the joint cavity to bring about temporary reduction of inflammation. This procedure is most often done to the knee joint, but it cannot be repeated too often because the drug itself may damage the cartilage.

Researchers recently discovered that in certain cases of inflammatory degenerative joint disease, tiny crystals of a substance called hydroxyapatite are present in the joint fluid. These crystals are shed from bone, presumably as the bony surfaces rub against each other; they are capable of causing inflammation. Those osteoarthritis patients whose joint inflammation is induced by such crystals may be temporarily relieved by inserting a needle into the joint space and withdrawing the fluid. This aspiration is followed by injection of a small amount of cortisone into the joint cavity.

Physical Therapy. Bed rest and traction or other physical therapy measures help relieve pain when nerves in the cervical or neck area are compressed. As the symptoms subside, a cervical collar may be prescribed to help bear the weight of the head and to restrict neck motion.

Treatment of degenerative joint disease of the lower back may require varying periods of complete bed rest and pelvic traction.

Surgery. When bed rest and traction fail to provide

satisfactory relief for degenerative joint disease of the lower back, surgery to remove the bony spurs may be performed.

Surgery to replace the joint may be indicated to treat incapacitating cases of degenerative joint disease of the hip or knee. This operation is remarkably successful and can be performed even on the elderly. Under certain circumstances, when the knee joint is not entirely destroyed, the surgeon may use a device called an arthroscope to remove some of the loose fragments within the joint, but the benefits of this procedure are usually very limited.

When degenerative joint disease involves the foot and ankle, there is relatively little that the surgeon can do except to fuse the joint; drugs remain the mainstay of treatment.

MALE/FEMALE DIFFERENCES

Although degenerative joint disease affects men and women equally, men may suffer symptoms earlier in life.

GOUT

DEFINITION

Gout is a type of arthritis in which disordered metabolic processes lead to deposits of uric acid crystals in one or more joints, causing severe inflammation and intense pain. An acute attack of gout is caused by the precipita-

tion, within the joint space, of sodium urate crystals. Although many joints can be attacked, the most common site is the big toe. These crystals produce severe inflammation leading to excruciating pain (see figures 25.6A and B). As the urate crystals increase within the joint, more and more inflammatory cells that respond to a "foreign invader" are drawn into the joint space in an effort to ingest and clear the fluid of the crystals. The ingestion of these crystals destroys some of the cells, and in a truly vicious cycle they release chemicals that further aggravate the inflammation. Painful attacks of acute gout may last days or even longer if not treated. Nonetheless, gout is one of the rheumatic diseases that can be discussed with great optimism. While the condition is not curable, highly effective drugs are available to alleviate acute attacks and prevent flare-ups.

In contrast to acute gout, chronic gout is characterized by deposits of uric acid in the tissues, which are called tophi. Some patients with chronic tophaceous gout may never have experienced an acute attack. In some cases, the initial evidence of the condition is the development of a kidney stone due to uric acid. Sometimes hyperuricemia (excess of uric acid in the blood) forms microscopic deposits of uric acid in the kidney tubules, resulting in severe kidney damage, even in the absence of symptoms. For this reason, patients with elevated uric acid should have periodic urine and blood tests to detect developing kidney damage. If so, the condition can be controlled with the use of urate-lowering drugs.

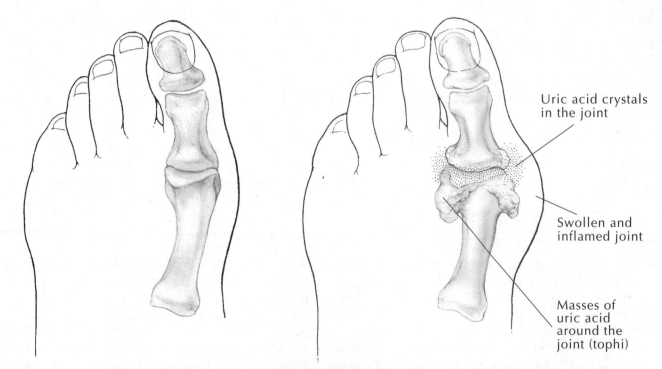

Figure 25.6A and B: (A) Normal big toe. (B) A big toe inflamed during an acute attack of gouty arthritis.

CAUSE

The excess uric acid that causes gout is a waste product derived from the metabolism of cell nuclei. More than one physiological imbalance may result in the buildup of uric acid in the blood and tissues. In primary gout it is due to either a metabolic fault resulting in overproduction of uric acid or a kidney impairment that prevents normal elimination or both. Some cases of gout combine both factors. There is an increasing incidence of secondary gout produced by certain drugs, most notably the diuretics used to treat high blood pressure and heart failure. These diuretics impair the ability of the kidneys to eliminate uric acid. Even aspirin, when taken regularly in low doses, may cause hyperuricemia and, sometimes, an erroneous diagnosis of gout.

Other conditions leading to hyperuricemia include diseases of the blood cells and blood-forming organs, certain cancers, and even psoriasis. All of these disorders involve an abnormally rapid breakdown of cell nuclei, resulting in excess uric acid. Elevated uric acid levels do not always lead to gout; there are many instances of hyperuricemia without symptoms of gouty arthritis.

DIAGNOSIS

The diagnosis of gout is based on the patient's symptoms, blood tests showing high levels of uric acid, and the finding of urate crystals in joint fluid. A trial of the drug colchicine (see "Treatment") also confirms the diagnosis.

TREATMENT

COLCHICINE

A number of drugs can successfully abort an acute gout attack. The most specific one is colchicine, which has been known since the time of Hippocrates.

Advantages. This drug is so specific for gout that if an acute attack of joint pain is dramatically relieved by colchicine, the diagnosis is almost surely gouty arthritis. During an acute attack, a tablet of colchicine is generally taken hourly until the pain is relieved or until nausea and/or diarrhea develops. These side effects can be very unpleasant, but often the colchicine must be taken until they occur in order for it to have its maximum beneficial effect. If the inflamed joint does not respond to colchicine, it often means that some disorder other than gout is responsible for the arthritis. After gout has been clearly diagnosed, acute attacks may be terminated by using any of the nonsteroidal anti-inflammatory drugs.

After the acute attack of gout has subsided, the treating physician should try to determine whether there are underlying, secondary causes for the hyperuricemia. For example, if a particular diuretic is causing the hyperuri-

cemia, alternative drugs may be prescribed. If there are no secondary factors, the problem can be assumed to be primary gout, which occurs mostly in men who often have a family history of the disease. After the first acute attack, the best policy is observation. It is impossible to predict when, if ever, another attack will occur.

If a patient experiences frequent, recurrent attacks, the next step is usually to prescribe colchicine as a preventive agent. This involves taking one or two colchicine tablets daily, indefinitely. This will often prevent acute attacks even though the colchicine has no effect on the blood uric acid level.

Disadvantages. Sometimes, colchicine will cause either nausea or diarrhea, even at very low dosages, or the drug may be well tolerated but may not succeed in preventing acute flare-ups. When colchicine is not tolerated, a drug to lower blood uric acid may be prescribed, although these are generally reserved for treatment of chronic gout. Such drugs fall into two general categories:

• **Uricosuric agents.** Drugs that promote excretion of uric acid by blocking its reabsorption as it filters through the kidney tubules. Uricosuric drugs include probenecid (Benemid) and sulfinpyrazone (Anturane).

• **Allopurinol (Zyloprim).** This drug reduces blood uric acid by blocking its production. The introduction of allopurinol marked a major advance in the treatment of hyperuricemia and gout. Sometimes both uricosuric agents and allopurinol are needed to normalize blood uric acid.

When urate-lowering therapy is first started, prophylactic colchicine or anti-inflammatory drugs must be continued for a time to prevent an acute attack of gout, which can be triggered by the administration of these agents. Indeed, any drug that rapidly lowers blood uric acid may paradoxically trigger an acute attack. After a normal uric acid level has been maintained for several months, colchicine or an anti-inflammatory prophylactic agent usually can be stopped without danger of inducing an acute attack. After that, only the urate-lowering drug will be needed.

Diet. Historically, the gout patient has been pictured (and caricatured) as an overweight, overindulgent, gluttonous person. Nonetheless, the basic cause of primary gout is not dietary excess, although foods rich in purine substances, which give rise to uric acid, may contribute to hyperuricemia. The modification of the diet to restrict purine-rich foods such as organ meats, sardines, anchovies, dried peas, and other legumes is not necessary if a person is taking medication to control uric acid.

Ideally, however, gout sufferers should restrict consumption of alcoholic beverages. Both wine and spirits in large amounts may impair the kidneys' ability to eliminate uric acid from the blood, which may result in an

PSEUDOGOUT

Pseudogout, like true gout, is characterized by deposits of crystals in and around the joints. But instead of uric acid, these crystals are formed from calcium pyrophosphate dihydrate (CPPD); the preferred medical term for the disorder is calcium pyrophosphate deposition disease.

An acute attack of pseudogout may be quite painful and last for 2 or more days. In about half of these attacks, the knee is the affected joint. Pseudogout also attacks the wrists, fingers, toes, hips, shoulders, elbows, and ankles. Surgery or severe illnesses such as a heart attack or stroke may bring on an attack of pseudogout. Very often, however, the disease progresses without acute attacks and causes chronic inflammation and calcification of the joint cartilage (chondrocalcinosis) and symptoms that may in some ways resemble those of rheumatoid arthritis.

Pseudogout may be mistaken for gout, as well as for inflammatory osteoarthritis, or it may accompany degenerative joint disease. Some patients may have pseudogout with relatively few symptoms or signs other than calcification of cartilage, which can be detected by x-ray studies. Pseudogout is differentiated from gout and other types of arthritis by the presence of calcium pyrophosphate crystals in the synovial fluid.

The treatment for pseudogout is not as well developed as that for true gout. There are no drugs that prevent the buildup of calcium pyrophosphate dihydrate crystals. Nonsteroidal anti-inflammatory drugs are usually effective in controlling the joint inflammation. An attack may be treated with cortisone injected into the joint after aspiration of the fluid containing the crystals. Oral use of colchicine is not as effective as it is for true gout.

acute attack. Until appropriate urate-lowering drugs have had a chance to work, alcohol must be used in moderation and "binge drinking" is prohibited.

Weight loss often alleviates gout in the severely obese, since the loss of body fat often normalizes serum uric acid without drug treatment. Weight reduction should be gradual, because a sudden, sharp deprivation in calories may result in secondary hyperuricemia and acute gouty attacks.

MALE/FEMALE DIFFERENCES

Gout is more common in men, but also occurs in women.

JUVENILE RHEUMATOID ARTHRITIS

DEFINITION

Juvenile rheumatoid arthritis (JRA), also known as juvenile chronic polyarthritis (JCP), is an inflammatory type of arthritis similar to adult rheumatoid arthritis in its tendency to be associated with systemic symptoms as well as symptoms in the joints. This condition afflicts about 200,000 children in the United States. Morning stiffness, swelling and tenderness of the affected joints, and varying degrees of pain are common signs of the disease. Fever, a characteristic rash, weight loss, and fatigue are other symptoms pointing to possible juvenile rheumatoid arthritis. Often, however, a child will not complain of symptoms until they seriously interfere with normal activities. The arthritis may affect many joints, usually in a symmetrical fashion, or be monarticular or pauciarticular, involving only one or two joints.

At least 75 percent of children with this disease eventually enter long remissions with little or no disability. Some may go on to develop adult rheumatoid arthritis or ankylosing spondylitis, but most do not. In some children, other organs, particularly the heart and eyes, may also be adversely affected.

CAUSE

The causes of juvenile rheumatoid arthritis are believed to be similar to those mechanisms involved in rheumatoid arthritis in adults.

DIAGNOSIS

There are no tests that specifically diagnose juvenile rheumatoid arthritis, and rheumatoid factor is often absent. The disease should be suspected in any child who has joint inflammation lasting more than 6 weeks. Since a number of other disorders produce symptoms similar to those of juvenile rheumatoid arthritis, diagnosis often involves eliminating the possibility of these other diseases, which include congenital abnormalities, infection, childhood cancer, and trauma.

TREATMENT

Drug Therapy. Treatment is similar to that for adult rheumatoid arthritis; aspirin is the basic therapy. Children who cannot tolerate aspirin may take nonsteroidal anti-inflammatory drugs. If these drugs inadequately control the disease, gold therapy, penicillamine, sulfasalazine, and even methotrexate may be required. In general, steroids are not recommended for children with juvenile rheumatoid arthritis except for those with severe disease, because daily administration of these drugs may retard growth.

Physical Therapy. Proper exercise and rest are

ARTHRITIS AND HLA-B27

In addition to ankylosing spondylitis, three other types of arthritis are often associated with the presence HLA-B27 antigen in the blood—an indication that some people have a hereditary predisposition to arthritis.

REITER'S DISEASE (REITER'S SYNDROME)

Definition
Reiter's is believed to be an infectious type of arthritis occurring primarily in young men. Its symptoms include inflammation of the large joints or only the spine and sacroiliac joint; inflammation of the eyes (usually conjunctivitis); urethritis, resulting in pain and burning upon urination; and skin eruptions involving the mouth, palms, soles of the feet, and sometimes the genitalia. Heel pain caused by inflammation of the Achilles tendon at its point of insertion also is common.

Cause
Reiter's is believed to be an infectious type of arthritis. It may be associated with sexual exposure, often without development of any known venereal disease, or with bacterial infections of the intestine.

Diagnosis
Because symptoms usually evolve over time, the true clinical picture of Reiter's disease may not be immediately apparent. Reiter's often coexists with ankylosing spondylitis.

Treatment
The primary treatment for Reiter's is NSAIDs given to ease inflammation and pain until the arthritis abates. Antibiotics are used only if there is evidence of chronic, persistent infection.

PSORIATIC ARTHRITIS

Definition
Psoriatic arthritis is a unique disease, with its own identifiable characteristics that are different from rheumatoid arthritis with psoriasis, which are two separate diseases that may coexist. Psoriatic arthritis most commonly affects the fingers and toes, with typical involvement of the adjacent nails and skin. There may be considerable pain and disability. The disorder can lead to a sausagelike deformity of the fingers and distortion of the nails.

Cause
The cause of this disease is unknown.

Diagnosis
Other joints may be involved symmetrically, and in some patients who have the HLA-B27 antigen there also may be inflammation of the spine.

Treatment
Entails taking aspirin or other anti-inflammatory drugs. Steroid injections may offer temporary improvement. In the more severe cases, injectable gold is helpful and may produce results as good as those achieved in rheumatoid arthritis. Methotrexate is highly effective against very aggressive forms of psoriatic arthritis but requires careful monitoring due to the risk of liver and bone marrow damage.

ENTEROPATHIC ARTHRITIS

Definition and Cause
An arthritic condition associated with inflammatory bowel disease such as ulcerative colitis and Crohn's disease. The joint inflammation may occur with the intestinal disorder or develop afterward. Sometimes, especially in Crohn's disease, it may precede the bowel symptoms.

Treatment
The arthritis may subside as the underlying intestinal disorder is controlled, and development of joint deformities or other permanent damage is unusual. About 10 percent of patients with chronic inflammatory disease of the intestine also develop ankylosing spondylitis—an association that is believed to be genetically determined because of the frequent finding of the HLA-B27 antigen.

important in treating juvenile rheumatoid arthritis. Night splints may be used to prevent deformity. The child should be encouraged to be self-sufficient, attending regular schools and leading as normal a life as possible.

MALE/FEMALE DIFFERENCES

Girls are more commonly affected by JRA than boys.

ANKYLOSING SPONDYLITIS

DEFINITION

Ankylosing spondylitis is a type of inflammatory arthritis that primarily affects the back, although, as in rheumatoid arthritis, systemic complications that affect other parts of the body may also occur. The term ankylosing spondylitis refers to what is usually considered this condition's most common feature, a spine with the vertebrae fused in a bent-over position. The most common target joint of spondylitis is the sacroiliac joint at the base of the spine, where the vertebral column joins the ilium (one of the pelvic bones). The sacroiliac is not a true joint since it has no motion; nonetheless, it can be the site of intense inflammation and pain. Although this disorder mainly involves the spine, it may attack certain peripheral joints as well, especially hips, shoulders, and rarely even the small joints of the hands and feet.

The predominant symptoms of ankylosing spondylitis—pain and stiffness—resemble those of any other inflammatory arthritis, but they are usually restricted to the back, especially the lower portion. Since these symptoms tend to worsen after prolonged inactivity, morning stiffness is a common problem. The disease also may cause systemic symptoms, such as a low-grade fever, lassitude, and easy fatigue, but usually patients with this disorder do not feel as generally ill as those with rheumatoid arthritis. Like so many arthritic disorders, spondylitis waxes and wanes in severity, with long periods of remission followed by flare-ups with no evident cause.

As ankylosing spondylitis progresses, fibrous connective tissue and ultimately, new bone gradually replaces the involved joints. This bony bridging immobilizes parts of the back, resulting in a stooping posture and rigidity. Disability from ankylosing spondylitis is more likely to be due to the spinal deformities, rather than the pain and stiffness that anti-inflammatory drugs can usually control.

This disease is most common in young adults, but, in some instances, it may occur in children, as a form of juvenile chronic polyarthritis, or start in middle age. It is often associated with other disorders, such as Reiter's syndrome or the arthritis accompanying ulcerative colitis, regional enteritis, or psoriasis.

CAUSE

There is a striking association between ankylosing spondylitis and a histocompatibility antigen, known as HLA-B27, which can be detected in the blood. HLA antigens are proteins present on cells believed to affect immune system responses, susceptibility to autoimmune disorders, and certain other diseases. Their presence is inherited. About 95 percent of white patients who have ankylosing spondylitis are HLA-B27 positive; in an otherwise healthy white population, only about 10 percent have HLA-B27. Although the association is weaker in blacks, it is still highly significant. This is perhaps the most dramatic evidence of the relationship of a genetic predisposition with the development of a rheumatic disease.

DIAGNOSIS

As with other types of inflammatory arthritis, ankylosing spondylitis is diagnosed based upon the medical history, physical examination, and laboratory tests, as well as x-rays of the spine and sacroiliac joints. Tests for HLA-B27 also are often performed, although a negative B27 test does not preclude the diagnosis.

FIBROMYALGIA SYNDROME (FMS)

Fibromyalgia is a complex disorder of unknown cause that appears to be more widespread than previously thought. It can be difficult to diagnose and treat. The term fibromyalgia means pain in the muscles, ligaments, and tendons that compose the fibrous tissues of the body. (The condition was formerly known as fibrositis, implying the presence of inflammation, which has not been shown to be accurate.) It can arise at any age, and more women than men are affected.

Routine laboratory tests in fibromyalgia are normal. Muscle pain, tenderness, and stiffness ebb and flow throughout the body, especially the back, shoulders, neck, and thighs. Patients are sensitive to pressure applied to certain areas of the body, called tender points. Fibromyalgia is often accompanied by mild to severe fatigue, chronic headaches, sleep problems, and irritable bowel syndrome. Symptoms may be aggravated by stress, anxiety, depression, hormonal fluctuations, cold or drafty environments, changes in weather, and other factors. Fibromyalgia may occur alone or in conjunction with other rheumatic disorders, especially osteoarthritis, rheumatoid arthritis, or lupus.

However, the drugs traditionally used to treat those diseases—from aspirin and other non-steroidal anti-inflammatories to potent steroids—seem to have little or no impact on fibromyalgia. Rather, the disorder often responds to treatment with antidepressant drugs. They are prescribed in low doses not for their antidepressive effects but because they appear to block endorphins, which are needed for transmission of pain messages.

In addition, recent research suggests benefits from regular aerobic exercise, including muscle stretching for flexibility, strengthening with light weights, and walking to raise the heart rate to 60 to 70 percent of target range. Exercisers experience a reduction in both muscle aches and tender points, possibly due to boosting levels of hormones called endorphins, which are the brain's natural painkillers. Improvement also may come from enhanced muscle fitness due to better blood circulation.

Some patients also may benefit from analgesic injections, physical therapy, acupuncture, and relaxation techniques.

Treatment

Drug Therapy. The pain and stiffness of spondylitis may be relieved by analgesics and nonsteroidal anti-inflammatory drugs, especially indomethacin (Indocin). Sulfasalazine and methotrexate may be necessary in severe cases. These drugs are important not only to relieve the symptoms but also to permit the patient to undergo appropriate physiotherapy.

Physical Therapy. Physical therapy is critical in treating ankylosing spondylitis to prevent the characteristic stooped posture as the spine begins to fuse. In addition, the joints where the ribs and vertebrae join also may be involved. If the ribs and spine become fused, breathing may be impaired due to a stiffening of the chest wall. Normally, the ribs flare in and out, like a bellows, as we inhale and exhale air. This action, which helps fill the lungs with air, is gradually lost in spondylitis unless preventive measures such as breathing exercises are followed. The exercises to help maintain a normal posture and breathing must be done daily—sometimes several times during the course of a day. This is why the physical therapist is an integral member of the treatment team in spondylitis.

Surgery. In severe cases of ankylosing spondylitis, when the spine has become badly deformed, surgery may be performed to straighten it and fuse it in a more acceptable alignment, but the need for this is infrequent.

Male/Female Differences

Ankylosing spondylitis differs from most other arthritic disorders in that it is far more common in men than women.

ARTHRITIS DUE TO INFECTION

Arthritis caused by bacteria or other infectious agents is the only kind of arthritis that truly may be cured. Typically, bacteria invade a joint, resulting in infection and inflammation that can be definitively treated by identifying the organism and then eliminating it with the proper antibiotic.

Time is the pivotal factor; the longer the infection persists, the greater the degree of joint damage. If the infection is not halted promptly, a secondary chronic arthritis that cannot be cured may result. In such circumstances, degeneration of the joint from the secondary condition may continue even after the infection has been eliminated.

Bacterial arthritis can be produced by a variety of bacteria and is usually associated with infection elsewhere in the body. For example, *Staphylococcus aureus,* or staph, is a common cause of infection, especially of the skin. People whose resistance is lowered by other circumstances—for example, long-term use of steroid drugs or certain other chronic diseases, such as diabetes—have an increased risk of having a localized staph infection spread to other parts of the body via the blood, a condition called bacteremia. There are other possible sources of joint infection, including bacterial seeding from the kidneys, lungs, or gallbladder. When bacteremia occurs, the joint seems to act as a filter, trapping the blood-borne bacteria and resulting in a secondary joint infection.

People whose joints have been damaged by rheumatoid arthritis also may be vulnerable to bacterial arthritis. An infection should be suspected in a rheumatoid patient when there is a persistent flare-up in a single joint. In such circumstances, a sample of joint fluid should be removed for laboratory study to see if an infectious agent is present.

Osteomyelitis is an infection of the bones that is more common in children than adults. When osteomyelitis occurs, the neighboring joint should be carefully studied for possible infection. Similarly, bones should be examined for possible infection in cases of infectious arthritis.

LYME DISEASE

Definition

Lyme disease, the newest infectious type of arthritis to be recognized, causes pain and swelling in multiple joints as well as problems in other body systems. Named after the Connecticut town where it was first identified in 1975, this disease is transmitted by the bite of a deer tick (Ixodes). At the site of the tick bite, a characteristic rash called erythema chronicum migrans is often found. This rash is unique to the disease: Typically, it is round and progressively clears in the center, creating an outer red ring that increases in diameter with each passing day. Other types of rash also may be found. In addition, vague symptoms like those of a flu, such as a low-grade fever, headache, malaise, and muscle aches, also may occur. If the disease is not recognized and effectively treated at this stage, it may subsequently develop into a generalized arthritis affecting many joints for months or even years. Other organs, including the heart, brain, and peripheral nervous system, also may be attacked. Nervous system involvement may cause Bell's palsy, which paralyzes part of the face.

Cause

The disease is caused by a microorganism called a spirochete—*Borrelia burgdorferi*—which is transmitted by the bite of several species of Ixodes ticks. Infected ticks are most commonly found in the Northeast, the upper Midwest, and the Northwest, including parts of California.

COMMON TYPES OF INFECTIOUS ARTHRITIS

Type	Cause	Comments
Gonococcal arthritis	Gonorrhea	Increasingly common due to recent rise in sexually transmitted diseases, gonococcal arthritis can lead to permanent joint destruction within a few days following the first sign of joint pain. When a person has undiagnosed gonorrhea without the characteristic symptoms of painful urination or discharge, gonococcal arthritis may not be suspected until permanent damage has occurred. If gonorrhea is a possible cause of joint inflammation, antibiotic treatment should be started immediately, even before confirmation of diagnosis.
Tuberculous arthritis	Tuberculosis	Attacks the large joints, such as knees and hips, and the spine. It is diagnosed by removing diseased joint tissue, examining it under the microscope, and subjecting it to special culture. The arthritis can be cured by long-term use of the antibiotics used to treat tuberculosis of the lung.
Rheumatic fever	Streptococcal infection	Rheumatic fever, which typically follows a strep throat, can be particularly damaging to the heart. One of the first signs may be a painful inflamed knee or other large joint. Aspirin usually controls the arthritis, and the disease almost never results in permanent damage to the joints. Prompt antibiotic therapy to prevent strep throat has markedly decreased the incidence of rheumatic fever and resulting heart damage.
Fungal arthritis	Fungal infections involving the lungs, skin, or other parts of the body	Those most vulnerable have a chronic disease that lowers resistance, or a history of alcoholism, drug addiction, long-term antibiotic or steroid therapy. In the U.S., the most frequent fungal (mycotic) infections causing joint inflammation are coccidioidomycosis, also called desert rheumatism or valley fever; sporotrichosis, which may be spread via the lymph system from a skin lesion or from inhaling the spores; blastomycosis, which may spread to the joints from the skin or lungs; and candidiasis. Diagnosis involves identifying the causative fungus followed by treatment with the appropriate antifungal drug.
Viral infections	Mononucleosis, rubella, etc.	Arthritis is a common component of viral infections. Arthritis usually subsides with the primary disease, but sometimes the joint inflammation may continue intermittently. Aspirin or other anti-inflammatory drugs are usually sufficient to control the pain.

DIAGNOSIS

Although several different types of blood tests are available, none is fully reliable. Most detect antibodies to the spirochete, and such an immune response may not be present for weeks or months after infection. Therefore, doctors in endemic areas are likely to diagnose the disease based on the characteristic symptoms, particularly if the patient is known to have suffered a tick bite.

Blood tests for Lyme disease cannot be used as a marker of a cure because they may remain positive even though adequate treatment has been given. Lyme disease may be looked upon as a model of nature, in which a known infective agent can lead to a chronic polyarthritis due to the initiation of an immune response to the invading germ, even though the inciting germ can no longer be found in the late stages of the disease.

TREATMENT

Drug Therapy. Antibiotic treatment with either tetracycline or doxycycline early in the course of the disease, when the characteristic rash is present, will generally result in a cure. Treatment later in the course of the disease, after developments such as generalized arthritis or other organ damage, may require large doses of intravenous penicillin or ceftriaxone (Rocephin) to eradicate the disease. The optimum duration for treatment of so-called late-stage Lyme disease is not yet known.

Patients with late Lyme disease may continue to suffer extreme degrees of depression, fatigue, generalized joint pain, and a continual sense of being unwell. Whether these symptoms stem from persistent infection or psychological reactions to having had the disease has not been clarified; physiological and psychological factors may be operative in different patients. Prolonged treatment for these symptoms, which may go on for several years, is probably not justified.

PREVENTION

Avoid exposure to ticks by walking on paved roads or sidewalks, rather than through brush in wooded and marshy areas. However, you may come in contact with ticks even when walking on grass. When spending time in infected areas, wear a long-sleeved shirt, long pants tucked into socks, closed shoes, and close-fitting hats. Spray insect repellents containing DEET on clothing and exposed skin. When you come indoors, examine yourself carefully, dressed and undressed. If you find a tick attached to your body, grasp it with a pair of tweezers as close to your skin as possible and tug gently to remove it.

Shower as soon as you come indoors. Ticks require several hours to attach themselves, and in the meantime can be washed away. Ticks removed within 48 hours of attachment are less likely to transmit infection. Save the tick in a closed jar for examination, and contact your physician promptly. (See First Aid for tick bites, chapter 14.)

COLLAGEN VASCULAR DISORDERS

SYSTEMIC LUPUS ERYTHEMATOSUS

DEFINITION

Systemic lupus erythematosus, also referred to as SLE or simply lupus, is a complicated disease affecting many organ systems. The term *lupus* means "wolflike" and refers to the characteristic butterfly rash that is seen over the cheekbones and gives the face a wolflike appearance. The rash is not always present, but when it is, it strongly suggests the likelihood of lupus. A variety of rashes almost anywhere on the body is another common finding in lupus. Many systemic lupus erythematosus patients also have Raynaud's syndrome, a blanching of the hands and feet on exposure to the cold, which disappears after warming.

Systemic lupus erythematosus is one of the most serious of all of the rheumatic diseases because it can involve the kidneys or other vital organs. It may strike at any age, from childhood into the 60s and 70s, but most patients with lupus will develop it when they are young adults. The symptoms largely depend upon the organs involved, and as the disease runs its course, usually over a period of years, different target organs may be affected. The degree of disease activity varies from potentially life-threatening flare-ups to complete remissions.

Joint disease that in many ways is almost identical to that of rheumatoid arthritis is often found in systemic lupus erythematosus. There is usually a considerable degree of synovitis, swelling, and inflammation of the joint tissues, but systemic lupus erythematosus patients only rarely develop deformities. Arthritis symptoms may be present for years before involvement of the skin or other internal organs becomes evident. Some patients diagnosed with uncomplicated rheumatoid arthritis ultimately are found to have systemic lupus erythematosus and, in retrospect, probably had it all along.

Since systemic lupus erythematosus may involve almost any vital organ, the various combinations of symptoms differ from patient to patient and from time to time during the evolution of the disease. Thus, a lupus patient may initially seek treatment for an emotional disturbance and, years later, develop arthritis and a characteristic rash. Or another may first consult a kidney specialist or a cardiologist. A false-positive blood test for syphilis, detected during a premarital physical examination, may be the first marker of lupus, preceding other manifestations by years (see box "The Anticardiolipin Syndrome"). Other symptoms may include severe fatigue, low-grade fever, hair loss, oral ulcers, swollen glands, appetite loss, nausea and vomiting, or other gastrointestinal disturbances.

CAUSE

The cause of systemic lupus erythematosus is not known, but certain facts have emerged as a result of years of intensive research. It appears that patients with systemic lupus erythematosus have a defect in their immune system, particularly with the regulation of the production of antibodies, the protein substances that

THE ANTICARDIOLIPIN SYNDROME

Some lupus patients have an antibody to a substance called cardiolipin, which causes a false-positive result in the blood test for syphilis. Consequently, lupus sufferers may be repeatedly treated with penicillin in the erroneous belief that they have a venereal disease. (In some cases, a false-positive test for syphilis may be the first manifestation of lupus.) It has been shown that the anticardiolipin antibody can be present for unknown reasons, as well as in association with other connective tissue diseases, and need not be restricted only to lupus patients.

The presence of anticardiolipin antibody is associated with a tendency to increased blood clot formation. This tendency may cause strokes or heart attacks in young people, recurrent phlebitis, multi-infarct dementia (a form of senile dementia due to multiple small strokes), and recurrent miscarriage. The test for anticardiolipin antibody is now routinely performed in anyone suffering these problems, and is particularly important for women who recurrently miscarry. The antibody is believed to cause miscarriage by stimulating thrombosis of the small veins in the placenta.

Anticardiolipin syndrome is treated with anticoagulant drugs, generally either low-dose aspirin or the Coumadin-type of anticoagulants, depending on the severity of the clinical manifestation and the duration for which the anticoagulation would have to be maintained. Pregnant women are given low-dose aspirin or, occasionally, heparin, since Coumadin would threaten the health of the fetus.

normally help to defend against infections. In systemic lupus erythematosus, many of these antibodies are defective or ineffective for their intended purpose, and are directed against one or more of the body's normal tissues. Sometimes, this "autoantibody" formation leads to damage to a vital tissue.

Damage to vital organs may be from a direct effect of antibody on a specific tissue, such as occurs when red blood cells or blood platelets are destroyed by an antibody that specifically attacks them, or indirectly as may occur in the kidney. In lupus, there are antibodies directed against certain of the protein components of cell nuclei, such as DNA. In some patients, DNA and antibody to DNA can be found circulating in the blood as immune complexes—an antigen and its antibody—similar to the immune complexes in the joint fluid in rheumatoid arthritis. In systemic lupus erythematosus, however, the complexes circulate throughout the body in the bloodstream. As the blood passes through the kid-

ney, these complexes may be trapped by the delicate filtration network that forms the basic structure of the kidney. Once caught, the complexes induce an inflammatory response in the kidney, ultimately leading to damage to the organ. A substance called complement is brought into the reaction, and it further contributes to the destructive inflammatory process, largely by attracting more inflammatory cells. In this sequence of events, there is no antibody directed against kidney tissue itself; instead, the organ is an "innocent bystander" that is injured simply as a result of performing its intended function, the filtration of the blood.

Immune complexes also may be found in the skin, central nervous system, and other vital organs, but only in the kidney is their relationship to the production of disease so well understood. We do not know the nature of the immunological defect that causes the body to make antibodies to its own DNA and other proteins, which leads to immune complex formation. Nor are the basic triggering factor(s) that initiate the antibody abnormality known. Some believe that a virus or other infective agent is responsible, but the proof is still lacking. Other research suggests that there is a basic genetic defect in the control of immunological responsiveness, which must be present in order for some external factor—virus, chemical, or drug, or ultraviolet light—to start the process. In some patients, for example, exposure to the ultraviolet rays found in sunlight can result in a flare-up of lupus, which is why they are advised to avoid any exposure to the sun. After even a mild sunburn, all of us may have an increase in free DNA from the injured skin, which is fed into the bloodstream and eliminated. In systemic lupus erythematosus, however, an antibody is produced against this DNA and gives rise in some patients to one type of circulating immune complex, which is trapped in the kidney. This is thought to be one possible mechanism by which ultraviolet light can cause a flare-up of the disease, or even induce the first attack. Other factors that seem to trigger incidents of lupus include fatigue, emotional stress, pregnancy, and infection, but they do not share the specific predictability of sun exposure.

DIAGNOSIS

When there are symptoms and signs of possible lupus, a number of diagnostic laboratory tests may be ordered. These include blood tests to detect antinuclear antibodies (ANA), anti-DNA antibodies, and serum complement levels, as well as urinalysis to detect protein.

TREATMENT

Drug Therapy. Corticosteroid drugs have greatly enhanced the prospects for survival in severe lupus.

Many researchers believe that these agents in high doses are capable of arresting and even reversing lupus kidney disease. In some cases, steroid drugs also appear to help patients with central nervous system and other life-threatening manifestations of lupus. Steroid drugs suppress the inflammation and consequent damage to internal organs. In high doses, they are also immunosuppressive, decreasing the amount of antibody and immune complexes. Hence, they attack the disease on two levels.

Perhaps one of the most serious steroid-induced complications in lupus patients is increased susceptibility to infection. Lupus patients are already infection-prone because their antibodies are often ineffective and they may have a decreased number of white blood cells. The corticosteroid drugs further aggravate the problem, but these risks must be taken to control the disease.

Sometimes, other drugs that suppress or kill certain cells that cause lupus inflammation and abnormal antibody formation may be used. These drugs, referred to as cytotoxic or immunosuppressive agents, may reduce the steroid requirement in some patients. Examples include azathioprine (Imuran) and cyclophosphamide (Cytoxan), which is of most value in lupus kidney disease. As with steroids, these cytotoxic drugs increase a person's susceptibility to infection, often from rare and unusual microorganisms.

As in other types of arthritis, most lupus patients take aspirin or NSAIDs to help reduce inflammation and ease pain. Antimalarial drugs, such as hydroxychloroquine and chloroquine, which were discussed in the section on rheumatoid arthritis, also may be applied in the treatment of lupus. These drugs are most effective when the lupus predominantly attacks the skin and joints and not internal organs, which require more potent therapies.

Despite the difficulties in treating lupus, patients today have a much better outlook than ever before. Sophisticated laboratory tests aid both in diagnosis and in the proper use of powerful drugs to treat the disease. Finally, our increasing understanding of the disease itself has further improved the chances for a normal, productive life despite the potential seriousness of the disease.

MALE/FEMALE DIFFERENCES

Similar to rheumatoid arthritis, lupus occurs predominantly in women for unknown reasons.

SCLERODERMA

DEFINITION

Scleroderma, also known as progressive systemic sclerosis, is a disorder characterized by excessive buildup of fibrous connective tissue. Initially scleroderma, which means thickening (sclero) of the skin (derma), was thought to involve only the skin. Recently, however, it has been recognized that vital internal organs also may be the targets of increased collagen deposits. Hence, the term progressive systemic sclerosis (PSS) is more accurate and will be used here except in situations involving only the skin, which will be referred to as scleroderma.

In progressive systemic sclerosis, there often is an associated arthritis even though the joints are not the main targets of the disease. In addition to mild joint inflammation, there are changes in the tissues around the joints due to deposition of excessive amounts of connective tissue, resulting in reduced mobility. With the progressive thickening and tightening of the skin about the fingers, motion becomes increasingly restricted. Larger joints such as the elbows and knees also may be involved.

Thickening of the skin may occur anywhere in the body, especially in the face. Scleroderma is usually chronic and progresses over a period of many years; however, there may be periods when the disease seems to be static. Occasionally, it may go into remission, either in certain localized areas or throughout the body. When this occurs, the skin appears to be perfectly normal, as though it had never been attacked by scleroderma.

Hair growth and sweating generally stop as the hair follicles and sweat glands are destroyed. Often the patient may experience intense itching as normal skin structures are replaced by excessive collagen. The superficial layers of the skin atrophy or shrink as their blood supply is decreased due to the strangulating effect on blood vessels of the dense new collagen in the underlying layers. The blood vessels themselves become narrowed. If the hands are affected, as they often are, tightening of the skin over the fingers results in a similar physical narrowing of the tiny blood vessels vital to their nourishment, and skin ulceration may develop on the fingertips and over the joints and bony prominences. These ulcers, which are usually painful and often become infected, are very difficult to treat and greatly interfere with the use of the hand. With progressive loss of blood supply, more distant tissues such as the ends of the fingers are unable to obtain adequate oxygen via the circulation and may gradually become shortened.

When the disease attacks internal organs, it may be life-threatening. In the lung, for example, progressive sclerosis may cause an increase in connective tissue in the delicate air sacs, a condition called pulmonary fibrosis. The normal process of oxygen transfer from the inhaled air to the blood is progressively blocked. As a result, blood is deprived of its normal oxygen content, leading to shortness of breath, which is often further aggravated by restriction in chest wall movement because of thickening of skin over the chest.

If the heart is affected, there may be a replacement of the pericardium, the membrane surrounding the heart, by increased fibrous tissue. This can encase the heart in a progressively tightening "shell" that restricts the normal pulsation and pumping of blood. More commonly, the actual heart muscle fibers themselves are replaced with ineffective scar tissue, leading to progressive heart failure.

In the gastrointestinal tract, progressive systemic sclerosis may cause difficulty in swallowing, malabsorption of digested food into the circulation, or severe constipation and possible intestinal obstruction, depending upon the structures that are affected. The kidney is still another vital organ progressive systemic sclerosis may attack, sometimes leading to a severe form of hypertension.

CAUSE

The immunological mechanisms underlying progressive scleroderma are still unknown, but may be similar to those involved in rheumatoid arthritis and other collagen vascular diseases, such as lupus, with both genetic and environmental factors playing a role.

For unknown reasons, the basic disease seems to be confined to the fibroblasts, the cells that make fibrous connective tissue or collagen. The processes that regulate these cells appear to go out of control. The fibroblasts behave almost as though they were continually stimulated to produce collagen. For example, when we cut ourselves, the wound heals with new connective tissue and new overlying skin. Once the cut is healed, the reparative process stops and new collagen ceases to be produced. In contrast, in scleroderma or progressive systemic sclerosis, fibrous tissue is produced at an accelerated rate, even without the stimulus of a wound. As a result, increasing amounts of young or immature collagen are continuously being laid down in the involved tissues, replacing the normal cells with connective tissue, as though it were a scar. This makes the skin, for example, thick and tight as the normal elastic tissue is replaced by dense fibrous tissue.

Because of the high incidence of Raynaud's syndrome (see chapter 16, Heart and Blood Vessel Diseases) and progressive systemic sclerosis, some researchers believe that the hypersensitivity of blood vessels to temperature change, and perhaps to other stimuli as well, may be responsible for causing some of the structural abnormalities in progressive systemic sclerosis.

DIAGNOSIS

Progressive systemic sclerosis and scleroderma are diagnosed based on classical changes in the skin, which are usually present, and blood tests, which show characteristic abnormal antibodies.

TREATMENT

Drug Therapy. No medication can significantly alter the natural course of PSS, although drugs may help alleviate specific symptoms. Medications include corticosteroids and penicillamine (discussed under "Rheumatoid Arthritis") and other immunosuppressive agents. Depending on the organ system involved, patients also may benefit from vasodilators or angiotensin-converting enzyme inhibitors to control hypertension and avoid kidney damage; antibiotics to control the overgrowth of intestinal flora; and antacids or cimetidine to alleviate other gastrointestinal problems.

Physical Therapy. Physical therapy is usually an important component of treatment that preserves muscle strength.

Surgery. If strictures develop in the esophagus, they may require periodic dilation. Severe gastroesophageal reflux may require surgery.

MALE/FEMALE DIFFERENCES

Progressive systemic sclerosis is about four times more common in women than in men.

Silicone breast implants have been incriminated as a possible cause of progressive systemic sclerosis, scleroderma, and lupus. Statistical studies thus far have shown no increased incidence of these diseases in women who have had silicone implants, when compared to a control group who had never received them. However, the number of cases that would be required to truly answer this question is greater than numbers studied in any of the published reports. As a result, the issue has not been fully and clearly resolved.

DERMATOMYOSITIS AND POLYMYOSITIS

DEFINITION

Dermatomyositis and polymyositis are connective tissue diseases in which arthritis is present but plays only a minor role compared to involvement of the muscles. The two disorders are very similar except that dermatomyositis involves the skin as well as the muscle, while polymyositis involves only muscles. Both have some features in common with rheumatoid arthritis, lupus, and progressive systemic sclerosis. The symptoms usually wax and wane in severity, but in some instances the disease progresses rapidly.

The major manifestation of polymyositis is inflammation, leading to destruction of muscle and increasing muscular weakness. As the disease progresses, the muscle tissue is replaced by functionless scar tissue. Muscles of the shoulders, arms, pelvis, and thighs are the most frequent targets, but the reasons for this are unknown.

As the disease spreads, other muscles may become involved. For example, the diaphragm and chest wall muscles, which are needed for breathing, may be attacked. The pharyngeal muscles, which are needed for swallowing, can be weakened to the point where swallowing solid foods becomes impossible. Heart muscle is still another potential target. This is particularly noteworthy because of the many similarities between the heart muscle fibers and those of the voluntary muscles, which move the limbs. When heart muscle is involved, there may be disturbances in the heart rhythm that require drug therapy.

Involvement of the skin is a major manifestation of dermatomyositis. There is a characteristic purplish rash, found mostly on the face and upper chest, although it may occur anywhere on the body. Associated with this rash, patients will often have swelling around the eyes, especially upon arising in the morning. There also may be scaly, reddened eruptions over the small joints of the fingers, sometimes over the eyelids, and occasionally on the shoulders or upper back.

CAUSE

Although the causes of dermatomyositis and polymyositis are unknown, it appears that abnormal immunological factors are responsible for at least part of the inflammatory attack against muscle tissue.

DIAGNOSIS

The skin eruptions seen in dermatomyositis, which may be somewhat itchy, are so specific that they almost always indicate the diagnosis. Diagnosis also depends on blood tests showing elevated muscle enzymes, the findings from muscle biopsy, and abnormal results on electromyography (test of the electrical activity of the muscles).

TREATMENT

Drug Therapy. Treatment may utilize corticosteroid drugs (see "Overview of Treatment"), although their effectiveness is less predictable in these disorders than in some other inflammatory diseases. As a result, many rheumatologists turn to one of the cytotoxic drugs to work in conjunction with the corticosteroids in attempting to suppress the muscle inflammation and to retard the destructive process. Usually, by combining the two classes of drugs, lower and safer doses of both can be used, thereby avoiding some of the more serious side effects that might be produced when either is used alone in higher doses.

Patients not helped by drugs may benefit from plasmapheresis, a technique that is used experimentally to treat several connective-tissue diseases. It involves removing large amounts of the patient's blood and putting it through a machine that separates it into its component parts. The red blood cells are returned to the body, and the plasma and often the lymphocytes are discarded. These plasma exchanges are usually done 2 or 3 times per week for 3 to 4 weeks, and may bring about a temporary but dramatic improvement in muscle strength. Sometimes, plasmapheresis will be so effective that the patients will respond to drugs that had previously failed to work.

Although plasmapheresis is still a research tool for this and the other autoimmune diseases, it is particularly appropriate to mention it here. Some researchers believe that there are substances circulating in the blood that contribute to the muscle weakness, and that these may be a by-product either of damaged muscle or of the immunological process that leads to the damage. The removal of these substances by plasmapheresis provides a new approach for this and other connective tissue diseases that fail to respond to conventional treatment.

Intravenous immunoglobulin (IVIG or intravenous gamma globulin) may be more effective than plasmapheresis and is replacing it in myositis and certain other autoimmune diseases as well. The gamma globulin is safe, virtually nontoxic, and carries no risk of transmitting the HIV or hepatitis viruses. It works as an immunosuppressant presumably by blocking antibody receptor sites on cells with normal gamma globulin, preventing abnormal autoantibodies from attaching to the cell and attacking it.

VASCULITIS

DEFINITION

Vasculitis is an inflammation of the blood vessels—both the arteries and the veins. Inflammation of a blood vessel, particularly a small artery, can cause a narrowing of its lumen (internal diameter). If the vessel completely closes, the tissue normally nourished by the diseased artery will die or be severely damaged. Diseases in this category are relatively rare and comprise some of the most baffling and poorly understood disorders in medicine. Polyarteritis nodosa and systemic necrotizing vasculitis are among the better defined examples. Very often, the diagnosis remains unsuspected for long periods because of the variable way in which these disorders behave.

Persons presenting with vasculitis, particularly when the disease involves widespread areas in the body, may be extremely ill with a generally poor prognosis. One type of vasculitis, which affects older people, involves inflammation of the cranial or temporal arteries, the vessels that serve a portion of the facial, jaw, and tongue muscles, the scalp, and most important, the retina. Cranial arteritis is the most common cause of sudden blindness in the elderly. Usually only one eye is involved, but sometimes it occurs in both.

Cranial arteritis is often associated with a syndrome of severe muscle pain and stiffness called polymyalgia rheumatica. This illness is also largely confined to the elderly. It is almost always associated with a very high sedimentation rate, a measure of the amount of inflammation. Polymyalgia may occur without cranial arteritis, but because of the association, arteritis should always be suspected in cases of polymyalgia.

Another form of vasculitis is called Wegener's granulomatosis. This is an extremely rare disorder that attacks the lungs, the nasal sinuses, and the kidney in a progressively destructive process.

People with generalized or systemic vasculitis will often have paralysis of a foot or a wrist as a result of loss of blood supply to the peripheral nerve serving that limb. The blood vessels of the lung may also be affected, resulting in symptoms like those of asthma. The development of asthma relatively late in life is very unusual, and may signify vasculitis.

The skin is another common site for vasculitis of all types. It shows up as areas of hemorrhage and death of superficial skin tissue due to loss of circulation.

Another type of vasculitis, known as Takayasu's disease, occurs almost exclusively in young women. The inflammation is largely restricted to the branches of the great artery that leaves the heart (the aorta). It has also been called "pulseless" disease, for the diseased arteries may be so narrowed that a pulse cannot even be detected at the wrist. Women with this disease will very frequently have symptoms of dizziness, light-headedness, weakness, and difficulty in using the arms, due to muscle pain from even slight physical effort. This is a direct result of lack of oxygen to the muscles, as the narrowed arteries are unable to deliver the increased amount of blood required during muscular effort.

CAUSE

The cause of most types of vasculitis remains unknown. Some forms of vasculitis are believed to result from an allergy or hypersensitivity, such as an adverse reaction to certain drugs. Sulfa drugs were very common causes of vasculitis, particularly in the early days of their use when the preparations were crude and the dosages given were higher than today. Viruses such as hepatitis B and HIV are examples of infectious causes of vasculitis.

DIAGNOSIS

Many types of vasculitis are difficult to diagnose because their onset and evolution may be vague and ill-defined. The more classic types are easier to identify, but because of their relative rarity, they are often not suspected until late in the course of the illness. Biopsy of an involved organ such as the kidney, muscle, or liver may be required in order to establish that a vasculitic process is indeed present.

A newly developed blood test called ANCA (antineutrophil cytoplasmic autoantibody) has helped in the diagnosis of the vasculitides. There are two types of antibody. One is an antibody to myeloperoxidase (P-ANCA), and the other reacts with proteinase (C-ANCA). These are both components of the cytoplasm of the neutrophil. The C-ANCA correlates best with classical Wegener's granulomatosis and microscopic polyarteritis, while the P-ANCA is less specific and may be found in some cases of Wegener's, as well as other types of vasculitis, lupus, rapidly progressive glomerulonephritis, inflammatory bowel disease, and infections.

TREATMENT

Drug Therapy

- *Cranial arteritis* can be successfully treated with corticosteroids, provided that treatment is started before there is significant loss of vision.
- *Polymyalgia rheumatica* usually responds dramatically to cortisone-type drugs in low doses.
- *Wegener's granulomatosis* was once invariably fatal, but now most patients can be treated successfully with cytotoxic or immunosuppressive drugs.
- *Takayasu's disease* is effectively treated with corticosteroid therapy, but the disease may go into remission without treatment.

SUMMING UP

In this chapter the more common forms of arthritis have been reviewed. Each year brings new advances in the diagnosis and treatment of the various types of arthritis and greater hope for the future. Now most arthritis patients can expect to live useful, relatively pain-free lives thanks to greater understanding of the diseases involved and new developments in drug therapy, surgery, and the more effective employment of physical therapy and rehabilitation.

26
Brain, Nerve, and Muscle Disorders

• • • • • • • • • • • • • •

JAMES R. MORRIS, M.D., PH.D., TIMOTHY A. PEDLEY, M.D., AND LEWIS P. ROWLAND, M.D.

Though modern medicine utilizes a sophisticated array of measuring instruments, computers, and laser technology and has compiled a vast knowledge of the maladies afflicting the human body, none of its devices match the overwhelming complexity of the brain and nervous system. This daunting conglomeration of gray matter, white matter, electrical impulses, and chemical transmitters is linked to the sprawl of peripheral nerves that activate muscles. The result is an awe-inspiring concoction of thought, emotion, and action.

Generations of researchers have tried to understand of this intricate system. Although research has not elucidated many of the brain's complexities, we do have a basic map of its fundamental properties.

The components of the brain and nervous system are wired together to maintain constant, body-wide communication. The brain and spinal cord (which links the brain to the rest of the body) constitute the central nervous system (CNS). Both are encased in bone for protection: the brain within the skull, the spinal cord within the vertebral canal. Nerve signals continuously traverse the spinal cord as they make their way out and back from the peripheral nervous system's (PNS) nerve connections to muscles and various organ systems (see figure 26.1).

The sections of the spinal cord and their emerging nerve roots are named according to their location at the spine's various levels: At the bottom of the spine are the sacral nerve roots; above these are, sequentially, the lumbar, thoracic, and cervical nerve roots.

AREAS OF THE BRAIN

The areas of the brain include:

• *The brain stem:* composed of the medulla, the pons, and the midbrain. The stem connects the spinal cord to the brain, maintaining vital functions such as breathing and circulation.

• *Cranial nerves:* paired nerves exiting from the brain stem that convey signals directing eye movements, facial muscles and tongue movements as well as the special senses of vision, hearing, balance, taste, and smell.

• *The cerebrum:* the top part of the brain, divided into left and right hemispheres (which, in turn, are further divided into lobes; see figure 26.2). The cerebral hemispheres control speech, memory, and intelligence.

The control for some of these functions, such as speech, is centered in specific, well-defined areas, while others, such as long-term memory and intelligence, seem to be spread over the entire cerebral hemispheres.

• *The cerebellum:* located under the cerebral hemispheres. Controls certain subconscious activities, including coordinated movement and maintenance of equilibrium.

• *The hypothalamus:* a major endocrine regulatory center influencing sleep, appetite, and sexual desire.

• *The thalamus:* a critical relay station linking the cerebral hemispheres to all other parts of the nervous system.

Supplying the brain and its components with oxygen and nutrients are two main sets of blood vessels, the paired carotid and vertebral arteries. These subdivide into smaller blood vessels, which supply different regions of the brain. A stroke occurs when blood supply to an area of the brain is interrupted, or when a blood vessel hemorrhages.

The brain and spinal cord are covered with three lay-

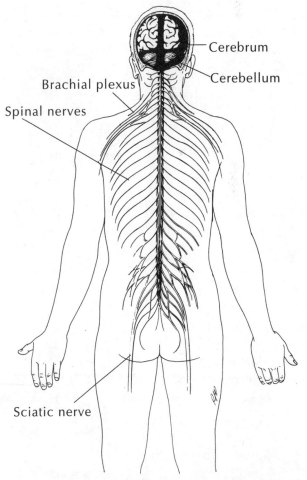

Figure 26.1: An overview of the central nervous system, showing the brain, spinal cord, and major nerve roots radiating from the spinal cord.

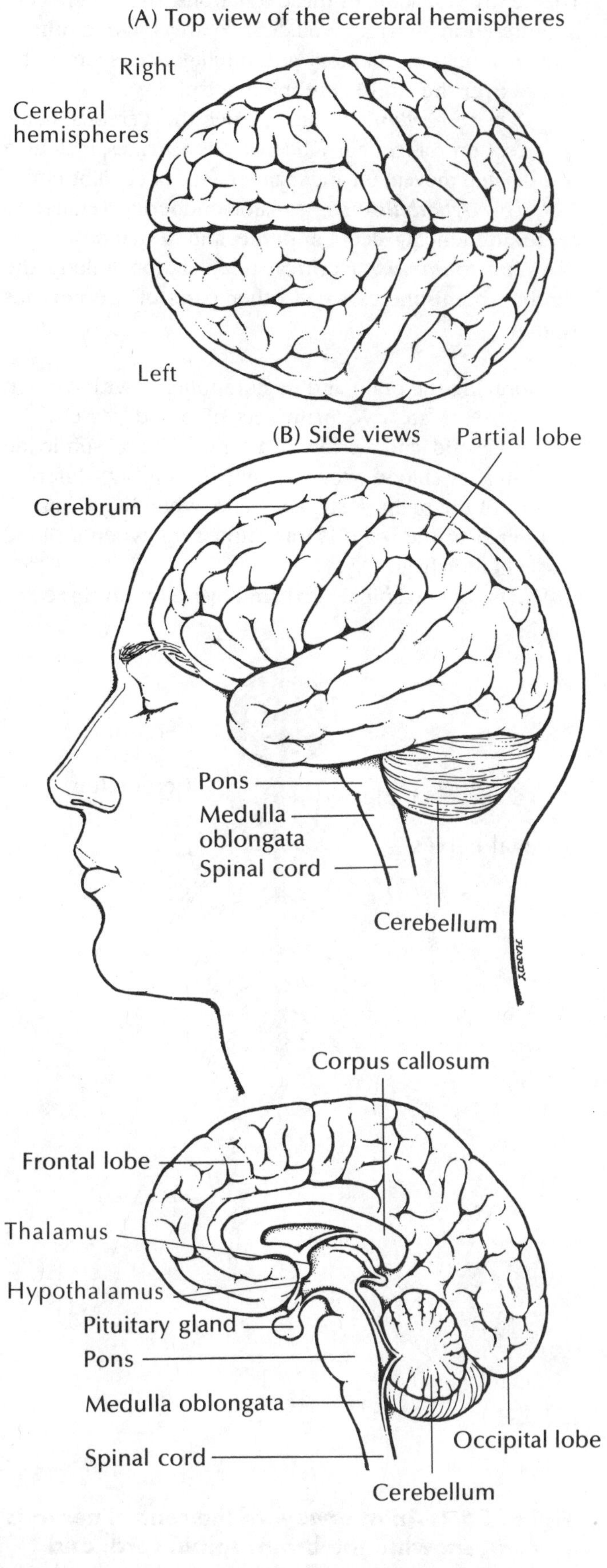

(A) Top view of the cerebral hemispheres

Right

Cerebral
hemispheres

Left

(B) Side views   Partial lobe

Cerebrum

Pons

Medulla
oblongata

Spinal cord

Cerebellum

Corpus callosum

Frontal lobe

Thalamus

Hypothalamus

Pituitary gland

Pons

Medulla oblongata

Spinal cord

Occipital lobe

Cerebellum

Figure 26.2: The brain, as seen from various views.

ers of membranes called meninges. The brain and spinal cord float in cerebrospinal fluid, a waterlike bath that insulates the soft nervous system structures from the encasing bones. Samples of cerebrospinal fluid are obtained by penetrating the subarachnoid space (between the middle and the innermost membranes) with a needle placed in the lumbar section of the spine. This procedure, known as a lumbar puncture or spinal tap, provides important clues about diseases that impair CNS function. (For more information, see chapter 12, Diagnostic Tests and Procedures.)

Disorders of the brain and spinal cord are treated by neurologists and neurosurgeons, doctors with several years of specialized, advanced training beyond medical school. The disorders they treat, with certain exceptions, are often very complex. One of the most spectacular advances in this field has been the application of molecular genetics to human neurological disease. Within the past decade, the techniques of molecular biology have transformed our understanding of several disorders. As research progresses, these developments will allow improved prenatal diagnosis, genetic counseling, and therapy of many previously "untreatable" diseases.

GENERAL SYMPTOMS

HEADACHE

Headache is one of the most ubiquitous of symptoms, experienced at one time or another by virtually everyone. Although the brain perceives pain felt by the body, the brain itself does not sense pain when it is touched or cut.

CAUSE

Among the many causes of headache, only a few are signs of a life-threatening disorder.

- *Tension headache:* the most common form, associated with contractions of head and neck muscles due to stress or other psychological factors. May be aggravated by changes in the environment, drugs, or factors unique to the individual.
- *Migraine:* caused by abnormally dilated blood vessels on the scalp, within the skull, about the eye, or in the neck. May be aggravated by changes in the environment or psychological factors unique to the individual.
- *Cluster headaches:* occur in runs, may be associated with dilated pupil, tearing from one eye, flushing of the face; more common in males.
- *Headache arising from structures outside the skull:* caused by pain originating in the scalp, exter-

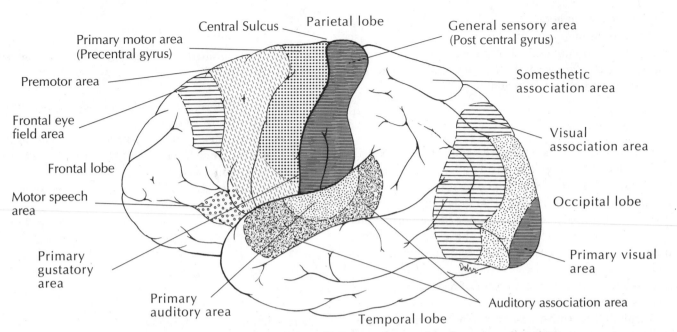

Figure 26.3: A map of the brain showing the major functional areas.

nal and middle ear, teeth, sinuses, blood vessels, and muscles of the face, head, and neck.

- *Headaches from pain-sensitive structures within the skull:* sources include the dura, which is the outermost layer of the meninges; the membranes surrounding the brain and spinal cord; the large arteries at the base of the brain; the cranial nerves; and the upper cervical nerves.

- *Extracranial headaches:* caused by muscular contraction, enlargement of the scalp arteries, and various inflammatory processes that affect sensitive areas of the head.

- *Headaches due to intracranial disease:* result from dilation or contraction of intracranial arteries, inflammation or stretching of the meninges, or pressure caused by tumors or other mass lesions.

In young people, headaches are most often caused by migraine and tension. Persistent headaches beginning after age 50 are more likely to have another cause, such as cranial arteritis (an inflammation of the blood vessels of the head), glaucoma, cerebrovascular disease, a brain tumor, or meningitis. A sudden, severe headache accompanied by loss of consciousness or decreased vision suggests the possibility of a hemorrhage beneath the middle meningeal layer or within the substance of the brain. Most chronic headaches, those that last unchanged for many months or even years, are caused by muscle disturbance tension or are manifestations of psychologic disturbance.

DIAGNOSIS

Determining the characteristics of head pain—quality, location, intensity, and duration—is an important step in diagnosis. For example, a throbbing quality, especially behind the eyes or on one side of the head, suggests pain arising from vascular structures. A throbbing, "sick" headache with nausea suggests migraine. Tension and muscular contraction headaches often cause a steady, nonthrobbing pressure as though a tight band were pulled around the head. Neuralgia (pain along the course of a nerve) is felt as a sharp, stabbing sensation. A headache's intensity does not necessarily indicate the seriousness of its cause: An anxiety headache may be severe while a life-threatening brain tumor may only produce mild discomfort.

Other symptoms accompanying the headache are also key to diagnosis. For example, migraine, unlike muscular contraction headaches, often causes nausea and visual symptoms including blind spots, sparkling points of light, jagged lines moving across the visual field, or sensitivity to light.

Headaches can also be linked to psychological factors or psychiatric disease, especially depression. But as a rule, all possible physical causes for headache should be investigated and eliminated before the headache is blamed on an emotional conflict or psychiatric disorder. Often a careful history and physical examination may rule out a physical basis of headache, but laboratory tests are sometimes necessary as well.

MALE/FEMALE DIFFERENCES

Studies show that migraine headaches are about 2.5 times more common in women than men in the United States, and tension headaches about 1.5 times more common in women. The reasons for these differences continue to be controversial. Age or hormonal fluctuations may be a factor in gender differences: Some studies suggest that both migraine and tension headaches increase in frequency in women before menstruation. Pregnancy and menopause are associated with a drop in headache frequency, particularly of migraine.

TREATMENT

Treatment of headache varies with the diagnosis. Nonaddictive analgesics relieve relatively mild pain; headaches associated with stress or tension may respond to psychotherapy or tranquilizing drugs. Migraine is best treated prophylactically by drugs that reduce the abnormal dilation response of blood vessels. These include ergotamine and its derivatives (e.g., Cafergot) and propranolol (Inderal). A relatively new medicine, sumatriptan (Imitrex), specifically limits the action of receptors on blood vessels that cause dilation.

Surgical Treatment. Surgery is not a common treatment for headaches. However, in rare instances, it may be necessary to treat headache caused by a vascular malformation or other intracranial mass.

HOME REMEDIES AND ALTERNATIVE TREATMENT

Biofeedback and acupuncture have successfully helped some patients control headaches linked to stress or tension.

DIZZINESS AND VERTIGO

DEFINITION

Dizziness is a word used to describe three different problems. One is a sense of light-headedness or an impending fainting spell. The second meaning is a feeling of imbalance and unsteadiness in walking. The third form of dizziness is *vertigo,* a sense that the person is moving or that the room is spinning or moving up and down. The symptom arises from disorders of the inner ear (the *vestibule*) and connections of the vestibular portion of the eighth cranial nerve in the brain. Vertigo sufferers may refuse to stand up and may minimize movement to avoid the characteristic nausea and spinning sensations. Many healthy people have occasional mild and brief episodes of dizziness that do not signify serious disease and usually do not require treatment.

Because of the proximity of the organs of balance and hearing, vertigo is sometimes accompanied by tinnitus, a buzzing or ringing sound, and by loss of hearing. These symptoms are caused by a disturbance in the cochlear portion of the auditory nerve, the part responsible for perception of sound. (For more information on problems in this part of the body, see chapter 31, Diseases of the Ear, Nose, and Throat.)

CAUSE

Many systems within the body contribute to your sense of equilibrium or balance:

- The sense of sight provides precise information about the body's location.
- The vestibular system (the structures of the inner ear and their nerves) reacts to movement and helps you keep your balance and equilibrium.
- The auditory system senses position relative to direct or reflected sounds
- Sense organs in the joints and muscles help determine posture in relation to the outside world.
- The sense of touch adds to the sense of equilibrium by providing tactile information about nearby objects.

The brain collects information from all these sensory inputs to determine the body's position and movement. Disturbances in any may cause dizziness and sometimes vertigo.

Dizziness is the sense of light-headedness associated with changes in blood flow to the brain, and may cause syncope (fainting) arising from transient impairment in the delivery of blood, oxygen, or glucose to the brain. The individual may pale, and, if standing, may need to sit or lie down. Vision may darken or "gray out," followed by loss of consciousness (usually regained within a minute or two).

In tracing the causes of dizziness or vertigo, doctors must rule out the disorientation, feelings of unreality, or brief lapses of memory caused by mild epileptic seizures, as well as conditions that cause loss of coordination of the legs, difficulty standing, and poor balance in walking. These problems may simulate dizziness, but have a different cause.

When dizziness is used to describe a sense of imbalance or unsteady gait, the problem is usually in the cerebellum (the back part of the brain), or the connections of the cerebellum or vestibular nerve in the brain stem. The resulting gait disorder, like that of a drunken person, is called *ataxia.* This is usually due to a neurological disorder involving the cerebellum or its connections. If ataxia persists, there may be a serious neurological disorder.

Intense vertigo with nausea is most often caused by a disorder of the vestibular system of the inner ear. This often begins abruptly and lasts days or weeks. When self-limited and not associated with other neurological problems, the condition is termed *labyrinthitis* or *vestibulitis.* Although the cause is unknown, viral inflammation is suspected in many cases.

Another condition, positional vertigo, occurs with a change in head position, such as leaning forward or backward, looking up or down, or turning quickly.

Attacks last several seconds. Positional vertigo is most common in middle-aged patients.

Vertigo may also occur immediately after head trauma or stroke. The cause is obvious in the former and other symptoms (i.e., pavalysis) are associated in the latter.

DIAGNOSIS

Accurate diagnosis requires defining the exact type of feeling—dizziness or vertigo—as well as the conditions under which they are felt and any accompanying neurologic or audiologic symptoms.

TREATMENT

If a transient drop in blood flow or pressure is suspected, medication, extra fluids, and additional diagnostic evaluation may be prescribed. Most commonly, labyrinthitis or positional vertigo may be successfully treated with antihistamines such as meclizine (Antivert) and diphenhydramine (Benadryl) among others. Alternatively, anticholinergenic drugs such as scopolamine may be used (commonly used to prevent seasickness). If nausea is a prominent complaint, phenothiazines such as promethazine (Phenergan) or chlorpromazine (Thorazine) may be effective. In some cases, a mild tranquilizer like diazepam (Valium) or hydroxyzine (Vistaril) may be used to reduce anxiety. Medication may be given for several weeks or only when symptoms are exacerbated. Reassuringly, labyrinthitis and positional vertigo are typically self-limited disorders.

HOME REMEDIES AND ALTERNATIVE TREATMENT

Some people with dizziness find relief by lying still in a dark room or by fixing their eyes on a spot to minimize the effects of uncontrolled eye movements.

LOW BACK PAIN

Low back pain can be a debilitating disorder and one of the most elusive to treat effectively.

CAUSE

Low back pain commonly results from muscular imbalance or misalignment of spinal vertebrae (the backbone). The underlying problem is often poor abdominal and back muscle tone, obesity, or degenerative changes in the vertebrae. Back pain of this type is often chronic, coming and going for months or years.

Intervertebral disks are composed of the shock-absorbing tissue between the vertebrae of the spinal column. These cause severe low back pain when they "herniate," and cartilage bulges out and may compress a nearby spinal nerve. Pain begins suddenly, often after heavy lifting, twisting, violent sneezing, or coughing. The patient may be unable to stand, but the pain subsides promptly when the patient lies down. When the herniated disk pinches a root of the sciatic nerve, pain radiates into one or both buttocks or down the back of the leg to the knee or foot in a pattern known as sciatica. The distribution of pain, numbness, or weakness indicates which nerve root is involved. (For more information on herniated disks see chapter 24.)

DIAGNOSIS

Physicians can often directly observe or feel muscle imbalances. A physical examination or x-ray may detect a curvature in the spinal column after an imbalance in muscle tension has persisted for years.

Diagnosing an isolated herniated disk with nerve compression is simplified when the patient experiences neurological problems that are caused by damage to a single spinal nerve. If such a condition is suspected, careful examination by a neurologist is the most important aspect of the evaluation to rule out more extensive disease. In addition, an MRI or CT scan (see "Brain Tumors" in this chapter) of the relevant area of the spine may show nerve root compression. Myelography (x-ray study of the spinal column after injection of a contrast medium) may also be used to determine if there is compression of the spinal cord. A neurologist may conduct electromyography or nerve conduction studies when muscle disease or general peripheral nerve disease is suspected.

TREATMENT

Treatment for low back pain includes muscle strengthening exercises, improved posture, weight loss, and use of chairs and beds that provide better back support when lying or sitting down.

Many people suffering a herniated disk can be successfully treated with strict bed rest. Anti-inflammatory and analgesic medications may also be helpful. Sometimes surgery is necessary to remove the portion of the disk that is pressing on a nerve. (For more information, see chapter 24, Disorders of the Musculoskeletal System.)

PREVENTION

The most effective preventive measures for low back pain include avoiding injurious movements at home and work such as carrying large weights. If you must pick up a heavy object, use your leg muscles rather than your back muscles while lifting. Follow a regular exercise program and keep your weight down. Unfortunately, large belts and other garments that claim to provide back support cannot guarantee protection against back injury and may provide the wearer a false sense of security. A physical or occupational therapist can offer detailed suggestions tailored to your particular situation and condition.

DISORDERS OF THE CENTRAL NERVOUS SYSTEM

DEMENTIA

DEFINITION

Dementia describes a progressive and sometimes irreversible loss of intellectual function that eventually impairs an individual's ability to work and socialize (this condition was previously called senility). Functions typically impaired in dementia include memory, learning ability, judgment, rational thought, personality, and capacity for abstract thought. The impairment may be mild at first, with problems in remembering appointments or misplacing objects. Over time, dementia may become so severe that the person is totally dependent upon others for normal activities of daily living (i.e., dressing, personal hygiene).

One million Americans over the age of 65 have dementia that is severe enough to require daily help and supervision to protect them from injury. About 2 million others have mild dementia and are able to care for themselves. Forty percent of people in nursing homes suffer from dementia, although it is not considered a normal part of the aging process.

Alzheimer's Disease. One type of dementia, Alzheimer's disease, has no known cure, but other types result from physical illnesses that can be treated and often cured if discovered early. Physical diseases associated with dementia include infection, stroke, trauma, multiple sclerosis, nutritional deficiency, and Parkinson's disease.

Alzheimer's disease is the most common of all primary dementias, affecting 2.5 to 4 million people in the United States. This disease usually develops in the later years and is marked by a gradual but inevitable deterioration of all mental processes. Widespread destruction of cells occurs in diverse areas of the brain. The course of deterioration can be viewed in these stages:

Normal (no impairment yet apparent)
Forgetfulness: difficulty remembering names or misplaces objects
Early Confusion: difficulty traveling, inadequate work performance
Early Dementia: forgets addresses, the date, names of close relatives
Middle Dementia: forgets name of spouse, major

> ### NEUROPHYSIOLOGIC TESTS
> **Electroencephalogram (EEG).** Determines electrical activity useful in diagnosing seizure disorder.
> **Positron Emission Tomography (PET Scan).** Uses specially prepared compounds to image metabolism and brain function.
> **Single Photon Emission Computerized Tomography (SPECT).** Measures cerebral blood flow and may be useful in diagnosing stroke.

events; suffers incontinence; experiences sleeping disturbances and personality changes, including anxiety, aggression, lack of concentration
Late Dementia: loses ability to walk, talk, eat, and maintain toileting skills

As the disease progresses, care can become psychologically, emotionally, and financially draining on the family. A collaborative effort involving several family members and a physician experienced with Alzheimer's is essential. Death may occur 5 to 15 years after onset.

CAUSE

The cause of Alzheimer's disease is unknown. Possibilities being considered include slow viruses, metallic toxins such as aluminum, genetic traits, and chemical abnormalities such as changes in brain acetylcholine levels.

OTHER DEMENTIAS

Multi-infarct dementia is caused by multiple strokes affecting both cerebral hemispheres. It accounts for 20 percent of all dementias and occurs in some people with multiple strokes that destroy brain tissue. In contrast to Alzheimer's, this condition may appear abruptly and grow progressively worse in a step-wise fashion. A different type of dementia is associated with Huntington's disease, a progressive hereditary disease with symptoms beginning as early as the 30s. Common early symptoms include irritability, impulsive behavior, and depression. Some patients develop a form of psychosis. Later in the course, characteristic spontaneous flowing movements (called chorea) develop. The disease is relentlessly progressive and no treatment is known.

Some dementias are reversible with early treatment of the underlying cause. These include dementia caused by infections (such as viral or bacterial meningitis, encephalitis, and syphilis); organic diseases such as brain tumors; liver disease and thyroid disorders; nutritional deficiencies (especially vitamin B_{12} and thiamine); head trauma; and drug and alcohol withdrawal.

BRAIN STRUCTURE IMAGING

Computerized Tomography Scan (CT Scan). Assesses the structure and anatomy of the brain. Strokes, tumors, and bleeding can be diagnosed this way.

Magnetic Resonance Imaging (MRI). Using a magnetic field, MRI can detect small brain abnormalities better than a CT scan.

DIAGNOSIS

Criteria for diagnosing dementia include:

1. Impairment in short- and long-term memory. Short-term impairment is the inability to learn new information. Long-term impairment is the inability to remember information that was known in the past, such as the name of the president or an individual's address.
2. At least one of the following is present:
   - Impairment in abstract thinking
   - Impaired judgment
   - Other disturbances of higher brain function, such as disorder of language, inability to carry out tasks, failure to recognize objects
   - Personality change from before the dementia
3. The presence of the first two criteria interferes with work, social activities, and relationships.
4. Mental disturbances are not associated with another mental illness, such as delirium and depression.

The diagnosis of dementia from underlying physical causes is made by a thorough medical and neurological evaluation and the process of elimination. If a search does not reveal another underlying disease as a cause for the dementia, a diagnosis of Alzheimer's disease is more likely. A conclusive diagnosis requires examination of the brain tissue for characteristic lesions—a study usually made only after death.

MALE/FEMALE DIFFERENCES

Men and women are affected equally in Alzheimer's disease. The ratio of men to women in other causes of dementia may vary, depending on the underlying disease.

TREATMENT

When dementia is discovered early and secondary to an underlying physical disease, treatment of that condition may reverse the impairment.

Because there is no cure for Alzheimer's disease, people with this disorder can only have their quality of life improved. Initially, when the impairment is mild, it is helpful for the affected person to stick to routine and

familiar surroundings, and keep lists of things to remember. Later, when such personality changes as depression, anxiety, insomnia, and agitation develop, medication can provide a degree of comfort. Support and education for caretaking families is essential. Often the physician can work with the family to determine when a person with Alzheimer's disease requires a nursing home.

HOME REMEDIES AND ALTERNATIVE THERAPIES

Isolation and waning communication skills are common in people with dementia. Nursing homes use dance therapy to increase social interactions and positive experiences. Other creative therapies such as music and art are effective when verbal communication is poor. People with dementia may also enjoy the companionship of a pet.

Exercise also benefits people with dementia who are commonly sedentary for most of the day. It provides a psychological lift as well as a physical improvement of the heart and the bones. Massage and hydrotherapy may alleviate agitation.

The effectiveness of herbal remedies used in Asia and Europe to improve mental function has not been proven. For example, a preparation made from the ginkgo tree is thought to act by increasing blood flow to the brain.

STROKE

DEFINITION

Stroke, formerly called a cerebrovascular accident (CVA), is a neurological disorder attributable to sudden interruption of the blood supply to part of the brain. Stroke occurs most often after age 65.

CAUSE

Several different mechanisms may result in stroke: thrombus formation, embolus, and hemorrhage. It is important to determine which mechanism is responsible because treatment and prognosis vary with each type (see figure 26.4).

- **Thrombosis.** An obstruction within an artery resulting from the gradual accumulation of plaque. Caused by arteriosclerosis, in which fat and cholesterol accumulate within the walls of arteries. These obstructions may restrict or completely block blood flow through the artery. Blockage of arteries supplying the brain causes stroke if alternative routes (collateral circulation) are not available to deliver an adequate blood supply.
- **Embolus.** An obstruction due to material formed elsewhere in the body (such as the heart) and in an artery

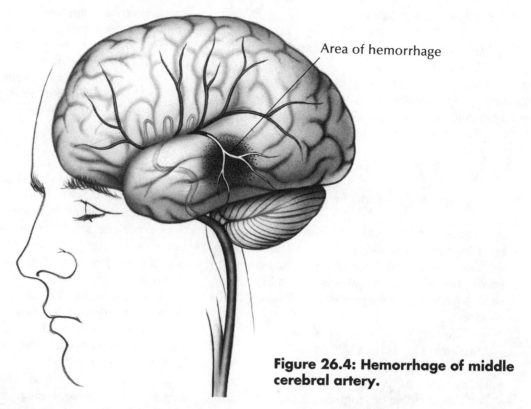

Area of hemorrhage

Figure 26.4: Hemorrhage of middle cerebral artery.

too small to permit its passage. Tissue downstream of the blockage is deprived of blood, resulting in stroke. Emboli may consist of blood clot fragments, clumps of platelets, fibrin, cholesterol, fat, or foreign matter.

• **Hemorrhage.** Results from a rupture of an intracranial blood vessel. Blood erupts at high pressure into the soft brain tissue or spaces surrounding the brain. Normal brain cells may be destroyed, and the presence of blood often results in severe headache, lethargy, or coma. When the blood ruptures primarily into spaces around the brain, the stroke is termed a subarachnoid hemorrhage. Rupture into the brain substance itself is termed an intracerebral, or intraparenchymal, hemorrhage. A blood vessel may burst as a result of high blood pressure or rupture of an aneurysm, a thin-walled balloon-like pocket that forms at a weak point in the wall of a cerebral artery.

DIAGNOSIS

The diagnosis of stroke is made after neurological examination and brain imaging. The patient experiences the sudden onset of a neurological problem attributable to dysfunction in a single location in the central nervous system. The symptoms depend on the artery involved and the brain area cut off from its blood supply. Strokes in brain areas supplied by the carotid artery or its branches commonly affect vision, cause aphasia (the inability to use language properly), partial blindness, hemiparesis (partial or complete paralysis of the face, arm, and leg), and/or loss of sensation. The hemiparesis

and sensory disturbance occur on the side of the body opposite the affected brain area. Strokes that involve the vertebral circulation may produce some combination of double vision, slurred speech, incoordination, difficulty swallowing, and various patterns of weakness or sensory loss that may involve parts of the body.

Following a neurological examination, brain imaging (usually a CT scan) determines if the stroke is due to vascular blockage or hemorrhage. A CT scan is the preferred imaging technique for detecting small amounts of bleeding quickly. Other diagnostic steps include evaluation of heart function (with an electrocardiogram and an echocardiogram), blood tests for coagulation disorders and inflammatory diseases, and a follow-up CT scan or MRI study to check changes from the initial findings. Some cases may require a cerebral angiogram if vasculitis, arterial dissection, aneurysm, venous thrombosis, or a vascular malformation is suspected. In other cases, a spinal tap is indicated. (For more information on these circulatory problems, see chapter 16, Heart and Blood Vessel Diseases.)

Significant risk factors for stroke include high blood pressure, diabetes mellitus, coronary artery disease, irregular heartbeat (especially atrial defibrillation), or a blood coagulation disorder. A stroke may be preceded by a warning sign—a brief episode of neurological impairment called a transient ischemic attack (TIA). (Ischemia is insufficient blood circulation.) As the name implies, transient ischemic attacks are only temporary (usually lasting from minutes to a few hours), and therapy must be started quickly to forestall a full-scale stroke and allow time to determine the cause of the TIA.

TREATMENT

Medications can help degrade blood clots (thrombi) or minimize platelet clumps forming in narrow blood vessels or the heart. Aspirin is a potent inhibitor of platelet aggregation, while warfarin (Coumadin) and heparin are widely prescribed anticoagulants that block some of the steps in the clotting process.

After a stroke, physical, occupational, and speech therapies help victims regain control of their bodies: Almost everyone recovers some degree of lost function, and many people make a full recovery. In general, disability that persists beyond 2 weeks without any improvement is more likely to be permanent. During the rehabilitation phase of treatment, the medical program also includes recommendations designed to reduce the risk of further stroke. (For more information, see chapter 16, Heart and Blood Vessel Diseases.)

Surgical treatment of blockage (usually in the carotid artery) is a procedure known as endarterectomy. A previously used surgical technique called bypass surgery involved connecting superficial arteries in the scalp directly to intracranial vessels. This has recently been proven ineffective for most stroke victims. In cases of hemorrhage due to an aneurysm, surgery may repair the tear and prevent further bleeding.

PREVENTION

Prevention of stroke preserves function much more effectively than treatment after it occurs. The most important preventive measures include:

- Control of blood pressure
- Weight reduction
- Quitting smoking
- Low-fat diet (see the chapter on nutrition)
- Exercise (a moderate walking program may reduce your chance of stroke)
- Recognition and early treatment of transient ischemic attacks (may interrupt the progression to a full-blown stroke)
- Annual check-up for an irregular heartbeat or other heart problems

MALE/FEMALE DIFFERENCES

The incidence of stroke is about 19 percent higher for males than for females; for males under age 65, the gender difference is even higher. However, about 87,000 women die of strokes each year, compared to about 57,000 male deaths, perhaps because women tend to live longer than men, and the risk of a fatal stroke increases with age.

PARKINSON'S DISEASE

DEFINITION

Parkinson's disease, sometimes called "shaking palsy," is a movement disorder characterized by progressive tremor at rest, stiff limbs and trunk (rigidity), slow movements (akinesia), quiet voice (hypophonia), loss of facial expression ("masked" face), loss of postural control that leads to frequent falls, and other symptoms.

CAUSE

The disease results from the deficiency of dopamine, a chemical vital to the transmission of nerve impulses in the basal ganglia. The basal ganglia, deep in the cerebral hemispheres, help regulate smooth, rapid movements of the limbs and other parts of the body. Within the basal ganglia, the neurotransmitters dopamine and acetylcholine normally operate in a chemical balance that enables nerve cells to relay accurate messages to each other. A dopamine deficiency disturbs this balance, allowing excessive acetylcholine activity.

DIAGNOSIS

Early symptoms of this disorder include diminished blinking and reduced spontaneity of facial expression, stiff postures, loss of ease in changing positions (such as attempting to sit or stand), and a tendency to remain in a single position for unusually long periods of time. A shaking tremor of the hands usually brings a Parkinson's disease sufferer to a physician. A neurologist often documents the signs of the disease and excludes other possible causes. The diagnosis of Parkinson's disease is often confirmed when medications that increase the level of dopamine alleviate symptoms.

TREATMENT

One goal of treatment is to restore the balance between dopamine and acetylcholine neurotransmission via medication. Most patients are now given L-dopa (Sinemet), a compound the body converts into additional dopamine. Other drugs, such as bromocriptine, that simulate the action of dopamine may also be prescribed.

At the same time as L-dopa is administered, other drug therapy may be used to counter the relative excess of acetylcholine. The most common of these agents are trihexyphenidyl (Artane) and benztropine mesylate (Cogentin). Early in the disease, the medication selegiline or deprenyl (Eldepryl) may improve symptoms by blocking dopamine breakdown. In recent experiments, researchers have attempted to restore normal biochemical and neurological function by transplanting tissue capable of producing dopamine into the brain.

Despite treatment, this disease is slowly progressive. The severity of symptoms at any time is directly related to the degree of dopamine deficiency. Nonetheless, drug treatments have substantially improved the functional capacity and survival time of patients with this disorder.

PREVENTION

There are no known controllable risk factors that reliably prevent the development of Parkinson's disease. However, avoiding activities that cause repeated head trauma (such as boxing) may prevent the development of Parkinson *syndrome,* in which the patient exhibits many of the symptoms of Parkinson's disease but shows no decrease in dopamine levels.

HUNTINGTON'S DISEASE

DEFINITION

Huntington's disease is a hereditary, progressive degeneration of the central nervous system.

CAUSE

Symptoms ensue from degeneration of nerve cells in the basal ganglia and cortex of the brain. Researchers do not know what kills these cells, but molecular biologists recently discovered that the abnormal gene linked to this condition is located on the short arm of chromosome 4 (the gene itself has not yet been identified). Huntington's disease is inherited as "autosomal dominant," which means that if one parent is affected, each child has a 50 percent chance of developing the disorder. Symptoms usually appear between ages 35 and 40 and the disease is fatal within 10 to 15 years.

DIAGNOSIS

The most striking sign of the disease is chorea: involuntary, abrupt, rapid, nonpatterned, and uncoordinated random movements of the face, trunk, arms, and legs. The disease also causes psychiatric symptoms and mental deterioration. Genetic research has created a blood test designed to identify individuals carrying the gene for the disease. The test has been administered to consenting adult patients for help in making family-planning decisions, but concerns about the test's reliability and confidentiality as well as ethical questions have kept it from being given to children or pregnant women.

TREATMENT

In the early stages of the disease, antipsychotic medication such as haloperidol (Haldol) or chlorpromazine (Thorazine) may be helpful because of their tranquilizing effects. Other medications used in an attempt to control the movement disorder include tetrabenazine and propranolol (Inderal and others) for tremor.

EPILEPSY

DEFINITION

Contrary to popular belief, epilepsy is not a specific disease, but a group of symptoms caused by many different conditions. These conditions all involve the tendency to excessive electrical excitability of the brain. This results in electrical discharges that are followed by sudden, recurrent, and transient changes of mental function or body movement. Common manifestations of epilepsy include impairment or loss of consciousness and muscle spasms or other involuntary motion.

The general categories of seizures are:

- **Generalized seizures:** seem to affect all of the brain from the outset.
- **Focal (partial) seizures:** begin locally in a part of the brain. When focal seizures spread to involve all of the brain, they are called secondarily generalized seizures.

The clinical pattern of attacks can be used to classify the specific types of epilepsy.

Absence, or Petit Mal, Seizures: short and generalized, lasting only a few seconds, beginning and ending abruptly. The manifestations include brief lapses of consciousness during which the person stares ahead and sometimes rhythmically twitches the eyelids or face muscles. Whatever activity or behavior is interrupted by the seizure can resume immediately when the seizure ceases. These brief seizures may occur up to several hundred times daily, are most common in children after the age of 2, and rarely begin after age 20. They may also stop after childhood.

Tonic-Clonic, or Grand Mal, Seizure: the most familiar form of generalized convulsion. Characterized by a sudden and complete loss of consciousness, the person falls and the arms and legs stiffen (the tonic phase), before beginning a rhythmic jerking (the clonic phase). A high-pitched cry may be heard at the outset of the fit as a result of air being forced through the vocal cords. The victim may bite the tongue and be incontinent. These events are swift—occurring within 2 minutes—followed by a more relaxed state of unconsciousness for another minute or so. Afterward, the patient will be confused, sleepy, and uncooperative for 15 minutes to several hours before full recovery.

Complex Partial Seizures, or Psychomotor Attacks: usually a consequence of electrical discharges involving the temporal lobe of the brain and varying considerably in their manifestations. Often the person experiences a warning, known as an aura, caused by the onset of seizure activity. The aura may be expressed as a disquieting sense that something is about to happen, or as fear, an unpleasant smell, abdominal sensation, or distortion in perception. Following the aura, consciousness is depressed, speech ceases, and the person performs automatisms—automatic movements such as chewing, repetitive swallowing, fidgeting of the hands, or purposeless moving from place to place. After the attack, the person suffers momentary confusion and cannot remember details of the episode.

Simple Partial Seizures: caused by seizure discharges affecting sections of the motor or sensory areas of the brain. In Jacksonian seizures (named for John Hughlings Jackson, the great English neurologist who first described them), hand or facial muscles on the side of the body opposite to the side of the brain showing abnormal electrical activity begin jerking movements. Nerve fibers controlling one side of the body originate on the opposite side of the brain and cross to the other side as they traverse the brain stem and extend into the body.)

CAUSE

Research has not disclosed why neurons discharge excessively, although some people apparently inherit a predisposition to develop a form of epilepsy. In others, a head injury scars in the brain are associated with seizures. Brain tumors and strokes also account for a small number of cases. But in half the people with chronic epilepsy, the cause is unknown. In these individuals, seizures typically begin early in life, usually before the age of 20, and continue for many years.

DIAGNOSIS

People with epilepsy need a careful physical examination by a neurologist, including a detailed seizure history. An electroencephalogram (EEG), measuring the electrical activity of the brain, is done in every case to document and define the nature of the electrical disturbance. Both a computed tomographic (CT) brain scan and magnetic resonance imaging (MRI) can provide useful information about the brain. (See "Brain Tumors" in this chapter.) The patient may also undergo blood tests and a lumbar puncture to obtain cerebrospinal fluid for analysis.

TREATMENT

Drugs. The vast majority of patients must take anticonvulsant drugs to control their condition. In general, carbamazepine (Tegretol), phenytoin (Dilantin), or phenobarbital is prescribed for partial and generalized tonic-clonic seizures, while valproate (Depakote) or ethosuximide (Zarontin) is appropriate for absence attacks. Several new drugs are undergoing clinical testing, and approval for use is anticipated. One recently approved drug, sabapentin (Neurotonin), is indicated for simple and complex partial seizures, or secondarily generalized seizures. Treatment with these drugs is tailored to each individual, and sometimes combinations of these medications (as well as others) are necessary.

Surgical Treatment. Some people whose seizures cannot be controlled with medication find relief after surgical removal of abnormal tissue initiating the seizure activity. Before surgery, a team of neurologists, surgeons, psychologists, radiologists, and technologists evaluate the patient's condition and define the location of abnormal tissue. The goal is to minimize risk to healthy regions of the brain during surgery.

Lifestyle Changes. Epilepsy is a chronic illness that requires accommodations in lifestyle even though medication allows the vast majority of people with epilepsy to live normal lives. Children can participate in sports with only minimal restrictions. Safety through careful supervision is still necessary. Adults can continue working, although those with active seizures must not drive, work at exposed heights, or operate dangerous machinery. Driving restrictions may not be necessary if someone with epilepsy demonstrates an extended period of seizure control through treatment. (Additional information about available services, education, and employment is available from the Epilepsy Foundation of America, listed in appendix B, Directory of Health Organizations and Resources.)

MULTIPLE SCLEROSIS

DEFINITION

Multiple sclerosis (MS) is a disease that destroys myelin, an insulating material that coats nerve fibers and is necessary for normal electrical conduction in the nervous system. As a result of this disease, an electrical short circuit inhibits normal electrical impulses from being conveyed by the nerves. Symptoms depend upon where in the brain or spinal cord the myelin is destroyed. Myelin has some regenerative ability. In MS, repeated incidents of inflammation cause scarring (sclerosis) and permanent abnormal function.

CAUSE

The cause of this disease is unknown. Evidence suggests it is caused by an autoimmune reaction because researchers have discovered antibodies and white blood cells that are active against myelin. Some researchers suspect a virus triggers this pathological immune response.

DIAGNOSIS

The diagnosis of multiple sclerosis depends upon the patient's history of disease, neurological examination, and/or other tests. There are no typical clinical findings in multiple sclerosis because almost any area of the central nervous system that contains myelin may be affected. MS sufferers usually have complaints that indicate malfunction in several different places in the CNS. Often, these problems appear and then vanish without any clear instigating factors. Common symptoms include:

- Loss of vision in one eye or double vision
- Loss of coordination and trembling of a hand
- Instability in walking and spasticity
- Loss of bladder control (incontinence or inability to void)
- Peculiar, spontaneous, nerve sensations such as a pins-and-needles feeling over part of the body (paresthesias)

In the early stages of MS, there may be only occasional symptoms. A physical examination at this time may appear to be completely normal and the patient's complaints dismissed as "psychosomatic" or "hysterical." As time passes, the recovery between attacks becomes less and less complete, leaving people progressively disabled.

Confirmatory tests include an MRI scan to search for lesions that indicate myelin destruction, spinal taps to examine cerebrospinal fluid and evoked potential studies to demonstrate dysfunction in CNS nerve pathways.

TREATMENT

While there is no cure for MS, the severity of attacks may be lessened by drugs that suppress inflammation (prednisone and ACTH) or blunt immune response (cyclophosphamide). Beta-interferon (Beta-seron) has been approved to treat a particular form of multiple sclerosis: Administered consistently even during remission, it slows the disease's progression and reduces the frequency of attacks. Beta-interferon is less effective in the steadily progressive form of MS. Physical therapy and rehabilitation are important in controlling symptoms and adapting to disability.

BRAIN TUMORS

The two major categories of brain tumor are: primary (those that develop in the brain) and metastatic (those originating elsewhere in the body but spreading to the brain secondarily). Both classifications include many different types of tumors, each with a unique prognosis and individualized treatment.

Almost nothing is known about the causes of primary brain tumors. While the prognosis for these tumors is usually bleak, some tumors can be cured. Except in rare conditions, hereditary factors do not appear to play a significant role.

DIAGNOSIS

Brain tumors can occur at any age and cause greatly diverse symptoms relatively independent of the exact tumor type. When the tumor increases pressure on the brain within the skull, victims may suffer headache, blurred vision, vomiting, and mental dulling. Localized signs of brain dysfunction may occur when a tumor destroys or compromises areas of the brain that regulate specific functions, such as language ability or motor control.

Laboratory tests can determine the location, type, and extent of a brain tumor. These tests are also used to rule out other diseases that cause many of the same symptoms, such as stroke, subdural hematoma (a hemorrhage beneath the outer meninges usually caused by head trauma), and infections. There is universal agreement that computerized imaging of the brain using either x-rays or magnetic resonance of brain molecules is the most valuable laboratory aid.

Computerized tomography (CT) uses a computer to reconstruct cross-sectional images of the brain, depicting both normal and abnormal structures. CT images can be enhanced by injecting a contrast agent into the bloodstream, which concentrates in or outlines some tumors. CT is relatively fast and can be used for patients who require ventilator support (or who have metallic prostheses). MRI reconstructs pictures of brain structures from a complex analysis of the energy state and magnetic fields of brain tissue molecules. The brain images created by MRI are similar to those of CT but may display structures in more detail. Because MRI creates an image based on magnetic properties, it more specifically identifies certain brain tumors than CT (although in certain instances CT is preferable). Other diagnostic tests include electroencephalography (EEG), which measures the electrical activity of the brain and assists in the location of seizure activity or tumors, and cerebral angiography, an x-ray examination of the cranial blood vessels able to define the blood supply of a tumor.

TREATMENT

Treatment of a tumor depends on the type, location, size, and whether it is benign or malignant. Skilled neurosurgeons can often completely remove benign tumors. For malignant brain tumors, surgery to remove as much of the tumor as possible to relieve pressure may precede radiation treatment. Researchers are still investigating the usefulness of chemotherapy in the treatment of malignant primary brain tumors.

ENCEPHALITIS

DEFINITION

Encephalitis is brain tissue inflammation.

CAUSE

Encephalitis most often results from a primary viral infection of the brain, or from the spread to the brain of an existing systemic viral infection, such as measles or mumps. In some cases, the brain may be infected without evidence of infection elsewhere in the body.

Encephalitis caused by the herpes simplex virus is a common and dangerous type. Sometimes fatal, herpes encephalitis begins abruptly and can cause seizures, mental changes, and rapid onset of coma. For a more complete discussion of diagnosis and treatment, see chapter 18.

MENINGITIS

DEFINITION

Meningitis is an inflammation of the meninges, the membranes covering the brain and spinal cord.

CAUSE

Viruses are the most common infectious agents, but bacterial infections also occur. In general, viral meningitis is more serious than bacterial meningitis. For a more detailed discussion of diagnosis and treatment, see chapter 18.

CEREBRAL PALSY AND RELATED MENTAL RETARDATION

DEFINITION

Cerebral palsy is impairment of motor function caused by brain damage in late pregnancy or just after birth—a period in which a child's brain is especially vulnerable to injury because nerve pathways are developing. When learning and reasoning functions are more severely affected, mental retardation may result. These disorders are termed static rather than progressive because they result from an injury that does not grow worse over time.

CAUSE

Cerebral palsy and related mental retardation result from a number of conditions, including:

- Inadequate blood or oxygen supply to the fetus
- Fetal infection
- Marked prematurity with intracranial bleeding
- Trauma during delivery
- Breech delivery
- Difficult and prolonged labor
- Multiple births

There are three types of cerebral palsy—spastic, dyskinetic, and ataxic—classified according to their major clinical signs. Two, or even all three, of these types may appear together and all three forms of cerebral palsy may occur with or without any degree of mental retardation. Although cerebral palsy is not progressive, the pattern of disability may change as the child matures, or in response to treatment.

Spastic Cerebral Palsy: may be characterized by

- Hemiparesis: partial paralysis of the arm and leg on one side
- Tetraparesis: partial but relatively equal paralysis of all four limbs
- Diparesis: partial paralysis of both legs with minimal or no apparent involvement of the arms

Besides being weak, spastic limbs caused by a birth injury may be thinner and smaller than normal extremities.

Dyskinetic Cerebral Palsy: characterized by abnormal involuntary movements such as writhing, twisting, or twitching of the limbs.

Ataxic Cerebral Palsy: uncommon and rarely the sole symptom of disability. Ataxia (lack or loss of control of skilled voluntary movements) can result from metabolic diseases such as phenylketonuria (PKU), a genetic disorder resulting from a deficiency of enzymes needed to digest certain protein components, or tumors. These conditions must be ruled out before a definitive diagnosis is made.

TREATMENT

Treatment of cerebral palsy and mental retardation is difficult because the underlying birth injury is irreversible. Motor function can be improved if treatment begins early. While no consensus exists about the best treatment methods, the goals of therapy are universally accepted: improvement of function, control of epileptic seizures if present, and guidance for parents to choose the most appropriate place and kind of education for children with palsy.

Therapy often utilizes physical and occupational therapy, speech therapy, and sometimes drugs to reduce spasticity. Failure to treat a spastic child may result in fixed joint and limb deformities and even more severe functional disability. School placement is especially critical; the primary criterion for placement should be the child's intellectual potential, not the physical limitations.

PREVENTION

Proper prenatal and obstetrical care could decrease the frequency of cerebral palsy and mental retardation by reducing the number of premature births.

ATTENTION DEFICIT HYPERACTIVITY DISORDER

DEFINITION

Children with attention deficit disorder (ADHD) have problems focusing their attention and learning new concepts, and frequently suffer impaired visual/spatial coordination. This condition, possibly related to cerebral palsy and retardation, is sometimes called minimal brain dysfunction or hyperactivity. For a more detailed discussion, see chapter 33.

TAY-SACHS DISEASE

DEFINITION

Tay-Sachs disease is a progressive genetic enzyme deficiency in infants and young children that results in neurological deterioration and leads to an early death.

CAUSE

The disease is caused by an abnormal gene sequence on chromosome 15 that occurs most often in individuals of Ashkenazi Jewish background. The abnormal gene causes a deficiency of an important enzyme (hexosaminidase), the loss of which permits abnormal accumulation in nerve cells of a destructive substance called GM2-ganglioside.

DIAGNOSIS

Tay-Sachs disease appears clinically most often at 5 or 6 months of age. A previously healthy baby begins to show signs of developmental regression, loss of vision, and myoclonus (sudden jerks of the limbs or whole body) in response to sudden sounds or otherwise being startled.

The child deteriorates to a vegetative state by the second year, and death usually occurs before age 4 or 5.

PREVENTION

Simple blood tests before pregnancy can determine whether a couple is at risk of having a child with Tay-Sachs. This prenatal carrier screening has made Tay-Sachs disease increasingly rare.

TREATMENT

Although there is currently no effective therapy for Tay-Sachs and similar diseases, advances in molecular genetics and increased knowledge about the biochemical deficiencies that produce these disorders give hope for future therapy or prevention.

NERVE DISORDERS

BELL'S PALSY

DEFINITION

Bell's palsy is the term used to describe paralysis of muscles on one side of the face.

CAUSE

The paralysis results from temporary damage to the facial nerve (the seventh cranial nerve). The severity of muscle paralysis depends on the extent of nerve damage. Although the cause is unknown, a viral infection is suspected. The facial nerve passes through a narrow hole (foramen) in the skull and it is thought that inflammation at this point compresses and blocks function of the nerve. The disorder occurs at all ages, but is most frequent between 30 and 60.

DIAGNOSIS

Bell's palsy occurs suddenly and is often first noticed when the patient wakes up and looks in the mirror. Normally there is no pain, but there may be a slight discomfort in the region of the jaw or behind the ear. Features of the syndrome include sagging of the muscles of the lower half of the face on one side. In mild cases, the facial weakness is noted only when the patient smiles. Sometimes, the eye cannot be fully closed on the affected side; when this is attempted, the eye elevates. Abnormal tearing from the eye may result when the weakened eyelid can no longer funnel tears into the lacrimal ducts.

Examination by a neurologist is important to exclude the possibility of injury to other nerves or the central nervous system. In some cases, electrophysiologic testing of facial nerve function may locate a lesion. Although this test is not required for diagnosis, it can offer a more detailed evaluation of the condition if weakness persists and recovery has not begun in 6 or more months.

TREATMENT

Fortunately, 90 percent of patients with Bell's palsy recover completely, or nearly completely, without treatment. Some physicians prescribe prednisone (a cortisone substance) to reduce inflammation if the diagnosis is made within the first 48 hours. Other physicians believe this is unnecessary. If eyelid function is compromised, the eye must be covered to prevent drying or inadvertent injury from foreign objects. (For more information, see chapter 31, Diseases of the Ear, Nose, and Throat.)

TRIGEMINAL NEURALGIA

DEFINITION

Trigeminal neuralgia (tic douloureux), the most frequent of all neuralgias, causes severe, stabbing paroxysmal pain on one side of the face. The condition results from dysfunction of the trigeminal nerve that runs from the brain stem to the face. Attacks of trigeminal neuralgia may be incapacitating and interfere with eating, but it is not fatal and causes no other symptoms.

CAUSE

The cause of this condition is unknown, but the disorder occurs most frequently in middle or old age.

DIAGNOSIS

The cardinal symptom is severe paroxysms of sharp, bulletlike pain in the gums, teeth, and lower face. Often a "trigger"—touching a particular part of the face, chewing, or a particular jaw motion—initiates the pain. In most instances, the pain is present for weeks or months and then ceases spontaneously for a variable period. As the patient grows older, the condition recurs more frequently. Diagnosis is based on the patient's medical history and a thorough examination that rules out other conditions.

TREATMENT

The drug carbamazepine (Tegretol), which stabilizes irritable nerve membranes, is effective for many individuals. Other useful medicines include phenytoin (Dilantin) and amitriptyline (Elavil). In some intractable cases, surgery on the nerve is required for pain relief.

PERIPHERAL NEUROPATHY

DEFINITION

Diseases that selectively damage the peripheral nerves without affecting the brain and spinal cord are termed peripheral neuropathy. The peripheral nervous system's motor nerves convey the brain's commands to the muscles of the body while the sensory nerves relay sensory information back to the brain. Peripheral neuropathy may involve either a single nerve (called mononeuropathy or mononeuritis) or many nerves and their terminal endings (called polyneuropathy).

CAUSE

Many diseases cause peripheral neuropathy. In the United States the most frequent causes include diabetes, chronic alcoholism, and malnutrition; leprosy is the most common cause throughout the rest of the world. The disorder is also associated with cancer and prolonged exposure to various toxic chemicals such as arsenic, mercury, and lead.

DIAGNOSIS

Serial examinations by a neurologist over time can be essential to diagnose the disease and suggest a prognosis. Symptoms of polyneuropathy usually begin gradually, over the course of a few months. Initially, numbness in the hands and feet (sometimes called a "stocking-glove distribution") is accompanied by a prickly pins-and-needles feeling, called paresthesia, in the same body areas. If the condition is untreated, loss of sensation grows increasingly severe and spreads up the legs and forearms. As sensory impairment worsens, the muscles of the feet, ankles, fingers, and hands weaken, and sometimes the skin becomes so sensitive that the merest touch causes pain. Diagnostic testing called nerve conduction studies, electromyography, or nerve/muscle biopsy may provide crucial information.

TREATMENT

Although there is no specific medical or surgical therapy to regenerate damaged nerves, proper treatment of the underlying disease may slow the disorder's progress.

CARPAL TUNNEL SYNDROME

DEFINITION

This common form of mononeuropathy causes pain and numbness in the fingers. The problem originates in a branch of the forearm's median nerve that is compressed as it passes through the tunnel formed by the wrist bones (carpals) and a ligament that lies just under the skin (see figure 26.5). Carpal tunnel syndrome occurs most often in middle age.

CAUSE

The syndrome is usually due to arthritis or other disorders affecting bones and ligaments or causing inflammation. Repetitive wrist motion such as typing on a computer keyboard can also cause the condition. Sometimes fluid accumulation (edema) or sudden weight gain (such as occurs in pregnancy) may also squeeze the nerve.

DIAGNOSIS

Initially intermittent, the symptoms eventually become constant. Numbness and tingling begin in the thumb and first two fingers; then the hand, and sometimes the whole arm, becomes painful. The pain may be severe enough to interrupt sleep. Gradual weakness and wasting of the thumb muscles can occur if the condition is not treated.

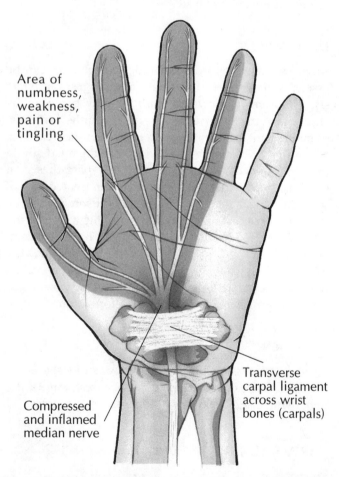

Area of numbness, weakness, pain or tingling

Compressed and inflamed median nerve

Transverse carpal ligament across wrist bones (carpals)

Figure 26.5: Repetitive hand motions, such as those used in typing, can cause Carpal Tunnel Syndrome, which is characterized by debilitating pain, numbness, or tingling in the hands.

MALE/FEMALE DIFFERENCES

For unknown reasons the syndrome affects more women than men.

PREVENTION

Weight loss can help alleviate the condition. Wrist rests for typists may help reduce the stress of using a keyboard.

TREATMENT

Relatively mild symptoms may be relieved by a wrist splint. Control of edema (usually with diuretics) and treatment of arthritis with aspirin or other antinflammatory medication may also decrease pain and numbness.

Surgical Treatment. If the symptoms progress despite medication or splinting (and especially if weakness appears) a simple surgical procedure cuts the ligament at the wrist and relieves pressure on the nerve.

GUILLAIN-BARRÉ SYNDROME

DEFINITION

The Guillain-Barré syndrome causes symmetric weakness in the limbs, sometimes progressing to total body paralysis. This condition usually occurs 1 to 2 weeks after a mild viral infection such as a sore throat, bronchitis, or flu.

CAUSE

The illness results from nerve inflammation and myelin destruction similar to that seen in multiple sclerosis, but while multiple sclerosis repeatedly attacks the central nervous system, Guillain-Barré syndrome affects the peripheral nerves and rarely recurs. The nerve damage is thought to be caused by an abnormal immune reaction directed against the myelin of the peripheral nervous system.

DIAGNOSIS

Weakness of the limbs develops over a few days, and the facial muscles may be paralyzed as well, making it impossible to swallow normally. Diagnosis is made by observation of these clinical features, characteristic changes in cerebrospinal fluid, and electromyography (EMG), electrical studies of the peripheral nerves and muscles.

TREATMENT

In severe cases, paralysis of respiratory muscles requires a tracheostomy and mechanical ventilation to maintain breathing. With intensive medical treatment and support, the majority of patients recover, but about one-third suffer residual weakness.

··

MUSCULAR DYSTROPHY AND OTHER MUSCLE DISEASES

Muscular dystrophy (MD) is a general term describing several inherited muscle diseases that cause progressive weakness and disability. The most common type is Duchenne dystrophy. Other relatively common types of MD are facioscapulohumeral, limb-girdle, and myotonic.

DUCHENNE DYSTROPHY

The most severe and probably most well-known type of MD. This condition almost invariably strikes children before age 3. Progressive disease usually confines its victims to wheelchairs by the teenage years.

CAUSE

Duchenne dystrophy is inherited. The genetic abnormality is located on a segment of the X-chromosome (called Xp21) that normally makes a muscle protein called dystrophin, which is absent in patients with Duchenne dystrophy.

DIAGNOSIS

Early manifestations of Duchenne include:

- Toe walking
- Running with excess limb motion and without much forward movement
- Frequent falls and difficulty rising from the ground
- Large (hypertrophic) calves
- Unusually straight posture

Later in the course of the disease, muscle wasting, a waddling gait, and curved posture also become evident.

In MD victims tests reveal elevated levels of muscle enzymes in the blood (due to degeneration of muscle). This may be found at birth. The best-known enzyme test is the one for creatine kinase (CPK). Biopsies of muscle tissue may show changes in the muscle characteristic of the disease.

MALE/FEMALE DIFFERENCES

Duchenne dystrophy is a sex-linked and recessive genetic disorder: Consequently, although women are carriers

of the gene, manifestation of the disorder is confined to males.

TREATMENT

There is no effective treatment, but gene therapy is being studied.

PREVENTION

Prenatal genetic counseling is an important consideration for women whose brothers or maternal uncles were victims of this condition.

Facioscapulohumeral Dystrophy: appears in adolescence, causing weakness of the face and arms. The illness progresses very slowly and, because the legs are only mildly affected, patients maintain the ability to walk.

Limb-Girdle Dystrophy: probably not a distinct disease, but thought to be a group of different muscle diseases that all cause weakness of the upper legs and arms.

Myotonic Dystrophy: unlike the other dystrophies, not only causes muscle weakness and wasting but also affects several other organ systems, including the eyes (cataract formation), the heart, and testes. The disorder's striking feature is myotonia, the failure of muscles to relax normally after sudden, vigorous use. The genetic abnormality causing myotonic dystrophy is now known to reside on chromosome 19.

POLYMYOSITIS

DEFINITION

Polymyositis is a muscle inflammatory disease causing fatigue and weakness.

CAUSE

Believed to be an autoimmune reaction, this disease may either occur by itself, in association with other autoimmune diseases such as systemic lupus erythematosus or rheumatoid arthritis, or with characteristic skin changes (called dermatomyositis). In older patients, especially men, polymyositis is often linked to cancer for unknown reasons.

DIAGNOSIS

Symptoms include weakness, especially of the shoulder and hip muscles, and aching and tender muscles. Patients have difficulty lifting, raising their arms overhead, and climbing stairs. In dermatomyositis, there is a characteristic purplish rash over the face (mainly nose and cheeks) and upper chest, with discoloration and swelling of the eyelids, skin around the nails, and skin overlying knuckles, elbows, and knees.

Medical evaluation must rule out the possibility of unrecognized malignancy.

TREATMENT

Steroid drugs (prednisone) are effective against this condition, but underlying or associated disorders (e.g., cancer or lupus) must also be treated.

MYASTHENIA GRAVIS

DEFINITION

This disease causes fluctuating muscle weakness, especially in muscles controlling eye movements, eye opening, facial mobility, and swallowing. In severe cases, the condition affects all muscles of the body, including those involved with respiration. The severity of weakness can vary from day to day or even in the course of a single day.

CAUSE

The disease is caused by a defect in neuromuscular transmission, in which the chemical signal between motor nerves and muscles is improperly transmitted. Antibodies interfere with muscle membrane receptors' response to acetylcholine, the neurotransmitter chemical released by motor nerve endings. The origin of these disruptive antibodies is unknown, but the thymus gland, located in the neck just under the sternum (breastbone), seems to be implicated in their production.

DIAGNOSIS

The earliest symptoms are usually double vision, drooping eyelids, inability to smile, slurred speech, and difficulty swallowing. Diagnosis depends on the distribution of weakness and the patient's medical history, which characteristically includes episodes of weakness during exertion followed by a relatively rapid recovery. The patient may also be given the tensilon test (if a drug that increases the strength of neuromuscular transmission improves the patient's condition, the disease is probably present). Additionally, patients may undergo electrophysiologic testing.

TREATMENT

Treatments include suppression of antibody formation or reduction of antibody concentration with steroids or other immunosuppressive drugs, as well as a special blood-filtering process called plasmapheresis. Another approach increases the amount of acetylcholine available to muscle receptors with enzyme-inhibiting drugs called anticholinesterases (pyrrdostigmine or Mestinon) and surgical removal of the thymus gland (thymectomy).

AMYOTROPHIC LATERAL SCLEROSIS (ALS)

DEFINITION

Sometimes called Lou Gehrig's disease after a famous patient, ALS is a disease of middle or late life that causes muscle weakness from progressive death of the nerve cells that control voluntary movement.

CAUSE

The cause is unknown.

DIAGNOSIS

Initial symptoms differ from person to person, but as the disease progresses every victim suffers difficulty walking due to leg weakness or stiffness, clumsiness of the hands, slurred speech, and difficulty swallowing. The muscles of the arms and legs waste away, and twitching of muscles (called fasciculations) may be observed under the skin (see figure 26.6). Eventually, walking is impossible, the hands become useless, and death occurs after respiratory muscles lose the strength to maintain breathing. Mental facilities remain normal throughout the course of the disease.

Diagnosis is made by assessing the patient's history, constellation of symptoms, and the exclusion of other causes. There is no specific medical test for ALS.

TREATMENT

No effective treatment presently exists for this condition. It is invariably fatal.

SLEEP DISORDERS

In the past 20 years, the recognition, understanding, and treatment of sleep disorders have advanced greatly. Consequently, an entire new field has emerged called chronobiology—the study of biological rhythms such as the wake-sleep cycle. Excessive daytime sleepiness is one of the most common complaints indicative of a sleep disorder. Despite getting nighttime sleep, sufferers complain of being unable to stay awake while driving a car or eating. The condition may cause injury or serious disruption of work efficiency, or interfere with leisure and family time. The two most frequently encountered medical disorders producing pathological somnolence are narcolepsy and sleep apnea (sometimes called the hypersomnia sleep apnea syndrome).

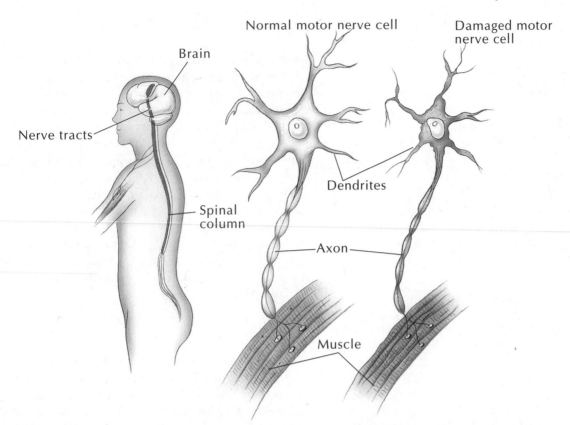

Figure 26.6: Amyotrophic lateral sclerosis (ALS), also known as Lou Gehrig's disease, causes degeneration of nerve cells connected to the brain that control voluntary motor functions.

NARCOLEPSY

DEFINITION

Narcolepsy is a sleep disorder whose victims are usually subject to falling asleep uncontrollably during the day.

CAUSE

The cause of narcolepsy is unknown.

DIAGNOSIS

Typically beginning in adolescence or early adulthood, this condition's two major symptoms are recurring periods of excessive and uncontrollable daytime sleepiness, and cataplexy (an episode of abrupt, short-duration muscle weakness occurring without loss of consciousness and usually triggered by an emotional reaction such as laughing). Other, less frequent characteristic symptoms include vivid visual hallucinations (especially when falling asleep), sleep paralysis (inability to perform voluntary movement when falling asleep or on awakening), and automatic behavior that cannot be recalled later. Most of these daytime symptoms are related to abnormal episodes of REM (rapid eye movement) sleep that inappropriately occur during the waking state. The diagnosis of narcolepsy can be supported with a characteristic electroencephalograph (EEG) study and other evaluations of sleep patterns.

TREATMENT

Stimulant drugs maintain wakefulness, and compounds such as imipramine (Tofranil) or protriptyline (Vivactil) prevent cataplexy. In some cases, gradual changes in the sleep-wake cycle are helpful.

SLEEP APNEA

DEFINITION

Sleep apnea is a breathing stoppage lasting a moment or longer. Prolonged apnea during sleep may be life-threatening.

CAUSE

Obstruction of the upper airway produces the short episodes of breathing stoppage that characterize apnea. More than half the sufferers are obese, a condition further compromising the normal flow of air. Less than complete obstruction causes loud snoring, and the breathing problem—and lack of air—may frequently wake up the sleep apnea victim during the night.

DIAGNOSIS

Sleep apnea's excessive daytime sleepiness is usually more pervasive and less episodic than the somnolence of narcolepsy. Nighttime symptoms include loud snoring recurring in regular cycles, restless sleep with frequent and brief arousals, and unusual sleep postures. Diagnosis is sometimes aided by audiotapes made of the patient's noisy nighttime breathing. In sleep study laboratories, obstruction of the airwaves may be confirmed by videotaping sleep and with a polysomnagram (a record of the heart, respiratory, and muscular movements while asleep).

MALE/FEMALE DIFFERENCES

For unknown reasons, men are affected 20 times more often than women. Most apnea sufferers are between the ages of 40 and 70.

TREATMENT

No drug has been shown to be consistently effective against apnea. Steps that reduce the airway obstruction and weight reduction often relieve some apnea symptoms. In severe cases, a tracheostomy may be performed to create an opening in the neck that allows breathing to bypass the obstruction.

HOME REMEDIES AND ALTERNATIVE TREATMENT

Some patients claim to have found relief through positive airway pressure (PAP). In this technique, the patient wears a face mask while asleep to create higher air pressure that supposedly helps keep the airway open. PAP's effectiveness is very controversial.

In addition, changing sleep position from the back to the side may decrease the obstruction in the throat and provide relief in sleep apnea. A simple technique to affect sleep posture is to pin a tennis ball to the back of the pajamas to ensure the sleeper lies on the side. Overweight people may benefit from weight reduction.

HEAD AND SPINAL CORD TRAUMA

HEAD INJURY

Head injury, especially from car and motorcycle accidents, is one of the most common causes of accidental injury and death in the United States.

DEFINITION

Head injuries can be divided into 3 major categories:

Closed Head Injury. The skull does not fracture. Brain damage results from bruising or swelling of brain tissue (called contusion), or internal hemorrhage. Injury to the brain is usually less severe than after obvious skull fractures. The mildest form of closed head injuries is a concussion, in which there is brief loss of consciousness at the time of trauma, but no permanent effects.

Depressed Skull Fractures. The outer skull may remain intact, but fragments of underlying bone are pushed down and can compress or lacerate the brain beneath. The degree of damage to the brain can vary greatly.

Compound Fractures. The outer tissues are torn, the skull opened, and the brain tissue exposed. Brain damage is likely.

DIAGNOSIS

The symptoms of a brain injury vary and are directly related to the location and severity of damage. Concussion may be followed by headache, dizziness, and amnesia about events immediately before and after the injury. More serious head injuries may cause speech difficulty, bleeding from the nose or ears, muscular weakness, paralysis, and long periods of altered awareness or coma. Serious injury may also cause convulsive seizures. Sometimes the effects of head injury are completely reversible; in other cases, some degree of neurological impairment may be permanent.

In more than a third of cases, even those with mild head injury, victims suffer a collection of sometimes vague symptoms known as posttraumatic or postconcussive syndrome. These symptoms, which may persist for weeks or longer, include headache, dizziness, insomnia, and such psychological disturbances as irritability, restlessness, inability to concentrate, personality change, and depression.

Anyone who loses consciousness following a head injury should be examined by a doctor. Even if the patient appears normal, a period called the "lucid interval" sometimes obscures a potential, fatal intracranial hemorrhage. Even slight bumps on the head that cause severe head or neck pain should be medically evaluated. More serious injuries producing any of the symptoms described above should be viewed as medical emergencies and the victim taken to a hospital emergency service at once. (For more information on first aid for head injuries, see chapter 14.)

The extent of injury is usually diagnosed by x-rays of the skull and CT scans. Electroencephalograms (EEGs) may also be used to determine the prognosis. (For more information, see chapter 12, Diagnostic Tests and Procedures.)

TREATMENT

Treatment depends on the extent of the injury and may range from bed rest and medical observation for 24 to 48 hours, to surgery and extended postoperative care including physical and occupational therapy.

Following the immediate treatment, the patient must be observed for late complications, including epilepsy and subdural hematoma (a blood clot between the layers of the tissue surrounding the brain), which may develop weeks or even many months later.

Reassurance and support by family members and medical personnel are vital to recovery; psychological counseling may also be necessary.

MALE/FEMALE DIFFERENCES

Head injuries are most common among young adult males because they have a higher rate of automobile accidents, a leading cause of head injury. Motor vehicle accidents cause an estimated 3 million head injuries annually.

PREVENTION

Many head injuries would be preventable if automobile drivers observed speed laws and both passengers and drivers wore seat belts. Motorcyclists and bicyclists should obey traffic laws and always wear helmets.

SPINAL CORD INJURY

DEFINITION

Accidents can stretch, crush, lacerate or sever spinal cords completely; consequently spinal cord injuries almost always result in permanent neurological damage. Today an estimated 150,000 persons in the United States, two-thirds of them under age 35, live with permanent damage caused by spinal cord injury.

The degree of disability caused by spinal cord injury depends not only on severity but also on location, since the brain's control of the area of the body below the injury site is most severely compromised. Injuries to the lumbar or thoracic region (low spinal cord) affect the function of the legs, bladder, and bowels; damage to the cervical end (high spinal cord) impairs control of the arms as well as other parts of the body.

CAUSE

Motor vehicle and motorcycle accidents, falls, and injuries involving sports such as diving, football, and tobogganing are the most frequent causes.

TREATMENT

Further damage can occur if an accident victim is improperly moved. **A patient with known or suspected neck injury should not be transported until the head and spinal column are immobilized and supported in a neutral position by trained emergency personnel.** Recently, some data suggest that high doses of steroids given soon after spinal cord injury improve recovery from spinal cord injury. (For more first-aid information concerning spinal injuries, see chapter 14.) After the patient is stabilized, physical and occupational therapy can help retrain partially paralyzed arm and leg muscles. Rehabilitation may also be necessary to assist with bowel and bladder control and restore sexual function.

Because the care and rehabilitation of people with spine injuries is long and complex, a number of major medical centers have developed separate units where equipment and teams of trained medical personnel specialize in this type of care.

Surgical Treatment. Surgery may be necessary to stabilize the spine or remove bone fragments.

PREVENTION

The number of spinal cord injuries would drop dramatically if more people used common sense in avoiding accidents (see safety tips, chapter 15) and never drove after drinking alcoholic beverages.

SUMMING UP

The brain and other parts of the nervous system control the body's most vital functions and are overwhelmingly complex. But even though these organs are extremely delicate, they are capable of withstanding serious injuries such as stroke, and after illness or accident frequently recover lost function completely. The nervous system is subject to a variety of disorders, including common, usually benign everyday conditions like headache, as well as complex diseases like Parkinson's disease and multiple sclerosis. Diagnosis is a critical step and careful evaluation by a neurologist is often essential. For some diseases, cause, treatment, and prognosis are clearly defined. For others, major advances in diagnostic procedures and medications still fall short of providing a cure.

27
Kidney and Urinary Tract Disorders

JAY I. MELTZER, M.D.

Kidneys have played a crucial role in the emergence of animal life from the sea to the land, allowing creatures to survive on land without dehydrating. While seawater nourishes the body cells of primitive ocean dwellers, inhabitants of dry ground use the kidneys to regulate an internal system of fluids—a kind of internal sea—that provides vital nutrients necessary for survival.

Among the kidney's hundreds of metabolic tasks, some of the most vital still preserve our ocean heritage: control of water balance, maintenance of the mild alkalinity of body fluids, and metabolic waste product removal. While performing these complex tasks, the kidneys are subject to numerous diseases, afflictions that affect 13 million Americans and kill 78,000 each year. Hypertension, which often devastates the kidney, afflicts still more.

But medical knowledge of the kidney now renders doctors capable of saving the life of virtually every kidney disease patient. The federal government recognizes the extraordinary nature of kidney disease by making it a special case under the Medicare/Social Security Law, providing complete care for almost everyone in end-stage renal failure, regardless of age, occupation, or socioeconomic status. The cost is enormous—over $3 billion yearly, primarily used to support chronic hemodialysis (artificial kidney machines) and kidney transplantation. Paradoxically, the very success of these two miracle treatments drives up the cost: Each year the number of patients enlisted and funded by these programs grows because of increased survival.

The large expenses necessary to treat the ravages of kidney disease have spurred prevention efforts. With a little applied knowledge of the kidney, we can all take commonsense measures to prevent kidney disease and keep our kidneys healthy.

KIDNEY ANATOMY

The kidneys receive more blood from the heart than any other organ of the body—almost one-quarter of the volume of every heartbeat goes to the kidneys. A complex system of blood circulation is necessary to handle this massive flow of blood—1½ quarts every minute—through an organ measuring only 4 inches high by 2 inches wide by 1 inch thick and weighing only 5 to 6 ounces. In fact, the blood vessel arrangement within the kidneys is the most complex by far of any in the body, allowing the enormous force of the blood to be moderated and controlled to a precise pressure and flow before it reaches the delicately thin membrane that filters the body fluids and makes urine (see figure 27.1). The glomerular basement membrane is so thin it must be magnified 25,000 times by an electron microscope to be clearly seen, yet it accepts the pressure of the circulating blood, pushing the body fluids through like a sieve as the membrane retains the cells and large protein molecules, and passing all the smaller chemicals in solution. After letting through both the useful and the waste chemicals, the kidney must retrieve most of what has already passed into the urine.

The kidneys' intricate filtering units consist of approximately 1 million nephrons, cuplike receptacles emptying into long, thin tubules lined by special cells with varying functions. Each long tubular unit empties into the center of the kidney, from which urine passes into the ureters and then to the bladder, to be expelled from the body through the urethra.

Every minute, the receptacles of the nephrons—the glomeruli—receive about 4 ounces into the urine's side of the filtering membrane, about 20 percent of the water content of the blood flowing through. As this large volume of "early" urine moves down the tubules, the lining cells begin to recover most of its precious water, nutrients, and salts, relinquishing mainly waste chemicals and retaining as much water as necessary to maintain the body fluids in a concentration similar to the primeval sea.

The nephrons usually reabsorb 99 percent of the water, salt, and vital nutrients initially filtered, an amount that may seem wasteful but which allows the nephrons the leeway for an enormous number of individual adjustments to the many components of our inter-

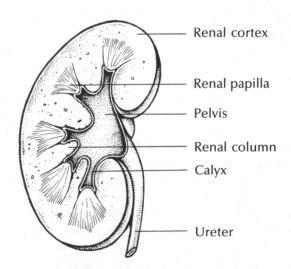

Renal cortex

Renal papilla

Pelvis

Renal column

Calyx

Ureter

Figure 27.1: Cross-sectional view of a normal kidney.

HYPERTENSION AND THE KIDNEY

Hypertension, or high blood pressure, the most common and most easily treated of the diseases affecting the kidneys, ensues only when the kidney's usual regulation of blood volume and blood vessel wall tension fails. The "tension" in hypertension describes the vascular tone of the smooth muscles in the artery and arteriole walls. While nervous tension may temporarily cause the blood pressure to rise—as it does with exertion, heavy mental exercise (such as solving a math problem), or sexual arousal—such transient rises are not harmful.

In a small percentage of cases, another disease or condition such as endocrine gland tumors, hormonal disorders, pregnancy, and birth control pills causes "secondary" hypertension (which is usually curable), but most hypertension is "essential" hypertension of unknown origin and treatable but not curable. Except in very rare cases of "malignant" hypertension, raised blood pressure by itself does no immediate harm and causes no acute symptoms for perhaps 10 to 15 years or more. Damage occurs gradually from years of wear and tear on blood vessel walls, mostly in the heart, brain, and kidneys; consequently, untreated hypertension greatly increases the risk of heart disease, kidney disease, and stroke. (For more information on the diagnosis and treatment of hypertension, see chapter 16, Heart and Blood Vessel Diseases.)

nal fluid, and allowing the kidney to cope with extreme changes in our environment such as lack of food or fluid, stress, or exposure to the elements.

The glomeruli are the tiny filtering units of the kidneys, each no more than 1 millimeter in diameter and forming one segment of a nephron, the basic functional unit of the kidney. (How tiny are these filters? Each of your kidneys, between 4 and 5 inches long, contains about 1 million nephrons.)

The glomerulus consists of a membrane with groups of capillaries on one side and nephron-lining cells on the other. Mesangial cells, which also take part in the body's immune surveillance system, lie in the middle. Specific kidney diseases affect the membrane and the cells in different ways. Although inflammation, scarring, or a decrease in membrane surface area lowers the amount of glomerular filtration, the kidney so effectively compensates that people rarely know they have lost kidney function until only 10 to 20 percent remains. High blood pressure and anemia may develop with increasing frequency after loss of 30 to 50 percent kidney function, but these signs develop so gradually they often produce no symptoms.

Because of its intimate relationship with such a large portion—up to 25 percent—of the circulating blood, the kidney plays the major role in the regulation of blood pressure. The kidney filters need to control large volumes of blood, reducing flow to a precise pressure against the delicate membrane, to protect it from breakage and hemorrhage that would clog the urine.

The key component of the kidney's blood pressure control mechanism operates from the center of the nephron, where a group of specialized cells senses the level of incoming blood pressure and responds by releasing renin, a chemical messenger that circulates to the entire body. (Renin, in turn, causes the blood to generate a chemical—angiotensin—so potent that one part per trillion raises the blood pressure.) If the pressure falls too low, the messenger causes the muscles in all the blood vessel walls to contract ever so slightly, raising blood pressure by narrowing the size of the blood compartment. If the pressure rises too high, the cells make less renin and the vascular compartment tends to relax.

Angiotensin plays a further vital role: It dispatches a separate message to the adrenal gland, an endocrine gland at the top of the kidney, to produce the hormone aldosterone, another chemical messenger. This second messenger circulates back to the kidney tubules, signaling the cells near the end to absorb more salt and water from the urine. This retention of salt and water by the body raises the volume of blood plasma, filling the blood compartment more completely, and raising the blood pressure. This blood pressure increase reduces the release of chemical messengers and allows a new equilibrium. Diseases of the kidney—or any disturbance in the kidney's delicate mechanism—can adversely influence blood pressure, and blood pressure, in turn, may alter kidney function.

INFLAMMATION OF THE KIDNEYS

Kidney inflammation, occurring either in the tubules (the long segments leading into the central urinary stream) or in the glomeruli (the filtering cups), is the most common kidney disease condition. This condition can be acute or chronic.

BACTERIAL PYELONEPHRITIS

DEFINITION

Bacterial pyelonephritis is inflammation of the tubules in the nephrons of the kidney caused by bacterial infection.

CAUSE

Most commonly, this infection is a result of bacteria from outside the body traveling back up the urinary stream through the urethra to the bladder and eventually to the kidneys, in which case it is known as an ascending infection. (Occasionally, the bacterial infection causing pyelonephritis arises elsewhere in the body and travels through the bloodstream to the space between the tubules—the tubulointerstitium.)

The backward flow of urine (reflux) may be caused by an anatomical defect (often inherited) or an obstruction. Reflux results when, as the bladder contracts during urination, the normally tight valve between the bladder and the ureter opens wide, allowing urine to flow in two directions, both out through the urethra (as it should) and back up through the ureters.

This defect is difficult to correct and can lead to repeated infections. Obstructions causing reflux in women commonly take the form of a stricture, or scar tissue formed from urethral infections or inflammation. In young men, such strictures form less often and usually are a consequence of a venereal infection. In older men, the prostate commonly obstructs the flow of urine.

Despite such obstructions, reflux backup into the kidneys is rare, and most urinary infections remain confined to the bladder, where they are less serious. Even severe obstruction by the prostate rarely causes kidney infection unless reflux is encouraged by the insertion of catheters or instruments such as cystoscopes for diagnosis or treatment. The introduction of any foreign body into an area of obstruction risks stimulating infection, which, because of obstruction, is doubly difficult to treat. So all such procedures must be carefully analyzed before being undertaken.

Acute bacterial infection, somewhat common in pregnancy (occurring in about 5 percent of cases), may result from the dilation of ureters and other structures, just as they are in obstruction conditions, although there is no visible obstruction.

DIAGNOSIS

Because the first symptoms of acute bacterial pyelonephritis may be severe: shaking, teeth-chattering chills accompanied by a high fever, and pain in the joints and muscles, kidney disease is often not suspected. The situation may be particularly difficult to diagnose in children, whose high fevers may bring on sudden seizures or a change in mental state, and in the aged, whose fevers may cause confusion and be accompanied by generalized aches and pains. Urinary frequency and discomfort with urination, common in bladder infections, are unusual in kidney infections.

In acute infections, the symptoms develop rapidly, the initial fever followed by possible changes in urine color and then tenderness in the flank. As the kidney grows more inflamed, pain, loss of appetite, headache, and general effects of infection ensue. Unlike the intermittent renal colic pain of kidney stones, this type of kidney pain is continuous, stays in one spot, and is made worse by movement.

While people with chronic pyelonephritis may suffer acute infections, sometimes no symptoms occur, or symptoms are too mild to notice: Hypertension or anemia or symptoms related to renal insufficiency, such as fatigue and nocturia (awakening in the night to urinate), may be the first indication of trouble. Consequently, infectious inflammatory disease may slowly progress undetected over many years until deterioration results in kidney failure and irreversible damage.

The diagnosis of acute pyelonephritis is based on symptoms and a manual examination over the kidney to reveal tenderness indicating inflammation. Microscopic examination of the urine reveals pus cells (white blood corpuscles) and active bacteria in large numbers. Culturing the bacteria and identifying the particular species confirm the diagnosis. While it is usually unnecessary to identify the microorganisms in bladder infections, kidney infections should be identified as precisely as possible and treated aggressively to forestall bacterial invasion of the bloodstream.

Routine urinalysis and cultures detect silent chronic pyelonephritis. When tests are positive, further checking for curable obstructions, stones, or neurologic abnormalities helps prevent chronic disease.

TREATMENT

Complete cure of acute infections is necessary to avoid possible chronic pyelonephritis. Several weeks' worth of antibiotics must be taken as directed by your physician, even if symptoms disappear after a few days. Follow-up urine tests confirm full eradication of the infectious bacteria.

If chronic disease has begun, the patient is treated for renal failure (see "Kidney Failure" later in this chapter).

HOME REMEDIES AND ALTERNATIVE THERAPIES

As a supplement to medical therapy, applying a heating pad to your flank may help ease pain. Drink at least 2 quarts of fluid daily—but no alcoholic beverages—during treatment for acute pyelonephritis.

MALE/FEMALE DIFFERENCES

Women, whose urethras are short and close to the anus, a potential source of bacteria, have four times as many cases of pyelonephritis as men. Women also may be at greater risk during pregnancy.

NONBACTERIAL TUBULOINTERSTITIAL DISEASE

DEFINITION

Nonbacterial tubulointerstitial disease, or interstitial nephritis, is inflammation of the nephrons in the area between the tubules due to injury to the tubules themselves. As the injury stimulates inflammatory cells locally, it also attracts others from the rich surrounding blood supply. The inflammation swells the kidney and, if severe, may impair kidney function and result in acute renal failure.

CAUSE

Drug reactions are the most common cause of acute interstitial nephritis (AIN), a distressing and increasingly common aspect of medical practice. Drugs are essentially foreign substances that the body expels. Since drugs dissolve in body solutions, the major method of elimination is filtration through the kidneys into the urine. Because renal urine formation collects wastes, the concentration of a drug in renal tissue may actually accumulate to many times that present in other fluids and trigger a toxic reaction.

The drug may also provoke an allergic reaction as the body's immune system's lymphocytes—the body's immunity warriors—attack the foreign substance. During this immune reaction, the lymphocytes may accumulate in the renal tubular cells, where the drug is often fixed during the act of excretion, causing interstitial nephritis.

These problems usually occur only while a drug is being taken, but sometimes continue afterward. As a result, careful surveillance of kidney health is crucial when taking drugs known to affect the kidney, especially for long periods. Continuing a drug that has already begun to cause kidney damage is particularly dangerous, whereas early discontinuation may completely prevent permanent damage and forestall acute renal failure.

Combinations of drugs are particularly troublesome for the kidney and sometimes our knowledge of drug interactions is sketchy. FDA tests of drug toxicity prior to release of drugs for public use are always single drug tests. Tests of every drug combination are not possible (even likely combinations may not be tested), and knowledge of the toxicity of drug combinations frequently comes only from clinical practice. This makes the public at large, in effect, a drug-testing ground that requires heightened surveillance on the part of both doctor and patient. Make sure your doctor is aware of all the medicines you take.

Drugs can interact in two ways that affect the kidneys:

1. Each drug may be individually nephrotoxic (toxic to the kidney) and the combination of drugs is additive or multiplicative.
2. While individually benign, drugs can combine to produce damage that would not result from either drug alone.

Potentially serious drug interactions include:

- ***Diuretics and prostaglandin inhibitors.*** This combination may produce acute renal failure and AIN. These widely used medications may be prescribed by different doctors, each unaware of the other's prescription. The risk of interaction has increased greatly because prostaglandin inhibitors are now available over-the-counter. The diuretics that can react are chlorothiazide, hydrochlorothiazide, chlorthalidone, and furosemide. The prostaglandin inhibitors are phenylbutazone, (indomethacin), ibuprofen, naprosyn, sulindac, and piroxicam. Prostaglandin inhibitors also tend to neutralize the antihypertensive effect of diuretics and other antihypertensive drugs.
- ***Diuretics—especially thiazides—taken with calcium supplements*** can cause hypercalcemia (too much calcium in the blood). Sometimes a physician prescribes calcium to treat postmenopausal osteoporosis without being aware that a woman may be taking diuretic hypertension medication.
- ***Analgesic (painkiller) combinations.*** One of the first known toxic drug combinations was the aspirin-phenacetin combination (with small doses of codeine or acetaminophen) popularized by such drugs as the original Anacin, which has been reformulated. Available over-the-counter, some people used them regularly, even daily, for decades. A significant number of daily users (and abusers) developed chronic renal failure from silent chronic interstitial nephritis, a disease so subtle that no troublesome indications arose, not even an abnormal urinalysis, until renal function deteriorated. When far enough along, this disease cannot be reversed.
- ***Chemotherapeutic agents.*** While the strong cell toxins used to kill cancer cells may cause damage to the kidney when excreted, much has been learned about how to protect the kidney by careful advance preparation, and this knowledge has been usefully applied to other drugs. Nevertheless, treating advanced cancer can sometimes necessitate kidney dialysis because of drug-induced renal failure.

Medications used in clinical situations—anesthetics, antibiotics, and antishock drugs—also may have renal consequences, and the stress on the kidney from blood loss or dehydration in these settings significantly increases the chance of drug toxicity. The complicated series of events that unfold in these circumstances usually make it impossible to tell precisely which factors provoked interstitial nephritis and other drug toxicity. As modern medical treatments grow more complex, and patients suffering from more than one disease require multiple drug regimens, the chances of drug-induced renal disease climb.

Despite the possible negative effects on the kidneys, these drugs and treatments must be used to save people's lives. However, in all cases, individuals taking medication must know, accept, and watch out for side effects of their prescriptions. (For more information, see chapter 34, Proper Use of Medications.)

Other drug reactions may not induce acute interstitial nephritis, but can cause a glomerulonephritis-like injury to the kidney called specific immune-induced drug injuries. These substances include:

- Gold salts (used to treat severe rheumatoid arthritis)
- Penicillamine (used to treat severe rheumatoid arthritis; Wilson's disease, a liver disorder characterized by a buildup of copper in the body; and cystinuria, a form of kidney stone disease)
- Captopril (an antihypertensive drug)

DIAGNOSIS

When the toxic reaction causing the disorder is confined to the kidneys, the symptoms vary with the severity of the reaction and whether the response is acute or chronic. Symptoms may include fever, painful urination, pus in the urine, and flank pain.

When kidney involvement is part of a general body reaction, fever, skin rash, and joint pains may appear. However, a chronic low-grade interstitial nephritis can proceed undetected and without symptoms for months, causing considerable, possibly irreversible, kidney damage.

A simple blood count usually reveals a large number of specialized white blood cells called eosinophils. They are also visible in a microscopic examination of a properly stained urine sample. (Routine urinalysis is not specific enough to spot this condition.) This type of examination is even more important in the chronic type, when no general body reaction is evident.

TREATMENT

In acute disease, discontinuation of the problem drug or drugs may resolve the problem. In other cases, prescription corticosteroid drugs can help resolve the inflammation. When irreversible kidney damage has already occurred, the patient must be treated for chronic kidney failure.

PREVENTION

Whenever drugs known to be potentially toxic to the kidney are prescribed, the patient should be informed of possible indications of kidney problems. Ask your doctor and pharmacist about the side effects of all medications. Drugs can cause kidney problems over the course of a few days or take years to do damage.

MALE/FEMALE DIFFERENCES

The classic drug-induced renal disease—phenacetin-induced interstitial nephritis—occurred predominantly in women possibly because of their increased use of analgesics. However, that problem has been eradicated by changing drug manufacture.

ACUTE POSTINFECTIOUS GLOMERULONEPHRITIS AND CHRONIC GLOMERULONEPHRITIS

DEFINITION

Acute postinfectious glomerulonephritis is the general term for all cases of inflammation of the filtering units of the kidney following an infection.

Up until the mid-1960s, chronic glomerulonephritis was the most common form of chronic renal failure. Thought to be caused by unresolved acute glomerulonephritis, there is no successful treatment for the chronic form of this disease.

CAUSE

Inflammation of the glomerulus is rarely caused directly by infection (and therefore cannot be treated with antibiotics, as can pyelonephritis), but infection in another part of the body induces this condition.

Poststreptococcal glomerulonephritis, for example, is an acute inflammation of the kidney that occurs about 10 days after a streptococcal infection. Since penicillin and other antibiotics effectively control strep infections, this type of nephritis has virtually disappeared in the United States, although it is still prevalent in tropical countries with poor hygiene and widespread untreated streptococcal skin infections.

Many common viral infections, such as mumps, chickenpox, and measles, the virus of infectious hepatitis and mononucleosis, and even malaria and syphilis, can cause postinfectious glomerulonephritis. The most common nephritis on earth is probably the one that afflicts the huge numbers of people who contract malaria. Glomerulonephritis is also seen frequently in patients with AIDS.

The widespread use of antibiotics and improved health measures that have reduced the number of strep infections in much of the world have dramatically reduced the incidence of chronic glomerulonephritis today.

DIAGNOSIS

The symptoms of acute nephritis include headache due to increased blood pressure, edema or swelling (especially of the face and ankles), and dark urine, the result of bleeding from the glomeruli. However, the chronic condition may cause no symptoms in the early stages. Dark-colored urine should be saved, refrigerated, and brought to a doctor as soon as possible for urinalysis.

Chronic inflammation of the glomeruli, or chronic nephritis, is usually discovered accidentally, either by routine urinalysis or during a routine physical when anemia, hypertension, or elevated serum creatinine and BUN (blood ureanitrogen) are discovered.

TREATMENT

Acute postinfectious glomerulonephritis is initially treated by curing the underlying infection. Edema and elevated blood pressure that cause fluid retention and decreased blood flow in the kidneys are first treated with salt restriction and decreased water intake and then with diuretics, or other antihypertensive drugs if necessary. Once the infection is under control, treatment is directed at the complications of the disease. In extreme cases where severe renal failure occurs, dialysis may be needed for a time. Almost all patients with acute postinfectious nephritis recover if the initiating disease is cured.

Unfortunately, there is no way to treat the underlying disease that causes chronic glomerulonephritis.

HOME REMEDIES AND ALTERNATIVE THERAPIES

Because this condition restricts the kidneys' excretion of salt, salt restriction is necessary to avoid fluid overload, and subsequent hypertension and heart failure. However, bed rest does not seem to be necessary for the healing process.

MESANGIAL GLOMERULONEPHRITIS

DEFINITION

This type of nephritis primarily damages the mesangium—the cells and matrix that support the glomerular capillary. Similar to acute nephritis, it may also follow infection (usually in 1 to 3 days) and cause bloody urine—often the only indication of disease—but differs in that initially there is no swelling, hypertension, or kidney failure.

The most common form of mesangial glomerulonephritis is Berger's disease, which follows infection (and causes bloody urine) more rapidly than acute postinfectious nephritis and, unlike postinfectious nephritis, initially does not cause proteinuria (protein in the urine), edema, hypertension, and renal failure. Although patients may suffer several attacks, fewer than 10 percent develop significant scarring and progression to renal failure. Many patients never experience an acute episode, and the condition is found only when urine is examined for an unrelated reason. This condition is often observed in children as an isolated abnormality of red cells in the urine.

CAUSE

The exact cause of this condition is not known, but is related to abnormalities in the immune mechanism involving immunoglobulin A antibodies.

DIAGNOSIS

Diagnosis is based on urinalysis and renal biopsy showing large deposits of antibodies in the inflamed areas. Although these deposits are assumed to cause the disease, it has not been conclusively proven.

GLOMERULONEPHRITIS ASSOCIATED WITH OTHER DISEASES

Because the kidney constantly filters more than 2,100 quarts of blood daily, it is especially vulnerable to injury from abnormalities in the passing cells and blood serum. The mesangium—the central core supporting the kidney's filtering system—contains cells closely allied to and communicating with the body's entire immune surveillance system so that it, too, is affected by other diseases that attack the body.

The collagen disease systemic lupus erythematosus most commonly causes this type of renal injury. Lupus, an immune system disorder in which antibodies attack normal tissue (including the kidney), may result in lupus nephritis, one of the most treatable of renal diseases. The treatment paradoxically uses immunosuppressive drugs to fight a disease noted for immune response suppression.

Possibly due to altered immune responses, lupus patients tolerate kidney transplants better than others, and active lupus rarely returns after transplantation, suggesting that the drugs used to control the effects of transplant may also control lupus.

TREATMENT

As with chronic glomerulonephritis, treatment is confined to control of complications and preservation of renal function.

MEMBRANOPROLIFERATIVE GLOMERULONEPHRITIS (MPGN)

DEFINITION

Similar to mesangial disease, MPGN produces proteinuria, decreased filtration, and hypertension. But it also resembles Berger's disease in that it is often seen in children as an isolated abnormality of red cells in the urine.

CAUSE

Unlike the other inflammatory kidney diseases, MPGN is commonly associated with a distinct immune system abnormality.

DIAGNOSIS

In addition to urinalysis, blood tests identify the immune system abnormality associated with MPGN.

TREATMENT

The course of this disease varies greatly, ranging from complete cure to progression to complete renal failure, and no proven therapy exists. Immunosuppressive drugs like cortisone, cyclophosphamide, and azathioprine have been used to treat this condition with sometimes serious side effects.

NEPHROTIC SYNDROME (NEPHROSIS)

DEFINITION

This disorder allows larger protein molecules, which should be retained in the blood during the kidney's filtering process, to suddenly leak into the urine. Within a few days, the blood proteins are markedly depleted and the flow back to the blood of normal tissue fluid is impaired, causing tissue to swell all over the body. The kidney cannot properly excrete salt, allowing massive retention of salt and water, further aggravating the situation.

Nephrosis is most common in young children and at its worst can produce an almost grotesque bloating of the face (especially around the eyes), hands, feet, and abdomen. While extremely uncomfortable, pure (primary) nephrosis does not curtail kidney excretory function and no inflammatory damage ensues. Without a complication such as infection or blood clots, it is not a life-threatening disease.

KIDNEY DISEASE AND CANCER

As cancer patients live longer, the chance for renal complications increases due to kidney damage from:

- Antibodies caused by the development of the tumors
- Injurious proteins produced during treatment
- Nephrotoxicity of chemotherapeutic agents

Thus, a patient surviving malignant cancer may develop renal failure and require dialysis.

CAUSE

The kidney's filtering membrane is constructed like a sieve that allows small molecules to pass through the blood while retaining larger protein molecules. In secondary nephrosis, the membrane is damaged by another illness—such as diabetes, lupus, lymphoma, leukemia, severe hypertension, or an injury—impairing normal filtration. In primary nephrosis, the cause is unknown but may be related to an immune system abnormality.

Unfortunately, primary nephrosis (which is treatable) occurs in pure form in only about 20 percent of adult cases, although 85 percent of juvenile cases are primary. When nephrosis occurs in association with other disease such as nephritis or diabetes, the prognosis is less hopeful.

DIAGNOSIS

Primary nephrotic syndrome is diagnosed based on a physical examination and blood and urine tests. However, in adults, it is not always possible to determine the cause without performing a renal biopsy.

TREATMENT

Primary nephrotic syndrome is one of the most treatable forms of nephritis and can usually be completely cured with a corticosteroid drug such as prednisone. Even relapses usually respond well to the drug.

For secondary nephrosis, the underlying disorder must be treated to heal the kidney as well as prevent a recurrence of kidney problems.

Adults with nephrosis of unknown origin who wish to avoid renal biopsy may sometimes be prescribed prednisone on a trial basis. (This should be thoroughly discussed by the patient and physician before proceeding.) For patients unresponsive to prednisone, fluid control may be problematic and may cause serious metabolic imbalance, especially if an individual becomes resistant to diuretics.

Home Remedies and Alternative Therapies

People with nephrotic syndrome must follow a special no-salt, high-protein diet with limited fluid intake, a very effective dietary control in chronic cases that requires a great deal of discipline.

Prevention

Patients who have any chronic illness associated with the development of nephrotic syndrome should receive regular medical supervision and follow self-care regimens scrupulously.

....

KIDNEY STONES

Definition

Kidney stones, also called renal calculi, are hard, rock-like deposits formed in the urinary tract. Few pains are as gripping as the pain caused by stones passing and blocking the kidney.

Cause

About 10 percent of kidney stones stem either from a problem of general metabolism affecting the entire body or from a structural or metabolic problem of the kidney itself. Structural problems (congenital defects as well as acquired defects, scars, and strictures) lead to poor drainage of the urine, stagnation, and bacterial infection. About 2 percent of kidney stones are due to medullary cysts in the center of the kidney, which disturb urine flow. These cysts and structural defects must be diagnosed by x-ray or ultrasound.

Metabolic problems include cystinuria, a birth defect that causes large amounts of the amino acid cystine to be excreted in the urine, and renal tubular acidosis, in which an alteration in acid-base chemistry leads to changes in the solubility of calcium and phosphorus, two chemicals that commonly form stones.

Diseases of general metabolism that cause kidney stones include gout, hyperparathyroidism, and abnormal intestinal absorption.

- Gout can cause excessive uric acid in the urine even when the uric acid level in the blood is normal, but raised blood levels increase the risk of stone formation. Uric acid stones may develop during certain treatments for gout unless precautions are taken to ensure that uric acid does not clog the urine.

- Hyperparathyroidism is a fairly common endocrine disorder characterized by a high level of calcium in the blood and excessive calcium excretion in the urine. Usually due to a small benign tumor in the parathyroid glands behind the thyroid glands in the neck, this condition is easily cured by surgery.

- Excessive intestinal absorption of oxalate usually occurs in people with reduced intestinal surface area, either from disease or surgical procedures, such as bowel resections used to treat regional enteritis. Their intestines cannot absorb fats normally, and calcium is bound in the intestinal fluids. This permits the remaining intestine to absorb large amounts of oxalate, which crystallizes into stones. While rare, excessive use of soda bicarbonate and milk for relief of excess stomach acidity can lead to high levels of calcium absorption and calcium stone formation.

The remaining 90 percent of stone disease is idiopathic (of unknown origin), resulting from some sort of imbalance in the biochemical forces in the final urine itself. Idiopathic stone disease affects all ages, is a cause of considerable disability, and, in the more serious cases, leads to eventual, progressive renal failure. Fortunately, stone disease is treatable, curable, and preventable. Although the percentage of serious cases is very low, the total number of stone patients is high, and a significant number require either dialysis or transplantation every year, making stone disease an important and expensive public health issue.

Worldwide, the incidence of stone disease in a particular geographic area is roughly proportional to the protein in the diet. Eskimos, whose diet is largely fat, and Amazon Indians, whose diet is totally vegetarian, rarely form stones. Although the relationship of protein to stone disease is not fully understood, protein may contribute to stone formation by increasing the acidity of urine, and increasing urinary excretion of uric acid, phosphorus, and calcium.

The role of salt intake in stone disease has not been fully explored, but there is a direct relationship between the amount of salt eaten and the amount of calcium excreted in the urine.

Diagnosis

Kidney stone pain is called colic because it often flares intermittently, brought on by stretching of the ureters and kidney pelvis as the stone blocks the normal flow of urine. While these pains make it agonizing to move (and still hurt when the person is motionless), there are usually no other symptoms.

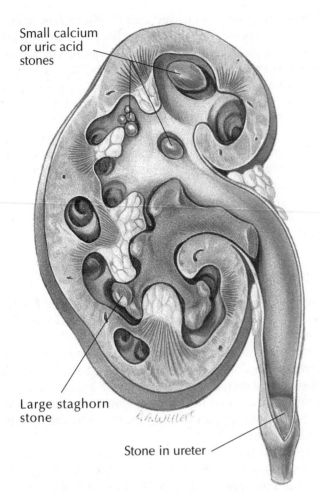

Small calcium
or uric acid
stones

Large staghorn
stone

Stone in ureter

Figure 27.2: Kidney stones.

In a significant minority of kidney stone cases, however, there may be distention of the intestines, nausea, and vomiting. The stone may irritate the lining of the kidney and its tubes, resulting in blood in the urine that may only be seen microscopically or may occasionally be sufficient to color the urine visibly.

Obstruction leading to infection is the most serious kidney stone complication (see figure 27.2). Infection causes shaking chills with high fever and represents a serious medical emergency demanding immediate medical attention at a hospital emergency room. Since the bladder may not be affected, there may be no other symptoms, such as frequency of or burning urination.

Renal colic in the absence of complications is not a serious problem if the pain is manageable. In the absence of infection, some kidney stone sufferers can safely wait weeks or even months to allow a small stone time to pass (as most people do). The colic will usually be intermittent, each episode nudging the stone along and causing pain that usually begins in the flank but which may be perceived as moving around to the front and down toward the groin and testicles. When the stone reaches the lower ureter, the bladder may be irri-

tated and there may be increased frequency of urination. Finally, once the stone enters the bladder, the pain stops and the stone is usually quickly passed during the next urination.

Stones may also pass out of the body after breaking up into tiny pieces resembling gravel or large grains of sand varying in chemical composition and color. These emerging lumps—small compared to the trouble they cause—represent only a portion of the stone. The stones inside the body consist of crystals held together in a matrix of a sugar-protein substance that often disintegrates when the crystals are passed.

The urine itself may appear normal when held to the light because, while one affected kidney is blocked, the other compensates by producing large volumes of normal urine. A microscopic examination is necessary to identify the source of pain, and chemical analysis of passed stones determines their composition.

Idiopathic stone disease (of no known origin) that causes no symptoms may be inadvertently discovered on an x-ray or sonogram of the abdomen performed for an unrelated condition.

TREATMENT

Even with standard diet therapy (as discussed below), some people pass many painful stones and resort to pharmaceutical relief. While some people prefer suffering 1 stone every 3 or 4 years (provided infection or complications are absent), others would rather take daily medication. The most appropriate course of action must be decided by each patient.

The key to sensible management of this condition is a careful assessment of stone activity. Inactive stone disease is common: The first stone may be the only one, or the second may not arrive for 20 years. Stones can be easily monitored and if growing insignificantly and causing no symptoms, treatment may be unnecessary. (In some cases, stones temporarily block the kidney for a day or two before passing and, with time, the body adapts to stone formation, allowing stones in the ureter without blockage.)

Stones that significantly block the kidney, cause persistent pain, and threaten function must be treated.

• If the stone is low enough, near the bladder, it can be reached via a cystoscope with a tiny basket-tipped catheter, which grasps the stone and extracts it. While this technique cures a great majority of cases, it fails in a significant minority, and the trauma of the procedure may require follow-up surgery.

• If the stone is high (in or near the pelvis), a tube may be inserted under local anesthesia through the skin and muscle into the kidney itself and the stone extracted. This requires leaving the tube in place for an extended period and, although safer than surgery, can cause infection and bleeding.

• If the stone is stuck in midureter or in the kidney and cannot be reached by any other method, surgery has traditionally been the only successful means of removal.

• As an alternative to surgery, underwater shock-wave treatment is proving to be a very effective and safe, nonsurgical means of disintegrating stones: Powerful shock waves generated while the patient is partially immersed in a special water tank breaks the stones. Although these waves have occasionally caused internal renal damage (and resulted in hypertension), newer local lithotripters (stone breakers) for stones near the bladder and accessible via cystoscope have reduced the risk.

As the technology of stone destruction advances, doctors may someday fully live up to the portion of the Hippocratic oath, which pledges "not to cut for the stone."

HOME REMEDIES AND ALTERNATIVE THERAPIES

For the majority of stone sufferers, decreasing dietary protein and increasing fluid (to increase urine flow) are all that is necessary to manage their condition. The necessary level of protein restriction has not been determined (nor is the minimum daily protein requirement agreed upon), but a safe, sufficient level of intake seems to be 1 gram (0.035 ounce) for every kilogram (2.2 pounds) of body weight for an adult. This reduction tends to protect kidney function and may lower cholesterol.

Since a reduction in calcium excretion is also desirable, salt restriction, or at least avoidance of high salt intake, is also wise, since this limits loss of calcium.

Capturing passed stones for chemical analysis is an important aid in diagnosis, treatment, and prevention. The smallness of the crystals may necessitate filtering urine through a fine mesh in order to find them.

PREVENTION

Analysis of a passed stone may identify specific chemicals such as calcium, which can be eliminated from the diet.

By ingesting more fluids, urine output can be increased to dilute the concentration of stone-forming substances. Often an output of at least 2 quarts a day is required. (Increased fluid intake should dilute the urine so that it is transparent without the normally characteristic yellow color.)

Research is under way to isolate the body's natural stone inhibitors. These inhibitors, which normally prevent mineral precipitation and stone formation when urine is very concentrated (as in cases of dehydration), are also produced and excreted by the cells lining the bladder and urinary tract to prevent stones in case of injury (damage to this area would otherwise stimulate stone formation). If these natural inhibitors can be isolated and their role more fully understood, they can be used to prevent stones.

HYPERCALURIA AND HYPERURICOSURIA

Whether hypercaluria (stone disease associated with too much calcium in the urine but a normal amount in the blood) is caused by excessive absorption of dietary calcium or is idiopathic can be determined by a special diet and urinalysis. Hypercaluria linked to calcium absorption is treated with a calcium-restricted diet, while diuretics (usually thiazides) are used to dilute the concentration of calcium in the urine in idiopathic cases. Whether this medication reduces stone formation more effectively than high fluid intake and diet remains to be proven. The benign nature of most stone disease and the extensive side effects of daily thiazide persuade many stone sufferers to avoid drugs and alter their diets.

Hyperuricosuria is a stone disease associated with excess uric acid in the urine, but a normal concentration in the blood and no gout. Although this condition is not well understood, some experts believe the level of uric acid excretion is linked to protein intake; a low-protein diet can decrease uric acid excretion. Daily doses of allopurinol, a drug commonly prescribed for gout, are also used to treat this disease. In this case, too, many stone sufferers alter their diets and abstain from drug treatment.

KIDNEY FAILURE

Since virtually all kidney disease can cause renal failure, the major focus of treatment in most cases is to preserve kidney function. We have far more kidney functioning power than necessary and most kidney diseases do not cause noticeable problems or symptoms until 90 percent of renal function is lost. The distinction between acute and chronic renal failure is crucial.

• **Chronic Renal Failure:** allows the body to adjust gradually, tolerating and compensating for the impaired function.

• **Acute Renal Failure:** occurs rapidly, in a matter of hours or a few days, and therefore causes serious metabolic disruptions.

DEFINITION

During kidney failure, the kidneys stop filtering the body's metabolic waste products properly. These products collect in the blood, a condition known as uremia.

CAUSE

The most common causes of acute renal failure are shock (usually from blood loss), infection, and drug reactions, often in combination. Most cases now occur in the hospital, where the condition is easily and promptly diagnosed and acute kidney dialysis units are ready to begin treatment.

Chronic renal failure is usually caused by glomerulonephritis, diabetes mellitus, hypertension, amyloidosis (accumulation of protein and starch in various organs), and other conditions that cause long-term kidney damage.

DIAGNOSIS

Although the acute and chronic forms of uremia are somewhat different, the major symptoms include:

- Upset stomach, varying from simple appetite loss to severe stomach pain, nausea, and vomiting (even vomiting of blood)
- Weakness, lack of energy, fatigue, and sleepiness
- Weight loss of fat and muscle tissue
- Dry, often itchy, skin
- Peculiar odor to the breath, reminiscent of urine
- Pallor, due to anemia
- Shortness of breath, due to heart muscle weakness, hypertension, and fluid retention
- Edema, or swelling
- In the very late stages, mental symptoms such as agitation, twitching, stupor, coma, or seizures

Because acute failure occurs suddenly and usually involves the entire kidney, the flow of urine is usually suppressed. Even when the urine flow is very low, however, few people notice the change or realize its significance. When a toxic substance or a drug has caused acute failure, the symptoms of uremia manifest themselves before the person is aware of the problem. The acute and total loss of kidney function does not allow the body to compensate, and symptoms may develop within a few days, usually indicated by swelling of the feet, shortness of breath, or headache. These symptoms stem from the acute retention of salt and water, sharply raising blood pressure, altering brain metabolism, and congesting the heart and lungs. Without treatment, more serious problems appear, including hyperkalemia, a buildup in the blood of potassium that is usually excreted in the urine. Potassium buildup can cause heart rhythm irregularity or stop the heart completely, with potentially fatal results.

Unlike acute renal failure, chronic renal failure does not shut down the entire kidney at once. As some nephrons become diseased, others compensate, enlarging and assuming a portion of the lost function. Since the body has time to adjust, the symptoms of chronic failure differ considerably from those of acute failure and the adjustments are so successful that symptoms rarely are perceived until 90 to 95 percent of kidney function is lost. (At the same time, another illness, surgery, or a complication of hypertension may limit effective compensation.)

Symptoms usually appear so gradually, the patients adjust to them unconsciously: rising at night to pass urine, sleeping more to cope with fatigue, and avoiding stairs, hills, and lifting to offset breathlessness. Only when a minimally acceptable level of function has deteriorated, or when an acute episode is precipitated by a complication like stroke, heart failure, inflamed stomach, colon, or heart sac, do people seek medical attention.

The simplest way to detect the fluid retention caused by acute renal failure is by a person's rapidly rising weight. Usually, the average urine flow is about 1 quart per day and when this fluid is not passed, it adds about 2 pounds to the total body weight.

TREATMENT

Acute renal failure is a medical emergency, but one that is rarely fatal and completely treatable with either medications or dialysis. Since acute failure today usually results from very serious disease elsewhere in the body, the outcome depends on the course of that disease. When the underlying kidney insult is corrected, most acute failure clears up in a few days with the help of medication. If it takes longer, dialysis may be needed until the kidneys heal, a process that may take 2 weeks to 2 months. Patients who do not respond to treatment may have to undergo long-term dialysis.

DIALYSIS

The most dramatic revolution in the treatment of chronic renal failure during the past 40 years has been the use of dialysis to treat chronic renal failure as well as acute. Although this may not seem revolutionary today, it represented a radically new idea in therapeutics.

Artificial kidneys generally filter the blood for 4 hours at a time, three times per week. Since these filters cannot perform any of the kidney's many metabolic functions, they cannot truly restore full health, but most patients manage to maintain varied and useful lives despite the chronic state of disease produced by maintenance hemodialysis.

Dialysis patients must:

- Adhere to rigid dialysis schedules
- Restrict fluid intake and follow strictly controlled diets
- Take daily medications
- Endure anemia, abnormal bone metabolism, chronic uremia, and diminished sexual function

Other possible complications of dialysis include high or low blood pressure, weakness, fatigue, cramps, weight loss, psychiatric disturbances, loss of nerve functions leading to muscle paralysis, and recurrent infections.

Still, for many the only alternative to dialysis is certain death, although at the time the first kidney machines were invented few expected the human body to endure dialysis so well. From the time the artificial kidney was invented in 1946 until 1961, these machines were only used to tide over patients with acute renal failure who would eventually recover.

When Dr. Belding Scribner first used dialysis to keep patients alive and reasonably well for a prolonged period, virtually the entire nephrology community considered it impossible, even immoral. Today, chronic dialysis is common, mainly because of government support, and the number of patients benefiting from it grows each year (the cost also grows).

- Over 90,000 people who would otherwise be dead are supported by kidney machines in hospitals, dialysis centers, or at home.
- Medicare pays the cost of dialysis for 93 percent of those requiring it. The cost of dialysis for the majority of the remaining 7 percent is paid for by either the Veterans Administration or Medicaid.
- The overall cost to the federal government for these programs is $3 billion annually.

Dr. Scribner first solved the technical problem of having to connect the dialysis machine to the same place again and again by constructing an external blood shunt worn on the forearm. Today, a minor operation creates an internal shunt allowing the veins to become like arteries, a development that led to the rapid growth and facility of chronic dialysis. When kidney machines were in short supply, this life-saving technological advance meant that many people died who could have been saved by dialysis. Today, with an unlimited supply of dialysis machines, few die for lack of technology, but many question the billions of dollars spent to save them when other diseases are in far more primitive states of conquest.

The kidney machine not only treats acute and chronic renal failure but is also vital to renal transplantation, the other treatment option for those with end-stage renal disease (see box on page 707). Transplant programs cannot exist without dialysis because most transplants do not function immediately, and the patient needs dialysis support during rejection episodes.

Who should have dialysis and who should receive a transplant are difficult questions to answer. But transplantation, despite the newest medications, is inherently risky. The suppression and alteration of immunity—necessary during transplantation—creates unique problems and risks. During the first year, transplants result in death far more than does dialysis. (In fact, transplant is often considered for those doing poorly on dialysis because the risk/gain ratio then favors transplant.)

But if a transplant patient survives the operation and the transplant is successful after 1 year, the risk decreases greatly.

HOME REMEDIES AND ALTERNATIVE THERAPIES

Those who are on dialysis need nutritional advice from a registered dietitian and also may benefit from counseling by a social worker or psychologist.

PREVENTION

The enormous financial burden of the dialysis/transplant treatment of end-stage renal failure has motivated nephrologists to greater efforts at preventing and curing chronic kidney failure. Disappointingly, few cases of end-stage renal failure can be cured and many are the consequences of the longer life span of people who suffer other diseases. Better overall medical treatment has led to much longer survival, long enough for people to outlive stroke, heart attack, or infection, and consequently develop kidney disease. Diabetes and hypertension now cause almost 50 percent of end-stage renal failure.

With few exceptions, the large amounts of time and money invested in immunology research on nephritis have produced few results. However, recent investigations by Dr. Barry Brenner and his colleagues at Harvard Medical School indicate that partial damage to a kidney as a result of disease strains the remaining nephrons, which must handle increased blood pressure and flow. The result is that they, too, begin a gradual but relentless progression toward total renal failure.

But the strain on the kidneys is not inevitable; rather, it seems to be related to several factors, including diet. Preliminary tests in animals have shown that limiting protein intake can prevent further damage (which would be relatively simple for people at risk to accomplish). Unfortunately, protein restriction in people does not always help the kidneys, since apparently not all renal diseases respond to this dietary measure. Still, most kidney specialists cautiously advocate protein restriction in most situations.

KIDNEY TRANSPLANTATION

For those with kidneys that no longer function, transplantation is the only treatment that restores reasonably normal health.

Transplants may originate from either related or unrelated donors. While the science of immunology has somewhat improved the art of matching kidneys to recipients, transplants involving blood relatives are the most successful, since more of the unknown immunologic factors may be matched. Although the gap in success rates between the two groups is narrowing all the time, people receiving kidneys from relatives generally survive longer and experience fewer complications than unrelated recipients.

For possible kidney donors, the value of donation must be weighed against the pain and possible complications of kidney removal. Donation usually bestows a new life to a loved one but entails medical uncertainties that should be discussed with a physician. However, the general shortage of cadaver kidneys and kidneys from unrelated donors and the difficulties of achieving a match in some patients put great pressure on relatives to donate.

The technical complications from transplantation surgery are now very rare, and the major early risk for transplant patients is infection. Since the body's normal immune response is suppressed by drugs meant to lower the possibility of organ rejection, infection can be life-threatening (although the use of the drug cyclosporine has reduced this risk). The administered doses of immunosuppressant drugs are also greatly decreased with time, so the risk of infection quickly falls.

However, immunosuppressant drugs also can cause cancer, and over a period of years, recurrence of the original kidney disease is also possible due to hypertension, nephritis, or diabetes but is not usually significant.

The requirements for kidney donation are very strict (or should be) and the number of end-stage kidney patients with willing, well-matched healthy related donors is small, probably less than 1 in 10.

Transplantation success depends on regional networks or centers that can rapidly identify and type potential donors.

- Special medical teams are needed to monitor accident cases or patients dying suddenly of other illness, protect the kidneys until they can be removed, and remove them after death.
- Kidneys taken from accident and disease victims can be stored about 24 hours.
- Patients waiting for kidneys need to be tissue-typed and tracked so they are ready to accept a kidney within 24 hours after one becomes available.

The larger the pool of donors, the more likely a specific kidney will be excellently matched. It is estimated that each available kidney will optimally match only 1 of 1,000 recipients. Considering the logistical problems involved, the achievements of the transplantation networks are substantial, commendable, and gratifying.

In the United States, thanks to the use of cyclosporine, people receiving donated kidneys from relatives have a 95 percent survival rate for 1 year; for kidneys from cadavers, the 1-year survival rate is over 75 percent. The 5-year survival rates are 75 percent for relatives and 60 percent for cadaver kidneys. These survival rates are boosted by the use of dialysis for patients whose transplants fail.

Not all authorities agree on how much protein is appropriate to preserve kidney function. The upper limit seems to be 1 gram per kilogram of body weight per day (but may be less). For those with a great deal of body fat, protein should probably be consumed at a lower level. In the kidney impaired with a high muscle-to-fat ratio, it may be advisable to reduce muscle mass. In any case, the recommended level of daily dietary protein is probably not less than 25 to 35 g daily.

Other preventive measures include:

• Reduction of phosphorus absorbed from the diet by taking either binding agents in pill form, such as Amphojel, which block phosphorus absorption by the stomach, or by increasing calcium intake with calcium carbonate. (Extra vitamin D will aid in calcium uptake.)

• Salt restriction: impaired kidneys excrete less salt, leading to hypertension.

• Protecting the kidneys from the ravages of high blood pressure with vasodilators or beta-blockers (for more information on these drugs see chapter 34). Diuretics for blood pressure control are not recommended, since they often interfere with glomerular filtration, renal blood flow, and uric acid excretion, which is already impaired.

• Good hygiene to lessen the risks of disease or infections. Since, to varying degrees, biologic functions may be already strained, a viral infection such as gastroenteritis with a fever, copious diarrhea, and fluid loss can have catastrophic results on damaged kidneys.

• The dosage of any medication taken for other conditions should be adjusted depending upon the degree of renal function. Drugs or drug combinations potentially toxic to the kidneys should be avoided.

POLYCYSTIC KIDNEY DISEASE

DEFINITION

Polycystic kidney disease is a hereditary condition in which numerous cysts form on individual nephrons and interfere with kidney function. Although it is not unusual to have one or two cysts within kidney tissue, in most cases they have no function and are harmless (although they may cause confusion and lead to unnecessary diagnostic procedures).

In polycystic kidney disease, virtually all the nephrons of both kidneys eventually become cystic or are compressed, distorted, and rendered increasingly ineffective by the pressure of adjacent cysts. In the process, the kidneys enlarge to three or four times normal size as function decreases. A person suffering this condition is unaware of the disease unless some complication—hypertension, blood in the urine, pain caused by bleeding into the kidney, a stone, or infection—calls attention to the kidney, usually long before kidney failure has developed. Eventually, the kidneys grow so large that it is possible to feel them through the skin. Although some patients with polycystic kidney live a normal life span and a significant group live long enough to die of something else, until the advent of dialysis and transplantation, many patients with the disease eventually died of uremic poisoning.

While some people who inherit the responsible genes do not encounter significant kidney damage from cysts until their 30s or 40s, others live into their 80s; the average age at which renal failure occurs is 50. Consequently, for carriers of these genes, choosing whether to have children is a difficult decision, but genetic counseling may be helpful.

CAUSE

This hereditary disease is brought on by a dominant gene, and there is a 50 percent chance that the children of those with the gene will inherit it.

DIAGNOSIS

Doctors are uncertain as to when diagnostic testing should be done for detection of the disease. The best test—ultrasound—is simple, and if and when a means of preventing or limiting cyst formation is found, early detection may become very important. Recent advances in genetics are close to identifying the specific gene that causes polycystic kidneys, thus providing a basis for genetic counseling and prenatal diagnosis.

TREATMENT

Since operative decompression of the cysts is of uncertain benefit, most treatment alleviates complications such as infection, stones, bleeding, and hypertension. General management of the disease is the same as for chronic renal failure, and it is important not to do any unnecessary procedures in dealing with this condition. Operations such as cyst puncture or removal designed to relieve pressure often worsens the condition. Cystoscopy is of little value and only introduces the possibility of infection, which can be devastating to patients with polycystic kidney disease.

Advances in the ability to control blood pressure safely, prevent stones, and cure infections have improved the prognosis for those with polycystic kidney disease. Special attention focuses on the use of converting enzyme-inhibitor drugs to hold down blood pressure since these substances may also inhibit cyst growth. (Increased plasma renin activity also influences this type of hypertension.)

Recent innovations in managing chronic renal failure have greatly aided patients with polycystic kidneys, but dialysis and transplantation have most dramatically improved their prospects. Because they do not have disease outside the kidney (with rare exceptions involving the liver and brain), people with polycystic kidneys are ideal candidates for dialysis and transplant, and they do better than those with other forms of kidney disease.

Discovery of several animals that can develop polycystic kidney has provided a basis for screening drugs to inhibit cyst growth and offers hope for improving treatment of the disease.

SUMMING UP

The kidneys play a crucial role in the body's circulatory and urinary systems by filtering waste products and toxins from the blood, while returning nutrients to the bloodstream and controlling blood pressure. Even though the kidneys are vital to sustaining life, only one is necessary for survival, which allows family members to donate healthy organs to relatives who suffer renal failure. However, the body's ability to compensate for reduced kidney function often allows severe kidney damage to occur before kidney disease becomes evident.

TABLE 27.1: UNCOMMON HEREDITARY KIDNEY DISORDERS

Condition	Causes	Symptoms	Risks	Treatment	Comments
Solitary kidney (only 1 kidney present)	Congenital defect; trauma, infection, other condition may destroy a kidney	Often none or urine abnormality may be noted	Special risk of decreased kidney function during pyelonephritis, trauma, cancer, stone attacks	None necessary unless remaining kidney becomes diseased; low protein intake may be advisable	Contact sports inadvisable; genetic counseling may be recommended for women before attempting pregnancy
Horseshoe kidney	Genetic defect; lower half of kidneys remain fused	Often none	Excessive pooling of urine may increase risk of infection or stones	None needed	Avoid unnecessary urologic procedures
Renal circulation anomalies	Genetic defect; creates 2 or more renal arteries, or arterial aneurysms	Often none; aneurysms may be detected by listening to kidneys with stethoscope	Extra arteries may cause problems if surgery needed; aneurysms may cause hypertension or rupture if large	None unless complications occur	A rare inherited disorder, von Recklinghausen's disease, may be associated with renal artery aneurysms
Floating (dropped) kidney	Possible genetic defect; right kidney not secured in space under rib, so it "floats" in area below liver	None; can be diagnosed by palpation	Often mistaken for a tumor, leading to unnecessary testing	None	More common in women; generally benign
Alport's syndrome	Genetic defect in glomerular basement membrane makes it thin, weak	None in early stages; possible blood in urine; eventually uremia develops; hearing loss, vision problems also may occur	Renal failure usually in 20s for men; women may never develop problems	No specific treatment for disorder	Women unaware of disorder may pass on gene to children without realizing it
Cystinuria	Metabolic defect in enzymes needed to recover the amino acid cystine from filtered urine	Pain if stones form	Because cystine lost in urine, stones may form, block kidney, causing renal colic, possible renal failure	Penicillamine may be given to help cystine dissolve	Attempts to dissolve massive levels of cystine by increasing, alkalizing urine flow usually unsuccessful
Nephrogenic diabetes insipidus	Genetic defect; kidney tubules do not respond to antidiuretic hormone in blood	Pervasive thirst quenched with high fluid intake leads to large urine volume, bed-wetting	Usually none	High fluid intake; if insufficient, salt restruction, thiazide diuretics, prostaglandin inhibitors	Recent genetic studies giving insight on exact biochemical defects offer hope for future treatment
Vitamin D–resistant rickets	Genetic defect; renal tubules unable to reabsorb phosphorus from filtered urine	Bowed legs, bone pain, short stature	Multiple bone deformities; convulsions	Phosphate improves resorption of calcium in intestine	More common, severe in males than females
Renal tubular acidosis	Genetic defect; impairs ability of renal tubules to reabsorb potassium	General failure to thrive; unusual early stone formation in body of kidney	Life-threatening potassium depletion	Soda bicarbonate	Early diagnosis, treatment essential

Major kidney disorders include hypertension, diabetic nephropathy, kidney stones, and inflammatory diseases of the nephrons and the glomeruli. When left untreated, the end result of many of these diseases is kidney failure.

Fortunately, treatment for kidney problems has greatly improved with the development of new drugs, a better understanding of the role of diet (particularly the benefits of restricting protein and sodium), and the availability of dialysis and kidney transplants.

Persons with kidney disease should play a major role in their own therapy by monitoring their blood pressure, carefully observing drug effects, and improving their diet.

28
Skin
Diseases

• • • • • • • • • • • • • • •

**ROBERT WALTHER,
M.D.**

BASIC FACTS ABOUT SKIN

The skin is the largest organ of the body. An average man's skin covers more than 2 square yards and weighs 10 pounds. In just 1 square inch of skin there are approximately 30 million cells, 100 fat glands, 600 sweat glands, 65 hairs, numerous muscles, and thousands of nerve endings. The human skin ranges in thickness from 0.5 millimeter in the eyelid to more than 2 millimeters in the palms and soles.

On and within this massive organ, disorders are rampant; at least 10 percent of all patients seen by primary-care physicians complain of skin problems. As the environment becomes increasingly polluted with toxic chemicals and irritants, skin sensitivity may increase. Because of skin's high visibility, unsightly diseases can have not only a physical effect but also a profound psychological effect on patients.

FUNCTION

The skin performs a complex role in human physiology:

- Protects the rest of the body from toxins, injuries, the sun, and temperature extremes in the external environment
- Preserves the stability of the body's inner environment and keeps it in place
- Helps the body to regulate heat
- Communicates information about physical and emotional states
- Provides identification through unique finger- and sole-prints

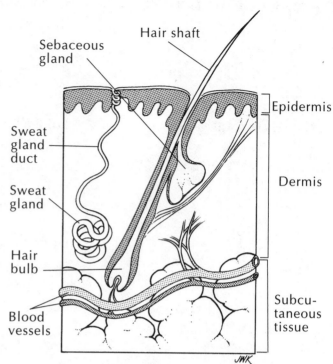

Figure 28.1: Anatomy of the skin.

STRUCTURE OF THE SKIN

The skin is usually described as having three layers (see figure 28.1). The outer layer is called the epidermis. Below that is the dermis, and underlying these is a layer of fat-producing cells called the subcutaneous tissue.

EPIDERMIS

Though paper thin, the epidermis is composed of many layers of cells. In the basal layer (the living epidermis), new cells are constantly being reproduced, pushing older cells to the surface (see figure 28.2). As skin cells move farther away from their source of nourishment, they flatten and shrink. They lose their nuclei, move out of the basal layer to the horny layer (the dead epidermis), and turn into a lifeless protein called keratin. After serving a brief protective function, the keratinocytes are imperceptibly sloughed off. This process of

a living cell's evolution, called keratinization, takes about 4 weeks.

Keratinocytes, or dead skin cells, constitute about 95 percent of the epidermal cells and function as a barrier, keeping harmful substances out and preventing water and other essential substances from escaping the body. The other 5 percent of epidermal cells are melanocytes, which manufacture and distribute melanin, the protein that adds pigment to skin and protects the body from ultraviolet rays. Skin color is determined by the amount of protein produced by these cells, not by the number of melanocytes, which is fairly constant in all races.

Hair and nails are specialized keratin structures and are considered part of the epidermis. While animals use fur and claws for protection and defense, these corresponding structures are largely cosmetic in humans. The skin, however, is uniquely human, since it can betray emotion by blushing (embarrassment), turning red (anger), blanching (fear), sweating (tension), and forming goosebumps (terror).

DERMIS

The dermis, or the "true skin," is composed of gel-like and elastic materials, water, and, primarily, collagen. Embedded in this layer are systems and structures common to other organs such as lymph channels, blood vessels, nerve fibers, and muscle cells, but unique to the dermis are hair follicles, sebaceous glands, and sweat glands.

Like the epidermis, the hair follicle manufactures a

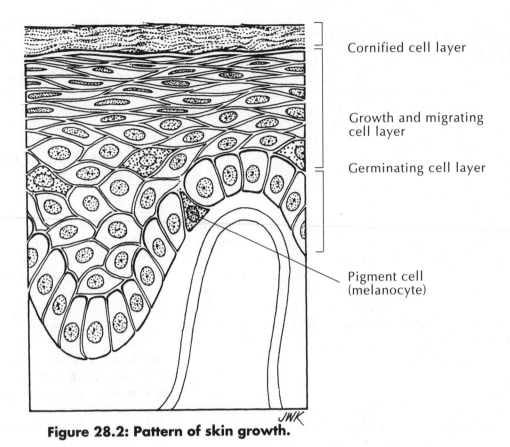

Cornified cell layer

Growth and migrating cell layer

Germinating cell layer

Pigment cell (melanocyte)

Figure 28.2: Pattern of skin growth.

keratin structure, hair. These follicles are found everywhere on the body except for the palms and soles, though most of the hairs produced are fine, light hairs that, quite unlike the hair of the scalp, are scarcely visible to the naked eye. The sebaceous glands are attached to the hair follicles and through the follicles excrete an oily substance called sebum, which both lubricates and protects the skin. On most of the skin surface sebum appears constantly and imperceptibly, but in areas with a higher concentration of sebaceous glands, such as the face and back, there are wide variations in the amount of sebum produced.

There are two distinctive sweat-producing glands, the apocrine and the eccrine. The apocrine gland is best known for producing body odor but otherwise has no known physiological function and is apparently a holdover from times past. In the ear it forms a portion of what we see as earwax. It is also present under the arms, around the nipples and navel, and in the anal-genital area.

The eccrine glands are an advanced and extensive system of temperature control. Several million of these glands are distributed over the entire body, with the highest concentration in the palms, soles, forehead, and underarms.

Sweat, a dilute salt solution, evaporates from the skin's surface to cool the body. Excessive sweating without replacement of lost water can cause heat stroke.

Eccrine glands sweat in response to physical activity and hot environments, but emotional stress and eating spicy foods can also cause perspiring.

The dermis also regulates heat through a network of tiny blood vessels. In hot weather these vessels dilate to give off heat, causing the skin to flush. In cold weather, they constrict, conserving heat, causing pallor. The blood in these vessels nourishes the skin and provides protection for the cellular and fluid systems. Like the eccrine glands, blood vessels in the dermis are responsive to emotional stress, causing the color changes mentioned previously.

Nerve endings in the dermis are the source of the body's sense of touch. They sense heat, cold, and pressure, providing both pain and pleasure.

SUBCUTANEOUS TISSUE

The subcutaneous tissue is another layer of connective tissue below the dermis, specializing in the formation of fat. It is unevenly distributed over the body, and there are wide individual differences in distribution. In addition to providing protection and insulation, the subcutaneous tissue serves as a depository for reserve fuel to be drawn upon whenever the amount of calories taken in is less than the amount burned up through activity. It is also instrumental in manufacturing vitamin D.

GENERAL PRINCIPLES OF SKIN AND HAIR CARE

Because the skin is the buffer zone for both internal and external environments, it is affected by conditions both within and outside the body. Factors that contribute to "good skin" include:

- Balanced diet.
- Exercise.
- Stress management.
- Sun avoidance: Daily moisturizing, sunscreens, protective clothing, umbrellas, and hats (especially for bald heads) all combat the sun's effects, but sun avoidance is best. Sunscreen labels should confirm UVA protection, and be rated 15 or above to provide the best protection against both short ultraviolet rays and the long ultraviolet rays that penetrate windows.

DRY SKIN

People of any age can have dry skin, but skin tends to dry out with age. To combat dry skin:

- Take tepid baths of at least 15 minutes soaking to rehydrate the skin.
- Use mild soaps and nonalkaline shampoos. Avoid deodorant soaps.
- Apply a moisturizer containing oil or 10 percent urea at least once a day, including immediately after bathing.
- Avoid astringents.
- Apply cosmetics with an oil base. Those who prefer a lighter feel may use moisturizing cosmetics containing urea.
- Wash less frequently (if you have dry hair) and use acid-based rinses and/or oil-based conditioners.

OILY SKIN

The regimen for people with oily skin should be quite different from those with dry skin.

- The more washing the better, at least three times per day for the face.
- Use astringents frequently.
- If more drying is needed, over-the-counter acne soaps may be useful. To avoid irritation, introduce these gradually.
- Wash the hair daily, or even twice daily, with an alkaline shampoo.
- Use cosmetics sparingly, and apply only water-based formulas.

As people differ in their sensitivity to various ingredients, trial and error is the best method for selecting appropriate cosmetics and cleansing products. Skin that is "normal," neither dry nor oily, should tolerate most products.

PROBLEMS AND DISEASES OF THE SKIN

ACNE

DEFINITION

Acne is a skin condition characterized by blackheads, pimples, and cysts resulting from clogged and inflamed oil (sebaceous) glands that normally exist to lubricate the skin. This outbreak is the single most common skin disorder. Acne frequently occurs among teenagers and is considered a normal part of development; it affects as many as 4 out of 5 adolescents. Acne may last for only a few weeks, but it often continues for as many as 10 years, extending from adolescence into early adulthood. In rare cases it continues throughout life.

CAUSE

Acne is generally not affected by a person's eating, bathing, or sleeping habits; it is not caused by dirty skin, and you cannot wash it away. The primary causes are mainly hormonal and genetic.

Androgens. During puberty, the increasing supply of these male sex hormones (produced by the testes or ovaries and adrenal glands of both men and women) creates conditions conducive to acne. As the amount of androgens builds, they stimulate increased growth and activity of the skin's sebaceous glands. These enlarged glands secrete excess sebum, the skin's oil designed to flow up through hair follicles to lubricate the skin. Acne forms when the sebaceous glands clog with sebum and keratin particles sloughed off in the hair follicles. To make matters worse, the irritation is sometimes complicated by the multiplication of the bacteria that reside on the skin. Pimples grow when sebum builds up inside clogged pores.

Oily Skin. Because oil contributes to acne formation, people whose skin naturally produces larger quantities of oil are more prone to acne than those with dry skin. But this is not always the case: Oily skin may be clear while dry skin may still suffer acne.

Heredity. A tendency to develop acne may be inherited; children whose parents had moderate or severe acne are also likely to have it. The mechanism for inheriting this tendency is not understood.

DIAGNOSIS

The blackheads, whiteheads, and cysts characteristic of acne are readily visible (see figure 28.3). Indeed, this visibility is the main complaint; though acne rarely causes dire physical effects, it can be emotionally destructive, often appearing at an emotionally fragile time of life (adolescence) when appearance can seem all-important.

Blackheads (Open Comedones). The mildest form of acne, blackheads form when sebum excreted by the sebaceous gland combines with skin pigments, not dirt, to plug the pores.

Pimples or Whiteheads (Closed Comedones). Clogged pores stuffed with sebum and scales beneath the surface of the skin form pimples or whiteheads. In severe cases, pressure builds up in these closed pores, and they rupture, spreading their contents under the skin. Bacteria in the injured area can cause widespread inflammation, and the resulting cysts can cause pain and scarring if not treated. The degree of scarring is thought to be at least partly determined by genetics.

Sebaceous Cysts. Often called wens, sebaceous cysts are saclike structures filled with a cheesy substance produced by the cells lining the sac. Occurring either separately or in conjunction with acne, they develop as little swellings on the face, scalp, or back, and at first can hardly be felt. When they remain very small, painless, and benign they are best left alone.

However, when the cysts may grow large and unsightly they may be prone to infection. Medical attention should be sought for any cyst that becomes red and tender, and steps should be taken to avoid infection.

The surgical removal of a sebaceous cyst is a simple outpatient procedure whereby an incision is made, the sac is removed, and the incision is stitched with nonabsorbent sutures that are removed about a week later. It is wise to have sebaceous cysts removed if they are troublesome.

TREATMENT

The general treatment strategy for dealing with acne is to keep your skin as free of oil as possible. To this end, you can use several effective medications to help dry out hyperactive oil glands and prevent the development of scarring pustules. Avoid oil-based cosmetics, which often exacerbate the problem. Despite myths that foods such as chocolate stimulate acne, no reliable research has shown that diet plays a significant role in causing or controlling acne.

Cleansing. For cases of mild acne, cleansing two or three times a day, shampooing frequently, and keeping greasy hair off the face will keep blackheads in check. Avoid irritating the skin by scrubbing too vigorously. Masks and facials may also be of help in controlling mild acne.

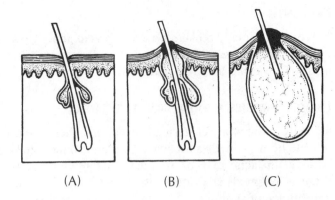

(A) (B) (C)

Figure 28.3: Development of acne. (A) normal sebaceous gland; (B) blackhead or small, open comedone; (C) cystic acne.

Blackhead Removal. Blackheads should be removed only with a specially designed surgical instrument wielded by a properly trained person. Do not pick, prod, or lance blackheads yourself; this can cause scarring.

Over-the-Counter Medications. If cleansing is insufficient treatment for your acne, creams, lotions, or gels containing benzoyl peroxide in a solution of between 2.5 and 10 percent can be useful in controlling pimples. Use benzoyl peroxide products as directed and in the mildest effective strength to avoid irritation. Drying agents (astringents), alone or in conjunction with benzoyl peroxide, may also be effective in mild cases.

Treatment by a Dermatologist. If acne is severe and unresponsive to over-the-counter medications, a dermatologist's help may be needed. Doctors may prescribe a peeling agent, a topical vitamin A derivative (Retin-A), a topical antibiotic cream, or an oral antibiotic.

The antibiotic tetracycline has been highly effective in preventing the development of scarring pustules. A full dosage is usually given for a few weeks, and then the amount taken is gradually reduced to about one-quarter normal strength. This reduced dosage may be taken for months or even years, with periodic interruptions to see if the acne recurs.

To suppress severe, recalcitrant cases of acne, oral 13-cis-retinoic acid (Accutane) may be used. Similar to but less toxic than other derivatives of vitamin A, this substance should be administered only by a dermatologist. Accutane and all vitamin A derivatives cause increased sun sensitivity, so use sunblock when going outdoors during treatment. Accutane can also cause severe birth defects and should be stopped at least three months before attempting pregnancy.

Dermabrasion, professional skin planing, can significantly improve the appearance of the skin in cases of severe scarring. Dermabrasion can be carried out only after the acne has subsided. Individual scars can also be raised with surgery, or filled with silicone or collagen.

PREVENTION

There are no totally reliable ways to prevent acne. However, to minimize its occurrence, follow cleansing instructions listed in "Treatment."

HOME REMEDIES AND ALTERNATIVE THERAPIES

Aside from following cleansing instructions, there are no reliable home remedies for acne. Although some naturopaths claim acne may be stimulated by refined foods, there is no medical evidence that diet influences the appearance of acne.

MALE/FEMALE DIFFERENCES

Acne is slightly more common and often more severe in men than in women, partly because men produce more androgens, the hormone triggering sebaceous gland activity. For women, it is not unusual for acne to first appear in their mid-20s or even mid-30s because of changes in underlying hormones throughout adulthood or following childbirth.

CORNS AND CALLUSES

DEFINITION

Corns and calluses are tough, thick spots that form where the foot or hand has been subjected to repeated friction or pressure.

CAUSE

On the feet, corns and calluses are usually caused by tight or ill-fitting shoes. Calluses on the hands are usually characteristic of a particular occupation: a laborer's callused joints, the calloused fingertips of a violinist, and a tennis player's thickened palms.

DIAGNOSIS

Corns and calluses may be seen and felt as thickened, horny spots in areas where friction occurs.

TREATMENT

A podiatrist or orthopedic surgeon can remove the thickened growth if home treatment is ineffective.

HOME REMEDIES AND ALTERNATIVE THERAPIES

Corns and calluses can usually be treated at home by following these procedures:

- Apply a plaster (40 percent salicylic acid) just larger than the affected spot.
- Apply a felt pad on top of the plaster to relieve pressure.
- Leave the plaster and pad in place for 1 to 7 days, depending on the thickness of the corn or callus. Trial and error will show how long is needed.
- Remove the plaster, and then remove the whitened, softened skin with a towel, pumice stone, or callus file.
- Repeat until the lesion is gone completely. Continued protection with a felt pad may help prevent recurrence.

PREVENTION

The only way to prevent corns and calluses from forming is by removing the cause of the friction. Wearing roomier shoes or abstaining from the activity that causes the thickening should prevent recurrence.

DERMATITIS

DEFINITION

Dermatitis, also called eczema, refers to any inflammation of the epidermis. The word *dermatitis* refers to the symptoms, not the cause of the irritation. Symptoms of dermatitis in the order in which they occur include:

- Itching
- Reddening (erythema)
- Swelling (edema) as in hives or rashes
- Blistering (vesication) and oozing
- Crusting and scabbing
- Thickening (lichenification) in chronic cases
- Peeling or chafing (excoriation)
- Color change: loss of pigmentation (hypopigmentation) or formation of pigmentation (hyperpigmentation)

Other forms of dermatitis may cause tightness and cracking of the skin rather than blisters. Itching may also be a sign of illness, including kidney, liver, or thyroid disease or internal cancer, environmental sensitivity, or psychological problems.

CAUSE

Dermatitis occurs when the skin reacts to an irritant. Irritants take many forms. Underlying causes of dermatitis include:

- Allergic reaction
- Toxic reaction
- Bacterial infection
- Viral infection
- Genetic predisposition

Specific episodes of dermatitis can be triggered by:

- Sweating
- Contact with toxic or allergenic irritants
- Reaction to ingested medications or allergens
- Clothing, especially wool or silk
- Extreme temperatures
- Emotional stress

Dermatitis is often exacerbated by the itch-scratch-itch cycle.

Some people's skin is more sensitive to irritants than others', so that the same irritant that causes dermatitis in one person may have no effect in another.

DIAGNOSIS

There are many forms of dermatitis, but most can be initially diagnosed by observing itching and/or reddening of the skin. The most common types of dermatitis include:

Atopic Dermatitis. Atopic dermatitis is sensitivity to common substances to which most people have no reaction; hence the name from the Greek *atopos:* "away from the place." An inherited condition, atopic dermatitis is often seen in conjunction with other atopic conditions, such as hay fever, asthma, or hives. It usually appears in infancy, and recurs at intervals into adult life. Early symptoms range from a red, blistering rash to thickening and discoloration of the skin often accompanied by intense itching.

After puberty, this condition predominantly causes dry, itchy patches, often in the folds of elbows or knees. Generally unrelated to food allergies, atopic dermatitis is usually accompanied by lowered resistance to wart infection and vaccinia viruses (used to inoculate against smallpox), but sufferers may be less likely than the general population to contract dermatitis from irritants such as poison ivy.

Because atopic dermatitis often seems to appear at random and can be most severe in the developmental periods of infancy and adolescence, it frequently harms emotional health, interfering with the mother-child relationship or with an adolescent's self-image.

Chronic Dermatitis. Chronic dermatitis is any form of dermatitis persisting for a prolonged period. Usually circumscribed, or limited to a well-defined area (as in lichen simplex), chronic dermatitis is often intensified by an itch-scratch-itch cycle. The affected area grows thick and leathery from continued irritation and the trauma of scratching. If the source of the initial itch is discovered and eliminated, the condition may be quickly relieved. Even if the source is never discovered, the treatment (described in "General Treatment for Dermatitis") can often reduce itching

and lichenification and bring about remission within several weeks.

Contact, Irritant Contact, and Allergic Contact Dermatitis. Contact dermatitis is an acute reaction to contact with a substance to which a person is sensitive or allergic. Irritant contact dermatitis is an occupational hazard to housewives, chemical workers, restaurant workers, doctors, and others whose work brings them into frequent proximity to irritants such as soaps, detergents, chemicals, and abrasives. These substances can either erode the protective oily barriers of the skin or physically injure its surface. With the exception of poison oak and ivy, most contact allergies produce sensitivities in only a few people. The most common contact allergies are to metals (especially nickel), rubber and elasticized garments, dyes, cosmetics (especially nail polish), and leather. But a person can become sensitized to anything, so the search for the offending substance causing this condition may be tedious and frustrating.

Hand Dermatitis. Popularly known as "dishpan hands" or "housewife's eczema," hand dermatitis is difficult to diagnose because it may be a manifestation of several causes, including atopic or nummular dermatitis, allergic contact dermatitis, irritant contact dermatitis, viral or fungal infections, psoriasis, excessive sweating, or nervous tension. Once viral and fungal infections are ruled out, treatment is the same as for contact dermatitis.

Nummular Dermatitis. Nummular dermatitis is eczema that appears in coin-shaped plaques. This ailment is most common in older people, those with extremely dry skin, and in children with atopic dermatitis. The plaques may appear on the backs of hands or the forearms, lower legs, and buttocks. Occasionally a dry environment, other skin diseases, or emotional stress triggers an outbreak. Nummular dermatitis is much more common in the winter, and often goes into remission in the summer.

Seborrheic Dermatitis. Dandruff is a common, mild form of seborrheic dermatitis. This condition, characterized by scaling of the scalp, is controlled by frequent shampooing with either regular or special dandruff shampoos, the most effective of which is determined by trial and error.

In more severe forms of seborrheic dermatitis, scaling and reddening occur not only on the scalp but also on the eyebrows, around the nose, behind the ears, in the underarm and anal-genital areas, and, in obese people, in almost any body fold. Sometimes a reddening and scaling of the eyelids and mild conjunctivitis are the only manifestations of the condition.

Seborrheic dermatitis is often exacerbated by physical or emotional stress. There is an increased incidence in those with Parkinson's disease or other neurologic disorders. Topical corticosteroid therapy is often the most effective treatment, although many patients have had improvements using systemic or topical ketoconazole.

Stasis Dermatitis. Seen primarily in middle age, often striking women who have borne several children, stasis dermatitis is a result of poor circulation. This malady usually first appears on the inside of the lower leg around the ankles forming red, scaly patches that do not itch. Pruritus and secondary infection may follow, and contact dermatitis may also develop.

A common treatment for uncomplicated cases is support stockings. Since the condition is often linked to varicose veins or thrombophlebitis of the legs, the dermatologist may suggest a consultation with a vascular specialist.

GENERAL TREATMENT FOR DERMATITIS

Treatment for dermatitis is designed to decrease trigger factors, reduce itching, suppress inflammation, lubricate the skin, and alleviate anxiety. If trauma caused by scratching complicates the condition, the affected area may be covered. Dermatitis sufferers may address many of these treatment goals themselves, at home. If dryness is a factor, the patient should follow the regimen for dry skin discussed earlier.

If self-treatment does not satisfactorily reduce the problem, medical treatment may be needed.

- *Corticosteroid (cortisone)* cream or ointment for milder cases. When steroid ointments are used around the eyes, regular checks on intraocular pressure are needed to detect glaucoma.
- *Corticosteroid injections* for acute conditions.
- *Phototherapy,* in which the affected area is exposed to strong ultraviolet light, sometimes following the ingestion of PUVA, a sensitizing agent.
- *Tar compounds* applied for prolonged, chronic conditions.
- *Antihistamines* to reduce itching.
- *Tranquilizers* taken before bed to help a patient sleep (without scratching), allowing the irritation to heal.

In cases of acute irritant dermatitis caused by contact with toxic substances, medical help should be sought immediately. Irrigate the affected area with water followed by treatment appropriate to burns (see chapter 14). The exact nature of the treatment depends on the irritant; the medical team treating the injury will need to know as much information as possible about the chemical composition of the irritant.

PREVENTION

Prevention methods vary depending on the type of dermatitis.

PREVENTION FOR ATOPIC DERMATITIS

- Follow "General Principles of Skin and Hair Care" for dry skin, described earlier.
- Apply prescribed medications or lotions immediately after bathing.
- Keep temperatures in your house as constant as possible.
- Avoid irritating fabrics such as wool, silk, and rough synthetics; wear absorbent fabric such as cotton next to the skin.
- Use mild laundry detergent and be sure that laundry is well rinsed.
- Promptly treat any infection of the skin.
- Avoid excess humidity.
- Vacation or live in a moderate climate.
- Maintain emotional stability.

PREVENTION FOR IRRITANT DERMATITIS

- Wear cotton gloves under rubber gloves for all wet work, or use a barrier cream two to three times a day and after handwashing.
- Avoid contact with harsh soaps, abrasives, and solvents.
- Avoid contact with allergenic substances.
- Use the mildest possible soap for bathing and handwashing.
- Use moisturizing cream or lotion frequently.
- Wash any area that comes in contact with an irritant as thoroughly and as quickly as possible after contact.

MALE/FEMALE DIFFERENCES

With the exception of stasis dermatitis, dermatitis occurs equally often in men as in women. Because of the circulatory stress that occurs with childbearing, stasis dermatitis occurs more frequently in women who have had children.

HOME REMEDIES AND ALTERNATIVE THERAPIES

Stress reduction techniques, such as yoga or meditation, are beneficial when dermatitis is triggered by anxiety and emotional turmoil. Evening primrose oil, oil from the seed of the plant, is taken orally for dermatitis. This oil may help some patients.

HAIR LOSS

DEFINITION

Male Pattern Baldness. This, the most common type of hair loss, may begin anytime after the midteens. First the hairline recedes at the temples, followed by some thinning on the top, with the crown becoming completely bald first. All the while, the hairline between the temples has been gradually receding, and finally the receding hairlines meet, leaving a bald pate with a fringe around the sides and back.

Telogen Effluvium. Telogen effluvium is a sudden, temporary hair loss caused by acute illness, surgery, stress, pregnancy, or cessation of birth control pills.

Alopecia Areata. Hair that falls out in patches is called alopecia areata. When only a few spots become bald, the hair often grows back of its own accord. In its most severe form (alopecia universalis) the individual loses all body hair including eyelashes, brows, and pubic hair.

Anagen Effluvium. This type of hair loss, often caused by the effects of drugs or other medical treatment, such as those used in conjuction with organ transplant or cancer therapy, usually takes place during the growing stage. The hair usually grows back when treatment is discontinued.

CAUSE

Some hair loss is a normal part of hair's growth cycle. Each of the roughly 100,000 hairs on a human head is going through a growth cycle independently of every other hair. About 90 percent of hairs at any given time will be in the first, or growing stage, which lasts 4 to 5 years. The other 10 percent will be in the resting phase, which lasts only a few months and ends when the hair falls out as a result of new growth underneath. Perhaps 50 hairs will fall out of an average head in an average day. Abnormal hair loss may be caused by many factors.

- *Metabolic disorders* may be initiated by starvation, sudden weight loss through dieting, iron deficiency caused by blood loss, diabetes, thyroid disease, or other disorders.
- *Hair shaft disorders* are often caused by chemical or physical treatments such as permanents or hair straightening done improperly or too frequently. May also be congenital.
- *Scalp disorders;* only very severe scalp problems produce significant hair loss.
- *Trauma* such as acute illness, surgery, stress, pregnancy, or cessation of birth control pills can cause the sudden temporary hair loss called telogen effluvium. These conditions may cause hair to stop growing and enter the resting phase. When growth resumes 1 to 3 months later, patients may be alarmed at their hair loss, but the underlying cause for the loss has already been corrected, so no treatment is needed.
- *Drugs or other medical treatment* can sometimes cause hair loss of anagen effluvium. In this case, the hair usually grows back after the treatment is discontinued.
- *Male pattern baldness* is caused by a combination of three factors interacting anytime after the midteens: heredity, androgen hormones, and aging.

A tendency toward baldness in the male members of either the father's or mother's family may indicate a predisposition to male pattern baldness.

DIAGNOSIS

Hair loss is usually diagnosed through observation, after which trigger factors may be sought. The source and pattern of hair loss will indicate the prognosis for its growing back.

TREATMENT

Alopecia Areata. When hair falls out in only a few patches it often grows back of its own accord. Corticosteroids may be given by mouth or injection to arrest or decelerate hair loss, but the treatment is not always successful.

Male Pattern Baldness. This condition has no known cure. Topical minoxidil offers some benefit in selected patients. Many people prefer to do nothing about it, allowing it to run its course. If remedy is desired, the condition can be disguised with no risk and little expense using artificial hairpieces and hair weaving. Many men, however, seek a more permanent solution. Transplanting hair from other regions of the scalp or surgically excising bald areas are the only such alternatives presently available. Artificial hair should never be used for hair transplants, as it will eventually be rejected and lead to infection and scarring.

HIVES

DEFINITION

Hives (urticaria) are itchy swellings of brief duration that affect about 20 percent of Americans at some point in their lives. Hives often appear as groups of bumps on the skin and usually disappear without a trace.

CAUSE

A single hive is usually a reaction to an outside irritant, such as an insect bite. Multiple hives are usually an allergic reaction to an internal agent. Common causes of hives are:

- Emotional stress.
- Sunshine.
- Food (especially shellfish, nuts, and berries).
- Heat or cold.
- Infections.
- Insect bites: A weal resulting from an insect bite normally subsides in a few hours. Severe local reactions may involve an unusual amount of swelling at the site. Toxic reactions, usually caused by ten or more simultaneous stings, may cause nausea, dizziness, headache, and fever. Immediate systemic reactions, called anaphylaxis or anaphylactic shock, are life-threatening and require immediate attention. Within minutes after the sting a patient will exhibit hives, swelling of the larynx, difficulty breathing and swallowing, cold sweats, abdominal cramps, and a sharp drop in blood pressure (for treatment of anaphylaxis, see chapter 14).
- Medications: Reactions to medications usually occur within an hour of ingestion. Swelling of the larynx may accompany hives. Late reactions may appear up to 3 days after administration, taking the form of a rash, hives, or an abnormal reaction of one of the organ systems. Drug-related rashes spread progressively from head to feet, and clear up in the same pattern over a 2-to-3-week period. In the presence of these symptoms, use of the drug should be discontinued.

TREATMENT

To treat the symptoms, a doctor may suggest cool compresses, soaking baths, lotions to alleviate itching, or antihistamines for itching and swelling. Antihistamines infrequently cause blurred vision or difficulty in urination.

For severe cases or when a patient is in danger of anaphylaxis, an injection of adrenaline is required immediately to raise the blood pressure and open up breathing passages. After adrenaline is injected and the immediate emergency passes, antihistamines and corticosteroids are given.

PREVENTION

The first line of preventive therapy is to find and eliminate the trigger factor. If the condition persists (chronic urticaria) there are probably multiple trigger factors. People who are known to be sensitive to bee stings should avoid areas populated by bees and should keep a syringe and dose of adrenaline on hand (and know how to inject themselves if they are stung). It

may also be possible to be desensitized to bee stings by an allergist, though this is a controversial procedure.

MOLES AND BIRTHMARKS

DEFINITION

Moles (pigmented nevi) and birthmarks are usually benign growths found in greater or lesser numbers on most people. Occasionally these growths may become malignant, so they need to be periodically checked for unusual changes in color and size (as indicated below).

CAUSE

Birthmarks, as their name states, are present at birth. The appearance of moles often begins in early childhood and is not well understood. So-called port wine stains and cherry-colored moles are caused by various abnormalities in capillary formation. Sun and age cause the skin to create a variety of spots and growths as well as wrinkles. Heredity interacts with the environment to influence how early these degenerative signs begin to appear.

DIAGNOSIS

These skin markings are identified by their physical appearance.

- *Sebborheic keratoses* are rough brown spots, either flat or slightly elevated. They run in families and increase with age. They are not dangerous but too many can be a nuisance.
- *Nevi (moles),* may start off flat at birth or in early childhood, but may become lighter and slightly raised as time passes. They sometimes darken during pregnancy.
- *Actinic keratoses (solar keratoses)* are flat, pink, scaly spots that grow on sun-damaged skin. They are more frequent and more numerous in fair-skinned individuals, and they are a type of growth that can become malignant.
- *Liver spots (lentigines)* are flat brown, liver-colored spots that are closely associated with sun-damaged skin. They are not actually related to liver function and pose no risk.

TREATMENT

Most moles, birthmarks, and keratoses are benign and require no treatment, although some are treated strictly for cosmetic reasons. In rare cases, an existing mole can become cancerous; changes in color, color irregularities, irregular shape, size greater than 6 millimeters in diameter, or changes in height should be checked by a dermatologist.

Actinic keratoses can become malignant and should be removed individually, or if they occur over a wide area the entire area may be treated with a 5-fluorouracil or masoprocol cream.

PITYRIASIS ROSEA

DEFINITION

Pityriasis rosea is a skin rash that appears primarily in adolescents and young adults. It starts on the trunk with one or two small red spots and spreads to cover all or part of the trunk and upper arms.

CAUSE

The cause of this rash is unknown.

DIAGNOSIS

Since the appearance of pityriasis rosea can be confused with secondary syphilis, a blood test should be performed in all patients to rule this out.

TREATMENT

There is no danger attached to this rash and it usually goes away on its own over a period of weeks. If it is itchy, the rash may be soothed with calamine lotion. If itching is severe, a doctor may prescribe antihistamine tablets or a steroid cream.

PSORIASIS

DEFINITION

Psoriasis is a skin condition in which itchy round or oval patches of skin break out on the scalp, elbows, knees, palms, or soles. The patches can also occasionally appear on the lower back or in folds of the skin, especially in the obese. When the nails are affected, the nail surface may become pitted or the dry, scaly material that separates the nails from the nail bed may build up. Psoriasis generally appears for the first time in early adulthood, but its initial appearance can occur late in life.

This malady is often chronic, erratic, and unpredictable. Striking about 1 percent of the total population, 1 of 20 people with psoriasis develops a type of arthritis different from rheumatoid arthritis, affecting the hands and, in severe cases, the back.

CAUSE

Psoriasis is linked to a defect in the production of the epidermal layer of the skin. Instead of taking the usual 26 to 28 days to form the epidermis, the process takes only 3 to 4 days. This causes an abnormal outer skin layer of red patches to form.

Heredity apparently plays a role in the development of psoriasis, but the disease is *not* contagious. Often, the condition appears after an injury to the skin or a generalized infection, and once it has appeared, an outbreak of psoriasis can be precipitated or aggravated by emotional stress, drug reactions, or a strep throat.

DIAGNOSIS

The presence of scaly patches distinguishes psoriasis from basic dermatitis. Occasionally, however, psoriasis begins as a group of little pimples instead of scaly patches. This is especially common when psoriasis is triggered by a streptoccocal infection such as a sore throat. In severe cases, the patches may run together and the body may be virtually covered with a red, bumpy rash. If psoriasis is present in warm, damp skin-fold areas, it will probably have no scales.

TREATMENT

With appropriate therapy, psoriasis can be rendered minimally annoying in the vast majority of cases. Many of the treatments for psoriasis are similar to those used in treatment of dermatitis.

- *Topical corticosteroid* cream, ointment, or shampoo is used as needed.
- *Coal tar* ointment or shampoo controls scaling in some cases.
- *Phototherapy* with ultraviolet light combined with coal tar ointment has been beneficial to sufferers of widespread psoriasis.
- *Acid gels* or creams remove scales.
- *Retinoids,* or derivatives of vitamin A and vitamin A acid, may also be effective, but they can have significant side effects, including birth defects.
- *PUVA* is a relatively new treatment in which a psoralen pill is taken prior to phototherapy to enhance the healing quality of the ultraviolet light. This treatment must be continuous to prevent relapse, and increased risk of skin cancer must be considered.
- *Methotrexate* and other internal drugs used in treating cancer should be used with caution and close medical supervision, since these substances can have serious side effects.
- *Vitamin D_3 and cyclosporine* are being investigated by medical researchers for their effectiveness in treating psoriasis.

PREVENTION

The unpredictable nature of psoriasis is the most difficult factor in its prevention and management. While about two-thirds of patients enjoy substantial periods of remission, neither the physician nor the patient can tell whether the remission will last a few weeks, a few months, years, or forever. Prevention is therefore tricky. Avoiding triggers such as emotional stress may helpful.

HOME REMEDIES AND ALTERNATIVE THERAPIES

Sauna baths to hydrate the skin are sometimes recommended for psoriasis but their effectiveness has not been proven. Naturopaths recommend fish oil supplements or a diet high in oily fish, but these measures have not been shown to be reliably effective.

ROSACEA

DEFINITION

Rosacea is a condition in which flushing of the skin in the areas of the forehead, nose, cheekbones, and chin becomes recurrent or permanent and marked.

DIAGNOSIS

Rosacea appears most often between the ages of 30 and 50. Fair-skinned people are more susceptible than people with dark skin. The reddened skin may show pustules, and in severe cases these pustules, especially on the nose, can be extremely tender. There may also be thickening of the affected skin. In some men there is a proliferation of reddish tumors on the nose, causing it to become grossly enlarged.

CAUSE

While the underlying cause is not known, rosacea is often triggered or worsened by the ingestion of hot liquids, spicy foods, or alcohol. Emotional stress, extreme temperatures, or sunlight may also set off a reaction.

TREATMENT

Treatment is similar to that used for acne. Tetracycline is given to control pustules, and topical medications are used to reduce active inflammation.

MALE/FEMALE DIFFERENCES

Women are three times as likely to be affected as men, but men are more likely to have the most severe form of rosacea.

PREVENTION

Avoiding triggers such as hot liquids, spicy foods, alcohol, emotional stress, extreme temperatures, and sunlight may lessen its occurrence.

SKIN CANCER

DEFINITION

Most skin cancer consists of tumors formed on the skin damaged by prolonged exposure to the sun. They rarely spread to other parts of the body, but if left untreated, they can invade other tissue.

Cancer of the skin is more common than all other forms of malignancy combined. Skin cancer is usually curable if caught in the early stages, but if left untreated some forms can spread to other parts of the body and can be lethal.

CAUSE

Skin cancer is often closely associated with excessive exposure to the sun. Severe sunburns can be particularly damaging to skin, but most skin cancers are related to the total amount of sunlight absorbed rather than to particular incidents of skin trauma. Exposure to chemicals, long-standing infection, and x-ray therapy can also contribute to the formation of cancerous skin lesions.

DIAGNOSIS

Unfortunately, skin cancer often looks like benign skin conditions and vice versa, so self-diagnosis is not always possible. Tests for malignancy require removal of cells from the suspect growth for microscopic examination. Even though most new growths are harmless, any growths or skin lesions that change size, shape, or color should be checked with a doctor. Lesions that bleed frequently, even with apparent cause, such as a shaving nick, should also be checked. "Better safe than sorry" is a good motto in this case.

There are three primary types of skin cancer:

- *Basal cell carcinoma,* the most common type of skin cancer, is most often seen in people over 40, and is linked to sun damage. Basal cell carcinoma rarely spreads to other parts of the body, but if left untreated it can invade other tissue.
- *Squamous cell carcinoma,* found most frequently on the head, face, and hands, is also associated with exposure to the sun. It can be cured if treated early and, though it can spread, is rarely life-threatening.
- *Malignant melanoma* is the leading cause of

death from skin diseases. Although it can arise from an existing mole, this is exceedingly rare; in the vast majority of cases, malignant melanoma starts in a new growth that is cancerous from inception. Characteristics of new growths that should be examined by a doctor include irregular, speckled, mixed coloration of various shades and hues; irregular shape; irregular surface; and rapid change or growth.

TREATMENT

Removal of basal and squamous cell carcinomas is localized and relatively easy. In malignant melanoma, the growth, along with a large amount of the surrounding and underlying skin, will be removed to get rid of any malignant cells that may have moved away from the original growth.

PREVENTION

The best way to avoid skin cancer is to stay out of the sun. If exposure to the sun is necessary, wearing a hat and applying strong sunblock on all exposed areas of the body is recommended. Children and adolescents in particular need extra protection.

SKIN INFECTIONS

The many forms of skin infections may be caused by viruses, bacteria, fungi, or mites. Superficial bacterial infections and common viral, fungal, and parasitic skin infections are discussed in this section; more complicated skin and soft tissue infections are covered in chapter 18, Infectious Diseases.

VIRAL INFECTIONS

FEVER BLISTERS AND COLD SORES

DEFINITION

Cold sores are caused by the herpes simplex Type 1 virus and are sometimes referred to as facial herpes. They are not related to herpes simplex Type 2 (genital herpes). The sores generally though not always appear on or around the lip, and they are contagious. They appear 3 to 12 days after exposure to the virus, and last 1 to 3 weeks, or an average of about 10 days for recurring cases.

At least 70 percent of the U.S. population has experienced fever blisters or cold sores by age 14. The first epi-

sode may be very painful and disabling, but recurrences are usually more annoying than anything else.

DIAGNOSIS

Cold sores can be diagnosed by physical examination. In addition to tenderness and blistering of the skin at the site of the blister or sore, the lymph nodes may be swollen and tender. There may also be a high fever and malodorous oozing from the affected site, and the patient may have difficulty eating.

CAUSE

Recurrent herpes can be triggered by overexposure to the sun, high fever or other infection in the body, trauma, menstruation, or emotional disturbance.

TREATMENT

Cold sores may be treated, and sometimes even prevented, with an antiviral compound, acyclovir, available in oral or topical preparations by prescription. Analgesics for pain and analgesic mouthwash may also ease the symptoms.

PREVENTION

Staying away from avoidable triggers of cold sores such as emotional turmoil or overexposure to sunlight will help prevent occurrences. But other triggers including menstruation and infection are not avoidable.

HOME REMEDIES AND ALTERNATIVE THERAPIES

Home remedies such as gargling with salt water or holding hot tea in the mouth may help soothe the pain but do not deal with the causative virus.

MOLLUSCA

DEFINITION, DIAGNOSIS, AND CAUSE

Mollusca are small viral growths that appear singly or in groups on the face, trunk, lower abdomen, pelvis, inner thighs, or penis. They are identified by appearance—skin-colored or pearly white pimples with a small depression in the center. Once found primarily on the face and trunk of children, they are now quite common in sexually active young adults.

TREATMENT

Mollusca may be treated by freezing, electrosurgery, excision with a curet, or applications of a blistering agent.

SHINGLES

DEFINITION

Shingles (herpes zoster), which usually only occurs once in a lifetime, appears as a rash (clusters of blisters with a red base). It is caused by the same virus responsible for chickenpox. For reasons that are not understood, the virus remains dormant after the chickenpox resolve until it is triggered and reappears.

CAUSE

Shingles is caused by the herpes zoster virus.

DIAGNOSIS

A physical examination is used to confirm shingles. The condition appears as a rash on one side of the body or face in an area supplied by one particular spinal nerve. Sometimes the rash is preceded by several days of tingling or prickling sensations. In a few cases, nerve pain (neuralgia) can persist for months or even years.

TREATMENT

As in herpes simplex, only the symptoms of shingles can be treated. A doctor may recommend anesthetic medication for the rash and analgesics for the nerve pain. Oral acyclovir therapy will lessen the severity of the eruption. Persistent neuralgia can often be treated with medications used for seizures or depression, but in general time offers the only cure.

HOME REMEDIES AND ALTERNATIVE THERAPIES

Acupuncture is sometimes recommended for postshingles neuropathy, nerve pain that persists long after the shingles rash clears up.

WARTS

DEFINITION AND CAUSE

Warts are a common, benign skin tumor caused by viral infection. They are contagious, but usually spread on the infected person rather than being passed on to someone else.

DIAGNOSIS

Warts are diagnosed with a physical examination. Hands and feet are the most common sites. On the hands, warts form the horny nodule usually associated with the name "wart." When they grow on the soles of feet, they may resemble small calluses, because the body's weight causes them to grow beneath the skin's surface rather than being raised. Except for plantar warts growing at pressure points on the heel or ball of the foot, most warts are not painful or itchy.

TREATMENT

Fifty percent of all warts disappear within 2 years with no therapy at all. There are several ways to remove warts, if removal is desired. A doctor can help choose the most appropriate treatment based on the size and location of the wart, the patient's age, and other factors.

WART REMOVAL TECHNIQUES

- *Superficial electrodesiccation* uses bursts of electric current to destroy the growth. This method is not recommended for anyone wearing a pacemaker, and it can cause scarring.
- *Curettage* involves cutting away the growth with a curet, an instrument with a small, loop-shaped cutting edge.
- *Cantharidin* is a poison that causes blistering, breaking, and crusting, eventually breaking down the growth without scars.
- *Cytotoxic agents,* which are poison to the infected cells. These are frequently used for warts in the anal-genital area.
- *Cryosurgery,* freezing the growth with liquid nitrogen. This is fairly quick therapy, usually requiring no anesthesia. Sometimes a small white dot remains at the site of the growth.
- *Laser cauterization,* in which heat produced by intense light is used to destroy the growth.

HOME REMEDIES AND ALTERNATIVE THERAPIES

If you have a wart you can treat it with an over-the-counter salicylic-lactic acid preparation. Other acids are not recommended.

Note: Regardless of therapy, there is a 25 percent chance that warts will recur after treatment.

SUPERFICIAL BACTERIAL INFECTIONS

INTERTRIGO

DEFINITION

Intertrigo is an eruption of the skin caused by the friction of two adjacent skin surfaces. It occurs most frequently in the underarms, groin, inner thighs, and below the breasts of obese people.

CAUSE

Friction between adjoining layers of skin combined with heat and sweat retained in generally covered areas of the body provide a perfect environment for the growth of the bacteria, fungi, and yeast that cause intertrigo. The presence of these organisms may cause ulcers, which may in turn be invaded by other organisms.

DIAGNOSIS

Diagnosis of intertrigo generally consists of a physical exam of the affected area of the body.

TREATMENT

To treat intertrigo, the opposing skin surfaces must be kept clean, free of friction, and open to the air to the extent possible. Any infectious organisms should be eliminated with the topical use of appropriate medications.

HOME REMEDIES AND ALTERNATIVE THERAPIES

In conjunction with medications to eliminate infectious organisms, absorbent powders should be applied to dry surfaces. A hair dryer on the cool setting is helpful in drying skin folds.

FOLLICULITIS

DEFINITION

Folliculitis is an infection of hair follicles on the face usually caused by shaving.

CAUSE

Folliculitis occurs when staph bacteria enter the hair follicle and cause a superficial infection, most frequently as a result of a razor passing over the hair follicle.

DIAGNOSIS

Diagnosis is by physical exam of the infection, which starts as a single pus-filled pimple and then quickly spreads to adjacent areas.

TREATMENT

Medical treatment usually consists of taking a prescribed antibiotic for 10 to 14 days.

HOME REMEDIES AND ALTERNATIVE THERAPIES

- Bathe frequently and pay special attention to keeping the nails short and clean.
- The family should use separate towels, washcloths,

bed linens, and clothing. These should be changed daily and laundered in soapy water.
- Before shaving, wash face with an antibacterial soap.
- After shaving, apply alcohol to the affected area. Then rub in antibacterial cream.
- Immerse razors in alcohol between shaves, and do not share razors.

FURUNCLES AND CARBUNCLES

DEFINITION

Furuncles are boils—infections of the deepest part of the hair follicles. Carbuncles are staph abscesses that are larger and deeper than boils.

CAUSE

Furuncles and carbuncles are caused by the invasion of microorganisms deep into hair follicles, where they inflame and infect surrounding tissue.

DIAGNOSIS

These growths can be identified from their characteristic appearance on the face, scalp, buttocks, or underarms. They can be extremely painful. When they occur on the eyelid, they are called sties. Carbuncles usually have several heads from which they drain, and are found on the neck, back, and thighs.

TREATMENT

They will often go away by themselves after several days. If they are very large, however, a doctor may drain them by making a small incision after they come to a head. If the boils cause significant inflammation of surrounding areas, if they are accompanied by a fever, or if they appear on the upper lip, nose, cheeks, or forehead, they should be treated by a physician.

HOME REMEDIES AND ALTERNATIVE THERAPIES

If the boils are not too large, they should be treated with moist heat only.

INFESTATIONS

HEAD AND BODY LICE

DEFINITION

These uncomfortable infestations are due to a tiny insect called the pediculus humanus. The first noticeable sign that lice are living on your skin or hair is usually an uncomfortable itch.

PARASITES

Lymphogranuloma venereum is a relatively rare, sexually transmitted disease caused by a parasite. It initially appears as a little pimple or blister 1 to 3 weeks after infection, and usually goes unnoticed at first. Two to 3 weeks after the appearance of the initial lesion, the lymph glands on one side of the groin become swollen and tender and the skin becomes tight and bluish red. The swelling may fester. Antibiotics are the usual treatment, and a doctor may also aspirate the inflamed gland. Another rare, parasite-related condition is *granuloma inguinale,* in which painless but malodorous ulcers form in the groin area, possibly accompanied by movable masses under the skin. Treatment is similar to that for lymphogranuloma venereum.

CAUSE

Head lice are transmitted through contact, clothing, or hairbrushes, while body lice are transmitted through bedding or clothing.

DIAGNOSIS

Diagnosis is through physical exam for the offending pest. Although adult head lice are difficult to find in the hair, nits (egg sacs) can more readily be found attached to the hair, especially around the ears and at the back of the head. They are extremely itchy, and are sometimes accompanied by hives, generalized itching, impetigo, or boils.

Body lice can rarely be found on the body, but they may be located in the seams of clothing or in bedding folds. On the body there may be scratch marks, hives, eczematous changes, and red pimples, especially on the back.

TREATMENT

To treat head lice, a pesticide shampoo is left on the scalp for a few minutes, then rinsed, and the hair is combed with a special comb to remove nits. For body lice, wash with a pesticide preparation, then wash all clothing and linen in very hot water and dry it on the hot cycle.

PUBIC LICE (PEDICULOSIS PUBIS)

DEFINITION

Pubic lice, usually known as crabs, are small, yellow-gray, wingless insects that attach themselves to the skin in the pubic area and lay their eggs (nits) on the pubic hair. They cause itching and sometimes hives.

CAUSE

Pubic lice are transmitted by sexual contact.

TREATMENT

Pubic lice may be eradicated by shampooing the affected area with one of several effective over-the-counter preparations. Clothing and linen should then be washed in very hot water and dried on the hot cycle.

SCABIES

DEFINITION

Scabies is a mite infestation that appears as little ridges or dotted lines ending in blisters.

CAUSE

Like crabs, scabies is acquired primarily through intimate personal contact, but it may also be transmitted through towels, linens, or clothing. Severe itching appears after 3 to 4 weeks and is at its worst just after going to bed.

DIAGNOSIS

Scabies can be identified with a physical examination. The characteristic rash is commonly found between the fingers, around the wrists, on the elbows, navel, nipples, lower abdomen, and in the genital area. Some people become sensitized to the mite and have hives, scaling, or other skin changes as well. It is not uncommon to see secondary skin infections and boils with scabies.

TREATMENT

Treatment involves using a pesticide shampoo for pubic hair and a cream or lotion for other parts of the body. The whole body must be treated for the cure to be effective. Clothing and linen must be washed in very hot water, as with crabs. Household members and people with whom sexual contact has been made should be treated even if they have no visible symptoms. Itching may continue for 1 to 2 weeks after successful eradication of the mite. The mite of canine scabies is also highly contagious and may be contracted through contact with a dog having mange. Canine scabies cause pimples or blisters without burrows and are found on the trunk, arms, and abdomen. One treatment with pesticide lotion is generally sufficient to eradicate the canine scabies mite.

29
Allergies

· · · · · · · · · · · · · · · ·

WILLIAM J. DAVIS, M.D.

GENERAL DEFINITION OF ALLERGIES

The word *allergy,* coined in 1906 by the Austrian pediatrician Clemens von Pirquet, comes from the Greek word *allos,* meaning "change in the original state." Allergy describes the altered or heightened response your immune system may display toward an otherwise harmless substance. Once you are sensitized to a particular substance, your immune system overreacts to it in future contacts, causing inflammation or irritation of the eyes, nose, throat, lungs, skin, digestive system, or other sensitive areas of the body. These distressing physical effects, stemming from hypersensitivity to a normally harmless substance, constitute an allergic reaction.

Allergies wreak havoc on the health of many people; an estimated 40 million people suffer allergy in the United States. Allergy keeps children out of school for more days than any other illness. And 10 million people suffer from asthma alone, which kills an estimated 3,000 annually.

A substance that produces an allergic reaction is known as an allergen. The symptoms and severity of allergies are extremely diverse, largely depending on the allergen and how it interacts with the antibodies the immune system releases against it. Respiratory allergens, such as dust, pollen, or animal dander, usually trigger relatively benign symptoms, including an itchy, sneezy, runny nose and irritated eyes. Other allergens, including wasp stings, penicillin shots, and some foods, can induce a life-threatening collapse known as anaphylactic shock in the hypersensitive.

Allergies develop at any age, but new ones rarely appear after age 40. Food allergies and asthma usually manifest themselves in childhood, while reactions to drugs are most common among young and middle-aged adults. Allergic symptoms generally diminish with age, and sometimes allergies to particular substances disappear completely with time.

GENERAL CAUSES OF ALLERGIES

The tendency to develop an allergy is inherited, but specific allergies are not. If you suffer an allergic condition you probably have a close relative with a type of hypersensitivity, but the specific allergens that trouble each of you are probably different.

No one knows why specific allergies develop, but the cause of allergies in general is clearly a misdirected response of the immune system (see figure 29.1). Normally, the immune system seeks, recognizes, and destroys bacteria, viruses, and other dangerous bodily invaders. The world is full of these intruders, known as antigens, and it is the job of the immune systems to prevent the body from being overwhelmed.

One of the main defenses against invaders are special molecules called antibodies, which match and counter antigens. The key soldiers of the immune system are lymphocytes, white blood cells manufactured by the millions in bone marrow. The lymphocytes interact with each antigen and release specific antibodies into the bloodstream, ready to attack antigens, defend the body against their harm, or make the invaders vulnerable to consumption by roaming scavenger cells called macrophages. Antibody-producing lymphocytes are called B cells.

Whenever lymphocytes are activated, some of them become "memory" cells, designed to remember antigens and be primed to destroy them if they ever reenter the body. (For a schematic illustration of the immune system, see chapter 18, Infectious Diseases.) This long-term memory is called acquired immunity, and is the reason most people don't get the same cold or the chickenpox twice.

Since we encounter so many varied substances every day, and ingest a wide variety of food, drink, and medications, the immune system is not designed to attack every foreign entrant. Rather, it selectively seeks out only those germs and invading antigens that are perceived as potential hazards, such as infectious agents or poisons. In this context, when you inherit the genetic tendency to develop allergies, the immune system selectively misreads foreign substances, mistaking benign substances for dangerous ones. Antibodies then react to what should be harmless food, chemicals, pollen, or other allergens.

The immune system produces five types of antibodies, but the principal class that participates in allergic reactions is immunoglobulin E, known as IgE. Every individual has various IgE antibodies, and each allergen stimulates production of a specific form of IgE. An IgE antibody designed to respond to ragweed pollen, for example, will react only to ragweed and not to oak, bluegrass, goldenrod, or any other type of pollen.

Within the body of allergy sufferers, IgE antibodies to specific allergens exist by the millions, attached either to a type of circulating white blood cell called a basophil, or to mast cells lining the respiratory tract, the gastrointestinal tract, or the subcutaneous layer of the skin. When IgE antibodies encounter the allergen they are designed to combat, they signal the basophils or mast cells to unleash histamine and other potent "mediating" chemicals into the site of allergen invasion.

These mediating chemicals—mainly histamine—instigate the distressful symptoms of allergic reactions. Histamine released in the nose, eyes, and sinuses, for example, stimulates sneezing, a runny nose, and itchiness; released in the lungs, it narrows and swells the lining of the airways and increases mucus secretion; in the

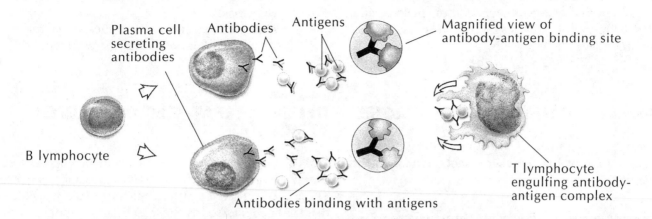

Figure 29.1: What happens during an allergic reaction. When an allergen is present, the body responds by producing a B lymphocyte, which in turn stimulates the plasma cells to secrete an antibody against that particular antigen. These antibodies bind to the antigen, forming an antibody-antigen complex. The complex is then engulfed by a T lymphocyte.

skin it raises rashes and hives; in the digestive system it provokes stomach cramps and diarrhea.

Some scientists believe that a single major gene controls an individual's IgE concentrations; others think that a more complex relationship exists. The intensity of an allergic reaction is directly related to several factors.

- Amount of histamine and other chemical mediators flooding the tissues
- Allergic person's state of health and genetic makeup
- Total level in the body of IgE to a particular antigen

GENERAL DIAGNOSIS OF ALLERGIES

Sneezing, wheezing, scratching, and itching are the allergic symptoms that most often bring patients to physicians for allergy evaluations. Diagnosis of an allergy can be difficult. Allergists say that two of every ten allergies get a "wastebasket diagnosis"—diverse, vague symptoms are attributed to all kinds of allergies but a specific identification pinpointing the exact cause is elusive. Diagnosis of specific allergies entails analysis of medical history, and patient interview, physical examination, and allergy tests and laboratory analyses.

The patient interview contributes significantly to deduction of the source of an allergy. The information elicited includes:

- The main discomfort
- Any present illness
- Past medical problems

- Family medical history
- Environmental history, including information on pets, workplace, household plants, etc.
- Complete food history
- Present and past social and emotional condition

If the information is inadequate for a diagnosis, the physician may ask the patient to start a diary of allergic reactions. If a reaction takes place only at a certain time of year, for instance, seasonal pollens or molds may be suspected. If a reaction occurs only when visiting people who own pets, animal dander may be the causative agent.

In the physical examination, the physician closely studies the allergy sufferer's skin, eyes, nose, ears, lungs, and abdomen. Topical reactions are also closely analyzed. Diagnostic tests may include:

- Blood counts
- X-rays of the lungs
- Pulmonary function tests
- Cultures to detect the presence of infectious agents
- Specific allergy tests such as bronchial challenge, or the radioallergosorbent (RAST) test (see Respiratory Allergies), and skin tests

Skin tests, in which small amounts of allergens are pricked into the skin, provide the basis for most diagnoses because they are generally accurate and comprehensive. However, a positive skin test is not absolute proof that an allergy exists or that an allergen is clinically relevant (causes a significant reaction in normal circumstances). Conversely, a negative skin reaction does not always rule out an allergic problem; thus, these tests must be interpreted cautiously and in conjunction with a patient's medical history. The most reliable skin tests are those for airborne allergens such as dust, pollens, and molds. The results of skin tests for food allergens are the most unreliable.

GENERAL TREATMENT FOR ALLERGIES

Standard allergy treatment consists of avoiding the allergen, desensitization through allergy shots, and treatment of symptoms.

ENVIRONMENTAL CONTROL OR REMOVAL OF ALLERGEN

If an allergen is easily isolated and removable from a person's life, elimination solves an allergy problem without need for further treatment. Examples of isolated allergy sources easy to avoid include down, animal dander, and cow's milk. In these cases, allergy sufferers switch to pillows and blankets of synthetic material, sell or give away pets (although this may be emotionally painful), and eliminate milk from the diet.

Many airborne pollutants that provoke or aggravate allergic reactions may be reduced by air filters.

ALLERGY SHOTS

Allergy shots are one of the most common approaches to long-term control of allergies. Injections of allergens in gradually increasing amounts stimulate production of a blocking antibody that interferes with the troublesome IgE molecule's interaction with the allergen. This agent prevents or curbs the release of histamine that the IgE would otherwise trigger. Several allergens can be combined in each injection.

Injections don't cure allergies; they desensitize the immune system and sometimes control symptoms to the point that they disappear. Weekly injections to attain maximum immunization may take anywhere from 12 weeks (for a ragweed allergy) to 2 to 3 years. After that, maintenance shots are given every 2 to 6 weeks, often for many years. Timing is important for seasonal pollen and mold allergies. Shots should be planned so the maximum dosage is reached by hay fever season. Shots are given on a year-round basis.

Allergy shots aid many people—6 million Americans receive them—but they have drawbacks:

- Inconvenience of visiting a physician repeatedly over an indefinite period of time.
- Expense of repeated visits to a physician.
- Time-consuming; many physicians ask patients to remain in the office for 20 minutes after the shot to

guard against rare instances of life-threatening anaphylactic reaction.
- Possible ineffectiveness: For some people allergy shots don't work, or offer only marginal relief.

GENERAL TREATMENT OF ALLERGY SYMPTOMS

Antihistamine drugs are the principal treatment for most allergy symptoms, particularly for inhalant allergies. These medications block the release of the histamine that has been released by the mast cells in response to an allergen.

For information on antihistamines, see Appendix A.

HOME REMEDIES AND ALTERNATIVE THERAPIES

Although a number of alternative therapies are promoted to alleviate allergies, most are of little benefit, and some can make matters worse. For example, if you have hay fever that is triggered by various pollens, be wary of herbal allergy remedies that may contain the same allergens that provoke your symptoms.

Also be wary of alternative practitioners who claim to treat allergies with high-dose vitamins. Allergies are not caused by nutritional deficiencies, and there is no evidence that supplements can alleviate or prevent symptoms.

ANAPHYLAXIS

DEFINITION

Anaphylaxis is the most frightening and severe, but infrequent, allergic reaction. Anaphylaxis begins minutes after exposure to an allergic agent and progresses rapidly. The most serious consequence is a constriction or narrowing of the airways and the dilation of blood vessels, resulting in difficult breathing, rapid pulse, a fall in blood pressure, and possible cardiovascular collapse, shock, and death.

CAUSE

Anaphylaxis can result from reactions to drugs like penicillin, insulin, aspirin, and contrast materials injected to improve x-ray images; horse serum (used in some vaccines); insect stings; and certain foods. Even everyday respiratory allergens like pollen sometimes provoke reactions that suddenly escalate into anaphylaxis.

TREATMENT

Anaphylactic shock is a life-threatening medical emergency in which a few minutes' delay in getting treatment can be disastrous (see chapter 14, Common First-Aid Procedures). Emergency therapy entails an immediate injection of epinephrine or adrenaline, which dilates the airways and constricts blood vessels. Other medications may be used to aid breathing or increase the blood pressure, including antihistamines, oxygen, steroids, and aminophylline.

PREVENTION

Obviously, but most importantly, anyone who knows they have a severe allergy should avoid the allergens that provoke their reactions. People known to have severe reactions to insect stings should avoid areas inhabited by stinging insects. They should carry and know how to use emergency kits containing epinephrine. (See "Insect Allergies" later in this chapter.)

ASTHMA

Asthma is a chronic respiratory disorder characterized by recurrent attacks of difficulty in breathing. Although allergies frequently trigger attacks, especially in adults, a number of other circumstances or conditions are also asthma triggers. For a more detailed discussion of both allergic and nonallergic asthma, see chapter 20, Respiratory Diseases and Lung Health.

DRUG ALLERGIES

DEFINITION

Drug allergies are heightened sensitivities to medications. As in other allergies, the body overreacts to an otherwise harmless substance as an invader or poison, in this case a drug.

CAUSE

Practically any medicine can stimulate an allergic reaction, but the penicillin group—including ampicillin and other related drugs—is a major allergen. Many people are also allergic to the contrast dyes injected into blood vessels to help outline organs in x-ray studies. About 3 percent of patients react to the organic iodine in these dyes, suffering hives, itching, asthmatic attacks, and even shock.

Other medications causing frequent allergic reactions include:

- Anticonvulsants
- Insulin
- Local anesthetics
- Sulfa drugs
- Barbiturates

About 1 million Americans react to aspirin with a pseudoallergenic reaction that is not a true immunologic response. Nearly one of four people with chronic hives, for example, suffers increased skin eruptions after taking aspirin, and a small percentage of asthmatics suffer acute bronchial spasm.

Ampicillin may also trigger a pseudoallergenic response, producing a nonallergenic skin rash frequently mistaken for allergic dermatitis.

DIAGNOSIS

Skin rash and hives, the two most common allergic drug responses, can both be diagnosed visually. These reactions usually appear within an hour of drug use, although delayed reactions may occur up to 3 days afterward. In the case of penicillin, the reaction called "serum sickness" may be delayed for up to 3 weeks and be characterized by fever, joint symptoms, skin eruption, and swelling of the lymph glands. In rare cases, penicillin, streptomycin, insulin, tetracycline, and contrast dyes can cause shock.

To trace the cause of allergic reactions, doctors rely strongly on patients' accurate and detailed recall of drug use—time, amount, the length of time before symptoms appeared, and other medications ingested. Too often patients fail to report laxative use, nose drops, tonics, cold remedies, vitamins, ointments, birth control pills, douches, suppositories, aspirin, antacids, and other over-the-counter products they don't realize are potent medications.

Once a person knows of an allergy to a drug, he or she should always pass that information along to a new physician during the initial visit. (For more information, see chapter 34, Proper Use of Medications.)

TREATMENT

Drug allergies are treated according to their symptoms. Cool compresses or a soaking bath relieves hives or skin rashes; lotions alleviate itching. The symptoms normally disappear on their own within a few weeks.

Warning: If someone appears to be going into shock after taking a drug, immediate medical attention is critically important. (See "Anaphylaxis .")

PREVENTION

For most drugs skin testing is ineffective and potentially dangerous for detecting drug sensitivity; only in a few cases such as penicillin can drug allergies be prevented with sensitivity tests and avoidance of reactive drugs. Skin testing can also forewarn of allergy to insulin. But with these exceptions, past experience is the most reliable means of uncovering sensitivity to the majority of

FOOD INTOLERANCE

Food intolerance is not an immunological reaction; it is a lack of one or more digestive enzymes. For example, the enzyme lactase helps digest one of the sugars in milk, and when it's absent the undigested milk fraction causes abdominal cramps and diarrhea. Many adults cannot tolerate milk or any product which contains milk or milk solids. (Many lactose-intolerant people can, however, consume hard cheeses and cultured dairy products like yogurt and sour cream, in which much of the lactose is predigested.) A blood test confirms lactose intolerance. People of northern European descent are generally not lactose intolerant.

Another common food intolerance is the glutamate in the food additive monosodium glutamate (MSG). Susceptible people experience dizziness, sweating, ringing in the ears, and a feeling of faintness shortly after eating MSG-laden foods. Because so many Chinese dishes traditionally call for MSG, this reaction is sometimes called "Chinese restaurant syndrome."

Some people have mild intolerance to vegetables, especially peas and broccoli, which cause intestinal gas. Others experience indigestion and diarrhea when they consume mushrooms and certain wines.

drugs. After a drug allergy is discovered, however, recurrence of the reaction may be prevented by:

Avoidance. Once a drug allergy is known, the allergenic drug that causes it must not be administered.

Desensitization. Some drugs such as penicillin or insulin are so important in modern medicine, people with known allergies are sometimes induced to tolerate them. The drug is given in slowly increasing doses until therapeutic levels are reached. In some patients, a desensitized immune system eventually tolerates the drug.

Attenuation. In the case of a known allergy, antihistamines and steroids may be taken prior to or simultaneously with the problem drug, to attenuate the reaction.

FOOD ALLERGIES

DEFINITION

Food allergies are antibody responses and sensitivity to particular foods. Unfortunately, much confusing misinformation has been published regarding food allergies, leading many people to blame food sensitivities for unrelated health problems. For instance, food intolerance and food allergy are frequently confused: Food intolerance denotes a lack of certain enzymes needed for digestion, but food allergy is an immunological antibody response to a particular food. (See the box "Food Intolerance.")

CAUSE

Foods most often causing allergies include:

- Milk
- Nuts (especially peanuts)
- Chocolate
- Corn
- Beans
- Eggs
- Fish or shellfish
- Wheat
- Berries
- Gum arabic (thickener)
- Soy

DIAGNOSIS OF FOOD ALLERGIES

A true food allergy produces a set of specific allergic symptoms repeatedly demonstrable. Classic symptoms include:

- Abdominal pain
- Diarrhea
- Nausea or vomiting
- Cramps
- Hives
- Eczema
- Swelling of the eyes, lips, face, and tongue
- Nasal congestion, runny nose

In some people, allergenic foods provoke a reaction almost as soon as they enter the mouth and thus are easy to identify. Most, though, are difficult to pinpoint, not only because of the delayed reaction but also because some provoke responses only at certain times or in certain quantities or with a certain frequency of consumption. Degree of cooking also modifies allergic responses, and additives—mainly vegetable gums used as thickeners and Yellow Dye No. 5—can sometimes provoke reactions instead of the food in which they are contained.

Avoiding food allergens can be as difficult as establishing an accurate diagnosis. Special allergen-free diets are often expensive, inconvenient to obtain, and difficult to prepare, especially if the allergen is milk, eggs, wheat, or other common ingredients in prepared foods. Allergy sufferers may have to stay on restricted diets for life.

Self-diagnosis of food allergies is often a process of elimination: A very restricted diet is followed for several days and then other foods are added back to the diet one by one. Alternatively, if certain foods are strongly suspected allergens, they must be eliminated for at least a week and then added back one at a time in excess quantity to observe the response.

Physicians usually begin their diagnostic sleuthing with a detailed questioning of the patient's diet and its relationship to the complaints. Some doctors will request that the patient keep a careful diary of the times, contents, and reactions to every meal, snack, and drink over a period of several weeks.

This history-taking will sometimes be supplemented with skin or blood tests, but medical tests have limited value. Many people react positively to the tests but fail to show reactions when they actually consume the suspected food. In one study, 60 percent of children whose skin tests indicated food allergies displayed no clinically significant symptoms when they ate the foods they were supposed to be allergic to.

Conversely, because the extracts used in skin tests tend to lose potency quickly, many people won't show test reactions to foods they are actually sensitive to.

One valuable but complicated way to confirm a food allergen is for the patient to be fed or "challenged" with food in a double-blind fashion in which neither the doctor nor the patient knows whether the suspect item has really been administered (a nurse or other third party tracks the tested substances). A dried preparation of suspected food is enclosed in opaque capsules. A repeated reaction to capsules with the test food but not to capsules with safe foods confirms the allergic response.

TREATMENT AND PREVENTION

Once a food is proven to be an allergen, it should be eliminated from the diet. If the allergic reaction has been a minor one, reintroduction of the food may be possible at some future time. Consulting with your doctor about this is important.

Sometimes, in spite of the best efforts of both doctor and patient, the cause of a suspected food allergy can never be found. In such cases, the doctor has to treat the symptoms with antihistamines and other drugs, since no drug is curative or preventive. Many food allergies, however, disappear as the patient grows older.

INSECT ALLERGIES

DEFINITION

An allergic reaction to an insect bite or sting is a hypersensitivity to insect venom or salivary protein. While for most people the bite or sting of a bee, wasp, ant, mosquito, or other angry insect causes momentary pain followed by redness, irritation, and itching around the

wound for a few hours, for people allergic to insects the results are a lot more discomforting and potentially life-threatening.

Symptoms of a reaction to an insect sting include:

- Exaggerated swelling around the bite
- Hives
- Itchy eyes
- Constricted throat and chest
- Dry cough
- Nausea
- Abdominal pain
- Vomiting
- Dizziness
- Breathing difficulties
- Slurred speech
- Blue skin
- Sense of confusion or impending disaster
- Collapse
- Shock

Note: Any or all of these symptoms may denote a medical emergency and the person should be brought to a hospital emergency room as soon as possible.

CAUSE

People are not allergic to insects per se, only to their venom. Toxic components of the venom cause the irritating local reactions that everyone develops, but the venom's other chemicals, which may provoke histamine release, cause allergic responses. In the United States, only a few stinging insects commonly cause serious allergic reactions.

- Honeybees
- Bumblebees
- Wasps
- Hornets
- Yellow jackets
- Fire ants

Of these, reactions to the yellow jacket and the honeybee are the most frequent. Mild reactions can be caused by:

- Biting flies
- Mosquitoes
- Ticks
- Spiders

A nasty newcomer to the list of troublesome insects is the fire ant. Introduced accidentally many years ago in Alabama, it has spread uncontrollably to at least a dozen southern states. The ant actually bites first and then, hanging on tenaciously, swivels about, stinging repeatedly. The potent venom is a very real hazard to those allergic to it, capable of causing severe systemic reactions.

DIAGNOSIS

A reaction to an insect sting can be immediate or delayed. In most cases, the sooner the reaction starts the more severe its consequences. Systemic responses usually begin in 10 to 20 minutes. Delayed reactions can occur several hours to several days later, producing a form of serum sickness—painful joints, fever, hives, and swollen lymph glands. Both immediate and delayed reactions can occur in the same person following a single sting.

If the insect is not available for examination, the doctor may be able to identify it from information about its appearance, mode of movement, and the time of day and place where the sting occurred. Some insects leave telltale mouth parts or a stinger in the skin, and others such as the fire ant make characteristic patterns of multiple bites.

A diagnosis is often confirmed with a skin test, but the test can't be administered until a few weeks after the sting, by which time the skin has replenished its supply of IgE antibodies used up during the allergic reaction. The arm is then usually tested with a series of venom dilutions beginning with a very mild solution.

A relatively new diagnostic technique is the blood test called the radioallergosorbent test (RAST). In this test, the patient's blood samples are exposed to specially prepared venom from the suspected insect to discover if the patient has produced an IgE antibody in response to the venom.

TREATMENT

The first treatment goal is to restrict the amount of venom in the blood. Honeybees abandon their stingers in the skin, and they should be removed immediately. Do not pull it straight out because it will release more venom. Instead, rub a card or fingernail over the surface of the sting to work the stinger out. (See chapter 14.) If the sting is on the arm or leg, a loose tourniquet should be tied above it and untied briefly every 10 minutes to maintain circulation. A cold pack will help reduce pain and swelling.

A serious allergic response is a medical emergency and the patient should be taken to a hospital emergency room as soon as possible. A double dose of antihistamine will decrease the severity of the reaction, but the most effective treatment is an injection of adrenaline or epinephrine. In acute shock or airway closure, intravenous fluids, oxygen, and a surgical opening in the windpipe

(tracheotomy) may be necessary. Steroids, which act more slowly than adrenaline, may be given for persistent swelling or hives.

For people with a known serious insect allergy, physicians recommend two precautionary measures:

- Wear a Medic Alert identification bracelet or tag or carry information on a wallet card stating the specific allergy.
- Carry an emergency kit (available only by prescription) containing epinephrine in a syringe or an Epipen, ready for injection, antihistamine tablets, a tourniquet, and alcohol swabs. The kit is not intended to replace medical help, but to aid the patient until arrival at an emergency room.

PREVENTION

Unfortunately, there's no way to predict who will react to an insect bite. Insect bite allergies appear just as frequently in people with allergies as in people who are otherwise allergy-free. Even experience from past stings is no sure predictor: About half the people with allergic reactions to stings previously may have had an entirely normal response.

Just as a series of allergy shots build up tolerance to pollens and other respiratory allergens, extracts of insect venom can be used for desensitization. At first, the weekly shots are very dilute, but gradually the strength of the extract builds until the patient can tolerate what might be a normal exposure to a sting or bite. Once the maintenance dose is reached, it is administered at 4- to 6-week intervals throughout the year. To be effective, maintenance shots must be continued indefinitely.

To minimize the possibility of a recurrent allergic reaction, susceptible people should avoid exposure to insects.

- Wear white clothing. Brown or black clothing may provoke bees.
- Do not use scented soaps, perfumes, suntan lotions, or cosmetics when outdoors.
- Do not wear loose-fitting clothes, which may trap insects between the material and the skin; bare as little skin as possible; wear shoes rather than sandals.
- Eschew picnics; they attract yellow jackets and ants.
- Keep garbage cans clean, sprayed with an insecticide, and tightly closed.
- Stay away from trees laden with ripe fruit.
- Keep car windows closed.
- Let someone else mow the lawn, trim the hedge, and tend the flower garden; avoid clover.

If an insect attack seems imminent, susceptible people should not swat at the bugs or flail their arms, but rather retreat slowly, keep calm, and make no sudden movement.

RESPIRATORY ALLERGIES

DEFINITION

Respiratory allergies are immunologic reactions triggered by substances inhaled from the air. These allergies are caused by pollen, mold, animal dander, and other inhaled allergens. Sufferers of inhalant allergies are usually allergic to more than one substance.

CAUSE

Pollen. Pollen cells from flowers, taxied from one plant to another by bees, are relatively large, waxy, and generally harmless to people. But the tiny, light, dry pollens thrown off in prodigious quantities by weeds, grasses, and trees, and carried by wind currents for up to 400 miles disrupt the breathing of the estimated 20 million Americans with hay fever (as well as to most asthma sufferers). One plant can generate a million pollen grains, and counts as low as 20 (grains per cubic meter of air) can provoke allergic reactions. Counts drop on rainy days and soar on hot, windy days. Pollen counts announced in the media are of limited value: Local airborne pollen levels vary greatly from place to place depending on local vegetation, wind direction and velocity, and other weather conditions.

After ragweed, the most significant sources of allergenic weed pollen are sagebrush, redroot pigweed, careless weed, spiny amaranth, Russian thistle or tumbleweed, burning bush, and English plantain. Next to weeds in producing troublesome pollen are grasses, notably timothy, redtop, Bermuda, orchard, sweet vernal, rye, and some bluegrasses. As for trees, almost every popular variety is a culprit, including elm, maple, oak, ash, birch, poplar, pecan, cottonwood, and mountain cedar. Trees generally shed pollen in the spring, grasses in the summer, and ragweed—the chief irritant east of the Rocky Mountains—in late summer. Citizens of warm, southern states are exposed to pollen 8 or 9 months annually.

Molds: These abundant, simple microscopic fungi live in the soil and on food, plants, leather, dead leaves, and other organic material. In the environment, molds are both troublesome and beneficial. These organisms spoil food and ruin clothes but they also speed decay of garbage and fallen trees, fertilize gardens, and help make foods like cheese. The antibiotic penicillin was derived from a mold that grows on bread.

Molds reproduce by shedding spores, or seeds, that cause hay fever–like symptoms in susceptible people (strictly speaking, hay fever refers only to pollen allergy). Like pollen, mold spores are borne by the wind and predominate in the summer and early fall. Molds thrive in warm climates, causing allergy problems at least three-quarters of the year in most of the southwestern and southern states. Indoors, molds living in damp cellars, mattresses, stuffed furniture, stuffed animals, fibers, wood, and wallpaper shed spores year-round.

Generally, you must be exposed to dry soil or composting plant debris and either cut grass or harvest crops or walk through tall vegetation to experience a significant allergic reaction to mold outdoors. Because of their occupations, however, some susceptible people—farmers, gardeners, botanists, grain-mill workers, furniture repairers, and handlers of fruit and vegetables—are plagued by repeat attacks.

Most mold allergy is caused by the spores of *Alternaria, Hormodendrum,* or *Claudosporium* fungi flourishing in the Midwest but scarce in dry regions. The most common indoor offenders are *Aspergillus, Penicillium, Mucor,* and *Rhizopus.*

Animal Dander. Dander consists of the scales shed from the skin, fur, hair, and feathers of birds and animals. Animal dander is a significant source of year-round allergy. In most cases, if you are allergic to pollen or molds you will develop sensitivity to animal dander. Consequently, many pet owners are forced to choose between breathing comfort and their cats, dogs, and birds. Cat saliva has also been identified as an important allergen; it can be minimized by bathing the cat weekly in plain water.

Dust. Although house dust harbors pollen, mold spores, and animal dander, its principal allergen component is thought to be mites, microscopic spiderlike creatures found worldwide. Mites live only during warm months, but allergic reactions to them worsen in winter. It is believed that in the colder months dead mite fragments enter the respiratory tract more easily than intact mites and cause increased respiratory distress.

Dust also contains disintegrated stuffing material from pillows, mattresses, toys, and furniture, as well as bits of fiber from draperies, blankets, and carpets. The breakdown of these materials apparently converts them into irritants for people with hay fever and asthma.

Miscellaneous Respiratory Irritants. There are scores of substances that exacerbate allergic reactions once they enter the respiratory tract, including smoke, mists, and fumes from commercial and industrial activities; smoke from pipes, cigars, and cigarettes; cosmetic and baby powder; and powdered laundry detergents. People allergic to pollen, mold spores, and dust are likely to be sensitive to one or more of these irritants, while people who have none of the major inhalant allergies are probably not bothered.

DIAGNOSIS

Pollen allergies are characterized by inflammation and swelling of the fragile lining of the nose and sinuses (allergic rhinitis) as well as of the eyelids and surface layer of the eyes (conjunctiva). Symptoms of pollen allergies include:

- Watery nasal discharge
- Violent sneezing
- Runny eyes
- Nasal congestion
- Itching in the nose, throat, and roof of the mouth

Some ultrasensitive people sneeze 10 to 50 times in a row several times a day, becoming too exhausted to work. Pollen allergies are seasonal, following the cycles of nature and influenced by the local geography.

Pinpointing specific causes of respiratory allergies is complex. The following steps may be taken to help identify allergens.

Keep a Diary. Careful notation of the times and places of allergic reactions may suggest which pollens or molds or other allergens are provoking reactions.

Skin Tests. Tiny amounts of suspected allergens are applied to the skin and the reactions are observed. Usually 6 to 12 substances are tested at the same time, each injected separately into the uppermost layer of the arm skin. Within 10 to 20 minutes, if any of the allergenic substances cause pale bumps, like hives or mosquito bites surrounded by angry red halos (erythemas), then the diagnosis is practically confirmed. In general, the bigger and more ragged-edged the bump, the greater the degree of allergic reaction, but this is not always the case. Skin tests are not always dependable. Some false positives appear, and if excess allergen is injected almost anyone will display allergic symptoms. Negative and positive test controls should be performed at the same time.

Radioallergosorbent Test (RAST). This diagnostic technique determines how much of a specific kind of IgE antibody the patient's blood contains. But the blood sample must be sent to a special laboratory, and fewer allergenic substances can be tested than with skin tests. RAST is less sensitive than skin tests, but it is also safer.

TREATMENT

No respiratory allergy can be cured, but the misery of these allergies can be greatly lessened by avoiding allergens (see "Prevention"). Treatment of respiratory allergens is similar to that of other allergens.

- **Antihistamines and decongestants** may adequately lessen symptoms if controlling the environment isn't feasible. Antihistamines are more effective when given prophylactically or at the first sign of an attack; some are sold over-the-counter, more potent ones are available by prescription. Many of the more effective antihistamines, such as hydroxyzine (Atarax), diphenhydramine (Benadryl), chlorpheniramine (Chlor-trimeton), or astemizole (Hismanal), carry an increased risk of causing drowsiness, dry mouth, and blurred vision. Others, such as terfenadine (Seldane) or loratadine (Laritin), cause less drowsiness. Cromolyn (Nasalcrom) is a topical antihistamine that prevents mast cells in the nasal passages from releasing histamines.

  Note: Antihistamines should not be taken by people with glaucoma.

- **Nasal steroids** are anti-inflammatories that reduce the mucosal damage caused by allergic reactions. These include beclomethasone (Beconase and Vancenase) and flunisolide (Nasalide).
- **Oral steroids,** more drastic drug therapy, are powerful anti-inflammatory agents that chemically resemble hormones. Dramatically effective, these medications cannot be used at high doses or for very long without serious side effects.
- **Allergy shots,** a form of immunotherapy or desensitization that involves the periodic injection of small amounts of the confirmed allergens over the course of several years. Injections may be used for long-term alleviation.

PREVENTION

No one subject to an inhalant allergy should smoke or spend much time in an environment contaminated with tobacco smoke.

Dust allergies may be prevented through dustproofing techniques applied at home, most important in the bedroom. The room should be rather spartan, with no dust-retaining upholstered furniture, carpeting, venetian blinds, bookshelves, or stuffed animals. Avoid bunk beds and canopy beds, and enclose mattresses, box springs, and pillows in allergen-proof coverings. Wet-dust the entire room daily, wiping all surfaces clean with a damp cloth. Always wash bedding in hot water.

Frequently wet-dust the entire house, and wash scatter rugs and furniture coverings weekly. If the allergic person does the cleaning, he or she should wear a disposable surgical mask covering the mouth and nose.

Animal dander can sometimes be reduced by bathing the pet regularly. Studies have shown that weekly or monthly bathing of a cat can significantly reduce the allergens shed from its fur. However, a person who is markedly allergic to cats still may not be able to tolerate having one in the home.

To minimize airborne allergens, a house should have a centralized system that heats, humidifies, cools, and filters the air throughout. The level of dust can further be reduced by attaching various air purifiers to the central unit. There are also air-purifying machines that can be used in the bedroom, but allergy sufferers should beware of exaggerated claims for these appliances.

SKIN ALLERGIES

DEFINITION

Skin allergies are allergic reactions manifested by changes in the skin, in the form of rashes, hives, itching, puffiness, blistering, and other reactions. Terms such as dermatitis and urticaria (hives) refer to these symptoms, rather than to the causes of skin allergies. While respiratory allergies and urticaria result from IgE antibody activity, skin allergies such as dermatitis are caused by T cells—immunity agents that attach themselves to antigens.

These skin conditions are widespread—for instance, one of five people occasionally suffers from hives and one of every two people is allergic to poison ivy.

CAUSE

Plants. About half of all people are allergic to poison ivy, oak, and sumac, with reactions ranging from slight to severe. The allergenic agent in all three plants is the oily resin urushiol that can spread by direct contact with the plant or indirectly by touching clothing or pets that have contacted it. Although a tiny amount may provoke a response, you must make contact with urushiol to experience a reaction; mere proximity to a plant will not cause a rash. And while scratching the rash and blisters may inflame the skin it will not spread the outbreak; there is no urushiol in the blister fluid.

Heliotrope, a desert plant with bluish purple flowers on a stem that coils into the shape of a fiddle neck, also causes contact dermatitis. These skin rashes are usually confined to the ankles and legs of persons walking through desert landscapes in the Southwest. The leaf and pollen of ragweed are other, though infrequent, causes of skin rashes; both contain a resin that dissolves in the natural oil of the skin. Other plants associated with skin rashes include sagebrush, wormwood, daisies, tulips, and chrysanthemums. Contact dermatitis may also result from handling such food plants as oranges, limes, celery, and potatoes.

Cosmetics. Cosmetics in general are quite safe, and allergic reactions are rare. For susceptible people, the most common allergens are hair dye, eye shadow and eye makeup, lipstick, and nail polish. Less frequently, antiperspirants, perfumes, and colognes cause reactions.

Chemicals and Metals. Formaldehyde, chlorine, phenol or carbolic acid, the various forms of alcohol, and other chemicals, and metals such as chrome, nickel, mercury, and beryllium can cause skin reactions among those who have developed a sensitivity after years of low-level exposure. Most often, the rash—accompanied by itching and swelling—appears within 24 to 48 hours of contact with the irritant and grows more severe for up to a week before gradually subsiding. Other allergens, such as film developers and rubber chemicals, can cause hives instead of the classic red rash and blisters.

Most allergy-generating exposure to chemicals and metals occurs in industrial occupations, but because the substances are used in many household products, ranging from furniture to insecticides to antifreeze to nylon, sensitivity can build up in the home as well. Of all the problematic chemicals, formaldehyde is by far the most ubiquitous. A highly active compound that exists in nature as a gas, it has little odor but can cause a burning sensation in the eyes and mucous membranes. Found in foam insulation, particle board, or wallboard (used in construction and in nearly all furniture), rugs, carpets, permanent-press clothing, waxes, dyes, polishes, plaster, and paper, this atmospheric pollutant is also a by-product of gasoline combustion.

Drugs. Agents that provoke contact dermatitis because of an allergic response are cocaine, Novocaine, and other local anesthetics; penicillin; neomycin; streptomycin; and the sulfa drugs. Reactions are largely confined to surgeons, dentists, and workers who manufacture the drugs. While aspirin and ampicillin often provoke systemic allergic reactions (see "Drug Allergies"), the skin rashes linked to these medications are not considered true allergic reactions.

Unidentified Allergies. Some skin allergies have no known cause. Atopic dermatitis (also known as eczema), whose cause is unknown, develops in up to 3 percent of infants. All atopic dermatitis sufferers have highly sensitive skin and most come from families prone to allergy. They also suffer from abnormal sweating, decreased skin oil production, and a low itch threshold; heat, abrasions, and psychological tension stimulate scratching. Children usually outgrow the disorder by age 6, with delayed improvement setting in at puberty.

DIAGNOSIS

Urticaria (Hives) and Angioedema. Urticaria is generally diagnosed by its visual characteristics: the rash is raised, reddened, swollen welts of various sizes that appear and vanish unpredictably. Welts may last for only a few minutes or for several days and typically recur in crops or bunches. Angioedema is a deeper swelling, usually in the face (eyes and lips), but often involving the hands and feet as well. Because the triggering agent of an outbreak is often elusive, a detailed history and a 2- or 4-week diary are crucial in evaluating urticaria.

Allergic Reaction to Plants. It usually takes 1 or 2 days for the skin reaction to poison ivy to begin, but in

HIVES

The cause of most hives is never identified, although allergists and dermatologists frequently collaborate in the search for the triggering agent. Almost anything can cause hives: foods, drugs, pollen and other inhalant allergens, physical agents, insect bites, infections, underlying illness, heredity, and even emotions. Among foods, berries, fish, shellfish, nuts, eggs, and milk are frequent allergens that cause hives. Penicillin and aspirin are the chief drug allergens, while even heat, light, and cold can instigate outbreaks.

Blood protein disorder: A rare hereditary form of hives, called hereditary angioedema (HAE), is a disorder of a blood protein that is part of the immune system. This condition causes nonitchy swelling and often leads to cramping, abdominal pain, and diarrhea. The condition can be dangerous if the throat swells (laryngeal edema). Treatment is with specialized hormones.

Hives due to physical allergy: Pressure on the hands or feet can cause swelling; vigorous exercise, emotional stress, or even a hot shower can provoke tiny hives called cholinergic urticaria; and cold urticaria can develop following rewarming of body parts exposed to cold air.

In some people, heat, cold, pressure, light, or sun rays can provoke allergic reactions. Those susceptible to physical allergy often have unusually sensitive skin—mere hand stroking will cause hives to form. If a blunt object is rubbed on this sensitive skin, a swelling or "weal" response begins within minutes.

the highly sensitive it may appear within 4 hours. At first, the exposed skin reddens and then bumps and blisters arise, usually accompanied by itching or swelling. The rash peaks after about 5 days and then disappears within 1 or 2 weeks even without treatment. Outbreaks rarely occur on the scalp, palms, or soles. Scratching the blisters may introduce bacteria into the open sores, causing secondary infection.

Allergic Reaction to Cosmetics. Because rash and inflammation due to a cosmetics allergy appear similar to other dermatologic conditions, many doctors use patch tests to confirm this diagnosis. Suspected allergens are applied to the skin, covered and left for 2 days to see if a reaction occurs. Patch tests are the single best means of confirming a cosmetic as an allergen.

Allergic Reaction to Chemicals and Metal Aller-gens. Specific chemical and metal allergens can be difficult or even impossible to isolate. Physicians have to ask detailed questions about work and leisure activities and do careful examinations of the rash to differentiate it from other skin disorders. The best means of confirming a suspected allergen is with a patch test.

TREATMENT

Atopic Dermatitis. Successful treatment disrupts the cycle of increased itching and scratching. The skin is kept moist and lubricated with creams and lotions. A Ph-neutral soap such as Dove is used for bathing (which should be done quickly about 3 times weekly). If the scratching persists, the physician may prescribe antihistamines, especially hydroxyzine (Atarax) and diphenhydramine (Benadryl). When the skin is oozing, wet dressings may provide some relief. Coal-tar ointments are effective with thickened, chronic eczema (lichenification). Topical therapy usually relies on the application of corticosteroid ointment or cream to the problem areas.

Hives (Urticaria). Hives may be treated with antihistamines, epinephrine, terbutaline, cimetadine, cromolyn, and, rarely, oral cortisone. A wide variety of drugs, including antibiotics, antifungals, antihistamines, diuretics, hypoglycemics, and tranquilizers, may also bring on hives. (For further information, see chapter 28, Skin Diseases.)

Physical Allergies. Most physical allergies are treated with strong antihistamines.

Contact Dermatitis. Treatments for the rashes of contact dermatitis only somewhat alleviate the symptoms; the best treatment is avoidance of the allergenic substances. The most common causes of contact dermatitis that must be avoided by the hypersensitive are:

1. Poison ivy, oak, and sumac
2. Paraphenylenediamine, used in hair and fur dye, leather, rubber, and printing
3. Nickel compounds
4. Rubber compounds
5. Ethylenediamine, a preservative in creams and ophthalmic solutions
6. Dichromates, used in textile ink, paints, and leather processing

Cosmetic Allergies. When allergy to cosmetics is suspected or confirmed, only cosmetics labeled "hypoallergenic" should be applied. A list of firms that make truly nonallergenic cosmetics is available without charge from the Asthma and Allergy Foundation of America in Bethesda, Maryland.

30

The

Eyes

● ● ● ● ● ● ● ● ● ● ● ● ● ●

ANTHONY DONN, M.D.

The eyes are the body's most sensitive tissues and the most important sensory structures, taking in up to four-fifths of our knowledge of the outside world through the sense of sight. Despite the vital role of the eyes in everyday life, few people know much about these orbs or how to protect them from injury or disease. Knowing when and whom to consult for professional eye care can prevent permanent loss of some aspects of vision caused by conditions such as amblyopia ("lazy eye") or glaucoma.

The eyes are very sensitive not only to sensory information but also to irritation. However, pain is not a reliable measure of the danger of eye disease; certain very painful conditions, such as damage to the cornea from ultraviolet light or contact lens overuse, quickly heal with a few days' rest. But other, far more serious sight-threatening conditions may cause no pain or symptoms at all in their early stages because they attack less sensitive structures deep within the eye.

For millennia, because of the eyes' importance and expressiveness, human beings have been fascinated at the sight of each other's eyes. New techniques and inventions of the past few decades promise that many more of us will enjoy clear sight for most or all of our lives.

The beginning of this chapter describes ocular structures within the eye and how they convey a picture of the world. It lists the different eye care specialists with the examinations they perform. The sections on eye care cover safety measures, including guidance for choosing sunglasses and protective goggles and first aid for injuries. The variations in eyeball shape and the different kinds of lenses used to correct eyesight impairment are described next. The causes and treatments for three major "thieves of sight"—amblyopia, glaucoma, and cataract—are discussed, as are the many ailments, trivial and serious, that cause painful, red eyes.

Eyelid problems and growths within the eyeball may also be serious or trivial, depending upon the cause. Damage to the retina, at the back of the eye, is among the leading causes of blindness in the United States. Diseases harming the retina are explained at the end of the chapter, along with the current treatments.

EYE EXAMINATIONS

Experts differ about the necessary frequency of routine eye examinations but there is some consensus.

Adults under the age of 40 should be examined only every 3 years, not annually as many people believe. Some experts maintain that young people without corrective lenses or symptoms can safely go 5 years between examinations.

People who wear corrective lenses may be reexamined every 18 months.

Note: Symptoms like a need to move the head to see distant or very close objects, blurring of vision, or any noticeable difference between the sight in the two eyes are good reasons for a checkup.

Children should have a first eye examination between the ages of 3 and 4, when they can give reliable responses, and a second one on starting school. Children often don't know what they're supposed to see, so parents should be alert for these signs of trouble.

- Frequent eye rubbing
- Closing or covering one eye
- Inability to do close work
- Blinking or squinting or complaining about bright lights
- Reddened, itchy, watery, or burning eyes

Any of these symptoms are good reasons for parents to consult an ophthalmologist. Nearsighted children will want to sit close to the blackboard, movie screen, or television. Obviously, any vision problem can interfere with education and possibly with social adjustment.

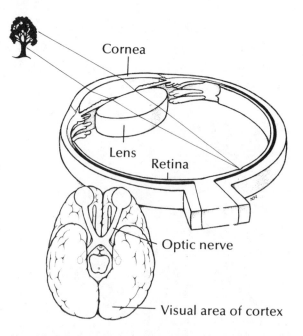

Figure 30.1: How the eye sees. A ray of light enters the eye through the cornea and lens and is transmitted to the retina, where the light impulses are transmitted to the optic nerve and then to the visual cortex, the area in the brain where the signals are interpreted.

THE EYE AND HOW IT WORKS

The eye is often compared to an extraordinarily sensitive camera. Figure 30.1 traces how light rays enter the eye and are turned into sensory signals interpreted by the brain as sight.

The main structures of the eye include:

The Orbit. This circle of bone—the eyebrow, cheekbone, and the bridge of the nose—safely nestles the eye away from most physical harm. The bony housing of the orbit continues around the back of the eye like a camera body.

The Eyelids. After the orbit, the eyelid forms the eye's second line of defense, protecting it from dust, intense light, and impact. From birth, the lid reflexively shuts tightly at the sight of an oncoming object. This reflex reaction often causes new contact lens wearers considerable difficulty learning to keep their eyes open while inserting their lenses.

Tear Glands. During our waking hours, the tear glands inside the upper lid secrete moisture that is pushed across the eyes every few seconds when we blink, like a windshield wiper cleaning our eyes. During sleep, the closed eyelid prevents harmful drying of the eye's surface. Tears usually collect in the lacrimal sac, connected to the nose; blowing your nose after crying empties these tears.

Conjunctiva. This single layer of tissue runs along the inside of the eyelid and turns to meet the sclera, the outside of the eyeball that is the white of the eye. Small blood vessels fill the conjunctiva and sclera; when these vessels enlarge or break because of irritation, infection, or injury, the eye reddens.

Eye Muscles. The coordinated action of six muscles attached to the eyeball under the conjunctiva turns the eye in any desired direction. These muscles move thousands of times a day, without any conscious effort, to concentrate the attention of both eyes on external objects. They continue to work when the body is asleep in the rapid eye movement associated with dreaming.

Cornea. In the center of the eye, the transparent membrane called the cornea covers the iris. By changing shape, this thin, tough, transparent section in front of the eyeball provides about two-thirds of the focusing power of the eye, while the lens supplies about one-third. Compared to the photographer's bulky zoom lens, which also contracts and expands in order to focus, the adjustable cornea is a marvelous example of compactness. It is also exquisitely sensitive to pain: A tiny piece of grit on its surface is disabling. Yet its outer layer regenerates very rapidly after injury, usually without scars that might impair vision.

Aqueous Humor. This clear, watery liquid fills the anterior chamber inside the cornea and cushions any impact to the eye. Normally, the aqueous humor flows from behind the iris (the colored part of the eye) through tiny ducts in the cornea. If this flow is blocked, the pressure in the eye climbs and glaucoma results, either acute or chronic, depending on the type of blockage. (See "Glaucoma.")

Iris. This part of the eye contains pigment. The amount of pigment in the iris determines the color of your eyes; the more pigment, the browner and darker each eye. Another function of the iris is its restriction of light entering the eye similar to the action of a camera's diaphragm.

Pupil. This opening in the iris plays the same role as a camera's aperture. Involuntary muscles control the pupil's size, constricting to as little as $\frac{1}{25}$ of its maximum size and enabling the eye to adjust to a wide variation of light intensity. Excitement and attractive sights cause pupils to dilate; many drugs also influence its size.

Lens. Situated behind the iris, the lens is shaped like the lentil seed that originally supplied its name. It consists of long, highly elastic fibers that expand and contract to focus the light rays from objects outside the eye onto the retina at the back of the eye. These expansions and contractions alter the outer curvature and change the angle at which the light passing through it is bent. The bending of light in this manner is called refraction.

Although devoid of blood vessels and nerves, the lens continually accumulates new fibers throughout life. The additional bulk restricts elasticity so that eventually the lens cannot focus on near objects. Consequently, many people who have never had vision problems find by middle age that they need reading glasses to accommodate this loss in focusing ability.

Vitreous Chamber. The largest section of the eye, the vitreous chamber forms the round space between the lens at the front and the retina at the back (see figure 30.2). It is filled with vitreous humor, a clear, colorless, gelatinous fluid. Opaque bits of debris in the vitreous humor—called floaters—may cause occasional "spots before the eyes" (see figure 30.3). They are usually leftover material from the prenatal growth of the eye. Hemorrhage or other events that cloud the vitreous humor can destroy vision. Fortunately, vitreous humor can sometimes be replaced, through a surgical procedure, with clear saline solution or aqueous humor.

Retina. Lining the back of the vitreous chamber, the retina looks like a pinkish net the thickness of onionskin. In its ability to react with light, the retina behaves like film emulsion. Within its 10 layers are the rod cells that perceive light, and the cone cells that perceive both light and color. The rods outnumber the cones by 20 to 1 and need far less light to register the black-and-white outlines of objects. The paucity of color-perceiving cone cells and their need for strong light makes discerning color difficult in dim light.

Rod and cone cells convert the light that strikes them into electric impulses carried by the optic nerve to the visual cortex, a region at the back of the brain that interprets these signals to create a picture of the world outside. Sometimes interference with the visual cortex can result in a visual illusion, as when a blow on the head makes the recipient "see" stars.

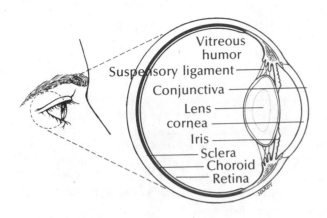

Figure 30.2: Structure of the eye.

Preschoolers should take an eye test provided by the National Society to Prevent Blindness. Parents can use it at home to discover whether a child needs a professional evaluation. The test is available free, in English and Spanish, from the Society, at 500 East Remington Road, Schaumburg, IL 60173.

THE EYE EXAM PROCEDURE

There is no one set formula for examining eyes. The eye doctor starts with a few basic tests and then uses the results to select from a menu of additional investigational techniques.

• A general medical history and a history of the patient's vision should begin the examination. The patient should recount any medications being taken; any eye problems, either long-standing or recent; and occupational and recreational activities, all of which can affect the examination.

• Testing of eye movement—both separately and together—is often the first part of the doctor's physical examination. Can both eyes focus on an object moving toward them? Do they move easily from side to side and up and down? How big are the pupils, and do they react quickly and adequately to changes in light?

• The slit-lamp microscope is then used to obtain a magnified view of the outer layers of the eye, which are carefully checked for signs of injury or disease.

• With an ophthalmoscope, a handheld device with a bright light, the examiner looks through the eye to the retina, checking the tiny blood vessels for damage due to high blood pressure or diabetes. Detachment of the retina from the back of the eyeball or blank spots on its surface will also be detected by the ophthalmoscope.

• When you read the eye chart—called a Snellen chart—the examiner checks for refractive errors.

• Your vision through a Phoropter, the black metal mask into which the examiner inserts different lenses, provides information about which corrective lenses are best for you. People sometimes worry about giving "wrong" answers to the examiner's questions about which lenses make the letters look clearest, but by checking the machine's focus on the retina, the examiner can obtain 95 percent of the data necessary to prescribe corrective lenses. The same lens that gives the examiner the clearest picture of the retina should give the patient the clearest view of the outside world. Answers from the eye patient merely confirm the physical information. If there is any contradiction, the doctor will repeat the question or use additional lenses to resolve the issue.

• Tests for peripheral vision utilize moving objects, and color vision is checked with a series of colored cards.

• A tonometer should be used on everyone over 35 or 40, to test for glaucoma. During this test, eye drops anesthetize the eye and a probe touches the eyeball to determine intraocular pressure. Tonometers that use a fast puff of air and do not require drops are sometimes

---

EYE "DOCTORS"—WHO THEY ARE, WHAT THEY DO

Although professional eye care can be provided either by an ophthalmologist or by an optometrist, only ophthalmologists are medical doctors licensed to treat many different eye diseases.

Ophthalmologist: a physician who specializes in diagnosis and treatment of eye diseases and conditions. Formally called an oculist, the ophthalmologist can also prescribe corrective lenses and perform surgery on the eyes. In some states, phthalmologists may give more complete examinations than other specialists because only ophthalmologists are licensed to insert certain diagnostic eye drops.

Optometrist: not a medical doctor, but a graduate of a school of optometry, with O.D. or D.O.S. after his or her name. Optometrists are trained to diagnose refractive errors and to prescribe lenses to correct them. They can detect signs of disease in the eye and diseases detectable through examination of the retina, but an ophthalmologist or other specialist must be consulted for a complete diagnosis and treatment.

Optician: specialist in filling the prescriptions of ophthalmologists and optometrists. They grind and dispense lenses, fitting them into frames, but do not examine the eyes for refractive errors or signs of disease.

used to screen large groups of people for glaucoma, but these devices are not as accurate.

Note: In the past, many eye examiners routinely inserted eye drops to enlarge the pupil and look into the eye. This is no longer considered necessary in all cases. Enlarged pupils can temporarily inconvenience the patient by making bright light uncomfortable. And the chemicals themselves may irritate the eye, making it difficult to determine the eye's normal functioning. Certain diseases—especially cataract and retinal disease—may necessitate drops. But the normal eye can be adequately examined without them.

• Besides diseases of the eye, the eye examination may also reveal the effects of diseases elsewhere in the body, including high blood pressure, diabetes, blood disorders, and tumors of the pituitary. Arthritis and other connective tissue disorders also affect the eye.

EVERYDAY EYE CARE

SAFETY

Approximately 35,000 Americans annually sustain eye injuries serious enough to warrant emergency room treatment. Most of these accidents occur in summer, when sports involving rackets, sticks, balls, bicycles, and pools as well as activities such as gardening, sunbathing, and do-it-yourself projects endanger eyes.

Modest precautions would prevent most of this eye damage. The National Society to Prevent Blindness estimates that 90 percent of all eye injuries that require hospitalization could be avoided simply through the use of devices such as inexpensive safety goggles.

SUN DAMAGE TO EYES

The two types of eye injuries caused by the sun are ultraviolet and infrared.

Ultraviolet Injuries. Ultraviolet light from the sun, reflected by snow, from a tanning lamp, or from welding equipment can damage the cornea. Often, the effect takes 12 to 24 hours to develop, and the person awakens in the middle of the night with searing pain and a feeling of sand or grit in the eyes.

DIAGNOSIS

An ophthalmologist can discern the cause of the problem by a physical examination and questioning of the circumstances causing the problem.

TREATMENT

The ophthalmologist will prescribe painkilling drugs, and the cornea usually regenerates after a few days under an eyepatch.

PREVENTION

Sunglasses can prevent ultraviolet damage. Many brands are labeled with light-transmission factors denoting the percent of light that penetrates the lenses. The most effective lens colors for sunglasses are gray, brown, or green, in that order. Prescription sunglasses are better than clip-on lenses. For active sports, sunglasses should have a strap going around the head or wires over the ears to avoid breakage and loss.

Test sunglasses' effectiveness by wearing the glasses in front of a mirror. Sunglasses should be dark enough to hide the eyes behind them. Besides normal dark lenses, other types of sunglasses include:

Gradient density lenses: These lenses are darker at the top and may be used to increase eye comfort on a sunny day.

Phototropic lenses: These lenses darken in sunlight and become pale indoors but are not usually effective against bright sun. The lenses take up to 10 minutes to change color, may not darken sufficiently to compensate for very bright sun, and never clear completely, so they cannot be used as a combination of regular prescription glasses and prescription sunglasses.

For optimal sun protection under most circumstances, sunglasses' light transmission factor should be 30 percent or less. For glare from sand, water, or snow, 10 to 15 percent light transmission is most effective. Polarized or mirrored lenses are the best protection against glare for skiers and yachtspeople. For tanning under a sunlamp (a device most dermatologists disapprove of), always use special goggles. A sunlamp's intense light can burn the cornea in just a few minutes, even through sunglasses and closed eyelids.

Eclipses and Solar Burns. People who stare directly at the sun during an eclipse can suffer infrared (heat) burns that damage the surface of the retina. The lens focuses destructive rays on rod and cone cells, causing permanent loss of vision. Avoiding solar burn is simple. Never look at the sun during an eclipse or otherwise through smoked glass, through exposed film, and especially not through optical instruments like telescopes that focus the sun's rays on the retina.

IMPACT AND WATER INJURY

Racket sports, bicycling, gardening, and home carpentry can all endanger the unprotected eye. Even today's man-

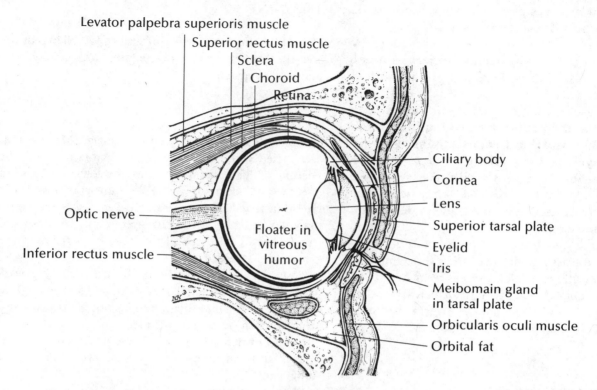

Figure 30.3: Anatomy of the eye.

datory impact-resistant prescription lenses can be broken by a projectile from a machine tool, lawn mower, or squash racket.

For optimal eye protection during special activities use:

Industrial safety glasses. Recommended by the National Society to Prevent Blindness to protect against impact injury. Industrial-quality safety glasses should have plastic lenses and bear the code number Z87.1, 1979, to show that they conform to the National Standard Practice for Occupational and Educational Eye and Face Protection. Safety glasses should be worn to trim shrubs, run a power lawn mower or carpentry tools, or spray pesticides or paint. These cost from about $15 to about $40 for models without prescription lenses. They can be obtained from opticians, eye doctors, and suppliers of safety equipment.

Sports eye protectors. The best sports eye protectors are goggles molded from optical-quality polycarbonate lenses designed to withstand severe blows. They can be purchased in stylish, lightweight wraparound models with clear or dark lenses; they are available at sporting goods stores.

Swim goggles. Goggles should be used to prevent mild chemical burns on the cornea from the chlorine used in pools. (These burns cause your eyes to feel dry and scratchy.) Because of corneal sensitivity, some people are unable to swim in pools at all. Besides keeping

chlorine off the eyes, goggles also help prevent infection in freshwater swimmers. Goggles should be watertight; they cost about $5. (Swimmers should also use only their own towels to lessen the chance of contracting or spreading eye infections.)

FIRST AID FOR EYES

Although protected in its circle of bone, the eye and surrounding areas are still vulnerable to blows, foreign particles, cuts, burns, and chemical irritants. In these cases, treatment during the first few moments after injury can be essential to saving sight.

FOREIGN BODIES

This category includes everything from relatively harmless eyelashes to destructive steel slivers.

To remove eyelashes or a speck of dust:

- Locate the object by looking in a mirror.
- If the object is visible, it can usually be removed by wiping it toward a corner of the eye with a moistened tip of a clean handkerchief. A few sharp blinks may be necessary to move the object off the sensitive cornea.

- If wiping is ineffective, pull the upper lid down over the lower lashes to wash the object out. Use the lower lashes to wipe the undersurface of the upper lid. If none of these actions removes the irritating object, go to a physician or emergency service.

For larger objects in the eye: More serious injuries are often due to small fragments of wood or metal that penetrate the eye during metalwork or carpentry. A splinter shot from a machine may enter the eyeball so quickly that it causes only mild pain and little external injury. However, a delayed reaction or infection may slowly destroy vision over the course of days, weeks, or even years.

Do not try to treat large objects that pierce the eye. This kind of injury should be covered with an eyepatch and referred to an ophthalmologist. Often a dangerous piece of metal can be removed easily by an expert with a magnet. (For further instructions see chapter 14.)

CUTS AND BRUISES

A black eye is a bruise of the cheek, eyelids, and eyebrow. A blow hard enough to produce a black eye may also damage the more sensitive eyeball and nerves, and warrants a complete evaluation by an ophthalmologist, especially if the patient has pain in the eye, or double or blurred vision. The same is true of cuts around the eye. External bleeding may be stopped by applying pressure, but bleeding behind the cornea may require hospitalization.

- Apply a cold compress to lessen bruising. An ice-bag is adequate (and neater and cheaper than a steak), but neither will reduce a black eye once the color is fully developed.
- Never force open an eye that has swollen shut after an injury, or press on it in any way. Sometimes the eyelid is the only thing holding a perforated eyeball together. As in any serious eye injury, take the person to an emergency service as soon as possible. There an ophthalmologist may be able to suture the eyeball back together but only if it arrives in the operating room intact.

DIAGNOSIS

After a serious eye injury, the ophthalmologist will perform a number of studies to evaluate the extent of eye damage, using painkillers if necessary.

TREATMENT

Injuries to the outer layers of the eye usually heal without medical intervention. Even hemorrhages under the conjunctiva, which appear as blood red patches in the white of the eye, will vanish on their own in a few weeks. Injuries to the cornea usually heal in a few days, although wounds due to wood splinters often take

EYE CARE, EYE MYTHS

EYESTRAIN

We use our eyes every moment they are open, but when we speak of overusing or straining our eyes we generally mean close work such as reading, sewing, or handicrafts, activities during which the eyes focus on an object 12 to 18 inches away for long periods of time. For this kind of work the optimum light is a 100-watt bulb a few feet away, behind the shoulder or on the side, positioned to avoid glare.

CAUSES

Reading in poor light or without glasses or for too long does not injure the eyes. But these habits may cause a headache as well as a strained, tired feeling in the eye muscles from holding the same position for too long.

TREATMENT

Since eyestrain is not really an injury, simply resting the eyes—closing them or performing an activity that does not require close focus—should relieve this condition.

PREVENTION

Eyestrain may be avoided by resting the eyes every half hour, gazing off into the distance or just letting the eyes unfocus. Frequent eyestrain may indicate the need for new glasses or a new prescription.

Over-the-counter eye drops will not help eyestrain, but they may be soothing to eyes irritated by dust, smoke, or air pollution. Insert eye drops while you are lying down. Squeeze a few drops into the corner of the eye and let them wash across the eyeball.

Many doctors feel these medications are overused. They sometimes provoke allergic reactions and are easily contaminated by bacteria. As with other drugs, never borrow or lend your eye drops to another, and discard them after a month or two. Their worst side effect, however, may be the fact that users mistakenly delay consulting a professional concerning serious eye problems.

longer. The doctor may prescribe an eyepatch, antibiotics, painkillers, or drops to prevent the eye from moving. Ice will limit pain and damage on the first day; heat will promote healing thereafter.

In rare cases of severe injury, the ophthalmologist and patient may be forced to contemplate removal of a lacerated, blinded eye to prevent a condition known as sympathetic ophthalmia. In this situation, leaving the injured eye in place for more than 12 days precipitates the loss of vision in the uninjured eye, resulting eventually in total blindness. Luckily, the tragedy is rare and becoming rarer, occurring in only 0.1 percent of cases, down from 2 to 4 percent during the early part of the 20th century.

CHEMICAL BURNS

Water is the most important first aid for injuries due to chemicals.

- Irrigate the injured eye with a spray nozzle from a kitchen sink, if available, or wash the irritant out of the eye with whatever water is at hand. As you wash the eyes, position the head with the more injured eye below the other.

- Using a gentle spray, rinse for at least 5 to 10 minutes. Do not try to "counteract" the irritant with another chemical.
- Take the injured person to an ophthalmologist or emergency service.

DIAGNOSIS

The ophthalmologist will evaluate the condition of the injured eye. If the damage is limited to the outer layer of the cornea, and the inner layers are still transparent, the injury, however painful, may heal after only a few days of rest.

TREATMENT

Even though the damage to a burned eye may heal on its own, antibiotics, analgesics, and drops to paralyze the eye muscles are often used to promote healing. A patch may also help the injured eye.

COMMON EYE SIGNS AND SYMPTOMS

Hemorrhage. Subconjunctival hemorrhages appear as sudden red blobs in the white of the eye. They usually form after a small injury to the eye, or sometimes as the result of a cough or a sneeze. Although these blobs look alarming, they are almost always harmless. Recurrences, however, may indicate a blood disease or high blood pressure. The blood in these formations is usually absorbed within 2 weeks; no special therapy is available to hasten its disappearance.

Spots. Trivial bits of debris floating in the vitreous humor usually cause "spots before the eyes," or floaters. While most are harmless, brown or red spots are often signs of vitreous hemorrhage, leakage of blood from the retina into the vitreous chamber. These spots are danger signs and may be followed by retinal detachment, a process that often begins with a shower of sparkling spots and the sensation of a curtain moving across the eyes. Retinal detachment is a medical emergency mandating an immediate trip to a hospital emergency room or emergency service. (See "Diseases of the Retina" in this chapter.)

Abnormal stimulation of the visual system may cause light spots or scintillating flashes. These are called "positive scotomas" and are often part of a migraine.

Pain. Pain in the eye is always an important symptom, not to be dismissed. Unless the cause is obviously trivial, like a speck of dust or a very minor injury, pain should be investigated by an ophthalmologist.

Pain due to bright light, however, is common, especially in fair-skinned persons. Dark glasses usually ensure comfort. But if sensitivity to light develops suddenly, it may indicate disease and should be investigated by a doctor.

Blind Spots. Many people who have blind spots, called negative scotomas, are unaware of their presence. However, blind spots warrant full medical investigation, as they may result from hemorrhage or optic nerve damage.

Protruding Eyes. An overactive thyroid may cause one or both eyes to protrude gradually, over a period of a month or more. Tumors also cause slow protrusion. Sudden protrusion of one eye usually signals a hemorrhage or inflammation in the orbit behind the eye.

Nystagmus (Rolling or Jerking Eyes). Nystagmus is a manifestation of brain dysfunction such as multiple sclerosis, use of drugs like alcohol or barbiturates, or other substances. Medical treatment for the underlying condition is essential.

Double Vision. Double vision, or diplopia, results when the brain cannot resolve the two pictures it receives from both eyes. Not simply blurred vision, this condition may result from injury, strabismus (squint or cross-eyes), or from palsy of the eye muscles. Both strabismus and ocular muscle palsy can be caused by serious ocular or neurologic disease, such as diabetes or aneurysm.

In more severe cases, the damage penetrates the cornea, making it opaque and white. When this occurs, the injury is usually irreversible. Corneal transplants are necessary to restore sight, and even this measure is not always successful in restoring the severely burned eye.

....

REFRACTIVE ERRORS

In order to see clearly, light striking the eye has to be refracted (bent) by the lens and cornea so that the rays come to a sharp focus on the retina. For this to happen, the refractive powers of the lens and cornea and the length of the eyeball must interact in a precise manner. In many people, however, heredity or environment—no one knows which—has created an imbalance, so that

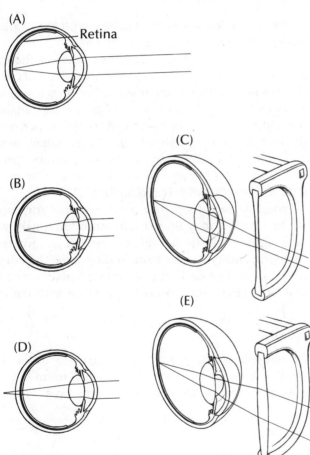

Figure 30.4: Common visual disorders. (A) Normal (20/20) vision, in which light rays focus sharply on the retina; (B) myopia (nearsightedness), in which light rays from a distance come to sharp focus in front of the retina; (C) myopia corrected by eyeglasses with concave lenses; (D) hyperopia (farsightedness), in which light rays from close objects come to sharp focus behind the retina; (E) hyperopia corrected by eyeglasses with convex lenses.

the rays do not focus on the retina. The three refractive errors that occur are:

- Nearsightedness: Light rays focus in front of the retina.
- Farsightedness: Light rays focus behind the retina.
- Astigmatism: Irregularities in the cornea cause only some of the light rays to focus on the retina.

In most cases, all three of these conditions are correctable with the proper lenses (see figure 30.4).

Refractive errors are described by numbers. The familiar "20/20" refers to normal vision, describing a person who sees at 20 feet what other people with normal vision see at the same distance. Farsighted people may have 20/10 vision (they see at 20 feet what normally is seen at 10 feet), but be unable to read print at the usual reading distance (see figure 30.5).

In most states, corrected vision of 20/40 or better is required for a driver's license. A person whose vision is around 20/60 may function adequately in normal household activities, but most people whose vision is less acute experience noticeable difficulty focusing their eyes. Most states define legal blindness as vision of 20/200 or worse that cannot be corrected with lenses. People with vision this poor can easily care for themselves, although they may be limited in many activities, such as reading or driving.

NEARSIGHTEDNESS

DEFINITION

Myopia, or nearsightedness, occurs when light rays are focused in front of the retina rather than on the retina itself.

CAUSE

Myopia usually begins in the school years, from the early grades through the late teens. Whether environmental factors or heredity—or some interaction of both—causes myopia is unknown. In any case, the growing eye becomes too long, so that rays of light from distant objects converge before the retina. The condition may develop rapidly in the teenage years, so that new glasses are needed every 6 months, but it often stabilizes in a person's 20s, necessitating little change in prescription until after age 40.

DIAGNOSIS

Signs of myopia in children include squinting, holding books close to the face, and needing to sit at the front of the classroom or theater. The inability to read an eye chart is most often used to initially diagnose this condition.

200 feet   20 feet

Figure 30.5: Meaning of 20/20 vision. In normal 20/20 vision, a person can see the 85 on the sign at a distance of 200 feet. In contrast a person with 20/200 vision must be 20 feet from the 85 to see it.

MALE/FEMALE DIFFERENCES

Both boys and girls develop myopia in equal numbers, and it often runs in families.

TREATMENT

Corrective treatment for nearsightedness almost always involves the use of eyeglasses or contact lenses. But public attention has recently been drawn to a new surgical procedure called radial keratotomy. This is an experimental operation in which the surgeon makes a series of cuts arranged like spokes of a wheel in the cornea, flattening its curvature and permanently correcting the myopia, if successful.

First developed in the Soviet Union, radial keratotomy has been performed in this country only in the past 10 years, so that the long-term results are still unknown. Serious risks with the procedure are very rare, but the short-term risks include infection, perforation of the cornea, and incomplete correction of the myopia. Even if over- or undercorrection of the myopia does not occur after this operation, you may notice a heightened sensitivity to glare. Only a few ophthalmologic surgeons are experienced in this operation, and they restrict it to highly motivated adult patients who absolutely cannot tolerate spectacles or contact lenses.

FARSIGHTEDNESS

DEFINITION AND CAUSE

Farsightedness is the inability to focus on objects that are close to the eyes. There are two refractive conditions that interfere with near vision:

Hyperopia. A usually congenital condition in which the eye is shortened so that rays of light cannot intersect on the retina. Most farsighted people with hyperopia do not need glasses until the age of 40 or so.

Presbyopia. An accumulation of fibers in the eye's lens that affects almost all people in their 50s and 60s. As the lens accumulates these fibers, it becomes less able to accommodate for near vision. Initially, you can adjust to this difficulty in focusing on nearby objects, perhaps at the cost of eyestrain or headache. But eventually almost everyone will need reading glasses. Some myopic people with presbyopia are able to see close objects by removing their glasses, but may require bifocals.

Note: Astigmatism, the asymmetrical formation of the cornea, may be present simultaneously with nearsightedness or farsightedness. In astigmatism, focusing ability is compromised because the cornea may be steeper or flatter in several places. See figure 30.6. This condition is correctable with lenses.

DIAGNOSIS

Farsightedness is diagnosed by the inability to focus on close objects. An ophthalmologist will confirm the diagnosis with a physical examination of the eyes.

TREATMENT

Farsightedness is almost always corrected with glasses. Many farsighted people need to wear glasses only when reading, sewing, or doing other work that necessitates looking at small, nearby objects. Those who are both nearsighted and farsighted may wear bifocals, glasses that compensate for both types of conditions (see below).

CORRECTIVE LENSES

Refractive errors cannot be corrected by eye exercises or diet. Curved lenses are necessary to compensate for the defect in the eye and make the light rays entering it focus on the retina.

Eyeglasses with handles or frames have been in use since the Middle Ages. But only since the industrial revolution have standardized, machine-ground lenses been available to most people.

- Convex lenses (thicker in the center) cause the light rays to converge, focusing on the retina of the farsighted eye.
- Concave lenses (thicker around the edge) spread the light rays, moving the focus back toward the retina of the nearsighted eye.
- Cylindrical lenses (with the thickness distributed along one axis) correct astigmatism.
- Bifocals, invented by Benjamin Franklin, combine two types of lenses: a prescription for correcting farsightedness at the bottom of the lens and another one for nearsightedness at the center and top of the lenses. They are usually worn by older people with presbyopia who prefer not to carry two pairs of glasses for near and far vision.
- Trifocals, with three prescriptions, for near, middle (1½ to 4 feet), and far distances, are also available for those who need them.
- Half-glasses can be useful for people who need only a reading prescription.
- "Invisible" bifocals (glasses that show no line where the two prescriptions join) are also available, but many people have trouble adjusting to them.

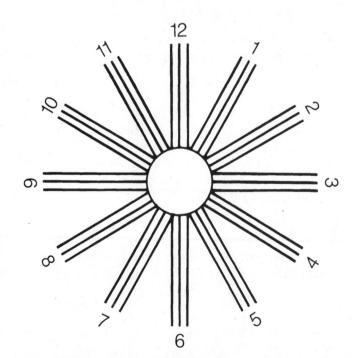

Figure 30.6: Test for astigmatism. Uneven curvature of the cornea causes these lines to be viewed as distorted.

Note: All of these glasses may be colored or coated for use as sunglasses.

CONTACT LENSES

Entertainers, athletes, cataract patients, people whose occupations require good peripheral vision free from eyeglass fogging, and people who just don't like wearing glasses can choose among several types of contact lenses. Fourteen million Americans now wear these curved disks of plastic on their corneas, and most delight in the convenience, improved appearance, and, in many cases, better vision. But unless contact lenses are carefully fitted and handled, they can be a waste of money or a threat to sight.

You may be unable to wear contact lenses if:

- Your eyes are severely irritated by allergies or occupational exposure to dust or chemicals.
- You suffer an overactive thyroid, uncontrolled diabetes, or severe arthritis of the hands.
- Your eyes are dry because of pregnancy, birth control pills, diuretics, antihistamines, or decongestants.
- In addition, parents of adolescents with myopia may prefer to wait until their children's eyes stabilize before paying for contacts that they may have to replace soon.

BUYING CONTACT LENSES

When shopping for contact lenses, seek out a well-trained professional ophthalmologist or optometrist skilled at fitting lenses and ready to spend sufficient time and effort helping you. Beware of the low-priced lenses ubiquitously advertised, which in the long run may not be a bargain: Hidden costs for appliances needed to clean the lenses and extra payments for visits after fitting may raise the final price. Even worse, cut-rate lenses may be so poorly fitted that they are unwearable and you eventually abandon them in your dresser drawer.

Contact lenses should be prescribed by an ophthalmologist or optometrist specializing in these lenses. The cost generally ranges from $125 to $500, depending on the type of lens and doctor. The fee should include a complete eye examination and checkups for up to a year after the contact lenses are fitted. Many people—especially hard-lens wearers—do not spend extra money to insure for loss of lenses.

Lenses that fit a given individual may be obtainable immediately, or they may have to be ordered or custom-made. Discomfort or constant awareness of new lenses is normal at first, but any significant pain during the break-in period should be referred to the eye doctor.

Checkups of new lenses are recommended after 1 week, 2 weeks, 1 month, 6 months, and 1 year. There is a risk of infection with the use of any contact lenses, but especially with extended-wear contacts when they are worn while sleeping.

CARE OF CONTACT LENSES

- Clean hands are essential for inserting or removing contact lenses.
- Do not wear lenses while swimming. Soft lenses absorb chemicals from the water; hard lenses float out of the eyes.
- Sleeping with lenses on will hurt the eyes by depriving the cornea of oxygen. And, unless absolutely necessary, wearing even extended-wear lenses while sleeping is not recommended (there is a slight increased chance of infection).
- Insert contact lenses before makeup is applied, and take them out before it is removed. Water-soluble makeup is best. "Lash-building" mascara may drop particles into the eyes, which is especially irritating with hard lenses. Eyeliner applied between the lashes and the eyes may discolor soft lenses permanently.
- Aerosol sprays and contact lenses don't mix. Sprays should be used before lenses are inserted—if at all.
- Burning, redness, pain, unusual light sensitivity, and hazy vision are all danger signs that should be referred to an ophthalmologist.
- Never put hard contact lenses in the mouth to moisten or clean them—this often causes infection.
- People who wear Medic Alert identification bracelets and others liable to lose consciousness should include the fact that they wear contact lenses on their medical information list.
- An extra empty lens case and an extra pair of lenses (or glasses) in case you lose your lenses may prevent a vacation or business trip from becoming a disaster.

HARD LENSES

Available since 1938, these are still the most popular type of contact lenses.

ADVANTAGES

- Hard contact lenses provide better visual correction than soft lenses, especially if you have severe astigmatism or irregular corneas.
- These lenses are less expensive than other types and easier to clean. They can be polished and reground when scratched or outgrown, thus saving the expense of a new pair.
- Bifocal hard lenses are available, with the reading

prescription either as a ring around the outside, or weighted to sink to the bottom of the lens. Fitting these can be difficult, however, and many people never adjust to them.
- Hard lenses are available with tints, either as sunglasses or for cosmetic reasons. They can even alter eye color.

DISADVANTAGES

- Relatively high level of initial discomfort.
- The break-in period takes at least 2 weeks to go from wearing the lenses half an hour to a full day.
- If lens-wearing is interrupted for a few days, the slow adaptation to wearing lenses must be repeated, so these lenses must be worn consistently and cannot be reserved for special occasions.
- Contacts cause an increased sensitivity to light and foreign particles in the eye. For this reason, new hard-lens wearers should invest in sunglasses—a dark pair for sunny days and a light pair to use as a windscreen.
- You may find hard lenses more uncomfortable during colds and allergic attacks.
- Compared with soft lenses, hard lenses are more easily dislodged from the cornea and the eye (although easier to find).
- You may have blurred vision after removing hard lenses to put on spectacles.

GAS-PERMEABLE LENSES

Unlike conventional hard lenses, these have openings to permit some of the oxygen and carbon dioxide in the air to reach the cornea.

ADVANTAGES

- Because gases can permeate these lenses, they are more comfortable than ordinary hard lenses.
- They may be worn by people with severe astigmatism or irregular corneal surfaces who cannot tolerate other hard lenses.

DISADVANTAGE

These lenses are much more expensive than conventional hard lenses.

SOFT LENSES

ADVANTAGES

- The major advantage of soft contact lenses is their comfort. Made of a water-absorbent plastic, they mold to the cornea.

- The adjustment period for new wearers is short: By the end of the first week of insertion, they can be worn for a whole day.
- Foreign objects do not intrude beneath the lens.
- The eyes do not become more light-sensitive.
- Soft lenses very rarely fall out and are easier to insert than hard lenses.
- They are available in bifocal and tinted models.

DISADVANTAGES

- Relatively expensive, both initially and in the upkeep.
- Because they absorb water, soft lenses must be sterilized by heat or chemicals every night.
- These lenses are more fragile than hard lenses, and proteins in tear fluid may cloud them after 2 years or so, necessitating replacement.
- If dropped, these contacts are difficult to find. They fall silently, stick to walls and floors, look like a drop of water or scrap of cellophane, and often dry out irrevocably before they can be found.
- Soft lenses absorb chemicals from the air and cosmetics from the hands and become irritating to the eyes.
- They may become uncomfortably dry under a hair dryer, in hot rooms, or in very windy or dry weather.

EXTENDED-WEAR LENSES

ADVANTAGES

- Unlike other types of contact lenses, extended-wear lenses can remain in the eye for 2 weeks at a time.
- They have a higher water content than other lenses and permit more oxygen to reach the cornea.
- Because they can be worn while sleeping, they offer instant clear vision upon awakening in the morning.
- Although they do have to be cleaned and sterilized periodically, they are most useful for people who cannot manage daily cleaning because of arthritis or other reasons, and people who need clear vision immediately upon awakening.

DISADVANTAGES

Research has shown that sleeping with these lenses causes an increase in the size of the endothelial tissue in the back of the eye, a development that may prove to be harmful. An increase in the incidence of eye infections has also been observed.

SURGICAL CORRECTION OF REFRACTIVE ERRORS

Keratorefractive Surgery. Numerous operations can be performed on the cornea to reduce or eliminate the need for spectacles. One procedure is called radial keratotectomy. The operation is not always successful. In some parts of the United States, many of these operations are performed, often with excellent results; at other times, the operation produces less satisfactory outcomes. The permanence of the refractive changes, the predictability of the changes, and the quality of vision following the surgery are matters that are still not fully resolved.

Photorefractive Keratectomy. Recently, new excimer lasers have been developed which have the ability to reshape corneas in an accurate and predictable manner. This modality of treatment is currently being evaluated by the FDA. The predictable results of this procedure seem dependable. However, some people experience a mild corneal haze and blurry vision within 6 months after the operation, a complication that researchers are working to minimize. Young people who have this operation to correct nearsightedness should be aware that they will probably need reading glasses after they reach age 40.

COLOR BLINDNESS

DEFINITION

Color blindness is an inability to clearly distinguish colors. Usually, the difficulty in perception is limited to telling apart reds and greens, which may both appear to be brown.

CAUSE

There are three types of cone cells, the structures in the retina that enable your brain to perceive color: red, blue, and green. Any of the three types may be defective, but most often the red-and-green-perceiving cones are the problematic structures; thus "color-blind" persons most often have trouble distinguishing reds from greens, especially in lighter shades of these colors. Difficulty in differentiating blues and yellows is another, much less common, form of color blindness.

Color blindness, which is almost never a significant handicap, is a hereditary defect carried on the mother's X chromosome.

DIAGNOSIS

The extent of color blindness can be determined with the use of a series of cards marked with multicolored dots. Those with difficulties in color perception will see different words or numbers than those with normal vision.

Figure 30.7: Warning sign of strabismus. In this drawing, the light reflected from a penlight is asymmetrical, with the pinpoint centered in the pupil in one eye, but off-center over the iris in the other.

MALE/FEMALE DIFFERENCES

Ten times as many men as women are affected: 6 percent and 0.6 percent of the population, respectively. Most types of color blindness are carried on the X chromosome and are expressed only when there is a Y chromosome present or, much less frequently, another carrier X chromosome. Women may therefore be unaffected carriers, transmitting the gene to their sons.

STRABISMUS AND AMBLYOPIA

DEFINITION

During the first few months when newborn babies learn to focus their eyes they often display strabismus, a general term for various types of cross-eye, walleye, or squint. But this condition is usually outgrown when the baby reaches the age of 6 months or so. If it is not, the child must have medical treatment—perhaps including surgery—or the sight of the wandering eye will be lost to a condition called amblyopia, or lazy eye.

CAUSE

Amblyopia occurs because the neural networks of the brain cannot function with double vision. If one eye sends signals that are much weaker, distorted, or inappropriate, because of refractive errors or lack of alignment, the brain will reject them and rely solely on signals from the stronger eye to make up its picture of the world. If this rejection is continued by a young brain, eventually the brain will become unable to interpret images from the weaker eye. By the age of 6 or 7, when the problem is discovered in school, it is often too late to restore sight to the weaker eye. Binocular vision, and with it depth perception, is permanently lost.

DIAGNOSIS

Parents should watch for any signs of strabismus in a child over 6 months old, even if only slight or occasional. Some children have broad folds on the sides of their noses, mak-

ing their pupils seem too close together (this is not harmful). To differentiate this from even slight strabismus, look at the reflection of a candle or penlight in the child's eye. In normal children, the spots of light may lie on either side of the pupil, but they will be symmetric. In a child with strabismus, one spot will be off center, and lie over the iris, not the pupil (see figure 30.7).

Other signs of amblyopia include rubbing the eye, tilting the head to see, covering one eye, and difficulty with games that require estimation of distances for catching or throwing a ball. Even small babies can be tested by covering one eye at a time. The baby with amblyopia will fuss and cry when the good eye is covered. However, amblyopia may occur without easily detectable signs; consequently, children should have a first eye examination before the age of 4.

TREATMENT

Amblyopia should be corrected as early as possible. If the amblyopic eye is weak because of a refractive error, special glasses will correct it: The child wears one corrective lens and one blackened one to force the brain to depend on the corrected weaker eye. Sometimes the child need only wear an eyepatch.

If the amblyopia is due to muscle weakness, however, special eye drops may be prescribed to force the child to rely on the weaker eye. Exercises may also help strengthen the eye muscles. In other cases, surgery to tighten one muscle or loosen another may help the child gain control of the wandering eye.

Treatment of amblyopia should begin when the child is 3 or 4; the longer the condition lasts, the less chance there is of conquering it. Exercises may help children as old as 7 or 8. After this age, however, even though surgery may make a squint less noticeable it will not restore binocular vision.

THE RED EYE

CONJUNCTIVITIS

DEFINITION

Conjunctivitis is an irritation and inflammation of the conjunctiva (the lining of the eyelid). The condition makes the eyes red and irritated with a sandy or burning feeling.

CAUSE

"Pinkeye" is caused by an allergy or an infection of the lining of the eyelid by bacteria or viruses. The disease may follow a cold or sore throat and is most common in children. Pinkeye is contagious and sometimes spreads through a whole grade school.

DIAGNOSIS

Sometimes pus is visible in the eye or causes the eyelids to stick together. The whites of the eyes may turn red and a discharge from the eyes or nose may also be present.

To aid in diagnosis, your doctor may order a lab test to accurately determine the cause of the condition.

TREATMENT

Conjunctivitis should be treated by a physician, who will prescribe antibiotics usually in the form of drops or ointment. Oral antibiotics may be used if the disease is related to a sore throat.

Allergic conjunctivitis may be helped by steroid eye drops, but this therapy has severe side effects, so the prescription must be followed exactly. Where no infectious agent is apparent, soothing drops may be prescribed until the discomfort subsides.

PREVENTION

When you suffer pinkeye, to avoid spreading it to others, stay home, wash your hands frequently, and don't share towels and face cloths. Linens should also be washed thoroughly.

In addition, old or borrowed eye makeup has also been implicated in the spread of conjunctivitis. Experts recommend not sharing eyeliners and discarding mascara after 4 to 6 months.

HERPES EYE INFECTIONS

Eye infections with the herpes virus are treated with the drug Acyclovir (Zovirax). For information on herpes, see Infectious Diseases, chapter 18.

CORNEAL INJURIES

DEFINITION

Since the cornea is at the front of the eye, it is particularly susceptible to environmental insult not always apparent at the time of initial injury. A person with corneal injury may go to sleep normally, unaware of the problem, only to wake a few hours later with a swollen, red, extremely painful eye.

CAUSE

There are two common causes of corneal injury: overuse of hard contact lenses and overexposure to ultraviolet light.

OTHER CAUSES OF RED EYES

Uveitis. An inflammation of the rearmost part of the globe of the eye, including the iris (iritis). This condition, whose cause is unknown, makes the eye painful, light-shy, and red, but not hard as in closed-angle glaucoma. Vision is poor. This condition is treated with atropine to dilate the pupil and prevent the iris from sticking to the lens. Steroids reduce the inflammation. Uveitis should be treated by an ophthalmologist.

Note: In persons suffering AIDS this condition is linked to cytomegalovirus (CMV), a severe, untreatable infection. (See chapters 18 and 19.)

Hemorrhage. Occurs when one of the tiny blood vessels in the eye breaks, spilling blood beneath the white of the eye. This frightening-looking red patch is not serious unless accompanied by pain; usually it clears within 2 to 3 weeks without treatment. Recurrent hemorrhages may signal a blood disorder or overuse of anticoagulant drugs.

Scleritis and Episcleritis. Inflammations of the outermost layers of the eye. Scleritis is often associated with rheumatoid arthritis or digestive diseases, and causes a dull pain. It is the more serious disease of the two; the sclera may become perforated. Both conditions are treated with anti-inflammatory drugs, taken orally or as eye drops. Episcleritis may clear up on its own.

DIAGNOSIS

Sometimes there are no initial signs of damage to the cornea. But the symptoms of corneal damage include swelling, redness, and pain. A doctor will closely examine the eye for signs of damage and may insert special eye drops that clarify the damaged area.

TREATMENT

The treatment consists of an eyepatch, painkilling drugs, and reassurance; the condition usually clears up in a few days.

PREVENTION

Whenever you work with tools, wear special goggles to keep splinters and flying objects from striking your eyes. If you sunbathe, sit under a sunlamp, or weld, you should don ultraviolet-proof goggles. In addition, limiting contact lens–wearing time will also prevent corneal injuries.

EYELID PROBLEMS

Eyelid problems are cared for by ophthalmologists. Most eyelid maladies are related to infections and are not serious. However, eyelids are subject to skin cancers, so any bump or change in a mole or birthmark deserves professional attention.

Blepharitis. An infection of the edges of the eyelids. Lids become red, sticky, and crusty, and sometimes you have to unstick them to see anything in the morning. The eyeball may also redden. Sometimes the infection is associated with dandruff or a *Staphylococcus aureus* infection like a boil.

Treatment: Usually consists of antibiotic drops or ointments. Any associated condition must be treated as well. More serious cases may require oral antibiotics for cure.

Stye. A pimple on the edge of the eyelid.

Treatment: A warm compress (a very clean lint-free cloth soaked in warm water and wrung out) held against the eye for 10 minutes, four times per day, hastens the disappearance of sties. A physician may prescribe an antibiotic ointment to apply under the lid. Occasionally, resistant sties may require lancing and drainage.

Chalazion. A smooth, round bump on the inside surface and some distance from the edge of the eyelid. These painless lumps occur when a gland in the lid becomes blocked.

Treatment: Chalazions sometimes disappear after a regimen of warm compresses and antibiotics like those used for sties. Unfortunately, they are more stubborn than sties. Although they do no harm if left in place, they can be removed surgically under local anesthesia in the ophthalmologist's office and require only the wearing of an eyepatch until the next morning.

Basal Cell Carcinoma. Any growth on the eyelid that does not vanish within a few days should be inspected by a physician, as it may be a basal cell carcinoma. This relatively common skin cancer often begins as a round, dimpled bump with a pearl-like sheen.

Treatment: Basal cell carcinomas are relatively slow growing and noninvasive, but should be removed as soon as possible. (See chapter 28.)

Xanthelasmae. Soft, yellowish skin growths that sometimes appear on the eyelids of persons with high cholesterol (hyperlipidemia) or diabetes.

Treatment: These growths are harmless and can easily be removed if you wish, although they may eventually grow back.

Note: Development of xanthelasmae is a sign that blood cholesterol should be measured.

Entropion and Ectropion. When the eyelid turns in, and the eyelashes scratch the surface of the eye, the condition is called entropion. The reverse problem (common in the elderly), when the lower eyelid becomes loose falling away from the eye and revealing the conjunctiva, is called ectropion.

Treatments: For entropion, a small piece of tape may be used to keep the eyelid in its proper position until an ophthalmologic surgeon can correct the condition. For ectropion, if the eyelid is very loose, tears intended to moisten the eye may flow out of the center, rather than cross to the tear duct next to the nose. This can be annoying enough to warrant surgery to tighten the lid.

Drooping Upper Lids. Very few people possess completely symmetrical facial features. Some children are born with an upper eyelid that droops over one eye, perhaps blocking the vision. This should be corrected early to avoid the development of amblyopia, or lazy eye. The surgery involves shortening the muscles that hold the lid up.

In adults, drooping eyelids, or ptosis, is a sign of eyelid muscle weakness. Sometimes the weakness results from old age. Ptosis may also occur when injury or a disease such as diabetes, myasthenia gravis, stroke, or aneurysm inside the skull damages nerves or muscles.

Treatment: A physician must be consulted to determine the true cause of ptosis. Treatment often necessitates treatment of the underlying cause. If the eyelid sags because of an injury, surgery can strengthen the muscle by shortening it, or the eyelid can be supported by specially designed eyeglasses or contact lenses.

CORNEAL INFECTIONS AND ULCERS

DEFINITION

An ulcer is an open sore. Corneal ulcers can be initiated by infections or foreign particles on the cornea.

CAUSE

Infections such as conjunctivitis can lead to corneal ulcers, which when caused by injuries due to foreign particles often become infected. As with conjunctivitis, the infecting organisms may be bacteria or viruses.

DIAGNOSIS

Symptoms are much more obvious in bacterial than in viral infections. In either case, the sensitive cornea is very painful, the eyeball becomes pink or red, and vision is blurred behind the ulcer. Bacterial ulcers generate pus; viral ulcers do not. A bacterial ulcer may be seen in the mirror as a whitish abrasion on the cornea. Viral ulcers of the cornea are usually caused by herpes simplex virus. The herpes ulcer is shaped like a tree branch (hence its name, dendritic ulcer), and is usually visible only by coating the eye with a fluorescent dye.

TREATMENT

Corneal ulcers demand prompt medical treatment. If neglected, they may permanently scar the cornea or even cut through it, infecting the entire eyeball and mandating surgery to close the opening. The ophthalmologist will prescribe antibiotics in the form of drops, ointments, or oral medicine. In severe cases, antibiotics may be injected near the eye. Viral ulcers are treated with antiviral drops or ointments, as often as once an hour. This controls the current ulcer, but like other herpes infections dendritic ulcers can recur.

If the cornea is badly damaged, a corneal transplant may be necessary to restore sight. In this case, the diseased or opaque cornea is removed and a healthy one from a donor who has recently died is sewn in its place. Formerly, the most common reason for doing a corneal transplant was scarring due to infection and injury, or developmental problems, for example, keratoconus (a displaced and protruding cornea that occurs most commonly in pubescent girls). With the growing elderly U.S. population, the most common reason for a corneal transplant has become corneal swelling or edema from old age or from surgical trauma. Because the cornea is not suffused with blood vessels and antigens from cornea transplant do not enter the bloodstream, they are rejected much less frequently than transplants of other tissue; between 80 and 90 percent of corneal transplants are successful.

GLAUCOMA

GENERAL DEFINITION

Glaucoma is the buildup of pressure in the aqueous humor, the liquid that fills the anterior of the eye. In 90 to 95 percent of cases, glaucoma occurs when the outflow of aqueous humor is blocked.

Usually glaucoma is inherited. Parents may be genetic carriers without developing the disease, however, so family history is not an infallible guide. Glaucoma usually occurs after the age of 40, but abnormal development of the eye may cause glaucoma in infants and toddlers. Injuries, cataracts, and bleeding in the eye may also precipitate glaucoma. Infants with congenital glaucoma will have an aversion to light, enlarged corneas, copious tear-

INFECTIONS OF THE TEAR GLANDS AND DUCTS

There are two kinds of tear gland infections:

Dacryocystitis. Infection, redness and swelling affecting the lower eyelid near the nose.

Dacryoadenitis. Infection of the tear glands above the outside corner of the eye (see figure 30.8). Pressure on the tear sac under the inside corner of the eye may produce a backflow of pus into the corner.

Treatment: Warm soaks and antibiotics. Antibiotics are in the form of eye drops for inflammation of the tear ducts, but in oral form for infected glands. Oral antibiotics may be used for stubborn infection of the tear ducts. If the infection continues, surgery may be necessary to clear out the passage from the eye to the nose.

ing, and big cloudy-looking eyes. Surgery may be necessary to save the infant's sight.

It is estimated that 1 out of every 25 Americans has glaucoma, but only half of these people are aware of the disease. More than 62,000 Americans are legally blind due to glaucoma, with an additional 5,350 losing their sight each year. The disease can cause extensive damage before the symptoms are noticed.

The damage of glaucoma can be contained by simple medications, but first the disease must be detected. For this reason, persons over 40 should be tested regularly, as described in the section on the eye examination.

NARROW-ANGLE OR CONGESTIVE GLAUCOMA

DEFINITION

This type of glaucoma is an immediate blockage of the flow of aqueous humor that causes the pressure in the eye to rise quickly and dramatically.

CAUSE

Narrow- or closed-angle glaucoma usually occurs when the iris dilates and severely blocks the outflow of aqueous humor. It is much rarer than open-angle glaucoma (see below), amounting to only 5 to 10 percent of total glaucoma cases.

DIAGNOSIS

Unlike open-angle glaucoma, this form of glaucoma is impossible to ignore: Within days, the eye becomes red, rock hard, and painful enough to cause nausea and vomiting. The cornea appears hazy, lights develop halos, and vision is poor. Closed-angle glaucoma is an obvious eye emergency.

TREATMENT

The ophthalmologist will first administer eye drops to constrict the pupil, hoping to move the surrounding iris away from the outflow ducts. Other drugs, administered intravenously or by mouth, will attempt to draw liquid out of the eye. Massaging the eye may also help break up the blockage.

Despite these measures, corrective surgery usually is necessary to prevent blindness and recurrences. Using a scalpel or laser, the ophthalmologist makes a wider outflow duct through the iris for the aqueous humor. The operation requires a brief hospital stay. Laser surgery may be performed on outpatients, with eye drops for anesthesia. The tendency to develop closed-angle glaucoma is inherited, and usually affects both eyes.

OPEN-ANGLE GLAUCOMA

DEFINITION

In open-angle glaucoma, the prevalent type of glaucoma, the drainage of the aqueous humor from the eye is slowed so that fluid and pressure in the eye build up gradually.

CAUSE

The structures that allow for drainage or absorption of aqueous humor fail, and the increased fluid pressure in the eyeball pinches the blood vessels that supply the optic nerve. Starved, the nerve slowly dies. Peripheral vision decreases, or the affected person may first notice halos around lights. Eventually, the eye can achieve only tunnel vision. If untreated, blindness results.

TREATMENT

Glaucoma may be diagnosed by an optometrist or ophthalmologist, but only the ophthalmologist is qualified to treat it. There are many forms of treatment, all aimed at reducing pressure in the eye.

Although glaucoma is defined as an intraocular pressure of more than 21 millimeters of mercury (mmHg), most doctors do not automatically begin treating every patient at this point. Different people have differing sensitivity to the pressure. The ophthalmologist must look into the eyes for signs of damage and test for loss of peripheral vision. Therapy should begin only when pressure is high enough to cause the individual damage. Patients with pressures above 21 but no visual loss should be retested every 6 to 8 months.

Most patients must take special eye drops or other medication every day for life.

- Timoptic (timolol maleate), eye drops taken once or twice a day, reduces fluid production and increases outflow.
- Pilocarpine, another form of eye drops, taken three or four times per day decreases the size of the pupil and thus increases outflow of aqueous humor.
- Diamox (acetazolamide), an oral medication that reduces fluid formation for those who have difficulty administering eye drops. These drugs may be taken singly or in combination.

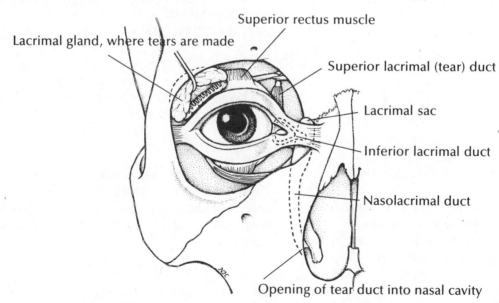

Figure 30.8: Where tears come from.

- Marijuana: also reduces intraocular pressure, but studies to determine the active ingredient and solve problems of drug tolerance are still not complete.

SURGICAL TREATMENTS

For the 10 percent of glaucoma patients who are not helped by medicine, surgery offers sight-saving alternatives. The traditional operation opens up drainage by removing a part of the iris; a newer procedure implants a tiny plastic valve to permit outflow of liquid. In addition, lasers are now being used to treat some cases of glaucoma.

Note: Patients with glaucoma should be aware that many medications increase ocular pressure, exacerbating the disease. These drugs include cold and allergy pills, antihistamines, tranquilizers, cortisone, and several remedies for stomach and intestinal problems. If you have glaucoma, be sure that any physician who treats you knows of this condition and does not prescribe anything that might worsen it.

....

GROWTHS WITHIN THE EYEBALL

Pinguecula. One or more soft yellow patches growing on either side of the eyeball, usually in a person over 35. The condition is benign and no treatment is necessary.

Ptyergium. A fleshy growth starting from either corner of the eye and moving toward the cornea. It is associated with exposure to wind and dust. It is also benign, but can be removed surgically for cosmetic reasons or if it impinges on the visual field.

RETINOBLASTOMA

DEFINITION

These malignant tumors of the eyes are the second most common form of childhood cancer, most often occurring in children under the age of 4.

CAUSE

This disease is frequently inherited; half the children of retinoblastoma patients also develop retinoblastoma.

DIAGNOSIS

The family often notices the first sign of retinoblastoma when the tumor appears in a child's pupil as a white reflection, like that of a cat's eye. Later stages of the disease cause pain, redness, and visual loss. In at least 20 percent of cases, both eyes are affected.

A physician thoroughly examines both eyes to determine the location and extent of the retinoblastoma tumor or tumors.

TREATMENT

Over 50 percent of retinoblastoma cases are curable with a combination of surgery and radiation. In some cases, as the tumor grows it may cut off its own blood supply and regress spontaneously. However, the possibility that the retinoblastoma may spread along the optic nerve toward the brain necessitates firm intervention.

Since retinoblastomas are very sensitive to radiation, radiation therapy to destroy the cancer in its early stages may save the eye. Small "plaques" of radioactive material are sewn to the outside of the eyeball over the tumor for a few days and then removed. The lens may be damaged, but vision is preserved in most early-stage cancers. Chemotherapy may also be used.

SURGICAL TREATMENT

If the eye cannot be saved with radiation and chemotherapy, the eye must be removed and an artificial one attached. The surgery is followed by a painless week in the hospital. A patch is worn for several weeks until a naturally moving false eye can be attached to the eye muscles. If both eyes are affected, the eye with the more advanced tumor is removed and the other eye treated with radiation to preserve vision. Laser therapy is a recently developed technique for precisely targeting destruction of retinoblastoma.

MELANOMA

DEFINITION

Most melanomas are skin cancers. However, these types of tumors also grow inside the eye, sometimes causing a form of glaucoma. Melanoma is an extremely fast-growing cancer, and the prognosis for a person with one so close to the brain is often poor.

CAUSE

Melanoma is generally associated with overexposure to sunlight, although there may also be an inherited susceptibility.

DIAGNOSIS

Sometimes a melanoma may appear as a dark spot in the white of the eye. If it lies on the back of the eye, it may cause no symptoms. When it is located in the center, vision may become unclear or objects may appear distorted. Immediate treatment is necessary.

TREATMENT

Surgical removal of the eyeball is the most common treatment. If one eye has already been removed, the other may be treated with radiation or removal of the tumor in an attempt to preserve sight. If only the iris is involved, it may be excised in an iridectomy, leaving the rest of the eye intact.

New forms of radiation using protons (hydrogen ions) and helium ions promise a higher rate of long-term survival for patients with melanoma of the eye. Although the studies are not complete (they lack data on long-term follow-up), the 18-month survival rates are quite high. Research is continuing at the University of California at San Francisco, Harvard University, and in Switzerland.

....

CATARACTS

Cataracts have been observed in the eyes of humans since the beginning of recorded history. Three thousand years ago, physicians in India left written descriptions of cataract operations. Today, almost half a million Americans annually undergo a basically similar procedure for clearing up lens opacity. It is estimated that one in seven people over the age of 65 have cataracts. Although 95 percent of cataract patients experience improved vision after surgery, ignorance and fear still motivate many to delay the operation. Consequently, many people become blind because they refuse to have this procedure.

DEFINITION

Cataracts are cloudy spots on the eye's lens that initially do not interfere with vision. But as the spots expand, sight grows grayer and mistier as though a series of veils were thrown across the visible world (see figure 30.9).

CAUSE

About three-quarters of cataracts are caused by age—these are called senile cataracts. The exact mechanism that causes this clouding is unknown.

German measles (rubella) during pregnancy may cause an infant to develop congenital cataracts; women of childbearing age who have not had rubella should receive rubella vaccine before becoming pregnant.

Galactosemia, a hereditary disease, causes cataracts in newborn infants. A special diet excluding galactose, a milk sugar, prevents this condition.

Cataracts may also appear after an eye is punctured or exposed to radiation, such as x-rays, microwaves, and infrared rays. Diseases such as uveitis or diabetes also may be responsible.

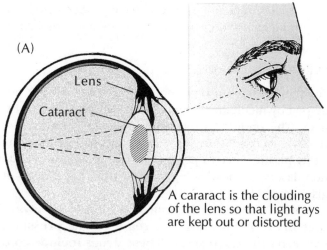

(A)

Lens

Cataract

A cararact is the clouding of the lens so that light rays are kept out or distorted

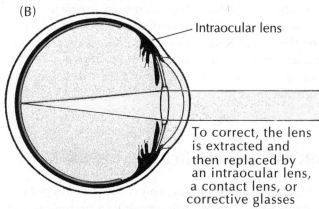

(B)

Intraocular lens

To correct, the lens is extracted and then replaced by an intraocular lens, a contact lens, or corrective glasses

Figure 30.9A and B: (A) Cataracts cloud the lens, reducing and distorting sight. (B) Cataracts are corrected by extracting the lens and either inserting an intraocular lens or using a contact lens or corrective glasses.

DIAGNOSIS

Initially, as your cataracts progress, you need brighter lights and stronger lenses for reading and you may experience double vision. Night driving becomes difficult as the glare from oncoming headlights is dispersed by the lens. After a while, new glasses no longer help.

But even before symptoms become apparent, an eye examination by a physician will reveal cataracts that have begun to form but do not yet interfere with vision.

TREATMENT

The only effective treatment for cataracts is surgery, not diet, drugs, or exercises. Advances in surgical techniques have made it unnecessary to wait until the cataract is "ripe," or completely opaque. It should be removed as soon as it interferes with your daily activities—at 20/40 vision in a diamond cutter, but as late as 20/200 if you are a retired person who rarely reads.

The operation should be performed by an ophthalmologic surgeon with extensive experience in removing cataracts. Since many different methods are available for anesthesia, hospitalization, correction of vision after cataract surgery, and removal of the cataract itself, you should discuss all these aspects of the operation thoroughly with your ophthalmologist before choosing a surgeon.

General anesthesia may be used, but local anesthesia is safer and simpler, especially for elderly or ill patients. An injection paralyzes the lid to prevent blinking during the surgery; another injection prevents eyeball movement. The 1 hour operation causes little or no pain.

Previously, cataracts were removed by extracting the entire lens and its capsule, usually by inserting a freezing probe (a cryoprobe) that stuck to the lens and drew it out. Today's most common operation excises the cataract but leaves the thin transparent capsule of the lens. In another common procedure, phacoemulsification, an ultrasonic vibrator breaks up the lens, which is then vacuumed up (aspirated) through a hollow needle. Children have very soft lenses, which can be aspirated without previous ultravibration. The cornea is then sutured together.

These techniques are increasingly available on an outpatient basis, but some physicians prefer to monitor their patients overnight or longer. A lengthy hospital stay is no longer necessary, except in unusual cases. Many patients return to normal activities soon after leaving the hospital.

When cataracts appear in both eyes and grow at different rates, the most severely affected eye is usually operated on first. Several months may pass to ensure complete healing without infection before the second cataract is removed.

REPLACING THE LENS

After cataract surgery, a new lens is needed to replace the removed one. Previously, glasses thick as bottle bottoms were worn to compensate for altered vision.

Aside from their undesirable appearance, thick glasses have significant disadvantages:

- They magnify your image of the world and restrict your field of view to the area straight ahead.
- When used on one eye, these glasses make it difficult for the brain to reconcile the magnified and unmagnified images.

After cataract surgery, most people prefer a lens that fits on or in the eyeball. Formerly, contact lenses that rest on the cornea have been the treatment of choice.

(See "Contact Lenses" in this chapter for a description of the different kinds.) They can be fitted about 6 weeks after surgery, but the wearer must be able to handle them properly and keep them clean. Today, however, ophthalmologists almost always implant intraocular lenses in patients who are over 40; these are now implanted after more than 90 percent of cataract removals in the United States.

Intraocular lenses are a vast improvement over previous treatments.

- They are implanted permanently into the eye during the same surgery that removes the cataract.
- You do not have to care for contact lenses; contact lens care is difficult for elderly people with arthritis of the hands.

In previous years, 50 to 60 percent of cataract implants were *anterior chamber implants:* The entire lens was removed and a plastic lens was placed in front of the iris. Today, virtually all doctors put in *posterior chamber implants:* The cataract is removed but the posterior lens capsule (a thin transparent membrane surrounding the lens) is preserved and the intraocular lens is placed in the capsular bag.

After cataract surgery, many patients are troubled by bright sunlight, which can cause serious burns of the eye. (For more on protection, see "Sunburn" in this chapter.) Because the normal crystalline lens absorbs a certain amount of ultraviolet light, its removal during cataract surgery can expose the retina to increased ultraviolet light. For this reason, many intraocular lenses incorporate an ultraviolet filter.

Although many people wonder if a laser will ever be used for cataract surgery, the laser's focused light is not suited for treating cataracts. Instead, lasers are used postoperatively after a significant number of posterior chamber implants. From 6 months to 10 years afterward, between 50 and 60 percent of these patients develop a fibrous membrane on the posterior capsule that blurs vision (the implant rests on the posterior membrane capsule). When this occurs, a laser is used to open this membrane, restoring vision in several days.

DISEASES OF THE RETINA

The rod and cone cells of the retina are the organs that actually perceive light and color. Any damage or derangement involving the retina therefore seriously threatens your vision. Among the most common causes of blindness are diseases that damage the retina and inherited conditions such as retinitis pigmentosa that compromise its ability to function.

MACULAR DEGENERATION

DEFINITION

The macula is the central part of the retina with the sharpest sight. A dense concentration of rods and cones helps us see fine details at the center of our field of vision. In almost 8,000 Americans each year, mostly older people, the surface of the macula degenerates enough to cause legal blindness.

CAUSE

The immediate cause for macular degeneration is not well understood, but a degenerative condition may be inherited. As degeneration progresses, central vision gradually and painlessly blurs in one or both eyes.

DIAGNOSIS

This ailment affects the central section of vision, so any noticeable changes in central vision necessitate a visit to the eye doctor. Physicians use fluorescein angiography to analyze the blood vessels in the eye. During this test, the doctor injects into a vein in the arm a dye that travels through the circulatory system to the eyes. The pattern revealed by this dye indicates the presence or absence of macular degeneration.

A simple self-test using the Amsler grid (see figure 30.10) can determine if the condition is worsening.

TREATMENT

In the early stages of the disease, magnifying glasses may help you read. Laser treatments seal leaks under the retina and reattach parts of it and in some cases will prevent the progression of senile macular degeneration. In the later stages, sharp central vision is lost completely. But the retention of outer vision allows most of the 58,000 Americans who are legally blind due to macular degeneration to care for themselves and get around easily.

DIABETES AND THE RETINA

More than 32,000 Americans are legally blind and about 4,700 lose their sight each year because of retinal damage caused by diabetes, or diabetic retinopathy (the medical term). The danger increases with the duration of the disease: After 15 years, two-thirds of people with diabetes show signs of eye damage, rising to 90 percent after 30 or 40 years.

DEFINITION

Diabetes can lead to several undesirable changes in the eyes. In each of these changes, sight may be threatened as the blood vessels in the eyes deteriorate and the supply of oxygen to the retina is restricted (diabetic retinopathy); or new blood vessels invade the eye (proliferative retinopathy), grow over the retina, and sometimes break, resulting in retinal detachment.

CAUSE

Vision problems usually start with changes in blood supply to the eyes. New blood vessels—often leaking blood—may form in the eye, interfering with sight. In addition, hemorrhages, visible as small red spots, can form, leading to scarring, which restricts vision.

DIAGNOSIS

The ophthalmologist will first notice the widening of the tiny veins in the retina, which often swell to pinch the arteries where they cross each other. The disease weakens the walls of the veins, causing outgrowths and expansions. When these break, their small hemorrhages may vanish or leave tiny white scars that mark areas where vision is lost.

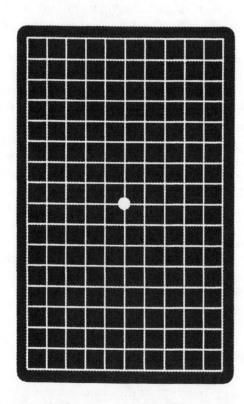

Figure 30.10: The Amsler grid. To monitor macular degeneration, patients are instructed to hold a card showing the Amsler grid about 10 to 12 inches from their eyes and look at it one eye at a time. Any blurring or distortion of the lines, or an inability to focus on the dot in the middle, signifies worsening degeneration.

As the disease progresses, new blood vessels grow over the retina and into the vitreous humor. These also swell and bleed, leading to the large hemorrhages that obscure sight. Sometimes they clear up without treatment, but their resorption can lead to retinal detachment (see below). The possibility of eyesight problems—and possible loss of sight—is an important reason for diabtetics to keep their diabetes under careful control.

TREATMENT

Medical care for this condition begins with good control of diabetes. In many patients, lasers can be used to coagulate the outgrowths and leaks in old blood vessels and stop the new blood vessels that threaten the retina. This procedure can be performed on outpatients under local anesthesia. Vision threatened by a blood-clouded vitreous humor can be restored by replacing the fluid with a clear saline solution, a surgical procedure called vitrectomy. (For more details, see chapter 21, Diabetes and Other Endocrine Disorders.)

HIGH BLOOD PRESSURE

DEFINITION

Hypertension, or high blood pressure, can cause hemorrhages and patches of scar tissue in the retina. Depending on whether the damage is due to a sudden peak in the blood pressure or to a long, steady rise, the tiny arteries in the retina become thin and tortuous, or so thick walled that the blood inside cannot be seen. "Floaters" (moving spots before the eyes) may appear in the vision, but often sight is normal.

CAUSE

The cause of the hypertension is in the circulatory system. Hypertension is not restricted to the eyes but may damage organs throughout the body.

DIAGNOSIS

The chief significance of this condition is that changes in the retina due to hypertension mirror serious changes elsewhere in the body, especially the kidneys and heart. Blood pressure taken at the arm will reveal hypertension affecting these other organs as well as the eyes.

TREATMENT

Treatment consists of lowering the blood pressure through diet or drugs, or both. This alone may correct the visual problems.

HOME REMEDIES AND ALTERNATIVE THERAPIES

In addition to medication for hypertension, weight loss and meditation may be used to help keep blood pressure down. Some people will also benefit from cutting back on sodium in their diet. (See chapter 16.)

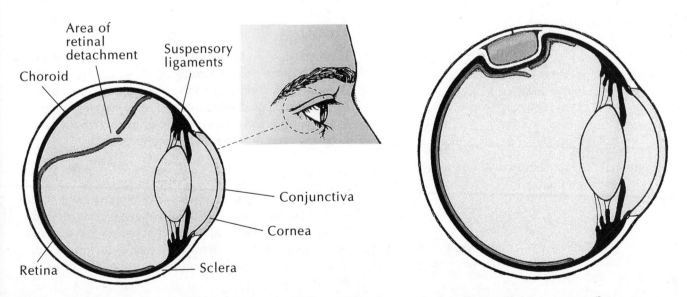

Figure 30.11: Detached retina. When the retina detaches, a hole allows fluid to enter the space between the choroid and the retina, allowing the retina to float free. To treat this problem, a silicon pad implanted in the pocket within the sclera reestablishes contact between the choroid and the retina while scar tissue cements the structures in place.

RETINAL DETACHMENT

DEFINITION

The retina receives oxygen and nutrients from the blood vessels at the back of the eyeball. When it breaks away from the back of the eyeball, it is said to be detached.

CAUSE

Occasionally (more often in an older person who is near-sighted) fluid leaks beneath the retina and it peels away from its backing like loose wallpaper (see figure 30.11). Sometimes detachment follows an injury to the eye.

DIAGNOSIS

The person sees dark spots or light flashes; a curtain may seem to blot out part of the field of vision, or the world may seem blurred or distorted.

TREATMENT

This is a genuine ophthalmologic emergency. If the retina is not reattached to its source of nutrients within a short period of time, the rod and cone cells will die and vision loss will be permanent. The ophthalmologist will use general anesthesia and one or more of the following techniques: draining the fluid under the retina; using a very cold instrument (a cryoprobe) to make the back of the eyeball stickier; pushing the back of the eyeball toward the retina with special instruments; sealing holes in the retina with a laser. Surgery is successful in about 90 percent of cases. The hospital stay usually lasts about 1 week.

RETINITIS PIGMENTOSA

DEFINITION

Retinitis pigmentosa is an inherited disease in which the retina degenerates in tiny patches. It affects about 1 million people in the United States.

CAUSE

Retinitis pigmentosa is a hereditary disease whose mechanism is poorly understood.

DIAGNOSIS

The patient first notices poor night vision, then loses peripheral vision, although central vision may be as good as 20/50 until middle age.

TREATMENT

There is no known treatment and eventually tunnel vision results. About 23,000 Americans are legally blind due to retinitis pigmentosa. Newly developed glasses employ precision optics to provide a horizontal widening of the field of vision. These experimental devices are odd-looking, heavy, and expensive (about $2,000), but they enable some retinitis pigmentosa patients to hold jobs and even drive.

PREVENTION

There is some evidence that taking large doses of vitamin A may slow the progression of this disease. At the same time, large doses of vitamin E may counteract the action of vitamin A. (For guidance on supplementing your diet with vitamins, see chapter 5, The Basics of Good Nutrition.) However, this has not been conclusively proven in long-term studies.

HOME REMEDIES AND ALTERNATIVE THERAPIES

Since retinitis pigmentosa may be related to sunlight exposure in the eye (although this has not been conclusively proven), covering one eye with an eyepatch after the initial onset of the disease may temporarily preserve eyesight in that eye. Then, after sight is lost in the uncovered eye, the other eye may be uncovered and used until sight is lost in that eye.

CHOROIDITIS

DEFINITION

The choroid is the layer of blood vessels that underlies and nourishes the retina. An inflammation of the choroid can spread to the retina and the resultant scars may permanently impair vision.

CAUSE

In many cases, choroiditis is due to infection with a microbe called *Toxoplasma gondii,* transmitted to children through contact with the feces of dogs or cats. The infection can also be transmitted by a pregnant woman to her baby, causing more severe disease. In many cases, however, the cause cannot be determined.

DIAGNOSIS

The condition is painless but causes blurred vision. Children who have the disease in one eye may develop amblyopia. In adults, the severity of the disease depends on the location of scarring: The closer to the macula, the more likely the loss of clear vision in the center of the field of vision.

TREATMENT

Prompt medical treatment is necessary to decrease the likelihood of scarring. Therapy consists of steroids to control the inflammation. In congenital infections, drugs to suppress the immune system may be necessary.

BLOCKAGES OF RETINAL BLOOD VESSELS

DEFINITION

The retina is nourished and cleansed by a set of tiny blood vessels, the retinal arteries and the retinal veins. Anything that interferes with blood flow through these vessels threatens the health of the retinal cells crucial to good vision.

CAUSE

Especially in older persons, these fine vessels sometimes become blocked with a blood clot (thrombosis) or fatty deposit (embolus).

DIAGNOSIS

The symptoms depend on the type of vessel being blocked. When an artery is obstructed, the retina it supplies stops functioning, causing blindness in part or all of one eye. Unlike retinal detachment, the vision loss often involves the upper or lower half of the field of vision. If the blocked blood vessel is a vein, it may rupture, spilling blood and fluid into the vitreous humor, blurring and clouding vision over the course of a few hours.

TREATMENT

Blockage of a retinal artery is an emergency, like retinal detachment. Without a blood supply, the rod and cone cells of the retina will die. Massage of the eyeball, drugs, or surgery may be necessary to dislodge the blockage. In many cases, vision can be only partially improved.

Retinal vein blockage is less dire. Especially in younger people, the spilled blood may be resorbed. There is no specific treatment, although complications such as overgrowth of new blood vessels may be halted through coagulation with a laser. Because blockage of a retinal vein may be undetectable to the affected person, regular eye examinations are essential so that treatment of underlying causes, like high blood pressure, can prevent further damage.

DISORDERS OF THE OPTIC NERVE

Atrophy of the optic nerve is another cause of blindness, responsible for about 2,000 new cases of legal blindness in the United States each year.

DEFINITION

An increase in pressure inside the skull presses against the optic nerve, causing it to atrophy (become dysfunctional).

CAUSE

The most common cause is an increase in pressure inside the skull. This may be caused by a growth or by very high blood pressure. The increased pressure causes swelling of the optic disk, the area in the back of the eye where the blood vessels and the optic nerve pass through to the brain. The optic disk becomes swollen and presses on the nerve.

DIAGNOSIS

A person with optic nerve atrophy may or may not see white or dark spots. As the optic nerve atrophies from the pressure, vision becomes poor. Part of the visual field may be lost. The condition is called papilledema.

TREATMENT

Treatment of papilledema must correct the causes of the increased cranial pressure. Vision usually returns to normal within 2 months.

SUMMING UP

Our eyes provide one of our most precious senses through which we learn an immense amount about the world around us. Yet many people endanger their sight through ignorance or carelessness. Regular, although not necessarily yearly, eye checkups are essential for both young and old. And simple eye protection during sports, work, and sun exposure prevents many injuries, pain, and disability, including blindness.

Today, a wide assortment of corrective lenses is available to compensate for nearsighted, farsighted, or astigmatic vision. Experienced professional medical attention is vital for getting the right prescription and the most comfortable contact lenses or glasses.

Doctors also have access to new techniques and devices for treating cataracts, detached retinas, and the damage due to diabetes. Glaucoma, the "sneak thief of sight," can be arrested through careful use of medications. With proper care, our eyes last as long as we do, and may even outlive us to serve others.

31
Diseases of the Ear, Nose, and Throat

• • • • • • • • • •

JONATHAN AVIV, M.D.

Parts of this chapter are adapted from the chapter by Malcolm H. Schvey, M.D., which appeared in the revised second edition.

Within the relatively small structure of the ears, nose, and throat are several very complex mechanisms that allow us not only to make sound but also to hear, to keep our balance, to smell, to breathe in and filter air, and to swallow food and water. These mechanisms are interrelated and generally carry out their functions without our being aware of the processes at work. Although these structures are complex, they are in many ways not far removed from the more primitive form in which they once existed—first in aquatic animals and later in more primitive land species. The doctor trained to diagnose and treat disorders of the ear, nose, and throat is the otolaryngologist (head and neck surgeon), sometimes referred to as an ENT specialist. The discipline is considered a subspecialty of surgery.

THE EAR

The ear is divided into three parts: the external ear, the middle ear, and the inner ear (see figure 31.1).

The *outer ear* consists of the auricle, or pinna (the cartilage and skin that we see on the outside of the skull), and the outer ear canal, which conducts sound to the middle ear. At the entrance to the middle ear is the eardrum, a thin membrane that is stretched across the end of the outer ear canal.

The *middle ear* is a cavity that contains three connected bones, collectively called the ossicles. Each is named for the object it resembles: the malleus (hammer), the incus (anvil), and the stapes (stirrup). Leading from the bottom of the middle ear cavity to the back of the nose is a narrow channel called the eustachian tube. When an individual swallows or yawns, the muscles attached to this tube pull on its edges and open it so that the air outside may replenish the air supply in the middle ear. The eustachian tube thus serves to equalize the air pressure on the inside of the eardrum with that on the outside.

The middle ear opens into the *inner ear* via the oval window, which is covered by the footplate of the stapes bone. On the inner ear of that plate, the stapes is bathed with the fluid of the vestibule, which is contiguous with the fluid of the cochlea. This structure, shaped something like a snail shell and lined with tiny hairs, is the major part of the hearing mechanism. The second part of the inner ear is the labyrinth, which is responsible for balance.

HEARING

Sound is essentially vibration. When the vibrations are very rapid and of a small amplitude, the sound is high-pitched; when they are slow and of a large amplitude, the sound has a low pitch. The ability to perceive vibration existed in very early forms of life found in an aquatic environment. Even now, the inner part of the human ear is virtually the same as the entire ear structure of many aquatic creatures, such as sharks. The later formation of the middle and outer ears has allowed the vibrations to

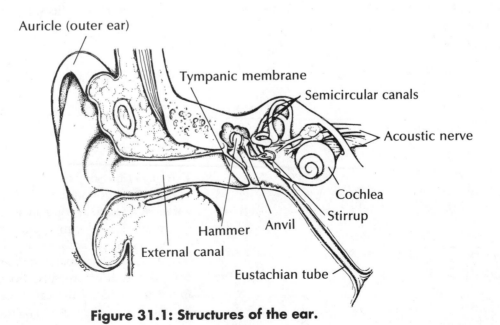

Figure 31.1: Structures of the ear.

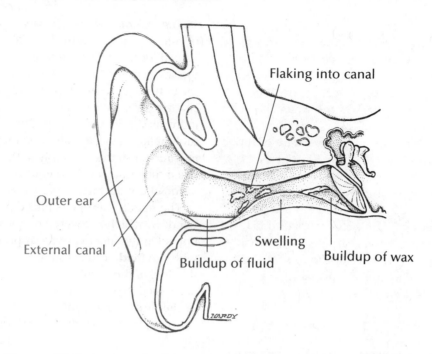

Figure 31.2: External otitis, inflammation of the external ear.

be augmented so that they can be perceived by humans and animals living in a gaseous environment, which does not carry vibrations as strongly as water does.

The vibrations, or sound waves from the air, are funneled by:

The outer ear and travel through the outer ear canal until they strike . . .

The eardrum: This drum vibrates, sending vibrations through . . .

The middle ear: Here the sound is magnified and transferred to the fluid of . . .

The inner ear cochlea: The tiny hairs lining the cochlea are stimulated by the waves and convey these stimulations to . . .

The auditory nerve: This nerve sends impulses to the brain, which perceives the messages as sounds.

The middle ear is basically designed for functioning on land, not for reentry into water. Consequently, one of the major sources of acquired ear disease is swimming. Nor is the middle ear designed to adapt to rapid changes in pressure or altitude. So a rapid change in pressure, such as that experienced in flying or scuba diving, is another important cause of middle ear disease in adults.

BALANCE

The second part of the inner ear is the labyrinth—two connected chambers and three connected, fluid-filled semicircular canals at right angles to one another. When the head or body is tilted, or moved up and down or back and forth, the fluid in these canals and chambers is set into motion or, if already in motion, is set to rest. The changes in motion or rest of these fluids produce the impulses enabling us to detect movement and provide information to the brain about the head's position. This information, along with sight and impulses from the muscles, helps determine what movements the body must make to maintain balance. Disorders or infections of the labyrinth often result in difficulties in balance and vertigo, which is a kind of dizziness that makes the individual feel as if he or his surroundings are spinning.

THE EXTERNAL EAR

EXTERNAL OTITIS AND FURUNCULOSIS

DEFINITION

External otitis, sometimes called swimmer's ear, is a generalized infection in the ear canal. It often occurs in the summer, especially after swimming in polluted water. Furunculosis, or recurring boils, is similar to external otitis, but only the hair follicles in the ear canal are infected.

External otitis usually starts with itching of the ear and may develop into very severe pain, caused by swelling of the tissue in the canal pressing against the bone. Furunculosis also results in painful swelling. In both conditions, there may be foul-smelling, yellowish pus oozing from the ear, or blocking it and affecting hearing (see figure 31.2).

CAUSE

External otitis usually results from eczema that develops in the ear canal. Once the skin is broken, germs, fungus, or bacteria can invade the tissues of the canal. Sometimes the *Pseudomonas aeruginosa* bacterium, which lives in the inadequately chlorinated water of a public pool, is the infecting agent. On rare occasions, external otitis is caused by a fungus, usually *Aspergillus niger,* which produces coal-black spores like those often seen on old bread. It may become so firmly entrenched that it remains even after the eczema is healed. Furunculosis is caused by an infection of a hair follicle in the ear canal.

DIAGNOSIS

The physician diagnoses these conditions by physical examination, observing the symptoms. *Aspergillus niger* infection is identified by the characteristic color of the spores in the ears. A culture can identify the bacteria.

TREATMENT

External otitis is usually treated with drops containing a steroid or cortisone derivative, along with a topical antibiotic to control the infection. *Aspergillus niger* is easily treated with a dusting of sulfanilamide powder. Furunculosis may be treated with systemic antibiotics as well as ear drops.

HOME REMEDIES AND ALTERNATIVE THERAPIES

No self-care can cure a serious infection, although self-care may suffice in mild cases (see chapter 18, Infectious Diseases). However, once medical treatment has begun, care should be taken not to get water in the ear while the infection is healing. In addition, applying a heating pad to the ear may help relieve pain.

PREVENTION

External otitis can be caused by substances other than water, such as hair spray or hair coloring dye. To help prevent this, place balls of lambswool in the ears while these substances are being used. Unlike cotton balls, which absorb liquid, lambswool tends to repel it.

BENIGN CYSTS AND TUMORS

DEFINITION

Sebaceous cysts are growths that usually contain a medium-thick fluid and often develop just behind the outer ear. Exostoses are benign tumors of the ear canal that arise about two-thirds of the way in toward the eardrum. Exostoses grow extremely slowly and rarely reach a size where they become a problem.

CAUSE

Sebaceous cysts result from fluid accumulation from skin glands. Exostoses result from an overgrowth of bone.

DIAGNOSIS

The physician diagnoses these growths based on physical examination of the lumps. If there is any doubt as to their benign nature, a fluid or tissue sample is taken for laboratory examination.

TREATMENT

Sebaceous cysts usually do not require treatment. However, if they become large or are prone to recurrent infection, they may be removed surgically. If exostoses become large enough to block the ear canal, they, too, will have to be removed surgically—a tricky procedure that requires that the skin covering be left intact because it is more resistant to infection than the tissue that may grow to replace it if removed.

FOREIGN BODIES

DEFINITION

A foreign body is anything that gets stuck in the ear, ranging from bugs to seeds, pieces of plastic or paper, and even earplugs that cannot be removed.

CAUSE

Foreign bodies most commonly get stuck in the ears of young children who experiment with putting small objects in their ears or noses.

DIAGNOSIS

The physician usually can see the object with the naked eye or, if deeper in the ear, with a lighted examining device.

TREATMENT

Removal is relatively easy with the right instrument, generally a special type of tiny forceps known as alligator forceps. Attempts to remove the object with the wrong instrument are difficult and even potentially dangerous.

HOME REMEDIES AND ALTERNATIVE THERAPIES

Attempts to remove a foreign object lodged in the ear by anyone other than an experienced physician using the appropriate instrument may drive the object farther into the ear. However, if an insect has become stuck in the ear (a particularly annoying occurrence) it is safe to try immobilizing it with drops of mineral oil until a physician can remove it.

PREVENTION

Teach children not to put foreign objects in their ears.

....

THE EARDRUM

TRAUMA

DEFINITION

Trauma to the eardrum is any accidental damage to the tympanic membrane. When the membrane is perforated, sudden severe pain occurs, followed by bleeding from the ear, hearing loss, and tinnitus.

CAUSE

Trauma can be caused by accidental laceration with a stick, pencil, bobby pin, or similar object—a condition that is painful and frightening to the patient. Another form of external trauma may result when someone is hit over the ear with an open hand. Unlike a closed fist, an open hand usually produces an air pocket with the ear canal, causing pressure against the eardrum that can actually rupture it inward.

DIAGNOSIS

The physician can see damage to the eardrum using a lighted examining device.

TREATMENT

Most traumatic perforations of the eardrum heal spontaneously if great care is taken to keep them dry. Even when the laceration is very large, if no external material is placed in the ear and no infection occurs, it will generally heal on its own. Antibiotics may be prescribed as a precautionary measure. If water gets in and an infection occurs, however, the hole in the eardrum is much less likely to heal spontaneously. If this occurs and the hole remains, it must be closed surgically at a later date.

PREVENTION

The standard adage, "Never put anything in your ear sharper than your elbow" remains sound advice for ear health.

BULLOUS MYRINGITIS (INFECTIOUS MYRINGITIS)

DEFINITION

Bullous myringitis, also known as infectious myringitis, is an inflammation of the eardrum in which little water blisters develop on the membrane, causing severe pain. The infection can be very painful, but is usually not very serious. In most cases the eardrum returns to normal in a week or so with proper treatment.

CAUSE

Bullous myringitis may be caused by bacteria or a virus, but the disease is not fully understood.

DIAGNOSIS

The physician diagnoses bullous myringitis based on observation of the infection.

TREATMENT

Systemic antibiotics or ear drops containing steroids and antibiotics, or both, are given to prevent infection of the vesicles as they break open. An analgesic also may be prescribed to alleviate pain.

RETRACTED EARDRUM

DEFINITION

If the eustachian tube is blocked completely, air in the middle ear is gradually reabsorbed and a vacuum will form, pulling the eardrum inward, causing pain and interfering with hearing. This condition is called a retracted eardrum. Sometimes the eustachian tube becomes blocked, but rather than a vacuum being formed, fluid accumulates, causing pain. Treatment is identical in either case.

CAUSE

An obstruction of the eustachian tube is the causitive factor. The blockage may be due to several conditions, but most commonly it stems from nasal congestion occurring with an upper respiratory infection or respiratory allergy.

DIAGNOSIS

The physician can observe a retracted eardrum using a lighted examining device.

TREATMENT

Nasal decongestants and antihistamines are prescribed to open the eustachian tube so that the pressure can be equalized. If this is not successful, the physician may make a little slit in the eardrum, a procedure known as a myringotomy. This allows air in, the vacuum disappears, and often the condition rights itself. However, if there is underlying chronic disease in the adenoids, the problem in the eardrum may also become chronic.

PREVENTION

Any upper respiratory infection or allergy should be treated promptly to help prevent eustachian tube blockage.

BAROTITIS MEDIA (BAROMETRIC OTITIS, BAROTRAUMA)

DEFINITION

When the eardrum is retracted by a change of atmospheric pressure while the eustachian tube is blocked, the condition is known as barotitis media. It is painful and usually reduces hearing temporarily, but it often responds easily to treatment and is seldom very serious. If the changes of air pressure are very great or if the eustachian tube is extremely blocked, the pressure may cause bleeding of the little capillaries in the middle ear. The blood filling the middle ear acts as a sound barrier, and there may be a considerable hearing loss, as well as a peculiar feeling of being under water.

CAUSE

Barotitis media often afflicts people who fly or scuba dive when they have a cold or stuffy nose.

DIAGNOSIS

The physician diagnoses barotitis media by direct observation of the condition using an otoscope.

TREATMENT

Generally the symptoms clear up spontaneously; otherwise treatment with antibiotics and decongestants, and possibly a myringotomy, may be necessary.

HOME REMEDIES AND ALTERNATIVE THERAPIES

Some people find that chewing gum or yawning helps equalize the pressure in their ears.

PREVENTION

Avoid flying when you have a cold. If air travel with a stuffy nose is unavoidable, nasal decongestants or antihistamines should be taken an hour before takeoff and, on long flights, again an hour before landing.

THE MIDDLE EAR

OTITIS MEDIA

DEFINITION

Otitis media is the general term used for a variety of middle ear infections that cause pain and, sometimes, hearing loss.

There are three basic *acute* types:

- Secretory otitis media: the mildest form; there is fluid in the ear, but no infection.
- Serous otitis media, the most severe form; there is fluid and infection.
- Acute purulent otitis media: pus forms and fills the middle ear (see figure 31.3). This infection—middle ear abscess—is common in infants and children, from 3 months to puberty. It produces a severe, persistent earache and may cause temporary hearing

---

EARWAX

Earwax, also known as cerumen, is produced by glands in the outer ear canal and serves as a protective mechanism against foreign matter. The amount of wax produced varies with the individual. In most people it is a small amount, and it gradually moves to the external opening, where it rolls out on its own. In some, however, an excessive amount forms, often hardening, and is the most common cause of hearing loss in people of all ages.

Cotton-tipped sticks should not be used to clean out earwax because they may pack it against the eardrum. Rather, earwax removal should be done by a physician, who may remove it with a curet (a scoop-shaped instrument) or wash it out. Occasionally, a suction device may be used. Softening agents may make the wax more difficult to remove, but sometimes their use is unavoidable.

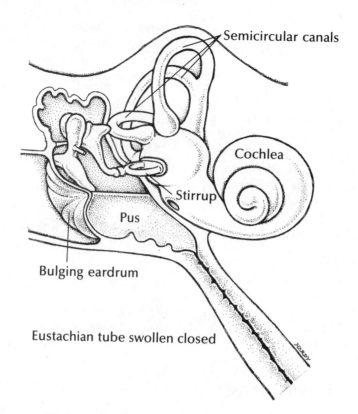

Figure 31.3: Otitis media, inflammation of the middle ear.

loss. If the eardrum ruptures, the discharge may be bloody at first and then become a thick pus. At the time of rupture, the pain abruptly stops.

Secretory otitis media may also be *chronic,* a condition most often found in children. Serous and purulent otitis media also can progress from acute to chronic problems. The infection spreads to the mastoid process, a honeycombed area of bone in the skull behind the ear that has few blood vessels.

CAUSE

Acute secretory otitis media is usually caused by obstruction of the eustachian tube or abnormal production of fluid in the middle ear. Acute serous otitis media can also be caused by an obstruction of the eustachian tube and is often secondary to some other upper respiratory infection or to enlarged adenoids, or both. If serous otitis media is not treated, it may lead to acute purulent otitis media.

Chronic secretory otitis media is frequently due to the presence of large amounts of adenoidal tissue. Sometimes it occurs in adults who have permanent or recurrent blockage of the eustachian tube, or recurrent changes in the consistency of the liquid that is produced in the middle ear, or both.

Although the causes of chronic serous and purulent otitis media are not clear-cut, the adenoids may play a significant role. Sometimes the attacks are not really recurrent, but a single one that is never completely cured; the infection spreads to the mastoid process. Because only a relatively small amount of blood reaches this area, antibiotics that travel through the bloodstream are less effective in fighting an infection there than in the middle ear itself, where the blood supply is rich. Therefore, a recurrent problem is often caused by insufficient antibiotic treatment, which results in a subclinical remnant of infection in the mastoid. When the antibiotics are stopped, the remnant in the mastoid reinfects the middle ear. This process may easily be mistaken for a new infection, rather than a recurrence.

DIAGNOSIS

The physician diagnoses otitis media based on a physical examination of the ears and your description of symptoms.

TREATMENT

Acute secretory otitis media is treated with decongestants and, if necessary, by myringotomy (surgical incision of the eardrum). Acute serous and purulent otitis media require heavy doses of antibiotics plus nasal decongestants and antihistamines. If it appears that the eardrum may rupture, the physician will probably perform a myringotomy rather than permit the eardrum to rupture on its own, because the surgical cut is clean and will almost always heal spontaneously, whereas the rupture may not. Myringotomy also relieves the pain and provides drainage, which in itself is important in the treatment of the disease.

Chronic secretory otitis media is usually treated with antihistamines and nasal decongestants. If these medications are ineffective, and the adenoids are enlarged, the best course in most cases is surgical removal, a simple procedure that usually ends the problem. In lieu of an adenoidectomy, or in cases when this surgical procedure is not effective, the alternative is to place a small plastic tube through the patient's eardrum so that the ear is inflated artificially and the fluid can drain from the middle ear. The major disadvantage of this method is that water must not get into the ear, meaning the patient must not swim and must be extremely careful when bathing, two difficult things to accomplish with young children over what may be a period of years.

HOME REMEDIES AND ALTERNATIVE THERAPIES

Although antibiotics are necessary to cure the infection, home remedies can help ease discomfort. The use of a heating pad on a low setting can reduce pain, as can acetaminophen. Never give aspirin to a child under the age of 18 with a possible viral infection because of its link to Reye's syndrome, a potentially fatal disease; use an acetaminophen such as Tylenol instead.

PREVENTION

Although difficult, acute otitis media may be prevented by avoiding exposure to people who have colds, flu, and other viral illnesses. Chronic otitis media often may be avoided by taking the full course of antibiotics prescribed by your doctor and using decongestants, antihistamines, and other drugs as prescribed to maintain a clear eustachian tube.

ACUTE MASTOIDITIS

DEFINITION

The mastoid process is a honeycombed section of bone located behind the outer ear and connected to the middle ear. If the mastoid process is severely infected and the bony honeycomb destroyed, the result is referred to as acute mastoiditis. Symptoms include ear pain, which tends to be throbbing, ear discharge, increasing hearing loss, and fever.

CAUSE

Acute mastoiditis develops from untreated or inadequately treated bacterial otitis media. When the middle ear becomes infected, the infection spreads to the mucous membrane covering the mastoid process and the walls of the bone itself.

DIAGNOSIS

The physician diagnoses acute mastoiditis based on a physical examination and your description of symptoms. If there are any doubts, a CT scan can reveal characteristic changes in the bone.

TREATMENT

Until the early 1950s, acute mastoiditis was a major cause of death in children, but now that acute purulent otitis media can be treated with antibiotics, acute mastoiditis is relatively uncommon. Should antibiotic treatment prove ineffective and acute mastoiditis develop, a simple mastoidectomy—surgical removal of all or part of the mastoid bone—may be required.

HOME REMEDIES AND ALTERNATIVE THERAPIES

Home remedies can help reduce discomfort but cannot cure the underlying disease. The use of a heating pad on a low setting eases pain, as can acetaminophen.

PREVENTION

Prompt antibiotic therapy for otitis media can prevent acute mastoiditis.

OTOSCLEROSIS

DEFINITION

Otosclerosis is a disease of ear bone degeneration that most commonly develops during the teen or early adult years. The composition of the sound-conducting bones of the ear changes from hard, mineralized bone to spongy, immature bone tissue. This can result in a buildup of inappropriate bone around the stapes footplate, fixing this bone and preventing the vibration that is necessary to conduct the sound to the inner ear.

CAUSE

Although the cause is unknown, the tendency to develop otosclerosis is familial.

DIAGNOSIS

Several tests, including hearing tests, are performed to determine the extent and nature of the hearing loss in order to diagnose otosclerosis.

TREATMENT

This disease is treated by a surgical procedure called a stapedectomy, which replaces the stapes with an artificial prosthesis and usually restores normal hearing. If surgery is not possible, a hearing aid may be used.

MALE/FEMALE DIFFERENCES

Otosclerosis occurs more frequently in women than in men.

CHOLESTEATOMA

DEFINITION

Cholesteatoma, a peculiar disorder that occurs in the mastoid and the middle ear, is a type of epithelial inclusion cyst—a cyst that fills with bits of dead surface skin cells (epithelium) that would normally be sloughed off. As the cyst enlarges, a process that is often rapid in children but may be slower in adults, it destroys the surrounding bone. Cholesteatomas are not malignant and do not metastasize (spread to other sites), but they can have serious consequences, possibly destroying the eardrum, the bones of the middle ear, and the facial nerve, and even invading the skull surrounding the brain. Symptoms include pain and drainage from the ear; hearing loss may also be present.

CAUSE

The origin of the disorder is not totally understood: It may be congenital or it may follow an infection.

DIAGNOSIS

The otolaryngologist diagnoses cholesteatoma by direct observation of the middle ear space, using an otoscope.

TREATMENT

The disorder is an ongoing, chronic condition that can be eradicated only after time-consuming and very meticulous surgery. Treatment often requires repeat procedures, either because small pieces of the cyst have remained or because the cyst has grown back. The surgery often involves rebuilding the bones of the middle ear with various plastic prostheses or with bits of the patient's cartilage. When it is successful (and this is more likely in adults than in children), normal hearing may be restored and the cavity closed off. Some patients have had three or four procedures and finally have been totally cured, with hearing restored. Others are discouraged and refuse further treatment after one or two operations. An alternative surgery is a radical mastoidectomy, which does not cure the problem but leaves an open cavity through which the physician can periodically clean out the debris that collects.

HOME REMEDIES AND ALTERNATIVE THERAPIES

After surgery, be sure to keep the ear dry. If drainage from the ear becomes foul smelling, call an otolaryngologist immediately.

PREVENTION

Since the underlying cause is often unknown, no preventive action other than prompt treatment of ear infections can be recommended.

THE INNER EAR

MÉNIÈRE'S DISEASE

DEFINITION

Ménière's is characterized by fluctuating hearing loss, vertigo, and tinnitus (ringing or buzzing in the ear). The vertigo consists of dramatic and debilitating attacks, during which the patient feels that either she or the room is moving. These attacks may be so severe that the patient cannot stand and often has nausea, retching, and vomiting. Symptoms are absent between flare-ups.

The condition may affect only one ear or, in 20 percent of cases, may grow to include both ears. The baseline hearing between attacks gradually gets lower and lower. The attacks vary considerably from one patient to another and from episode to episode. One person may have weekly attacks lasting 4 hours; another may have attacks lasting 1 hour twice a year; a third may have three attacks a day; and a fourth, one attack in 6 years.

CAUSE

The exact cause of Ménière's disease is not known. It is believed to involve an increase of fluid in the labyrinth that puts pressure on the membrane of the labyrinth wall and affects both balance and hearing. Historically, accountants, dentists, otolaryngologists, and watchmakers—people who do fine, meticulous work that requires great concentration and control of the hands for long periods of time—are more prone than others to develop this condition. In fact, it was originally called watchmaker's disease.

DIAGNOSIS

Diagnosis is based on the patient's description of symptoms and audiometry testing, in which the patient's ability to hear sounds of various frequencies conducted both through the air and through the bones in the head is evaluated.

TREATMENT

The only proven, reliable treatment for Ménière's disease is surgery, which selectively destroys the balance mechanism or the nerve responsible for the sense of balance. Alternatively, a prosthesis may be implanted to help drain the excess fluid that accumulates in the ear as an attack starts. If there is no hearing left and the only problem is dizziness, the physician may choose to destroy the entire inner ear via a safe and easy surgical procedure. Since there is no hearing, there is nothing to lose by this method, because the balance function can still be handled by the other ear, as well as by sight and muscle impulses.

Drug therapy usually can provide only symptomatic relief. Vertigo can be eased by anticholinergic agents, such as atropine or scopolamine, by antihistamines such as diphenhydramine or meclizine, or by barbiturate drugs such as pentobarbital that provide general sedation. The use of diuretics to reduce salt and water retention in the body also helps some patients.

For patients with bilateral Ménière's disease, treatment is more difficult. Sometimes surgical intervention on the most problematic ear will stop the majority of attacks. In the past, the antibiotic streptomycin was sometimes used in exceptionally large doses, which had the effect of destroying the balance mechanism while not affecting the hearing. Some patients are willing to endure having to use their tendon reflexes and their eyes to achieve balance (meaning they have no sense of balance in a completely dark room) in order to stop the attacks of vertigo.

HOME REMEDIES AND ALTERNATIVE THERAPIES

Some patients have found that lifestyle modifications, especially quitting smoking, can help decrease the frequency and severity of Ménièrre's attacks. Restricting fluid intake, by limiting water and other fluids to 6 or fewer glasses a day, may reduce fluid in the labyrinth and decrease attacks. A low-sodium diet and reduction of caffeine intake has helped some people.

MALE/FEMALE DIFFERENCES

The condition seems to be more common in women than in men.

ACOUSTIC NEURINOMA

DEFINITION

A neurinoma is a tumor that arises from the cells of the thin sheath that covers a nerve. In the case of an acoustic neurinoma, the tumor arises on the vestibular rather than the acoustic nerve, and grows very slowly, often taking many years to mature. It may present only mild, transient dizziness and unsteadiness, tinnitus (ringing in the ear), and eventually a gradual loss of hearing in the affected ear. The tumor is not malignant.

CAUSE

The cause of acoustic neurinoma remains unknown.

DIAGNOSIS

Diagnosis is accomplished based on audiometry, brain stem response testing, and magnetic resonance imaging.

TREATMENT

If found while it is still small, an acoustic neurinoma can often be removed surgically with no damage to the facial nerve and the remaining hearing can be preserved. If the growth is too large to remove completely, partial removal may still be possible.

PRESBYCUSIS

DEFINITION

Presbycusis is a type of sensorineural hearing loss that occurs gradually as people age. In some cases, there may be a loss of ability to discriminate sounds. That is, a person may be able to hear sounds, but may not be able to make words out of them. Presbycusis generally begins to affect people between ages 55 and 65, but may not occur until much later.

CAUSE

Tiny inner-ear hair cells (sensory neuroreceptor cells) degenerate, leading to a gradual loss of hearing. These cells send electrical sound impulses to the brain where sounds are received and processed.

DIAGNOSIS

Presbycusis is diagnosed based on the patient's report of the type of hearing loss experienced and several tests, including audiometry.

TREATMENT

Presbycusis cannot be cured. However, hearing aids usually can restore useful hearing.

HOME REMEDIES AND ALTERNATIVE THERAPIES

Learning to lip read can enhance understanding in those with moderate hearing loss.

PREVENTION

The onset and severity of presbycusis may be related to the degree of excessive noise exposure the patient has experienced in life. To protect yourself, wear earplugs in all noisy environments, avoid overamplified concerts, and use proper protective equipment when exposed to occupational noise such as heavy machinery.

MALE/FEMALE DIFFERENCES

Men are affected more often and more severely than women.

LABYRINTHITIS

DEFINITION

Labyrinthitis is an infection of the inner ear. It produces extreme vertigo—a feeling that the person or his surroundings are spinning—and often nausea and vomiting.

CAUSE

Bacterial infection secondary to acute otitis media or to purulent meningitis can cause the condition. So can a viral infection, either arising independently or secondary to an upper respiratory illness such as a cold or flu. When the disease is caused by bacteria, there is a total loss of hearing on the affected side. However, if tuberculosis or syphilis is to blame, the hearing loss may be only partial.

DIAGNOSIS

Clinical examination of the ear and the patient's description of symptoms form the basis for a diagnosis of labyrinthitis.

TREATMENT

Treatment of bacteria-caused labyrinthitis consists of heavy doses of antibiotics. The viral form is usually self-limiting, and there is some difference of opinion among physicians about the existence of a viral form; often, the symptoms are ascribed to another cause. The only treatment for the viral form is bed rest, tranquilizers, and a medication such as Antivert to combat the dizziness.

HOME REMEDIES AND ALTERNATIVE THERAPIES

Keeping lights dim and remaining as still as possible can help ease the dizziness and nausea.

PREVENTION

Get prompt treatment for any middle-ear or respiratory infection. If your nose is congested, don't blow too hard since this can push infectious material into the inner ear.

VESTIBULAR NEURONITIS

DEFINITION

Vestibular neuronitis is characterized by a sudden loss of the balance mechanism in one ear. The person is so violently dizzy that he or she usually cannot walk for several days or weeks, and may be unable to get up and move around at all. If the loss is total, the individual should be seen by a doctor at once.

CAUSE

Vestibular loss may be precipitated by a virus (viral neuronitis) or a tiny blood clot in the arterial system that brings blood to the balance mechanism. These blood vessels are so small that they can be blocked by a microscopic clot of no more than four or five red cells clumped together.

DIAGNOSIS

Diagnosis is based on symptoms, a physical examination, and several tests, including audiometry, electronystagmography, and magnetic resonance imaging of the head.

TREATMENT

Treatment, about which there is considerable difference of opinion, may depend on whether the loss of balance is total or partial and on whether it is treated within the first 24 hours or later. Anticoagulants (to thin the blood and perhaps dissolve the clot) are sometimes used at times in conjunction with vasodilators to expand the blood vessels and allow the clot to pass. These seem to work best when used in the first 24 hours. Corticosteroids may be used when the condition is thought to be caused by a virus. Other drugs may be prescribed to alleviate the discomfort of the vertigo, as in Ménière's disease (see earlier in chapter).

If the loss is only partial, the chance for spontaneous recovery is quite good. If the loss is total, the chance of spontaneous recovery is poor. With time, however, the balance mechanism of the other ear will compensate and the symptoms will disappear. Continuing symptoms indicate that the damage to the vestibular system is still in flux, preventing compensation by the other side.

HOME REMEDIES AND ALTERNATIVE THERAPIES

As with the vertigo of labyrinthitis, remaining very still in a darkened room can help ease dizziness.

HEARING PROBLEMS AND HEARING LOSS

Hearing loss may be partial or total. A good test of whether a hearing loss affecting only one ear is total or partial is to hold a telephone receiver to that ear. If a dial tone can be heard, the loss is only partial.

Hearing loss may develop gradually or suddenly. Sudden hearing loss—the usually instantaneous loss of hearing in one ear or, rarely, both—is like vestibular loss in that it may be precipitated by a virus or by a tiny blood clot and is treated similarly to vestibular neuronitis (see above). Total sudden hearing loss is an acute emergency, and the individual should be examined by a doctor at once.

There are two basic types of hearing loss—conductive loss and sensorineural (or perceptive) loss—that are easily differentiated by hearing tests.

CONDUCTIVE HEARING LOSS

Conductive hearing loss refers to hearing problems created by an interference with the mechanism of conduction that carries the sound waves from the air to the fluid medium. The cause can be as simple as earwax, fluid in the ear, a torn eardrum, or an exostosis (see "Benign Cysts and Tumors" in this chapter) in the ear canal, or it may be due to otosclerosis (see above). In most, if not all, cases, once the cause is found and removed or treated, hearing returns.

SENSORINEURAL (PERCEPTIVE) HEARING LOSS

Sensorineural hearing loss derives from problems in the inner ear, in the nerve from the inner ear to the brain, or in the brain. Unlike conductive losses, these cannot be corrected surgically. Aging is the most common cause of this hearing loss, in the form of presbycusis (see above), but the degree of loss varies greatly from person to person. Acoustic trauma can cause similar damage. The trauma may come from a blow to the ear or from excessive noise due to living near an airport, working with or near heavy machinery, listening to excessively loud music, and so on. "Rock and roll deafness" is an increasing problem, causing hearing loss in some young people who attend concerts where sound is overamplified or who listen to music with earphones at high volume. Teenagers should be taught that if the sound at concerts hurts their ears it is loud enough to do permanent damage, and they should leave immediately.

HEARING AIDS

Hearing aids are helpful in certain types of perceptive hearing losses, but not in others. They must be fitted by an audiologist, a professional trained in conducting tests that measure hearing and indicate the cause of a hearing loss, and in fitting hearing aids. The ability to obtain comfortable hearing often depends on the individual patient and his pattern of perceptive hearing loss, as well as the skill of the audiologist.

If the perceptive hearing loss is rather flat, that is if it is at the same level throughout all frequencies, a hearing

TINNITUS

Tinnitus, or the sensation of sound in the ear when there is no sound, is an annoying, extremely common symptom. It may take the form of ringing, buzzing, whistling, or hissing. It may be intermittent or continuous. It is usually, although not necessarily, associated with hearing loss.

Tinnitus may be caused by a wide variety of factors, ranging from earwax to disease in the cortex of the brain, although the cause is not always clear. Tinnitus may be a symptom of an ear disorder, but it may also be a symptom of anything from cardiovascular disease to hyperthyroidism. If it is due to something as simple as earwax, removing the wax will relieve it. Treating the underlying disease may or may not stop the tinnitus.

Some patients tolerate the condition better than others. Some may find that the tinnitus is easier to tolerate if they play music to mask the sound. In fact, there is a device called a tinnitus masker, worn like a hearing aid, which produces a neutral sound that acts in the same way as music.

aid may function well, allowing the patient to have good hearing and discrimination with it. This is often the case in Ménière's disease.

In presbycusis, the hearing loss is often in the high frequencies. Special hearing aids are made that magnify the high frequencies only, but the magnification sometimes leads to excessive sensitivity to noise or sound (known as hyperacusia), a sensitivity that makes the hearing aid almost useless. Hearing aids may also be difficult to fit people suffering recruitment, a phenomenon wherein soft sounds cannot be heard but higher volume sounds are perceived normally.

THE NOSE AND THE PARANASAL SINUSES

THE NOSE

Air begins its journey to the respiratory system through the nose, which filters, warms, and moistens our inhalations before they pass through the pharynx, larynx, and trachea into the bronchi and the lungs. For this purpose, the external nose contains a septum (the wall dividing the two nostrils) composed of cartilage and bone covered by a layer of mucous membrane, and six or eight turbinates (see figure 31.4).

The turbinates are thin curlicues of bone, also covered by thick mucous membranes, that curve from the outer part of the nose in toward the septum. Under the mucous membrane is erectile tissue that is sensitive to temperature and causes tissues of the area to swell with the influx of blood when there is an abundance of cold, dry, or contaminated air. This narrows the passages and thus slows the incoming air, allowing the turbinates to warm and humidify it. When the turbinates become erect they give rise to large amounts of mucus, which is why noses tend to run on cold days.

The sticky mucous lining of the nose and nasal passages acts as a filter, trapping bacteria and airborne dirt particles. The mucus is then moved by the action of hairlike cilia either to the front of the nose where it can be blown out, or to the back of the nose where it enters the throat and is swallowed.

The nose also contains the organ of smell, which in turn affects taste. Odors are detected by the very fine and sensitive hairlike ends of the olfactory nerve, which begins with the olfactory bulb in the brain and ends in the nose. The nerve endings pick up scents and transmit this information to the brain, which matches it against stored information from past experience, and thus perceives and identifies smells. Since 95 percent of the ability to taste

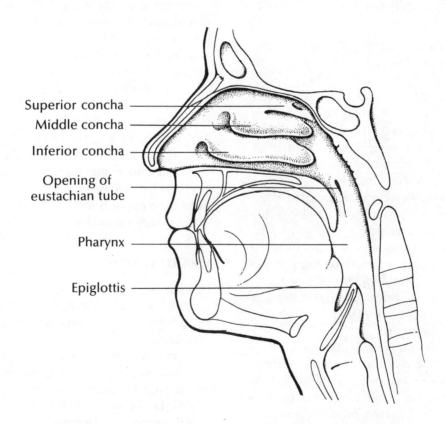

Superior concha
Middle concha
Inferior concha
Opening of eustachian tube
Pharynx
Epiglottis

Figure 31.4: Structure of the nose and nasal passages.

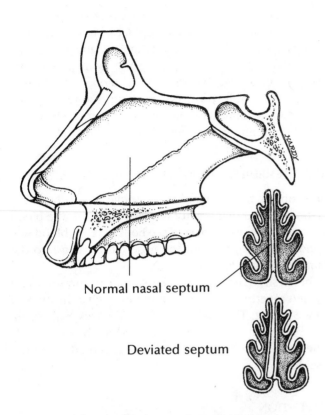

Normal nasal septum

Deviated septum

Figure 31.5: Deviated septum.

relies on the ability to smell, a loss of sense of smell will greatly diminish taste and thus enjoyment of food.

DEVIATED SEPTUM

DEFINITION

A deviated septum is an internal nose deformity in which the bone that separates the two nostrils is not straight. This condition does not always lead to health problems (see figure 31.5).

CAUSE

About 5 percent of infants are born with a subluxation, in which the lower half of the septum deviates to one side. In other cases, the septum may be damaged by injury, with or without any external sign of deformity.

DIAGNOSIS

A physician can detect a deviated septum by physical examination. More important to the decision to treat is whether health problems are present. A deviated septum can cause breathing problems leading to mouth breathing or unusual snoring. In others, it may cause nasal congestion and infection due to reduced airflow through one nostril, which provides a haven for bacte-

ria, pollen, and other substances. Such problems may be more severe in people who have asthma, hay fever, and other allergies.

TREATMENT

No one has a nasal septum that is exactly in the midline, and every septum is deviated to some degree. But if the deviation is severe and there is a history of recurrent illness associated with it, surgical corrective treatment may be appropriate. Septoplasty for a deviated septum may be performed by an otolaryngologist. Sometimes the procedure is performed at the same time as rhinoplasty, a procedure to reshape the external nose. These procedures may be done with either local or general anesthesia, either in the surgeon's office or a hospital-based ambulatory surgery unit.

PREVENTION

Trauma to the nose may be prevented by safe driving and sports habits, including the use of seat belts and protective headgear and masks when appropriate.

RHINOPHYMA

DEFINITION

Rhinophyma is a condition in which the epithelium—the upper layer of skin on the external surface of the nose—thickens greatly and the nose assumes a large, bulbous appearance.

CAUSE

Although the condition has often been associated with alcohol abuse and does indeed occur in some people who are heavy drinkers, it affects nondrinkers as well. It

RHINOPLASTY

Rhinoplasty is a surgical procedure used to change the structure of the external nose, either to repair it after a fracture or simply to improve its appearance. The bones may be fractured and brought closer to the midline to give the upper part of the nose a thinner appearance. Then the cartilage below is trimmed so that it will be suited to the appearance of the newly shaped upper part. Sometimes, only the cartilage is reshaped. Depending on the hospital and often the geographical area, the operation may be performed by an otolaryngologist, a plastic surgeon, or a general surgeon.

is sometimes preceded by rosacea, a chronic inflammatory skin disorder.

DIAGNOSIS

The diagnosis is made by clinical examination of the skin.

TREATMENT

Treatment entails surgery in which the excess epithelium is sliced off from the outside and the nose usually resumes its natural shape.

PREVENTION

Avoidance of excessive alcohol and proper treatment of rosacea can prevent some cases of rhinophyma.

EPISTAXIS (NOSEBLEED)

DEFINITION

A nosebleed occurs when blood drips, dribbles, or runs from the nostrils. It is usually bright red blood and may or may not be mixed with mucus or other secretions.

CAUSE

Simple nosebleeds not obviously caused by a blow to the nose are often caused by picking it. Or they may result from continually breathing very dry air, which causes the nasal mucous membranes to dry out, crack, and bleed. Sometimes, they are caused by hypertension, when the blood pressure is high enough to rupture the wall of the thin vessels in the mucous membranes. Nosebleeds are also commonly found in people who drink excessive amounts of alcohol, perhaps because alcohol has a tendency to dilate the blood vessels. Since the mucous membranes of the nose contain blood vessels that are relatively large and exposed to the external environment, spontaneous bleeding can easily take place if the membranes are disturbed or altered in any way.

TREATMENT

The overwhelming majority of nosebleeds are not serious and are easy for individuals to take care of themselves as described below. On rare occasions, a nosebleed is more serious and may not respond to simple pressure. It may be posterior, well behind the fleshy area, causing a lot of the blood to run down the back of the throat and be swallowed or spit out, even when the patient is sitting up. This is often a sign that the nosebleed will not stop on its own.

If the nosebleed does not stop easily or recurs frequently, the patient should see a doctor, who will sometimes pack the nose with petroleum jelly and gauze for a day or two, if the bleeding is in the front part of the nose. Posterior nosebleeds require more complicated and uncomfortable postnasal packing. Cauterizing the site of the bleeding with electrocautery or silver nitrate is another common treatment.

HOME REMEDIES AND ALTERNATIVE THERAPIES

The simplest way to handle a nosebleed is to have the person sit up so that gravity will slightly lower the blood pressure in the upper part of the body and the blood will be more likely to run out the nose rather than into the mouth to be swallowed.

The fleshy part of the nose should be grasped and pinched together for about 5 minutes to give the blood a chance to clot. The use of ice and cold packs is questionable. Although cold does constrict the blood vessels somewhat, it probably will not have much effect on the nosebleed.

PREVENTION

Try to avoid sports and driving accidents. Do not drink alcohol excessively or pick your nose. If you live or work in a dry environment, use a humidifier. If you have hypertension, seek proper treatment.

CHRONIC RHINITIS

DEFINITION

Rhinitis is an inflammation of the membrane lining the nose and may result from a number of causes. Ordinary chronic rhinitis, of unknown origin, consists of inflamed nasal mucous membranes, red and enlarged turbinates, excess production of mucus, and sometimes pus and a postnasal drip, all of which make the patient miserable. In vasomotor rhinitis, there is some swelling of the mucous membranes, but they do not become red or inflamed. The turbinates, however, are in a continual state of erection, resulting in a stuffy nose, a postnasal drip, and susceptibility to sinusitis. Chronic allergic rhinitis results when the nose sets up a defense system to an inhaled substance to which the body is allergic. It produces a mucous discharge that is very thin and watery, and the turbinates enlarge and become very pale, almost blue-white.

CAUSE

Chronic rhinitis may be occupational, afflicting those who manufacture or work with chemicals, such as house painters and photo developers; or it may be environmental, afflicting, for example, those who swim in a chlorinated indoor pool; or it may be neither. Allergic rhinitis results from an abnormal response of the immune system to substances that cause no problems for most people.

TREATMENT

Treatment consists of trying to eliminate the irritant and of local treatment on the inside of the nose, possibly with local injections of steroids. If one or more allergy-producing substances can be isolated—if, for example, the patient's problem begins and ends at a specific time of the year, suggesting a pollen allergy—the patient can be desensitized. If the condition lasts throughout the year, the patient is probably allergic to a number of things, and attempts at desensitization may be long, arduous, expensive, and often futile. Some people find relief by injecting small amounts of long-acting steroids directly into the turbinates. Antihistamines and nasal decongestant tablets are also used, and if they don't work steroids may be prescribed.

When the allergic rhinitis is seasonal, the patient is probably best treated by an allergist; when it is perennial, however, he or she is probably best treated by the otolaryngologist. (For more information, see chapter 29, Allergies.)

HOME REMEDIES AND ALTERNATIVE THERAPIES

Using a vaporizer to increase humidity may help ease discomfort.

PREVENTION

Chronic rhinitis can often be prevented by identifying and avoiding the offending irritants or allergens.

ATROPHIC RHINITIS (OZENA)

DEFINITION

Atrophic rhinitis is an inflammation of the membrane lining the nose that produces thick crusts of dried material and may be accompanied by loss of the sense of smell and recurrent and severe nosebleeds. Eventually the crusts may become so bad that they begin to decompose and stick, producing a noxious odor. The disease seems to occur more frequently in people of southeastern European origin. Although not particularly hazardous to health, it may become extremely uncomfortable.

CAUSE

Atrophic rhinitis may be caused by a lack of activity of the mucous glands in the nasal mucous membrane or a thinning of the membrane, or it may be due to excessive size of the nasal chambers.

DIAGNOSIS

The condition is diagnosed by direct observation of the nasal passages by the otolaryngologist.

TREATMENT

The condition may be treated with saline irrigation in which the doctor flushes a saline solution through the nasal cavities. Another approach is to inject or topically apply steroids to the afflicted area. Not all cases respond to treatment.

HOME REMEDIES AND ALTERNATIVE THERAPIES

Avoid the use of over-the-counter decongestant nasal sprays such as Afrin. A vaporizer may ease some discomfort.

PARANASAL SINUSES

The sinuses—air-filled cavities in the bones surrounding the nose—are divided into four pairs: frontal, ethmoid, sphenoid, and maxillary. Like other parts of the nasal passages, they are lined with sticky mucus.

SINUSITIS

DEFINITION

Any infection or allergic reaction that causes an inflammation of the lining of the sinuses is called sinusitis. The inflammation may partially or totally obstruct the flow of air and mucus into the nose, and may be accompanied by pus (see figure 31.6). In *acute* sinusitis, a bacterial infection may be accompanied by large amounts of pus, which may not be able to drain into the nose by itself. True *chronic* sinusitis is a relatively uncommon disease; more likely, when something is wrong, it is chronic rhinitis (see above).

CAUSE

Acute sinusitis is caused by a bacterial, viral, or fungal infection or an allergic reaction, although a severely deviated nasal septum may predispose the patient to recurrent attacks of acute sinusitis. Chronic sinusitis is usually secondary to an anatomical deformity that is

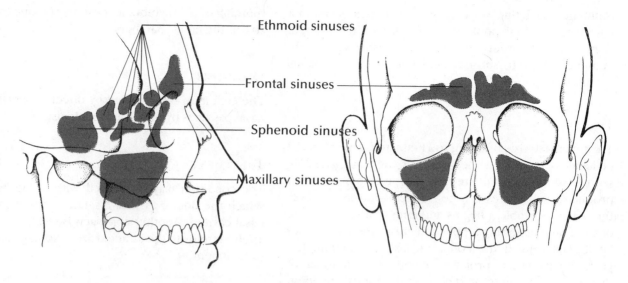

Figure 31.6: Sinuses of the nasal passages.

either congenital or was produced during the course of multiple attacks of acute sinusitis. Often after many attacks of acute sinusitis the openings of the sinus into the nose become narrowed or closed completely, leaving no possibility of drainage from the sinus. A deviated septum is often the cause of chronic frontal sinusitis, since drainage of the frontal sinuses depends almost entirely on gravity moving the contents of the sinuses down through a small opening that may be totally or partially blocked by the deviation.

TREATMENT

Acute sinusitis requires treatment with antibiotics to cure the bacterial infection and nasal decongestants. If the affected sinuses are blocked the doctor may be able to facilitate drainage through irrigation: injecting fluid with a large needle through an area of the sinus that is easily accessible and then allowing the fluid to drain out through the nose. If an anatomical malformation is the cause of recurrent acute or chronic sinusitis, it must be corrected. For example, if the openings of the sinus into the nose have become narrowed or closed, surgery is necessary either to reopen the natural openings of the sinuses or to create an artificial opening through which the sinuses may drain.

HOME REMEDIES AND ALTERNATIVE THERAPIES

Although antibiotics are necessary to cure bacterial infections, home care can also help clear sinusitis inflammation. Keep air in the bedroom moist with a humidifier. To promote drainage, use steam inhalation, with a vaporizer or in a hot shower, as well as hot beverages such as chicken soup and tea.

PREVENTION

Chronic sinusitis usually can be prevented by vigorous treatment of acute sinusitis.

NASAL POLYPS

DEFINITION

Nasal polyps are not true polyps in the sense that they do not result from growth of a new or abnormal type of tissue. They are really swollen sinus-lining tissue that protrudes into the nasal cavity (see figure 31.7). Nasal polyps may appear singly or in clusters and look something like pearly grapes. Although they are benign and most never cause any problems, they may grow to obstruct nasal passages, making breathing difficult and affecting the sense of smell.

CAUSE

Nasal polyps tend to grow when there is an overproduction of fluid in cells in the mucous membranes. Therefore, they may arise in people who have allergies, vasomotor rhinitis, or frequent respiratory infections.

DIAGNOSIS

The physician can visually see the polyps using a lighted device to examine the nasal passages.

TREATMENT

Polyps that arise after a respiratory infection may shrink and disappear by themselves. In other cases, a doctor may prescribe a corticosteroid spray that may shrink and

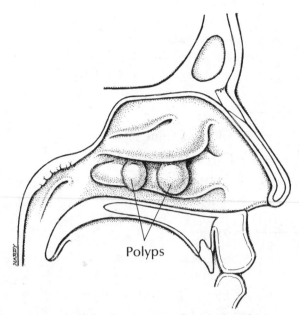

Figure 31.7: Development of nasal polyps.

banish the polyps. However, polyps that are caused by a chronic condition usually require surgical removal if they interfere with breathing or seem to contribute to chronic sinusitis.

PREVENTION

If you have frequent allergies or respiratory infections, discuss with your doctor the use of antihistamines or decongestants to help keep nasal passages dry.

THE THROAT

THE PHARYNX

The throat, or pharynx, is ringed by muscle and cartilage and contains two important passageways—for air into the lungs and food into the digestive system—as well as the mechanism for producing sounds. Air travels from the nose and the mouth down through the trachea, or windpipe, into the bronchi and the lungs, while food and water travel from the mouth into the esophagus and then to the stomach.

Located in the pharynx between the mouth and the trachea are the tonsils, adenoids, and the larynx (or voice box), which contains the vocal cords. The epiglottis, a lidlike structure at the top of the larynx, closes during swallowing to deflect food and water

away from the windpipe and into the esophagus (see figure 31.8).

The tonsils, located in the folds of the throat between the tongue and the palate, are usually rather large in infants. Unlike adenoids, which normally shrink throughout childhood and virtually disappear by puberty, tonsils shrink to about the size of almonds in adults, but do not disappear. Tonsils and adenoids begin as protective mechanisms, acting as sieves or filters to keep disease from entering the body, but they lose this function about the time the child is 3 years old. Occasionally, a child's tonsils and adenoids will become so enlarged that he or she is not able to eat or even breathe properly, or they will block the opening to the eustachian tube and result in secondary middle-ear disease, either an accumulation of fluid in the ear or acute otitis media.

PHARYNGITIS

DEFINITION

Pharyngitis, which may be acute or chronic, is simply a sore throat, which may be accompanied by fever, and if the throat is particularly inflamed may cause difficulty in swallowing. It may be a symptom of an infection elsewhere or a chronic problem.

CAUSE

The acute forms of pharyngitis may be due to *Streptococcus, Staphylococcus,* or other bacteria, or to a virus such as those that cause colds and flu. Local irritation, from smoking or excessive consumption of liquor, can also cause pharyngitis, as can air pollutants.

DIAGNOSIS

A sore throat can easily be identified by observing the red swollen tissue. To determine the cause, the physician uses a swab to collect a sample of throat cells and secretions for laboratory examination.

TREATMENT

With either bacterial or irritant pharyngitis, resting the voice and taking aspirin may help relieve the pain. Bacterial pharyngitis, especially strep throat, requires prompt treatment with antibiotics. Viral and irritant pharyngitis are usually self-limiting. If not treated, the infection may lead to more serious conditions. (See chapter 18, Infectious Diseases.)

HOME REMEDIES AND ALTERNATIVE THERAPIES

Sore throat pain may be eased by gargling with warm salt water and sucking anesthetic throat lozenges. Some peo-

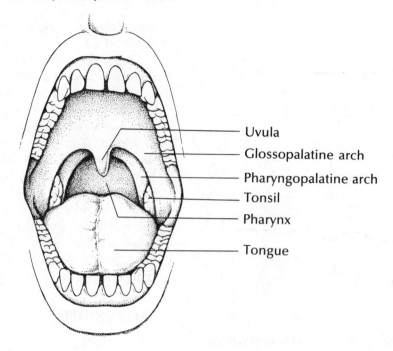

Figure 31.8: Structure of the mouth and throat.

ple get relief from sipping hot beverages such as tea and broth, while others prefer contact with cold, such as eating ice cream or sucking ice chips. Avoid acidic or spicy foods and beverages that can increase irritation.

PREVENTION

If you smoke, quit; smoking makes you more susceptible to respiratory infections. To avoid catching infections from others, never share eating utensils or beverage containers. Be sure to wash your hands frequently, especially after contact with others.

TONSILLITIS

DEFINITION

Tonsillitis is an acute inflammation or infection of the tonsils, causing a sore throat. If infection also is present, a fever, headache, and vomiting may occur.

CAUSE

Sometimes, the tonsils are overwhelmed by the disease microorganisms they are trying to filter out and they become greatly enlarged and inflamed. More commonly, tonsillitis is caused by bacterial or viral infection.

DIAGNOSIS

Tonsillitis can easily be diagnosed by observing the enlarged, red, and inflamed tissue. To determine the cause of the tonsillitis, the physician uses a swab to collect a sample of cells from the tonsils for laboratory examination.

TREATMENT

Before the advent of penicillin and other antibiotics, infected tonsils were removed almost routinely. Tonsillectomies are now performed only when infected tonsils are an obvious source of difficulty for the child or adult. As a rule of thumb, if there are three or more attacks of tonsillitis with high fevers within a year, removal is warranted. Once removed, tonsils do not grow back.

HOME REMEDIES AND ALTERNATIVE THERAPIES

While antibiotics are necessary to treat infected tonsils, home care similar to that for sore throats can help ease discomfort. A soft diet of soup, pudding, and ice cream may be necessary until inflammation subsides.

PREVENTION

No preventive techniques other than tonsillectomy are available.

PERITONSILLAR ABSCESS (QUINSY)

DEFINITION

Peritonsillar abscess is the formation of a collection of pus between the infected tonsil and the tissue of the soft palate. The infection may spread, before it abscesses, into a fairly large area of the soft palate, and when the abscess finally forms, it may include a good portion of that side of the soft palate. The abscess may displace the tonsil, and cause pain, fever, and difficulty in swallowing. Spread of the infection to spaces in the neck and down into the chest can lead to a number of complications, including infection of the tissue between the lungs or the lining covering the heart. It may even be fatal if the resultant inflammation is severe enough to push the tongue upward and cause strangulation. Peritonsillar abscess is much more likely to be seen in young adults than in children.

CAUSE

Peritonsillar abscess is a complication of tonsillitis.

DIAGNOSIS

Like tonsillitis, peritonsillar abscess can easily be diagnosed by observing the enlarged, red, and inflamed tissue and the collection of pus.

TREATMENT

The abscess must be drained surgically and the infection treated promptly with antibiotics. Since the condition tends to recur, it is usually advisable to remove the tonsils after the acute infection subsides.

HOME REMEDIES AND ALTERNATIVE THERAPIES

Home care similar to that for tonsillitis can help ease discomfort and supplement medical and surgical care.

PREVENTION

Prompt and proper treatment of tonsillitis can help prevent peritonsillar abscess.

JUVENILE ANGIOFIBROMA

DEFINITION

Juvenile angiofibroma is a benign tumor of the nasopharynx region that occurs primarily at puberty. Nosebleeds are the major symptom, although it may grow to obstruct the nasal cavity and inhibit nasal breathing. While the tumor has a natural tendency to diminish after puberty, it can grow rapidly and invasively and if untreated may infiltrate the bones at the base of the skull.

CAUSE

The cause of juvenile angiofibroma remains unknown.

DIAGNOSIS

The physician can usually see the growth in the nasal cavity, but special x-rays such as a CT scan or MRI are necessary to determine the extent of the tumor.

TREATMENT

Treatment may be by embolization, surgical excision, or both. With embolization, the doctor (using x-ray visualization) injects small pellets of plastic or gluelike material through a catheter into some of the blood vessels in order to block them off. Without the blood supply, the tumor has a tendency to shrink. If allowed to grow unchecked, the tumor may become so extensive that it is almost impossible to remove, and the result can be fatal. Even if treatment is instituted early, it is complicated by serious bleeding from the large number of blood vessels within the tumor.

MALE/FEMALE DIFFERENCES

Juvenile angiofibroma is seen almost exclusively in boys, and on rare occasion in girls.

THE LARYNX

The larynx, or voice box, contains two flaps of tissue called the vocal cords. The larynx is controlled by muscles that open and close it, allowing the passage of air and the tensing of the vocal cords. As air passes over the tensed cords, they vibrate, producing sounds that are then shaped by the mouth and tongue into words.

LARYNGITIS

DEFINITION

Laryngitis is an inflammation of the larynx. The primary symptoms are hoarseness, pain when swallowing or speaking, and loss of voice.

CAUSE

Acute laryngitis is caused by an infection, usually a virus but occasionally a bacterium. Chronic laryngitis is usually caused by irritation. One of the most common causes is excess intake of alcohol, which is relatively toxic to the larynx. People who drink a great deal may develop a condition called pachydermia, in which the folds of the vocal cords take on the appearance of elephant skin. They become extremely hoarse, developing a voice which is often hardly understandable. Other irritants can also cause chronic laryngitis. People who work in paint factories, with paint remover, or at any job involving heavy exposure to organic chemicals are prone to this condition. On rare occasions, chronic laryngitis precedes cancer of the larynx.

DIAGNOSIS

The physician can diagnose laryngitis by hearing your symptoms and using a lighted device to examine the throat.

TREATMENT

Acute viral laryngitis is generally self-limiting, but those cases caused by a bacterial infection must be treated by antibiotics and can be more damaging to the larynx. In chronic laryngitis, the underlying cause must be treated.

HOME REMEDIES AND ALTERNATIVE THERAPIES

Whatever the cause of laryngitis, complete voice rest and warm fluids are essential supplemental treatments to ease discomfort and facilitate healing of the irritation.

PREVENTION

Avoid excessive use of alcoholic beverages and other irritants that can precipitate laryngitis. If you smoke, quit.

POLYPS AND NODULES

DEFINITION

Vocal cord polyps result from swelling of the loose connective tissue directly below the mucous membrane of the vocal cords (see figure 31.9). The bulge that is produced becomes larger and initially appears like a half-moon on the edge of the cord. With continued use of the voice without treatment, the polyps will develop

into globular structures connected to the vocal cord by thin stalks. Nodules, which are somewhat different from polyps, are composed of epithelium, the covering surface of skin or mucous membrane; they could be compared to a corn on the toe.

CAUSE

People who abuse their voices through excessive improper use (such as screaming, shouting, or speaking in an unnaturally low frequency) sometimes develop polyps on their vocal cords. Nodules are seen in singers, speakers, and people who often abuse their voices.

DIAGNOSIS

The physician can diagnose polyps and nodules by using a lighted device to examine the vocal cords.

TREATMENT

Speech therapy by a speech pathologist often can successfully treat vocal cord nodules. If not, nodules as well as polyps can be easily removed by laryngoscopy, in which a metal tube with a light on the end is passed through the mouth and into the throat, and a small, sharp, cup-shaped punch is threaded through the tube and used to clip off the polyp. Although nodules also can easily be removed, they will return if the patient continues to use his or her voice improperly. Voice therapy is

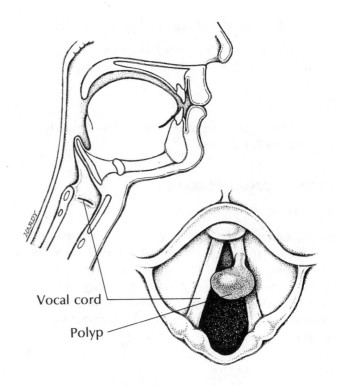

Vocal cord

Polyp

Figure 31.9: Vocal polyps.

usually recommended and may begin before the surgery and continue afterward.

PREVENTION

Do not abuse your voice by excessive use at unnatural frequencies. If you are a singer or must do a lot of public speaking, get voice therapy to learn to use your voice most effectively.

CONTACT ULCERS

DEFINITION

Contact ulcers are sores that appear on the vocal cords where the two cartilages that act as an anchor for the muscle portion of the vocal cords touch each other.

CAUSE

Contact ulcers are caused by voice abuse and overuse.

DIAGNOSIS

The physician can diagnose contact ulcers by using a lighted device to examine the vocal cords.

TREATMENT

Contact ulcers are often difficult to eliminate, and will recur even after surgical removal. Voice rest and retraining are usually the best treatment.

HOME REMEDIES AND ALTERNATIVE THERAPIES

Voice rest and humidification using a vaporizer may sometimes alleviate contact ulcers.

PREVENTION

Speech therapy can be helpful for those who must use their voices extensively and may help prevent contact ulcers.

JUVENILE PAPILLOMAS

Juvenile papillomas are warts, thought to be caused by a virus, that grow on the vocal cords of children, often diminishing spontaneously at puberty. Although the papillomas are benign (degenerating to cancer only very rarely), their excessive growth can obstruct breathing and make them potentially fatal if not treated.

CAUSE

Warts are believed to be caused by a virus.

DIAGNOSIS

The physician can diagnose juvenile papillomas by using a lighted device to examine the vocal cords.

TREATMENT

Juvenile papillomas are extremely difficult to remove completely without damaging the larynx, and the rate of recurrence is very high. Recently, laser treatment has proved more satisfactory than traditional surgical methods.

MALE/FEMALE DIFFERENCES

Juvenile papillomas primarily occur in boys.

32
Maintaining Oral Health

••••••••••••••••

STEPHEN M. ROSER, D.M.D., M.D.

Parts of this chapter are adapted from the chapter by Irwin D. Mandel, D.D.S., which appeared in the revised second edition.

Americans are taking better care of their teeth. In the past decade, tooth decay has dropped by one-third in children ages 5 to 17 and the number of children without cavities has risen by 15 percent. At the same time, the number of denture wearers declined from 35 percent to less than one-quarter of the adult population. These encouraging changes are due to a number of factors:

- The fluoridation of municipal water supplies, which began in the 1950s, that now covers more than half of the United States population.
- Increased use of fluoride toothpastes and mouthwashes (especially in school-based programs), as well as applications of fluoride directly onto the teeth, and the use of sealants for permanent teeth in children.
- Improved oral hygiene as a result of educational campaigns in schools and clinics and efforts on the part of private dentists.
- Improved tools and materials for dental restorations
- Increasing numbers of people are availing themselves of regular dental care.
- Improved diet and the increased use of low- or nonfermentable sweeteners in candy, chewing gum, and soft drinks.

Reflecting an awareness of the importance of dental health, dental care insurance as an employment benefit has expanded rapidly and more than 90 million people are now covered by some form of pre-paid dental coverage, mostly through group plans offered by unions or employers. Insurance policies favor prevention; full coverage is usually provided for diagnostic services and preventive care, while other treatment is often only partially covered.

Nevertheless, the nation spends more than $32 billion annually on dental care. (The average yearly family bill is now over $200.) In addition, dental disease is responsible for the loss of some 32 million working days per year. And, these costs do not reflect the effect of dental disease on the quality of life—in pain, discomfort, tooth loss, poor self-image, and the psychological distress associated with wearing dentures.

DENTAL CHECKUPS

Although the number of people who visit their dentists regularly—at least once per year—has risen over the past three decades, only about half the population visits a dentist in any given year. Some people still fear the dentist, others cannot afford dental care, and a large number simply do not understand the need for regular care and the importance of dental health for general well-being. They seek treatment only when pain or discomfort strikes, or when seeking an improvement in appearance.

Dental checkups should begin in early childhood and continue throughout adult life. The frequency of the examination should be determined on an individual basis, increasing with accelerated decay, progressive periodontal disease, and the presence of full dentures. In general, dentists recommend that the mouth be reexamined according to the following schedule.

EVERY 3 MONTHS

- Everyone with a high decay rate (6 or more cavities per year)
- Adults whose oral home care is poor, even if the decay rate is low

EVERY 6 MONTHS

- Anyone with a low to moderate decay rate (1 or 2 cavities per year) and adequate oral hygiene
- Denture wearers or adults over 35 who use tobacco and alcohol

ONCE A YEAR

- Adults experiencing no decay, whose oral home care is excellent, and who do not use tobacco or alcohol
- Denture wearers who are experiencing no problems and do not use tobacco or alcohol

DENTAL X-RAYS

X-rays are used in dentistry, as in other medical fields, to aid in the diagnosis of disease. X-rays can reveal the extent of decay, cavities hidden between the teeth or under the gumline, bone damage from periodontal disease, tumors, fractures in the teeth or jawbone, impacted teeth, and abscesses. They are therefore an essential diagnostic tool in dentistry, but should be used only periodically. In the absence of conditions requiring more frequent x-rays, a full-mouth x-ray series, or panoramic radiographs, need not be made more than once every 5 years. Two to four "bite-wing" x-rays often suffice for diagnosis of decay.

The radiation dosage of dental x-rays is extremely small, but as a precautionary measure, all patients should be protected with a lead apron. This is particularly important during pregnancy and for women of childbearing age in general. In children especially, the

JUDGING A DENTIST

You can use many sources for referral to a qualified dental general practitioner: a family doctor, local pharmacist, local dental society, a hospital, or a university with a dental school. Specialists are especially good sources of recommendation: Orthodontists, periodontists, endodontists, and oral and maxillofacial surgeons are keenly aware of the quality of work of the general dental practitioners in the area.

On the first visit, a dentist should:

1. Take a complete medical and dental history.
2. Take blood pressure and pulse.
3. Examine the mouth and associated structures.
4. Determine and discuss your treatment plan.
5. Emphasize prevention and give appropriate advice on home oral health techniques.
6. Explain treatments and fees clearly and be willing to provide written estimates and itemized bills.
7. Give emergency care when necessary.
8. Discuss alternative treatments and possible complications.

lead apron should include a collar to protect the thyroid gland, which is particularly vulnerable to x-rays.

ALLEVIATING ANXIETY

For many patients, dental visits cause high anxiety. Tape-recorded relaxation instruction, hypnosis, and biofeedback training effectively reduce anxiety during routine dental treatment; listening to music does not appear to have a significant effect. Biofeedback is most effective, and after a short period of training—as little as 8 minutes—patients can learn control of muscle tension and anxiety reduction by observing a display of their muscle activity on a TV-like screen. Some dentists may prescribe medication prior to the visit to reduce anxiety. Sedation may also be administered (by specially trained dentists) in the office.

SPECIAL DENTAL CONCERNS

PREGNANCY

Experts dismiss the adage "a tooth is lost for every child," arguing that tooth decay in new mothers is probably due to neglect of teeth during pregnancy and in the months following delivery. Contrary to popular belief, calcium is not absorbed from the mother's teeth for the benefit of the fetus, and pregnancy as such is not responsible for caries. The nutrients required for the proper formation of the primary teeth in a fetus—calcium, phosphorus, protein, iron, and vitamins A, C, and D—are provided by a well-balanced diet, although sugar intake should be kept to a minimum for the sake of both mother and child.

In the first trimester of pregnancy, electric dental treatment should be avoided if it will require the patient to take medication such as analgesics, which may possibly damage the fetus. Local anesthesia has not been shown to be harmful to the fetus. A history of miscarriage or other problems associated with pregnancy may make it advisable to postpone any dental treatment except for emergency care until after delivery. During the last 2 or 3 months of pregnancy, a woman may find sitting or reclining in the dentist's chair uncomfortable, and may wish to avoid extensive treatment for that reason. Nonetheless, routine oral hygiene, especially of the soft tissues, is important because gingivitis (gum inflammation) can be a problem during pregnancy. Gum inflammation can become severe and result in growths called pregnancy tumors, which may have to be removed surgically.

Sedation and general anesthesia can expose the fetus to the danger of oxygen deficiency and should be given only in emergency situations by trained individuals. Consultation between the dentist and the patient's obstetrician should occur if any medications are used or prescribed. Valium, for example, which is frequently used to help control pain and anxiety during dental procedures, is linked to fetal damage if administered in the first trimester of pregnancy. Dental x-rays should be done only when absolutely necessary.

INFANCY AND EARLY CHILDHOOD

TEETHING

Babies have a tendency to keep a hand or finger constantly in the mouth and may drool excessively right before the emergence of primary teeth. In many children, some degree of gum inflammation and flushed cheeks also accompanies teething and a child may suffer general disturbances: loss of appetite, irritability, disturbed sleep, or a rash around the mouth. The symptoms of teething may be relieved by gently massaging the baby's gums or giving the baby a teething ring or a hard, unsweetened biscuit to chew on. Understanding the problem should allay parental fears that the child's agitation is more serious.

ORAL HYGIENE

Once the teeth have emerged, parents should clean them with a soft toothbrush and a pea-sized dab of toothpaste. Children can begin to learn to brush their own teeth by the age of 2 or 3, but close supervision is necessary until the age of 6 to 8 to ensure an adequate performance and to prevent the child from swallowing excessive amounts of toothpaste, especially if it contains fluoride. Flossing should be part of the child's regular oral hygiene routine from the age of 6 or 7, depending on the manual dexterity of the child.

Healthy primary teeth are necessary for proper chewing, clear speech, and an attractive appearance, and these early teeth reserve room for the permanent teeth, allowing them to grow into their appropriate spaces. To prevent neighboring teeth from drifting into the space left by a prematurely lost primary or secondary molar, space maintainers (fixed metal bands) may be fitted. Maintaining this space may eliminate or minimize the need for later orthodontic treatment.

NURSING BOTTLE MOUTH

DEFINITION

Nursing bottle mouth is severe tooth decay sometimes seen in infants and young children.

CAUSE AND DIAGNOSIS

This condition can be recognized as the decay of the front teeth in infants. In extreme cases, only the roots of the front teeth in the upper jaw remain. This condition is the result of giving children a bottle of sweetened water, juice, milk, or formula at bedtime or naptime. The long-term presence of sugar in the mouth, combined with lack of salivation during sleep and the tendency of liquid to pool around the front teeth, results in rampant dental decay.

TREATMENT AND PREVENTION

Plain water only should be given if a baby requires a bottle for comfort before falling asleep.

THE FIRST DENTAL VISIT

At the age of 2 or 2½ children should have their first dental visit (after all the primary teeth have emerged). Parents should not delay dental care until a child develops a toothache or some other painful problem. Dental treatment following a night of toothache is a frightening experience for a young child and may lead to an association—perhaps a permanent one—between the dentist and pain.

An essential part of preventive dentistry is the gradual education of the young child about the importance of oral health. The first visit to the dentist should represent a natural extension of the education already begun at home. Started early, preventive treatment (examination of the teeth, cleaning, polishing with a fluoride preparation) gives the child confidence in the dentist and a sense of familiarity with the equipment in the dental office. In this way, if caries develops, it can be treated with reduced distress for the child and parents.

THE DISABLED

Almost 15 percent of the American population (some 33 million people) have some sort of chronic physical, mental, or emotional condition that to some extent inhibits self-care. Periodontal disease, untreated tooth decay, and premature loss of teeth are particularly prevalent among this segment of the population. For the disabled, dental health is often neglected because of other pressing health problems or inability to care for themselves sufficiently.

In addition, some disabilities come with inherent dental problems. For example, Down syndrome is associ-

EMERGENCY TREATMENT FOR TRAUMATIZED TEETH

Adults' or children's teeth completely displaced in an accident should be replaced in their sockets as soon as possible. The patient must be seen by a dentist immediately. If the tooth cannot be replaced, it should not be cleaned but should be placed in a glass of water with ½ teaspoon of salt or wrapped in a wet cloth. If neither of these are available, and the patient is cooperative, the tooth should be placed in the person's mouth under the tongue. A dentist should be contacted immediately. If the tooth is replaced in its socket within 30 minutes, there is a good chance of successful reattachment. However, baby teeth or primary teeth should not be replaced. (If there is a question as to whether the tooth is primary or permanent, it should be replaced and a dentist consulted.)

If a tooth has been broken and the pulp exposed, it will be very painful, especially upon contact with hot and cold fluids and air. As soon as possible, the tooth must be treated by a dentist, who will cover the area with medication and will put a temporary restoration or crown on it. If treatment is delayed, or if a large portion of the pulp has been exposed, the pulp will die, resulting in the need for a root canal procedure.

DIRECTORY OF DENTAL SPECIALISTS

About 80 percent of all dentists are general practitioners and the remaining 20 percent are specialists.

Endodontists deal with the diagnosis and treatment of diseases of the tooth pulp and injuries involving the pulp and supporting tissues.

Oral pathologists specialize in the interpretation and diagnosis of the changes caused by disease in the tissues of the oral cavity.

Oral and maxillofacial surgeons treat diseases, injuries, and defects of the jaw, mouth, and face, using surgery and other treatments. They also perform extractions.

Orthodontists are concerned with the guidance and correction of the growing or mature dentofacial structure; they treat conditions that require moving the teeth or correcting malformations or poor relationships of teeth and jaws.

Pediatric dentists specialize in the dental problems of children from birth through adolescence; they also care for patients beyond adolescence who have special mental, emotional, or physical problems.

Periodontists specialize in treating disease of the tissues supporting and surrounding the teeth.

Prosthodontists are concerned with the design and fitting of dentures, bridges, and other replacements for missing teeth.

Any licensed dentist can practice any area of dentistry, but specialized work should be undertaken by a specialist with the education and background to perform an expert job. Board-certified specialists satisfy requirements of training and experience designed to ensure competence. Each dental specialty program requires two to three years of postgraduate training, while oral surgery requires at least four years.

ated with congenitally missing teeth, malocclusion (bad bite), and periodontal disease.

In both children and adults, oral health can be affected by medications and treatment. Radiation therapy, certain antidepressants, and some hypertension medications reduce salivation, which in turn can increase decay. Dilantin, a drug that controls epilepsy, may cause an enlargement of the gingiva, or the soft tissues around the teeth.

Most oral problems of the disabled are caused by the diseases that affect the population generally: caries and periodontal disease. The responsibility for preventive care of the teeth and gums of these people must often be assumed by parents and family members. Caregiving in this area is extremely important, especially as the patient gets older and becomes more susceptible to loss of teeth due to periodontal disease.

DEVELOPMENT OF THE TEETH AND JAWS

By the end of the third month of fetal life, the jaws are well formed and tooth development advanced. The primary (deciduous) teeth begin as groups of cells in the developing jaws, each group corresponding to the tooth. The first evidence of calcification of the teeth (the enamel and dentin) is found in about the fourth month of pregnancy.

Six or seven months after birth, the first teeth start to erupt in the front of the mouth. There is a variation in time and pattern of eruptions, but in general the primary teeth in the lower jaw (the mandible) emerge before those in the upper (the maxilla), and the incisors emerge before the molars. By the age of 3 years, the full set of 20 primary teeth, 10 in the maxilla and 10 in the mandible, is usually in place.

The permanent teeth develop in a similar way, but form somewhat later. The first permanent molars often begin to calcify before birth; most of the permanent canines and incisors begin to calcify in the early months of childhood.

The first permanent molars erupt behind the primary teeth in the back of the mouth at about 6 years of age, and are often mistaken for primary teeth. Other perma-

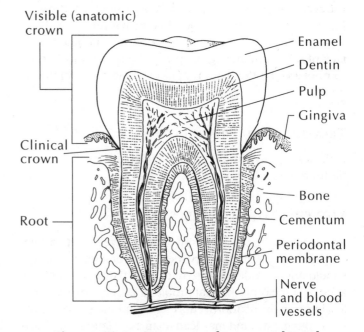

Figure 32.1: Structure of a normal tooth.

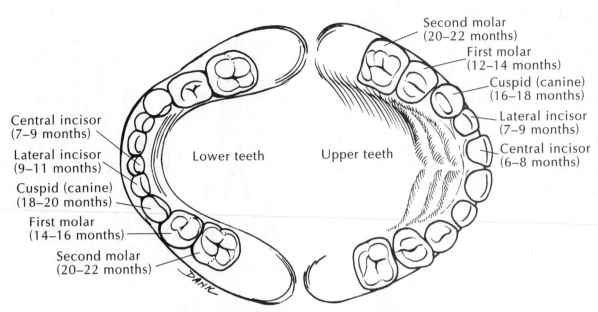

Figure 32.2A: The primary or "baby" teeth.

nent teeth toward the front of the mouth erupt as the primary teeth become loose and fall out, usually painlessly. By the age of 14, all 28 permanent teeth have usually emerged, and only the last four third molars (the wisdom teeth) are still to erupt if enough room in the jaws exists.

TOOTH STRUCTURE AND TYPE

Each tooth, whether primary or permanent, has a crown visible in the mouth above the level of the gum (gingiva) and a root embedded in a socket in the jaw (see figure 32.1). The incisors and canines normally have only one root; the premolars or bicuspids have one

or two, and the molars two or three or, occasionally, four. The roots of the primary teeth are thinner than those of the permanent teeth. Primary and secondary teeth are similar in structure, although the primary teeth have relatively larger pulp chambers and thinner enamel and dentin. Enamel, the hardest tissue in the body, is insensitive and incapable of self-repair. It protectively covers the tooth crown. Dentin—the bulk of the tooth structure—consists of millions of tiny cells arranged in tubules that extend from the pulp to the junction between the enamel and the dentin. It has nerve endings and though as hard as bone is softer than enamel. The pulp chamber, which occupies the space in the center of the crown and runs through the rootar

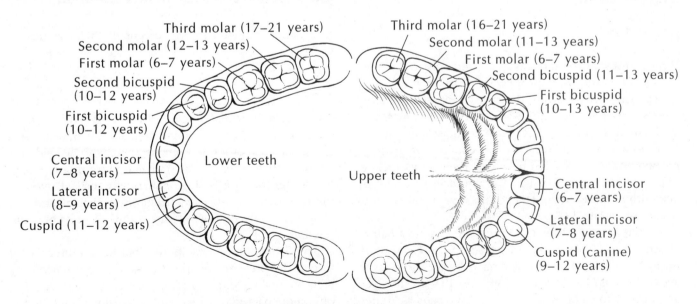

Figure 32.2B: The secondary or permanent teeth.

roots, contains the living tissue of the tooth. This pulp contains nerves and blood vessels that supply the cells extending into the dentin. The nerves and blood vessels enter the tooth at the end, or apex, of the root. The root itself is covered with cementum, a hard, bonelike tissue in which fibers are embedded to attach the tooth to its bony socket (the periodontal ligament).

Although similar in structure, teeth vary in shape according to their different functions. The incisors have sharp, chisel-shaped crowns that cut, or incise, food, whereas the canines, with single-pointed cusps, tear food. The premolars, located behind the canines, crush and tear what is eaten, while the multicusped molars in the back of the mouth grind food before it is swallowed (see figures 32.2A and 32.2B).

SUPPORTING STRUCTURES

Attached close to the area where the enamel and the cementum meet, the gum surrounds the neck of the tooth and forms a firm cuff around the crown. In healthy gums, a shallow crevice (the gingival crevice) between the gum and tooth is barely evident. At the base of the crevice, the gum tissue merges into the periodontal ligament, a thin layer of tissue lying between the cementum and the jawbone (alveolus) and attached firmly to both. The fibers of the periodontal ligament support the tooth in its socket, and bind the gum firmly against the tooth. Both the gums and the periodontal ligament are well supplied with blood vessels and nerves (see figure 32.1).

··

COMMON ORAL PROBLEMS

DENTAL CARIES

DEFINITION

Dental caries, or tooth decay, is second only to the common cold as the most prevalent disease in the United States. This progressively destructive disease primarily affects children and young adults, but continues as a problem throughout adult life. Recent studies in fact point to a marked increase in root caries among adults. As people keep their teeth longer, their gums recede, exposing the root surface. This surface, covered by cementum rather than enamel, is very vulnerable to decay (see figure 32.3).

Despite recent advances in prevention, almost half of all American children experience some degree of tooth decay by the age of 3 years, and many by age 2. The average 12-year-old has four tooth surfaces that are decayed and filled, and eight by the age of 17. As many as 70 percent of the children of low-income families may never go

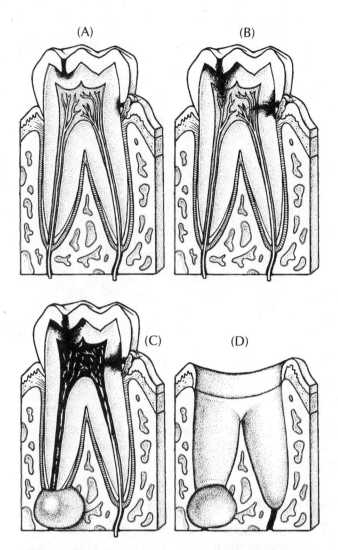

Figure 32.3: Development of dental caries. (A) Decay breaks through enamel and attacks dentin; (B) pulp is invaded; (C) pulp is destroyed and abscess forms; (D) tooth is extracted.

to a dentist, and up to 85 percent of their cavities go unfilled.

CAUSE

Caries is a bacterial disease. Laboratory studies have established that experimental animals can transmit this disease to each other. In humans, there is some evidence showing that caries can be transmitted from one person to another through kissing or sharing utensils. However, because caries is so extraordinarily prevalent and not life-threatening, few people take steps to prevent transmission.

The formation of a cavity results from an interplay of forces: the presence of specific bacteria, a predisposing dietary intake, and a susceptible tooth surface. The offending bacteria, which are normally found in the mouth, come in contact with the teeth in plaque, a gela-

HOW TO BRUSH AND FLOSS YOUR TEETH

Although a number of toothbrushing methods are acceptable, the American Dental Association suggests these steps for home dental hygiene:

1. Place the head of the toothbrush against the teeth, with the bristle tips angled against the gumline at a 45° angle.
2. Moving the brush back and forth with a short (half a tooth wide) stroke in a gentle scrubbing motion; brush the outer surfaces of each tooth, upper and lower, keeping the bristles angled against the gumline.
3. Using the same motion, brush the inside surfaces of the teeth.
4. Scrub chewing surfaces of all teeth, using a light pressure, letting the bristles reach into the grooves of the teeth.
5. To clean the inside of the front teeth, tilt the brush vertically and make several gentle up and down strokes with the "toe" (the front part) of the brush over the teeth and gum tissue of the upper and lower jaws.
6. Brush the tongue to freshen the breath.

Only the tips of the bristles actually clean. It is important to use a light pressure so as not to bend the bristles. The position of the toothbrush should be changed frequently.

HOW TO CHOOSE A TOOTHBRUSH

Choose a brush with soft, end-rounded or polished bristles, which is generally less likely to injure gum tis-

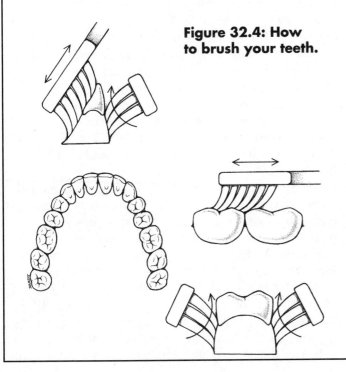

Figure 32.4: How to brush your teeth.

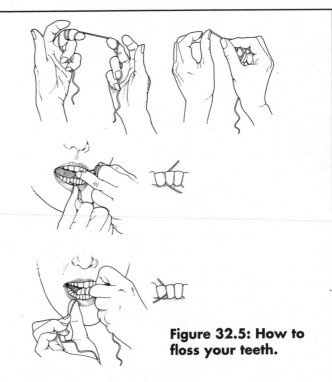

Figure 32.5: How to floss your teeth.

sues than a hard-bristled brush. Replace toothbrushes often—every 3 or 4 months. Brushes are available in children's and adults' sizes. Choose one that fits comfortably in the mouth.

A little practice is necessary to develop skill in flossing, but once learned, it takes but a few minutes.

1. Break off about 18 inches of floss and wind most of it around the middle finger of one hand. Wind the rest around the middle finger of the opposite hand, to take up the floss as it is used.
2. With the thumb of one hand and the forefingers of the other, guide an inch of floss between the teeth. Hold the floss tightly and use a gentle sawing motion.
3. When the floss reaches the gumline, curve it into a C-shape against one tooth and slice it into the space between the tooth and the gum until you feel resistance.
4. Holding the floss tightly against the tooth, move it away from the gum, scraping the side of the tooth.
5. Wind the floss around the middle finger, so that a fresh section is in position, and repeat for all teeth. (It is helpful to think of the mouth as consisting of four sections and to floss one at a time.)

When you begin flossing daily, your gums may bleed and become slightly sore. As the plaque is broken up, however, the gums should heal and the bleeding will stop. If bleeding does not stop after 4 or 5 days, consult your dentist. Improper flossing can injure the gums.

tin-like mat that adheres to specific sites on the teeth, principally in the pits and the fissures on the grinding surface of the molars and the premolars (the occlusal surfaces) and on the area along the gumline. (Plaque also adheres to dental restorations of all kinds.) Plaque sticks to these areas when it is not cleared by the action of the lips or cheeks, tongue movement, the flow of saliva, or brushing and flossing.

The plaque bacteria live primarily off the sugars they encounter in the mouth. In the course of metabolizing these sugars, the bacteria produce acids, which are strong enough to dissolve the enamel and dentin.

A number of different kinds of sugars (sucrose, glucose, fructose, maltose, lactose) can nourish the plaque bacteria and lead to the formation of plaque acids. In addition, starch, which is converted to maltose and glucose by enzymes in the mouth, can cause decay. But the sugars vary in the amount of decay they cause. Sucrose (common table sugar) is indisputably the most conducive to dental decay.

• Each time sugar is ingested, plaque bacteria produce acid. The greatest tooth damage occurs within the first 20 minutes after sugar enters the mouth. Repeated cycles of acid generation will in time (usually within 1 to 2 years) cause the first visible signs of decay: an opaque white or brown spot on the surface of the enamel. At this stage, the outer layer is relatively intact, although the subsurface layer of enamel is partly demineralized. Later, the surface breaks down and becomes roughened and stained.

• As soon as the bacteria break through the enamel, these microorganisms invade and destroy the softer dentin beneath and spread, widely undermining the enamel. (Consequently, a large cavity may appear quite small on the surface.)

• When the undermined enamel chips or fractures, the cavity becomes visible. As the bacteria and their products pass deep into the tooth through the tiny tubules in the dentin, pain is experienced, especially when sweet foods or hot or cold liquids are consumed.

• Continuing deeper into the tooth, the bacteria and their irritant products inflame the pulp tissue, causing more pain. Blood vessels in the pulp dilate, but the pulp cannot swell enough to accommodate the increased fluid (as would be the case with a boil on the skin) because it is completely surrounded by rigid tooth structure.

• The swelling blocks the tiny opening at the end of the root, impairing the blood supply to the pulp. Rampant infection and impaired blood supply combine to kill the pulp unless the infection is treated quickly, in which case the pulp may recuperate.

• The death of the pulp can result in severe pain, although at times pulp death is painless. After pulp death, the pain disappears because of the death of the

nerve tissue, and there will be no more perceived problems unless the "dead" tooth abscesses, which is very likely, perhaps several years later.

• An abscess forms when the bacteria and their products pass out of the end of the root canal into the surrounding bone and soft tissue. The blood vessels in these tissues become inflamed and infected and often cause persistent, throbbing pain that can become excruciating. The tooth becomes extremely sensitive to pressure and touch. Further progression of the infection from the root can result in a cellulitis of the soft tissues of the face or oral cavity. The infection can further spread and become life-threatening (see figure 32.3).

Fortunately, these destructive stages in tooth decay are not set in motion every time we ingest sugar. Protective components of the teeth and saliva can usually prevent the demineralization process. Moreover, this inherent resistance can be augmented by a number of preventive approaches.

DIAGNOSIS

Caries may appear as white or brown spots on the teeth, and x-rays may be used to examine parts of the teeth that cannot be observed superficially. A catch felt by the tongue on a tooth may indicate a cavity. Pain to hot or cold stimuli may also indicate a carious lesion, whereas constant pain and sensitivity to pressure may indicate an infected tooth.

TREATMENT

Depending on the extent of the decay, cavities are treated with restorations (fillings), root canal therapy, or extraction. Fillings are done on living teeth. If the caries involves the pulp and causes inflammation (pulpitis), treatment requires removing the caries and applying medication over the affected pulp. This can facilitate healing, after which the dentist can reseal the pulp. When the decay is so extensive that it has caused the pulp of the tooth to die, the only options are root canal therapy or extraction—regardless of whether the tooth has abscessed or not.

Restorations. Before a tooth is filled, decay must be completely removed and the resulting cavity shaped to retain the filling material. During this procedure, any pain is usually controlled with local anesthesia.

The ideal filling material should match the tooth tissue in resistance, strength, and, when desirable, in color. It should also react as the tooth does to chewing forces and to changes of temperature within the mouth. Therefore, different materials are chosen according to the requirements and functions of the different teeth.

So-called silver, or amalgam, fillings are most common. They are composed of an alloy of mercury and a variety of metals in addition to silver. Recently, the conventional mixture has been markedly improved with the inclusion of additional copper.

Plastic composite materials can be matched very closely in color to the tooth, are easy to use, and do not dissolve in the mouth fluids. Composites are now strong enough for use in the back teeth, which are subject to heavy biting forces.

Root Canal Therapy. Root canal therapy is a multiphase procedure designed to save a badly diseased tooth.

- All traces of pulp tissue are removed from the pulp chamber and the canals.
- The canals are mechanically shaped and cleaned of all bacteria.
- The canals are carefully and completely filled, usually with a form of gutta-percha material. A perfect seal is imperative to avoid reinfection and the need to remove the tooth.

After root canal therapy, the tooth needs to be restored and protected, as the teeth can become more brittle. (See box Crowns and Bonding.)

Extraction. When root canal therapy is not feasible, a permanent dead tooth must be extracted. Abscessed primary teeth may be saved using a procedure called a pulpotomy, in which only the pulp is removed. If a primary tooth is extracted and the permanent tooth does not emerge for 6 months, space maintainers should be considered. The extracted tooth can be replaced with a fixed bridge, a partial denture, or an implant supported prosthesis.

Dental pain accompanied by swelling or fever is an emergency; immediate care must be sought. The family dentist, an oral and maxillofacial surgeon, dental emergency service, or hospital emergency room all should have 24-hour coverage.

PREVENTION

Current knowledge of caries suggests a three-part strategy for prevention:

Combating Bacteria. Plaque with a high concentration of acid-producing bacteria (especially *Streptococcus mutans*) is necessary for caries to develop. Techniques to interfere with plaque deposit include removing the plaque through good oral hygiene practices (see box How to Brush and Floss Your Teeth, and figures 32.4 and 32.5). Still in the experimental stage are the use of antibacterial agents directed toward the microorganisms in the plaque, and a vaccine to prevent the bacteria from adhering to the teeth.

Regular toothbrushing effectively removes plaque in

SNACK FOODS THAT ARE NOT CARIOGENIC

FOOD GROUP	SNACKS
Bread and cereal	Popcorn (unsalted)
Fruits and vegetables	All raw fruits and vegetables, unsweetened juices
Dairy	Cheddar cheese
Meats and proteins	All meats
	Hard-boiled eggs
	Bean dips
	Nuts (unsalted)
Other	Sugarless gum
	Sugarless candy
	Sugarless soft drinks
	Coffee or tea without sugar

Taken with sweetened foods, milk can help wash sugar from the mouth.

Because some fruits—oranges, pineapples, peaches—are very high in natural sugar, frequent fruit snacks can be damaging to the teeth (although less harmful than candy bars). Dried fruits such as raisins are sweet and stick to teeth, and should be avoided as between-meal snacks.

---

those areas the brush reaches. The use of dental floss can remove plaque from between teeth. Five to 10 minutes of thorough brushing and flossing daily, supplemented by regular cleaning by a dentist or oral hygienist, can be very effective on all but the occlusal surfaces (the biting surfaces of the molars and premolars).

Plastic sealants placed on the occlusal surfaces after the teeth appear in the mouth (6 to 12 years) are effective in preventing plaque formation and enamel breakdown in this vulnerable area. Application of the sealant to the molars is quick and simple and usually takes less than an hour.

In a recent study, 95 percent of the teeth treated retained their sealants for years. In a 10-year study, sealant was completely or partially retained in 78 percent of the teeth treated. Research indicates that the use of sealants reduces decay by about 50 percent.

Modifying the Diet. The form and frequency of sugar ingestion is more influential on caries formation than the amount of sugar consumed. A "sweet tooth" gratified by between-meal snacks of foods high in sucrose is extremely conducive to tooth decay. Reducing overall sugar intake—of sucrose in particular—and limiting sugar to mealtimes will reduce tooth decay in most people. (See box Snack Foods That Are Not Cariogenic.)

Some foods seem to protect against caries: Cocoa and

CROWNS AND BONDING

Several conditions necessitate covering the entire tooth surface above the gumline with a replacement crown (also known as a cap):

- To cover severe damage from decay.
- To protect a tooth that has been heavily filled.
- To protect thin sections of the teeth that have had root canal treatment.
- To cosmetically improve front teeth that are unsightly due to decay or injury.

Crowns

A tooth is prepared for a crown by removal of all its enamel, together with enough of the underlying dentin to provide for a sufficiently substantial crown. Impressions (molds) are taken of the tooth, as well as of the neighboring and opposing teeth, to ensure a precise and functional fit. Gold or an alloy has been traditionally used for crowns on the back teeth, where strength is required, often with plastic or porcelain facings. On the front teeth, a combination of gold and porcelain is used to make a crown both strong and attractive (the porcelain can match the tooth color almost exactly). Increasingly, porcelain alone is used as a crown for a single tooth, since new, stronger porcelain materials are now available.

Bonding is an increasingly popular alternative to a crown for a tooth that is chipped, or has stains, cracks, or flaws in the enamel. Bonding takes place in three steps:

- The enamel is lightly etched with an acid solution to improve retention.
- A paste made of plastic combined with finely ground quartz, glass, or silica matched as closely as possible to the tooth color is applied in layers until the imperfection is repaired or the stain covered.
- The restoration is set or "cured" by means of a chemical process that often uses ultraviolet or visible light.

Veneers

In badly chipped or misshapen front teeth, for which the bonding is inadequate, thin acrylic shells or veneers can be bonded directly to the front surface of the teeth via acid etching. Unlike a crown, bonding and veneers are not permanent and the procedure may have to be repeated after several years of wear.

rice hulls, for example, contain a still unidentified anti-cariogenic substance, and phosphates in foods have similar protective qualities. Cheddar cheese eaten at the end of a meal generates a protective response, neutralizing mouth acids and helping to remineralize the tooth.

Contrary to popular belief, fibrous foods such as fruits and vegetables are not natural toothbrushes; instead, they protect by stimulating salivation, a natural mouth rinse that combats caries. Conversely, caries may become more prevalent when salivation decreases during sleep or is suppressed due to diseases of the salivary glands or as a side effect of certain drugs.

Increasing Resistance to Decay. The recent drop in caries among children is credited largely to fluoride supplementation or addition to drinking water, since there has been no apparent decrease in the prevalence of decay-producing bacteria and no decrease in sugar consumption. During early childhood, fluoride is incorporated into the enamel of developing teeth, modifying their crystal structure and making them more decay-resistant.

Over half the population in the United States—123 million people—drink fluoridated water (at a concentration of 1 part per million) either because the local water is naturally high in fluoride or because the municipal water supply is fluoridated. But while fluoridated communities have experienced a 50 percent decrease in caries, the wide-scale use of fluorides such as dentrifices and mouthwashes has also reduced the rate of caries by between 25 and 50 percent. It is estimated that every dollar spent on fluoridation saves $50 in dental bills.

In parts of the country without fluoridated water, fluoride can be prescribed as a dietary supplement during the period of tooth formation (that is, until about 14 years of age) and will produce a level of protection similar to that of fluoridated water. The supplement is available as drops, tablets, or a vitamin-fluoride combination. Taking the proper amount is crucial, since too much fluoride causes white spots or discolorations on teeth known as fluorosis.

- Children from birth to 2 should take 0.25 mg daily.
- Children 2 to 3 need 0.5 mg daily.
- Children 3 to 14 should take 1.0 mg/day until a year after all the permanent molars have appeared.

Pregnant women do not need to take fluoride supplements; it is in the first months of infancy that fluoride begins to help children's teeth.

The proper use of fluoride has no side effects and no effects other than dental fluorosis, or discoloration of the enamel, with elevated levels: More than 40 years of research in many countries attest to the safety and value of fluoridated water and fluoride supplements. Speculation that fluoride is responsible for cancer, birth defects, or any other condition is totally unfounded. The only recognized concern is for patients on hemodialysis, who should use demineralized or distilled water so as not to build up a high concentration of fluoride (and other ions) in their blood.

The regular use of fluoride toothpaste and mouthwashes at any age reduces decay yet further on a topical basis, that is, in interaction with the tooth surface. For children, the topical application of fluoride gels or solutions in the dental office provides additional benefit. People who use multiple forms of fluoride therapy can build a high enough level of fluoride on the surface enamel to virtually defy acid attack.

PERIODONTAL DISEASE

DEFINITION

Periodontal disease affects the periodontium: the gums (gingivae), the periodontal ligament, and the alveolar bone that together make up the supporting structure of the teeth. The several types of periodontal disease all lead to destruction of the structures supporting the teeth (see figure 32.6). As with caries, bacterial plaque is an underlying cause of periodontal disease, although this condition involves different bacteria and destructive process.

Gingivitis is a superficial inflammation of the gum tissue, due to irritation by bacteria products in the plaque. It usually first manifests itself at puberty and then persists at a chronic level throughout life, in differing degrees of severity. The first sign of gingivitis—red, swollen gums that bleed easily when subjected to pressure—is especially noticeable with toothbrushing (the "pink toothbrush" is almost always the first symptom). Because gum inflammation may cause little discomfort and progresses slowly, gingivitis is often neglected until it is far advanced and requires extensive treatment.

Unless reversed by successful treatment, gingivitis usually progresses to periodontitis (formerly known as pyorrhea from the Greek for "a flow of pus"). During long-term gingivitis, the continuing formation of irritating bacterial products causes a pocket to form between the tooth surface and the gums. Plaque continually builds up in this pocket that cannot be reached with a toothbrush. This leads to increased inflammation and in turn a deepening pocket—a vicious circle that can be reversed only through effective treatment. The progressive inflammation destroys the periodontal ligament as the margin of the gums detaches from the teeth and pus oozes from the periodontal pockets. The adjacent bone becomes affected and progressive bone loss leads to loosening teeth, which may eventually fall out. In general, the younger you are at the onset of bone loss, the greater the effort required to save the teeth. Periodonti-

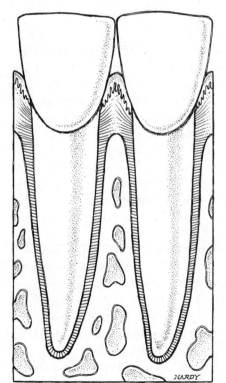
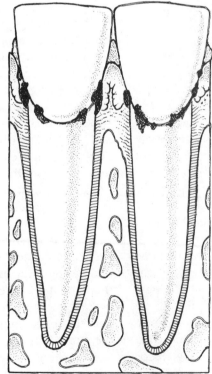
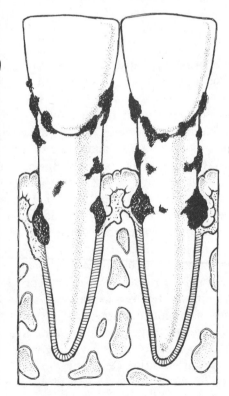

Figure 32.6: Inflamed gingiva with increase in depth of gingival pocket.

tis itself, however, is usually painless unless an acute infection (such as an abscess in one or more of the pockets) occurs along with the chronic condition.

Necrotizing ulcerative gingivitis (trench mouth or Vincent's infection) usually affects young adults, although it can strike at any age. In this form of periodontal disease (which can be mild or severe, acute or chronic) the gums usually hurt and bleed profusely at the slightest provocation. The gum points (papillae) between the teeth are destroyed, leaving craters that collect food debris and plaque, and the affected area is covered with a whitish layer of decomposing gum tissue. This infection is strongly associated with emotional stress.

Localized juvenile periodontitis (LJP), formerly known as periodontosis, is a particularly rapid and destructive form of periodontal disease that affects a small segment of the teenage and young adult population (1 to 3 percent). This condition causes marked destruction of the bone around the front teeth and first molars.

Periodontal disease is responsible for most loose teeth and much of the tooth loss after age 40. It has been estimated that 100 million Americans suffer from periodontal disease to some degree. These conditions affect all who possess any natural teeth (except the very young). Seventy-five percent of those 45 and older suffer from its most severe form (periodontitis with pockets), and there is a steady increase in severity with increasing age. Experts believe these conditions are not integral degenerative aspects of aging but are the cumulative effect of bacterial plaque on the periodontal tissue over the years.

CAUSE

Bacterial plaque causes gingivitis. The accumulation of plaque is usually heaviest near the gum margin and between teeth, areas that are not self-cleaning. The inflammation of the gums that results is mainly a result of the toxins and enzymes produced by bacteria. At the same time, plaque can mineralize to form tartar, or calculus. Calculus most commonly forms in those parts of the mouth that are closest to the salivary glands: inside the lower front teeth, on the outer surface of the upper molars. It also forms in the periodontal pockets. If not adequately removed, the plaque and calculus build up in layers, increasing the bacteria in the mouth and leading to further gum inflammation. While periodontal disease generally results from poor dental hygiene, it can be aggravated by overhanging rough margins or fillings, which accumulate plaque, and by poorly aligned, or maloccluded, teeth that don't come together correctly and may generate abnormal biting forces. The nervous habit of grinding or clenching the teeth during sleep, called bruxism, can also overload the periodontal structure and contribute to the breakdown of the supporting tissues. Smoking is a further aggravating factor, and smokers tend to have more periodontal problems than nonsmokers.

People suffering systemic chronic conditions such as diabetes, thyroid disorders, and a variety of blood conditions may have a higher risk of developing advanced periodontal disease. Deficiencies of vitamin C and (possibly) folic acid also contribute to an increasing rate of periodontal breakdown.

Hormones may also play a part in periodontal disease, since gingivitis is often particularly marked during puberty and again during pregnancy. At these times, plaque bacteria are able to utilize the increased hormonal levels available in the fluid adjacent to the gingiva. In pregnancy, noticeably swollen gums that bleed easily are common as early as the second month. After delivery, however, the gingiva usually return to the prepregnancy condition.

DIAGNOSIS

Periodontal disease can be recognized by its characteristic tender, swollen gums that are red and irritated. Other signs and symptoms might include bleeding gums on stimulation, or teeth that are loose or have shifted, leaving spaces between the front teeth. There may also be a bad taste in the mouth. X-rays will show bone loss. The depth of the pockets in the gums is measured with a periodontal probe.

TREATMENT

In the earlier stages of the disease, treatment usually involves regular prophylaxis (cleaning teeth, removing plaque and calculus), root planing, and curettage under the gum margins. Along with lifting calculus and plaque from the tooth surfaces, inflamed tissue is taken from the pockets around the teeth by use of a curet, a spoon-shaped instrument. When the bacterial colonies and the mechanical and chemical irritants that cause inflammation are removed, the gum usually reattaches itself to the tooth or constricts enough to eliminate the pocket. In most early cases, subgingival curettage and good oral hygiene are all that is required for satisfactory treatment.

In more advanced cases, pockets are eliminated by a surgical procedure called gingivectomy, which is usually done using local anesthesia. A dressing is used to cover the wound for a week or so while it heals. A similar procedure, the gingivoplasty, is used to remove excessive gum tissue and to provide a new and healthier shape for the gums, helping them to stay self-cleaning.

In situations where there has been bone loss, a procedure may be required in which a gum flap is lifted away from the teeth, and the underlying infected tissue and calculus are removed. The bone is recontoured and the gum flap is then replaced in its proper position, sutured, and allowed to heal.

For advanced cases, osseous (bone) surgery may be performed to correct defects in the bone structure caused by the periodontal disease.

Other treatments may be necessary, depending on the nature of the periodontal problem. Occlusal adjustment involves the reshaping of the chewing and biting surfaces of the teeth so that the pressures sustained by the teeth are distributed evenly. Orthodontic treatment can be used to improve the bite and to reduce trauma to malpositioned teeth. Jaw surgery may be necessary to significantly improve the bite when the jawbones are mismatched in size. For habitual tooth grinders, appliances can be worn at night to protect the teeth from wear and excessive pressure.

HOME REMEDIES AND ALTERNATIVE THERAPIES

A recommended nonsurgical treatment for periodontal disease (named for its developer, Dr. Paul Keyes) entails, in addition to careful scaling and curettage in the dental office, assiduous daily home care using such antibacterial agents as salt, baking soda, and hydrogen peroxide to suppress the infection. The results of this home care are monitored by microscopic examination of the bacterial debris under the gums, and if necessary antibiotic treatment is administered.

Keyes's treatment, which has received much publicity, is not a substitute for conventional treatment but an adjunct that may be appropriate for some people.

The same meticulous removal of tooth deposits is required for Keyes's method as for any other treatment, and once this has been done, the maintenance of periodontal tissues becomes in large degree the responsibility of the patient. Indeed, recent studies indicate that Keyes's treatment may be no more effective than conventional properly carried out home care.

PREVENTION

Thorough brushing and flossing of teeth will keep bacterial plaque and calculus formation to a minimum. For some people, dentists also advise the use of special toothpicks, interproximal brushes, or an interdental stimulator to reach between teeth. The rubber or plastic tip found on many toothbrushes is not a cleaning instrument (although it can be used as one); rather, it is designed to massage the gum tissue between the teeth.

Irrigating devices such as a Water Pik can supplement cleaning techniques in areas of the mouth difficult to reach with a toothbrush. Irrigation does not remove plaque; rather it flushes out plaque's toxic products.

Even the best oral hygiene does not completely prevent plaque formation, nor remove calculus that has already formed and firmly attached to the teeth at the gumline and below. Calculus must be removed professionally by scaling the teeth with a sharp instrument or the more modern ultrasonic device that vibrates the calculus off the teeth. The combination of personal plaque control and appropriately scheduled office visits is the key to preventing periodontal disease.

Several personal products are now available to supplement mechanical and professional plaque and calculus control.

• Antitartar (calculus) dentifrices, now approved by the Council on Dental Therapeutics of the American Dental Association, reduce the rate of calculus buildup above the gumline. These products are helpful if used on a daily basis after professional tooth cleaning. They have no effect, however, on tartar that has already formed.

• Antiplaque, antigingivitis mouthwashes, approved by the council, should be used twice daily after brushing and flossing. (Peridex [chlorhexidine gluconate] is available on a prescription basis.)

PROSTHODONTICS—REPLACING MISSING TEETH

A dislodged permanent tooth should always be replaced or else the teeth on either side of the space gradually tilt toward the gap, and the teeth in the opposite jaw begin to slip vertically (supererupt) toward the space. These teeth are at risk of caries and periodontal disease. Several options are available.

• **Fixed bridge:** can be used if generally healthy teeth are present adjacent to the space where the tooth (or teeth) has been lost. Crowns are made for these supporting teeth and the replacement tooth or teeth (pontics) are soldered onto the crowns. The bridge is then cemented permanently onto the prepared supporting teeth. A fixed bridge lasts many years, looks good, and is not removable. However, it requires extra care to keep clean, and the supporting teeth may be more prone to periodontal disease. If additional teeth are lost, they cannot be added to the existing bridge. When teeth are missing in several areas in the same jaw, additional stability may be obtained by joining the bridges together.

• **Removable partial denture:** usually replaces multiple missing teeth when there are insufficient natural teeth to support a bridge. This device rests on the soft tissues of the jaws, and is held in place with clips (clasps) or supports. Partial dentures greatly increase the surface area in the mouth that is subject to plaque formation and must therefore be meticulously cleaned.

Fortunately, this is easy. Over time, the pressure produced by the retaining clips of a partial denture can loosen the supporting teeth. However, this should not happen if the denture is well constructed and remade as necessary. It is considerably less expensive than a fixed bridge, and additional teeth can usually be added to it.

• **Full denture:** made to restore both the teeth and the underlying bone if all the teeth are missing in an arch. While dentures are quite satisfactory, the lower denture can be problematic when the amount of bony surface available is limited. In this situation, the lower denture tends to become dislodged while chewing, or even, on occasion, while speaking.

• **Implant-supported prosthesis:** Implants may be surgically placed in the jaw to replace missing teeth.

• **Immediate dentures:** Three to 6 months are required for the implants to heal after they are placed in the jaw. After healing, a small second surgical procedure is necessary to expose the implant and connect a piece to it which will be used by the restorative dentist to hold the crown or bridge. Cylinder implants made of titanium are almost always used. Implants in both the upper and lower jaw enjoy about a 90 percent success rate.

The feasibility of implantation depends on the amount, shape, and quality of bone available in the jaw where the implant is to go (although extra bone may be grafted from other parts of body to aid the implant).

Implants can support either a single tooth or multiple teeth. They are especially useful to replace a front tooth because they do not require other front teeth to be prepared for crowns.

Also, implants can be connected with a bar and a denture fitted with clips, which clip onto the bar. This clip bar is very secure, and can be made with limited palatal coverage, which requires fewer implants than a bridge.

In a growing number of cases, an implant-supported prosthesis is the best choice for restoration of a missing tooth or teeth, for example, in the replacement of a central incisor in a teenager who lost it in an accident. Another situation in which an implant-supported bridge is the best option is the restoration of missing posterior teeth (molars and premolars) on only one side of the maxillary or mandibular arch. The field is rapidly evolving with new techniques and procedures using implants. As it should be in any situation, the person must have confidence in the clinician's experience, in this case in the use of implants. The person should inquire about the surgeon's and restorative dentist's experience with implants and seek a second opinion if further information is needed.

To spare people the potential embarrassment and inconvenience of temporary toothlessness, some dentures are prepared prior to the removal of natural teeth and inserted into the mouth immediately following extraction. These dentures, however, must be refitted when the jaw heals. If healing results in extensive change, new dentures must be made.

Because the bony base of the jaw continually shrinks, dentures require regular relining to prevent movement that encourages further shrinking of the tissues, mouth ulcers, or excessive growth of the tissues adjacent to the dentures. Despite some inevitable loss in chewing ability, most people function well with dentures.

• **Overdenture:** a variation of a full denture. Where possible, two to four teeth in the arch are saved and their crowns ground down to small stubs. Gold thimbles are cemented to these stubs and the denture is prepared to fit over these pegs and the bony ridge.

Overdentures are particularly successful in the mouth's lower arch, where retention of full dentures is often a problem. Care must be taken, however, to protect the stubs with good oral hygiene and the use of fluorides if root surfaces become exposed.

• More common than prepared teeth, implants are being used to support an overdenture. Two implants are connected by a bar, to which the denture is attached. The stability and retention achieved by this system compared to a standard denture are excellent. Although implant-supported overdentures are more expensive, improvement in function is usually considered to be worth the cost. The procedure used to place the implants is described in the previous section.

ULCERS OF THE LIPS AND ORAL CAVITY

DEFINITION

Ulcers—or sores—are commonly found on the lips and in the mouth. Single ulcers in the mouth are usually the result of trauma, although a single ulcer on the lip is often caused by a herpes simplex virus. The most common ulcers in this part of the body are canker sores, or apthous ulcers. These can occur singly or in groups inside the mouth, on the inside surface of the cheeks and lips, on the tongue, the soft palate, and the base of the gums.

The painful ulcers resemble craters and range in size from $\frac{1}{8}$ inch to more than 1 inch in diameter. They can interfere with eating and talking and most recurrent episodes of these ulcers occur two to three times per year or may even be present continually.

CAUSE

Lip ulcers are often caused by the herpes simplex virus, which, when not causing discomfort, remains dormant in the epithelial cells of the mucosa of the lip. Trauma, such as exposure to the sun, or a cold or fever (hence the popular names of fever blister and cold sore) can activate the virus and cause an ulcer. Initial episodes of mouth ulcers may occur at a young age and cause a fever and mouth pain. This condition, known as primary herpetic gingivostomatis, may cause swollen glands and dehydration because it is painful to eat and drink.

Allergies (sometimes to toothpaste, mouthwash, or food) can cause mouth ulcers that are often small and spread throughout the mouth.

Cancer chemotherapy and radiation treatments can cause mouth ulcers that are painful and cause difficulty eating.

Skin diseases such as Stevens Johnson syndrome or lichen planus also cause ulcers.

DIAGNOSIS

These ulcers are always painful. The center of an ulcer is gray and the border a bright red. Bleeding is rare. Infection of the ulcer can increase its pain and duration. If the ulcer becomes infected, it can become more painful and last longer.

TREATMENT

Oral and lip ulcers heal without treatment and, except for a condition called recurrent apthous stomatitis, leave no scars. Treatment is symptomatic and eases discomfort. Topical anesthetics such as diclonine can be used to numb the area. Various other medications are available to stop the pain. Steroids such as hydrocortisone can be injected into long-standing ulcers to promote healing. In severe cases, systemic steroids are necessary to reduce the inflammation.

When infection delays healing, antibiotics, usually oral penicillin, can be used to treat significantly infected ulcers. Tetracycline mouthwash can be used when systemic antibiotics are not indicated.

Some evidence shows that acyclovir (Zovirax) ointment can be used successfully to treat herpes sores on the lips if this medication is applied early in their development. If used before the ulcer forms, the size, pain, and duration of the ulcer can be diminished. Once the ulcer itself has formed, however, Acyclovir ointment does not seem to have any beneficial effects.

HOME REMEDIES AND ALTERNATIVE THERAPIES

Warm salt rinses (½ teaspoon of salt in a glass of warm water) can be used to cleanse ulcers and reduce the possibility of infection. To relieve some of the discomfort of mouth ulcers, a mixture of kaolin (Kaopectate) and Benadryl exilir in a 50:50 mixture can help. After holding the mixtue in the mouth for 50 seconds, it should be spit out. It can be used as often as necessary.

TEMPOROMANDIBULAR DISORDERS

DEFINITION

Temporomandibular disorders (TMD) are a group of disorders that involve pain upon opening the jaw, clicking or grinding noises with jaw movement, jaw fatigue and stiffness, and locking of the jaw that impairs lower jaw movement.

TMD includes disorders such as myofacial pain dysfunction syndrome, synovitis, and other inflammatory conditions of the temporomandibular joint, degenerative disorders (osteoarthritis of the temporomandibular joint), and others.

CAUSES

Because a number of conditions are included in the TMD grouping, no one etiology exists for all of them. Trauma to the joint, either acute or chronic, perhaps from heavy clenching or grinding, or an unstable joint that puts stress on the muscles of the jaw because the ligaments of the joint are loose, are two findings that are common to many of the conditions. Stress, either physical, emotional, or both, is also another finding in many people with TMD who are asymptomatic. The joint and its associated structures or the jaw muscles, alone or together, can produce symptoms of pain and/or dysfunction. Effective management relies upon a correct diagnosis with clarification of the causative factors.

Diagnosis is based on a thorough history and a complete examination. Laboratory tests for arthritis and imaging studies such as an x-ray or MRI may be ordered. No one should be treated for TMD based on the results of an MRI or other imaging study alone. A number of testing devices are being promoted as important diagnostic tools. Not all of them are, however, and patients should be wary of something they do not understand.

DIAGNOSIS

Diagnosis is based on symptoms of TMD as well as other diagnostic techniques, which may include x-rays, an MRI, or a CT scan. If you do not have pain or difficulty with your jaw, an x-ray or other imaging technique should not be accepted as a sign of TMD. Similarly, you may suffer TMD symptoms and have TMD even if your x-rays appear normal.

Be wary of expensive gadgetry alleged to assist in the diagnosis of TMD. Many of these devices have not been widely accepted by the medical and dental professions.

TREATMENT

Treatments for TMD can be grouped into nonsurgical and surgical treatments. Nonsurgical treatment should be used as the primary approach to treatment in most situations, as it may eliminate the need for the more invasive procedures. Nonsurgical treatment includes:

- Anti-inflammatory medication to reduce inflammation.
- Muscle relaxants to reduce muscle spasms.
- Appliance therapy to increase joint space, reduce muscle spasms, and dampen the deleterious effects of jaw clenching and teeth grinding.
- Physical therapy to reduce pain, spasm, and strengthen jaw muscles.
- Psychiatric therapy

Surgical treatment should be considered when non-surgical treatment fails to provide relief. This includes:

- Arthroscopic temporomandibular joint surgery: Looking into the joint with a small instrument (without incisions) and performing surgery depending on observances.
- Open temporomandibular joint surgery: Removing scar tissue and adhesions and repositioning jaw structures.
- Orthograthic surgery to reposition the jaws into a better relationship to each other if the malocclusion (bad bite) has been shown to be a cause of the pain.

Because nonsurgical TMD symptoms sometimes resolve by themselves, therapy should be tried first for about 3 months. If symptoms improve, nonsurgical therapy can be discontinued or modified. But if symptoms are not relieved by nonsurgical therapy, are significant to the patient, and a condition exists for which surgery can be helpful to treatment, surgery should be considered. Many surgeons believe that a conservative arthroscopic surgical procedure with a joint irrigation is the best first step in surgical therapy. Based on the arthroscopic findings and other information, an open joint procedure may be indicated.

Home Remedies and Alternative Therapies

Moist heat or ice can be used to reduce the pain of tender muscles and joints. Stress management techniques or psychiatric treatment may also ease muscle tension. Physical therapy and exercises can help reduce muscle spasms and maintain and increase jaw motion.

....

DEVELOPMENTAL ABNORMALITIES

Developmental abnormalities are dental conditions present at birth or developing during childhood.

MALOCCLUSION

Definition

Malaligned teeth are overcrowded or have gaps between them and produce malocclusion, or bad bite. This condition may cause dental and general health problems, as well as an unfavorable appearance. Malaligned teeth are difficult to clean and may be especially susceptible to caries and periodontal disease. Chewing and speech may be abnormal.

Cause

Many factors contribute to poor occlusion.

- Inherited conditions that cannot be prevented, such as crowded teeth, wide spacing, and incorrect relationships of the jaws.
- Thumb-sucking that persists after the permanent incisors have emerged may open up lasting spaces between the teeth.
- Persistence of an infantile swallowing reflex, in which the tongue is thrust against the teeth during swallowing, speaking, and even at rest can result in creating or maintaining an opening between the front teeth.

While mouth breathing and lip biting may be also associated with this condition, they are probably not causes.

Diagnosis

Observation of the teeth and their relative position when the mouth is open and closed reveals malocclusion. In most cases, the poor spacing or overcrowding associated with this condition is evident even on casual examination.

Treatment

Orthodontic therapy. Although it is estimated that 90 percent of all children ages 12 to 17 with correctable malocclusions are not treated, some 400,000 new patients start orthodontic treatment each year. The majority are in their early teens, but some are younger and 15 to 25 percent are adults, a percentage steadily on the rise.

Active orthodontic treatment (movement) takes an average of 2 years, followed by a similar, sometimes longer period of stabilization (retention) of the teeth in their new position. In adults, whose bone is more dense than that of adolescents, the treatment may take somewhat longer.

Dental and cosmetic considerations determine the orthodontic choice of treatment. The health and stability of the teeth in their projected new positions and the facial contours that will result from repositioning the teeth are all considered.

In some situations (cases with a marked overbite, for example) some teeth may be extracted while others are repositioned with a fixed appliance (braces). This procedure may occur in this way:

• Four bicuspids are extracted, one from each quadrant of the mouth, in a single session under either local or general anesthesia.

• Stainless steel bands are then fitted and cemented onto the teeth. Tubes in which the arch wires will be anchored are welded onto the bands on the terminal teeth, usually a molar in each quadrant; the other teeth receive brackets. Increasingly, transparent plastic is being used in place of steel, and frequently brackets and tubes are bonded directly to the teeth.

• Flexible wires are inserted. By adjusting these arch wires, steady horizontal or vertical pressure can be maintained on the tooth surface and transmitted through the periodontal ligament to the bone. Gradually, the bone resorbs and the tooth drifts into the created space. On the side where tension is applied, meanwhile, new bone builds. This alternation of resorption and deposit is the basic orthodontic process.

While give-and-take displacement of this kind effectively straightens individual teeth, when all the teeth in one jaw or even the jaw itself must be moved, other means of applying force must be found. Frequently, the necessary anchorage is found in the opposing jaw. If the upper teeth protrude, elastic bands are attached to link the front part of the appliance in the upper jaw with the back part of a similar appliance in the lower jaw. The upper teeth are pulled back and the lower one tends to come forward. In some cases, anchorage is needed outside the mouth: The elastic force of "night braces," for example, is anchored on the top of the head or the back of the neck.

Serial extraction is a preventive measure used in cases of severe overcrowding of the teeth.

• Selected primary teeth are extracted at intervals to allow the permanent teeth to emerge in their proper places in the dental arch.

• Permanent teeth for which there is no room are extracted when (or before) they appear.

• This procedure is usually supplemented with mechanical orthodontic treatment.

After even the most successful orthodontic treatment, relapse may occur as the teeth return to their original position. Consequently, the retention phase of orthodontic treatment is as important as the movement phase. Various devices forestall relapse.

• Retainers: removable plates carrying wires that press on the front teeth
• Lingual arches: rigid bands between the lower bicuspids
• Positioners: rubber mouthpieces, representing ideal models of the patient's tooth structure, worn 4 hours each day

In both the movement and the retention phases of treatment, the patient's cooperation is essential. Since adolescents are often unreliable in their use of night braces, removable appliances, and rubber bands, many orthodontists prefer to start treatment before adolescence, when children are generally more cooperative. The increasing use of transparent plastic in place of steel, and appliances worn on the inside of the teeth, may improve compliance among adolescents.

Orthognathic surgery. In cases in which conventional orthodontic measures will not be effective because there is a mismatch of the jaws, orthognathic surgery is indicated. For example, protrusion of the lower jaw can be corrected by a procedure in which the jaw is sectioned and the remaining portion is set back in the correct position. Surgery can also be performed in the maxilla or upper jaw to correct open or closed bites that would never respond to orthodontic force. Incisions are usually performed within the mouth, so there is no visible scarring.

The need for a surgical procedure is determined by an examination and an analysis using cephalometric trays (facial measurement-taking devices) and dental models. Computer imagery can be used to help predict outcome. The best result in appearance and occlusion is usually obtained using both orthodontics and surgery rather than either alone.

The decision to undertake surgery in conjunction with orthodontic treatment is made by the team of the orthodontist, the oral and maxillofacial surgeon, and the patient. The practitioners should be familiar with each other as well as the patient's needs. Although there are exceptions, surgery is usually delayed until the growth of the lower jaw—the last bone to grow in the facial skeleton—is completed, which is in the range of 15–16 years in females and 16–17 years in males. Since some people will grow until the age of 21, bone-age x-rays can be useful but are not always reliable. If surgery is undertaken early and further growth occurs, further orthodontic treatment, and perhaps surgery, needs to be considered to correct the change in bite.

IMPACTED TEETH

DEFINITION

Both the primary and permanent teeth develop in the jaws below the surface of the bone and gum. As the teeth develop they push toward the bone surface (erupt). But when the permanent teeth are either partially or completely prevented from erupting, they are said to be impacted. Over the years as the human diet has become more refined and both our mouths and teeth have grown smaller, the shrinking of our jaws has proceeded more rapidly than the reduction of tooth size. Therefore our teeth are often crowded and impacted.

Although any tooth can become impacted, the third molars (wisdom teeth) or permanent upper canines are most commonly affected. If the wisdom teeth are not fully erupted by age 18 or 19, they are unlikely to erupt further and are considered impacted. Limited space for normal eruption in the front of the mouth can crowd the canine teeth, which are the last of the front teeth to erupt.

DIAGNOSIS

Frequently, in the late teens or early twenties, the tissue overlying a partially impacted third molar, usually one of the lower third molars, becomes inflamed and infected. This usually causes pericoronitis, a condition causing mild to moderate pain for five to seven days and may result in fever, enlarged lymph nodes on the side of the neck, and trouble swallowing. (Enlarged nodes on both sides of the neck may be a sign of mononucleosis infection or numerous other disorders.) Pericoronitis usually clears up by itself but may need to be treated.

Cysts may form around impacted teeth. These are painless but can enlarge and destroy a considerable amount of bone before causing symptoms. Often a cyst develops in an area not seen in routine dental radiographs and will be detected only by a panoramic radiograph that displays the entire upper and lower jaw (a type of dental x-ray you should have every 5 to 10 years). Impacted teeth can also trap debris at the base of the second molar crown, resulting in serious caries damage or periodontal problems.

Impacted teeth are either not visible or only partly visible in the mouth.

TREATMENT

A dentist should make every effort to encourage impacted canine teeth in children to grow in properly. Early removal of deciduous canines and/or molar teeth may create enough room to allow blocked canines to erupt. This may require orthodontic treatment to bring the canines into the dental arch. Treatment may be delayed until all the primary teeth have fallen out. It entails surgical exposure of the impacted canine, bonding of a bracket to the exposed crown, and attachment of the bracket to a wire connected to an orthodontic appliance on the rest of the teeth.

Impacted third molars should be removed soon after diagnosis to prevent damage to adjacent teeth or bone and to minimize the chance of surgical complications that increase with age. If all four third molars are impacted, they should all be removed at the same time by a practitioner experienced in this procedure.

MALFORMED TEETH

DEFINITION

Malformed teeth possess pitted or grooved crowns, enamel of abnormal color, or abnormal dentin.

CAUSE AND DIAGNOSIS

The great majority of malformed teeth are the result of some infectious or febrile illness in infancy or early childhood. The 6-year molars and the eight front teeth are most often involved, since these are the teeth developing during these years. A medical history and examination of the teeth confirm the diagnosis.

TREATMENT

Severely malformed teeth may require crowns for appearance's sake and to protect against wear. Bonding or laminates are also used to restore these teeth.

TETRACYCLINE STAINING

DEFINITION

Tetracycline staining is a discoloration of the enamel and dentin that varies from yellow to dark gray-brown, depending on the type of tetracycline used and the length of treatment.

CAUSE AND DIAGNOSIS

Tetracycline antibiotics administered to women in late pregnancy or to children under 7 years of age are incorporated into the enamel and dentin of the forming teeth and may lead to discoloration.

TREATMENT

Bonding, laminates, and capping cover discolored teeth.

PREVENTION

Tetracycline staining has become less common since doctors became aware of this side effect. Alternative antibiotics should always be prescribed during risk periods to prevent staining of the teeth.

CLEFT LIP AND PALATE

DEFINITION

Clefts of the lip and palate, which affect about 1 child in 1000, occur when the embryo's facial folds fail to unite in the palate or upper lip region. They may involve the upper lip or the palate, or both. If untreated, cleft lip and/or palate will cause disfigurement, swallowing problems, speech difficulties, and significant malocclusions. The cleft of the lip may be on one side (unilateral) or both sides (bilateral). The palatal cleft can be of the hard palate, the soft palate, or both.

CAUSE AND DIAGNOSIS

Although the causes are not well understood, it appears that some cases of cleft palate are due to a genetic predisposition combined with a specific agent such as rubella (German measles) or drugs (for example, the antiepileptic drug Dilantin or corticosteroids) taken during the first trimester of pregnancy.

TREATMENT

A cleft lip is usually repaired in the third month of birth by a simple surgical procedure. A cleft palate is usually repaired at 12 to 18 months. Surgery to repair the lip and nose is done later.

Prior to surgery, a removable device is inserted to temporarily close the palate and ensure proper feeding and normal speech development. In some situations, because of continuing growth, use of this device is alternated with surgery several times.

PREVENTION

Pregnant women should avoid exposure to rubella and avoid all drug use unless absolutely necessary and prescribed by a doctor.

....

SALIVARY GLAND DISEASE

SALIVARY GLAND DISEASE

DEFINITION

Three pairs of major salivary glands and myriad minor salivary glands excrete saliva into the mouth. The largest pair—the parotid glands, which are next to the ears—empty into the oral cavity next to the upper first molars via Stenson's ducts. The second largest pair, the submandibular glands, secrete saliva under the tongue through Wharton's ducts. The smallest of the major salivary glands are beneath the tongue and excrete saliva along the margins of the Wharton's ducts through the ducts of Ravini. Numerous other small salivary glands are within the lips, palate, cheeks, and oropharynx.

Saliva contains mucus, antibodies, and enzymes. This liquid lubricates the mouth, fights dental caries (decay) and periodontitis, and helps digest food. Insufficient saliva, a condition called xerostomia, causes dry mouth, dental decay, foul-smelling breath (halitosis), and an altered sense of taste.

CAUSE

Several diseases can compromise salivary gland function, causing xerostomia and painful glands. Infection of the salivary glands (sialoadenitis) can result from viral infections (such as mumps) and bacterial infection (from bacteria normally present in the mouth that multiply due to dehydration or blockage of the salivary ducts by salivary stones).

Salivary glands can also be affected by autoimmune diseases (such as Sjogren's disease) and tumors, most of which are benign. Many drugs also decrease a flow of saliva.

DIAGNOSIS

Diagnosis of salivary gland disease should be made by a specialist—a qualified oral and maxillofacial surgeon. The doctor uses medical history, physical exam and specialized x-rays (called sialograms), and chemical analysis of the saliva to make the diagnosis.

TREATMENT

Therapy treats the underlying disease that causes salivary gland symptoms, such as removal of stones or treatment with steroids for autoimmune disease. Acute bouts of sialoadenitis are treated with hydration (you must drink plenty of fluids or are given fluids intravenously), antibiotics, and sometimes artificial saliva.

....

DENTAL RESEARCH

ANTIBACTERIAL AGENTS

There has been little success in developing agents to control all the potentially cariogenic bacteria in plaque. Scientists have therefore turned their attention to a search for agents that affect *S. mutans,* one particular, major decay-producing bacterium. While researchers believe that preparations of antimicrobial agents in slow-release devices attached to the teeth may someday effectively fight decay, this technique has not yet proven satisfactory.

A number of antibacterial agents hold promise for combating the bacteria involved in gingivitis and periodontal disease.

- Chlorhexidine, widely used in Europe, has become available as an antiplaque, antigingivitis agent in a prescription product.
- Listerine has been shown to be a helpful supplement to brushing and flossing. (A number of other antiplaque, antigingivitis agents are under active clinical testing.)
- Tetracycline is becoming more widely used as a supplement to treatment of progressive periodontal disease with pocket formation. Techniques for incorporating the antibiotic in special fibers and other devices for placement locally are under study.

ANTICARIES VACCINE

A vaccine directed against *S. mutans* has been effective in markedly reducing new decay in animal experiments. In one study, people who ingested one type of vaccine—capsules of modified *S. mutans*—over a 10-day period developed elevated levels of antibodies in their saliva, and significantly fewer bacteria were able to establish themselves in the oral cavity. However, this technique has not been shown to be safe and more research is necessary.

OTHER RESEARCH

Studies of the association of specific bacteria with some forms of periodontal disease have suggested the possibility of a vaccine against these conditions. However, the involvement of the immune system in the progression of periodontal disease complicates this research. A number of diagnostic tests are now available to identify areas of the mouth in which the periodontal disease is in an active and progressive rather than quiescent phase. These diagnostic tools are helping dentists determine the most appropriate treatment.

Active research is also under way in the development of biological materials to fill in jaw defects, to stimulate bone formation, and to "glue" together teeth and bone weakened by periodontal disease. New procedures are being developed to increase the possibility of tissue regeneration and reattachment of tissue to tooth roots, as an element of periodontal treatment in advanced disease.

Researchers are also learning that deficits in salivary flow, or the body's various defense systems, make some people more prone to tooth decay than others. For these caries-prone people, a slow-release fluoride implant may prove beneficial. Attached to a molar, the tiny device will release fluoride continuously into the saliva, providing sustained fluoride protection. For people with xerostomia (dry mouth) resulting from diseases of the salivary glands or as a side effect of medication or radiation, there is hope that new artificial salivas will offer some comfort and protection.

33
Mental and Emotional Health

JOHN M. OLDHAM, M.D.

Parts of this chapter are adapted from the chapter by Donald S. Kornfeld, M.D., and Philip R. Muskin, M.D., which appeared in the revised second edition.

People's personalities incorporate unique combinations of strengths and vulnerabilities that determine different patterns of thinking, feeling, and behaving. These personality fingerprints determine our capacity to deal with life's demands and reflect our state of mental health. While we all face stress and pain on a regular basis, we differ in our resiliency and ability to cope. When we are unable to function at home or at work, to achieve personal goals, or to attain satisfactory relationships, we may have made the transition to mental illness. Genetic, biochemical, and environmental factors endow the brain with an astonishing capacity to deal effectively with life's challenges and stresses, but these same factors may render us susceptible to mental disorders.

Different areas of the brain control specific functions. Innovative brain imaging techniques such as position emission tomography (PET) and single photon emission computerized tomography (SPECT), which identify metabolic activity, can picture locations of brain function. Using these scanning methods, areas of the brain can be seen "lighting up" after they have been stimulated. For example, asking a person to name a series of objects will cause an increased activity in a different part of the brain than does exposure to music. As a result of these brain images, we are increasingly able to match areas of the brain with their biological functions, and researchers have used these techniques to connect mental illnesses with specific areas of brain dysfunction.

Abnormalities in certain brain locations cause both mental and physical symptoms. For instance, if the blood supply ceases to an area of the brain known as the frontal lobe, a stroke may occur, resulting in a frontal lobe syndrome that produces memory problems and personality changes, as well as weakness or paralysis of parts of the body.

In some cases, mental problems occur secondarily, following traumatic body injury that causes physical disability, or after a natural disaster that injures or kills loved ones and destroys personal possessions. While depression may be triggered by such stressful events (or apparently occur spontaneously), its development is usually facilitated by a genetic vulnerability to depression. A combination of genetic predisposition and environmental stress can precipitate other mental illnesses, some of which are better understood and more successfully treated than others. Depression, for instance, can be successfully treated with a combination of medications and psychotherapy about 80 percent of the time.

Unfortunately, despite the fact that new medical findings have enabled doctors to treat mental illness as successfully as they treat other medical illness, mental illness is still seen as a sign of moral weakness or failing. People who could be effectively treated are often reluctant to seek help because of the stigma attached to acknowledging mental problems. This chapter reviews common mental disorders in adults and children, and discusses their causes, symptoms, warnings, diagnoses, and treatments.

AIDS

Although acquired immune deficiency syndrome (AIDS) is not a mental illness per se, it has psychological manifestations. Some people with mental illness may engage in high-risk behaviors, such as substance abuse, that increase their risk of contracting HIV. Alternatively, AIDS may make a person vulnerable to depression, anxiety, suicide, and dementia.

High-risk behavior. AIDS can be transmitted through unprotected sexual intercourse, exchange of blood products, and sharing needles—all of which may be exacerbated by mental illness. For example, people with borderline personality disorder may be sexually promiscuous, and some with depression are more likely to abuse drugs. Treatment of underlying mental illness and education about transmission are both necessary to slow the transmission of HIV.

Substance abuse. In many ways, infection with HIV may influence increased substance abuse among people with a history of drug problems. The ability to cope with a fatal disorder occurring in the prime of life largely depends on individual personality style. Some patients find ways to increase support systems and mobilize resources, while others become vulnerable and isolated, making them more likely to abuse drugs or alcohol. Not only are these behaviors unhealthy for the individual, but they also may be an obstacle to effective medical care.

Depression, anxiety, and suicide. As with substance abuse, the stress of a chronic illness such as AIDS can worsen depression, anxiety, or other mental disorders and increase the risk of suicide. Medical problems, medication side effects, and problems at home can exacerbate emotional problems and should not be overlooked, as they are often treatable.

Dementia. The brain can be affected by HIV, resulting in dementia. AIDS dementia can be the first sign of HIV infection and ultimately affects one-half to two-

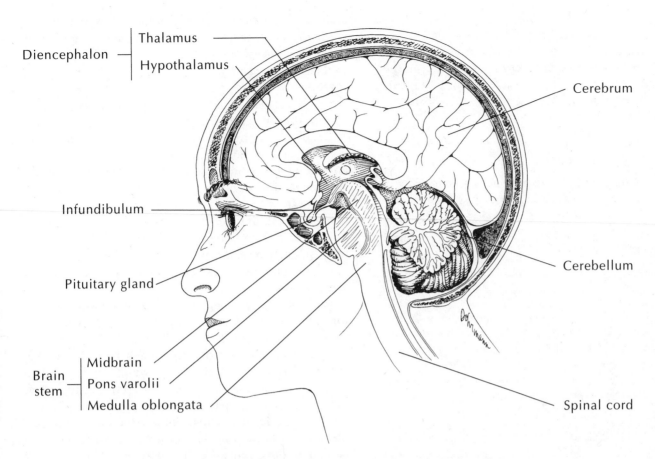

Diencephalon — Thalamus
Hypothalamus

Cerebrum

Infundibulum

Pituitary gland

Cerebellum

Brain stem — Midbrain
Pons varolii
Medulla oblongata

Spinal cord

Figure 33.1: The brain and its major structures.

thirds of all AIDS patients. Symptoms include mild changes in memory, weakness in the legs, loss of interest in life, confusion, disorientation, and in late stages, inability to speak and paralysis. Treatment includes practical measures such as lists and memory aids in addition to medication such as AZT and methyphenidate (Ritalin). (See section on dementia for more on treatment; see chapter 19 for a more detailed discussion of AIDS.)

People with AIDS and their caregivers have many resources for counseling and support, including community-based organizations and professional mental health care. For a list of organizations see appendix B, Directory of Health Organizations and Resources.

DEMENTIA AND ALZHEIMER'S DISEASE

Dementia (previously called senility) describes a progressive and sometimes irreversible loss of intellectual function and memory, usually accompanied by changes in personality and behavior, that eventually impairs a person's ability to engage in work and other daily activities.

The most common type of dementia is Alzheimer's

disease. This disease, which affects 2.5 to 4 million Americans, usually strikes in the later years and is incurable. It involves progressive brain cell destruction and produces a characteristic course of mental deterioration beginning with minor confusion and difficulty remembering names of acquaintances, leading ultimately to forgetting even a spouse's name and losing the ability to talk and care for oneself. A person with the disease may display personality disturbances such as anxiety, aggression, and lack of concentration.

Other causes of dementia may include stroke, brain tumors, or injuries, and less commonly, infectious diseases of the brain. For a complete discussion of dementia and Alzheimer's disease, see chapter 26, Brain, Nerve, and Muscle Disorders.

ANXIETY DISORDERS

DEFINITION

Anxiety, a normal reaction to a threatening situation, is part of the "fight-or-flight" response that caused our ancestors to flee animals or seek shelter during storms. The feeling of anxiety results from an increase in the

DIAGNOSTIC TESTS

The procedures and laboratory tests listed below can supplement the data obtained from a person's psychiatric history and physical examination by a doctor.

MENTAL STATUS EXAMINATION

An assessment by a health professional of emotional state and cognitive function. The test is based on appearance, behavior, speaking manner, affect or emotion, thought process, thought content, and intellectual function.

MEDICAL TESTS

Used to determine if a physical cause, most importantly a treatable disease, is responsible for a psychiatric symptom. Blood tests may measure electrolytes, thyroid function, hormone levels, complete blood count, and drug levels. An individual may also be tested for infectious diseases such as syphilis, tuberculosis, HIV, Lyme disease, and hepatitis. (See chapter 12, "Diagnostic Tests and Procedures.")

NEUROPSYCHIATRIC TESTS

Electroencephalogram (EEG). Determines electrical activity useful in diagnosing seizure disorder.

Computerized Tomography Scan (CT Scan). Assesses the structure and anatomy of the brain. Strokes, tumors, and bleeding can be diagnosed this way.

Magnetic Resonance Imaging (MRI). Using a magnetic field, MRI can detect small brain abnormalities better than CT scan.

Positron Emission Tomography (PET Scan). Uses specially prepared compounds to image metabolism and brain function.

Single Photon Emission Computerized Tomography (SPECT). Measures cerebral blood flow and may be useful in diagnosing stroke.

PSYCHOLOGICAL TESTING

These tests evaluate an individual's personality, coping resources, and emotional difficulties. They include IQ tests, neuropsychological test batteries (e.g., Halstead-Reitan battery), other psychological tests (e.g., Minnesota Multiphasic Personality Inventory), projective psychological tests (e.g., Rorschach test), and standard rating scales.

amount of adrenaline (epinephrine) from the sympathetic nervous system, which speeds the heart and respiration rate, raises blood pressure, and diverts blood flow to the muscles, among other responses. These physical reactions are appropriate for escaping from danger, but when they cause anxiety in many situations throughout the day they may prove detrimental.

People with physical disease often suffer from anxiety, and anxiety can be an early symptom of many psychiatric illnesses, including schizophrenia, depression, and sexual disorders. In addition, alcohol and drug use are prevalent in people with anxiety because of the temporary calming effect and escape they may provide.

When a person persistently overreacts to a situation, he or she may be suffering an anxiety disorder. The two most common disorders in our society are panic attacks and phobias.

Panic attacks can begin with a feeling of intense terror and impending doom followed by physical symptoms of anxiety (see below). They can last for minutes to hours, and the person experiencing the panic may not be aware of the cause. The symptoms may be so severe that the person goes to the emergency room thinking it is a heart attack. Agoraphobia, fear of going outside, can develop when the person fears being in a place far from help in the event of an attack. About 6 percent of the population will experience a panic attack at some time in their lives.

Phobias are unreasonable fears of objects, activities, or situations that result in avoidance or intense anxiety. People with phobias are aware of their irrational fear but are unable to do anything about it. Phobias fall into three categories: social phobia, simple phobia, and agoraphobia. Examples of social phobias are fear of public speaking and socializing due to a fear of humiliation. Social phobias affect 3 to 5 percent of the population. Simple phobias are common and include fear of snakes, spiders, and heights, among others. Agoraphobia is a fear of being trapped in a place outside the person's home, such as a supermarket or restaurant. People with extreme agoraphobia may become prisoners in their homes.

CAUSE

Biological and psychological causes may contribute to anxiety disorders. As in all illnesses, the physical body and the mind probably act in concert.

- *Hereditary factors.* Panic disorder tends to run in families. If an identical twin experiences panic attacks, 80 percent of the time the other twin suffers them as well.
- *Metabolic factors.* Three neurotransmitters—norepinephrine, gamma-aminobutyric acid (GABA), and serotonin—act as signals between brain cells

and may play a role in anxiety. Drugs that change the level of these neurotransmitters are useful in the treatment of anxiety.

- *Hyperventilation.* Rapid shallow breathing can cause a decrease in carbon dioxide in the blood, which has been associated with the feeling of anxiety. People with anxiety may not know they are hyperventilating. The anxiety and hyperventilation can be relieved by holding the breath or breathing into a paper bag, which causes carbon dioxide to increase in the blood.
- *Psychological factors.* Psychodynamic theory suggests that anxiety results from unconscious conflict, that is, a tension between certain wishes and desires, and counteracting guilt associated with these desires.
- *Past experience.* Learning theory links fearful situations in childhood to anxiety-provoking situations later. This has been used to explain agoraphobia, in which the fear of being abandoned in the past may lead to fear of public places.

DIAGNOSIS

Criteria used by the American Psychiatric Association to diagnose panic disorder include:

- More than four unexpected panic attacks in a 4-week period, or a 1-month period of persistent fear of an attack followed by an actual attack.
- Four or more of the following symptoms must be present during the attack: pounding heart, difficulty breathing, dizziness, chest pain, shaking, sweating, choking, nausea, depersonalization, numbness, fear of dying, flushes, fear of going crazy.

Some of these symptoms can be caused by drugs such as caffeine and amphetamines, or illness such as heart attack, hyperthyroidism, or an adrenal tumor. A thorough history and physical examination are important to identify an underlying disorder.

American Psychiatric Association criteria for diagnosing a social phobia include:

- A persistent fear of a situation because of fear of humiliation.
- Avoidance of a situation that provokes anxiety. This avoidance often interferes with work or social activities, such as speaking or eating in public. Despite the anxiety and fear, the person is still aware that it is unreasonable.

Criteria for a simple phobia are the same as for social phobia, except this fear of a situation or object excludes fear of humiliation.

American Psychiatric Association criteria for agoraphobia include:

- Fear of being alone in public places, particularly in situations from which a rapid exit would be difficult.
- The feared situations are avoided or endured with marked distress or anxiety about having a panic attack.

MALE/FEMALE DIFFERENCES

Panic disorder occurs equally in men and women. Agoraphobia is twice as common in women. Social phobia is slightly more common in males.

TREATMENT

Medication and psychotherapy are used to treat anxiety disorders. Benzodiazepines, (mild tranquilizers that include diazepam [Valium]) are the mainstay of drug therapy for panic attacks. These drugs (see box) can lead to physical dependence or withdrawal symptoms if stopped abruptly after long-term use; thus, they should be used under the guidance of a physician. Another class of drugs, beta-adrenergic blockers such as propranolol (Inderal and others), can prevent symptoms of pounding heart, shaking, and fear and are very useful for performers and public speakers who suffer from stage fright or social phobia.

Insight-oriented psychotherapy may help a person understand the origin and the response to the phobia. It is most effective when used with treatments that relieve anxiety symptoms.

HOME REMEDIES AND ALTERNATIVE THERAPIES

As you might imagine, there are many alternative therapies for anxiety, an affliction that has been around for ages. Self-help techniques such as meditation, deep breathing, imagery, and self-hypnosis all make us step back from the anxiety and can have lasting benefits. Meditation has been shown to counteract the fight-or-flight response in the brain that occurs in response to stressful situations. One technique called the relaxation response, named by Dr. Herbert Benson, a Harvard cardiologist, combines breathing and meditation to alleviate immediate as well as chronic symptoms of anxiety. (See description of relaxation techniques later in this chapter.)

A practical treatment for phobias is a behavioral technique called desensitization. Desensitization is the practice of confronting a specific fear gradually, starting with the least frightening situation and working up to the most frightening. For example, if you are afraid of enclosed spaces, start with standing in a small room with the door open. If the time comes when the anxiety diminishes, try

BEONZODIAZEPINES

The benzodiazepines are often called minor tranquilizers and are used to treat anxiety. The sedative property of some has made them popular for use in insomnia.

GENERIC NAME	(BRAND NAME)
alprazolam	(Xanax)
chlordiazepoxide	(Librium)
clonazepam	(Klonopin)
clorazepate	(Tranxene)
diazepam	(Valium)
flurazepam	(Dalmane)
lorazepam	(Ativan)
oxazepam	(Serax)
prazepam	(Centrax)
temazepam	(Restoril)
triazolam	(Halcion)

closing the door. If this becomes comfortable after some practice, enter a closet first with the door open then closed, and so on. Relaxation and breathing techniques as well as psychotherapy may be required in combination with desensitization to relieve the anxiety.

Exercise, yoga, t'ai chi, and other movement therapies are also effective in relieving anxiety. They can increase energy, concentration, and a feeling of well-being in addition to reducing stress. Hydrotherapy, or the use of water of varying temperatures, is an old home remedy that is being used in stress reduction. Mineral springs and spas are gaining popularity as sources of hydrotherapy.

Massage is still another popular relaxation technique. Other potentially helpful alternative therapies include music, dance, and other creative therapies, as well as pet therapy.

MENTAL DISORDERS IN CHILDREN

It is almost impossible to define what constitutes a "normal" child at each stage of growth and development, but in general, a child who functions well at home, in the neighborhood, and at school is unlikely to be suffering psychological problems. Nor does a transient problem with a teacher or an occasional fight with another child necessarily represent a mental health problem. Instead, parents should watch for behaviors that occur on a daily basis or last for a significant period of time. Children who fail to seek friends or are not sought as a friend among other children the same age may have emotional or psychological problems.

A family doctor is an excellent counselor for consultation on behaviors and problems—he or she knows the child and can help choose a mental health professional if necessary. A teacher who can assess grades as well as the child's behavior with peers may be helpful in identifying problems. (Mental disorders in children and adolescents are discussed below.)

MENTAL RETARDATION

DEFINITION

Developmental milestones are used as an approximate guide to normal functioning for children. At a certain age most children will respond to a parent's voice or learn to walk. Guidelines for age-appropriate behavior are not strict and if your child walks or talks a little later or earlier than other children it may not represent a problem. Standardized testing to evaluate mental retardation should be done if there is a concern of a delay in development. About 1 percent of children are found to be mentally retarded.

Many mentally retarded children are born with other physical abnormalities such as seizures, impaired hearing, or heart problems. They are also three to four times more likely to suffer from other mental disorders such as learning disabilities and bed-wetting than the general population.

MALE/FEMALE DIFFERENCES

The ratio of mentally retarded boys to girls is 3:2.

CAUSE

A cause of mental retardation is identified in less than half of all cases. Mild mental retardation is more common in lower socioeconomic classes, but moderate and severe mental retardation are similar in all classes. Negative influences in the home such as child neglect and lack of social and language stimulation may be factors in the development of milder cases.

Hereditary disorders are found in 25 percent of mentally retarded children and usually are associated with severe retardation. Down syndrome is the most common hereditary form of mental retardation. It is caused by a chromosomal abnormality and occurs in 1 in 700 births in the United States. Although women of any age can have a child with Down syndrome, the risk rises dramatically after age 35. This disorder, along with many other hereditary and congenital disorders, can be diagnosed in utero with ultrasound or amniocentesis. Children with Down syndrome have distinctive facial features from birth and are developmentally delayed in speech and muscle coordination, among other skills.

Many illnesses contracted during pregnancy can cause

mental retardation, especially during the first few weeks when organ systems are being formed, emphasizing the importance of early prenatal care. Maternal infections such as rubella (German measles), syphilis, and cytomegalovirus are among those that can cause retardation.

Childhood illness and injury can also cause mental retardation after birth. The most prevalent of these are encephalitis and meningitis, which affect the brain directly. Other causes are trauma to the head from child abuse injuries, motor vehicle accidents, and other mishaps.

DIAGNOSIS

Psychological testing may be performed before school age to determine mental retardation. Because of the many variations in child development, very young children may develop more slowly than their peers but not be mentally retarded.

American Psychiatric Association criteria of mental retardation include:

- Significantly subaverage IQ (70 or below)
- Concurrent deficits in adaptive functioning in areas of social skills, responsibility, communication, independence, daily living skills, and self-sufficiency for age
- Onset before age 18

TREATMENT

Prevention of mental retardation through improved maternal prenatal care and infection control is the best treatment. Once mental retardation is diagnosed, a child's social and intellectual functioning can be improved by programs designed to stimulate development. School programs are now available for speech and language training, play therapy, and teaching social skills.

Parents may find it very demanding and psychologically difficult to care for a mentally retarded child. Parental counseling is essential to help with the stresses and can identify anger and guilt that may be present in these situations.

HOME REMEDIES AND ALTERNATIVE THERAPIES

Dance and music therapy have been used in children with mental retardation, as well as other disabilities, to improve social interaction. A child who is unable to communicate with words may find pleasure in these activities.

PREVENTION

Proper prenatal care may prevent infections leading to mental retardation in unborn children.

EVALUATION BY A MENTAL HEALTH PROFESSIONAL

History. Information is obtained about cultural background, the marriage, other children, and the child's development.

Evaluation techniques. Mental health professionals spend time with the child drawing, playing with toys, and telling stories in order to observe the child's usual behavior, thinking, and interaction with others.

Psychological testing. Tests are available for children of all ages to assess intelligence, language, and attention span.

Medical exam. A physical exam can diagnose many conditions, including malnutrition, lead poisoning, and impaired hearing, which can cause learning and behavior problems.

TREATMENT

Parental involvement. Parents are always a part of the treatment of children. The parents may also receive counseling to cope with stress or improve family interactions.

Play therapy. Therapists often use games and stories to act out emotions and teach coping.

Psychotherapy. This is helpful in certain situations, especially for older children. Supportive therapy may be used to deal with stressful situations, such as a parent's divorce. A behavioral technique that is often employed is "time out": The child knows he or she will be removed to a specific area for a brief time when a certain behavior occurs. This gives the child a chance to calm down and see that problem behavior is not appropriate. Family therapy can also be helpful, especially for rebellious teenagers.

Medication. Drugs are used in conjunction with psychotherapy for certain disorders such as attention deficit hyperactivity disorder and depression. Children should be taken off the drugs periodically to minimize side effects and to see if the underlying disorder has improved. Most drugs should be tapered over time to prevent withdrawal symptoms.

AUTISM

DEFINITION

An autistic child has severe problems with social interaction, communication, and imagination. These children do not bond or emotionally connect to parents even when they are held. Having an autistic child is very difficult for parents, who often suffer from stress, frustration, and guilt.

Autistic disorder occurs in about 4 of 10,000 children. About two-thirds of autistic children do not improve function and communication in adulthood, and are dependent on others for the activities of daily living. There is a better prognosis for children who can communicate with language.

CAUSE

In the past autism was blamed on parental neglect, but studies have failed to support this. Now it is thought that certain conditions predispose to autism, such as maternal rubella infection, encephalitis, lack of oxygen during birth, and certain hereditary diseases. Siblings of autistic children are more likely to suffer autism and mental retardation, suggesting a genetic component to this condition.

MALE/FEMALE DIFFERENCES

Autistic disorder is three to four times more common in boys.

DIAGNOSIS

The American Psychiatric Association specifies that at least eight of the following characteristics must be present to diagnose autism.

IMPAIRMENT IN SOCIAL INTERACTION

- Lack of awareness of the existence or feelings of others
- Abnormal seeking of or response to comfort at times of distress
- Impaired imitation, such as waving good-bye
- Abnormal social play and preference for solitary activities
- Gross impairment in ability to make friendships

IMPAIRMENT IN VERBAL AND NONVERBAL COMMUNICATION AND IN IMAGINATION

- No language, facial expression, or other communication

- Abnormal nonverbal communication, as in eye-to-eye gaze, facial expression, body posture
- Absence of imagination or fantasy
- Abnormalities in the production of speech (e.g., monotonous tone or high pitch)
- Repetitive speech, use of "you" when "I" is meant, or irrelevant remarks
- Impairment in the ability to sustain a conversation with others despite adequate speech

RESTRICTED ACTIVITIES AND INTERESTS

- Stereotyped body movements (e.g., spinning, head-banging)
- Preoccupation with parts of objects or attachment to unusual objects
- Marked distress over changes in trivial aspects of environment
- Unreasonable insistence on following routines in detail
- Restricted range of interest (e.g., interested only in lining up objects)
- Onset during infancy or childhood

TREATMENT

There is no cure or medication for this disorder. Most autistic children require daily care throughout their lives, but some individuals can function in work and the community.

Autistic children function best in a highly structured environment. Classroom training for language and communication skills and approaches to improve disruptive behaviors are helpful. Controlling problem behaviors is important both for family function and social interaction.

HOME REMEDIES AND ALTERNATIVE THERAPIES

Creative art therapies such as painting, sculpture, dance, and music are helpful in bringing these children out of social withdrawal and isolation. These therapies are innovative attempts to break down the communication barriers that exist in autism. Special education programs using dolphins, horses, farm animals, and household pets also have been helpful in some cases.

SEPARATION ANXIETY

DEFINITION

Strangers and new situations can be scary to a young child. While most children eventually become comfortable in these situations, the child with separation anxiety disorder fears separation from the parent more than the new situation. He or she may choose to stay at home instead of playing with other children or going to school. Some children have trouble sleeping without being next to their parents, while others develop physical symptoms such as headache or stomachache at the thought of separation. These are signs of a more serious problem, and professional help may be necessary.

School phobia is a type of separation anxiety disorder that can occur in a child who previously went to school. Children may scream or make excuses not to get out of bed just to be able to stay at home.

MALE/FEMALE DIFFERENCES

This disorder occurs equally in boys and girls.

CAUSE

Separation anxiety often develops after stress such as the death of a parent or pet, illness, or change in environment. In the background may be an overprotective parent who gives the message to a child that the world is a dangerous place.

Hidden behind separation anxiety disorder often is a complex set of unconscious and subconscious reactions. The disorder may actually be a way of dealing with the hostility to the parent who has prevented the child from having a normal relationship with peers. For the parent, being overprotective may cover up hidden hostility against the child and the desire to be free of him or her. By preventing dangers to the child through overprotection, the parent has found a socially acceptable way to resolve his or her hostility. The child may also harbor hostility to the parent and in separation from the parent he or she cannot be sure that the things secretly wished for have not actually happened to the parent. Therefore the child feels compelled to stay at home to keep a watch on the parent.

DIAGNOSIS

This condition is characterized by excessive anxiety concerning separation from those to whom the child is attached lasting at least 2 weeks and occurring before age 18. According to the American Psychiatric Association criteria, three of the following conditions should be present to make a diagnosis:

- Unrealistic and persistent worry about possible harm befalling caregivers or fear that they will leave
- Unrealistic and persistent worry that the child will be separated from the caregiver either through accident, death, or kidnapping
- Persistent refusal to go to school in order to stay at home

- Persistent refusal to go to sleep without being near a major caregiver or to sleep away from home
- Persistent avoidance of being alone
- Repeated nightmares about separation
- Complaints of physical symptoms on school days
- Recurrent signs of excessive anxiety when separated from home or caregivers

TREATMENT

Simple separation anxiety does not require medical treatment. A pediatrician may be able to treat mild cases of school phobia, but a child with a persistent problem should receive psychotherapy.

HOME REMEDIES AND ALTERNATIVE THERAPIES

Reinforcing the child's self-esteem through love and approval goes a long way in building social confidence. If a child is slow to warm up, introducing new situations slowly and with reassurance can decrease the anxiety level. There is more than one way to make friends and participate, and each child's pace should be respected.

Treatment of school phobia begins with the rule that the child must go to school every day. Only by regularly attending school will the child gain the independence necessary for normal maturation.

BED-WETTING (ENURESIS)

DEFINITION

Most children start toilet training at age 2 or 3 (girls may start before boys), but most experts are not concerned about a child of 4 or 5 who still wets the bed. In a child who is usually dry at night, accidents and periods of wetting may recur especially during stress. By puberty most children no longer wet at night, but the problem persists in an unknown number of adults.

MALE/FEMALE DIFFERENCES

At age 5, 7 percent of boys and 3 percent of girls are affected.

CAUSE

Several theories exist to explain bed-wetting. A genetic component is supported by the 75 percent incidence of bed-wetting among other family members. Bed-wetting can also be a sign of physical illness such as urinary tract infection, seizure, or diabetes. Bed-wetting in some children may be due to a lag in development of the nervous system's controls on elimination.

Stress such as childhood hospitalization or the birth of a sibling may be a factor. Even when bed-wetting is not psychological in origin, it can cause emotional problems. The embarrassment of bed-wetting may prevent a child from going to parties or away to camp, and the child may be the target of ridicule from friends.

DIAGNOSIS

American Psychiatric Association criteria for a diagnosis of bed-wetting include:

- Repeated urination during the day or night into bed or clothes
- At least one event per month after age 6, two events per month between 5 and 6
- Chronological age at least 5, mental age at least 4
- Not due to a physical disorder such as diabetes or infection

TREATMENT

The large majority of children eventually outgrow bed-wetting. In the meantime the self-help techniques outlined below may help. In refractory cases, medications to help bladder muscles can be effective. The drug imipramine (Tofranil) sometimes resolves the problem by increasing contraction of the urethral sphincter.

HOME REMEDIES AND ALTERNATIVE THERAPY

Treatment starts with reassurance from the parents and praise for each dry night. Parents should be aware that the bed-wetting child cannot help himself and that punishment will only make the situation worse. Although most children will stop bed-wetting after a period of time, early treatment is recommended to limit psychological and social consequences.

A simple treatment effective in about one-third of cases is based on the fact that salt retains water in the body. The parents should restrict the child's intake of liquids after supper while providing salty snacks such as pretzels and potato chips. While this dietary treatment is not a cure, it may give the child a feeling of control over the problem.

A bedwetting alarm is very effective for about two-thirds of children. At the first appearance of moisture the alarm wakes the child so he or she can go to the bathroom. The theory behind this device is that the child will associate the sound of the alarm with urination and lead to better control in the future. Successful treatment usually takes 1 month. However, it may not be easy for the family to tolerate the alarm, as many bed wetters

are heavy sleepers and the rest of the family may respond while the child remains asleep.

When none of these methods cures bed-wetting, the child should be encouraged that he will most likely outgrow the problem.

ELIMINATION DISORDERS (ENCOPRESIS)

DEFINITION

Children can develop bowel control problems such as constipation and/or passage of feces in inappropriate places. One percent of children age 5 have this disorder and need professional help. (Some children with elimination problems also are bed wetters.)

CAUSE

When children have problems with involuntary soiling it may be related to constipation and overflow around it (part of the stool may be liquid). Constipation can develop for several reasons, including anxiety, dehydration, or painful defecation from an anal fissure. Children may enter a cycle of constipation leading to rectal enlargement, lack of pressure sensation in the rectum, and pain. This cycle leads to physical and psychological suffering for the child and parents.

Many children with feces problems have been abused or neglected, and this condition may be a way of expressing anger.

Rarely, infections and congenital abnormalities cause rectal enlargement and difficulty with bowel movements. These conditions should be and can be diagnosed by a pediatrician.

DIAGNOSIS

Criteria for diagnosing encopresis:

- Repeated passage of feces in inappropriate places whether involuntary or intentional
- At least one event per month for 6 months
- Age at least 4
- Not due to a physical disorder

TREATMENT

The pediatrician should become involved early in this condition if a child has difficulty with the bowels. Treatment is a slow process and may consist of enemas, stool softeners, and adding fiber to the diet. A mental health professional can help both child and parents with underlying stresses and psychological consequences of the situation.

MALE/FEMALE DIFFERENCES

The disorder is more common in boys than girls.

ATTENTION DEFICIT HYPERACTIVITY DISORDER (ADHD)

DEFINITION

Attention deficit hyperactivity disorder, also known as hyperactivity, is one of the most common behavioral disorders of childhood. Children with this condition display a limited attention span, impulsiveness, and excessive movement during the day and night. School can be especially difficult because long periods of quiet and sitting are expected. The child may be punished by parents and teachers for overactivity that he cannot control.

CAUSE

While researchers have tried to link hyperactivity to cerebral palsy, epilepsy, and toxins in the environment, there is no established cause for this condition. In some cases the children may be victims of child abuse or neglect.

DIAGNOSIS

Criteria for diagnosing hyperactivity (at least eight of the following must be present for at least 6 months), as established by the American Psychiatric Association, stipulate that the child:

- Often fidgets or squirms in seat
- Has difficulty remaining seated when required to do so
- Is easily distracted
- Has difficulty awaiting turns in games or group situations
- Often blurts out answers to questions before they have been completed
- Has difficulty following through on instructions from others
- Has difficulty sustaining attention in tasks or play activities
- Often shifts from one uncompleted activity to another
- Has difficulty playing quietly
- Often talks excessively
- Often interrupts
- Often does not listen to what is being said to him or her
- Often loses things necessary for school or home (e.g., toys, pencils, books)

- Often engages in physically dangerous activities without considering possible consequences
- Onset before age 7

A professional evaluation is necessary to diagnose normal but active behavior or medical illness such as thyroid disease. The diagnosis of hyperactivity is made only after the behavior has been present for more than 6 months and it interferes with the child's intellectual and social development.

MALE/FEMALE DIFFERENCES

The condition occurs 10 times more in boys than girls.

TREATMENT

Medications that stimulate the central nervous system such as methylphenidate (Ritalin), dextroamphetamine (Dexedrine), and pemoline (Cylert) are successful in up to 80 perent of hyperactive children. Even though they are stimulants, these medications decrease motor activity and increase attention span in children. Side effects occur in less than 5 percent of children and include insomnia, weight loss, and headaches.

Psychotherapy and counseling for the child and family may improve relationships and help with the social or school-related consequences of the disorder. Counseling should be used along with medication.

Hyperactive children grow up to lead normal lives more than half the time, but there is an increased tendency for some to have problems with antisocial behavior. Adults with persistent hyperactivity can also benefit from medication, psychotherapy, and choosing a profession that does not require long periods of attention.

HOME REMEDIES AND ALTERNATIVE THERAPIES

Numerous nondrug treatments have been proposed for hyperactivity, but none has been proven more effective than medication. The most well-documented therapy is restricting food additives in the child's diet. Although studies suggest this is far less effective than stimulant medication, a carefully constructed diet may be worth trying, either alone or in combination with drug treatment. Contrary to media claims, there is little or no evidence that restricting sugar intake can help to control hyperactivity.

Some studies suggest that reducing the variety of sensory stimuli may help hyperactive children to focus on educational tasks. However, behavior modification techniques that attempt to control hyperactivity are very time-consuming, and labor intensive, and there is no evidence that their effects endure. Even more dubious "remedies" include a program of exposure to fluorescent light, heavy metal chelation therapy, and megavitamin treatments. Large doses of vitamins should be avoided due to the possibility of adverse side effects.

LEARNING DISABILITIES

DEFINITION

Children who learn below the level that is expected in reading, language, or arithmetic are labeled "learning disabled." This category includes about 15 percent of school-age children. Learning difficulties can be mild, disappearing with time, or they can be severe, having a lasting impact on the child's future. A learning difficulty may also be the result of a medical problem such as hearing or vision impairment. Any child suspected of having learning difficulty should be evaluated by a professional to distinguish these possibilities and start a program of instruction tailored to the child's needs.

Reading problems—formerly called dyslexia—are the most common learning disabilities. Children with reading problems read more slowly, have poor comprehension, and may have trouble writing and speaking aloud. Attention deficit hyperactivity disorder may accompany a reading disorder.

CAUSE

There is no known cause of learning disabilities. Children with neurologic problems or prenatal injury are more likely to develop a learning disability. If a child is below the expected level in school, there is a possibility that a physical problem such as poor vision or hearing or an emotional problem such as depression is responsible.

MALE/FEMALE DIFFERENCES

Most learning disabilities are more common in boys than girls.

DIAGNOSIS

Criteria for diagnosing this type of developmental disorder:

- Reading, writing, or arithmetic skills, as measured by a standardized, individually administered test, are markedly below the expected level, given the child's schooling and intellectual capacity.
- The disturbances above significantly interfere with academic achievement or activities of daily living.
- Not due to a defect in vision or hearing or a neurological disorder.

TREATMENT

Special education for children with learning disabilities is required by law in public schools, and it is essential for a child to be tested in a standardized way so he or she can receive these services. One technique to improve reading uses phonetics or the association of sounds with written letters. Others encourage reading aloud while tracing letters to overcome the difficulty in visually perceiving words. Tutoring should focus on the child's strengths to preserve self-esteem and motivation.

The success of treatment depends on the child's intelligence and the quality of the treatment. Many children can learn to compensate and become high achievers.

HOME REMEDIES AND ALTERNATIVE THERAPIES

Creative art therapies such as painting, sculpture, dance, and music may be helpful and a boost to self-esteem in some children with learning disabilities. They offer new ways to communicate outside of reading and writing.

ADOLESCENT MENTAL HEALTH

Adolescence is marked by turmoil, a young adult's struggle to establish independence and a unique personality. Rebellious attitudes and mood swings are part of normal development and are not cause for concern. The desire to fit in with peers is a healthy sign at this age.

Some adolescent problems have their roots in childhood. Signs of abnormal behavior can be found in home, school, and leisure activities. Poor grades, a lack of interests or hobbies, violence, truancy, drug and alcohol use, and sexual promiscuity should be taken seriously by parents. Problems such as depression and talk of suicide require immediate help.

EATING DISORDERS

DEFINITION

There are two major forms of eating disorder, anorexia nervosa (severe self-starvation) and bulimia (binge eating and purging). The prevalence of these conditions has increased dramatically in recent decades. (Both conditions occur much more frequently in girls.) Anorexia nervosa affects 1 in 100 to 200 girls between ages 12 and 18. The problem begins when a girl is unhappy with her appearance and starts dieting. She may say she feels fat and continue to diet, when she is in fact underweight. Almost all teenage girls diet at one time, but most do not develop anorexia nervosa.

When a girl becomes profoundly underweight, physical symptoms may develop, including sensitivity to cold, constipation, weakness, leg swelling, and growth of fine body hair. Menstruation may cease after more weight loss. Most symptoms disappear when weight returns to normal. There is a risk of death in 5 to 18 percent of people with anorexia nervosa.

Peculiar behaviors may develop as a result of starvation, perhaps because people with anorexia nervosa still feel hungry. For example, an anorexic may prepare elaborate meals for others and not eat them herself, or she may collect recipes. Anxiety begins to surround any situation where food is present while the anorexic denies that there is a problem.

Bulimia starts in late adolescence and can continue to the mid-30s. At one time it was estimated the 5 to 10 percent of women in college suffered from bulimia. A person with bulimia eats large amounts of high-calorie foods secretly and then vomits, exercises to excess, or takes laxatives and diuretics to keep weight down. Someone suffering from bulimia lives in fear of gaining weight. Despite bingeing and purging, most bulimics are of normal weight, making this disease very difficult to recognize.

In rare cases bulimia can cause death from electrolyte imbalances and dehydration. More commonly, laxatives and vomiting can cause dental problems, constipation, and rupture of the esophagus. Peculiar behaviors may also develop to enable the person with bulimia to obtain a large amount of food, for example, hoarding or stealing food.

MALE/FEMALE DIFFERENCES

Anorexia occurs 20 times more commonly in women than men and bulimia occurs 10 times more commonly in women than men.

CAUSE

Anorexia nervosa is more common in women with low self-esteem, family members with the disease, and depression. Less commonly, it develops in young dancers or athletes, such as gymnasts or runners whose coaches stress slimness. The problem usually begins at a time when a girl becomes concerned about emerging sexuality and bodily changes. She becomes convinced that she is too fat and restricts her eating, sometimes to emaciation. There is also sometimes a power struggle that develops in the home, which may be a reflection of difficulty with separation from parents.

Factors that produce bulimia are often similar to those for self-starvation. Obesity in adolescence may also predispose to this disorder.

DIAGNOSIS

Criteria for diagnosing anorexia nervosa, as established by the American Psychiatric Association, include:

- Refusal to maintain body weight over a minimal normal weight for age and height, for example, 15 percent below expected; or failure to make expected weight gain during period of growth
- Intense fear of gaining weight or becoming fat, even though underweight
- Disturbance in the way a person sees her body weight, size, or shape, for example, the person claims to feel fat even when emaciated
- In females, absence of at least three consecutive menstrual cycles when there is no other explanation

Criteria for diagnosing bulimia nervosa, as established by the American Psychiatric Association, include:

- Recurrent episodes of binge eating (rapid consumption of food in a discrete period of time)
- A feeling of lack of control over eating behavior during the eating binges
- Regularly engaging in either self-induced vomiting, use of laxatives or diuretics, strict dieting or fasting, or vigorous exercise in order to prevent weight gain
- A minimum average of two binge-eating episodes a week for at least 3 months
- Persistent overconcern with body shape and weight

TREATMENT

Women with anorexia nervosa can be very difficult to treat because of the large component of denial about their weight loss and body size. Ideally, treatment should be sought when the first signs of self-starvation appear and before weight loss has become dramatic or dangerous. The starvation state itself may cloud the anorexic's ability to understand what is happening or participate in therapy. The longer the disorder goes untreated, the more likely it is to become chronic.

Parents should discuss concerns about abnormal eating behavior, even before significant weight loss, with a physician. The first step in treatment is weight gain, as it is difficult to deal with emotional problems while weight is dangerously low. Hospitalization is required when low weight is dangerous—at about 25 percent below the person's normal weight.

Individual psychotherapy is essential for successful treatment and resolution of the underlying issues. Family psychotherapy and family support groups may also be needed. Some suggestions for the family are: do not feel guilty, do not give excess sympathy, do not make food an issue, be open and communicative, and maintain family normalcy.

Treatment for bulimia differs in that the focus is on altering the eating behavior. People with bulimia should keep a record of their binges and learn to recognize situations that make them vulnerable, such as stress, loneliness, or hunger. They should learn to develop methods to deal with the situations, such as exercise, work, or calling a support person. Once the behavior is resolved, individual or group psychotherapy and consultations with a support group for people with eating disorders can be beneficial.

HOME REMEDIES AND ALTERNATIVE THERAPIES

Exercise from early adolescence may be beneficial in preventing these disorders if done in moderation. Keeping a fit and strong body at any age may improve self-esteem and prevent the cycle of yo-yo dieting that can lead to food cravings and excessive weight loss.

DEPRESSION AND SUICIDE IN ADOLESCENTS

Adolescents suffer from depression similar to adults, but it can be more difficult to recognize because mood swings are normal and common at this stage. Signs of depression include social isolation, tearfulness, change in weight or sleep, and destructive behavior. (Also see "Depression and Other Mood Disorders.")

Persistent depression can lead to suicide attempts. While suicide occurs in all age groups, it is the third leading cause of death among teenagers. Other problems associated with increased teenage suicide are aggression and conduct disorder, drug and alcohol abuse either in the adolescent or the parents, and conflict in the home.

Treatment with psychotherapy and medication is helpful for depression in adolescence. Hospitalization may be necessary if there is a significant risk of suicide. Special attention should be given to problems of drug and alcohol addiction, including the need for detoxification in a hospital setting if necessary.

DEPRESSION AND OTHER MOOD DISORDERS

DEFINITION

Depression affects millions of people each year in our society and is a major cause of work-related disability, utilization of medical services, and drug use. In the public mind, depression is often confused with unhappiness or a reaction stemming from a death of a loved one. These are natural emotions but do not represent a psychiatric illness. Depression, on the other hand, is a dis-

order that affects both the mind and the body in profound ways. A person with depression experiences great distress and is often inconsolable. He or she may suffer from sadness and guilt leading to outbursts of crying or lack of pleasure in all activities. In some cases there are tragic consequences, such as inability to eat or drink and suicide.

The two basic categories of mood disorders are: major depressive disorder and bipolar, or manic-depressive, disorder. Major depression is marked by persistent, extreme, and inappropriate low mood, while bipolar depression is much less common and is marked by periods of excited states as well as periods of depression.

Mood disorder is one of the most common and currently most treatable forms of mental illness. It is estimated that 23 percent of people will have two or more symptoms of depression, and 6 percent will have major depression or dysthymia (a mild form of depression) at some point in their lifetime. About 1 percent of the population has had bipolar disorder. At all ages it is important to seek help for symptoms of depression because of the risk of suicide.

CAUSE

In many cases there is no identifiable cause; in others a distressing event such as the death of a loved one or a life stress such as the loss of a job may trigger depression. Biological and psychosocial factors may interact and produce a mood disorder in a vulnerable person.

There is evidence that a biochemical imbalance of the chemical messengers (neurotransmitters) that transmit signals between brain cells is associated with depression (chemical imbalance may also play a role in other mental disorders, such as schizophrenia). Specifically, a deficiency of the neurotransmitters norepinephrine and serotonin may be present. Antidepressants mitigate depression be-

SUICIDE

Suicide, the most dangerous consequence of depression, may be a result of the person's hopelessness or the feeling that life is not worth living. Suicidal thoughts are most common among the elderly, adolescents, men, alcoholics, and people who live alone. A family history of suicide or previous suicide attempt indicates an increased risk. A doctor should inquire about thoughts of suicide, since they are common reflections of the pain and anguish that depressed people experience. Suicidal thoughts always merit immediate and special care, with hospitalization as necessary to ensure the safety of the patient.

cause they increase the supply of these neurotransmitters, thereby correcting the imbalance. Hormonal imbalance is also related to some forms of depression. For example, changes in cortisol seem to be related to sleep disturbance, which is present in most types of depression.

A genetic link to depression is supported by adoption and twin studies, which indicate that vulnerability to mood disorders is inherited in certain people. Major depression is 1.5 to 3 times more common in close relatives of people with this disorder than in the general population. Bipolar disorder shows a higher rate of genetic transmission than unipolar illness.

Personality traits such as passivity and dependency may increase some people's risk of developing depression. Other risks for depression may be borderline personality disorder and alcohol or drug abuse.

MALE/FEMALE DIFFERENCES

Bipolar disorder is equally common in men and women. Major depression is estimated to be twice as common in women as men.

DIAGNOSIS

Criteria used by the American Psychiatric Association to diagnose a major depressive episode include:

1. At least five of the following symptoms have been present during a 2-week period and represent a change from previous functioning; at least one of the symptoms is either depressed mood or loss of interest or pleasure.
   - Depressed mood most of every day
   - Diminished interest or pleasure in almost all activities most of every day
   - Significant weight loss or weight gain when not dieting
   - Insomnia or hypersomnia nearly every day
   - Restlessness or slowing down nearly every day
   - Fatigue or loss of energy nearly every day
   - Feelings of worthlessness or excessive guilt nearly every day
   - Diminished ability to think or concentrate nearly every day
   - Recurrent thoughts of death or suicide, with or without a plan
2. A physical illness or reaction to the death of a loved one is not responsible for the reaction.

American Psychiatric Association criteria to diagnose a manic episode include:

1. A distinct period of abnormally and persistently elevated or irritable mood.

2. During the period of mood disturbance, at least three of the following symptoms have persisted.
   - Inflated self-esteem
   - Decreased need for sleep
   - Pressure to keep talking
   - Racing thoughts
   - Easily distractable
   - Excessive involvement in pleasurable activities that have a high potential for painful consequences, (e.g., buying sprees, sexual promiscuity)
3. Mood disturbance severe enough to cause impairment in work, social activities, or relationships, or to necessitate hospitalization to prevent harm to self or others.

Criteria for diagnosing bipolar disorders, as established by the American Psychiatric Association, include:

1. Bipolar Disorder, Mixed
   - Current episode involves symptoms of both manic and major depressive episodes intermixed and alternating every few days
   - Prominent depressive symptoms lasting at least a full day
2. Bipolar Disorder, Manic
   - Currently in a manic episode
3. Bipolar Disorder, Depressed
   - Has had one or more manic episode
   - Currently in a major depressive episode

Criteria for seasonal affective disorder (SAD; depression that recurs at a particular time of year):

- A temporal relationship between the onset of an episode of depression and a particular 60-day period of the year
- Full remissions occurring within a particular 60-day period of the year
- At least three episodes of mood disturbance that have demonstrated this temporal seasonal relationship

Dysthymia, a milder form of depression, is a chronic state that lasts for years. Individuals with this disorder can suffer many of the same symptoms as depression but in a less intense way. People with dysthymia are at risk for anxiety, eating, personality, and substance abuse disorders.

Symptom checklists like the Hamilton Rating Scale for Depression can be helpful to the health care professional in distinguishing "the blues" from depression (many family doctors fail to diagnose depression). People may be misdiagnosed because they present predominantly physical symptoms or may be reluctant to mention moods or feelings because of the social stigma attached to mental

DRUGS TO TREAT DEPRESSION

TRICYCLIC ANTIDEPRESSANTS

Imipramine (Tofranil)
Desipramine (Norpramin)
Nortriptyline (Pamelor)
Amytriptyline (Elavil)
Doxepin (Sinequan)

Indication: First-line treatment of depression.

Side Effects: The most common side effects are constipation, dry mouth, blurry vision, impotence, and urinary problems. Some of these drugs, such as Elavil, can cause sedation. In the elderly memory loss, low blood pressure on standing, and heart rhythm problems can occur. Most people can find simple solutions to side effects, such as using a stool softener to relieve constipation.

Interactions with Food or Medication: Any time you start a new medication your doctor should advise you on possible drug interactions with other medications you may be taking. Other substances to avoid are alcohol, sedatives, and oral contraceptives.

MONOAMINE OXIDASE (MAO) INHIBITORS

Tranylcypromine (Parnate)
Phenelzine (Nardil)
Isocarboxazid (Marplan)

Indication: These medications are used if tricyclic antidepressants are not effective. Although MAO inhibitors are very effective and act more quickly, they have potentially more serious side effects.

Side Effects: These drugs can cause a life-threatening elevation in blood pressure when combined with certain foods and wines. They also can cause insomnia, low blood pressure on standing, and impotence.

Interactions with Food or Medication: Foods rich in tyramine should be avoided completely while taking this medication and until 2 weeks after stopping treatment. Tyramine-rich foods include certain red wines (e.g., Chianti), aged cheese, liver, and pickled meats. (A complete list should be provided by your doctor.) Medications to avoid are those used for asthma, narcotics (especially Demerol), selective serotonin reuptake inhibitors, amphetamines, cocaine, or over-the-counter cold formulas with dextromethorphan.

SELECTIVE SEROTONIN REUPTAKE INHIBITORS

Fluoxetine (Prozac)
Sertraline (Zoloft)
Paroxetine hydrochloride (Paxil)

Indications: Used for depression, these drugs have gained in popularity because of limited side effects and can be used either as first-line treatment or after failure of other medication.

Side Effects: The most common side effects are nausea, insomnia, headache, and weight changes.

Interactions with Food or Medication: People on these medications should avoid monoamine oxidase inhibitors, alcohol, sedatives, and oral contraceptives.

LITHIUM

Indications: This is the drug of choice for mania, or bipolar disorder, used in combination with either an antipsychotic or antidepressant medication.

Side Effects: Common adverse affects include weight gain, tremor, fatigue, and frequent urination.

Interactions with Food or Medication: Avoid most diuretics (used in treating high blood pressure) and over-the-counter anti-inflammatory medication, which can increase the level of lithium in the blood.

ANTICONVULSANT

Carbamazepine (Tegretol)
Valproic acid (Depakote)

Indications: In lithium-resistant patients carbamazepine (first) and valproic acid (second) can be tried for the treatment of bipolar disorder.

Side Effects: The most common side effects of carbamazepine and valproic acid are nausea, drowsiness, dizziness, and blurred vision. With carbamazepine there is a minor risk of liver toxicity and a small (1 in 50,000) but serious risk of the disorder aplastic anemia.

Interactions with Food and Medication: Carbamazepine and valproic acid should not be taken with alcohol. Other anticonvulsant medication can alter the levels of these drugs in the blood.

illness. In addition, some people do not seek help for depression because of lack of insurance coverage. Education of health care providers about diagnosis and treatment may help correct these problems.

TREATMENT

Episodes and recurrences of depression can be limited and in some cases cured with therapy. The three basic treatments are medication, psychotherapy, and electroconvulsive therapy (ECT), which are used alone or in combination, depending on the severity and duration of symptoms.

Medications. Antidepressant medications correct an imbalance in neurotransmitters and fall into three categories: tricyclic antidepressants, monoamine oxidase (MAO) inhibitors, and selective serotonin reuptake inhibitors. Lithium is the drug of choice for mania and bipolar disorder. The drugs are prescribed in gradually increasing dosages and may take several weeks to be effective. If there is no improvement or if side effects are a problem, a new drug may be added or substituted. Treatment generally lasts at least 6 months. (See the box "Drugs to Treat Depression," on the opposite page, for information on medications.)

Before prescribing an antidepressant drug a doctor should perform a physical exam (these medications can pose a risk for people with certain medical conditions). An infrequent but serious side effect of MAO inhibitors is sudden hypertension brought on by interaction with foods containing tyramine. This is a life-threatening state, and your doctor should provide a list of symptoms to watch for and foods to avoid. Less serious side effects may occur and should also be discussed with a doctor in an effort to find a medication that permits a good quality of life.

Electroconvulsive therapy (ECT) is a safe, painless, and effective treatment for depression and bears no resemblance to the "shock therapy" of the past. During this treatment an electric current is passed through the brain and the only visible sign is twitching of the eyelids. It is used when rapid results are vital, such as with acutely suicidal patients or those in whom drug treatments have failed or cannot be administered. Treatments are generally given three times a week for 2 weeks. The only common side effect is temporary memory loss.

Psychotherapy is generally used in conjunction with either ECT or medication. Many forms are available and should be tailored to individual needs. After the medication begins to take effect, psychotherapy can help the person understand the factors that contributed to the depression. For some people low self-esteem is a major issue, whereas others need to expose angry feelings. Many depressed people also benefit from making new social contacts and developing new activities.

HOME REMEDIES AND ALTERNATIVE THERAPIES

Many therapies outside of medication and psychotherapy are used for treatment of depression. These alternative treatments can help treat anxiety, low self-esteem, lack of energy, and isolation.

Exercise and yoga may partially relieve depression and boost confidence, perhaps by generating chemicals in the brain called endorphins, which may contribute to feelings of well-being and energy that can persist even after exercise ends.

Relaxation and meditation have been shown to reduce the anxiety that may be prominent in some people with depression. Imagery techniques have been shown to boost self-esteem. In guided imagery, depressed people may be helped to envision situations in which they receive praise from someone they admire and then use the imagined praise to improve feelings of self-worth.

Creative art therapies such as dance, painting, and sculpture can open communication and break down barriers when talking is too difficult for depressed people. Pet therapy, in which a person establishes a connection with another living creature, also may be helpful.

Light therapy (treatment with special kinds of bright lights) has been shown to be beneficial for seasonal affective disorder.

PERSONALITY DISORDERS

DEFINITION

Personality is the unique combination of attitudes, thoughts, behaviors, and temperament that each person develops in interaction with the environment. These characteristics are both inherited and shaped by life events and experiences. Personality disorders may develop when personality is too rigid or inflexible, leading to unhappiness or poor functioning at work and in relationships. People with these disorders may lack empathy, have difficulty with intimate relationships, or be very annoying. Manifestations of personality disorders usually begin in adolescence, the age when the personality stabilizes and matures.

CAUSE

Genes and environment shape our personality styles. Consequently, when one identical twin has a personality disorder the other may be more likely to have it than would be predicted in the general population. Some personality disorders have been studied more extensively than others. For example, people with antisocial personality disorder are more likely to have family members with other personality disorders or alcoholism. A family history of depression may predispose one to borderline and obsessive-compulsive personality disorders.

Children who must adapt in a disturbed environment under unreasonable demands may appropriately develop coping mechanisms for self-preservation. These coping mechanisms can alleviate the pain, anxiety, and depression that may develop in a child who is abused or neglected. However, this setting may lead to a disordered personality in the child if he or she relates to the rest of the world expecting always to be mistreated in similar ways.

Children with conduct disorders and attention deficit hyperactivity disorder are also at risk for developing antisocial personality disorder.

DIAGNOSIS

Distinguishing between personality styles such as being organized, outgoing, shy, or emotional and personality disorders is a matter of degree. For example a normal individual may enjoy being alone as a preferred style of behaving, while someone with a schizoid personality disorder has no friends and actively avoids contact with family members without justification.

The distinction between normal personality style and disorder can be made by assessing personality function in six main areas: work, interpersonal relationships, feelings, self-identity, reality testing, and impulse control. There are ten distinct personality disorders.

PARANOID PERSONALITY DISORDER

This disorder is characterized by a consistent expectation that others are trying to demean, harm, or threaten. These individuals refuse to confide in others for fear that information will be used against them. Difficulty in the workplace is common among people with this disorder.

MALE/FEMALE DIFFERENCES

This disorder is more common in men.

SCHIZOID PERSONALITY DISORDER

This disorder exhibits a pattern of indifference to social relationships. People with this disorder are loners who prefer solitary activities, rarely marry, have little desire for sexual experience and rarely experience strong emotion such as anger or joy.

SCHIZOTYPAL PERSONALITY DISORDER

Peculiarities of thinking, appearance, and behavior characterize people with this disorder. They may have odd beliefs, extreme superstitiousness, unusual mannerisms, odd appearance, and suspiciousness. In addition, extreme social anxiety with unfamiliar people is common.

ANTISOCIAL PERSONALITY DISORDER

Manifestations of a conduct disorder are usually present before age 15 and included truancy, physical fighting, cruelty to animals or people, arson, stealing, or lying. Irresponsible and antisocial behavior follow, as indicated by an inability to abide by society's rules, aggressive behavior, getting into trouble with the law, and a lack of remorse. In everyday language these individuals are often referred to as sociopaths.

MALE/FEMALE DIFFERENCES

This disorder is much more common in men.

BORDERLINE PERSONALITY DISORDER

Unstable mood, chaotic interpersonal relationships, impulsiveness (e.g., sexual promiscuity, shoplifting, and reckless driving) and poor self-image mark this condition. There are often periods of depression, anxiety, anger, and self-destructive behavior, including suicide gestures.

MALE/FEMALE DIFFERENCES

This disorder is more common in women.

HISTRIONIC PERSONALITY DISORDER

Attention seeking and being overly emotional in a given situation is typical of this disorder. Specific behaviors include constantly seeking approval, inappropriately seductive appearance, and temper tantrums.

MALE/FEMALE DIFFERENCES

This disorder is more common in women.

NARCISSISTIC PERSONALITY DISORDER

This is characterized by an underlying fragile sense of self-esteem and a subsequent preoccupation with success and power. Patients lack empathy, require constant attention, and often react with rage or humiliation to negative criticism. This results in poor interpersonal relationships.

AVOIDANT PERSONALITY DISORDER

Avoidance of social interactions with others is typical of this disorder due to excess concern over being judged inadequate and fear of being embarrassed. As a result the people with this disorder have few close friends and avoid social situations while wishing to be with others at the same time.

DEPENDENT PERSONALITY DISORDER

This condition is characterized by dependency and submissiveness, inability to make everyday decisions, a need for excessive reassurance, and feelings of helplessness when alone. A person with this disorder will often attach closely to another individual and try inordinately to please that person.

OBSESSIVE-COMPULSIVE PERSONALITY DISORDER

This disorder is characterized by a pattern of perfectionism and inflexibility, with pronounced fear of making mistakes. The result is inability to make decisions, difficulty completing a task, preoccupation with details, excessive devotion to work at the exclusion of leisure activities, and a tendency to be stingy.

MALE/FEMALE DIFFERENCES

This disorder is more frequently diagnosed in men.

TREATMENT

Personality disorders can be extremely disabling and difficult to change without professional help. Often a person with a personality disorder does not recognize how the behavior is related to failing relationships, career problems, or general unhappiness. As a result, he or she may ask for treatment only at the insistence of a friend or loved one. Despite the deeply ingrained, maladaptive patterns, treatment can be beneficial for many types of personality disorders.

The commonly used therapies are medications and psychotherapy, tailored to each personality disorder. In general, medications are aimed at periods of disabling symptoms that can occur in these patients. For example, antidepressants, antipsychotics, antianxiety, and impulse-stabilizing medications may be helpful at times.

Psychotherapy is almost always helpful in these disorders. Long-term treatment is usually necessary to make the painful and difficult connections between events of the past and the development of maladaptive behavior and emotion in the present.

Behavioral therapy can be useful in some cases by helping people interrupt their habitual patterns while learning new coping strategies within a supportive environment. Self-help groups, which often provide caring and a substitute family, may also be helpful.

SCHIZOPHRENIA AND PSYCHOSIS

DEFINITION

Psychosis is a loss of contact with reality due to a disorder of thinking and/or mood. Psychosis is a symptom of schizophrenia, but it can occur in other mental illness as well. In addition to psychosis, a person who develops schizophrenia will usually experience a decline in function both at work and in social situations.

A common misconception about schizophrenia is the belief that it refers to "split personality." While the Greek root *schizo* does mean split, it derives from a split between the mind and soul, and should not be confused with the disorder psychiatrists call multiple personality.

Most often, schizophrenia occurs in adolescence and continues through life with exacerbations and remissions. It affects about 1 in a 100 people, a number that is constant across many societies and is more common in lower socioeconomic groups. During an active phase of the illness, bizarre thought patterns such as delusions or hallucinations occur.

Between schizophrenic episodes some people can care for themselves while others lose their ability to work, participate in social interactions, or maintain personal hygiene.

CAUSE

The cause of schizophrenia is unknown, although several factors are thought to contribute to its development.

• Socioeconomic: Schizophrenia affects both rich and poor but is more prevalent in lower socioeconomic groups. Some argue that this is a result of poverty's increased stress, while others believe that the illness itself results in loss of education and social opportunity.

• Genetic: Schizophrenia tends to run in families, with five to ten times the likelihood of developing schizophrenia in family members of someone with schizophrenia. An identical twin has about a 50 percent chance of developing schizophrenia if the other twin has it. Environment and other factors may help explain its multiple incidence in some families.

• Biological: Brain structure, brain metabolism, and brain chemistry are abnormal in people with schizophrenia. Research in this area is growing rapidly, and in the future it may be possible to locate specific areas of the brain that are responsible for schizophrenia.

Brain structure has only recently been analyzed using the technology of CT scans and MRI. Researchers have found differences in the amount of brain tissue and the size of brain cavities in schizophrenia. Studies on brain metabolism have revealed that the brain activity in the area of the frontal lobe is less active than aver-

SYMPTOMS OF PSYCHOSIS

People with schizophrenia have symptoms of psychosis that fall into five basic categories: thought disorder, false beliefs, false perceptions, emotional disturbance, and behavior disorders. The distinction between normal and abnormal thoughts may not always be clear. When someone says "The IRS is after me," it may be true or a psychotic belief. A mental health professional can often help to diagnose psychotic thoughts.

- **Thought Disorder.** The thinking process becomes disorganized, so that statements do not seem connected or logical.
- **False Beliefs.** Delusions are false beliefs that are persistent, organized, and cannot be shaken by a logical argument.
- **Perception Disorder.** Unusual sensory experience, like hearing voices that aren't there (auditory hallucinations). A dangerous consequence of hearing voices can be a command hallucination, when a voice tells someone to perform a life-threatening act.
- **Emotional Disorder.** A lack of emotion or interest in life events. Social withdrawal and apathy can result, sometimes seen as a hallmark of this disease.
- **Behavior Disorders.** Unusual behavior such as repetitive movement (e.g., rocking), catatonic behavior (e.g., lack of movement), and, rarely, unpredictable assaultive behavior.

age. In addition, alterations in brain chemistry among neurotransmitters, the messengers between brain cells, are found in patients with schizophrenia. (Similar imbalances are present in depression and other mental illness.)

In schizophrenia and other illnesses with psychosis, the neurotransmitter dopamine may be present in excess in certain areas of the brain. The drugs used to treat schizophrenia, which have been used for many years, are now known to work by blocking excess dopamine.

- Environmental: In the past, an abnormal parent-child interaction was thought to contribute to this condition, but this connection is not supported by studies on the development of schizophrenia. Stress may be a factor in the development of schizophrenia in a susceptible person or may influence the course of the illness once present. Other factors being studied include viral infections and maternal malnutrition during a critical period of pregnancy with a vulnerable child.

DIAGNOSIS

American Psychiatric Association criteria for diagnosing schizophrenia include:

1. Psychotic symptoms (see box) for at least 1 week
   - Two of the following: delusions, persistent hallucinations, incoherent speech, catatonic behavior, flat affect (or no range of emotion)
   - Bizarre delusions
   - Prominent hallucinations
2. Work, social relations, and personal hygiene below pre-episode levels
3. Signs of the disturbance for at least 6 months

Symptoms of schizophrenia can be classified as positive or negative: Positive symptoms include delusions, hallucinations, and thought disorder. Negative symptoms describe apathy and social withdrawal. The forms of schizophrenia are described as paranoid schizophrenia (delusions are prominent), catatonic schizophrenia (immobility), and undifferentiated schizophrenia.

Other illnesses and conditions can cause psychosis and mimic symptoms of schizophrenia, including drug abuse with cocaine, crack, amphetamines, and PCP. Head injury, illness such as brain tumors, and other psychiatric disorders such as manic-depression with psychosis can cause schizophrenic-type symptoms. However, odd or eccentric behavior such as speaking to the spirit of a deceased person or joining a religious cult may reflect differences in cultural values or systems of belief rather than symptoms of schizophrenia.

Testing for drug use, a physical and neurological exam, and observation for a period of 6 months can differentiate between schizophrenia and other conditions.

TREATMENT

With the advent of medication and new forms of rehabilitation, people with schizophrenia can usually live with families or in community settings instead of living in psychiatric institutions for extended periods of time. People with schizophrenia differ in their need for assistance in daily activities of dressing, grooming, and supervision. Antipsychotic medication and education of families about caring for family members with schizophrenia help keep these people out of psychiatric institutions.

In general, psychiatric hospitalization is now used mainly to diagnose schizophrenia, stabilize the person on medication, prevent suicidal or homicidal behavior, and provide support and referral services for those unable to take care of daily needs. Antipsychotic drugs control schizophrenia but do not cure it. Very effective in preventing relapses as well as returning patients to normal function, they are thought to work by blocking the neurotransmitter dopamine in the brain. Newer antipsychotics, such as clozapine or risperidone, may not only reduce positive schizophrenia symptoms but also help counteract the negative symptoms (apathy, social withdrawal).

One of the most common and serious side effects of the antipsychotic drugs is a movement disorder called tardive dyskinesia. Unpredictable and causing involuntary, repetitive movements of the mouth, tongue, and body, tardive dyskinesia affects up to one-third of patients and may be irreversible even after the medication is stopped. To date there is no treatment for tardive dyskinesia.

Although this side effect can be quite unwelcome, it is generally not dangerous and may be worth the risk if the benefit of the medication eradicates extreme and persistent psychosis. Other side effects include dry mouth, constipation, blurred vision, inhibition of ejaculation, and a feeling of faintness on rising quickly from a chair or bed. The most recently discovered antipsychotics seem to cause tardive dyskinesia less often than older medications. However, clozapine, in 1 to 2 percent of cases, can cause a dangerous lowering of the white blood cell count; therefore, people on this drug require frequent blood test monitoring. In addition, a rare but potentially lethal side effect of antipsychotic medication is neuroleptic malignant syndrome (NMS), which causes muscle rigidity, fever, and kidney damage. If symptoms of NMS appear, all antipsychotic medication must be stopped and emergency medical care provided.

Psychiatric rehabilitation programs teach skills required for work, social interaction, and personal hygiene. Behavioral treatments focus on improving social skills and self-sufficiency through the use of praise and rewards for desired behavior while group therapy reduces social isolation and deepens relationships. Family therapy and individual psychotherapy are also utilized.

HOME REMEDIES AND ALTERNATIVE THERAPIES

Music and pet therapy can be effective in breaking down the barriers of social isolation surrounding patients with schizophrenia. These communication methods, as well as painting, sculpture, and drama, help people with schizophrenia express thoughts and emotions.

....

SLEEP DISORDERS

DEFINITION

Sleep disorders are persistent sleep disturbances. Healthy people display a wide range of sleeping patterns; some people feel rested with only 5 hours of sleep, while others require 10. Normally, five separate phases of sleep occur in cycles several times every night. Stages 1 through 4 are progressively deeper stages of sleep, whereas REM sleep (rapid eye movement) is a dream phase. Children spend more time in the deeper stages of sleep, whereas the elderly spend more time in lighter sleep stages.

Most people have an occasional disturbance in sleeping (either too little or too much), but when it lasts for an extended period of time a problem exists. Sleep disorders are classified as insomnias, hypersomnias, sleep-wake schedule disorders, and parasomnias.

INSOMNIA

Insomnia is the inability to fall asleep. People who suffer from insomnia do not get enough quality sleep to feel rested the next day. It is one of the most common complaints—an estimated 25 million Americans are affected.

CAUSE

Lack of sleep can be caused by physical or psychological problems. Any disease that causes pain or discomfort (e.g., asthma, palpitations, indigestion, or cancer) can make it difficult to fall asleep. Nutritional, hormonal, and neurological disorders may act directly on the brain to hamper sleep. Medications that interfere with sleep include decongestants, barbiturates, benzodiazepines (when used for a long time), and alcohol.

In addition, psychiatric disorders such as schizophrenia, depression, and anxiety often cause insomnia that usually resolves when the underlying illness is treated.

Transient insomnia due to any psychological or physical stress can become chronic, and after several sleepless nights the bed can become a place of fear, compounding the insomnia and possibly preventing the return of a normal sleep pattern.

MALE/FEMALE DIFFERENCES

Insomnia is more common in females than males.

DIAGNOSIS

American Psychiatric Association criteria for diagnosing insomnia include:

1. The predominant complaint is difficulty in initiating or maintaining sleep.
2. The sleep disturbance occurs at least three times a week for at least 1 month and results in significant daytime fatigue or some symptom that is attributable to the sleep disturbance, for example, irritability.

TREATMENT

Medication and behavioral therapy are both useful in the treatment of insomnia. The behavioral approach emphasizes good sleep habits: No matter how sleepy, the person suffering insomnia should not nap during the day.

Insomniacs should also never go to bed unless tired, should get up after 20 minutes of unsuccessfully trying to fall asleep to do something quiet such as reading a book, and should set an alarm clock to go off at the same time 7 days a week.

Sleeping pills, helpful during a period of crisis or illness, should be used only on a short-term basis to establish a normal sleep pattern. Benzodiazepines and sedative hypnotics, the most effective and commonly prescribed drugs for sleep, should be used with caution because of side effects such as impaired coordination and the risk of addiction. Over time they lose their effectiveness and may interfere with normal sleep cycles. In addition, rebound insomnia, which may be worse than the initial disturbance, can occur after the medication is discontinued.

HOME REMEDIES AND ALTERNATIVE THERAPIES

Exercise during the day helps increase sleepiness at bedtime. Relaxation techniques that include breathing exercises and muscle relaxation may also be helpful to reduce anxiety prior to bedtime. Acupuncture, massage, and music therapy are felt to have calming effects for the insomniac. There are electronic devices available that deliver a constant background or "white" noise, which can create a soothing environment.

While minerals such as calcium and magnesium and herbs such as lemon balm and chamomile are thought by some to improve sleep, no scientific evidence has established their effectiveness.

HYPERSOMNIAS

People suffering from hypersomnias feel sleepy despite a normal number of hours of sleep. These conditions include sleep apnea and narcolepsy. These conditions occur in 1 to 2 percent of the population. For a detailed discussion of these disorders, see chapter 26.

DISTURBANCE OF SLEEP-WAKE CYCLE

All human beings have inborn clocks that regulate a variety of functions such as sleep, temperature, and hormone production. Disturbance of the sleep-wake cycle occurs in people who maintain a sleep schedule that is unsynchronized with their internal rhythm.

CAUSE

Anyone who has taken a plane flight through several time zones knows the best modern example of sleep-wake cycle disturbance: jet lag. Similar sleep disruptions occur in people who work the night shift. In a few rare cases, an individual's internal clock may be set incorrectly for unknown reasons.

DIAGNOSIS

This condition is diagnosed by observing insomnia or hypersomnia caused by a mismatch between the normal sleep-wake schedule for a person's environment and his or her sleep-wake pattern.

TREATMENT

In travelers with jet lag, specialists recommend going to sleep at the usual home time to combat sleepiness. Medications to induce drowsiness may also be helpful. Light therapy and exercise may improve sleep in travelers suffering jet lag.

Persons working a night shift should choose an appropriate bedtime and sleep for only 5 hours a day. After a few days, sleep should be extended by 15 minutes each night until the new bedtime is reached.

PARASOMNIAS

Activities such as walking, talking, and urinating associated with being awake but occur during sleep are called parasomnias. Sleepwalking is the most common parasomnia, occurring more commonly in children than adults. Sleepwalkers stare ahead, apparently seeing, and are difficult to arouse. In the morning sleepwalkers do not remember the event. It is estimated that 1 to 6 percent of children are sleepwalkers.

Nightmares and night terrors are common parasomnias in children. Nightmares are frightening dreams from which the sleeper awakens, frightened but alert. Night terrors, on the other hand, are sudden attacks of panic that often cause the sleeper to awake in terror, screaming, sweating, and with a pounding heart but not remembering the cause of the terror. It may take 10 to 15 minutes before she calms down and falls back asleep.

Bruxism or grinding the teeth at night is thought to affect 15 percent of the population at some time in their lives. The sleeper is not aware of this behavior. The effects of bruxism include wearing down the teeth, gum disease, facial pain, and headache.

MALE/FEMALE DIFFERENCES

Nightmares are more common in women. Sleepwalking and night terrors are more common in men.

CAUSE OF PARASOMNIAS

Sleepwalking is thought to have a genetic component: If one identical twin sleepwalks, the other is six times as likely to sleepwalk as other siblings. Sleepwalking is not considered abnormal but in rare cases is a symptom of a psychological conflict, medical, or neurologic disorder. A complete medical evaluation should be obtained.

Nightmares and night terrors can be normal in children. Persistent and frequent episodes can be provoked by drug withdrawal, alcohol use, or use of prescription drugs such as beta-blockers and antidepressants. In addition, they can be caused by unresolved conflicts and are a common symptom of posttraumatic stress disorder.

Bruxism may be caused by several factors including genetic predisposition, stress, and poor tooth alignment.

DIAGNOSIS

American Psychiatric Association criteria for diagnosing sleepwalking include:

1. Repeated episodes of arising from bed during sleep and walking about, usually during the first third of the sleep period.
2. While sleepwalking, the person has a blank face, is unresponsive to communication by others, and can be awakened only with great difficulty.
3. On awakening, the person has no memory of the episode.
4. There is no impairment of mental activity or behavior within several minutes of awakening.

American Psychiatric Association criteria for diagnosing sleep terror include:

1. Recurrent episodes of abrupt awakening from sleep characterized by screaming.
2. Intense anxiety and symptoms of rapid breathing and sweating during each episode.
3. Unresponsiveness to comforting during the episode, with confusion and disorientation.

American Psychiatric Association criteria for diagnosing nightmares include:

1. Repeated awakenings with detailed recall of extremely frightening dreams, usually involving threats to survival or self-esteem.
2. On awakening the person rapidly becomes oriented and alert.
3. The dream causes significant distress.

TREATMENT

The immediate environment of the sleepwalker should be safe from obstacles, open windows, and stairs. Treatment is not usually necessary in children, as most outgrow it with time. In adults medications such as benzodiazepines or anticonvulsants are frequently prescribed.

Frequent nightmares and night terrors can be treated initially with psychotherapy when contributing stress or trauma is present. Medication (same as above) may also

be helpful.

A dental evaluation and mouth guard is the only effective treatment for bruxism.

SEXUAL DISORDERS

Sexual behavior is a complicated interaction of physical, psychological, and environmental factors. Although society may accept a wide range of sexual behaviors as normal, each person's individual tastes, peer groups, and families influence the perceived acceptability of various sexual behaviors. When sexual preferences and behavior are at odds with those of our family, friends, and mates, internal conflict may result.

Sexual disorders describe dissatisfaction during sexual interactions, rather than define normal or abnormal sexual behavior. Sexual dysfunction occurs when one does not feel aroused or fulfilled by sexual activity. Other sexual disorders, called paraphilias, involve acting on fantasies that may be disturbing to others and to society, such as an adult having sex with a child.

SEXUAL DYSFUNCTIONS

DEFINITION

The sexual response cycle as described by Dr. William Masters and Virginia Johnson includes the excitement phase, orgasmic phase, and resolution phase. Sexual dysfunctions occur when dissatisfaction is felt with any of these phases during sexual relations. Sexual dysfunction is extremely common in our society, and one study found as many as 40 percent of men had premature ejaculation or difficulty maintaining an erection, and 77 per-

HOMOSEXUALITY

Homosexuality is not a sexual disorder. In recent years the social stigma attached to homosexuality has lessened, making it easier for homosexuals to display affection in public and share their private lives with their families. However, it can be difficult for some homosexuals to come to terms with their sexual orientation, whether as a result of a conflict with strict upbringing or feared ostracism from their religious group, friends, or family. If, as a homosexual, any of these issues affects your ability to function at a high level, inhibits enjoyment of social and sexual relationships, or causes pain and suffering, then it may be helpful to seek professional advice.

cent of women had difficulty becoming aroused or experiencing an orgasm.

During sexual relations people may have problems with:

- *Excitement disorders:* impotence (difficulty in achieving or maintaining an erection) and female sexual arousal disorder.
- *Orgasm disorders:* inhibited female orgasm, premature ejaculation, and inhibited male orgasm.
- *Desire:* Persistent loss of sexual desire and persistent aversion to all sexual activity. In women, dyspareunia or recurrent genital pain during intercourse can occur.

CAUSE

Sexual functioning depends on the nervous system, the blood supply, hormones, and the mind to act in concert. A problem or disease in any one of these systems can lead to sexual dysfunction.

When there is a problem with sexual function it is important to establish in which phase of the sexual cycle it occurs. Excitement problems including impotence or female sexual arousal disorder can result from medication side effects, psychological illness, anxiety, and inhibitions. In addition, medical illnesses such as atherosclerosis, diabetes, and trauma from surgery or violence can damage the nerves and blood vessels and lead to impaired arousal. Some medications that cause impotence are high blood pressure pills, antihistamines, antidepressants, and antipsychotics. In addition, people who use drugs such as alcohol, cocaine, heroin, or caffeine may suffer from inhibited arousal.

Disorders in achieving orgasm may be caused by medical illness, injury, or psychological factors listed above. In women, insufficient exploration or stimulation, known as foreplay, is a common cause of inability to achieve orgasm. Painful sex is more common in women and can result from physical problems such as vaginal scarring, endometriosis, urinary tract infection, and tumors. Psychological factors such as trauma can lead to involuntary muscle spasm called vaginismus.

Subtle factors that many of us experience at one time or another include anxiety about sex, performance anxiety, cultural inhibitions, insufficient stimulation, history of sexual trauma, life stress, and problems in the relationship. Treatment for sexual dysfunction is targeted to both the cause and the problem.

MALE/FEMALE DIFFERENCES

Each sexual dysfunction affects men and women differently. For example, inhibited orgasm is more common in females whereas impotence can occur only in males.

DIAGNOSIS

Diagnosing sexual dysfunction depends on the type of problem experienced causing sexual dissatisfaction.

- *Sexual aversion disorder:* aversion or avoidance of all genital sexual contact.
- *Female sexual arousal disorder:* either persistent or recurrent failure to attain or maintain the lubrication-swelling response of sexual excitement until completion of sexual activity or persistent or recurrent lack of sexual excitement and pleasure during sexual activity.
- *Premature ejaculation:* persistent or recurrent ejaculation with minimal sexual stimulation and before the person wishes it.
- *Inhibited female orgasm:* persistent or recurrent delay or absence of orgasm during normal sexual excitement. A clinician must determine that the sexual activity is adequate in focus, intensity, and duration. In some women orgasm may result during coitus and in others from manual clitoral stimulation; both are normal female sexual responses.
- *Inhibited male orgasm:* persistent or recurrent delay or absence of orgasm during normal sexual excitement as determined by a clinician.
- *Dyspareunia:* recurrent or persistent genital pain in either a man or woman before, during, or after sexual intercourse.
- *Vaginismus:* recurrent or persistent involuntary spasm of the musculature of the vagina that interferes with coitus.

TREATMENT

Treatment can deal with both physical and psychological causes of sexual dysfunction.

Biological Therapies. These are being used in men who have erectile dysfunction usually as a result of disease such as diabetes or trauma after surgery. Surgically implanted penile prostheses, vacuum devices, and medication injected into the penis all can cause erection. These therapies do not restore natural erection or orgasm to the man once it has been lost. Counseling is necessary before undergoing these treatments to address expectation and possible disappointment of both partners.

Dual Sex Therapy. Developed by Masters and Johnson, both partners participate in discussion, communication, and intimacy exercises even if the dysfunction appears to be centered in one person. The intimacy exercises, known as sensate focus exercises, reduce anxiety by emphasizing intimate contact and warmth, taking the focus off intercourse. Partners begin by giving pleasure through nongenital touch and eventually progress to sexual intercourse over time. Giving and receiving pleasure rather than performance is the goal. These exercises can be used in several types of sexual dysfunction, including erectile/arousal, premature ejaculation, inhibited female orgasm, and low sexual desire.

A technique called the stop-start technique treats premature ejaculation by helping men tolerate high levels of excitement without ejaculation by withholding sexual activity when the feeling of ejaculation comes on. When the feeling subsides, sexual activity is resumed.

Therapy. Sex therapy and couples therapy may be useful in many sexual disorders to explore guilt, fears, and anxieties about sex and address problems in the relationship.

HOME REMEDIES AND ALTERNATIVE THERAPIES

Many cultures have used herbal and natural remedies to heal sexual ills. Aphrodisiacs such as anise and ginseng have been used to enhance sexual arousal, although scientific studies have not established their effectiveness. If anxiety or lack of energy contributes to sexual dysfunction, meditation, exercise, and massage may be helpful. Listening to music, watching an adult movie, or indulging in erotic fantasies are among the many self-help techniques.

PARAPHILIAS

DEFINITION

Paraphilias, formerly known as perversions, are sexual fantasies involving nonhuman objects, suffering or humiliation of a sexual partner, or children or nonconsenting persons. These fantasies often begin in adolescence and persist into adulthood. Paraphilia is diagnosed only when fantasies are acted upon or if they are distressing to the person.

In our society, pedophilia, sexual activity with children, is the most common paraphilia, with 10 to 20 percent of children having been molested by age 18. It is difficult to estimate the occurrence of other paraphilias, since this kind of behavior is recorded only when it comes to the attention of the police.

MALE/FEMALE DIFFERENCES

Almost all paraphilias are diagnosed exclusively in men except sexual masochism, which is 20 times more common in men than women.

CAUSE

Several theories have been proposed to explain the cause of paraphilias. Psychoanalytical models focus on the fear of castration by the father and separation from the mother as anxieties that in abnormal development can lead to paraphilia. Another theory attributes the development of paraphilia to the nature of the first sexual experience. For example, someone molested as a child may be predisposed to becoming a child molester or alternatively the subject of sexual humiliation as an adult. Some have tried to identify physical differences in paraphiliacs such as abnormal hormone levels and genetic abnormalities, but these studies have been inconclusive.

DIAGNOSIS

All diagnoses of paraphilia require that the person either is markedly distressed by or has acted on the paraphilic urge.

Exhibitionism: recurrent intense sexual urges and fantasies over a period of at least 6 months involving the exposure of one's genitals to an unsuspecting stranger.

Fetishism: recurrent intense sexual urges and fantasies over at least 6 months involving nonliving objects.

Frotteurism: recurrent intense sexual urges and fantasies over at least 6 months involving touching and rubbing against a nonconsenting person.

Pedophilia: recurrent intense sexual urges and fantasies over at least 6 months involving sexual activity with a prepubescent child by a person at least 16 years old and at least 5 years older than the child.

Sexual Masochism: recurrent intense sexual fantasies and urges over at least 6 months involving the act of being beaten, humiliated, bound, or made to suffer.

Sexual Sadism: recurrent intense sexual urges and fantasies over at least 6 months involving acts in which the psychological or physical suffering of the victim is sexually exciting to the person.

Voyeurism: recurrent intense sexual urges and fantasies over at least 6 months involving the act of observing an unsuspecting person who is naked, in the process of disrobing, or engaging in sexual activity.

TREATMENT

Psychotherapy and behavioral therapies are the most common approaches to dealing with paraphilia. The goal is to find acceptable ways for a person with paraphilia to achieve sexual fulfillment through increased self-esteem and understanding of the cause of paraphilia. Treatment can be difficult, as the roots of these disorders often go back to childhood.

HOME REMEDIES AND ALTERNATIVE THERAPIES

Self-help groups and 12-step programs may be beneficial for men who are addicted to certain types of sexual behaviors. This approach should be combined with psychotherapy.

VI

Drugs and Their Use

34

Proper Use of Medica- tions

**NORMAN KAHN, D.D.S.,
Ph.D., AND ANDREW L.
WITT, Ph.D.**

Parts of this chapter
are adapted from the
one by Hamilton
Southworth, M.D.,
which appeared in the
revised second edition.

American doctors currently write approximately 56.9 billion prescriptions per year, according to the Pharmaceutical Manufacturers Association. In addition, Americans annually spend more than $50 each on nonprescription medications—so-called over-the-counter (OTC) drugs.

According to the Food and Drug Administration, there are more than 5,000 prescription drugs. The list grows constantly, with about five prescription drugs added every month. The OTC drugs constitute half a million products, from medicated shampoos to corn plasters for the feet. Besides the prescription drugs they take after professional diagnosis of a disease, people treat themselves for myriad ailments: insomnia, drowsiness, cold and flu symptoms, constipation, diarrhea, headaches, stomachaches, and skin problems. And many people seem unaware that some of their favorite beverages also contain drugs: alcohol and caffeine.

The ways to misuse drugs seem almost as numerous as the drugs themselves. All drugs—even aspirin—can have unpleasant side effects in some people. The chances of unwanted side effects can multiply when two or more drugs are combined. Drugs sometimes interact with food and drink: The combination may intensify a drug's effect or neutralize it. Or the combination may cause new, unforeseen side effects not predictable from the action of each drug considered separately.

Ignorance deprives many people of the benefits of drugs. Taken improperly, medicines may lose their effect, lead to relapse, or cause adverse reactions. Nor are doctors immune to error. They can prescribe unnecessary drugs or the wrong drugs, exposing the patient to side effects without the possibility of benefit.

Just as drug sales are big business—more than $50 billion for prescription drugs in 1993, and over $13 billion in OTC remedies (source: Neilsen Marketing Research)—misuse of medicines and adverse reactions to them are a major part of health care costs. Approximately 300,000 Americans each year are hospitalized because of reactions to drugs; 18,000 hospitalized patients die from side effects. To avoid these ill effects, people need to know as much as possible about the drugs they are taking.

INFORMATION AND THE DOCTOR: A TWO-WAY EXCHANGE

In every field of life, correct decision-making depends on accurate information. Yet decisions about medications are sometimes made without proper information, in a lack of communication involving both patient and doctor. To dispel this ignorance, both need to ask a barrage of questions, on everything from other medications to lifestyle of the patient, to effects and interactions of the proposed therapy. Only then can the optimum treatment in the optimum amounts be prescribed. And this information is necessary not only for physicians but also for dentists, nurse practitioners, podiatrists, and nutritionists.

What to Tell the Doctor. The doctor needs to know:

- All other drugs (prescription, OTC, vitamins, nutritional supplements, etc.) that you are currently taking.
- Your medical history. Do you suffer from a chronic illness? Kidney or liver disease, high blood pressure, heart disease, glaucoma?
- If you are pregnant, planning to become pregnant, or breast-feeding (many drugs can pass into the fetus and the mother's milk).
- Any allergies you may have.
- Any bad reactions you have experienced from taking a drug in the past, as well as any side effects you experience while taking the drug.
- If you drink alcohol or caffeinated beverages, or if you smoke tobacco.

What to Ask the Doctor. A recent poll showed that less than 30 percent of the general population considered itself "well informed" about prescription drugs. About 80 percent wanted more information on safety and efficacy. Other important areas of information were "proper home use, general health issues, misuse and dependency, and cost and value."

The problem of doctor-patient miscommunication is nothing new. In 1982, the American Medical Association began distributing patient information sheets about disease and treatments. Drug manufacturers, medical publishers, insurance companies, and individual doctors themselves prepare information kits for patients and the general public. However, many people still feel that they are not receiving the kind of information they require to become full partners in their own medical care. Two surveys commissioned by the Food and Drug Administration pinpointed the source of the problem.

- Very few patients—only 2 to 4 percent—questioned their doctors or pharmacists about their prescriptions.
- Doctors interpreted the patients' silence to mean satisfaction with the information received.
- Most doctors and almost all pharmacists said that they provided written materials—from an illustrated brochure to a typed prescription label for the medicine bottle.

- Only 6 percent of patients said they received written information at the doctor's office; 15 percent said they had received written materials at the pharmacy.

Many factors inhibit patients from asking questions. They don't know what questions to ask. They are in awe of the doctor, or feel that questions may be taken as mistrust of the doctor's ability. They don't want to seem impudent or take up the doctor's time. Or they may be too stunned and confused by the diagnosis to comprehend what the doctor is saying. They may even feel that it is somehow wrong for them to know more than the doctor has told them. None of these is a good reason to remain silent and uninformed. Ultimately, you will have to live with the effects of anything taken—or not taken—into your body.

Below is a list of questions each person should ask the doctor about any medicines prescribed. A pencil and paper will help you keep the answers straight, especially if you are taking more than one drug.

- What is the name of the drug? Many drugs have two names, the brand name and the generic name. It helps to know both.
- What is it supposed to do? When should this effect become noticeable? What should you do if no effect is seen? How will the effect change the course of the disease?
- How and when should it be taken? For how long?
- Can the drug be prescribed in a generic form, instead of under a more expensive brand name? Many new drugs are not available in generic form, and the doctor may prefer a particular brand for a good reason (see below for further information).
- What are the most common side effects? Which should be reported immediately if they occur, and which are trivial? Some drugs, for example, turn the urine startling colors. Knowing this in advance can spare you unnecessary consternation; if you are well informed, you will be able to recognize the first symptoms of any serious reactions. However, many doctors fear that patients may develop symptoms by power of suggestion.
- What foods, drugs, drinks, or activities should be avoided while taking the drug? Many drugs can be inactivated or have their onsets-of-action delayed by food in the stomach; others must be taken with food to avoid irritating the stomach. A number of drugs can make you drowsy and should not be taken before driving. Some drugs may have their effects multiplied by alcohol or other drugs.
- Is there any written information about the drug? If this material is available, it will reinforce the doctor's oral instructions and your notes. Book, pamphlets, and even magazine articles can be most helpful.
- Are there any alternatives to use of drugs? Mild hypertension (high blood pressure), for example, can sometimes by relieved by weight loss, exercise, the reduction of salt in the diet, or a combination of these measures. A determined person might want to try modifying his or her lifestyle before embarking on a possibly lifelong course of antihypertensive drugs.

Pharmacists are also aware of all this information. The pharmacist will type all instructions from the prescription form onto the label. Problems may arise if the physician does not write them on the prescription. In this case, the patient can ask the pharmacist to call the physician for more precise instructions.

An FDA study concluded that the only way for the doctor-patient and pharmacist-patient communications to improve was for the patient to ask more questions. Patients should feel free to call the doctor's office or pharmacy if additional questions come to mind after the office or pharmacy visit. If the health care professional seems too busy to inform the patient adequately, the patient should consider finding another one who is not.

FILLING THE PRESCRIPTION

Besides their notorious handwriting, doctors use a traditional set of Latin abbreviations to convey information to the pharmacists, and then to the drug consumer. Most of these concern dosing and are listed in the box, A List of Abbreviations, in this section.

Usually, the name of the drug is the first word on the prescription. Next is its form—tablets, capsules, liquid—and the strength, expressed by weight (250 milligrams, for example). The quantity covered by the prescription follows: 20 capsules, or 10 fluid ounces, for instance. Last come the directions for use, usually in Latin abbreviations. The prescription will also contain instructions on whether and how often it can be refilled.

The patient should read over the prescription in the doctor's office and ask questions about anything not readily understood.

AT THE PHARMACY

- Have all prescriptions filled at one pharmacy (this helps you avoid potentially dangerous interactions with other drugs you are taking).
- Containers with childproof caps are often difficult to open (especially if you are elderly or have arthritis). Feel free to request a container that is

A LIST OF ABBREVIATIONS

aa	Equal amounts of each
aq	Water (aqua)
b.i.d.	Twice a day
coch or	
cochl	Spoonful
ea	Each
g	Gram
gr	Grain
gt	Drop (plural; gtt)
l.a.s.	Label as such, i.e., label with the name of the drug. The AMA recommends this practice unless there is a reason to leave the patient in ignorance.
p.r.n.	As needed
q.2 h.	Every 2 hours, similarly, q.3 h., etc.
q.d.	Every day
q.i.d.	Four times a day
t.i.d.	Three times a day
ut dict	As directed. The AMA counsels against this abbreviation on prescriptions and recommends that instructions for taking medicine be written on the label.
d.a.w.	Dispense as written. Used in some states to prevent generic substitution.

easier to open if you do not have young children in your household.
- Even if you have a prescription filled at another pharmacy, make sure your primary pharmacist enters it in your drug profile. Also let your pharmacist know if you take vitamin and mineral supplements and OTC medications.

LABELS AND PACKAGE INSERTS

The following information should be on the label of every container of prescription medicine.

- Name, address, and phone number of the pharmacy
- Prescription name
- Patient's name
- How often and when to take the drug
- How much to take in each dose
- Any special instructions on storage or preparation
- Name of the physician
- Date the prescription was filled
- Name of the drug (if the doctor or state law indicates it should be written on the label)

The patient should check to make sure all these are clearly written on the label and ask any questions of the pharmacist before leaving the drugstore. Certain drugs, especially oral contraceptives and estrogens, come with an FDA-mandated leaflet describing the risks and benefits of these products. These contain helpful information and warrant careful reading. Again, any questions should be referred to the doctor or pharmacist.

SAVING MONEY ON DRUGS

The cost of medicines makes up a substantial part of the cost of medical care. There are several ways for the consumer to reduce the expense of drugs, both prescription and over-the-counter forms. They include:

- **Generics.** When pharmaceutical companies develop new drugs (a process that can take up to 12 years and can cost hundreds of millions of dollars), they are granted a 17-year patent so that they can recoup some of their investment. When the patent expires, other companies may manufacture and sell the drug under its generic name, which refers to the primary active substance in the drug. Generic drugs are basically copies of brand-name drugs. They have the same active ingredients as the brand name and those ingredients are identical in strength, dosage, and mode of administration. On

CHOOSING A PHARMACY

Many factors determine which pharmacy a patient should use. They include:

- **Nearness and Convenience.** A pharmacy around the corner may be best for patients who don't drive, parents scrambling to fill a prescription to combat a child's high fever, or anyone who needs a pain reliever in a hurry. Sometimes the 24-hour, open-on-Sundays pharmacy is the only one in town. Home delivery may also be essential to get the drugs to the patient.
- **Cost.** Comparison shopping may result in substantial savings. On the other hand, lower prices may mean fewer services. (See the section, "Saving Money on Drugs," above, for other suggestions.)
- **Record Keeping.** Many pharmacies can clarify many questions about medications, recommend nonprescription drugs, and help evaluate symptoms, but only if the customer feels comfortable discussing medical problems. The pharmacist should ask the same kinds of questions as would a physician before recommending a medication or course of action.

average, generics cost 30 percent less than their brand-name counterparts.

If you are prescribed a brand-name drug, you can safely take a generic version instead, unless your doctor specifically indicates that substitution is not permissible. Most generic drugs are just as effective as their brand-name counterparts, but in a few cases generic drugs are not "bioequivalent." This means that the body handles them differently from the proprietary product. Different filler, coating, or manufacturing processes may be responsible. In these cases substitution may be unwise. In some states, pharmacists are required, when possible, to substitute a generic formulation for the proprietary form unless the physician specifies otherwise. In any case, the cost-conscious patient can ask the doctor if generic forms of prescribed drugs are available.

• **Shopping Around.** Different pharmacies charge different prices for the same products. In many states, pharmacies can now advertise their prices on prescription products as well as nonprescription drugs. Some will cite prices over the telephone. In some states, pharmacies are required to post prices of the most common prescription drugs.

• **Buying in Bulk.** Buying a year's supply of a drug taken regularly—for instance, an oral contraceptive—may save money. But the patient should consult with the doctor or pharmacist first. Many drugs do not maintain their potency with time, but deteriorate or decompose within weeks. All drugs now carry an expiration date and should not be used after that date.

• **Checking Your Policy.** Some medical insurance plans pay all or part of drug costs. Also, some employers—chiefly hospitals and universities—have a pharmacy where employees may buy drugs at cost. These may provide considerable savings to the customer.

• **Mail-order Pharmacies.** Mail-order is a good way to save money on drugs you are taking on an ongoing basis (i.e., antihypertensives, hormones).

Taking Medication. Before taking a new medication, you should always read the label/package insert to familiarize yourself with the drug, and use medicine only for the condition for which it was prescribed.

For medication safety in general:

• Keep medicines in original containers; if you must transfer medication to another container, make sure you clearly label it with the name of the drug and the dosage information.
• Never mix two different drugs in the same container.
• Take correct dose at correct times; follow instructions to the letter.
• Never take drugs in the dark; turn on the light and check the label.

SPECIAL CARE FOR CHILDREN

• Consult your doctor before buying OTC medicine for children.
• Keep all drugs out of children's reach.
• Keep the childproof caps on all medicines.
• Don't give children under the age of 18 aspirin or aspirin-containing drugs if they have a viral illness.
• Don't refer to medicine as "candy."
• Don't take medicine in front of children, as they love to imitate grown-ups.

TIPS ON GIVING MEDICINES THAT TASTE BAD

• Beforehand, give your child a Popsicle or an ice cube to suck to partially numb the tongue.
• Serve the medicine cold to reduce its taste.
• Mix the drug with fruit juice (cranberry, apple, orange) to conceal the offending taste.
• Mix the drug, whether it be a liquid or crushed pill, with applesauce, cereal, dessert pudding, or any other baby food.
• After administration, give a "chaser" of water, juice, or a Popsicle.
• If your child is nauseated, give an unfizzed carbonated beverage (e.g., ginger ale), as it's easier on the stomach. Defizzing is accomplished by transferring the drink from one glass to another and back again until there is no more fizz.

• Don't break tablets unless they are scored.
• Enteric-coated tablets, which contain thin outer layers that delay absorption, shouldn't be taken with milk or antacids; otherwise they may dissolve prematurely in the stomach.
• Don't chew, crush, or dissolve enteric-coated or sustained-release preparations.
• Don't stop taking your medication prematurely; talk to your doctor before discontinuing it.
• Never share medication.
• Don't save leftover prescription medication.
• All drugs have expiration dates; throw out all old medication.
• Have the name and telephone number of your family physician, the police, the ambulance, the nearest hospital, and the local poison control center handy in case of an emergency.
• When traveling abroad with controlled substances—e.g., opiates or benzodiazepines—always keep them in their original labeled containers.

MANAGING A COMPLICATED DRUG SCHEDULE

For most people, it is easy to remember to take a drug once a day, perhaps in the morning or at bedtime. Problems arise, however, when numerous medications must be taken more often, and on different schedules. These problems are compounded if the patient is senile, busy, forgetful, or travels frequently. Here are some suggestions to make your drug therapy a little easier.

- Familiarize yourself with the drugs you are taking (what they look like, what they're for, how and when they should be taken). Put the answers in writing, if necessary, and refer to it whenever you need a little refreshing.
- Set up a drug schedule. Similar to an appointment calendar, a drug schedule is a written checklist, organized by the hour, that enumerates when each drug should be taken.
- If you are elderly and frail, or are physically or mentally unable to manage your own drug therapy, then perhaps a close family member, friend, or a nurse can assist you.

THE DOSING SCHEDULE

When a drug should be taken depends on how long it takes to reach the bloodstream, how long it remains active in the blood, whether or not a constant level of the drug is needed, and how the drug interacts with food or the stomach. The following factors are taken into consideration when establishing dosage and medication schedules.

HOW MUCH?

In general, doctors try to prescribe the least amount of medication needed to combat a disease or condition. More specifically, however, various factors come into play that determine the dosage for each individual case.

AGE

The Elderly. As one grows older, kidney function declines and one metabolizes drugs more slowly. If a drug remains in the body longer, a lower dose should be used.

Children. Since children are smaller and generally need smaller doses, their dosages are usually based on height and weight. In addition, there are many drugs, like tetracycline, that should not be given to young children, as they are known to adversely affect growth and development. Even greater caution is needed when giving drugs to babies.

WEIGHT

Often, a very large person needs a higher dose of a drug than a small person in order for it to be effective. Also, fatty tissue absorbs certain medications differently from lean muscle—faster for some drugs, slower for others. For this reason, a person's body fat content might also be taken into consideration when determining the dosage of a drug.

MEDICAL HISTORY

If your kidney or liver function is impaired, lower doses are often required, as these organs play a key role in the elimination and metabolism of drugs. If too high a dose is taken, dangerously high levels of the drug can accumulate in the blood. Specific drugs have their own specific precautions. People with diabetes, for example, must proceed with caution when using certain antihypertensives, and anyone with a gastrointestinal problem should use extra care when taking any nonsteroidal anti-inflammatory drug. Be sure to inform your doctor of any and all medical problems you are experiencing or have experienced in the past. This way, your doctor will have the knowledge needed to ensure a safe and effective drug therapy.

WHEN?

With Meals. Certain drugs should be taken with meals because if taken on an empty stomach, they can cause nausea or abdominal discomfort. Aspirin is a common example of a drug that should be taken with food. Also, a large volume of food present in the stomach after a meal can often diminish the unpleasant side effects of the drug. For a few drugs, absorption of the drug from the GI tract is even enhanced when taken with meals because of bile secretion from the gallbladder.

On an Empty Stomach. Other drugs should be taken on an empty stomach because they may be inactivated by foods or their absorption may be significantly delayed. Thus, these drugs should be taken long before or in between meals.

At Bedtime. Drugs that cause drowsiness or dizziness (i.e., sedatives and some antihypertensives) can often be taken at bedtime to minimize this sometimes hazardous side effect.

HOW OFTEN?

The body metabolizes different drugs at different speeds. Some drugs remain in the bloodstream for days, while others leave the body only a few hours after they enter. The shorter this time is, the more often a drug must be taken in order to be effective.

ENDING DRUG TREATMENT

- Continue taking your medication until the physician approves its termination.
- Never end drug treatment on your own.
- The disappearance of symptoms is not enough to ensure that the drug has completed its work. Antibiotics, for example, may relieve the symptoms of an infection after a few days, but often they must continue to be taken for about 10 days to ensure that the invading microorganisms are all gone.
- Do not discontinue taking a drug because you don't think it is working. Some medications need weeks to achieve their beneficial effects.
- Do not discontinue your medication because of unpleasant side effects. Discuss the problems with your doctor, who may lower the dosage or inform you that your body will adjust to the drug after a couple of days and the side effects will simply disappear. Or, perhaps a substitute drug will produce fewer side effects.

As Needed. For example, you may take aspirin or acetaminophen when you have a headache (but never more frequently than the label recommends).

On an Ongoing Basis. Often, a drug must be taken at regular intervals for an extended period of time to achieve the desired effect (i.e., antihypertensives, antidepressants).

Four Times a Day. This can mean "at meals and bedtime" or "every 6 hours on the dot." Ask your doctor to specify.

WHAT IF I MISS A DOSE?

Almost everyone forgets to take their medicine at one time or another; the more drugs a person takes the more likely this is to occur. For some drugs, the missed dose should be taken as soon as it is remembered. For others, the dose should just be skipped altogether because it might result in a dangerously high concentration of the drug when the next dose is taken. In still other cases, special precautions need to be taken to avoid a poor result of therapy. For example, if a woman forgets to take one dose of her oral contraceptive, she should take it as soon as she remembers and then take the next dose at the regular time. If she misses 2 pills in a row, she should take 2 pills on each of the next 2 days and use an additional method of contraception for the rest of the cycle. The precautions vary with different oral contraceptives.

If you have a complicated drug schedule or you habitually forget to take your medicines, inform your doctor; perhaps there are ways to simplify your treatment.

FORMS OF MEDICATION

Drugs come in many different forms: tablets, drops, ointments, injections, and skin (transdermal) patches, to name a few. A single drug is often available in different formulations: cimetidine (Tagamet), an anti-ulcer agent, for example, is available as a tablet, liquid, and injection.

Various factors determine which form of a drug will be used.

- The speed at which it is needed
- The area of the body it will act upon
- Chemical properties of the medication
- Ease of administration by medical personnel or the individual being treated
- The age of the patient
- The patient's medical history

PILLS, TABLETS, CAPSULES, AND SUPPOSITORIES

ORAL MEDICATIONS

Pills, tablets, and capsules are taken simply by swallowing or chewing them. (A **pill** is a round mass of medication; **tablets** are flatter.) Sometimes pills and tablets are coated with a thin layer to protect your stomach (as with buffered aspirin) or to protect the drug from stomach acids.

Capsules are torpedo-shaped containers usually made of gelatin that enclose a powdered form of the drug. Controlled-release capsules contain pellets of a drug in a protective coating that dissolves slowly in the intestinal tract. This allows for prolonged, steady absorption into the bloodstream. Controlled-release drugs can remain active in the body for hours, days, or, when given in a repository (long-acting intramuscular injection) form, even months.

RECTAL/VAGINAL MEDICATIONS

A **suppository** is a large, bullet-shaped tablet that is inserted either rectally or vaginally. It melts at body temperature and then enters the bloodstream. It is used when a person cannot take a drug orally (e.g., if you are vomiting, unable to swallow, unconscious, or if the drug would be destroyed by the stomach's acids). Creams and ointments are also available for rectal use. Rectal administration is sometimes useful for young children.

LIQUID MEDICATIONS

For some people, these medications are easier to swallow than pills. Things to remember when taking a liquid drug include:

If liquid is in **suspension,** it may have to be shaken before taken. Some must be refrigerated.

Drops are commonly used for eye or ear infections.

INJECTIONS

Injections are necessary to administer medication that cannot pass through skin, that does not reach sufficient blood levels when taken orally, or is irritating to the stomach.

Used when a rapid response is needed.

Intravenous (IV). Injected into a vein. It is the quickest means of taking a drug and is, therefore, used in emergency situations.

Intramuscular (IM). Injected into a muscle (usually the thigh, upper arm, or buttock). This results in relatively fast drug action.

Subcutaneous (SQ). Injected beneath the surface of the skin (usually into the fat pads on the abdomen, the upper arms and thighs, and the upper hips). If subsequent injections are needed, different injection sites must be used in order to avoid leftover deposits of unabsorbed drug.

ABSORBED THROUGH SKIN OR MUCOUS MEMBRANES

Ointments. Applied to skin (such as nitroglycerin ointment for angina).

Transdermal Patch. Medicinally impregnated adhesive bandage that gradually releases drug. Examples include nitroglycerin for angina, scopolamine for motion sickness, nicotine for quitting smoking, and estrogen for hormone replacement.

Implants. Capsule implanted under the skin that releases its drug into the body for an extended period. Norplant, an effective form of long-term birth control, is the only commercially available implant today.

Sublingual Tablets. Drug is held under the tongue for rapid absorption into the bloodstream (i.e., nitroglycerin capsules).

Buccal Tablets. Drug is placed between the cheek and the gum, where it is quickly absorbed into the bloodstream.

SPRAYS, AEROSOLS, AND GASES

These are inhaled into the lungs, where they are then absorbed into the bloodstream.

Aerosol. A suspension of drug particles in air or gas, used for various respiratory conditions. In a fixed-dose aerosol, each squirt contains a specific dose of the drug. In a nonfixed-dose aerosol, each squirt contains an unmeasured amount.

Spray. Consists of drug particles dissolved in water. It is used for local effects in the nose, throat, and lungs.

Gas. Used for general anesthetic effects.

CREAMS, LOTIONS, AND OINTMENTS

These are applied directly to the skin and are used to treat local skin infections (i.e., insect bites, acne, hemorrhoids).

SIDE EFFECTS AND DRUG ALLERGIES

Side effects are adverse reactions to drugs taken properly—at normal doses and without other complicating factors such as use of other drugs. Before drugs appear on the market, the FDA usually mandates testing in healthy people as well as treatment of people suffering from the disorder. Then the benefits of the drug are compared with the risks, and guidelines for its use are drawn up. However, this testing may not reveal side effects that occur in less than 1 out of 1,000 cases, only in special cases (e.g., adverse effects during pregnancy), or only after long use of the drug or as a delayed reaction.

Adverse reactions to drugs can range from a change in laboratory results, noticeable only with sensitive testing, to life-threatening allergic reactions. They can affect any organ or organ system, and often, confusingly, mimic new or exacerbated symptoms of the disease they were prescribed to cure.

There are several forms of adverse reactions to drugs. Physicians distinguish among intolerance, idiosyncrasy, and allergy to any given drug. Intolerance occurs when a patient shows undesirable effects like those of overdosage at normal therapeutic dosage levels. Idiosyncrasy occurs when a patient's metabolism handles a drug in an unusual, unpredictable way. These two forms of adverse reaction do not depend on previous exposure to the drug.

In drug allergy, which does depend on previous expo-

REDUCING SIDE EFFECTS

In some cases, side effects can be minimized or avoided by:
Reducing the dosage
Changing the route of administration
Taking the drug at bedtime
Changing your diet

sure, the reaction may be immediate, especially if the drug is taken intravenously, or the reaction may take a week to develop. Common allergic reactions to drugs such as insulin, penicillin, and barbiturates include low fever, itchy rashes, and hives. Treatment consists of discontinuing the medication.

Probably the most drastic drug reaction is anaphylaxis, a violent form of drug allergy (see below). The first symptoms are all-over itchiness, especially on the soles of the feet and the palms. The skin of the face and ears may swell, mimicking a bad sunburn. The bronchial muscle (the muscle in the airway leading to the lungs) constricts, and the patient struggles for breath. The blood vessels dilate, blood pressure drops, and the patient faints. Deprived of oxygen, the brain and nervous system cannot narrow the blood vessels again, and the body cannot recover without immediate medical aid. Treatment consists of epinephrine, a drug that constricts blood vessels and dilates the bronchioles to open the airway. Steroid drugs may be given for a few days to aid recovery.

Other signals of allergy or serious adverse reaction to drugs include bleeding, wheezing, vomiting, impaired sight or hearing, and muscle weakness. Hives (itchy red lumps on the skin), headache, rashes, nausea, and drowsiness are less serious side effects. A physician should be consulted when side effects occur. Often another drug can be substituted; sometimes the patient must learn to tolerate the unpleasantness.

A person who has experienced an allergic reaction to a drug should carry a wallet card or wear an ID necklace or bracelet with the information even if the initial reaction was slight. Subsequent exposure to the drug may provoke more severe reaction.

TYPES OF ALLERGIC REACTIONS

MILD ALLERGY

- Itching
- Rash or hives
- Headache
- Nausea and other GI symptoms
- Drowsiness

Antihistamines can be used to prevent certain allergic responses. However, because of their slow onset, they are not very effective in treating reactions already underway.

ANAPHYLACTIC SHOCK

This is a life-threatening allergic response that occurs within 1 hour (usually within minutes) of taking a drug. Emergency treatment is necessary. Treatment consists of

an injection of epinephrine (adrenaline), which opens the blood vessels and airways, antihistamines, and sometimes steroids.

Symptoms include:

Extensive itchiness (especially on the soles of the feet and the palms)
Severe swelling of the eyes, lips, or tongue
Swelling of the throat, causing difficulty in breathing
Hives
Extensive dizziness
Nausea and vomiting
A rapid drop in blood pressure that can lead to fainting and even death

SERUM SICKNESS

This usually appears 1 to 3 weeks after the drug is taken, and disappears within a week after discontinuation. Symptoms include:

Skin rash
Fever
Nausea
Vomiting
Aching muscles and joints

DRUG INTERACTIONS

In the human body, 2 plus 2 does not always make 4. When drugs are taken together, they usually have an additive effect, but other results are possible. When the combined effects are greater than one would expect from adding the two drugs, the result is said to be synergistic. For example, trimethoprim and sulfamethoxazole are two antibiotics that can act synergistically and are commonly combined in one pill.

Some drug interactions are not beneficial. Drugs may counteract each other, canceling or diminishing any benefits, or the combination may produce too strong an effect as when alcohol is combined with a sedative. (For a complete list of drug interactions, see the chart in appendix A.)

TRAVELING WITH DRUGS

Unfortunately, vacationers cannot leave their illnesses at home when they travel. Following are some tips that make it easier to take your medication while traveling.

- If you are taking medication, don't forget to pack it. Bring enough to cover the whole trip, plus extra in case of delay or loss.
- Carry the drugs in their original containers, and keep a copy of the prescription for emergency refills, if needed.
- For foreign travel, know the drug's generic name and trade names in the countries you will visit. Foreign trade names are available in the *Merck Index.*
- For a large amount of drugs or any controlled substance, federal authorities recommend that you have a letter from the doctor explaining why and how the drugs are used.
- Pack a first-aid kit. (See chapter 15, The Basics of Safety.) Anticipate any medical problems you may encounter on your journey (i.e., diarrhea, muscle soreness, headache) and bring along the appropriate medications.
- If you are traveling with a child, bring Band-Aids and children's Tylenol.
- Many drugs conveniently come in smaller travel sizes. Check with your pharmacist.
- If traveling by plane, keep your medicine bag in your carry-on luggage. A lost suitcase might not be recovered quickly.

DRUG CLASSIFICATIONS

Drugs can be classified in many different ways: OTC versus prescription versus controlled drugs (R.G., narcotics, and others that can be prescribed for only a limited time); by chemical structure; by the dosage form—oral medications versus injectable products versus drugs applied to the skin or body surface. In this section, prescription medications will be discussed by therapeutic classes, with descriptions of what the drugs are intended to accomplish inside the body. Many of these classes also contain nonprescription drugs.

Over-the-Counter Drugs (OTC). There are more than 300,000 different nonprescription remedies that are taken for myriad ills from the serious to the nonexistent. Almost everyone uses them. OTC drugs are currently being reviewed by special panels of the Food and Drug Administration, but the FDA cannot protect the consumer from taking the wrong pill, or the right pill improperly. Only the consumer can do that.

The first step to becoming an intelligent user of OTC medications is to read the label before buying. The label must state all directions for use: what symptoms the drug treats, the dosage, who should not use the drug, the list of ingredients, possible side effects, and precautions. All these will directly help the consumer decide whether the drug is suitable.

Follow the directions on the label. These drugs are real medicines. Overdosage, side effects, and drug interactions are just as likely as with prescription drugs.

Consult a doctor if symptoms persist after a reasonable period of time. The label will state how long is reasonable. Seemingly trivial symptoms may be signs of a serious underlying disease.

Do not mix drugs or use alcohol in addition to drugs, unless a physician or pharmacist approves the mixtures. Also, do not buy more than you can use. These drugs can become outdated and should be discarded.

HOME MEDICINE CHEST

If you have the following items in your home, you should be sufficiently prepared for many of life's minor medical emergencies.

- **Allergy medicines:** a decongestant and antihistamine (for hives, hay fever, eye allergies)
- **Antibiotic cream** (Neosporin)
- **Antiseptic solution:** Betadine
- **Bandages:** adhesive-strip bandages, adhesive tape and sterile gauze pads (several sizes), Ace bandage, elastic bandages, surgical bandages (Steri-Strips)
- **Cotton balls**
- **Cough suppressant/syrup**
- **GI medicines** (Pepto-Bismol, milk of magnesia, antacid, antidiarrheals)
- **Hydrocortisone, calamine, or other anti-itch lotion** (for itchy skin conditions such as mosquito bites and poison ivy)
- **Hydrogen peroxide** (for cleaning wounds)
- **Ice bag** (for injured muscles, bones, and joints)
- **Pain relievers and fever reducers:** aspirin, acetaminophen, ibuprofen
- **Rubbing alcohol** (for cleaning the skin or needles/tweezers)
- **Skin cream/lotion** (for sunburn and dry skin)
- **Sunscreen** (cream and lip balm)
- **Thermometer, oral** (and a rectal if you have children)
- **Tweezers**

SOME HELPFUL HINTS REGARDING YOUR HOME MEDICINE CHEST

- It should be kept in a cool, dark place, away from heat, humidity, and bright light.
- It should be far out of children's reach.
- Narcotics and other medicines that could be toxic in an overdose should be kept under lock and key.

- Some drugs (i.e., insulin, allergy vaccines, certain antibiotics) that need to be kept in the refrigerator should be kept separate from the food.

PAIN AND FEVER MEDICATIONS

Aspirin. At an estimated 85 to 90 million dosages per day, aspirin is America's most widely used drug. Found in medicine chests, desk drawers, kitchen cabinets, and handbags, aspirin is both overused (taken in doses too large for inappropriate ailments) and underused (slighted in favor of less-effective narcotics for pain relief).

Aspirin (technically acetylsalicylic acid) is a very effective pain reliever. For example, it is sometimes more effective than propoxyphene (Darvon) or codeine against pain of inoperable cancer or postoperative dental pain. It is best for mild to moderate pains such as muscle aches, backaches, toothaches, and headaches. It should be used for short periods only; chronic or recurrent pains should be referred to a physician. Frequent headaches due to stress or tension, often depicted in TV commercials, may respond better to avoidance of stress than to painkillers.

Aspirin's second most important effect is its ability to lower fever. It also has an important anti-inflammatory effect, making it a major drug for the treatment of arthritis and rheumatic fever. Both these conditions should be monitored by a physician; however, aspirin can control arthritis pain but does not prevent the inflammatory progress of the disease. By acting on platelets aspirin also reduces the formation of blood clots; for this reason it has been recommended as a preventive measure against heart attacks and stroke. (This should be supervised by a physician.)

The antiplatelet activity of aspirin is an important side effect. People taking anticoagulants and those with liver disease, vitamin K deficiency, or hemophilia should avoid aspirin, as should pregnant women and patients expecting surgery. Conversely, many doctors now recommend a low dosage of aspirin—usually a baby aspirin or one regular tablet a day—to prevent clots that may cause a heart attack or stroke.

The most common side effect of aspirin is gastrointestinal irritation. For this reason, people with ulcers should not take aspirin. Taking aspirin after a meal may lessen stomach irritation. A full glass of water or milk afterward also helps, but buffering the acid with antacids may not reduce injury to the stomach lining. Enteric coatings—thin outer layers that delay absorption of aspirin until it reaches the intestines—seem best for those whose stomachs are irritated by regular aspirin.

Aspirin is a potent drug: Overdoses can be fatal, especially to young children, and some people are allergic to this substance. It has been associated with Reye's syndrome, a rare but dangerous illness that occurs in children under the age of 18 who have taken aspirin for relief of viral illness symptoms.

Note: Children under the age of 18 should never be given aspirin if they have or have had a cold or other viral illness.

Acetaminophen. Acetaminophen is very similar to aspirin in its effects against pain and fever. It has little effect on inflammatory disorders such as rheumatoid arthritis or on blood clotting. It has fewer side effects: no stomach irritation and few allergic reactions. However, massive overdoses can cause fatal liver damage; heavy use for several weeks can also injure the liver. For this reason, people with liver disease and heavy drinkers should avoid acetaminophen. In time, chronic acetaminophen use may also damage the kidneys, especially if it is taken in combination with aspirin.

Ibuprofen. Ibuprofen is a nonsteroidal anti-inflammatory drug. Like aspirin, it effectively relieves mild to moderate pain, fever, and inflammation. It was originally developed for the treatment of arthritis and sold by prescription only. It is available by prescription (Motrin, Rufen) for mild to moderate pain of rheumatoid arthritis and osteoarthritis and menstrual pain, and over-the-counter (Nuprin, Advil, Motrin, Midol 200) for fever, menstrual cramps, headaches, toothaches, backaches, muscle aches, and the minor aches and pains of arthritis and colds.

Ibuprofen can cause gastrointestinal distress, but this appears to be less of a problem than with aspirin. In some people, however, it can be severe. To minimize possible heartburn or upset stomach, it should be taken with food or milk. It should not be taken by anyone who has had a hypersensitivity reaction to aspirin, or who has experienced any serious reactions while taking other nonprescription analgesics. Ibuprofen can cause kidney failure in patients who have diminished fluid volume. It should not be taken in combination with either nonprescription (including aspirin) or prescription non-opiate analgesic drugs or given to children under 12 except under a doctor's supervision. Because ibuprofen may cause developmental problems in the fetus or complications during delivery, a woman should not take ibuprofen during pregnancy, especially in the last 3 months, unless directed by a physician.

Combination and Extra-Strength Pain Relievers. The active ingredient in a cup of coffee seems to boost the painkilling power of aspirin or acetaminophen, and for this reason caffeine is added to some brands. However, many people cannot tolerate caffeine, especially in the evening, and should look for another means to enhance the effect of the analgesic drugs.

The usual dose of aspirin or acetaminophen is 650 mg, or two regular tablets. There is some evidence that 1000 mg of acetaminophen may be more effective than the smaller dose, with little risk of additional toxicity.

For most purposes, however, aspirin is still given at the 650 mg dose because many people cannot tolerate the 1000 mg. Much larger doses of aspirin are used for rheumatoid arthritis, thereby increasing the risk of toxicity.

COLD AND COUGH REMEDIES, ALLERGY MEDICATIONS

According to an old saying, the common cold lasts 7 days, but modern medical care can shorten it to a week. This is still true. Over-the-counter drugs only relieve symptoms, and even antibiotics are useless against viral infections like cold and flu. Physicians recommend resting at home, breathing moist air from a vaporizer, and drinking plenty of fluids. A person wanting relief from symptoms should decide which are most bothersome and find a specific remedy rather than using a shotgun approach with an all-in-one capsule.

Cough Suppressants/Coughing can be useful if it brings up mucus and secretions from the lungs. Asthmatics and people with emphysema or other lung diseases may need to cough for these reasons. For others with a dry, nonproductive cough, effective cough-suppressing ingredients include codeine (a narcotic) and dextromethorphan.

Expectorants. These are supposed to thin out phlegm, mucus, and sputum so that they can be coughed away. Unfortunately, most preparations sold have not been proven to be very effective.

Nasal Decongestants. The kind applied directly to the nose are quite effective at clearing up stuffiness, but using them too long (more than about 4 days) can cause a rebound effect in which the nasal blood vessels enlarge tremendously as the previous dose wears off. Effective ingredients include oxymetazoline (for long action) and phenylephrine. Phenylpropanolamine and pseudoephedrine are two oral agents with similar effects.

Antihistamines (H₁ blockers). These drugs block some of the effects of histamine, a natural body substance that stimulates among other things the fluid-producing cells of the nose, eyes, lungs, and skin. Some of the effects of antihistamines against the runny nose of colds may be due to an anticholinergic effect, which will tend to dry up secretions. Some of them are useful against motion sickness. However, some have major side effects: drowsiness, which makes it unwise to operate machinery or drive after taking these drugs, and dry mouth. Different antihistamines have different potential for causing drowsiness, however, and the amount differs from person to person. The drowsiness effect can be aggravated by alcohol.

Newer antihistamines, for example, terenadine (Seldane) and astemizole (Hismanal) have no demonstrable sedative or mouth-drying effects and are now widely prescribed. An example of how a side effect can be used as a therapeutic effect is seen with diphenylhydramine. This excellent anti-allergy medication produced sedation too frequently. It is now widely used in OTC sleep remedies such as Sominex.

The older antihistamines below are safe and effective for use against some allergy symptoms.

Low risk of drowsiness: brompheniramine maleate, chlorpheniramine maleate
High risk of drowsiness: diphenhydramine hydrochloride, doxylamine succinate

DRUGS TO TREAT INFECTIONS

Each year, more drugs are prescribed to combat infections than for any other reason. These comprise over 182 million prescriptions, or over 13 percent of all prescription drugs, according to a study reported in the *Journal of the American Medical Association.* These include antibiotics such as the penicillins, erythromycin, the tetracyclines, cephalosporins, and aminoglycosides, which operate against bacteria and some fungi.

Antibiotics, however, have no effect against certain forms of infection. To treat some parasitic infections such as those caused by amoebae, there are synthetic compounds available. Viruses are very resistant to available antibiotics. There are drugs that may help prevent some viral infections (for example, amantadine for some forms of influenza) or may ameliorate the severity of an infection. The agents used in the treatment of genital herpes, for instance, do not cure the underlying disease but are helpful in controlling individual infections. Another example of this is the drug AZT, which may be useful in creating a better quality of life for people with AIDS.

Other drugs in this class are used against tuberculosis, malaria, leprosy, and parasitic infections such as hookworm and roundworm.

CARDIOVASCULAR DRUGS

The second most frequently prescribed category of drugs is the medications that affect the heart and blood vessels. If diuretics (used to promote the excretion of sodium and water and often prescribed for hypertension and heart failure) were included, it would be the largest category.

Cardiovascular drugs are those used to treat congestive heart failure, irregular heartbeat, angina pectoris, and hypertension. Digitalis, in one of its many forms, is an important drug used against congestive heart failure, but this condition may also be treated with a vasodilator—a drug to dilate blood vessels. Digitalis may also be used to slow some types of overly rapid heartbeat. Other drugs used to regulate heartbeat include beta-blockers (drugs that prevent some of the excitatory effects of the sympathetic nervous system), various forms of quinidine (a quinine derivative), local anesthetic derivatives, calcium channel blockers, and many other medications.

Beta-adrenergic-blocking agents are also used to prevent angina. The most widely prescribed class of drugs for the treatment of angina is the nitrates: These may be placed under the tongue, rubbed into the skin, worn in an impregnated skin patch, or even tucked into the cheek. Long-acting forms of nitrates are also used to prevent angina. A third line of defense against angina are the calcium-channel blockers, a group of chemically unrelated medications that prevent spasms of the smooth muscle in the walls of the blood vessels supplying the heart.

Hypertension, or high blood pressure, is also treated with beta-blockers, calcium-channel blockers, diuretics (see chapter 16, Heart and Blood Vessel Diseases), ACE (angiotensin converting enzyme) inhibitors, and other drugs. These include alpha-adrenergic blockers, which modify the effect of the sympathetic nervous system on blood vessels; vasodilators, described above; and a number of drugs that decrease activity of the sympathetic nervous system.

Agents now available for dissolving clots that block arteries include tissue plasminogen activator (TPA), a product of genetic engineering, and streptokinase, a bacterial enzyme. A number of studies show aspirin to be effective in helping to prevent second heart attacks and strokes.

PSYCHOTHERAPEUTIC DRUGS

This class of drugs includes medications used to treat psychoses such as schizophrenia and other severe personality disorders, mood disorders such as depression, and forms of substance abuse including alcoholism. This group includes antianxiety drugs (tranquilizers) and drugs used to treat attention deficit hyperactivity disorder.

Antianxiety drugs constitute a major portion of the drugs taken in the United States, including alprazolam (Xanax) and diazepam (Valium). These compounds suppress anxiety and produce sleep. By themselves they are relatively safe but can be extremely dangerous when combined with alcohol or other central nervous system depressants.

Antipsychotic or neuroleptic drugs are used to control the symptoms of acute psychoses: hallucinations, failure of logic, severe excitement, aggression, and delusions. These symptoms may be the result of acute mania, schizophrenia, paranoia, and other psychotic disorders.

Drugs Used in Affective Disorders. Affective disorders are the imbalances of mood more commonly known as manic or depressive illnesses. Unless treated with drugs or electroconvulsive therapy, severe affective disease may persist for 6 months or longer. Tricyclic antidepressants trazodone (Desyrel) and fluoxetine (Prozac) are most often used against depression. If they are ineffective or cause intolerable side effects, monoamine oxidase inhibitors are prescribed.

The use of monoamine oxidase inhibitors is complicated by the need for rigid dietary control and avoidance of other drugs, especially stimulants, dextromethorphan, beer, wine, and caffeine. (See "Drug Interactions.") Lithium is most often used for patients with manic-depressive disorders. It has also been used to treat depression.

Other Mental Disorders. An adjunct in the treatment of alcoholism is a drug called disulfiram, or Antabuse. (See chapter 33.) Attention deficit hyperactivity disorder is a childhood syndrome of inattentiveness and impulsiveness. This condition is, paradoxically, treated with stimulants. (See chapter 33.)

Appendix A

COMMONLY PRESCRIBED DRUGS

ANALGESICS

Generic (Brand Names)	Common Side Effects	Drug Interactions	Precautions
NONNARCOTIC acetaminophen (aspirin-free Anacin, Bufferin AF, Excedrin, Feverall, Liquiprin, Midol, Panadol, Percogesic, Phenaphen, aspirin-free St. Joseph, Tempra, Tylenol) OTC		Heavy drinking of **alcohol** may increase risk of liver damage.	Not recommended for use for more than 3 days for fever or 10 days for pain. Overdose can cause liver failure; prolonged use can damage kidneys.
aspirin (Anacin, Ascriptin, Bayer, Bufferin, Empirin, St. Joseph) OTC (Easprin) RX	Nausea/vomiting; indigestion; possible GI bleeding.	May increase effect of **anticoagulants** and **oral antidiabetic** agents. May decrease effect of **gout** medications (especially **allopurinol**). Use with **NSAIDs, corticosteroids,** or **alcohol** increases risk of stomach irritation.	Taking high doses during pregnancy may lead to birth defects. Taken near term may delay labor. Breast-feeding not recommended. Prolonged use can cause stomach bleeding and stomach ulcers.
NARCOTIC butalbital, aspirin + caffeine (Fiorinal) C-III **butalbital, acetaminophen + caffeine** (Esgie, Fioricet)	Dizziness/light-headedness; intoxicated feeling; drowsiness; nausea; abdominal pain	**CNS depressants** (i.e., narcotics, tranquilizers, antianxiety) increase CNS depression. Use with **MAO inhibitors** increases risk of CNS depression and may increase blood pressure. Use with **anticoagulants** increases risk of bleeding. Use with **oral antidiabetics/insulin** increases risk of hypoglycemia. Use with **NSAIDs** increases risk of stomach ulcer and stomach bleeding. Decreases effectiveness of **gout** medications (i.e., **probenecid, sulfinpyrazone**).	Use caution in elderly and if have head injury, peptic ulcer, or liver/kidney impairment. Use not recommended in child less than 12 or when breast-feeding. Avoid driving or any other activity requiring mental alertness or physical coordination. Drug dependence may develop.
hydrocodone + acetaminophen (Anexsia, Hydrocet, Hy-Phen, Lortab, Vicodin, Zydone) C-III **codeine + acetaminophen** C-III, **hydrocodone + aspirin** (Azdone, Lortab ASA) C-III	Nausea/vomiting; light-headedness/dizziness; sedation/drowsiness	**CNS depressants** (other narcotics, sedatives, hypnotics, antianxiety, antidepressants) and **MAO inhibitors** increase CNS depression. **Antinauseants** alter hydrocodone's effect. **Anticholinergic** agents increase risk of bowel disorders. Avoid **alcohol**.	Should not be used during pregnancy or while breast-feeding. Use caution if elderly, have pulmonary disease, liver/kidney impairment, hypothyroidism, Addison's disease, or enlarged prostate. Drug dependence may develop. Avoid driving and other potentially hazardous activities, as mental alertness and physical coordination may be impaired.

ANALGESICS

Generic (Brand Names)	Common Side Effects	Drug Interactions	Precautions
oxycodone + acetaminophen (Percocet, Roxicet, Roxicodone, Tylox) C-II **oxycodone + aspirin** (Percodan)	Light-headedness; dizziness; sedation; nausea/vomiting	**CNS depressants** increase CNS depression. Oxycodone increases effect of **tricyclic antidepressants** and **MAO inhibitors.** Use with **anticholinergic agents** increases risk of bowel obstruction. Avoid **alcohol.**	Use caution if elderly and if have severe kidney/liver impairment, head injury, hypothyroidism, Addison's disease, or enlarged prostate. Not for use in child under 6; use caution in child 6 or older. Drug dependence may develop. Avoid driving and other potentially hazardous activities, as mental alertness and physical coordination may be impaired.
propoxyphene (Darvocet-N, Darvon, Dolene, Doxaphene, Wygesic) C-IV	Dizziness/drowsiness; nausea/vomiting; intoxicated feeling	**Tricyclic antidepressants, barbiturates, other CNS depressants, oral anticoagulants,** and **MAO inhibitors** increase CNS depression. Use with **carbamazepine** can cause severe adverse reactions, including coma. Avoid **alcohol.**	Use caution if elderly or if have kidney/liver disease; reduced dose may be necessary. Should not be used during pregnancy. Use in children not recommended. Avoid driving or operating heavy machinery, as mental capacity and physical coordination may be impaired. Drug dependence may develop.

ANTIBIOTICS

Generic (Brand Names)	Common Side Effects	Drug Interactions	Precautions
CEPHALOSPORINS **cefaclor** (Ceclor)	Diarrhea; itching; rash; joint pain/swelling	**Probenecid** may increase cefaclor blood levels. Use with **aminoglycoside** antibiotics may increase risk of kidney damage.	Use caution if have history of drug allergies (especially to penicillin) or of GI problems. Safety and effectiveness not established in children less than 1 month old. If kidney is impaired, close monitoring is advised.
cefadroxil (Duricef, Ultracef)	Rash; diarrhea; genital itching	**Probenecid** increases cefadroxil blood levels.	Use caution if have a history of drug allergies (especially to penicillin) or GI problems (i.e., colitis). Large doses may trigger seizures if kidney is impaired.
cefuroxime (Ceftin, Kefurox, Zinacef)	Headache; dizziness; diarrhea; nausea/vomiting; rash	**Probenecid** increases cefuroxime blood levels. Use with **aminoglycosides** and potent **diuretics** increases risk of kidney damage.	Use caution if have a history of drug allergies (especially to penicillin) or of GI problems (i.e., colitis). Large doses may cause seizures if kidney function is impaired.
ERYTHROMYCIN **erythromycin** (EES, E-Mycin, ERYC, Eryped, Ery-Tab, Erythrocin, Ilosone, Ilotycin, PCE)	Nausea/vomiting; diarrhea; rash/itching	May increase action or side effects of **theophylline, carbamazepine, digoxin, oral anticoagulants.** Use with **cyclosporine** can increase risk of kidney damage.	Avoid or use with caution if liver/kidney function is impaired or if have syphilis. Prolonged use increases risk of liver damage.

ANTIBIOTICS

Generic (Brand Names)	Common Side Effects	Drug Interactions	Precautions
PENICILLINS amoxicillin (Amoxil, Augmentin, Larotid, Polymox, Trimox, Wymox)	Rash; nausea/vomiting; fatigue/weakness; diarrhea; itching	May decrease effectiveness of **oral contraceptives** and increase risk of breakthrough bleeding. Use with other **antibiotics** lowers effectiveness of amoxicillin. **Probenecid** increases amoxicillin blood levels and may cause toxicity.	Use caution if have history of allergies (especially to cephalosporins).
Penicillin V (Betapen-VK, Ledercillin VK, Pen-Vee K, V-cillin K, Veetids)	Nausea/vomiting; diarrhea; rash; black, hairy tongue	**Probenecid** increases penicillin blood levels and may cause toxicity.	Use caution if have history of allergies (especially of cephalosporins). Prolonged use may increase risk of yeast infections and diarrhea. Continue taking drug for entire length of treatment (usually 10 days).
QUINOLONES ciprofloxacin (Cipro)	Headache; rash; nausea/vomiting; diarrhea; abdominal pain/discomfort; light-sensitivity; tremor; restlessness; light-headedness; confusion	Increases the effect of **warfarin**. **Probenecid** increases ciprofloxacin blood levels. Use with **fenoprofen** increases risk of seizures and CNS stimulation. Use with **theophylline** increases risk of serious reactions (i.e., cardiac arrest, seizures). Taken with certain **antacids** lowers the effect of ciprofloxacin.	Safety not established in children under 18. Adjust dosage if liver or kidney function is impaired. Use caution if have convulsive disorder. Take 2 hours after meals.
TETRACYCLINES tetracycline (Achromycin, Achromycin V, Panmycin, Robitet, Sumycin, Topicycline)	Nausea/vomiting; diarrhea; light-sensitive rash; rash/itching	May decrease effectiveness of **oral contraceptives** and increase risk of breakthough bleeding. Tetracycline interferes with action of **penicillins** and increases action of **oral anticoagulants** and **lithium. Antacids, iron, and dairy products** interfere with the absorption of tetracycline.	Pregnant and nursing women should not use. Not recommended for use in children younger than 8 years old. Use caution if have syphilis. Lower doses are necessary if kidney is impaired. Avoid UV light.
OTHER ANTI-INFECTIVES nitrofurantoin (Furadantin, Macrodantin)	Loss of appetite; nausea/vomiting; muscle fatigue; diarrhea; rash; difficulty breathing	**Probenecid** increases nitrofurantoin blood levels. Use with **nalidixic acid** or **magnesium trisilicate** lowers the effect of nitrofurantoin.	If pregnant, do not use at term. Passes into milk; use with caution. Not for infants less than 1 month; reduce dose in older children. Use with caution in anyone with anemia or diabetes mellitus. Take with food. Used only for urinary tract infections.
ANTIFUNGAL AGENT Miconazole (Monistat 3, Monistat-Derm) RX (Micatin, Monistat 7) OTC	Irritation/burning/itching; rash; hives; pelvic cramps; headaches	May increase effect of **anticoagulants** and **phenytoin.** Use with **oral antidiabetics** increases risk of low blood sugar. Lowers the antifungal action of **amphotericin B.**	Avoid using diaphragm if taking suppositories.

ANTIBIOTICS

Generic (Brand Names)	Common Side Effects	Drug Interactions	Precautions
ANTIVIRAL AGENT **acyclovir** (Zovirax)	Burning/ stinging/ itching; rash (ointment); rash; nausea/ vomiting; headache; dizziness; diarrhea; constipation; loss of appetite (capsules); itching/rash/hives; nausea/vomiting; lethargy (injection)	**Probenecid** increases acyclovir blood levels. Acyclovir increases risk of kidney damage when used with drugs that are potentially harmful to kidneys. Use of injectable acyclovir with **interferon** and **methotrexate** may increase risk of adverse reactions of the nervous system.	Use caution during pregnancy and if kidney is impaired. Used only for the treatment of herpes.
VAGINAL **ANTI-INFECTIVE** **terconazole** (Terazol)	Burning/itching; headaches; body pain; abdominal pain; fever (cream); genital pain; headache (suppositories)	None known.	Breast-feeding not recommended. Do not use diaphragm when taking suppositories. Use only for yeast infections.

ANTICOAGULANTS

Generic (Brand Names)	Common Side Effects	Drug Interactions	Precautions
warfarin (Coumadin)	Internal bleeding resulting in pain; difficulty breathing or swallowing; headache	Many drugs interact with warfarin to either increase or decrease anti-clotting effect (i.e., **antibiotics, barbiturates, diuretics, laxatives, oral contraceptives**). Large doses of **aspirin** significantly increase warfarin's effect.	Use caution if elderly, if kidney/ liver is impaired, or if have high blood pressure, diabetes, edema, high cholesterol level, hypothyroidism, hyperthyroidism, cancer, collagen disease, heart problems, diarrhea, fever, hepatitis, jaundice, or are malnourished. Use caution in child under 18. Should not be used during pregnancy.

BRONCHIAL THERAPY

Generic (Brand Names)	Common Side Effects	Drug Interactions	Precautions
ANTIHISTAMINES **astemizole** (Hismanal)	Fatigue; increased appetite; dry mouth; weight gain	Use with **antiarrythmics, terfenadine,** and **diuretics** that affect electrolyte balance increases risk of heart problems.	Use caution if have asthma, electrolyte abnormalities, kidney/liver damage. Use caution in child under 12.
clemastine (Tavist) OTC	Sleepiness, dizziness; indigestion; ringing in ears	**Alcohol, barbiturates, narcotics, sedatives,** other **CNS depressants,** and other **antihistamines** increase risk of severe CNS depression. Use with **MAO inhibitors** increases anticholinergic effects.	Use caution if elderly or if have glaucoma, peptic ulcer, hyperthyroidism, cardiovascular disease, high blood pressure, or asthma. Do not use if breast-feeding. Use caution in child under 12. Do not drive or engage in other potentially hazardous activities until you know how the drug affects you.

BRONCHIAL THERAPY

Generic (Brand Names)	Common Side Effects	Drug Interactions	Precautions
promethazine (Anergan, Mepergan, Phenazine, Phenergan, Phenergan D, Prorex)	Drowsiness; dizziness; nausea; drowsiness	**Alcohol, barbiturates, narcotics, sedatives,** other **CNS depressants,** and other **antihistamines** increase risk of severe CNS depression. **Antacids** lower the effect of promethazine; take at least 1 hour apart.	Use caution if liver is impaired, if have peptic ulcer, a convulsive disorder, heart disease, glaucoma, asthma or other lower respiratory tract condition, or history of sleep apnea. If pregnant, discontinue use 2 weeks before delivery. Not for use in child under 2. Do not drive or engage in other potentially hazardous activities until you know how the drug affects you.
terfenadine (Seldane, Seldane-D)	Insomnia; headache; drowsiness; fatigue; dizziness; palpitations; rash; nausea; indigestion; dry mouth/nose/throat; blurring of vision	Increases effect of **sedatives, antidepressants,** and **antipsychotics.** Lowers effect of some **antihypertensives.** Use with **MAO inhibitors** increases risk of dangerous rise in blood pressure. Used with **erythromycin** or **ketoconazole** increases risk of rare but serious heart-related side effects.	Use caution if elderly, if liver is damaged, or if have hypertension, diabetes, heart disease, glaucoma, enlarged prostate, or hyperthyroidism. Do not use if breast-feeding or in a child under 12.
BRONCHODILATORS albuterol (Proventil, Ventolin)	Palpitations, increased blood pressure; nervousness, tremor; headache; dizziness, drowsiness, weakness; nausea, indigestion, vomiting, loss of appetite	**MAO inhibitors** and **tricyclic antidepressants** increase risk of dangerously high blood pressure. Other **sympathomimetic agents** increase toxicity. **Beta-blockers** lower effect of both drugs.	Use caution if elderly or if have heart problems, hyperthyroidism, diabetes, or a convulsive disorder. Use caution in child under 12. Don't stop drug treatment on your own.
NASAL CORTICOSTEROID beclomethasone (Beclovent, Beconase, Beconase AQ, Vancenase, Vancenase AQ, Vanceril)	Nasal irritation, nose bleeds, sneezing; headache, nausea, light-headedness; dry mouth	None known.	Avoid if have had nasal ulcers or nasal surgery recently. Use extreme caution if have tuberculosis or other viral infection. Do not use if have asthma, chickenpox or measles. Not for use for child younger than 6.
XANTHINES theophylline (Aerolate, Constant-T, Bronkodyl, Bronkolixir, Elixophyllin, Marax, Quibron, Quibron-T, Respbid, Slo-Bid, Slo-Phyllin, T-Phyl, Tedral, Theo-24, Theobid, Theochron, Theo-Dur, Theolair, Theolair-SR, Theo-Organidin, Theovent, Theo-X, Uniphyl)	Nausea/vomiting; restlessness; dizziness	**Cimetidine, ciprofloxacin, erythromycin, propranolol, allopurinol,** and **oral contraceptives** increase theophylline blood levels. **Barbiturates, rifampin, lithium, phenytoin,** and **nicotine** lower theophylline blood levels.	Use caution in person over 55 and child younger than 1. Use caution if kidney/liver impaired, or if have sustained high fever, high blood pressure, arrhythmia, severe asthma, flu or other viral infection, flu immunization, or history of heart problems, or peptic ulcer. Should not breast-feed. Don't stop taking drug on your own. Blood levels should be monitored.

DERMATOLOGICS

Generic (Brand Names)	Common Side Effects	Drug Interactions	Precautions
TOPICAL ANTIFUNGAL betamethasone + clotrimazole (Lotrisone)	Skin irritations; itching; burning/stinging	None known.	During pregnancy, do not over apply, or use in large amounts, or for prolonged periods. Breast-feeding not recommended. Safety and effectiveness not established in children under 12 yrs. old. Not recommended for diaper rash; apply smallest amount necessary; chronic use may interfere with child's development.
TOPICAL ANTI-INFECTIVES mupirocin (Bactroban)	Burning/stinging; rash; itching	None known.	Continued or prolonged use may cause growth of a resistant strain of bacteria, possibly leading to secondary infection.
ACNE PREPARATION tretinoin (Retin-A)	Burning/stinging; blistering; peeling of skin; redness	None known.	Avoid/minimize exposure to UV light. Skin-drying products (i.e., soaps, cleansers, cosmetics) increase risk of dryness and skin irritation. If you have a sunburn, avoid use until fully recovered. Use caution if you have eczema. Avoid contact with eyes, mouth, and nose.
HAIR RESTORAL AGENT minoxidil (Rogaine)	Skin irritation; nausea/vomiting; headache	None known.	Use caution if have heart problems or high blood pressure. Safety not known in child under 18. Use not recommended if pregnant or breast-feeding.

ANTIDIABETIC DRUGS

Generic (Brand Names)	Common Side Effects	Drug Interactions	Precautions
glipizide (Glucotrol)	Dizziness, drowsiness; headache; allergic skin reactions; nausea, diarrhea, constipation; hypoglycemia	Many drugs decrease effect of glyburide (**corticosteroids, hormones, diuretics, rifampin, phenobarbital, antipsychotics, phenytoin**). Many drugs increase effect of glyburide (**insulin, dicumarol, probenecid, oral anticoagulants, MAO inhibitors, sulfonamides, aspirin**). Use with **alcohol** can cause hypoglycemia.	Use caution in elderly, malnourished. Use caution if liver, kidney, adrenal or pituitary gland is impaired. If using during pregnancy, discontinue at least 1 month prior to delivery date. Should not breast-feed. Glucose tests should be performed frequently during therapy.
glyburide (DiaBeta, Glynase, Micronase)	Nausea; heartburn; bloating; itching, other allergic skin reactions; liver function abnormalities; hypoglycemia	Many drugs decrease effect of glyburide (**corticosteroids, hormones, diuretics, rifampin, phenobarbital, antipsychotics, phenytoin**). Many drugs increase effect of glyburide (**insulin, dicumarol, probenecid, oral anticoagulants, MAO inhibitors, sulfonamides, aspirin**). Use with **alcohol** can cause hypoglycemia.	Use caution in elderly, malnourished. Use caution if liver, kidney, adrenal or pituitary gland is impaired. If using during pregnancy, discontinue 2 weeks prior to delivery date. Should not breast-feed. Glucose tests should be performed frequently during therapy.

DIURETICS

Generic (Brand Names)	Common Side Effects	Drug Interactions	Precautions
DIURETIC COMBINATIONS triamterene + hydro-chlorothiazide (Dyazide, Maxzide)	Weakness, fatigue, dizziness, headache; nausea, vomiting; muscle cramps	**Alcohol, barbiturates, narcotics, beta-blockers,** and other **antihypertensives** increase antihypertensive effect. **Indomethacin** and other **NSAIDs** increase risk of renal failure. Risk of **lithium** toxicity. **ACE inhibitors** increase potassium levels.	Use caution if elderly, if kidney/liver is impaired, or if have diabetes. Use caution if pregnant or breast-feeding. Monitor kidney function and levels of body salts. Don't discontinue drug therapy on your own.
LOOP DIURETIC bumetanide (Bumex)	Hypotension; dizziness, headache; nausea; muscle cramps	**Antihypertensives** increase antihypertensive effect. **Indomethacin, probenecid,** and **NSAIDs** lower effects of bumetanide. Risk of **lithium** toxicity. Use with **aminoglycoside antibiotics** increases risk of hearing problems. Avoid **alcohol.**	Use caution if elderly, if kidney is impaired, or if have liver cirrhosis, ventricular arrhythmia, prostate trouble, or diabetes. Use caution in child under 18. Monitor kidney function. Don't discontinue drug therapy on your own. Decreased potassium levels may occur; supplements may be needed; eat plenty of fruits and vegetables.
furosemide (Lasix)	Dizziness	**Alcohol, barbiturates, narcotics,** and other **antihypertensives** increase antihypertensive effect. **Indomethacin** and **NSAIDs** decrease effect of furosemide. Risk of **lithium, digitalis,** and **salicylate** toxicity. Use with **aminoglycoside antibiotics** increases risk of hearing problems. Lowers effect of **oral hypoglycemics.**	Use caution if elderly, if kidney is impaired, or if have liver cirrhosis, gout, prostate trouble, or diabetes. Monitor kidney function. Don't discontinue drug therapy on your own. Decreased potassium, salt, and calcium levels may occur; supplements may be needed; eat plenty of fruits and vegetables.
POTASSIUM SUPPLEMENT potassium chloride (K-Dur, K-Lor, K-Norm, K-Tab, Kaochlor, Kaon-Cl, Kay Ciel, Klotrix, Klorvess, Micro-K, Slow-K, Ten-K)	Nausea, vomiting; abdominal pain; possible GI bleeding	Many drugs interact to either increase or decrease potassium levels (i.e., **ACE inhibitors, diuretics, laxatives**).	Use caution if kidney is impaired or have adrenal insufficiency. Take with meals to avoid GI irritation. Monitor potassium levels.
THIAZIDE DIURETICS hydrochlorothiazide (Aldactazide, Aldoril, Esidrix, HydroDIURIL, Moduretic, Oretic, Thiuretic)	Leg cramps	**Alcohol, barbiturates, narcotics,** and other **antihypertensives** increase antihypertensive effect. **NSAIDs** lower diuretic effect. Risk of **lithium** and **digitalis** toxicity. Dosages of **insulin** and **oral hypoglycemics** need adjusting. **Corticosteroids** increase potassium loss.	Use caution if kidney/liver is impaired or if have diabetes or lupus. Decreased potassium, salt, and calcium levels may occur; supplements may be needed; eat plenty of fruits and vegetables.
chlorothiazide (Diuril)	Dizziness; loss of appetite; headache; abdominal pain	**Alcohol, barbiturates, narcotics,** and other **antihypertensives** increase antihypertensive effect. Dosages of **insulin** and **oral hypoglycemics** need adjusting. Risk of **digitalis** toxicity. **NSAIDs** lower diuretic effect.	Use caution if kidney/liver is impaired, or if have diabetes or lupus. Decreased potassium, salt, and calcium levels may occur; supplements may be needed; eat plenty of fruits and vegetables.

CARDIOVASCULAR DRUGS

Generic (Brand Names)	Common Side Effects	Drug Interactions	Precautions
ACE INHIBITORS **captopril** (Capoten, Capozide)	Dizziness, weakness; hypotension, chest pain, palpitations; rash, itching; diminution/loss of taste; cough	Other **antihypertensives** increase risk of hypotension. **Indomethacin, other NSAIDs,** and **vasodilators** lower the antihypertensive effect. Increases risk of **lithium** toxicity. Use with **potassium-sparing diuretics** and **potassium supplements** increases potassium blood levels. Use with **cimetidine** increases risk of adverse reactions and lowers effect of captopril.	Use caution if elderly, if kidney is impaired, or if have diabetes. Avoid rapid increase in physical activity. Avoid during pregnancy, especially in 2nd and 3rd trimester. Breast-feeding not recommended. Avoid driving or other potentially dangerous activities until you know how the drug affects you. Do not stop taking drug on your own.
enalapril (Vasotec)	Hypotension, fainting; dizziness, headache, weakness; rash; nausea; cough	Use with **diuretics** and other **antihypertensives** can lead to excessive hypotension. Increases risk of **lithium** toxicity. Use with **potassium-sparing diuretics** and **potassium supplements** increases potassium blood levels. Avoid **alcohol**.	Use caution if kidney is impaired, or if have diabetes or heart problems. Avoid during pregnancy, especially 2nd and 3rd trimesters. Breast-feeding not recommended. Avoid driving or other potentially dangerous activities until you know how the drug affects you. Do not stop taking drug on your own.
lisinopril (Prinivil, Zestril)	Hypotension, chest pain; dizziness, headache; fatigue, numbness/tingling; rash; diarrhea, nausea, vomiting, indigestion; impotence; cough, breathing difficulties, nasal congestion	**Diuretics** and other **antihypertensives** can lead to excessive hypotension. Use with **indomethacin** can decrease antihypertensive effect. Increases risk of **lithium** toxicity. Use with **potassium-sparing diuretics** and **potassium supplements** increases potassium blood levels. Avoid **alcohol**.	Use caution if elderly, if kidney is impaired or if have diabetes or heart problems. Avoid during pregnancy, especially 2nd and 3rd trimesters. Breast-feeding not recommended. Avoid driving or other potentially dangerous activities until you know how the drug affects you. Do not stop taking drug on your own.
ALPHA-ADRENERGIC BLOCKERS **terazosin** (Hytrin)	Palpitations, hypotension; dizziness, headache; drowsiness; numbness, tingling, nervousness; nausea; impotence; fluid retention; painful extremities, back pain; blurred vision; nasal congestion, breathing difficulties, sinusitis	Use with other **antihypertensives** increases risk of hypotension and of fainting.	Avoid driving and other potentially hazardous activities as mental alertness and physical coordination may be impaired. Take at bedtime to alleviate some of the side effects.
ANTIANGINAL **isosorbide dinitrate** (Dilatrate-SR, ISMO, Iso-Bid, Isordil, Sorbitrate, Sorbitrate-SA)	Headache, dizziness, light-headedness; itching; nausea, vomiting	**Calcium-channel blockers** and **vasodilators** increase hypotensive effect. Avoid **alcohol**.	Use caution if elderly, if kidney/liver is impaired, or have heart problems, low blood pressure, or blood abnormalities. Avoid driving and other potentially dangerous activities until you know how the drug affects you. Do not stop taking drug on your own; drug must be tapered off gradually.

CARDIOVASCULAR DRUGS

Generic (Brand Names)	Common Side Effects	Drug Interactions	Precautions
nitroglycerin (Deponit, Minitran, Nitro-Bid, Nitro-Dur, Nitrodisc, Nitrogard, Nitroglyn, Nitrol, Nitrolingual, Nitrostat, Tridil)	Headache; hypotension, fainting; increased angina; light-headedness	**Alcohol, antihypertensives, calcium-channel blockers,** and other **vasodilators** increase hypotensive effect.	Use caution if have glaucoma, heart problems, thyroid disease, or blood disorders. Avoid driving or other potentially dangerous activities until you know how the drug affects you. Don't discontinue treatment on your own. Monitoring blood pressure is recommended.
BETA-ADRENERGIC BLOCKERS atenolol (Tenoretic, Tenormin)	Muscle fatigue; dizziness, light-headedness	**hydralazine, methyldopa, prazosin,** and **thiazide-type diuretics** increase antihypertensive effect. Use with **reserpine** can cause hypotension and/or bradycardia. Use caution if also taking **digitalis, clonidine,** or other **drugs causing myocardial depression.** Use with **antacids** lowers the effect of atenolol (take 1 hour apart).	Use caution if elderly, if kidney is impaired, or if have congestive heart failure, diabetes, a lung disorder (i.e., asthma, bronchitis), or thyroid disease. Breast-feeding is not recommended. When ending treatment, drug must be withdrawn gradually.
metoprolol (Lopressor, Toprol XL)	Weakness; itching, rash; shortness of breath; depression; cold hands and feet	Use with **indomethacin** lowers metoprolol's effect. **Cimetidine** increases metoprolol's blood levels. Use with **nifedipine** can lead to dangerously low blood pressure. Use with **ergotamine** may worsen circulation in hands and feet.	Use caution if elderly, if kidney/liver is impaired, if have heart problems, or if have lung problems (i.e., asthma, bronchitis) or diabetes. Avoid in late pregnancy. Avoid driving and other potentially dangerous activities until you know how the drug affects you. Do not stop taking drug on your own.
nadolol (Corgard, Corzide)	Dizziness, fatigue; changes in heartbeat; changes in behavior; cold hands and feet	Alters effect of **insulin** and **sulfonylureas. Indomethacin** lowers effect of nadolol. Use with **reserpine** increases risk of vertigo, fainting, and abnormally low blood pressure. Use with **anesthetics** increases risk of hypotension.	Use caution if kidney/liver is impaired, if have diabetes, a lung disorder (i.e., asthma, bronchitis), or a history of congestive heart failure. Don't stop drug treatment on your own.
CALCIUM-CHANNEL BLOCKERS diltiazem (Cardizem CD, Cardizem SR, Dilacor XR)	Fluid retention; flushing; headache, dizziness, weakness; rash; nausea, indigestion, loss of appetite	Increases effects of **digoxin** and **cimetidine.** Use with **antihypertensives** increases hypotensive effect. Avoid **alcohol**.	Use caution if kidney/liver is impaired or if have sick sinus syndrome or congestive heart failure. Breast-feeding not recommended. Avoid driving or other potentially dangerous activities until you know how the drug affects you. Do not stop taking drug on your own. Monitor liver function.

CARDIOVASCULAR DRUGS

Generic (Brand Names)	Common Side Effects	Drug Interactions	Precautions
nifedipine (Procardia XL)	Palpitations; headache; fatigue; sleeplessness; numbness/tingling; fluid retention; rash, itching; constipation, nausea, abdominal pain, diarrhea; impotence; leg cramps; chest pain; weakness, flushing	Increases **digoxin** blood levels. Use with **beta-blockers** increases risk of severe hypotension, congestive heart failure, and worsening of angina. Use with **cimetidine** increases nifedipine blood levels. Use with **fentanyl** increases risk of severe hypotension. Avoid **alcohol**.	Use caution if elderly, if kidney/liver is impaired or if have angina, diabetes, or heart problems. Avoid driving or other potentially dangerous activities until you know how the drug affects you. Do not stop taking drug on your own; dosage must be decreased gradually.
verapamil (Calan, Calan SR, Isoptin, Isoptin SR, Verelan)	Hypotension; fluid retention; congestive heart failure, pulmonary edema; flushing; dizziness, headache, fatigue; constipation, nausea; breathing difficulties; rash	Increases blood levels of **carbamazepine, cyclosporin, digoxin, quinidine,** and **theophylline.** Use with **beta-blockers** increases risk of heart problems. Use with **cimetidine** and **phenobarbital** increases effects of verapamil. Effect of **lithium** is increased. Use with **nitrates** increases antianginal effect. Avoid **alcohol**.	Use caution if elderly, if kidney/liver is impaired, or if have muscular dystrophy or history of heart failure. Do not use if have Wolff-Parkinson-White or Lown-Ganong-Levine syndrome. Take sustained-release with food. Avoid driving or other potentially dangerous activities until you know how the drug affects you. Do not stop taking drug on your own; dosage must be decreased gradually.
CARDIAC GLYCOSIDE/ ANTIARRHYTHMIC digoxin (Lanoxicaps, Lanoxin)	Headache; drowsiness; nausea, loss of appetite; confusion; visual disturbances; palpitations	Many drugs (**antiarrhythmics, benzodiazepines, tetracyclines, verapamil**) increase effects of digoxin. Various drugs (**antacids, anticholinergics, methotrexate**) lower effects of digoxin. **Diuretics** increase risk of adverse reactions.	Use caution if kidney/liver is impaired or a history of thyroid dysfunction. Young infants are especially sensitive to digoxin. Avoid cheeses, yogurt, and ice cream for 2 hours before and after taking drug. Eating fruits and vegetables is recommended to replenish potassium levels. Monitoring of blood levels of digoxin and body salts is recommended.
CENTRAL ALPHA-ADRENERGIC AGONIST guanfacine (Tenex)	Weakness, fatigue; dizziness, drowsiness; headache; insomnia; constipation; dry mouth	**Phenothiazines, barbiturates, benzodiazepines, other CNS depressants,** and **alcohol** increase CNS depression and can lead to dangerous sedation.	Use caution if kidney/liver is impaired or if have heart problems. Safety not established in children under 12. Avoid driving and other potentially hazardous activities that require mental alertness and physical coordination until you know how the drug affects you. Do not discontinue abruptly; drug must be tapered off gradually.

ANTIARTHRITIS/NONSTEROIDAL ANTI-INFLAMMATORY DRUGS (NSAIDS)

Generic (Brand Names)	Common Side Effects	Drug Interactions	Precautions
diflunisal (Dolobid)	Dizziness, drowsiness, insomnia; rash; nausea, vomiting, indigestion, diarrhea, constipation; ringing in the ears; headache; fatigue	Increases toxicity of **cyclosporine** and **methotrexate**. Lowers effect of **antihypertensives** and **diuretics**. Various drugs (**oral anticoagulants, corticosteroids, other NSAIDs, aspirin**) increase risk of bleeding and peptic ulcers.	Use caution if elderly, if have kidney impairment, heart problems, high blood pressure, blood disorder, or history of GI problems. Use caution in child younger than 12. Avoid during pregnancy, especially in 3rd trimester.
flurbiprofen (Ansaid)	Indigestion, abdominal pain, diarrhea, nausea/vomiting, constipation; GI bleeding; rash; headache, dizziness, anxiety, insomnia, tremor, amnesia, lethargy, depression; blurred vision; ringing in the ears; edema/fluid retention	Increases drug action of **cimetidine** and **furosemide**. Decreases effect of **aspirin** and **propranolol**. Use with **anticoagulants** increases risk of bleeding. Use with **oral hypoglycemic** agents decreases blood glucose levels. **Antacids** lower the rate of flurbiprofen absorption.	Use caution if elderly, if have kidney/liver damage, high blood pressure, heart problems, or history of GI problems (i.e., ulcer). Avoid during late pregnancy.
ibuprofen (Haltran, Medipren, Midol IB, Motrin IB, Pamprin-IB) RX (Advil, Nuprin, Motrin, Pediaprofen, Rufen) OTC	Diarrhea; constipation; nausea/vomiting	Various drugs (**oral anticoagulants, corticosteroids, other NSAIDS, aspirin**) increase risk of bleeding and peptic ulcers. Ibuprofen increases effect of **lithium** and **oral antidiabetic** agents. Ibuprofen lowers effectiveness of **antihypertensives** and **diuretics**. Avoid **alcohol**, may increase risk of stomach disorders.	Taken late in pregnancy may result in birth defects and prolonged labor. Not recommended in children under 12. Prolonged use increases risk of bleeding from peptic ulcers and in bowel.
ketoprofen (Orudis)	Headache; drowsiness, nervousness, insomnia, dizziness; rash; indigestion; diarrhea, constipation, loss of appetite, nausea, vomiting; fluid retention; blurred vision; ringing in the ears	Increases blood levels of **oral antibiotics, lithium,** and **methotrexate**. Increases effect of **oral antibiotics**. Use with **oral anticoagulants, corticosteroids, other NSAIDs,** or **aspirin** increases risk of bleeding and stomach ulcers. Use with **diuretics** increases risk of renal failure. Avoid **alcohol**.	Use caution if elderly or if have history of kidney problems, heart failure, high blood pressure, fluid retention, or GI problems (i.e., ulcer). Prolonged use increases risk of bleeding from peptic ulcers in the bowel. Stomach discomfort can be minimized by taking drug with food, milk, or antacid.
piroxicam (Feldene)	Dizziness, drowsiness, headache; rash, itching; nausea, loss of appetite, constipation, indigestion, diarrhea; edema; ringing in the ears	May lower effect of **antihypertensives, diuretics,** and **oral antidiabetics**. Use with **oral anticoagulants, corticosteroids, other NSAIDs,** and **aspirin** increases risk of bleeding and peptic ulcers. Increases **lithium** blood levels.	Regular use increases risk of GI bleeding. Use caution if have kidney/liver problems, heart disease, or hypertension. Avoid driving or other potentially dangerous activities until you know how the drug affects you.

PSYCHOTHERAPEUTIC DRUGS

Generic (Brand Names)	Common Side Effects	Drug Interactions	Precautions
ANTIANXIETY alprazolam (Xanax) C-IV	Drowsiness, fatigue, impaired coordination, light-headedness, dizziness; insomnia, headache, anxiety, weakness, depression; blurred vision; palpitations; sweating, rash; dry mouth, constipation, nausea, vomiting, diarrhea; nasal congestion; fluid retention; change in appetite/weight	**Sedatives, anticonvulsants, antihistamines, alcohol, narcotics,** and other **CNS depressants** increase CNS depression and risk of dangerous sedation.	Use caution if elderly, if kidney/liver is impaired, or if have history of seizures or pulmonary disease. Use caution in children under 18 and in addiction-prone individuals. Do not use during pregnancy; increased risk of congenital abnormalities. Breast-feeding not recommended. Drug dependence may develop. Avoid driving or engaging in other potentially dangerous activities. Do not stop taking drug on your own. A gradual reduction may be necessary.
buspirone (Buspar)	Dizziness, nervousness, insomnia, light-headedness, headache, decreased concentration; palpitations; rash; nausea, dry mouth, indigestion, diarrhea; blurred vision; ringing in ears; sore throat	Use with **MAO inhibitors** increases blood pressure. Avoid **alcohol**.	Use caution in child under 18 and if kidney/liver is impaired. Breast-feeding not recommended. Avoid driving or engaging in other potentially dangerous activities until you know how the drug affects you.
diazepam (Valium, Valrelease) C-IV	Drowsiness, fatigue, light-headedness	**Alcohol, barbiturates, sedatives, MAO inhibitors,** and other **CNS depressants** increase CNS depression, lower blood pressure, and increase muscular weakness. Use with **cimetidine** increases adverse reactions of diazepam.	Use caution if elderly, if kidney/liver is impaired, and if have epilepsy. Not for use during pregnancy, especially 1st trimester. Do not breast-feed. High risk of drug dependence; severe withdrawl reactions have occurred. Avoid driving or engaging in other potentially dangerous activities. Do not end drug treatment on your own; drug may need to be stopped gradually. Periodically monitor blood and liver function.
lorazepam (Ativan) C-IV	Sedation, dizziness, weakness, unsteadiness	**Alcohol, tricyclic antidepressants, sedatives, MAO inhibitors,** and other **CNS depressants** increase CNS depression and risk of dangerous sedation.	Use caution in child under 12, if elderly, if addiction-prone, or if kidney/liver is impaired. Not for use during pregnancy, especially in 1st trimester. Breast-feeding not recommended. Drug dependence can develop. Avoid driving or engaging in other potentially dangerous activities. Blood and liver function tests are recommended during prolonged therapy. To end treatment on your own, dosage must be reduced gradually.

PSYCHOTHERAPEUTIC DRUGS

Generic (Brand Names)	Common Side Effects	Drug Interactions	Precautions
ANTIDEPRESSANTS **fluoxetine** (Prozac)	Headache, nervousness, anxiety, tremor, dizziness, lightheadedness, decreased concentration, fatigue, insomnia; drowsiness; sweating; nausea, vomiting, diarrhea, dry mouth, loss of appetite, indigestion, constipation; visual disturbances; upper respiratory tract infection; nasal congestion; weakness, fever	**Alcohol, barbiturates, sedatives,** and other **CNS depressants** increase CNS depression and risk of dangerous sedation. Use with **MAO inhibitors** can result in serious/fatal reactions. Use with **tryptophan** can result in agitation and GI distress.	Use caution if kidney/liver is impaired or if have history of seizures, depression, or heart/blood disorders. Drug dependence can develop. Avoid driving or other potentially dangerous activities. Don't discontinue drug treatment on your own; a gradual reduction in dosage may be necessary.
nortriptyline (Aventyl, Pamelor)	Dizziness, headache, anxiety; diarrhea, nausea, vomiting, dry mouth, loss of appetite; urinary frequency; restlessness, tremors, sweating	**Alcohol, barbiturates, sedatives,** and other **CNS depressants** increase CNS depression and risk of dangerous sedation. Use with **MAO inhibitors** can result in serious/fatal reactions. Reduces antihypertensive effect of **guanethidine** and **reserpine.** Use with **sympathomimetic** agents can result in severe hypertension or high fever. Use with **anticholinergic agents** increases risk of glaucoma. Use with **cimetidine** increases nortriptyline blood levels. Use with **thyroid** increases nortriptyline blood levels and risk of arrhythmia. Use may decrease oral contraceptive efficacy.	Use with caution if you have a history of seizures, urinary retention, glaucoma, or cardiovascular disease, or if you take thyroid medication. Don't discontinue use on your own. Avoid driving or operating dangerous machinery.
MUSCLE RELAXANTS **cyclobenzaprine** (Flexeril)	Drowsiness, dizziness, fatigue, weakness, headache; dry mouth, nausea, constipation, indigestion; blurred vision	**Alcohol, barbiturates, sedatives,** and other **CNS depressants** increase CNS depression and risk of dangerous sedation. Use with **MAO inhibitors** can result in serious/fatal reactions. Reduces antihypertensive effect of **guanethidine** and **clonidine.** Increases effect of **anticholinergic** drugs.	Use caution if have glaucoma, arrhythmia, overactive thyroid, or history of heart problems or urinary retention. Use caution in child younger than 15. Avoid driving or engaging in other potentially dangerous activities. Don't stop taking drug on your own. Use for more than 2 weeks not recommended.

PSYCHOTHERAPEUTIC DRUGS

Generic (Brand Names)	Common Side Effects	Drug Interactions	Precautions
SEDATIVE/ HYPNOTIC triazolam (Halcion) C-IV	Dizziness, drowsiness, headache; nervousness; nausea, vomiting; coordination problems	**Alcohol, barbiturates, sedatives,** other **CNS depressants, anticonvulsants,** and **antihistamines** increase CNS depression and risk of dangerous sedation. Use with **cimetidine** increases triazolam blood levels.	Use caution if elderly, if kidney/ liver is impaired, or if have history of seizures or respiratory dysfunction. Use caution in child under 18. Do not use during pregnancy; possibility of birth defects. Breast-feeding not recommended. Drug dependence may occur. Avoid driving or other potentially dangerous activities. Don't stop taking drug on your own; a gradual reduction in dosage may be necessary.
ABUSE DETERRENT nicotine polacrilex (Nicorette gum)	Dizziness, light-headedness, insomnia, headache; nausea, vomiting, indigestion, loss of appetite; sore mouth/throat, jaw muscle ache, excessive salivation, hiccups	Smoking while using this may cause harmful rise in blood pressure.	Use caution if have a heart problem, hyperthyroidism, diabetes, peptic ulcer, or dental problems. Not for children. Avoid during pregnancy. Breast-feeding not recommended. Drug dependence may develop.
nicotine (Habitrol, Nicoderm, Nicotrol, Prostep) (transdermal patch)	Sweating; diarrhea, indigestion, dry mouth; itching at patch site; fluid retention; muscle fatigue; insomnia, nervousness	Smoking while using these products may cause a harmful rise in blood pressure.	Use caution if elderly, if kidney/ liver is impaired, or if have hyperthyroidism, diabetes, peptic ulcer, hypertension, a heart problem, or certain skin disorders. Not for children's use. Not recommended during pregnancy or if breast-feeding. Avoid smoking (benefits of drug vs. risk of continued smoking must be weighed).

Appendix B

DIRECTORY OF HEALTH ORGANIZATIONS AND RESOURCES

CONDITIONS

AGING

American Association of Retired
People (AARP)
601 E Street NW
Washington, DC 20049
(202) 434-2277

American Geriatric Society
770 Lexington Avenue,
Suite 300
New York, NY 10021
(212) 308-1414

American Society on Aging
833 Market Street, Suite 512
San Francisco, CA 94103
(415) 882-2910

CAPS (Children of Aging
Parents)
1609 Woodbourne Road,
Suite 302A
Levittown, PA 19057-1511
(215) 945-6900

National Council of Senior
Citizens, Inc.
1331 F Street NW
Washington, DC 20004
(202) 347-8800

The National Council on Aging
409 Third Street SW
Second Floor
Washington, DC 20024
(202) 479-1200

National Institute on Aging
Building 21, Room 5C27
Bethesda, MD 20892
(301) 496-1752

AIDS/HIV

AIDS Hotline
(800) 342-AIDS
(202) 245-6867 (call collect if in
Alaska or Hawaii)

Gay Men's Health Crisis
(GMHC)
(212) 807-6664
Women's AIDS Network
(415) 864-4376
(800) FOR-AIDS

National AIDS Information
Clearinghouse
P.O. Box 6003
Rockville, MD 20850
(800) 458-5231
(800) 342-AIDS
(800) 334-7492 (Spanish
speakers)
(800) 243-7889 (TDD—Deaf
access)

ALCOHOLISM AND SUBSTANCE ABUSE

Addiction Treatment Providers
2082 Michelson Drive,
Suite 304
Irvine, CA 92715
(714) 992-1677

Al-Anon Family Group
Headquarters
1372 Broadway
New York, NY 10018
(212) 302-7240

Alcoholics Anonymous
475 Riverside Drive
New York, NY 10015
(212) 870-3400

American Council on Alcohol
Problems, Inc.
3426 Bridgeland Drive
Bridgeton, MO 63044
(314) 739-5944

Association of Halfway House
Alcoholism Programs of
North America
680 Stuart Avenue
St. Paul, MN 55102
(612) 227-7818

Children of Alcoholics
Foundation
Grand Central Station,
P.O. Box 4185
New York, NY 10163-4185
(800) 359-COAS

Do It Now Foundation
6423 South Ash Avenue
P.O. Box 27568
Tempe, AZ 85283-7568
(602) 257-0797

DRUG ABUSE AND NARCOTIC ADDICTION

Cocaine Abuse Hotline
(800) COCAINE
(201) 522-7055 (in Alaska or
Hawaii)

Drug Abuse Clearinghouse
Room 10A53
5600 Fishers Lane
Rockville, MD 20857
(301) 443-6500

Mothers Against Drunk Driving
(MADD)
511 E. John Carpenter Freeway
Irving, TX 75062-8187
(800) 438-MADD

National Association of
Children of Alcoholics, Inc.
11426 Rockville Pike, Suite 100
Rockville, MD 20852
(301) 468-0985

National Clearinghouse for
Alcohol and Drug
Information
P.O. Box 2345
Rockville, MD 29847
(301) 468-2600

National Council on Alcoholism
and Drug Dependence, Inc.
12 West 21st Street
New York, NY 10010
(212) 206-6770
(800) 622-2255

National Drug Abuse and
Treatment Hotline
(800) 662-HELP
(800) 66-AYUDA (Spanish
speakers)

National Institute on Alcohol
Abuse and Alcoholism
Willco Building, Suite 400
6000 Executive Boulevard,
Suite 409
Rockville, MD 20892-7003
(301) 443-3860

National Institute on Drug
Abuse
(800) 638-2045
(301) 443-2450 (in Alaska,
Hawaii, or Maryland)

New York State Division of
Substance Abuse
Information Line
(800) 522-5353

ANOREXIA NERVOSA AND OTHER EATING DISORDERS

American Anorexia Nervosa
Association, Inc.
133 Cedar Lane
Teaneck, NJ 07666
(201) 836-1800

Anorexia Nervosa and
Associated Disorders
Box 7
Highland Park, IL 60035
(708) 831-3438

Help Anorexia, Inc.
P.O. Box 2992
Culver City, CA 90231
(213) 558-0444

National Institute of Child
Health and Human
Development
Building 31, Room 2A32
Bethesda, MD 20892
(301) 496-5133

National Institute of Diabetes
and Digestive and Kidney
Disease
National Institutes of Health
Building 31, Room 3A18B
Bethesda, MD 20892
(301) 496-7823

National Institute of Mental
Health
5600 Fishers Lane, Room 5CO5
Rockville, MD 20857
(301) 443-4515

ALLERGIES, ASTHMA, AND RESPIRATORY DISORDERS

Allergy Research Group
400 Preda Street
P.O. Box 480
San Leandro, CA 94577
(800) 545-9960

American Lung Association
432 Park Avenue South
New York, NY 10016
(212) 889-3370

Asthma and Allergy Foundation
of America
1125 15th Street NW, Suite 502
Washington, DC 20005
(202) 466-7643

Emphysema Anonymous, Inc
P.O. Box 3224
Seminole, FL 34642
(813) 391-9977

National Asthma Education
Program
4733 Bethesda Avenue,
Suite 350
Bethesda, MD 20814
(301) 495-4484

National Jewish Center for Immunology and Respiratory Medicine
1400 Jackson Street
Denver, CO 80206
(800) 222-LUNG

National Institute of Allergy and Infectious Disease
Building 31, Room 7A32
Bethesda, MD 20892
(301) 496-5717

ARTHRITIS

The Arthritis Foundation
550 Pharr Road, Suite 550
Atlanta, GA 30305
(404) 237-8771

National Institute of Arthritis and Musculoskeletal and Skin Diseases
Box AMS
Bethesda, MD 20814
(301) 495-4484

AUTISM

Autism Society of America
7910 Woodmount Avenue, Suite 650
Bethesda, MD 20814
(301) 657-0881

BIRTH DEFECTS

American Genetic Association
P.O. Box 39
Buckeystown, MD 21717
(301) 695-9292

March of Dimes/Birth Defects Foundation
1275 Mamaroneck Avenue
White Plains, NY 10605
(914) 428-7100

National Institute of Child Health and Human Development
Building 31, Room 2A32
Bethesda, MD 20892
(301) 496-5133

Spina Bifida Association of America
3080 Ogden Avenue, Suite 103
Lyle, IL 60532
(708) 637-1050

BLINDNESS AND VISION PROBLEMS

American Council for the Blind
1155 15th Street NW, Suite 720
Washington, DC 20005
(800) 424-8666
(202) 467-5081 (in Alaska, Hawaii, or DC)

American Foundation for the Blind
15 West 16th Street
New York, NY 10011
(212) 620-2000

American Printing House for the Blind
1839 Frankfort Avenue
Louisville, KY 40206
(502) 895-2405

Associated Blind, Inc.
135 West 23rd Street
New York, NY 10011
(212) 255-1122

The Association for the Education and Rehabilitation of the Blind and Visually Impaired
204 North Washington Street, Suite 320
Alexandria, VA 22314
(703) 548-1884

Association for Macular Diseases, Inc.
210 East 64th Street
New York, NY 10021
(212) 605-3719

Fight for Sight
160 East 56th Street
New York, NY 10022
(212) 751-1118

Guiding Eyes for the Blind, Inc.
611 Granite Springs Road
Yorktown Heights, NY 10598
(914) 245-4024
(information on guide dogs)

National Association for the Visually Handicapped (Partially Sighted)
3201 Balboa Street
San Francisco, CA 94121
(415) 221-3201

National Eye Institute
Building 31, Room 6A32
Bethesda, MD 20892
(301) 496-5248

National Library Service for the Blind and Physically Handicapped
The Library of Congress
1291 Taylor Street NW
Washington, DC 20542
(202) 707-5100

National RP Foundation Fighting Blindness
(800) 638-2300
(301) 655-1011 (in Maryland call collect)

National Society to Prevent Blindness
500 East Remington Road
Schaumburg, IL 60173
(708) 843-2020

National Society to Prevent Blindness
160 East 56th Street
New York, NY 10022
(212) 980-2020

Recording for the Blind, Inc.
20 Roszel Road
Princeton, NJ 08540
(609) 452-0606

The Seeing Eye, Inc.
P.O. Box 375
Morristown, NJ 07963-0375
(201) 539-4425

BLOOD DISEASES

Leukemia Society of America, Inc.
600 Third Avenue
New York, NY 10016
(212) 573-8484

National Hemophilia Foundation
110 Greene Street, Suite 303
New York, NY 10012
(212) 219-8180

National Sickle Cell Disease Branch Division of Blood Diseases and Resources
National Heart, Lung, and Blood Institute
Room 504, Federal Building
7550 Wisconsin Avenue
Bethesda, MD 20892
(301) 496-6931

BONE AND MUSCLE DISORDERS

Ankylosing Spondylitis Association
P.O. Box 5872
Sherman Oaks, CA 91413
(800) 777-8189
(310) 652-0609

National Arthritis and Musculoskeletal and Skin Diseases Information Clearinghouse
P.O. Box AMS, 9000 Rockville Pike
Bethesda, MD 20892
(301) 495-4484

National Osteoporosis Foundation
2100 M Street NW, Suite 602
Washington, DC 20037
(202) 223-2226

CANCER

American Cancer Society, Inc.
National Headquarters
1599 Clifton Road NE
Atlanta, GA 30329
(404) 320-3333

Cancer Counseling and Research Center
P.O. Box 7237
Little Rock, AR 72217
(501) 224-1933

Cancer Information Clearinghouse
National Cancer Institute
Building 31, Room 10A24
9000 Rockville Pike
Bethesda, MD 20892
(800) 4-CANCER
(808) 524-1234 (in Hawaii)

Cancer Response System
(800) ACS-2345

The Candlelighters Childhood Cancer Foundation
7910 Woodmount Avenue, Suite 460
Bethesda, MD 20814
(301) 657-8401

Corporate Angel Network, Inc.
Westchester County Airport, Building One
White Plains, NY 10604
(914) 328-1313

Damon Runyon–Walter Winchell Cancer Fund
131 East 36th Street
New York, NY 10016
(212) 532-3888

Mammatech Corporation
930 NW Eighth Avenue
Gainsville, FL 42601
(800) MAM-CARE
(for information on centers teaching the Mammacare self-examination methods)

Ronald McDonald Houses
c/o Golin Harris Communications, Inc.
500 North Michigan Avenue
Chicago, IL 60611
(312) 836-7129

Rose Kushner Breast Cancer Advisory Center
P.O. Box 224
Kensington, MD 20895

United Ostomy Association
36 Executive Park, Suite 120
Irving, CA 92714
(714) 660-8684

Y-ME
National Organization for Breast Cancer Information and Support
18220 Harwood Avenue
Harwood, IL 60430
(800) 221-2141
(708) 799-8228 (Illinois only)

YWCA
ENCORE
726 Broadway
New York, NY 10003
(212) 614-2827

CARDIOVASCULAR DISEASE

American Heart Association
(Mended Hearts Club)
7320 Greenville Avenue
Dallas, TX 75231
(214) 373-6300

Citizens for Public Action on
Blood Pressure and
Cholesterol
7200 Wisconsin Avenue,
Suite 1002
Bethesda, MD 20814
(301) 907-7790

Coronary Club, Inc.
9500 Euclid Avenue, Room
E4-15
Cleveland, OH 44195
(216) 444-3690

National Heart, Lung, and
Blood Institute
Building 31, Room 4A21
Bethesda, MD 20892
(301) 496-4236

National High Blood Pressure
Education Program
Information Center
National Institutes of Health
7200 Wisconsin Avenue,
Suite 500
Bethesda, MD 20814
(301) 951-3620

The Sister Kenny Institute
800 East 28th Street
Minneapolis, MN 55407
(612) 863-4457

CEREBRAL PALSY

United Cerebral Palsy
Association, Inc.
120 East 23rd Street
New York, NY 10010
(212) 979-9700

National Institute of
Neurological Disorders
and Stroke
Building 31, Room 8A06
Bethesda, MD 20892
(301) 496-5751
(800) 352-9424

CHILD ABUSE AND NEGLECT

National Clearinghouse for
Child Abuse and Neglect
Information
P.O. Box 1182
Washington, DC 20013
(800) FYI-3366

American Humane Association
63 Inverness Drive East
Inglewood, CA 80112
(303) 792-9900

CALM (Child Abuse Listening
Mediation, Inc.)
1236 Chapala Street
Santa Barbara, CA 93101
(805) 965-2376

National Child Abuse Hotline
(800) 422-4453

National Council on Child
Abuse and Family Violence
1155 Connecticut Avenue NW,
Suite 20036
Washington, DC 20036
(202) 429-6695

CHILDBIRTH/ MATERNITY CARE

The Compassionate Friends,
Inc.
101 Shelter Road, Suite B-103
Lincolnshire, IL 60069
(708) 990-0010

International Childbirth
Education Association, Inc.
P.O. Box 20048
Minneapolis, MN 55420
(612) 854-8660

La Leche League International
Box 1209, 9616 Minneapolis
Avenue
Franklin Park, IL 60131
(800) LA LECHE
(708) 455-7730

Maternity Center Association
48 East 92nd Street
New York, NY 10128
(212) 369-7300

CYSTIC FIBROSIS

Cystic Fibrosis Foundation
2250 North Druid Hills Road,
Suite 275
Atlanta, GA 30326
(404) 325-6973
(800) 638-8815

DIABETES AND OTHER HORMONAL DISORDERS

American Diabetes Association,
Inc.
149 Madison Avenue
New York, NY 10016
(212) 725-4925

The Juvenile Diabetes
Foundation International
432 Park Avenue South
New York, NY 10016
(212) 889-7575

National Diabetes Information
Clearinghouse
9000 Rockville Pike, Box NDIC
Bethesda, MD 20892
(301) 654-3327

Thyroid Foundation of America
Ruth Sleeper Hall, RSL 350
40 Parkman Street
Boston, MA 02114-2698

DIGESTIVE DISEASE

Crohn's and Colitis Foundation
of America, Inc.
444 Park Avenue South
New York, NY 10016
(800) 343-3637
(212) 685-3440

National Digestive Disease
Education and Information
Clearinghouse
1555 Wilson Boulevard,
Suite 600
Rosslyn, VA 22209

National Foundation for Ileitis
and Colitis, Inc.
386 Park Avenue South
New York, NY 10016
(212) 685-3400
(800) 343-3637

DOWN SYNDROME AND MENTAL RETARDATION

National Down Syndrome
Society
(800) 221-4602
(212) 460-9330 (in New York)

American Association on
Mental Retardation
444 North Capitol Street NW,
Suite 846
Washington, DC 20001
(202) 387-1968

American Association on
Mental Deficiency
(800) 424-3638
(202) 387-1968
(in Washington, DC)

Association for Retarded
Citizens
500 East Border Street,
Suite 300
Arlington, TX 76010
(817) 261-6003

Kennedy Child Study Center
151 East 67th Street
New York, NY 10021
(212) 988-9500

EPILEPSY

Epilepsy Foundation of America
4351 Garden City Drive,
Suite 406
Landover, MD 20785
(301) 459-3700

Epilepsy Institute
257 Park Avenue South
New York, NY 10010
(212) 677-8550

FAMILY PLANNING/SEX INFORMATION

The Alan Guttmacher Institute
120 Wall Street, 21st Floor
New York, NY 10005
(212) 248-1111

Family Life Information
Exchange
P.O. Box 37299
Washington, DC 20013
(301) 585-6636

Planned Parenthood
Federation of America, Inc.
810 Seventh Avenue
New York, NY 10019
(212) 541-7800

Population Council, Inc.
One Dag Hammarskjold Plaza,
9th Floor
New York, NY 10017
(212) 339-0500

Sex Information and
Educational Council of the
United States
130 West 42nd Street,
Suite 2500
New York, NY 10036
(212) 819-9770

FERTILITY

American Fertility Society
1209 Montgomery Highway
Birmingham, AL 35216
(205) 978-5000

RESOLVE, Inc.
1310 Broadway
Somerville, MA 02114
(617) 623-0744

GENETIC DISEASES

March of Dimes/Birth Defects
Foundation
1275 Mamaroneck Avenue
White Plains, NY 10605
(914) 428-7100

National Tay-Sachs and Allied
Disease Association, Inc.
92 Washington Avenue
Cedarhurst, NY 11516
(516) 569-4300
or
2001 Beacon Street
Brookline, MA 02146
(617) 277-4463

GROWTH DISORDERS

National Institute of Diabetes
and Digestive and Kidney
Diseases
Building 31, Room 9AO4
Bethesda, MD 20892
(301) 496-3583

HEAD INJURIES

The National Head Injury
Foundation, Inc.
1140 Connecticut Avenue NW,
Suite 812
Washington, DC 20036
(800) 444-NHIF
(202) 296-6443

HEARING AND SPEECH DISORDERS

Alexander Graham Bell
Association for the Deaf
3417 Volta Place NW
Washington, DC 20007-2778
(202) 337-5220

American Humane Association
63 Inverness Drive East
Inglewood, CA 80112
(303) 792-9900
(resource center for information on hearing dogs)

American Tinnitus Association
P.O. Box 5
Portland, OR 97207
(503) 248-9985

Dogs for the Deaf
10175 Wheeler Road
Central Point, OR 97502
(503) 826-9220

American Speech-Language-
Hearing Association
10801 Rockville Pike
Rockville, Md 20852
(301) 897-5700
(800) 638-8255

Deafness Research Foundation
9 East 38th Street, 7th Floor
New York, NY 10016
(212) 684-6556 National
Association for Speech and
Hearing Action
(800) 638-TALK
(301) 897-8682 (in Alaska,
Hawaii, or Maryland)

National Association of the Deaf
814 Thayer Avenue
Silver Spring, MD 20910
(301) 587-1788
(301) 587-1789 (TDD)

National Information Center on
Deafness
Gallaudet University
800 Florida Avenue NE
Washington, DC 20002
(202) 651-5051
(202) 651-5052 (TDD)

National Hearing Dog Project
American Humane Association
Box 1266
Department BHG
Denver, CO 80201

Self-Help for Hard of Hearing
People, Inc.
7910 Woodmont Ave,
Suite 1200
Bethesda, MD 20814
(301) 657-2248

KIDNEY DISEASE

American Association of Kidney
Patients
111 South Parker Street,
Suite 405
Tampa, FL 33606
(813) 251-0725

National Kidney Foundation,
Inc.
30 East 33rd Street, 11th Floor
New York, NY 10016
(212) 889-2210
(800) 622-9010

LEARNING DISABILITIES

Association for Children with
Learning Disabilities
4156 Library Road
Pittsburgh, PA 15234
(412) 341-1515

LUPUS ERYTHEMATOSUS

National Institute of Arthritis,
Musculoskeletal, and Skin
Diseases
Box AMS
Bethesda, MD 20892
(301) 495-4484

American Lupus Society
23751 Madison Street
Torrance, CA 90505
(213) 373-1335

MENTAL HEALTH

American Mental Health
Foundation
2 East 86th Street
New York, NY 10028
(correspondence by mail only)

National Association for
Mental Health
66 Canal Center Plaza, Suite 302
Alexandria, VA 22314
(703) 139-9333

National Institute of Mental
Health
Public Inquiries Section
Room 15 C-05
5600 Fishers Lane
Rockville, MD 20857
(301) 443-4513

MINORITY HEALTH ISSUES

National Black Women's Health
Project
1237 Ralph Davis Abernathy
Boulevard NW
Atlanta, GA 30310
(404) 758-9590

Office of Minority Health
Resource Center
P.O. Box 37337
Washington, DC 20013
(800) 444-6472

NEUROLOGIC DISORDERS

Association for Alzheimer's and
Related Diseases
919 North Michigan Avenue,
Suite 1000
Chicago, IL 60611-1676
(800) 621-0379
(312) 335-8700

NEUROMUSCULAR DISORDERS

National Multiple Sclerosis
Society
733 Third Avenue
New York, NY 10017
(212) 986-3240

Muscular Dystrophy
Association of America, Inc.
342 Madison Avenue,
Room 1426
New York, NY 10173
(212) 557-8450

Myasthenia Gravis Foundation,
Inc.
61 Gramercy Park North
New York, NY 10010
(212) 533-7005

PAIN RELIEF

American Chronic Pain
Association, Inc.
P.O. Box 850
Rocklin, CA 95677
(916) 632-0922

American Council for Headache
Education
875 Kings Highway, Suite 200
West Deptford, NJ 08096
(800) 255-ACHE
(609) 845-0322

American Pain Society
5700 Old Orchard Road
Skokie, IL 60077
(708) 966-5595

Chronic Pain Support Group
P.O. Box 148
Peninsula, OH 44264
(216) 657-2948

Committee on Pain Therapy
American Society of
Anesthesiologists
520 North Northwest Highway
Park Ridge, IL 60068
(708) 825-5586

International Association for
the Study of Pain
909 N.E. 43rd Street, Suite 306
Seattle, WA 98015-6020
(206) 547-6409

National Chronic Pain Outreach
Association
7979 Old Georgetown Road
Bethesda, MD 20814
(301) 652-4948

National Headache Foundation
5252 North Western Avenue
Chicago, IL 60625
(800) 843-2256
(312) 878-7715

PARKINSON'S DISEASE

American Parkinson's Disease
Association
116 John Street
New York, NY 10038
(212) 685-2741

National Parkinson's
Foundation
(800) 327-4545
(800) 433-7022 (in Florida)
(305) 547-6666 (in Miami)

Parkinson's Disease Foundation
650 West 168th Street
New York, NY 10032
(212) 923-4700

The Parkinson Support Group
of America
11376 Cherry Hill Road,
Suite 204
Beltsville, MD 20705
(301) 937-1545

United Parkinson Foundation
800 West Washington
Boulevard
Chicago, IL 60607
(312) 733-1893

PSORIASIS

National Psoriasis Foundation
6600 South West 92nd Avenue,
Suite 300
Portland, OR 97223
(503) 244-7404

SEXUALLY TRANSMITTED DISEASES

National Sexually Transmitted
Disease Hotline
P.O. Box 13827
Research Triangle Park, NC
27709
(800) 227-8922

VD National Hotline
(800) 227-8922
(800) 982-5883 (in California)

SLEEP DISORDERS

American Narcolepsy
  Association
425 California Street, Suite 201
San Francisco, CA 94104-6230
(800) 222-6085
(415) 788-4793

American Sleep Apnea
  Association
P.O. Box 3893
Charlottesville, VA 22908

The American Sleep Disorders
  Association
1610 Fourteenth Street NW,
  Suite 300
Rochester, MN 55901
(507) 287-6006

SMOKING

Action on Smoking and Health
  (ASH)
2013 H Street NW
Washington, DC 20006
(202) 659-4310

Centers for Disease Control
  Office on Smoking and
  Health Public Information
  Branch
Mail Stop K-50
1600 Clifton Road, NE
Atlanta, GA 30333
(404) 488-5705

National Center for Health
  Promotion
Smoke Stoppers Program
3920 Varsity Drive
Ann Arbor, MI 48108
(313) 971-6077

Seventh-Day Adventists
Community Health Services
P.O. Box 1029
Manhasset, NY 11030
(Ask for "How to Stop
  Smoking" pamphlet)

Smokenders
1430 East Indian School Road,
  Suite 102
Phoenix, AZ 85014
(800) 828-4357

STROKE

American Paralysis Association
P.O. Box 187
Short Hills, NJ 07078
(800) 255-0292
(201) 379-2690

Courage Center
Courage Stroke Network
3915 Golden Valley Road
Golden Valley, MN 55422
(800) 553-6321
(612) 520-0466 (in Minnesota)

National Aphasia Association
P.O. Box 1887, Murray Hill
  Station
New York, NY 10156-0611
(800) 922-4NAA

National Stroke Association
8480 East Orchard Road,
  Suite 1000
Englewood, CO 80111
(303) 771-1700
(800) STROKES

The Stroke Foundation
898 Park Avenue
New York, NY 10021
(212) 134-3434

SUDDEN INFANT DEATH SYNDROME (SIDS)

New York City Program for
  Sudden Infant Death
520 First Avenue
New York, NY 10016
(212) 686-8854

Sudden Infant Death Syndrome
  (SIDS) Resource Center
8201 Greensboro Drive,
  Suite 600
McClean, VA 22102
(703) 821-8955 Ext. 249

URINARY TRACT DISORDERS

American Foundation for
  Urologic Disease
1120 North Charles Street
Baltimore, MD 21201
(800) 242-AFUD

American Urological
  Association
1120 North Charles Street
Baltimore, MD 21201
(410) 727-1100

Bladder Health Council
1120 North Charles Street
Baltimore, MD 21201
(410) 727-2896

Continence Restored, Inc.
785 Park Avenue
New York, NY 10021
(212) 879-3131

Help for Incontinent People
P.O. Box 544
Union, SC 29373
(800) BLADDER
(803) 579-7900

National Kidney and Urologic
  Diseases Clearinghouse
P.O. Box NKUDIC
9000 Rockville Pike
Bethesda, MD 20892

WOMEN'S HEALTH

HERS (Hysterectomy
  Educational Resources and
  Services)
422 Bryn Mawr Avenue
Bala Cynwyd, PA 19004
(215) 667-7757

National Black Women's Health
  Project
1237 Ralph David Abernathy
  Boulevard NW
Atlanta, GA 30310
(404) 758-9590

The PMS and Menopause
  Self-Help Center
101 First Street, Suite 441
Los Altos, CA 94022
(415) 964-7268

National Women's Health
  Network
1325 G Street NW
Washington, DC 20005
(202) 347-1140

MISCELLANEOUS DISORDERS

Jaw Joints and Allied Musculo-
  Skeletal Disorders
  Foundation, Inc. (JJAMD)
Forsyth's Research Institute
140 Fenway
Boston, MA 02115
(617) 262-5200, Ext. 360

National Information Center for
  Orphan Drugs and Rare
  Diseases
P.O. Box 1133
Washington, DC 20013-1133
(800) 456-3505
(301) 656-4167

....

ALTERNATIVE MEDICINE

ACUPUNCTURE

American Association of
  Acupuncture and Oriental
  Medicine
4101 Lake Boone Trail,
  Suite 201
Raleigh, NC 27607

American Academy of Medical
  Acupuncture
2520 Milvia Street
Berkeley, CA 94704
(415) 841-3220

ALEXANDER TECHNIQUE

North American Society of
  Teachers of the Alexander
  Technique
P.O. Box 3992
Champagne, IL 61826-3992

AROMATHERAPY

Aromatherapy Institute and
  Research (AIR)
P.O. Box 2354
Fair Oaks, CA 95628

BIOFEEDBACK TRAINING

Association for Applied
  Psychophysiology and Bio-
  feedback
Biofeedback Certification
  Institute of America
10200 West 44th Avenue,
  Suite 304
Wheat Ridge, CO 80033
(303) 420-2902

CHIROPRACTIC

American Chiropractic
  Association
1701 Claredon Boulevard
Arlington, VA 22209
(703) 276-8800

HERBAL MEDICINE

The American Botanical
  Council
P.O. Box 201660
Austin, TX 78720
(512) 331-8868

The Herb Research Foundation
1007 Pearl Street, Suite 200
Boulder, CO 80302
(303) 449-2265

HYPNOTHERAPY

American Council of
  Clinical Hypnosis
2200 East Devon Avenue,
  Suite 291
Des Plaines, IL 60018
(312) 297-3317

International Society for
  Professional Hypnosis
1 Lincoln Street, P.O. Box 452
North Haven, CT 06473
(203) 239-7046

Society for Clinical and
  Experimental Hypnosis
128-A King Park Drive
Liverpool, NY 13090
(315) 652-7299

MASSAGE

American Massage Therapy
  Association
National Information Office
820 Davis Street
Evanston, IL 60201
(312) 761-2682

International Institute of
  Reflexology
P.O. Box 12642
St. Petersburg, FL 33733

Rolf Institute
P.O. Box 1868
Boulder, CO 80306
(303) 449-5903

MEDITATION

Insight Meditation Society
1230 Pleasant Street
Barre, MA 01005

MOVEMENT THERAPIES

The American Dance Therapy
Association
2000 Century Plaza, Suite 108
Columbia, MD 21044
(301) 997-4040

American Yoga Association
3130 Mayfield Road
Cleveland Heights, OH 44118

A Taste of China (T'ai Chi)
111 Shirley Street
Winchester, VA 22601

Himalayan International
Institute of Yoga Science
and Philosophy of the U.S.A.
RR1, Box 400
Honesdale, PA 18431

MUSIC THERAPY

National Association for Music
Therapy
8455 Colesville Rd, Suite 930
Silver Spring, MD 20910
(301) 589-3300

VISUALIZATION AND IMAGERY

Academy for Guided Imagery
P.O. Box 2070
Mill Valley, CA 94942
(415) 389-9324

·····························

GENERAL HEALTH INFORMATION AND ORGANIZATIONS

American Red Cross
17th and D Street NW
Washington, DC 20006
(908) 737-8300

Centers for Disease Control and
Prevention
1600 Clifton Road NE
Building 1 SSB249, MS A 34
Atlanta, GA 30333
(404) 639-3492

Food and Drug Administration
Center for Biologics
Evaluation and Research
8800 Rockville Pike
Building 29-NIH Campus
Bethesda, MD 20852
(301) 295-8228

Office of Disease Prevention
and Health Promotion
(ODPHP)
National Health Information
Center
P.O. Box 1133
Washington, DC 20013-1133
(800) 336-4797

DYING

Choice in Dying (Living Wills)
200 Varick Street, Suite 1001
New York, NY 10014-4810
(212) 366-5540

FITNESS

Aerobics and Fitness
Foundation
15250 Ventura Boulevard,
Suite 310
Sherman Oaks, CA 91403
(800) BE-FIT-80

President's Council on Physical
Fitness and Sports
707 Pennsylvania Avenue NW,
Suite 250
Washington, DC 20004
(202) 272-3430

HOME CARE AND HOSPICE

The National Association for
Home Care
519 C Street NE
Washington, DC 20002
(202) 547-7424

Hospice Education Institute
Hospicelink
P.O. Box 713
5 Essex Square, Suite 3-B
Essex, CT 06426
(800) 331-1620
(203) 767-1620

National Hospice Organization
1901 North Moore Street,
Suite 901
Arlington, VA 22209
(800) 658-8898
(703) 243-5900

INSURANCE

National Association of
Insurance Commissioners
120 West 12th Street,
Suite 1100
Kansas City, MO 64105
(816) 842-3600

National Underwriters
Company
505 Guest Street
Cincinnati, OH 45203
(513) 721-2140

INSURANCE FOR NURSING HOMES

National Citizens' Coalition for
Nursing Home Reform
1224 M Street NW, Suite 301
Washington, DC 20005
(202) 393-2018

Nursing Home Information
Service
National Council of Senior
Citizens
National Senior Citizens
Education and Research
Center
925 15th Street NW
Washington, DC 20005
(202) 347-8800 Ext. 340

JOB DISCRIMINATION

Department of Health and
Human Services
200 Independence Avenue SW
Washington, DC 20201
(202) 619-0257

Office of Federal Contract
Compliance Programs
Department of Labor
200 Constitution Avenue NW
Washington, DC 20210
(202) 401-8818

MEDIC ALERT

Medic Alert Foundation
International
P.O. Box 1009
Turlock, CA 95381-1009
(209) 668-3333
(800) ID-ALERT
(800) 344-3226

NATIONAL SELF-HELP SERVICE

National Self-Help
Clearinghouse
Graduate School and University
Center of the City University
of New York
33 West 42nd Street,
Room 1227
New York, NY 10037
(212) 840-1259

NURSING HOMES

American Assocation of Homes
for the Aging
901 E Street NW, Suite 500
Washington, DC 20004
(202) 783-2242

American Health Care
Association
1201 L Street NW
Washington, DC 20005
(202) 842-4444

ORGAN DONATION

The Living Bank
P.O. Box 6725
Houston, TX 77265
(800) 528-2971
(713) 528-2971

United Network for Organ
Sharing
P.O. Box 13770
1100 Boulders Parkway,
Suite 500
Richmond, VA 23225-8770
(800) 24-DONOR

SEX THERAPY

Center for Human Sexuality
Department of Psychiatry,
Box 1203
Downstate Medical Center
450 Clarkson Avenue
Brooklyn, NY 11203
(718) 270-2576

Impotence Foundation
(800) 221-5517

Impotence Institute of America
119 South Ruth Street
Maryville, TN 37801
(800) 669-1603
(615) 983-6064

The Male Sexual Dysfunction
Clinic
4940 Eastern Avenue
Baltimore, MD 21224
(410) 550-2329

Recovery of Male Potency
27211 Lahser Road, Suite 208
Southfield, MI 48034
(800) 835-7667
(313) 357-1216

The Sexual Behaviors
Consultation Unit
550 North Broadway, Suite 114
Baltimore, MD 21205
(410) 955-6318

SURGERY

American College of Surgeons
Office of Public Information
55 East Erie Street
Chicago, IL 60611
(312) 644-4030

American Society of Plastic
and Reconstructive
Surgeons
444 East Algonquin Road
Arlington Heights, IL 60005
(708) 228-9900

Non-Emergency Surgery
Hotline
(800) 638-6833
(800) 492-6603 (in Maryland)

TRAVELERS

Centers for Disease Control
Information Resource
Management Office
Mail Stop C-15, 1600 Clifton
Road, NE
Atlanta, GA 30333
(404) 332-4555

Health Guide for Travelers
Healthcare Abroad
107 West Federal Street
P.O. Box 480
Middleburg, VA 22117
(800) 237-6615

The International Association
for Medical Assistance to
Travelers
417 Center Street
Lewiston, NY 14092
(716) 754-4883

International SOS Assistance
P.O. Box 11568
Philadelphia, PA 19116
(800) 523-8930
(215) 244-1500 (in
Pennsylvania)

Runaway Hotline
(800) 231-6946
(800) 392-3352 (in Texas)

REHABILITATION ORGANIZATIONS

ADVOCACY ORGANIZATIONS

American Coalition of Citizens
with Disabilities
1201 15th Street NW, Suite 201
Washington, DC 20005

Center for Concerned
Engineering
1707 Q Street NW
Washington, DC 20009

National Center for Law and the
Deaf
Gallaudet College
7th Street and Florida
Avenue NE
Washington, DC 20002

National Center for Law and the
Handicapped, Inc.
1235 North Eddy Street
South Bend, IN 46617

Paralyzed Veterans of America
801 18th Street NW
Washington, DC 20006
(202) 872-1300

AMPUTEES

Amputees' Service Association
6613 North Clark Street
Chicago, IL 60626
(312) 583-3949

The National Amputation
Foundation, Inc.
73 Church Street
Malverne, NY 11565
(516) 887-3600

GENERAL REHABILITATION

American Paralysis Association
Spinal Cord Injury Hotline
2201 Argonna Drive
Baltimore, MD 21218
(800) 526-3456

Disabled American Veterans
National Headquarters
P.O. Box 14301
Cincinnati, OH 45250
(606) 441-7300

Federation of the Handicapped
211 West 14th Street
New York, NY 10011
(212) 727-4200

Goodwill Industries of America
2200 South Dakota Avenue
Washington, DC 20018
(202) 636-4225

Human Resources Center
I.U. Willets Road
Albertson, NY 11507
(516) 747-5400

The National Easter Seal Society
230 West Monroe Street,
Suite 1800
Chicago, IL 60606
(312) 726-6200

National Information Center for
Handicapped Children and
Youth
P.O. Box 1492
Washington, DC 20013-1492
(202) 416-0300

National Rehabilitation
Association
633 South Washington Street
Alexandria, VA 22314
(703) 836-0850

National Rehabilitation
Information Center
8455 Colesville Road, Suite 935
Silver Spring, MD 20910
(800) 346-2742
(301) 588-9284

National Spinal Cord Injury
Association
600 West Cummings Park,
Suite 2000
Woburn, MA 01801
(617) 935-2722
(800) 962-9629

National Study Center of
Emergency Medical Systems
701 West Pratt Street—001
Baltimore, MD 21201
(410) 328-5085
Spinal cord injury hotline:
(800) 526-3456

Paralyzed Veterans of America
801 18th Street NW
Washington, DC 20006
(202) 872-1300

People-to-People Committee for
the Handicapped
1020 Ashton Road
Ashton, MD 20861
(301) 774-7446

Rehabilitation International
The International Society for
Rehabilitation of the
Disabled
25 East 21st Street
New York, NY 10010
(212) 420-1500

LEISURE ACTIVITIES FOR THE HANDICAPPED

ARTS, DANCE, AND MUSIC

Music Services Unit
National Library Service for the
Blind and Physically
Handicapped
Washington, DC 20542
(202) 287-9256

Very Special Arts USA
The John F. Kennedy Center for
Performing Arts, Education
Office
Washington, DC 20566
(800) 933-8721
(202) 737-0645 (TDD)

NATURE STUDY

The National Audubon Society
700 Broadway
New York, NY 10003
(212) 979-3000

SPORTS

American Alliance for Health,
Physical Education,
Recreation, and Dance
Program for the Handicapped
1900 Association Drive
Reston, VA 22091
(703) 476-3400

National Wheelchair Athletic
Association
3617 Betty Drive, Suite S
Colorado Springs, CO 80917
(303) 597-8330

National Wheelchair Basketball
Association
University of Kentucky
110 Seaton Building
Lexington, KY 40506-0219
(606) 275-1623

TRAVEL

Flying Wheels Travel
143 West Bridge
P.O. Box 382
Owatonna, MN 55060
(800) 533-0363
(800) 722-9351 (in Minnesota)

Society for the Advancement of
Travel for the Handicapped
26 Court Street
Brooklyn, NY 11242
(send self-addressed envelope
and specify type of
handicap)
(718) 858-5483

SOURCES OF EQUIPMENT AND AIDS FOR THE HANDICAPPED

SUPPLIERS

Guardian Products
P.O. Box 2744
Oshkosh, WI 54901
(414) 231-7970

G. E. Miller, Inc.
540 Nepperhan Avenue
Yonkers, NY 10701
(914) 969-4036

Maddakk, Inc.
661 Route 23 South
Wayne, NJ 07440
(201) 628-7600

Rehabilitation Equipment, Inc.
1513 Olmstead Avenue
Bronx, NY 10462
(718) 829-3800

GOVERNMENT ASSISTANCE FOR THE HANDICAPPED

Sherri Lynn, Acting Chief
Branch of Exceptional
    Education
Office of Indian Education
    Programs
Bureau of Indian Affairs
Department of the Interior
Washington, DC 20240
(202) 208-6675

Office of Special Education
    Programs
Switzers Building, Room 3090
330 C Street SW
Washington, DC 20201
(202) 724-4172

Commissioner
Rehabilitation Services
    Administration
330 C Street SW
Mail Stop 2312
Washington, DC 20202

STATE AND TERRITORIAL OFFICES

Kenneth Wison, Assistant
    Superintendent
Exceptional Children and
    Youth
State Department of Education
P.O. Box 302101
Montgomery, AL 36130
(205) 242-9700

Director
Office of Special Services
801 West 10th Street, Suite 200
Juneau, AK 99801-1894
(907) 465-2970

Deputy Associate
    Superintendent
Special Education
1535 West Jefferson
Phoenix, AZ 85007
(602) 542-5057

Diane Sydoriak
Special Education Section
State Education Building C
Room 105-C
Little Rock, AR 72201
(501) 371-2161

Director
California Department of
    Education
Special Education Division
721 Capitol Mall, Room 610
Sacramento, CA 95481
(916) 323-4753

Fred Smokoski
Colorado Department of
    Education
201 East Colfax
Denver, CO 80203
(303) 866-6600

Tom B. Gillung
Bureau of Special Education and
    Pupil Education
Connecticut State Department
    of Education
25 Industrial Park Road
Middletown, CT 06457
(203) 566-5497

Martha Brooks
Exceptional Children and
    Special Programs Division
Department of Public
    Instruction
P.O. Box 1402
Dover, DE 19903
(302) 739-5471

Constance Clark
D.C. Public Schools
Division of Special Education
215 E Street NE
Washington, DC 20002
(202) 724-4801

Diane Gillespie
Bureau of Education of
    Exceptional Students
Florida Department of
    Education
Knott Building
Tallahassee, Fl 32399
(904) 487-1785

Joan A. Jordan
Georgia Department of
    Education
Program for Exceptional
    Children
Twin Towers East, Suite 1970
Atlanta, GA 30334
(404) 656-2446

Evangeline Barney
Special Needs Branch
State Department of Education
3430 Leahi Avenue
Honolulu, HI 96815
(808) 737-3720

Fred Balcom
Special Education Section
State Department of Education
Len B. Jordan Building
650 West State Street
Boise, ID 93720
(208) 334-3940

Gayle Leiberman
Specialized Educational
    Services
Illinois State Board of Education
100 North First Street
Springfield, IL 62777
(217) 782-6601

Paul Ash
Indiana Division of Special
    Education
229 State House
Indianapolis, IN 46204
(317) 232-0570

Bureau Chief of Education
Special Education Division
Department of Education
Grimes State Office Building
Des Moines, IA 50319-0146
(515) 281-3176

Betty Withers
Kansas State Department of
    Education
Special Education Outcomes
120 South East 10th Avenue
Topeka, KS 66612-1182
(913) 296-3869

Ken Warlick
Department of Education
Office of Education for
    Exceptional Children
Capitol Plaza Tower, 8th Floor
Frankfort, KY 40601
(502) 564-4970

Leon Barne, Jr.
Louisiana Department of
    Education
P.O. Box 44064
Baton Rouge, LA 70804
(504) 342-3633

David Noble Stockford
Division of Special Education
State Department of
    Educational and Cultural
    Services
State House, Station 23
Augusta, ME 04333
(207) 287-5953

Director
Division of Special Education
State Department of Education
200 West Baltimore Street
Baltimore, MD 21201
(410) 659-2489

Director
Special Education Division
State Department of Education
350 Main Street
Malden, MA 02148

Richard Baldwin
Michigan Department of
    Education
Special Education Services
P.O. Box 30008
Lansing, MI 48909
(517) 373-9433

Wayne Erickson
Minnesota Department of
    Education
Capitol Square Building,
    Room 813
350 Cedar Street
St. Paul, MN 55101
(612) 296-1793

Carolyn Black
State Department of Education
P.O. Box 771
Jackson, MS 39205
(601) 359-3498

John Allan
Division of Social Education
Department of Elementary and
    Secondary Education
P.O. Box 480
Jefferson City, MO 65201
(314) 751-2965

Robert Runkel
Office of Public Instruction
P.O. Box 202501
Helena, MT 59620-2501
(406) 444-4429

Gary M. Sherman
Special Education Branch
Nebraska Department of
    Education
Box 94987
301 Centennial Mall South
Lincoln, NE 68509
(402) 471-2471

Gloria Dopf
Special Education Branch
Division of Special Education
Nevada Department of
    Education
400 West King Street, Capitol
    Complex
Carson City, NV 89710
(702) 687-3140

Nathan Norris
State Department of Education
101 Pleasant Street
Concord, NH 03301
(603) 271-3741

Jeffery V. Osowski
Office of Special Education
    Programs
State Department of Education
CN 500
Trenton, NJ 08625
(609) 292-0147

Linda Wilson
Special Education Unit
State Department of Education
Educational Building
Sante Fe, NM 87501-2786
(505) 827-6541

Thomas Neveldine
Office for Education of Children
    with Handicapping
    Conditions
New York State Department of
    Education
1 Commerce Plaza, Room 1610
Albany, NY 12234
(518) 474-5548

Lowell Harris
Division for Exceptional
    Children
State Department of Public
    Instruction
Raleigh, NC 27601
(919) 715-1563

Gary Gronberg
Department of Public
    Instruction
State Capitol
Bismarck, ND 58505-0164
(701) 224-2277

John Herner
Division of Special Education
933 High Street
Worthington, OH 43085-4087
(614) 466-2650

John Carpolongo
Special Education Section
State Department of Education
2500 North Lincoln, Suite 411
Oklahoma City, OK 73105
(405) 521-3351

Director
Special Education and Students
    Services
State Department of Education
700 Pringle Parkway SE
Salem, OR 97310
(503) 378-3569

Michelle Desera
Bureau of Special Education
Pennsylvania Department of
    Education
333 Market Street, 7th Floor
Harrisburg, PA 17126-0333
(717) 783-6913

Robert M. Pryhoda
Rhode Island Department of
    Education
Roger Williams Building,
    Room 209
22 Hayes Street
Providence, RI 02908
(401) 277-3505

Director, Office of Programs for
    the Handicapped
South Carolina Department of
    Education
1429 Senate Street, 5th Floor
Columbia, SC 29210
(803) 734-8500

Deborah Barnett, Director
Office of Special Education
Kneip Office Building
700 Governor's Drive
Pierre, SD 57501
(605) 773-4689

Joseph Fisher
Division of Special Education
Department of Education
Gateway Plaza, 8th Floor
710 James Robertson Parkway
Nashville, TN 37243-0380
(615) 741-2851

Jill Gray
Department of Special
    Education
Texas Education Agency
1701 North Congress
Austin, TX 78701
(512) 463-9734

Steven J. Kukic
Utah State Office of Education
Special Education Department
250 East 500 South
Salt Lake City, UT 84111
(801) 538-7700

Dennis Cane
Division of Special and
    Compensatory Education
Department of Education
State Capitol Office Building
120 State Street
Montpelier, VT 05620-2501
(802) 828-3141

Patricia Abrams, Administrative
    Director
Office of Special and
    Compensatory Education
Department of Education
P.O. Box 2120
Richmond, VA 23216
(804) 225-2402

Priscilla Stridiron
Division of Special Education
Department of Education
44-46 Kongens
St. Thomas, VI 00802
(809) 774-0100

Judith Billings
Office of the Superintendent of
    Public Instruction
Old Capitol Building,
    P.O. Box 47200
Olympia, WA 98504-7200
(206) 753-6733

Director, Office of Special
    Education Administration
West Virginia Department of
    Education
1900 Kanawha Boulevard East
Charleston, WV 25305
(304) 553-2691

Juanita Polsch
Division for Handling Children
    and Pupil Services
Wisconsin Department of
    Public Instruction
P.O. Box 7841
Madison, WI 53707-7841
(608) 266-1649

Appendix C

DIRECTORY OF REGIONAL POISON CONTROL CENTERS

Compiled by the American Association of Poison Control Centers
(All phone numbers are for emergency purposes only)

ALABAMA

Regional Poison Control Center
The Children's Hospital of
 Alabama
1600 7th Avenue South
Birmingham, AL 35233-1711
(205) 939-9201
(800) 292-6678
(205) 933-4050

ARIZONA

Arizona Poison and Drug
 Information Center
Arizona Health Sciences Center,
 Room #3204-K
1501 North Cambell Avenue
Tucson, AZ 85724
(800) 362-0101
(602) 626-6016

Samaritan Regional Poison
 Center
Teleservices Department
1441 North 12th Street
Phoenix, AZ 85006
(602) 253-3334

CALIFORNIA

Fresno Regional Poison Control
 Center of Fresno
 Community Hospital and
 Medical Center
2823 Fresno Street
Fresno, CA 93721
(800) 346-5922
(209) 445-1222

San Diego Regional Poison
 Center
UCSD Medical Center: 8925
200 West Arbor Drive
San Diego, CA 92103-8925
(619) 543-6000
(800) 876-4766

San Francisco Bay Area Regional
 Poison Control Center
San Francisco General Hospital
1001 Potrero Avenue,
 Building 80, Room 230
San Francisco, CA 94110
(800) 523-2222

Santa Clara Valley Medical
 Center Regional Poison
 Center
750 South Bascom Ave,
 Suite 310
San Jose, CA 95128
(408) 299-5112
(800) 662-9886

Unversity of California, Davis,
 Medical Center Regional
 Poison Control Center
2315 Stockton Boulevard
Sacramento, CA 95817
(916) 734-3692
(800) 342-9293

COLORADO AND MONTANA

Rocky Mountain Poison and
 Drug Center
645 Bannock Street
Denver, CO 80204
(303) 629-1123

DISTRICT OF COLUMBIA

Georgetown University
 Hospital
3800 Reservoir Road NW
Washington, DC 20007
(202) 625-3333
(202) 784-4660 (TTY)

FLORIDA

The Florida Poison Information
 Center and Toxicology
 Resource Center
Tampa General Hospital
P.O. Box 1289
Tampa, FL 33601
(813) 253-4444 (Tampa)
(800) 282-3171 (Florida)

GEORGIA

Georgia Poison Center
Grady Memorial Hospital
80 Butler Street SE
P.O. Box 26066
Atlanta, GA 30335-3801
(800) 282-5846 (GA only)
(404) 616-9000

INDIANA

Indiana Poison Center
Methodist Hospital of Indiana
1701 Senate Boulevard
P.O. Box 1367
Indianapolis, IN 46206-1367
(800) 382-9097 (Indiana only)
(317) 929-2323

MARYLAND

Maryland Poison Center
20 Pine Street
Baltimore, MD 21201
(410) 528-7701
(800) 492-2414

National Capitol Poison Center
 (DC suburbs only)
Georgetown University
 Hospital
3800 Reservoir Road NW
Washington, DC 20007
(202) 625-5333
(202) 784-4660 (TTY)

MASSACHUSETTS

Massachusetts Poison Control
 System
300 Longwood Avenue
Boston, MA 02215
(617) 232-2120
(800) 682-9211

MICHIGAN

Poison Control Center
Children's Hospital of Michigan
3901 Beaubien Boulevard
Detroit, MI 48201
(313) 745-5711

MINNESOTA

Hennepin Regional Poison
 Center
Hennepin County Medical
 Center
701 Park Avenue
Minneapolis, MN 55415
(612) 347-3141
(612) 337-7387 (pets)
(612) 337-7474 (TDD)

Minnesota Regional Poison
 Center
St. Paul-Ramsey Medical Center
640 Jackson Street
St. Paul, MN 55101
(612) 221-2113

MISSOURI

Cardinal Glennon Children's
 Hospital Regional Poison
 Center
1465 South Grand Boulevard
St. Louis, MO 63104
(314) 722-5200
(800) 366-8888

NEBRASKA

The Poison Center
8301 Dodge Street
Omaha, NE 68114
(402) 390-5555
(800) 955-9119

NEW JERSEY

New Jersey Poison Information
 and Education System
201 Lyons Avenue
Newark, NJ 07112
(800) 962-1253

NEW MEXICO

New Mexico Poison and Drug
 Information Center
University of New Mexico
Alburquerque, NM 87131-1076
(505) 843-2551
(800) 432-6866

NEW YORK

Hudson Valley Poison Center
Nyack Hospital
160 North Midland Avenue
Nyack, NY 10960
(800) 336-6997
(914) 353-1000

Long Island Regional Poison
 Control Center
Winthrop University Hospital
259 First Street
Mineola, NY 11501
(516) 542-2323, -2324, -2325,
 -3813

New York City Poison Control
 Center
N.Y.C. Department of Health
455 First Avenue, Room 123
New York, NY 10016
(212) 340-4494
(212) POISONS
(212) 689-9014 (TDD)

OHIO

Central Ohio Poison Center
700 Children's Drive
Columbus, OH 43205-2696
(614) 228-1323
(800) 682-7625
(614) 228-2272 (TTY)

Cincinnati Drug and Poison Information Center and Regional Poison Control System
231 Bethesda Avenue, M.L. 144
Cincinnati, OH 45267-0144
(513) 558-5111
(800) 872-5111 (Ohio only)

OREGON

Oregon Poison Center
Oregon Health Sciences University
3181 S.W. Sam Jackson Park Road
Portland, OR 97201
(503) 494-8968
(800) 452-7165

PENNSYLVANIA

Central Pennsylvania Poison Center
University Hospital, Milton S. Hershey Medical Center
Hershey, PA 17033
(800) 521-6110

The Poison Control Center (serving greater Philadelphia metropolitan area)
One Children's Center
Philadelphia, PA 19104-4303
(215) 386-2100

Pittsburgh Poison Center
3705 Fifth Avenue
Pittsburgh, PA 15213
(412) 681-6669

RHODE ISLAND

Rhode Island Poison Center
593 Eddy Street
Providence, RI 02903
(401) 277-5727

TEXAS

North Texas Poison Center
5201 Harry Hines Boulevard
P.O. Box 35926
Dallas, TX 75235
(214) 590-5000
(800) 441-0040 (Texas Watts)

Texas State Poison Center
The University of Texas Medical Branch
Galveston, TX 77550-2780
(409) 765-1420 (Galveston)
(713) 654-1701 (Houston)

UTAH

Utah Poison Control Center
410 Chipeta Way, Suite 230
Salt Lake City, UT 84108
(801) 581-2151
(800) 456-7707

VIRGINIA

Blue Ridge Poison Center
Blue Ridge Hospital, Box 67
Charlottesville, VA 22901
(804) 924-5543
(800) 451-1428

National Capital Poison Center (Northern Virginia and Washington, DC only)
Georgetown University Hospital
3800 Reservoir Road NW
Washington, DC 20007
(202) 625-3333
(202) 784-4660 (TTY)

WEST VIRGINIA

West Virginia Poison Center
3110 MacCorkle Avenue SE
Charleston, WV 25304
(800) 642-3625
(304) 348-4211

Appendix D

FAMILY MEDICAL RECORDS

FORM 1   FAMILY TREE

Name _____   Soc. Sec. No. _____

Great-Great-Great Grandparents

Great-Great Grandparents

Great-Grandmother Great-Grandfather Great-Grandmother Great-Grandfather   Great-Grandparents   Great-Grandmother Great-Grandfather Great-Grandmother Great-Grandfather

Grandmother Grandfather   Grandparents   Grandmother Grandfather

Mother   Father

You

Genealogical Chart

© Personal Health Profile, Inc.

FORM 2 FAMILY MEDICAL HISTORY

Name _____   Soc. Sec. No. _____

Mark the appropriate space with a check ( ) or insert the name of specific medical problem.

Problem	Mother	Father	Maternal grandmother	Maternal grandfather	Paternal grandmother	Paternal grandfather
Birthplace						
Occupation						
Alcoholism						
Allergies						
Blood/Circulation						
Bones/Joints (where)						
Cancer						
Diabetes						
Digestive system						
Drug sensitivities						
Eye disorder						
Hearing disorder						
Heart disorder						
Kidney disorder						
Liver disorder						
Mental disorder						
Nerves/Muscles						
Reproductive system						
Respiratory system						
Stroke						
Urinary problem						
Major surgery						
Other						
Age/Cause of death						

FORM 3 RECORD OF MAJOR MEDICAL PROBLEMS

Name _____   Soc. Sec. No. _____

For quick review, major medical problems are separated from minor ones. Major problems are those that caused hospitalization, surgery, or an emergency. In the third column, summarize treatment and also refer to other pertinent charts (e.g., medications or x-rays).

Date	Major medical problem	Treatment, other forms

FORM 4 RECORD OF MINOR MEDICAL PROBLEMS

Name _____   Soc. Sec. No. _____

Minor medical problem—any accident or medical problem requiring treatment..

Date	Minor medical problem	Treatment, other forms

FORM 5 YOUR INFANT PROFILE

Name _____ Male _____ Female _____

Date of birth _____ Day of week _____ Time _____

Place of birth _____ Birth certif. no. _____
               City   County   State

Hospital _____ Address_____

Obstetrician _____ Address_____

Pediatrician _____ Address_____

Weight at birth _____ Length _____ Blood type _____ Rh factor _____

Color of eyes _____ Color of hair_____

Mother's maiden name _____

Mother's birthplace_____

Father's name _____

Father's birthplace _____

Birth defects, if any _____

_____

_____

Other information _____

_____

_____

_____

_____

_____

_____

_____

_____

_____

FORM 6 RECORD IMMUNIZATIONS AND INFECTIOUS DISEASES

Name _____   Soc. Sec. No. _____

A. Record of Immunizations

Immunization for	Age	Date	Booster		Booster		Booster	
			Age	Date	Age	Date	Age	Date
Diphtheria								
Pertussis								
Tetanus								
Polio								
Smallpox								
Typhoid								
Rubella (Ger. measles)								
Mumps								
Measles								
TB								
Other								

B. Record of Infectious Diseases

Disease	Age	Date	Remarks
Chickenpox			
Measles			
Rubella (Ger. measles)			
Hepatitis			
Mumps			
Polio			
Pneumonia			
Pertussis			
Scarlet Fever			
Other			

FORM 7 RECORD OF DOCTORS' VISITS

Name _____ Soc. Sec. No. _____

Date _____ Age _____ Cost of visit _____

Doctor's name _____ Specialty _____

Reason for visit _____

Treatment prescribed _____

Comments _____

_____

FORM 8 RECORD OF PRESCRIPTIONS AND MEDICATIONS

Name _____ Soc. Sec. No. _____

Date	Medicine prescribed	Rx No.	Pharmacy	Doctor	Cost

FORM 9 RECORD OF HOSPITAL ADMISSIONS

Name _____ Soc. Sec. No. _____

Date admitted_____ Date discharged _____ Age _____

Hospital _____ Tel. _____

Address _____

Hospital chart no._____ Length of stay _____ Cost _____

Reason for admission _____

Doctor's name _____ Tel. _____

Discharge plan _____

© Personal Health Profile, Inc.

Glossary

UNDERSTANDING THE LANGUAGE OF MEDICINE

by Rita A. Charon, M.D.

INTRODUCTION

The work of medicine is intimately connected to its language. Although the technology of health care gets more and more sophisticated, it is clear that the center of medicine is still the dialogue between the health care provider and the patient. Medical interviews are complex conversations in which uncertainties, fears, hopes, and information are shared. The success of this conversation is crucial for both doctor and patient.

One thread of the conversation is a narration of the patient's life. During the dialogue between a doctor and a patient, which may take place over years or decades, the story of a life unfolds. Patients talk about their childhoods, their families, their activities, their plans. Many aspects of patients' lives enter into caring for their health.

A more specific level of the conversation is the reporting of symptoms. Patients must put their physical sensations into words, a task that challenges the most literate of us. Doctors must learn to understand the difference between a "pushing" pain and a "pressing" pain, or a "cramp" and a "stitch."

The quality of the symptom can help to diagnose its cause; this is why patients are often urged to describe their sensations in detail. "Is the pain sharp or dull? Is it there all the time or does it come and go? Does it move around or does it stay in one place?" are all questions that most patients have been asked by their doctors.

The major part of the medical interview is the sharing of information. Patients tell about past hospitalizations, allergies, medications they take, and current medical problems. Doctors tell about what the symptoms may signify, what the diagnoses mean, what further tests need to be done, and what treatment can be offered. They give instructions about medicine, diet, and exercise, and referrals to other health care providers.

Interwoven into this dialogue is a thread of feelings. Because of the intimacy and the meaning of the topics discussed, many emotions are involved. Patients may be fearful or concerned. Doctors must deal with the uncertainty they face, for so much is not known and not understood in medicine even now. The feelings themselves may have brought the patient to seek medical attention, for a high proportion of visits to medical doctors are said to be prompted by anxiety, depression, or worry. Patients often talk with their doctors about troubles with families, with work, with money, or at home.

During the medical conversation, feelings between doctor and patient are expressed. They might be supportive, open, and helpful or they can be distant, hostile, and abrupt. The doctor may be able to empathize with the patient in distress, or might be perceived as ignoring the concerns expressed by the patient.

Finally, there is a shape to the conversation between doctor and patient. Who does most of the talking? Who interrupts whom? Are the topics chosen by one person most of the time? Do they reach agreement on what to focus on? Who decides when the conversation is over? All these features reveal facts about the control of the doctor-patient relationship. It seems sometimes that there are two different conversations going on at the same time, one about the patient's world and one about the world of medicine.

The medical conversation, then, is a dynamic and complicated event. When all these levels are working well, the interview is smooth and effective. Patients and doctors learn about each other on a personal level. The health problems are described clearly, and the medical information is offered coherently. Emotional problems are openly addressed, and a supportive relationship is established. In this case, the doctor and the patient are talking the same language with mutual understanding and shared control. When the conversation goes badly, the opposite occurs. Patients may not be clear in presenting their problems, doctors may not listen. Information may be given in scientific terms with no explanation. The real reason for the visit may not be expressed at all. One person may do most of the talking and prevent dialogue altogether. In this case, neither participant in the conversation feels heard. The work of medicine can't progress.

Studies are showing that the nature of the conversation between doctor and patient can have drastic effects on health care. Patients are more likely to follow advice and to keep return appointments when they feel that their doctors listen to them, understand their concerns, and convey interest in them. Even more important, we now think that good communication can improve the actual health condition of the patient. In some studies, patients who were allowed to ask questions and to clarify their understanding of their problems reached better control of their medical diseases.

We don't know how successful most doctors and patients are in talking with each other. There is active research in this field among medical doctors and social scientists who study language. We are learning that problems are widespread and that both doctors and patients are very troubled by the gaps in communication.

Fortunately, there is much that can be done to improve medical conversations by both doctors and patients. Medical schools have realized how important it is to teach their students how to talk with patients. Schools offer courses in medical interviewing skills, stressing the importance of listening to patients, recognizing the emotional issues raised, and responding in supportive and helpful ways. Because doctors spend so much time talking to each other, they have to be reminded how to speak in ordinary language about bodies and medical topics.

Patients are learning more and more about the language of medicine. Many health centers and doctors' offices have active programs in health education where patients can learn about diseases' treatments and preventive health care. Patient self-help groups have been formed to share information about specific health problems like the Reach to Recovery group for women who have had breast surgery. These groups can make a big impact on the ability of a patient to deal with a disease and the changes it brings to his or her life. Health reporting on television and in the press has become quite sophisticated, giving medical news in ways that help people understand their own bodies. There is a growing library of books offered to the general audience about health and medicine topics.

This chapter gives you a glossary of medical terms to add to your knowledge of medical language. The dictionary is arranged to teach you about specific words and also to teach you how to interpret words by understanding smaller parts of them. You will see a list of prefixes and suffixes that will enable you to decode what many more complex words mean.

At Columbia University's College of Physicians and Surgeons, we believe that informed patients can be healthier patients. We offer this textbook to help patients be better informed, with this chapter as a road map. Together, doctors and patients can improve their communication with each other. Patients will be empowered through education and sharing of control of health events.

Doctors will grow in their ability truly to listen to patients, and to be not only diagnosticians and interveners but also supportive presences in their patients' lives. We hope that doctors and patients are approaching a common language.

....

PREFIXES

a-, an-, Without, absent, deficient, not. Example: anaerobic (without oxygen).

ad-, Near, toward. Example: adrenal glands (glands located on top of the kidneys).

ambi-, Both. Example: ambidextrous (having equal dexterity in both hands).

anti-, Against. Example: antitoxin (substance that acts against a poison).

bi-, Two. Example: bicuspid (having 2 points or protrusions).

brady-, Slow. Example: bradycardia (slow heartbeat).

co-, con-, Together, in contact. Example: conjunctiva (the membrane that connects the eyeball to the eyelid).

con-, contra-, Against. Example: contraception (methods to prevent conception).

cyan-, cyano-, Blue. Example: cyanosis (the dark blue color of deoxygenated blood).

de-, Away, without, down from, out of. Example: dementia (state of being "out of one's mind").

dia-, Through, completely, across. Example: dialysis (separation of particles from liquid through a straining device).

dys-, Difficult, bad. Example: dyspepsia (indigestion).

ect-, ecto-, Outside. Example: ectopic (displaced).

en-, endo-, Inside, within, inner. Example: endoscopy (internal examination).

epi-, On, over, next to. Example: epidermis (the outer layer of skin).

erythro-, Red. Example: erythrocyte (red blood cell).

eu-, Good, well. Example: euphoria (extreme elation).

ex-, Out of, away from. Example: exanthem (the appearance of lesions on the skin).

hemi-, Half. Example: hemiplegia (paralysis of one side of the body).

hetero-, Different. Example: heterogeneous (made up of differing components).

homo-, Alike, similar, the same. Example: homograft (transplant of tissue from one organism to another of the same species).

hyper-, Excessive, increased. Example: hypertension (high blood pressure).

hypo-, Insufficient, below. Example: hypotension (low blood pressure).

inter-, Between. Example: intertrigo (chafing between 2 skin surfaces).

intra-, Within. Example: intrauterine (inside the uterus).

leuk-, leuko-, White. Example: leukocyte (white blood cell).

lig-, Binding. Example: ligament (band of tissue that connects bones).

macro-, Large. Example: macrocyte (a large cell).

mega-, Large. Example: megacolon (an enlarged large intestine) or cardiomegaly (an enlarged heart).

melan-, melano-, Black, dark. Example: melanin (dark pigment).

met-, meta-, Change in, between, after. Example: metabolism (the total of all the chemical changes in the body).

micro-, Small. Example: microbe (very small living organism).

mono-, One. Example: monosaccharide (simple sugar).

myc-, myco-, mycet-, Fungal, relating to fungus. Example: mycotic infection (disease caused by a fungus).

ne-, neo-, New. Example: neoplasm (new growth, tumor).

olig-, oligo-, Scanty, little. Example: oliguria (deficient urine secretion).

ortho-, Erect, straight. Example: orthodontics (straightening of teeth).

osteo-, Bone. Example: osteomalacia (softness of the bones).

pachy-, Thick. Example: pachyderm (thick skin).

pan-, Whole, entire. Example: pandemic (epidemic affecting entire area).

para-, Alongside of. Example: parasite (organism that lives on or in another organism).

patho-, Disease. Example: pathology (study of disease).

peri-, Around, surrounding. Example: pericardium (the membrane surrounding the heart).

phlebo-, Vein. Example: phlebitis (inflammation of a vein).

pneumo-, Air, lung. Example: pneumonia.

poly-, Many, more than normal. Example: polydactyly (having more than the usual number of fingers).

post-, After. Example: postmortem (after death).

pre-, Before. Example: prenatal (before birth).

procto-, Pertaining to the anus or rectum. Example: proctoscope (instrument to examine the anus and rectum).

proto-, First, earliest. Example: prototype.

re-, retro-, Again, back, behind. Example: repression (pressing back feelings into the subconscious).

retro-, Behind, past. Example: retroversion (turning back of).

rhino-, Nose. Example: rhinoplasty (plastic surgery of the nose).

schisto-, schizo-, Split. Example: schizophrenia ("split personality").

sclera-, Tough, hard. Example: scleroderma (hardening of the skin and connective tissue).

sub-, Under, less than. Example: subacute (less than acute).

super-, supra-, Above. Example: suprapubic (above the pubis).

syn-, syl-, sym-, Together. Example: syndrome (occurring together).

tachy-, Abnormally fast. Example: tachycardia (very fast heartbeat).

tri-, Three, third. Example: trimester (one-third of pregnancy).

trichi-, tricho-, Hairy, hairlike. Example: trichiasis (ingrown hair).

ultra-, Beyond. Example: ultrasound (sound waves out of the range of human hearing).

xanth-, Yellow. Example: xanthoma (yellow patch on the skin).

xero-, Dryness. Example: xeroderm (dry skin).

SUFFIXES

-alg, -algia, Pain. Example: myalgia (pain in the muscles).

-cele, Swelling. Example: varicocele (swollen vein in the spermatic cord).

-cide, Capable of killing. Example: spermicide (agent capable of killing sperm).

-ectomy, Surgical removal. Example: splenectomy (surgical removal of the spleen).

-gen, -genic, Producing, indicating origin. Example: allergen (substance capable of producing an allergic reaction).

-gram, -graph, -graphy, Record, recording device, recording process. Examples: cardiogram, cardiography.

-ia, -iasis, Indicating diseased condition.

-itis, Inflammation. Example: tonsillitis (inflammation of the tonsils).

-lysis, Breaking down. Example: hydrolysis (breakdown of a substance by the addition of water).

-oid, Resembling, similar to. Example: adenoid (organ similar to a gland).

-ologist, one who studies, specialist in a branch of medicine.

-ology, the science or study of.

-oma, Tumor, not necessarily malignant.

-osis, Diseased condition.

-ostomy, Surgical creation of an opening.

-otomy, Incision.

-penia, Scarcity, deficiency.

-plasia, -plasm, Formation, growth. Example: neoplasm (tumor).

-poiesis, Production.

-rhag, -rhagra, Excessive discharge. Example: hemorrhage.

-rrhea, Flow. Example: leukorrhea (whitish discharge of mucus from the vagina).

-scope, Instrument for viewing. Example: cystoscope (instrument for viewing the interior of the bladder).

ROOTS

aden, adeno, Pertaining to a gland. Example: adenitis (inflammation of a gland).

andro, andros, Male. Example: android (resembling a male).

angi, angio, Vessel, usually a blood or lymph vessel. Example: angiography (x-ray study of blood vessels or lymphatic system).

arthr, Pertaining to a joint. Example: arthritis (inflammation of a joint).

bleph, Pertaining to the eyelid. Example: blepharitis (inflammation of the eyelids).

bronch, broncho, From the Greek word for windpipe. Example: bronchitis (inflammation of the bronchi, or airway).

cardio, Pertaining to the heart. Example: cardiovascular.

cephal, Pertaining to the head. Example: encephal (inside the head, brain).

cerebr, cerebri, Pertaining to the brain. Example: cerebral.

chol, chole, Pertaining to bile. Example: cholecystectomy (removal of the gallbladder, where bile is stored).

cyst, Pertaining to a bladder or sac. Example: cystoscopy (examination of the interior of the bladder).

cyt, cyto, Pertaining to cells. Example: cytology (cell biology).

dent, dont, Pertaining to teeth, or to a tooth.

derm, derma, dermo, Pertaining to the skin. Example: dermatology.

enter, entero, Pertaining to the intestines.

gastr, gastro, Pertaining to the stomach. Example: gastroenteritis (inflammation of the stomach and intestines).

gloss, Pertaining to the tongue. Example: glossoplegia (paralysis of the tongue).

gnath, Pertaining to the jaw. Example: gnathalgia (pain in the jaw).

gyn, gyne, Pertaining to women. Example: gynecology.

hema, hemo, Pertaining to blood. Example: hematoma (a blood-filled swelling).

hepar, hepat, Pertaining to the liver. Example: hepatoma (tumor of the liver).

hyster, Pertaining to the uterus. Example: hysterectomy (surgical removal of the uterus).

iatro, Pertaining to a physician, doctor. Example: iatrogenic (caused by a doctor).

idio, Peculiar to a specific individual. Example: idiosyncrasy.

lipo, Fat, fatty. Example: lipid (fatty substance).

lith, Stone, sandy calcification. Example: lithiasis (formation of gallstones or kidney stones).

mamma, mast, Pertaining to the breast. Example: mammary gland (milk-secreting gland of the breast).

men, meno, Pertaining to menstruation (monthly cycle).

metr, metro, Pertaining to the uterus. Example: metrorrhagia (bleeding from the uterus other than normal menstrual flow).

my, myo, Pertaining to the muscles. Example: myopathy (a disease of the muscles).

myelo, Pertaining to the marrow. Example: myeloma (tumor of the bone marrow).

necro, Pertaining to death. Example: necropsy (autopsy).

nephro, Pertaining to the kidneys. Example: nephrolith (kidney stone).

neuro, Pertaining to nerves. Example: neuralgia (pain along the course of a nerve).

ocul, oculo, Pertaining to the eyes.

odont, odonto, Pertaining to the teeth.

orchi, Pertaining to the testes. Example: orchitis (inflammation of the testicles).

oro, os, Pertaining to the mouth or an opening.

ortho, Straight, upright. Example: orthopnea (a condition in which one is able to breathe only when standing erect).

os, oste, osteo, Pertaining to bones. Example: ossification (the process of becoming bone).

ot, oto, Pertaining to the ear. Example: otitis (inflammation of the ear).

path, patho, pathy, Suffering or disease.

ped, 1. Pertaining to the foot or feet. 2. Pertaining to children (pediatrics).

phag, Pertaining to eating or swallowing. Capable of consuming. Example: phagocyte (cell capable of engulfing bacteria or debris).

phleb, Pertaining to a vein. Example: phlebitis (inflammation of a vein).

plast, Formation or reconstruction. Example: plastic surgery.

plegia, Paralysis. Example: quadriplegia (paralysis of both arms and both legs).

pnea, Pertaining to breathing. Example: dyspnea (difficulty breathing).

pneumo, Pertaining to the lungs. Example: pneumonia (infection of the lungs).

presby, Pertaining to old age, the aging process. Example: presbyopia (the progressive degeneration of the eyes associated with getting older).

psych, psycho, Pertaining to the mind. Example: psychogenic (originating in the mind).

pur, pus, pyo, Pertaining to pus. Example: purulent (containing pus).

pyelo, Pertaining to the pelvis (urine-collecting basin) of the kidney.

pyr, pyret, Indicating fever. Example: pyrexia (fever).

ren-, Pertaining to the kidneys. Example: renin (an enzyme produced in the kidneys).

rhin, rhino, Pertaining to the nose. Example: rhinoplasty (plastic surgery of the nose).

scler, sclero, Hard, stiff. Example: sclerosis (abnormal stiffening of a tissue).

sicca, Dry, dryness.

somat, somato, Pertaining to the body.

stom, stomato, Pertaining to the mouth.

thor, Pertaining to the chest.

thromb, Pertaining to a blood clot. Example: thrombosis (formation of a blood clot in the blood vessels).

tract, tracto, Pertaining to pulling or extending. Example: traction (continuous pulling of a body part using weights and pulleys).

ur, uro, Pertaining to urine.

veni, veno, Pertaining to veins.

....

GLOSSARY OF MEDICAL TERMS

Abortion The interruption of pregnancy through expulsion of the fetus before it can survive outside the uterus (generally before the 20th week of pregnancy). Abortion may be either induced (also called therapeutic) or spontaneous.

Abscess A localized buildup of pus due to the breakdown of tissue by bacteria.

Acidosis A disrupted acid/alkaline balance due to a depletion of the body's alkali supplies or a production of acid. The condition is linked with several disorders, such as diabetes.

Acne The inflammation of the sebaceous (oil) glands due to a buildup of sebum, a fatty substance discharged through the pores to lubricate the skin. The condition is associated with the hormonal changes of adolescence, but may occur at any age.

Addiction Physical and emotional dependence on a drug due to the body's adaptation to its presence.

Addison's anemia See Pernicious anemia.

Addison's disease A disorder caused by insufficient secretion of aldosterone and cortisol from the adrenal glands, resulting in a variety of serious symptoms.

Adhesion The abnormal union of body surfaces caused by fibrous scars formed when tissues heal.

Adolescence The stage of development between puberty and full maturity.

Adrenal glands Endocrine glands that are situated just above the kidneys and which secrete important hormones. Among the hormones secreted are epinephrine (adrenaline), which affects heart rate and blood circulation and is instrumental in the body's response to physical stress, and cortisone, a natural anti-inflammatory. See also Epinephrine, Cortisone.

Adrenaline See Epinephrine.

Adrenocorticotropic hormone (ACTH) A hormone produced by the pituitary gland in order to induce the secretion of corticoids from the adrenal glands.

Afterbirth The collection of special tissues that are associated with fetal development and which are expelled after the delivery of the body. See also Placenta.

Agalactia The inability to produce milk after childbirth.

AIDS (acquired immune deficiency syndrome) An incurable disease that attacks and weakens the body's immune system, leaving the patient open to opportunistic infections and disorders that are normally warded off.

Albumin A protein found in animals, plants, and egg whites; the presence of albumin in the urine could indicate kidney disease.

Alcoholism Dependence on or addiction to alcohol. A poisoning of the body with alcohol. Physical damage can occur in the liver, heart, and kidneys as a result of alcohol poisoning. It can also lead to decreased resistance to infections.

Alkali Opposite and neutralizer of acid. Bicarbonate is the body's chief alkali.

Allergen Any agent that produces an allergic reaction. Common allergens include animal fur, pollen, dust, and certain foods. See also Allergy.

Allergy A hypersensitive or exaggerated reaction to exposure to certain substances (see also Allergen) or conditions (such as sun rays). Manifestations of allergies include rashes, coldlike symptoms, headaches, gastrointestinal symptoms, and asthma.

Alveoli The microscopic air sacs in the lungs through which oxygen and carbon dioxide are exchanged.

Amenorrhea The failure to menstruate. Amenorrhea is a symptom of many diseases and conditions.

Amino acid The nitrogen-containing components of protein used by the body to build muscle and other tissue. Some essential amino acids must be supplied by eating high-protein foods while others are synthesized in the body.

Amnesia Memory loss.

Amniocentesis The extraction and examination of a small amount of the amniotic fluid in order to determine genetic and other disorders in the fetus. See also Amniotic fluid.

Amnion The bag of waters in which the fetus and the amniotic fluid are contained during pregnancy.

Amniotic fluid The fluid surrounding the fetus.

Amphetamine A drug that stimulates the central nervous system.

Analgesic Any substance that gives temporary relief from pain.

Androgen Hormones, such as testosterone and androsterone, that are produced in the testes and are responsible for male characteristics. They are also produced normally in small amounts in females.

Androsterone One of the male sex hormones.

Anemia A deficiency in the hemoglobin, the number of red blood cells, or in the amount of blood. Anemia is usually a symptom of an underlying disorder.

Anesthesia Loss of sensation or feeling. General anesthesia involves the whole body while local anesthesia involves a particular area.

Anesthesiology The branch of medicine dealing with anesthesia and the application of anesthetic agents in surgery and pain relief.

Aneurysm A sac filled with blood that forms as a result of an abnormal widening of a vein or artery.

Angina Intense pain that produces a feeling of suffocation. The term is commonly used to refer to chest pains (angina pectoris) that are usually a result of an interruption of the oxygen supply to the heart muscle.

Angiography Examination of the interior blood vessels by injecting radiopaque substances so that any disorder or abnormality shows up on x-ray film. The record of pictures is called an angiogram.

Anoxia Oxygen deficiency.

Antacid An acid-neutralizing substance.

Antibiotic An antibacterial substance derived from bacteria, molds, and other substances. Penicillin is a common antibiotic.

Antibody The components of the immune system that eliminate or counteract foreign substances (antigens) in the body.

Anticoagulant An agent that retards the blood-clotting process.

Antidote An agent that counteracts the effects of a poison.

Antigen A substance, usually a protein found in germs or foreign tissue, that stimulates the production of antibodies.

Antihistamine A drug that blocks histamine action. Since histamines are often produced in large amounts in response to allergens, they cause many of the symptoms associated with allergies; antihistamines are often used to relieve allergic reactions, such as hay fever or hives. Antihistamines also may be prescribed to counter nausea.

Antihypertensive Any drug that lowers blood pressure.

Antiseptic Any substance that prevents or slows the proliferation of germs or bacteria.

Antitoxin An antibody produced by or introduced into the body to counteract a poison.

Anus The opening at the end of the rectum (the last segment of the large intestine) through which fecal waste passes.

Anvil One of the tiny bones in the middle ear (also called the incus).

Anxiety Feelings of apprehension and undue uneasiness. Appropriate anxiety may occur in the face of identifiable danger. In contrast, clinical anxiety is the feeling of apprehension or fear, even in the face of no identifiable hazards.

Aorta The body's largest artery, it carries blood pumped from the left ventricle of the heart and distributes it to all parts of the body.

Aphasia Loss of the ability to speak or to understand speech due to brain damage. The organs of speech may be unimpaired.

Apnea The absence of breathing.

Appendicitis An inflammation of the appendix that results in severe pain on the lower right side, fever, and nausea or vomiting. Appendicitis calls for immediate medical attention, usually requiring removal of the appendix.

Aqueous humor The fluid in the anterior part of the eyeball.

Areola A round pigmented area around a raised center, such as the nipple of a breast.

Arrhythmia Any deviation from the regular heartbeat rhythm.

Arteriole A tiny artery that joins another artery to the capillaries.

Arteriosclerosis Also called hardening of the arteries, this condition involves a thickening of the arterial walls resulting in a loss of elasticity. *See also* Atherosclerosis.

Artery A blood vessel that transports oxygenated blood away from the heart to the rest of the body.

Arthritis Inflammation of a joint.

Ascorbic acid Vitamin C.

Asphyxia Suffocation due to lack of oxygen or overabundance of carbon dioxide.

Aspiration The removal of fluids from the lungs or other body cavities. A suction or siphoning implement is used.

Aspirin Acetylsalicylic acid. A drug used to relieve pain and lower fever. It is also an anti-inflammatory drug and anticoagulant.

Asthma A disorder of the respiratory system due to bronchial spasm that results in breathing difficulties.

Astigmatism A defect in one of the eye's surfaces that leads to an inability to focus the eye correctly.

Atherosclerosis A form of arteriosclerosis in which, in addition to the thickening and reduced elasticity of the arteries, a fatty substance (plaque) forms on the inner walls of the arteries, causing obstruction of blood flow.

Athlete's foot *See* Tinea pedia.

Atrophy Wasting; degeneration of a body part through lack of activity or nourishment.

Auscultation A method of examining the body by listening, usually using a stethoscope.

Autoimmune disease Any disease in which the body manufactures antibodies against itself. The body regards its own tissue as a foreign body and acts accordingly to eliminate it.

Bacilli Rod-shaped bacteria.

Bacteria One-celled microscopic organisms. Some cause disease, others are harmless, and some are beneficial.

Bag of waters *See* Amnion.

Barbiturate A drug that produces sedation, hypnosis, anesthesia, or sleep.

Barium tests Diagnostic tests using barium, a metallic element that does not permit x-rays to pass through and therefore makes internal organs visible on x-ray films. Common barium tests are the barium swallow (upper GI series) and the barium enema (lower GI series).

B cell A specialized type of white cell (lymphocyte) that works as part of the immune system by providing antibodies that attack foreign agents such as bacteria or viruses.

Bedsore Decubitus ulcer; an ulcerlike sore on the skin as a result of the pressure of the bed against the body.

Bell's palsy A paralysis of the face muscles due to the inflammation of the facial nerve.

Benign Harmless or innocent. Term is used to describe a nonmalignant tumor that will not spread or grow back after removal.

Bile The bitter alkaline fluid secreted by the liver to aid in digestion. Bile is greenish yellow until it is stored in the gallbladder, where it becomes darker.

Biofeedback A behavior modification therapy by which a patient is taught to control involuntary body functions such as blood pressure.

Biopsy The examination of a small sample of tissue taken from a patient's body, usually used to determine if a growth is cancerous.

Birth control *See* Contraception.

Birthmark A colored patch or skin blemish that is present at birth.

Blackhead An open comedo, in which a follicle is clogged by fatty substances secreted by the sebaceous glands. Its black coloration is caused by exposure to air, not dirt as is commonly assumed.

Bladder A sac that contains fluid or gas.

Bladder infection *See* Cystitis.

Blastomycosis A fungal disease usually affecting the lungs but sometimes the whole system.

Blind spot The spot where the optic nerve and the retina connect. It is not light sensitive.

Blister An accumulation of fluid causing a raised sac under the surface of the skin.

Blood The body fluid circulated by the heart through a network of arteries, veins, and capillaries to provide oxygen and nutrients to all body cells and to remove carbon dioxide and wastes from them.

Blood clotting The process of blood coagulation in which blood platelets and proteins join together to close up a break in the circulatory system.

Blood corpuscle Either a red blood cell (erythrocyte) or a white blood cell (leukocyte).

Blood count The amount of red and white blood cells in the blood.

Blood plasma The part of the blood that is composed mostly of water (over 90 percent). The other constituents include electrolytes, nutrients, wastes, clotting agents, antibodies, and hormones.

Blood pressure The force exerted by the blood against the arterial walls. A sphygmomanometer measures both the systolic pressure (when the heart is at maximum contraction) and diastolic pressure (when the heart is relaxed between beats).

Blood serum The liquid that separates from the blood when it clots. It is the plasma without the clotting agents and is yellowish in color.

Blood sugar The glucose that is circulated in the blood. It is the end product of carbohydrate metabolism (although protein and some fat also may be converted to glucose) and is the body's major fuel.

Blood transfusion The intravenous replacement or replenishment of a patient's blood with healthy, compatible blood from an outside source.

Blood type Grouping of hereditary factors in the blood. The four major groupings are O, A, B, and AB. It is essential to determine if the donor's and recipient's blood types are compatible before a transfusion is administered.

Blood vessel A vein or artery.

Boil A round, painful, pus-filled bacterial infection of a hair follicle, usually caused by staphylococci (also called furuncle).

Bone graft Transplantation of bone from one person to another or from one part of the body to another.

Boric acid A mild antiseptic powder that is poisonous if swallowed. It was once considered a useful household first-aid item, but it is no longer recommended because of its limited effectiveness and potential toxicity.

Botulism A dangerous form of food poisoning caused by the toxin produced by botulinus bacteria. The toxin attacks the nervous system causing headache, weakness, constipation, and paralysis. The causative bacterium grows in anaerobic (without oxygen) conditions and therefore is found in improperly canned or improperly refrigerated fresh foods.

Bowel Intestine, gut.

Brain The central organ of the nervous system consisting of the cerebrum, cerebellum, pons varolii, midbrain, and medulla.

Breast The mammary (milk-producing) gland and the fat and connective tissue around it.

Breech delivery (or presentation) Delivery of a baby with either the feet or buttocks instead of the head emerging first.

Bright's disease A term formerly used to describe nephrosis, a disease affecting the kidney's filtering units (nephrons).

Bromides A group of drugs once used as anticonvulsants because of their sedative effects on the central nervous system. They have been replaced by newer, more effective drugs that do not have as high a risk of adverse reactions.

Bronchi The two tubes branching off at the lower part of the trachea (singular: bronchus).

Bronchiole Subdivision of a bronchus that leads to the alveoli in the lungs.

Bronchitis Inflammation of the bronchi.

Bronchopneumonia Bacterial infection that results in the inflammation of the bronchioles.

Bruise Damage to the subcutaneous blood vessels resulting in the escape of blood into the other tissues. Characteristic features are pain, swelling, and discoloration of the skin. A bruise in which the outer layer of skin is not broken is called a contusion. An abrasion or laceration is a bruise in which the skin is broken.

Bulimia Excessive appetite. Also refers to the binge/purge syndrome, in which deliberate overeating is compensated for through self-induced vomiting, laxative use, excessive exercise, or starvation.

Bunion A deformity of the big toe resulting from an inflammation of the joint that connects the toe to the foot.

Bursa A fibrous, fluid-filled sac in the joints that aids movement by decreasing friction.

Bursitis A painful condition involving inflammation of the bursa, a fluid-filled sac in a joint.

Caffeine A substance that stimulates the central nervous system. It is present in coffee, tea, chocolate, and certain soft drinks.

Calamine lotion A compound containing zinc oxide used to treat skin rashes, irritations, and other skin disorders.

Calcium An essential mineral. Calcium is the main material in teeth and bones and vital to proper function of the heart, other muscles, and other body tissues.

Calculus Abnormal stone formation in certain parts of the body such as the gallbladder or kidneys. Calculi are composed of minerals, cholesterol, bile pigments, or other substances, depending upon their location (plural: calculi).

Callus 1. An area where the skin has become thick in order to protect itself against repeated friction. 2. The partly calcified tissue that forms around a broken bone in the healing process.

Calorie Measure of energy (heat) used in physics and in nutrition.

Cancer A general term referring to the abnormal reproduction of cells in the body. The term covers more than 100 different malignant tumors and conditions.

Candidiasis A yeast infection caused by the *Candida* fungus. Also called moniliasis or thrush.

Canker sore An ulcerlike sore on the mucous membrane of the mouth or lips.

Capillary Minute thin-walled blood vessel, in a network that facilitates the exchange of substances between the surrounding tissues and the blood.

Carbohydrates Organic compounds of carbon, hydrogen, and oxygen. They include starches, cellulose, and sugars and are divided into three groups: monosaccharides (simple sugars), disaccharides (containing two different sugars), and polysaccharides (complex sugars).

Carcinogen Any agent that is capable of causing cancer.

Carcinoma The type of cancer that originates in the epithelial cells located in glands, skin, and mucous membranes.

Cardiac Pertaining to the heart.

Cardiograph A device for tracing the movements of the heart. The record produced is called a cardiogram or electrocardiogram.

Cardiopulmonary Pertaining to the heart and lungs.

Cardiovascular Pertaining to the heart and blood vessels.

Carditis Inflammation of the heart.

Caries Tooth or bone decay.

Cartilage The white, elastic tissue located in joints, the nose, and the outer ear.

Cast Fibrous material that has collected in body cavities and hardens to the shape of them.

Castor oil An oil derived from a poisonous bean plant and that acts as a purgative or cathartic.

Castration The removal of ovaries or testes.

Cataract An opacity or clouding of the eye lens, which can eventually lead to loss of vision as progressively less light is filtered through the lens to the retina.

Cathartic Any substance that stimulates rapid intestinal activity resulting in bowel evacuation (also called purgative).

Catheterization Any procedure in which a small flexible tube is inserted into the body for the purpose of withdrawing or introducing substances.

Caustic Having the ability to destroy or corrode organic tissue.

Cauterization The application of caustic chemicals or electrically heated devices for the purpose of eliminating infected, unwanted, or dead tissue.

Cavities 1. Extension of dental decay through enamel. 2. Hollow spaces.

Cell A minute mass of protoplasm containing a nucleus; the structural unit of body tissue.

Cellulose A polysaccharide carbohydrate (starch) found in plant cells. It is indigestible by humans but aids in the overall digestive process by providing roughage.

Cerebellum The movement-coordinating part of the brain.

Cerebral cortex The convoluted outer surface of the brain.

Cerebrum The largest part of the brain, containing two hemispheres and the cerebral cortex, which controls thinking, feeling, and voluntary activities.

Cervix The neck; also the narrow part of the uterus.

Cesarean section Delivery of a baby through the abdominal wall by means of a surgical procedure.

Chancre The highly infectious ulcerated sore that is the first sign of syphilis.

Chemotherapy The use of chemicals to treat disease with minimal damage to the patient. Use in the treatment of cancer is widespread and has increased life expectancy of patients.

Chilblains Painful and itchy swelling of skin due to exposure to the cold.

Cholera An epidemic disease characterized by diarrhea, vomiting, thirst, and cramps. It is spread through polluted water.

Cholesterol A crystalline fatlike substance found in all animal cells. It is synthesized in the liver and is essential in the production of sex hormones, nerve function, and a number of other vital processes. Excessive consumption of dietary cholesterol (found only in animal products) is thought to contribute to heart disease.

Chorea A disease of the nervous system manifested by spasmodic movements of the body.

Chromosome Any one of the rod-shaped bodies in the nucleus of a cell that carry hereditary factors.

Cirrhosis Chronic inflammation and hardening of an organ, usually the liver, but occasionally the heart or kidneys are involved.

Cleft palate Congenital defect of the mouth in which the palate bones fail to fuse and result in a groove in the roof of the mouth. Harelip is often associated with cleft palate.

Climacteric Menopause.

Clitoris A small organ situated at the front of the vulva that is one source of the female orgasm. It contains erectile tissue and is the female counterpart of the male penis.

Colic Spasmodic pain in the abdomen.

Colitis Inflammation of the colon (large intestine), characterized by bowel spasms, diarrhea, and constipation. Ulcerative colitis is a more serious form of the disease, and is characterized by open sores in the lining of the colon and the passage of diarrhea streaked with blood and mucus.

Colon Large intestine extending from the small intestine to the rectum. Undigested food that is not absorbed by the body passes from the small intestine into the colon; water is extracted from the waste and it is eventually eliminated from the body in the form of a bowel movement.

Colostomy Surgical procedure to create an artificial anus in the abdominal wall.

Colostrum The pale yellow "first milk" secreted by women in the late stages of pregnancy and just after delivery.

Colposcope A magnifying device used to examine the cervix and vagina.

Coma State of unconsciousness from which one cannot be awakened.

Communicable disease Transmissible to other persons.

Conception Impregnation of the ovum by the sperm.

Concussion Injury resulting from a severe blow or shock to the head.

Congenital Existing at birth or before.

Congestive heart failure A condition in which the heart is unable to pump strongly enough to maintain normal blood circulation. As a result, blood backs up in the lungs and veins leading to the heart. Often accompanied by accumulation of fluid in various parts of the body.

Conjunctiva The transparent membrane lining the front of the eyeball and eyelid.

Conjunctivitis Inflammation of the conjunctiva.

Constipation A condition of infrequent and difficult bowel movements.

Contraception Prevention of conception; birth control.

Contraceptive An agent used in preventing conception.

Contusion A bruise; bleeding under the skin.

Convulsions Involuntary spasms due to abnormal cerebral stimulation.

Cornea The transparent membrane that protects the outer surface of the eye.

Corn A patch of thickened skin (callus) usually occurring around the toes and caused by friction or pressure.

Coronary Related to the coronary arteries, the blood vessels that supply the heart muscle with blood.

Coronary artery disease Progressive narrowing of the coronary arteries, usually due to a buildup of fatty plaques (atheromas) along the vessel walls. The most common cause of angina pectoris and heart attacks. *See also* Heart attack.

Coronary thrombosis The blockage of a coronary artery with a clot (thrombus), a common cause of heart attacks.

Corpuscle A small mass of protoplasm. Red corpuscles are called erythrocytes and white corpuscles are called leukocytes.

Cortisol A principal hormone produced by the adrenal gland.

Cortisone Hormone preparation closely related to cortisol that acts as an anti-inflammatory agent and is used in treating various diseases; corticosteroid.

Coryza Acute upper respiratory infection lasting only a short while; head cold.

Cowpox A viral disease of cattle used to vaccinate against smallpox in humans. Since the worldwide elimination of smallpox, vaccination against this disease is no longer necessary.

Cranium The section of the skull that encases the brain.

Curettage A scraping out of tissue from an organ (particularly the uterus) for diagnostic purposes with a forklike instrument called a curet.

Cuspid Canine tooth; tooth having only one point.

Cuticle The epidermis (outer layer of skin); dead skin, especially that which surrounds fingernails and toenails.

Cyanosis A condition in which tissue takes on a bluish tinge due to lack of oxygen.

Cyst An abnormal cavity or sac enclosing a fluid, gas, or semisolid substance.

Cystic fibrosis A hereditary respiratory disease occurring in early childhood. It is characterized by the buildup of mucus in the lungs and other abnormalities affecting the exocrine system (glands that secrete directly into their target organs, such as the sweat glands).

Cystitis Infection and inflammation of the urinary bladder.

Cystoscopy A diagnostic procedure involving examination of the bladder with a cystoscope inserted through the urethra.

Cytology The study of the origins, structures, and functions of cells.

Dandruff A common condition in which white scales and flakes of dead skin appear on the scalp.

Debility Lessened ability; weakness.

Decubitus ulcer Bedsore.

Defibrillation Cessation of fibrillation (tremor or twitching of cardiac muscle) and resumption of normal heart rate through electric shock (defibrillator) or drugs.

Deficiency disease Disorder resulting from a nutritionally deprived diet or inability of the body to absorb needed nutrients.

Degenerative disease A group of diseases characterized by deterioration of body part(s) and resulting in progressive disability.

Dehydration Inadequate amount of fluids in the body caused by removal, abnormal loss, or failure to ingest fluids.

Delirium Mental disorder characterized by delusions or hallucinations. May be caused by disease, high fever, or drug use.

Delirium tremens Delirium suffered by chronic alcoholics as a result of withdrawal. Characterized by vivid hallucinations, uncontrollable trembling of hands, confusion, and nausea.

Delusion A false belief that persists even in the presentation of contrary evidence.

Dementia Deterioration of mental faculties due to irreversible organic causes.

Dementia praecox Schizophrenia.

Dendrite One of the threadlike branches of the nerve cell that transmits an impulse to the cell body.

Dentin The calcified tissue that encloses the tooth's pulp cavity.

Deoxyribonucleic acid (DNA) The fundamental component of all living matter that controls and transmits the hereditary genetic code.

Depilatory An agent that removes hair.

Depressant An agent that produces a calming, sedative effect, slowing down body functions.

Depression An organic disease characterized by profound feelings of sadness, discouragement, and worthlessness unexplained by life's events. Depression is often recurring and interrupted by feelings of extreme euphoria, a condition referred to as bipolar depression or manic-depressive state.

Derma or dermis The skin.

Dermatitis Inflammation of the skin.

Desensitization (immunotherapy) Neutralization of allergies by periodic exposure to progressively larger doses of the allergen.

Dextrose A form of glucose, a simple sugar.

Diabetes mellitus A chronic condition characterized by an overabundance of blood sugar due to insufficient insulin production in the pancreas or inability of the body to utilize insulin.

Dialysis A technique for separation of waste products or toxins from the bloodstream. Used in cases of kidney failure and overdose.

Diaphragm 1. The large muscle between the chest and the abdomen. 2. A dome-shaped rubber cap inserted vaginally to cover the cervix in order to prevent conception.

Diastole The interval between contractions of the heart (heartbeat) in which the heart relaxes. The diastolic reading obtained in blood pressure measurement is the lower number.

Diethylstilbestrol (DES) Synthetic estrogen hormone once used to prevent miscarriage. Its use is believed to have resulted in a higher incidence of vaginal and reproductive abnormalities, including difficulty in achieving or maintaining a pregnancy, among daughters born to women who took it. Sons may also suffer reproductive abnormalities. DES is also used to prevent conception if given promptly after unprotected intercourse (the so-called morning-after pill). Since it causes severe nausea and vomiting and other adverse effects, its use is limited primarily to rape victims.

Digestion The process by which food is transformed into absorbable nutrients.

Digit Finger or toe.

Dilation Enlargement or expansion of an organ, a passageway (e.g., blood vessel or the pupil of the eye). May be artificially induced for therapeutic or diagnostic purposes.

Diplopia Double vision.

Disk (vertebral) The cartilage cushions between the vertebrae.

Dislocation The displacement of a bone from its normal position in a joint.

Diuretic Any substance that increases the flow of urine and excretion of body fluid.

Diverticula Pouchlike sacs protruding from the wall of an organ.

Diverticulitis Inflammation of diverticula.

Diverticulosis A disorder in which diverticula develop. Most commonly seen in the intestinal tract.

Dominant A term used in genetics to describe the stronger of two hereditary traits.

Dorsal Pertaining to the back.

Down syndrome A congenital condition that may include mental retardation and physical malformations caused by abnormal chromosomal distribution. Also called trisomy 21. Formerly called mongolism.

Dropsy *See* Edema.

Duodenum The portion of the small intestine closest to the stomach.

Dura mater The outermost layer of fibrous membrane covering the brain and spinal cord. One of three types of meninges.

Dysentery Infectious inflammation of the bowel characterized by diarrhea with passage of blood and mucus and severe abdominal cramps.

Dyslexia Learning disability characterized by impaired reading ability and tendency to reverse characters.

Dysmenorrhea Painful menstruation or cramps.

Dyspareunia Painful sexual intercourse.

Dyspepsia Indigestion.

Dysphagia Difficulty in swallowing.

Dyspnea Difficulty in breathing.

Dystrophy Wasting, usually due to defective metabolism or nutrition.

Dysuria Painful urination.

Echography The use of ultrasound waves in detecting and diagnosing abnormalities. The results are called an echogram.

Eclampsia A sudden convulsive attack caused by toxemia during pregnancy.

Ectopic pregnancy Pregnancy in which the fertilized egg begins to develop outside the uterus, usually in the fallopian tubes.

Eczema Skin rash characterized by itching and scaling.

Edema Swelling of body tissue caused by a buildup of fluid.

Effusion An accumulation of fluid between body tissues or in body cavities.

Ejaculation Emission of semen from the penis during the male orgasm.

Electrocardiography A diagnostic procedure in which metal plates (electrodes) are placed on body surfaces for the purpose of detecting and tracing electrical impulses from the heart. The resulting graph is called an electrocardiogram (EKG or ECG).

Electroencephalography A diagnostic procedure in which the electrical impulses from the brain are traced and recorded through metal plates (electrodes) attached to the head. The resulting graph is called an electroencephalogram (EEG).

Electrolysis Decomposition or destruction by means of electricity.

Electroshock therapy (EST) The use of a controlled amount of electric current in treatment of severe depression. The electric shock is administered through electrodes placed on the head.

Embolism Obstruction of a blood vessel by a solid body, called an embolus. Common emboli include blood clots, fat globules, or air bubbles.

Embryo The term used to refer to the fetus in the first 8 weeks after conception.

Emetic Agent that induces vomiting.

Emission Discharge of fluid.

Emphysema A respiratory disease characterized by progressive loss of elasticity of lung tissue, making it difficult to exhale stale air fully. Most commonly caused by smoking.

Empyema Accumulation of pus in a body cavity, usually the lungs.

Encephalitis Inflammation of the brain due to virus infection, lead poisoning, or other causes.

Endocrine system The physiological network of ductless glands that secrete hormones into the bloodstream to control the digestive and reproductive systems, growth, metabolism, and other processes.

Endometriosis A gynecological disease in which tissue normally found in the uterus grows in other areas.

Endometrium The lining of the uterus in which the fertilized ovum is implanted and which is shed during menstruation if conception has not taken place.

Endoscopy Diagnostic procedure using an illuminating optical instrument to examine a body cavity or internal organ.

Enema Fluid injected through the rectum to the lower bowel. Used to induce bowel movement or diagnose bowel disorders (barium enema).

Enteritis Inflammation of the intestine.

Enuresis Inability to control urination while sleeping; bed-wetting.

Enzyme A substance, usually protein, that causes a chemical reaction; a catalyst.

Epidermis Outermost layer of skin.

Epiglottis The flap of cartilage that covers the larynx in the act of swallowing and aids in directing food to the esophagus.

Epilepsy A disease of the nervous system characterized by convulsive seizures as a result of an imbalance in the electrical activity of the brain.

Epinephrine (also called adrenaline) The hormone produced by the medulla (inner core) of the adrenal glands. It is secreted in stressful situations in order to increase the body's capacity to respond or to speed up bodily processes.

Episiotomy An incision made in the final stages of childbirth from the vagina downward toward the anus.

Erection The stiffening or swelling of the penis or other erectile tissue as it becomes filled with blood.

Erysipelas A severe infectious skin disease caused by a streptococcal organism and characterized by swelling and redness.

Erythema Reddening of the skin due to dilation of the capillaries under the skin.

Erythroblastosis fetalis The anemic condition in infants due to Rh incompatibility between mother and child.

The condition is seen in Rh-positive babies born to Rh-negative women.

Erythrocyte Red blood corpuscle.

Esophagus Tube that transports food from the mouth to the stomach.

Estrogen A primarily female sex hormone produced by the ovary, adrenal gland, and placenta. In women, it controls development of secondary sex characteristics, menstruation, and pregnancy. A small amount of estrogen is produced in the testes of the man, and also in fat tissue.

Eustachian tube The tube that connects the middle ear to the pharynx.

Exophthalmos Protruding eyeballs, sometimes due to diseases of the thyroid gland.

Expectorant A drug that promotes the coughing of sputum.

Faint Brief loss of consciousness due to insufficient blood in the brain.

Fallopian tubes The two tubes extending one from each side of the uterus through which an egg must pass after release from the ovary. Also called oviducts.

Farsightedness Also called hyperopia. A disorder of the eyes that causes difficulty in focusing on an object close up.

Fascia Thin connective tissues that join the skin to underlying tissues.

Fat An essential nutrient of animal or plant origin. May be saturated or unsaturated.

Fauces The opening from the throat to the pharynx.

Feces The waste matter discharged from the bowels.

Femur Thigh bone.

Fertility The ability to conceive.

Fertilization Impregnation of ovum by sperm cell.

Fetus An unborn baby after the eighth week of pregnancy.

Fever Abnormally high body temperature. Generally above 98.6°F or 37°C.

Fiber 1. Body tissue composed mainly of fibrils, tiny threadlike structures. 2. The plant cell components that are indigestible by humans; dietary fiber; roughage.

Fibrillation Uncoordinated tremors or twitching of cardiac muscle resulting in an irregular pulse.

Fibrin Protein formed in blood during clotting process.

Fibroid A benign tumor of fibromuscular tissue, usually occurring in the uterus.

Fibula The long, thin bone found in the lower leg.

Fission Splitting.

Fistula An abnormal connection between two body cavities.

Flat foot A congenital or acquired deformity in which there is only a slight, or no, arch between the toes and the heel of the foot.

Flatulence An overabundance of gas in the stomach or intestines.

Fluorine A chemical that in small amounts prevents tooth decay.

Fluoroscope A special x-ray that projects images on a screen. Used to observe the organs or bones while in motion.

Folic acid A B-complex vitamin, used to promote blood regeneration in cases of folate deficiency. Occurs naturally in liver, kidney, green vegetables, and yeast.

Follicle A small sac or tubular gland.

Fontanel A membranous spot on a baby's head where skull bones have not yet come together.

Foramen An opening. Usually used in reference to the opening in a bone through which blood vessels or nerves pass.

Forceps Surgical instrument used to grasp or compress tissues.

Fracture A crack or break in a bone.

Frontal Pertaining to the front of a structure.

Frostbite Freezing of the skin as a result of exposure to extreme cold. Affected area may become red and inflamed.

Fulminating Developing quickly and with great severity.

Fungicide Any substance that eliminates fungi.

Fungus A low form of vegetable life including some that can cause disease. Fungal infections.

Furuncle (boil) A round, painful, pus-filled bacterial infection of a hair follicle.

Gallbladder A membranous sac that is situated below the liver and condenses and stores the bile drained from the liver.

Gallstones Stonelike masses that form in the gallbladder. May be composed of calcium, bile pigment, and/or cholesterol.

Gamma globulin The type of blood protein that contains antibodies to fight infection. Gamma globulin can be separated from the other constituents in the blood and used to prevent or treat infections.

Ganglion 1. A mass of nerve tissue, a nerve center. 2. A cystic tumor in a tendon sheath.

Gangrene Death of body tissue usually due to loss of blood supply. Affected area becomes shrunken and black.

Gastrectomy Surgical removal of a part or all of the stomach.

Gastric Pertaining to the stomach.

Gastric juice Acidic secretion of the stomach containing enzymes and hydrochloric acid to aid in digestion.

Gastric ulcer A peptic ulcer that forms in the stomach.

Gastritis Inflammation of the stomach.

Gastroenteritis Inflammation of the mucous membranes of the stomach and intestines.

Gastroenterology Study of the stomach and intestines and the diseases affecting them.

Gastrostomy Surgically formed fistula between the stomach and abdominal wall.

Gene A part of the chromosome that determines hereditary characteristics.

Genetics The study of heredity.

Genitals, genitalia Reproductive organs.

Geriatrics The branch of medical science devoted to diseases of the aged.

Germ Microorganism usually associated with causing disease.

Germicide Germ-killing agent.

Gerontology The study of aging and the diseases associated with it.

Gestation Pregnancy.

Gingivitis Inflammation of the gums.

Gland Any organ that produces and secretes a chemical substance used by another part of the body. Ductless, or endocrine, glands secrete into the bloodstream. Secretions of exocrine glands are transported through ducts or excreted directly to a particular location.

Glandular fever Infectious mononucleosis.

Glans penis The head of the penis.

Glaucoma A disease of the eye in which increased pressure within the eye damages the retina and optic nerve. Leads to impaired sight and sometimes blindness.

Globulin The portion of blood protein in which antibodies are formed.

Globus hystericus The feeling of "a lump in the throat" due to hysteria, anxiety, or depression. Sometimes accompanied by difficulty in swallowing.

Glomerulus (glomeruli) A small tuft of blood capillaries in the kidney, responsible for filtering out waste products.

Glucose (dextrose or blood sugar) The most common monosaccharide (simple sugar) and the main source of energy for humans. It is stored as glycogen in the liver and can be quickly converted back into glucose.

Glucose tolerance test Test to determine body's response to a glucose challenge. Used to detect hypoglycemia or diabetes.

Glycogen Animal starch. The form in which glucose is stored in the liver. Glycogen is easily converted into glucose for body use as energy.

Glycosuria Sugar in the urine.

Goiter Enlargement of the thyroid gland, which causes swelling on the front of the neck.

Gonad Primary sex gland. Ovary in the female; testes in the male.

Gonococci Kidney-shaped gonorrhea-causing bacteria.

Gonorrhea A common venereal disease caused by the gonococcus bacterium and characterized by inflammation of the urethra, difficulty in urination (in males), and inflammation of the cervix (in females).

Gout A metabolic disorder in which an overabundance of uric acid causes urate crystals to form in the joints and sometimes elsewhere.

Graafian follicles Tiny vesicles in the ovaries that contain ova before release (ovulation).

Graft Transplantation of tissue or skin from one part of the body to another.

Gram-negative or gram-positive Method of classifying bacteria according to how they are affected when stained with alcohol.

Grand mal A severe epileptic attack in which convulsions are accompanied by loss of consciousness.

Granulation The new skin tissue containing capillaries, blood vessels, and reparative cells that forms in a wound's healing process.

Granulocytes White blood cells (leukocytes) containing granules. They are manufactured in the bone marrow to digest and destroy bacteria.

Granuloma A tumor or growth containing granulation tissue.

Granuloma inguinale A contagious venereal disease characterized by ulcers on the genitals.

Gravel Fine, sandlike particles composed of the same substance as kidney stones but usually passed in the urine without notice.

Graves' disease One form of hyperthyroidism or an overactive thyroid gland, usually accompanied by abnormalities of the eyes and skin.

Gravid Pregnant.

Greenstick fracture Incomplete fracture due to the pliability of the bone.

Usually occurs in children whose bones are still growing.

Grippe Influenza.

Gristle *See* Cartilage.

Groin The lower abdominal area where the trunk and thigh join. Also called the inguinal area.

Gumma A fibrous tumor filled with a rubberlike substance that occurs in the brain, liver, or heart in the late stages of syphilis.

Gynecology The branch of medical science that deals with the normal functioning and diseases of women's reproductive organs.

Gynecomastia Abnormal enlargement of the male breasts.

Halitosis Technical term for bad breath.

Hallucination A false perception believed to be real but actually having no basis in fact.

Hallucinogen Agent capable of producing hallucinations; psychedelic drug.

Hallus valgus *See* Bunion.

Hallux The big toe.

Hammertoe A permanent hyperextension of the toe, which cannot be flattened out.

Hamstring Group of tendons at the back of the knee.

Harelip Congenital defect of the lip due to a failure of bones to unite and causing a split from the margin of the lip to the nostril.

Hay fever An allergic reaction to pollen in which mucous membranes of the eyes, nose, and throat become inflamed.

Hearing aid Device used to amplify sounds for those with hearing difficulties.

Heart The muscular organ that pumps blood through the body. It is situated between the two lungs and behind the sternum.

Heart attack Myocardial infarction. Damage to part of the heart muscle caused by interruption of the blood circulation in the coronary arteries.

Heart block A condition in which an abnormality in the tissues connecting the heart chambers interferes with the normal transmission of electrical impulses and may lead to disturbances in the heart's rhythm or pumping action.

Heartburn Burning sensations in the upper abdomen or behind the sternum. Usually caused by the regurgitation of gastric juices into the esophagus.

Heart failure *See* Congestive heart failure.

Heart-lung machine An apparatus that takes over for the heart during open-heart surgery. The blood bypasses the heart and is oxygenated in the machine and pumped back into the body.

Heart murmur Any of various sounds heard in addition to the regular heartbeat. Often associated with a diseased heart valve, but may also have a benign or harmless cause.

Heat exhaustion Collapse, with or without loss of consciousness, due to extreme heat conditions and loss of salt through sweating. In attempts to cool down the body surface, blood accumulates close to the skin, thus depriving the vital organs of full blood supply.

Heat stroke An emergency condition in which the sweating mechanism of the body fails, resulting in an extremely high body temperature.

Hemangioma A malformation of blood vessels that appears as a red, often elevated mark on the skin. It may be present at birth and may require treatment if it fails to disappear on its own.

Hematemesis Vomiting of blood.

Hematology The scientific study of blood.

Hematoma A blood-filled swelling resulting from blood vessels injured or ruptured by a blow.

Hematuria The presence of blood in the urine.

Hemiplegia Paralysis affecting one side of the body.

Hemochromatosis Abnormal accumulation of iron deposits in the body as a result of a metabolic disturbance. Symptoms include a bronzing of the skin, diabetes, and cirrhosis of the liver.

Hemodialysis Removal of waste materials from the blood. The artificial kidney performs this function.

Hemoglobin The red pigment contained in red blood cells and combining the iron-containing heme with the protein-containing globin. Hemoglobin is responsible for transporting oxygen to body tissue and removing carbon dioxide from body tissue.

Hemolysis Breaking down of red blood cells.

Hemophilia An inherited blood disorder in which the blood is unable to clot, causing severe bleeding from even minor wounds. The disease affects primarily males but is passed on by female carriers.

Hemoptysis Spitting up blood.

Hemorrhage Abnormal bleeding due to rupture of a blood vessel.

Hemorrhoids (piles) Varicose veins in and around the rectal opening. Hemorrhoid symptoms include pain, bleeding, and itching.

Hemostat An instrument that prevents bleeding by clamping a blood vessel.

Heparin Anticoagulant substance that is found in the liver and other tissues. It is sometimes administered to prevent blood clots. It also may be used to treat a threatened stroke, thrombophlebitis, and various clotting diseases.

Hepatitis Inflammation of the liver, usually due to a viral infection but can also be the result of alcoholism and other conditions. Hepatitis B is transmitted through blood contact (e.g., contaminated hypodermic needles or transfused blood from a hepatitis B carrier). Hepatitis A is transmitted through fecal contact, usually from contaminated food. Hepatitis C (formerly non-A, non-B) is not as well understood as the other two.

Hepatoma Tumor of the liver.

Heredity The transmission of traits from parents to offspring. Genetic information is carried by the chromosomes.

Hermaphrodite An individual possessing both the male and female sex organs.

Hernia The abnormal protrusion of part or all of an organ through surrounding tissues.

Heroin An addictive narcotic drug derived from opium and a form of morphine (diamorphine).

Herpes simplex Recurring infection caused by herpesvirus. Type 1 involves blisterlike sores usually around the mouth and referred to as "cold sores" or "fever blisters." Type 2 usually affects the mucous membranes of the genitalia and can be spread by sexual contact, although either type can cause genital or oral sores.

Herpes zoster (shingles) A painful viral infection resulting in inflammation and blisters following the path of a nerve. It is caused by the same virus that causes chickenpox, which remains in the body in a latent form and may erupt many years later in an attack of shingles.

Hiatal hernia A disorder in which a portion of the stomach protrudes through the esophageal opening of the diaphragm and may cause symptoms of indigestion, heartburn, or regurgitation of food.

Hiccups (hiccoughs) An involuntary

spasm of the diaphragm followed by the sudden closing of the glottis, which coincides with the intake of a breath.

High blood pressure *See* Hypertension.

Histamine A chemical found in body tissue and released to stimulate production of gastric juices for digestion. In an allergic reaction, excessive amounts of histamine are produced and cause surrounding tissue to become inflamed. Antihistamines are thus prescribed for relief from allergic attacks.

Hives (urticaria) Itchy red and white swellings that appear on the skin usually in an allergic reaction.

Hodgkin's disease A serious disorder of the lymphatic system in which the lymph nodes enlarge. Type of cancer.

Homograft Tissue or organ transplantation from one individual to another of the same species.

Homosexuality Sexual desire for those of one's own sex.

Hormone Secretion from an endocrine gland transported by the bloodstream to various organs in order to regulate vital functions and processes.

Hyaline A glasslike substance that occurs in cartilage or the eyeball.

Hyaline membrane disease (respiratory distress syndrome) A condition affecting newborn premature infants in which the air sacs in the lungs are immature and clogged with hyaline, a crystalline material that makes effective breathing difficult or impossible.

Hydrocele An abnormal accumulation of fluid, usually in the sac of the membrane that covers the testicle.

Hydrocephalus ("water on the brain") An abnormal increase in cerebral fluid resulting in an enlarged head.

Hydrochloric acid An acid, composed of hydrogen and chlorine, secreted by the stomach in the process of digestion.

Hydrolysis Division into simple substance(s) by the addition of water.

Hydrotherapy Treatment of disease or injury by use of baths or wet compresses.

Hymen The membrane partially covering the entrance to the vagina.

Hyperchlorhydria Excessive amounts of hydrochloric acid in the gastric juice.

Hypercholesterolemia Excessive amounts of cholesterol in the blood.

Hyperemesis Excessive vomiting.

Hyperemesis gravidarum Excessive vomiting during pregnancy, commonly referred to as morning sickness.

Hyperglycemia Excessive amounts of sugar in the blood. One of the indications of diabetes.

Hyperhidrosis Excessive sweating.

Hyperinsulinism A condition in which excessive amounts of insulin cause abnormally low blood sugar. Similar to insulin shock.

Hyperkinesis Hyperactivity; excessive movement or activity.

Hyperopia Farsightedness.

Hyperplasia Overgrowth of an organ caused by an increase in the number of normal cells.

Hypertension High blood pressure; a major risk factor for stroke and heart attack.

Hyperthyroidism Overactivity of the thyroid gland. Symptoms include weight loss, restlessness, and sometimes goiters.

Hypertrophy Increased size of a body tissue or organ usually in response to increased activity.

Hypnosis A trancelike state in which a person's consciousness is altered to make him/her susceptible to suggestion.

Hypnotic A drug that induces sleep.

Hypochondria Excessive anxiety about and preoccupation with illness and supposed ill health.

Hypoglycemia Low blood sugar. Hypoglycemic shock due to insulin overdose is another term for insulin shock.

Hypophysis The pituitary gland.

Hypospadias A congenital malformation of the urethra.

Hypotension Low blood pressure.

Hypothalamus The part of the brain just above the pituitary gland. It has a part in controlling basic functions such as appetite, procreation, sleep, and body temperature and may be affected by the emotions.

Hypothyroidism Abnormal inactivity or decrease in activity of the thyroid.

Hysterectomy Surgical removal of the uterus.

Hysteria A neurosis, usually due to mental conflict and repression, in which there is uncontrollable excitability or anxiety.

Iatrogenic disease Any disorder or disease caused as an unintentional side effect of a physician's prescribed treatment.

Ichthyosis A congenital disorder in which the skin is dry and scaly.

Icterus Jaundice.

Idiopathic Peculiar to an individual or originating from unknown causes.

Ileitis Inflammation of the ileum (lower portion of the small intestine); Crohn's disease.

Ileum The lower portion of the small intestine.

Ilium Broad upper part of the hipbone.

Immobilization Making a bone or joint immovable in order to aid in correct healing.

Immunity State of resistance to a disease. Active immunity is acquired by vaccination against it or by previous infection. Passive immunity is acquired from antibodies either from the mother through the placenta during gestation or from injection of serum from an animal that has active immunities.

Immunization The procedure by which specific antibodies are induced in the body tissue.

Impacted Wedged in tightly and abnormally immovable.

Imperforate Without normal opening.

Impetigo Highly contagious inflammatory pustular skin disease caused by staphylococci or streptococci.

Impotence Inability of the male to achieve penile erection and engage in sexual intercourse.

Incisors The eight sharp cutting teeth, four in each jaw.

Incontinence Inability to control release of urine or feces.

Incubation period The interval of time between contact with disease organisms and first appearance of the symptoms.

Incubator A temperature- and atmosphere-controlled container in which premature or delicate babies can be cared for. Also a container in which bacteria or other organisms are grown for cultures.

Incus The small bone of the middle ear that conducts sounds to the inner ear.

Indigestion An abnormality in the digestive process; dyspepsia.

Induration Hardening of tissue.

Infarct An area of dead tissue as a result of a total blockage of the blood supply.

Infertility Inability to reproduce.

Inflammation The reaction of tissue to injury, infection, or irritation. Affected area may become painful, swollen, red, and hot.

Influenza (flu) A contagious viral infection that occurs in epidemics.

Inguinal Pertaining to the groin.

Inoculation The intentional introduction of a disease agent to the body in order to induce immunity by causing a mild form of the disease.

Inoperable Not treatable by surgery.

Insemination Introduction of semen into the vagina either through sexual intercourse or artificially.

Insomnia Inability to sleep. Can be chronic or occasional.

Insulin The hormone produced and secreted by the beta cells of the pancreas gland. Insulin is needed for proper metabolism, particularly of carbohydrates, and the uptake of sugar (glucose) by certain body tissues. Diabetes mellitus is a deficiency of insulin or the inability of the body to use insulin.

Insulin shock Loss of consciousness caused by an overdose of insulin.

Integument The skin.

Intention tremor Involuntary trembling triggered or intensified when movement is attempted.

Interferon A complex natural protein that causes cells to become resistant to infection.

Intertrigo (chafing) Superficial inflammation of opposing skin surfaces that rub together.

Intestines The section of the digestive tract extending from the stomach to the anus.

Intima The innermost lining of an artery.

Intracutaneous test Introduction of allergens into the skin in order to test sensitivity to particular substances.

Intrauterine contraceptive device (IUD) Device made of stainless steel, silkworm gut, or plastic that is inserted by a physician into the uterus to prevent pregnancy.

Intravenous Into or within a vein.

Intravenous feeding Nourishment through a glucose solution and other nutrients injected directly into a vein.

Involution of uterus Shrinking of the uterus to normal size after childbirth.

Iris The round, colored portion of the eye that surrounds the pupil.

Iritis Inflammation of the iris.

Iron The essential mineral micronutrient of hemoglobin.

Iron lung A respirator. A machine that artificially expands and contracts to facilitate breathing for patients with paralyzed respiratory muscles.

Irreducible Incapable of being replaced to normal position. Applied to fractured bones or to hernia.

Ischemia Localized blood deficiency, usually as a result of a circulatory problem. For example, cardiac ischemia results when a coronary artery is so occluded that it cannot

deliver sufficient blood to the heart muscle.

Islets of Langerhans The groups of cells (alpha and beta) in the pancreas that secrete endocrine hormones; the alpha cells produce glucagon and the beta cells produce insulin.

Isotope A chemical element similar in structure and properties but differing in radioactivity or atomic weight.

Jaundice Yellow discoloration of the skin and eyes caused by excessive amounts of bile pigments in the bloodstream.

Jejunum Part of the small intestine situated between the duodenum and the ileum.

Jigger Sand flea that burrows into skin in order to lay eggs, causing itching and inflammation (also called chigger).

Jock itch *See* Tinea cruris.

Joint The point where two or more bones connect.

Jugular veins The two veins on the sides of the neck that carry blood from the head to the heart.

Keloid An overgrowth of scar tissue after injury or surgery.

Keratin Substance that is the chief constituent of the horny tissues, such as the outer layer of skin, nails, and hair.

Keratitis Inflammation of the cornea.

Ketogenic diet A diet that results in the excessive burning of fat, which can lead to ketosis.

Ketosis The buildup of ketone bodies, highly acidic substances, in the body. This condition is often associated with diabetes and can lead to a fatal coma.

Kidneys The two bean-shaped glands that regulate the salt, volume, and composition of body fluids by filtering the blood and eliminating wastes through production and secretion of urine.

Kinesthesia Perception of movement, position, and weight. Muscle sense.

Klinefelter's syndrome Chromosomal abnormality in which an individual has 2 X and 1 Y sex chromosomes. As a result, the individual appears to be male but has oversized breasts, underdeveloped testes, and is sterile.

Kneecap Patella.

Knee jerk Reflex reaction in which the foot kicks forward in response to a tap on the ligament below the kneecap.

Kwashiorkor A disease caused by protein deficiency due to malnutrition; occurs mostly in underdeveloped countries. Symptoms include growth retardation, apathy, anemia, and abnormal distention of the abdomen.

Kyphosis A rounding of the shoulders or hunchback caused by poor posture or disease, such as osteoporosis.

Labia Liplike organs. Labia majora: two folds of skin and fatty tissue that encircle the vulva. Labia minora: the smaller folds inside the labia majora that protect the clitoris.

Labor (parturition) The rhythmic muscle contraction in the uterus in the process of childbirth.

Laceration A wound caused by the tearing of tissue.

Lacrimal ducts (tear glands) The gland at the inner corner of the eye that secretes tears.

Lactation Production and secretion of milk by the breasts.

Lactic acid Acid produced by the fermentation of lactose; a waste product from the muscles.

Lactose A sugar contained in milk.

Lactovegetarian Vegetarian who eats dairy products.

Lancet Small double-edged knife used in surgery.

Lanolin Fat derived from wool and used as an ointment or lotion base.

Laryngitis Inflammation of the larynx characterized by hoarseness or complete loss of voice.

Larynx Voice box. A cartilaginous structure containing the apparati of voice production: the vocal cords and the muscles and ligaments, which move the cords.

Laser Light Amplification by Stimulated Emission of Radiation.

Laser beam A beam of intense controlled light that can sever, eliminate, or fuse body tissue.

Laxative Any agent that encourages bowel activity by loosening the contents.

Lead poisoning Intoxication from ingestion of lead.

Lecithin A waxy, fatty compound found in cell protoplasm.

Lens The transparent tissue of the eye that focuses rays of light in order to form an image on the retina.

Leprosy An infectious skin disease caused by bacteria and affecting the nerves and skin with ulcers.

Leptospirosis (infectious jaundice) An infectious disease spread to humans by urine of infected animals. Symptoms include jaundice.

Lesion Any breakdown of tissue, i.e., wound, sore, abscess, or tumor.

Leukemia A group of diseases of the blood-forming organs in which a proliferation of bone marrow and lymphoid tissue produces an overabundance of white blood cells (leukocytes) and disrupts normal production of red blood cells. A form of cancer.

Leukocytes White blood cells instrumental in fighting infection.

Leukocytosis Abnormal increase in the amount of white blood cells in the body, often due to the physiological response to infection.

Leukopenia Abnormal deficiency of white blood cells.

Leukorrhea Vaginal discharge of mucus. When discharge is heavy, it may be a sign of infection or disease.

Libido Term used by Freud for the desire for sensual satisfaction. Commonly used to mean sexual desire.

Ligament The tough, fibrous band of tissue that connects bones.

Ligature A thread of silk or catgut or wire used to tie off blood vessels to prevent bleeding during surgery.

Lipid Fat or fatlike substance such as cholesterol or triglycerides.

Lipoma A benign tumor composed of fat cells.

Lithiasis Formation of gallstones or kidney stones (calculi).

Litholapaxy Method of crushing a stone and removal of fragments from the urinary bladder through a catheter.

Lithotomy Removal of stone by cutting into the bladder.

Lithuresis Elimination of gravel in the urine.

Liver The largest internal organ of the body. Among its many functions are secreting bile and digestive enzymes, storing glycogen, neutralizing poisons, synthesizing proteins, producing several blood components, and storing certain vitamins and minerals.

Lobotomy Surgical disconnection of nerve fibers between the frontal lobe and the rest of the brain. Once commonly used to calm uncontrollable mental patients.

Lochia Vaginal discharge of blood, mucus, and tissue after childbirth.

Lockjaw *See* Tetanus.

Lordosis Swayback. Condition in which the inward curve of the lumbar spine is exaggerated.

Low blood sugar Hypoglycemia.

Lues Syphilis.

Lumbago Lower back pain.

Lumbar Lower back between the pelvis and the ribs.

Lungs Two organs of spongelike tissue that surround the bronchial tree to form the lower respiratory system. Are vital to oxygenation of blood and expulsion of gaseous waste from the body.

Lupus erythematosus An inflammatory autoimmune disease. Systemic lupus erythematosus involves deterioration of the body's connective tissues.

Lymph Transparent yellowish fluid containing lymphocytes and found in lymphatic vessels. Lymphatic fluid.

Lymph nodes Oval-shaped organs located throughout the body that manufacture lymphocytes and filter germs and foreign bodies from the lymph.

Lymphocytes A disease-fighting type of leukocyte manufactured in the lymph nodes and distributed in the lymphatic fluid and blood.

Lymphogranuloma venereum A sexually transmitted viral disease that causes sores around genitals and swollen lymph nodes in the male groin.

Lymphosarcoma Malignant tumor of lymphatic tissue.

Maceration The softening of tissue in contact with fluid.

Macula Spot of discolored skin.

Macula lutea The small, yellow round spot on the retina. Center of color perception and clearest vision.

Malabsorption Defective absorption of nutrients in the small intestine. Malabsorption syndrome is characterized by steatorrhea (loose fatty stool) or diarrhea, weight loss, weakness, and anemia. May be caused by lesions on the intestine, metabolic deficiencies, or surgery.

Malacia Softening of a part.

Malaise A general feeling of illness and discomfort. Tiredness, irritability, and listlessness.

Malaria A tropical parasitic disease spread by mosquitoes. Symptoms include chills, fever, and sweating.

Mal de mer Seasickness.

Malignant Harmful, life-threatening. Used mostly in reference to a cancerous tumor.

Malingering Deliberate feigning of illness.

Malleus The largest of the three bones in the inner ear.

Malnutrition Insufficient nourishment due to poor diet or defect in body's assimilation.

Malocclusion Failure of the upper teeth to mesh properly with lower teeth.

Malpresentation Any abnormal position of the fetus in the birth canal.

Mammary gland Milk-secreting gland of the breast.

Mammography Diagnostic x-ray examination of the breasts.

Mandible Lower jawbone.

Mania Mood of undue elation and excitability often accompanied by hallucinations and increased activity.

Manic-depressive psychosis A mental illness characterized by alternating periods of depression and mania.

Manubrium The handle-shaped upper part of the breastbone.

Marijuana The hemp, or cannabis, plant. A hallucinogenic drug.

Marrow The soft substance present in bone cavities. Red marrow is responsible for red blood cell production. Yellow marrow is marrow that is no longer involved in making blood cells.

Massage Rubbing, kneading, and pressing the parts of the body for therapeutic purposes. Massage can stimulate circulation, reduce tension, relax muscles, and reduce pain.

Mastectomy Surgical removal of breast tissue.

Mastication Chewing.

Mastitis Inflammation of the breast.

Mastoid cells Hollow areas (air cells) located in the middle ear.

Mastoiditis Inflammation of the mastoid cells usually as a consequence of an untreated ear infection.

Masturbation Manipulation of the genitals for the purpose of deriving sexual pleasure.

Materia medica The study of the origin, preparation, and use of medicinal substances.

Maxilla Upper jaw.

Measles An acute infectious disease characterized by fever, rash, and inflammation of mucous membranes. It is caused by a virus.

Meatus Passage or opening.

Meconium The greenish pasty discharge from the bowels of a newborn baby.

Mediastinum The space that separates the two lungs and contains the heart, thymus, esophagus, and trachea.

Medicine 1. Science of healing. 2. A therapeutic substance.

Medulla The center of an organ, gland, or bone.

Medulla oblongata The brain part connected to the spine.

Megalomania Delusions of grandeur. Symptom of insanity characterized by an exaggerated self-image.

Melanin Dark pigment found in hair, skin, and choroid of the eye.

Melanoma Tumor composed of cells containing melanin. Mostly benign but malignant melanoma is a rare and serious form of skin cancer.

Membrane A thin layer of lining of tissue.

Menarche Commencement of first menstrual period.

Meninges Membranes covering the brain and spinal cord.

Meningitis Inflammation of the meninges.

Menopause The period of time in which menstruation decreases and finally stops. The change of life after which a woman is no longer able to reproduce.

Menorrhagia Unusually heavy menstrual bleeding.

Menstruation The discharge of blood and tissue from the uterus every 28 days and lasting 4 or 5 days.

Mescaline A hallucinogen.

Mesencephalon The midbrain; the region between the cerebrum and the cerebellum.

Mesentery The folds in the abdominal lining between the intestine and the abdominal wall. They support the abdominal organs and supply them with blood and nerves.

Metabolism The combination of chemical and physical changes in the body essential for maintaining life processes. Basal metabolism is the minimum amount of energy required to sustain life while resting.

Metastasis The spread of disease from one body part to another usually by transfer of cells or germs through the blood or lymph.

Methadone An addictive synthetic narcotic used instead of morphine and administered in drug treatment centers to heroin addicts. Also may be used as a painkiller under some circumstances.

Metritis Inflammation of the uterus.

Metrorrhagia Bleeding from the uterus between menstrual periods.

Microtome A surgical instrument for cutting thin slices of body tissue for study.

Micturition Urination.

Migraine Periodic severe headaches typically affecting one side of the head and often accompanied by nausea or vomiting, light sensitivity, and visual distortions. Also referred to as vascular headaches.

Miliaria Prickly heat, heat rash. Sweat trapped under skin because of gland obstruction. Produces itching, prickling pimples on the skin.

Miosis Contraction of the pupil of the eye.

Miscarriage *See* Abortion.

Mitosis Cell division.

Mitral valve The valve that allows oxygenated blood into the left ventricle from the left atrium.

Molar teeth The grinding teeth at the back of both jaws.

Mongolism *See* Down syndrome.

Moniliasis Yeast infection usually caused by *Candida albicans* and affecting the mucous membranes such as the lining of the vagina, mouth, and gastrointestinal tract and the skin and nails.

Monocyte The largest type of white blood cell.

Mononucleosis, infectious A communicable disease in which the number of monocytes in the bloodstream increases. Symptoms include fever, swollen lymph nodes, and general malaise.

Mons veneris (or mons pubis) The pad of fatty tissue that covers the pubic bone of the female.

Morning sickness Nausea during the early stages of pregnancy.

Morphine A pain-relieving narcotic derived from the opium plant.

Motor Pertaining to movement; action.

Mountain sickness A temporary onset of symptoms of difficult breathing, headache, thirst, and nausea brought on by decreased oxygen in air at high altitudes.

Mucous Pertaining to mucus.

Mucous colitis Usually a functional disorder of the bowel characterized by mucus in the stool.

Mucous membrane Thin layers of tissue containing mucus-secreting glands.

Mucus The viscid secretion of mucous glands that moistens body linings.

Multiple sclerosis A degenerative disease affecting the central nervous system and brain, characterized by increasing disability.

Mumps A contagious disease affecting mostly children. Symptoms include painful swollen glands.

Muscle Body tissue that has the ability to contract.

Muscular dystrophy A disease appearing in childhood and characterized by a wasting of the muscles.

Myalgia Pain in the muscles.

Myasthenia Muscle fatigue or weakness. Myasthenia gravis is a chronic, progressive disease characterized by weakness of the voluntary muscles, especially those of the eyelids.

Mydriasis Abnormal dilation of the pupil.

Myelin The white fatty substance that covers most nerves like a sheath.

Myelitis Inflammation of the spinal cord or bone marrow.

Myeloma Malignant tumor of the cells derived from the bone marrow.

Myocardial infarction *See* Heart attack.

Myoma A tumor of muscle tissue.

Myopathy Any disease of the muscle.

Myopia Nearsightedness.

Myringitis Inflammation of the eardrum.

Myxedema Thyroid deficiency characterized by a slowdown in metabolism and body function. *See* Hypothyroidism.

Myxoma A tumor of the connective tissue containing mucoid cells.

Narcolepsy Neurological disorder characterized by an irresistible tendency to sleep.

Narcosis Unconsciousness and insensibility to pain brought on by a drug (narcotic).

Narcosynthesis A method for treating psychoneurosis in which a hypnotic drug is injected into the patient for the purpose of reviving suppressed memories.

Nares Nostrils.

Nasopharynx The part of the pharynx situated over the roof of the mouth.

Nausea A feeling of sickness in the stomach; sometimes followed by vomiting.

Navel Umbilicus.

Nearsightedness (myopia) A defect of the eye in which the eyeball is too convex. This causes light rays to focus in front of the retina, resulting in an inability to see objects clearly at a distance.

Necropsy Autopsy. Examination after death.

Necrosis Death and deterioration of tissue surrounded by living healthy tissue.

Neonatal Pertaining to the newborn (up to 1 month old).

Neoplasm A new and abnormal growth.

Nephrectomy Surgical removal of a kidney.

Nephritis Inflammation of a kidney.

Nephrolith Kidney stone.

Nephron The unit of the kidney in which waste is removed from the blood and urine is formed.

Nephrosis Kidney degeneration without inflammation.

Nerve A bundle of fibers that carries impulses between the nerve center (the brain and spinal cord) and the other parts of the body. There are five kinds of nerves: cranial, mixed, motor, sensory, and spinal.

Neuralgia Sharp, stabbing pain in a nerve or along its course. The pain is short-lived but recurring.

Neurasthenia A nervous condition in which one suffers from fatigue and loss of initiative. Usually accompanied by oversensitivity, restlessness, and uncalled-for irritability.

Neuritis Inflammation of a nerve.

Neurofibroma Tumor of nervous and connective tissues.

Neurofibromatosis A condition in which multiple tumors (neurofibroma) form under the skin or along the course of a nerve.

Neurology The branch of medicine dealing with the nerves and the central nervous system.

Neuron A nerve cell.

Neurosis A nervous disorder, usually related to anxiety, in which there is no functional degeneration of tissue.

Nevus A congenital pigment or elevated portion of skin; birthmark.

Nictation (or nictitation) Wink. Rapid blinking of eyelid.

Nightblindness (nyctalopia) Reduced ability to see at night.

Nitrous oxide Laughing gas; an inhalant that induces euphoria and dulls the sensation of pain. Often used in dentistry.

Nocturia Urination at night.

Node A small protuberance or swelling; a knoblike structure; nodule.

Nucleus The center part of any cell that is essential for cell growth, nourishment, and reproduction. Except for red blood cells, all human body cells have nuclei.

Nutrient A substance that provides materials the body needs; provides nourishment.

Nutrition The combination of processes by which the body or organism receives and uses materials essential for growth and maintenance.

Nystagmus Involuntary and repetitive oscillation of the eyeballs.

Obesity Excessive weight; body weight more than 20 percent above the average for one's age, height, and bone structure.

Obstetrics The branch of medical science dealing with pregnancy, childbirth, and neonatal care.

Occipital Pertaining to the back of the head.

Occlusion Used in reference to a closure of ducts and blood vessels. In dentistry, it refers to the fitting together of the upper and lower teeth.

Occult Undetectable by the naked eye.

Ocular Pertaining to the eye.

Olfactory Pertaining to the sense of smell.

Oligomenorrhea Infrequent or scanty menstrual flow.

Oligospermia Abnormally deficient spermatazoa in the semen.

Oliguria Deficient urine production.

Omentum A fold of the peritoneum (membrane lining of the abdomen) that covers and connects the abdominal organs.

Omphalitis Inflammation of the navel.

Oncology The scientific study of tumors.

Onychia Inflammation of the nail matrix, the tissue from which the nail grows.

Onychopagy Nail-biting.

Ophthalmitis Inflammation of the eye.

Ophthalmology The branch of medical science dealing with the eyes and their care.

Ophthalmoplegia Paralysis of eye muscles.

Ophthalmoscope An instrument for examining the interior of the eye.

Opiate Narcotic containing opium. Opiate drugs are used as painkillers, sedatives, or to slow gastric motility.

Optic nerve The fiber that transmits optic impulses from the retina to the brain.

Orbit Eye socket.

Orchiectomy (or orchectomy) Surgical removal of the testicles.

Orchitis Inflammation of the testicles.

Orgasm Climax of sexual intercourse.

Orthodontics The branch of dental science dealing with prevention and correction of teeth irregularities and malocclusions.

Orthopedics The branch of surgery dealing with diseases, disorders, and injuries to the locomotor system.

Orthopnea Condition in which breathing can only be facilitated when sitting or standing up.

Orthostatic Exacerbated by standing erect.

Osmosis The transfer of substance from one solution to another through a porous membrane that separates them.

Osseous Composed of or resembling bone tissue.

Ossicle A tiny bone. The three bones in the inner ear are ossicles.

Ossification The process of becoming bone or the change of cartilage to bone.

Osteitis Inflammation of bone.

Osteochondritis Inflammation of bone and cartilage.

Osteoma Tumor of bone tissue.

Osteomalacia A condition in which bones become soft, brittle, flexible, and painful due to a lack of calcium and vitamin D. Similar to childhood rickets.

Osteomyelitis Inflammation of the bone and marrow resulting from infection.

Osteopathy A system of treating disease that emphasizes massage and bone manipulation.

Osteoporosis A condition in which bones become porous, resulting in increased fragility. Associated with the aging process.

Otitis Inflammation of the ear.

Otorhinolaryngology Branch of medical science that deals with the ear, nose, and throat.

Ovariectomy Surgical removal of an ovary or ovaries.

Ovary The female reproductive gland whose function is to produce the eggs (ova) and the sex hormones estrogen and progesterone.

Oviduct *See* fallopian tubes.

Ovum The egg cell. The female sex cell, which, when fertilized by the male sperm, grows into a fetus. The egg contains 23 chromosomes that pair off with 23 chromosomes in the sperm to make a complete set needed to start a new life.

Oxygen The colorless, odorless gas that is essential for life. Oxygen makes up about 20 percent of the air.

Oxygenation The saturation of a substance with oxygen.

Oxyhemoglobin Oxygen-carrying hemoglobin.

Oxytocin A pituitary hormone that is secreted during childbirth for the stimulation of uterine contractions and milk secretion. A synthetic form of oxytocin is administered sometimes to induce or hasten labor.

Ozone A form of oxygen that is used as a disinfectant.

Pacemaker (sino-atrial node) A small knot of tissue (node) in the right atrium of the heart from which the contraction of the heart originates. Artificial or electronic pacemakers are small, battery-operated devices that can substitute for a damaged pacemaker.

Pachydermia Abnormal thickening of the skin.

Paget's disease 1. A type of breast cancer in which the nipple becomes sore and ulcerated. 2. Osteitis deformans. A chronic bone disease in which rates of bone production and bone loss are increased, leading to thickened and softened bones.

Palate The roof of the mouth.

Palliative Any agent that relieves pain and symptoms of disease but does not actually cure it.

Palpate Examine by feeling with the hand.

Palpitation Rapid, throbbing heartbeat.

Palsy Paralysis.

Pancarditis Inflammation of all the structures of the heart.

Pancreas The gland situated behind the stomach that secretes pancreatic juice and enzymes to aid in food digestion. Also contains groups of specialized cells (islets of Langerhans) that secrete insulin and glucagon hormones that regulate blood sugar levels.

Pancreatitis Inflammation of the pancreas.

Pantothenic acid One constituent of the vitamin B complex.

Papanicolaou smear (Pap test) The microscopic examination of cells shed from body surfaces; used routinely to screen for cancer of the cervix or uterus.

Papilla A small conical or nipple-shaped elevation.

Papilloma A tumor, usually benign, of the skin or mucous membrane.

Papule Small abnormal solid elevation on the skin.

Paralysis Loss of nervous function or muscle power due to injury or disease of the nervous system.

Paranoia A mental illness characterized by delusions of being persecuted or conspired against.

Paraplegia Paralysis affecting both legs, usually due to disease of the spinal cord or injury.

Parasite An organism that lives in or on another organism (host).

Parathyroid glands Four small glands embedded in the thyroid gland. The hormones secreted by the parathyroids control the body's calcium and phosphorus levels.

Paratyphoid fever An infectious disease whose symptoms resemble those of typhoid fever but are less severe.

Paregoric An opium compound that slows gastric action, thereby relieving cramps or diarrhea.

Parenchyma The parts of an organ that are directly related to the function of the organ (as opposed to supporting or connective tissues).

Parenteral A substance administered by injection or directly in the bloodstream rather than orally.

Paresis Slight paralysis.

Parkinson's disease (Parkinsonism) A disorder in which the patient suffers from tremors, stiffness, and slowness of movement.

Paronychia Infection of the tissues surrounding a nail.

Parotid gland One of the salivary glands located near the ear.

Parotitis Mumps; a viral disease characterized by the swelling of the parotid glands.

Paroxysm A sudden but temporary attack of disease or symptoms.

Parrot fever *See* Psittacosis.

Parturition Childbirth.

Pasteurization A process in which disease-causing bacteria in milk or other liquids are destroyed by heat.

Patch test A diagnostic procedure in which a suspected allergen is injected (in a diluted form) into the skin.

Patella Kneecap.

Pathogen Any disease-causing agent.

Pathology The science dealing with disease, its nature, and causes.

Pectoral Pertaining to the chest.

Pediatrics The branch of medical science dealing with children and the diseases affecting them.

Pedicle Stem of a tumor.

Pediculosis Lice infestation.

Pellagra A disease due to a lack of vitamin B_2 (nicotinic acid). Symptoms include skin rashes, weakness, and mental confusion.

Pelvis 1. A basin-shaped cavity, such as that of the kidney. 2. The bony basin-shaped cavity formed by the hip bone and the lower bones of the back.

Pemphigus A serious skin disease in which groups of large blisters on the skin rupture.

Penis The external male sex organ through which urine is passed and semen is ejaculated.

Pepsin A protein-digesting enzyme secreted by the stomach in gastric juices.

Peptic Pertaining to pepsin.

Peptic ulcer Ulcer in the stomach, duodenum, or esophagus that is related to pepsin.

Percussion A method of physical diagnosis by tapping or thumping a body part to produce sounds that indicate the size, density, and position of organs.

Perforation A hole or puncture, usually made by injury or infection (as of the eardrum) or by an ulcer.

Pericarditis Inflammation of the pericardium.

Pericardium The two-layer membranous tissue covering the heart. The layer closest to the heart is called the visceral layer. The other is the parietal layer.

Perineum The area between the anus and the genitals.

Periodontal membrane The tissue around the teeth covering the roots and connecting them to the jaw.

Periodontitis Inflammation of the periodontal membrane.

Periosteum The tough, fibrous membrane covering nearly all bone surfaces.

Peristalsis A wave of muscular contractions that push materials along the digestive tract.

Peritoneum The serous membrane that lines the abdominal organs.

Peritonitis Inflammation of the peritoneum.

Perleche A condition in which the corners of the mouth become cracked, raw, and thickened due to vitamin deficiency, bacterial infection, or other causes.

Pernicious Deadly, life-threatening.

Pernicious anemia Anemia caused by a deficiency of vitamin B_2 or an inability of the body to absorb vitamin B_2.

Perspiration Sweat; the secretion of the sweat gland through the pores of the skin.

Pertussis Whooping cough.

Pessary 1. A device placed in the vagina to support the uterus or correct uterine displacements. 2. A vaginal suppository.

Petechiae Small hemorrhages under the skin.

Petit mal A form of epilepsy or seizure in which the person does not lose consciousness.

Phagocyte A cell that is capable of engulfing bacteria and debris.

Phalanx One of the bones in the finger or toe.

Phallus Penis.

Pharyngitis Sore throat; inflammation of the pharynx.

Pharynx The mucous membrane–lined cavity at the back of the mouth. It extends to the esophagus.

Phimosis A condition in which the foreskin tightens so it prevents retraction over the head of the penis.

Phlebectomy Surgical removal of a vein.

Phlebitis Inflammation of a vein.

Phlegm Mucus, sputum.

Phobia An abnormally excessive and irrational fear. Some common phobias are acrophobia, fear of high places; agoraphobia, fear of open places; algophobia, fear of pain; claustrophobia, fear of closed places; ocholophobia, fear of crowds; triskaidekaphobia, fear of the number 13; and xenophobia, fear of strangers.

Physiology The study of cells, tissues, and organs; their functions and activities.

Pia or pia mater The innermost layer of the meninges that covers the brain and spinal cord.

Pica The craving or consumption of unusual substances that ordinarily are not food, such as dirt, chalk, or paint chips.

Pigment Any coloring matter.

Piles *See* Hemorrhoids.

Pimple Common term for a pustule or papule.

Pineal body A small gland, conical in structure, located on the back of the midbrain. Its function is not fully understood, but it may be concerned with regulation of growth or of the sex glands.

Pinkeye Contagious conjunctivitis.

Pituitary gland The pea-size gland located at the base of the brain. It is controlled by the hypothalamus, and it in turn controls the hormone productions in many other endocrine glands.

Pityriasis A skin disease in which patches of skin become red and scaly.

Placebo A substance without medicinal properties that is administered for psychological benefit or as part of a clinical research study.

Placenta The structure developed on the uterine wall about the third month of pregnancy. Through the placenta, the fetus receives nourishment and oxygen and eliminates waste products. It is expelled from the mother after childbirth. The afterbirth.

Plague Any deadly contagious epidemic disease.

Plantar Pertaining to the sole of the foot.

Plaque Patch or film of organic substance on tissues, such as teeth or in arteries.

Plasma The fluid part of blood. *See* Blood plasma.

Platelet (thrombocyte) The colorless bodies in the blood instrumental in blood clotting.

Pleura The membrane lining the chest cavity and covering the lungs.

Pleurisy Inflammation of the pleura.

Plumbism Lead poisoning.

Pneumococcus The oval-shaped bacterium responsible for diseases such as pneumonia, meningitis, and otitis media.

Pneumonia Infection of the lungs.

Pneumonitis Inflammation of lung tissue.

Pneumothorax Lung collapse due to air or gas in the chest cavity.

Pollinosis An allergic reaction to plant pollens inhaled with the air.

Polyarteritis Inflammation of a number of arteries.

Polycythemia An overabundance of red blood cells in the blood.

Polydipsia Excessive thirst, such as that which occurs in untreated diabetes.

Polyopia Seeing multiple images of a single object.

Polyp A nodular tumor, usually benign, that grows on a mucous membrane.

Polyphagia Excessive eating.

Postpartum After childbirth.

Preeclampsia A toxic condition of pregnancy characterized by high blood pressure, edema, and kidney malfunction.

Premenstrual syndrome (PMS) A variety of symptoms, both physical and emotional, associated with the menstrual cycle.

Prepuce The foreskin of the penis.

Presbycusis The normal decrease in hearing ability as one gets older.

Presbyopia Increasing inability to see objects close up. Normal condition of midlife and getting older.

Prickly heat (miliaria) Skin irritation or rash caused by perspiration.

Proctitis Inflammation of the membranes of the rectum.

Proctoscope A tubular instrument for examination of the interior of the rectum.

Progesterone The female sex hormone that causes the thickening of the uterine lining and the other body changes before conception.

Prognosis Prediction or forecast of the probable course and/or results of a disease.

Prolactin Hormone secreted by the pituitary that stimulates the breasts to produce milk.

Prolapse Downward displacement of an organ from its usual position.

Prophy1axis Prevention of disease or its spread.

Prostaglandins Hormonelike substances, secreted by a wide range of body tissues, that perform varying functions in the body.

Prostatectomy Surgical removal of all or part of the prostate gland.

Prostate gland The male sex gland located at the base of the bladder.

Prosthesis An artificial replacement for a missing body part.

Proteins Complex nitrogen compounds made up of amino acids. Most of the tissues of body, especially the muscles, are composed primarily of protein.

Prothrombin A substance in the blood that forms thrombin, an enzyme essential to blood coagulation.

Protoplasm "The stuff of life" in cells. The essential jellylike substance in all living cells.

Protozoa One-celled organisms, the smallest type of animal life. Amoeba and paramecia are protozoa. Some protozoa can cause disease.

Prurigo A chronic skin disease characterized by small papules and intense itching.

Pruritis Itching.

Psittacosis (parrot fever) A disease similar to pneumonia and transmitted to humans by birds, such as pigeons.

Psoriasis A chronic skin disease characterized by an overgrowth of the epidermis in which scaly lesions appear on various parts of the body.

Psychiatry The branch of medical study dealing with mental health.

Psychoanalysis A method developed by Sigmund Freud for the diagnosis and treatment of mental illness. The patient recalls past, perhaps forgotten, events in order to gain insight into the unconscious mind.

Psychogenic Originating from the mind.

Psychology The study of the mind and behavior.

Psychomotor Voluntary movement.

Psychoneurosis A mild emotional or mental disturbance, usually a defensive overreaction to unresolved conflicts.

Psychopathy Any disease of the mind.

Psychosis A mental illness originating in the mind itself rather than from environmental factors.

Psychosomatic Any condition either caused or exacerbated by emotional factors.

Psychotherapy Treatment of mental disorders based on verbal communication with the patient.

Ptomaine A poisonous substance produced by the decay of protein.

Ptosis A drooping, especially of the eyelid.

Ptyalin An enzyme contained in the saliva that initiates the breakdown of starch.

Puberty The age at which secondary sex characteristics develop and reproductive organs become functionally active. In girls, puberty is marked by the onset of menstruation and in boys by the discharge of semen and the change of voice.

Puerperium The period of time directly after childbirth until the time when the uterus has returned to its normal state.

Pulmonary Pertaining to the lungs.

Pulse The expansion and contraction of

an artery as a response to the expansion and contraction of the heart.

Pupil The opening in the middle of the iris of the eye that allows the passage of light to the retina.

Purgative A drug inducing evacuation of the bowels. A cathartic or strong laxative.

Purpura A disorder in which hemorrhages of tiny blood vessels cause purple patches to appear on the skin and mucous membranes.

Purulent Containing pus.

Pus A thick, yellowish fluid containing bacteria and white blood cells. Formed in some types of infection.

Pyelitis Inflammation of the kidney pelvis.

Pyorrhea The discharge of pus, usually from the teeth sockets.

Pyrexia Fever.

Pyrosis Heartburn.

Pyuria Pus in the urine.

Q fever A mild infectious disease caused by a rickettsia germ. It is usually transmitted from cows and sheep to humans by contaminated milk, tick bites, or contaminated food products.

Quadriplegia Paralysis of the arms and legs.

Quarantine The isolation of persons who might be sick with or have come in contact with a communicable disease.

Quickening The stage of pregnancy in which the first fetal movements are felt by the mother, usually around the 18th week of pregnancy.

Quinsy Acute inflammation of the tonsils accompanied by abscess.

Rabbit fever *See* Tularemia.

Rabies A deadly disease of the central nervous system caused by the rabies virus and spread by the bite of an infected (rabid) dog or other animal. Hydrophobia.

Radiation sickness Nausea and diarrhea caused by exposure to moderate radiation. Exposure to massive doses is extremely serious and perhaps fatal.

Radioactive Giving off penetrating energy waves to produce electrical or chemical effects.

Radioisotope An element whose atomic number is the same as another but whose atomic weight differs. Radioisotopes can be injected into the body and traced with monitors for diagnostic purposes.

Radium A highly radioactive metal used to treat cancer.

Rales Abnormal sounds from the lungs or bronchi.

Rash Eruption on the skin.

Rat-bite fever An infectious disease caused by bacteria spread to humans by rat bites.

Raynaud's disease A disease in which blood vessels of the fingers and toes constrict on exposure to cold, causing numbness and pallor. Blood vessels then expand, causing the area to tingle and become red or purple as the blood returns.

Recessive A term used in genetics to describe the weaker of two hereditary traits.

Rectum The portion of the large intestine closest to the anal opening. It consists of the rectal canal and the anal canal.

Reflex An unconscious, automatic response to a stimulus.

Refractory Not reacting to treatment.

Regeneration Repair or renewal of tissue.

Regurgitation Backflow.

Relapsing fever Recurrent fever as a symptom of infection caused by bacteria carried by lice and ticks.

Remission An easing of the symptoms of disease.

Renal Pertaining to the kidneys.

Renin An enzyme found in the kidney and capable of raising blood pressure.

Rennin The enzyme contained in the gastric juice that digests milk.

Repression The refusal of the conscious mind to acknowledge unacceptable or conflicting thoughts, feelings, or ideas.

Resection Removal of a part of an organ or tissue by means of surgery.

Respiration Breathing.

Respiratory distress syndrome *See* Hyaline membrane disease.

Resuscitation Restoration of breathing or heartbeat to one who is apparently dead or threatened with death.

Reticuloendothelial system A network of tissues containing cells (phagocytes) capable of taking up bacteria and foreign bodies in the bloodstream.

Retina The layered lining of the eye that contains light-sensitive receptors (the rods and cones) and conveys images to the brain.

Retinoblastoma A malignant tumor of the retina occurring in infants and children only.

Retinopathy An injury or disease of the retina, particularly common in insulin-dependent diabetes.

Retractors Devices used to pull back the edges of a wound.

Rh factor A group of antigens in the blood. Some people lack the Rh factor and are therefore designated as

Rh negative. Complications can occur if an Rh-negative mother conceives and has an Rh-positive baby. *See* Erythroblastosis fetalis.

Rheumatoid factor Abnormal protein in the blood of most people afflicted with rheumatoid arthritis or other autoimmune diseases.

Rhinitis Inflammation of the mucous membrane of the nose, usually as a symptom of the common cold or allergies.

Rhinoplasty Plastic surgery of the nose.

Rhinovirus Any of the more than 100 viruses that cause the common cold.

Rhodopsin The visual purple in the rods of the retina. It becomes bleached when exposed to light and requires vitamin A for regeneration.

Riboflavin Vitamin B_2.

Rickets A childhood disease caused by a deficiency of vitamin D. Symptoms include improper development of bones and teeth because of a calcium/phosphorus imbalance.

Rickettsia Disease-causing microorganisms, smaller than bacteria but larger than viruses. Usually transmitted to humans by the bites of fleas, lice, and ticks.

Rickettsial pox A rickettsial disease spread by the bites of mites. Symptoms include a poxlike rash, headache, and fever.

Ringworm A fungal infection affecting the tissues of the skin, hair, nails, and scalp. Dermatophytosis is the general medical name and examples of ringworm infections are tinea pedis (athlete's foot) and tinea capitis of the scalp.

Rocky Mountain spotted fever A rickettsial disease spread by ticks. Symptoms include fever, headache, muscle pain, and rash.

Rods Cylindrical nerve structures in the retina. They contain rhodopsin, and together with the cones they perceive the images of light, dark, and color, which are transmitted to the brain.

Roentgen rays X-rays.

Root canal The nerve-containing passageway through the root of the tooth.

Rose fever An allergic reaction to roses; term often used to describe pollen and/or mold allergies that occur during the spring as opposed to hay fever, which is in the fall.

Roseola Any pink eruption on the skin.

Roughage Indigestible matter (such as fiber).

Roundworms Parasites found in contaminated feces. In humans, roundworms cause ascariasis, a condition whose symptoms include disruption of the digestive system and abdominal pain.

Rubella German measles.

Rubeola Measles.

Rupture A tearing or bursting of a part. Also, a hernia.

Saccharin A sugar substitute derived from coal tar.

Sacroiliac The joint connecting the base of the spine to the upper part of the hip bone.

Sacrum The triangular bone just above the coccyx, near the lower end of the spine. It is composed of five vertebrae that have fused together. Together with the bones of the pelvis it forms the sacroiliac joint.

St. Anthony's fire *See* Erysipelas.

St. Vitus' dance *See* Chorea.

Saline Salty.

Saliva The secretion of the salivary glands. Lubricates the mouth and throat and initiates the digestion of food with enzymes.

Salivary glands The three glands on each side of the face. The sublingual gland and submaxillary gland secrete saliva onto the floor of the mouth. The parotids are situated near the ears and secrete saliva through passageways in the back of the mouth.

Salmonella A group of bacteria primarily responsible for the gastrointestinal disturbances of food poisoning.

Salpingectomy Surgical removal of the fallopian tubes; tubal ligation; a method of sterilization.

Salpingitis Inflammation of the fallopian tubes.

Sarcoma A malignant tumor from connective tissue.

Scabies Infestation of the skin by parasites (scabies mites) that burrow under the skin surface to lay their eggs. "The itch."

Scapula The shoulder blade.

Schick test A skin test for immunity to diphtheria.

Schizophrenia Dementia praecox. A group of mental illnesses classified as psychotic (rather than neurotic). Patient's thought patterns become disturbed and disorganized, and hallucinations or delusions are common symptoms.

Sciatica Pain extending along the path of the sciatic nerve. Can be caused by a slipped disk or by a muscle spasm.

Sciatic nerve The largest nerve in the body. It branches out from the base of the spinal cord (where it is attached) to form the motor and sensory nerves of the legs and feet.

Sclera The fibrous outer coat of the eye.

Sclerosis Abnormal hardening or thickening of a tissue.

Scoliosis Curvature of the spine.

Scorbutus Scurvy.

Scotoma Any (normal or abnormal) blind spot in the field of vision.

Scrotum The pouch that holds the testicles in the male.

Scurvy A disease caused by a deficiency of vitamin C. Symptoms include anemia, weakness, and bleeding gums.

Sebaceous glands The oil glands that secrete sebum, a fatty substance to lubricate the skin.

Seborrhea Overactivity of the sebaceous glands resulting in a greasiness of the skin.

Sebum The fatty substance secreted by the sebaceous glands.

Secretion Any substance formed or emitted by glands or tissue. Various secretions perform various functions for the body.

Sedative An agent that calms and reduces excitability.

Semen The thick, whitish secretion produced by the male testes and sex glands and containing the male reproductive cells, the spermatozoa.

Semicircular canals The three membranous canals of the inner ear that control the sense of balance.

Seminal vesicles The two glands that store the spermatozoa.

Senescence The process of aging; growing old.

Senility Abnormal deterioration of mental function associated with increasing age. Many physical diseases, such as arteriosclerosis, may be associated with senility.

Sepsis The state of being infected by germs in the blood or tissues.

Septicemia Blood poisoning. The presence of living bacteria in the bloodstream.

Septum A dividing wall between two compartments or cavities.

Serum The fluid formed in the clotting of blood. Contains antibodies and is injected in vaccines to build up immunities to specific diseases.

Serum sickness An allergic reaction (usually hives and fever) to the injection or administration of serum.

Shingles (herpes zoster) A virus infection of nerve endings characterized by pain and blisters along the course of the nerve. Caused by a latent form of the same virus that causes chickenpox, usually years after that disease.

Shock A condition in which the body processes slow down in response to injury or extreme emotion. Symptoms include rapid pulse, low blood pressure, paleness, and cold, clammy skin.

Sickle cell anemia A hereditary type of anemia caused by malformed (crescent-shaped) red blood cells.

Siderosis Chronic inflammation of the lungs caused by inhaling iron particles. An excess of iron in the circulating blood.

Silicosis Inflammation and damage of the lung caused by silicon dioxide. It is an occupational disease associated with sand blasting and stone cutting.

Sinus A cavity, hollow space, especially of the nasal passages.

Sinusitis Inflammation of a sinus.

Smegma Thick sebaceous secretion that accumulates beneath the prepuce and clitoris.

Solar plexus A network of nerves in the abdomen.

Somnambulism Sleepwalking.

Somniloquy Talking in sleep.

Spasm Sudden and severe involuntary contraction of a muscle.

Speculum An instrument used to dilate a body passage in order to examine the interior, such as the examination of the vagina and cervix during a pelvic examination.

Spermatocele Enlargement of the scrotum due to the development of a fluid-filled sac (cystic dilation) of the tubules.

Spermatozoa Male reproductive cell. *See* Ovum.

Spermicide An agent that kills spermatozoa.

Sphincter A ring of muscle that encircles and controls the opening of an orifice.

Sphygmomanometer An instrument used to measure blood pressure.

Spina bifida A congenital defect in which some of the vertebrae fail to close and therefore expose the contents of the spinal canal.

Spinal canal The central hollow formed by the arches of the vertebrae that contains the spinal cord.

Spinal column The structure formed from the 33 vertebrae (spinal bones); the backbone.

Spinal cord The cord or column of nerve tissue extending from the brain, enclosed in the spinal canal.

Spinal nerves 31 pairs of nerves that pass out of the spinal cord and carry impulses to and from all parts of the body.

Spinal tap The withdrawal of cerebrospinal fluid for the purpose of diagnosis or relief of pressure on the brain; lumbar puncture.

Spirochete Spiral-shaped bacterium. Syphilis is caused by a spirochete.

Spleen A large lymphoid organ behind the stomach on the lower left side of the rib cage. Its function includes cleansing the blood of parasites and manufacturing lymphocytes.

Spondylitis Inflammation of the spine.

Spore A life stage in the cycle of certain microorganisms in which they become inactive and highly resistant to destruction. A spore can become active again.

Sprain Injury to the soft tissue around a joint.

Sprue A chronic malabsorption disorder in which the body cannot absorb fats. Symptoms include diarrhea, indigestion, weight loss, and soreness in the mouth.

Sputum Discharge from the lungs and throat composed of mucus and saliva.

Stapes A tiny stirrup-shaped bone in the inner ear.

Staphylococci Spherical bacteria occurring in clusters. Responsible for food poisoning and skin infections; staph infections.

Steatorrhea Pale, bulky stools containing undigested fats.

Stenosis A narrowing of a body passage, tube, or opening.

Sterile 1. Germ-free. 2. Unable to reproduce.

Sternum The breastbone. The bone in the middle of the chest.

Steroids (corticosteroids, cortisone) Natural hormones or synthetic drugs that have many different effects. Some steroids are anti-inflammatory and are used to treat arthritis, asthma, and a number of autoimmune disorders.

Stethoscope An instrument that amplifies bodily sounds.

Stillborn Term used to describe a baby born dead after the 20th week of pregnancy.

Stomach The pouchlike organ into which the food flows from the esophagus. Digestion takes place here by means of enzymes and hydrochloric acid and also the churning action of the stomach muscles.

Stomatitis Inflammation of the soft tissues of the mouth; canker sore.

Stool Feces. Evacuation of the bowels.

Strabismus An eye disorder in which both eyes are unable to focus simultaneously; cross-eyed.

Strain Injury caused by misuse or overuse of a muscle.

Strawberry tongue A bright red tongue with enlarged papillae; associated with scarlet fever.

Streptococci Spherical bacteria that grow in chains. They are responsible for infections like scarlet fever and strep throat.

Striae Stripes, narrow bands. Stretch marks are a common example.

Stroke An interruption of the blood flow to the brain causing damage to the brain. Depending on the severity and location of the stroke, it may result in partial or complete paralysis or loss of some bodily function, or death.

Stroma The supporting tissue of an organ as opposed to the functioning part. See Parenchyma.

Stupor A state of impaired but not complete loss of consciousness and responsiveness.

Sty Infection of one of the sebaceous glands of the eye.

Subconscious The contents of the mind not in the range of consciousness.

Subcutaneous Under the skin.

Sulfonamides Sulfa drugs. A group of medicines that were the first antibiotic drugs.

Sunstroke Failure of the body's temperature control system as a result of overexposure to high heat and humidity. Body temperature rises to a very high degree, leading to coma and death. See Heat stroke.

Suppository Medicated substance in solid form for insertion into a body opening, usually the vagina or rectum. It melts inside the body to release the medicine.

Suppuration Pus formation.

Suprarenal glands See Adrenal glands.

Suture 1. To join two surfaces by stitching. 2. The threadlike substance used to join two surfaces.

Sympathectomy Surgical removal of part of the sympathetic nervous system.

Sympathetic nervous system Part of the autonomic nervous system. A chain of spinal nerves whose functions include contraction of blood vessels, increase of heart rate, and regulation of glandular secretions.

Synapse The point of communication between nerve endings.

Syncope Fainting.

Syndrome A group of symptoms that occur together, presumably originating from the same cause.

Synovia The viscid fluid that lubricates joints.

Systole The contraction of the heart muscle. Systolic pressure is the greater of the two blood pressure readings (the other is diastolic).

Systolic murmur An abnormal sound heard during the contraction of the heart.

Tachycardia Excessively rapid heartbeat.

Talipes (clubfoot) Congenital deformity in which the foot is twisted out of the normal position.

Tampon A plug of cotton or other absorbent material that is inserted into a body cavity in order to soak up discharge, such as vaginal tampons to absorb menstrual flow.

Tartar Calcified deposits on the teeth that are from a buildup of plaque.

Tay-Sachs disease A congenital disease affecting the fat metabolism and the brain and characterized by progressive weakness, disability, and blindness, and finally death. Also known as amaurotic familial idiocy.

T cells A specialized type of white blood cell (lymphocyte) that works as part of the immune system by attaching itself directly to an invading organism, such as a parasite or fungus, and destroying it. See B cell.

Temple The portion of the head between the eye and the ear.

Tendinitis Inflammation of a tendon.

Tendon A white fibrous band that connects muscle to bone.

Tenesmus Urgent desire to evacuate the bowel or bladder with painful and ineffectual straining to urinate or to move the bowels.

Tensor A muscle that stretches or tenses.

Testicles, testes The pair of primary male sex glands enclosed in the scrotum. They produce the male sex hormone testosterone and the spermatozoa.

Testosterone The male sex hormone that induces the secondary sex characteristics.

Tetanus (lockjaw) A serious and acute infection caused by the invasion of toxic microorganisms into an open wound.

Tetany Muscular spasms and cramps due to muscular hypersensitivity. Causes include gastrointestinal disorders or calcium deficiency.

Thalamus An egg-shaped mass of gray matter at the base of the cerebrum.

Thermometer Instrument used to measure temperature.

Thiamine (vitamin B_1) One of the B-complex vitamins.

Thoracic Pertaining to the chest.

Thorax The chest.

Thrombin An enzyme that converts fibrinogen into fibrin, which is necessary in order for blood to clot.

Thrombocyte Blood platelet, necessary for the process of blood clotting.

Thrombosis The formation of a blood clot that partially or completely blocks the blood vessel.

Thrombus A blood clot formed in a blood vessel.

Thrush A fungal infection (candidiasis) of the mouth, often occurring in infancy, but also in immunocompromised people whose resistance to disease is lowered.

Thymus A gland active in childhood and located behind the breastbone. It plays a part in defending the body against infection.

Thyroidectomy Surgical removal of the thyroid.

Thyroid gland The ductless gland located in the neck. The secretions of the thyroid gland control the rate of metabolism, among other functions.

Thyroxin The primary hormone secretion of the thyroid gland.

Tibia The shinbone. The larger (inner) of the two bones of the lower leg.

Tic Involuntary spasmodic movements or twitching.

Tick A blood-sucking parasite that is associated with the spread of disease.

Tincture A medicinal mixture of alcohol and a drug.

Tinea (ringworm) Fungus infection of the skin, and depending upon the location, the cause of barber's itch, jock itch, scalp ringworm, or ringworm of the foot.

Tinea cruris. Fungal infection of the groin area. Commonly called jock itch. .

Tinea pedia (athlete's foot) A fungal infection of the foot characterized by itching, small sores, and cracks on the skin.

Tinnitus Ringing, buzzing, or other perceived noises that originate inside the head rather than from outside stimuli.

Tissue A group of cells or fibers that perform similar functions and together form a body structure.

Tonsillectomy Surgical removal of the tonsils.

Tonsillitis Inflammation of the tonsils.

Tonsils The two masses of lymphoid tissue covered by a mucous membrane that are located one on each side of the back of the throat.

Topical Local.

Torticollis (wry neck) A condition in which the (sternocleidomastoid) muscle on one side of the neck contracts and pulls the head into an abnormal position.

Toxemia (blood poisoning) A condition in which poisonous compounds (toxins) are present in the bloodstream. Toxemia of pregnancy is another term for eclampsia.

Toxic Poisonous.

Toxic shock syndrome (TSS) An acute form of blood poisoning caused by the *Staphylococcus aureus* bacteria. It is associated with the use of superabsorbent tampons during menstruation but has been identified in children and men as well.

Toxin A poisonous substance produced by bacteria that may have serious effects in humans. Examples include toxic shock syndrome or botulism.

Toxoid A toxin that has been altered so that it is no longer poisonous but still stimulates antibody production. Used in vaccinations.

Toxoplasmosis A disease transmitted from animals (especially cats) to humans by parasite-infected feces or by eating undercooked meat containing the parasite. Infection during pregnancy can cause birth defects or fetal death.

Trachea The windpipe; the tube that extends from the larynx to the bronchi.

Tracheitis Inflammation of the trachea.

Tracheobronchitis Inflammation of the trachea and the bronchi.

Tracheotomy A surgical operation in which an artificial slit is made in the trachea in order to bypass an obstruction and allow air into the lungs.

Trachoma A contagious virus disease of the eye in which the conjunctiva and other mucous membranes become infected. May lead to blindness.

Traction Continuous pulling of a body part using weights and pulleys. Used in treatment of dislocations, deformity, and severe muscle spasm.

Tranquilizers A category of drugs used to relieve anxiety or calm disturbed behavior. "Minor" tranquilizers (such as Valium) are used to alleviate anxiety in stressful situations. "Major" tranquilizers (such as Thorazine) are used to reduce psychotic symptoms.

Transfusion The injection of fluids (usually blood or its components) into the circulatory system.

Transplantation The transference of an organ or tissue from one part of the body to another or from one individual to another.

Trauma Injury to the body or emotional shock.

Tremor Involuntary quivering or trembling. May have nervous, congenital, or organic origin or may result from certain drugs.

Triceps The muscle that extends the forearm.

Trichinosis A disease caused by ingestion of parasites often found in raw or insufficiently cooked pork.

Trichomoniasis Inflammation, usually of the vagina but also may affect the urethra in males, caused by a protozoan (single-celled) parasite, *Trichomonas vaginalis.*

Tricuspid valve The heart valve through which blood passes from the right atrium to the right ventricle.

Trigeminal nerve The fifth cranial nerve. Its three branches serve the face, the tongue, and the teeth.

Triglycerides The most common lipid found in fatty tissue. A high level of triglycerides may increase the risk of blood vessel or heart disease.

Truss A device used to hold a hernia or organ in place.

Trypsin An enzyme produced in the pancreas to digest proteins.

Tubal ligation (salpingectomy) Method of sterilization in which the fallopian tubes are tied or cut so that the sperm is unable to meet the ovum.

Tubal pregnancy The most common form of ectopic pregnancy in which the fertilized egg starts to develop in the Fallopian tubes rather than in the uterus.

Tubercle 1. A nodule on a bone. 2. The lesion characteristic of tuberculosis.

Tuberculin test A skin test used to detect tuberculosis or tuberculosis sensitivity. An extract of tubercle bacilli is injected into the skin and a positive reaction indicates possible tuberculosis or a previous exposure to the disease.

Tuberculosis An infectious disease affecting the lungs most often but also other parts of the body. It is caused by the tubercle bacillus and symptoms include cough, chest pains, fatigue, sweating, and weight loss. Commonly referred to as TB.

Tubule A small tube.

Tularemia Rabbit fever. A disease of small animals that is spread to humans by direct contact (e.g., handling the meat of an infected animal) or by the bite of a vector, such as a tick or flea. Symptoms include chills, fever, and swollen lymph nodes.

Tumefaction Swelling.

Tumor An abnormal growth of tissue similar to normal tissue but without function. May be benign (harmless) or malignant (cancerous).

Tympanic membrane The eardrum.

Tympanum The middle ear.

Typhoid fever A bacterial infection spread through contaminated water, milk, or food, especially shellfish. Symptoms include fever and diarrhea and disease may cause fatal dehydration.

Typhus A rickettsial disease transmitted by lice to humans. Symptoms include headache, chills, pain, and fever.

Ulcer An open sore on the skin or in a body cavity. Term commonly refers to intestinal or peptic ulcers, which form in the digestive tract.

Ulcerative colitis An inflammation of the colon and rectum in which ulcers in the digestive tract cause bloody stool.

Ulna The larger bone of the forearm.

Ultrasound Sound waves of very high frequency used for diagnostic purposes. The echoes of the ultrasound are registered with devices that construct pictures showing internal organs.

Umbilical cord The tube that connects the fetus to the placenta and through which the fetus is nourished and wastes are disposed.

Umbilicus The navel. The round scar in the middle of the abdomen left by the cutting of the umbilical cord after birth.

Undulant fever (brucellosis, or Malta fever) A disease transmitted from animals to humans through contaminated, unpasteurized milk products. Symptoms include fatigue, chills, joint pains, and a fever that undulates between near normal and extremely high (104°F).

Urea The nitrogen-containing waste product of protein breakdown that is excreted as the main component of urine.

Uremia A condition in which toxic substances remain in the blood due to the failure of the kidneys to filter out and excrete them.

Ureter One of the two tubes connecting the kidneys to the bladder and through which urine passes (by means of muscle contractions) into the bladder.

Urethra The tube through which the urine passes from the bladder to the outside. In the female, it is about 1½ inches long; in the male, it is 8 to 9 inches long.

Urethritis Inflammation of the urethra.

Uric acid An acid that is the waste product of metabolism. It is usually excreted in the urine; a buildup of it is characteristic of gout.

Urinalysis Examination and analysis of the urine for diagnostic purposes.

Urination (micturition) The discharge of liquid waste through the urethra.

Urine The amber-colored liquid produced in the kidneys from waste products filtered out of the blood. It is released through the ureters to the bladder, where it is stored temporarily before excretion. The urine is discharged from the bladder through the urethra during urination.

Urogenital Pertaining to the urinary and genital organs.

Urology The branch of medical science that deals with disorders of the urinary tract of the female and the urogenital system of the male.

Urticaria (hives) An allergic reaction in which itchy elevations (wheals or welts) appear on the skin. May be due to a food allergy, drugs, or other substances. Antihistamines may be prescribed in serious or recurring cases, but most hives disappear in a few days with no treatment.

Uterus (womb) The hollow, pear-shaped muscular organ where the fertilized ovum develops during pregnancy. It normally weighs about 2 ounces but enlarges to 30 ounces in pregnancy.

Uvea The pigmented parts of the eye.

Uvula The small tag of tissue that hangs from the center of the soft palate at the back of the throat.

Vaccination Inoculation of an antigenic substance in order to stimulate immunity to disease.

Vaccine Dead or weakened microorganisms that prevent disease by stimulating artificial immunity.

Vaccinia Cowpox.

Vagina The muscular canal lined with mucous membrane that extends from the vulva to the uterus. Sometimes referred to as the birth canal.

Vaginismus Painful contractions of the muscles of the vagina; often responsible for painful intercourse.

Vaginitis Inflammation of the vagina, accompanied by discharge and discomfort.

Vagus The 10th cranial nerve that extends from the brain to serve the stomach, intestines, esophagus, larynx, lungs, and heart.

Varicella Chickenpox.

Varicocele Varicose or swollen veins in the spermatic cord.

Varicose veins Abnormally swollen, dilated veins in which the valves are weakened and therefore allow the backflow of blood. Areas most commonly affected are the lower legs and the rectum. *See also* Hemorrhoids.

Variola Smallpox.

Vas deferens The duct of the testes through which the spermatozoa must pass in ejaculation.

Vascular Pertaining to, or supplied with, vessels, usually blood vessels.

Vasectomy A method of sterilization of the male. The passageway of the vas deferens is cut off so that the spermatozoa cannot enter the semen.

Vasoconstrictor Any agent that causes the blood vessels to narrow or to contract.

Vasodilator Any agent that causes the blood vessels to widen or enlarge.

Vasomotor Having the ability to contract or enlarge the blood vessels.

Vector An animal, insect, or person that carries disease.

Vein The vessels that carry deoxygenated blood from all parts of the body back to the heart.

Venereal diseases Diseases transmitted through sexual contact.

Venesection (bloodletting) Cutting a vein for the withdrawal of blood.

Venipuncture Puncturing a vein for the withdrawal of blood.

Venous Pertaining to the veins.

Ventral Pertaining to the front of the body; the abdomen.

Ventricle A small cavity, especially the two lower muscular chambers of the heart and the four cavities of the brain.

Venule A small vein that serves as a link between the arterial and venous systems.

Verruca A wart.

Vertebra One of the 33 flat, roundish bones that make up the spinal column.

Vertigo Dizziness.

Vesicle A small sac or bladder.

Viable Capable of survival.

Vibrios Hooklike bacteria.

Villus A microscopic finger-shaped projection such as those found in the mucous lining of the stomach walls.

Viral Pertaining to a virus.

Virulent Poisonous; disease-producing.

Virus A submicroscopic organism that causes disease and is capable of reproduction only within the living cells of another organism (such as a plant, animal, or human). Viruses cause many diseases of humans, ranging from mild ailments (such as the common cold) to serious, even fatal, diseases.

Viscera The internal organs (viscus—an internal organ).

Visual purple *See* Rhodopsin.

Vitreous humor The jellylike substance that is found between the lens and the retina and that supports the interior parts of the eye.

Vocal cords Two ligaments in the larynx, the vibrations of which produce the sounds of the human voice.

Volvulus A twist or knot in the intestine that blocks passage.

Vomit Ejection of matter from the stomach through the mouth.

Vulva The external genitalia of the female, including the clitoris and vaginal lips.

Vulvovaginitis Bacteria-caused inflammation of the vulva and the vagina.

Walleye An eye condition in which the cornea is whitish and opaque instead of clear; term also used to describe a form of divergent strabismus (crossed eyes) in which the images are slanted in different directions instead of merging into one.

Wart Small, harmless growths on the skin caused by a virus.

Wasserman test A blood test used to detect syphilis.

Wen A sebaceous cyst caused by the obstruction of an oil gland of the skin.

Wheal A temporary skin elevation, usually a result of an allergic reaction.

White blood cell *See* Leukocytes.

Widal test A blood test used to detect typhoid fever.

Windpipe *See* Trachea.

Womb *See* Uterus.

Xanthoma An accumulation or nodule of cholesterol that forms under the skin and appears as an elevated yellow patch.

Xeroderm Dry skin.

Xerophthalmia A dryness of the membranes of the eyelids and eye, associated with vitamin A deficiency.

Xerosis Abnormal dryness.

Xiphoid The sword-shaped piece of cartilage at the lower edge of the breastbone.

X-rays Electromagnetic radiation waves of very short length that are capable of penetrating some substances and producing shadow pictures showing structures of differing densities.

Yaws (frambesia) A tropical disease very similar to syphilis and caused by a spirochete resembling syphilis organisms.

Yellow fever An acute disease caused by a virus spread by insect bites. Usually seen in South America and Africa.

Zoonoses Any disease transmitted by an animal to humans.

Zoster *See* Herpes zoster; Shingles.

Zygote The fertilized egg before division.

Index